Fromm

Central America

1st Editio

by Nicholas Gill, Patrick
Greenspan, Charlie O'M

Here's what the cri

"Amazingly

"De

"H

Published by:

WILEY PUBLISHING, INC.

111 River St.
Hoboken, NJ 07030-5774

Services

obtain technical support, please 800/762-2974, outside the U.S. at

ntent that appears in

CONTENTS

4 BELIZE 84

5 GUATEMALA 152

6 EL SALVADOR 222

9 COSTA RICA 536

10 PANAMA 636

LIST OF MAPS

ABOUT THE AUTHORS

Apart from having authored numerous travel guides to Latin American destinations, writer and photographer **Nicholas Gill** (Honduras)—based in Brooklyn, New York, and Lima, Peru—has contributed to publications such as *Islands, Caribbean Travel & Life,* World Hum, *Forbes Traveler,* and the *Columbus Dispatch.* Visit his website, www.nicholas-gill.com, for more information.

Patrick Gilsenan (El Salvador) is a Washington, D.C.–based freelance writer with a passion for travel and Latin America. He's made friends, danced in the streets, and hopefully learned something in nearly every country from Mexico to the tip of Argentina. After earning his early chops in newspaper journalism, he traded city council and zoning board meetings for a backpack and border crossings. He has since coauthored a cycling guidebook published by Globe Pequot Press and written countless travel and adventure stories.

Eliot Greenspan (Belize, Costa Rica, and Guatemala) is a poet, journalist, and travel writer who took his backpack and typewriter the length of Mesoamerica before settling in Costa Rica in 1992. Since then, he has traveled seemingly ceaselessly around Latin America, writing articles and guidebooks to feed his travel habit. He feels particularly at home in the Neotropics—in their rain and cloud forests, on their rivers, and under their seas. Eliot is the author of *Frommer's Belize, Frommer's Costa Rica, Frommer's Guatemala,* and *Frommer's Ecuador,* as well as the chapter on Venezuela in *Frommer's South America.*

Charlie O'Malley (Nicaragua, Central America in Depth) is an Irishman working and living in South America, based in the Argentine wine region Mendoza. He is also the author of the Argentina, Bolivia, Paraguay, and Uruguay chapters in *Frommer's South America* and has helped put together *Frommer's Argentina.* He edits his own magazine called *Wine Republic* in Mendoza.

Jisel Perilla (Panama) has written about, lived in, and traveled throughout much of Latin America, and is the author of the Colombia chapter in *Frommer's South America.* She currently resides in the Washington, D.C., area.

ACKNOWLEDGMENTS

The editor would like to thank all the Central America authors for their contributions to the Best of Central America, Central America in Depth, Planning Your Trip to Central America, and the appendix chapters.

AN INVITATION TO THE READER

In researching this book, we discovered many wonderful places—hotels, restaurants, shops, and more. We're sure you'll find others. Please tell us about them, so we can share the information with your fellow travelers in upcoming editions. If you were disappointed with a recommendation, we'd love to know that, too. Please write to:

Frommer's Central America, 1st Edition
Wiley Publishing, Inc. • 111 River St. • Hoboken, NJ 07030-5774

AN ADDITIONAL NOTE

Please be advised that travel information is subject to change at any time—and this is especially true of prices. We therefore suggest that you write or call ahead for confirmation when making your travel plans. The authors, editors, and publisher cannot be held responsible for the experiences of readers while traveling. Your safety is important to us, however, so we encourage you to stay alert and be aware of your surroundings. Keep a close eye on cameras, purses, and wallets, all favorite targets of thieves and pickpockets.

FROMMER'S STAR RATINGS, ICONS & ABBREVIATIONS

Every hotel, restaurant, and attraction listing in this guide has been ranked for quality, value, service, amenities, and special features using a **star-rating system.** In country, state, and regional guides, we also rate towns and regions to help you narrow down your choices and budget your time accordingly. Hotels and restaurants are rated on a scale of zero (recommended) to three stars (exceptional). Attractions, shopping, nightlife, towns, and regions are rated according to the following scale: zero stars (recommended), one star (highly recommended), two stars (very highly recommended), and three stars (must-see).

In addition to the star-rating system, we also use **seven feature icons** that point you to the great deals, in-the-know advice, and unique experiences that separate travelers from tourists. Throughout the book, look for:

Finds	Special finds—those places only insiders know about
Fun Facts	Fun facts—details that make travelers more informed and their trips more fun
Kids	Best bets for kids and advice for the whole family
Moments	Special moments—those experiences that memories are made of
Overrated	Places or experiences not worth your time or money
Tips	Insider tips—great ways to save time and money
Value	Great values—where to get the best deals

The following **abbreviations** are used for credit cards:

AE	American Express	DISC	Discover	V	Visa
DC	Diners Club	MC	MasterCard		

FROMMERS.COM

Now that you have this guidebook to help you plan a great trip, visit our website at **www.frommers.com** for additional travel information on more than 4,000 destinations. We update features regularly to give you instant access to the most current trip-planning information available. At Frommers.com, you'll find scoops on the best airfares, lodging rates, and car rental bargains. You can even book your travel online through our reliable travel booking partners. Other popular features include:

- Online updates of our most popular guidebooks
- Vacation sweepstakes and contest giveaways
- Newsletters highlighting the hottest travel trends
- Podcasts, interactive maps, and up-to-the-minute events listings
- Opinionated blog entries by Arthur Frommer himself
- Online travel message boards with featured travel discussions

The Best of Central America

Whether you're an archaeology buff, an outdoor adventurer, or a partyer in search of a good time, Central America presents so many diverse travel options that it'll make your head spin. There are so many rainforests to hike, volcanic peaks to climb, coral reefs to scuba dive, and there's so much colonial splendor to see, that you can't possibly see and do everything that Central America has to offer in one trip. You can certainly make a good go of it, though. Below are some of our personal favorites to get you started.

1 THE MOST UNFORGETTABLE TRAVEL EXPERIENCES

- **Snorkeling at Shark-Ray Alley & Hol Chan Marine Reserve** (Northern Cayes and Atolls, Belize): These two very popular sites are threatened with overcrowding but still live up to their billing. Shark-Ray Alley guarantees a close encounter with schools of large stingrays and nurse sharks. The experience provides a substantial adrenaline rush for all but the most nonchalant and veteran divers. Hol Chan Marine Reserve is an excellent snorkeling spot comprised of a narrow channel cutting through a rich and well-maintained shallow coral reef. See chapter 4.
- **Riding an Inner Tube through the Caves Branch River Cave System** (Cayo District, Belize): Strap on a battery-powered headlamp, climb into the center of an inflated car inner tube, and gently float through a series of limestone caves, your headlamp illuminating the stalactites and the occasional bat. The entire sensation is eerie and claustrophobic at times, but fun nonetheless—especially if you go with a small group on a day when the caves are not crowded. See chapter 4.
- **Watching the Sunrise from the Top of a Pyramid in Tikal** (Guatemala): A visit to Tikal is a remarkable experience on its own, but our favorite way to start a visit here is by catching the sunrise from the top of one of the pyramids. In addition to the ruins and sunrise, the surrounding jungle comes to life with the cries of howler monkeys and the frenzied activity and calls of awakening birds. See chapter 5.
- **Paying Your Respects to Maximón** (Guatemala): A syncretic saint worshiped by Guatemala's Maya and Catholic alike, Maximón is the bad boy of the religious pantheon. Maximón supposedly responds well to gifts, and has very specific tastes, so be sure to bring some rum or a cigar as an offering. Many towns across Guatemala have a carved idol of Maximón, or San Simon, although only a few really keep the practice of his daily worship alive. The towns with the most elaborate Maximón rituals and traditions include Santiago de Atitlán and Zunil. See chapter 5.

- **Touring the Towns & Villages around Lake Atitlán** (Guatemala): While Lake Atitlán is exceedingly beautiful in and of itself, the true charm of the lake is its ability to let you visit a half-dozen or more lakeshore towns via local water-taxi services. The water taxis run regular routes throughout the day, stopping at the villages of Santiago de Atitlán, San Pedro de la Laguna, San Marco, San Antonio Palopó, and more. You can hop on and off the taxis at your whim, and stay as long as you like before heading on to the next place or back home to your hotel. See chapter 5.
- **Exploring the 35km (22 miles) of Winding Mountain Road & Villages of the Rutas de Las Flores** (El Salvador): If you're tight on time, this route offers an excellent sample of what El Salvador has to offer. The route is known primarily for its small towns, each offering something different, from the furniture craftsmen of Nahuizalco, to Juayua's weekend food and craft festival, to the artsy vibe and cool restaurants of Ataco. The route also offers amazing views of thousands of flowering coffee plants and one of the country's highest and longest zip-line canopy tours. See chapter 6.
- **Seeing Suchitoto** (El Salvador): This is one of El Salvador's most beautiful and unique towns and well worth the easy, 1-hour drive north of San Salvador. After a turbulent history during El Salvador's civil war, Suchitoto has reemerged as one of El Salvador's leading international arts and cultural centers, with the country's most luxurious boutique hotels and a famous international arts festival. But despite its international flair, Suchitoto is still very much a distinctly El Salvadoran town, close to the historic town of Cinquera, home to a weekend artisans market, and surrounded by amazing mountain views. See chapter 6.
- **Eating a Baleada** (Honduras): The iconic snack food of Honduras, served in streetside stalls and sit-down restaurants all over the country, is a folded wheat tortilla stuffed with refried beans, crumbled *queso blanco* (white cheese), sour cream, and occasionally egg, chicken, beef, avocado, onions, or tomatoes. It's so delicious that, after tasting one, you might never want to leave the country. See chapter 7.
- **Seeing the Still-Smoking Flor de Copán Factory** (Santa Rosa de Copán, Honduras): The Flor de Copán tobacco factory is world-renowned for its production of fine cigars like the Don Melo line. A tour here involves a walk through of the factory's heady drying and deveining rooms and witnessing the country's most skilled rollers working firsthand. Even if you hate smoking, this is a great chance to mingle with real Hondurans, outside the standard tourist industry. See chapter 7.
- **Visiting Volcán Masaya** (Masaya, Nicaragua): The Spanish called this volcano the "Gates of Hell" and you can understand why when you see its boulder-spitting craters and glowing red lava fields. Volcán Masaya is easily one of the most accessible and scariest live volcanoes in the region—it's also one of the most exciting to see up close. Also worth a climb or look are Volcán Maderas and Volcán Concepcion. See chapter 8.
- **Turtle-Watching in San Juan del Sur** (San Juan del Sur, Nicaragua): After a spot of sun worshiping on Nicaragua's beaches, come out at night and see one of nature's true wonders—massive turtle hatchings on the very beautiful Playa La Flor. The best time to see turtles nesting is August and September. See chapter 8.
- **Gaping at Arenal Volcano/Soaking in Tabacón Hot Springs** (near La Fortuna, Costa Rica): When the skies are

clear and the lava is flowing, Arenal Volcano offers a thrilling light show accompanied by an earthshaking rumble that defies description. You can even see the show while soaking in a natural hot spring and having a drink at the swim-up bar at **Tabacón Grand Spa Thermal Resort** (p. 608). If the rushing torrent of volcano-heated spring water isn't therapeutic enough, you can get a massage here, as well. See chapter 9.

- **Touring the Osa Peninsula** (Southern Costa Rica): This is Costa Rica's most remote and biologically rich region. **Corcovado National Park,** the largest remaining patch of virgin lowland tropical rainforest in Central America, takes up much of the Osa Peninsula. Jaguars, crocodiles, and scarlet macaws all call this place home. Whether you stay in a luxury nature lodge in **Drake Bay** or outside of **Puerto Jiménez,** or camp in the park itself, you will be surrounded by some of the most lush and most intense jungle this country has to offer. See chapter 9.
- **Hiking Sendero Los Quetzales** (Volcán Barú National Park, Panama): Panama's foremost day hike takes visitors around the northeastern flank of Volcán Barú and through primary and secondary tropical forest and cloud forest that provides a dazzling array of flora and fauna. The trail's namesake resplendent quetzal lives here, too. The trail is mostly downhill from the Cerro Punta side to Boquete, and this is the recommended direction unless you really crave a workout. What's unique about this trek is that travelers lodging around Cerro Punta can send their luggage to their next hotel in Boquete, and walk there. See chapter 10.
- **Looking for More than 500 Species of Birds along Pipeline Road in Soberanía National Park** (Panama): This is the country's "celebrity" bird-watching trail for the immense number of species found here. In fact, for several years Pipeline Road has set the world record for 24-hour bird counts. Even nonbirders can't help getting caught up in the action with so many colorful show birds fluttering about, such as motmots, trogons, toucans, antbirds, colorful tanagers, and flycatchers. The farther you walk or bike along the rainforest trail, the better your chances are of spotting rare birds. See chapter 10.

2 THE BEST SMALL TOWNS & VILLAGES

- **Caye Caulker,** Belize: The official slogan here is "Go Slow." Even going slow, you can walk from one end of this small island to the other in under 20 minutes. The fastest moving vehicles, in fact, are bicycles, although lazier souls roam around in golf carts. The town itself is a small and funky Caribbean beach burg, with a lively mix of restaurants, bars, and tour operators to keep you busy and interested. See chapter 4.
- **Flores,** Guatemala: In addition to serving as the gateway to Guatemala's greatest Maya ruin, Tikal, the small island town of Flores has ample charms of its own. The small island is great for walking, and you'll find plenty of fine restaurants, bars, and small hotels here. In addition, the town is loaded with small boats eager to give you a tour of nearby attractions, or simply a sunset cruise on the lake. See chapter 5.
- **Perquín & Mozote,** El Salvador: Exploring the history and tragedy of the towns of Perquín and Mozote should provide unique insight into the troubled history of this complex nation. Perquín is a small town tucked into the

high eastern mountains, which formed the base of the people's FMLN organization during the civil war. The nearby village of Mozote was the site of one of Latin America's worst modern wartime atrocities; the square and church now feature the well-known Mozote memorial and the names of the townspeople who were killed. See chapter 6.

- **Barra de Santiago,** El Salvador: Santiago is a protected reserve and largely undeveloped fishing village along the country's far western coast. The best thing about the place is its isolation and natural beauty; it's surrounded by wide, nearly deserted, sandy beaches and mangrove-filled estuaries where majestic white egrets glide low over the water. And the entire place sits immediately in front of a miles-long line of volcanoes that seem to rise from the palm-tree-lined estuary shores. You can fish, swim, surf, paddle, spot sea turtles laying their eggs, or just do nothing and enjoy the view. See chapter 6.
- **Miami,** Honduras: Set on a narrow sandbar between the Caribbean and the Los Micos lagoon in Parque Nacional Jeanette Kawas, this Garífuna village, just a small collection of thatched huts, has remained unchanged for a couple of hundred years. Get there while you can though, as development around Tela Bay is a serious threat to this and other communities nearby. See p. 377.
- **San Juan del Sur,** Nicaragua: This small, colorful fishing village of clapboard houses is slowly morphing into a party town with excellent hotels and restaurants. It sits amid a string of great beaches offering surfing, fishing, sailing, or just glorious idling. See chapter 8.
- **Tortuguero Village** (on the Caribbean coast, Costa Rica): Tortuguero Village is a small collection of rustic wooden shacks on a narrow spit of land between the Caribbean Sea and a dense maze of jungle canals. It's been called Costa Rica's Venice, but it actually has more in common with the South American Amazon. As you explore the narrow canals here, you'll see a wide variety of herons and other water birds, three types of monkeys, three-toed sloths, and caimans. If you come between June and October, you might be treated to the awe-inspiring spectacle of a green turtle nesting—the small stretch of Tortuguero beach is the last remaining major nesting site of this endangered animal. See chapter 9.
- **Bocas del Toro,** Panama: There are plenty of surfing hot spots along the Pacific Coast of Panama, especially at Santa Catalina, but Bocas is where surfers find everything from beginner-friendly waves to monster, Hawaii-style waves that reach more than 6m (20 ft.). What's special about Bocas, too, is that the water is clear blue, allowing you to see the reef as you race over it, and there are lots of lodging options, restaurants, and thumping nightlife, unlike in Santa Catalina. See chapter 10.

3 THE BEST BEACHES

- **Placencia,** Belize: This is the hippest little beach town in Belize. In a Caribbean country decidedly lacking in long stretches of beach, Placencia offers nearly 26km (16 miles) of white sand fronting a shimmering turquoise sea. You can wander up and down the length of this long beach, or hang out near the little creole village, whose main thoroughfare and directional reference point is a narrow strip of concrete running north to south and known simply as "the sidewalk." See chapter 4.

- **Playa los Cóbanos,** El Salvador: Who knew? El Salvador happens to be home to some of Central America's best Pacific diving. Specifically, El Salvador's Playa los Cóbanos features a 161-sq.-km (62-sq.-mile) reef system filled with tropical fish and a half-century-old shipwreck to explore. See chapter 6.
- **West Bay Beach,** Roatán, Honduras: The crystal-clear water and powdery white sand have led many to call this one of the top beaches in the entire Caribbean. Don't forget your snorkel gear; the world's second-largest barrier reef is just offshore See chapter 7.
- **The Corn Islands,** Nicaragua: You won't lack company while taking a dip and exploring the coral reefs around these classic Caribbean treasure islands: Spider crabs, parrot fish, and baby barracuda among others will dart before your eyes in the pristine blue waters here. See chapter 8.
- **Manuel Antonio,** Costa Rica: The first beach destination to become popular in Costa Rica, Manuel Antonio retains its charms despite burgeoning crowds and mushrooming hotels. The beaches inside the national park are idyllic, and the views from the hills approaching the park are enchanting. This is one of the few remaining habitats for the endangered squirrel monkey. Rooms with views tend to be a bit expensive, but many a satisfied guest will tell you they're worth it. See chapter 9.
- **Playa Montezuma,** Costa Rica: This tiny beach town at the southern tip of the Nicoya Peninsula has weathered fame and infamy, but retains a funky sense of individuality. European backpackers, vegetarian yoga enthusiasts, and UFO seekers choose Montezuma's beach over any other in Costa Rica. The waterfalls are what set it apart from the competition, but the beach stretches for miles, with plenty of isolated spots to plop down your towel or mat. Nearby you can explore the **Cabo Blanco National Park.** See chapter 9.
- **Isla Bastimentos National Park,** Bocas del Toro, Panama: Cayos Zapatillas, or the "Slippers Islands" (so-called because they resemble footprints), not only fulfill the beach lover's fantasy with their soft sand backed by a tangle of jungle; they are also surrounded by a rich display of coral that attracts hordes of fish, providing good snorkeling. The park's main island, Isla Bastimentos, offers terrific beaches with clean sand and blue water, which can be reached by a short walk or hike, or by boat during the calm-water season from August through October. See chapter 10.

4 THE BEST OUTDOOR ADVENTURES

- **Scuba Diving or Snorkeling on the Belize Barrier Reef** (Belize): Running the entire length of the country's coastline, the Belize Barrier Reef is the second-longest continuous barrier reef in the world. Here you will find some of the best snorkeling opportunities and scuba-diving sites in the world. Whether it's shallow water snorkeling over multicolored fan and staghorn coral, or scuba diving with whale sharks off of Gladden Spit, the opportunities are nearly endless and almost always amazingly rewarding. See chapter 4.
- **Horseback Riding through the Cayo District** (Belize): The Cayo District is a perfect area to explore on horseback. Rides can be combined with visits to jungle waterfalls and swimming holes, as well as nearby Maya ruins. **Mountain Equestrian Trails** (© **669-1124;** www.metbelize.com) has one of the

better stables and horse-riding operations in the Cayo District. See chapter 4.

- **Climbing an Active Volcano** (Guatemala): Guatemala's mountainous terrain is predominantly volcanic, and many of these volcanoes are still active. There's nothing as primal as climbing the flanks of an active volcano or peering down into an erupting crater. Both of these experiences are possible on a climb to the summit of **Pacaya** volcano. Once Pacaya's whetted your appetite, there are numerous other volcanoes here to scale, including **Santa María, Tajumulco, Agua,** and **Acatenango.** See chapter 5.
- **Mountain Biking Rural Back Roads** (Guatemala): The back roads and dirt paths of rural Guatemala are perfect for fat tire explorations. Whether you choose to take a ridge ride between small villages or a more technically challenging ascent or descent of a volcano, there is something for all ability levels. **Old Town Outfitters** (**✆ 502/5399-0440;** www.bikeguatemala.com) is one favorite operator, and has excellent guides and equipment, and a wide range of tours and trips. See chapter 5.
- **Hiking & Swimming in Parque Nacional El Imposible** (El Salvador): Parque Imposible is one of El Salvador's largest, most lush, and richest-in-wildlife national parks, and it's dotted with streams, waterfalls, and natural swimming holes that are perfect for swimming. Tacuba, the small town just outside the park, serves as a great base camp for hiking trips. See chapter 6.
- **Trekking through La Mosquitia** (Honduras): Rich with wildlife and home to ethnic groups like the Miskito, Pech, Garífuna, and Tawahkas, Central America's largest tract of rainforest is nothing less than spectacular. Community-based tourism initiatives, run directly in the indigenous villages themselves, can assist in your exploration of the swamps, wetlands, grasslands, lagoons, and beaches here. See chapter 7.
- **Bird-Watching in Honduras:** Trogons, motmots, tanagers, scarlet macaws, boat-billed herons, resplendent quetzals, and toucans are only a small fraction of the avian life you will encounter in places such as Lancetilla, Lago de Yojoa, Pico Bonito, Cerro Azul, and Celaque. Some areas of the country have recorded as many as 400 species. See chapter 7.
- **Kayaking around Isla Juan Venado** (Nicaragua): Pelicans and herons step over crocodiles, iguanas, and caimans as you paddle through a labyrinth of channels and waterways in this protected mangrove swamp on the Pacific coast, close to León. See chapter 8.
- **Hiking through Miraflor Nature Reserve** (Nicaragua): Miraflor is a slice of Eden in the northern highlands of Nicaragua. Orchids bloom amid begonias and moss-draped oak trees, while toucans and parakeets hide among the foliage. Hike La Chorrera trail as far as a 60m-high (197-ft.) waterfall, going past ancient caves and prehistoric mounds. See chapter 8.
- **Trying the New Adventure Sport of Canyoning** (Costa Rica): While far from standardized, canyoning usually involves hiking along and through the rivers and creeks of steep mountain canyons, with periodic breaks to rappel down the face of a waterfall, jump off a rock into a jungle pool, or float down a small rapid. **Pure Trek Canyoning** (**✆ 2461-2110;** www.puretrekcostarica.com) in La Fortuna, and **Psycho Tours** (**✆ 8353-8619;** www.everydaycostarica.com) near Puerto Jiménez, are two of the prime operators in Costa Rica. See chapter 9.
- **Kayaking around the Golfo Dulce** (Costa Rica): Slipping through the waters of the Golfo Dulce by kayak gets you intimately in touch with the raw

beauty of this underdeveloped region. Spend several days poking around in mangrove swamps, fishing in estuaries, and watching dolphins frolic in the bay. **Escondido Trex** (✆ **2735-5210;** www.escondidotrex.com) provides multiday custom kayaking trips out of Puerto Jiménez on the Osa Peninsula. See chapter 9.

- **White-Water Rafting & Kayaking the Chiriquí & Chiriquí Viejo Rivers** (Panama): Depending on which section you raft, these two rivers produce serious white-water ranging from technical Class 3 to Class 5, some portions of which are so difficult they've been named "Fear" and "Get Out If You Can." There are plenty of tamer floats on Class 2 rivers, such as the Esti, for families and beginners. Virtual solitude, beautiful views, and lush surroundings are part of the tour, too. Contact **Chiriquí River Rafting** (✆ **720-1505;** www.panama-rafting.com) in Boquete or, for kayaking, **Panama Rafters** (✆ **720-2712;** www.panamarafters.com). See chapter 10.
- **Swinging through the Treetops on a Canopy Tour** (Panama and throughout Central America): This unique adventure is becoming quite the rage. In most cases, after a strenuous climb using ascenders, you strap on a harness and zip from treetop to treetop while dangling from a cable. There are canopy tours all around Panama, and throughout Central America for that matter. Check the various destination sections to find a canopy tour operation near you.

5 THE MOST INTRIGUING HISTORICAL SITES

- **Caracol** (Belize): Caracol is the largest known Maya archaeological site in Belize, and one of the great Maya city-states of the Classic era. Located deep within the Chiquibil Forest Reserve, the ruins are not nearly as well excavated as Tikal. However, this is part of Caracol's charm. The main pyramid here, Caana or "Sky Palace," stands some 41m (136 ft.) high; it is the tallest Maya building in Belize and still the tallest man-made structure in the country. See p. 134.
- **Tikal** (El Petén, Guatemala): In our opinion, Tikal is the most impressive of all the ancient Maya ceremonial cities. Not only is the site massive and meticulously excavated and restored, it's set in the midst of a lush and lively tropical jungle. The peaks of several temples poke through the dense rainforest canopy, toucans and parrots fly about, and the loudest noise you'll hear is the guttural call of howler monkeys. In its heyday, the city probably covered as many as 65 sq. km (25 sq. miles) and supported a population of more than 100,000. See p. 178.
- **Joya de Cerén** (outside of San Salvador, El Salvador): Joya de Cerén isn't El Salvador's most visually stunning ruin, but it offers one of Central America's most accurate glimpses into the lives of the region's Maya ancestors in the form of the remains of a Maya village, frozen in time 1,400 years ago when the village was buried beneath the ash of a violent volcanic eruption. Still standing and preserved are the local shaman's house, a community sauna, and private sleeping rooms. See p. 244.
- **Copán** (Honduras): Often referred to as the Paris of the Maya world, these majestic ruins will take you on a dramatic journey through the Maya civilization. The secret to understanding the Copán Ruins is a large square block of carved stone known as the Altar Q, which represents the dynastic lineage of 16 kings whose rule spanned nearly 4 centuries. See p. 356.

- **Huellas de Acahualinca** (Managua, Nicaragua): Six thousand-year-old footprints of men, women, and children beg the question; were they fleeing a volcanic eruption or just going for a swim? One thing is for sure, the footprints on display here are some of the oldest pieces of evidence of human activity in Central America. This intriguing site can be visited in a northern suburb of Managua. See p. 448.
- **León** (Nicaragua): This cradle of the revolution has been bombed, besieged, and washed away by hurricanes. Every street corner tells a story, and it's highly recommended that you take a city tour of this fascinating university town with its vibrant murals, tiny plazas, and the biggest cathedral in Central America. Nearby is León Viejo, the original, abandoned colonial city at the feet of its destroyer—Volcán Momotombo. See p. 460.
- **Casco Viejo** (Panama City, Panama): This UNESCO-designated Panama City neighborhood is renowned for its Spanish, Italian, and French-influenced late-18th-century architecture and its narrow streets, bougainvillea-filled plazas, and breezy promenade. But Casco Viejo is also home to some of the country's top historical landmarks, such as La Catedral Metropolitana, the charred remains of the Iglesia de Santo Domingo, Casa Gongora, the best preserved example of a Spanish colonial home, and the UNESCO-designated Salon Bolivar, the site of the famous 1826 congress organized by Bolivar to discuss the unification of Colombia, Mexico, and Central America.

6 THE BEST MUSEUMS & CHURCHES

- **Iglesia La Merced** (Antigua, Guatemala): In a city awash in Catholic churches, convents, and monasteries, Iglesia La Merced reigns supreme. It's no small coincidence—nor small honor—that the principal procession of the Holy Week celebrations leaves from this church. The ornate baroque facade is painted bright yellow and white, and the interior is full of art and sculptures. The ruins of the attached convent are also worth a visit. See p. 182.
- **Iglesia de Santo Tomás** (Chichicastenango, Guatemala): Dating from 1540, this modest church serves simultaneously as a place for Catholic worship and ancient Maya rituals. The exterior steps, which possess a privileged perch over the town of Chichicastenango, are believed to represent the 18 months of the Maya calendar. Today, these steps are constantly in use as an altar for Maya prayer and offerings. It was in the attached convent that the oldest known version of the Popol Vuh was discovered. See p. 207.
- **Museo de Arte** (San Salvador, El Salvador): This 2,267-sq.-m (24,400-sq.-ft.), six-room museum of rotating and permanent exhibits offers the visitor an insightful, visual glimpse into the character of the country. Exceptionally interesting is the art of the country's civil war period. Museo de Arte de El Salvador also features the famous towering stone mosaic Monument to The Revolution, which depicts a naked man whose outstretched arms are thought to symbolize freedom and liberty. See p. 241.
- **Chiminike** (Tegucigalpa, Honduras): This modish children's museum in the country's capital isn't shy about making sure kids are entertained: a human body room complete with fart sounds, a crawl through an intestinal tract, and a graffiti prone VW Beetle are all on exhibit. Kids might not realize it, but

every quirk is part of the museum's ingenious way to get young people to learn. See p. 334.

- **Antiguo Convento San Francisco** (Granada, Nicaragua): Though the Antiguo Convento San Francisco has a remarkable collection of pre-Colombian statues, it's not the only attraction in this beautiful city. One great way to see all the sites, including the Antiguo Convento, is to take a horse-and-carriage ride through Granada's charming cobbled streets. See p. 477.
- **Museo Nacional de Costa Rica** (San José, Costa Rica): In addition to housing a comprehensive collection of historical and archaeological artifacts, Costa Rica's National Museum occupies a former army barracks that was the scene of fighting during the civil war of 1948. The exterior of the building still shows the pockmarks from bullets used in the street battles of the country's last civil war. See p. 555.
- **Miraflores Visitors Center** (Canal Zone, Panama): This top-notch museum is the best land-based platform from which to see the Panama Canal at work. The four-floor museum features an interactive display, a theater, and exhibits providing information about the canal's history and its impact on world trade. Helpful information is provided in English and Spanish, and the museum is well organized and maintained. Best of all are the excellent views of gigantic cargo ships transiting the canal. See p. 673.

7 THE BEST SMALL & MODERATELY PRICED HOTELS

- **San Pedro Holiday Hotel** (Ambergris Caye, Belize; ✆ **501/226-2014;** www.sanpedroholiday.com): This brilliantly white three-building complex with painted purple and pink trim sits in the center of San Pedro town. This was the first hotel on Ambergris Caye when Celi McCorkle opened it over 40 years ago, and it's still one of the best. Grab a room with an oceanview balcony and you'll be in tropical vacation heaven. See p. 116.
- **Tree Tops Guest House** (Caye Caulker, Belize; ✆ **501/226-0240;** www.treetopsbelize.com): While the best rooms here actually fall into the moderately priced category (and are some of the best rooms on Caye Caulker), the whole place offers such good value for your money that it's getting a listing here. See p. 128.
- **La Casa del Mundo** (Jaibalito, Lake Atitlán, Guatemala; ✆ **502/5218-5332;** www.lacasadelmundo.com): Set atop an isolated rocky outcropping jutting into Lake Atitlán, this hotel offers a few rooms with shared bathrooms that are a real steal (even the ones with private bathrooms are a bargain), with stupendous views of the lake. A lakeside fire-heated Jacuzzi and several open-air terraces make this place really special. See p. 198.
- **Casa Mañen** (Quetzaltenango, Guatemala; ✆ **502/7765-0786;** www.comeseeit.com): This is my favorite hotel in Quetzaltenango. The rooms are all decorated with a range of local arts and craft works, the service is excellent, and the owners are very knowledgeable about the various local tour options. The large rooftop terrace offers wonderful panoramic views of the city. See p. 205.
- **Los Almendros de San Lorenzo** (Suchitoto, El Salvador; ✆ **503/2335-1200;** www.hotelsalvador.com): This six-room Suchitoto hotel is a rare taste

of luxury in a rural mountain village. It's owned by former Paris fashion convention organizer Pascal Lebailly, who spent 17 months with 30 workers transforming a 200-year-old house into an oasis of style. He applied his eye for fashion to create an interior-design that's magazine-ready, with a gorgeously lit stone pool, glass-enclosed French restaurant, and walls filled with some of El Salvador's best art. You won't find a more romantic or casually elegant hotel in the country. See p. 285.

- **The Lodge at Pico Bonito** (La Ceiba, Honduras; © **888/428-0221;** www.picobonito.com): While you can tour the wonderful Parque Nacional Pico Bonito near La Ceiba in a number of ways, few would argue that one of the best is by staying at luxurious Pico Bonito Lodge. This property has its own set of trails, a butterfly farm, a resort-style pool, spa facilities, and a gourmet restaurant, in addition to great rooms. Guided hikes bring you through former cacao fields, across several levels of tropical forest, and to swimming holes and waterfalls that are ideal for taking soaks in. See p. 389.
- **La Posada Azul** (San Juan del Sur, Nicaragua; © **505/568-2524;** www.laposadaazul.com): This delightful boutique hotel will make you feel like you've stepped into a García Márquez novel—it's old-school charm is that authentic. High ceilings grace neat wooden interiors and an old-world living room, and a veranda runs the length of the house to a lovely flower garden with a fountain and small pool. See p. 498.
- **Hotel Grano de Oro** (San José, Costa Rica; © **2255-3322;** www.hotelgranodeoro.com): San José boasts dozens of old homes that have been converted into hotels, but few offer the plush accommodations or professional service found at the Grano de Oro. All the guest rooms have attractive hardwood furniture, including old-fashioned wardrobes in some rooms. When it's time to relax, you can soak in a hot tub or have a drink in the rooftop lounge while taking in San José's commanding view. See p. 562.
- **Amor de Mar** (Montezuma, Costa Rica; ©/fax **2642-0262;** www.amordemar.com): Clean, spacious, and comfortable rooms set on a sloping lawn that leads down to a rocky coastline, with a natural pool carved into the rocks, all add up to my idea of a tropical paradise. What's more: you get this all at a great price. See p. 590.
- **Arco Iris Lodge** (Monteverde, Costa Rica; © **2645-5067;** www.arcoirislodge.com): This small lodge is right in Santa Elena, and it's by far the best deal in the Monteverde area. The rooms are cozy and immaculate, and the owners are extremely knowledgeable and helpful. See p. 599.
- **The Coffee Estate Inn** (Boquete, Panama; © **720-2211;** www.coffeeestateinn.com): Gorgeous views of Volcán Barú, cozy bungalows with full kitchens, and owner-managed, friendly service tailored to your needs are the hallmarks of the Coffee Estate Inn. The bungalows are enveloped in native forest, fruit trees, and flowers that attract myriad birds. The romantic ambience is ideal for honeymooners. See p. 689.

8 THE BEST LUXURY HOTELS & ECOLODGES

- **Turtle Inn** (Placencia, Belize; © **800/746-3743** in the U.S., or 501/824-4912; www.turtleinn.com): Building on the experience gained from his Blancaneaux Lodge, and constructing upon the ruins of a hotel destroyed by

Hurricane Iris, director Francis Ford Coppola has upped the ante on high-end beach hotels in Belize. The individual villas here are perhaps the most beautiful and luxurious in Belize. The hotel is set right on an excellent stretch of beach, and the service and dining are top-notch. See p. 147.

- **Chaa Creek** (Cayo District, Belize; ✆ **501/824-2037;** www.chaacreek.com): A pioneer nature lodge in Belize, this collection of individual and duplex cottages was also an innovator in the whole concept of rustic luxury. Cool terra-cotta tile floors, varnished wood, thatched roofs, and beautiful Guatemalan textiles and handicrafts are elegantly yet simply combined. The property is set on a steep hillside over the lovely Macal River. Service is very friendly and personable, and the lodge provides easy access to a wealth of natural adventures and ancient Maya wonders. See p. 137.
- **Mesón Panza Verde** (Antigua, Guatemala; ✆ **502/7832-1745;** www.panzaverde.com): This elegant and artistic Antigua hotel offers large suites and superb service, and one of the best restaurants in the country. The old building is loaded with artwork and interesting architectural details, and there's a wonderful, mazelike rooftop terrace with panoramic views. See p. 186.
- **Palacio de Doña Leonor** (Antigua, Guatemala; ✆ **502/7832-2281;** www.palaciodeleonor.com): Although it's located in an old colonial mansion—just off Antigua's main plaza—that once belonged to Pedro de Alvarado's daughter, this hotel also offers up all the modern conveniences you could ask for. The suites have massive flatscreen televisions and Jacuzzis. Yet, the decor and ambience is decidedly colonial and decadent. See p. 186.
- **Hotel Atitlán** (Panajachel, Guatemala; ✆ **502/7762-1441;** www.hotelatitlan.com): This fabulous hotel is set on the shores of Lake Atitlán, with a stunning view of the lake and its surrounding volcanoes. Beautiful rooms, lush gardens, ample amenities, impeccable service, and a great restaurant make this a complete package. See p. 196.
- **Las Olas Beach House** (Balsamo Coast, El Salvador; ✆ **503/2411-7553**): If you like the ocean and adventure, Los Olas Beach House along El Salvador's gorgeous Balsamo Coast is for you. This upscale adventure resort is perched atop a rocky cliff rising from the Pacific with unrivaled ocean views, a cliff-side infinity pool, and an excellent restaurant. But what really makes this place special are the English-peaking owners and managers who live the life they sell. They will take you surfing, snorkeling, sea kayaking, and off-road motorcycling, as well as on more sedate hiking and horseback riding tours. See p. 302.
- **Hotel Telamar** (Tela, Honduras; ✆ **504/269-4414;** www.hoteltelamar.com): This neighborhood of pastel-colored stilted villas formerly owned by Tela Railroad Company executives is situated on Tela's best beach. They recently added a few posh buildings with hotel-style rooms, a few restaurants, and a 90m-long (300-ft.) pool, transforming it into Tela's first resort. Even the old villas have been remodeled and are being rented out. See p. 378.
- **Hotel Plaza Colon** (Granada, Nicaragua; ✆ **505/552-8489;** www.hotelplazacolon.com): The Plaza Colon hits just the right balance between exuding colonial authenticity and matching the modern traveler's expectations. A wide, polished balcony overlooks the boisterous plaza, and exquisite tiled floors lead

to a majestic inner balcony that runs around a glorious courtyard and blue mosaic pool. Everything is luxurious and elegant, and the service is prompt and reliable. See p. 479.

- **La Perla** (León, Nicaragua; ✆ **505/311-3125;** www.laperlaleon.com): La Perla sets a new standard for accommodations in Nicaragua, with impeccable rooms and a palatial interior boasting high ceilings, a spectacular central courtyard, and contemporary Nicaraguan art. See p. 467.
- **Four Seasons Resort Costa Rica** (Papagayo Peninsula, Costa Rica; ✆ **800/819-5053** or 2696-0000; www.fourseasons.com/costarica): This was the first major resort to really address the high-end luxury market in Costa Rica. Within its first month of operation, Michael Jordan and Madonna were notable guests. A beautiful setting, wonderful installations, a world-class golf course, and stellar service continue to make this the current king of the hill in the upscale market. See p. 588.
- **Flor Blanca Resort** (Playa Santa Teresa, Costa Rica; ✆ **2640-0232;** www.florblanca.com): The individual villas at this intimate resort are some of the largest and most luxurious in the country. The service and food are outstanding, and the location is breathtaking, spread over a lushly planted hillside steps away from Playa Santa Teresa. See p. 588.
- **Arenas del Mar** (Manuel Antonio, Costa Rica; ✆/fax **2777-2777;** www.arenasdelmar.com): With large and ample rooms, excellent service and amenities, a beautiful little spa, and arguably the best beach access and location in Manuel Antonio, this hotel has a lot to offer. See p. 618.
- **The Bristol Panama** (Panama City, Panama; ✆ **265-7844**): This hotel exudes buttoned-up luxury with its conservative decor, but the ambience at the Bristol somehow manages to feel cozy rather than stuffy. The Bristol is particularly known for its bend-over-backwards service and fine dining at Las Barandas Restaurant. See p. 663.
- **Canopy Tower** (Soberanía National Park, Panama; ✆ **264-5720**): Birders flock to this ecolodge for its focus on bird-watching and its location in a habitat that's friendly to a wide range of species. The Canopy Tower, a remodeled military radar station in thick jungle, is a cross between a stylish B&B and a scientific research center. It's just 25 minutes from Panama City but feels worlds away, and the 360-degree observation deck here provides stunning views and a platform with scopes. See p. 679.

9 THE BEST LOCAL DINING EXPERIENCES

- **Rojo Lounge** (Ambergris Caye, Belize; ✆ **501/226-4012**): The folks at Azul Resort, an isolated little place on Northern Ambergris Caye, serve very creative and well-prepared fusion cuisine, in a relaxed and inviting open-air ambience. The menu features some of the more creative fusion items to be had on the island—no mean feat given the competition—and there are also nightly specials. See p. 120.
- **The French Connection** (Placencia, Belize; ✆ **501/523-3656**): This place created an immediate buzz when it first opened in Placencia, and quickly outgrew its first location. At once elegant and relaxed, the food here is a creative take on contemporary bistro fare. See p. 149.
- **Tamarindos** (Guatemala City, Guatemala; ✆ **502/2360-2815**): The chef at this trendy Zona Viva restaurant is

wowing Guatemala City with her eclectic fusion cooking. It's easy to overdo or miscalculate when combining ingredients and techniques from various world cuisines, but Tamarindos hits all the right notes. The menu is long, and touches many bases, with culinary influences from Asia, Italy, and many places in between. Be sure to ask about daily specials, as this is where the chef really shines. See p. 175.

- **Kacao** (Guatemala City, Guatemala; ✆ **502/2237-4188** or 2377-4189): This popular restaurant takes Guatemalan cuisine and polishes it up a bit. The cooking is fairly traditional, with signature dishes from around the country, but the service, ambience, and presentation are far more refined than you'll find at almost any other place specializing in Chapin cuisine. Although they do a brisk lunch business, I prefer to come for dinner, when the thatch roof is illuminated by candles and other strategically placed lighting. See p. 175.
- **Alo Nuestro** (San Salvador, El Salvador; ✆ **503/2223-5116**): San Salvador is packed with excellent restaurants offering cuisines from around the world. But even in that crowded market, Alo Nuestro stands out for its simply delicious food. The restaurant has been open since 1999 and has built a quiet word-of-mouth following among locals and international travelers. The frequently changing menu is a fusion of San Salvador's many ethnic restaurants, with an emphasis on local ingredients. The service is top-notch and the ambience is formal but comfortable. See p. 251.
- **Hacienda San Lucas** (Copán Ruinas, Honduras; ✆ **504/651-4495;** www.haciendasanlucas.com): On a hillside overlooking the Copán valley, this rustic 100-year-old, family-owned hacienda dishes out an authentic Maya Chortí five-course candlelit dinner focusing on fresh, local ingredients. Their tamales, corn chowder, and fire-roasted chicken with *adobo* sauce do not disappoint. See p. 363.
- **El Colibri** (San Juan del Sur, Nicaragua; ✆ **505/863-8612**): Set within a funky colored clapboard house with a large veranda overlooking a lovely garden, this enchanting restaurant is a piece of art put together from recycled materials. Mosaic-framed mirrors hang between stained-glass lamps and African face masks, while small colored stones hold down your place mats lest the sea breeze carry them away. The international, mostly organic fare, is a work of art, too. See p. 500.
- **La Casita** (Estelí, Nicaragua; ✆ **505/713-4917**): At this part-farmhouse restaurant and part coffeehouse, you can enjoy great local coffee, fresh bread, cheeses, and yogurts in a garden by a beautiful stream with relaxing music in the background. Also on sale are local crafts and herbal medicines. See p. 534.
- **Grano de Oro Restaurant** (San José, Costa Rica; ✆ **2255-3322**): This stylish little hotel has an elegant restaurant serving delicious Continental dishes and decadent desserts. The open-air seating in the lushly planted central courtyard is delightful, especially for lunch. See p. 568.
- **Playa de los Artistas** (Montezuma, Costa Rica; ✆ **2642-0920**): This place is the perfect blend of refined cuisine and beachside funkiness. There are only a few tables, so make sure you get here early. Fresh, grilled seafood is served in oversize ceramic bowls and on large wooden slabs lined with banana leaves. See p. 591.
- **La Pecora Nera** (Puerto Viejo, Costa Rica; ✆ **2750-0490**): I'm not sure that a tiny surfer town on the remote Caribbean coast of Costa Rica deserves such fine Italian food, but it's got it. Your best bet here is to allow yourself to be

taken on a culinary roller-coaster ride with a mixed feast of the chef's nightly specials and suggestions. See p. 632.

- **Panamonte Inn Restaurant** (Boquete, Panama; ✆ **720-1324**): This sanctuary of gourmet cuisine is located within the clapboard walls of the oldest hotel in Boquete. The food is inventive and consistently good, and service is attentive and courteous. You can bypass their more formal dining area for a comfy seat in their fireside bar and still order off the main menu. See p. 692.

10 THE BEST MARKETS & SHOPS

- **Nim Po't** (Antigua, Guatemala): A massive indoor space with a soaring ceiling houses this local craft-and-textile cooperative warehouse. Textiles, woodcarvings, and ceramic wares from across the country are available here. The quality varies greatly, but if you know what to look for, you can find some fine works without having to venture into the farther reaches of rural Guatemala. See p. 185.
- **Chichicastenango's Market** (Chichicastenango, Guatemala): Guatemala's Maya people are world-famous for their incredible arts and crafts, which they sell predominantly at local and regional open-air markets. There's a reason Chichi's twice-weekly open-air market is so famous. The abundance and variety of wares for sale and the semicontrolled frenzy of the entire operation are not to be missed. You may find better bargains and products around the country, but you'll never see so much in one place at one time. See p. 206.
- **Diconte Artisans Shop** (Ataco, El Salvador): This five-room shop in the town of Ataco along the Rutas de Las Flores offers unique whimsical paintings, woodcarvings, and crafts in the surrealistic style of Ataco's two main artists, as well as a room full of colorful textiles made on-site by artisans working five old-style looms. You can also watch the artisans work from the shade of a small garden-side coffee and dessert cafe here. See p. 272.
- **Mercado Central** (San Salvador, El Salvador): Mercado Central near San Salvador's central plaza is the antimercado. It's a sprawling, seemingly chaotic warren of shouting vendors, blaring horns, and old women in traditional clothes chopping vegetables in the street. Its biggest attraction is that it's *not* an attraction. Instead, it's the place to visit if you want to see a slice of unfiltered El Salvadorian life. See p. 246.
- **Guamilito Market** (San Pedro Sula, Honduras): Products from around the country, as well as El Salvador and Guatemala, fill up literally hundreds of small stalls at this market. You'll find everything from hammocks, T-shirts, and Lenca pottery to cigars, Maya figurines, jewelry, coffee, Garífuna coconut carvings, and tortilla stands. See p. 346.
- **Mercado Viejo** (Massaya, Nicaragua): The Gothic, palm-lined walls of Masaya's block-size Old Market offer an endless array of tempting souvenirs such as intricate pottery, handsome woodcarvings, sturdy leather ware, and beautiful hand-woven hammocks. They are all made in the surrounding city and hilltop villages known as Pueblos Blancos. See p. 489.
- **Galería Namu** (San José, Costa Rica): This is my favorite gallery and gift shop in downtown San Jose, with an excellent collection of art and craft selections. These folks specialize in finding some of the better and more obscure

works done by Costa Rica's indigenous communities. See p. 560.

- **Mercado de Mariscos** (Calidonia, Panama City): This bustling market is *the* distribution headquarters for fresh seafood from the Pacific and the Caribbean. Even if you're not here to buy any fish, this is a fascinating place to see the everyday hustle and bustle of a typical Panamanian market and check out the often weird and mysterious seafood selection. You can get some of the best seviche in the city from vendors located at the entrance to the market. The Mercado de Mariscos Restaurant on the second level serves tasty and authentic seafood dishes. See p. 661.

11 THE BEST OF CENTRAL AMERICA ONLINE

Below are some good Internet sources for each country, along with the recommendations on sites that cover the region in general. Each chapter in this book has more country-specific websites.

COUNTRY-SPECIFIC SITES

- **www.toucantrail.com**: This is an excellent site about Belize geared toward budget travelers, with extensive links and comprehensive information.
- **www.travelbelize.org**: This is the official site of the Belize Tourist Board. It has its fair share of information and links, although you'll probably end up being directed to other sites.
- **www.revuemag.com**: This is an excellent Guatemalan-based English-language monthly magazine geared toward tourists and expatriates. The entire magazine, as well as past issues, is available online.
- **www.xelawho.com**: A slightly irreverent English-language magazine produced in Quetzaltenango, Guatemala, and directed at the town's large population of foreign-language students, this site has honest reviews and a wealth of useful information.
- **www.corsatur.gob.sv**: This great English-language website groups information about El Salvador's attractions into the headings of nature/adventure/culture/and the beach. The site also provides a country map outlining El Salvador's 14 departments with demographic information for each.
- **www.letsgohonduras.com**: This is the official site of the Honduras Tourist Board. It has a variety of roundup articles that are good for planning, and lists a decent range of basic information on the major towns, attractions, and national parks in the country.
- **www.intur.gob.ni** and **www.visitanicaragua.com**: The Nicaragua Tourist Board, or NTB, has two sites that are entirely in Spanish, with very limited information but some gorgeous imagery.
- **www.vianica.com**: This independent site about Nicaragua is much more informative than other sites and has data in English on the country, as well as some nifty features such as distance calculators and wildlife lists with photos.
- **www.ticotimes.net**: The English-language *Tico Times* makes it easy for *norteamericanos* (and other English speakers) to see what's happening in Costa Rica. It features the top story from its weekly print edition, as well as a daily update of news briefs, a business article, regional news, a fishing column, and travel reviews. There's also a link to current currency-exchange rates.
- **www.panamainfo.com**: This excellent website provides hotel, restaurant, and attraction information, as well as information on retiring, living, and doing business in Panama.

- **www.visitpanama.com**: The Panamanian Institute of Tourism regularly updates this website, which provides culture, history, and destination-specific information.

CENTRAL AMERICAN SITES

- **www.latinworld.com**: This is a search engine specializing in Central America, providing information, resource links, and other websites.
- **www.latinamericabureau.org**: An independent website promoting better awareness of Central America, especially regarding human rights.
- **www.planeta.com**: This site deals with ecotourism and has some excellent content regarding Central America, including a directory of ecofriendly hotels and travel agencies.
- **www.bbc.co.uk**: The British broadcaster has an excellent world service section that covers in detail past and current affairs in the Americas.
- **www.lcweb2.loc.gov**: The library of Congress has detailed profiles of each country, including history and culture.
- **www.oas.org**: The Organization of American States is about the closest you will get to unity in the region. This site is not just for political animals but worth visiting for updates on ongoing issues and up-and-coming cultural events throughout the region.
- **www.lanic.utexas.edu**: The Latin America Network Information Center is a University of Texas initiative that provides an extensive directory and database. Primarily used for academic research, it also facilitates education programs.
- **www.alfatravelguide.com**: A small independent website that gives good listings for hotels and travel agents all over Central America, including contact information.
- **http://lanic.utexas.edu/la/ca**: This site houses a vast collection of information about Central America, and is hands-down the best one-stop shop for browsing, with helpful links to a diverse range of tourism and general information sites.

2

Central America in Depth

When one thinks of Central America, a region that comprises a jumble of countries along a slim, rugged isthmus connecting the two colossal continents of North and South America, what might first come to mind is the jungle. Add its standing as a tropical dead-end zone to its tumultuous history of war, poverty, crime and corruption, and natural disasters and it's no wonder the region has often been overlooked as a travel destination. Yet in the past few years, Central America has finally begun to step out of the shade and into the sunlight. As more and more travelers head to the region, it's becoming recognized as a safe and adventurous getaway, one that just happens to have a sorry knack for getting bad press.

Now for some good press: The region has a diverse climate and geography that offers everything from sun-kissed Caribbean islands to lush cloud forests. It also has a rich native-Indian heritage, mixed with a history of ostentatious Spanish colonialism, both of which have led to a vibrant music-and-art scene that frequently spills out onto the streets in the form of festivals and parades. But perhaps the region's biggest asset is its friendly, kind-hearted people, who may not have much but insist of sharing it with others anyway.

It's also now easier and more comfortable than ever to travel around the region. In the past few years, as millions of visitors have discovered this gem of a destination, airline links have improved drastically and some first-rate ecolodges and mountain refuges have opened up. If you are no longer content with just a pool and beach, and want to climb volcanoes, hike through rainforests, visit towering Maya ruins, take Spanish classes, volunteer, and go scuba diving and surfing—in addition to lounging by some stellar pools and beaches—Central America will not disappoint.

1 CENTRAL AMERICA IN 2 WEEKS OR MORE

Two weeks will fly by when you're traveling around Central America. Though it is possible to visit three to four countries in this time frame, you will unfortunately have to sacrifice some amazing places on the way. Below are two suggested itineraries, one visiting the northern four countries and the second touring the southern three. There are of course numerous other combinations for tours in the region—you might want to mix and match the suggestions below to create your own itinerary. The following itineraries were also designed with the presumption that you'll be taking private shuttles and taxis. Those on a tighter budget will have to slow right down, to allot more time for traveling between destinations.

Central America in 2 Weeks

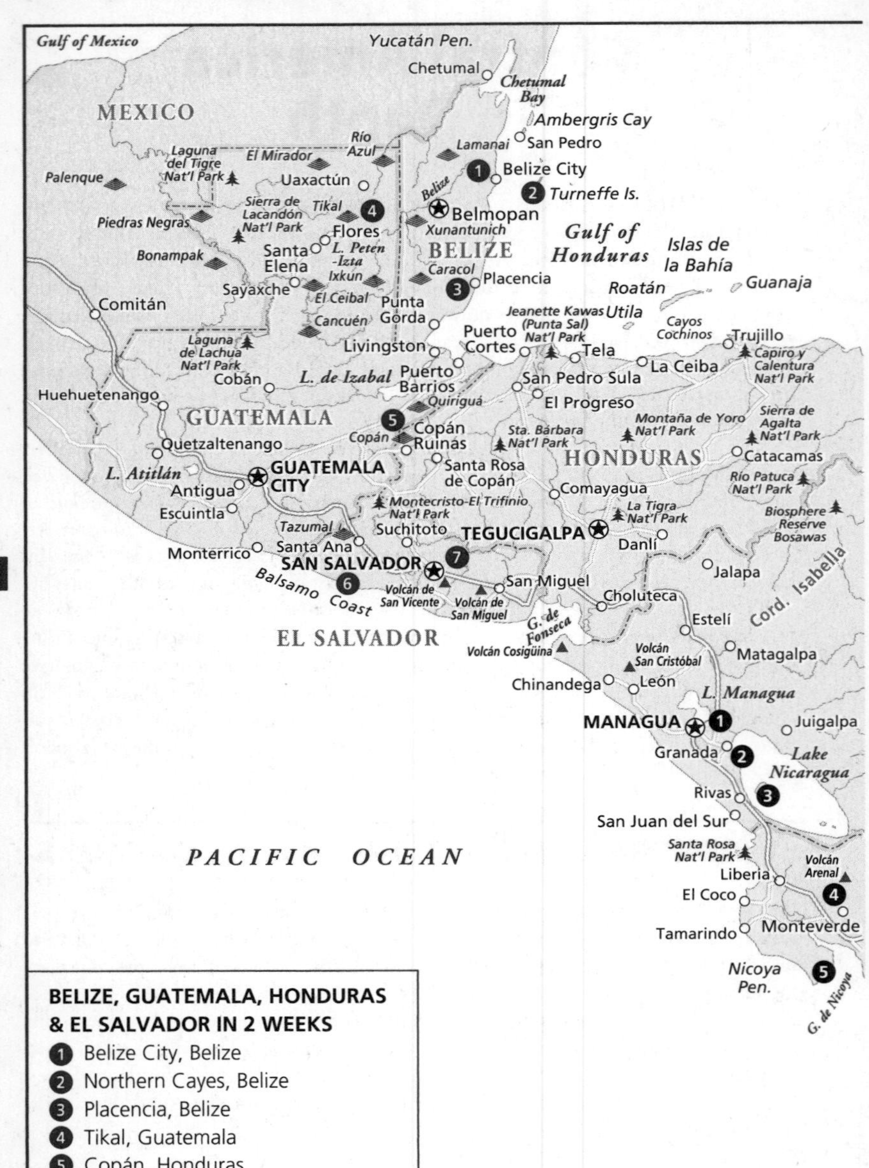

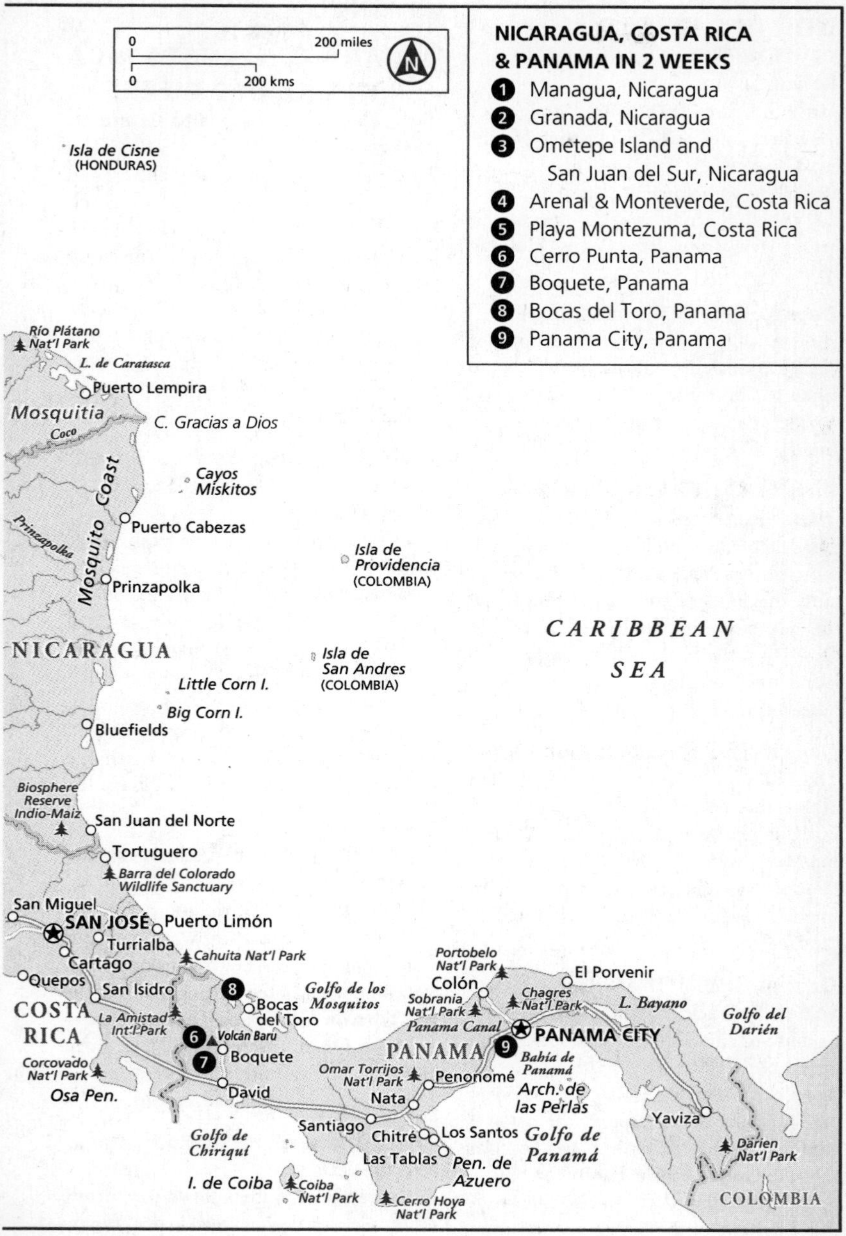

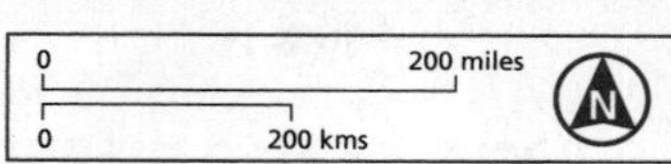

NICARAGUA, COSTA RICA & PANAMA IN 2 WEEKS

1. Managua, Nicaragua
2. Granada, Nicaragua
3. Ometepe Island and San Juan del Sur, Nicaragua
4. Arenal & Monteverde, Costa Rica
5. Playa Montezuma, Costa Rica
6. Cerro Punta, Panama
7. Boquete, Panama
8. Bocas del Toro, Panama
9. Panama City, Panama

Isla de Cisne
(HONDURAS)
Río Plátano Nat'l Park
L. de Caratasca
Puerto Lempira
Mosquitia
Coco
C. Gracias a Dios
Cayos Miskitos
Mosquito Coast
Puerto Cabezas
Prinzapolka
Prinzapolka
Isla de Providencia
(COLOMBIA)
CARIBBEAN SEA
NICARAGUA
Isla de San Andres
(COLOMBIA)
Little Corn I.
Big Corn I.
Bluefields
Biosphere Reserve Indio-Maiz
San Juan del Norte
Tortuguero
Barra del Colorado Wildlife Sanctuary
San Miguel
SAN JOSÉ
Puerto Limón
Turrialba
Cahuita Nat'l Park
Cartago
Quepos
San Isidro
COSTA RICA
La Amistad Int'l Park
Corcovado Nat'l Park
Osa Pen.
Volcán Baru
Boquete
David
Bocas del Toro
Golfo de los Mosquitos
Portobelo Nat'l Park
Colón
El Porvenir
Sobrania Nat'l Park
Chagres Nat'l Park
L. Bayano
Panama Canal
PANAMA CITY
Golfo del Darién
PANAMA
Bahía de Panamá
Omar Torrijos Nat'l Park
Penonomé
Arch. de las Perlas
Nata
Santiago
Chitré
Los Santos
Las Tablas
Pen. de Azuero
Golfo de Panamá
Golfo de Chiriquí
I. de Coiba
Coiba Nat'l Park
Cerro Hoya Nat'l Park
Yaviza
Darien Nat'l Park
COLOMBIA

BELIZE, GUATEMALA, HONDURAS & EL SALVADOR IN 2 WEEKS

Days ❶ & ❷: The Northern Cayes, Belize

Arrive in Belize City and head straight for the beach, in this case the pristine Northern Cayes, where you can spend 2 days snorkeling with friendly sharks in Shark-Ray Alley. Then enjoy the spectacular ocean view from **San Pedro Holiday Hotel** (p. 116).

Days ❸, ❹ & ❺: Placencia, Belize

Head south to the hip little beach town of Placencia. Soak up some rays on this white sandy paradise and feel like a film star by staying at Francis Ford Coppola's **Turtle Inn** (p. 147).

Days ❻, ❼ & ❽: The Maya Ruins of Tikal, Guatemala

Tan suitably topped, it's now time to grab some culture. Take a taxi from Belize and cross the border into Guatemala. Enjoy the awe-inspiring temples of Tikal and then go on a sunset cruise around the island town of Flores. See chapter 5 for hotel recommendations in the area.

Days ❾, ❿ & ⓫: Copán, Honduras

The laid-back colonial town of Copán across the border in Honduras offers intriguing ruins regarded as the "Paris of the Maya world," as well as hot springs, a famous cigar factory, **Flor de Copán** (p. 367), and an excellent boutique resort, the **Hacienda San Lucas** (p. 363).

Days ⓬, ⓭ & ⓮: The Balsamo Coast to San Salvador, El Salvador

Round your holiday off with some more beach bliss, this time Pacific side, at El Salvador's Playa los Cóbanas. Here you can go scuba diving around the colorful tropical reef before retiring to the cliff-top **Las Olas Beach House** (p. 302). Spend your final day enjoying the magnificent views of the Balsamo Coast from the cliff-side infinity pool, trying not to think of your flight home from San Salvador the next day.

NICARAGUA, COSTA RICA & PANAMA IN 2 WEEKS

Days ❶ & ❷: Managua to Granada, Nicaragua

Fly into Managua, but don't hang around the bewildering, shabby capital of Nicaragua—instead, depart right away to the radiant colonial city of Granada. Sip a rum on the rocks from the gigantic balcony of the **Hotel Plaza Colon** (p. 479) overlooking the colorful plaza. Catch a horse and carriage ride through the city's enchanting cobbled streets and take a short boat tour of **Las Isletas** archipelago.

Days ❸ & ❹: Tour Ometepe Island & Arrive in San Juan del Sur, Nicaragua

Take a day tour of the twin peak jungle island of Ometepe before transferring to the beach town of San Juan del Sur. Stay at the lovely villa known as **Posada Azul** (p. 498) and eat in the artful garden of **El Colibri** (p. 500). The following day, catch a water taxi up the coast to some beautiful, secluded beaches or, if your timing is right, opt for a night excursion to watch the spectacular turtle hatching in **Playa La Flor** (p. 497).

Days ❺ & ❻: Arenal & Monteverde, Costa Rica

Get up early to make the journey across the border to Costa Rica, where you can watch molten lava flowing from Arenal Volcano, while safely sitting poolside at the **Tabacón Grand Spa Thermal Resort** (p. 608). On your second day, take a day trip to the Monteverde Cloud Forest Reserve if you're feeling adventurous.

Days ❼, ❽ & ❾: Playa Montezuma, Costa Rica

Grab a cab and go south down the Nicoya Peninsula until you reach the funky, hippie hangout that is Playa Montezuma. Stay at the relaxing **Amor de Mar** (p. 590), which boasts beautiful gardens on the Pacific coast.

Days ⑩ & ⑪: The Quetzal Trail, Panama

Enough lazing around—it's time to cross the border into Panama and make your way to the town of **Cerro Punta.** Send your baggage on ahead while you take a 1-day hiking tour around the Barú Volcano through a tropical paradise known as the Quetzal Trail. Take a break and keep your eyes peeled for the beautiful but elusive bird of the same name. Catch up with your luggage at the town of Boquete and stay at the **Coffee Estate Inn** (p. 689), where you can relax in bungalows surrounded by romantic fruit gardens.

Days ⑫, ⑬ & ⑭: Bocas del Toro to Panama City, Panama

Nearby Boquete is the party-beach town of Bocas del Toro. Here you'll find excellent surfing on crystal blue Caribbean seas, and you can explore the nearby island utopias known as Cayos Zapatillas. Then retire to your thatched-roof lodge high up in the forest canopy at the **La Loma Jungle Lodge** (p. 697). The next day, transfer to Panama City for your flight home.

2 CENTRAL AMERICA PAST & PRESENT

The Americas were first populated by humans when Asians crossed the Bering straits into Alaska some 20,000 years ago. These tribes soon fanned southward and funneled into South America through the Central American isthmus. The period around 3000 B.C. saw the arrival of one of the greatest civilizations of the pre-Columbian New World, the Maya culture, which spread its influence from southern Mexico to El Salvador. By A.D. 750, 10 million Maya people lived in elaborate stone cities such as Tikal, Palenque, and Copán. Both savage and sophisticated, the Maya developed hieroglyphics and calendars yet were also fond of human sacrifice to appease the gods. Their empire mysteriously collapsed around A.D. 900. Drought, war, and overpopulation are blamed, but new theories for the civilization's demise appear all the time.

The Spanish came here in 1502 and they brought with them gunpowder, horses, and disease. In return, they discovered a paradise that became a living hell for its own people. By the time the conquistadors stepped off their boats, the great Maya cities had been abandoned and lost in the jungle and the population decimated into small, isolated tribes. These remaining scattered tribes put up some resistance, but were eventually subjugated and enslaved by the conquistadors.

Independence from Spain came in 1821, and the five states that existed then (Guatemala, El Salvador, Honduras, Nicaragua, and Costa Rica) were briefly united in a federation that eventually fell apart in 1838. What happened next—indigenous massacres, military dictatorships, left-wing revolutions, war, utter poverty, and blatant U.S. intervention—meant that the region remained united in misfortune only throughout much of the 19th and 20th centuries.

Peace treaties in the 1990s allowed for a new dawn of democracy in this region. Many ex-combatants from the right and left are now fighting out their differences on congress floors, rather than on city streets. The region is still dreadfully poor, however, and plagued with high unemployment, crime, and rampant corruption, not to mention earthquakes and hurricanes. Development continues at a slow pace. More and more people are abandoning subsistence farming and moving to the cities for low-paid factory jobs. Emigration north is often the only way to break

Maya History

Before the arrival of the first Europeans, Mesoamerica was the land of the ancient Maya. Here, mathematicians came up with the concept of zero, astronomers developed a solar calendar accurate to a single day every 6,000 days, and scribes invented an 850-word hieroglyphic vocabulary that scholars consider the world's first advanced writing system. Some of this civilization's practices were less than civil: The Maya built extensive ball courts to play a game called "pok a tok," where the losing team could be executed.

Evidence of human presence in the Maya region dates as far back as the 10th millennium B.C. Maya history is often divided into several distinct periods: Archaic (10,000–2000 B.C.), Pre-Classic (2000 B.C.–A.D. 250), Classic (A.D. 250–900), and Post-Classic (900–1540). Within this timeline, the Classic period itself is often divided into Early, Middle, Late, and Terminal stages. At the height of development, as many as 10 million Maya may have inhabited what are now Guatemala, Belize, Mexico's Yucatán Peninsula, and parts of Honduras and El Salvador. No one knows for sure what led to the decline of the Classic Maya, but somewhere around A.D. 900, their society entered a severe and rapid decline. Famine, warfare, deforestation, and religious prophecy have all been cited as possible causes. See Jared Diamond's bestseller *Collapse* (Penguin, 2005) for more information and speculation.

Unlike the Incas of Peru, the Maya had no centralized ruler. Instead, the civilization consisted of a series of independent city-states, usually ruled by hereditary kings, often at war with one another. The most famous city-state is Tikal, in the northern Petén region, whose massive stone temples are the principal draw for tourists in Guatemala. In A.D. 562, Tikal was defeated in battle by the kingdom of Caracol, in what is now the Cayo District of western Belize.

According to the Popol Vuh, the sacred Maya book of creation myths and predictions, the world as we know it will end on December 21, 2012. While some New Age analysts have dire predictions for the date, more optimistic prognosticators foresee a day of positive human evolution. Hotels around Tikal and other major Maya ceremonial sites are already booking up for this date.

free from the region's poverty, and many families are dependent on remittances from relatives in the United States. Some countries are doing much better than others, Costa Rica and Panama being the best examples. A real-estate and tourism boom there means more jobs but also raises some important questions about the state of the environment. Sustainable and ecofriendly tourism is often seen as Central America's greatest economic hope, and for good reason.

In this section, we´ll give you a little bit of background on the history and culture of the countries we cover in this guide. See the individual country chapters for more on both subjects.

BELIZE

A Look at the Past

Before the arrival of the first Europeans, Belize was a major part of the Maya Empire. River and coastal trade routes connected dozens of cities and small towns throughout Belize to each other and to major ceremonial and trading cities in Mexico and Guatemala. At the height of development, as many as two million Maya may have inhabited the region that is today known as Belize. No one knows for sure what led to the decline of the Classic Maya, but somewhere around A.D. 900, their society entered a severe and rapid decline. Nevertheless, Belize is somewhat unique in that it had several major ceremonial or trading cities still occupied by Maya when the first Spanish conquistadors arrived.

Christopher Columbus sailed past the Belize coast in 1502, but he never anchored or set foot ashore here, and the Spanish never had much success in colonizing Belize. In fact, they met with fierce resistance from the remaining Maya. Part of their problem may have come from Gonzalo Guerrero, a Spanish sailor who was shipwrecked off the coast of Belize and the Yucatán in the early years of the 16th century. Originally pressed into slavery, Guerrero eventually married the daughter of a Maya ruler, and became an important warrior and military advisor in the Maya battles with the Spanish. Though the Spanish led various attacks and attempts at conquest and control of the territory that is present-day Belize, by the mid-1600s, they were forced to abandon all permanent settlements and attempts at colonialism in the country, and began concentrating their efforts on more productive regions around Central and South America and the Caribbean Sea.

The lack of Spanish colonial might left the door pretty wide open in Belize, and an assortment of pirates, buccaneers, and other unsavory characters were among the first to fill that void and make this their base of operations. These pirates and buccaneers used the Belize coastline and its protected anchorages as hide-outs and bases following attacks on Spanish fleets transporting gold and silver treasures from their more productive colonies.

By the mid–17th century, British loggers were settling along the coast and making their way up the rivers and streams in search of mahogany for shipbuilding and other types of wood for making dyes. Proud and independent, these early settlers called themselves "Baymen" (after the Bay of Honduras). Politically, the Baymen treaded a delicate balance between being faithful British subjects and fiercely independent settlers. A steady stream of Spanish attacks, however, forced the Baymen to seek more and more support from the British. Diplomatic and military give and take between Spain and Britain ensued until 1798, when the Baymen won a decisive military victory over a larger Spanish fleet, just off the shores of St. George's Caye. The Battle of St. George's Caye effectively ended all Spanish involvement and claim to Belize, and it solidified Belize's standing within the British Empire.

In 1862, with more or less the same borders it has today, Belize was formally declared the colony of British Honduras. This small colonial outpost became a major source of hardwood and dyewood for the still-expanding British Empire. The forests were exploited, and agriculture was never really encouraged. The British wanted their colony to remain dependent on the mother country, so virtually all the necessities of life were imported.

Throughout the 18th and 19th centuries, African slaves were brought to British Honduras. The slave period was marked by several revolts and uprisings. Black Caribs, today known as Garífuna, migrated here from the Bay Islands of Honduras, although they originally hail from the Caribbean island of St. Vincent. Beginning in the early 1800s, the Garífuna established their own villages along the southern coast.

Moreover, during the mid–19th century, many Mexican and Guatemalan refugees of the bloody Caste Wars fled across the borders into British Honduras and founded such towns as Corozal and Benque Viejo. Further waves of Guatemalan, El Salvadoran, and Honduran refugees, who were fleeing civil wars and right-wing death squads, immigrated to Belize during the 1970s and 1980s.

In the early 1960s, groundwork was laid by the People's United Party (PUP) for granting British Honduras independence. In 1973, the country's name was officially changed to Belize. However, it was not until September 21, 1981, that Belize finally gained its independence, making it Central America's newest nation. The delay was primarily due to Guatemala's claim on the territory. Fearful of an invasion by Guatemalan forces, the British delayed granting full independence until an agreement could be reached with Guatemala. Although to this day no final agreement has actually been inked, tensions cooled enough to allow for the granting of full sovereignty in 1981. The country is still a member of the Commonwealth.

Belize Today

Belize is a developing nation, plagued with a small economy, a tiny industrial base, a huge trade deficit, and a historic dependence on foreign aid. These problems have been compounded by the British pullout and a universal reduction of international largesse. Sugar and citrus are the principal cash crops, though bananas and seafood exports also help. However, tourism is the most promising emergent source of income, and it has become an important engine in the economy. This trend is sure to continue.

Belize held its first parliamentary elections in 1984. Since then, power has ping-ponged back and forth between the United Democratic Party (UDP) and the People's United Party (PUP). The former is a more conservative, free-market oriented party, while the latter champions a more liberal, social-democratic agenda. In the August 1998 elections, PUP won 26 of the 29 parliamentary seats, while the UDP managed to win just three. However, by 2005 discontent with the PUP over tax increases and money mismanagement had grown widespread and there were even some public demonstrations and disturbances. The UDP pummeled them in 2006 municipal elections, and again in the 2008 national elections, electing Dean Barrow as the country's first black prime minister, and maintaining a strong majority of parliamentary seats.

It was big news when oil was discovered near the Mennonite community of Spanish Lookout in 2005. Currently, some 5,000 barrels of oil are being extracted each day. This matches the nation's daily import of crude oil. And, it is projected that as many as 50,000 barrels may someday be produced.

GUATEMALA

A Look at the Past

Much of Guatemala's early history was lived by the Maya, and they've left ample legacy in words, artifacts and stone. You'll see the evidence of this legacy all over Guatemala, particularly in the great ceremonial city of Tikal. See p. 22 for more information on the Maya.

While Christopher Columbus never set foot on Guatemala, his oversight did not save the country from Spanish conquest. Conquistador Pedro de Alvarado was sent by Hernán Cortés to Guatemala in 1523. In a ruthless campaign, Alvarado pitted different Maya tribes against each other, and then turned on his unwitting accomplices. According to legend, when Alvarado killed the Quiché king Tecún Umán at the Battle of Quetzaltenango in 1524, the quetzal (Guatemala's national bird) swooped down into the vast pools of blood and gained its red breast.

By 1525, Alvarado had completely subdued the western highlands, but the Spanish subsequently met with fierce resistance from many Maya tribes. Multiple invasions of the Petén failed, and the Kekchí in the central highlands held out as well. Unable to control the Kekchí by force, the Spanish allowed a group of Franciscan friars under the leadership of Fray Bartolomé de las Casas to attempt the "humane" conversion of the tribe to Christianity. The friars succeeded, the population converted, and the area was given its Spanish name, "Verapaz" or "true peace." A human rights advocate until his death, Las Casas also successfully convinced the Spanish crown to pass the *New Laws* in 1542, awarding some basic protections to the *indígenas.*

During Spanish colonial rule, Guatemala was a Captaincy General, part of the Viceroyalty of New Spain. The Spanish established Guatemala's capital at Ciudad Vieja in 1527, but moved to what is now Antigua (then called Santiago de Guatemala) in 1543 after the old capital was buried in a massive mudslide from the Volcán de Agua. For 200 years, Antigua was the center of political and religious power of the entire "Audiencia de Guatemala," including the provinces of Costa Rica, Nicaragua, El Salvador, Honduras, and Chiapas in Mexico. After severe earthquakes ravaged Antigua in 1773, the crown decided to move the capital to safer ground, and chose the site of the ancient city of Kaminal Juyú, today's Guatemala City.

In colonial society, racial divisions were enshrined in law. *Peninsulares,* or Spanish-born Spaniards living in the New World, were at the top of the economic and political pyramid, followed by *criollos* (descendants of Spaniards born in the New World), *mestizos* (of mixed Spanish and Amerindian ancestry), *mulattos* (mixed Spanish and black), Amerindians, *zambos* (mixed Amerindian and black), and blacks. Individuals from the latter three groups were often enslaved outright.

Discontent with the exclusive rule of *peninsulares* reached a boiling point in the early 19th century, and a mood of reform swept across New Spain. Most of the fighting for independence took place in Mexico, where an unlikely coalition of conservatives and liberals eventually prevailed.

On September 15, 1821, Gabino Gainza, the captain general of Central America, signed the Act of Independence, breaking the region's ties with Spain. By 1840, the Central American Federation had dissolved in civil war, instigated by the conservative dictators who had seized power in most of the nations, such as Rafael Carrera, a charismatic 23-year-old swineherd-turned-highwayman who, in Guatemala in 1838, raised an army, seized control, declared Guatemala independent, and promptly reversed decades of liberal reforms. With the adoption of a constitution in 1851, Carrera officially became independent Guatemala's first president.

Over the course of the next century, power continued to change hands by military rather than democratic means. Liberal reformers traded off with conservative reactionaries, but one entity saw its influence grow fairly consistently: the United Fruit Company. United Fruit, nicknamed "El Pulpo" (The Octopus) for its sweeping influence, first arrived in Guatemala in 1901, when it purchased a small tract of land to grow bananas. The company built its own port, Puerto Barrios, and after being awarded a railway concession leading inland from the port, had a virtual monopoly on long-distance transportation in the country. United Fruit's rise to prominence coincided with the successive and enduring dictatorships of Manuel José Estrada Cabrera and Jorge Ubico. Collectively, these two men ruled, with great deference to United Fruit Company, from 1898 to 1941.

In 1941, a band of disgruntled military men, joined by students, labor leaders, and liberal political forces, overthrew Ubico, and ushered in a period popularly referred to as "The Ten Years of Spring." Marked by moves to encourage free speech and liberal reforms, this time saw the election of Guatemala's first civilian president of modern times, Juan José Arévalo.

In 1951, Guatemala held its first-ever universal-suffrage election, bringing retired army colonel and political reformer Jacobo Arbenz to power. Confronting a vast gap between rich and poor, Arbenz fought for the passage of the 1952 Agrarian Reform Law, which redistributed thousands of acres of unproductive land to some 100,000 rural families. United Fruit was furious, having lost half its land. In 1954, the CIA, whose director sat on United Fruit's board, sponsored a coup d'état. Guatemala's new government, largely drawn from the ranks of its military, was flown into the capital aboard a U.S. Air Force plane.

The new U.S.-sponsored regime eliminated the constitutional reforms of the previous decade, reinstituting rule by and for the *ladino* minority. In the early 1960s, a guerrilla war began between government forces and Marxist rebels, who drew their strength largely from indigenous communities and were headquartered in the highlands.

For the next 30 years, a succession of authoritarian rulers were brought to power by rigged elections or coups d'état. They largely followed the maxim of president and army colonel Arana Osorio, who said, "If it is necessary to turn the country into a cemetery in order to pacify it, I will not hesitate to do so." An estimated 200,000 people died or disappeared during the conflict, most of them indigenous. Death squads roamed the cities and highlands killing those suspected of rebel activity. Professors, students, union leaders, and priests were especially prone to attack.

Following the recommendations of the 1987 Central American Peace accords, Guatemalan President Alvaro Arzú negotiated a peace agreement with the URNG (as the united rebel factions were known) in December 1996. The agreement ended the 36-year-old civil war, with the government promising to support a Truth Commission led by the UN Mission to Guatemala, MINUGUA. The constitution was also amended to allow for greater indigenous rights.

Guatemala's security situation improved after the end of the war, but great challenges remained. First, the military still wielded significant power, and did its best to cover up its involvement in the atrocities of the war. In 1998, days after delivering a report on human rights that blamed 80% of the abuses on the military, Catholic Bishop Juan Geradi was bludgeoned to death in his home in Guatemala City. Government and judicial officials were too afraid of suffering the same fate to investigate the crime.

Guatemala Today

A millennium of Maya civilization, 3 centuries of Spanish colonial rule, and almost 4 decades of guerrilla war have left Guatemala's economy, politics, crafts, architecture, languages, and religions with one common trait: profound variety. Home to nearly 13 million people, Guatemala is by far the most populous country in Central America, and its residents are extremely diverse. Less than a decade after the end of a long and brutal civil war, Guatemala is still writing its own history at a dizzying pace. The country seems poised between following a rising path to prosperity, democracy, and justice, and taking a precipitous fall into crime, chaos, and continued impunity.

The Guatemalan economy is still heavily agricultural, based on the production of sugar cane, coffee, and bananas, with tourism and manufacturing playing increasingly important roles. Despite gradual economic growth since the 1996 peace agreement, the country's war-torn past continues to cast a long shadow on its economy and society. The gap between rich and poor is wide. Up to 75% of the population lives below the poverty line. As much as 30% of the population lives on less than $2 (£1) per day. The country's levels of infant mortality and illiteracy are some of the worst in the Americas. And, crime continues to be a major problem. Violent gangs, or *maras,* are having a noticeable impact across Guatemala, particularly in poor urban areas, and drug-trafficking and money laundering are considered to be major problems. Lawlessness pervades many parts of the country, and impunity is rampant. As a result, vigilante groups, frustrated at the lack of police presence, often take justice into their own hands. A succession of governments have failed to address any of the country's major problems. Moreover, President Alvaro Colom, elected in 2007, is getting off to a rocky start. After a year in power, his administration and the government in general are embroiled in corruption scandals and largely deemed ineffective.

EL SALVADOR

A Look at the Past

El Salvador's earliest residents on record were Paleo-Indian peoples whose history in the country is thought to stretch back 10,000 years and is evidenced by indigenous paintings found near the village of Morazán. The next residents to arrive were the more advanced Olmecs, Mesoamericans who moved into the region around 2000 B.C. The Olmecs held power until roughly 400 B.C. when they were largely replaced by the Maya. The Maya dynasty is responsible for the country's Classic pyramid ruins such as Tazumal and Casa Blanca—these show evidence not only of contact with other Maya from around what is now Central America but also point to how El Salvador acted as a vital trading center in the Maya world.

Around the 11th century, the Maya dynasty was replaced by what remains of El Salvador's largest indigenous population, the Nahuat-speaking Pipil, who were part of the nomadic Mexican Nahua tribe and dominated the western part of the country. At the same time, the Lenca tribe, with its own Aztec-based language, settled into and controlled the eastern region of the country, where its descendants remain today. Both the Maya and Lenca dynasties held power until the arrival of the Spanish in 1524 and both waged ultimately futile efforts to stop the invading conquistadors.

When Spaniard Pedro de Alvarado attempted to claim this territory for Spain in 1524, his army was thwarted by Pipil fighters. Alvarado tried again the following year, however, and was able to bring the region under the Spanish flag. Alvarado then named the region El Salvador or "The Savior."

For roughly the next 3 centuries, El Salvador remained under Spanish control. In 1821, El Salvador, along with four other Central American countries, declared its independence from Spain. The first couple of years of freedom, however, weren't easy. In 1822, El Salvador decided against joining Mexico and other provinces in a Central American union and had to fight off troops sent to bring the country in line. The country went so far as to request statehood from the United States government. Ultimately, however, El Salvador was able to expel the troops and joined a more equitable union of Central American states, known as the Central American Federation, in 1823.

Things remained relatively calm until 1832, when El Salvador's poor staged the first of what would be numerous uprisings to protest unfair land distribution. Like later uprisings, the 1832 effort resulted in little change. In 1838 the Central American Federation dissolved and El Salvador became a fully independent country.

During the 19th century, El Salvador's system of land-based oligarchy, presided over by a famous set of "14 families" (actually a few dozen), flourished as the coffee industry grew. During that time, the country's much-amended constitution was again restructured to give the majority of its 72 legislative seats to landowners. The head of each department was also appointed by the president. The system allowed wealthy coffee-plantation owners simply to incorporate much of the country's deedless common land into their coffee farms and to maintain a stranglehold over the landless masses.

This obviously didn't sit well with the landless masses, who rose up numerous times to try to force change but were largely powerless against the wealthy elite and their military bidders. One of the largest of these early uprisings, later named "La Matanaza" (The Massacre), took place in 1932 and was led by Farabundo Martí, for whom the people's FMLN organization was later named. It was a failed and brutal uprising, which resulted in the deaths, imprisonment, or deportation of 30,000 indigenous people and government opponents.

Over the next nearly 5 decades, El Salvador's poor suffered under successive repressive governments that occasionally offered token land reforms, allowing for large-scale armed conflict to be largely avoided. The country did engage, however, in a short 5-day war from July 14 to July 18, 1969, with Honduras over immigration issues, which came to be known as the Soccer War (see p. 31 for more info).

Though the Soccer War quickly became a memory, the anger of El Salvador's poor farmers did not, and by the 1970s, sporadic and violent insurgencies against the government began. The government responded with a largely useless land reform bill in 1976 that did little to improve lives or ease the anger of the *campesinos* (peasant farmers). Some held out hope for improvements when a slightly more moderate group took control in 1979, but that group quickly dissolved under its own political strife and targeting by the military death squads. Many say the final straw came in 1980, with the government's assassination of beloved human rights champion Monseñor Oscar Romero, who was gunned down in the middle of Mass. After four of the country's leading guerilla groups merged into the cohesive and organized Farabundo Martí National Liberation Front, or FMLN, later in 1980, the stage was set for war.

The FMLN staged its first large-scale military offensive on January 10, 1981, in which it gained control over the areas around Chalatenango and Morazán. All ages, including children and the elderly, and both sexes joined in the guerilla movement. The El Salvadoran government's response was brutal, particularly at the 2-day, December 1981 Mozote Massacre, when military soldiers executed more than 1,000 men, women, and children in the eastern mountain village of Mozote. The war raged on and off over the next 11 years, with international powers viewing the battle as an ideological struggle between democracy and communism. Cuba supported the guerillas, and the United States—to a total of $7 billion (£3.5 billion)—supported the El Salvadoran military government. More than 70,000 people were killed during the war's brutal run, including many who were executed and mutilated by government troops, who then dumped the bodies near town squares in order to warn against terrorism. More than 25% of the country's population was displaced by the war by its end.

By 1991, both sides had had enough of the long stalemate and a spirit of compromise emerged. In 1992, a truce was declared and a peace deal signed. A new constitution was drafted that enacted a number of land reforms and did away with the military death squads in favor of a national civil police; in addition, the FMLN became a legal political party that remains active today. Amnesty for war crimes, of which there were many, was declared in 1993.

El Salvador Today

Today, El Salvador continues to struggle. The plight of its campesinos and civil war deaths have been replaced by one of Latin America's highest homicide rates, due mainly to the presence of the notorious street gang Mara Salvatrucha or MS-13. Though MS-13 began on the streets of Los Angeles in the 1980s, heavy deportation of U.S.-based gang members has steadily increased the gang's influence in El Salvador. Continuing government efforts to break up the gang have had small, sporadic impacts, but crime remains a central issue of El Salvadoran life.

In 1989, El Salvador was hit by catastrophic Hurricane Mitch, which killed 374 people, left 55,000 homeless, and stalled the economy. Mitch was followed in 2001 and 2005 by more massive earthquakes that killed over a thousand people, left thousands more homeless, and severely damaged thousands of buildings—many of which remain under repair today, including San Salvador's majestic National Theater.

Since 1992, however, the country's new constitution and cooperation of the two main political parties has allowed El Salvador to remain politically peaceful. In 2006, former TV sports presenter Tony Saca became president of El Salvador under the conservative ARENA party, and he remains president at press time even though his presidency has witnessed an underperforming economy with high inflation.

Despite rising inflation and other problems, El Salvador's economy has grown steadily in the last decade—the percentage of El Salvadorans living in poverty has been reduced from 66% in 1991 to just over 30% in 2006. Still, many El Salvadorans think the Central America Free Trade Agreement, which the country joined in 2006, is causing economic woes. As a result, the FMLN party is currently on the upswing and looks likely to win the 2009 presidential elections with its candidate Mauricio Funes, a popular and respected TV journalist. He has toned down his party's left-wing rhetoric, promising to stick with dollarization and keep a friendly distance from Hugo Chavez.

HONDURAS

A Look at the Past

Prior to the arrival of the Spanish, Honduras was inhabited by the Maya, who drifted down from Mexico and Guatemala to settle in the highlands and valleys throughout the western half of the country. In A.D. 426, they founded the city-state of Copán, considered one of the intellectual capitals of the Maya for its rich architecture and design until, around A.D. 800, the Maya civilization mysteriously began to collapse. While pockets of the Mayas' descendants remained in the region after this collapse, other indigenous groups, such as the Lencas, the Miskito, and the Pech, eventually developed as well.

On July 30, 1502, during his fourth and final voyage to the Americas, Christopher Columbus reached the pine-covered island of Guanaja, becoming the first European to set foot on Honduran soil. Eventually, Columbus would set sail for the northern mainland coast, stopping in Trujillo on August 14 and soon after in Puerto Castilla, where the first Catholic Mass in Honduras took place. The Honduran coast was ignored for several decades until after Hernán Cortés's conquest of the Aztecs, when the Spanish exploration of the mainland began. In 1523, conquistador Gil Gonzáles de Avila reached the Golfo de Fonseca, but was quickly captured by rival Spaniard Cristóbal de Olid a year later, who founded the colony of Triunfo de la Cruz. Olid's soldiers turned on him, though, and he was swiftly executed. Cortés learned of the power struggle and sent trusted Francisco de las Casas to intervene and establish a colony at Trujillo in 1525.

In the 1530s, gold and silver were discovered in the country's western highlands and an influx of Spaniards quickly arrived on the scene, leading to the founding of the cities of San Pedro de Puerto Caballos, now San Pedro Sula, and Gracias a Dios. In answer to this, a Lenca chief named Lempira unified rival tribes to launch attacks on the Spanish from his fort at Cerquín. The Spanish waged a fierce assault on the fort for more than 6 months, but to no avail. So the Spanish initiated peace talks with Lempira, only to murder him upon his arrival. After his death, significant resistance from the native groups was slowed and eventually stopped.

The Spanish, now that they were in full control of the territory, proceeded to decimate the native population via enslavement and harsh treatment—they wiped out as much as 95% of the indigenous population within a few decades. To make up for the labor shortage, African slaves were brought in during the 1540s. For the next few centuries, more colonies were founded, and a provincial capital was established in Gracias a Dios, though it was quickly moved to Comayagua. Mining fueled the economy until the collapse of silver prices forced the Spaniards to turn to agricultural endeavors such as tobacco farming and raising cattle.

During the 1600s, the Spanish began looting the riches of the South American continent and sent ships up the Central American coast on their return to Spain. French and English pirates, like the legendary Henry Morgan and John Coxen, began using the Bay Islands as their base for expeditions to plunder these Spanish ships, and they set up semipermanent settlements there. When in 1739 war erupted between England and Spain, the British took control over the islands and established a fort at Port Royal in Roatán. The treaty of Aix-la-Chapelle returned the islands to Spain, though the British reclaimed them during another war in 1779; in 1797, descendants of Carib Indians and African slaves from the Cayman Islands, called the Garífuna, were dumped in Roatán by the British. More waves of Garífuna arrived from the Caymans in the 1830s and began permanent settlements on the islands, as well as along the north coast of the mainland.

In 1821, Honduras declared independence from Spain, along with the Central American territories of Guatemala, El Salvador, Costa Rica, and Nicaragua. After a brief period as part of independent Mexico, it joined the United Provinces of Central America in 1823. Infighting among the provinces brought upon the collapse of this federation in 1838, leaving the members to form independent countries. On November 15th of that year, most of current-day Honduras became a separate nation. The Bay Islands gained sovereignty from Britain in 1859.

Over the next 150 years, the country was plagued by political unrest that saw various rebellions, civil wars, coups, rigged elections, invasions, and changes of government. In one of the more unusual events, American William Walker attempted to conquer Central America with his own army but was executed that same year (see the "The Wars of William Walker" box on p. 36 for info).

In the early 19th century, U.S. companies such as the Tela Railroad Company, a subsidiary of United Fruit, now Chiquita, and Standard Fruit, now Dole, established banana plantations along the north coast and held sway over politics in the country. Bananas became the chief product in the country, accounting for as much as 80% of exports in 1929. The bribing of politicians and unjust labor practices marred the industry for much of the 20th century and kept the country from developing its own business elite, which was protested during a 2-month strike by plantation workers in 1954.

In 1956, the country's first military coup took place. A new constitution put the control of the military in the hands of the top general, not in the president, and this began a period of military rule of the country. In 1963, only days before the next election, the military, headed by Colonel López Arellano, seized power and canceled the election. Two years later, he was elected on his own and then served a 6-year term. A year after the next election, he again took control during another military coup. When it was discovered that Arellano took a $1.25-million bribe from the United Brands Fruit Company, previously known as United Fruit, he was removed from office. In his place came General Juan Alberto Melgar Castro, whose reign was rocked by a scandal involving using the military for drug trafficking. Next came General Policarpo Paz García, who would return the country to civilian rule in 1980 with the election of a president and congress.

During the end of the 19th century and much of the 20th century, the two main political parties in Honduras, liberals (who preferred a free-market economy like in the U.S.) and conservatives (who desired an aristocratic-style regime) wrestled power from each other again and again. From 1821 to 1982, the constitution was rewritten an astounding 17 times.

Political conflict was not all internal, however. In 1969, more than 300,000 undocumented El Salvadorans were believed to be living in Honduras, and the government and private groups increasingly sought to blame them for the country's economic woes. During a World Cup preliminary match in Tegucigalpa, a disturbance broke out between fans on both sides, followed by a more intense incident during the next game in San Salvador. El Salvadorans living in Honduras began to be harassed and even killed, leading to a mass exodus from the country. On June 27, 1969, Honduras broke off diplomatic relations with El Salvador, and on July 14, the El Salvadoran air force began an assault on Honduras and took control of the city of Nueva Ocotepeque, marking the start of what would be called the Soccer War. Though the war lasted only 5 days and ended in a stalemate of sorts, in the end, between 60,000 and 130,000 El Salvadorans were expelled or fled from Honduras, and more than 2,000 people, mostly Hondurans, were killed. While a peace treaty was signed between the two countries in 1980, even to this day relations between them remain strained.

Civil wars broke out in every country neighboring Honduras in the late 1970s and 1980s. El Salvador, Guatemala, and Nicaragua all saw wide-scale political upheaval, assassinations, and all-out civil unrest. To the surprise of many, Honduras, despite its shaky governments, scandals, and economic problems, escaped any major turmoil during this period—the one exception being protests over U.S. military involvement in the country. During the 1980s, the U.S. provided aid to the country, in exchange for using it as a base for counter-insurgency movements (led by the CIA-trained group the Contras) against the Sandinistas in Nicaragua. Student and opposition leaders in Honduras organized massive protests of the U.S. military influence, to which the Honduran military responded by kidnapping and killing protestors. The protests only grew, however, and eventually the country was forced to reexamine its policies on U.S. operations in Honduras—especially after it was revealed in 1986 that the Reagan administration had sold arms to Iran to support the anti-Sandinistas in Honduras. In 1988, the military agreement with the U.S. was not renewed and the Nicaraguan Contras ended up leaving the country entirely by 1990, when the Contra war concluded.

During the late 1980s and into the 1990s, struggles to maintain the value of the lempira against the dollar resulted in rapid inflation. Because wages remained the same, many Hondurans simply became poorer than they already were. When Carlos Roberto Flores Facusse became president in 1988, he initiated wide-scale currency reforms and took steps to modernize the economy. Things looked like they were about to change for the better. And then came Hurricane Mitch.

Honduras Today

In October 1998, the most powerful Atlantic hurricane ever recorded at the time decimated the country. Wind speeds as high as 180 mph caused billions of dollars in damage throughout the country. In the end, more than 6,000 people were killed and more than 1.5 million people were displaced, 70% of roads and bridges were destroyed, 70% of all crops were lost, and entire towns were destroyed by this storm. Relief poured in from the world community, although funds quickly dried up or never materialized (such as $640 million from various European organizations). Though the country has by now recovered greatly from the hurricane, to this day, many economic woes are still blamed on Mitch.

In 2006, Manuel Zelaya Rosales, a rancher from Olancho, was elected president after promises of doubling the police force, re-educating gang members, and lowering petroleum prices. Soon after, the Central America and Dominican Republic Free Trade Agreement (CAFTA-DR) went into effect in Honduras amid protests throughout Central America. The pact will eliminate tariffs on goods and services traded between both countries, in the hopes that it will open up markets to U.S. businesses and provide manufacturing jobs that would otherwise go to Asia. Some feel it will go the way of NAFTA and only hurt small farmers and business owners. In addition to such growing economic concerns, the first years of Zelaya's presidency have been marred by corruption scandals involving members of the government.

NICARAGUA

A Look at the Past

Evidence of human life in Nicaragua dates back 8,000 years, in the form of shells collected by a tribe called Los Concheros on the Caribbean coast. In the 13th century, the Corotega and Nicarao tribes also settled in the country, when they fled south from Aztec Mexico and found refuge around the country's two great lakes. These same people gave the Spanish a taste of their fighting spirit when the Europeans first landed in 1519. The tribal leaders Nicaroa and Diriangén engaged the conquistador Gonzalez in a brief battle, after which the Spanish retreated.

The Spanish explorer Francisco Hernández de Córdoba first established a permanent colonial foothold in the country in 1524. The tribes were defeated and, despite the occasional rebellion over the next century or so, were eventually subdued and subjugated by the Europeans. Nicaragua became the domain of the Spanish Empire for the next 300 years, with Granada becoming a major merchant city because of its access to the Atlantic. As in other parts of the region, Nicaragua's prosperity led to frequent raids from British, French, and Dutch pirates sailing up the Río San Juan in search of loot and fortune, using the Atlantic coast as their base.

After a period of struggle, Nicaragua won independence from Spain in 1821 along with the rest of Central America. It was briefly a province of Mexico before becoming a part of the short-lived Central America Federation. It eventually emerged as an independent nation in 1838. The English still retained their presence in the Caribbean, however, controlling the San Juan estuary from the port of Greytown until 1860. In that year, the British signed a treaty surrendering the Caribbean territory to Nicaragua, though in fact the region remained largely autonomous until 1893.

Quick to fill this power gap was America, which influenced Nicaraguan history from the late 1800s on. Nicaragua was of particular interest to the U.S. because it seemed like a good candidate for building a water channel between the Atlantic and Pacific. Plans for such a canal are still being considered to this day. When the steamship magnate Cornelius Vanderbilt pioneered a land, river, and sea route that saw thousands of North Americans passing up the river San Juan as part of the Californian Gold Rush in the 1850s, the country gained even more importance in the eyes of America.

In addition to growing American influence, the 19th century was dominated by a vicious rivalry centered in the cities of Granada and León that continues in some way to this day. During this period, Granada emerged as the establishment capital, favored by landowners and merchants who had little desire to reform the feudal system that existed. León became the center for liberal bourgeoisie who were inspired by the Enlightenment and the American and French revolutions. Such was their rivalry that a national government was not declared until 1845, and the country was rocked by a civil war that went on intermittently throughout the rest of the century.

The country's political landscape was transformed by another American when mercenary and filibuster William Walker was hired by the León liberals to help in their latest skirmish with Granada. His private army of 300 roughnecks won the battle but had no intention of going home. Walker declared himself president in 1855 (with the support of the U.S. government) and soon instituted policies such as reestablishing slavery and declaring English as the official language. These policies did not go down well with the locals, and the Leoneses soon united with the conservatives to defeat Walker at the battle of San Jacinto in 1856. See the box on p. 36 for more info.

A disgraced liberal class then surrendered to 36 years of mediocre conservative rule. The fishing village of Managua was declared the country's capital as a compromise. A nationalist general, José Santos Zelaya, took power in 1893 and marched his troops to the Atlantic coast to finally lay claim to what until then was Nicaragua's on paper only. The liberal-leaning Zelaya antagonized the Americans by threatening to rival the planned Panama canal with a foreign-financed waterway of his own. He was ousted with the aid of American marines in 1909. Three years later, a rebellion led by Benjamin Zeledón was crushed by an invasion of American marines that basically took over the country. For the next 12 years, there were 10 such uprisings against American-backed, conservative governments. After U.S. interests acquired some of Nicaragua's main businesses, Nicaragua soon found itself in hock to the United States and locked into an agreement where no other country could finance a canal that would interfere with Washington´s plans in Panama.

A glimmer of hope came in 1924 when the liberals and conservatives finally agreed to a form of power sharing and the Americans withdrew their military presence. But the pact collapsed when conservative Emilio Chamorro staged a coup d'état and the Constitutional War broke out. Fearing a liberal victory, the U.S. again stepped in and negotiated a settlement that was opposed by one liberal general called Augusto C. Sandino. He held out in the northern highlands despite an American offensive that included the first recorded bombing of a civilian town, Ocotal.

In 1933, the American-trained National Guard was created, led by Anastasio Somoza Garcia. The Americans withdrew, handing power to Juan Bautista Sacasa. Sandino accepted the government's invitation to negotiate but instead was assassinated by the National Guard in 1934 in Managua. The murder was followed by a vicious clampdown by Somoza, who eventually took complete control in 1937.

What followed was 42 years of iron rule by a family dynasty that in the end owned everything worth owning in Nicaragua. The Somoza family became fabulously wealthy and all-powerful. They installed the occasional puppet president for appearance's sake and, with the help of the National Guard, rigged elections. When Anastasio Somoza Garcia was assassinated by the poet Rigoberto López Pérez in 1956, he was swiftly replaced by his son Luís "Tacho" Somoza Debayle and the regime continued as usual. The only good things to come out of such ravenous, profit-driven rule were huge public works such as the Pan-American Highway (Carretera Panamericana) and the Lake Apanás hydroelectric plant. There were several attempts on Somoza's life, including a Cuban-style insurrection in 1959 that petered out after 2 weeks.

The Somoza regime showed its gratitude for American patronage in 1961 by allowing its Atlantic coast to be used as the launching pad for the disastrous Bay of Pigs operation. In 1963, a new organization called the Frente Sandinista de Liberación Nacional (FSLN) made its presence be known by staging an uprising in the North. Led by the Marxist Carlos Fonseca Amador, the Sandinistas were to prove a thorn in the side of an increasingly repressive regime. Tacho lost an election in 1963 and retired from politics. The new president Renée Schick was soon ousted by Anastasio "Tachito" Somoza in 1967. This younger brother of Tacho proved to be the cruelest and greediest of all the Somozas. He plundered reconstruction funds for the 1972 earthquake disaster and arranged the murder of newspaper editor and critic of the regime, Pedro Joaquin Chamorro, in 1978. Based on his orders, the national guard massacred hundreds in Masaya and pitched battles broke out in the capital in which the air force bombed its own people. Despite the killing of their leader, Fonseca, in 1976, the Sandinistas gained the upper hand. The northern town of Matagalpa fell to the FSLN, followed by Estelí, and eventually the capital on July 19, 1979. Somoza fled to Paraguay, where he was eventually killed by a rocket attack in 1980.

The Sandinista revolution brought radical land reform and interventionist economics, policies that made the elite flee to Miami. While the economy collapsed, the poor became educated in hugely popular literacy drives. The new Reagan administration watched with dread what it perceived as a new front in the Cold War. Aid was halted in 1981 and an economic embargo was imposed in 1985, putting the economy into free-fall. A new insurgency appeared in the north, this time by a right-wing group called the Contras, financed and trained by the CIA. The Sandinista government had to divert badly needed money toward this new war, as well as impose unpopular policies such as a draft and rationing.

By the end of the 1980s, both sides of this battle were exhausted. The Iran-Contra scandal (p. 47) had dried up support for the counterinsurgents and the collapse of the Soviet Union was a serious blow to the revolution. A peace accord was proposed by Nicaragua's Central American neighbors (though opposed by the U.S.) and the Sandinistas accepted. Elections were held in 1990, and to the surprise of many, the government lost. A further surprise was a peaceful handover of power with the Sandinistas relinquishing control, but not before a shameful last grab of property and assets.

Violeta Barrios de Chamorro became the president of this new Nicaragua. The widow of the slain editor and leader of a loose coalition known as UNO, Doña Violeta introduced policies aimed at ending the war, reconciling all sides, and kick-starting the economy, with limited success. Meanwhile the Sandinistas embraced democracy and became the main opposition party, led by veteran Daniel Ortega. Despite strong support, Ortega lost the 1996 election to a corrupt, right-wing politician called Arnoldo Alemán, leader of the Partido Liberal Constitucionalista (PLC). Alemán's tenure was rocked by endless kickback scandals and further tarnished by a disgraceful political pact with Ortega that basically divided power, pushed smaller parties out, and guaranteed immunity from prosecution for both leaders.

When Hurricane Mitch struck in 1998, wreaking havoc across the country and killing thousands, Alemán's appallingly slow reaction sealed his fate as a one-term president. His vice president, Enrique Geyer Bolaños, came to power in 2002, trouncing Ortega with 56% of the vote.

Nicaragua Today

Once in office, Bolaños, acting on his anticorruption campaign pledges, turned on his own party, stripped Alemán of immunity, and had him jailed for 20 years for embezzlement and money laundering. Such justice is a rare thing in Central American politics and Bolaños paid for his crusade by being virtually paralyzed in a congress made up of disaffected and begrudging colleagues, who retaliated by trying to convict him in turn for illegal funding.

In the 2006 election, the Sandinistas were able to capitalize on this infighting and a general downturn in the economy; Ortega won the election with 37% of the popular vote. The initial reaction was a sudden dip in foreign investment, as people feared the country would return to the 1980s-style economy of hyperinflation and debt default. Ortega has however softened his Marxist image and declared himself to be market friendly. Nevertheless, his popularity is low, due to a stalled economy and rising food prices. Both sides of the political spectrum are currently disaffected, with members on the right saying that Ortega has become a crony of Hugo Chavez and members on the left accusing him of selling out. The next elections are due in November 2011, but Ortega has his work cut out for him if he wants to remain in power.

COSTA RICA

A Look at the Past

Precious little is known of Costa Rica's history before the Spanish conquest. The pre-Columbian Indians who made their home here never developed the large cities or advanced culture that flowered farther north in present-day Guatemala, Belize, and Mexico. However, ancient artifacts indicating a strong sense of aesthetics have been unearthed from scattered excavations around the country. Beautiful gold and jade jewelry, intricately carved grinding stones, and artistically painted terra-cotta objects point to a small but highly skilled population.

In 1502, on his fourth and last voyage to the New World, Christopher Columbus anchored just offshore from present-day Limón. Whether he actually gave the country its name—"the rich coast"—is open to discussion, but the Spaniards never did find much gold or minerals to exploit here.

Despite their small numbers, scattered villages, and tribal differences, the original indigenous inhabitants of Costa Rica fought fiercely against the Spanish, until overcome by superior firepower and European diseases. When the fighting ended, the Spanish conquistadors found very few Indians left to force into servitude. Settlers were thus forced to till their own lands, a situation unheard of in other parts of Latin America. Few pioneers headed this way because they could stake their claims in other parts of the Spanish crown, where large slave workforces were available. Costa Rica was nearly forgotten, as the conquest looked elsewhere for riches to plunder and souls to convert.

The Wars of William Walker

In 1856, Costa Rica was invaded by William Walker, a soldier of fortune from Tennessee who, with the backing of U.S. President James Buchanan, was attempting to fulfill his grandiose dreams of presiding over a slave state in Central America (before his invasion of Costa Rica, he had invaded Nicaragua and Baja California). The people of Costa Rica, led by their own president, Juan Rafael Mora, chased Walker back to Nicaragua. Walker actually surrendered to a U.S. warship in 1857, but in 1860, he attacked Honduras, claiming to be the president of that country. The Hondurans, who had had enough of Walker's shenanigans, promptly executed him.

The few Spanish settlers that did make a go of it headed quickly for the hills, where they found rich volcanic soil and a climate that was less oppressive than in the lowlands. Cartago, the colony's first capital, was founded in 1563, but it was not until the 1700s that additional cities were established in this agriculturally rich region. In the late 18th century, the first coffee plants were introduced, and Costa Rica had its first major cash crop.

In 1821, Spain granted independence to its colonies in Central America. Costa Rica joined with its neighbors to form the Central American Federation; but in 1838, it withdrew to form a new nation and pursue its own interests. By the mid-1800s, coffee was the country's main export. Free land was given to anyone willing to plant coffee on it, and plantation owners soon grew wealthy and powerful, creating Costa Rica's first elite class.

Until 1890, coffee growers had to transport their coffee either by oxcart to the Pacific port of Puntarenas or by boat down the Río Sarapiquí to the Caribbean. In the 1870s, a progressive president proposed a railway from San José to the Caribbean coast to facilitate the transport of coffee to European markets. It took nearly 20 years for this plan to reach fruition, and more than 4,000 workers lost their lives constructing the railway, which passed through dense jungles and rugged mountains on its journey from the Central Valley to the coast. Partway through the project, as funds were dwindling, the second chief engineer, Minor Keith, proposed an idea that not only enhanced his fortunes but also changed the course of Central American history. Banana plantations would be planted along the railway right of way (land on either side of the tracks). The export of this crop would help to finance the railway, and, in exchange, Keith would get a 99-year lease on 1,976,000 hectares (800,000 acres) of land with a 20-year tax deferment. The Costa Rican government gave its consent, and in 1878 the first bananas were shipped. In 1899, Keith and a partner formed the United Fruit Company, a business that eventually became the largest landholder in Central America and caused political disputes and wars throughout the region.

In 1889, Costa Rica held what is considered the first free election in Central American history. The opposition candidate won the election, and the control of the government passed from the hands of one political party to those of another without bloodshed or hostilities. Thus, Costa Rica established itself as the region's only true democracy. In 1948, this democratic process was challenged by Rafael Angel Calderón, who had served as the country's president from 1940 to 1944. After losing by a narrow margin, Calderón, who had the backing of the communist labor unions and the Catholic church, refused to concede the country's leadership to the rightfully elected president, Otillio Ulate, and a civil war ensued. Calderón was eventually defeated by José "Pepe" Figueres. In the wake of this crisis, a new constitution was drafted; among other changes, it abolished Costa Rica's army so that such a revolution could never happen again.

In 1994, history seemed to repeat itself—peacefully this time—when José María Figueres took the reins of government from the son of his father's adversary, Rafael Angel Calderón.

Costa Rica Today

The battle-worn traditional two-party system is increasingly under threat in Costa Rica, in large part thanks to major corruption scandals. Two former presidents are currently under house arrest (Miguel Angel Rodríguez and Rafael Angel Calderón), and another (José María Figueres) is in Switzerland refusing a legislative call to return and testify. All are implicated, as well as a long list of other high-level government employees and deputies, in one way or another, in various financial scandals or bribery cases. While it's unclear how these various scandals and trials will play out in the courts, they have already had a profound effect on the country's political landscape.

In 2006, former president Oscar Arias Sánchez, a Nobel Peace Prize laureate who had presided over the country during the mid-1980s, was reelected, defeating Otton Solís of the upstart Citizen's Action Party (PAC) by an incredibly slim margin. If this election is any precedent, it is likely that the 2010 presidential elections will signal the end of the two-party system in Costa Rica.

A series of "Free Zones" and high-tech investments and production facilities have dramatically changed the face of Costa Rica's economy. Intel, which opened two side-by-side assembly plants in Costa Rica, currently accounts for more than 15% of the country's exports, compared with traditional exports such as coffee (3%) and bananas (8%). However, while Intel and other international companies are used to trumpet a growing gross domestic product, very few of the profits actually make their way into the Costa Rican economy.

Tourism is the nation's principal source of income, surpassing both cattle ranching and exports of coffee, pineapples, and bananas. Nearly two million tourists visit Costa Rica each year. Increasingly, Ticos whose fathers and grandfathers were farmers and ranchers find themselves hotel owners, tour guides, and waiters. Although most have adapted gracefully and regard the industry as a source of new jobs and opportunities for economic advancement, restaurant and hotel staff can seem gruff and uninterested at times, especially in rural areas. And, unfortunately, an increase in the number of visitors has led to an increase in crime, prostitution, and drug trafficking. Common sense and street savvy are required in San José and in many of the more popular tourist destinations.

Today, Costa Rica is the most technologically advanced and politically stable nation in Central America, and it has the largest middle class. Even the smallest towns have electricity, the water is mostly safe to drink, and the communications system is relatively advanced. Still, the gap between rich and poor has been widening for years. The roads, hospitals, and school systems have been in a slow but steady state of decay for decades. And there are no immediate signs of this condition changing.

In a public referendum held in October 2007, Costa Ricans approved, again by a slim margin, a free trade agreement with the United States. It's too soon to tell how this agreement will affect the economy and politics of the nation.

PANAMA

A Look at the Past

Little is known about the ancient cultures that inhabited Panama before the arrival of the Spanish. The pre-Columbian cultures in this region did not build large cities or develop an advanced culture like the Maya or the Incas did, and much of what was left behind has been stolen by looters or engulfed in jungle. We know that the most advanced cultures came from central Panama, such as the Monagrillo (2500–1700 B.C.), who were one of the first pre-Columbian societies in the Americas to produce ceramics. Excavation of sites such as Conte, near Natá, have unearthed elaborate burial pits with *huacas* (ceremonial figurines) and jewelry, which demonstrates an early introduction to metallurgy during the 1st century, as well as trade with Colombia and even Mexico.

The first of many Spanish explorers to reach Panama was Rodrigo de Bastidas, who sailed from Venezuela along Panama's Caribbean coast in 1501 in search of gold. His first mate was Vasco Nuñez de Balboa, who would return later and seal his fate as one of Panama's most important historical figures. A year later, Christopher Columbus, on his fourth and final voyage to the New World, sailed into Bocas del Toro and stopped at various points along the isthmus, one of which he named Puerto Bello, now known as Portobelo.

Meanwhile, Balboa had settled in the Dominican Republic but had racked up huge debts. In 1510, he escaped his creditors by hiding out as a stowaway on a boat bound for Panama. In the years since Columbus's failed attempt, many other Spaniards had tried to colonize the coast, but were thwarted by disease and indigenous raids. Balboa suggested settling at Antigua de Darién, where he became a tough but successful administrator who both subjugated Indians as well as befriended conquered tribes. Having listened to stories by Indians about another sea, Balboa set out in 1513 with Francisco Pizarro and a band of Indian slaves, and hacked his way through perilous jungle for 25 days until he arrived at the Pacific coast, where he claimed the sea and all its shores for the king of Spain. Balboa was later beheaded by a jealous new governor, Pedro Arias de Avila (Pedrarias the Cruel), on a trumped-up charge of treason.

In 1519, Pedrarias settled a fishing village called Panama, which meant "plenty of fish" in the local language, and resettled Nombre de Dios on the Atlantic to create a passageway for transporting Peruvian gold and riches from the Pacific to Spanish galleons in the Caribbean Sea. The trail was called the Camino Real, or Royal Trail, but later a faster and easier route was established, called the Camino de las Cruces. The land portion of this trail was two-thirds shorter, and met with the Chagres River, which could be sailed out to the Caribbean Sea. This trail can be walked today, and portions of the stone-inlaid path still exist.

By the mid–17th century, dwindling supplies of silver and gold from the Peruvian mines and ongoing pirate attacks precipitated a severe decline in the amount of precious metals being transported to Spain. In 1671, the notorious Welsh buccaneer Henry Morgan sailed up the Chagres River, crossed the isthmus, and overpowered Panama City, sacking the city and leaving it in flames. Those who escaped the attack rebuilt Panama City, 2 years later, at what is now known as Casco Viejo.

Spain finally abandoned the isthmus crossing and Portobelo after the city was attacked by the British Admiral Edward Vernon, and returned to sailing around Cape Horn to reach Peru. Spain granted independence to its Central America colonies in 1821, and Panama was absorbed into "Gran Colombia," a union led by liberator Simón Bolívar that included Colombia, Venezuela, and Ecuador. Panama attempted to split from Colombia three times during the 19th century, but wouldn't be successful until the U.S.-backed attempt in 1903.

Having been a colonial backwater since the pullout of the Spanish in the late 17th century, Panama was restored to prosperity from 1848 to 1869 during the height of the California Gold Rush. Given that crossing from the Atlantic to the Pacific of the U.S. was a long, arduous journey by wagon and prone to Indian attacks and other pitfalls, gold-seekers chose to sail to Panama, cross the Las Cruces trail, and sail on to California. In 1855, an American group of financiers built the Panama Railroad, greatly reducing the travel time between coasts.

Travel time would be reduced even further by the Panama Canal, the history of which dates from 1539, when King Charles I of Spain dispatched a survey team to study the feasibility of a canal (which was deemed impossible). The first real attempt at construction of a canal was begun in 1880 by the French, led by Ferdinand de Lesseps, the charismatic architect of the Suez Canal. De Lesseps had been convinced that a sea-level canal was the only option. Once workers broke ground, however, engineers soon saw the impracticality of a sea-level canal but were unable to convince the stubborn de Lesseps, and for years rumors flew, financial debts mounted, and nearly 20,000 workers perished before the endeavor collapsed. Few had anticipated the enormous challenge presented by the Panamanian jungle, with its mucky swamps, torrential downpours, landslides, floods, and, most debilitating of all, mosquito-borne diseases such as malaria.

Meanwhile, Panama was embroiled in political strife and a nonstop pursuit to separate itself from Colombia. Following the French failure with the canal, the U.S. expressed interest in taking over construction but was rebuffed by the Colombian government. In response, the U.S. backed a growing independence movement in Panama that declared its separation from Colombia on November 3, 1903. The U.S. officially recognized Panama, and sent its battleships to protect the new nation from Colombian troops, who turned back home after a few days.

A French canal engineer on the de Lesseps project, Philippe Bunau-Varilla, a major shareholder of the abandoned canal project, had been grudgingly given negotiating-envoy status by the Panamanian government for the new U.S.-built canal. His controversial Hay-Bunau-Varilla Treaty gave the U.S. overly generous rights that included the use, occupation, and sovereign control of a 16km-wide (10-mile) swath of land across the isthmus, and was entitled to annex more land if necessary to operate the canal. The U.S. would also be allowed to intervene in Panama's affairs.

The French had excavated two-fifths of the canal, built hospitals, and left behind machinery and the operating railway, as well as a sizeable workforce of Afro-Caribbeans. For the next 10 years, the U.S., having essentially eradicated tropical disease, pulled off what seemed impossible in terms of engineering: carving out a path through the Continental Divide, constructing an elevated canal system, and making the largest man-made lake in the world.

A stormy political climate ensued in Panama for the following decades, with frequent changes of administration. Presidents and other political figures were typically *rabiblancos,* or wealthy, white elites loathed by the generally poor and dark-skinned public. Increasingly, Panamanians were discontented with the U.S. presence and, in particular, its control of the canal. In 1964, several U.S. high-school students in the Canal Zone raised the American flag at their school and ignited protests by Panamanian college students. The protests culminated in the deaths of more than two dozen Panamanians, an event that is now called "Día de los Mártires," or Martyrs Day.

By 1974, the U.S. had begun to consider transferring the canal to Panama. Arias was once again voted into power and after strong-arming the National Guard, he was deposed in a military coup led by Omar Torrijos Herrera, a colonel of the National Guard. Torrijos was an authoritarian leader but a champion of the poor who espoused land redistribution and social programs—a "dictatorship with a heart," as he called it. His most popular achievement came in 1977, with the signing of a treaty with then-president Jimmy Carter that relinquished control of the canal to Panama on December 31, 1999. Also part of the treaty was the closing of U.S. military bases and the U.S. right to intervene only if it perceived a threat against the security of the canal. On July 31, 1981, Torrijos died in a plane accident.

By 1983, the National Guard, now renamed the Panamanian Defense Forces (PDF), was firmly controlled by Colonel Manuel Antonio Noriega, and continued to dominate political and everyday life in Panama. Noriega created the so-called Dignity Battalions that aimed to stifle citizen dissent through force, and terrorize anyone who opposed the PDF. For the next 6 years, Noriega kept the Panamanian public in a state of fear, running the country through presidents he had placed in power via rigged elections, killing and torturing his opponents, and involving himself in drug trafficking.

The U.S. imposed tough economic sanctions on Panama that included freezing government assets in U.S. banks, and withholding canal fees, spurning widespread protests against Noriega across Panama City. In 1989, a fresh set of presidential elections pitted the Noriega-picked candidate against Guillermo Endara. When Endara won, Noriega annulled the election amid widespread claims by foreign observers of fraud on the part of the Noriega regime.

With Panama veering out of control, the U.S. began sending troops to bases in the Canal Zone. On December 20, 1989, the U.S. launched Operation Just Cause, led by 25,000 soldiers who pounded the city for 6 days, leaving anywhere from 500 to 7,000 dead, depending on whom you asked. Noriega fled and hid in the offices of the Vatican *nuncio,* where he asked for asylum. He later surrendered and was flown to the U.S., where he was tried, charged, and sentenced to 40 years in prison. The sentence was later reduced and Noriega was due be released in 2007, but a French extradition request for money laundering meant he remained in a Florida prison at press time. Though Noriega will serve jail time in Panama if he returns, Panamanians are justifiably nervous about his release.

In the wake of Noriega's extradition, Guillermo Endara was sworn in as president of a country racked by instability. In 1994, a former Torrijos associate, Ernesto Pérez Balladares, took over the presidency and instituted sweeping economic reforms and worked to rebuild Panama's relationship with the U.S., which still had control of the canal. The same year, the constitution was changed to ban the military in Panama.

Balladares was followed by Mireya Moscoso in 1999, the ex-wife of Arias and Panama's first female president. During her 5 years in power, however, her approval ratings dropped to less than 30%; she was generally viewed as grossly incompetent and prone to cronyism and corruption. Moscoso oversaw the much-anticipated handover of the canal. Despite decades of protest against the U.S. presence, many Panamanians in the end expressed ambivalence about the pullout when faced with the economic impact on businesses and the loss of jobs. Still, the handover has defied everyone's expectations, and the canal is run today as well, if not better, than before.

Panama Today

Panama has a dollarized economy whose major natural resources are its rainforests, beaches, and oceans, making this country an irresistible draw for tourism—though it hasn't really taken off yet. Panama's principal source of income is derived from the services sector, including the Panama Canal, the Colón Free Trade Zone, banking, and flagship registry among other "export" services, all of which total about three-quarters of the country's GDP. The withdrawal of U.S. canal workers and military personnel in 2000 had a devastating effect on Panama City's local economy, but a growth explosion in the construction sector is currently underway thanks to juicy tax incentives, and glitzy skyscrapers seemingly shoot up overnight like mushrooms along the city's shoreline.

Recently, Panama has also effectively sold itself as a retirement haven. Foreign investors lured by get-rich-quick schemes are snapping up property in a real-estate boom that has locals grumbling about the soaring value of land.

On the legislative side, the Panamanian government has reformed its tax structure, opened its borders to free trade with key nations like the U.S., and implemented a social security overhaul. Yet money laundering, political corruption, and cocaine transshipment continue to be problems, as is widespread unemployment, with indigenous groups and Colón residents faring the worst. As the nation grows economically, the split between the rich and the poor widens. Today, about 40% of the population is under the poverty level and lacks adequate housing, access to medical care, and proper nutrition.

The current president of Panama is Martín Torrijos, a member of the center-left Democratic Revolutionary Party and son of the late populist dictator Omar Torrijos, but election season is underway and a new president will be elected in May 2009. The candidate leading the polls is a left-wing ex-housing minister named Balbina Herrera. Meanwhile Torrijos maintains a political balance between free-trade economic incentives and fiscal responsibility on the one hand, and, on the other, embracing his father's populist past and reaching out to the poor. One week he's shaking hands with Fidel Castro, the next he's fishing with former U.S. president George H. W. Bush.

In 2007, a $5.5-billion expansion of the Panama Canal got underway, a move that caused much controversy and discussion, but that ultimately, promises to keep the canal relevant.

3 A CENTRAL AMERICAN CULTURAL PRIMER

Central America's population of 40 million people comes from diverse backgrounds: indigenous, European, African, and West Indian. Because of the history of Spanish influence in this region, *mestizos* (people of both Amerindian and Spanish ancestry) are in the majority. As you head from Panama north, the population of Central America becomes more indigenous. *Mestizos* are in the majority until you reach Guatemala, which has a predominantly Maya culture. Belize also has a tiny population of 4,000 Mennonites who migrated from Mexico in the 1950s. And along the Atlantic coast, there's a strong African presence that is more West Indian than Latin American in spirit. Most of the communities along this coast are English-speaking.

Though there is much variety, there are some constants in Latin American society. One is an acute wealth gap, with 50% of the population living below the poverty

Architecture 101

If you're looking for Classic monumental architecture, head to Guatemala, Belize, or Honduras. The creative Maya masons who constructed stone pyramids in these countries built them to last—they've even survived the daily swarms of tourists who scamper all over them—though it's not clear how long they can endure an existence unprotected by guide ropes. The most famous Maya ceremonial cities are **Tikal** in Guatemala, **Tazumal** in El Salvador, **Copán** in Honduras, and **Caracol** in Belize, but visitors can tour a host of other lesser sites around these countries.

A number of colonial buildings of any interest survive in the region, but many have succumbed to the ravages of time or were destroyed in major hurricanes. Guatemala and Nicaragua are perhaps most awash in architectural wonders. **Antigua, Guatemala,** is a fabulously preserved colonial city, as is **Managua, Nicaragua.** Many of these towns' colonial-era churches and buildings have survived several major earthquakes.

Clapboard houses built on stilts are the most typical architectural feature along the coast, and quite a few of these buildings, often painted in the pastel colors that are so popular throughout the Caribbean, can be seen around the region. Outside the coast and cities, much of the rest of the region's architecture is pretty plain. Most residential houses are simple concrete-block affairs, with zinc roofs.

level. The other is a pervasive *machista* attitude. Women are very much still tied to the home, though this attitude is gradually changing and women (especially those in cities) are becoming more independent. Finally, innate racism is unfortunately prevalent in all countries. The lighter your skin, the more educated, sophisticated, and richer you are thought in everyone's eyes.

Most of Central America is also primarily a Roman Catholic society, and family is an integral part of the culture here. Offspring, especially daughters, often remain with their families until they're married and even then multiple generations frequently continue to live in the same house. Most small towns offer little nightlife, since restaurants and shops shutter at dark. Instead, evenings are spent at home or in the town square—nearly every major town in the region is built around a central square that serves as a meeting spot for that community. In most Central American countries, *fútbol,* or soccer, competes with baseball as the leading sport. In countries such as Nicaragua, there is a baseball stadium in even the smallest towns.

One thing you'll find about Central Americans is that they are a warm and outgoing people who are eager to help strangers. Though most folks across the region no longer indulge in afternoon siestas, you will also notice that things move at a languid pace. Take for granted that any informal meeting will start 30 minutes late. This is not true regarding tourism—tour buses, for example, are expected to leave on time.

Below is a more detailed country-by-country cultural background of this region.

BELIZE

Belize has a population of some 297,000, roughly half of whom live in one of the six major towns or cities, with the rest living in rural areas or small villages. About 45% of the population is considered *mestizo,* descendants of mixed Spanish, Mexican, and/or Maya blood. Making up 30% of the population are the creoles, predominantly black descendants of slaves and the early British colonists. Belize's three Maya tribes—Yucatec, Mopan, and Kekchi—make up around 10% of the population. The Garífuna constitute approximately 6.5% of the population, while a mix of whites of British descent, Mennonites, Chinese, and East Indians fill out the rest.

With its tiny population and relative isolation from the outside world, Belize lacks the vibrant cultural scene found in larger, more cosmopolitan countries. Still, if you poke around, you'll find some respectable local music, literature, art, and architecture to enjoy. For current information about the arts and what might be happening while you're in Belize, contact the **Belize Arts Council** (**© 227-2110**), which is housed in the Bliss Institute for the Performing Arts (p. 106) in Belize City.

Belizean artists range from folk artists and artisans working in a variety of forms, materials, and traditions to modern painters, sculptors, and ceramicists producing beautiful representational and abstract works. Out in the western Cayo district, the traditional Maya arts are kept alive by several talented artisans working in carved slate bas-reliefs. Of these, the García sisters, who run a gallery and small museum in the Mountain Pine Ridge area, are the prime proponents.

Perhaps the most vibrant place to look for modern art is in southern Belize, where Garífuna painters like Benjamín Nicholas and Pen Cayetano have produced wonderful bodies of work depicting local life in a simple style. Walter Castillo is another excellent modern painter.

Belize doesn't have a strong literary tradition. However, most gift shops and bookstores around the country have a small collection of locally produced short stories, poetry, fiction, and nonfiction. In recent years, there has been a trend to resuscitate and transcribe the traditional Maya and Garífuna tales and folklore, along with the publication of modern pieces of fiction and nonfiction either set in Belize or written by Belizeans. Perhaps the best modern Belizean author is Zee Edgell, and you'll be able to find her works at gift shops around the country.

The most distinctive and popular form of Belizean music you will come across is Punta and Punta Rock. Punta is similar to many Afro-Caribbean and Afro-pop music forms, blending traditional rhythms and drumming patterns with modern electronic instruments (Punta is usually more rootsy and acoustic than Punta Rock, which features electric guitars and keyboards). Pen Cayetano is often credited as being the founder of Punta Rock; you will find his discs for sale throughout Belize, as well as those by his successors Andy Palacio, Peter Flores (aka Titiman), and Chico Ramos. Punta music is usually sung in the Garífuna dialect, although the latest incarnations feature lyrics in English and even Spanish. Dancing to Punta and Punta Rock is sensuous and close, often settling into a firm butt-to-groin grind.

You might want to rent a copy of *The Mosquito Coast* (1986), which was filmed in Belize, though it's set in Honduras (see p. 47 for info). Other films shot in Belize include *Dogs of War,* which features Christopher Walken, and *Heart of Darkness,* with John Malkovich.

GUATEMALA

Long-lasting Maya and Spanish empires produced an ethnically, linguistically, and economically divided Guatemala. Around half of the population is *mestizo* (known as *ladino* in Guatemala), or mixed Spanish-Amerindian heritage. The other half belongs to one of 23 indigenous Maya groups, each with their own language and customs. The largest group is the Ki'che, who live around Lake Atitlán and make up around 10% of the country's population—which totals almost 13 million. Other Maya groups include the Cakchiquel, Tz'utujil, Mam, and Kekchi; and on the Caribbean coast live the Garífuna, descendants of former slaves and Carib Indians.

Racial tensions can be strong between these groups, especially between *ladinos* and the Maya in the cities, and between *ladinos* and Garífuna on the Caribbean coast. Subsurface religious tensions also exist between the vast-majority Catholic population and the fast-growing Evangelical Protestant movement, which draws its greatest support within indigenous communities.

Guatemala's best-known art and craft works are indigenous woven tapestries and clothing. Artisans use natural dyes extracted from the *clavel* and *heraño* flowers, then mix in the crushed bodies of mosquitoes to keep the colors from running. The fabrics are woven on huge looms or simple, portable back-strap looms. Traditional dress for women includes a *huipil* (blouse) and *corte* (skirt), often fastened to the waist with a rope belt. Handicrafts are far from the only art in Guatemala, though. Several top-notch galleries in Guatemala City and Antigua carry a wide range of contemporary local art.

Guatemala's literary tradition dates from pre-Columbian Maya civilization, when Ki'che authors wrote the holy book Popol Vuh. The book traces the history of the Ki'che people beginning with their creation myth, linking the royal family with the gods in order to reaffirm its legitimacy. The book's exact age is unknown; the Spanish first recorded its existence in Chichicastenango in 1701.

Apart from the Popol Vuh, Guatemala's most famous literary works come from the Nobel Prize–winning poet, playwright, and ambassador Miguel Angel Asturias. Considered one of the fathers of magical realism, Asturias authored such works as *El Señor Presidente* (1946), *Viento Fuerte* (1950), and *Hombres de Maíz* (1967).

Literature can't be discussed without mentioning Maya activist Rigoberta Menchú, who won international acclaim with her autobiography, *I, Rigoberta,* first published in 1982. Other Guatemalan authors to look out for, both in Spanish and occasionally in translation, include the wonderful short story writer Augusto Monterroso, as well as the poets Luis Cardoza y Arragon, Otto Rene Castillo, and Humberto Ak'Abal.

In Guatemalan folk music, both *mestizo* and Maya, the marimba is king. *Mestizo* forms reflect their Spanish roots with marimba bands and Spanish-language folk songs influenced by the mariachi and ranchero traditions. Maya music may also prominently feature flute and drum, as with the Ki'che and Cakchiquel, or violins and harps, as with the Kekchi. A favorite contemporary Guatemalan musician is Ricardo Arjona, a rocking songster and lyricist of the first order. Songs such as "Ella y El" ("She and He") and "Si el Norte Fuera el Sur" ("If North Were South") are smart works of social and political satire with very catchy melodies.

The Guatemalan film industry is still in its infancy. However, the country has had subtle appearances in mainstream American productions. The 11th season of *Survivor* was filmed at the Maya ruins of Yaxhá, and the tribes were named after ancient ceremonial cities. More recently, *Looking for Palladin,* featuring Ben Gazzara and Talia Shire, was shot on location in Antigua. Going back a bit in time, the 1935 film *The New Adventures of Tarzan* was filmed in the rainforests of Guatemala, with the fabulous Atlantic coast waterfalls of Siete Altares playing a feature roll.

EL SALVADOR

El Salvador's culture is not a simple one to grasp. This small country is about the size of Massachusetts, with a population of roughly six million—making it the most densely populated Central American nation. It's a place where the beauty of its people stands in stark contrast to the violence of its history. Having suffered through decades of oppression, a bloody civil war, crushing poverty, and horrendous crime, the people of El Salvador have every right to be bitter. But somehow they're not—though the civil war of the 1980s very much remains part of the national psyche, many of the 2.5 million El Salvadorans who have migrated to the United States aim to one day return to their beloved El Salvador.

Of El Salvador's roughly six million residents, 90% identify themselves as *mestizo,* or of mixed race. Nine percent identify as white, with most either of Spanish descent or from elsewhere in Europe. Exact figures vary on the indigenous population and range from 1% to 5%. But whatever the exact number, the majority of El Salvador's indigenous people are descendants of the Pipil, who were part of the nomadic Mexican Nahua tribe that replaced the Maya as El Salvador's dominant population around the 11th century. Today, the greatest concentration of indigenous communities can be found in the southwestern department of Sonsonate, where a dwindling few continue to speak the native Nahuat language. A smaller indigenous population descended from the Lenca (Honduras' largest indigenous population) and are found mainly in El Salvador's eastern region. Though more than a third of El Salvadorans live in San Salvador, the majority of El Salvadorans live in rural areas. The country has a relatively young population, with 36% under the age of 15.

You won't find as obvious a culture here of art, literature, music, or film as you will in nearby Mexico or Guatemala. Rural village markets throughout the country, particularly those in La Palma, do offer traditional arts and crafts called "artesania," though, and the artist Fernando Llort (p. 247) has developed a reputation throughout the world for his art workshop in San Salvador, from which he encourages locals to express themselves through art.

Perhaps the most famous work of literature that hails from the country is *La Diáspora,* an award-winning novel by one of El Salvador's leading contemporary writers, Horacio Castellanos Moya. It chronicles the struggles of exiles from El Salvador's civil war.

Native indigenous music, using instruments like the marimba, flute, and drums, was repressed in the early 20th century but has miraculously survived and can be

Shopping Tips

International laws prohibit trade in endangered wildlife, so don't buy any plants or animals, even if they're readily for sale. Do not buy any kind of sea-turtle products (including jewelry); wild birds; lizard, snake, or cat skins; corals; or orchids (except those grown commercially). No matter how unique, beautiful, insignificant, or inexpensive it might seem, your purchase will directly contribute to the further hunting of endangered species.

At most stores and shops, sales and import taxes have already been figured into the display price, and it is not normal to haggle. You can however bargain a price down (within reason) in more informal settings such as city markets.

heard today through performers such as Paquito Palaviccini. El Salvador also has its very own take on Colombian *cumbia,* and the country dances to popular musical forms such as salsa, reggaeton, and hip-hop. There is even a form of hybrid El Salvadoran rock called *guanarock.*

Arguably the country's most heralded film is the 2004 movie *Film Voces Inocentes,* which tells the story of the El Salvadoran civil war through the eyes of an 11-year-old child and is based on the childhood of El Salvadoran filmmaker Oscar Torres, who fled El Salvador for the United States in the midst of the war.

HONDURAS

The vast majority (an estimated 85%–90%) of Honduras' 7.5 million or so people are ***mestizos*** or *ladinos,* which means they are of mixed American Indian and Spanish descent. The *mestizo* population therefore dominates the country's cities and the economic and political landscape of the country.

There are also eight other major ethnic groups that are concentrated in various regions around the country, the largest being the **Lenca,** who reside in the southwest, particularly the mountains and valleys near Gracias, and number around 100,000. The Lencas are descended from Chibcha-speaking Indians who came to Honduras from Colombia and Venezuela several thousand years ago. Nearby in the Copán Valley and along the border with Guatemala the **Chortí-Maya** is another indigenous group numbering between 4,000 and 5,000. They are the descendants of the ancient Maya.

The second-largest ethnic group in the country is the **Garífuna,** descendants of Carib and Arawak Indians who mixed with escaped African slaves and now populate the entire North Coast and the Bay Islands and number around 95,000. The British forcibly transplanted the Garífuna from the Cayman Islands to the island of Roatán in 1787 and from there they moved to other islands and to the mainland. The Garífuna still populate the Bay Islands, though they share the land with the Bay Islanders—another ethnic group descended from pirates and blacks from elsewhere in the Caribbean—and an increasing number of North Americans who are buying property and calling the islands home.

In the department of Yoro in the central highlands, the **Tolupan** inhabit scattered communities isolated among the mountains there. Three other indigenous groups can be found in the La Mosquitia (Mosquito Coast) region of the country. The lack of roads and transportation in this region has allowed the small pockets of **Miskitos, Pech,** and **Tawahkas** to maintain their cultural identities far better than most other indigenous groups in Central America, who have sometimes been engulfed by mainstream society. While the Miskitos are not a straight indigenous group—but rather a cultural mishmash of an unknown tribe, English pirates, and escaped African slaves—the Pech and Tawahkas have remained practically unchanged since preconquest.

Although Honduras has often been overshadowed by the impressive arts emerging from neighboring countries, the country's vibrant and diverse population has led to a number of achievements in the fine arts. Honduras has a thriving folk art scene. Best known are the country's primitivist painters, such as José Antonio Velásquez (1906–83) and Pablo Zelaya Sierra (1896–1933). The Lencas are also known throughout Central America for their pottery and ceramics. Finally, the artisans in Valle del Angeles are prized for their wood and leather work, while the Santa Bárbara area is known for producing excellent junco-palm hats, baskets, and mats.

The country has also been blessed with many gifted writers, including journalist Rafael Heliodoro Valle, poet Juan Ramón

Molina, and novelist Ramón Amaya Amador. Medea Benjamin's *Don't Be Afraid, Gringo: A Honduran Woman Speaks From The Heart: The Story of Elvia Alvarado* is the story of a poverty-stricken peasant in rural Honduras that's a favorite read of many volunteers and Peace Corps workers. *Banana Cultures: Agriculture, Consumption, and Environmental Change in Honduras and the United States,* by John Soluri, covers the history and growth of Honduras' banana industry along with the consumer mass market in the United States, while Ramón Amaya Amador's novel *Prisión Verde* gives an unsettling account of life on a banana plantation through the eyes of a worker.

Several well-known writers from abroad have also found inspiration here. William Sydney Porter, aka O'Henry, spent a year or so in Trujillo and Roatán while escaping embezzlement charges in the U.S., after which he coined the term "Banana Republic," and wrote *Cabbages and Kings,* a collection of stories revolving around the fictitious Central American town of Coralio, Anchuria.

Garífuna music has probably caught on more on the international scene than any other form of Honduran music. Top albums include Aurelio Martinez's *Garífuna Soul* and Andy Palacios' critically acclaimed Wátina. While musicians in both La Ceiba and San Pedro Sula are peddlers of Latin America's ever-present pop, rock, rap, and reggae mix of reggaeton, none has particularly caught on outside of their local followings. Along the North Coast and Bay Islands, the Garífuna have won acclaim for their dance and music, particularly punta, or *bangidy,* an intense dance performed by pairs amid the beats of drums, maracas, and other instruments.

Few notable films have been produced about Honduras. Perhaps the best is *The Mosquito Coast,* the 1986 movie starring Harrison Ford, River Phoenix, and Helen Mirren that was based on the 1982 novel by Paul Theroux. The film focuses on an egotistical inventor, Allie Fox, who is disgusted with American society and moves with his wife and four children from the U.S. to the north coast of Honduras. They set up their own society in the jungle while battling Christian missionaries, guerillas, and the harsh environment of La Mosquitia.

NICARAGUA

Most Nicaraguans refer to themselves as *pinoleros,* in reference to the popular corn drink *pinol.* This reveals the country's strong rural culture, one in which even the cities' shantytown dwellers are tied to the land. The vast majority of the population of 4.5 million are *mestizo* and 45% work in agriculture, much of it subsistence related. In recent years, there has been a strong shift to the cities and currently 55% of the population live in an urban area, though. Nicaragua is the poorest country in Central America and the second poorest in the Western Hemisphere, after Haiti. The national poverty rate is 50%, though that rate is often higher in rural areas.

The majority of Nicaraguans are Catholic, though there is a burgeoning minority of evangelicals here. Nicaragua is also one of the central places for liberation theology—a third-world take on Catholicism that portrays Jesus as a revolutionary. In addition, traditional Indian beliefs and folklore figures are very much alive and can be seen on parade at any of the country's famous weekend festivals.

Despite bad blood with the U.S. because of the Contra war in the 1980s, very few ordinary Nicaraguans associate American tourists with that country's foreign policy. Indeed, many have relatives in the U.S. and harbor a wish to get there someday themselves. This friendly attitude toward the U.S. is further highlighted by Nicaragua's obsession with baseball. There is a stadium in every town and the public follows the leagues avidly. Even in the smallest village, you'll find a scruffy pitch with a gang of kids in rags, using wooden planks as bats.

The written word is all-important here—Nicaraguans are famous throughout the Spanish-speaking world for being a country of great poets and writers. (Despite this, many poor people have only recently achieved literacy and most Nicaraguans cannot afford a book.) It is a source of great national pride that one of the finest poets in Spanish literature, Rubén Darío, hailed from León. *Songs of Life and Hope* is an excellent collection by Darío, or try the anthology *Ruben's Orphans,* translated into English by Marco Morelli.

The Country Under My Skin: A Memoir of Love and War is by one of Nicaragua's best-known writers and poets, Giaconda Belli, and covers her experience as a woman and Sandinista during the revolution. *The Jaguar Smile* by Salman Rushdie gives a poetic and humorous account of a trip he made to Nicaragua in 1986 to experience the revolution firsthand. *Blood of Brothers,* by *New York Times* journalist Stephen Kinser, is generally regarded as the best and most evenhanded chronicle of modern Nicaragua.

Poetic folk music is very popular in Nicaragua, and the Mejia brothers are perhaps the country's most famous troubadours. They use the guitar and accordion to sing of love and revolution. Over on the Caribbean coast (where Kenny Rogers is phenomenally popular), old-fashioned country-and-western music rules. Finally, you'll find it hard to avoid the cheerful rhythms of marimba (a wooden xylophone), which play on almost every city plaza.

Most films that are available in English about Nicaragua inevitably dwell on the recent wars. *Under Fire* stars Nick Nolte as a photojournalist covering the Sandinista revolution, uttering the immortal words, "I don't take sides, I take pictures." *Carla's Song* is a gritty and realistic movie about a Glaswegian bus driver taking a Nicaraguan refugee home to her country. *Walker—A True Story* has Ed Harris playing the American filibuster. *The World Is Watching* is an acclaimed documentary about the media coverage of the Contra war, and *The World Stopped Watching* is a just-as-fascinating sequel.

COSTA RICA

Costa Rica has a population of some four million, more than half of whom live in the Central Valley and are considered as urban. Nearly 96% of the Tico population (Costa Ricans are often referred to as "Ticos") is of Spanish or otherwise European descent, and it is not at all unusual to see fair-skinned and blond Costa Ricans. This is largely because the indigenous population in place when the first Spaniards arrived was small and thereafter was quickly reduced to even more of a minority by wars and disease. There are still some remnant indigenous populations, primarily on reservations around the country; the principal tribes include the Bribri, Cabécar, Boruca, and Guaymí. In addition, on the Caribbean coast and in the big cities, there is a substantial population of English-speaking black creoles who came over from the Antilles to work on the railroad and on the banana plantations. Racial tension isn't palpable, but it exists, perhaps more out of simple ignorance and fear rather than any organized or articulated prejudice.

Roman Catholicism is the official religion of Costa Rica, although freedom to practice any religion is guaranteed by the country's constitution. More than 90% of the population identifies itself as Roman Catholic, yet there are small but visible evangelical Christian, Protestant, and Jewish communities.

A small and provincial country, Costa Rica's culture and arts are somewhat similarly limited in size and scope. Though Costa Rica's literary output is sparsely translated and little known outside of Costa Rica, there are some notable authors to look out for, especially if you can read in Spanish. **Carlos Luis Fallas's** 1941 tome, *Mamita Yunai,* is a stark look at the impact of the large banana giant United Fruit on the country. More recently, **Fernando Contreras** takes up where his predecessor left off in *Unico Mirando al Mar,* which describes the conditions of the poor, predominantly children, who scavenge Costa Rica's garbage dumps.

Several musical traditions and styles meet and mingle in Costa Rica. The northern Guanacaste region is a hotbed of folk music that is strongly influenced by the *marimba* (wooden xylophone) traditions of Guatemala and Nicaragua, while also featuring guitars, maracas, and the occasional harp. On the Caribbean coast you can hear traditional calypso sung by descendants of the original black workers brought over to build the railroads and tend the banana plantations. Roving bands play a mix of guitar, banjo, washtub bass, and percussion in the bars and restaurants of Cahuita and Puerto Viejo.

There's also a healthy contemporary music scene. The jazz-fusion trio **Editus** has won two Grammy awards for their work with Panamanian salsa giant (and movie star and tourism minister) **Rubén Blades.** Meanwhile, **Malpaís,** the closest thing Costa Rica has to a supergroup, is a pop-rock outfit that is tearing it up in Costa Rica and around Central America.

Costa Rica has a budding and promising young film industry. Local feature films like ***Tropix, Caribe,*** and ***Passport*** are all out on subtitled DVD. In 2008, ***El Camino (The Path),*** by Costa Rican filmmaker Ishtar Yasin Gutiérrez, was screened at the Berlin Film Festival. And several other feature films are expected to be produced in 2009 and 2010, including ***Del Amor y Otros Demonios,*** based on a novel by Gabriel García Márquez.

PANAMA

Panama has 3.2 million residents, and collectively more than a third live in Panama City, Colón, and David, the country's three largest cities. The remaining population is concentrated mostly in small towns and villages in central Panama and the Azuero Peninsula. Roughly 70% of the population is *mestizo;* 14% are of African descent, 10% are white and other immigrant races, and 6% are Amerindian. About 30% of the population is under the age of 14.

There are seven indigenous groups in Panama who, despite foreign influences and modern advancements, have to differing degrees held onto their culture and languages. Ethnic tribes such as the **Kuna,** who live along the central Caribbean coast, are a semiautonomous and insular society that has hardly changed over the last century. However, the eastern Kuna community, near the Darién, has adapted to modern society, wears Western clothing, and practices few native traditions. The **Ngöbe** and **Buglé** are two tribes that are culturally similar and collectively referred to as Guaymí. Ngöbe-Buglés live in the highlands of western Panama (as well as eastern Costa Rica), and are the country's largest indigenous group; many travel nomadically and make their living in coffee production. Eastern Panama is home to two indigenous groups, the **Emberá** and the **Wounaan**—several Emberá communities are close enough to Panama City to be visited for the day. Tiny populations of **Teribe** (also called Naso) and **Bri Bri** live scattered around mainland Bocas del Toro.

People of African descent first came to Panama as slaves of the Spanish during the 16th century, and many escaped into Darién Province where they settled and became known as ***cimarrones.*** In and around Portobelo and the eastern Caribbean coast, they call themselves **Congos.** During the 19th century, jobs in canal

Etiquette Tips

Always greet Central Americans with a cheerful *buenos días* in the morning and *buenos tardes* in the afternoon. Excuse yourself from company by saying "permiso." Don´t get too hung up on whether you address people formally *(usted)* or informally (*tu* or *vos*). Most locals make allowances for the fact that you are a foreigner, speaking a strange tongue, and won't get offended by such subtleties. Medical professionals like to be called "Doctora" and it is always wise to address a policeman as "Señor Policia."

Also be careful with your hand gestures. Central Americans use gestures that are often the opposite of what you may be used to. For example, a beckoning index finger is regarded as vulgar. A downward shooing gesture actually means "come here!" The universal finger wag is however the same everywhere and can be used in all sorts of situations from haggling to arguments. In addition, Central Americans are not as outwardly affectionate as their South American cousins. Females are sometimes kissed on the cheek, but if in doubt, a handshake will suffice.

Most Central Americans dress in a conservative manner; this is less true for the younger generation who are more casually fashionable. The torpid weather will compel you to wear light clothes and shorts (and that's perfectly fine in most restaurants and attractions), but be aware that this mode of dress is not acceptable in churches. Also, while most Maya craftspeople are more than happy to see foreigners purchase their goods, for some indigenous people, seeing tourists walking the streets in native garb can be insulting—especially when women unknowingly wear traditional men's clothing, or vice versa. Use caution, and when in doubt, don't model your purchases in any but the most touristy towns or settings until you get home.

building and banana plantations lured immigrants from Jamaica, Barbados, and Colombia, who settled along the western Caribbean coast and are commonly referred to as **Afro-Caribbeans** or *creoles.*

One notable book about Panama is ***Emperors in the Jungle,*** by John Lindsay-Poland, which digs deep into the history of U.S. military involvement in Panama during the past century. ***Panama,*** by Kevin Buckley, is a gripping read by a former *Newsweek* correspondent who vividly describes the events leading to the overthrow of Manuel Noriega. Another probing insight into the failure of U.S. policy that led to the rise of Noriega and the invasion is ***The Noriega Mess: The Drugs, the Canal, and Why America Invaded,*** by Luis E. Murillo. ***Path Between the Seas: The Creation of the Panama Canal, 1870–1914,*** by David McCullough, brings the epic history of the building of the canal to life with McCullough's meticulously researched book.

Ruben Blades may be Panama's current minister of tourism, but he is better known as Panama's best-known salsa singer. He's made dozens of CDs, but you might want to check out *Maestro de la Fania,* his latest creation, and *Lo Mejor vol. 1 and 2,* featuring his greatest hits over his decades-long career.

The Panama Deception is an interesting documentary featuring Elizabeth Montgomery and Abraham Alvarez among others that aims to tell the truth about the 1989 invasion of Panama by the U.S. *The Tailor of Panama* (2001) is an excellent spy-thriller staring Pierce Brosnan, Geoffrey Rush, and Jamie Lee Curtis, which centers around the transfer of power of the canal from the Americans to the Panamanian people during the post-Noriega years.

4 THE LAY OF THE LAND

At 518,000 sq. km (200,000 sq. miles), the seven Central American countries of Belize, Guatemala, Honduras, El Salvador, Nicaragua, Costa Rica, and Panama are squeezed into a narrow landmass (the distance from west to east is a mere 30km/19 miles at the narrowest point of Panama). That's approximately the same surface area as the states of California and New York put together. Yet with 4,500km (2,790 miles) of coastland, numerous mountain ranges, 300 volcanoes, and four tectonic plates crunching into each other, the area is much more of a geological hot spot, with some of the most varied natural diversity in the world.

On one side of the isthmus that is Central America, the muddy swamps and deltas of the Caribbean coast descend onto a narrow shelf of limestone rock that extends several miles out to sea. Here you'll find numerous islands and the second-longest barrier reef in the world, whose rich coral grounds stretch along the coasts of Belize and Honduras. On the other side of the isthmus, the dark Pacific pounds black volcanic beaches up and down the coast, which lead to narrow plains of agricultural land, tropical dry forest, and large freshwater lakes such as Lago de Nicaragua. The Pacific coast is generally less humid, and it's sheltered from the easterly trade winds by a rugged spine of mountains that hold cloud forests and pine valleys.

Earthquakes are common throughout Central America, as are belching, lava dribbling volcanoes such as **Arenal** in Costa Rica and **Masaya** in Nicaragua. Such a volatile, churning landscape also means the land is dotted with plenty of hot thermal springs and underground cave systems.

CENTRAL AMERICA'S ECOSYSTEMS

Central America's **lowland rainforests** are true tropical jungles. Some are deluged with more than 200 inches of rainfall per year, and their climate is hot and humid. Trees grow tall and fast, fighting for sunlight in the upper reaches. In fact, life and foliage on the forest floor are surprisingly sparse. The action is typically 30m (98 ft.) up, in the canopy, where long vines stream down, lianas climb up, and bromeliads grow on the branches and trunks of towering hardwood trees. Classic examples of lowland rainforests are found along the **southern Pacific coast** of Costa Rica, the **La Mosquita** region of Honduras, along the **Río Dulce** in Guatemala, and the **Laguna de Perlas** in Nicaragua.

At higher altitudes, you'll find Central America's famed **cloud forests.** Here the steady flow of moist air meets the mountains and creates a nearly constant mist. Epiphytes—resourceful plants that live cooperatively on the branches and trunks of other trees—grow abundantly in the cloud forests, where they must extract moisture and nutrients from the air. Because cloud forests are found in generally steep, mountainous terrain, the canopy here is lower and less uniform than in lowland rainforests, providing better chances for viewing elusive fauna. The region's most spectacular cloud forests can be experienced at **Monteverde Biological Cloud Forest Reserve** in Costa Rica, **Parque Nacional Celaque** in Honduras, **Reserva Natural Miraflor** in Nicaragua, and **the Chiriqui highlands** of Panama.

At the highest reaches, the cloud forests of this region give way to **elfin forests** and ***páramos.*** More commonly associated with the South American Andes, a *páramo* is characterized by a variety of tundralike shrubs and grasses, with a scattering of twisted, windblown trees. Reptiles, rodents, and raptors are the most common residents here. Typical examples of *páramo* can be found at **Chirripó National Park** in **Costa Rica** and parts of the **Guatemalan highlands.**

On the Pacific side of the highlands, you'll still find examples of the otherwise vanishing **tropical dry forest.** During the long and pronounced dry season (late Nov to late Apr), no rain relieves the unabated heat. To conserve much-needed water, the trees drop their leaves but bloom in a riot of color: purple jacaranda, scarlet *poró,* and brilliant orange flame-of-the-forest are just a few examples. Then, during the rainy season, this deciduous forest is transformed into a lush and verdant landscape. Because the foliage is not that dense, the dry forests are excellent places to view a variety of wildlife, especially howler monkeys and *pizotes* (coati). The best examples of dry forests are found in **Santa Rosa** and **Guanacaste** national parks in Costa Rica and parts of northern Belize.

Along the coasts, primarily where river mouths meet the ocean, you will find extensive **mangrove forests** and **swamps.** Around these seemingly monotonous tangles of roots exists one of the most diverse and rich ecosystems in the region. Birdlife includes pelicans, storks, and pink flamingos, and reptiles such as crocodiles and caimans also thrive in this environment.

In any one spot in Central America, temperatures remain relatively constant year-round. However, they vary dramatically according to altitude, from tropically hot and steamy along the coasts to below freezing at the highest elevations.

FLORA & FAUNA

For millennia, this land bridge between North and South America served as a migratory thoroughfare and mating ground for species native to the once-separate continents. Perhaps its unique location between both continents explains why the region comprises only .05% of the earth's landmass, yet it is home to 7% of the planet's biodiversity. More than 15,000 identified species of plants, 900 species of birds, 9,000 species of butterflies and moths, and 500 species of mammals, reptiles, and amphibians are found here. And that is just what has been cataloged. Scientists calculate there is much more to be discovered. The key to this biological richness lies in the many distinct life zones and ecosystems found in Central America. It might all seem like one big mass of green to the untrained eye, but the differences are profound.

All sorts of fish and crustaceans live in the brackish tidal waters off the coast, primarily in the Caribbean but also parts of the Pacific. Caimans and crocodiles cruise the maze of rivers and unmarked canals. There are many snakes, but very few are poisonous. Watch out for the tiny coral snake and the bigger barba amarilla. Another creature worth avoiding is the poisonous arrow frog.

Hundreds of herons, ibises, egrets, and other marsh birds nest and feed along the region's silted banks, as well. Mangrove swamps are often havens for water birds like cormorants, frigate birds, pelicans, and herons. Farther out, both coastal waters are alive with marine life that includes turtles, barracudas, stingrays, marlins, dolphins, and red snappers. Nicaragua boasts the only freshwater shark in the world on Lago de Nicaragua, while the

Río San Juan that joins it to the Caribbean is famous for a giant silver fish called a tarpon. Keep an eye out for whales along the Costa Rican coast.

The jungle teems with wildlife, particularly birds. Macaws, parrots, hummingbirds, and toucans are just some of the many reasons why Central America is a birder's paradise. The larger birds tend to nest up high in the canopy, while the smaller ones nestle in the underbrush. Count yourself lucky if you catch sight of the beautiful quetzal, Guatemala's national bird, or one of the region's elusive big cats, including jaguars, puma, and ocelots. A little easier to spot are howler monkeys and their simian brethren the spider and squirrel monkeys. Other mammals to look out for on the jungle floor include anteaters, deer, and sloths.

Plant life in this region is very much determined by altitude and climate. The Pacific dry forest is home to hardy species of thorny shrubs that lose their leaves in the high season and burst into flower in April and May. Higher up, the landscape is dominated by pines, oaks, and evergreens. Above 1,600m (5,248 ft.), the flora becomes lusher with orchids, mosses, and ferns all growing abundantly on giant trees.

SEARCHING FOR WILDLIFE

Forest animals throughout Central America are predominantly nocturnal. When they are active in the daytime, they are usually elusive and on the watch for predators. Birds are easier to spot in clearings or secondary forests than they are in primary forests. Unless you have lots of experience in the Tropics, your best hope for enjoying a walk through the jungle lies in employing a trained and knowledgeable guide.

Tips to keep in mind include **listening carefully and keeping quiet**—you're most likely to hear an animal before seeing one. Also, it helps to **bring binoculars and dress appropriately.** You'll have a hard time focusing your binoculars if you're busy swatting mosquitoes. Light, long pants and long-sleeved shirts are your best bet. Comfortable hiking boots are a real boon, except where heavy rubber boots are necessary (a real possibility, if it's been raining). Avoid loud colors; the better you blend in with your surroundings, the better your chances are of spotting wildlife. Finally, **be patient.** The jungle isn't on a schedule. However, your best shots at seeing forest fauna are in the very early-morning and late-afternoon hours.

5 EATING & DRINKING IN CENTRAL AMERICA

TYPICAL MEALS

Rice and beans are the bases of most Central American meals—all three of them. At breakfast, they're called *gallo pinto* and come with everything from eggs to steak to seafood. At lunch or dinner, rice and beans are an integral part of a *casado* (which translates as "married" and is the name for the local version of a blue-plate special). A *casado* usually consists of cabbage-and-tomato salad, fried plantains (a starchy, banana-like fruit), and a chicken, fish, or meat dish of some sort. On the Caribbean coast, rice and beans are called *rice 'n' beans,* and are cooked in coconut milk.

However, you don't have to look too far to see that the region boasts an abundant variety of other local dishes to sample, which incorporate unique vegetables, fruits, and grains. Though rice and beans will be on almost all menus, in coastal areas, you'll also come across an incredible amount of seafood, especially lobster and shrimp. There is a growing controversy around eating lobster, due to overfishing and the extreme danger lobster pickers are put through for very little money. Avoid eating *huevos de paslama* (turtle eggs), since turtles are an endangered species.

In the highlands, you'll find more beef on the menu in the form of *caldos* (stews) served with yucca (manioc root or cassava in English), along with chicken dishes—just don't be too surprised if your chicken comes with the feet still attached. Everywhere you will find corn-based treats like *tamales* (stuffed cornmeal patties wrapped and steamed inside banana leaves), along with *patacones* (fried green plantain chips), often served streetside.

On the whole, you'll find vegetables surprisingly lacking in the meals you're served throughout Central America—usually nothing more than a little pile of shredded cabbage topped with a slice or two of tomato. For a much more satisfying and filling salad, order a *palmito* (hearts of palm salad). The heart (actually the stalk or trunk of these small palms) is first boiled and then chopped into circular pieces and served with other fresh vegetables, with a salad dressing on top. If you want something more than this, you'll have to order a side dish such as *picadillo,* a stew or purée of vegetables with a bit of meat in it.

Central America has a wealth of delicious tropical fruits. The most common are mangoes, papayas, pineapples, melons, and bananas. Other fruits include *marañón,* which is the fruit of the cashew tree and has orange or yellow glossy skin; *granadilla* or *maracuyá* (passion fruit); *mamón chino,* which Asian travelers will recognize as rambutan; and *carambola* (star fruit).

Fruit is often served as dessert throughout this region, but there are some other options for sweets. *Queque seco,* literally "dry cake," is the same as pound cake. *Tres leches* cake, on the other hand, is so moist that you almost need to eat it with a spoon. Flan is a typical custard dessert. It often comes as either *flan de caramelo* (caramel) or *flan de coco* (coconut). Numerous other sweets are available, many of which are made with condensed milk and raw sugar. *Cajetas* are popular handmade candies, made from sugar and various mixes of evaporated, condensed, and powdered milk. They are sold in differing-size bits and chunks at most *pulperías* (general stores) and streetside food stands.

See "Tips on Dining" in the individual country chapters throughout this book for more info.

BEVERAGES

Central America produces some of the best rum in the world, especially Nicaragua and Belize. The best Nicaraguan rum is called Flor de Caña, and the best Belize version is One Barrel. Zacapo Centenario is generally regarded as the best rum from Guatemala, with Ron Botrán Añejo coming a close second. The national alcoholic drink in Panama is called *seco.* Like rum, it is made from sugar cane but has milk and ice added to the mix. The whole region is known for *chicha,* a sweet, fermented corn beverage, and an even stronger variation known as *chicha brava. La cususa,* a crude cane liquor that's often combined with a soft drink or tonic, is popular in Nicaragua; a *guaro* is the Costa Rican version of this same drink.

You can find imported wines at reasonable prices in the better restaurants throughout the region. You can usually save money by ordering a Chilean wine over a Californian or European one. Cashew wine is popular in Belize, though you may find it to be too strong and vinegary. *Cerveza* (beer) can be found everywhere, and every country has its most popular native brands.

Popular nonalcoholic drinks include *pinol,* which is toasted, ground corn with water, and *tiste,* a variation made with cocoa beans and corn. Soda in the form of *gaseosa* is everywhere, as are vendors selling small bags of ice-cold mineral water—

much more environmentally friendly than bottles. Look out for excellent fruit juices called *liquadas* that can be served with milk or water. Among the more common fruits used in these shakes are mangoes, papayas, blackberries, and pineapples. Order *un fresco con leche sin hielo* (a *fresco* with milk but without ice) if you're avoiding untreated water.

If you're a coffee drinker, you might be disappointed here. Most of the best coffee has traditionally been targeted for export, and Central Americans tend to prefer theirs weak and sugary. Better hotels and restaurants are starting to cater to American and European tastes and are serving superior blends. If you want black coffee, ask for *café negro;* if you want it with milk, order *café con leche.* For something different, ask for *agua dulce,* a warm drink made from melted sugar cane and served with either milk or lemon, or straight.

Although water in parts of the region is safe to drink, bottled water is readily available and is a good option if you're worried about an upset stomach. If you like your water without bubbles, request *aqua mineral sin gas,* or *agua en botella.*

DINING CUSTOMS

The region's capital cities have the best choices regarding restaurants, with everything from Italian, Brazilian, and Chinese eateries to chains like T.G.I. Friday's. For cheap meals, buffet-style restaurants are very popular, as are street grills on the side of the road. Every country has a different term for these informal types of restaurants, so consult the individual chapters for info.

Outside the region's major tourist destinations, your options get very limited very fast. In fact, many beach destinations are so remote that you have no choice but to eat in the hotel's dining room. Even on the more accessible beaches, the only choices aside from the hotel dining rooms are often cheap local places or overpriced tourist traps serving indifferent meals. At remote jungle lodges, the food is usually served buffet or family style and can range from bland to inspired, depending on who's doing the cooking, and turnover is high.

Throughout Central America, people sit down to eat lunch at midday and dinner at 7pm. Some downtown restaurants in big cities are open 24 hours; however, expensive restaurants tend to be open for lunch between 11am and 3pm and for dinner between 6 and 11pm. At even the more expensive restaurants in the region, it's hard to spend more than $50 (£25) per person unless you really splurge on drinks.

3

Planning Your Trip to Central America

The country chapters in this guide provide specific information on traveling to and getting around individual Central American countries. In this chapter, we provide you with region-wide tips and general information that will help you plan your trip.

1 VISITOR INFORMATION

See "The Best of Central America Online" (p. 15) for info on country-specific tourist board and other helpful websites. Also see the "Visitor Information" sections throughout this book's country chapters for info; note that a number of small towns throughout this region do not have tourist board offices.

In the United States or Canada, you can get basic information on Central America by checking out the **CIA World Fact Book** (www.odci.gov) or the U.S. State Department's travel advisory section on http://state.gov. In addition to this official site, you'll be able to find a wealth of Web-based information on Central America with a few clicks of your mouse.

The **American Automobile Association** (www.aaa.com) produces a decent road map for the region, but perhaps the best map of Central America is the *Travelers Reference Map of Central America,* produced by ITM and available in larger bookstores.

2 ENTRY REQUIREMENTS

The passport and visa information in this section is for quick reference; see individual country chapters for complete details about the entry requirements for your destination.

Due to concerns about parental abductions, there are special requirements for children visiting many foreign countries, including those in Central America. If you are a lone or single parent or a guardian, you must bring a copy of the child's birth certificate and a notarized consent document from the parent(s). For single parents, a decree of sole custody or a parental death certificate will also do. Ask your airline what's required when you book the ticket; also check the State Department's "Foreign Entry Requirements" page at http://travel.state.gov.

BELIZE No visas are required for citizens of the United States, the European community—including Great Britain and Ireland, South Africa, Australia, or New Zealand. Visitors from these countries do require a current and valid passport. Nationals of certain other countries need a visa or consular permission to enter Belize. For a current list, see the Belize Tourism Board website (www.travelbelize.org) or call the nearest Belize consulate or embassy.

GUATEMALA Citizens of the United States, Canada, Great Britain, all European Union nations, Ireland, Australia, and New Zealand may visit Guatemala for

Coming & Going

In 2006, Guatemala entered into an immigration and border control treaty with El Salvador, Honduras, and Nicaragua. This agreement, which allows free travel between the countries to all nationals of these signatory nations, creates a single 90-day entry visa for foreign visitors. What this means is that if you travel between these four countries, your total stay cannot exceed 90 days without seeking an extension from the immigration authorities in the country you are visiting. If you want to "renew" your Guatemalan visa by exiting the country for 72 hours and then returning on a new tourist visa, it must be to a country not covered in this agreement.

a maximum of 90 days. No visa is necessary, but you must have a valid passport.

HONDURAS Citizens of the United States, Canada, Australia and New Zealand, and the European Union require just a passport to enter Honduras and may stay for up to 90 days. The passport must be valid for at least 6 months after the date of entry and you must pay a $2 (£1) entrance fee to get a tourist card. Residents from Israel, South Africa, and China require $10 (£5) visas.

EL SALVADOR Citizens of the United States, Canada, Great Britain, and most European nations may visit El Salvador for a maximum of 90 days. No visa is necessary, but you must have a valid passport, which you should carry with you at all times while you're in the country. There is a $10 (£5) charge on your tourist card upon entry. Citizens of Australia and New Zealand require a visa.

NICARAGUA Citizens of the United States, Canada, Australia and New Zealand, and the European Union require just a passport to enter Nicaragua and may stay for up to 90 days. The passport must be valid for at least 6 months after the date of entry.

COSTA RICA Citizens of the United States, Canada, Great Britain, and most European nations may visit Costa Rica for a maximum of 90 days. No visa is necessary, but you must have a valid passport, which you should carry with you at all times while you're in Costa Rica. Citizens of Australia, Ireland, and New Zealand can enter the country without a visa and stay for 30 days, although once in the country, visitors can apply for an extension.

PANAMA Citizens of the United States, Canada, Great Britain, and most European nations may visit Panama for a maximum of 90 days. No visa is necessary, but you must have a valid passport and a $5 (£2.50) tourist card, which can be paid for when entering by land or at the airline counter before your departure.

PASSPORT INFORMATION

To apply for a passport, residents of the United States can download passport applications from the U.S. State Department website at http://travel.state.gov, or call the **National Passport Agency** at ✆ **202/647-0518.**

Canadian residents should visit www.ppt.gc.ca or call ✆ **800/567-6868.**

British citizens should contact the **United Kingdom Passport Service** at ✆ **0870/521-0410** or on the Web at www.ukpa.gov.uk. Residents of Ireland can call ✆ **01/671-1633,** or visit www.irlgov.ie/iveagh.

Australian citizens should contact the **Australian Passport Information Service** at ✆ **131-232,** or visit www.passports.gov.au. Residents of New Zealand should call the **Passports Office** at ✆ **0800/225-050** or 04/474-8100, or log on to www.passports.govt.nz.

For more information on how to obtain a passport, see **"Passports"** in the appendix.

CUSTOMS

For information about what you can bring with you upon entry, see the "Customs" section in individual country chapters.

What You Can Bring Home

Returning **U.S. citizens** who have been away for at least 48 hours are allowed to bring back, once every 30 days, $800 worth of merchandise duty-free. You'll pay a flat rate of duty on the next $1,000 worth of purchases. Any dollar amount beyond that is subject to duties at whatever rates apply. On mailed gifts, the duty-free limit is $200. Be sure to keep your receipts or purchases accessible to expedite the declaration process. ***Note:*** If you owe duty, you are required to pay on your arrival in the United States—either by cash, personal check, government or traveler's check, or money order (and, in some locations, a Visa or MasterCard).

With some exceptions, you cannot bring fresh fruits and vegetables into the United States. For specifics on what you can bring back, download the invaluable free pamphlet *Know Before You Go* online at **www.cbp.gov**. (Click on "Travel," and then click on "Know Before You Go! Online Brochure.") Or contact the **U.S. Customs & Border Protection (CBP),** 1300 Pennsylvania Ave. NW, Washington, DC 20229 (✆ **877/287-8667**), and request the pamphlet.

For a clear summary of **Canadian** rules, write for the booklet *I Declare,* issued by the **Canada Border Services Agency** (✆ **800/461-9999** in Canada, or 204/983-3500; www.cbsa-asfc.gc.ca). Canada allows its citizens a C$750 exemption, and you're allowed to bring back duty-free one carton of cigarettes, one can of tobacco, 40 imperial ounces of liquor, and 50 cigars. In addition, you're allowed to mail gifts to Canada valued at less than C$60 a day, provided they're unsolicited and don't contain alcohol or tobacco (write on the package "Unsolicited gift, under $60 value"). All valuables should be declared on the Y-38 form before departure from Canada, including serial numbers of valuables you already own, such as expensive foreign cameras. ***Note:*** The $750 exemption can only be used once a year and only after an absence of 7 days.

U.K. citizens returning from **a non-E.U. country** have a Customs allowance of: 200 cigarettes; 50 cigars; 250 grams of smoking tobacco; 2 liters of still table wine; 1 liter of spirits or strong liqueurs (over 22% volume); 2 liters of fortified wine, sparkling wine or other liqueurs; 60cc (ml) perfume; 250cc (ml) of toilet water; and £145 worth of all other goods, including gifts and souvenirs. People under 17 cannot have the tobacco or alcohol allowance. For more information, contact **HM Customs & Excise** at ✆ **0845/010-9000** (from outside the U.K., 020/8929-0152), or consult their website at www.hmce.gov.uk.

The duty-free allowance in **Australia** is A$400 or, for those under 18, A$200. Citizens can bring in 250 cigarettes or 250 grams of loose tobacco, and 1.125 milliliters of alcohol. If you're returning with valuables you already own, such as foreign-made cameras, you should file form B263. A helpful brochure available from Australian consulates or Customs offices is *Know Before You Go.* For more information, call the **Australian Customs Service** at ✆ **1300/363-263,** or log on to www.customs.gov.au.

The duty-free allowance for **New Zealand** is NZ$700. Citizens over 17 can bring in 200 cigarettes, 50 cigars, or 250 grams of tobacco (or a mixture of all three if their combined weight doesn't exceed 250g); plus 4.5 liters of wine and beer, or 1.125 liters of liquor. New Zealand currency does not carry import or export restrictions. Fill out a certificate of export, listing the valuables you are taking out of the country; that way, you can bring them back without paying duty. Most questions are answered in a free pamphlet available at New Zealand consulates and Customs offices: *New Zealand Customs Guide for Travellers, Notice no. 4.* For more information, contact **New**

Zealand Customs, The Customhouse, 17–21 Whitmore St., Box 2218, Wellington (✆ **04/473-6099** or 0800/428-786; www.customs.govt.nz).

3 WHEN TO GO

Central America remains consistently hot throughout the year, unless you spend a night in the chilly highlands. The **rainy season** runs from April to early December, but the region still experiences plenty of sunshine during this period. The **hurricane season** rains down in September to October and can cause flooding everywhere, though it can be particularly bad on the Caribbean coast. The **dry season** runs from Christmas to Easter and this is the tourist peak season. Easter is a particularly good time to go to Central America as the whole region goes crazy for *Semana Santa*. Make sure you book ahead, and expect higher hotel prices during this time of year. The low season means fewer people, lower prices, and you can still have glorious weather. ***A drawback:*** Some of the region's rugged roads become downright impassable without four-wheel-drive during the rainy season.

HOLIDAYS

Latin Americans love a good street party—even ones devoted to celebrating chaste Catholic saints exude a wild exuberance. Christmas is colorful but Easter is the wildest celebration; during Easter week, some countries virtually shut down as the locals head for the beach for a week (be careful of canceled buses during this period). The best place to celebrate Carnaval is in Panama.

Whatever time of year you go, there's bound to be a small town somewhere celebrating its patron saint with parades, bullfights, and firecrackers. Many of the region's celebrations have a strong indigenous flavor, and employ folklore and traditional dances to honor things like famous battles or thwarted volcanic eruptions. Below are just some highlights. Consult each individual country chapter for more details on all the revelry.

CALENDAR OF EVENTS

JANUARY

Festival of San Sebastián, Masaya, Nicaragua. Drums, whistles, and chanting reverberate around the streets of Masaya during this festival celebrating Saint Sebastian. The town of Diriamba (30km/19 miles southwest of Masaya) is generally recognized as throwing an even more colorful and authentic parade, too, with a lively mix of pagan satire and colonial pomp. Last 2 weeks in January.

Fiesta de Palmares, Costa Rica. One of the best organized of the country's traditional *fiestas,* the Fiesta de Palmares includes bullfights, a horseback parade *(tope),* and many concerts, carnival rides, and food booths. First 2 weeks in January.

Feria de las Flores y del Café (Flower and Coffee Festival), Boquete, Panama. This festival is one of the grandest celebrations of flowers in the world, drawing thousands of people to Boquete for 10 days. Expect lush flower displays, food stands, live music, amusement rides, handicrafts booths, and hotel rooms booked far in advance. Mid-January.

FEBRUARY

Carnaval. Panama's most revered holiday is Carnaval, the 4 days that precede Ash Wednesday. The largest celebrations take place in Panama City and the

Azuero Peninsula, with parades, floats, drinking, costumes, and music.

International Permanent Festival of Art and Culture. This 15-year-old international arts festival in Suchitoto, El Salvador, was founded by retired but once world-renowned cinematographer Alejandro Cotto and is one of the country's premier arts events, attracting visual and performing artists from around Latin America and the world. Dates vary in February.

March

Baron Bliss Day (Nationwide, Belize). While not officially the nation's patron Saint, Baron Henry Edward Ernest Victor Bliss is certainly Belize's foremost patron and benefactor. The day is marked with nationwide celebrations. The greatest festivities are held in Belize City, which hosts a regatta, as well as horse and footraces. March 9.

National Orchid Show, San José, Costa Rica. Orchid growers throughout the world gather to show their wares, trade tales and secrets, and admire the hundreds of species on display. Contact the Costa Rican Tourist Board (www.visitcostarica.com) for location and dates in 2009 and 2010. Mid-March.

April

Holy Week, throughout Central America. Religious processions are held in cities and towns throughout Central America during *Semana Santa,* and it is a fantastic time to visit the region. León in Nicaragua throws a particularly colorful event with elaborate sawdust pavement paintings. Antigua in Guatemala is also famous for its celebrations and carpet-lined streets. Holy Week celebrations in Comayagua are one of the biggest festivals in Honduras and feature a week of elaborate processions. Celebrations take place the week before Easter, which sometimes falls in late March rather than April.

Garífuna Day (The Bay islands and north Coast, Honduras): Dancing, drinking, music, and other cultural feats take place to celebrate the arrival of the Garífuna on Roatán in 1797. April 12.

May

Cashew Festival, Crooked Tree Village, Belize. Celebrating the cashew harvest, this weekend festivity features booths selling everything possible under the sun made with this coveted nut, including cashew wine and cashew jelly. Live music and general revelry accompany the celebrations. First weekend in May.

Feria de San Isidro (La Ceiba, Honduras): Hundreds of thousands of revelers flock to this north coast town for the Honduran version of Carnaval. Parades march through the downtown streets, the constant beating of drums is everywhere, and all-night partying occurs on the beaches. The week preceding the third Saturday of May.

June

Festival Corpus Christi, La Villa de Los Santos, Panama. This Panamanian town explodes with activity for a 2-week religious festival known for its elaborate dances led by men in devil masks. Forty days after Easter.

Lobster Festival (Placencia, Belize). You'll get your fill of this tasty crustacean during this extended weekend celebration of the opening of lobster season. In addition to gorging on lobster, you can also take in concerts and street parties and an arts fair. Check www.placencia.com for the latest details. Late June.

Feria Juniana (San Pedro Sula, Honduras). The last week of June sees a series of parades and live events celebrating the city's founding. There is a large agricultural fair that attracts thousands and the week culminates with a huge, colorful parade down the main thoroughfare on June 29.

JULY

Fiestas Julias, July, Santa Ana. Fiestas Julias, also known as Fiestas Patronal, is a month-long celebration in the city of Santa Ana, El Salvador, featuring parades, music, and carnival rides honoring Santa Ana's patron saint. Throughout July.

Fiesta of the Virgin of the Sea, Puntarenas, Costa Rica. A regatta of colorfully decorated boats carrying a statue of Puntarenas's patron saint marks this festival. A similar event is held at Playa de Coco. Saturday closest to July 16.

La Fiesta Nacional Indígena de Guatemala, Cobán, Guatemala. This is one of Mesoamerica's greatest celebrations of Maya culture. The city of Cobán features a steady stream of street fairs, concerts, parades, and parties. This is celebrated for 2 solid weeks in late July, sometimes extending into early August.

Festival Patronales de La Virgen de Santa Librada, Las Tablas, Panama. This is famous for its **Festival de la Pollera** on July 22, which showcases the region's most beautiful pollera dresses and elects the "Queen of the Pollera" for that year. July 20 to July 22.

AUGUST

Fiesta de la Virgen de la Asunción, Guatemala. The Virgin of the Assumption is the patron saint of Guatemala City and, by extension, the entire nation. There are celebrations, parades, and small fairs across the country, but the largest celebrations are held in Guatemala City. August 15.

Fiesta of the Virgin of Los Angeles, Cartago, Costa Rica. Each year, on August 2, Costa Rica's patron saint is celebrated with a massive pilgrimage to the country's only basilica in the former capital city of Cartago, 24km (15 miles) outside of San José, to the basilica in Cartago.

Costa Maya Festival, San Pedro, Ambergris Caye, Belize. This is perhaps the largest festival in the country. Drawing participants from the neighboring countries of El Salvador, Mexico, Guatemala, and Honduras, this celebration features a steady stream of live concert performances, street parades, beauty pageants, and water shows and activities. Early August.

SEPTEMBER

Costa Rica's Independence Day, celebrated all over Costa Rica. One of the most distinctive aspects of this festival is the nighttime marching band parades of children in their school uniforms, who play the national anthem on steel xylophones. September 15.

Festival de la Mejorana, Guararé, Panama. This nationally famous folkloric festival features hundreds of dancers, musicians, and singers coming together for a week of events and serious partying. Last week of September.

Belize Independence Day, celebrated throughout Belize. Patriotic parades and official celebrations are mixed with street parties, beauty pageants, and open-air concerts. September 21.

Fiestas Patronales, Masaya, Nicaragua. The handicrafts capital of Nicaragua finds reason to celebrate year-round. The biggest festival date is September 20, though, with the opening of the Fiestas Patronales, weekend parties in different neighborhoods that carry on until December.

OCTOBER

Festival del Cristo Negro (Black Christ Festival), Portobelo, Panama. Thousands of pilgrims come to pay penance and perform other acts of devotion at the Iglesia de San Felipe, home to a wooden black Christ effigy that is paraded around town on this day. October 21.

NOVEMBER

Día de los Muertos (All Saints' Day), Guatemala. The most famous celebration in Guatemala is the "drunken horse race" in the mountain town of

Todos Santos. Guatemalans also fly giant, colorful kites to communicate with the dead in the village of Santiago Sacatepéquez. November 1.

Garífuna Settlement Day, Belize, Honduras, Guatemala, Nicaragua. Garífunas from across the Caribbean coast of Central America gather to commemorate their arrival from St. Vincent in 1832. Street parades, religious ceremonies, and dance and drumming performances are all part of the celebrations throughout this zone. November 19.

December

Día de la Purísima Concepción, León, Nicaragua. This celebration is known as the *Gritería* (shouting), a type of religious trick-or-treat. Groups of people walk around, shouting up to households, in order to obtain sweets. The following day is the Día de la Concepción de María, when the whole country goes parade crazy. December 7.

Quema del Diablo (Burning the Devil), Guatemala. Huge bonfires fill the streets throughout the country as trash, tires, old furniture, and effigies of Satan are burned in a symbolic ritual cleansing. December 7.

El Tope and Carnaval, San José, Costa Rica. The streets of downtown belong to horses and their riders in a proud recognition of the country's important agricultural heritage. The next day, those same streets are taken over by carnival floats, marching bands, and street dancers. December 26 and 27.

Boxing Day, Belize. While Christmas Day is predominantly for the family in Belize, Boxing Day is a chance to continue the celebration with friends, neighbors, and strangers. Dances, concerts, horse races, and general festivities are put on around the country. December 26.

4 GETTING THERE & GETTING AROUND

GETTING THERE

By Plane

Every country in Central America now receives international flights, mostly from the U.S. and Mexico. Below is a quick country-by-country glance. See the individual country chapters for more detailed information. For additional help in booking your air travel, please turn to the "Fast Facts, Toll-Free Numbers & Websites" appendix on p. 703.

To Belize

The following carriers offer service to Belize City's **Philip S. W. Goldson International Airport (BZE).**

FROM THE U.S. American Airlines, Continental, Grupo Taca (via San Salvador), and US Airways.

The only direct flights from Canada are seasonal winter charters. There are no direct flights to Belize from Europe, Australia, or New Zealand.

To Guatemala

Most international flights land at **La Aurora International Airport (GUA)** in Guatemala City. A few international and regional airlines fly directly into **Flores Airport (FRS)** near Tikal.

FROM THE U.S. & MEXICO American Airlines, Continental, Delta, Mexicana, United Airlines, US Airways, and Grupo Taca.

There are no direct flights from Europe, Australia, or New Zealand but it is easy to get a connection from New York or Miami.

To Honduras

The following carriers fly to San Pedro Sula's **Ramón Villeda Morales International Airport (SAP),** Tegucigalpa's

Toncontín International Airport (TGU), or **Roatán International Airport (RTB):**

FROM NORTH AMERICA Air Canada, American, Continental, Delta, United, Taca, and Spirit.

FROM THE U.K. & EUROPE There are no direct flights, but Delta, Continental, and American Airlines connect through the U.S.

FROM AUSTRALIA & NEW ZEALAND There are no direct flights, but connections can be made in North American gateway cities.

To El Salvador

The following carriers fly into San Salvador's **Comalapa International Airport (SAL):**

FROM NORTH AMERICA American, Continental, Delta, and Taca.

FROM THE U.K., EUROPE, AUSTRALIA & NEW ZEALAND There are no direct overseas flights from the U.K., Australia, or New Zealand. You'll need to fly first into the U.S., with many European flights routing out of Miami and Houston to San Salvador.

To Nicaragua

The following carriers offer service to Managua's **Augusto C Sandino International Airport (MGA):**

FROM THE U.S. American Airlines, Continental, Delta, United Airlines, Spirit, and Taca.

FROM MEXICO Aeroméxico.

FROM EUROPE Iberia (via Miami).

To Costa Rica

International flights land in San José's **Juan Santamaría International Airport (SJO)** and to a lesser extent Liberia's **Daniel Oduber International Airport (LIR);** there are no direct flights from Australia or New Zealand.

FROM THE U.S. Air Canada, American Airlines, Continental, Delta, Frontier, Grupo Taca, Mexicana, Spirit Air, and US Airways.

FROM EUROPE Iberia and Martin Air.

To Panama

The following airlines fly into **Tocumen International Airport (PTY)** in Panama City:

FROM THE U.S. & MEXICO American Airlines, Copa, Delta, Mexicana, and Taca.

FROM THE U.K. & EUROPE Iberia (via Costa Rica), American Airlines (via Miami), British Airways (via Miami), Continental (via Orlando or Houston), and Delta (via Atlanta).

FROM AUSTRALIA & NEW ZEALAND Qantas and Air New Zealand (both via Los Angeles).

By Cruise Ship or Ferry

Luxury cruise liners now sail frequently along the Caribbean and Pacific coast via the Panama Canal. Two reputable companies are Miami-based **Seabourn Cruise Line** (**© 800/929-9391;** www.seabourn.com) and Californian-based **Princess Cruises** (**© 845/075-0031;** www.princess.com).

Some key international ferry crossings are between Punta Gorda, Belize, and Puerto Barrios, Guatemala. You can cross into Flores, Guatemala, from Palenque in Mexico. There is a river crossing between San Carlos, Nicaragua, and Los Chiles, Costa Rica.

BY CAR

It's possible to travel to Central America by car, but it can be difficult. After leaving Mexico, the Pan-American Highway (Carretera Panamericana), which is also referred to as the Interamerican Highway, passes through Guatemala, El Salvador, Honduras, Nicaragua, and Costa Rica before reaching Panama. All of these countries can be problematic for travelers for a variety of reasons, including internal violence, crime, corrupt border crossings, and visa formalities. If you decide to undertake this adventure from the U.S., take the **Gulf**

Coast route from the border crossing at Brownsville, Texas, because it involves traveling the fewest miles through Mexico. You might also try to find a copy of *Driving the Pan-Am Highway to Mexico and Central America,* by Audrey and Raymond Pritchard.

Anyone driving into Central American countries needs to show a passport, country or international driver's license, proof of vehicle ownership, such as registration card, and proof of insurance. Cars are normally granted 30-days visitation. Many consulates also offer prevalidation of driver's documents, which can quicken the process at the border.

GETTING AROUND

The most frustrating and stressful part of traveling in Central America is getting from point A to point B. The roads are awful and, though there are plenty of local buses, they are usually decrepit and packed and take forever. It is often wise to spring for a private shuttle, especially if you are traveling with other people. (The international bus companies that travel between Central America countries have much better standards.). Because car-rental agencies don't allow cars to be taken across international borders, it's very difficult to drive from country to country. And there is zero train service.

See individual country chapters for complete details on getting around within each country.

BY PLANE

Copa (✆ **800/359-2672;** www.copaair.com) offers the most comprehensive plane service in Central America. The Panama-based airline travels between all the capital cities and is a strategic partner with Continental Airlines. **Grupo Taca** (✆ **800/400-8222;** www.taca.com), also has several routes between Central American countries.

Many countries offer "puddle jumper" or propeller-airline flights. These flights are not for the fainthearted, as you literally sit right behind the pilots and it can get a little claustrophobic. As you are checking in, the plane's crew will weigh your bags and then weigh you so as not to overload the aircraft—you'll want to pack light.

No matter what flight you book, always be sure to reconfirm your flight upon arrival.

BY BUS

Though they're a hassle, a bus journey in Central America will likely be one of the lasting memories of your trip. (They're also by far the cheapest way to get around.) Chaotic bus stations, pushy touts, hordes of vendors, and buses packed with people and with livestock will, at the very least, truly allow you to feel that you have left home.

There are different types of buses throughout Central America and each country may use different terms, but they generally fall into the following categories: **Local buses,** otherwise known as "chicken buses," are the cheapest and slowest; they stop frequently and are generally an old, dilapidated American school bus with colorful clientele that may include small farm animals. Many of these buses are intercity or urban buses that service the satellite towns of a particular city. **Expreso buses** are like chicken buses, in that they are cheaper and slower, but they do not stop (in theory) between cities. They also run much less frequently than the local buses.

Probably the most inconvenient aspect of local bus travel in Central America is that many towns or cities have no central bus stations. In lieu of that, the "stations" are dirty platforms beside busy markets on the city outskirts, where overly enthusiastic touts literally grab tourists' bags and run them to the next departing bus. Many bus lines therefore do not have ticket offices, so you'll have to buy your ticket on the bus.

The Art of Addresses in Central America

Addresses are an inexact science throughout Central America. Larger cities sometimes list building numbers in addresses but not always, and small-town addresses remain a simple set of directions usually mentioning the street, the neighborhood, a nearby landmark, the city, the state (or "departmento"), and the country. A typical small-town address might read, "4 Avenida Norte, Barrio El Centro across from the cathedral, La Paz, El Salvador." But most of the time, all you'll need is the name of the hotel, restaurant, or attractions to get you where you need to go.

Route numbers are very rarely used on road signs in Central America, although there are frequent signs listing the number of kilometers to various towns or cities. Your best bets for on-road directions are billboards and advertisements for hotels. It's always a good idea to know the names of a few hotels at your destination, just in case your specific hotel hasn't put up any billboards or signs. When taking a taxi, always try and have the address of your destination in Spanish so there are no misunderstandings with the driver.

International buses run between major cities; these tend to be newer units and more comfortable, although very few are so new or modern as to have bathroom facilities, and they sometimes operate only on weekends and holidays. One advantage is they have their own private terminals so you avoid the chaos of heading to a local market to catch a bus. There are several express bus companies that provide services between Central American countries. **Tica Bus** (✆ **529/62-626-2880** in Mexico, or 507/314-6385 in Panama; www.ticabus.com) is one of the most reputable and travels from Mexico to Panama. **King Quality** (✆ **505/228-1454;** www.kingqualityca.com) does not go as far north as Mexico but has a reputation for having more comfortable buses. **Trans Nica** (✆ **505/277-2104** in Nicaragua) and **Central Line** (✆ **505/254-5431** in Nicaragua) are two other well-known companies.

If traveling with another person, it is often wise to have one person in charge of luggage while the other secures the bus, tickets, and seats. It is also best to hold onto your bags when boarding and store them above your head where you can see them. Another good tip is when arriving at a terminal (if there is one), check out the departing timetable and book your seat (if you can) for when you plan to leave in a few days.

An alternative busing option is **microbuses.** These are small minivans that depart as soon as they fill up with passengers, which usually means every 20 minutes. Their main advantage is they depart from city-center locations. However, they can get crowded and are not recommended for long journeys, especially when traveling with luggage.

Pickup trucks are a popular form of public transport in rural areas. Bumpy and uncomfortable, they are often covered in canvas to protect the mostly local passengers from the elements.

Shuttle buses are becoming more and more popular, too. These are privately organized tourist transfers between cities, usually operated by a tour agency or hotel. Much more comfortable and faster than local transport, they are also a lot more expensive.

For a sense of distance, to travel south between all capital cities starting at Belize and ending in Panama is approximately 1,400km (868 miles) and would take 4 days of nonstop traveling.

BY TAXI

There is no shortage of taxis in all major towns and cities. There are some differences to how they operate, however. For example, in some countries, taxis have no meter. If this is the case, make sure you agree on a price before climbing in and ascertain whether the price is per person or trip. Sharing with strangers is another frequent occurrence, and you may find yourself waiting while the driver stops along the way to pick up more people. This practice should be avoided at night.

In general, taxis are cheap, but keep in mind that the increasing price of gas is making transportation more expensive throughout the region, so prices quoted in this book are subject to change.

Central America's taxis are usually safe to hail from the street without going to special taxi stations. At night you'll need to call a cab from your hotel or restaurant, as many big-city streets are not safe to walk after dark. Never get into an unmarked car claiming to be a taxi.

BY BOAT

The Caribbean provides many opportunities to travel by small boat. Small, local water taxis travel to the Bay Islands in Honduras, Caye Caulker in Belize, Bocas del Toro in Panama, and the Corn Islands in Nicaragua. In general, the shorter the ride, the smaller and more uncomfortable the boat will be. Some ferries are rusting hulks, such as the one that carries people, livestock, and cars to Isla Ometepe in Nicaragua. Larger boats, like the ones that cross Lago Nicaragua from Granada to San Carlos, may have first- and second-class seating but that's often on a first-come, first-served basis. First-class passengers generally get a sheltered bench below deck, while second-class passengers get seating on the exposed deck above. A hammock is invaluable on such extended voyages.

Note that boats can be particularly crowded around holiday time, especially Easter week, and common safety precautions should be taken during any trip.

BY CAR

Renting a car in Central America is no idle proposition. The roads are riddled with potholes, most rural intersections are unmarked, and, for some reason, sitting behind the wheel of a car seems to turn peaceful Central Americans into homicidal maniacs. But unless you want to see the country from the window of a bus or pay exorbitant amounts for private transfers, renting a car might be your best option for independent exploring. (If you don't want to put up with any stress on your vacation, it might be worthwhile springing for a driver, though.)

Be forewarned, however: Although rental cars no longer bear special license plates, they are still readily identifiable to thieves and are frequently targeted. (Nothing is ever safe in a car in Central America, although parking in guarded parking lots helps.) Transit police also seem to target tourists; never pay money directly to a police officer who stops you for any traffic violation.

Before driving off with a rental car, be sure that you inspect the exterior and point out to the rental-company representative every tiny scratch, dent, tear, or any other damage. It's a common practice with many Central American car-rental companies to claim that you owe payment for minor dings and dents that the company finds when you return the car. Also, if you get into an accident, be sure that the rental company doesn't try to bill you for a higher amount than the deductible on your rental contract.

These caveats aren't meant to scare you off from driving in Central America. Thousands of tourists rent cars here every year, and the large majority of them encounter no problems. Just keep your wits about you and guard against car theft and you'll do fine. Also keep in mind that four-wheel-drives are particularly useful in the rainy season (May to mid-Nov) and for navigating the bumpy, poorly paved roads year-round.

Among the major international agencies operating in Central America are **Alamo, Avis, Budget, Hertz, National, Payless,** and **Thrifty.** For a complete list of car-rental agencies and their contact information, see "Appendix: Fast Facts, Toll-Free Numbers & Websites," p. 703, as well as the "Getting Around" sections of country chapters.

Generally speaking, speed limits in the region are about 60 to 80kmph (37–50 mph) on major roadways and slower on secondary roads. You'll want to stick to this limit, as police speed traps are common, and you don't want a speeding ticket to put a damper on your trip.

It's sometimes cheaper to reserve a car in your home country rather than book when you arrive. If you know you'll be renting a car, it's always wise to shop around and reserve it well in advance for the high season because the rental fleet often can't match demand.

Note: Estimated driving times are listed throughout this book, but bear in mind that it might take longer than estimated to reach your destination during the rainy season or if roads have deteriorated.

5 MONEY & COSTS

High inflation in many Central American countries means the dollar remains strong in the region. El Salvador has scrapped its own currency and made the U.S. dollar its official currency. The dollar is also the official currency in Panama, although it is used in conjunction with the *balboa*. In other Central American countries, you can expect the local currency to fluctuate while you're there, usually resulting in a better exchange rate for foreigners.

Note that most vendors prefer small bills and exact change. It's almost impossible to find someone who has change for a large bill. Many ATMs give out money in multiples of one or five, so try to request odd denominations of money. For larger sums, try to withdraw in a multiple of 500 instead of 1,000, for instance.

Here's a general idea of what things cost throughout Central America: a taxi from the airport to downtown cities runs $12 to $18 (£6–£9); a double room at a budget hotel with private bathroom, $20 to $50 (£10–£25); a double room at a moderate hotel, $80 to $120 (£40–£60); a double room at an expensive hotel, $150 to $250 (£75–£125); a small bottle of water, 50¢ (25p); a cup of coffee, $1 to $1.50 (50p–75p); admission to most national parks $10 (£5); lunch at a simple restaurant, $3 to $6 (£1.50–£3); and a three-course dinner for one without wine at a fancier restaurant, $15 to $25 (£7.50–£13).

CURRENCY

In most countries in Central America, you can use American dollars without much of a problem. But if you're traveling in rural areas, it's always useful to have the local currency on hand. A list of currencies for all the countries in this guide is below.

Some prices throughout this book, particularly hotel rates, are quoted in U.S. dollars since local currencies can fluctuate, though we also give you prices in British pounds (at a ratio of .50 U.S. dollars to 1 U.K. pound). ***Note:*** Because of high inflation and volatile exchange rates, prices quoted here may vary greatly in accuracy.

BELIZE The Belize dollar, abbreviated BZ$, is the official currency of Belize. It is pegged to the U.S. dollar at a ratio of 2 Belize dollars to 1 U.S. dollar, or 4 Belize dollars to the U.K. pound. Both currencies are acceptable at almost any business

Central American Currency Conversions

	US$1	C$1	UK£1	AUS$1	NZ$1
Belizean dollar	0.51	0.52	0.26	0.54	0.67
Costa Rican colón	0.0019	0.0019	0.00098	0.002	0.0025
Guatemalan quetzal	0.13	0.136	0.068	0.14	0.17
Honduran lempira	0.52	0.53	0.26	0.054	0.69
Nicaraguan córdoba	0.051	0.052	0.026	0.054	0.068

Note: Panama and El Salvador use the U.S. dollar.

or establishment around the country. Denominations include 50¢ and $1 coins, while notes come in 2, 5, 10, 20, 50, and 100 denominations.

GUATEMALA The unit of currency in Guatemala is the **quetzal.** In June 2008, there were approximately 7.4 quetzales to the American dollar, or 14.8 quetzales to the U.K. pound, but because the quetzal does fluctuate, you can expect this rate to change. There are 1 quetzal coins and paper notes in denominations of 1, 5, 10, 20, 50, and 100 quetzales.

EL SALVADOR El Salvador uses the **U.S. dollar** as its national currency. Prices in that chapter are quoted in American and British currency only.

HONDURAS The Honduran unit of currency is called a **lempira.** It currently hovers at approximately 19 to 1 with the American dollar, and 38 to 1 with the U.K. pound. It comes in paper denominations of 1, 2, 5, 10, 20, 100, and 500 lempiras. There are 100 centavos in a lempira and they come in coin forms of 1, 2, 5, 10, 20, and 50 centavos.

NICARAGUA The official Nicaraguan currency is the **córdoba** (it is sometimes referred to as a peso). It currently rates at approximately 19 to 1 with the American dollar, and 38 to 1 with the U.K. pound. It is made up of 100 **centavos.** Money is denominated in notes of 10, 20, 50, 100, and 500 córdobas. Coins are made of 1 and 5 córdobas and 50 centavos.

COSTA RICA The unit of currency in Costa Rica is the **colón.** In June 2008, there were approximately 520 colones to the American dollar and 1,040 colones to the British pound. *Because of this high exchange rate, prices in the Costa Rica chapter are quoted only in American and British currency.* The colón is divided into 100 **céntimos.** Currently, two types of coins are in circulation. The older and larger nickel-alloy coins come in denominations of 10, 25, and 50 céntimos and 1, 2, 5, 10, and 20 colones; and newer, gold-hued 5-, 10-, 25-, 50-, 100-, and 500-colón coins. There are paper notes in denominations of 1,000, 2,000, 5,000, and 10,000 colones.

PANAMA The unit of currency in Panama is the U.S. dollar, but the Panamanian balboa, which is pegged to the dollar at a 1:1 ratio, also circulates in denominations of 5¢, 10¢, 25¢, and 50¢ coins. (U.S. coins are in circulation as well.) Balboa coins are sized similarly to their U.S. counterparts. Prices in the Panama chapter are quoted in American and British currency only.

ATMS

The easiest and best way to get cash throughout Central America is from an ATM (automated teller machine). The

Cirrus (✆ **800/424-7787;** www.mastercard.com) and **PLUS** (✆ **800/843-7587;** www.visa.com) networks work here; look at the back of your bank card to see which network you're on, then call or check online for ATM locations at your destination. Be sure you know your personal identification number (PIN) and daily withdrawal limit before you depart—you'll need a four-digit PIN throughout much of this region. ***Note:*** Remember that many banks impose a fee every time you use a card at another bank's ATM, and that fee can be higher for international transactions (up to $5/£2.50 or more) than for domestic ones (where they're rarely more than $2/£1). In addition, the bank from which you withdraw cash may charge its own fee. For international withdrawal fees, ask your bank.

You can also use your credit card to receive cash advances at ATMs. Keep in mind that credit card companies protect themselves from theft by limiting maximum withdrawals outside their home country, so call your credit card company before you leave home. And know that you'll pay interest from the moment of your withdrawal, even if you pay your monthly bills on time.

TRAVELER'S CHECKS

Traveler's checks are something of an anachronism from the days before the ATM made cash accessible at any time. They're also hard to cash outside major Central American cities, and even in those cities, you may still have problems doing so. Your best bet for exchanging traveler's checks is by heading to *casas de cambio* (money-exchange houses), though they usually change checks for a significant fee. Many banks will not exchange traveler's checks, and those that do often have long lines.

If you do choose to carry traveler's checks, keep a record of their serial numbers separate from your checks in the event that they are stolen or lost. You'll get a refund faster if you know the numbers.

CREDIT CARDS

Credit cards are another safe way to carry money throughout this region. They provide a convenient record of all your expenses, and they generally offer relatively good exchange rates. You can also withdraw cash advances from your credit cards at banks or ATMs, provided you know your PIN. If you don't know yours, call the number on the back of your credit card and ask the bank to send it to you. It usually takes 5 to 7 business days, though some banks will provide the number over the phone if you tell them your mother's maiden name or some other personal information.

Keep in mind that many banks now assess a 1% to 3% "transaction fee" on *all* charges you incur abroad (whether you're using the local currency or U.S. dollars). But credit cards still may be the smart way to go when you factor in things like exorbitant ATM fees and the higher exchange rates and service fees you'll pay with traveler's checks.

Visa, MasterCard, American Express, and Diners Club are all commonly accepted in Central America.

IF YOUR WALLET IS LOST OR STOLEN

Be sure to tell all of your credit card companies the minute you discover your wallet has been lost or stolen, and file a report at the nearest police precinct. Your credit card company or insurer may require a police report number or record of the loss. Most credit card companies have an emergency toll-free number to call if your card is lost or stolen; they may be able to wire you a cash advance immediately or deliver an emergency credit card in a day or two. Emergency numbers for each country are listed in the "Money" section of country chapters.

STAYING HEALTHY

For general information about health issues in Central America, log on to the **Centers for Disease Control and Prevention**'s website at **www.cdc.gov/travel**. In addition to the recommendations below, the CDC advises visitors to Central America to protect themselves against hepatitis A and B. Consult your doctor for more information about these vaccinations.

Before You Go

It can be hard to find a doctor you can trust when you're in an unfamiliar place. Try to take proper precautions the week before you depart to avoid falling ill while you're away from home. Amid the last-minute frenzy that often precedes a vacation, make an extra effort to eat and sleep well.

Pack prescription medications in their original labeled containers in your carry-on luggage. Also, bring along copies of your prescriptions in case you lose your pills or run out. Carry written prescriptions in generic form, in case a local pharmacist is unfamiliar with the brand name. If you wear contact lenses, pack an extra pair or your glasses.

If you worry about getting sick away from home, you may want to consider **medical travel insurance** (see "Travel Insurance," in the appendix).

If you suffer from a chronic illness, consult your doctor before your departure. For conditions such as epilepsy, diabetes, or heart problems, wear a **MedicAlert identification tag (✆ 888/633-4298;** www.medicalert.org), which will immediately alert doctors to your condition and give them access to your records through MedicAlert's 24-hour hot line.

Contact the **International Association for Medical Assistance to Travelers (IAMAT; ✆ 716/754-4883,** or 416/652-0137 in Canada; www.iamat.org) for tips on travel and health concerns in the countries you're visiting, and lists of local, English-speaking doctors.

General Availability of Healthcare

Not surprisingly, most of the region's best hospitals and healthcare centers are in the big cities, but service varies widely. If you do get sick, it's best to contact your home country's consulate or embassy. They all have health departments with staff who can recommend the best English-speaking doctors and hospitals in the area.

Common Diseases & Ailments

DIETARY DISTRESS It's unfortunate, but many travelers to Central America do suffer from some sort of food or water-borne illness. Most of this is just due to tender northern stomachs coming into contact with slightly more aggressive Latin American intestinal flora. Symptoms vary widely—from minor cases of diarrhea to debilitating flulike illnesses. To minimize your chances of getting sick, be sure to always drink bottled or boiled water and avoid ice. In high altitudes, you will need to boil water for several minutes longer before it is safe to drink. If you don't have access to bottled water, you can treat it with iodine or chlorine, with iodine being more effective. You can buy water purification tablets at pharmacies and sporting-goods stores. You should also be careful to avoid raw food, especially meats, fruits, and vegetables. If you peel the fruit yourself, you should be fine.

If you do suffer from diarrhea, it's important to keep yourself hydrated. Many pharmacies sell Pedialyte, which is a mild rehydrating solution. Drinking fruit juices or soft drinks (preferably without caffeine) and eating salted crackers are also good remedies. In extreme cases of diarrhea or intestinal discomfort, it's worth taking a stool sample to a lab for analysis. The results will usually pinpoint the amoebic or parasitic culprit, which can then be readily treated with available over-the-counter medicines.

Typhoid Fever is a food- or waterborne illness that occurs throughout Central America (it's caused by salmonella). Long-term travelers should seriously consider taking a typhoid fever vaccine before setting off, as the malaria-like symptoms are very unpleasant.

Hepatitis A is another viral infection acquired through water and food (it can also be picked up off infected people), this time attacking the liver. Usually the symptoms of fever, jaundice, and nausea will pass but it can in some cases cause liver damage. There is an effective vaccine that you can take before the trip.

TROPICAL ILLNESSES **Yellow fever** is no longer a problem in Central America. However, if you are traveling from South America or Africa you will require a vaccination certificate to enter Nicaragua, El Salvador, Honduras, Guatemala, and Belize.

Malaria does exist in Central America, especially in rural areas. To protect yourself, wear mosquito repellent with DEET, wear long-sleeved shirts and trousers, and use mosquito nets. You can also take antimalaria drugs before you go; consult your doctor about the pros and cons of such medications. Be sure to ask whether a recommended drug will cause you to be hypersensitive to the sun; it would be a shame to come down here for the beaches and then have to hide under an umbrella the whole time. Because malaria-carrying mosquitoes usually come out at night, you should do as much as possible to avoid being bitten after dark. Also be aware that symptoms such as high fever, chills, and body aches can appear months after your vacation.

Dengue fever, transmitted by an aggressive daytime mosquito, is a risk in tropical environments and densely populated urban areas. As with malaria, the best prevention is to avoid mosquito bites; there is no vaccine available. Dengue is also known as "bone-break fever" because it is usually accompanied by severe body aches. The first infection with dengue fever will make you very sick but should cause no serious damage. However, a second infection with a different strain of the dengue virus can lead to internal hemorrhaging and could be life threatening. If you are unfortunate enough to get it, take some paracetamol and lots of fluids.

BEES, BUGS & BITES **Snakes, scorpions,** and **spiders** rarely bite without provocation. Keep your eyes open and never walk barefoot. If you're in the jungle or rainforest, be sure to shake your clothes and check your shoes before putting them on. Africanized bees (the notorious "killer bees" of fact and fable) are common in this region, but there is no real danger of being attacked unless you do something silly like stick your hand into a hive. Other than mosquitoes, the most prevalent and annoying biting insect you are likely to encounter, especially along the coast, is sand flies. These tiny biting bugs leave a raised and itchy welt, but otherwise are of no significant danger. They tend to be most active around sunrise and sunset, or on overcast days. Your best protection is to wear light long-sleeved shirts and long pants.

The chances of contracting **rabies** while traveling in Central America are unlikely but not completely impossible. Most infected animals live in rural areas. If you are bitten by an infected dog or bat, wash the wound and get yourself to a hospital as quickly as possible. There is a prevacation vaccine that requires three injections but you should only get it if you are planning a high-risk activity such as cave exploring. Treatment is effective but must be given promptly.

RIPTIDES Many of the Pacific coast beaches have riptides: strong currents that can drag swimmers out to sea. A riptide occurs when water that has been dumped on the shore by strong waves forms a channel back out to open water. These channels have strong currents. If you get caught in a riptide, you can't escape the current by swimming toward shore; it's like trying to swim upstream in a river. To break free of the current, swim parallel to shore and use the energy of the waves to help you get back to the beach. ***Note:*** Lifeguards are a rarity in the region.

7 SAFETY

Central America's reputation for gang violence and drug running are not entirely unwarranted. However, such a well-publicized (and sensationalized) crime image will contrast strongly with your experience of the region's friendly, peace-loving people. Travelers rarely experience anything more untoward than being pickpocketed or distracted in some way and relieved of a backpack (and even this is rare). Gun crime is usually confined to the shantytowns and poor barrios and rarely effects tourists. In my experience, the more budget-oriented you are, the more vulnerable you are—a public chicken bus is not as safe as a private shuttle.

Before you depart, check for travel advisories from the **U.S. State Department** (www.travel.state.gov), the **Canadian Department of Foreign Affairs** (www.voyage.gc.ca), the **U.K. Foreign & Commonwealth Office** (www.fco.gov.uk/travel), and the **Australian Department of Foreign Affairs** (www.dfat.gov.au/consular/advice).

Once you're in the region, keep some common-sense safety advice in mind: Stay alert and be aware of your surroundings; don't walk down dark, deserted streets; and always keep an eye on your personal belongings. Keep your passport and credit cards on your person (but not stuffed in your back pocket). Theft at airports and bus stations is not unheard of, so be sure to put a lock on your luggage. Rental cars generally stick out, and are easily spotted by thieves (see "Getting Around: By Car" for more info).

Public intercity buses are also frequent targets of stealthy thieves. Never check your bags into the hold of a bus if you can avoid it. If this can't be avoided, when the bus makes a stop, keep your eye on what leaves the hold. If you put your bags in an overhead rack, be sure you can see the bags at all times.

See the individual chapters in this book for more specific safety advice.

8 SPECIALIZED TRAVEL RESOURCES

TRAVELERS WITH DISABILITIES

Central America is not well equipped for travelers with disabilities. Where elevators exist, they are often tiny. Many city streets are crowded, narrow, and badly maintained and public buses so frenetic that even able-bodied people have scarcely time to board before the driver roars off. The nature of the terrain means climbing in and out of small buses, boats, and planes, and that will be challenging for travelers with disabilities.

Nevertheless, a disability shouldn't stop anyone from traveling. There are more resources out there than ever before. Some of the best include **MossRehab** (www.mossresourcenet.org), which provides a library of accessible-travel resources online; the **Society for Accessible Travel and Hospitality** (**SATH; © 212/447-7284;** www.sath.org), which offers a wealth of travel resources for all types of disabilities and informed recommendations on destinations, access guides, travel agents, tour operators, vehicle rentals, and companion services; and the **American Foundation for the Blind** (**© 800/232-5463;** www.afb.org), which offers a referral resource for the blind or visually impaired that includes information on traveling with Seeing Eye dogs.

For more on organizations that offer resources to travelers with disabilities, go to Frommers.com.

GAY & LESBIAN TRAVELERS

Central America is Catholic and conservative. Public displays of same-sex affection are rare and considered somewhat shocking. There are some openly gay or lesbian bars in the bigger cities but most are rather low-key. Gay and lesbian travelers should choose their hotels with care, and be discreet in most public areas and situations.

Many agencies offer tours and travel itineraries to Central America that are specifically targeted at gay and lesbian travelers. **Above and Beyond Tours** (**© 800/397-2681;** www.abovebeyondtours.com) is the exclusive gay and lesbian tour operator for United Airlines. **Now, Voyager** (**© 800/255-6951;** www.nowvoyager.com) is a well-known San Francisco–based gay-owned and -operated travel service. Another well known agency is **Olivia Cruises & Resorts** (**© 800/631-6277;** www.olivia.com).

For more gay and lesbian travel resources visit Frommers.com.

SENIORS

Although it's not common policy in Central America to offer senior discounts, don't be shy about asking for one anyway. You never know. Always carry some kind of identification, such as a driver's license, that shows your date of birth, especially if you've kept your youthful glow.

Members of **AARP** (formerly known as the American Association of Retired Persons), 601 E St. NW, Washington, DC 20049 (**© 888/687-2277;** www.aarp.org), get discounts on hotels, airfares, and car rentals. AARP offers members a wide range of benefits, including *AARP The Magazine* and a monthly newsletter. Anyone over 50 can join.

Many reliable agencies and organizations target the 50-plus market. **Elderhostel** (**© 800/454-5768;** www.elderhostel.org) arranges Costa Rica study programs for those ages 55 and older. **ElderTreks** (**© 800/741-7956,** or 416/558-5000 outside North America; www.eldertreks.com) offers small-group tours to Costa Rica, restricted to travelers 50 and older.

Frommers.com offers more information and resources on travel for seniors.

FAMILIES

"Children not Allowed" is a rare concept in Central America—family values are very important here, so if you're traveling with your whole family, you can expect locals to welcome you with open arms.

A handful of hotels give discounts for children 11 and under, or allow children under 3 or 4 years old to stay for free. Discounts for children and the cutoff ages vary according to the hotel, but in general, don't assume that your kids can stay in your room for free.

Many hotels also offer rooms equipped with kitchenettes or full kitchen facilities. These can be a real money-saver for those traveling with children. Hotels offering regular, dependable babysitting service are few and far between, however. If you will need babysitting, make sure your hotel offers it before you make your reservation.

To locate Central American accommodations, restaurants, and attractions that are particularly kid-friendly, refer to the "Kids" icon throughout this guide.

STUDENTS

Although you won't find any discounts at the national parks, most museums and other attractions around Central America do offer discounts for students. It always pays to ask.

You'd be wise to arm yourself with an **International Student Identity Card (ISIC),** which offers substantial savings on rail passes, plane tickets, and entrance fees. It also provides you with basic health and life insurance and a 24-hour help line. The card is available for $22 (£11) from **STA Travel** (✆ **800/781-4040;** www.sta.com), the biggest student travel agency in the world. If you're no longer a student but are still under 26, you can get an **International Youth Travel Card (IYTC)** for the same price from the same people, which entitles you to some discounts (but not on museum admissions).

Travel CUTS (✆ **800/667-2887** or 416/614-2887; www.travelcuts.com) offers similar services for both Canadians and U.S. residents. Irish students should turn to **USIT** (✆ **01/602-1600;** www.usitnow.ie).

WOMEN TRAVELERS

For lack of better phrasing, Central America is a typically "macho" part of the world. Single women can expect a nearly constant stream of catcalls, hisses, whistles, and car horns, especially in big cities. Women should be careful walking alone at night throughout the country.

For general travel resources for women, go to Frommers.com.

SINGLE TRAVELERS

Many people prefer traveling alone. Unfortunately, the solo traveler is often forced to pay a premium price for the privilege of sleeping alone. On package vacations, single travelers are often hit with a "single supplement" to the base price. To avoid it, you can agree to room with other single travelers on the trip, or you can find a compatible roommate before you go from one of the many roommate locator agencies.

GAP Adventures (✆ **800/708-7761** in North America, or 44/870-999-0144 in the United Kingdom; www.gapadventures.com) is an adventure tour company with a good range of regular and varied tours in Central America. As a policy, they do not charge a single supplement and will try to pair a single traveler with a compatible roommate.

9 SUSTAINABLE TOURISM

Central America is one of the planet's prime ecotourism destinations. Many of the isolated nature lodges and tour operators around the country are pioneers and dedicated professionals in the ecotourism and sustainable tourism field. Many other hotels, lodges, and tour operators are simply "green-washing," using the terms "eco" and "sustainable" in their promo materials, but doing little real good in their daily operations. **Responsible Travel** (www.responsibletravel.com) is a great source of sustainable travel ideas with listings on Central America; the site is run by a spokesperson for ethical tourism in the travel industry. **Sustainable Travel International** (www.sustainabletravelinternational.org) promotes ethical tourism practices, and manages an extensive directory of sustainable properties and tour operators around the region.

Deforestation is the main threat to Central America's fragile ecosystem. Farming has virtually wiped out most of the region's dry tropical rainforests, while logging is a major threat to the cloud forest. Thirty percent of Central America is forest today, which is half of what existed 50 years ago. Such destruction has been devastating to many species, including man

It's Easy Being Green

Here are a few simple ways you can help conserve fuel and energy when you travel:

- Each time you take a flight or drive a car greenhouse gases release into the atmosphere. You can help neutralize this danger to the planet through "carbon offsetting"—paying someone to invest your money in programs that reduce your greenhouse gas emissions by the same amount you've added. Before buying carbon offset credits, just make sure that you're using a reputable company, one with a proven program that invests in renewable energy. Reliable carbon offset companies include **Carbonfund** (www.carbonfund.org), **TerraPass** (www.terrapass.org), and **Carbon Neutral** (www.carbonneutral.org).
- Whenever possible, choose nonstop flights; they generally require less fuel than indirect flights that stop and take off again. Try to fly during the day—some scientists estimate that nighttime flights are twice as harmful to the environment. And pack light—each 15 pounds of luggage on a 5,000-mile flight adds up to 50 pounds of carbon dioxide emitted.
- Where you stay during your travels can have a major environmental impact. To determine the green credentials of a property, ask about trash disposal and recycling, water conservation, and energy use; also question if sustainable materials were used in the construction of the property. The website **www.greenhotels.com** recommends green-rated member hotels around the world that fulfill the company's stringent environmental requirements. Also consult **www.environmentallyfriendlyhotels.com** for more green accommodations ratings.
- At hotels, request that your sheets and towels not be changed daily. (Many hotels already have programs like this in place.) Turn off the lights and air conditioner (or heater) when you leave your room.
- Use public transport where possible—trains, buses, and even taxis are more energy-efficient forms of transport than driving. Even better is to walk or cycle; you'll produce zero emissions and stay fit and healthy on your travels.
- If renting a car is necessary, ask the rental agent for a hybrid, or rent the most fuel-efficient car available. You'll use less gas and save money at the tank.
- Eat at locally owned and operated restaurants that use produce grown in the area. This contributes to the local economy and cuts down on greenhouse gas emissions by supporting restaurants where the food is not flown or trucked in across long distances.

himself, in the form of displaced indigenous tribes, and has led to drinking-water shortages, flash flooding, and mud slides.

Fortunately, some countries, particularly Costa Rica, have taken great strides toward protecting the region's rich biodiversity.

Thirty years ago, it was difficult to find a protected area anywhere in Costa Rica, but now more than 11% of that country is protected within the national park system. Another 10% to 15% of the land enjoys moderately effective preservation as part of private and public reserves, Indian reserves, and wildlife refuges and corridors. Still, Costa Rica's precious tropical hardwoods continue to be harvested at an alarming rate, often illegally, while other primary forests are clear-cut for short-term agricultural gain. Many experts predict that Costa Rica's unprotected forests will be gone within the early part of this century.

Belize, Guatemala, and Honduras have commendable environmental records, with 40% of those countries protected. Belize has the best environmental policy of these three countries, with 40% of the country protected. Although Honduras still has significant forest cover (41%), it is losing 3% year after year; Guatemala is losing 1.7% a year, with 10% of its land classified as highly degraded and 60% at risk.

El Salvador has the worst environmental record in Central America, with only 2% of its original forest left, while Nicaragua is losing 150,000 hectares (370,500 acres) of forest per year. Fifty-seven percent of Panama is covered in forest but the country is losing 6,900 hectares (1,704 acres) a year.

Though environmental awareness is growing, solving the region's huge environmental problems, including not just deforestation but the effects of overpopulation and industrial pollution, clearly remains an uphill struggle.

Volunteer travel has become increasingly popular among those who want to venture beyond the standard group-tour experience to learn languages, interact with locals, and make a positive difference while on vacation in Central America. Volunteer options in are listed under "Special-Interest Trips," below, as well as in this guide's country chapters.

Animal-Rights Issues

For information on animal-friendly issues throughout the world, visit **Tread Lightly** (www.treadlightly.org). For information about the ethics of swimming with dolphins, visit the **Whale and Dolphin Conservation Society** (www.wdcs.org).

10 PACKAGES & ESCORTED TOURS

Package tours are simply a way to buy the airfare, accommodations, and other elements of your trip (such as car rentals, airport transfers, and sometimes even activities) at the same time and often at discounted prices.

One good source of package deals is the airlines themselves. Most major airlines offer air/land packages, including **American Airlines Vacations** (✆ 800/321-2121; www.aavacations.com), **Delta Vacations** (✆ 800/654-6559; www.deltavacations.com), **Continental Airlines Vacations** (✆ 800/301-3800; www.covacations.com), and **United Vacations** (✆ 888/854-3899; www.unitedvacations.com). Several big **online travel agencies**—Expedia, Travelocity, Orbitz, and Lastminute.com—also do a brisk business in packages.

Travel packages are also listed in the travel section of your local Sunday newspaper. Or check ads in national travel magazines such as *Arthur Frommer's Budget Travel Magazine, Travel + Leisure, National Geographic Traveler,* and *Condé Nast Traveler.*

For more information on package tours and for tips on booking your trip, see Frommers.com.

ESCORTED TOURS

Escorted tours are structured group tours with a group leader. The price usually includes everything from airfare to hotels, meals, tours, admission costs, and local transportation.

Despite the fact that escorted tours require big deposits and predetermine hotels, restaurants, and itineraries, many people derive security and peace of mind from the structure they offer. Escorted tours—whether they're navigated by bus, motorcoach, train, or boat—let travelers sit back and enjoy the trip without having to drive or worry about details. They take you to the maximum number of sights in the minimum amount of time with the least amount of hassle. They're particularly convenient for people with limited mobility, and they can be a great way to make new friends.

On the downside, you'll have little opportunity for serendipitous interactions with locals. The tours can be jampacked with activities, leaving little room for individual sightseeing, whim, or adventure—plus they often focus on the heavily touristy sites, so you miss out on many a lesser-known gem.

TOUR OPERATORS SPECIALIZING IN CENTRAL AMERICA

Organizing a hassle-free tour in Central America is a challenge. Transport is the main problem, as the roads and public buses are shabby to say the least. The language barrier is something else to consider when trying to piece together a preplanned itinerary. Often it's best to leave the logistics to the experts. The tour companies below have connections throughout the region, and their staffs can make all of your travel arrangements for you.

- **Ladatco Tours** (✆ **800/327-6162;** www.ladatco.com) has been providing "pampered adventure" since 1966. The company will put together a personalized tour of any country in Central America, including an epic 12-day tour of the region. It also organizes air-only packages.
- **Far Horizons** (✆ **800/552-4575;** www.farhorizon.com) offers cultural and archaeological tours of the region and are the experts if you want to unlock the secrets of the Maya civilization.
- **Tara Tours, Inc.** (✆ **800/327-0080;** www.taratours.com) is one of the most experienced agencies offering package tours to Central America. Tours are personalized based on your interests; some of the specialties here include archaeology and spiritual journeys. In general, the company's package tours are great deals.
- **Condor Journeys and Adventures** (✆ **01700/841-318;** www.condorjourneys-adventures.com) is a British company that offers tour packages and active vacations throughout Central America. They also arrange fixed-group tours for individual travelers.
- **Latin Discover** (✆ **506/2290-4017;** www.latindiscover.com) is a small, high-end operator based in Costa Rica, though it offers tours of the entire region. The company caters to all types of travelers, including honeymooners and independent self-drivers.
- **Tropical Discovery** (✆ **305/593-8687;** www.tropicaldiscovery.com) conducts private and custom-made tours up and down Central America. You can choose between 1-day volcano hiking or 11-day all-inclusive country tours.
- **Journey Latin America** (✆ **020/8747-8315;** www.journeylatinamerica.co.uk) is a premier British travel agency offering trips to Central America. The company can arrange airfare and tour packages throughout the region.
- **Adventure Associates** (✆ **02/9389-7466;** www.adventureassociates.com) is the best source in Australia for high-end package tours to Central America.

11 SPECIAL-INTEREST TRIPS

Many outdoor activities can be arranged easily and cheaply upon arrival in Central America. Local operators will have everything you need and can arrange guides and even companions. The quality of tours can vary greatly, and you will find paying a little extra gets you away from the herd. It is strongly advisable to hire knowledgeable guides to get the most out of your visit. See individual chapters throughout this book for specific tour operator info.

BIRD-WATCHING Resplendent quetzals, tropical kingbirds, social flycatchers, and keel-billed toucans are just some of the many marvelous feathered creatures that inhabit the jungles, savannas, and coastal rocks of Central America. You do not have to venture far from your hotel to catch sight of some creature that will have you fumbling for your camera. Some of the best birding spots are Costa Rica's Parque Nacional Corcovado, Nicaragua's Reserva Natural Miraflor, Belize's Crooked Tree Wildlife Sanctuary, and Panama's Volcán Barú.

HIKING Where to start? At the foot of a cone-shaped volcano or the lake of a rainforest reserve? Central America has numerous hiking possibilities with its many natural parks, cloud forests, lava fields, and deserted beaches offering a truly breathtaking variety of experiences. If you plan on camping, bring your own gear, as there is little in the way of equipment rental.

DIVING & SNORKELING The Atlantic coast is where the best diving takes place, particularly around the Bay Islands in Honduras and Caye Caulker in Belize. The Corn Islands are the next big thing in Caribbean coral treasure islands. All the well-known diving zones offer short dives and instructor training. The Pacific is not as popular as the Caribbean because its waters are darker and rougher. You can catch some good dives in places like San Juan del Sur in Nicaragua.

MOUNTAIN BIKING The region's best biking opportunities are in the cooler highland areas, particularly in Guatemala. There are plenty of outfitters in most cities but be careful that you get a road-worthy bike. Expect poor roads and dangerous drivers. This is definitely a pursuit best suited to the dry season (Nov–Apr).

RIVER RAFTING There is nothing quite like capering down a fast, tropical river. White-water rafting is becoming more and more popular in a region that has plenty of rivers offering Class 2 to Class 4 rafting. Costa Rica is ahead of everybody else when it comes to adventure companies and places. Guatemala and Honduras are slowly becoming known for excellent river floating, too, though.

KAYAKING A little more civilized than river rafting, kayaking is one of the most enriching experiences in Central America. Whether you are paddling on a crater lake or gliding through a Caribbean swamp, kayaking is a great way to break away from the crowd and creep up on some spectacular wildlife. Sea kayaking is popular in Belize and Costa Rica. Las Isletas in Nicaragua is a popular kayaking spot, as is the Chiriquí River in Panama and the Río Cangrejal in Honduras.

SURFING All along the rolling Pacific you'll find big waves and excellent breaks. It was surfers who first put Nicaragua's San Juan del Sur on the map and now El Salvador's Punta Roca is also making itself known among wave riders. Costa Rica has the most established surfers' hangouts, particularly around Playa del Coco and Parque Nacional Santa Rosa. Don't fancy getting your feet wet? Try volcano surfing in León, Nicaragua—this involves sliding

Studying Spanish & Staying with a Local Family

Studying the local language in a foreign country is all the rage, and Central America is the perfect place to study Spanish. In addition to the wonderful surroundings and bargain prices, the Central American accent is one of the cleanest and easiest Spanish accents to master (there's far less difference in regional accents here than in Spain, for instance). Many of the region's major tourist destinations also have Spanish schools, each of which offers the option of living with a local family while you study. Antigua, Guatemala, is particularly known for its Spanish-language classes and homestays, while Estelí in northern Nicaragua is gaining a reputation for such classes. See the boxes on Spanish schools throughout this book for info, or you can prearrange courses and homestays with organizations like **AmeriSpan** (✆ **0800/879-6640;** www.amerispan.com) or **Spanish Abroad** (✆ **602/778-6791;** www.spanishabroad.com). Wherever you decide to study, shop around and carefully examine the options, as some academies are much better organized than others.

down the side of black volcano on a waxed surfboard. It's strenuous (especially the walk back up), but great fun.

FISHING Sportfishing is popular all along the Atlantic coast with lots of marlin, sailfish, tarpon, and snook ready to catch. The Pacific coast also has big-game fishing, with giant dorado and yellowtail tuna. To catch such big fish requires chartering a boat from one of the many outfitters in the region, or you could just do what the locals do and stand in the tide throwing nets at the shoals.

VOLUNTEER VACATIONS

Here's a list of companies offering educational and volunteer opportunities in Central America; see individual country chapters for specific volunteer options.

- **AmeriSpan** (✆ **800/879-6640** or 215/751-1100; www.amerispan.com) helps students arrange programs that combine language study, travel, and volunteer opportunities throughout Central America.
- **Amigos de las Américas** (✆ **800/231-7796** or 713/782-5290; www.amigoslink.org) is always looking for volunteers to promote public health, education, and community development in rural areas of Central America.
- **Earthwatch Institute** (✆ **800/776-0188** or 978/461-0081; www.earthwatch.org) supports sustainable conservation efforts of the earth's natural resources. The organization can always use volunteers for its research teams in Central America.
- **Habitat for Humanity International** (✆ **229/924-6935,** or check the website for local affiliates; www.habitat.org) needs volunteers to help build affordable housing in more than 79 countries in the world, including most countries in Central America.
- **Spanish Abroad, Inc.** (✆ **888/722-7623** or 602/778-6791; www.spanishabroad.com) organizes intensive language-study programs throughout Central America.
- **Building New Hope** (✆ **412/421-1625;** www.buildingnewhope.org) is a Philadelphia-based organization always looking for volunteers for its numerous projects, especially in Nicaragua.
- **i-to-i** (✆ **0800/011-1156;** www.i-to-i.org) is a company that specializes in "meaningful travel." It has an extensive

range of programs all over the region that are particularly targeted toward gap-year students.

- **Global Volunteers** (✆ **0800/487-1074;** www.globalvolunteers.org) organizes volunteer vacations throughout Central America.
- **Enforex** (✆ **34091/594-3776;** www.enforex.com) is a Madrid-based Spanish-language company that organizes study-abroad programs in several Central American countries.

12 STAYING CONNECTED

TELEPHONES

Central America's phone systems differ in quality. For example, Costa Rica's system is much more efficient than that in Nicaragua. A local call generally costs just a few pennies per minute. Calls to cellphones or between competing phone companies can be much more expensive. Public phones are very rare, although calling cards are sold in most grocery and general stores. Your hotel is usually your best bet for making calls or sending and receiving faxes, although it may charge exorbitant rates for international faxes.

Your best, cheapest bet for making international calls it to head to any Internet cafe with an international calling option. These cafes have connections to Skype, Net2Phone, or some other **VoIP service.** International calls made this way can range anywhere from 5¢ (3p) to $1 (50p) per minute—much cheaper than making direct international calls or using a phone card. If you have your own Skype or similar account, you just need to find an Internet cafe that provides a computer with a headset.

See the "Fast Facts" sections throughout this guide's country chapters for tips on dialing.

Note that a number of establishments like shops and bars in smaller towns throughout this region do not have working land lines—these have been listed wherever possible.

USING A CELLPHONE

The three letters that define much of the world's wireless capabilities are GSM (Global System for Mobiles), a big, seamless network that makes for easy cross-border cellphone use throughout Central America and dozens of other regions worldwide. In the U.S., T-Mobile, AT&T Wireless, and Cingular use this quasi-universal system; in Canada, Microcell and some Rogers customers are GSM, and all Europeans and most Australians use GSM. Unfortunately, per-minute charges on roaming phone calls can be high—usually $1.50 to $3.50 (75p–£1.25) in this region.

For many, **renting** a phone is a good idea. (Even world phone owners will have to rent new phones if they're traveling to non-GSM regions, such as Japan or Korea.) While you can rent a phone from any number of overseas sites, including kiosks at airports and at car-rental agencies, we suggest renting the phone before you leave home. North Americans can rent one before leaving home from **InTouch USA** (✆ **800/872-7626;** www.intouchglobal.com) or **RoadPost** (✆ **888/290-1606** or 905/272-5665; www.roadpost.com). InTouch will also, for free, advise you on whether your existing phone will work overseas; simply call ✆ **703/222-7161** between 9am and 4pm EST, or go to **http://intouchglobal.com/travel.htm**.

Buying a phone can be economically attractive, as many Central American nations have cheap prepaid phone systems. Once you arrive at your destination, stop by a local cellphone shop and get the cheapest package; you'll probably pay less than $100 (£50) for a phone and a starter calling card. Local calls may be as low as

 **Where Are You @?**

The @ symbol is hard to find on a Latin American keyboard. You must keep your finger on the "Alt" key and then press "6" and "4" on the number pad to the right. If you're still unsuccessful and at an Internet cafe, ask the assistant to help you type an *arroba*.

10¢ (5p) per minute, and in many countries incoming calls are free.

Wilderness adventurers, or those heading to less-developed parts of Central America, might consider renting a **satellite phone** ("satphone"). It's different from a cellphone in that it connects to satellites and works where there's no cellular signal or ground-based tower. You can rent satellite phones from RoadPost (see above). InTouch USA (see above) offers a wider range of satphones but at higher rates. Per-minute call charges can be even cheaper than roaming charges with a regular cellphone, but the phone itself is more expensive. As of this writing, satphones were outrageously expensive to buy, so don't even think about it.

INTERNET ACCESS AWAY FROM HOME

Without Your Own Computer

It's hard nowadays to find a major city in Central America that *doesn't* have a few cybercafes. Although there's no definitive directory for cybercafes—these are independent businesses, after all—two places to start looking are at **www.cybercaptive.com** and **www.cybercafe.com**.

Aside from formal cybercafes, most **youth hostels** and hotels nowadays have at least one computer you can get to the Internet on, and many provide at least 15 minutes free.

If you need to access files on your office computer, look into a service called **GoToMyPC** (www.gotomypc.com). The service provides a Web-based interface for you to access and manipulate a distant PC from anywhere—even a cybercafe—provided your "target" PC is on and has an always-on connection to the Internet (such as with Road Runner cable). The service offers top-quality security, but if you're worried about hackers, use your own laptop rather than a cybercafe to access the GoToMyPC system.

With Your Own Computer

More and more hotels, cafes, and retailers in Central American cities are signing on as Wi-Fi (wireless fidelity) "hot spots." Mac owners have their own networking technology: Apple AirPort. iPass providers (www.ipass.com) also give you access to a few hundred wireless hotel lobby setups. To locate other hot spots that provide **free wireless networks** in cities around the world, go to **www.personaltelco.net/index.cgi/WirelessCommunities**. For dial-up access, most business-class hotels throughout Central America offer dataports for laptop modems.

Wherever you go, bring a **connection kit** of the right power and phone adapters, a spare phone cord, and a spare Ethernet network cable—or find out whether your hotel supplies them to guests.

13 TIPS ON ACCOMMODATIONS

Upscale travelers are finally starting to get their due in Central America. It has taken time, but spurred on by the example and standards of several international chains, service and amenities have been improving across-the-board, particularly in the upscale market. The region's strong suit is still its moderately priced hotels, though. In the \$60-to-\$125 (£30–£63) price range, you'll find comfortable and sometimes outstanding accommodations almost anywhere in the region. However, room size and quality vary quite a bit within this price range, so don't expect the kind of uniformity that you may find at home. Almost all the big hotels have free parking lots, while the smaller, budget hotels have street parking.

If you're budget- or bohemian-minded, you can find quite a few good deals for less than \$50 (£25) a double. ***But beware:*** Budget-oriented lodgings often feature shared bathrooms and either cold-water showers or showers heated by electrical heat-coil units mounted at the shower head, affectionately known as "suicide showers." If your hotel has one, do not adjust it while the water is running. ***Note:*** Air-conditioning is not necessarily a given in many midrange hotels and even some upscale joints. In general, this is not a problem. Cooler nights and a well-placed ceiling fan are often more than enough to keep things pleasant, unless we mention otherwise in the hotel reviews. And although power outages aren't a regular issue (at least in the region's cities) anymore, it is always wise to check out if your hotel has a backup generator in case things get uncomfortable.

Another welcome hotel trend in the area is the renovation and conversion of old homes into small hotels or B&Bs. Central America is still riding the ecotourism wave, and you'll find small nature-oriented ecolodges throughout the region, too. These lodges offer opportunities to see wildlife (including sloths, monkeys, and hundreds of species of birds) and learn about tropical forests. They range from spartan facilities catering primarily to scientific researchers, to luxury accommodations that are among the finest in the country. Keep in mind that although the nightly room rates at these lodges are often quite moderate, prices start to climb when you throw in transportation (often on chartered planes), guided excursions, and meals. Also, just because you can book a reservation at most of these lodges doesn't mean that they're not remote. Be sure to find out how you get to and from the ecolodge, and what tours and services are included in your stay. Then think long and hard about whether you really want to put up with hot, humid weather (cool and wet in the cloud forests); biting insects; rugged transportation; and strenuous hikes to see wildlife.

A couple of uniquely Central American lodging types that you might encounter are the *apartotel* and the *cabina.* An apartotel is just what it sounds like: an apartment hotel where you'll get a full kitchen and one or two bedrooms, along with daily maid service. *Cabinas* are the region's version of cheap vacation lodging. They're very inexpensive and very basic—often just cinder-block buildings divided into small rooms; some come with kitchenettes. A *posada* is a small, usually family-run hotel, not unlike a B&B.

Wherever you choose to stay, make sure you keep your doors closed or you might have some unwanted hairy visitors. Pack a flashlight for those midnight runs to the kitchen, bathroom, or beach. If you're visiting an ecolodge or hotel in any area near the jungle, most accommodations have either screened-in windows or provide mosquito nets. The exceptions are the bare-bones beach shacks along the coast and rustic huts in the jungle.

Hotels listed as "expensive" throughout this book often offer much cheaper rates for travelers booking through their websites. Your best bet throughout this region is negotiating directly with the hotels themselves, especially the smaller hotels.

However, be aware that response times might be slower than you'd like, and many of the smaller hotels might have some trouble communicating back and forth in English. Rates quoted throughout the book reflect double occupancy, and differences between low- and high-season rates are noted wherever possible. (Note that there are some bargains to be had during the low or rainy season.)

Also see "Tips on Accommodations" in the country chapters throughout this book for info. For tips on surfing for hotel deals online, visit Frommers.com.

4

Belize

by Eliot Greenspan

Belize proves the cliché that big things come in small packages. This tiny Central American country has the longest continuous barrier reef in the Western Hemisphere; the largest known Classic Maya city, Caracol; and the highest concentration per square mile of the largest new-world cat, the jaguar. It also has one of the most extensive and easily accessible cave systems for amateur and experienced spelunkers alike, as well as a nearly endless supply of some of the world's best snorkeling and scuba-diving opportunities. "You'd betta Belize it!" goes the common local exclamation. The best part about all the world-class attractions and experiences to be found in Belize is that the country's compact size makes it easy to sample a wide range of them in a short period of time.

Belize is the second-youngest nation in the Western Hemisphere, having been granted independence from Britain in 1981. It's also a decidedly sparsely populated country, with just under 300,000 citizens and no large cities. Belize is the only country in Central America where English is the official and predominant language.

Originally a major part of the ancient Maya empire, Belize was next settled by pirates and then colonized by the British, using slave labor. The descendants of each of these groups are woven into the historical lore and cultural fabric of modern Belize. Add to the mix the independent Garífuna people, who settled along the remote southern shore in the early part of the 19th century, and the more recent waves of Mexican, Chinese, and East Indian immigrants, and you have an idea of the cultural meld that constitutes this unique Central American country. Surprisingly, Belizeans of all cultural stripes tend to get along a lot better and with far fewer outward and untoward shows of racism than citizens of most other nations. This is a small country. The sense of community is strong and, even in the big city, people tend to know their neighbors and almost everyone is somehow related.

1 THE REGIONS IN BRIEF

Bordered to the north by Mexico, to the south and west by Guatemala, and to the east by the Caribbean sea, Belize is a small nation, about the size of the state of Massachusetts.

BELIZE CITY Belize City is a modest-size coastal port city located at the mouth of the Belize River. Although it's no longer the official governmental seat, Belize City remains the most important city—culturally, economically, and historically—in the country. It is also Belize's transportation hub, with the only international airport, an active municipal airport, a cruise-ship dock, and all the major bus line and water taxi terminals. Belize City has a reputation as a rough and violent urban center, and visitors should exercise caution and stick to the most popular tourist areas of this small city.

NORTHERN BELIZE Anchored on the south by Belize City, this is the country's business and agricultural heartland. Orange Walk Town and Corozal Town are small cities with a strong Spanish feel and influence, having been settled largely by refugees from Mexico's Caste War. The Maya also lived here, and their memories live on at the ruins of Altun Ha, Lamanai, Cerros, and Santa Rita, all in this zone. Toward the western section of this region lies the Río Bravo Conservation Area, a massive tract of virgin forest, sustainable-yield managed forest, and recovering reforestation areas. Northern Belize has some of the country's prime destinations for bird-watchers, including the Shipstern Nature Reserve and Crooked Tree Wildlife Sanctuary.

THE NORTHERN CAYES & ATOLLS This is Belize's primary tourist zone. Hundreds of palm-swept offshore islands lie between the coast of the mainland and the protection of the 298km (185-mile) Barrier Reef. This reef offers some of the world's most exciting snorkeling, scuba diving, and fishing. The most developed cayes here, Ambergris Caye and Caye Caulker, have numerous hotels and small resorts, while some of the less developed cayes maintain the feel of fairy-tale desert isles. In addition, there are two open-ocean atolls here, Turneffe Island Atoll and Lighthouse Reef Atoll. For those whose main sport is catching rays, not fish, it should be mentioned that the cayes, and Belize in general, lack wide, sandy beaches. Although the water is as warm and clear blue as it's touted to be, most of your sunbathing will be on docks, deck chairs, or imported patches of sand fronting a sea wall or sea-grass patch.

SOUTHERN BELIZE Southern Belize encompasses two major districts, Stann Creek and Toledo. The former includes the Cockscomb Basin Wildlife Sanctuary and the coastal towns of Dangriga, Hopkins Village, and Placencia. Placencia boasts what is arguably the country's best beach. Farther south, the Toledo District is Belize's final frontier. The inland hills and jungles are home to numerous Kekchi and Mopan Maya villages. Hidden in these hills are some lesser known and less visited Maya ruins, including Lubaantun and Nim Li Punit. Off the shores of southern Belize lie more cayes and yet another midocean atoll, Glover's Reef Atoll.

THE CAYO DISTRICT & WESTERN BELIZE This mountainous district near the Guatemalan border has become Belize's second-most popular destination. Here you'll find some of Belize's most beautiful countryside and most fascinating natural and man-made sights. The limestone mountains of this region are dotted with numerous caves, sinkholes, jagged peaks, underground rivers, and waterfalls. There are clear-flowing aboveground rivers that are excellent for swimming and canoeing, as well as mile after mile of unexplored forest full of wild animals and hundreds of bird species. Adventurers, nature lovers, and bird-watchers will definitely want to spend some time in the Cayo District. This is also where you'll find Belize's largest and most impressive Maya ruins.

2 THE BEST OF BELIZE IN 1 WEEK

The timing is tight, but this itinerary packs a trio of Belize's best destinations into 1 week. It allows for a chance to visit a major Maya ruin, snorkel on the barrier reef, ride an inner tube on an underground river, and relax a bit on the beach.

Belize in 1 Week

Day ❶: Arrive & Head to Placencia ★★

Arrive into **Belize City** and grab a quick connecting flight to **Placencia.** Spend the afternoon strolling along the beach and the town's famous sidewalk. Head back to the sidewalk after dark, and enjoy some time mingling with locals and tourists alike at the **Barefoot Beach Bar** ★ (p. 149).

Day ❷: Way Down Upon the Monkey River

Take a tour on the **Monkey River** ★ (p. 146), where you're sure to see a rich array of wildlife. In the afternoon you can treat yourself to a spa treatment, get some snorkeling in, or try a seaweed shake. For dinner, head to the **French Connection** ★★★ (p. 149).

Day ❸: Cayo Calling

Fly back to Belize City and pick up a rental car for the drive to the **Cayo District** ★★. Stop at the **Belize Zoo** ★★ (p. 101) or for a cave tubing adventure near Jaguar Paw en route. Settle into one of the hotels in San Ignacio or one of the lodges located out on the way to Benque Viejo. If there's time, take an afternoon tour to the ruins at **Xunantunich** ★★ (p. 133).

Day ❹: Climbing Caana

Wake up very early and head to the Maya ruins at **Caracol** ★★ (p. 134), stopping at the **Río On Pools** ★★ and **Río Frío Cave** (p. 135) on your way back to San Ignacio.

Days ❺ & ❻: Fly to the Cayes

Head for the cayes. Choose between **Caye Caulker** ★★★, with its intimate funky charm, or **Ambergris Caye** ★, with its wide choice of hotels, resorts, and restaurants. A whole range of activities and adventures await you here. Be sure to try the snorkel trip to **Hol Chan Marine Reserve** ★★ and **Shark-Ray Alley** ★★ (p. 112). You can also just chill in the sun and sand.

Day ❼: Going Home

Return to **Belize City** in time for your international connection. If you have time, stop off at the **Belize Tourism Village** (p. 100) to do some last-minute shopping before you go.

3 PLANNING YOUR TRIP TO BELIZE

VISITOR INFORMATION

The **Belize Tourism Board,** 64 Regent St. (P.O. Box 325) in Belize City, will mail you a basic information packet. You can order this packet on their website at **www.travelbelize.org**. Alternatively, folks in the United States and Canada can call the Belize Tourism Board toll-free at ✆ **800/624-0286.** Travelers from the United Kingdom, Australia, and New Zealand will have to rely primarily on the website, or dial direct to Belize (✆ **501/227-2430**), as the Belize Tourism Board does not have offices or a toll-free number in these countries.

In addition to the official website listed above, you'll be able to find a wealth of Web-based information on Belize with a few clicks of your mouse. Here are a few good places to begin your clicking:

- **http://lanic.utexas.edu/la/ca/belize**: The University of Texas Latin American Studies Department's database features an extensive list of useful links.
- **www.belizeforum.com**: These are active and informative forums on living in and traveling around Belize.
- **www.toucantrail.com**: This is an excellent site geared toward budget travelers, with extensive links and comprehensive information.

Telephone Dialing Info at a Glance

Belize has a standardized seven-digit phone numbering system. There are no city or area codes to dial from within Belize; use the country code, 501 (not to be confused with the area code for the state of Arkansas), only when dialing a Belizean number from outside Belize.

- **To place a call from your home country to Belize,** dial the international access code (011 in the U.S. and Canada, 0011 in Australia, 0170 in New Zealand, 00 in the U.K.), plus the country code (501), plus the seven-digit phone number.
- **To place a local call within Belize,** dial the seven-digit local number.
- **For directory assistance:** Dial ✆ **113** if you're looking for a number inside Belize, and for numbers to all other countries dial ✆ **115** and (for a charge) an operator will connect you to an international directory assistance operator.
- **For operator assistance:** If you need operator assistance in making a call, dial ✆ **115,** whether you're trying to make a local or an international call.
- **Toll-free numbers:** Numbers beginning with 0800 and 800 within Belize are toll-free, but calling a 1-800 number in the States from Belize is not toll-free. In fact, it costs the same as an overseas call.

Tour Operators

Local travel agencies are another good source of information. Two in Belize City to try are **Discovery Expeditions,** 5916 Manatee Dr., Buttonwood Bay (✆ **501/223-0748;** www.discoverybelize.com), and **S&L Travel and Tours ★**, 91 N. Front St. (✆ **501/227-7593;** www.sltravelbelize.com).

ENTRY REQUIREMENTS

A current passport, valid through your departure date, is required for entry into Belize. Driver's licenses and birth certificates are not valid travel documents. In some cases you may be asked to show an onward or return plane ticket.

No visas are required for citizens of the United States; the European community—including Great Britain and Ireland; South Africa; Australia; or New Zealand. Nationals of certain other countries do need a visa or consular permission to enter Belize. For a current list, see the Belize Tourism Board website (www.travelbelize.org) or call the nearest Belize consulate or embassy.

Tourists are permitted a maximum stay of 30 days. The **Belize Department of Immigration and Nationality** in Belmopan (✆ **501/822-2423**) will sometimes grant an extension of up to 3 months. These extensions are handled on a case-by-case basis and cost BZ$100 ($50/£25) per month.

Belizean Embassy Locations

In the U.S. & Canada: 2535 Massachusetts Ave. NW, Washington, DC 20008 (✆ **202/332-9636;** www.embassyofbelize.org).

In the U.K.: Belize High Commission, 22 Harcourt House, 45 Crawford Place, London, W1H 4LP (© **020/7723-3603**).

In Australia & New Zealand: 5/1 Oliver Rd., Roseville NSW (© **02/9905-8144**).

CUSTOMS

Visitors to Belize may bring with them any and all reasonable goods and belongings for personal use during their stay. Cameras, computers, and electronic equipment, as well as fishing and diving gear for personal use, are permitted duty-free. Customs officials in Belize seldom check arriving tourists' luggage.

MONEY

The Belize dollar, abbreviated BZ$, is the official currency of Belize. It is pegged to the U.S. dollar at a ratio of 2 Belize dollars to 1 U.S. dollar, or 4 Belize dollars to the U.K. pound. Both currencies are acceptable at almost any business or establishment around the country. As long as you have U.S. dollars or U.S. dollar–based traveler's checks, it is entirely unnecessary to change for Belize dollars in advance of your trip. However, travelers from Canada, Europe, Australia, and New Zealand will want to change a sufficient amount of their home currency to U.S. dollars before traveling.

Once you are in Belize, the change you receive will most likely be in Belize dollars, although it is not uncommon for it to be a mix of both currencies. However, do try to have some small-denomination bills for paying taxis, modest meal tabs, and tips.

Tip: Be careful to note whether or not the price you are being quoted is in Belize or U.S. dollars. Many hotels, restaurants, and tour operators actually quote in U.S. dollars. If in doubt, ask. At a two-to-one ratio, the difference can be substantial.

ATMS You'll find internationally accessible ATMs in all major cities or towns and tourist destinations, including Belize City, San Pedro, Caye Caulker, Placencia, Punta Gorda, San Ignacio, Belmopan, Dangriga, and Corozal Town. Still, it's wise to bring some spending cash, and charge the rest of your bills. Try not to rely on your ATM card for an emergency cash bailout.

CREDIT CARDS Most major credit cards are accepted in Belize, although MasterCard and Visa are much more widely accepted than American Express, especially by smaller hotels, restaurants, and tour operators. While there are some exceptions, Diners Club and Discover have made minimal inroads around Belize.

To report lost or stolen credit cards or traveler's checks, call the following numbers: **American Express,** © **1-336/393-1111** collect from Belize; **Diners Club,** © **1-303/799-1504** collect from Belize; **MasterCard, 1-636/722-7111** collect from Belize; and **Visa, 1-410/581-9994** collect from Belize.

WHEN TO GO

PEAK SEASON Belize's high season for tourism runs from late November to late April, which coincides almost perfectly with the chill of winter in the United States, Canada, and Great Britain. The high season is also the dry season. If you want some unadulterated time on a tropical beach and a little less rain during your rainforest experience, this is the time to visit. During this period (and especially around the Christmas and Easter holidays), the tourism industry operates at full tilt—prices are higher, attractions are more crowded, and reservations need to be made in advance.

CLIMATE The weather in Belize is subtropical and generally similar to that of southern Florida. The average daytime temperature on the coast and cayes is around 80°F (27°C), although it can get considerably warmer during the day during the summer months. During the winter months, when northern cold fronts extend their grip south, it can get downright nippy. In fact, from late December to February, "northers" can hit the coastal and caye areas hard, and hang around for between 3 and 5 days, putting a severe crimp in any beach vacation. The best months for guaranteed sun and fun are March through May.

The rainy season runs from June to mid-November, while the hurricane season runs from July to October, with the most active months being August, September, and October. For the most part, the rainy season is characterized by a dependable and short-lived afternoon shower. However, the amount of rainfall varies considerably with the regions. In the south, there may be more than 150 inches of rain per year, while in the north, it rarely rains more than 50 inches per year. Usually there is also a brief dry period in mid-August, known as the *mauger.* If you're skittish about rain and hurricanes, don't come to Belize between late August and mid-October, the height of both the rainy and hurricane seasons.

The Cayo District and other inland destinations tend to be slightly cooler than the coastal and caye destinations, although since there is generally little elevation gain, the differences tend to be slight.

PUBLIC HOLIDAYS Official holidays in Belize include **January 1** (New Year's Day), **March 9** (Baron Bliss Day), Good Friday, Holy Saturday, Easter Sunday, Easter Monday, **May 1** (Labour Day), **May 24** (Commonwealth Day), **September 10** (St. George's Caye Day), **September 21** (Independence Day), **October 12** (Pan American Day), **November 19** (Garífuna Settlement Day), **December 25** (Christmas Day), **December 26** (Boxing Day), and **December 31** (New Year's Eve).

HEALTH CONCERNS

Staying healthy on a trip to Belize is predominantly a matter of being a little cautious about what you eat and drink, applying sunscreen, and using common sense. See p. 70 in "Planning Your Trip to Central America" for more info on avoiding and treating illness.

COMMON AILMENTS None of the major tropical illnesses are epidemic in Belize, and your chance of contracting any serious tropical disease in the country is slim. Although **malaria** is found in Belize, it's far from epidemic. It is most common along the coastal lowlands, as well as in some of the more remote southern inland communities. Of greater concern may be **dengue fever,** which seems to be most common in lowland urban areas; Belize City and Dangriga have been the hardest hit cities in Belize. See p. 70 in "Planning Your Trip to Central America" for more info on treating and avoiding these diseases.

DIETARY RED FLAGS Even though the water around Belize is generally safe, particularly in most of the popular tourist destinations, and even if you're careful to buy and drink only bottled water, you still may encounter some intestinal difficulties. Most of this is just due to tender northern stomachs coming into contact with slightly more aggressive Latin American intestinal flora.

VACCINATIONS No specific vaccinations are necessary for travel to Belize, although it is recommended that you be up-to-date on your tetanus, typhoid, and yellow-fever vaccines. It is also a good idea to get a vaccination for hepatitis A and B.

GETTING THERE

By Plane

Belize's international airport is Belize City's **Philip S. W. Goldson International Airport** (**BZE; ✆ 501/225-2045**), which is 16km (10 miles) northwest of the city on the Northern Highway. See p. 96 for info on getting from the airport into town or to other destinations in Belize.

FROM NORTH AMERICA **American Airlines, Continental, Delta, Grupo Taca,** and **US Airways** all have regular direct service to Belize from the U.S. Flying time from Miami is just over 2 hours. From Canada, the only direct flights are seasonal winter charters. See the appendix for phone numbers and websites.

FROM THE REST OF THE WORLD There are no direct flights to Belize from Europe, Australia, New Zealand, mainland Asia, or Africa. To get to Belize from any of these points of origin, you will have to connect through one of the major U.S. hub cities, used by the airlines mentioned above.

By Bus

Belize is connected to both Guatemala and Mexico by regular bus service.

Two separate bus lines, **Línea Dorada** (**✆ 502/7926-0070;** www.tikalmayanworld.com) and **San Juan Travel** (**✆ 502/7926-0042;** sanjuantravel@hotmail.com.gt), make the run between Belize City and Guatemala's Petén district. Both can be contacted in Belize at **✆ 501/223-0457** or 223-1235. Alternatively, you can take one of the many buses from Belize City (or from San Ignacio) to the Guatemalan border.

Buses (**✆ 501/227-2255**) connect Belize City to Corazal and the Mexican border. The Mexican border town is Chetumal. From here buses leave roughly every half-hour between 5:30am and 7:30pm.

By Boat

Fast water taxis connect Belize to Livingston and Puerto Barrios, Guatemala, as well as the Bay Islands of Honduras. These boats arrive at and depart from both Placencia and Punta Gorda. Ask around the docks at either one of these small towns and you'll be able to find out current schedules and fares.

GETTING AROUND

BY PLANE Traveling around Belize by commuter airline is common, easy, and relatively economical. Two local commuter airlines serve all the major tourist destinations around Belize. The carriers are **Maya Island Air** (**✆ 501/223-1140;** www.mayaairways.com) and **Tropic Air** (**✆ 800/422-3435** in the U.S. and Canada, or 501/226-2012 in Belize; www.tropicair.com). Both operate out of both the **Philip S. W. Goldson International Airport** (p. 96) and the Belize City **Municipal Airport** (p. 96). In both cases, flights are considerably less expensive into and out of the Municipal Airport.

BY BUS Belize has an extensive network of commuter buses serving all of the major villages and towns, and tourist destinations in the country. However, this system is used primarily by Belizeans. The buses tend to be a bit antiquated, and buyouts and bankruptcies within the industry have left the status of the local bus network in a state of confusion and limbo. See the destination sections for specific details on schedules, and be sure to check in advance, or as soon as you arrive, as schedules do change regularly. Rates run between BZ$4 ($2/£1) and BZ$28 ($14/£7).

BY CAR There are only four major roads in Belize: the Northern, Western, Southern, and Hummingbird highways. All are just two-lane affairs, and all actually have speed bumps as they pass through various towns and villages along their way. Belize is only about 113km (70 miles) wide, and around 403km (250 miles) long. Renting a car is an excellent way to see the country. If you are going to the Mountain Pine Ridge area of the Cayo District, you will certainly need a four-wheel-drive vehicle. However, if you're just visiting the major towns and cities like San Ignacio or Placencia, you'll probably be fine in a standard sedan. It's always nice, however, to have the extra clearance and off-road ability of a four-wheel-drive vehicle, particularly during the rainy season (June through mid-Nov).

Among the major international agencies operating in Belize are **Avis, Budget, Hertz,** and **Thrifty;** see "Appendix: Fast Facts, Toll-Free Numbers & Websites" for info. **Crystal Auto Rental** ★ (✆ **800/777-7777** toll-free in Belize; www.crystal-belize.com) is a local company, with an excellent fleet and good prices.

Prices run between BZ$120 and BZ$240 ($60–$120/£30–£60) per day for a late-model compact to a compact SUV, including insurance. Most of the rental companies above have a 25-year-old minimum age requirement for renting, although Crystal Auto Rental will rent to 21- to 24-year-olds, but with twice the deductible.

Often included in the price, car-rental insurance runs about BZ$24 to BZ$40 ($12–$20/£6–£10) per day with an average deductible of around BZ$1,500 ($750/£375), although sometimes for a few extra dollars per day you can get no-fault, no-deductible coverage.

BY TAXI There's no standardized look or color to taxis in Belize. Many are old, gas-guzzling American models, although newer Japanese sedans are starting to appear more frequently. Most taxis are clearly marked in some form or other, usually with a roof ornament. Very few taxis use meters, so be sure to negotiate your fare in advance.

BY BOAT While it's possible to fly to a few of the outer cayes, most travel between mainland Belize and the cayes and atolls is done by high-speed launch. There are regular water taxis between Belize City and Ambergris Caye and Caye Caulker. Hotels and resorts on the other islands all either have their own boats, or can arrange transport for you.

TIPS ON ACCOMMODATIONS

Belize has no truly large-scale resorts or hotels. While the Radisson and Best Western chains have one property each in Belize City, there are no other chain hotels in Belize. Upscale travelers looking for over-the-top luxury have few options here. True budget hounds will also find slim pickings, especially in the beach and caye destinations. What the country does have is a host of intimate and interesting **small to midsize hotels** and **small resorts.** Most of these are quite comfortable and reasonably priced, although nowhere near as inexpensive as those in neighboring Mexico and Guatemala.

Belize is a noted ecotourism and bird-watching destination, and there are small nature-oriented **ecolodges** across the inland portion of the country. These lodges offer opportunities to see wildlife and learn about tropical forests. They range from spartan facilities catering primarily to scientific researchers to luxury accommodations that are among the finest in the country.

TIPS ON DINING

Belizean cuisine is a mix of Caribbean, Mexican, African, Spanish, and Maya culinary influences. Belize's strongest suit is its **seafood.** Fresh fish, lobster, shrimp, and conch are widely available, especially at the beach and island destinations. **Rice and beans** are another major staple, served as an accompaniment to almost any main dish. Often the rice and beans are cooked together, with a touch of coconut milk.

Keep in mind that there are seasons for lobster and conch. Officially, lobster season runs from July 15 to February 14, while conch is available from October 1 to June 30. Local restaurants and fishery officials have struck a deal to allow lobster to be served in the off season. Supposedly this is lobster caught and frozen during the open season, and not while they are mating in the formerly closed season.

There is an additional 10% GST tax, and a 10% service charge is often added on to all restaurant bills. Belizeans rarely tip, but that doesn't mean you shouldn't. If the service was particularly good and attentive, you should probably leave a little extra.

TIPS ON SHOPPING

You won't be bowled over by shopping options in Belize, and very few people come to Belize specifically to shop. You will find a modest handicraft industry, with different specialties produced by the country's various ethnic communities. The creole populations of the coastal area and outer cayes specialize in coral and shell jewelry, as well as woodcarvings with maritime (dolphins, turtles, and ships) themes. The Belizean Maya population produces replicas of ancient petroglyphs and different modern designs on varying sized pieces of slate. Finally, the Garífuna peoples of the southern coastal villages are known for their small dolls.

My favorite gift item in Belize continues to be **Marie Sharp's Hot Sauce ★★**, which comes in several heat gradations, as well as some new flavors. The original blend of habanero peppers, carrots, and vinegar is one of my all-time favorite hot sauces. The company also produces mango chutney and an assortment of pepper jams. You can pick up Marie Sharp products at any supermarket and most gift shops; I recommend you stick to the supermarkets, though, to avoid price gouging. In addition to Marie Sharp's, Lizette's brand of hot sauces is also a good bet.

Fast Facts Belize

American Express American Express Travel Services is represented in Belize by **Belize Global Travel Services Ltd.,** 41 Albert St. (✆ **501/227-7185;** www.belizeglobal.bz), which can issue traveler's checks and replacement cards, and provide other standard services. They are open Monday through Friday from 8am to noon and 1 to 5pm, and on Saturday from 8am to noon. To report lost or stolen Amex credit card or traveler's checks within Belize, call the local number above, or call collect to ✆ **336/393-1111** in the U.S.

Business Hours Banks are generally open Monday through Friday from 8am to 4:30pm. However, in many small towns, villages, and tourist destinations, bank hours may be limited. In very few instances, banks have begun opening on Saturday. Belizean businesses tend to be open Monday through Friday from 8am to noon, and from 1 to 5pm. Some businesses do not close for lunch, and some open on Saturday. Most bars are open until 1 or 2am, although some go later.

Drugstores There are a handful of pharmacies around Belize City, and in most of the major towns and tourist destinations. Perhaps the best-stocked pharmacy in the country can be found at **Belize Medical Associates,** 5791 St. Thomas Kings Park (✆ **501/223-0303;** www.belizemedical.com) in Belize City.

Embassies & Consulates The **United States Embassy** is located in Belmopan on Floral Park Road (✆ **501/822-4011;** www.belize.usembassy.gov). The **British High Commission** is located in Belmopan, at Embassy Square (✆ **501/822-2146**). You can contact the **Canadian Honorary Consul** in Belize City at 80 Princess Margaret Dr. (✆ **501/223-1060**). **Australia** and **New Zealand** do not have an embassy or consulate in Belize.

Emergencies In case of any emergency, dial ✆ **90** from anywhere in Belize. This will connect you to the police. In most cases, ✆ **911** will also work.

Hospitals **Belize Medical Associates,** 5791 St. Thomas Kings Park, Belize City (✆ **501/223-0303;** www.belizemedical.com), is a modern, 24-hour private hospital, with emergency care and numerous private practice physicians. The country's main public hospital, the **Karl Heusner Memorial Hospital,** Princess Margaret Drive, Belize City (✆ **501/223-1548**), is also open 24 hours and has a wide range of facilities and services.

Language English is the official language of Belize, and it is almost universally spoken. However, Belize is a very polyglot country, and you are likely to hear Spanish, Patois, and Garífuna.

Newspapers & Magazines Belize has no daily newspaper. There are four primary weeklies: *Amandala,* the *Reporter, Belize Times,* and the *Guardian.* Most come out on Friday, and all are relatively similar in terms of content, although with some differing and usually obvious political leanings. A couple, most notably *Amandala* and the *Reporter,* actually publish twice weekly. *Belize First* is a periodic book-style magazine aimed at the tourist trade.

Police The police in Belize are generally helpful; there is a dedicated tourism police force in Belize City. Dial ✆ **90** or **911** in an emergency. You can also dial ✆ **501/227-2222.**

Post Offices & Mail Most hotels will post a letter for you, and there are post offices in the major towns. It costs BZ$.80 (US40¢/20p) to send a letter to the United States, and BZ$1 (US50¢/25p) to send a letter to Europe. Postcards to the same destinations cost BZ$.40 (US20¢/10p) and BZ$.50 (US25¢/13p) respectively.

If your postal needs are urgent, or you want to send anything of value, several international courier and express-mail services have offices in Belize City, including **DHL,** 38 New Rd. (✆ 501/223-1070; www.dhl.com); **FedEx,** 1 Mapp St. (✆ 501/224-5221; www.fedex.com); and **Mail Boxes Etc.,** 166 N. Front St. (✆ 501/227-6046; www.mbe.com). All can arrange pickup and delivery services to any hotel in town, and sometimes in the different outlying districts.

Safety Belize City has a reputation for being a rough and dangerous city. While things have improved somewhat in recent years, the reputation was earned for a reason. Tourist police do patrol the busiest tourist areas during the day and early evenings. Still, while most populous downtown areas and tourist attractions are quite safe during the daytime, travelers are strongly advised to not walk around very much at night, except in the best-lit and most popular sections of downtown. Basic common sense and street smarts are to be employed. Don't wear flashy jewelry or wave wads of cash around. Be aware of your surroundings, and avoid any people and places that make you feel uncomfortable.

Outside of Belize City, things get a lot better, but you should still exercise common sense—make sure your valuables are securely stored and don't venture away from major tourist areas by yourself or after dark.

Rental cars generally stick out and they are easily spotted by thieves, who know that such cars are likely to be full of valuables. Don't ever leave anything of value in an unattended parked car.

Taxes There is a $35 (£18) departure tax that must be paid in cash at the airport upon departure. There is a 9% hotel tax added on to all hotel bills, and there is a 10% GST tax on all goods and services. A 10% service charge is sometimes added to restaurant bills. Take this into account when deciding how much to tip.

Telephone & Fax If you have an unlocked 1900MHz GSM phone, **DigiCell** (**© 501/227-2017;** www.digicell.bz) sells local prepaid SIM chips with a local number. The chip and initial activation costs BZ$54 ($27/£14), including BZ$10 ($5/£2.50) of calls. You can buy subsequent minutes in the form of scratch-off cards in a variety of denominations. The SIM chips and calling cards are sold at their desk at the airport or at one of their many outlets around Belize. Their website also has information on setting up your home phone for roaming in Belize. But be careful, the rates are quite high. Also see p. 80 in "Planning Your Trip to Central America" and the "Telephone Dialing Info at a Glance" box earlier in this chapter for info.

Tipping Most Belizeans don't tip. Many restaurants add a 10% service charge. However, if the service is particularly good, or if the service charge is not included, tipping is appropriate.

4 BELIZE CITY

Despite a reputation for crime and violence, periodic devastation from passing hurricanes, and the loss of its capital status, Belize City remains the urban heart and soul of Belize. Most visitors treat Belize City merely as a transition point and transportation hub. This is probably what you'll want to do, too. But if you've got a day or two to burn on a layover here, Belize City is a good place to walk around, admire the fleet of working wooden fish sloops, do some craft and souvenir shopping, and stock up on Marie Sharp's Hot Sauce to bring home with you.

Long ago stripped of its status as the country's capital, Belize City remains Belize's business, transportation, and cultural hub. With a population of some 71,000, Belize City is surrounded on three sides by water, and at high tide it is nearly swamped. It's a dense warren of narrow streets and canals (the latter being little more than open sewers, and pretty pungent in hot weather), modern stores, dilapidated shacks, and quaint wooden mansions, coexisting in a seemingly chaotic jumble.

Getting There

BY PLANE All international flights into Belize land at the **Philip S. W. Goldson International Airport** (**BZE; ✆ 501/225-2045;** www.pgiabelize.com), which is located 16km (10 miles) northwest of the city on the Northern Highway.

In the baggage claim area, there's an information booth maintained by the **Belize Tourist Board.** This booth supplies maps and brochures, and will often make a call for you if you need a hotel or car-rental reservation. Inside the international departure terminal is a branch of **Belize Bank** (**✆ 501/225-2107**), open daily from 8:30am to 4pm. Across the parking lot, you'll find car-rental and tour-agency desks, open daily from 8am to 9:30pm. A taxi into town will cost BZ$50 to BZ$60 ($25–$30/£13–£15).

If you fly in from somewhere else in Belize, you might land at the **Municipal Airport** (**TZA**; no phone), which is on the edge of town. A taxi from here costs just BZ$10 ($5/£2.50). There's no bank or any other services at the municipal airport, although most car-rental agencies can arrange to have a car there for you.

BY BUS If you arrive in town by bus, you'll probably end up at the main **bus terminal** on West Collet Canal Street. A taxi from the bus station to any hotel in town will cost around BZ$8 ($4/£2).

Orientation

Belize City is surrounded on three sides by water, with Haulover Creek dividing the city in two. The Swing Bridge, near the mouth of Haulover Creek, is the main route between the two halves of the city, as well as the city's principal landmark. At the south end of the bridge is Market Square and the start of Regent Street and Albert Street. This is where you'll find most of Belize City's banks, shops, and offices. To the west and east of these two major roads is a grid of smaller roads lined with dilapidated wooden houses. On the north side of the bridge and to the right is the Fort George area. From the southern side of the city, Cemetery Road heads out of town to the west and becomes the Western Highway, while from the northern side of the city, Freetown Road becomes Haulover Road and then the Northern Highway.

Getting Around

BY TAXI Taxis are plentiful and relatively inexpensive. A ride anywhere in the city should cost between BZ$6 and BZ$14 ($3–$7/£1.50–£3.50). If you need to call a cab, ask at your hotel or try **Belize Marine Terminal Land Taxi Association** (**✆ 501/223-5850**), **Cinderella Plaza Taxi Stand** (**✆ 501/203-3340**), **Taxi Garage Services** (**✆ 501/227-3031**), or **Majestic Taxi** (**✆ 501/203-4465**).

ON FOOT Belize City's downtown hub is compact and easy to navigate on foot. However, the city has a rather nasty reputation for being unsafe for visitors, and you'd be wise to stick to the busiest sections of downtown and obvious tourist districts. You can easily walk the entire Fort George neighborhood, as well as the compact business area just south of the Swing Bridge. If you need to venture any farther, take a taxi. Be careful when you walk, as sidewalks are often in bad shape and sometimes quite narrow. And don't walk anywhere at night, except perhaps around the downtown hub of budget hotels and restaurants and the Fort George area.

BY BUS While Belize has an extensive network of bus connections to most cities and rural destinations, there is no metropolitan bus system in Belize City.

BY CAR There is little need to navigate Belize City in a car. If you do find yourself driving around Belize City, go slow, as pedestrians can appear out of nowhere, and pay attention to the general flow of traffic and a wealth of one-way streets. Despite being a former British colony, cars drive on the right-hand side of the road, and road distances are listed in miles. Most rental car agencies are based at the Philip S. W. Goldson International Airport, although a couple have offices downtown or at the Municipal Airport, and almost all will arrange to deliver and pick up your vehicle at any Belize City hotel. See p. 66 for rental-car agency info.

Visitor Information

The **Belize Tourist Board** (✆ **800/624-0686** toll-free in the U.S. and Canada, or 227-2430 in Belize; www.travelbelize.org) has its main office at 64 Regent St., in the heart of the business district of Belize City. If you missed their desk at the airport, they have another information desk here with regional brochures, basic maps, and a score of hotel and tour fliers; the office is open Monday through Friday from 8am to 5pm. Local travel agencies are another good source of information. Two in Belize City to try are **Discovery Expeditions,** 5916 Manatee Dr., Buttonwood Bay (✆ **501/223-0748;** www.discoverybelize.com), and **S&L Travel and Tours,** 91 N. Front St. (✆ **501/227-7593;** www.sltravelbelize.com).

FAST FACTS There are several banks located within a few blocks of each other along Regent and Albert streets, just south of the Swing Bridge. The main post office (✆ **501/227-2201**) is located at the corner of Queen and North Front streets, across from the Swing Bridge.

Belize Medical Associates, 5791 St. Thomas Kings Park (✆ **501/223-0303;** www.belizemedical.com), is a modern, 24-hour private hospital, with emergency care and numerous private practice physicians. The city's main public hospital, the **Karl Heusner Memorial Hospital,** Princess Margaret Drive (✆ **501/223-1548**), is also open 24 hours and has a wide range of facilities and services.

Most hotels listed here either have Wi-Fi or a small business center with Internet connections. You can also find Internet cafes scattered around the principal business and tourist districts of Belize City. Rates run between BZ$2 and BZ$10 ($1–$5/50p–£2.50) per hour. Alternatively, **BTL** (✆ **0800/112-4636;** www.btl.net), the state Internet monopoly, sells prepaid cards in denominations of BZ$10 ($5/£2.50), BZ$25 ($13/£6.50), and BZ$50 ($25/£13) for connecting your laptop to the Web via a local phone call. In addition, you can buy a 24-hour period of Wi-Fi access from BTL for BZ$34 ($17/£8.50), which will work at a number of "hot spots" around the city.

Most folks rely on their hotel's laundry and dry cleaning services, although these can be expensive. Alternatively, you can try the **C.A. Coin Laundromat,** 114 Barrack Rd. (✆ **501/203-3063**), **Belize Dry Cleaners & Laundromat,** 3 Dolphin St. (✆ **501/227-3396**), or **Southside Coin Laundromat,** 6 Neal's Pen Rd. (✆ **501/207-0301**).

For restrooms, head to the little cruise-ship tourist village on Fort Street in the Fort George section of Belize City. (Most hotels and restaurants will let tourists use their facilities, too.)

WHAT TO SEE & DO

There really isn't much reason to take a guided tour of Belize City. The downtown center is extremely compact and lends itself very easily to self-directed exploration. There are only a handful of interesting attractions, and all are within easy walking distance of the

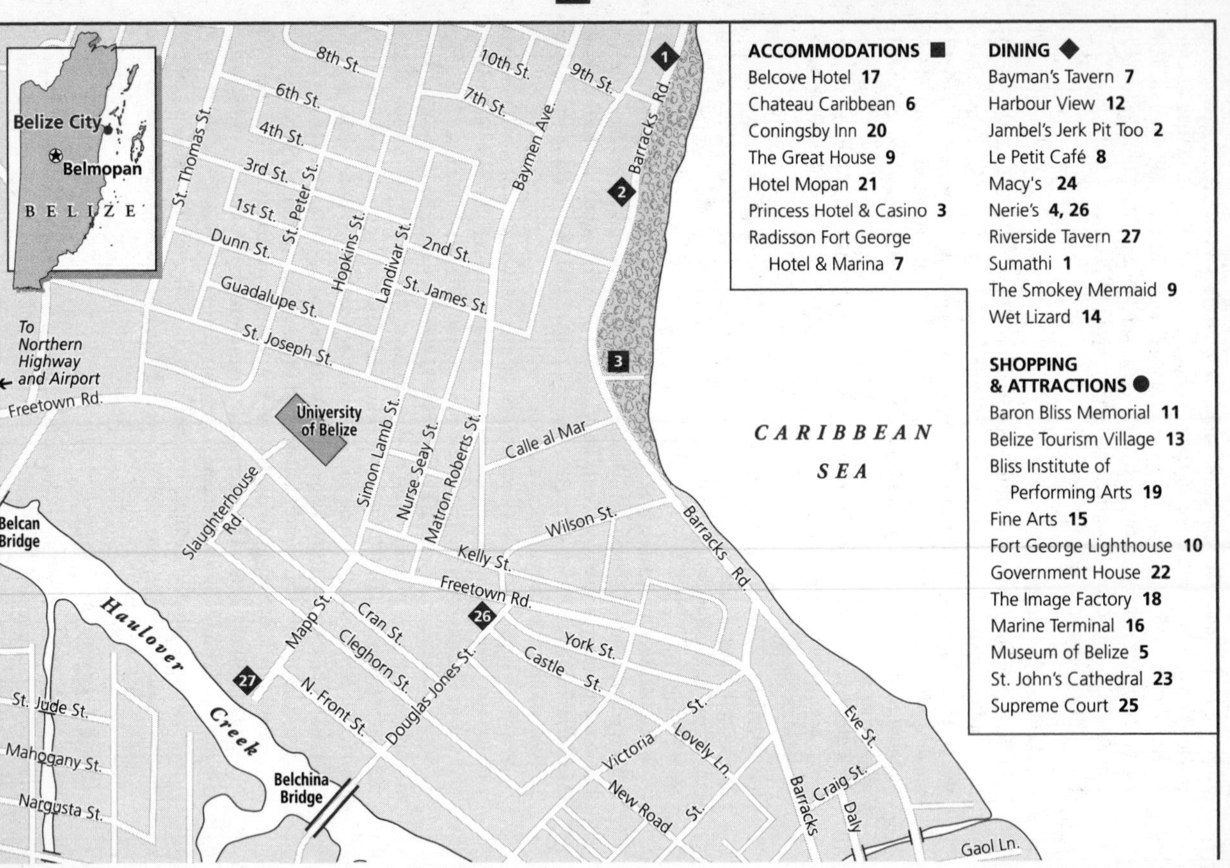
ACCOMMODATIONS
Belcove Hotel 17
Chateau Caribbean 6
Coningsby Inn 20
The Great House 9
Hotel Mopan 21
Princess Hotel & Casino 3
Radisson Fort George Hotel & Marina 7
DINING
Bayman's Tavern 7
Harbour View 12
Jambel's Jerk Pit Too 2
Le Petit Café 8
Macy's 24
Nerie's 4, 26
Riverside Tavern 27
Sumathi 1
The Smokey Mermaid 9
Wet Lizard 14
SHOPPING & ATTRACTIONS
Baron Bliss Memorial 11
Belize Tourism Village 13
Bliss Institute of Performing Arts 19
Fine Arts 15
Fort George Lighthouse 10
Government House 22
The Image Factory 18
Marine Terminal 16
Museum of Belize 5
St. John's Cathedral 23
Supreme Court 25
CARIBBEAN SEA
Belize City
Belmopan
BELIZE
8th St.
10th St.
9th St.
6th St.
7th St.
4th St.
3rd St.
1st St.
St. Peter St.
St. Thomas St.
Baymen Ave.
Barracks Rd.
Dunn St.
Hopkins St.
Landivar St.
2nd St.
Guadalupe St.
St. James St.
St. Joseph St.
To Northern Highway and Airport
Freetown Rd.
University of Belize
Simon Lamb St.
Nurse Seay St.
Matron Roberts St.
Calle al Mar
Slaughterhouse Rd.
Wilson St.
Belcan Bridge
Kelly St.
Freetown Rd.
Haulover Creek
Mapp St.
Cran St.
Cleghorn St.
York St.
Castle St.
N. Front St.
Douglas Jones St.
St. Jude St.
Mahogany St.
Nargusta St.
Belchina Bridge
Victoria St.
Lovely Ln.
New Road St.
Barracks
Craig St.
Daly
Eve St.
Gaol Ln.

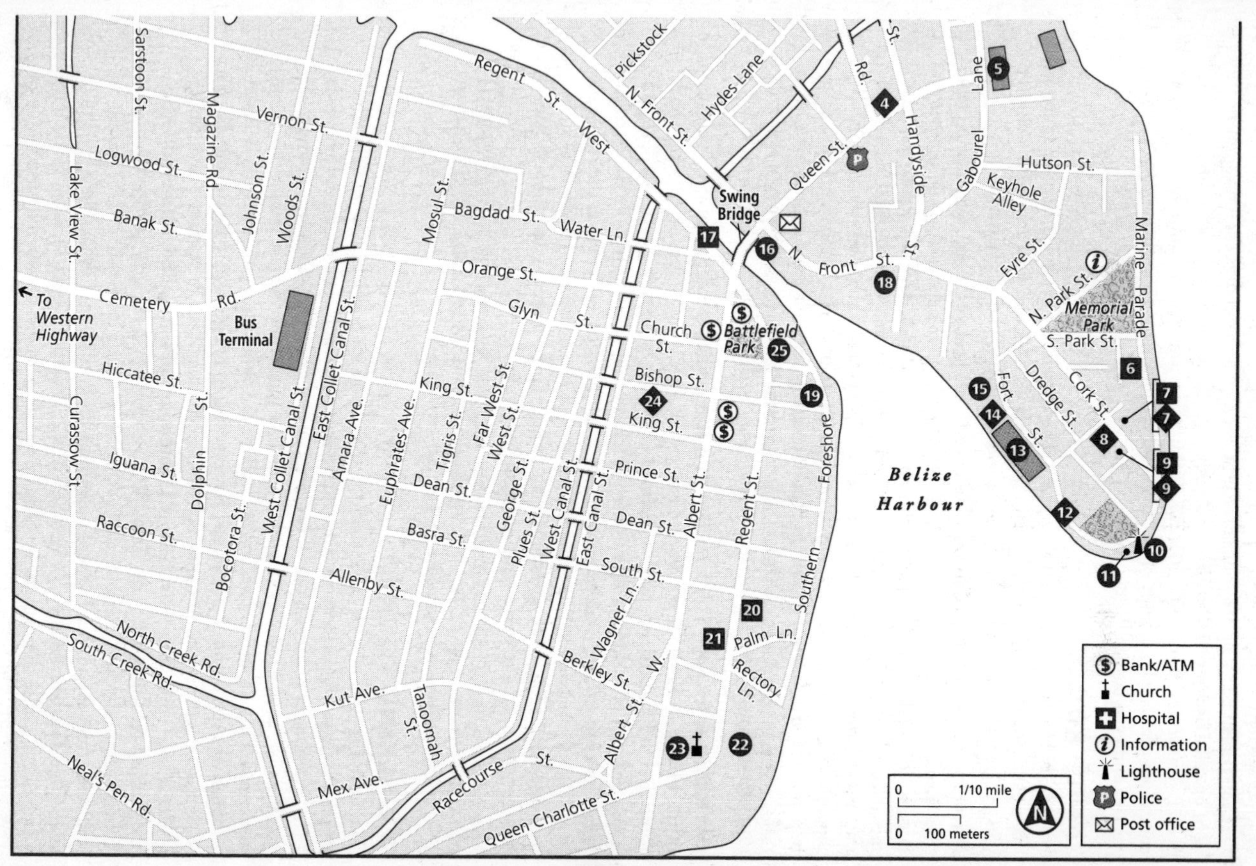
Belize Harbour
Swing Bridge
Bus Terminal
To Western Highway
Memorial Park
Battlefield Park
Marine Parade
N. Park St.
S. Park St.
Cork St.
Dredge St.
Fort St.
Eyre St.
Hutson St.
Keyhole Alley
Gabourel Lane
Handyside St.
Queen St.
Rd.
St.
N. Front St.
Hydes Lane
Pickstock
Regent St. West
Water Ln.
Bagdad St.
Mosul St.
Orange St.
Glyn St.
Church St.
Bishop St.
King St.
Prince St.
Dean St.
South St.
Albert St.
Regent St.
Foreshore
Southern
Palm Ln.
Rectory Ln.
W. Albert St.
Wagner Ln.
Berkley St.
East Canal St.
West Canal St.
Plues St.
George St.
West St.
Far West St.
Tigris St.
Euphrates Ave.
Basra St.
Allenby St.
Amara Ave.
East Collet Canal St.
West Collet Canal St.
Tanoomah St.
Kut Ave.
Mex Ave.
Racecourse St.
Queen Charlotte St.
Vernon St.
Logwood St.
Johnson St.
Woods St.
Banak St.
Magazine Rd.
Sarstoon St.
Lake View St.
Cemetery Rd.
Hiccatee St.
Dolphin St.
Iguana St.
Bocotora St.
Raccoon St.
Curassow St.
North Creek Rd.
South Creek Rd.
Neal's Pen Rd.
0 1/10 mile
0 100 meters
N
Bank/ATM
Church
Hospital
Information
Lighthouse
Police
Post office

central Swing Bridge. Below you'll find reviews of the most interesting attractions, as well as a walking tour of the city.

If you really need a guided tour of the city, ask at your hotel desk for a recommendation, or call **Discovery Expeditions** (© **501/223-0748;** www.discoverybelize.com) or **S & L Travel and Tours** (© **501/227-7593;** www.sltravelbelize.com). Both of these companies offer a whole range of day trips and combinations to the attractions close to the city and even farther afield.

The Top Attractions

Belize City is very light on true attractions. The museums mentioned below are quite quaint and provincial by most international standards, although they are worth a visit if you are spending a day getting to know the city, residents, and local history.

Museum of Belize Housed in what was once "Her Majesty's Prison," this museum features a collection of historical documents, photographs, currency, stamps, and other artifacts, as well as exhibits of Maya pottery and archaeological finds. Although somewhat small, the collection of Maya ceramic, jade, and both ornamental and functional pieces is worth the price of admission. There are also traveling exhibits, and a room featuring attractively mounted insects from Belize. Just so you won't forget the building's history, a prison cell has been restored to its original condition. Plan on spending between 1 and 2 hours here.

Gabourel Lane, in front of the Central Bank bldg. © **501/223-4524.** Admission BZ$10 ($5/£2.50), BZ$4 ($2/£1) for students, free for children. Mon–Fri 9am–5pm.

Old Belize ★★ Kids This attraction aims at providing a comprehensive experience of the natural, cultural, and political history of Belize, with exhibits re-creating everything from a rainforest, to a Maya ceremonial cave, to a logging camp, to a Garífuna home. Admission includes a 45-minute guided tour, but you'll probably want to stay longer, to explore some exhibits on your own, visit the gift shop, or eat at the restaurant here. There's even a decent little beach here, with a water slide and children's play area, and separate zip-line cable adventure. Plan on spending between 1 and 2 hours here—more if you're going to eat or hang out at the beach.

Mile 5, Western Hwy. © **501/222-4286.** www.oldbelize.com. Admission BZ$30 ($15/£7.50), BZ$15 ($7.50/£3.75) for children 6–12, for full-access package; BZ$5 ($2.50/£1.75) adults, BZ$3 ($1.50/75p) children for just the museum. Tues–Sat 8am–4pm; Sun–Mon 10am–4pm.

A WALKING TOUR

The following walking tour covers both the north and south sides of Belize City, which together comprise the entire historic downtown center. For most of its length, you'll be either right on the water or just a block or two away. As described, the walking tour should take you anywhere from 2 to 4 hours, depending on how much time you take visiting the various attractions. The only major attraction not right on the route below is the Museum of Belize, although it's only a 4-block detour east from the Swing Bridge. The route laid out on this walking tour is pretty safe during daylight hours, but should not be attempted after dark.

Begin your stroll at the **Fort George Lighthouse** and **Baron Bliss Memorial,** out on the northeastern tip of the city. A small slate stone marks the grave of Henry Edward Ernest Victor Bliss (see "Baron Bliss," below). After soaking up the view of the Caribbean and some fresh sea air, head toward downtown on Fort Street. On your left, you'll find the **Belize Tourism Village** (© **501/223-2767**), which was built to accommodate the rising tide of cruise-ship passengers. Stop in and shop, or just browse the variety of local and regional arts and crafts.

Baron Bliss

Henry Edward Ernest Victor Bliss, the fourth Baron Bliss of the Kingdom of Portugal, anchored his yacht *Sea King* off of Belize City on January 14, 1926. Within 2 months, the baron would be dead, never having set foot on Belizean soil. Nonetheless, the eccentric Baron Bliss is this tiny country's most beloved benefactor. His time spent anchored in Belize Harbour was enough to convince him to rewrite his will and leave a large chunk of his estate—nearly $2 million at the time—to the country of Belize (then British Honduras). The trust he set up stipulated that the principal could never be touched, and only the interest was to be used. The ongoing bequest has funded numerous public works projects around the country, and today it's hard to miss the baron's legacy. There's the Baron Bliss Memorial, Bliss Institute of Performing Arts, and the Bliss (Fort George) Lighthouse. Every year on March 9, a large regatta is held in Belize Harbour in his honor.

As you continue, Fort Street becomes North Front Street. Just north of the Belize Tourism Village you'll find **Fine Arts** and the **Image Factory,** by far the two best galleries and fine arts gift shops in the country. Just before reaching the Swing Bridge, you'll find the **Marine Terminal,** where you can pick up water taxis to Ambergris Caye and Caye Caulker.

Now, cross the **Swing Bridge** and head south. On your left is the **Commercial Center.** Wander through the stalls of fresh vegetables, butcher shops, and fish stands. You'll also find some gift shops and souvenir stands here. The **Supreme Court building,** off the small **Battlefield Park** (or Market Sq.) just a block south of the Swing Bridge, is a real prize of English colonial architecture with the city's only clock tower.

Down at the southern end of Regent Street, you'll find the **Government House** and **St. John's Cathedral,** also known by its more official-sounding moniker, the Anglican Cathedral of St. John the Baptist. Both of these buildings were constructed with slave labor in the early 19th century, and they remain the most prominent reminders of the 3 centuries of British colonial presence here. The Government House has been converted into a **House of Culture** (✆ **501/227-3050**), with the mission of encouraging and sponsoring local participation in the arts, music, and dance.

An Attraction Outside Belize City

Founded as part of a last-ditch and improvised effort to keep and care for a host of animals that were being used in a documentary film shoot, the **Belize Zoo ★★**, Western Highway, Mile Marker 29 (✆ **501/220-8003;** www.belizezoo.org), is a national treasure. Gentle paths wind through 12 hectares (29 acres) of land, where the zoo houses over 125 animals, all native Belizean species, and all either orphaned, born at the zoo, rehabilitated, or sent to the Belize Zoo as gifts from other institutions. All the exhibits have informative hand-painted signs accompanying them. It's best to visit early in the morning or close to closing time, when the animals are at their most active and the Belizean sun is at its least oppressive.

The entrance is 180m (600 ft.) in from the Western Highway. Any bus traveling between Belize City and Belmopan or San Ignacio will drop you off at the zoo entrance. Admission is BZ$16 ($8/£4) for adults and BZ$8 ($4/£2) for children, and the zoo is open daily from 8am to 5pm.

Outdoor & Wellness Activities

Due to the crime, chaos, and often oppressive heat and humidity, you'll probably want to get out of the city, or on to the water, before undertaking anything too strenuous. But if you want to brave the elements, there are a few outdoor activities for you to try in and around Belize City.

FISHING While most serious fishermen head to one of the cayes or southern Belize destinations, it's possible to line up fishing charters out of Belize City. The marinas at the **Radisson Fort George Hotel & Marina** (✆ **501/223-3333**), **Old Belize** (✆ **501/222-4129**), and **Princess Hotel & Casino** (✆ **501/223-2670**) all have regular sport charter fleets and can arrange a variety of options. You could also check in with the folks at the **Belize River Lodge** (✆ **501/225-2002;** www.belizeriverlodge.com). Expect to pay around $1,200 to $1,800 (£600–£900) per day for a boat that can accommodate up to four fishermen.

SCUBA DIVING & SNORKELING The Belize barrier reef lies just off the coast from Belize City. It's a short boat ride to some excellent scuba diving and snorkeling. It is possible to visit any number of excellent sites on day trips from Belize City, including the Blue Hole and Turneffe and Lighthouse atolls. Check in with **Hugh Parkey's Belize Dive Connection** (✆ **501/223-5086;** www.belizediving.com).

SPAS & GYMS **Best Western Belize Biltmore Plaza** (✆ **501/223-2302**) and **Princess Hotel & Casino** (p. 104) have small gym facilities and offer basic spa services. However, neither of these hotels allows nonguests use of their facilities.

SWIMMING A few of the higher-end hotels in Belize City have pools. Of these, **Radisson Fort George Hotel & Marina** (✆ **501/223-3333**), is your best bet, allowing nonguests to use their pool facilities for BZ$10 ($5/£2.50) per day.

Alternatively, you can head out to the **Cucumber Beach** ★ at Old Belize (p. 100). The beach here has an open-water section, as well as an enclosed, and hence calmer, lagoon. There's also a water slide and children's playground, as well as chaise longues and palm thatch shade shelters. Admission is BZ$5 ($2.50/£1.25) for beach access, and BZ$10 ($5/£2.50) for both the beach and water-slide privileges. Children are charged half price.

Shopping

Most shops in the downtown district are open Monday through Saturday from about 8am to 6pm. Some shops close for lunch, while others remain open. Since the cruise ships are such a big market for local merchants, many adjust their hours to specifically coincide with cruise-ship traffic and their particular shore times. By far the largest selection of gift shops and souvenir stands can be found at the **Belize Tourism Village** (8 Fort St.; ✆ **501/223-2767**), which is a harborside collection of shops geared toward visiting cruise-ship passengers.

Fine Arts ★★ This is the best gallery and gift shop I've found in Belize. They have a large selection of original artworks in a variety of styles, formats, and sizes. Browse primitivist works by Walter Castillo and Pen Cayetano, alongside more modern abstract pieces, traditional still lifes, and colorful representations of Belize's marine, natural, and human life. 1 Fort St., next to the Belize Tourism Village. ✆ **501/223-7773.** www.fineartsbelize.com.

Maya Jade ★ This place bills itself as a museum and gallery, and while there is a whole room of museum-style displays explaining the history of Mesoamerican Maya jade use and artistry, this is nonetheless predominantly a retail operation. That said, the small selection here includes some very well done necklaces and earrings that you won't find elsewhere. 8 Fort St. ✆ **501/203-1222.**

WHERE TO STAY

Belize City is small, and your options on where to stay are limited, especially for a capital city. The most picturesque and safest neighborhood by far is the area around the Fort George Lighthouse. Here you'll find most of the city's best shopping, dining, and accommodations. When getting a price quote from or negotiating with a hotel in Belize, be careful to be clear whether or not you are being quoted a price in Belize or U.S. dollars.

Expensive

The Great House ★★ Finds This stately colonial-style small hotel is aptly named. Set a block from the water, near the Fort George Lighthouse, this three-story resort and converted mansion was originally built in 1927. All rooms are on either the second or third floor, and there are no elevators, if that is an issue for you. The rooms on the top floor are my favorites, with high ceilings, wood floors, and a large, shared wraparound veranda. In fact there are wraparound verandas on both the second and third floors. While the rooms vary in size, most are very spacious; room no. 1 is one of the largest. Room no. 8 is the smallest room, but it just may have the best view.

13 Cork St. (opposite the Radisson Fort George), Belize City. ✆ **501/223-3400.** Fax 501/223-3444. www.greathousebelize.com. 16 units. BZ$300 ($150/£75) double. AE, DISC, MC, V. Free parking. **Amenities:** Restaurant; lounge; concierge; laundry service; nonsmoking rooms. *In room:* A/C, TV, fridge, hair dryer, Wi-Fi.

Radisson Fort George Hotel & Marina ★ Kids This is Belize City's best business-class and luxury hotel. The best rooms here are located in the six-story Club Tower; those on the higher floors have the best views. All are spacious and relatively modern, and feature marble floors and plush furnishings. The Club Tower also has one junior suite on each floor. The Colonial rooms, all of which are nonsmoking, are also large and comfortable. Rooms on the ground floor come with a small private garden terrace, while some of those on the higher floors offer enticing ocean views. The poolside bar here is one of the more popular spots in town, and often features live music. The hotel also features a full-service marina and dive shop.

2 Marine Parade, Belize City. ✆ **800/333-3333** in the U.S., or 501/223-3333 in Belize. Fax 501/227-3820. www.radisson.com. 102 units. BZ$278–BZ$348 ($139–$174/£70–£87) double. Rates slightly lower in the off season. AE, DISC, MC, V. Free parking. **Amenities:** 3 restaurants; 2 bars; lounge; babysitting; concierge; small gym; laundry service; nonsmoking rooms; 2 midsize outdoor pools; room service. *In room:* A/C, TV, hair dryer, minibar, Wi-Fi.

Moderate

In addition to the hotel listed below, the **Chateau Caribbean** (✆ **501/223-0800;** www.chateaucaribbean.com) is an atmospheric, although somewhat long-in-the-tooth, option located right on the water in the Fort George neighborhood.

Princess Hotel & Casino This is the largest hotel in Belize City, and the only one with a resort feel to it. The massive lobby area lets out into the hotel's casino, two movie theaters, a shopping arcade, an eight-lane bowling alley, a salon, and various restaurants and bars. The hotel is set right on the water's edge a little bit north of downtown and is built as one long six-story structure, so that every room has an ocean view. The rooms are all come with either one king-size bed or two full-size beds, a working desk, large bathrooms, and bathrobes. The junior suites are a little bit larger and have private oceanfront balconies. The Princess also has a full-service marina and dive shop. The Radisson is definitely more elegant and better maintained, but the Princess does have a little bit more in the way of facilities and nightlife.

Barracks Rd., Belize City. ✆ **888/790-4264** in the U.S., or 501/223-0638 in Belize. Fax 501/223-3148. www.princessbelize.com. 181 units. BZ$240 ($120/£60) double; BZ$300–BZ$600 ($150–$300/£75–£150) suite; BZ$1,000 ($500/£250) presidential suite. Rates include breakfast buffet. AE, DISC, MC, V. Free parking. **Amenities:** 2 restaurants; 2 bars; lounge; concierge; fitness center; laundry service; nonsmoking rooms; large outdoor pool; room service. *In room:* A/C, TV, hair dryer, Internet.

Inexpensive

In addition to the hotel reviewed in full below, you might check out the **Belcove Hotel** (✆ **501/227-3054;** www.belcove.com) a funky riverside option just north of the Swing Bridge, or **Hotel Mopan** (✆ **501/227-7351;** www.hotelmopan.com; 55 Regent St.), a long-standing and humble little hotel that's a good option in downtown Belize City.

Coningsby Inn (Value) Housed in a converted old home toward the western end of Regent Street, the rooms here are compact and rather nondescript. Still, they are clean and comfortable. I prefer those on the second floor, although don't choose one of these for the view, which is over an abandoned lot. I would definitely recommend a splurge for one of the air-conditioned rooms. There's a convivial hostel-like vibe to this operation, and the second-floor bar and lounge area is the social hub of the joint.

76 Regent St., Belize City. ✆ **501/227-1566.** Fax 501/227-3726. www.coningsby-inn.com. 10 units. BZ$100 ($50/£25) double without A/C; BZ$120 ($60/£30) double with A/C. MC, V. Free street parking. **Amenities:** Bar; laundry service. *In room:* TV.

Near the Airport

The area around the airport is decidedly undeveloped and of little interest to visitors. Few international flights arrive late enough or leave early enough to necessitate a stay near the airport. Your best bet nearby it is the **Belize River Lodge** (✆ **888/275-4843** in the U.S. and Canada, or 501/225-2002 in Belize; www.belizeriverlodge.com), an upscale fishing lodge on the banks of the Belize River, just a few miles from the airport.

WHERE TO DINE

Despite its small size, Belize City actually has an excellent and varied selection of dining options open to visitors. While Belizean cuisine and fresh seafood are most common, you can also get excellent Chinese, Indian, and other international fare at restaurants around the city. Note that when the cruise ships are in town, the restaurants in the Fort George area can get extremely crowded, especially for lunch.

Expensive

Harbour View ★★ INTERNATIONAL This is the most expensive and creative restaurant in town. I like the Parasol of Reddened Shrimp, which are coated in an Asian-style sweet-and-pungent glaze and served atop a rice palau. Another excellent choice is the Picasso Pork Tenderloin, which comes with a delicious jalapeño relish. You can also get thick cuts of steak, and a host of other dishes. The main dining room is a second-floor space with large picture windows opening onto Belize Harbour. When the weather's right, I recommend grabbing one of the outdoor tables on the wooden wraparound veranda. There's often live jazz music in the evenings. During the day, they feature a more modest menu with a selection of salads and sandwiches.

Fort St., next to the Belize Tourism Village. ✆ **501/223-6420.** Reservations recommended. Main courses BZ$32–BZ$80 ($16–$40/£8–£20). AE, DISC, MC, V. Mon–Fri 11:30am–3pm; daily 5–11pm.

Moderate

In addition to the place listed below, you can get good burgers and bar food at the **Bayman's Tavern** at the Radisson Fort George Hotel (see above). To add some spice to your life, head to either **Sumathi** (✆ **501/223-1172**) or **Jambel's Jerk Pit Too** (✆ **501/223-1966**). Both are toward the north end of Newtown Barracks Road.

Riverside Tavern ★★ INTERNATIONAL One of the most popular spots in Belize City, this large place has both indoor and outdoor seating on a spot overlooking Haulover Creek. The restaurant specializes in hefty steaks and delicious ribs. But you can also get seared tuna, grilled snapper, coconut shrimp, or jerk shrimp. The lunch menu features pizzas, pastas, sandwiches, and rolls. The burgers here are rightly famous, and served for both lunch and dinner. There are TVs showing sporting events, and at times this place can get quite boisterous. There's actually a bit of a dress code here, and shorts, sleeveless shirts, and sandals are discouraged after dark.

2 Mapp St. ✆ **501/223-5640.** Lunch BZ$15–BZ$36 ($7.50–$18/£3.75–£9); main courses BZ$22–BZ$55 ($11–$23/£5.50–£12). DISC, MC, V. Tues–Wed 11am–midnight; Thurs–Fri 11am–2am; Sat noon–2am; Sun noon–midnight.

The Smokey Mermaid ★ INTERNATIONAL I love the open-air brick courtyard setting of this semi-elegant yet relaxed restaurant. There are a couple of raised decks and gazebos and a few fountains, spread out among heavy wooden tables and chairs under broad canvas umbrellas in the shade of large seagrape and mango trees and a wealth of other lushly planted ferns and flowers. An equally pleasant choice for breakfast, lunch, or dinner, the menu here ranges from Jamaican jerk pork to shrimp thermidor to chicken Kiev. I recommend the yuca-crusted catch of the day. The desserts here are excellent, with their signature sweet being the Decadent Ecstasy, a chocolate-coconut pie swimming in ice cream, nuts, and chocolate sauce.

13 Cork St., in The Great House. ✆ **501/223-4722.** Reservations recommended. Main courses BZ$24–BZ$72 ($12–$36/£6–£18). AE, MC, V. Daily 6:30am–10pm.

Inexpensive

In addition to the place listed below, **Nerie's,** which has two locations (124 Freetown Rd., ✆ **501/224-5199;** and at the corner of Queen and Daly sts., ✆ **501/223-4028**), is another simple restaurant specializing in Belizean cuisine, and it's very popular with locals. For breakfast, a light bite, or a coffee break, head to **Le Petit Café** (✆ **501/223-3333**) at the Radisson Fort George Hotel. For authentic Belizean cooking and a down-home funky vibe, you can't beat **Macy's** (✆ **501/207-3419**) at 18 Bishop St.

Wet Lizard ★ Finds BELIZEAN Boasting a prime setting on a second-floor covered deck overlooking the Swing Bridge and Belize City's little harbor, this raucous restaurant is one of the hottest spots in town. The menu is simple, with an emphasis on sandwiches, burgers, and American-style bar food. Start things off with some coconut shrimp, conch fritters, or fried calamari, before tackling one of the hearty sandwiches or wraps. You can also get tacos, nachos, fajitas, and quesadillas, as well as a daily special or two. If you like sweets, save room for the banana chimichanga. The best seats here are the small tables and high stools ringing the railing and overlooking the water. Everything is painted in bright primary colors, and the walls are covered with graffiti and signatures from guests. When the cruise ships are in town, this place is overrun and even serves a separate menu, so be sure to ask for their full menu.

1 Fort St. ✆ **501/223-5973.** Reservations not accepted. Main courses BZ$10–BZ$24 ($5–$12/£2.50–£6). AE, MC, V. Tues–Sat 11am–9:30pm.

BELIZE CITY AFTER DARK

Belize City is a small, provincial city in an underdeveloped country, so don't expect to find a raging nightlife scene. The most popular nightspots—for both locals and visitors alike—are the bars at the few high-end hotels in town.

PERFORMING ARTS It's really the luck of the draw as to whether or not you can catch a concert, theater piece, or dance performance—they are the exception, not the norm. To find out if anything is happening, ask at your hotel, read the local papers, or check in with the **Bliss Institute of Performing Arts** (✆ **501/227-2110**), on Southern Foreshore, between Church and Bishop streets.

THE BAR SCENE The bar and club scene in Belize City is rather lackluster. The most happening bar in town is the **Riverside Tavern** ★ (✆ **501/223-5640**). This is especially true on weekends, and whenever there's an important soccer, basketball, or cricket match on.

Travelers and locals alike also tend to frequent the bars at the major hotels and tourist traps. The liveliest of these are the bars at the **Radisson Fort George Hotel & Marina,** the **Best Western Belize Biltmore Plaza,** and the **Princess Hotel & Casino,** all of which often have a live band on weekend nights. Of these, I prefer the **Club Calypso** ★ (✆ **501/223-2670**), an open-air affair built over the water at the Princess Hotel & Casino, although it's sort of a crapshoot as to which bar will be hopping on any given night.

CASINOS For gaming, the **Princess Hotel & Casino** (see above) is the only game in town, and the casino here is large, modern, and well equipped. While it's not on the scale of Vegas or Atlantic City, the casino is certainly respectable, with enough gaming tables, slots, and other attractions to make most casual gamblers quite happy to drop a few dollars.

SIDE TRIPS FROM BELIZE CITY

Given the fact that Belize is so small, it is possible to visit any of the country's major tourist destinations and attractions as a side trip from Belize City. Most are easily reached in less than 2 hours by car, bus, or boat taxi. Other attractions are accessible by short commuter flights. All in all, you can visit almost any destination or attraction described in this chapter as a day trip, except for the far southern zone.

For a listing of active adventures that make good day trips, see the various descriptions of activities and attractions throughout this chapter. Possible destinations for side trips out of Belize City include **Caye Caulker** and **Ambergris Caye,** dive excursions to the nearby reefs, and even to the more isolated dive destinations like the **Blue Hole** and the **Lighthouse** and **Turneffe atolls** ★★. **Cave tubing** excursions are quite popular, and you can also visit the Maya ruins of **Altun Ha, Lamanai, Xunantunich, Cahal Pech,**

Volunteer & Learning Opportunities in Belize

Below are some institutions and organizations that are working on ecology and sustainable development projects.

Cornerstone Foundation ★★ (✆ **501/824-2373;** www.peacecorner.org/cornerstone.htm), based in San Ignacio in the Cayo District, is an excellent and effective nonreligious, nongovernmental peace organization with a variety of volunteer and cultural exchange program opportunities. Programs range from AIDS education to literacy campaigns to renewable resource development and use. Apart from the US$100 (£50) application fee, costs are extremely low, and reflect the actual costs of basic food, lodging, and travel in country.

International Zoological Expeditions ★★ (✆ **800/548-5843;** www.ize2belize.com) has two research and educational facilities in Belize, on South Water Caye and in Blue Creek Village. IZE organizes and administers a variety of educational and vacation trips to these two stations, for both school groups and individuals. A 10-day program usually costs about US$1,150 to US$1,700 (£575–£850).

Maya Research Program at Blue Creek ★ (✆ **817/257-5943** in the U.S.; www.mayaresearchprogram.org) runs volunteer and educational programs at an ongoing Maya archaeological dig. Two-week sessions allow participants to literally dig in and take part in the excavation of a Maya ruin. The cost is US$1,250 for the 2-week program; discounts are available for longer stays.

Monkey Bay Wildlife Sanctuary ★ (✆ **501/820-3032;** www.monkeybaybelize.org) is a private reserve and environmental education center that specializes in hosting study-abroad student groups. They also run their own in-house educational programs and can arrange a variety of volunteer stays and programs, including homestays with local Belizean families.

Toledo Institute for Development and Environment ★ (✆ **501/722-2274;** www.tidebelize.org) is a small, grass-roots environmental and ecotourism organization working on sustainable development and ecological protection issues in the Toledo District. Contact them directly if you are interested in volunteering.

and even **Caracol** and **Tikal.** All are popularly sold as day tours, often in various mix-and-match combinations.

Most hotels can arrange any of the day trips suggested above. In addition, you can check in with **Discovery Expeditions** (✆ **501/223-0748;** www.discoverybelize.com) or **S & L Travel and Tours** (✆ **501/227-7593;** www.sltravelbelize.com). Prices range from about BZ$100 to BZ$280 ($50–$140/£25–£70) per person, depending on the tour, means of transportation, and the attraction(s) visited. ***Note:*** Most of the tours and activities mentioned here and earlier in this chapter are also sold to visiting cruise-ship passengers. When the cruise ships are in town, a cave tubing adventure, snorkel trip to Hol Chan Marine Reserve and Shark-Ray Alley, or a visit to either Altun Ha or Lamanai ruins can be a mob scene. If you are organizing your tour or activity with a local operator, mention that you want to avoid the cruise-ship groups, if at all possible.

5 AMBERGRIS CAYE ★

58km (36 miles) N of Belize City; 64km (40 miles) SE of Corozal Town

Ambergris Caye is Belize's principal sun-and-fun destination. Though Ambergris Caye continues to attract primarily scuba divers and fishermen, it is today popular with a wide range of folks who like the slow-paced atmosphere, including an increasing number of snowbirds, expatriates, and retirees. While certainly not akin to big-city traffic, golf carts and automobiles are proliferating on Ambergris Caye and constantly force pedestrians and bicycle riders to the sides of the road. In fact, the ongoing boom has actually led to gridlock. During peak hours, the downtown area of San Pedro is a jumble of golf carts, cars, bicycles, and pedestrians, all moving at a rather slow pace. Development has reached both ends of Ambergris Caye, and steady construction appears destined to fill in the blanks from north to south.

Ambergris Caye is 40km (25 miles) long and only 1km (1/2 mile) wide at its widest point. Long before the British settled Belize, and long before the sun-seeking vacationers and zealous reef divers discovered Ambergris Caye, the Maya were here. In fact, the Maya created Ambergris Caye when they cut a channel through the long thin peninsula that extended down from what is now Mexico. The channel was cut to facilitate coastal trading and avoid the dangerous barrier reef that begins not too far north of San Pedro.

Despite the fact that much of the island is seasonally flooded mangrove forest, and despite laws prohibiting the cutting of mangroves, developers continue to clear cut and fill this marginal land. Indiscriminate cutting of the mangroves is already having an adverse effect on the nearby barrier reef: Without the mangroves to filter the water and slow the impact of waves, silt is formed and carried out to the reef where it settles and kills the coral. There is still spectacular diving to be had just off the shore here, but local operators and long-term residents claim to have noticed a difference.

ESSENTIALS

Getting There

You've got two options for getting to and from Ambergris Caye: sea or air. The trip is usually beautiful by either means. When the weather's rough, it's bumpy both ways, although it's certainly quicker by air, and you're more likely to get wet in the boat.

BY PLANE There are dozens of daily flights between Belize City and **San Pedro Airport (SPR;** no phone) on Ambergris Caye. Flights leave from both Philip S. W. Goldson International Airport (p. 96) and Municipal Airport (p. 96) roughly every hour. If you're coming in on an international flight and heading straight for San Pedro, you should book a flight from the international airport. If you're already in Belize City or in transit around the country, it's cheaper to fly from the municipal airport, which is also closer to downtown, and quicker and cheaper to reach by taxi. During the high season, and whenever possible, it's best to have a reservation. However, you can usually just show up at the airport and get a seat on a flight within an hour.

Both **Maya Island Air** (✆ **501/223-1140** in Belize City, or 226-2435 in San Pedro; www.mayaairways.com) and **Tropic Air** (✆ **800/422-3435** in the U.S. or Canada, 501/226-2012 in Belize; www.tropicair.com) have 11 flights daily between Goldson International Airport and San Pedro Airport. Flight time is around 15 minutes. These flights actually originate at the Belize City Municipal Airport 10 minutes earlier. When you're ready to leave, flights from San Pedro to Belize City run from 7am to 5pm. Most

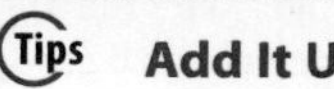

Add It Up

Because a taxi into Belize City from the international airport costs BZ$50 to BZ$60 ($25–$30/£13–£15), and the boat to Ambergris Caye costs BZ$20 to BZ$30 ($10–$15/£5–£7.50), it is only slightly more expensive to fly if you are heading directly to the cayes after arriving on an international flight.

of these flights stop first at Caye Caulker and then at the international airport, before continuing on to the municipal airport. Almost any of the above Tropic Air and Maya Island Air flights can be used to commute between Caye Caulker and San Pedro. Flight duration is just 10 minutes.

Connections to and from all the other major destinations in Belize can be made via the municipal and international airports in Belize City.

BY BOAT Regularly scheduled boats ply the route between Belize City and Ambergris Caye. All leave from somewhere near the Swing Bridge. Most boats leave directly from the **Marine Terminal,** which is located right on North Front Street just over the Swing Bridge; and are associated with the **Caye Caulker Water Taxi Association** (© **501/223-5752;** www.cayecaulkerwatertaxi.com). Most are open speedboats with one or two very powerful engines. Most carry between 20 and 30 passengers, and make the trip in about 75 minutes. Almost all of these boats drop off and pick up passengers in Caye Caulker on their way, and on St. George's Caye and/or Caye Chapel when there's demand. Find out at the Marine Terminal just where and when they stop. The schedule is subject to change, but boats for Ambergris Caye leave the Marine Terminal roughly every 90 minutes beginning at 8am, with the last boat leaving at 4:30pm. The fare is BZ$20 ($10/£5) one-way, BZ$40 ($20/£10) round-trip between Belize City and Ambergris Caye; and BZ$15 ($7.50/£3.75) one-way between Caye Caulker and San Pedro. All the boats dock on Shark's Pier, near the center of town.

It is possible to purchase a seat in advance by visiting the Marine Terminal personally. This is a good idea in the high season, although in most cases, you'll need to purchase the ticket in cash upfront. Some Belize City hotels provide this service or can get you a confirmed reservation by phone.

In addition to the Caye Caulker Water Taxi Association, the ***Triple J*** (© **501/223-3464**) leaves from Courthouse pier near the Marine Terminal every day at 8 and 10:30am, noon and 3 and 4:40pm, returning from the Texaco dock on Ambergris Caye at 7, 8, and 10:30am, and 1, 2:30, and 3:30pm. The rates for the ***Triple J*** are similar to those listed above.

Getting Around

The downtown section of San Pedro is easily navigated by foot. Some of the hotels located on the northern or southern ends of the island can be quite isolated, however.

Most hotels arrange pickup and drop-off for guests, whether they are arriving or departing by air or sea. Taxis are waiting for all flights that arrive at the airport, and are available for most trips around the island. If your hotel can't call you one, try **Amber Isle Taxi** (© **501/226-4060**), **Felix Taxi** (© **501/226-2041**), or **Island Taxi** (© **501/226-3125**). Fares run between BZ$4 and BZ$15 ($2–$7.50/£1–£3.75) for most rides.

Golf carts are available for rent from several outlets on the island. Rates run around BZ$120 to BZ$160 ($60–$80/£30–£40) per day for a four-seat cart, and BZ$160 to BZ$240 ($80–$120/£40–£60) for a six-seat cart. Hourly rates are between BZ$20 and BZ$40 ($10–$20/£5–£10). One of the largest and most dependable outfits is **Moncho's Rental** (© **501/226-3262;** www.monchosrentals.com). Other dependable options include **Cholo's Golf Cart Rental** (© **501/226-2406**) and **Ultimate Cart Rental** (© **501/226-3326;** www.ultimaterentalsbelize.com).

You can also rent scooters for around BZ$90 to BZ$120 ($45–$60/£23–£30) per day. **Island Scooters** (© **501/226-4152**) has a couple of stands and outlets around the island.

I think the best way to get around here is on a bicycle. Most hotels have their own bikes, available either for free or a small rental fee. If your hotel doesn't have a bike, call or head to **Joe's Bike Rental** on the south end of Pescador Drive (© **501/226-4371**). Rates run around BZ$20 to BZ$30 ($10–$15/£5–£7.50) per day.

Depending on where your hotel is located, a water taxi may just be your best means for commuting between your accommodations and the restaurants and shops of San Pedro. **San Pedro Water Taxi** (© **501/226-2194**) and **Island Ferry** (© **501/226-3231**) both run regularly scheduled launches that cover the length of the island, cruising just offshore from north to south and vice versa. The launches are in radio contact with all the hotels and restaurants, and they stop to pick up and discharge passengers as needed. Rates run around BZ$10 to BZ$40 ($5–$20/£2.50–£10) per person for a jaunt, depending on the length of the ride. Chartered water taxis are also available, and usually charge around BZ$80 to BZ$240 ($40–$120/£20–£60) depending on the length of the ride and size of your group.

Orientation

San Pedro (the only town on the island of Ambergris Caye) is just three streets wide. The streets, from seaside to lagoon side, are Barrier Reef Drive (Front St.), Pescador Drive (Middle St.), and Angel Coral Street (Back St.). The airport is at the south end of the busy little downtown. The island stretches both north and south of San Pedro. Less than a mile north of San Pedro there is a small channel, or cut, dividing the island in two. The northern section of the island is much less developed, and is where you will find more of the higher-end isolated resorts. A bridge connects the north and southern sections of Ambergris Caye. Pedestrians and bicycles can cross the bridge for free, but golf carts and other vehicles must pay a toll of BZ$5 ($2.50/£1.25) each way.

Visitor Information

There's no real tourism information office on Ambergris Caye. Your best source of information will be your hotel desk, or any of the various tour operators around town.

FAST FACTS For the local **police,** dial © **911,** or 501/226-2022; for the **fire department,** dial © **501/226-2372.** In the case of a medical emergency, call the **San Pedro Health Clinic** (© **501/226-2536**).

Atlantic Bank (© **501/226-3527**) and **Belize Bank** (© **501/226-2482**) are both on Barrier Reef Drive in downtown San Pedro. The **post office** (© **501/226-2250**) is on Barrier Reef Drive; it's open Monday through Friday from 8am to noon and from 1 to 5pm. There are plenty of Internet cafes on the island, and most hotels provide connections. One of the best and longest standing Internet cafes on the island is **Caribbean Connection Internet Café** (© **501/226-2573**) at 55 Barrier Reef Dr.

Most hotels also provide laundry service, but pricing varies widely, so ask first. **Nellie's Laundromat** (© **501/226-2454**) is located on Pescador Drive toward the south end of town. They charge around BZ$15 ($7.50/£3.75) per load, and they even offer pickup and delivery service.

WHAT TO SEE & DO

Fun on & Under the Water

First off, you should be aware that there really isn't much beach to speak of on Ambergris Caye: There is a narrow strip of sand for much of the length of the island, where the land meets the sea, but even at low tide it isn't wide enough for you to unroll a beach towel on in most places. Many beachfront hotels create their own beaches by building retaining walls and filling them in with sand. You'll find the best of these at the resorts on the northern part of the island, and at Victoria House.

Likewise, swimming is not what you might expect. For 90m (300 ft.) or more out from shore, the bottom is covered with sea grass. In a smart move that prioritizes the environment over tourism, the local and national government have decided to protect the sea grass, which supports a wealth of aquatic life. Beneath the grass is a layer of spongy roots and organic matter topped with a thin layer of white sand. Walking on this spongy sand is somewhat unnerving; there's always the possibility of a sea urchin or stingray lurking, and it's easy to trip and stumble. Swimming is best off the piers, and many of the hotels here have built long piers out into the sea.

FISHING Sportfishing for tarpon, permit, and bonefish is among the best in the world around these cayes and reefs, and over the years a few record catches have been made. If you prefer deep-sea fishing, there's plenty of tuna, dolphin, and marlin to be had beyond the reefs. **Fishing San Pedro** (© **501/607-9967;** www.fishingsanpedro.com), the **Rock** (© **501/226-3200;** www.belizefishfinder.com), and **Excalibur Tours** (© **501/226-3235**) all have respectable guides and equipment.

Hard-core fishermen might want to check out one of the dedicated fishing lodges, like **El Pescador** ★ (© **800/242-2017** in the U.S. and Canada, or 501/226-2398; www.elpescador.com) on Ambergris Caye, or **Turneffe Flats** ★★ (© **888/512-8812** in the U.S.; www.tflats.com) out on the Turneffe Island Atoll.

SAILING The crystal-clear waters, calm seas, and isolated anchorages and snorkeling spots all around Ambergris Caye make this an excellent place to go out for a sail. Your options range from crewed yachts and bareboat charters for multiday adventures, to day cruises and sunset sails. A day cruise, including lunch, drinks, and snorkeling gear, should run between BZ$200 and BZ$320 ($100–$160/£50–£80) per person. Most hotels and tour operators around town can hook you up with a day sail or sunset cruise.

SCUBA DIVING & SNORKELING Just offshore of Ambergris Caye is the longest coral reef in the Western Hemisphere. Snorkeling, scuba diving, and fishing are the main draws here. All are consistently spectacular.

Within a 10- to 20-minute boat ride from the piers lie scores of **world-class dive sites** ★★, including **Mexico Rocks, Mata Rocks, Tackle Box, Tres Cocos, Esmeralda, Cypress Tunnel,** and **Rocky Point.** A day's diving will almost always feature a mix of steep wall drops and coral caverns and tunnels. You'll see brilliant coral and sponge formations, as well as a wealth of colorful marine life.

There are scores of dive operators in San Pedro, and almost every hotel can arrange a dive trip, either because they have their own dive shop or they subcontract out. For reliable scuba-diving service and reasonable rates, contact **Amigos del Mar** (© **501/226-2706;** www.amigosdive.com), **Aqua Dives** (© **800/641-2994** in the U.S. and Canada, or 501/226-3415; www.aquadives.com), or **Patojo's Scuba Center** ★

The Perfect Plunge

If you're hesitant to take a tank plunge, don't miss a chance to at least snorkel. There's good snorkeling all along the protected side of the barrier reef, but some of the best is at **Shark-Ray Alley ★★** and **Hol Chan Marine Reserve ★★**, which are about 6km (4 miles) southeast of San Pedro. Shark-Ray Alley provides a nice adrenaline rush for all but the most nonchalant and experienced divers. Here you'll be able to snorkel above and between schools of nurse sharks and stingrays. *Hol chan* is a Mayan term meaning "little channel," which is exactly what you'll find here—a narrow channel cutting through the shallow coral reef. The walls of the channel are popular with divers, and the shallower areas are frequented by snorkelers. Most combination trips to Shark-Ray Alley and Hol Chan Marine Reserve last about 2½ to 3 hours, and cost around BZ$60 to BZ$100 ($30–$50/£15–£25). There is a BZ$20 ($10/£5) park fee for visiting Hol Chan, which may or may not be included in the price of boat excursions to the reserve.

(© **501/226-2283;** patojos@btl.net). Most of these companies, as well as the individual resorts, charge BZ$100 to BZ$140 ($50–$70/£25–£35) for a two-tank dive, with equipment rental running around BZ$30 to BZ$60 ($15–$30/£7.50–£15) for a complete package. You should be able to get deals on multiday, multidive packages.

For more adventurous and truly top-rate diving, you'll probably want to head out to the **Turneffe Island Atoll ★★**, **Lighthouse Reef ★★**, and **Blue Hole ★★**. Most of the dive operations on the island offer this trip, or will subcontract it out. You'll definitely want to choose a seaworthy, speedy, and comfortable boat. Most day trips out to Turneffe Island or Lighthouse Reef and Blue Hole run around BZ$280 to BZ$500 ($140–$250/£70–£125) per person, including transportation, two or three dives, and tanks and weights, as well as lunch and snacks. All the above-mentioned operators offer day and multiday trips to the outer atoll islands and reefs. Prices average around BZ$600 to BZ$900 ($300–$450/£150–£225) for a 2-day trip, BZ$800 to BZ$1,200 ($400–$600/£200–£300) for a 3-day trip.

Ambergris Caye is also a great place to learn how to dive. In 3 to 4 days, you can get your full open-water certification. These courses run between BZ$700 and BZ$1,000 ($350–$500/£175–£250), including all equipment rentals, class materials, and the processing of your certification, as well as four open-water and reef dives. All of the above-mentioned dive centers, as well as many of the individual resorts here, offer these courses.

There are a host of boats offering snorkeling trips, and most of the above dive operators also offer snorkel trips and equipment rental. Trips to other sites range in price from BZ$30 to BZ$60 ($15–$30/£7.50–£15) for short jaunts to half-day outings, and BZ$100 to BZ$140 ($50–$70/£25–£35) for full-day trips. One of the operators who specialize in snorkeling trips here is the very personable Alfonse Graniel and his launch ***Li'l Alfonse*** (© **501/226-2992;** lilalfonse@btl.net). Snorkel gear is available from most of the above operators and at several other sites around town. A full set of mask, fins, and snorkel will usually cost BZ$16 to BZ$24 ($8–$12/£4–£6) per person per day.

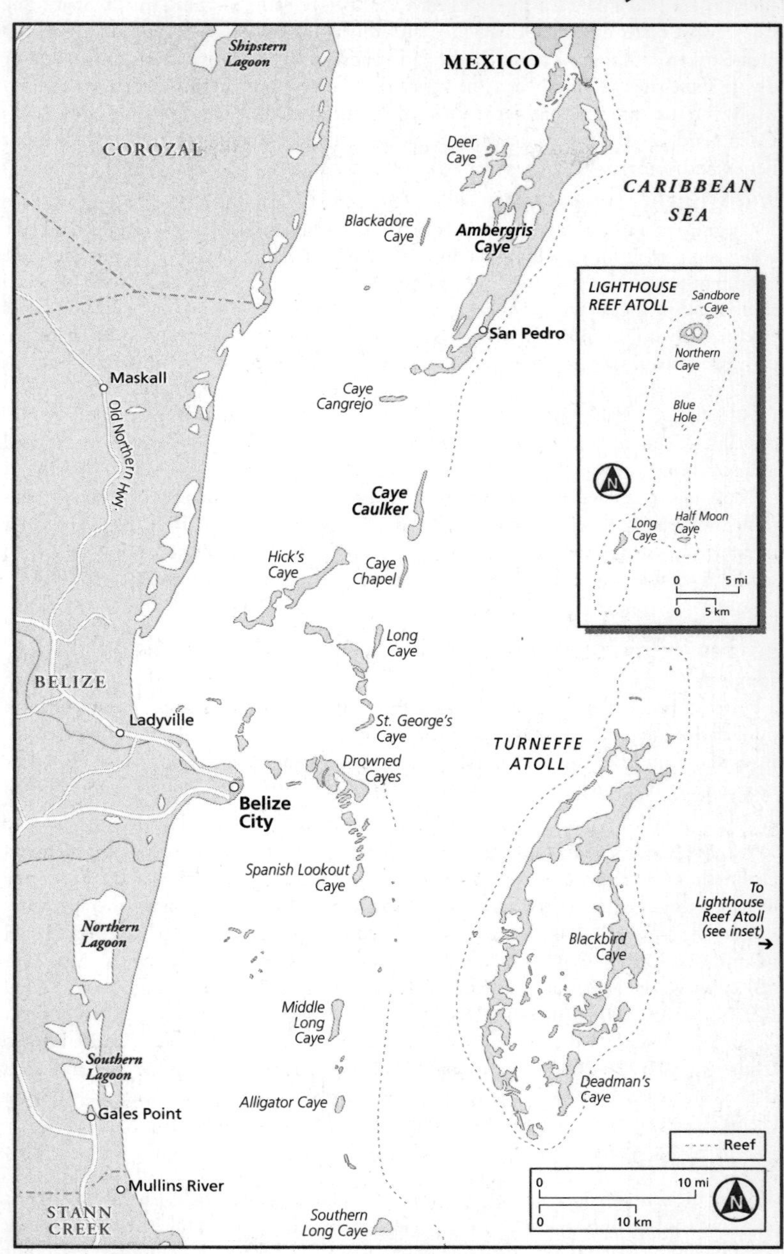
Shipstern Lagoon
MEXICO
COROZAL
Deer Caye
CARIBBEAN SEA
Blackadore Caye
Ambergris Caye
LIGHTHOUSE REEF ATOLL
Sandbore Caye
Northern Caye
Blue Hole
Half Moon Caye
Long Caye
0 5 mi
0 5 km
San Pedro
Maskall
Old Northern Hwy.
Caye Cangrejo
Caye Caulker
Hick's Caye
Caye Chapel
Long Caye
BELIZE
Ladyville
St. George's Caye
TURNEFFE ATOLL
Drowned Cayes
Belize City
Spanish Lookout Caye
To Lighthouse Reef Atoll (see inset)
Northern Lagoon
Blackbird Caye
Middle Long Caye
Southern Lagoon
Deadman's Caye
Alligator Caye
Gales Point
Reef
Mullins River
0 10 mi
0 10 km
STANN CREEK
Southern Long Caye

Tip: Hol Chan and Shark-Ray Alley are extremely popular. If you really want to enjoy them, try to find a boat leaving San Pedro at or before 8am, and head first to Shark-Ray Alley. Most boats dive Hol Chan first, and this is the best way to get a dive with the greatest concentration of nurse sharks and stingrays. By all means, avoid snorkeling or diving these sites at times when the cruise ships are running excursions there. Alternatively, you may want to consider visiting a different snorkeling site, such as Mexico Rocks Coral Gardens, Tres Cocos, or Mata Rocks, where the snorkeling is just as good, if not better, and you're more likely to have the place to yourself.

WINDSURFING, PARASAILING & WATERCRAFT Ambergris Caye is a good place for beginning and intermediate windsurfers. The nearly constant 15- to 20-knot trade winds are perfect for learning on and easy cruising. The protected waters provide some chop, but are generally pretty gentle on beginning board sailors. If you're looking to do some windsurfing, or to try the latest adrenaline boost of kiteboarding, your best bet is to check in with the folks at **Sail Sports Belize** (✆ **501/226-4488;** www.sailsportsbelize.com). Sail board rentals run around BZ$44 to BZ$54 ($22–$27/£11–£14) per hour, or BZ$144 to BZ$164 ($72–$82/£36–£41) per day. Kite board rentals run BZ$120 ($60/£30) for a half-day, and BZ$180 ($90/£45) for a full day. Weekly rates are also available. These folks also rent out several types of small sailboats for cruising around close to shore.

Most resort hotels here have their own collection of all or some of the above-mentioned watercraft. Rates run around BZ$40 to BZ$70 ($20–$35/£10–£18) per hour for a Hobie Cat, small sailboat, or windsurfer; and BZ$60 to BZ$80 ($30–$40/£15–£20) per hour for a jet ski. If not, **Sail Sports Belize** (see above) is your best bet.

Fun on Dry Land

BUTTERFLY GARDEN About 7.2km (4½ miles) north of the bridge, **Butterfly Jungle** ★ (✆ **501/226-2911;** www.butterflyjungle.bz) is a pleasant little attraction with a butterfly breeding program and covered butterfly enclosure. A visit here includes an informative tour and explanation of the butterfly life cycle, as well as a visit to the enclosure, where anywhere from 15 to 30 species may be in flight at any one time. This place is open daily 10am to 5pm, and admission is BZ$20 ($10/£5) for adults, free for children 11 and under.

SPAS, FITNESS & BODYWORK While there are no full-scale resort spas or high-end facilities on Ambergris Caye, you can certainly get sore muscles soothed and a wide array of pampering treatments at a series of day spas and independent massage-therapy storefronts. The best of these include the **Art of Touch,** at the entrance to the Sunbreeze Hotel (✆ **501/226-3357;** www.touchbelize.com), and **Asia Garden Day Spa** ★ (✆ **501/226-4072;** www.asiangardendayspa.com), across from Ramon's Village. Rates run around BZ$140 to BZ$200 ($70–$100/£35–£50) for an hour-long massage.

For a work out, try the modest health club and gym at the **San Pedro Family Fitness Club** (✆ **501/226-2683**). These folks also offer aerobic, Pilates, Tae Bo, and yoga classes, and even have a couple of lit tennis courts. This place is a bargain—BZ$30 ($15/£7.50) gets you a full-day pass and access to all their facilities.

SHOPPING

Most of the shopping on Ambergris Caye is typical tourist fare. You'll see tons of T-shirts and tank tops, with dive logos and silk-screen prints of the Blue Hole. Beyond this, the best buy on the island is handmade jewelry sold by local Belizean artisans from makeshift display stands along Barrier Reef Drive. I'd be wary of black coral jewelry, though. Black coral is extremely beautiful, but as with every endangered resource, increased demand just leads to increased harvesting of a slow-growing coral.

Inside Fido's Courtyard at **Belizean Arts** ★ (✆ **501/226-3019;** www.belizeanarts.com), you'll find the island's best collection of original paintings and crafts. Of special note are the prints and paintings of co-owner Walter Castillo, a Nicaraguan-born artist whose simple, but bold, style captures the Caribbean color and rhythm of Belize.

Another shop at Fido's Courtyard worth checking out is **Ambar** ★★ (✆ **501/226-3101**). The owner and artisan here sells handmade jewelry, with a specialty in amber. The stuff here is a significant cut above the wares you'll find in most other souvenir shops and street stands.

To get your fill of jade, head to the small **Ambergris Maya Jade & History Museum,** Barrier Reef Drive (✆ **501/226-3311**), which has a nice collection of jade artifacts and jewelry, and really functions as the draw to get folks into their retail store.

WHERE TO STAY

In & Around San Pedro

There's a score of hotel options right in the heart of San Pedro town. Most are geared towards budget travelers, although a few of these are quite comfortable and charming. Most of the more upscale resorts are located a little bit farther north or south of town.

Very Expensive

Victoria House ★★★ (Finds) This elegant and exclusive island retreat features a varied collection of rooms, suites, and villas. Everything is done with a refined sense of style and attention to detail. The resort is set on an expansive piece of land a couple of miles south of San Pedro, with lush tropical gardens and a surprisingly good section of soft white sand fronting it. The plantation rooms and suites are spread through several buildings, and there's a string of individual casitas aligned around a grassy lawn facing the sea. The villas and suites are large, and feature flatscreen televisions and plush furnishings. Some have kitchenettes, and others are duplex units that can be joined or rented separately. Service is attentive yet understated. A full range of tours and activities are offered, and the restaurant here is one of the finest on the island.

Beachfront, 3km (2 miles) south of San Pedro (P.O. Box 22, San Pedro), Ambergris Caye. ✆ **800/247-5159** or 713/344-2340 in the U.S., or 501/226-2067 in Belize. www.victoria-house.com. 42 units. BZ$360 ($180/£90) double; BZ$596–BZ$620 ($298–$310/£149–£155) casita or plantation room; BZ$750–BZ$1,316 ($375–$658/£188–£329) suite; BZ$1,330–BZ$3,500 ($665–$1,750/£333–£875) villa. Rates higher during peak weeks, lower in the off season. AE, MC, V. **Amenities:** Restaurant; bar; free bicycles for guests; full-service dive shop; golf cart rental; laundry service; 2 midsize outdoor pools; watersports equipment rental; free Wi-Fi. *In room:* A/C, no phone, safe.

Expensive

The **Blue Tang Inn** (✆ **866/881-1020** in the U.S. and Canada, or 501/226-2326 in Belize; www.bluetanginn.com) is another good option in this category.

Ramon's Village ★ This place is one of the original resorts on Ambergris Caye, and it's grown over the years. The handiwork of local son Ramón Núñez, this place is appropriately named, as there is a small-village feel to the collection of thatch-roofed bungalows and suites. At the center of the complex is a small but inviting free-form pool, surrounded by palm trees and flowering plants. Rooms vary a bit in size, and are classified as beachfront, seaside, and garden view, with the beachfront units having the best unobstructed views of the water. Some of the older units are a bit dark and too close to the road and airstrip for my taste. Most have a private or shared balcony with a sitting chair or hammock. There are a few suites, which are larger and provide more room to roam and relax. Ramon's has one of the longer and prettier beaches to be found in San Pedro, as well as a very long dock jutting into the sea, and a wide range of watersports equipment and activities to choose from.

Coconut Dr. (southern edge of town), San Pedro, Ambergris Caye. ✆ **800/624-4215** or 601/649-1990 in the U.S., or 501/226-2067 in Belize. Fax 501/226-2214. www.ramons.com. 60 units. BZ$290–BZ$370 ($145–$185/£73–£93) double; BZ$430–BZ$800 ($215–$400/£108–£200) suite. Rates slightly higher during peak weeks, lower in the off season. AE, MC, V. **Amenities:** Restaurant; bar; bike and golf cart rental; full-service dive shop; laundry service; small outdoor pool; room service; watersports equipment rental. *In room:* A/C, hair dryer, no phone.

Sunbreeze ★★ For my money, this is the best hotel right in San Pedro town. This two-story seafront hotel is built in a horseshoe around a simple garden area, with a small pool at its core. The superior rooms are all spacious, contemporary, and nonsmoking. The standard rooms have slightly small bathrooms, but are otherwise quite acceptable. The five deluxe units feature Jacuzzi tubs and the best views. This hotel is very ideally located in the center of town, with its own dive operation and a small arcade of shops. One of the nicest features here is a covered open-air hammock area built over the restaurant and bar. The hotel is directly across from the airstrip, and quite convenient if you are arriving and departing by air.

Coconut Dr. (P.O. Box 14) San Pedro, Ambergris Caye. ✆ **800/688-0191** in the U.S., or 501/226-2191 in Belize. Fax 501/226-2346. www.sunbreeze.net. 42 units. BZ$306–BZ$372 ($153–$186/£77–£93) double; BZ$340 ($170) deluxe; rates lower in the off season. AE, MC, V. **Amenities:** Restaurant; bar; bike rental; full-service dive shop; laundry service; nonsmoking rooms; small outdoor pool; room service; watersports equipment rental. *In room:* A/C, TV.

Moderate

In addition to the hotel reviewed below, you might want to try **Tides Beach Resort** (Boca del Río Dr., San Pedro; ✆ **501/226-2283;** www.ambergriscaye.com/tides), a three-story oceanfront hotel that's popular with scuba divers and dive groups.

San Pedro Holiday Hotel ★ (Finds You can't miss this brilliantly white three-building complex with painted purple and pink trim in the center of town. Every room comes with air-conditioning, and most have excellent ocean views and small refrigerators. Get a room on the second floor and you'll have a wonderful balcony—you won't want to leave. Celi McCorkle opened this hotel over 40 years ago, the first on the island, and it's continued to keep pace with the times and tourism boom. This hotel lacks some of the amenities of other options in this price range—there's no swimming pool and not all rooms have televisions—but it makes up for that with its funky island vibe and friendly service.

Barrier Reef Dr. (P.O. Box 61), San Pedro, Ambergris Caye. ✆ **501/226-2014.** Fax 501/226-2295. www.sanpedroholiday.com. 17 units. BZ$220–BZ$250 ($110–$125/£55–£63) double; BZ$350 ($175/£88) apt. AE, MC, V. **Amenities:** 2 restaurants; bar; bike rental; full-service dive shop; laundry service; watersports equipment rental. *In room:* A/C, no phone.

Inexpensive

There are quite a few budget options on Ambergris Caye, and almost all of them are concentrated in the compact downtown area of San Pedro. True budget hounds should just walk around and see who's got the best room for the best price. I list my favorite below.

Ruby's (Value Most of the rooms at Ruby's overlook the water. The best ones have air-conditioning and a private balcony overlooking the sea. The floors are wooden, the rooms are simply furnished with a couple of beds and little else, and the showers and bathrooms are clean. You can't beat the location at this price in San Pedro. Downstairs you'll find Ruby's Deli, which is a good place for breakfast or a casual midday meal. These folks also have a separate hotel on the lagoon side of the island, with clean, spacious, simple rooms at even lower prices. After years of mixed messages, it seems like the owners here have settled on spelling Ruby's with a "y" and not "ie" at the end.

Barrier Reef Dr. (P.O. Box 56), San Pedro, Ambergris Caye. ✆ **501/226-2063.** Fax 501/226-2434. www.ambergriscaye.com/rubys. 21 units. BZ$80–BZ$120 ($40–$60/£20–£30) double. MC, V. **Amenities:** Restaurant; laundry service. *In room:* No phone.

On North Ambergris Caye

This is where you'll find most of the larger, more isolated, and more upscale resorts on Ambergris Caye. If you stay here, you will have to rely on your hotel or on the local water taxis to get to and from San Pedro town.

Very Expensive

The individual villas at **Azul Resort** (✆ **501/226-4012;** www.azulbelize.com) and **Capricorn Resort** (✆ **501/226-2809;** www.capricornresort.net) are also good selections.

Captain Morgan's Retreat ★★ Kids Captain Morgan's is a large, lively, and well-equipped resort on a long and lovely section of beach. The rooms are either individual beachfront casitas, or one- or two-bedroom villas set in a series of two-story units. All feature thatch roofs and wood construction, as well as attractive Guatemalan bedspreads and varnished wood furnishings. Every room comes with a private balcony or veranda, and all are modern, comfortable, and plenty spacious. I prefer the casitas, which are named after famous pirate captains, for their sense of privacy, although if you want more space and amenities, choose one of the second-floor villas. The villas all come with a fully equipped kitchenette.

Oceanfront, 5km (3 miles) north of the cut on northern end of Ambergris Caye. ✆ **888/653-9090** or 307/587-8914 in the U.S., or 501/226-2207 in Belize. Fax 501/226-4171. www.belizevacation.com. 26 units. BZ$398 ($199/£100) casita; BZ$498 ($249/£125) 1-bedroom villa; BZ$840 ($420/£210) 2-bedroom villa. Rates lower in the off season; higher during peak periods. AE, MC, V. **Amenities:** Restaurant; 2 bars; lounge; 2 outdoor pools; complimentary bike use; full-service dive shop; laundry service; spa services; watersports equipment rental. *In room:* A/C, fridge, free Wi-Fi.

Mata Chica ★★ This is one of the hippest resorts on Ambergris Caye. There's a sense of rustic luxury throughout. Artistic details abound, with an eclectic mix of fabrics, sculptures, ceramics, and paintings from around the world. Every room here is actually a private bungalow or villa, and all can be considered junior suites or better. My favorites are the casitas, which are the closest to the ocean, and feature a large sitting area, a king-size bed on a raised platform, and an interior garden shower. At the back of the property, set high on raised stilts, are two very large villas, and one immense mansion. The latter is over 465 sq. m (5,000 sq. ft.), and features three bedrooms, a full kitchen, three full bathrooms, a huge living room, and ample deck areas and views. There's a small outdoor pool surrounded by shady palm trees, in addition to a large outdoor Jacuzzi. There's also a small spa, with a full list of treatments and cures, as well as a full-service tour desk.

Oceanfront, northern end of Ambergris Caye. ✆ **501/223-0002** reservations, or 220-5010 at the hotel. Fax 501/220-5012. www.matachica.com. 14 units. BZ$560–BZ$830 ($280–$415/£140–£208) double; BZ$1,450–BZ$2,090 ($725–$1,045/£363–£523) villa. Rates include continental breakfast and transfers to and from San Pedro airport. Rates slightly lower in the off season. AE, MC, V. **Amenities:** Restaurant; bar; Jacuzzi; complimentary kayak use; laundry service; small outdoor pool; small spa. *In room:* A/C, no phone, free Wi-Fi.

An Island of Your Own

Cayo Espanto ★★★ *Finds* Whether you're a bona fide member of the jet set or you just want to feel like one, this is the place for you in Belize. Six individual bungalows are spread across this private island. Each bungalow is luxurious and elegantly appointed and set on the edge of the Caribbean Sea, and each comes with a private butler. All but one of the bungalows has a private plunge pool, and all have a private pier jutting out into the ocean. All have wide French doors and windows that open on to private decks and verandas and stunning views. All meals are served in your villa, or out on your own private deck or dock area. Service is very attentive and pampering, and the food is excellent.

Cayo Espanto. ✆ **888/666-4282** in the U.S. and Canada. www.aprivateisland.com. 6 units. BZ$2,390–BZ$4,590 ($1,195–$2,295/£598–£1,148) double. Rates include 3 meals, all drinks (except wine and champagne), all nonmotorized watersports equipment usage, and transportation to and from San Pedro during daylight hours. Rates slightly higher during peak weeks. AE, MC, V. **Amenities:** Full-service dive operation; small exercise room; laundry service; 5 small outdoor pools; room service; spa services. *In room:* A/C, TV, fridge, hair dryer, free Wi-Fi.

WHERE TO DINE

In & Around San Pedro

Expensive

For an elegant dining experience, with fabulous food, setting, and service, it's hard to beat the **Palmilla ★★** (✆ **501/226-2067**) at the Victoria House (see above).

Blue Water Grill ★★ INTERNATIONAL/ASIAN This place has a broad and extensive menu, as well as a lovely setting overlooking the ocean and piers from the waterfront in the heart of San Pedro. While there's a good selection of pizzas, pastas, and such hearty dishes as grilled beef tenderloin with a creole mustard and black-pepper sauce; or chicken breasts served with fresh herbs, walnuts, and blue cheese, the real reason to come here is for their inspired Asian fare. Start things off with crispy coconut-battered shrimp sticks with a sweet and spicy black-bean dipping sauce. For a main course, I recommend the Japanese spiced grouper with a sesame vinaigrette, or the massive surf and turf. These folks also have sushi nights every Tuesday and Thursday. If you come for sushi, be sure to try their spicy scallop hand roll.

At the Sunbreeze hotel, on the waterfront. ✆ **501/226-3347.** www.bluewatergrillbelize.com. Reservations recommended. Main courses BZ$30–BZ$54 ($15–$27/£7.50–£14). AE, MC, V. Daily 7–10:30am, 11:30am–2:30pm, and 6–9:30pm.

Moderate

Casa Picasso ★★★ INTERNATIONAL/TAPAS The odd angles of the walls give this chic place its name, and the creative decor and eclectic music lend a comfortable and captivating ambience. The menu features a wide selection of tapas, both traditional and more modern choices. I recommend the mini crab cakes with a chili-lime dipping sauce, as well as the chicken marinated in sangria and served with an orange-raisin-walnut salsa. For heartier fare, there are several pasta dishes to choose from. Casa Picasso also has great desserts, and I definitely recommend saving room for their flourless chocolate cake. They also have an extensive list of creative martinis and coffee drinks, as well as a good wine selection.

Sting Ray St., south of town on lagoon side of island. ✆ **501/226-4507.** Reservations recommended. Tapas BZ$14–BZ$24 ($7–$12/£3.50–£6); main courses BZ$28–BZ$32 ($14–$16/£7–£8). MC, V. Mon–Sat 5:30–10pm.

Wild Mangos ★★ INTERNATIONAL/FUSION After establishing a reputation at Palmilla, and winning the Taste of Belize competition twice, chef Amy Knox has set up shop at this down-home open-air joint. The menu is fairly broad and quite creative. Start things off with the Fire and Ice Ceviche, sushi-grade chunks of raw tuna marinated in a coconut milk broth spiced with fresh chilies. For a main course I like the bacon-wrapped shrimp grilled with a rum glaze, or the Conchinita Pibil, a traditional Maya pork dish slow cooked in banana leaves. There are often nightly specials, and the desserts are delectable. There's also a streamlined lunch menu featuring sandwiches, wraps, tacos, and burritos, as well as salads and other treats.

On the beach, just north of the Sunbreeze Hotel. ✆ **501/226-2859.** Reservations recommended. Main courses BZ$27–BZ$52 ($14–$26/£7–£13). AE, MC, V. Mon–Sat noon–9pm.

Inexpensive

In addition to the places below, **Jambel's Jerk Pit** (✆ **501/226-3515**) is right on Barrier Reef Drive, and serves the same excellent Caribbean fare you'll find at its sister restaurant in Belize City (p. 105). **Ruby's Cafe** and **Celi's Deli,** on the ground floors of Ruby's hotel (p. 116) and the San Pedro Holiday Hotel (p. 116) respectively, are good places to pick up a light meal, and both specialize in fresh-baked breads and pastries, and sandwiches to go.

Other dependable options include **Ambergris Delight** (✆ **501/226-2464**), which is a popular local joint; **Caramba** (✆ **501/226-4321**), which serves a mix of Belizean, Mexican, and Caribbean fare; and **Ali Baba** (✆ **501/226-4042**), which specializes in Middle Eastern cuisine. For a seafront seat in the sand, it's hard to beat **Lily's Treasure Chest** (✆ **501/226-2650**) or **Estel's Dine By the Sea** (✆ **501/226-2019**), both of which are great for breakfast, lunch, or dinner.

Elvi's Kitchen ★★ *Finds* BELIZEAN/SEAFOOD/INTERNATIONAL Local legend Elvia Staines began selling burgers out of a takeout window in 1974. Today, Elvi's is the most popular and renowned restaurant on Ambergris Caye. Even after having enlarged the dining room, they still can't keep up with the dinner crowds that flock here for the lively ambience, substantial servings, fresh ingredients, and food cooked to order. The restaurant is a thatched, screened-in building with picnic tables, a large flamboyant tree growing up through the roof, and a floor of crushed shells and sand. You can get everything from Belizean stewed chicken to shrimp in watermelon sauce. For lunch, there are still burgers, including traditional beef burgers, although I prefer the shrimp and fish burgers. There's live music every night, with Caribbean night on Thursday, Maya night on Friday, and Mexican night on Saturday. Food specials complement the musical selections.

Pescador Dr., San Pedro. ✆ **501/226-2176.** www.elviskitchen.com. Reservations recommended. Main courses BZ$16–BZ$50 ($8–$25/£4–£13); fresh fish, seafood, and lobster priced according to market. AE, MC, V. Mon–Sat 11am–2pm and 5:30–10pm.

On North Ambergris Caye

Despite its relative isolation, the northern section of Ambergris Caye has perhaps the island's greatest concentration of truly superb eateries. In addition to the places listed below, you will find contemporary fusion-style food, with a heavy Pacific Rim influence, at **Pinki Knox** (✆ **501/622-6991**), located a little bit north of the bridge; and contemporary Thai and French fare at **Rendezvous Restaurant & Winery** (✆ **501/226-3426**) located about 7km (4½ miles) north of the bridge connecting the two sections of Ambergris Caye.

If you're staying in San Pedro or on the southern half of the island, you'll need to take a water taxi. Most of these restaurants will usually be able to arrange this for you, often at a reduced rate from the going fare.

Expensive

In addition the restaurant reviewed below, you might check out **Mambo** (at Mata Chica, on the northern end of Ambergris Caye; ✆ **501/220-5010**), a restaurant with an eclectic menu that touches on a wide range of world cuisines.

Rojo Lounge ★★★ (Finds) FUSION Self-taught chef and owner Jeff Spiegel and his partner, Vivan Yu, have created an elegant and ultrahip open-air restaurant, adjacent to their luxury two-villa resort. The lighting and decor are heavily red, hence, the name—Rojo. There are traditional chairs, as well as couch and plush chair seating, on a broad open deck facing the sea. It's always wise to try the nightly specials, but whatever you do, don't miss the chorizo, shitake, and shrimp pot stickers. The guava-glazed baby back ribs are also spectacular. If you're more interested in seafood, there are both crab and grouper cakes, or you could get some homemade conch sausage on a fresh pizza. This place has an extensive wine list, as well as a fabulously stocked bar.

At Azul Resort, on the northern section of Ambergris Caye. ✆ **501/226-4012.** Reservations necessary. Main courses BZ$34–BZ$68 ($17–$34/£8.50–£17). MC, V. Tues–Sat 6–9pm, by reservation only.

Moderate

Sweet Basil Gourmet Café ★ INTERNATIONAL This breezy, two-story wood-frame house with a bright paint job and gingerbread trim is a great spot for lunch or dinner. A wide range of specialty items and imported goods, from cheeses to olives to deli meats, are used to create an extensive menu of interesting salads, sandwiches, and pasta dishes. The burgers are especially good. A selection of more substantial dinner options are also offered daily. While there's seating on the first floor, you'll definitely want to grab a seat on the open-air second-floor veranda, with views to both the lagoon and Caribbean Sea.

Just across the cut, on the northern section of Ambergris Caye. ✆ **501/226-2113.** Reservations recommended during high season. Sandwiches BZ$20–BZ$32 ($10–$16/£5–£8); main courses BZ$30–BZ$38 ($15–$19/£7.50–£9.50); lobster priced according to market. AE, MC, V. Wed–Mon 11am–9pm.

AMBERGRIS CAYE AFTER DARK

Ambergris Caye is a popular beach and dive destination, and as such it supports a fairly active nightlife and late-night bar scene. I recommend starting things off at one of the beachside bars such as the **Pier Lounge** (✆ **501/226-2002**) at the Spindrift Hotel, or a bar built out over the water like **Wet Willy's ★** (✆ **501/226-4136**), located off the center of town, or the **Palapa Bar ★** (✆ **501/226-3111;** www.palapabarandgrill), about 1.6km (1 mile) north of the cut on the northern half of the island. Two other popular choices are **Fido's Courtyard** (✆ **501/226-2056**), which has live music every night of the week, and the **Purple Parrot** (✆ **501/226-2071**) in Ramon's Village, which claims to be a favorite haunt of Jimmy Buffet.

For dancing and late-night action, your best options are the two traditional San Pedro discos, **Jaguar's Temple Club** (no phone) and **Big Daddy's** (no phone), which are within a stone's throw of each other on Barrier Reef Drive, near the basketball court and the church. Just south of downtown on Coconut Drive, you might try the huge **Barefoot Iguana ★** (✆ **501/226-2927**), which features everything from hot new DJs, to mud wrestling, to sporting events shown on a giant screen.

If you're the betting type, try **Casino Belize** ★ (✆ **501/226-2777**), at the Belize Yacht Club, just south of the airstrip.

SIDE TRIPS FROM AMBERGRIS CAYE

If you've been on the island for a while or just want to see more of Belize, a host of tour operators on Ambergris Caye offer excursions to all of the major attractions and destinations around the country, including Altun Ha, Lamanai, Xunantunich, Mountain Pine Ridge, and even Tikal. You can also go cave tubing in the Caves Branch region. Most of these tours involve a flight in a small charter plane.

One of the most popular day trips is to the Maya ruins at Altun Ha. This is also one of the most economical, as it doesn't require a flight. This begins on a powerful little boat that will whisk you over to the mainland. You'll then take a taxi to the ruins and have lunch before returning to San Pedro. Most operators offering the Altun Ha trip include a lunch stop at Maruba Resort, with the option of adding on a decadent jungle spa treatment. Prices for these trips run around BZ$140 to BZ$200 ($70–$100/£35–£50). A similar trip by boat and land is offered to the ruins at Lamanai.

For trips involving a flight, prices range from BZ$200 to BZ$400 ($100–$200/£50–£100) per person, depending on the distance traveled and number of activities and attractions crammed into 1 day. Most hotels on the island can book these tours, or you can contact **Excalibur Tours** (✆ **501/226-3235**), **SEAduced** (✆ **501/226-2254;** www.seaducedbybelize.com), or **Sea Rious Adventures** (✆ **501/226-4202**).

6 CAYE CAULKER ★★★

32km (20 miles) N of Belize City; 16km (10 miles) S of Ambergris Caye

Caye Caulker is no longer the secret hideaway of a handful of happy hippie backers and a few chosen cognoscenti. That said, this remains the epitome of a small, isolated, and laid-back Caribbean getaway. Unlike neighboring San Pedro, you won't find any gridlock traffic here, or be constantly run off the road by cars and golf carts. In fact, golf-cart traffic is still relatively light, with flip-flops and bicycles fulfilling most of the transportation needs. I hope it stays that way. Still, Caye Caulker has begun to experience some of the effects of the amazing boom going on just to the north on Ambergris Caye. There's more and more development on either end of the island, and the long-neglected northern section of Caye Caulker—across the Split—is starting to be developed.

ESSENTIALS

Getting There

As with Ambergris Caye, you've got two options for getting to and from Caye Caulker: sea or air. When the weather's rough it's bumpy both ways, although it's certainly quicker by air, and you're more likely to get wet in the boat.

BY PLANE Dozens of daily flights run between Belize City and **Caye Caulker Airport** (**CUK;** no phone). Flights leave from both Philip S. W. Goldson International Airport and Municipal Airport roughly every hour. If you're coming in on an international flight and heading straight for Caye Caulker, you should book a flight from the international airport. If you're already in Belize City or in transit around the country, it's cheaper to fly from the municipal airport, which is also closer to downtown.

Fun Facts **What's in a Name?**

The Spanish called this little island "Cayo Hicaco." *Hicaco* is Spanish for the coco plum palm. Some say the name comes from the fact that ships used to be caulked in the shallow calm waters off the backside of this island, hence Caye Caulker. However, a third theory notes that the island appears as Caye Corker on several early British maps. This line of reasoning claims that early sailors and pirates stopped to fill and then "cork" their water bottles with the abundant fresh water found here.

Both **Maya Island Air** (✆ **501/223-1140;** www.mayaairways.com) and **Tropic Air** (✆ **800/422-3435** in the U.S. and Canada, or 501/226-2012 in Belize; www.tropicair.com) have 11 flights daily between Goldson International Airport and Caye Caulker. The flights depart every hour beginning at 7:40am, with the last flight at 5:40pm. Flight time is around 10 minutes. These flights actually originate at the Belize City Municipal Airport 10 minutes earlier. From the municipal airport, the fare should be a bit cheaper. These flights take around 20 minutes, because they stop en route to pick up passengers at the international airport. When you're ready to leave, flights from San Pedro to Belize City run from 7:10am to 5:10pm.

Almost all of the above flights originating in Belize City continue on to San Pedro on Ambergris Caye. Similarly, almost all the return flights originate in San Pedro. The flight between the two islands takes 10 minutes, and the fare is BZ$63 ($32/£16). Connections to and from all the other major destinations in Belize can be made via the municipal and international airports in Belize City.

BY BOAT Regularly scheduled boats ply the route between Belize City and Caye Caulker. All leave from somewhere near the Swing Bridge, and the majority leave directly from the **Marine Terminal,** which is right on North Front Street just over the Swing Bridge, and are associated with the **Caye Caulker Water Taxi Association** (✆ **501/226-0992;** www.cayecaulkerwatertaxi.com). Most are open speedboats that carry between 20 to 30 passengers, making the trip in about 45 minutes. If you're going to Ambergris, St. George's, or Caye Chapel from Caye Caulker, these boats all will take you there. Find out on Caye Caulker just where and when they stop. The schedule is subject to change, but boats for Caye Caulker leave the Marine Terminal roughly every 90 minutes beginning at 8am, with the last boat leaving at 4:30pm. The fare is BZ$20 ($10/£5) one-way, BZ$40 ($20/£10) round-trip between Belize City and Caye Caulker; and BZ$15 ($7.50/£3.75) one-way between Caye Caulker and San Pedro.

In addition to the Caye Caulker Water Taxi Association, the ***Triple J*** (✆ **501/223-3464**) leaves from Courthouse pier near the Marine Terminal every day at 8 and 10:30am, noon and 3 and 4:40pm, returning from the Texaco dock on Ambergris Caye at 7:30, 8:30, and 11am, and 1:30, 3, and 4pm.

Getting Around

Caye Caulker is small. You can easily walk from one end of the island to the other in around 20 minutes. If you want to cover more ground quickly, a bicycle is your best bet. Many hotels have their own for guests to use free of charge or for a slight rental fee. If not, you can rent a bicycle from one of several stores on Front Street.

While I think it's really unnecessary, you can also rent a golf cart from **Caye Caulker Golf Rentals** (✆ **501/226-0237**), **C & N Golf Carts** (✆ **501/226-0252**), or **Jasmine Cart Rentals** (✆ **501/206-0212**). Rates run around BZ$120 to BZ$160 ($60–$80/ £30–£40) per day for a four-seat cart.

Orientation

Most boats dock at the pier jutting off Front Street at a spot called Front Bridge—so named because this is the front side of the island facing the reef (east). The town extends north and south from here. As you debark, if you kept walking straight ahead, you'd soon come to the western side of the island and the Back Bridge or dock, where some of the boats dock. Caye Caulker consists of two or three main north-south sand roads, a few cross streets, and numerous paths. The closest street to the water on the east side of the island is Front Street. The next street in is called either Middle Street or Hicaco Avenue, and the next street to the west is called alternately Back Street or Langosta Avenue. The small Caye Caulker airstrip is on the southern outskirts of town. At the north end of town you'll find the Split or Cut. Much of Caye Caulker is uninhabited. The small town and inhabited sections are quite concentrated.

Visitor Information & Fast Facts

For the local **police,** dial ✆ **911,** or 501/226-2022; for the **fire department,** dial ✆ **501/226-0353.** In case of a medical emergency, call the **Caye Caulker Health Clinic** (✆ **501/226-0166**).

Atlantic Bank (✆ **501/226-0207**) is located on Back Street, near the center of the island, and has an ATM that accepts international credit and debit cards. The **post office** (✆ **501/226-2325**) is also located on Back Street; it's open Monday through Friday from 8am to noon and from 1 to 5pm. There are several **Internet cafes** on the island; just walk along Front Street and find one with an open terminal. I like **Caye Caulker Cyber Café,** which serves drinks—and even has a popular happy hour with reduced rates on drinks and Internet usage. They also have a good book-swap library.

WHAT TO SEE & DO

The main activities on Caye Caulker itself are strolling up and down the sand streets, and swimming and sunbathing off the docks. The most popular spot is at the north end of the island by the **Split** ★. The Split was formed in 1961 when Hurricane Hattie literally split the island in two. Take care when swimming off the docks here. The split is an active channel with regular boat traffic. Also, when the tides are running strong, there's quite a bit of current through the split and it's easy to get dragged along for a few hundred yards or so. If you do get caught in this current, treat it like any riptide: Don't panic, and swim diagonally across the current to get out of it.

Aside from the split, there is not much beach to speak of on the rest of the island. There is a narrow strip of sand for much of the length of the island, where the land meets the sea, but even at low tide it isn't wide enough for you to unroll a beach towel on in most places. In fact, along most of its length this is a small bike and footpath that is probably the busiest thoroughfare on Caye Caulker. Several of the hotels have built long piers out into the sea, with steps down into the water, and swimming is best here.

On & Under the Water

KAYAKS & OTHER WATERCRAFT The calm protected waters just offshore are wonderful for any number of watersports vehicles. Several hotels and tour operators around

Chocolate & the Manatees

On Caye Caulker, when someone mentions "Chocolate," they are almost inevitably referring to pioneering guide and boat captain Lionel "Chocolate" Heredia. Chocolate began his career as a fisherman, but he soon dedicated himself to the fledgling business of taxiing folks by speedboat back and forth between Belize City and Caye Caulker. Chocolate was also probably the first guide to introduce the popular day trip to see manatees and do some snorkeling at remote cayes. He and his wife, Annie, also led the battle to protect these gentle sea mammals and their feeding grounds, finally seeing the dedication of the Swallow Caye Manatee Reserve (www.swallowcayemanatees.org) in 1999.

Chocolate (✆ **501/226-0151;** chocolateseashore@gmail.com) still leads manatee and snorkel tours. These tours begin with a stop at the manatee-feeding site on Swallow Caye, before heading to either Geoff's or Sergeant's Cayes, which are little more than football field–size patches of sand with a few palm trees. The afternoons are usually spent snorkeling in the clear waters off these cayes, and lunching on the sand. These trips, which are also offered by most other tour operators on the island, include all transportation, lunch on one of the cayes, and several snorkel stops, and cost between BZ$120 and BZ$160 ($60–$80/£30–£40).

Caye Caulker have various types of watercraft for guest use, or general rental. Rates run around BZ$20 to BZ$30 ($10–$15/£5–£7.50) per hour for a kayak; BZ$40 to BZ$60 ($15–$30/£7.50–£15) per hour for a Hobie Cat or small sailboat; and BZ$60 to BZ$80 ($30–$40/£15–£20) per hour for a jet ski.

KITESURFING & SAILBOARDING With strong, steady, but not overpowering winds, Caye Caulker is a great place to learn or practice kitesurfing. The folks at **Kitexplorer** (✆ **501/602-9297;** www.kitexplorer.com) rent out both kitesurfing and sailboarding equipment. They also offer an intensive 9-hour course in kitesurfing for BZ$720 ($360/£180) that is guaranteed to get you up and skimming across the sea.

SAILING The crystal-clear waters, calm seas, and excellent snorkeling spots around Caye Caulker make this an excellent place to go out for a sail. Unlike on Ambergris Caye, there's no organized bareboat charters available here, but you can go out on any number of different vessels for a half- or full-day sail, a sunset cruise, a moonlight cruise, or a combined sailing and snorkeling adventure. A day cruise, including lunch, drinks, and snorkeling gear should run between BZ$100 and BZ$220 ($50–$110/£25–£55) per person; a half-day tour including drinks, a snack, and snorkeling gear should cost between BZ$70 and BZ$120 ($35–$60/£18–£30). Most hotels and tour operators around town can hook you up with an appropriate captain and craft. Or you can head out on the Shark-Ray Alley and Hol Chan tour with **Raggamuffin Tours** ★ (see above).

SCUBA DIVING & SNORKELING There's excellent diving and snorkeling close to Caye Caulker. Within a 5- to 20-minute boat ride from the pier lie a couple of world-class dive sites, including **Caye Caulker North Cut, Coral Gardens, Pyramid Flats,**

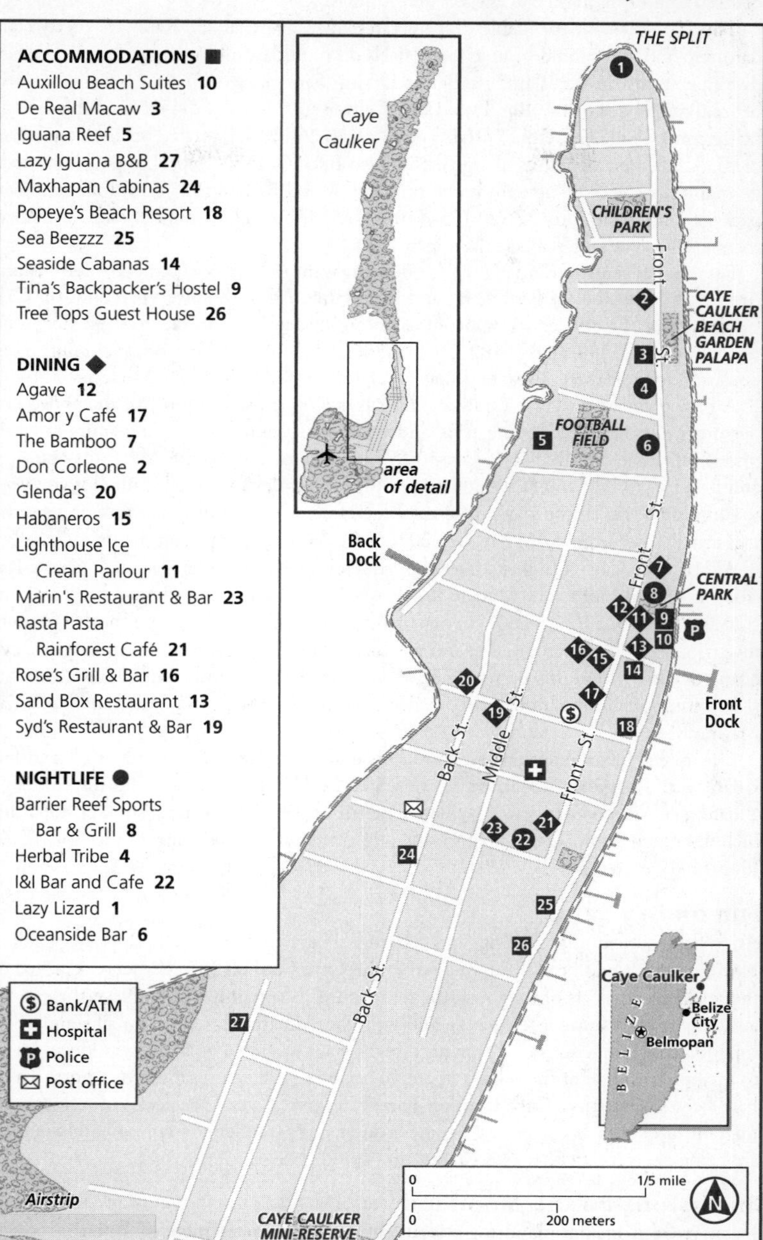
ACCOMMODATIONS
Auxillou Beach Suites 10
De Real Macaw 3
Iguana Reef 5
Lazy Iguana B&B 27
Maxhapan Cabinas 24
Popeye's Beach Resort 18
Sea Beezzz 25
Seaside Cabanas 14
Tina's Backpacker's Hostel 9
Tree Tops Guest House 26
DINING
Agave 12
Amor y Café 17
The Bamboo 7
Don Corleone 2
Glenda's 20
Habaneros 15
Lighthouse Ice Cream Parlour 11
Marin's Restaurant & Bar 23
Rasta Pasta Rainforest Café 21
Rose's Grill & Bar 16
Sand Box Restaurant 13
Syd's Restaurant & Bar 19
NIGHTLIFE
Barrier Reef Sports Bar & Grill 8
Herbal Tribe 4
I&I Bar and Cafe 22
Lazy Lizard 1
Oceanside Bar 6
Bank/ATM
Hospital
Police
Post office
Caye Caulker
area of detail
THE SPLIT
CHILDREN'S PARK
CAYE CAULKER BEACH GARDEN PALAPA
FOOTBALL FIELD
CENTRAL PARK
Back Dock
Front Dock
Front St.
Middle St.
Back St.
Airstrip
CAYE CAULKER MINI-RESERVE
Caye Caulker
Belize City
Belmopan
BELIZE
0
1/5 mile
200 meters
N

 Sponge Avenue, and **Amigos Wreck.** A day's diving here will almost always feature a mix of steep wall drops and coral caverns and tunnels.

There are several dependable dive operators on Caye Caulker. Rates are pretty standardized, and you should be able to get deals on multiday, multidive packages. The best dive operations on the island are **Belize Diving Services ★** (✆ 501/226-0143; www.belizedivingservice.com), **Big Fish Dive Center** (✆ 501/226-0450; www.bigfishdivebelize.com), and **Frenchie's Diving** (✆ 501/226-0234; www.frenchiesdivingbelize.com). All of these operators charge BZ$100 to BZ$160 ($50–$80/£25–£40) for a local two-tank dive, with equipment rental running around BZ$50 ($25/£13) for a complete package, and BZ$12 to BZ$20 ($6–$10/£3–£5) for a mask, snorkel, and fins. All of them also offer a range of certification courses.

For more adventurous diving, you'll probably want to head out to the **Turneffe Island Atoll ★★**, **Lighthouse Reef ★★**, and **Blue Hole.** All of the dive operations on Caye Caulker offer this trip or will subcontract it out. Most day trips out to these dive spots run around BZ$300 to BZ$400 ($150–$200/£75–£100) per person, including transportation, two or three dives, tanks, and weights, as well as lunch and snacks.

A host of boats on Caye Caulker offer snorkeling trips, and most of the above dive operators also offer snorkeling trips and equipment rental. Snorkeling tours range in price from BZ$30 to BZ$60 ($15–$30/£7.50–£15) for short jaunts to half-day outings, and BZ$100 to BZ$160 ($50–$80/£25–£40) for full-day trips—a bit more if you want to jump on a trip all the way out to the Blue Hole. A full set of mask, fins, and snorkel will usually cost from BZ$12 to BZ$20 ($6–$10/£3–£5) per person per day.

All of the Caye Caulker dive and snorkel operators offer trips to **Shark-Ray Alley ★★** and **Hol Chan Marine Reserve ★★**. These trips cost between BZ$90 and BZ$240 ($45–$120/£23–£60) per person, depending on whether it is a snorkel or scuba dive trip, how long the tour lasts, and whether or not there is a stop on Ambergris Caye. Many of these include a stop for lunch and a quick walk around town in San Pedro. See p. 112 for more information and a detailed description of Shark-Ray Alley and Hol Chan Marine Reserve.

One of my favorite options for snorkelers is a day cruise to Shark-Ray Alley and Hol Chan with **Raggamuffin Tours ★** (✆ **501/226-0348;** www.raggamuffintours.com) aboard a classic wooden Belizean sloop. The trip makes three distinct snorkel stops, and includes lunch on board the boat, snorkeling gear, and the park entrance fee for BZ$90 ($45/£23) per person.

Fun on Dry Land

Aside from sunbathing, reading, and relaxing, there's very little to do on Caye Caulker. However, you could head south of town to the **Caye Caulker Mini-Reserve.** Located on the southern outskirts of the town, the term "mini" is certainly fitting. Nevertheless, this local endeavor features a few gentle and well-cleared paths through a small stand of littoral forest. More serious bird-watchers might want to grab a boat and a guide and head to the northern half of the island, where 40 hectares (100 acres) on the very northern tip have been declared the **Caye Caulker Forest Reserve.** Over 130 species of resident and migrant birds have been spotted on and around Caye Caulker. So far, no admission fees are being charged at either reserve, but that could change.

Excursions on the Mainland

If you've been on the island for a while or just want to see more of Belize, a host of tour operators on Caye Caulker offer excursions to all of the major attractions and destinations around the country, including Altun Ha, Lamanai, Xunantunich, Mountain Pine Ridge, and even Tikal. You can also go cave tubing in the Caves Branch region. Most of these tours involve a flight in a small charter plane.

One of the most popular day trips is to the Maya ruins at Altun Ha. This is also one of the most economical, as it doesn't require a flight. This begins on a powerful little boat that will whisk you over to the mainland. You'll then take a taxi to the ruins and have lunch before returning to San Pedro. Most operators offering the Altun Ha trip include a lunch stop at Maruba Resort, with the option of adding on a decadent jungle spa treatment. Prices for these trips run around BZ$140 to BZ$200 ($70–$100/£35–£50). A similar trip by boat and land is offered to the ruins at Lamanai.

For trips involving a flight, prices range from BZ$200 to BZ$400 ($100–$200/£50–£100) per person, depending on the distance traveled and number of activities and attractions crammed into 1 day. Most hotels on the island can book these tours, or you can contact **Tsunami Adventures** (✆ **501/226-0462;** www.tsunamiadventures.com) a good, all-purpose operator with an extensive list of offerings on and under the water, and all around the cayes and mainland, as well.

WHERE TO STAY

Accommodations on Caye Caulker have improved over the years, but there are still no resorts or real luxury options to be had. In my opinion, this adds to the charm of the place. Budget and midrange lodging options are abundant, and some of these are quite comfortable.

Expensive

In addition to the below recommendation, **Auxillou Beach Suites** ★ (✆ **501/226-0370;** www.auxilloubeachsuites.com) are well-equipped oceanfront units, right near the center of town.

Iguana Reef ★★ This is the closest thing to a resort hotel on Caye Caulker. The spacious rooms are housed in several two-story concrete block structures. Most rooms come with two queen-size beds. All have air-conditioning, a stocked minibar, and a programmable safe. The deluxe units have a sitting area, a stereo CD player, and a semi-private veranda. A continental breakfast is served in a pleasant open-air dining area overlooking the water. Iguana Reef, which is on the lagoon or back side of the island, has a large and comfortable sandy area for lounging, with a pier leading off to a nice swimming spot. This is also arguably the best spot on the island to catch a sunset.

Back St. (P.O. Box 31), Caye Caulker. ✆ **501/226-0213.** Fax 501/226-0087. www.iguanareefinn.com. 12 units. BZ$270–BZ$330 ($135–$165/£68–£83) double; BZ$750 ($375/£188) penthouse. Rates include continental breakfast. Rates slightly higher during peak weeks, lower during the off season. DISC, MC, V. **Amenities:** Bar; laundry service; small outdoor pool. *In room:* A/C, stocked fridge, no phone, safe.

Moderate

In addition to the places listed below, **Popeye's Beach Resort** (✆ **501/226-0032;** www.popeyesbeachresort.com) and **Lazy Iguana B & B** (✆ **501/226-0350;** www.lazyiguana.net) are other good options in this price range.

Seaside Cabanas ★★ Rising from the ashes of a devastating fire, this hotel was rebuilt from scratch, and is better than ever. The whole complex is set in a horseshoe around a small rectangular pool, with a broad wooden deck around it. All the rooms are spacious and painted in lively yellows and reds, and feature modern decorative touches. Four of the rooms come with a private rooftop lounge areas with hammocks strung under an open-air thatch roof. These are by far my favorite rooms. There's no restaurant, but they have a great bar and an excellent tour desk.

Front St. (P.O. Box 39), Caye Caulker. ✆ **501/226-0498.** Fax 501/226-0125. www.seasidecabanas.com. 17 units. BZ$210–BZ$260 ($105–$130/£53–£65) double. Rates slightly higher during peak weeks, lower during the off season. AE, MC, V. No children under 10 allowed. **Amenities:** Bar; laundry service; outdoor pool. *In room:* A/C, TV, fridge, no phone.

Inexpensive

There are scores of budget options on Caye Caulker. I list my favorite and the most dependable choices below. In addition to these, **Tina's Backpacker's Hostel** (✆ **501/226-0351;** tinashostel.blogspot.com) is probably the best of the rock-bottom budget options, while both **Maxhapan Cabinas** (✆ **501/226-0118;** maxhapan04@hotmail.com) and **Sea Beezzz** (✆ **501/226-0176;** www.geocities.com/seabeezzz) get high marks for their intimate vibes and service.

De Real Macaw Value This place is located just north of the center of town, across from a little sandy park and the ocean on Front Street. The two "beachfront" rooms are the best rooms here, but all are very clean and well kept, with tile floors, tiny television sets, and a front porch or balcony. Most of the rooms come with air-conditioning, but you'll pay more for it. The two-bedroom "condo" and separate beach house both come with a full kitchen, and these folks also rent out fully furnished apartments on a weekly basis, located a little bit away towards the center of town.

Front St., north of Front Bridge, Caye Caulker. ✆ **501/226-0459.** Fax 501/226-0497. www.derealmacaw.biz. 7 units. BZ$50–BZ$110 ($25–$55/£13–£23) double with no A/C; BZ$120–BZ$140 ($60–$70/£30–£35) double with A/C; BZ$240–BZ$260 ($120–$130/£60–£65) condo or beach house. Rates lower in the off season. MC, V. *In room:* TV, fridge, safe, no phone.

Tree Tops Guest House ★ Set just off the ocean in the heart of town, this converted three-story home offers clean, spacious, and cool rooms. There are four rooms on the ground floor. Each comes with tile floors, high ceilings, a standing fan, a cable TV, and a small refrigerator. Two of these share a common bathroom down the hall, but each has a vanity sink in the room itself. However, the best rooms here are the two top-floor suites. Each comes with a king-size bed, cable television, air-conditioning, minifridge, telephone, and private balcony. The Sunset Suite is the best of these, with the largest balcony, and views to both the lagoon and the ocean. If you opt for one of the standard rooms, however, you can still enjoy the view from the rooftop lounge area, which features several hammocks hung under a shade roof.

On the waterfront south of Front Bridge (P.O. Box 29), Caye Caulker. ✆ **501/226-0240.** Fax 501/226-0115. www.treetopsbelize.com. 6 units (4 with private bathroom). BZ$94 ($47/£24) double with shared bathroom; BZ$120–BZ$184 ($60–$92/£30–£46) double with private bathroom. MC, V. *In room:* TV, fridge, no phone.

WHERE TO DINE

In addition to the places listed below, I've received good reports about the **Bamboo** (✆ **501/625-0339**) a beachfront restaurant serving a mix of Cajun and Caribbean–inspired fare, while **Agave** (✆ **501/226-0403**) is another excellent restaurant serving fusion cuisine. For fancy Italian fare, head to **Don Corleone** (✆ **501/226-0025**). Finally, while the food is good but unremarkable, you can't beat the location and ambience of **Rainbow Grill & Bar** (✆ **501/226-0281**), which is built out over the water.

Also, be sure to stop in at some point at the **Lighthouse Ice Cream Parlour** on Front Street, for a cone or scoop of some fresh, homemade ice cream.

Moderate

Habaneros ★★★ Finds INTERNATIONAL Although the name suggests a Mexican joint, the menu ranges far and wide. You can get homemade pastas and Thai coconut curries, as well as Brazilian pork. You can also get spicy fajitas made of beef, chicken, or jerk pork. The nightly specials tend to be inventive takes on whatever fresh fish and seafood has been caught that day. Heavy wooden tables are spread across the pleasant open-air wraparound veranda of this raised-stilt wooden home right on Front Street. There's also indoor seating, but you'll really want to try to grab one of the outdoor spots. Margaritas and sangria are served by the pitcher, and there's a pretty good wine list for Caye Caulker.

On Front St., near the center of town. ✆ **501/226-0487.** Reservations recommended during the high season. Main courses BZ$12–BZ$42 ($6–$22/£3–£11). MC, V. Daily 5:30–10pm.

Rasta Pasta Rainforest Café ★★ INTERNATIONAL There's a reason this place is perennially popular. The food is excellent, the menu eclectic, the portions huge, and the prices right. Appetizers include fabulous conch fritters and deep-fried crab rolls. There are several namesake pasta dishes, as well as Thai curries, and everything from chicken to conch and lobster is served grilled, blackened, or with a spicy Jamaican jerk sauce. Vegetarians are well cared for here as well, with various dishes to choose from. Save room for some of their B-52 Cheesecake, flavored with Bailey's and Kahlúa and baked in an Oreo cookie crust. If you like the food, be sure to pick up some of their homemade "Genesis in the Jungle" spice packages.

Front St., towards the south end of town. ✆ **501/206-0356.** Reservations recommended during the high season. Main courses BZ$12–BZ$30 ($6–$15/£3–£8). MC, V. Thurs–Tues 7am–10pm.

Inexpensive

Perhaps the best cheap eats on Caye Caulker are the various outdoor grills that set up nightly all along Front Street, offering up chicken, shrimp, beef, and lobster (in season) at very reasonable rates. In addition, there are several simple local restaurants serving fresh fish, seafood, and Belizean standards at very economical rates. The best of these are **Sand Box Restaurant** (✆ **501/226-0200**), **Syd's Restaurant & Bar** (✆ **501/206-0294**), and **Marin's Restaurant & Bar** (✆ **501/226-0104**). However, my favorite of these local joints is **Rose's Grill & Bar** (✆ **501/226-0085**), on the side street next to Habaneros. For breakfast, head to **Amor y Café** (✆ **501/601-4458**); to check out one of Caye Caulker's most popular spots, head to **Glenda's** (in back of Atlantic Bank; ✆ **501/226-2148**), which specializes in simple Mexican fare.

CAYE CAULKER AFTER DARK

For evening entertainment, you can stargaze, go for a night dive, or have a drink in one of the island's handful of bars. Periodically, one of the bars will crank up the music. In general, the scene is so small that most folks will congregate at one or two bars. Which one or two bars is happening might shift from night to night; ask a local or two, and you'll certainly be directed to the current hot spot. My favorite bar is the open-air **I&I Bar and Cafe ★**, which features rustic wooden plank swings for most of its seating. The bar itself takes up the second and third floors of this thatch-roofed wooden structure and is located on a cross street on the southern end of town. Right in the center of town on Front Street, the **Oceanside Bar** often has either live music or karaoke; the new **Barrier Reef Sports Bar & Grill** has a raucous vibe most nights; while out by the Split, there's sometimes a crowd at the **Lazy Lizard.** Finally, you might stop in to check out the scene and the music videos projected onto the large outdoor screen at **Herbal Tribe.**

GETTING OUT THERE: THE OUTER ATOLLS

Roughly due east of the northern cayes, out beyond the barrier reef, lie two of Belize's three open ocean atolls, Turneffe Island Atoll and Lighthouse Reef Atoll. The reef and island rings of tranquillity in the midst of the Caribbean Sea are stunning and pristine places. The outer island atolls are popular destinations for day trips out from Belize City, Ambergris Caye, and Caye Caulker. However, if you really want to experience their unique charms, you should stay at one of the few small lodges located right on the edge of one of them, or on one of the live-aboard dive boats that ply these waters.

Exploring the Atolls

Most folks come out here to do one of two things: fish or dive. Some do both. Both activities are truly world-class. In broad strokes, fishermen should head to Turneffe Island Atoll, while dedicated and serious divers would probably want to choose Lighthouse Reef Atoll, although there's great diving to be had off Turneffe.

TURNEFFE ISLAND ATOLL ★★ This is the largest of Belize's three ocean atolls, and the largest in the Caribbean Sea. Both the diving and fishing here are excellent, but the fishing gets a slight nod. The extensive mangrove and saltwater flats are perfect territory for stalking permit, bonefish, snook, and tarpon. Most fishing is done with fly rods, either wading in the flats or from a poled skiff. Turneffe Island Atoll also boasts scores of world-class wall, coral, and sponge garden, and drift dive sites. Most of these sites are located around the southern tip of the atoll. Perhaps the most famous dive site here is the **Elbow ★★★**, a jutting coral point with steep drop-offs, huge sponges, and ample fish life. Another popular site is **Rendezvous Point ★★**, which features several grottoes that divers can swim in and out of, and there's a small modern wreck, the ***Sayonara,*** sitting in about 9m (30 ft.) of water.

LIGHTHOUSE REEF ATOLL ★★ Boasting nearly 81km (50 miles) of wall and reef diving, including some of the best and most coveted dive sites in all of the Caribbean, this is a true scuba-diving mecca. As the atoll farthest from shore, its waters are incredibly clear and pristine. The central lagoon of this atoll is some 48km (30 miles) long and around 13km (8 miles) wide at its widest point. In the center, you'll find the world-famous **Blue Hole ★★**, a perfectly round mid-atoll sinkhole that plunges straight down to a depth of over 120m (400 ft.). You'll see postcards, photos, and T-shirts all over town showing off aerial views of this perfectly round hole in the ocean. Nearly 300m (1,000 ft.) across, the Blue Hole's eroded limestone karst walls and stalactite formations make this a unique and justifiably popular dive site. However, some of the wall and coral garden dives around the outer edges of the atoll are even better. Of these, **Half Moon Caye Wall ★★** and **North Long Caye Wall ★★** are consistently considered some of the best clear-water coral wall dives in the world.

Water conditions here are amazingly consistent, with an average water temperature of around 80°F (27°C), while visibility on the outer atoll walls and reefs easily averages over 30m (100 ft.).

Where to Stay on the Outer Atolls

The lodgings out on the outer atolls are isolated, plush, and pricey. The two main lodges are both located on Turneffe Island Atoll, but at widely different spots. Both offer diving and fishing packages, with all transportation, meals, lodging, and activities included. If this is what you're looking for, check out **Turneffe Flats ★★** (✆ **888/512-8812** in the U.S.; www.tflats.com) or **Turneffe Island Lodge ★★** (✆ **800/874-0118** in the U.S.; www.turneffelodge.com).

Getting There These are remote and isolated destinations. Aside from the lodges, which all offer their own transportation, there is no regularly scheduled transportation out here. However, private water taxis and charter flights can be arranged.

Turneffe Island Atoll is a 1½- to 2-hour boat ride from Belize City. The lodges listed above provide their own transportation to and from Belize City as part of their vacation packages.

The quickest and easiest way to get out to these atolls is by helicopter. **Astrum Helicopter** (✆ **501/222-5100;** www.astrumhelicopters.com) will take you out here for BZ$2,500 ($1,250/£625) in a helicopter that will hold four passengers, and BZ$3,750 ($1,875/£938) in a six-passenger bird.

7 SAN IGNACIO & THE CAYO DISTRICT ★★

116km (72 miles) W of Belize City; 32km (20 miles) W of Belmopan; 14km (9 miles) E of the Guatemalan border

Western Belize, from the capital city of Belmopan to the Guatemalan border, is a land of rolling hills, dense jungles, abundant waterfalls, clear rivers, extensive caves, and numerous Maya ruins. This region was the heart of the Belizean Maya world, with the major ruins of **Caracol, Xunantunich,** and **El Pilar,** as well as lesser sites like **Cahal Pech.** At the height of the Classic Maya period, there were more residents in this area than in all of modern Belize.

Today, the Cayo District is the heart of Belize's ecotourism industry. There are a host of national parks and protected areas. The pine forests and rainforests here are great for hiking and bird-watching; the rivers are excellent for canoeing, kayaking, and inner tubing; and the dirt roads are perfect for horseback riding and mountain biking.

The cave systems of the Cayo District were sacred to the ancient Maya, and many of them are open for exploration by budding and experienced spelunkers alike. Some of the more popular underground attractions include **Actun Tunichil Muknal, Barton Creek Cave, Chechem Ha, Crystal Cave,** and the **Río Frío Cave.** Of particular interest is the **Caves Branch River,** which provides the unique opportunity to float on an inner tube, kayak, or canoe through a series of caves.

In the foothills of the mountains close to the Guatemalan border lie the sister towns of Santa Elena and San Ignacio, which are set on either side of the beautiful Macal River. For all intents and purposes, San Ignacio is the more important town, both in general terms and particularly for travelers. Just north of town, the Macal and Mopan rivers converge to form the Belize River.

ESSENTIALS

Getting There

BY BUS San Ignacio has very frequent bus service from Belize City. Buses to San Ignacio leave roughly every half-hour from the main bus station on West Collet Canal Street between 5am and 8pm. Return buses to Belize City leave the main bus station in San Ignacio roughly every half-hour between 4am and 6pm. The fare is BZ$10 ($5/£2.50). The trip takes 2½ hours. Most of the western-bound buses continue on beyond San Ignacio to Benque Viejo and the Guatemalan border. There is no regular direct bus service to the Mountain Pine Ridge area from Belize City.

For Short

The name "Cayo" is used to refer to both the Cayo District as well as to the city of San Ignacio.

BY CAR Take the Western Highway from Belize City. It's a straight shot all the way to San Ignacio. You'll come to the small town of Santa Elena first. Across the Macal River lies San Ignacio. If you're heading to San Ignacio and points west, a well-marked detour will lead you through the town of Santa Elena to a Balley bridge that enters San Ignacio towards the north end of town. The more prominent and impressive Hawksworth Bridge is solely for traffic heading east out of San Ignacio towards Santa Elena, Belmopan, and Belize City.

If you're driving to the Mountain Pine Ridge area, the first turnoff is at Georgeville, around Mile Marker 61. This is the quickest route if you're going deep into the Mountain Pine Ridge area and to Caracol. There's another turnoff in the town of Santa Elena that will take you through Cristo Rey and San Antonio villages, as well as to some of the lodges listed below. Whichever of these routes you take, the roads merge around Mile Marker 10, where you will come to the entrance to the Mountain Pine Ridge Forest Reserve. A guard will ask you where you are going, and if you have a reservation, but there is no fee to enter the reserve.

Getting Around

San Ignacio is quite compact and easily navigated by foot. If you want to visit any of the attractions listed below, you'll probably have to find transportation. Frequent buses (see above) will take you to the entrances to most of the hotels listed below on Benque Viejo Road, as well as within walking distance of the Xunantunich ruins. Infrequent buses (ask around town or at the bus station; ✆ **501/824-3360**) do service the Mountain Pine Ridge area. However, if you don't have your own vehicle, you will probably need to take some taxis or go on organized tours.

You can rent a car from **Cayo Rentals** (✆ **501/824-2222;** www.cayoautorentals.com) or **Matus Car Rental** (✆ **501/824-2005;** www.matuscarrental.com). A small four-wheel-drive vehicle here should run you around BZ$150 to BZ$200 ($75–$100/£38–£50) per day.

If you need a cab, call the **Cayo Taxi Association** (✆ **501/824-2196**) or **San Ignacio Taxi Stand** (✆ **501/824-2155**). Taxi fares around the Cayo District should run you as follows: BZ$6 ($3/£1.50) around town; BZ$55 ($23/£11) between San Ignacio and Chaa Creek or duPlooy's; and BZ$80 to BZ$120 ($40–$60/£20–£30) between San Ignacio and Mountain Pine Ridge. Collective taxis run regularly between downtown San Ignacio and the border at Benque Viejo; the fare is BZ$6 ($3/£1.50) per person.

Visitor Information & Fast Facts

There are several banks right in the heart of downtown San Ignacio: **Atlantic Bank,** at Burns Avenue and Columbus Park (✆ **501/824-2347**); **Scotiabank,** at Burns Avenue and Riverside Street (✆ **501/824-4190**); and **Belize Bank,** 16 Burns Ave. (✆ **501/824-2031**).

To reach the **police,** dial ✆ **911** or 501/824-2022; for the **fire department,** dial ✆ **501/824-2095.** The **San Ignacio Hospital** is on Simpson Street, on the western side of town (✆ **501/824-2066**). The **post office** (✆ **501/824-2049**) is on Hudson Street, near the corner of Waight's Avenue.

If you need to log on, head to **Eva's Restaurant,** 22 Burns Ave. (✆ **501/804-2267**); or the **Café Sol,** Far West St. (✆ **501/824-2166**). Both offer a few computers with high-speed Internet connections. Eva's is one of the most popular restaurants and meeting places in town, while the Café Sol also offers free Wi-Fi.

There are no towns, banks, or general services in the Mountain Pine Ridge, although most hotels in the area do have Internet service.

WHAT TO SEE & DO

The Cayo District is Belize's prime inland tourist destination. There's a lot to see and do in this area, from visiting Maya ruins and caves to a broad range of adventure activities. Most hotels in the area either have their own tour operations or can hook you up with a reputable local operator. In addition, there are several long-standing tour agencies based in San Ignacio. Some of the best of these include **Cayo Adventure Tours** (✆ **501/824-3246;** www.cayoadventure.com), **Pacz Tours** ★★ (✆ **501/824-2477;** www.pacztours.net) and **Yute Expeditions** ★★ (✆ **501/824-2076;** www.inlandbelize.com). All of these companies offer virtually all of the options listed in this chapter and more, including multiday tours and adventures.

Maya Ruins

The Cayo District is in the heart of the Maya highlands, with several major ruins and cave systems used by the ancient residents of this region. The most impressive are **Xunantunich** ★★ (on Benque Viejo Rd.) and **Caracol** ★★. Close by, in Guatemala, lies **Tikal** ★★★, perhaps one of the best excavated and most impressive Maya cities in Mesoamerica. See chapter 5 for complete coverage.

XUNANTUNICH ★★ Although you may have trouble pronouncing it (say "Zoo-nahn-too-*neetch*"), Xunantunich is an impressive, well-excavated, and easily accessible Maya site. The name translates as "maiden of the rocks." The main pyramid here, El Castillo, rises to 38m (127 ft.) and is clearly visible from the Western Highway as you approach. It's a steep climb, but the view from the top is amazing—don't miss it. You'll be able to make out the twin border towns of Benque Viejo, Belize, and Melchor de Menchos, Guatemala. On the east side of the pyramid, near the top, is a remarkably well-preserved stucco frieze.

Down below in the temple forecourt, archaeologists found three magnificent stelae portraying rulers of the region. These have been moved to the protection of the small, on-site museum, yet the years and ravages of weather have made most of the carvings difficult to decipher. Xunantunich was a thriving Maya city about the same time as Altun Ha, in the Classic Period, about A.D. 600 to 900.

The visitor center at the entrance contains a beautiful scale model of the old city, as well as a replica of the original frieze. Open daily from 8am to 4pm, the site charges an admission of BZ$10 ($5/£2.50). Xunantunich is 10km (6$^1/_2$ miles) past San Ignacio on the road to Benque Viejo. To reach the ruins, you must cross the Mopan River aboard a tiny hand-cranked car ferry in the village of San José Succotz. After crossing the river, it's a short, but dusty and vigorous, uphill walk to the ruins. If you've got your own vehicle, you can take it across on the ferry and drive right to the ruins. To get here by bus, take any bus bound for Benque Viejo and get off in San José Succotz.

Fun Facts **Sky Scraper**

The largest pyramid at Caracol, **Caana** or "Sky Palace," stands some 41m (136 ft.) high, and is the tallest Maya building in Belize, and still the tallest man-made structure in the country.

CARACOL ★★ Caracol (www.caracol.org) is the largest known Maya archaeological site in Belize, and one of the great Maya city-states of the Classic era (A.D. 250–950). At one point, Caracol supported a population of over 150,000. Caracol, which means "shell" in Spanish, gets its name from the large number of snail shells found here during early explorations.

Caracol has revealed a wealth of informative carved glyphs that have allowed archaeologists to fill in much of the history of this once powerful city-state. Glyphs here claim Caracol defeats of rivals Tikal in A.D. 562 and Naranjo in 631. One of the earliest temples here was built in A.D. 70, and the Caracol royal family has been officially chronicled since 331. The last recorded date on a glyph is 859, and archaeologists conclude that by 1050 Caracol had been completely abandoned.

Caracol is open daily from 8am to 4pm; admission is BZ$15 ($7.50/£3.75). There's a small visitor center at the entrance, and a guide can sometimes be hired here, although most visitors come with their own guide as part of an organized tour. Caracol is about 81km (50 miles) along a dirt road from the Western Highway. Actually, the final 16km (10 miles) in to the park are paved. Plan on the drive taking about 2 hours, or more if the road is in bad shape. A visit to Caracol is often combined with a stop at the Río On Pools, or some of the other attractions in the Mountain Pine Ridge area.

Will Natural Wonders Never Cease?

WATERFALLS Waterfalls are abundant in this region. Perhaps my favorite is the falls found at the **Río On Pools ★★**. This is a series of falls and pools somewhat reminiscent of Ocho Ríos in Jamaica. There's an entrance hut and parking lot when you enter the area. From here, some concrete steps lead straight down a steep hill to the base of the falls. While the views and swimming are fine at the bottom, it's a very strenuous hike back up, and I think you'll find better pools and views by hiking a few minutes upstream. Here you'll find numerous pools and rapids flowing between big rocks. Many of these rocks are perfect for sunbathing. The Río On Pools are located at around Mile Marker 18½ of the Pine Ridge Road. There's no entrance fee.

You can also visit the **Five Sister Falls ★★**, a lovely series of cascading falls, that divide into five distinct side-by-side cascades just above the riverside beach and bar area of the Five Sisters Lodge. If you are not staying at the lodge, you may visit the falls for BZ$5 ($2.50/£1.25). For an extra charge of BZ$6 ($3/£1.50), a funicular will take you to and from the base of the falls, where the hotel has a little beach area and several natural swimming holes. There are some nature trails you can hike, and a small snack bar, restrooms, and changing facilities. You'll even find a wonderful open-air thatch palapa on the banks of the river strung with hammocks—a compelling spot for an afternoon siesta.

BARTON CREEK CAVE ★ This is one of the area's easier and more relaxing caves to explore. The trip is conducted entirely by canoe, and while there are a few tight squeezes and areas with low ceilings, in general you won't get as wet (you'll stay dry) or claustrophobic here as you will at some of the other caves in Belize. Located beside a small Mennonite community, Barton Creek is navigable for nearly a mile inside the cave. Along the way, by the light of headlamps and strong flashlights, you'll see wonderful natural formations, a large gallery, and numerous Maya artifacts, including several skeletons believed to be the remains of ritual sacrifices.

There's a BZ$10 ($5/£2.50) fee to visit the site, but that doesn't include the canoe trip or transportation. If you drive there yourself, you can hire a canoe that holds two passengers, plus the guide, for around BZ$30 to BZ$40 ($15–$20/£7.50–£10). Tours out of San Ignacio average around BZ$60 to BZ$120 ($30–$60/£15–£30) per person, not including the entrance fee. Barton Creek Cave is located just off the Pine Ridge Road, about 6km (4 miles) from the Western Highway.

RÍO FRIO CAVE This high vaulted cave is about 180m (600 ft.) long and open at both ends, with a lazy creek flowing through it. There's a path leading through the cave, and several hiking trails through the forests surrounding it. Along the neighboring trails you will find other caves that you can venture into. However, be careful and be sure to have a good flashlight. To reach the Río Frío Cave, drive the Pine Ridge Road to Douglas Da Silva Village at about Mile Marker 24. Do not follow the turnoff for Caracol, but head into the little village. Here you will see signs for the turnoff to the cave. The cave is about a mile outside the village. There's a small parking area very close to the mouth of the cave and a couple of picnic tables and benches along the river. No admission is charged to visit here.

BUTTERFLIES The **Green Hills Butterfly Ranch & Botanical Collection** (**© 501/820-4017;** www.green-hills.net) is a lovely project where you'll get to see numerous butterfly species and a range of tropical flora. These folks raise dozens of species of butterflies, and visitors get to see them up close and personal. Located near Mile Marker 8 of the Pine Ridge Road, the ranch offers guided tours (BZ$10/$5/£2.50) daily, between 8am and 3:30pm. Reservations are recommended.

Just off the main road at Mile Marker 71½ near the village of San José Succotz, **Tropical Wings Nature Center** (**© 501/823-2265**) similarly features an enclosed butterfly garden with scores of brightly colored and varied species flitting about. There's also a butterfly breeding center, as well as an open-air medicinal plant nature trail. Hummingbird feeders ensure that you'll be buzzed by these frenetic flighty creatures. This place is open daily from 9am to 5pm; admission is BZ$6 ($3/£1.50).

BOTANICAL GARDENS ★★ Located next to duPlooy's and run by the same family, the **Belize Botanic Gardens ★★** (**© 501/824-3101;** www.belizebotanic.org) is a sprawling collection of local and imported tropical fauna. They have an excellent mix of fruit trees, palms, bromeliads, and bamboos, all well laid out whether or not you are taking a self-guided or guided tour. The orchid house is not to be missed, with its beautiful collection of orchids and sculpted waterfall wall. The gardens are open daily from 7am to 5pm. Admission is BZ$10 ($5/£2.50). Guided tours cost BZ$20 ($10/£5) per person, including the entrance fee. You can buy a helpful self-guided tour booklet, or take a leisurely horse-and-buggy ride through the lovely gardens.

Located directly between the Chaa Creek and the Macal River Jungle Camp, the **Rainforest Medicine Trail ★** (**© 501/824-2037**) is the former Ix Chel Farm, which was set up by Drs. Rosita Arvigo and Greg Shropshire. Rosita studied traditional herbal medicine with Don Elijio Panti, a local Maya medicine man and a folk hero in Belize. The farm boasts a small gift shop that features local crafts, T-shirts, and several relevant books, including a couple by Arvigo. You'll also find Ix Chel's line of herbal concentrates, salves, and teas called Rainforest Remedies. Self-guided visits to the Medicine Trail, along with a tour of Chaa Creek's Natural History Museum, and a visit to their Blue Morpho Butterfly Breeding project, cost BZ$18 ($9/£4.50). You can easily spend 3 hours visiting all three attractions.

Other Adventure Activities

HORSEBACK RIDING The terrain here is wonderful for horseback riding. Most horseback tours will take you to one or more of the major attractions in this area, or at least to some quiet swimming hole or isolated waterfall. Most of the hotels here offer horseback riding tours. Or, you can contact the folks at **Mountain Equestrian Trails** ★ (✆ **501/820-4041;** www.metbelize.com), who have one of the better horse-riding operations in the Cayo District. A half-day trip including lunch costs BZ$122 ($61/£31) per person; a full-day trip costs BZ$166 ($83/£42).

MOUNTAIN BIKING This region lends itself equally well to mountain biking. The same trails and dirt roads that are used by cars and horses are especially well suited for fat-tire explorations. Most of the hotels in the region have bikes for rent or free for guests. If not, you'll probably have to have them arrange it for you, or contact an agency in San Ignacio.

RIVER TRIPS For much of Belize's history, the rivers were the main highways. The Maya used them for trading, and British loggers used them to move mahogany and logwood. If you're interested, you can explore the Cayo District's two rivers—the Macal and Mopan—by canoe, kayak, and inner tube.

Most tours put in upstream on one of the rivers and then float leisurely downstream. The trip can take anywhere from 1 to 3 hours, depending on how much time you spend paddling, floating, or stopping to hike or swim.

In addition to the tour operators listed above, you can contact **Toni's River Adventures** (✆ **501/824-3292**) or **David's Adventure Tours** (✆ **501/824-3674**). If you want to go inner tubing, contact the folks at the **Trek Stop** (✆ **501/823-2265;** www.thetrekstop.com).

Shopping

If you're in the area, be sure to stop at the **Tanah Mayan Art Museum** ★ (✆ **501/824-3310;** daily 8am–5pm), run by the Garcia Sisters, some of the premier artisans working in carved slate. While it's a stretch to call their little shop and showroom a museum, you will find a nice collection of the Garcia sisters' carvings, as well as other Maya artifacts and handicrafts. This place is located at about Mile Marker 8 of the Cristo Rey Road, about 1.6km (1 mile) before you reach the village of San Antonio. Inside the village, you should stop at the **Magaña Zaactunich Art Gallery** (no phone), which carries a range of local craftworks and specializes in woodcarvings.

WHERE TO STAY

While San Ignacio is the regional hub and makes a good base, the real attractions in this area are up the rivers and in the forests. Just north of San Ignacio are several lodges set somewhat off the beaten path, where you can canoe down clear rivers, ride horses to Maya ruins, hike jungle trails, and spot scores of birds. Out on the road to Caracol and Mountain Pine Ridge, there are more of these lodges. Except for the true budget traveler, I recommend that you stay at one of these lodges if you can. All offer a wide range of active adventures and tours to all the principle sites in the area.

Very Expensive

Blancaneaux Lodge ★★ This remote lodge was built with style and grace, which is fitting, as the owner is director Francis Ford Coppola. The lodge is set on a steep pine-forested hillside, overlooking the Privassion River and a series of gentle falls. The individual *cabañas* here are all comfortable and intimate, with wood floors, a private balcony or deck, and a mix of furnishings and decorations from around the world that blend together in a sort of chic world fusion. My favorite *cabañas* are the riverfront "honeymoon" units, which have private plunge pools. Most of the villas are two-bedroom, two-bathroom affairs. The best feature of these is their large, open-air central living area, which flows into a forest and river-view deck. There are two restaurants and two pools here, as well as a full-service riverside spa. The masseuses are from Thailand, and provide Thai massage, alongside a host of other treatments.

Mountain Pine Ridge Reserve (P.O. Box B, Central Farm), Cayo District. ✆ **800/746-3743** in the U.S., 501/824-4912 reservations office in Belize, or 824-3878 at the lodge. Fax 501/824-3919. www.blancaneaux.com. 20 units. BZ$520–BZ$990 ($260–$495/£130–£248) double cabin; BZ$1,000–BZ$1,350 ($500–$675/£250–£338) 2-bedroom villa. Rates include continental breakfast. Rates lower in the off season, higher during peak weeks. AE, MC, V. **Amenities:** Restaurant; bar; lounge; airstrip; bike rental; horse stables; laundry service; outdoor pool; small spa. *In room:* Safe, no phone, free Wi-Fi.

Chaa Creek ★★★ (Finds) This is the premier lodging choice in this neck of the woods, and one of the best hotels in the country. Much loving care has gone into creating the beautiful grounds and cottages here. Located on a high, steep bank over the Macal River, all of the thatched-roof cottages are artistically decorated with local and Guatemalan textiles and handicrafts. Each comes with a quiet porch or balcony area set amid the flowering gardens. My favorite rooms are the large treetop suites, which feature a queen-size bed, a sunken living-room area, and a wraparound deck fitted with a sunken Jacuzzi. Canoes and mountain bikes are available, and horseback rides can always be arranged. Over 250 bird species have been spotted within a 8km (5-mile) radius of the lodge. The guides here are well trained and knowledgeable, and much of the food served is organically grown on the hotel's own farm.

Off the road to Benque Viejo (P.O. Box 53, San Ignacio), Cayo District. ✆ **501/824-2037** reservations office, or 820-4010 at the lodge. Fax 501/824-2501. www.chaacreek.com. 23 units. BZ$600 ($300/£150) double; BZ$500–BZ$1,150 ($350–$575/£175–£288) suite or villa. AE, MC, V. To reach Chaa Creek, drive 8km (5 miles) west from San Ignacio and watch for the sign on your left. It's another 3.2km (2 miles) down a rough dirt road from the main highway. **Amenities:** Restaurant; bar; lounge; bike rental; laundry service; nonsmoking rooms; midsize outdoor pool; small, well-equipped spa; free Wi-Fi. *In room:* No phone.

Expensive

In addition to the places listed below, the **San Ignacio Resort Hotel** ★ (✆ **800/822-3274** in the U.S.; www.sanignaciobelize.com) is a plush option right in the town of San Ignacio, while **Five Sisters Lodge** (✆ **800/447-2931** in the U.S.; www.fivesisterslodge.com) is a good choice out in Mountain Pine Ridge, at the site of the impressive Five Sisters Falls. **Hidden Valley Inn** ★★ (✆ **866/443-3364** in the U.S., or 501/822-3320 in Belize; www.hiddenvalleyinn.com) is an isolated mountain resort situated in a beautiful setting, close to the Hidden Valley, or Thousand Foot Falls, the tallest waterfall in Belize.

duPlooy's ★ This family-run lodge overlooks the Macal River, with jungle-covered limestone cliffs opposite. This stunning location, combined with personalized attention, make duPlooy's one of Cayo's most popular jungle lodges. My favorite rooms here are the spacious bungalows, which come with a king-size bed, futon couch, and large wooden veranda. The lodge's open-air bar features a spacious deck overlooking the river. There's a beach on the river, as well as several trails through the forest. Horses and canoes are available for rent. One of the nicest features here, though, is an elevated walkway running at the level of the forest canopy, which connects much of the complex and also juts out into the forest, offering up wonderful opportunities for bird-watching. Neighboring **Belize Botanic Gardens ★★** provides even greater bird-watching opportunities, in addition to an abundance of tropical flora.

Off the road to Benque Viejo (P.O. Box 180, San Ignacio), Cayo District. ✆ **501/824-3101.** Fax 501/824-3301. www.duplooys.com. 19 units. BZ$360–BZ$450 ($180–$225/£90–£113) double; BZ$520-BZ$580 ($260–$290/£130–£145) casita or suite. Rates include breakfast. AE, MC, V. To get here, head out of town on the road to Benque Viejo; the turnoff for duPlooy's is the same as that for Chaa Creek, and it is well marked. DuPlooy's is a bit farther on the same dirt road, but be sure to take the right fork and follow the signs. **Amenities:** Restaurant; bar; lounge; laundry service; small spa. *In room:* No phone.

Moderate

In this price range, the **Cahal Pech Village Resort** (✆ **888/790-5264** in the U.S. and Canada, or 501/824-3740 in Belize; fax 501/824-2225; www.cahalpech.com), on the outskirts of San Ignacio, is worth considering, as are the two riverside options: **Clarissa Falls Resort** (✆/fax **501/824-3916;** www.clarissafalls.com) and **Macal River Jungle Camp** (✆ **501/824-2037;** www.belizecamp.com).

Black Rock Jungle River Lodge ★ Finds So, you *really* want to get away from it all? Well, this is the place. The setting, on a high bluff overlooking the Macal River, is one of the nicest in the area. Swimming and inner tubing on the river from the lodge are excellent. The deluxe *cabañas* are beautiful, with stone floors, two queen-size beds, plenty of large screened windows, and views of the valley and river below from a private veranda. The standard *cabañas* and shared bathroom units are quite comfortable and beautifully situated as well. Meals are served in the large open-air dining room and main lodge area, which also has a fabulous view of the river below and forests all around.

Off the road to Benque Viejo (P.O. Box 48, San Ignacio), Cayo District. ✆ **501/824-2529** reservations office, or 501/820-3929 at the lodge. www.blackrocklodge.com. 14 units (1 with shared bathroom). BZ$140 ($70/£35) double with shared bathroom; BZ$220–BZ$350 ($110–$175/£55–£88) double. Rates lower in the off-season; higher during peak periods. MC, V. If you're driving, take the turnoff for Chaa Creek and duPlooy's, and then follow the signs to Black Rock. **Amenities:** Restaurant; laundry service. *In room:* No phone.

Inexpensive

There are a host of good budget options right in San Ignacio. During the high season, reservations are recommended for the more popular places. At other times, backpackers might prefer to arrive in town early enough to visit a few places, and see which place gives the best bang for the buck. Of the backpacker-geared options, I like the **Hi-Et,** 12 West St. (✆ **501/824-2828**), with its hostel-like vibe and playful name. For a few more dollars and some more comfort, check out the **Casa Blanca Guest House,** 10 Burns Ave. (✆/fax **501/824-2080;** www.casablancaguesthouse.com).

Martha's Guest House This cozy guesthouse is located in the heart of San Ignacio, above a popular restaurant. The vibe here is somewhere between that of a home stay and a youth hostel. All of the rooms are immaculate. The more expensive rooms are larger and have minifridges and coffeemakers. There are also a couple of common lounge and balcony areas, where guests can hang out and read a book or chat. The fourth-floor First Lady suite is huge, and features a large balcony with wonderful views of the town. These folks also have a separate option a few blocks away that they are calling the Inn at Martha's, with fully equipped studio apartments.

10 West St. (P.O. Box 140), San Ignacio, Cayo District. ✆ **501/804-3647.** Fax 501/804-2917. www.marthasbelize.com. 10 units. BZ$80–BZ$110 ($40–$55/£20–£23) double; BZ$120–BZ$160 ($60–$80/£30–£40) suite. AE, MC, V. **Amenities:** Restaurant; bar; 2 lounges; laundry service. *In room:* TV, no phone.

The Trek Stop This rustic little outpost is geared towards backpackers and adventure travelers. The accommodations are spread around a broad garden and backed by dense forest, and range from campsites, to simple cabins, to a couple of newer cabins with private bathrooms. Most of the wooden cabins are quite small, but they do come with a private little front porch, where you can sit and read. Guests can either eat at the little restaurant here, or cook their own food in the communal kitchen. A wide range of tours and activities are offered, and inner tubing on the Mopan River is one of their specialties. They also have a 9-hole Frisbee golf course, which is free for guests, and costs BZ$6 ($3/£1.50) per person for visitors.

Benque Viejo Rd., Mile Marker 71½, San José Succotz, Cayo District. ✆ **501/823-2265.** www.thetrekstop.com. 10 units (8 with shared bathroom). BZ$76 ($38/£19) double cabin; BZ$48–BZ$56 ($24–$28/£12–£14) double with shared bathroom; BZ$10 ($5/£2.50) per person camping. MC, V. **Amenities:** Restaurant; laundry service; mountain-bike rental; free Wi-Fi. *In room:* No phone.

WHERE TO DINE

Moderate

Running W Steak House ★★ STEAK/BELIZEAN This restaurant is located in the San Ignacio Resort Hotel and is affiliated with Belize's largest beef and cattle operation, its namesake. Try the Mayan Steak, marinated strips of tenderloin grilled and served with fresh tortillas. If you want something more traditional, order the 16-ounce porterhouse. There are also fish and chicken dishes, as well as some Belizean standards. The dining room is large and comfortable, with plenty of varnished wood. A few wrought-iron tables line an outdoor patio and make a great place to have lunch with a jungle view, or dinner under the stars.

18 Buena Vista St., in the San Ignacio Resort Hotel. ✆ **501/824-2034.** Reservations recommended. Main courses BZ$16–BZ$50 ($8–$25/£4–£13). AE, MC, V. Daily 7am–11pm.

Inexpensive

In addition to the places listed below, **Hannah's,** 5 Burns Ave. (✆ **501/824-3014**), is the place to go for Indian and Pan-Asian food, while **Martha's Restaurant & Pizza House,** 10 West St. (✆ **501/804-3647**), is a friendly hangout serving local food and pizzas. You might also want to take the adventure of finding **Sanny's Grill,** 23rd Street (✆ **501/824-2988**), which is tucked away in a residential neighborhood, but serves up excellent seafood and grilled meats. For inexpensive eats in a large outdoor setting, you can try **Hode's Place Bar & Grill** (✆ **501/804-2522**), on the northern end of town.

Café Sol ★ Finds INTERNATIONAL/VEGETARIAN This homey restaurant and coffeehouse features an eclectic menu ranging from a Thai noodle salad to jerk chicken to soy burgers. You can also get burritos and quesadillas, and a range of pasta dishes, as well as hearty sandwiches on fresh baked focaccia. Be sure to check the chalkboard for daily specials. I like the tables on the covered front porch; inside, you'll find a small Internet cafe and a helpful corkboard with a variety of tour and hotel info. This is a great place for everything from breakfast to a coffee break to a filling meal.

Far West St. ✆ **501/824-2166.** Main courses BZ$12–BZ$20 ($6–$10/£3–£5). MC, V. Tues–Sat 7am–9pm; Sun 7am–2:30pm.

Eva's Restaurant & Bar *Finds* BELIZEAN/INTERNATIONAL Above and beyond dishing up good economical meals, Eva's serves as San Ignacio's central meeting place and unofficial tourist bureau. Hotel and tour advertisements cover the walls here, and brochures are abundant. The social scene is the main draw, but you can also get hearty servings of well-prepared Belizean and Mexican standards. If you want to get a group of people together to rent a taxi or canoe or to defray the costs of a tour, this is a good place to find other like-minded folks.

22 Burns Ave. ✆ **501/804-2267.** Main courses BZ$6–BZ$18 ($3–$9/£1.50–£4.50). MC, V. Daily 7am–midnight.

SAN IGNACIO AFTER DARK

San Ignacio is a pretty sleepy town. Many travelers end up at **Eva's Restaurant & Bar,** trading tales and planning adventures with new friends. Several bars are around the downtown area, though. Most nights, but especially on weekends, the most happening spot in town can be found up the hill at the **Stork Club** (✆ **501/824-2034**), which is in the San Ignacio Resort Hotel. This place has karaoke on Thursday nights, and live bands often on the weekends. On the north end of town, **Hode's Place Bar & Grill** (✆ **501/804-2522**) is a massive spot that is very popular with locals. They have a tiny casino, as well as a large video arcade, and pool and foosball tables.

If you're the gambling type, you'll want to head to the **Princess Casino** (✆ **501/824-4099**), which is also in the San Ignacio Resort Hotel. I'd definitely choose this one over the very little casino at **Hode's Place** (✆ **501/804-2522**).

CAVE EXCURSIONS FROM THE CAYO DISTRICT

The ancient Maya believed that caves were a mystical portal between the world of the living and the underworld of spirits and the dead. From their earliest days, there is evidence that the Maya made extensive use of caves for ritual purposes, as well as for more mundane and rudimentary things as keeping dry, storing grains, and gathering water. They called this mystical realm **Xibalba.**

Belize is literally riddled with caves. In almost every explored cave to date, some evidence of use by the Maya has been uncovered. Fire pits, campsites, burial mounds, and ritual altars have all been found. Numerous pieces of pottery and abundant bones and artifacts have also been encountered. Belize offers many unique and easily accessible opportunities to explore this fascinating world, on foot, by kayak or canoe, or by floating on an inner tube. Don't miss it.

Caves Branch River Cave System ★★★

The Caves Branch River is a gently flowing body of water coming down off the Mountain Pine Ridge. It really should be called a creek in most places. However, what makes the Caves Branch River unique is the fact that it flows in and out of a series of long limestone caves that are easily navigable on inner tubes and in kayaks.

There are two major entry points along the river for visits to the Caves Branch caves: One is at **Ian Anderson's Caves Branch** jungle lodge (Mile Marker 41½ Hummingbird Hwy; ✆ **501/822-2800;** www.cavesbranch.com), and the other is just above **Jaguar Paw,** a luxury hotel built on the banks of the river (Mile Marker 37 Western Hwy; ✆ **501/820-2023;** www.jaguarpaw.com). In general terms, travelers looking for more adventurous and gritty trips into the caves should head to Ian Anderson's place; those seeking a more luxurious excursion into the underworld should head to Jaguar Paw. Still,

 **For the Most Enjoyable Experience**

The Caves Branch River cave system is a very popular tourist attraction, and it can get crowded at times, especially in the three caves closest to Jaguar Paw and the public entrance. When the cruise-ship groups are in the caves, it's downright overcrowded. Whatever tour operator you use, try to time it so that you avoid other large groups if possible. I also highly recommend hiking the extra 15 minutes or so upstream to get to the fourth cave. However, if you choose to do the tour with Ian Anderson's Cave's Branch outfit, you are assured of avoiding the crowds. Also, wear plenty of insect repellent, as the mosquitoes can be fierce here (only on the hike—once you're in the caves there are none).

for anyone looking for some serious cave adventures and explorations, both of the aforementioned lodges offer a host of guided tours to much less commonly explored caves, including the fabulous **Crystal Cave ★★**, located just off the Jaguar Paw grounds.

By far, most visitors go either directly through Jaguar Paw or use the same section of the river. Either way, you will have to hike upstream to a put-in. Depending on the tour you choose and the amount of hiking you want to do, you will eventually climb into your inner tube and begin a slow float through anywhere from one to four caves. You will be equipped with a headlamp, and little else.

Cave tubing tours cost between BZ$60 and BZ$220 ($30–$110/£15–£55), depending on the length of the tour. The most inexpensive way to go is to drive yourself to the government parking area below Jaguar Paw and hire one of the local guides there for around BZ$30 to BZ$60 ($15–$30/£7.50–£15). However, you'll generally get better guides, better service, and better equipment if you go with one of the more established operators.

Actun Tunichil Muknal ★★

Actun Tunichil Muknal means "Cave of the Crystal Sepulcher," and the site was featured in the 1993 National Geographic Explorer film *Journey Through the Underworld.* This is one of the most adventurous and rewarding caves you can visit in Belize. The trip involves a 45-minute hike through dense forest to the entrance of the cave. A midsize stream flows out of the beautiful entrance. From here you wade, crawl, and scramble, often up to your waist in water. There are some tight squeezes. Inside, you'll come to several ceremonial and sacrificial chambers. Fourteen skeletons and burial sites have been found inside here, as well as numerous pieces of pottery and ceramic shards. There are even two rare slate stelae, believed to have been used by Maya religious and political leaders for ritual bloodletting ceremonies. Many of the skulls, skeletons, and pieces of pottery have been encased in calcium, creating an eerie effect, while others are very well maintained, making it hard to imagine that they are over a thousand years old. Moreover, given its remote location and relatively recent discovery, Actun Tunichil Muknal has been spared much of the serious looting that has plagued many other Maya cave sites. Only licensed guides can take visitors into this cave. Most hotels and tour agencies in the Cayo District can arrange these tours.

8 PLACENCIA & SOUTHERN BELIZE ★★

242km (150 miles) S of Belize City; 89km (55 miles) NE of Punta Gorda

Southern Belize has only two major towns, **Dangriga** and **Punta Gorda,** and one popular beach village, **Placencia ★★**. For years, this was the least developed region of Belize, but that's changing quickly. Placencia is arguably the hottest and fastest growing destination in Belize. And the tiny Garífuna settlement of **Hopkins Village ★★** is also booming. Both Placencia and Hopkins Village offer some of the longest and finest sand beaches to be found in the country.

Placencia is at the southern tip of a long, narrow peninsula that is separated from the mainland by a similarly narrow lagoon, and boasts nearly 26km (16 miles) of white sand fronting a calm turquoise sea and backed by palm trees. Placencia attracts everyone from backpackers to naturalists to hard-core divers to upscale snowbirds.

For years, the village's principal thoroughfare was a thin concrete sidewalk. Once listed in the *Guinness Book of World Records* as the narrowest street in the world, the sidewalk still runs through the heart of the village parallel to the sea. However, the ongoing construction and development boom have made the main road through town (called "the Back Road") actually the town's busiest thoroughfare most days.

Offshore, you'll find some of Belize's most beautiful cayes and its most remote atoll, **Glover's Reef Atoll ★★**. The cayes and barrier reef down here are as spectacular as that found farther north, yet far less developed and crowded. You can literally have an island to yourself down here. Much of the offshore and underwater wonders are protected in reserves, such as the **Southwater Caye Marine Reserve, Glover's Marine Reserve, Sapodilla Cayes Marine Reserve,** and **Laughing Bird Caye National Park.**

ESSENTIALS

Getting There

BY PLANE **Maya Island Air** (**© 2501/23-1140** in Belize City, or 501/523-3475 in Placencia; www.mayaairways.com) and **Tropic Air** (**© 800/422-3435** in the U.S. and Canada, 501/226-2012 in Belize City, or 501/523-3410 in Placencia; www.tropicair.com) both have around 10 flights daily between Belize City and Placencia. The first flight leaves at 8:10am and the last flight is at 5pm. Flight time is 35 minutes, with a brief stop in Dangriga. On each airline, there are somewhat fewer flights from the Municipal airport.

Flights to and from Punta Gorda on Maya Island Air and Tropic Air stop in **Placencia Airport** (**PLJ;** no phone) to pick up and drop off passengers. On both airlines, flights are sometimes added during the high season or suspended during the low season, so check in advance. Flight time runs between 25 and 50 minutes, depending on whether there is an intermediate stop or two. See "Getting Around," below, for info on getting from the airstrip into town.

BY BUS **James Bus Line** (**© 501/702-2049**) and **National Transport** (**© 501/227-2255**) have regular service throughout the day between Belize City and Dangriga, roughly every half-hour between 6:30am and 5:30pm from either the main bus terminal on West Collet Canal Street (National Transport), or the nearby Shell gas station on Cemetery road (James). The fare is BZ$20 ($10/£5). The ride takes about 3 hours. Direct buses leave Dangriga for Placencia daily at 10:30 and 11:30am, and 4 and 5:15pm. The fare is BZ$10 ($5/£2.50). Buses leave Placencia for Dangriga, with onward connection to Belmopan, San Ignacio, and Belize City, daily at 5:30 and 6am, and at 1:30 and 2pm.

Most independent and bus travelers will want to reach Placencia via Independence Village and Mango Creek, using the *Hokie Pokie* ferry (✆ **501/523-2376**). This short 30-minute boat ride cuts a lot of bumpy miles off the road trip. The ferry fare is BZ$12 ($6/£3). All north- and southbound bus traffic along the Southern highway stops in Independence Village, near the ferry dock. Ferries to Placencia leave daily at 6:30, 7:30, 8, and 11am, and at noon and 2:30 and 4:30pm. Return ferries from Placencia to Independence Village leave at 6:45 and 10am, and at 12:30, 2:30, 4, 5, and 6pm.

In order to get to Independence Village, you'll need to take any bus heading south to Punta Gorda. **James Bus Line** (✆ **501/207-3937** in Belize City, or 702-2049 in Punta Gorda) and **National Transport** (✆ **501/227-2255**) have service throughout the day between Belize City and Punta Gorda. Buses leave at irregular intervals between 4:30am and 5pm, with at least 15 different buses making the run throughout the day. The one-way fare is BZ$24 ($12/£6).

BY CAR From Belize City, head west on Cemetery Road, which becomes the Western Highway. Take this all the way to Belmopan, where you will connect with the Hummingbird Highway heading south. Ten kilometers (6 miles) before Dangriga, the Hummingbird Highway connects with the Southern Highway. Take the Southern Highway towards Placencia and Punta Gorda. After 37km (23 miles) on the Southern Highway, turn left onto the road to Riversdale and Placencia. From this turnoff, it's another 32km (20 miles) to Placencia. The drive from Belize City should take around 3 hours.

The road for almost the entire length of the peninsula—save for small patches of pavement—is a hard-packed red dirt, sand and gravel affair that can often be very dusty and bumpy. They've been talking about paving it for over a decade now. Given the amount of development going on here, it seems inconceivable that this hasn't happened, yet. Locals swear it might actually happen sometime soon. Currently, the road is paved from the airstrip into the center of the village.

Getting Around

Placencia Village itself is tiny, and you can walk the entire length of the sidewalk, which covers most of the village, in about 10 to 15 minutes. If you need a taxi, call **Cobo's Taxi** (✆ **501/661-2370**), **J's Taxi Service** (✆ **501/623-4137**), **S&M Taxi** (✆ **501/523-3524**), or **Peninsula Star Taxi** (✆ **501/523-4017**). Fares within the village run around BZ$4 to BZ$6 ($2–$3/£1–£1.50) per person. A trip from the airstrip to the village costs BZ$12 ($6/£3) for one person, or BZ$6 ($3/£1.50) per person for two or more.

If you want to rent a car or golf cart while in Placencia, **Barefoot Rentals** (✆ **501/523-3438;** www.barefootrentals.net) is your best option, charging around BZ$130 ($65/£33) per day for a golf cart, and between BZ$150 and BZ$180 ($75–$90/£33–£45) per day for an SUV. Alternately, you can rent a golf cart from **Caribbean Tours** (✆ **501/523-3047**) for similar rates.

Visitor Information

For most of the peninsula there is only one road. As the road reaches the end of the peninsula and the village of Placencia, it basically dead-ends at the Shell station and some boat docks. Just before this, a dirt spur turns right just beyond the soccer field and heads for a few hundred yards towards the lagoon.

Hotels and resorts are spread all along the length of the Placencia peninsula. To make it easier to understand where a hotel or resort is, the peninsula is broken up into three broad sections: Maya Beach, Seine Bight, and Placencia Village. Maya Beach is the northernmost section of the peninsula, and the hotels and resorts here are quite spread out, with few other services or businesses. More or less anchoring the center of the peninsula is the tiny Garífuna village of Seine Bight. Just to the north and south of Seine Bight village are several other isolated resorts. Down at the southern end of the peninsula is Placencia Village itself.

The helpful **Placencia Information Center** (✆ **501/523-4045;** www.placencia.com) is towards the end of the road, in a minimall across from the soccer field.

FAST FACTS For the local **police,** dial ✆ **911** or 501/503-3142; you can also reach the **tourist police** at ✆ 501/603-0374. If you need any medical attention, the **Placencia Medical Center** (✆ 501/523-3326) is behind the school in the center of the village.

There's a **Scotiabank** (✆ 501/523-3277) on the main road near the center of the village, as well as an **Atlantic Bank** (✆ 501/523-3431). Scotiabank has an ATM that accepts international cards. There's a **pharmacy** attached to Wallen's Market (✆ 501/523-3128), in the center of the village. The **post office** is above the Fishermen's Co-op, near the start of the sidewalk.

If you need to use the Internet, there are a host of options. If you want Wi-Fi or some food or drink to go along with your surfing, I recommend the **Purple Space Monkey** (✆ **501/523-4094**). The **Placencia Office Supply** (✆ **501/523-3205**), which is on the main road and has high-speed connections, is another good option, as is the **Live Oak Plaza,** a small strip mall just south of the airstrip with free Wi-Fi.

WHAT TO SEE & DO IN PLACENCIA

On & Under the Water

FISHING Fishing around here is some of the best in Belize. There's excellent bonefishing in flats in this area. Anglers can also go for tarpon, permit, and snook, or head offshore for bigger game, including grouper, yellowfin tuna, king mackerel, wahoo, mahimahi, and the occasional sail or marlin. Experienced guides can help you track any of the above fish, and many are taking their guests out fly-fishing for them as well. The folks at **Kingfisher Adventures** ★ (✆ **501/523-3323;** www.tarponcayelodge.com) are some of the more reputable fishing guides, specializing in fishing for permit and tarpon. They even have a small fishing lodge on the remote Tarpon Caye. You can also try **Trip 'N Travel** (✆ **501/523-3614**), another long-standing local operation with well-regarded guides.

KAYAKING Several hotels and tour operators in town rent out sea kayaks. The waters just off the beach are usually calm and perfect for kayaking. However, the lagoon is probably a better choice, offering up more interesting mangrove terrain and excellent bird-watching opportunities.

If you're looking for a guided tour, the best kayak operator in Placencia is **Toadal Adventures** ★ (✆ **501/523-3207;** www.toadaladventure.com). These folks offer several different multiday kayaking trips, both out on the ocean and on inland rivers. Custom trips can also be designed.

SAILING The crystal-clear waters, calm seas, and isolated islands surrounding Placencia make this an excellent place to go out for a sail. Your options range from crewed yachts and bareboat charters for multiday adventures to day cruises and sunset sails. A

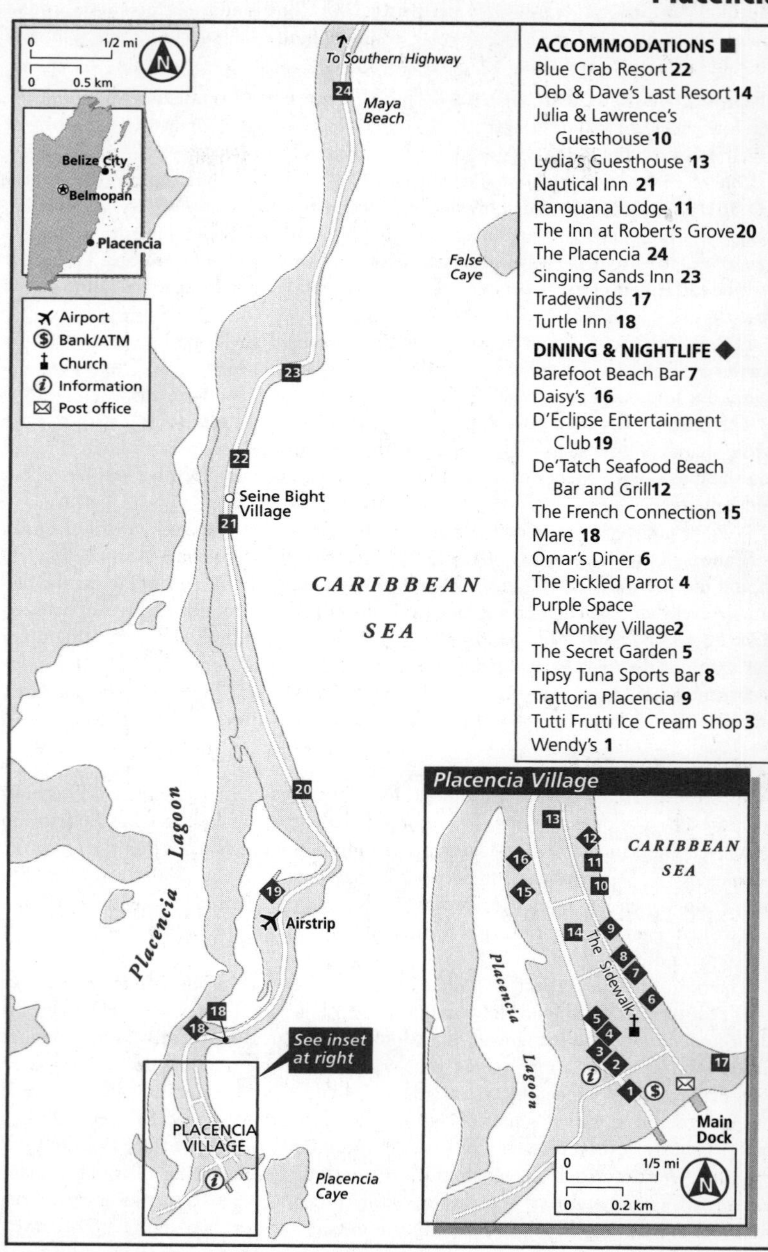
0
1/2 mi
0
0.5 km
N
Belize City
Belmopan
Placencia
Airport
Bank/ATM
Church
Information
Post office
To Southern Highway
Maya Beach
False Caye
Seine Bight Village
CARIBBEAN SEA
Placencia Lagoon
Airstrip
See inset at right
PLACENCIA VILLAGE
Placencia Caye
ACCOMMODATIONS
Blue Crab Resort 22
Deb & Dave's Last Resort 14
Julia & Lawrence's Guesthouse 10
Lydia's Guesthouse 13
Nautical Inn 21
Ranguana Lodge 11
The Inn at Robert's Grove 20
The Placencia 24
Singing Sands Inn 23
Tradewinds 17
Turtle Inn 18
DINING & NIGHTLIFE
Barefoot Beach Bar 7
Daisy's 16
D'Eclipse Entertainment Club 19
De'Tatch Seafood Beach Bar and Grill 12
The French Connection 15
Mare 18
Omar's Diner 6
The Pickled Parrot 4
Purple Space Monkey Village 2
The Secret Garden 5
Tipsy Tuna Sports Bar 8
Trattoria Placencia 9
Tutti Frutti Ice Cream Shop 3
Wendy's 1
Placencia Village
CARIBBEAN SEA
Placencia Lagoon
The Sidewalk
Main Dock
0
1/5 mi
0
0.2 km
N

day cruise, including lunch, drinks, and snorkeling gear, should cost between BZ$160 and BZ$300 ($80–$150/£40–£75) per person. Most hotels and tour operators around town can arrange a sail or cruise, or you can simply head to the docks, or check in with the folks at **Next Wave Sailing** (✆ **501/523-3391**).

SNORKELING & SCUBA DIVING There's often decent snorkeling right off the beach, especially if you head north a mile or so. The water's clear and you'll see plenty of fish and bottom life in the sea grass and along the sand bottom.

One of the more popular snorkel excursions is to the nearby **Laughing Bird Caye** (✆ **501/523-3565;** www.laughingbird.org). Just a few miles offshore from Placencia, Laughing Bird Caye is a national park. It's a tiny little island measuring roughly 11×105m (35×350 ft.). There's good snorkeling and swimming offshore, and a beautiful little beach. A host of tour operators take folks here, and then serve a picnic lunch on the beach.

However, if you're serious about diving or snorkeling, you'll want to get out to the **barrier reef** and its dozens of little offshore cayes. It's between 16 and 40km (10–25 miles) out to the reef here, making it a relatively quick and easy boat ride.

The offshore **Gladden Spit ★★** site is a world-renowned spot to dive with massive whale sharks. Whale shark sightings are fairly common here from late March through June, and to a lesser extent during the months of August through October and December and January.

If you're not staying at a hotel with a dedicated dive operation, check in with the folks at **Seahorse Dive Shop ★** (✆ **501/523-3166;** www.belizescuba.com). A snorkeling trip should cost between BZ$60 and BZ$160 ($30–$80/£15–£40), depending on the distance traveled and whether or not lunch is included. Rates for scuba diving run between BZ$120 and BZ$300 ($60–$150/£30–£75) for a two-tank dive, also depending upon the length of the journey to the dive site and whether or not lunch is included. Equipment rental should cost from BZ$15 to BZ$30 ($7.50–$15/£3.75–£7.50) for a snorkeler, and BZ$30 to BZ$60 ($15–$30/£7.50–£15) for a scuba diver.

Guided Day Trips

While the ocean and outlying cayes are the focus of most activities and tours in Placencia, there are a host of other options. The most popular of these include tours to Cockscomb Basin Wildlife Sanctuary, the Maya ruins of Lubaantun and Nim Li Punit, and up the Monkey River. Day trips can run between BZ$100 and BZ$300 ($50–$150/£25–£75) per person, depending upon the distance traveled and the number of activities offered or sites visited. Almost every tour agency in town offers these trips, or ask at your hotel for a recommended guide or operator.

The most popular "inland" trip offered out of Placencia is up the **Monkey River ★**, and most of it is actually on the water, anyway. About a half-hour boat ride down the coast and through the mangroves, the Monkey River area is rich in wildlife. If you're lucky, you might spot a manatee on your way down. Once traveling up the river, keep your eyes peeled for crocodiles, green iguana, wild deer, howler monkeys, the occasional boa constrictor, as well as scores of bird species. These tours can be done entirely in a motor launch, or may allow you to kayak on the Monkey River portion; I recommend the latter. Most tours include lunch in the quaint little Creole fishing village of Monkey River itself, as well as a short hike through a forest trail. Monkey River trips cost between BZ$90 and BZ$120 ($45–$60/£23–£30) per person.

WHERE TO STAY

There are a host of accommodations options in and around Placencia. In general, the town's budget hotels and guesthouses are located in the village proper, either just off the sidewalk, or around the soccer field. As you head north to the broader and more isolated beaches, prices tend to rise.

Very Expensive

In addition to the places listed below, there's the **Placencia ★★** (✆ **501/520-4110;** www.theplacencia.com) up north at Maya Beach.

The Inn at Robert's Grove ★★★ Kids A full-service resort, the Inn at Robert's Grove features two restaurants, three pools, an in-house spa, professional dive and fishing operations, a tennis court, and a host of tour and activity options. All of the rooms are roomy and comfortable, and come with a host of modern amenities. Rustic red-tile floors, Guatemalan textiles, and Mexican ceramic accents abound. All come with a private balcony, hung with a hammock. There are six—count 'em—six Jacuzzis spread around the resort. The rooftop ones are particularly inviting for late-night stargazing and soaking. Guests enjoy unlimited free use of the hotel's sea kayaks, Windsurfers, Hobie Cat sailboats, tennis court, and bicycles, as well as free airport transfers. The hotel also owns and manages two small private islands, Ranagua Caye and Robert's Caye.

Placencia, on the beach north of the airstrip. ✆ **800/565-9757** in the U.S., or 501/523-3565 in Belize. Fax 501/523-3567. www.robertsgrove.com. 52 units. BZ$480–BZ$520 ($240–$260/£120–£130) double; BZ$630–BZ$1,070 ($315–$535/£158–£268) suite. Rates lower in the off season, higher during peak weeks. AE, MC, V. **Amenities:** 2 restaurants; 3 bars; lounge; babysitting; full-service dive shop; exercise room; laundry service; all rooms nonsmoking; 3 outdoor pools; room service; small spa; lit outdoor tennis court; complimentary watersports equipment and bike use; free Wi-Fi. *In room:* A/C, TV, fridge, hair dryer.

Turtle Inn ★★★ Finds This is Francis Ford Coppola's fanciest resort in Central America. You get your choice of a one- or two-bedroom private villa here. Either way you go, you're going to have plenty of space, including a large living room and a spacious bathroom that lets out on to a private interior rock garden, with its own open-air shower whose fixture is a piece of bamboo. Tons of beautiful woodwork, and a heavy dose of Asian decor and furnishings, dominate the rooms. All of the villas are set on the sand just steps from the beach, but not all have ocean views, hence the price variations. There are two separate pools on the grounds, as well as a small spa and full-service dive operation across the street on the lagoon side of the peninsula.

Placencia Village, on the beach north of the center of the village. ✆ **800/746-3743** in the U.S., or 501/824-4912 central reservation number in Belize, or 523-3244 at the hotel. Fax 501/523-3245. www.turtleinn.com. 25 units. BZ$690–BZ$930 ($345–$465/£173–£233) 1-bedroom double; BZ$1,000–BZ$1,250 ($500–$625/£250–£313) 2-bedroom double; BZ$3,600 ($1,800/£900) Coppola Pavilion. Rates include continental breakfast. Rates lower in the off season, higher during peak weeks. AE, MC, V. **Amenities:** 3 restaurants; 2 bars; babysitting; complimentary bikes and kayaks; concierge; full-service dive shop; laundry service; outdoor pool; room service; watersports equipment rental; free Wi-Fi. *In room:* Hair dryer, minibar.

Moderate

This is a price range with tons of options. In addition to the hotel listed below other good choices include: **Singing Sands Inn ★** (✆ **501/523-8017;** www.singingsands.com) on Maya Beach; and **Blue Crab Resort** (✆ **501/523-3544;** www.bluecrabbeach.com) and **Nautical Inn ★** (✆ **501/523-3595;** www.nauticalinnbelize.com), both just outside of Seine Bight Village.

Ranguana Lodge (Value) The five individual cabins at this small family-run hotel are all clean and cozy. In the two older cabins, nearly everything is made of hardwood—walls, floors, ceilings, even the louvered windows. These rooms feature a full kitchenette. The three oceanfront cabins are the newest, and while they are right in front of the sea and have air-conditioning, they are a little smaller and have a little less character. All of the cabins are just steps from the ocean, and all come with a private balcony or porch area.

Placencia Village, on the beach in the center of the village. ✆ **501/523-3112.** Fax 501/523-3451. www.ranguanabelize.com. 5 units. BZ$160–BZ$168 ($80–$84/£40–£42) double. Rates include taxes. AE, MC, V. *In room:* Fridge, no phone.

Inexpensive

If the place listed below is full, you can simply walk around the village and see what's available, or head to either **Julia & Lawrence's Guesthouse** (✆ **501/503-3478;** www.juliasrooms.com), **Lydia's Guesthouse** (✆ **501/523-3117;** lydias@btl.net), or **Deb and Dave's Last Resort** (✆ **501/523-3207;** debanddave@btl.net), both located just off the sidewalk towards the center of the village.

Tradewinds (Finds) You can't beat the setting of Tradewinds. Perched right on the ocean's edge towards the southern end of the village, the eight individual cabins here are just a few feet from the water. All are comfortable, roomy, and come with a very inviting porch, hung with a hammock overlooking the waves, where I predict you'll spend most of your time. The less expensive rooms here are set a bit farther back from the sea in a simple triplex building, although each comes with its own little veranda. Everything is painted in lively pastels, and there's a friendly family-like vibe to the whole operation.

Placencia Village, on the beach, south end of the village. ✆ **501/523-3122.** Fax 501/523-3201. www.placencia.com. 11 units. BZ$80–BZ$140 ($40–$70/£20–£35) double. Rates slightly lower in the off season, higher during peak weeks. MC, V. *In room:* Fridge, no phone.

WHERE TO DINE

In addition to the places mentioned below, the main restaurant at the **Inn at Robert's Grove** (see above) is consistently top-notch, as is the Italian restaurant **Mare** at **Turtle Inn** (see above). For simpler Italian fare and homemade pastas in a beachfront setting, try **Trattoria Placencia** (✆ **501/623-3394**), about midway along the sidewalk. Finally, as you wander around town in the heat of the day, be sure to stop in at **Tutti Frutti Ice Cream Shop** for some fresh, homemade ice cream or gelato. Tutti Frutti is on the main road in the Placencia Village Square shopping center, across from the soccer field. **Daisy's,** on the main road near the center of town, also serves up fresh, homemade ice cream, as well as breakfasts, lunches and dinners.

Moderate

De'Tatch Seafood Beach Bar & Grill ★ BELIZEAN/SEAFOOD This funky open-air beachfront joint is one of the most popular spots in town. Traditional Belizean breakfasts here are hearty and inexpensive. You can get excellent seafood or shrimp burritos or tacos for lunch or dinner. There's an Internet cafe off to one side, and the sea is just steps away. The second-floor open-air deck can get hot in the daytime, but is especially nice on starry nights.

Placencia Village, on the ocean just off the Sea Spray Hotel towards the center of the village. ✆ **501/503-3385.** Reservations not accepted. Breakfast and lunch main courses BZ$6–BZ$16 ($3–$8/£1.50–£4); dinner main courses BZ$12–BZ$36 ($6–$18/£3–£9); lobster BZ$34–BZ$50 ($17–$25/£8.50–£13). MC, V. Thurs–Tues 7am–10pm.

The French Connection ★★★ *Finds* FRENCH/FUSION For a standout and memorable meal, it's hard to beat this place. The menu changes regularly, according to what seasonal ingredients are available and the chef's whim. I recently got to start things off with a fabulous onion tartlet, topped with goat cheese, sun-dried tomatoes, and tapanade. For a main, the offerings included roasted grouper in a smoked chili beurre blanc, and a pinot-noir braised lamb shank. Presentations are relatively simple—no high towers here—and the servings are ample. These folks have an excellent and fairly priced wine list. Owners Anna and Marcus Perigo are engaging and amiable hosts as well.

Placencia Village, on the lagoon, south end of town. ✆ **501/523-3656.** Reservations recommended. Main courses BZ$36–BZ$40 ($18–$20/£9–£10). MC, V. Fri–Wed 6–10pm.

Inexpensive

Other good choices around town include **Omar's Diner** (✆ **501/523-4094**), the **Secret Garden** ★ (✆ **501/523-3617**), **Wendy's** (✆ **501/523-3335**), and the **Pickled Parrot** ★ (✆ **501/604-0278;** www.pickledparrotbelize.com), all located just off the sidewalk in Placencia Village.

Purple Space Monkey Village ★ INTERNATIONAL This is Placencia's central meeting place for travelers, expatriates, and locals alike. The heavy wrought-iron tables and chairs here are a rainbow of primary colors. The food is well prepared, abundant, and reasonably priced. I like to start the day with their fryjacks stuffed with eggs and cheese. The lunch menu tends towards burgers, sandwiches, wraps, and burritos, whereas their dinner menu gets more creative and extensive. Specialties include fresh blackened fish, and chicken or shrimp served in a mango-teriyaki sauce. There's free Wi-Fi, four complementary computer workstations, and a lending library.

Placencia Village, in front of the soccer field. ✆ **501/523-4094.** Reservations not necessary. Main courses breakfast and lunch BZ$10–BZ$15 ($5–$7.50/£2.50–£3.75), dinner BZ$26–BZ$40 ($13–$20/£7.50–£10). MC, V. Daily 7am–10pm.

PLACENCIA AFTER DARK

Two of the most popular spots in town are the **Barefoot Beach Bar** ★ (✆ **501/523-3515**) and the **Tipsy Tuna Sports Bar** (✆ **501/523-3480**), two neighboring establishments; I prefer the relaxed vibe and outdoor setting of the Barefoot Beach Bar, while the Tipsy Tuna is more of a late-night place, with pool tables, and regular live music and karaoke. For real late-night action, there's the **D'Eclipse Entertainment Club** (✆ **501/523-3288**); it's located just north of the airstrip so the noise and crowds won't bother residents of the town's hotels and houses.

A SIDE TRIP TO HOPKINS VILLAGE

Hopkins Village is a midsize coastal Garífuna community located 53km (33 miles) north of Placencia. It is a picturesque village with colorfully painted raised clapboard houses. It is also my preferred destination for getting a true taste of and some direct contact with this unique culture. This is a great place to wander around talking with children, fishermen, and elderly folks hanging out in front of their homes.

Hopkins Village is set on a long curving swath of beach, which in addition to Placencia is one of the few true beaches in the country. In recent years, several beach and dive resorts have opened on the stretch of sand south of the village, while in the village itself you'll find a hodgepodge of budget lodgings and simple restaurants.

Essentials

The access road from the Southern Highway heads right into the heart of Hopkins Village. If you continued straight, you'd be in the Caribbean Sea. The village itself spreads out for a few hundred yards in either direction.

Getting There

BY CAR The turnoff for Hopkins Village is on the Hummingbird Highway, about 13km (8 miles) south of Dangriga. From here, it's 6km (4 miles) on a graded gravel road. A few miles farther south on the Southern Highway is the entrance to Sittee River Village; however, you can also enter at Hopkins and head south from there along the coast, as it's really just a small loop.

BY BUS In theory, Hopkins Village is serviced by all of the buses heading north and south along the Hummingbird Highway. However, only a couple of the buses each day make the loop through Hopkins Village and Sittee River. Be sure to ask before you get on the bus if it will drop you off in the village. If not, you will be let off on the Southern Highway, at the entrance to Hopkins, but still some 6km (4 miles) away. If this is the case, you will hopefully have arranged pickup with your hotel in advance. Otherwise, you'll have to hitchhike into town.

Getting Around

Hopkins Village itself is tiny and you can easily walk the entire town. If you're staying south of town or want to explore, a bicycle is the preferred means of transportation. Most of the hotels will either lend you a bike or rent you one for a few dollars per day. There are no official taxi services, but if you ask around town or at your hotel, you should be able to hire someone for small trips or excursions.

Visitor Information

Hopkins Village has no banks, or major stores or services. There are, however, a couple of Internet cafes, and you can get gas at the little marina.

What to See & Do

This is a very isolated and underdeveloped area. All the hotels here can help you arrange scuba diving, snorkeling, and fishing outings, as well as tours to attractions such as Cockscomb Basin Wildlife Sanctuary, Sittee River canoeing, Blue Hole National Park, the Mayflower Maya ruins, and cultural tours of Dangriga. If you really want to get a taste of the local culture, sign up for classes at the **Lebeha Drumming Center ★** (✆ **501/608-3143;** www.lebeha.com), which is on the northern edge of the village. The folks here teach traditional Garífuna drumming and dancing.

Where to Stay

There are several upscale resorts and condo options in Hopkins. My two favorites are **Hamanasi ★★** (✆ **877/552-3483** in the U.S.; www.hamanasi.com) and **Jaguar Reef Lodge ★★** (✆ **800/289-5756** in the U.S.; www.jaguarreef.com). Both are full-service resorts with in-house dive operations and a host of tour and activity options. In addition to these places, there are also a score of simple guesthouses and small inns. The best of these are **Hopkins Inn** (✆ **501/523-7283;** www.hopkinsinn.com), **Jungle Jeanie's By The Sea ★** (✆ **501/523-7047;** www.junglebythesea.com) and **Tipple Tree Beya** (✆/fax **501/520-7006;** http://tippletree.net).

Where to Dine

Even if you're staying at one of the large resorts around here, it's worth heading into town to try a meal at one of the simple, local-run restaurants on the main street. Of these, **King Kassava** (✆ **501/608-6188**), **Iris's Restaurant** (✆ **501/523-7019**), and **Innies Restaurant** (✆ **501/523-7026**) are perennial favorites. All serve excellent fresh seafood, and will usually have some *hudut* and other Garífuna dishes on hand. A similar option, which I prefer for its seafront location, is **Laruna Hati** ★ (✆ **501/661-5753**), which is towards the north end of the village. For something different, try **Taste of India** ★ (✆ **501/660-0971**), which serves authentic Indian fare.

5

Guatemala

by Eliot Greenspan

A millennium of Maya civilization, 3 centuries of Spanish colonial rule, and nearly 4 decades of guerrilla war have left Guatemala's economy, politics, crafts, architecture, languages, and religions with one common trait: profound variety.

For visitors, the country's charms are nearly as varied as the riotous colors woven into its famed fabrics. From the Maya ruins of Tikal and the colonial splendor of Antigua—both exquisitely preserved through the centuries—to the breathtaking natural beauty of Lake Atitlán, there are a range of destinations and attractions here to please just about any type of traveler.

A trip to Guatemala can focus on the art and culture, natural beauty, ancient archaeology, or a combination of the above. You can also partake in a variety of adventure sports or spend some time brushing up on your Spanish.

1 THE REGIONS IN BRIEF

Guatemala sits at the northwestern tip of Central America. It's bordered by Mexico to the north, Belize and the Caribbean Sea to the east, Honduras and El Salvador to the southeast, and the Pacific Ocean to the southwest. The country covers an area of 100,000 sq. km (just more than 40,000 sq. miles). Almost two-thirds of the country is covered by mountains, most of which are volcanic. Of these, quite a few are active, including Volcán Pacaya, Volcán Santiaguito, and Volcán Fuego.

Most visitors stick close to a well-defined tourist trail that encompasses Guatemala City, Antigua, Lake Atitlán, and the Western Highlands, with a side trip to Tikal and the Petén. Those with more time, or a more adventurous spirit, can explore the Caribbean Lowlands (its main attractions include Lago Izabal and the small Garífuna village of Livingston), the Pacific coast (which is becoming well known as a sportfishing hot spot, and place for surfers to head for uncrowded waves), and the central region (which is the place to head for a mix of adventure activities, wildlife viewing, and cave adventures, and to visit the beautiful waterfalls and forests of Semuc Champay, as well as Las Verapaces and El Oriente).

GUATEMALA CITY Guatemala City is the largest city in the country and its capital. With a population of more than three million, the city is a sprawling, congested, confusing, and polluted urban center. The city sits on a high, broad plateau, at an elevation of 1,469m (4,897 ft.) above sea level, and enjoys moderate temperatures year-round. Guatemala City serves as a de facto transportation hub for most, if not all, visitors, with the country's principal international airport and bus connections to all other points.

ANTIGUA This small colonial city lies just 40km (25 miles) southwest of Guatemala City. For a couple hundred years, it was the nation's capital, until a series of major earthquakes forced its evacuation. Antigua is set in a valley surrounded by towering volcanic mountain peaks. The entire colonial city is little more than 10 blocks by 10 blocks, with a bit more modern urban sprawl around the edges. The city is one of the most well-preserved examples of a colonial city in the Americas. The city core features rough cobblestone streets, ruined and restored colonial-era churches, convents, and monasteries, and a few newer constructions that maintain the colonial style and feel.

PANAJACHEL & LAKE ATITLÁN Lake Atitlán is technically part of the Western Highlands, but for our purposes, and in the minds of most travelers, it is a world unto itself. Lake Atitlán is a beautiful mountain lake that is actually the filled-in crater of a massive volcano. It's hard to imagine this, since today, several more volcanoes rise from around the shores and tower over the lake. More than 16km (10 miles) across at its widest point, Lake Atitlán has a series of small villages and a few major towns lining its shores. The principal means of transport between the various towns and villages is by boat and boat taxi. The main town and gateway to Lake Atitlán is **Panajachel,** which sits on the northern shore of the lake. Other major towns include **Santa Catarina Palopó** and **San Antonio Palopó** to the east of Panajachel, and **Santiago de Atitlán** and **San Pedro La Laguna** across the lake to the south.

THE WESTERN HIGHLANDS The area to the west and northwest of Guatemala City is widely referred to as the Western Highlands, or Altiplano (the "Highlands" in Spanish). This is the heart of Guatemala's rural Maya population. The Western Highlands are populated with a dense patchwork of small, rural farming communities spread around the rough, steep, mountainous region. The towns and cities of **Chichicastenango, Quetzaltenango,** and **Huehuetenango** serve as central market and commercial centers for the smaller surrounding communities. The Western Highlands are home to Guatemala's greatest artisans, and are the best place in the country to purchase a wide array of arts, crafts, carvings, and textile products. Perhaps the most famous place to buy these goods is the twice-weekly market held in Chichicastenango.

TIKAL & EL PETÉN The Petén, or El Petén, is Guatemala's largest and least populated province. It occupies the entire northeastern section of the country. It's an area of lush primary tropical rainforest, within which lies an immense natural wealth of flora and fauna, as well as many of Mesoamerica's most amazing archaeological treasures. The only major population centers of note in El Petén are the sister cities of **Santa Elena** and **Flores.** In addition to the world-renowned ruins of **Tikal,** visitors to the Petén can visit the archaeological sites of **Yaxhá, El Ceibal, El Mirador,** and **Uaxactún,** to name just a few.

2 THE BEST OF GUATEMALA IN 1 WEEK

One week will allow you enough time to visit (and actually enjoy) four of Guatemala's prime destinations. This itinerary takes you to the best of Guatemala, and includes a colonial city, a breathtaking natural wonder, an extensive traditional market, and spectacular ancient Maya ruins.

Day ❶: Antigua ★★★

Once you arrive into Guatemala City, head straight to Antigua, check into your hotel, and hit the streets. Get familiar with the city by starting out at **Plaza Mayor** ★★ (p. 170) in the center of town. End the night with dinner at **Hector's** ★★ (p. 188). If the weather's nice, be sure to grab a table near the pool.

Day ❷: The Colonial Core

Start your morning by visiting the major attractions around the city's colonial core. There are almost too many sights to see, and it may be hard to choose. Your best bet is to sign up for a walking tour with **Antigua Tours** ★★ (p. 181). Many of their tours are led by longtime resident and well-known author Elizabeth Bell.

Spend the afternoon shopping at Antigua's fabulous shops, galleries, and local markets.

Don't miss the opportunity to have dinner, and perhaps catch a little jazz, at **Mesón Panza Verde** ★★★ (p. 186).

Day ❸: Lake Atitlán ★★★

Since this is a relatively tight itinerary, I recommend you stay in or around **Panajachel** (p. 190). Spend the day walking around town, and be sure to visit the **Museo Lacustre Atitlán** ★ (p. 192). For a good hike through some beautiful foliage, head to the **Reserva Natural Atitlán** ★ (p. 192). Splurge for dinner with a meal at **Hotel Atitlán** ★★★ (p. 196).

Day ❹: Around the Lake

Set aside the whole day to visit some of the other cities and towns around Lake Atitlán. Sign up for an organized tour, or head down to the docks and climb aboard one of the public boat taxis. You won't have time to visit the more than half-dozen towns and villages around the lake, but you must visit **Santiago de Atitlán** ★★ (p. 197). After that, and as time allows, I recommend **Santa Catarina Palopó** (p. 193), **San Marcos La Laguna** ★ (p. 192), and **San Pedro La Laguna** ★ (p. 192).

Day ❺: Chichicastenango

Take a day trip to the **market in Chichicastenango** ★★★ (p. 178). Chichicastenango, or Chichi, is a little more than an hour's drive from Panajachel, and all of the local tour agencies and hotel tour desks in Panajachel can arrange a guided tour or simple transfer. Even if you come here just to shop, be sure to take some time to visit the **Iglesia de Santo Tomás** ★★ (p. 207).

You'll get back to Panajachel with plenty of time to enjoy the evening. Head to the **Sunset Café** (p. 199) for a namesake cocktail, and then journey over to **El Bistro** ★ (p. 199) for dinner. End your evening with a drink at the **Circus Bar** ★★ (p. 199).

Note: Chichicastenango's market is only open on Thursday and Sunday. Feel free to swap this day of the itinerary with any of the other 2 days around Lake Atitlán to match the market day schedule.

Days ❻ & ❼: Tikal ★★★

In my opinion, **Tikal** (p. 207) is the most impressive ancient Maya city in all of Mesoamerica. You'll probably have to leave Panajachel at an ungodly hour to catch your flight to Tikal, but it'll be worth it. I suggest spending 1 night in the Tikal area, and true Maya buffs will want to stay at one of the hotels right at the archaeological site, which will allow you extra hours to explore. Those with a more passing interest will be better off staying in Flores or at one of the hotels on the lake.

Early international flights from Aurora International Airport in Guatemala City are hard to catch if you're flying from Tikal the same date, so you may have to adjust your itinerary to allow an overnight in either Antigua or Guatemala City before your flight home.

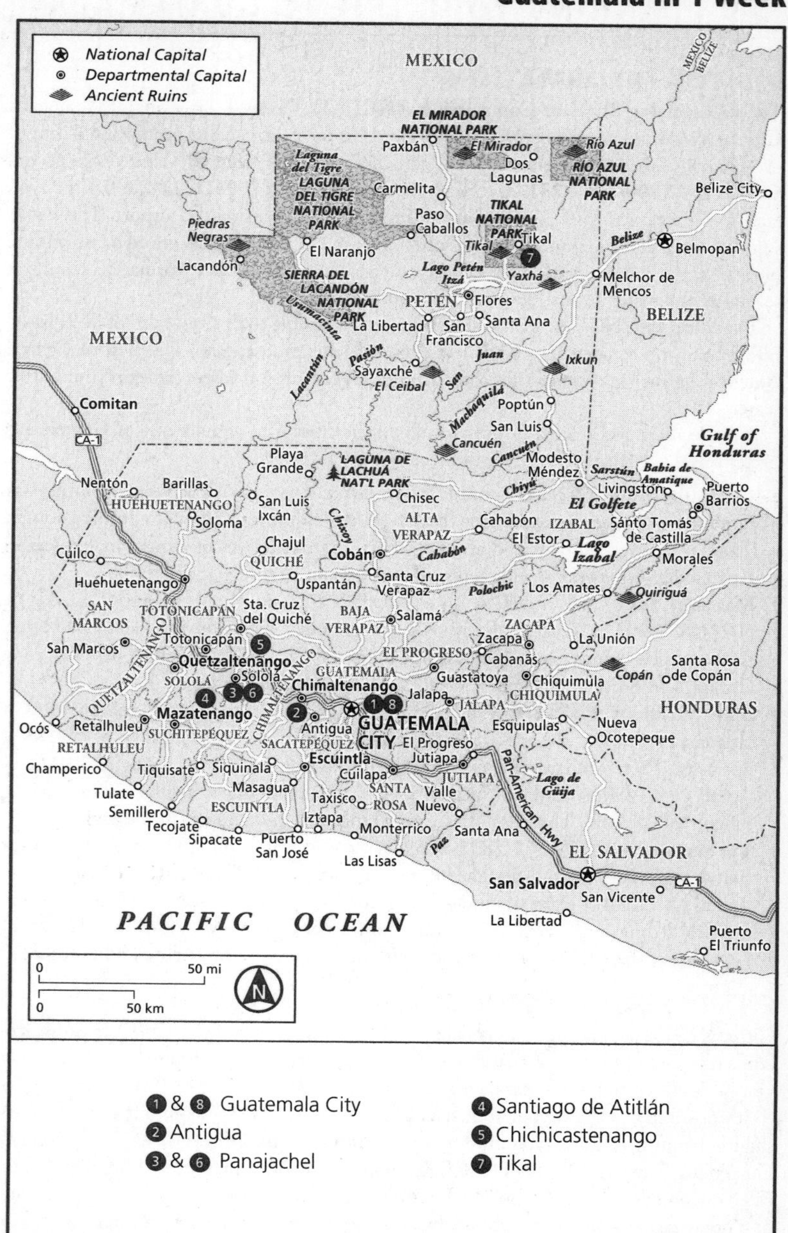

1 & 8 Guatemala City
2 Antigua
3 & 6 Panajachel
4 Santiago de Atitlán
5 Chichicastenango
7 Tikal

VISITOR INFORMATION

The **Guatemalan Tourism Commission (INGUAT),** 7a Av. 1-17, Zona 4, Guatemala City (www.visitguatemala.com), is the principal informational and promotional arm of the Guatemalan government. You can call them toll-free from the United States and Canada at ✆ **800/464-8281,** or directly in Guatemala at ✆ **502/2421-2800.** Once you land in Guatemala, INGUAT has an information booth inside the airport. The booth supplies maps and brochures, and will often make a call for you if you need a last-minute hotel or car-rental reservation. INGUAT also maintains offices or information booths at several of the major tourist destinations around the country.

In addition to INGUAT's official website, you'll be able to find a wealth of Web-based information on Guatemala with a few clicks of your mouse. See "The Best of Central America Online" in chapter 1 for some helpful suggestions on where to begin your online search.

For specific travel-related information, your best bet is to contact one of Guatemala's better travel agencies. Here is a list of some of my favorites:

- **Clark Tours** (✆ **502/2412-4848;** www.clarktours.com.gt) has been operating for more than 70 years in Guatemala, making it the oldest tour company in the country. They have several offices and are the official representatives of American Express in Guatemala. They offer a wide range of custom and fixed departure tours.
- **Martsam Tour and Travel** ★ (✆ **866/832-2776** in the U.S. and Canada, or 502/7867-5093 in Guatemala; www.martsam.com). Based on the island of Flores, these guys are hands down the best operators for Tikal and the Petén, although they also have an office in Antigua and can book tours for the entire country.
- **Maya Vacations** ★ (✆ **866/498-5333** in the U.S. and Canada, or 502/2426-1400 in Guatemala; www.mayavacations.com) is a small agency run by very knowledgeable local operators. Their standard itineraries run the gamut from a 4-day/3-night circuit of Guatemala City, Antigua, and Chichicastenango to an 8-day/7-night highlight tour covering much more ground. They also offer a wide range of active and adventure tours.
- **Via Venture** ★★ (✆ **502/7832-2509;** www.viaventure.com). This well-run operation specializes in custom-designed itineraries using the finest hotels in the country, as well as an excellent team of guides and ground transport services. They are also particularly strong in the area of adventure tourism and theme vacations. In addition to Guatemala, these folks run trips and combined itineraries into Belize and Honduras.

ENTRY REQUIREMENTS

Citizens of the United States, Canada, Great Britain, all European Union nations, Ireland, Australia, and New Zealand may visit Guatemala for a maximum of 90 days. No visa is necessary, but you must have a valid passport.

It's possible to extend your tourist visa for an additional 90 days, but the process is slightly tedious. To do so, you must go to the **Immigration Office,** 6a Av. 3-11, Zona 4, Guatemala City (✆ **502/2411-2407**). The process involves presenting several authenticated documents and photocopies. Moreover, these documents will need a lawyer's stamp or a notarization from your embassy. Even though the official fee for an extension is just $15 (£7.50), the whole process can take as long as a week, and cost between $20 and $50 (£10–£25).

Telephone Dialing Info at a Glance

The country code for Guatemala is 502, which you use only when dialing from outside the country. In this chapter, telephone numbers include this prefix because most businesses' published phone numbers include the prefix.

- **To place a call from your home country to Guatemala:** Dial the international access code (011 in the U.S. and Canada, 0011 in Australia, 0170 in New Zealand, 00 in the U.K.), plus the country code (502), followed by the eight-digit number. For example, a call from the U.S. to Guatemala would be 011+502+XXXX+XXXX.
- **To place a call within Guatemala:** There are no area codes inside Guatemala. To make a call, simply dial the eight-digit number.
- **To place a direct international call from Guatemala:** Dial the international access code (00), plus the country code of the place you are dialing, plus the area code and the local number.
- **To reach an international operator:** Dial ✆ **147-120.** For **directory assistance,** call ✆ **2333-1524.**

Guatemala is also part of a 2006 border control agreement with Honduras, El Salvador, and Nicaragua, allowing travel between the four countries under one tourist card. See p. 56 for info.

Guatemalan Embassy Locations

If you need a visa or have other questions about Guatemala, you can contact any of the following Guatemalan embassies or consulates: in the **United States,** 2220 R St. NW, Washington, DC 20008 (✆ **202/745-4952**); in **Canada,** 130 Albert St., Ste. 1010, Ottawa, Ontario K1P 5G4 (✆ **613/233-7237**); and in **Great Britain,** 13 Fawcett St., London, England SW10 9HN (✆ **020/7351-3042**). There are no Guatemalan embassies in Australia or New Zealand, but you could try contacting the embassy in **Japan,** 38 Kowa Bldg. 9F, no. 905, 4-12-24 Nishi Azabu, Tokyo 106-0031 (✆ **81/3400-1830**).

CUSTOMS

Visitors to Guatemala may bring all reasonable goods and belongings for personal use during their stay. Cameras, computers, and electronic equipment, as well as fishing and diving gear for personal use, are permitted duty-free. Customs officials in Guatemala seldom check arriving tourists' luggage.

MONEY

The unit of currency in Guatemala is the **quetzal.** In June 2008, there were approximately 7.5 quetzales to the American dollar, or 15 quetzales to the U.K. pound, but because the quetzal does fluctuate, you can expect this rate to change. To check the very latest exchange rates visit **www.xe.com/ucc**.

The quetzal is theoretically divided into 100 ***centavos.*** However, because of their insignificant value, you will rarely see or have to handle *centavos.* If you do, there are coins in denominations of 1, 5, 10, 25, and 50 *centavos.* There are also 1 quetzal coins, which are quite common and handy. There are paper notes in denominations of 1, 5, 10, 20, 50, and 100 quetzales. This can be a bit of a problem for travelers, since the bill with the largest denomination is worth only around $13 (£6.50). In late 2009, the government is expected to introduce a 200-queztales note.

ATMS ATMs are fairly common throughout Guatemala, particularly in Guatemala City and Antigua, and at most major tourist destinations around the country. You'll find them at almost all banks and most shopping centers. Still, make sure you have some cash at the start of your trip; never let yourself run totally out of spending money, and definitely stock up on funds before heading to any of the more remote destinations in the country. Most ATMs accept cards from both the **Cirrus** and **PLUS** networks, but some can't deal with PINs that are more than four digits. Before you go, make sure that your PIN fits the bill.

CREDIT CARDS MasterCard and Visa are accepted most everywhere. American Express and Diners Club are less common, but still widely accepted. To report a lost or stolen **American Express** card from inside Guatemala, you can call ✆ **336/393-1111** collect in the U.S.; for **MasterCard,** ✆ **1800/999-1480,** or call ✆ **636/722-7111** collect in the U.S.; for **Visa,** ✆ **1800/999-0115,** or call ✆ **410/581-9994** collect in the U.S.; and for **Diners Club,** call ✆ **502/2338-6801,** or call collect to ✆ **303/799-1504.**

WHEN TO GO

PEAK SEASON & CLIMATE The tourist high season runs December through March, coinciding with the winter months in most northern countries. It also coincides with Guatemala's dry season. Throughout this season, and especially around the Christmas and Easter holidays, hotels can be booked solid well in advance, so be sure to have a reservation. Easter and Holy Week are major holidays in Guatemala and in Antigua specifically. Hotels in Antigua are booked solid as much as a year in advance.

Guatemala is a tropical country and has distinct wet and dry seasons. However, some regions are rainy all year, and others are very dry and sunny for most of the year. Temperatures vary primarily with elevations, not with seasons: On the coasts it's hot all year, while up in the mountains and highlands, it can be quite cool at night and in the early morning, before the sun heats things up, any time of year. At the highest elevations (3,500–4,000m/11,500–13,120 ft.), frost is common.

Generally, the **rainy season** (or *invierno,* winter) is May through October. The **dry season** (or *verano,* summer) runs from November to April. Along the Pacific coast, the dry season lasts several weeks longer than in other places. Even in the rainy season, days often start sunny, with rain falling in the afternoon and evening. On the Atlantic coast, the weather is less predictable, and you can get rain year-round, though this area gets less rain in July and August than the rest of the country. The rainforests of the Petén get the heaviest rainfall, and the rainy season here lasts at least until mid-November.

In general, the best time of year to visit weather-wise is in December and January, when everything is still green from the rains, but the sky is clear. If you want to avoid the crowds, I recommend traveling during "shoulder" periods, near the end or beginning of the rainy season, when the weather is still pretty good.

PUBLIC HOLIDAYS Official holidays in Guatemala include **January 1** (New Year's Day), Thursday and Friday of Holy Week, **June 30** (Armed Forces Day), **July 1** (Day of Celebration), **August 15** (Virgen de la Asunción), **September 15** (Independence Day), **October 20** (Commemoration of the 1944 Revolution), **November 1** (All Saints' Day), **December 24** and **25** (Christmas), and **December 31** (New Year's Eve).

HEALTH CONCERNS

Guatemala's public healthcare system is overburdened, under-funded, and outdated. Throughout the chapter, I've listed the nearest public hospital and, when available, private hospital or clinic. Still, when you're in Guatemala, your hotel or local embassy will be your best source of information and aid in finding emergency care or a doctor who speaks English. Most state-run hospitals and walk-in clinics around the country have emergency rooms that can treat most conditions. However, I highly recommend that you seek out a specialist recommended by your hotel or embassy if your condition is not life-threatening and can wait for treatment until you reach one of them.

Common Ailments

Your chance of contracting any serious tropical disease in Guatemala is slim, especially if you stick to the well-worn tourist destinations. However, malaria and dengue fever both exist in Guatemala. **Malaria** is found in rural areas across the country, particularly in the lowlands on both coasts and in the Petén. There is little to no chance of contracting malaria in Guatemala City or Antigua. See p. 70 in "Planning Your Trip to Central America" for tips on how to treat and avoid such ailments.

Guatemala suffers from periodic outbreaks of **cholera,** a severe intestinal disease whose symptoms include severe diarrhea and vomiting. However, these outbreaks usually occur in predominantly rural and very impoverished areas. Your chances of contracting cholera while you're in Guatemala are very slight. Other food and waterborne illnesses can mimic the symptoms of cholera and are far more common. These range from simple traveler's diarrhea to salmonella. See p. 70 in "Planning Your Trip to Central America" for tips on how to treat and avoid such ailments.

No specific vaccines are required for traveling to Guatemala. That said, many doctors recommend vaccines for hepatitis A and B, as well as up-to-date booster shots for tetanus.

GETTING THERE

By Plane

Most international flights land at **La Aurora International Airport** (**GUA;** ✆ **502/ 2332-6086**). A few international and regional airlines fly directly into **Flores Airport** (**FRS;** no phone) near Tikal. If you're only interested in visiting the Maya ruins at Tikal and touring the Petén, this is a good option. However, most visitors will want to fly in and out of Guatemala City.

FROM NORTH AMERICA **American Airlines, Continental**, **Delta, Grupo Taca, Iberia, Mexicana, Spirit,** and **United** all have regular flights from a variety of North American hub cities. Presently, there are no direct flights from Canada to Guatemala, so Canadians will have to take a connecting flight via the United States. See the appendix for phone numbers and websites.

FROM THE U.K. & EUROPE There are no direct flights to Guatemala from the U.K., although **Iberia** (✆ **2332-0911;** www.iberia.com) does have a direct flight from Madrid. Otherwise. you will have to fly via a major U.S. hub city and connect with one of the airlines mentioned above.

FROM AUSTRALIA & NEW ZEALAND To get to Guatemala from Australia or New Zealand, you'll first have to fly to Los Angeles or some other U.S. hub city, where you can connect with one of the airlines mentioned above.

By Bus

Guatemala is connected to Mexico, Belize, El Salvador, and Honduras by regular bus service. If at all possible, it's worth the splurge for a deluxe or express bus.

From Mexico, the principal border crossing is at La Mesilla, north of Huehuetenango. From Honduras, the main border crossing is at El Florido, on the route from Copán. From El Salvador, the main border crossing is at San Cristobal, along the Pan-American Highway (Carretera Panamericana). And from Belize, the main border crossing is at Melchor de Mencos, in the Petén district.

There are several bus lines with regular daily departures connecting the major capital cities of Central America. **Tica Bus Company** (✆ **502/2221-0006;** www.ticabus.com) has buses running from Mexico all the way down to Panama, while **Pullmantur** (✆ **502/2367-4746;** www.pullmantur.com) connects Guatemala with daily service to San Salvador, El Salvador, and Tegucigalpa, Honduras.

GETTING AROUND

BY SHUTTLE For most of the major destinations in Guatemala, tourist shuttles or a private car and driver are your best means for getting around. There are a couple of major tourist shuttle services in the country, and almost every hotel tour desk and local tour agency can book you a ride to just about any major tourist destination in the country either on a regularly scheduled shuttle or with a private car and driver.

The main tourist shuttle company is **Atitrans** ★ (✆ **502/7832-3371** 24-hr. reservation number; www.atitrans.com) which offers both regularly scheduled departures to most of the major tourist destinations in the country, as well as private cars or vans with drivers. Or you can contact **Clark Tours** (✆ **502/2412-4848;** www.clarktours.com.gt), **Maya Vacations** (✆ **502/2426-1400;** www.mayavacations.com), or **Via Venture** (✆ **502/7832-2509;** www.viaventure.com).

Shuttle rates from Guatemala City or Antigua to or from other major destinations run between Q90 and Q375 ($12–$50/£6–£25) depending upon the destination. A private car or van with driver should cost between Q600 and Q1,500 ($80–$200/£40–£100) per day, depending on the size and style of the vehicle and how many passengers are traveling.

BY BUS This is by far the most economical way to get around Guatemala. Buses are inexpensive and go nearly everywhere in the country. There are two types: **Local buses** are the cheapest and slowest; they stop frequently and are generally very dilapidated. They also tend to be overcrowded, and you are much more likely to be the victim of a robbery on one of these. These buses are commonly referred to as **"chicken buses"** because the rural residents who depend on these buses often have chickens and other livestock as luggage. For all but the most adventurous types, I recommend you avoid these buses.

Warning: Guatemalan buses are often the targets of crime, both violent and nonviolent. Do not arrive by bus at night if at all possible, as the bus terminals and surrounding areas are very dangerous at night. If you do, hop in a cab immediately after you arrive.

Express or **deluxe buses** run between Guatemala City and most beach towns and major cities; these tend to be newer units and much more comfortable. They also tend to be direct buses, and thus are much quicker. Most have working bathrooms, and some have televisions equipped with DVD players showing late-run movies.

BY CAR In general, I don't recommend renting a car in Guatemala. The roads are often dangerous. Guatemalan drivers, particularly bus and truck drivers, have apparently no concern for human life, their own or anybody else's. A brutal Darwinian survival of the fittest attitude reigns on Guatemala's roads. Passing on blind curves seems to be the national sport. Pedestrians, horses, dogs, and other obstacles seem to appear out of nowhere. In addition, theft is an issue. I highly recommend you avoid driving at night at all costs. While rare, there have been armed robberies of tourists and Guatemalans along the highways and back roads of Guatemala, particularly at night. Moreover, the inherent dangers of oncoming traffic and unseen obstacles are heightened at night.

These caveats aren't meant to entirely scare you off from driving in Guatemala. Thousands of tourists rent cars here every year, and the large majority of them encounter no problems. Renting a car is a good option for independent exploring, and it does provide a lot more freedom and save a lot of time over bus travel. Just keep your wits about you.

Among the agencies operating in Guatemala are: **Avis** (© **800/331-1212** in the U.S., or 502/2239-3249 in Guatemala; www.avis.com), **Budget** (© **800/527-0700** in the U.S., or 502/2232-7744 in Guatemala; www.budgetguatemala.com.gt), **Hertz** (© **800/654-3131** in the U.S., or 502/2470-3737 in Guatemala; www.hertz.com), **National** (© **800/227-7368** in the U.S., or 502/2362-3000 in Guatemala; www.natcar.com), and **Thrifty** (© **800/367-2277** in the U.S., or 502/2379-8747 in Guatemala; www.thrifty.com). **Tabarini** (© **502/2331-9814;** www.tabarini.com) is a good Guatemalan company with offices in Guatemala City, Antigua, and Tikal.

Rates run between Q263 and Q750 ($35–$100/£18–£50) per day, including unlimited mileage and full insurance.

BY PLANE Guatemala still doesn't have a very extensive network of commuter airlines. The only major destination regularly serviced by commuter traffic is Tikal. **TACA Regional Airline** (© **502/2470-8222;** www.taca.com) and **TAG Airlines ★** (© **502/2380-9401;** www.tag.com.gt) both have daily service to Tikal. For information on schedules, see p. 208.

BY TAXI In most tourist destinations, taxis are plentiful, safe, and inexpensive, and while they're supposed to use meters, most don't, especially outside of Guatemala City. It's always best to ask before taking off whether it will be a metered ride, and if not, to negotiate the price in advance. Most short rides cost between Q15 and Q30 ($2–$4.10/£1–£2.05). Where possible, I've listed taxi phone numbers throughout the book. Still, in most popular destinations it's usually quite easy to flag one down in the street, or have your hotel or restaurant call you one.

TIPS ON ACCOMMODATIONS

With the exception of a few large business-class hotels clustered in Guatemala City's Zona Viva, Guatemala has no truly large-scale resorts or hotels. What the country does have is a wealth of intimate and interesting **small to midsize hotels** and **resorts.** A few very classy luxury boutique hotels are scattered around the country, and are found with relative abundance in Antigua and around Lake Atitlán. Real budget travelers will find a glut of very acceptable and very inexpensive options all across the country.

A hotel is sometimes called a *posada* in Guatemala. As a general rule, a *posada* is a smaller, more humble and less luxurious option than a hotel. However, there are some very serious exceptions to this rule, particularly in Antigua, where some of the finest accommodations are called *posadas.*

Unless otherwise noted, rates given in this book do not include the 12% IVA and 10% hotel tax. These taxes will add considerably to the cost of your room.

TIPS ON DINING

With the exception of some regional specialties, the most common and prevalent aspects of Guatemalan cuisine are rather unimpressive. Handmade fresh corn tortillas are the basic staple of Guatemalan cooking. Tortillas, along with refried black beans, are usually served as an accompaniment to some simply grilled meat or chicken. Very few vegetables are typically served at Guatemalan meals.

You will find excellent restaurants serving a wide range of international cuisines in Guatemala City, Antigua, and Panajachel. However, outside the capital and these major tourist destinations, your options get limited very fast.

If you're looking for cheap eats, you'll find them in little restaurants known as ***comedores,*** which are the equivalent of diners in the United States. At a *comedor,* you'll find a limited and very inexpensive menu featuring some simple steak and chicken dishes, accompanied by rice, refried beans, and fresh tortillas.

Keep in mind that the 12% IVA tax added onto all bills is not a service charge. A tip of at least 10% is expected, and sometimes it is automatically added to your bill.

TIPS ON SHOPPING

In many respects, Guatemala City is a great place for shopping, particularly if you're interested in Guatemalan arts and crafts. While it's much more fun and culturally interesting to visit one of the traditional markets, like that in Chichicastenango, you can find just about anything made and sold throughout Guatemala on sale at gift shops in all of the major tourist destinations around the country. Moreover, you can find these arts and crafts in large, expansive markets, as well as in small, boutique shops. ***Note:*** It is illegal to export any pre-Columbian artifacts out of Guatemala.

The best-known crafts are indigenous woven tapestries and clothing. The fabrics are woven on huge looms or simple, portable back-strap looms. Traditional dress for women includes a *huipil* (blouse) and *corte* (skirt), often fastened to the waist with a rope belt. In recent years, mass-produced machine-woven fabrics have begun replacing the more traditional wares. To spot a fake, look for gold or synthetic threads woven into the cloth, and for overly neat stitching on the back.

Other common handicrafts found in gift shops and markets across Guatemala include carved-wood masks and carved stone and jade. For high-end arts, crafts, jewelry, and clothing, Antigua is your best bet. Here you'll find a wide range of excellent small shops and galleries.

In addition to the arts, crafts and clothing, Guatemala's **Zacapa rum** ★★★ is one of the finest rums in the world. The 23-year-old Zacapa Centenario is as rich and smooth as a fine cognac. Zacapa rums also come in 15- and 25-year aged varieties. You can get Zacapa rum at liquor stores and supermarkets across the country. However, you'll find good prices right at the airport. It's convenient to know you can save that last bit of shopping until the last minute.

Fast Facts Guatemala

American Express **Clark Tours** (✆ **502/2412-4848;** www.clarktours.com.gt) is the representative of American Express Travel Services in Guatemala. Their main offices are in Guatemala City at Clark Plaza, 7a Av. 14-76, Zona 9. They also have desks at the downtown Westin and Marriott hotels. To report lost or stolen Amex traveler's checks within Guatemala, dial ✆ **800/288-0073,** or call ✆ **801/964-6665** collect in the U.S.

Business Hours Banks are usually open Monday through Friday from 9am to 4pm, although many have begun to offer extended hours. Offices are open Monday through Friday from 8am to 5pm (many close for 1 hr. at lunch). Stores are generally open Monday through Saturday from 9am to 6pm (many close for 1 hr. at lunch). Stores in modern malls generally stay open until 8 or 9pm and don't close for lunch. Most bars are open until 1 or 2am.

Doctors Contact your embassy for information on doctors in Guatemala, or see "Hospitals," below.

Embassies & Consulates All major consulates and embassies, where present, are in Guatemala City. **Canada,** 13a Calle 8-44, Zona 10 (✆ **502/2363-4348;** www.guatemala.gc.ca); **United Kingdom,** Avenida de la Reforma and 16a Calle, Torre Internacional, Zona 10 (✆ **502/2367-5425**); and the **United States,** Av. de la Reforma 7-01, Zona 10 (✆ **502/2326-4279**). **Australia** and **New Zealand** do not have an embassy or consulate in Guatemala.

Emergencies In case of any emergency, dial ✆ **1500** from anywhere in Guatemala. This will connect you to **Asistur,** which will have a bilingual operator, who in turn can put you in contact with the police, fire department, or ambulance service, as necessary. Alternately, you can dial ✆ **110** for the National Police; and ✆ **125** for the Red Cross (Cruz Roja, in Spanish). Moreover, ✆ **911** works as an emergency number from most phones in Guatemala.

Hospitals The country's best hospitals are in Guatemala City. **Hospital Centro Médico,** 6a Av. 3-47, Zona 10 (✆ **502/2279-4949**), is an excellent private hospital, with English-speaking doctors on staff. Alternately, the **Hospital General San Juan de Dios,** 1a Avenida and 10a Calle, Zona 1 (✆ **502/2220-8396**), is the biggest and best equipped public hospital in the city.

Language Spanish is the official language of Guatemala. English is spoken at most tourist hotels, restaurants, and attractions. Outside of the tourist orbit, English is not widely spoken, and some rudimentary Spanish will go a long way. Some 23 Mayan dialects are also widely spoken around the country. In many rural areas, many residents speak their local dialect as their primary language, and a certain segment of the population may speak little or no Spanish.

Newspapers & Magazines *La Prensa Libre* is the country's most highly regarded daily newspaper, with an outstanding investigative reporting staff. The lower-brow *Nuestro Diario* has the highest circulation. There are several other daily papers, including *Siglo XXI*. There are currently no English-language newspapers. The free, monthly, English-language **Revue Magazine** (www.revuemag.com) is the most valuable information source for most tourists, with museum, art gallery, and theater listings. It is widely available at hotels and other tourist haunts around the country.

Police In case of an emergency, dial ✆ **1500** from anywhere in Guatemala. This will connect you to a bilingual operator at Asistur who can put you in contact with the police, fire department, or ambulance service. Dial ✆ **110** or **120** for the **National Police,** and ✆ **125** for the **Red Cross** (**Cruz Roja,** in Spanish). As in the U.S., ✆ **911** works as an emergency number from most phones in Guatemala.

Post Offices & Mail A post office is called *correo* in Spanish. Most towns have a main *correo,* usually right near the central square. In addition, most hotels will post letters and cards for you. It costs around Q5 (65¢/35p) to send a letter to the U.S. or Europe. Postcards to the same destinations cost Q3 (40¢/20p). Most post offices are open Monday to Friday from 8am to 5pm. Some are open Saturday from 8am to noon. However, it's best to send anything of any value via an established international courier service. **DHL,** 12a Calle 5-12, Zona 10 (✆ **502/2379-1111;** www.dhl.com), **UPS,** 12a Calle 5-53, Zona 10 (✆ **502/2231-2421;** www.ups.com), and **FedEx,** Diagonal 6 12-20, Zona 10 (✆ **502/2411-2100;** www.fedex.com) all have offices in Guatemala City, with nationwide coverage for pickup and delivery. DHL also has offices in Antigua and Panajachel.

Safety Safety is serious issue in Guatemala. In Guatemala City, I highly recommend that you stick to the most affluent and touristy sections of town highlighted in this book. Basic common sense and street smarts are to be employed. Don't wear flashy jewelry or wave wads of cash around. Be aware of your surroundings, and avoid any people and places that make you feel uncomfortable. Basically, it is unwise to walk almost anywhere except the most secure and heavily trafficked tourist zones after dark. Rental cars generally stick out and are easily spotted by thieves, who know that such cars are likely to be full of expensive camera equipment, money, and other valuables. Don't ever leave anything of value in an unattended parked car.

Taxes A Q225 ($30/£15) tax must be paid upon departure. This is often included in your airline ticket price. Be sure to check in advance. If not, you will have to pay the fee in cash at the airport. There is an additional airport security fee of Q20 ($2.65/£1.35).

A 12% IVA (value added) tax is tacked on to the purchase of all goods and services. An additional 10% tax, on top of the 12% IVA, is added to all hotel rooms and lodgings.

Telephone & Fax Guatemala has a modern and extensive telephone network. Several competing cellphone companies vie for new clients. All of these companies sell prepaid GSM chips that can be used in any unlocked tri-band GSM cellphone. Moreover, all sell activated new phones for as little as Q100 ($13/£6.65). See the "Telephone Dialing Info at a Glance" box above for more info.

Tipping While there is a 12% IVA tax on all goods and services, none of this counts as a tip. In restaurants, a minimum tip of 10% is common and expected. Tip more if the service was exemplary. Taxi drivers do not expect, and are rarely given, a tip.

4 GUATEMALA CITY

Guatemala City is the country's capital and largest city. In fact, with a population of nearly three million, it's the largest city in Central America. Guatemala City was founded as the country's third capital in 1776, following the destruction of two earlier attempts by natural disasters—earthquakes and mudslides. Christened with the unwieldy name of La Nueva Guatemala de La Asunción de la Valle de la Ermita by Spain's King Charles III, it's most commonly known by its simple abbreviation, Guate. Long before the Spaniards moved their capital here, this was the site of the pre-Classic Maya city of Kaminaljuyú, whose ruins you can still visit.

Despite its well-deserved reputation as a sometimes violent and dangerous place, Guatemala City has a lot to offer travelers. The principal commercial and tourist zones are full of fine hotels and excellent restaurants, and the nightlife found in Zona Viva and Cuatro Grados Norte is the best in the country. The city also boasts theaters, art galleries, and several worthwhile museums.

ESSENTIALS

Getting There

For more information on arriving in Guatemala City, see "Getting There" in "Planning Your Trip to Guatemala," earlier in this chapter.

BY PLANE All flights into Guatemala City land at **La Aurora International Airport (GUA; ✆ 502/2332-6086)**, which is located in Zona 13 on the edge of the city center and about 25km (16 miles) from Antigua.

There is an **INGUAT** (Guatemalan Tourism Commission; www.visitguatemala.com) information booth inside the airport, which is open to meet all arriving flights. There are also a couple of banks inside the airport that will exchange dollars and some European currencies, and cash traveler's checks. They are usually open whenever there are arriving or departing flights. An ATM is located near the baggage claim area.

You'll find various shuttle companies offering hotel transfers as you exit either the national or international terminal. These companies charge between Q30 and Q60 ($4–$8/£2–£4) to any hotel in Guatemala City, and between Q75 and Q113 ($10–$15/£5–£7.50) to Antigua. Many of the larger hotels also have regular complimentary airport shuttle buses.

If you don't want to wait for the shuttle to fill or sit through various stops before arriving at your hotel, there are always taxis lined up at the airport terminal exits. A taxi downtown will cost around Q45 to Q75 ($6–$10/£3–£5).

Avis, Budget, Hertz, National, Tabarini, and **Thrifty** all have car-rental desks at the airport. See "Getting Around: By Car" below, for more information.

BY BUS Guatemala's bus system is a chaotic mess. Scores of independent companies provide service to just about every nook and cranny in the country. However, there is little rhyme or reason to their terminal locations. If you arrive in town by bus, you may end up at the large and hectic main bus terminal and market area in Zona 4, or at any number of private terminals around the city, often in Zona 1. It's always easy to find a taxi near any of the bus terminals, and I recommend taking one to your final destination in the city, which should cost Q45 to Q75 ($6–$10/£3–£5).

Orientation

Guatemala City is divided into 21 zones or "*zonas.*" The *zonas* are numbered sequentially in a spiral pattern beginning with Zona 1, the most central and oldest zone in the city. In general, the city is laid out on a standard grid, with *avenidas* (avenues) running roughly north-south, and *calles* (streets) running east-west. Of the 21 zones, there are only a few that you're likely to visit, as they hold the majority of the city's hotels, restaurants, and major attractions.

Fun Facts Breaking the Code

Guatemalan addresses may look confusing, but they're actually easy to understand. All addresses are written beginning with the *avenida* or *calle* that the building, business, or house is on, followed by the nearest cross street and actual building number, written out as a two-number hyphen combination. This is then followed by the zone. For example, the INGUAT Office on 7a Av. 1-17, Zona 4 is located at no. 17, on Avenida 7, near the cross street of 1a Calle in Zona 4. Be very careful, first and foremost, that you're in the correct zone. 7a Av. 1-17, Zona 4; and 7a Av. 1-17, Zona 10, are two radically different addresses.

Zona 1 is the historic center and colonial core of the city. Zonas 9 and 10 are two neighboring upscale neighborhoods where you will find just about all the major hotels, restaurants, shops, travel agencies and services of note. Zona 10 is commonly referred to as Zona Viva, though only the small section of Zona 10 with the greatest concentration of hotels, restaurants, and shops falls under this category. Zona 4 is a central area, which is home to the INGUAT offices, immigration, the national court system, and a major bus terminal. This is also where you'll find Cuatro Grados Norte, a pedestrian-friendly and safe section of bars, restaurants, shops, and discos. The airport and area around it are Zona 13.

Getting Around

Guatemala City has an extensive network of metropolitan buses, but a vast number of assaults take place on them at all times of day and night. I highly recommend you take a taxi instead.

BY TAXI Taxis are plentiful and relatively inexpensive, and while they're supposed to use meters, many don't. It's always best to ask before taking off whether it will be a metered ride, and if not, to negotiate the price in advance. A ride anywhere in the city should cost between Q15 and Q75 ($2–$10/£1–£5).

If you need to call a cab, ask your hotel or try **Taxi Amarillo Express** (© **502/2470-1515**), **Taxi Blanco y Azul** (© **502/2440-8789**), **Taxis 2000** (© **502/2433-9984**), or **Taxis Las Americas** (© **502/2362-0583**). Express cabs all use meters.

ON FOOT Guatemala City is not very conducive to exploring by foot. The city is spread out, and many of the major attractions are far from one another. Plus street crime is a problem. It's relatively safe to walk around zonas 1, 4, 9, 10, and 13 by day. However, with few exceptions, you should never walk around Guatemala City at night. Those few exceptions include the most developed parts of Zona 10, or the Zona Viva; and the hip, strip of bars and restaurants in Zona 4, known as Cuatro Grados Norte.

BY CAR Driving in Guatemala City falls somewhere between a headache and a nightmare. There is little need to navigate Guatemala City in a car. I highly recommend you take taxis and leave the driving to others. If you do find yourself driving around Guatemala City, go slow, as pedestrians and vehicles can appear out of nowhere. See p. 66 for rental car info.

Visitor Information

The **Guatemalan Tourism Commission (INGUAT; © 502/2421-2800;** www.visitguatemala.com) has an airport booth for arriving tourists, as well as a main office at 7a Av. 1-17, Zona 4. This office is open Monday through Friday from 8am until 4pm, and can provide maps and brochures. They can also make a call for you if you need a hotel or car-rental reservation. To get tourist assistance and information from anywhere within Guatemala, dial **© 1500.**

Hotel concierges, tour desks, and local travel agencies are another good source of information. There are scores of tour agencies around Guatemala City. I recommend **Clark Tours,** 7a Av. 14-76, Zona 9, inside Clark Plaza (**© 502/2412-4848;** www.clarktours.com.gt), and **Maya Vacations,** 11 Av. 7-15, Zona 13 (**© 502/2426-1400;** www.mayavacations.com).

FAST FACTS In case of an **emergency,** call **© 1500** or **911.** You can reach the **Cruz Roja (Red Cross)** by dialing **© 125.**

Hospital Centro Médico, 6a Av. 3-47, Zona 10 (**© 502/2279-4949**), is an excellent private hospital, with English-speaking doctors on staff. Alternately, the **Hospital General San Juan de Dios,** 1a Avenida and 10a Calle, Zona 1 (**© 502/2220-8396**), is the biggest and best equipped public hospital in the city.

Clark Tours, Clark Plaza, 7a Av. 14-76, Zona 9 (**© 502/2412-4700;** www.clarktours.com.gt), is the official representative of American Express Travel Services. They also have desks at the downtown Westin and Marriott hotels.

Internet cafes are ubiquitous in Guatemala City; particularly in the Zona Viva and Zona 1 neighborhoods. Rates run between Q3 and Q15 (40¢–$2/20p–£1) per hour. Many hotels either have their own Wi-Fi network or Internet cafe where guests can send and receive e-mail.

The main **post office,** 7a Av. 12-11, Zona 1 (**© 502/2232-6101**), is a beautiful building. It costs around Q7 (95¢/45p) to send a letter to the U.S. or Europe. Postcards to the same destinations cost Q5 (65¢/35p).

WHAT TO SEE & DO

While it's easy to visit all of these attractions on your own by taxi, many travelers like the convenience and built-in guide offered by organized city tours. **Clark Tours,** 7a Av. 14-76, Zona 9, inside Clark Plaza (**© 502/2412-4848;** www.clarktours.com.gt), offers several different city tours. Most of these combine a tour around the principal attractions of Zona 1 and the colonial core, with stops at the **Museo Popul Vuh, Museo Ixchel del Traje Indígena,** and one of the city's large markets.

Zona 1

Catedral Metropolitana (Metropolitan Cathedral) ★★ This stately, blue-domed, earthquake-resistant cathedral was completed in 1868 after 86 years of construction. The neoclassical structure inspires both austerity and awe, with its stone floors, colonial paintings, lofty arches, and bursts of gold at its altars. Perhaps the cathedral's most striking feature is the entrance, which is supported by 12 pillars, each of which is inscribed with the names of hundreds of Guatemalans who died or "disappeared" during the civil war. The interior is large and filled with religious icons, carvings, and artworks. You can tour the cathedral in about 20 minutes.

8a Calle and 7a Av., Zona 1. No phone. Free admission. Daily 8am–8pm.

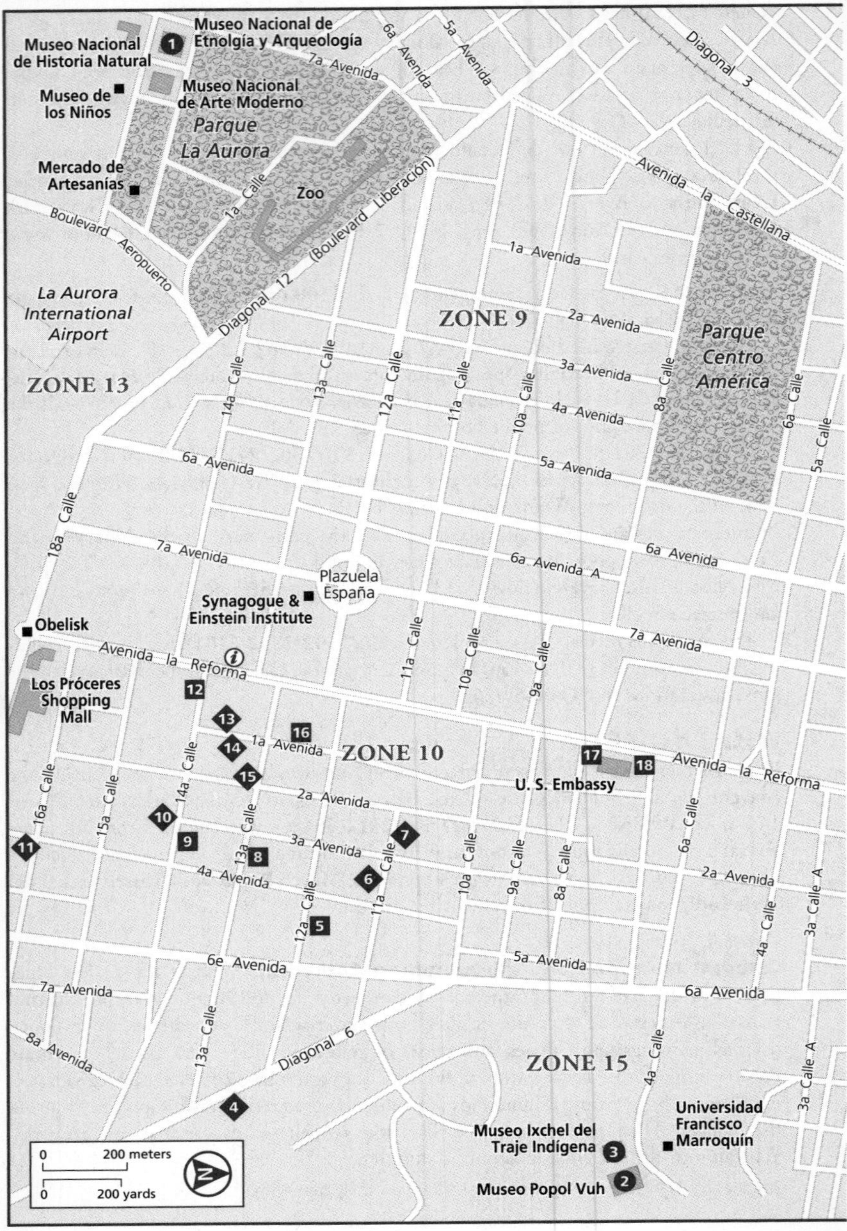

Museo Nacional de Etnolgía y Arqueología
Museo Nacional de Historia Natural
Museo de los Niños
Museo Nacional de Arte Moderno
Parque La Aurora
Mercado de Artesanías
Zoo
1a Calle
7a Avenida
6a Avenida
5a Avenida
Diagonal 3
Avenida la Castellana
Boulevard Aeropuerto
Diagonal 12 (Boulevard Liberación)
La Aurora International Airport
ZONE 13
ZONE 9
1a Avenida
2a Avenida
3a Avenida
4a Avenida
5a Avenida
6a Avenida
6a Avenida A
7a Avenida
Parque Centro América
14a Calle
13a Calle
12a Calle
11a Calle
10a Calle
9a Calle
8a Calle
6a Calle
5a Calle
18a Calle
Plazuela España
Synagogue & Einstein Institute
Obelisk
Avenida la Reforma
Los Próceres Shopping Mall
ZONE 10
U. S. Embassy
16a Calle
15a Calle
2a Avenida
3a Avenida
4a Avenida
6e Avenida
7a Avenida
8a Avenida
Diagonal 6
4a Calle
3a Calle A
ZONE 15
Universidad Francisco Marroquín
Museo Ixchel del Traje Indígena
Museo Popol Vuh
0 200 meters
0 200 yards
N

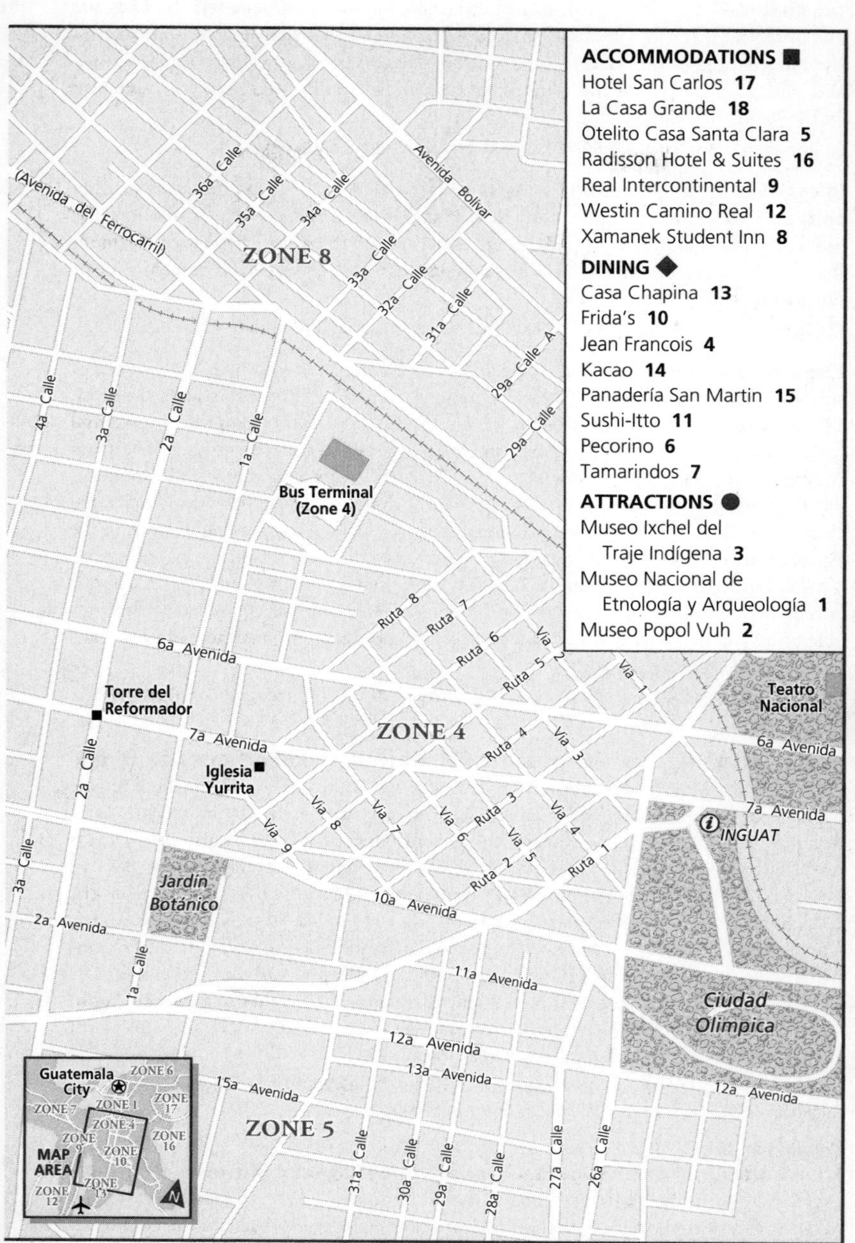
ACCOMMODATIONS
Hotel San Carlos 17
La Casa Grande 18
Otelito Casa Santa Clara 5
Radisson Hotel & Suites 16
Real Intercontinental 9
Westin Camino Real 12
Xamanek Student Inn 8
DINING
Casa Chapina 13
Frida's 10
Jean Francois 4
Kacao 14
Panadería San Martin 15
Sushi-Itto 11
Pecorino 6
Tamarindos 7
ATTRACTIONS
Museo Ixchel del Traje Indígena 3
Museo Nacional de Etnología y Arqueología 1
Museo Popol Vuh 2
ZONE 8
ZONE 4
ZONE 5
(Avenida del Ferrocarril)
Avenida Bolivar
36a Calle
35a Calle
34a Calle
33a Calle
32a Calle
31a Calle
29a Calle A
29a Calle
4a Calle
3a Calle
2a Calle
1a Calle
Bus Terminal (Zone 4)
Ruta 8
Ruta 7
Ruta 6
Ruta 5
Ruta 4
Ruta 3
Ruta 2
Ruta 1
Vía 1
Vía 2
Vía 3
Vía 4
Vía 5
Vía 6
Vía 7
Vía 8
Vía 9
6a Avenida
7a Avenida
Torre del Reformador
Iglesia Yurrita
Teatro Nacional
INGUAT
Jardín Botánico
2a Avenida
10a Avenida
11a Avenida
12a Avenida
13a Avenida
15a Avenida
Ciudad Olimpica
31a Calle
30a Calle
29a Calle
28a Calle
27a Calle
26a Calle
Guatemala City
ZONE 6
ZONE 7
ZONE 1
ZONE 17
ZONE 4
ZONE 9
ZONE 10
ZONE 16
MAP AREA
ZONE 13
ZONE 12
N

Iglesia La Merced (La Merced Church) ★ Not to be confused with its more famous sister church of the same name in Antigua, this lovely baroque-style building has one of the most ornate facades of any Catholic church in Guatemala City. The interior is quite stunning as well, and features an extensive collection of religious art, sculpture, and relics. Originally built and administered by the order of La Merced, it was taken over by the Jesuits in the early 19th century.

5a Calle and 11a Av., Zona 1. ✆ **502/2232-0631.** Free admission. Daily 6am–6pm.

Iglesia San Francisco (San Francisco Church) ★★ The namesake Franciscan order built this baroque church in the early 19th century. The main altar is an impressive piece of work, at almost 91m (300 ft.) tall and 12m (40 ft.) wide. The church is famous for its woodcarvings, which include its main altar and a couple of beautiful pieces donated by King Charles V of Spain.

13a Calle and 6a Av., Zona 1. ✆ **502/2232-6325.** Free admission. Daily 6am–5pm.

Plaza Mayor ★★ Called the "center of all Guatemala," the Plaza Mayor brings together the great powers of Guatemalan society: the government, the church, the army, and the people. It consists of two large plazas, the Parque del Centenario with its central fountain, and the Plaza de las Armas, intended as a military parade ground. The Plaza Mayor was first laid out and designed in 1778, just 2 years after the city was founded. The impressive buildings surrounding the plaza include the Catedral Metropolitana, the Palacio Nacional, and the National Library. Next to the Guatemalan flag in front of the Palacio Nacional burns an Eternal Flame dedicated to the "anonymous heroes of peace." Crowds gather here to celebrate holidays, protest, and sell their goods. The makeshift market here is busiest on Sundays, when vendors offer a wide variety of crafts at reasonable prices, though you might be able to find better deals in the small towns along Lake Atitlán or in Quetzaltenango.

Btw. 6a Calle and 8a Calle, and btw. 5a Av. and 7a Av., Zona 1. No phone. Free admission. Daily 24 hr.

Zona 10

Museo Ixchel del Traje Indígena (Ixchel Museum of Indigenous Dress) ★★ Ixchel was the Maya goddess of fertility and weaving, and she certainly inspired artistic talent in her people. A collection of textiles from approximately 120 indigenous communities is on display here, providing a good introduction to and history of the crafts travelers are likely to see on their journey across the country. The museum also has two permanent exhibitions of paintings: 61 watercolors of Maya traditional dress from the collection of Carmen de Pettersen, and 48 oil paintings of the Cakchiquel artist Andrés Curruchiche. Three 13-minute videos are shown by request on the second floor. I recommend you ask to see the one on traditional fabrics even before you tour the museum.

Since you're already here, I also recommend visiting the neighboring **Museo Popul Vuh** (✆ **502/2361-2301;** www.popolvuh.ufm.edu), which features several rooms worth of exhibits of Maya archaeology, art, and artifacts.

Universidad Francisco Marroquín, end of 6a Calle, Zona 10. ✆ **502/2331-3622.** www.museoixchel.org. Admission Q35 ($4.65/£2.35). Mon–Fri 9am–5pm; Sat 9am–1pm.

Zona 13

Museo Nacional de Etnología y Arqueología (National Museum of Ethnology and Archaeology) ★ The National Ethnology and Archaeology Museum houses the most important collection of Maya archaeological artifacts in the country. It traces indigenous history over the centuries and through the present day, using several hundred Maya artifacts to tell the story. (Unfortunately the only written descriptions are in Spanish.) Exhibits include a room dedicated to Maya technology (paper, and ceramic, shell, and bone tools), as well as a display of indigenous clothing. The highlight of the collection is the jade exhibit, with earrings, bracelets, masks, and an impressive scale model of Tikal.

5a Calle and 7a Av., Finca La Aurora, Local 5, Zona 13. ✆ **502/2475-4010.** www.munae.gob.gt. Admission Q30 ($4/£2). Tues–Fri 9am–4pm; Sat 9am–noon and 2–4pm.

Outdoor & Wellness Activities

Guatemala City is a hectic, somewhat dangerous, congested urban center, and not a particularly inviting place to pursue most outdoor activities. If you want to exercise or get out into nature, you're best off leaving the city.

BIKING Though you can forget about riding a bicycle in Guatemala City, several tour companies organize mountain biking trips in the hills, mountains, and volcanoes just outside the city. Your best bet is to contact **Old Town Outfitters ★★** (✆ **502/5399-0440;** www.bikeguatemala.com), which is based in Antigua and can arrange transportation for you to join any of their daily mountain bike rides.

JOGGING As is the case with biking, Guatemala City is not very amenable to jogging. There are no public parks or outdoor spaces I can recommend as safe and secure for a foreigner to go jogging, and the busy streets of the secure Zona 10 district are not suitable. If you want to run, try the **Grand Tikal Futura** (✆ **502/2410-0800;** www.grandtikalfutura.com.gt), which has a small outdoor jogging track.

SPAS & GYMS You can certainly burn some calories or get a nice pampering massage while in Guatemala City. Most of the high-end business hotels in town have some sort of spa or exercise room, which vary widely in terms of quantity and quality. The best equipped hotel spas I've found include those at the **Real InterContinental** (✆ **502/2413-4444;** www.interconti.com), the **Westin Camino Real** (✆ **502/2333-3000;** www.westin.com), and the **Grand Tikal Futura** (✆ **502/2410-0800;** www.grandtikalfutura.com.gt).

SWIMMING The tropical daytime heat makes a cooling dip quite inviting. Several of the higher-end hotels in Guatemala City have pools, but none of them will let outside guests use their facilities, even for a fee. If you really want to have access to a swimming pool, check the listing information under "Where to Stay," below, and make sure you choose a hotel with a swimming pool.

TENNIS The **Westin Camino Real** (✆ **502/2333-3000;** www.westin.com) and the **Grand Tikal Futura** (✆ **502/2410-0800;** www.grandtikalfutura.com.gt) are the only downtown hotels with tennis courts. If you're a die-hard tennis player and must play while in town, you should stay at one of these hotels. There are no other public facilities open to tourists downtown. Alternatively, you can contact any of the golf and country clubs listed above; all of these have multiple tennis courts, and will allow outside guests to play with advance reservations.

Shopping

There are two main markets in Guatemala City, the **Mercado Central,** or Central Market, in Zona 1, and **Mercado de Artesanías (Artisans' Market),** in Zona 13. Both are massive and stocked with a wide range of arts, crafts, textiles, and souvenirs available throughout the country. Aside from these, the greatest concentration of shops can be found in the Zona Viva. These shops tend to be higher-end, and you'll often pay a premium price for the same goods available at the markets. However, the markets are often flooded with low-quality items, which are weeded out from the offerings at the higher-end shops.

Carlos Woods Arte Antiguo y Contemporáneo ★★ After several generations of focusing on antiques and classic artwork, this family-run gallery moved into a larger space and began adding contemporary works to their repertoire. The lighting, architecture, and well-thought-out displays make this place feel as much like a museum as a gallery. 10a Av. 5-49, Zona 14. © **502/2366-6883.**

Colección 21 ★ This is an excellent shop and gallery with a wide range of arts, crafts, textiles, and jewelry of generally high quality. They also have a collection of contemporary painting, as well as some antiques. 12a Calle 4-65, Zona 14. © **502/2363-0649.**

Lin Canola ★★ This popular store features a massive selection of Guatemalan cloth and textile products, as well as other arts and crafts items. This is a great place to buy local fabrics in bulk. Originally operated out of the Mercado Central, they now have this downtown outlet, as well as their even newer sister storefront, **In Nola,** in the upscale Zona 10 neighborhood. 5 Calle 9-60, Zona 1. © **502/2253-0138.** www.lin-canola.com.

Mercado Central (Central Market) ★ Value This massive indoor market takes up several floors, covering a square city block in a building just behind the Catedral Metropolitana. This is your best bet for getting good deals on native wares. Offerings range from clothing and textiles to housewares and handicrafts. This market is actually frequented by Guatemalans more than tourists. Be careful of pickpockets. 9a Av. btw. 6a Calle and 8a Calle, Zona 1. No phone.

Sophos ★★ This hip and contemporary bookstore and cafe would fit right into the landscape in Seattle, New York, or Paris. They carry a wide selection of titles in Spanish and English, and feature rotating art exhibits and regular workshops, performances, readings, and book signings. Av. La Reforma 13-89, Zona 10. © **502/2334-6797.** www.sophosenlinea.com.

WHERE TO STAY

While Zona 11 is not typically a hot spot for tourists, the **Grand Tikal Futura ★★**, Calzada Roosevelt 22-43, Zona 11 (© **502/2410-0800;** www.grandtikalfutura.com.gt), is a well-equipped modern option, well suited for those having a rental car dropped off before driving out to Antigua or the Western Highlands.

Zonas 9, 10, 13 & Environs

These side-by-side zones contain the greatest concentration of hotels, restaurants, bars, and shops in the city, and heavy police presence makes them relatively safe for strolling and exploring on foot. Most of the hotels here are high-end business-class affairs, but there are actually options to fit all budgets. This area, particularly Zona 10, is often referred to as Zona Viva, or the "Alive Zone," because of all the dining and nightlife options.

Very Expensive

In addition to the hotel listed below, the **Westin Camino Real ★★**, 14a Calle and Avenida La Reforma, Zona 10 (© **800/228-3000** in the U.S. and Canada, or 502/2333-3000 in Guatemala; www.westin.com), is another excellent high-end hotel.

Real InterContinental ★★★ This is my favorite of the high-end, business-class hotels in this area. The rooms, facilities, and service are a notch above the competition, though most of the hotels in this class do a very good job. Rooms are spacious and in great condition, and all are carpeted and feature firm beds and 25-inch flatscreen televisions. Rooms on the InterClub floors have separate check-in desks, butler services, and a private lounge with regularly replenished snacks, free continental breakfast, and daily complimentary cocktail hour. There's an attractive pool area with a large Jacuzzi nearby. The hotel is situated on a busy corner in the Zona Viva, with scores of good restaurants, bars, and shops just steps away.

14a Calle 2-51, Zona 10. ✆ **502/2379-4446.** Fax 502/2379-4447. www.interconti.com. 239 units. Q940–Q2,007 ($126–$269/£64–£137) double; Q1,575–Q2,543 ($210–$339/£105-£)170) junior suite. AE, DISC, MC, V. Free valet parking. **Amenities:** 2 restaurants; 2 bars; babysitting; car-rental desk; well-equipped gym and spa; Jacuzzi; laundry service; nonsmoking rooms; pool; room service; salon; tour desk. *In room:* A/C, TV, hair dryer, Internet, minibar, safe.

Expensive

In addition to the hotels listed below, the **Radisson Hotel & Suites ★★**, 1a Av. 12-46, Zona 10 (✆ **800/333-3333** in the U.S. and Canada, or 502/2421-5151 in Guatemala; www.radisson.com), is a top-notch business-class option, while **Otelito Casa Santa Clara ★★**, 12a Calle 4-51, Zona 10 (✆/fax **502/2339-1811;** www.otelito.com), is a hip and intimate boutique choice.

Hotel San Carlos (Finds) Located right on the busy Avenida La Reforma, this charming three-story hotel features a Tudor exterior that's a little out of place in this Central American country. The British influence is carried over to the rooms, which feature antique furniture or knockoffs. My favorite rooms have plenty of space and varnished wood floors. This place is very similar in feel to La Casa Grande (below), but trumps it in terms of amenities and comfort. The hotel has a small lap pool in a pretty garden area.

Av. La Reforma 7-89, Zona 10. ✆ **502/2332-6055.** Fax 502/2331-6056. www.hsancarlos.com. 17 units. Q675 ($90/£45) double; Q938–Q1,313 ($125–$175/£63–£88) suite. Rates include continental breakfast. AE, DC, MC, V. Free parking. **Amenities:** Restaurant; bar; lounge; laundry service; pool; room service. *In room:* TV, hair dryer, Internet.

Moderate

La Casa Grande (Kids) This small boutique hotel harkens back to an earlier time. With whitewashed walls and a red-clay tile roof, this two-story building is an anomaly in an area of high-rise glass and steel buildings. Rooms feature antique tile floors and Victorian-style furnishings and decor. Even though the main building is set back from the street, the rooms closest to the street can be noisy. La Casa Grande has several pleasant courtyard and interior sitting areas.

Av. La Reforma 7-57, Zona 10. ✆/fax **502/2332-0914.** www.casagrande-gua.com. 28 units. Q563–Q750 ($75–$100/£38–£50) double. AE, DISC, MC, V. Free parking. **Amenities:** Restaurant; bar; laundry service; room service. *In room:* TV, coffeemaker, hair dryer, minibar.

Inexpensive

With the opening of **Xamanek Student Inn,** 13 Calle 3-57, Zona 10 (✆ **502/2360-8345;** www.mayaworld.net), backpackers finally have an excellent option in the heart of the Zona Viva.

Zona 1

While this area is convenient for visiting the city's colonial-era attractions, it is much less secure and tourist friendly than the *zonas* listed above. If you do stay here, be particularly careful after dark, when I recommend you take a taxi, even for short trips.

Moderate

Hotel Royal Palace ★ Finds This is the most atmospheric option in the Old Town. From the crystal chandeliers in the grand lobby to the well-maintained rooms, this classic hotel maintains all the charm and ambience of a bygone era. The rooms are large and stylish, some with carpeting and others with antique tile floors. My favorite rooms are those with balconies overlooking the street, where you can watch the daily parade from the comfort of your own room. (The trade-off for this great people-watching is more street noise.)

6a Av. 12-66, Zona 1. ✆ **502/2220-8970.** Fax 502/2238-3715. www.hotelroyalpalace.com. 74 units. Q413 ($55/£28) double; Q488 ($65/£33) junior suite. Rates include 22% tax. AE, DISC, MC, V. Free parking. **Amenities:** Restaurant; bar; concierge; gym; laundry service; room service; sauna. *In room:* TV.

Inexpensive

In addition to the place listed below, **Hotel Colonial,** 7a Av. 14-19, Zona 1 (✆ **502/2232-6722;** www.hotelcolonial.net), is another good choice.

Posada Belén ★ Value If you're looking for a charming, family-run bed-and-breakfast at a very reasonable price, this should be your first choice in Zona 1. The converted colonial-era home that houses this hotel was built in 1873, and features a lush and beautiful interior garden. Rooms are decorated in a mixed style with rustic wood furniture, checkerboard tile floors, washed walls, and local arts and crafts. The hotel is set on a short transited street, so its rooms are quieter than many of the downtown options. This place advertises itself as a "museum," and they have a very extensive collection of Maya artifacts and colonial-era art and carvings. The owners and their in-house guides and drivers are very friendly and knowledgeable.

13a Calle A10-30, Zona 1. ✆ **866/864-8283** in the U.S. and Canada, or 502/2253-4530 or 2232-9226 in Guatemala. Fax 502/2251-3478. www.posadabelen.com. 11 units. Q425 ($57/£29) double. Rates include full breakfast. AE, DC, DISC, MC, V. Free parking. **Amenities:** Restaurant; laundry service; lounge; room service. *In room:* No phone.

Zona 13 (Near the Airport)

There are a couple of hotel choices right near the airport. However, given the fact that hotels in zonas 9 and 10 are less than 10 minutes away from the airport by taxi, this is a very limited advantage and minor consideration. You'll enjoy much better access to restaurants, bars, and shopping if you stay at any of the hotels listed above. Still, if you really want to stay close to the airport, the **Crowne Plaza ★**, Av. Las Ameritas 9-08, Zona 13 (✆ **502/2422-5000;** www.crowneplaza.com) should be your top high-end choice, while **Dos Lunas Guest House,** 21a Calle 10-92, Zona 13 (✆ **502/2332-5691;** www.hoteldoslunas.com) is good for those watching their budgets.

WHERE TO DINE

Guatemala City has some excellent restaurants. As with the hotels, the best and most varied selection of restaurants is to be found in zonas 9 and 10. Likewise, there are some good restaurants in Zona 1, particularly for lunch, as the area can be a little sketchy at night. One excellent exception is the 2-square-block pedestrian mall area of Zona 4 known as **Cuatro Grados Norte,** which is full of bars, restaurants, shops, and art galleries.

Zonas 9 & 10

In addition to the places listed below, the restaurant at the boutique hotel **Otelito Casa Santa Clara,** 12a Calle 4-51, Zona 10 (✆ **502/2339-1811**), and **Jake's,** 17a Calle

10-40, Zona 10 (© **502/2368-0351**), are two excellent, upscale fusion restaurants with many local fans. For French food, try **Jean François,** Diagonal 6 13-63, Zona 10 (© **502/2333-4786**), and for sushi, try **Sushi-Itto,** 4a Av. 16-01, Zona 10 (© **502/2368-0181**). Refined Italian food can be found at **Pecorino,** 11a Calle 3-36, Zona 10 (© **502/2360-3035**), while **Casa Chapina,** 1a Av. 13–42, Zona 10 (© **502/2337-0143**), serves good traditional Guatemalan fare in a cozy ambience. And, for margaritas and Mexican cuisine, try **Frida's,** 3a Av. 14-60, Zona 10 (© **502/2367-1611**).

Expensive

Tamarindos ★★★ Finds INTERNATIONAL/FUSION This restaurant offers a perfect blend of creative and artful cooking, accompanied by attentive service and a very attractive ambience. Inside you'll find several different dining rooms, each with its own decor. All feature subdued lighting combined with a minimalist modern aesthetic. The menu is long and eclectic, running the gamut from steak with a chili poblano sauce to moo shu duck. Italy and Asia are the dominant culinary influences, as seen in everything from sushi to risotto, but there are some traditional Continental dishes, as well as nightly specials, on the menu as well. Save room for dessert; their molten *bomba de chocolate* (chocolate bomb) is superb.

11a Calle 2-19A, Zona 10. © **502/2360-2815.** Reservations recommended. Main courses Q75–Q225 ($10–$30/£5–£15). AE, DC, MC, V. Mon–Sat noon–4pm and 7:30–10:30pm.

Moderate

Kacao ★★ Finds GUATEMALAN This elegant restaurant is *the* place to come for traditional Guatemalan cooking prepared and presented with style and flare. Various regional specialties include *pepian,* chicken in a pumpkin seed and tomato sauce from the Western Highlands, and *tapado,* spicy Caribbean seafood soup in coconut milk. The silky black-bean soup is finished off in a clay bowl and baked in the oven. There are a host of steak, poultry, and seafood options. For dessert, try the fried apple rings served with a vanilla-rum sauce. The restaurant decor is as traditional as the menu. Waiters wear traditional Maya garb, and the tablecloths are old *huipiles.*

2a Av. 13-44, Zona 10. © **502/2237-4188** or 2377-4189. Reservations recommended. Main courses Q40–Q150 ($5.35–$20/£2.65–£10). AE, DC, MC, V. Daily noon–4pm and 6–11pm.

Inexpensive

Panadería San Martin Value CAFE/BAKERY Set on a busy corner in the heart of the Zona Viva, this place is busy throughout the day. Folks come here for breakfast, lunch, or a coffee break, and the San Martin handles them all well. Breakfasts are excellent, and you can't beat the lunch special of soup alongside a half-sandwich and a half-salad for Q45 ($6/£3). These folks have a bakery on premises, and a wide selection of sweets and gourmet coffees. The indoor seating is a bit too sterile for me, with its high-backed booths and Formica tables. I prefer to grab a seat in the shady outdoor patio or on the front veranda.

13a Calle 1-62, Zona 10. © **502/2385-4929.** Reservations not accepted. Main courses Q25–Q45 ($3.35–$6/£1.65–£3). AE, DC, MC, V. Daily 6am–8:30pm.

Zona 1

For a taste of Spanish food that fits in perfectly with the Spanish colonial charms of the Old City, try **Restaurante Altuna,** 5a Av. 12-31, Zona 1 (© **502/2251-7185;** www.restaurantealtuna.com).

Inexpensive

Arrin Cuan ★ Kids GUATEMALAN This is my favorite restaurant in Zona 1. The rambling old building that houses the classic Guatemalan eatery is a quiet retreat in this busy area. The main dining room features wood tables crammed around the edges of a small interior garden. The menu is heavy on Guatemalan classics, with such regional dishes as *kac ik,* a filling turkey soup from the Alta Verapaz. If you want to sample something really exotic, order the *tepezquintle,* a large rodent served grilled over hot charcoal. This place has a children's play area, and plenty of free parking in a guarded lot across the street. They also have a branch in the Zona Viva at 16a Calle 4-32, Zona 10 (✆ **502/2366-2660**), but I prefer this original site. A marimba band plays most days during lunch and dinner.

5a Av. 3-27, Zona 1. ✆ **502/2238-0242.** www.arrincuan.com. Main courses Q45–Q75 ($6–$10/£3–£5). AE, DC, MC, V. Daily 7am–10pm.

GUATEMALA CITY AFTER DARK

Guatemala City is a large, metropolitan city. However, its after-dark pleasures are somewhat limited. Part of this is due to the famously dangerous nature of much of the city, especially after dark. Many of the late-night offerings are confined to a couple of very concentrated and centralized "safe" areas, which gives the scene a little bit of an apartheid feel.

For visitors and locals alike, there are two main after-dark destinations—the Zona Viva and Cuatro Grados Norte. Both offer a broad range of bars, restaurants, and clubs in a compact area that's safe and pedestrian-friendly.

Your best bet for finding out what's going on is to ask your hotel concierge, or pick up a copy of the free monthly ***Revue Magazine*** (www.revuemag.com), which is widely available at hotels and other tourist haunts around the country. If you can read Spanish, ***Recrearte*** (www.revistarecrearte.com) is another good source of information, with local listings for theater, concerts, and art galleries.

BARS & PUBS For a mellow scene and a cozy place to catch a game or shoot some pool, head to **Cheers** (✆ **502/2368-2089;** 13a Calle 0-40, Zona 10). Another bar popular with tourists and expatriates is **Shakespeare Pub** (✆ **502/2331-2641;** 13a Calle and 1a Av., Torre Santa Clara II, Zona 10). To mingle with some Guatemalans, try heading to **Rattle 'N' Hum** (✆ **502/2366-6524;** 4a Av. 16-11, Zona 10).

In Cuatro Grados Norte, I like **Del Paseo** (✆ **502/2385-9046**) and **Kloster** (✆ **502/2334-3882**) for drinks and socializing, and **Trovajazz** (✆ **502/2334-1241**) as a place to catch some live music. Still, the entire area is perfectly suited to a simple bar-crawl or scouting stroll, where you can choose which place most suits your fancy.

Most bars don't charge a cover unless there's a live act, in which case the cover is anywhere from Q15 to Q75 ($2–$10/£1–£5).

DANCE CLUBS Perhaps the best dance club in town is **Kahlua ★**, 1a Av. 15-06, Zona 10 (✆ **502/2333-7468**), a large complex with a hip young crowd and music and decor to match. Discos and dance clubs often have a cover of between Q15 and Q45 ($2–$6/£1–£3).

THE PERFORMING ARTS The greatest number of high-quality performances take place at the **Centro Cultural Miguel Angel Asturias ★★**, 24a Calle 3-81, Centro Cívico, Zona 1 (✆ **502/2232-4041**), which features the country's largest, most modern and most impressive theater. Offerings range from local and visiting ballet companies and symphonies to theater and modern dance. Another principal venue for the performing

Volunteer & Learning Opportunities in Guatemala

There are plenty of options for active, adventure, special-interest, or theme vacations to Guatemala. Popular themes and activities include bird-watching, Maya archaeology, cave explorations, and mountain biking. In many cases, you may want to add on a specific theme tour or partake in some adventure activity as an a la carte option within the broader scope of your trip to Guatemala. However, some of you may want to build your entire itinerary around a specific theme or activity.

- **Art Workshops in Guatemala** (✆ **612/825-0747** in the U.S. and Canada; www.artguat.org). This group offers many creative opportunities, including nearly every genre of writing, plastic arts, and even yoga. While there are opportunities to try your hand at Maya weaving, that class watches the real experts at work and visits the markets where their works are sold. Ten-day tours run around Q12,000 to 13,500 ($1,600–$1,800/£800–£900) per person, plus airfare, depending on the workshop.
- **Entre Mundos** (✆ **502/7761-2179;** www.entremundos.org), which is based in Quetzaltenango, functions as a bridge between a host of nongovernmental organizations and community projects. They specifically work to connect foreign volunteers with appropriate community, social, health, and educational projects.
- **Habitat for Humanity International** (✆ **502/7763-5308** in Guatemala; www.habitat.org) has several chapters in Guatemala and sometimes runs organized Global Village programs here. Their Global Village trips are large, group-escorted trips that include work on a Habitat for Humanity building project, as well as other cultural and educational experiences. The costs range from Q7,500 to Q11,250 ($1,000–$1,500/£500–£750), not including airfare, for a 9- to 14-day program.
- **Jim Cline Photo Tours** (✆ **877/350-1314** in the U.S. and Canada; www.jimcline.com) is guided by a professional photographer who teaches participants to see Guatemala through the camera lens. The 10-day "Living Maya" tour, limited to nine people, focuses on colonial architecture, colorful markets, small villages, the natural beauty of Lake Atitlán, and the Maya people. Cost is around Q16,500 ($2,200/£1,100) per person, plus airfare.

arts is the theater at the **Instituto Guatemalteco Americano** ★ (**IGA;** ✆ **502/2422-5555;** www.iga.edu), which is at 9a Av. 0-51, Zona 4, on the outskirts of Cuatro Grados Norte. These folks maintain a steady schedule of events that range from children's and traditional theater to art-film cycles and dance performances. The **Centro Cultural de España,** Vía 5, 1-23, Zona 4 (✆ **502/2385-9066;** www.centroculturalespana.com.gt), is right on the main drag of Cuatro Grados Norte, close to the IGA. In addition to their small gallery space, they have a regular schedule of artistic, literary, and cultural events.

Ticket prices can range from Q30 to as high as Q375 ($4–$50/£2–£25) depending on the event and the clout of the main act.

SIDE TRIPS FROM GUATEMALA CITY

Several side trips out of Guatemala City are possible, ranging from day trips and tours to multiday excursions. I highly recommend you take any of these trips as part of an organized tour. All of the major hotels have tour desks that can arrange these for you. Alternatively, you can contact **Clark Tours,** 7a Av. 14-76, Zona 9, inside Clark Plaza (© **502/2412-4848;** www.clarktours.com.gt), or **Maya Vacations,** 11 Av. 7-15 Zona 13 (© **502/2426-1400;** www.mayavacations.com).

Top Tours & Excursions

ANTIGUA ★★★ The fabulous colonial city of Antigua is just 45 minutes away from Guatemala City by car or bus. All of the local tour companies offer half- and full-day tours to Antigua. I definitely recommend you sign up for a full-day tour if possible. Antigua is *that* beautiful, and there is *that* much to see. Half-day tours cost Q263 to Q375 ($35–$50/£18–£25), including lunch and entrance fees to all attractions. Full-day tours cost Q375 to Q600 ($50–$80/£25–£40), including lunch. For more information on Antigua, see below.

CHICHICASTENANGO ON MARKET DAY ★★★ If you're in Guatemala City with a free Thursday or Sunday, you'll want to take a day trip to the fabulous market in Chichicastenango. These tours also hit Panajachel and Lake Atitlán on the way back, so you get to kill two or more birds with one stone. This is a full-day tour, with a fair amount of travel time, but it's worth it. These tours cost between Q340 and Q675 ($45–$90/£23–£45), and include lunch. For more information on Chichicastenango and its market, see later in this chapter.

TIKAL ★★★ Perhaps the most popular day tour out of Guatemala City is to the amazing Maya ruins of Tikal. These tours generally involve a very early morning flight and even earlier hotel pickup. The tours give you a good, full day in Tikal. However, if you've got the time, I seriously recommend you add at least a 1-night extension to the tour. These tours run around Q2,100 to Q2,625 ($280–$350/£140–£175), including round-trip airfare, park entrance fee, and a guide. Budget an additional Q375 to Q1,125 ($50–$150/£25–£75) per person per day for multiday excursions, depending on the level of accommodations chosen. For more information on Tikal, see later in this chapter.

5 ANTIGUA ★★★

40km (25 miles) SW of Guatemala City; 108km (67 miles) SE of Chichicastenango; 80km (50 miles) SE of Panajachel

Simply put, Antigua is a gem, an enchanting blend of restored colonial-era architecture and rugged cobblestone streets, peppered with ruins and brimming with all the amenities a traveler could want—beautiful boutique hotels, fine restaurants, and plenty of shopping and activity options. Antigua sits in a small valley surrounded by towering volcanoes, which are clearly visible over the red tile roofs and church bell towers that dominate the small city's skyline.

Antigua was Guatemala's capital from 1543 until 1776. It was founded after mudslides and flooding destroyed the country's first capital, in what is today Ciudad Vieja, in 1541. Originally christened La Muy Noble y Muy Leal Ciudad de Santiago de los Caballeros de Goathemala (The Very Noble and Very Loyal City of Santiago of the Knights of Guatemala), it was for centuries perhaps the New World's finest city. In fact, it was declared the Capitancy General, which in effect granted it status as the government seat for all of Mexico and Central America. Antigua flourished throughout the 17th and on into the 18th centuries, with the massive wealth generated by the Spanish conquest being poured into the construction of churches, government buildings, universities, convents and monasteries, private homes, and military garrisons.

Many of those impressive buildings were knocked down in a steady string of earthquakes, and after a massive earthquake in 1773 destroyed most of the city, the government seat was relocated to present-day Guatemala City. There was great resistance to the move, and in 1777, the government actually instituted a law making it illegal to live in Antigua. Eventually, the city was almost entirely abandoned and stayed that way until the 20th century. In 1944, Antigua was declared a National Monument by the Government of Guatemala, and in 1979, UNESCO named it a World Heritage Site.

Antigua has the most elaborate and stunning **Holy Week celebrations ★★★** in all of Guatemala, and perhaps even the Americas. During Holy Week, the streets are decorated with intricate and beautiful *alfombras* (rugs) made of colored sawdust and flower petals. A steady stream of religious processions parade through the streets and over these *alfombras,* which are quickly replaced with new ones.

ESSENTIALS

Getting There

BY PLANE The nearest airport to Antigua is **La Aurora International Airport (GUA; ✆ 502/2332-6086)** in Guatemala City. Since Antigua is so close to Guatemala City, many visitors book their first and last nights—and often a few more—in Antigua. Once you've made it through Customs, you can be settled into your hotel in Antigua in less than an hour, if you don't hit too much traffic.

BY SHUTTLE The most common way to get to and from Antigua is on a minivan shuttle. Several companies operate regular minivan shuttles between Antigua and most major tourist destinations, including the airport, downtown Guatemala City, Lake Atitlán, and Chichicastenango. If you're coming to Antigua directly from the airport, you'll find several kiosks for these shuttles after clearing Customs. All charge between Q75 and Q90 ($10–$12/£5–£6) per person, and will leave as soon as they are full, which shouldn't take more than a few minutes.

If you're already in Guatemala City, or arriving from any other destination, ask your hotel or any tour agency about booking a shuttle to Antigua. Alternately, you can book directly with **Atitrans** (**✆ 502/7832-3371;** www.atitrans.com).

Rates between Antigua and other popular destinations run around Q90 to Q113 ($12–$15/£6–£7.50) for Panajachel; Q135 to Q150 ($18–$20/£9–£10) for Chichicastenango; and Q300 to Q375 ($40–$50/£20–£25) for Flores/Tikal.

BY TAXI A taxi is the fastest, safest, and easiest way to get from the airport or Guatemala City to Antigua. A taxi should cost between Q188 and Q300 ($25–$40/£13–£20). Expect to pay the higher rate, maybe even a little more, after dark.

BY BUS Buses from Guatemala City to Antigua leave from the El Trebol intersection in Zona 8. Buses leave every 15 minutes or so, usually as they fill up, between 5am and 9pm, with more sporadic service from around 4am to about 11pm. The fare is Q10 ($1.35/70p) for the 1-hour ride. The main bus terminal in Antigua is at the end of 4a Calle Poniente, next to the Municipal Market. Buses leaving Antigua for Guatemala City follow roughly the same schedule. Safety is a serious concern on these buses, and I recommend you take a taxi or shuttle.

BY CAR The best route to Antigua from Guatemala City is to take the Calzada Roosevelt out of town. The Calzada Roosevelt heads northwest out of Guatemala City, through Zona 11 (passing right in front of the Tikal Futura Hotel), before turning into the Pan-American Highway (Carretera Panamericana). Take this and exit at San Lucas. From here you'll take the new, well-paved, windy highway (RN10) into Antigua. The ride takes about 40 to 45 minutes with no traffic.

Getting Around

ON FOOT Antigua is walkable, and cars and taxis are unnecessary to explore the colonial core of the city. The entire downtown section of Antigua, which is where most tourist attractions are, extends less than 10 blocks in any direction from the Plaza Mayor. However, watch your step—several hundred years and a few serious earthquakes have made Antigua's streets and sidewalks rather treacherous at places.

BY TAXI Taxis and tuk tuks are plentiful in Antigua. A ride anywhere in the city should cost between Q20 and Q30 ($2.65–$4/£1.30–£2). Most of the taxis in Antigua use meters, but if the one you get into doesn't, be sure to negotiate a firm price beforehand. If you need to call a cab, ask your hotel, or try **Taxis Antigua** (✆ **502/7832-2360**).

BY CAR While you won't need a car to explore Antigua, you may want one for a trip to Chichicastenango, Lake Atitlán, or other nearby towns. In Antigua, try **Tabarini,** 6a Av. Sur, #22 (✆ **502/7832-8107;** www.tabarini.com).

Visitor Information

The Guatemala Tourism Commission, **INGUAT,** 4a Calle between 4a and 5a avenidas, inside "Casa El Jaulon" (✆ **502/7832-0763;** www.visitguatemala.com), has a helpful bilingual staff, and offers regional brochures, basic maps, and a score of hotel and tour fliers. The office is open Monday through Friday 8am to 5pm, and Saturday through Sunday 9am to 5pm.

Local travel agencies and hotel tour desks are another good source of information. There are numerous travel agencies all over town. Some of the best include **Lax Travel Antigua** ★, 3a Calle Poniente, #12 (✆ 502/7832-1621); **Sin Fronteras** ★, 5a Av. Norte, #15A (✆ 502/7720-4400; www.sinfront.com); **Rainbow Travel Center** ★, 7a Av. Sur, #8 (✆ 502/7832-4202; www.rainbowtravelcenter.com); and **Via Venture** ★★, 2a Calle Oriente, #22 (✆ 502/7832-2509; www.viaventure.com).

FAST FACTS Many banks have branches right on the Plaza Mayor or within a 2-block radius, including **Banquetzal,** 4a Calle Poniente and 5a Avenida Norte (✆ **502/7832-1111**); **Banco Industrial,** 5a Av. Sur, #4 (✆ **502/2420-3000**); and **Bancafé,** 4a Calle Poniente, #1A (✆ **502/7832-4876**). All of these have ATMs, will change money, and make cash advances against a credit card. The main post office (✆ **502/7832-2164**) is located at 4a Calle Poniente and Alameda Santa Lucía.

The best hospital in Antigua is **Hospital Privado Hermano Pedro,** Av. La Recolección, #4 (✆ **502/7832-1190**), a modern 24-hour private hospital offering a wide range of services, including emergency and trauma units.

There are scores of *farmacias* around Antigua, and you can probably find one simply by walking around. **Farmacia Fénix,** 6a Calle Poniente, #35 (✆ **502/7832-5337**), offers free delivery and has several outlets.

There are a host of Internet cafes around Antigua, and a growing number of hotels and restaurants are offering Wi-Fi. **Conexiones,** 4a Calle Oriente, #14 (✆ **502/**

7832-3768; www.conexion.com), or the **Funkey Monkey,** 5a Av. Sur, #6 (© **502/7832-7181**) are two good bets.

The main Antigua police station is at the Palacio de los Capitanes Generales (© **502/7832-2266**), on Plaza Mayor. The **tourism police** (© **502/7832-7290**) is a division of the larger police force with bilingual officers trained specifically to deal with tourists. Their office is around the corner on 4a Avenida Norte, and is open 24 hours.

WHAT TO SEE & DO

Antigua is a fabulous city for a leisurely stroll, and along the way you can visit a museum or do some shopping. There are also a number of tour agencies in town, and most hotels have a tour desk. All of these offer a standard city tour, as well as visits to volcanoes, Chichicastenango market, Lake Atitlán, and 1-day and multiday trips to Tikal. If you're not happy with the offering at you hotel's tour desk, try **Lax Travel Antigua ★**, 3a Calle Poniente, #12 (© 502/7832-1621); **Sin Fronteras ★**, 5a Av. Norte, #15A (© 502/7720-4400; www.sinfront.com); or **Rainbow Travel Center ★**, 7a Av. Sur, #8 (© 502/7832-4202; www.rainbowtravelcenter.com).

The best city tours are the walking tours offered by **Antigua Tours ★★** (© **502/7832-5821;** www.antiguatours.net). They offer a wide range of tour and hotel booking options, but are best known for their walking tours with longtime resident and author Elizabeth Bell, whose books about Antigua include *Antigua Guatemala: The City And Its Heritage* (Antigua Tours, 2005). The 3-hour tour leaves daily and costs Q150 ($20/£10). On days when Bell is not available, other well-trained and personable guides lead the tour. These folks have an office on the west side of the main plaza, inside the Café El Portal.

MAJOR ATTRACTIONS

The **Plaza Mayor ★★** is the central axis of all Antigua. In colonial times, this was the city's main market and meeting area. Today, it's a great place to grab a shady seat and watch the parade of life pass before you. The current park was built in the 20th century, and covers a full city block with towering trees, well-tended gardens, various pathways lined with sturdy benches, and a beautiful fountain at its core.

The most distinguishing architectural feature north of Plaza Mayor—even more so than the Convento de las Capuchinas and the Iglesia La Merced (see below)—is the **Arco de Santa Catalina (Santa Catalina Arch).** This high arch spans 5a Avenida Norte, about 3 blocks north of the Plaza Mayor. The arch was built in the mid–17th century to allow nuns to pass from one part of the Santa Catalina Convent to the other without being seen. In the 19th century, a clock was added to a large cupola atop the center point. Today, 5a Avenida Norte is often called Calle del Arco.

Casa del Tejido Antiguo ★ This museum will tell you everything you ever wanted to know about textiles. It has a sizeable collection of typical clothing from various regions of Guatemala. The exhibits of colorful, vintage *cortes* and *huipiles* are complemented by ample information on how they're woven, the history of the process, and the broader cultural significance of Maya cloth. Informative placards explain the exhibits, but guided tours are available and recommended if you're deeply interested in the subject. A gift shop has various handmade items for sale. The selection is good, and the products are guaranteed to be authentic, but you'll probably find better prices elsewhere.

1a Calle Poniente, #51, btw. Ruínas Recolección and San Jerónimo. © **502/7832-3169.** www.casadeltejido.org. Admission Q5 (70¢/35p). Mon–Sat 9am–5:30pm.

Catedral San José ★ Vowing to learn from the destruction of the cathedral during the earthquakes of 1583, the city began construction of a new, more complex, and supposedly stronger cathedral in 1669. The structure, completed in 1680, contained seven entrances, five naves, 78 arches, 18 chapels, a main sacristy, and a main chamber. Unfortunately, seismology tends to repeat itself, and that cathedral was leveled in the great earthquake of 1773. You can visit the ruins from the south gate on 5a Calle Oeste. The entire structure was rebuilt in the 19th century (the sacrarium is the only piece used from the original). The interior is not notably impressive, but houses a statue of Christ carved by Quirio Cataño, famous for carving the "Black Christ" of Esquipulas.

4a Av. Norte, on the east side of Plaza Mayor. No phone. Admission Q10 ($1.35/70p) to visit the ruins; free for the main cathedral. Daily 9am–5pm.

Convento de las Capuchinas ★★ The Capuchins are a Roman Catholic order who seek sanctification through a life of work, privation, and continual penitence. Unlike other convents of old, the Convento de las Capuchinas did not require women to donate a dowry to join, though in Antigua that egalitarian outlook kept their ranks at fewer than 28 nuns. Completed in 1736, the impressive convent was abandoned after an earthquake in 1773 scared the nuns to safer ground. Fortunately the damage was relatively minor, and the well-preserved courtyards, gardens, bathing halls, and nuns' private cells are now open to the public. Mannequins occupy some of those cells, demonstrating cloistered life. The roof is a great spot to take in a good view of the city.

2a Av. Norte and 2a Calle Oriente. ✆ **502/7832-0184.** Admission Q30 ($4/£2), Q15 ($2/£1) students and children 11 and under. Daily 9am–5pm.

Iglesia La Merced ★★★ This church's central plaza is one of the most important launching points for processions during Holy Week. Built in a baroque style and adorned with stucco pilasters, it's also one of the best restored and preserved in the city. Architect Juan de Dios began work on the building in 1749, and completed it in 1767. The facade of the yellow temple is adorned with amazing detail, and several impressive paintings can be found inside, including the well-known work "Jesus Nazareno." The previous incarnation of the church had, like all the others in town, been destroyed by an earthquake some years before. This incarnation was to suffer the same fate, though it has recently been restored after years of abandonment.

1a Calle Poniente and 6a Av. Norte. No phone. Free admission to the church; Q5 (70¢/35p) to visit the convent ruins. Daily 9am–6pm.

SPANISH & OTHER EDUCATIONAL CLASSES

There are a host of Spanish-language schools in Antigua. Most offer small group or individual immersion-style classes between 4 and 5 hours daily, as well as various other activities and guided trips and tours. Most offer the option of a homestay with a local family, or a booking at any one of many hotels around the city. Schools I recommend include **Academia de Español Guatemala ★**, 7a Calle Oriente, #15 (✆ **502/7832-5057;** www.acad.conexion.com); **Centro Lingüístico Maya ★**, 5a Calle Poniente, #20 (✆ **502/7832-0656;** www.clmmaya.com); and **Escuela de Español San José el Viejo ★★**, 5a Av. Sur, #34 (✆ **502/7832-3028;** www.sanjoseelviejo.com). Rates run Q1,125 to Q2,250 ($150–$300/£75–£150) per week including classes, excursions, homestay, and airport transfers.

An alternative educational experience can be had at the **Antigua Cooking School,** 5a Av. Norte, #25B (✆ **502/5944-8568;** www.antiguacookingschool.com). Located right under the Santa Catalina Arch, the school offers regular 4-hour classes in preparing local

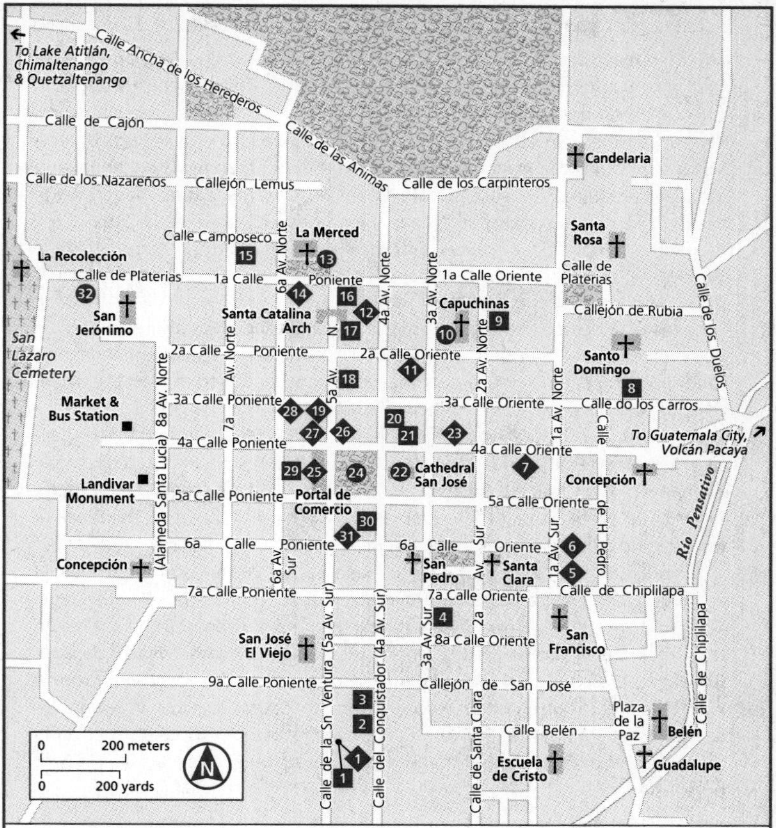

To Lake Atitlán, Chimaltenango & Quetzaltenango
Calle Ancha de los Herederos
Calle de Cajón
Calle de las Animas
Candelaria
Calle de los Nazareños
Callejón Lemus
Calle de los Carpinteros
Calle Camposeco
La Merced
Santa Rosa
La Recolección
Calle de Platerias
1a Calle Poniente
6a Av. Norte
4a Av. Norte
3a Av. Norte
1a Calle Oriente
Calle de Platerias
Calle de los Duelos
San Jerónimo
Santa Catalina Arch
Capuchinas
Callejón de Rubia
San Lazaro Cemetery
2a Calle Poniente
7a Av. Norte
5a Av. N.
2a Calle Oriente
2a Av. Norte
Santo Domingo
Market & Bus Station
8a Av. Norte
3a Calle Poniente
3a Calle Oriente
1a Av. Norte
Calle do los Carros
4a Calle Poniente
4a Calle Oriente
To Guatemala City, Volcán Pacaya
Cathedral San José
Concepción
Landivar Monument
5a Calle Poniente
Portal de Comercio
5a Calle Oriente
Calle de H. Pedro
Río Pensativo
(Alameda Santa Lucia)
6a Calle Poniente
6a Calle Oriente
6a Av. Sur
Av. Sur
1a Av. Sur
San Pedro
Santa Clara
Concepción
7a Calle Poniente
7a Calle Oriente
Calle de Chiplilapa
San Francisco
San José El Viejo
3a Av. Sur
2a
8a Calle Oriente
Calle de Chiplilapa
9a Calle Poniente
Callejón de San José
Plaza de la Paz
Calle Belén
Belén
Guadalupe
Escuela de Cristo
Calle de la Sn Ventura (5a Av. Sur)
Calle del Conquistador (4a Av. Sur)
Calle de Santa Clara
0 200 meters
0 200 yards
N

ACCOMMODATIONS ■

Black Cat Inn **29**
Casa Azul **20**
Casa Capuchinas **9**
Casa Encantada **3**
Casa Santo Domingo **8**
The Cloister **17**
Hotel Palacio Chico **30**
Hotel Posada de Don Rodrigo **18**
Hotel Posada La Merced **15**
Mesón Panza Verde **1**
Posada Asjemenou **16**
Posada del Angel **2**
Palacio de Doña Leonor **21**
Posada San Pedro **4**

DINING ◆

Café Condesa **25**
Café Mediterraneo **31**
Café Sky **5**
Doña Luisa Xicoteneatl **23**
El Sabor del Tiempo **19**
El Sereno **12**
Hector's **14**
La Cocina de Lola **11**
La Fonda de la Calle Real **26, 27, 28**
Mesón Panza Verde **1**
Nokiate **6**
Welten **7**

ATTRACTIONS ●

Casa del Tejido Antiguo **32**
Catedral San José **22**
Convento de las Capuchinas **10**
Iglesia La Merced **13**
Plaza Mayor **24**

N
Tikal
MEXICO
BELIZE
Livingston
L. Izabal
Lake Atitlán
HOND.
Antigua
Guatemala City
EL SAL.

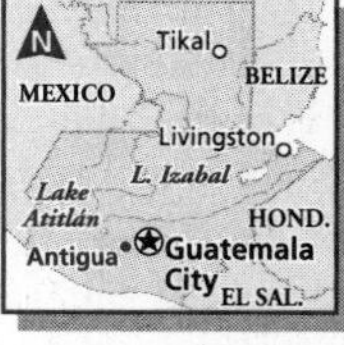

Semana Santa (Holy Week)

The Christian **Semana Santa ★★★** celebrations in Antigua are an extravagant mix of religious fervor, civic pride, and artistic achievement. Throughout the week there are a score of Masses, vigils *(velaciones)*, and public processions. The processions can vary in size, and are often made up of hundreds of worshipers, who include men in regal purple robes, women in white linens and lace, and ubiquitous incense carriers. Other processions feature men in white hooded costumes (whose style was later borrowed by the Ku Klux Klan), women in somber black dresses (as if in mourning), and the occasional horseback-riding members. Most carry large floats *(andas)* with sculptures of Jesus Christ, Mary Magdalene, and other saints.

Some of the *andas* are enormous (as much as 3 tons) and require as many as 100 men to carry them on their shoulders. Individual processions can last for many hours, and you'll notice a complex choreography used to keep the shoulders and legs of those carrying them fresh.

Although the celebrations officially begin on Ash Wednesday, the real spectacle begins on Palm Sunday and peaks on Good Friday. Throughout the week, elements of the Passion, Crucifixion, and Resurrection are reenacted and celebrated. The sheer scope of the celebrations are hard to describe. The smell of incense and a thick smoke often hang heavy over the whole city.

If you plan on coming during Semana Santa, book your room well in advance, as much as a year or more in some of the more popular hotels here. The real score during Holy Week is rooms overlooking some of the streets on the processional routes. Of the hotels listed below, **Hotel Posada de Don Rodrigo** and **Posada del Doña Leonor** both have choice second-floor rooms with balconies fronting one or more of the processional routes. ***Warning:*** Be careful as you enjoy the Semana Santa celebrations. Pickpockets and petty thieves thrive in the crowded streets. Leave your money and valuables in your hotel safe.

cuisine. Each class tackles one of five different menus and costs Q375 ($50/£25) per person. Discounts are available for groups and multiple classes.

Shopping

Antigua is probably the best city for shopping in all of Central America. Options range from high-end jewelry and clothing stores to fine-art galleries and open-air street vendors selling locally produced crafts and textiles. There are shops to fit all budgets and tastes.

In general, prices are higher in Antigua than anywhere else in Guatemala. The higher-end stores have set prices, and rarely budge on them. However, the handicraft and souvenir outlets, as well as the larger markets and street vendors, will all bargain.

Casa de Artes ★★ If you're looking for the best, this is it—but you'll pay for it. This is probably the art and handicraft shop with the highest end selection. Different rooms are dedicated to woodcarvings, traditional textiles, ceramics, jewelry, and paintings.

Open Monday to Saturday 9am to 1pm and 2:30 to 6:30pm, and by appointment. 4a Av. Sur, #11. ✆ **502/7832-0792.** www.casadeartes.com.gt.

Chocotenengo You'll have to search for this place (it's in the back of a simple convenience store), but it's worth the effort. The homemade chocolates, in particular their truffles, are seriously decadent and delicious. On any day, there may be a dozen or more truffle varieties to choose from. It's open daily from 9am to 6pm. 3a Calle Poniente, #2. ✆ **502/5500-2457.**

Jades S.A. These folks are pioneers of Guatemala's jade industry, and their main factory (listed here) is a museum of their impressive history and dedication to quality production. Wares range from jewelry and replica masks to assorted gift items and sculptures. They have two other storefronts in Antigua, in addition to outlets at the Hotel Casa Santo Domingo and the Marriott and Camino Real hotels in Guatemala City. It's open daily from 9am to 6:30pm. 4a Calle Oriente, #34. ✆ **502/7832-3841.** www.jademaya.com.

Joyería del Angel ★★ Finds Custom-made one-of-a-kind pieces are the forte of this place. Though many of the pieces are quite expensive, there are some more moderately priced works, as well as the occasional sale items. It's open daily from 9am to 6pm. 4a Calle Oriente, #5A. ✆ **502/7832-3189.**

Mercado de Artesanías y Compañía de Jesús ★ This clean and modern facility was built to give a semi-permanent home to the many street vendors who had set up shop around Antigua. It features a tightly packed maze of small souvenir stands selling standard, mass-produced fare aimed at the unsuspecting tourist market. However, there are a few vendors selling quality wares, but you'll have to know your stuff and sift through a lot of junk to get to anything good. It's open daily from 8am to 7pm. 4a Calle Poniente. ✆ **502/7832-5599.** www.munideantigua.com.

Nim Po't ★★★ Value This large indoor market works as a sort of consignment warehouse for local craft and textile cooperatives selling arts, crafts, and textiles from around Guatemala. The prices here are very fair, but the quality of the merchandise varies greatly. Still, you can find excellent *huipiles* and carved masks. It's open daily from 9am to 7pm. 5a Av. Norte, #29. ✆ **502/7832-2681.** www.nimpot.com.

Wer ★★ Finds Owned by local artist Alejandro Wer, this converted 250-year-old home houses a massive collection of contemporary Guatemalan art by more than 100 artists in several of its rooms. It's open daily from 9am to 5:30pm. 4a Calle Oriente, #27. ✆ **502/7832-7161.**

Tips Before You Buy

If you're planning to head to the large and hectic markets—whether here, in Chichicastenango, or around the country—to bargain and shop, it's good to get an idea of what to look for before you dive in. I recommend visiting **Casa de Artes** or **Nim Po't** before setting out in search of any arts, crafts, or textiles. The folks at Casa de Artes carry high-end pieces, and their staff is very knowledgeable, so you can learn the difference between a quality piece of work and something that's mass produced. Be sure to ask where the different styles are from, and see if any specific town or region strikes your fancy.

Whether you're looking for a budget room in which to plop down your backpack or a top-notch luxury inn in which to kick up your feet, your choices are endless.

Very Expensive

In addition to the places listed below, you can't go wrong at either **Palacio de Doña Leonor ★★** (✆ **502/7832-2281;** www.palaciodeleonor.com), housed in the old home of Pedro de Alvarado's daughter Leonor, or **Posada del Angel ★★** (✆ **502/7832-5303;** www.posadadelangel.com), which has hosted a fair number of dignitaries and stars over the years.

Casa Santo Domingo ★★ (Finds) This grandiose hotel lives up to the hype. The hotel is a tourist attraction in and of itself, spread over massive grounds that include the colonial-era ruins of an old convent, a working chapel, several museum-quality display areas, and a large amphitheater. The rooms are all top-notch with comfortable beds, stately decor, and a host of amenities. Most have working fireplaces, and the best have balconies with volcano and sunset views. Even if you're not staying here, be sure to visit the Casa Santo Domingo, particularly around sunset. The grounds and facilities are impressive, and they have a sunset terrace with a perfect view of the nightly setting behind Volcán de Agua. Stick around for a drink or dinner as night falls, and the whole place is transformed into a candlelit fantasy.

3a Calle Oriente, #28. ✆ **502/7820-1220.** Fax 502/7820-1221. www.casasantodomingo.com.gt. 128 units. Q1,125–Q1,358 ($150–$181/£75–£91) double; Q1,815–Q2,625 ($242–$350/£121–£175) suite. AE, DC, MC, V. Free parking. **Amenities:** Restaurant; bar; Jacuzzi; laundry service; large outdoor pool; room service; sauna. *In room:* TV, hair dryer, minibar.

Mesón Panza Verde ★★★ (Finds) Although this place is not nearly as massive in scale, I find it every bit as captivating and special as the Casa Santo Domingo. The standard rooms are certainly acceptable, with small private garden terraces. However, the rest of the rooms, which are all suites, are why this place is so wonderful. All are quite spacious and beautifully decorated, with an eclectic mix of furnishings, artwork, and design touches from Guatemala and around the world. My favorite rooms here are nos. 9 and 10, which are ground-floor suites with large private garden patios and huge bathrooms. The restaurant (see review below) is one of the best in Antigua. There's also a small lap pool, art gallery, and wonderful rooftop terrace that winds around the building with several different places to sit and admire the view.

5a Av. Sur, #19. ✆ **502/7832-1745.** Fax 502/7832-2925. www.panzaverde.com. 12 units. Q675 ($90/£45) double; Q1,125 ($150/£75) suite; Q1,275–Q1,875 ($170–$250/£85–£125) master suite. Rates include full breakfast and taxes. Rates lower in the off season and for extended stays; higher during peak periods. AE, DC, MC, V. Free parking. **Amenities:** Restaurant; bar; laundry service; small lap pool. *In room:* TV.

Expensive

Other good options in this price range include **Casa Capuchinas ★** (✆/fax **502/7832-0121;** www.casacapuchinas.com); the **Cloister ★** (✆ **502/7832-0712;** www.thecloister.com); and **Hotel Posada de Don Rodrigo ★** (✆ **502/7832-0291;** www.hotelposadadedonrodrigo.com).

Casa Encantada ★★ (Finds) Although most rooms at this refined boutique B&B are rather compact, what they lack in size they make up for in comfort and style. The best room here is the large, rooftop suite, which has plenty of space and a private Jacuzzi. However, my favorite room is no. 7, which is tucked in the back of the hotel and reached by a rock walkway over a small pool. At night this pathway is lit with candles and is quite romantic. Breakfast is served on the delightful open-air rooftop, with great views of the red-tile roofs and the surrounding hills and volcanoes.

9a Calle Poniente Esquina, #1. ✆ **866/837-8900** toll-free in the U.S. and Canada, or 502/7832-7903 in Guatemala. www.casaencantada-antigua.com. Q750–Q1,088 ($100–$145/£50–£73) double; Q1,313–Q1,763 ($175–$235/£88–£118) suite. Rates include full breakfast. These are weekend rack rates. Rates lower midweek and off season; higher during peak periods. AE, DC, MC, V. Parking nearby. **Amenities:** Bar; laundry service; small pool; free Wi-Fi. *In room:* TV, hair dryer, minibar.

Moderate

For a more traditional and colonial feel than the place listed below, you could try **Hotel Palacio Chico** (✆/fax **502/7820-0406;** www.palaciochico.enantigua.com).

Casa Azul ★ Unlike the other hotels in Antigua, this place has a modern and eclectic style, with an array of furniture styles from Art Deco to contemporary. The rooms all have very high ceilings, especially those on the second floor. My favorite room in the house is no. 8, a second-floor corner unit with lots of space and great views over the rooftops of Antigua. Casa Azul is very well located, just a half-block from the Plaza Mayor. There's no restaurant here, but breakfast is served, and a host of restaurants are located nearby.

4a Av. Norte, #5. ✆ **502/7832-0961.** Fax 502/7832-0944. www.casazul.guate.com. 14 units. Q720–Q825 ($96–$110/£48–£55) double. Rates lower in the off season, higher during peak periods. AE, DC, MC, V. Parking nearby. **Amenities:** Jacuzzi; laundry service; small outdoor pool; sauna. *In room:* TV, minibar.

Inexpensive

There are a host of cut-rate backpacker hotels and hostals around town, or you could also try **Posada San Pedro** (✆/fax **502/7832-3594;** www.posadasanpedro.net) or **Posada Asjemenou** (✆ **502/7820-2670**). Of the hostals, I recommend the **Black Cat Inn** (✆ **502/7832-1229;** www.blackcathostels.net).

Hotel Posada La Merced Kids This economical option is located right near La Merced church. The rooms are spread around a sprawling, converted colonial-style home, and all open on to one of two central courtyard areas. The rooms are simple, clean, and homey. A modest amount of local artwork and neo-colonial wooden furniture livens up the rooms. There are a couple of apartments with kitchenettes for longer stays, and two-bedroom/one-bathroom "suites" that are good for families. There's also a large communal kitchen for all of the guests to use. The owner and staff here are quite personable and helpful.

7a Av. Norte, #43A. ✆ **502/7832-3197** or 7832-3301. www.merced-landivar.com. 23 units. Q300–Q450 ($40–$60/£20–£30) double; Q600–Q750 ($80–$100/£40–£50) suite or apt. Rates lower in the off season; higher during peak periods. Rates include taxes. V. Parking nearby. **Amenities:** Laundry service; free Wi-Fi.

WHERE TO DINE

Matching Antigua's abundance of top-notch hotels, boutique inns, and B&Bs, the city has a wide range of excellent dining options. In addition to the places listed below, **Café Mediterráneo** (✆ **502/7832-7180;** 6a Calle Poniente, #6A) and **El Sabor del Tiempo** (✆ **502/7832-0516;** 3a Calle Poniente and Calle del Arco) are both excellent Italian restaurants. **La Cocina de Lola** (✆ **502/7832-6616;** 2a Calle Poniente, #3) is great for Spanish cuisine, and **Nokiate** (✆ **502/7821-2896;** 1a Av. Sur, #7) serves sushi and Pan-Asian treats. For a view, you can't beat the rooftop terrace dining at **Café Sky** (✆ **502/7832-7300;** 1a Av. Sur, #15).

Expensive

Other long-standing and dependable high-end dining options in town include **El Sereno ★** (✆ **502/7832-0501;** 4a Av. Norte, #16) and **Welten ★★** (✆ **502/7832-0630;** 4a Calle Oriente, #21). Both feature excellent international and continental fare in elegant and refined settings.

Mesón Panza Verde ★★★ Finds INTERNATIONAL/FUSION This is perennially one of the top restaurants in Antigua, for good reason. The ambience is fabulous, the service professional and attentive, and the food superb. Chef Christophe Pache blends traditional French techniques and training with a wide range of world influences. Tables are spread around several open-air terraces, assorted rooms, and nooks; my favorite seats are poolside under a vaulted stone roof. Enjoy live jazz Wednesday through Friday nights, and Sunday during brunch. This place has an extensive and reasonably priced wine list, as well as some good top-shelf cognacs, tequilas, rums, and single-malt whiskeys.

5a Av. Sur, #19. ✆ **502/7832-1745.** www.panzaverde.com. Reservations recommended. Main courses Q75–Q130 ($10–$17/£5–£8.50). AE, DC, MC, V. Mon–Sat noon–3pm and 7–10pm; Sun 10am–4pm and 7–10pm.

Moderate

Hector's ★★ Finds INTERNATIONAL Almost always bustling, this new and tiny little restaurant serves excellent bistro-style fare in a cozy and amiable space. There are only six or so tables and a few chairs at a small bar, which fronts the open kitchen. There are always daily specials, a pasta option, and some regular favorites, like beef bourguignon. I recommend the seared duck breast served over a potato and carrot gratin, with some balsamic roasted grapes along for the ride. There's no sign here, and owner/chef Hector Castro says the place really doesn't have an official name, but you'll be able to find it, right across from the La Merced Church.

1a Calle Poniente #9A. ✆ **502/7832-9867.** Main courses Q45–Q120 ($6–$16/£3–£8). AE, MC, V. Thurs–Sun 12:30am–10pm; Mon–Wed 6–10pm.

La Fonda de la Calle Real ★ GUATEMALAN This is *the* place to come in Antigua for authentic Guatemalan cuisine, but don't expect a quiet, laid-back joint. It's become so popular, in fact, that they now have three branches in town—all within a block of one another. The menu features a range of classic Guatemalan dishes from *pepian,* a spicy chicken dish, to *kac ik,* a filling turkey soup from the Cobán region. All of the branches do a good job of re-creating a sense of colonial ambience with wood furniture and tall-backed chairs. I like the second-floor seating at the original outlet listed below, but the location at 3a Calle Poniente, #7, is much more spacious.

5a Av. Norte, #12. ✆ **502/7832-0507.** Main courses Q45–Q100 ($6–$13/£3–£6.50). AE, MC, V. Daily 8am–10pm.

Inexpensive

Similar to the place listed below in terms of offerings, **Doña Luisa Xicoteneatl** (✆ **502/7832-2578;** 4a Calle Oriente, #12) is a simple restaurant and bakery, and one of the original, and still going strong, backpacker hangouts in town.

Café Condesa Value INTERNATIONAL Located just off the central park, this place is a great choice for breakfast, coffee, or a light lunch. The sandwiches are very creative and come on homemade bread. I like the vegetarian La Tara, with homemade herb garlic cheese and tomato pistou. You can also opt for one of several quiche options or a large salad, and finish with one of the fresh pies or desserts. Sundays feature an all-you-can-eat brunch. Even when this place is packed, which it often is, the service is extremely fast. The restaurant is tucked in the back of a small collection of shops, inside the Casa del Conde.

5a Av. Norte, #4. ✆ **502/7832-0038.** Breakfast Q25–Q40 ($3.35–$5.35/£1.70–£2.70); salads and sandwiches Q25–Q50 ($3.35–$6.65/£1.70–£3.35); dessert Q15–Q20 ($2–$2.65/£1–£1.35). AE, DC, MC, V. Daily 7am–9pm.

Antigua After Dark

You'll find plenty of bars and clubs in Antigua, but overall, the nightlife scene is pretty mellow. In fact, by city ordinance, all bars and clubs must shut down by 1am. Adaptive as always, what follows are several nightly "private" after-hours parties, which are safe for tourists to attend. The parties shift around, and you'll almost certainly be handed a flier "inviting" you to one if you are still hanging around any of the bars in Antigua as the witching hour approaches.

My favorite bar in town is **Café No Sé** (✆ **502/5501-2680;** 1a Av. Sur, #11C, between 5a Calle and 6a Calle) a laid-back, bo-ho joint with occasional live music. For a more elegant wine-bar and tapas scene, try Sangre (✆ 502/5656-7618; 5a Av. Norte, #33A). Nice rowdy bars popular with tourists and locals alike include the nearly neighboring Reilly's (✆ 502/5640-9860; 5a Av. Norte, #31) and Frida's (✆ 502/7832-1296; 5a Av. Norte, #29), as well as Monoloco (✆ 502/7832-4235; 5a Av. Sur, #6).

For dancing, you'll want to try either **Casbah** (✆ 502/7832-2640; 5a Av. Norte, #30), Café 2000 (✆ 502/7832-2981; 6a Av. Norte, #2) or La Sala (✆ 502/7882-4237; 6a Calle Poniente, #9).

Outdoor Activities & Side Trips from Antigua

Most visitors come to Antigua for the history, culture, dining, and shopping, but outdoor enthusiasts will find there's something here for them, too. If you're looking for adventure, your best bet is to contact **Old Town Outfitters ★★** (✆ **502/5399-0440;** www.adventureguatemala.com), who offer a range of mountain biking, hiking, and other activities around Antigua and the country.

VOLCÁN PACAYA ★★ About 1½ hours from Antigua is the country's most popular volcano destination, **Volcán Pacaya.** Rising to 2,552m (8,370 ft.), Pacaya is in a near constant state of eruption. Tours tend to leave either very early in the morning or around 1pm. I recommend the later tours, especially in the dry season, as you may get to see some of the lava glowing red against the night sky. More likely you'll be treated to the sight, sound, and smell of volcanic gases and steam.

Most ascents of Volcán Pacaya begin at San Francisco de Sales, where you must pay the Q30 ($4/£2) national park entrance fee. From here you'll hike for about 1½ hours to reach the base of the crater's rim, where the steep hiking trail gives way to a solid slope of loose debris made of lava rocks and ash. This final stretch is a steep and arduous scramble, with loose footings and many small rock slides—don't climb directly behind anyone else in your group. On the way down, more adventurous and athletic hikers can "ski" down.

Those who make it to the summit will encounter an otherworldly scene of smoke and gas, with the occasional volcanic belch. Some of the rocks will be very hot to the touch. Very infrequently, Pacaya will let loose with a spectacular eruption. When the skies are clear, the views are amazing.

Be sure to come well prepared. Sturdy, closed-toe hiking shoes or boots are necessary. You'll also want to bring water, a warm sweatshirt, and (if it's in the forecast) rain gear.

Finally, if you're coming on one of the later tours, be sure to either bring a flashlight or make sure your tour agency provides one. Before you go, get current safety information, in terms of both volcanic and criminal activity, from your tour agency, INGUAT, or the Antigua tourism police. It's sometimes possible to camp here, which is your best chance of seeing the nighttime lava show. If this interests you, many of the tour agencies listed above also offer camping options.

Tour prices range between Q75 and Q225 ($10–$40/£5–£20) depending on the size of your group and whether or not lunch and the park entrance are included.

6 PANAJACHEL & LAKE ATITLAN ★★★

115km (71 miles) W of Guatemala City; 37km (23 miles) S of Chichicastenango; 80km (50 miles) NW of Antigua

Aldous Huxley famously claimed that **Lake Atitlán ★★★** was "the most beautiful lake in the world," and that Italy's Lake Como paled in comparison. Formed thousands of years ago in the crater of a massive volcano, Lake Atitlán is more than 16km (10 miles) across at its widest point. It sits at nearly 1.6km (1 mile) high in altitude, and is surrounded on all sides by steep verdant hills, picturesque Maya villages, and massive volcanoes with striking pointed cones. The views from the lakeshore, the hillsides above the lake, and the boats plying its waters are all stunning, and seemingly endlessly varied, as the light and cloud cover shift constantly throughout the day.

The shores of Lake Atitlán are populated with a series of small villages and a few larger towns connected by rugged roads and frequent boat traffic. Panajachel is the gateway to Lake Atitlán. It's the largest city on the lake's shore and the most easily accessible by car and bus from the rest of Guatemala.

ESSENTIALS

Getting There

BY SHUTTLE Panajachel is connected to Guatemala City, Antigua, and Chichicastenango by regular tourist shuttle buses. These range from minivans to standard buses. Fares between Panajachel and Guatemala City run around Q188 to Q270 ($25–$36/£13–£18); between Panajachel and either Antigua or Chichicastenango is about Q135–Q270 ($18–$36/£9–£18). Any hotel tour desk or local tour agency can book you one of these shuttles, or you can contact **Atitrans ★** (✆ **502/7832-3371;** www.atitrans.com).

BY CAR To drive to Panajachel and other cities along the lake, take the Pan-American Highway (Carretera Panamericana) to the junction at Los Encuentros. A few miles north of Los Encuentros is the turnoff to Sololá. In Sololá, follow the signs and flow of traffic to the road to Panajachel. The drive takes a little more than 2 hours from Guatemala City.

Getting Around

Panajachel is compact, so it's fairly easy to walk anywhere in town. In fact, most people spend most of their time walking up and down the long strip that is Calle Santander. If you need a taxi or tuk-tuk, they are plentiful and can almost always be flagged down anywhere in town.

If you want to rent a motorcycle, scooter, or bicycle, ask at your hotel or at any of the many tour agencies around town.

BY BOAT Panajachel is connected to all the towns and villages ringing the lake by regular boat taxi service. There are two separate dock areas. The docks below the end of Calle Santander are used by boats heading east around the lake, as well as those going directly to Santiago de Atitlán. The docks at the end of Calle del Embarcadero are used by the boats heading west around the lake, as well as those going directly to San Pedro La Laguna.

There are several types of boats providing service around the lake. The least expensive boats are large and slow, and follow a regular schedule. However, smaller, faster boat taxis leave throughout the day—some by regular schedule, others as they fill up—and are definitely worth the few extra dollars. The slower boat taxis take about an hour to go from Panajachel to either San Pedro La Laguna or Santiago de Atitlán. The smaller, faster boats cut that time in half.

The boats operate roughly from around 5am until 6pm. However, if you're coming back to Panajachel from any of the villages across the lake, you should try to grab a boat by around 3pm, as service after that becomes less frequent and less reliable. Schedules change according to demand, but you should never have to wait more than an hour to find a boat heading in your direction.

Boat taxis, their captains, and street touts almost always try to gouge tourists. There is a de facto price differential between what locals pay and what tourists pay, and it's often hard to get a firm sense of what the official rates are or should be. Always ask your hotel or the INGUAT office about current fares before heading to the docks, and then try to be polite but firm in sticking to those guidelines.

In general, a small, fast boat taxi between Panajachel and San Pedro La Laguna or Santiago de Atitlán should cost around Q25 ($3.35/£1.70) each way; between San Pedro and Santiago, or between San Pedro and San Marcos, about Q15 ($2/£1). The slow water taxi between Panajachel and either San Pedro or Santiago should cost Q20 ($2.65/£1.30). ***Note:*** Pay only for the leg of the ride you are actually taking. There is absolutely no reason to reserve a return trip in advance, and you run the risk of not meeting up with that specific boat or captain at the appointed time and losing your fare.

Orientation

Panajachel sits on the north shore of Lake Atitlán. As you enter Panajachel from the Pan-American Highway (Carretera Panamericana) and Sololá, you'll be on Calle Principal (also known as Calle Real), which continues on around the lake toward Santa Catarina Palopó. Soon after you enter Panajachel, you'll come to a major intersection at Calle Santander. The actual center of the town, called the Old Town, or Ciudad Vieja, is about 3 blocks from this intersection and about 10 or so blocks from the lakeshore. By far the majority of the action in Panajachel is centered on Calle Santander, which runs from this intersection directly toward the lake, where it dead-ends. The sidewalks are crowded with street vendors and are such a jumble that most people walk in the center of the street, making way, as necessary, for the sporadic traffic.

Visitor Information

There's an **INGUAT** (Guatemala Tourism Commission) office (© **502/7762-1392**) on Calle Santander 1-87, in the Centro Comercial San Rafael. It's open Monday through Friday from 9am to 5pm. They can give you a map of Panajachel and the Lake Atitlán area, and help you with hotel reservations and figuring out the current bus and boat taxi schedules.

FAST FACTS There are a host of banks on Calle Principal and around the Old Town, including **Banco de Comercio, Banco Industrial,** and **Banco G&T.** There are also scores of Internet cafes around Panajachel, both in the Old Town and along Calle Santander. The **post office** is at the corner of Calle Santander and Calle 15 de Febrero. There's a small health clinic (✆ **502/7762-1258**) on Calle Principal in Panajachel. The nearest hospital is the **Hospital Nacional Sololá** (✆ **502/7762-4121**) in Sololá. To contact the local **police,** dial ✆ **502/7762-1120.**

WHAT TO SEE & DO

In Panajachel

The principal activities in Panajachel are strolling along Calle Santander and the lakeshore, shopping, and hanging out in one of the cafes, bars, or restaurants.

The main **Catholic church,** in the heart of the Old Town, dates from 1567, and was meticulously restored in 1962. The old stone facade looks almost whitewashed, and the diminutive plaza in front of the church is a major meeting place for locals.

Museo Lacustre Atitlán ★ Kids A series of excellent and informative displays explain the geology and geography behind the formation of the lake. The museum also showcases a collection of ceramic pieces discovered in the area, many of which were brought up from the depths of the lake by scuba divers.

At the Posada Don Rodrigo. At the south end of Calle Santander, Zona 2. ✆ **502/7762-2326.** Admission Q35 ($4.65/£2.35), free for children 11 and under. Mon–Fri 8am–6pm; Sat–Sun 8am–7pm.

Reserva Natural Atitlán ★ A couple of nature trails, a butterfly garden, and botanical gardens are the offerings at this reserve. The trails pass through some areas of dense forest, and feature a few high-hanging bridges to get you up into the canopy. You'll certainly see a range of tropical bird species, and if you're lucky you may see a monkey or two. The reserve has a visitor center, restaurant, and small section of private beach. There's also a zip-line canopy tour here.

In the San Buenaventura valley, just down the road from the Hotel Atitlán (see below). About .5km (¼ mile) before Panajachel, on the road in from Sololá. ✆ **502/7762-2565.** www.atitlanreserva.com. Admission Q45 ($6/£3), Q25 ($3.35/£1.70) for students and children 11 and under includes a guided tour through the butterfly garden and breeding exhibit; Q150 ($20/£10) canopy tour. Daily 8am–5pm.

Around the Lake

There are perhaps a dozen or more small towns and villages set on the shores around the lake. The two most significant towns are **San Pedro La Laguna ★** and **Santiago de Atitlán ★★**, both pretty much south across the lake from Panajachel. Other towns of note and interest to visitors include **San Marcos La Laguna, Santa Cruz La Laguna, Santa Catarina Palopó,** and **San Antonio Palopó.** Almost all of these towns are more popularly known by their abbreviated names of San Pedro, Santiago, San Marcos, and so on.

San Pedro is probably the most popular of these towns. It features a host of language schools and budget hotels, and has earned a reputation as a hippie and backpacker haven.

Santiago ★★ is a picturesque Tz'utujil town with a distinct character and fiercely independent streak. Santiago de Atitlán was the site of a horrible massacre during the civil war and one of the first villages to organize against the paramilitary and military forces. The Santiago de Atitlán *huipil* and men's pants are unique and highly prized by

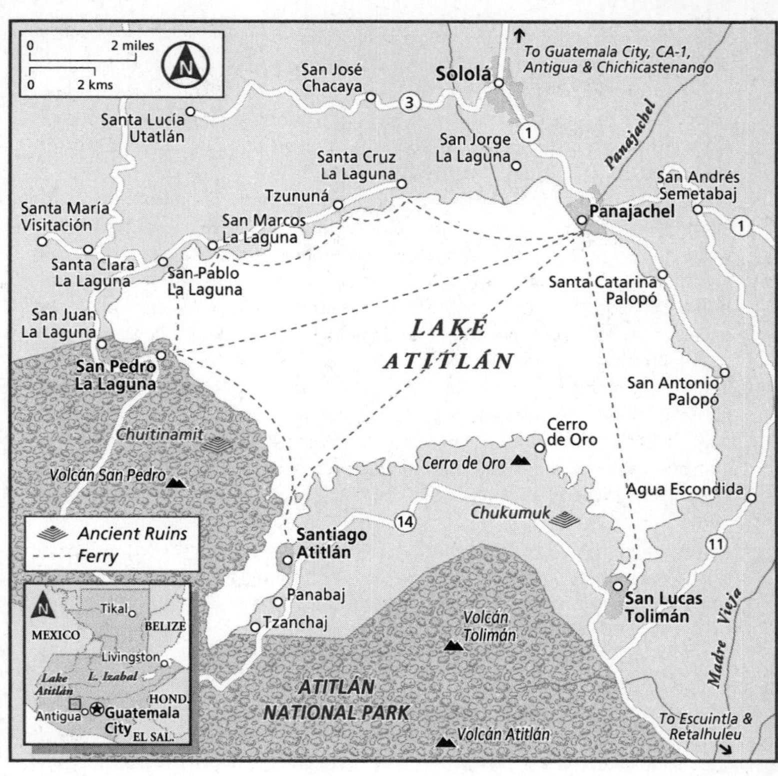

foreigners buying indigenous textiles. The cult of Maximón (see the box, below) is very strong in Santiago, and as soon as you step off any boat here, you'll be met with offers from local kids and touts to take you to see him. You'll definitely want to visit Maximón, but don't feel obligated to go along with the first person who approaches you.

San Marcos ★ and **Santa Cruz ★** are two small communities on the northwestern shores of Lake Atitlán. Both are set on hillsides above the lakeshore. However, each has a selection of small hotels spread along the water's edge. For some reason, these two towns have developed as hot spots for yoga retreats and holistic getaways, with several hotels in each town catering to this niche. The most popular and long-standing yoga retreats and meditation centers in the area are **Las Pirámides** (**© 502/5205-7151;** www.laspiramidesdelka.com) and **Villa Sumaya** (**© 502/5617-1209;** www.villasumaya.com).

Santa Catarina Palopó and **San Antonio Palopó** are two Kaquichel Maya towns on the northeastern shore of the lake connected to Panajachel by a well-paved road. **Santa Catarina** is particularly well known for its distinctive *huipil* of dark blues and greens with intricate embroidery. The brilliantly whitewashed church in San Antonio is especially pretty, with an enviable perch and fantastic view over Lake Atitlán.

Maximón

The Maya introduction to Catholicism often came with the threat of immolation, hanging, or beheading, and they soon rationalized that this new religion could easily be superimposed with their own. When they saw the statue of Mary crushing a snake under her foot, they prayed to Gukumatz, the creator snake god.

The Maya also brought their own saint to their brand of Catholicism. Maximón (pronounced "Mashimon") was a pre-Columbian Maya god of the underworld known as Maam, or Grandfather. The modern name is a blend of Maam and his other name, San Simon. Maximón symbolizes male sexual virility and brings rain to fertilize the earth. He's known as the saint of gamblers and drunkards, and is thought to give wealth and worldly success to his followers.

Despite the Catholic church's attempt to demonize the dark-skinned Maximón by equating him with Judas, he is still found in churches, shops, and homes across Guatemala. He is now depicted as a 20th-century mustached man wearing a black suit, red tie, and wide-brimmed hat, and is represented in life-size wood statues, small dolls, or pictures on votive candles. He's given offerings of tobacco, alcohol, Coca-Cola, and a tropical plant with orange-red berries.

Maximón's feast day is October 28. On this day, and on the Wednesday of Holy Week, he's carried through the streets on the shoulders of his followers. In some villages he's hung from the main church's cross at the end of the ceremony. Maximón's more scandalous side forces most followers to keep him out of public view for the rest of the year, for fear that his famed sexual desires may run amok. He is kept in the house—and sometimes the outhouse—with his whereabouts changing regularly. In most towns with strong Maximón traditions (including Santiago de Atitlán and Zunil), locals will bring you to see him for a small tip. If you go, be sure to bring a cigar or some rum to leave in offering. In most cases, you'll have to pay a small fee for each photo you take.

Spanish Classes

There are a half-dozen or more language schools in San Pedro. Most offer either individual or small-class intensive instruction combined with a homestay with a local family and various organized activities and tours. Try **Corazón Maya Spanish School** (© **502/7721-8160;** www.corazonmaya.com), or **San Pedro Spanish School** (© **502/5715-4604;** www.sanpedrospanishschool.com). In Panajachel, you can try **Jardín de América Spanish School** ★ (© **502/7762-2637;** www.jardindeamerica.com). Rates run around Q750 to Q1,125 ($100–$150/£50–£75) per week for 4 hours of class per day and a homestay with a local family. More adventurous students might want to learn a local Mayan dialect. Ask at any of the language schools, and they'll be able to set you up with a local instructor.

Outdoor Activities

In addition to the attractions listed above, Panajachel and Lake Atitlán are good bases for active adventures. Most hotels have a tour desk that can arrange any of the activities listed below, and then some. Or you can book through **Hunab Kú Travel & Adventure** (✆ **502/7762-1626;** www.hunabkutours.com), or **Atitrans** (✆ **502/7762-0146;** www.atitrans.com), both with offices on Calle Santander.

In addition to the activities listed below, you might ask around and try your hand at fishing on the lake, or sign up for a mountain bike tour. For something completely different, head underwater with **ATI Divers** (✆ **502/5706-4117;** www.laiguanaperdida.com), which offers daily scuba dive tours.

BOATING **Boat tours** ★★ on the lake are one of the most popular activities in the area. All the hotel tour desks and tour agencies in town offer organized tours, most of which depart in the morning and make stops at various towns around the lake. The tours generally last around 5 to 6 hours. Most cost between Q50 and Q100 ($6.65–$13/£3.30–£6.50), which gets you the guaranteed boat ride and an hour to 90-minute layover in each town. You can also sign on for a more elaborate tour, including a bilingual guide and lunch. These generally run between Q225 and Q375 ($30–$50/£15–£25) per person.

If you prefer to do it yourself, it's easy; see "Getting Around: By Boat" above. As soon as the boat lands in each town, you'll be met by local touts and tour guides offering to show you around. For example, in Santiago de Atitlán, they offer to take you to see Maximón; in Santa Catarina Palopó, they'll take you to see some weaving. Feel free to wave them off and just explore on your own.

HIKING At 3,020m (9,905 ft.), **Volcán San Pedro** is a great hike. The trail is generally wide and well-maintained, and the round-trip hike should take between 5 and 6 hours. Tour desks all around the lake offer guided hikes to the summit for around Q40 to Q115 ($5–$15/£2.50–£7.50) per person. Other popular hikes include **La Nariz del Indio (Indian's Nose),** another lookout spot, near San Pedro, that allegedly looks like a Maya profile from afar.

HORSEBACK RIDING & MOUNTAIN BIKING The countryside here is beautiful and horseback and mountain bike tours can be set up by any hotel tour desk tour agency. In Santiago de Atitlán, longtime residents **Jim & Nancy Matison** (✆ **502/5811-5516;** wildwestgua@yahoo.com) have very well-cared-for horses, and offer a range of rides in the area, as well as various treks and hikes.

KAYAKING & CANOEING You can rent canoes and kayaks from a variety of hotels and operators in most towns around the lake. Just ask around. Rates run around Q10 ($1.35/70p) per hour and Q30 to Q40 ($4–$5.35/£2–£2.70) per day. If you're in good shape, you can paddle to one of the nearby towns or villages. Remember that the winds and chop tend to kick up in the afternoon.

SWIMMING The lakeshore along the front of Panajachel is filled with public beaches. You'll often find local kids and, to a lesser extent, tourists swimming here. However, I think the boat and foot traffic and pollution make it unappealing. If you want to swim in the lake, I recommend heading to the beach at the Reserva Natural Atitlán (see above) or in front of one of the smaller villages around the lake.

Tips **Be Careful**

The beautiful countryside and volcanic peaks around Lake Atitlán are quite enticing to climbers and hikers. However, due to the current security situation, poverty, and a history of violence, it's often not safe for tourists to be on isolated trails or back roads. It's best to sign up for a guided tour if you want to scale a volcano or hike to one of the nearby villages or lookouts.

SHOPPING

Calle Santander and the road ringing the lakeshore are crammed with street vendors selling all sorts of Guatemalan handicrafts, ranging from clothing and other textile products to stone and woodcarvings and leather goods. There are also a fair number of stalls selling handmade jewelry and trinkets, but these are relatively run-of-the-mill works that have no real connection to the land or its people.

The nearby towns of **Santiago de Atitlán, Santa Catarina Palopó,** and **Sololá** have deep and highly developed arts, crafts, and textile traditions. It's worth taking a trip to one or all of these towns to shop for the local wares. In addition, Panajachel makes a perfect base for visiting nearby **Chichicastenango** (p. 206) on market day. All of the tour operators in town offer day trips to Chichi on Thursdays and Sundays.

Note: It's become common practice to take old *huipiles* and dip them into a large dye vat of either blue or ocher. This gives the *huipil* an interesting look, but it's very far from traditional, and often serves to mask an inferior piece of work.

WHERE TO STAY

In Panajachel

Expensive

Hotel Atitlán ★★★ Finds Beautiful and luxurious rooms, fabulous grounds, impeccable service, and an excellent restaurant make this the top choice in Panajachel. The hotel is jampacked with colonial-era and local art, sculpture, and religious iconography. The rooms are all distinct and come with a private balcony or garden-front patio. Ask for a third-floor room to get the best lake and volcano views. The extensive botanical gardens and aviary are true treasures, and the lake-view pool and infinity-edge Jacuzzi may make it hard for you to get up the impetus to tour the lake, towns, and markets just off the hotel's grounds.

Finca San Buenaventura. ✆ **502/7762-1441** or 7762-2060 reservations office. Fax 502/7762-0048. www.hotelatitlan.com. 62 units. Q900 ($120/£60) double; Q1,275 ($170/£85) junior suite; Q1,500 ($200/£100) master suite. AE, DC, MC, V. **Amenities:** Restaurant; bar; lounge; babysitting; small gym; Jacuzzi; laundry service; nonsmoking rooms; outdoor pool; unlit outdoor tennis court; Wi-Fi. *In room:* TV, hair dryer.

Posada Don Rodrigo ★ Kids This lakefront property at the end of Calle Santander is a great choice in the heart of Panajachel. The sprawling grounds, tasteful rooms, fabulous terrace views, and in-house attractions set it apart from the competition. The standard rooms feature dark, colonial decor with heavy wood furniture, stucco walls, and a fireplace. The lakefront rooms are a bit more spacious and worth the modest splurge, which gets you a small private balcony and shared lawn. The pool, with a big spiral slide, and a very well-done museum (Museo Lacustre Atitlán) make this an excellent choice for families.

At the south end of Calle Santander, Zona 2. © **502/7762-2326** or 7762-2329. Fax 502/2331-6838. www.hotelposadadedonrodrigo.com. 39 units. Q750–Q825 ($100–$110/£50–£55) double. Rates include full breakfast. AE, DC, MC, V. **Amenities:** Restaurant; bar; lounge; babysitting; laundry service; outdoor pool; room service. *In room:* No phone.

Moderate

Other good midrange options include **Hostal Real Santander** (© **502/7762-2915;** necos@itelgua.com) and **Hotel Regis** (© **502/7762-1149;** www.hotelregisatitlan.com).

Hotel Dos Mundos ★ Value Not as stylish or fancy as the Don Rodrigo (above), this is still an excellent option right on Calle Santander. The rooms, as well as the pool and gardens, are set back off the main drag. All the rooms are spacious and well kept. I prefer room nos. 11 through 23, which front the pool and garden area and share a veranda. The other rooms are a bit closer to the street, though not so close that noise is a problem. The hotel has a popular Italian restaurant, as well as a separate cafe and bar.

Calle Santander 4-72, Zona 2. © **502/7762-2078** or 7762-2865. Fax 502/7762-0127. www.hoteldosmundos.com. 22 units. Q495 ($66£33) double. AE, DC, MC, V. **Amenities:** Restaurant; bar; lounge; laundry service; outdoor pool; room service. *In room:* TV.

Inexpensive

Posada de los Volcanes (© **502/7762-0244;** www.posadadelosvolcanes.com) is another good budget choice in Pana.

Hotel Primavera Value This small hotel is a step above the score of budget options on Calle Santander. Most of the rooms are on the second floor and feature bay windows that overlook the street. The rooms are relatively small and standard, but they are kept immaculate. I like no. 9, which has a private staircase and balcony, and is set back from the busy street.

Calle Santander. © **502/7762-2052.** Fax 502/7762-0171. www.primaveratitlan.com. 10 units. Q300 ($40/£20) double. AE, DC, MC, V. **Amenities:** Restaurant; laundry service. *In room:* TV, no phone.

WHERE TO STAY AROUND THE LAKE

In San Pedro La Laguna

Hotel Mansión del Lago (© **502/7721-8041;** www.hotelmansiondellago.com) is another well-located option in this small town, as is **Casa Elena** (7a Av. 8-61, Zona 2; © **502/5980-4400**).

Hotelito El Amanacer Sak'cari ★ Value The second-floor rooms, with a shared veranda overlooking the lake, are your best bet at this semi-modern hotel. Only three of the rooms have queen-size beds, so be sure to request one of these if you're traveling as a couple. The hotel also has a large, clean steam bath. The name is a little redundant since "amanacer" and "sak'cari" mean sunrise in Spanish and Tz'utujil, respectively.

7a Av. 2-10, Zona 2. © **502/7721-8096** or 5512-0038. www.hotelsakcari.com. 16 units. Q195 ($26/£13) double. AE, DC, MC, V. **Amenities:** Laundry service; steam bath. *In room:* No phone.

In Santiago de Atitlán

Located even farther outside of the town center, **Posada de Santiago** (© **502/5784-9111;** www.posadadesantiago.com) is another pretty lakeside hotel.

Bambú Hotel & Restaurant ★ Finds This is my favorite hotel in Santiago de Atitlán. Rooms include two bungalows with private patios overlooking the lake and those in the two-story building set a bit farther back from the lake. Both options are spacious and cozy with warm earth tones and pretty artwork. The hotel has a pool and an excellent Nuevo Spanish-influenced restaurant with lake and volcano views. The town is just a

 15-minute walk or short cab ride away, and any of the boat taxis from Panajachel or San Pedro will drop you off at the hotel's private dock.

Carretera San Lucas Toliman, Km 16. ✆ **502/7721-7332.** Fax 502/7721-7333. www.ecobambu.com. 11 units. Q450 ($60/£30) double. Rates include full breakfast. AE, DC, MC, V. **Amenities:** Restaurant; bar; laundry service; midsize outdoor pool; sauna. *In room:* No phone.

In Other Villages

Casa Palopó ★★★ This small, artsy hotel exudes elegance. Most of the rooms have king-size beds, large bathrooms with beautiful Mexican majolica sinks, and large terraces with gorgeous views. There's a private villa above the main building with two gorgeous master suites, a Jacuzzi, a full kitchen, dining and living rooms, and a private infinity-edge pool. The villa also comes with a personal butler and cook. Back down at the hotel, the restaurant is worth a visit even if you're not a guest here, and the pool with wood gazebo is a good place to unwind.

Carretera a San Antonio Palopó, Km 6.8, Santa Catarina Palopó. ✆ **502/7762-2270.** Fax 502/7762-2721. www.casapalopo.com. 8 units. Q1,260–Q1,545 ($168–$206/£84–£103) double; Q1,650–Q1,973 ($220–$263/£110–£132) suite; Q6,975 ($930/£465) villa. Rates higher during peak periods, lower during the off season. AE, DC, MC, V. No children 14 and under allowed. **Amenities:** Restaurant; bar; small gym; laundry service; small outdoor pool. *In room:* Minibar.

La Casa del Mundo ★ Finds This hotel sits at the top of several steep flights of steps on a rocky outcropping that juts into the lake. The rooms' distinctive decor mixes local arts and crafts with a European sense of style. Every room has a view of the lake, and a few have private balconies with lake and volcano views. There are also several open-air tiled terraces spread around the grounds, all with great views. On one of these terraces, down near the water, is the hotel's wood-fired hot tub, wonderfully located to allow you to alternate between the hot tub and the cool lake.

Jaibalito. ✆ **502/5218-5332.** www.lacasadelmundo.com. 15 units (9 with private bathroom). Q233 ($31/£16) double with shared bathroom; Q458–Q510 ($61–$68/£31–£34) double with private bathroom. Rates slightly higher during peak periods. AE, DC, MC, V. **Amenities:** Restaurant; bar; kayak rentals; laundry service. *In room:* No phone.

Villa Sumaya ★★ Finds If you're looking for spiritual and physical rejuvenation, this is the place for you. The individual cabins are beautifully done with tile floors, soft cotton comforters, local crafts, and a large veranda with several chairs and a hammock. All rooms face the lake, with the towering silhouettes of volcanoes in the background. The hotel's Blue Tiger Temple is a wonderful wood-floored yoga and meditation room that often attracts visiting instructors and retreat guests, and there's always a massage therapist on call. There's a good beach for swimming, and the grounds are lush with tropical flowers.

San Marcos La Laguna. ✆ **502/5617-1209** or ✆/fax 5810-7199. www.villasumaya.com. 14 units. Q375–Q750 ($50–$100/£25–£50) double. AE, DC, MC, V (5% surcharge). **Amenities:** Restaurant; bar; laundry service; sauna. *In room:* No phone.

WHERE TO DINE

Panajachel is the only town here with a real dining scene and variety of restaurants. In most cases, at the other towns and villages, you'll probably be eating mostly at your hotel or posada. San Pedro is a slight exception to that rule. In San Pedro, do try the laid-back atmosphere and mostly vegetarian cooking offered at **Zoola ★** (✆ **502/5534-3111**) and the varied international fare at **Restaurant Jarachik** (✆ **502/5571-8720**).

Back in Pana, in addition to the places listed below, **Guajimbo's** (✆ **502/7762-0063**) is a popular Uruguayan-style steakhouse that often has live music; **Las Chinitas** (✆ **502/7762-0063**) is the town's most popular Asian restaurant, with a mix of Chinese, Thai, and Indian options; and **La Terraza** (✆ **502/7762-0041**) is a relaxed and slightly refined place serving tapas and Continental cuisine. All of these are located on Calle Santander. For something fancier, head to **Hotel Atitlán** (see above), and for something simpler, try one of the lakefront restaurants spread over the hill above the main boat docks.

Moderate

El Bistro ★ ITALIAN This place serves excellent pastas and entrees in a convivial open-air setting. While there's some indoor seating, the best tables are found in a large covered courtyard just off Calle Santander that's lined with plants, palms, and bamboo. Homemade fettuccine is available with more than 15 different sauces, and other pasta options include lasagna and cannelloni. For something heartier, opt for grilled fish, chicken parmigiana, or steak pizzaola. When you order, the waiter will ask if you want your pasta "al dente" or "normal." "Normal" would be overcooked for most people accustomed to good Italian cooking.

Southern end of Calle Santander. ✆ **502/7762-0508.** Reservations recommended. Pasta Q45–Q50 ($6–$6.65/£3–£3.30); main courses Q45–Q75 ($6–$10/£3–£5). AE, DC, MC, V. Tues–Sun 7:30am–10pm; Mon noon–10pm.

Sunset Café GUATEMALAN/MEXICAN As the name suggests, sunset is a good time to come here. The wonderful view makes the standard Mexican fare more memorable. I like the *fajitas de pescado* (fish fajitas) and *enchiladas verdes* (chicken enchiladas in a green tomatillo sauce). There's live music here most nights, so grab a drink, a plate of nachos, and a seat under the tree (heavily hung with orchids and bromeliads) that grows through the thatch roof.

Calle Santander and Calle del Lago. ✆ **502/7762-0003.** Reservations recommended for large groups. Main courses Q30–Q80 ($4–$11/£2–£5.50). AE, DC, MC, V. Daily 11am–midnight.

Inexpensive

Café Bombay ★ Value INDIAN/VEGETARIAN The name of this place indicates that they dish out Indian cuisine, which you will find here, but you'll also get everything vegetarian from pad Thai and tacos to lasagna and falafel. In addition, excellent sandwiches, soups, and smoothies are served, as well as vegan fare. The atmosphere is casual, and on a nice day you can grab a seat on one of the umbrella-covered tables just off Calle Santander.

Calle Santander. ✆ **502/7762-0611.** Reservations not accepted. Main courses Q40–Q60 ($5.35–$8/£2.70–£4); sandwiches Q15–Q30 ($2–$4/£1–£2). No credit cards. Wed–Mon 11am–10pm.

LAKE ATITLÁN AFTER DARK

Panajachel has a fairly active nightlife. For nearly 20 years, my favorite place has been the **Circus Bar** ★★, which has a relaxed vibe, simple menu, and decor to match the joint's name. They also frequently have live music. Circus Bar is located in what's considered Panajachel's mini–Zona Viva. Of the bars on Calle Santander, I like **Maktub'ar Café,** which has a relaxed, almost beach-bar feel, and **Pana Rock Café,** which is a takeoff on the Planet Rock chain. For loud and late-night dancing, try **Sócrates Disco** or **El Chapiteau Discoteque.**

Over in San Pedro, **El Barrio,** the **Buddha,** and **Freedom Bar** are the top spots. The latter two often feature live music.

All of the above nightlife picks are located on the winding street connecting the two main docks in town, and known locally as "Gringo Alley."

7 QUETZALTENANGO & THE WESTERN HIGHLANDS ★

201km (125 miles) NW of Guatemala City; 90km (56 miles) S of Huehuetenango

The rugged geography of Guatemala's Western Highlands is a dense patchwork of volcanic mountains and lakes populated mostly by small, and often isolated, villages of the country's many Maya people. Some of the primary tribes who call this area home include the Ki'che, Mam, Kekchi, Tz'utujil, Ixil, Kaqchiquel, and Jacaltec. Most still practice small-scale plot farming on *milpas,* which are usually predominantly sown with corn. Locals live on a mix of subsistence farming and bartering. Aside from the food they grow, they also produce intricately designed and brightly colored woven textiles. In Spanish, the Western Highlands are called the Altiplano.

The highland burg of **Quetzaltenango** is the largest city and commercial hub in the Altiplano, and the second-largest city in Guatemala, with a population of more than 300,000. This was and still is a principal center of the Maya Ki'che of Guatemala—and many locals still refer to the city by its Ki'che name **Xelajú.** In fact, most people simply call the place **Xela** (pronounced "*sheh*-la"). Xelajú is close to the sight where Ki'che King Tecún Umán was killed in battle against the Spanish conquistador Pedro de Alvarado. Following Tecún Umán's defeat in 1524, the city was renamed Quetzaltenango, or "place of the Quetzal," which is what Alvarado's Nahuatl mercenaries called it.

Thanks to the presence of a large national university and scores of language schools and foreign volunteer programs, there's a college-town vibe to the city, and you'll find several good coffee shops and used bookstores in Xela, and even a couple of art-movie houses. You'll also find more nightlife here than anywhere else in the country outside of Guatemala City.

Quetzaltenango makes an excellent base for visiting a host of nearby towns and attractions, including **hot springs,** small villages with impressive **markets and churches,** and towering **volcanoes** waiting to be hiked.

ESSENTIALS

Getting There

BY BUS Several bus lines provide regular service in comfortable modern buses throughout the day between Xela and Guatemala City. **Líneas Dorada** (**© 502/2220-7990** in Guatemala City, or 7767-5198 in Xela) has express buses leaving from 16a Calle and 10 Avenida, Zona 1 in Guatemala City, at 8am and 3pm. The return buses leave Xela from 12 Avenida and 5a Calle, Zona 3 at 4am and 2:30pm.

Transportes Galgos (**© 502/2253-4868** in Guatemala City, or 7761-2248 in Xela) has buses leaving Guatemala City for Xela at 8:30am and 2:30 and 5pm. The return buses leave Xela from Calle Rodolfo Robles 17-43, Zona 1, at 4 and 8:30am, and at 12:30pm.

The trip on either bus line takes about 4 to 5 hours. The fare is around Q50 to Q70 ($6.65–$9.35/£3.30–£4.70) each way.

BY CAR To drive to Quetzaltenango, take the Pan-American Highway (Carretera Panamericana) north out of Guatemala City. At Cuatro Caminos, take the turnoff for Quetzaltenango, which lies 13km (8 miles) to the southwest, after the small city of Salcajá. The trip takes about 4 hours from Guatemala City. Quetzaltenango is also connected to the southern Pacific Coast Highway, which visitors can use to go down to Retalhuleu and the Pacific beaches.

Getting Around

Taxis and tuk tuks are plentiful in Xela. You can always find one around Parque Centro America. Fares around town should run between Q15 and Q30 ($2–$4/£1–£2). If you can't flag one down, have your hotel call one for you, or call **Taxi Catedral** (✆ **502/7761-8472**). If you want to rent a car for the day, or longer, contact **Tabarini** (✆ **502/7763-0418;** www.tabarini.com).

Orientation

The long, narrow **Parque Centro América** is the central hub of Xela. You'll find most of the hotels, restaurants, language schools, and offices, and the main Catholic church either right on this central plaza or within a few blocks. You can see the massive cone of the Santa Maria Volcano 3,677m (12,256 ft.) towering over the southern horizon from almost anywhere in town. Xela sits at 2,334m (7,656 ft.) above sea level. The climate here is relatively cool, and sometimes damp, particularly from May through mid-November. Be sure to have a light jacket or sweater for the evenings.

Visitor Information

There's an **INGUAT** office (✆ **502/7761-4931**) fronting the Parque Centro America in the Edificio Casa de la Cultura. They can provide you with a city map and basic information on tours and attractions in and around Xela. The main **post office** (✆ **502/7761-7608**) is about 4 blocks west of the central park at 4a Calle 15-07, Zona 1.

FAST FACTS **Banco de Occidente, Banrural,** and **Banco Industrial** all have branches right on Parque Centro America, and there are dozens of other bank branches around town. Since this is a university and language school city, you'll also find an abundance of Internet cafes in Xela. If your hotel doesn't provide the service, there are several coin-operated and self-service laundromats, and most of these will also wash and fold for you. I like **Pila's Laundry,** 15a Av. 3-51, Zona 1, inside the Plaza Centro (✆ **502/5515-2877**), which has three locations around the city.

In the event of a medical emergency, the **Hospital La Democracia,** 13a Av. 6-51, Zona 3 (✆ **502/7763-5671**), is a well-equipped, modern hospital. You might also try **Hospital Privado Quetzaltenango,** Calle Rodolfo Robles 23-51, Zona 1 (✆ **502/7761-4381**), a well-equipped private hospital. To reach the **National Police** dial ✆ **502/7765-4987.** However, for most tourist needs, whether it be for information or an emergency, you should call **Asistur** (✆ **1500**), which is a toll-free call.

WHAT TO SEE & DO

It won't take you long to visit Quetzaltenango's principal attractions. The **Parque Centro América ★**, with its open-air gazebo, is the town's focal point. On the southeastern side of the park you'll find the **Catedral Metropolitano de los Altos,** which is actually two churches. Fronting the park is the ornate facade of the **Catedral del Espíritu Santo ★**, which is all that remains of the city's original 16th-century baroque church. Behind this facade is the more modern, and much larger, **Catedral de la Diócesis de los Altos,** which was inaugurated in 1899.

On the south side of the park sits the **Casa de la Cultura,** 7th Calle 11-09, Zona 1 (✆ **502/7761-6031**), a large building that houses the INGUAT offices and the Museo de Historia Natural (Natural History Museum), which, in my opinion, can be missed. It gets a fair amount of press in the local tourist propaganda, and is housed in the popular Casa de la Cultura, next to the INGUAT office. Should you decide to visit the exhibits, which include dinosaur bones, Maya artifacts, and a room dedicated to the marimba (a large wooden xylophone and the bands that play them), the museum is open Monday through Friday from 8am to noon and 2 to 6pm and Saturday from 9am to 1pm. Admission is Q10 ($1.35/70p).

North of the park and town center is the **Teatro Municipal (Municipal Theater)** ★, 14a Avenida and 1a Calle (✆ **502/7761-2218**), a wonderfully restored theater built between 1884 and 1908. The theater hosted its first concert in 1903 and is still functioning today. It's worthwhile to catch a show if there's one while you're in town. Just across from the Teatro Municipal is the equally well-restored **Teatro Roma,** 14a Avenida A (✆ **502/7761-4950**), the city's first cinema. While they no longer show movies here, they do have occasional performances, which are worth a visit.

SPANISH CLASSES Quetzaltenango offers a number of Spanish schools, most with immersion-style lessons, small classes, excursions, and homestay accommodations with a local family. The best among the choices are **Celas Maya Spanish School,** 6a Calle 14-55, Zona 1 (✆ **502/7761-4342;** www.celasmaya.edu.gt); **Proyecto Lingüístico Quezalteco** ★, 5a Calle 2-40, Zona 1 (✆ **502/7765-2140;** www.plqe.org); and **Ulew Tinimit Spanish School** ★, 4a Calle 15-23, Zona 1 (✆ **502/7763-0516;** www.spanishguatemala.org). Rates run between Q1,125 and Q1,500 ($150–$200/£75–£100) per week, including homestay, most meals, and some organized excursions.

TOURS, TREKS & ATTRACTIONS AROUND QUETZALTENANGO

While there is little to see in Xela itself, there are a host of tour and activity options within easy reach of the town. All of the hotels and tour agencies listed in this section can arrange any of the tours or excursions listed below.

The best and longest-running agencies in Xela include **Adrenalina Tours** ★ (✆ **502/7761-4509;** www.adrenalinatours.com), which has its offices in the Pasaje Enriquez building just off Parque Centro America; **Altiplano's Tours** (✆ **502/7766-9614;** www.altiplanos.com.gt); and **Quetzal Trekkers** ★, Casa Argentina at 12a Diagonal, 8-37, Zona 1 (✆ **502/7765-5895;** www.quetzaltrekkers.com). In addition to the hikes and treks mentioned below, you can also sign on for a 6-day trip through **Nebaj** and **Todos Santos Chuchumatán;** a 3-day hike from **Xela** to **Lake Atitlán;** and a 2-day trek to the summit of **Tajumulco** volcano—at 4,220m (13,842 ft.), it's the highest point in all of Central America.

Zunil & Fuentes Georginas

Zunil ★ is a picturesque little town on the shores of the Salamá River and is surrounded by verdant agricultural fields. It has a beautiful whitewashed church and narrow, cobblestone streets that wind up the hills from the river. Zunil is famous for its worship of Maximón (p. 194), who is known as San Simon here in Zunil. San Simon is housed in different local homes at different times, and you can ask anyone in town where to find him. A small tip is expected for taking you to see the saint's statue. Monday is market day in Zunil, and while small, it's still a colorful and vibrant market.

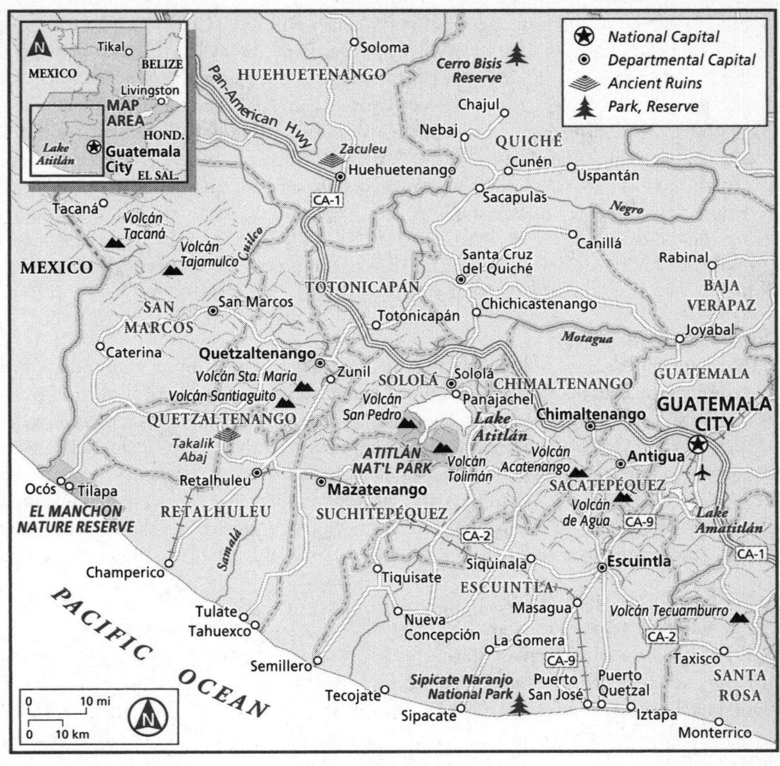

Hot springs can be found in several places on the way to Zunil, including Los Vahos, El Recreo, and Los Cirilos, but they all pale in comparison to **Las Fuentes Georginas** ★ (✆ **502/5704-2959**), a hot springs complex just beyond Zunil. The large pool here is set in rock and surrounded by steep hills. The hottest water is found closest to the hillside, and gets cooler as you move farther away. There's a restaurant, some changing rooms, and a few basic cabins for overnight stays, but I don't recommend them, as they're very musty and in desperate need of upkeep. Las Fuentes Georginas is open daily from 8am to 6:30pm. Admission is Q20 ($2.65/£1.30) for adults, Q10 ($1.35/70p) for children 11 and under.

Zunil is located 9km (5½ miles) south of Xela on the road to Retalhuleu and the Pacific coast. Las Fuentes Georginas is another 8km (5 miles) beyond Zunil up a beautiful, winding road that heads into the mountains. A taxi from Xela to the hot springs should charge around Q100 ($13/£6.50) each way. The fare is a bit less if you're only going to Zunil. Alternately, **Adrenalina Tours** (see above) runs a twice daily shuttle to Las Fuentes Georginas, leaving Xela at 8am and 2pm, and returning at noon and 6pm. The cost is Q40 ($5.35/£2.70).

Volcán Santa Maria ★★

The skyline south of Quetzaltenango is dominated by the 3,677m (12,256-ft.) **Volcán Santa María.** All of the tour agencies listed above lead hikes to the summit, and most leave Xela before dawn for the town of Llanos del Pinal. From here it takes between 3 and 4 hours of strenuous hiking to reach the summit. On a clear day, you can see as far as Mexico. You can also see a host of other Guatemalan volcanoes, including Tajumulco, Siete Orejas, and Acatenango, as well as the volcanoes surrounding Lake Atitlán and the volcanoes Fuego and Agua just outside of Antigua. The best view here, however, is of the crater of Santa María's very active sister volcano, **Santiaguito.** Santiaguito is in an almost constant state of eruption, belching out gases, volcanic ash, and molten lava. Guided tours run between Q75 and Q225 ($10–$30/£5–£15) per person, depending upon group size. During the dry season, it's possible to camp near the summit, which is worth it for the amazing sunrise and sunset views.

San Andres Xecul

The ornate church here is definitely worth a visit. Try to come in the afternoon, when the sun hits the church's facade, as it's much harder to get a good photo in the morning, when the sun is behind the church. Up the hill from the main church is a much smaller church worth a visit for two reasons. First, the high perch here offers a wonderful view of the main church and town. Second, this church, and the plot of land beside it, are still actively used for Maya ritual prayers and ceremonies, and you can almost always find local Maya worshiping here. San Andrés Xecul is 9km (5½ miles) from Xela, just beyond Slacajá, and off the road to Cuatro Caminos.

San Francisco El Alto

While Chichicastenango's market gets most of the press and acclaim, insiders know that **San Francisco El Alto's Friday market ★★** is the largest traditional market in Guatemala. As in Chichi, San Francisco's central plaza is taken over on market day and packed with merchants from all over the highlands. However, far fewer tourists come here. Instead, large wholesalers and local barterers are the principal buyers. The goods are far more geared to everyday Guatemalans, and you'll have to hunt to find the textiles and arts and crafts. Animal activists should be aware that part of the market here is reserved for live animals—everything from dogs and cats to pigs and chickens. You'll also see caged birds and the occasional captured monkey. San Francisco El Alto is 17km (11 miles) from Xela beyond Cuatro Caminos on the way to Huehuetenango.

Shopping

The shopping scene is rather uninspired in Xela, but because of the large university and language school presence here, there are several good used bookstores in town, with selections of both English- and Spanish-language books. **Vrisa Bookshop,** 15a Av. 3-64, Zona 1 (✆ **502/7761-3237**), and **North & South Bookstore,** 8a Calle and 15 Av. 13-77, Zona 1 (✆ **502/7761-0589**), are both good choices. For Guatemalan textiles or craftwork, head to the Friday market at San Francisco El Alto (see above).

WHERE TO STAY

Moderate

If you want amenities that include a pool and Jacuzzi, try **Hotel Bonifaz** (✆ **502/7765-1111;** bonifaz@intelnet.net.gt) at 4a Calle 10-50, Zona 1.

Casa Mañen ★★ Finds The immaculately restored building that houses this B&B might be pushing 200 years, but it's still my top choice in Xela. The rooms all feature thick, antique terra-cotta floors, heavy hand-woven wool blankets and rugs, firm and comfy beds, and a wealth of local art and craft works for decoration; most also have working fireplaces. I prefer the second- and third-floor rooms, which are above the street and away from the action. The hotel's terrace offers great views of the city.

9a Av. 4-11, Zona 1. ✆ **502/7765-0786.** Fax 502/7765-0678. www.comeseeit.com. 9 units. Q375–Q488 ($50–$65/£25–£33) double; Q525–Q750 ($70–$100/£35–£50) suite. Rates include full breakfast. AE, DC, MC, V. **Amenities:** Laundry service. *In room:* TV.

Inexpensive

In this category, **Hotel Modelo** (✆ **502/7761-2529;** 14a Av. A 2-31, Zona 1) is another good choice. Backpackers and real budget hounds should head to the **Black Cat** (✆ **502/ 7765-8951;** www.blackcathostels.net; 13 Av. 3-33, Zona 1).

Casa Doña Mercedes Value There are tons of budget options in Xela, but I prefer this joint. The converted old home is located just 2 blocks from the Parque Centro America. The rooms are cheerful and immaculate, there's a shared kitchen, and the service is friendly and efficient.

6a Calle and 14a Av. 13-42, Zona 1. ✆ **502/5569-1630** or 7765-4687. www.geocities.com/guest_house_mercedes. 3 units. Q175 ($23/£12) double with shared bathroom; Q278 ($37/£19) double with private bathroom. No credit cards. **Amenities:** Laundry service; free Wi-Fi. *In room:* No phone.

WHERE TO DINE

It's hard to beat the views from **El Balcón de Enríquez,** 4a Calle 12-33, Zona 1 (✆ **502/ 7761-4212**), which I like for breakfast or a light meal. Other options for a light meal or simple coffeehouse include **Café La Luna ★**, 8a Av. 4-11 (✆ **502/7761-2242**), with its hodgepodge of antiques; **Casa Antigua,** 12a Av. 3-26, Zona 1 (✆ **502/7765-8048**), with its more elegant decor; or **Café Bavaria,** 5a Calle 13-14, Zona 1 (✆ **502/7763-1855**), which has a wonderful Sunday brunch featuring live jazz.

For good Indian and vegetarian fare, head to **Sabor de la India ★**, 2a Calle and 15a Av. A 19, Zona 1 (✆ **502/7761-9957** or 5280-1869); for ribs, steaks and excellent Tex-Mex fare, grab a table at **Restaurante y Cantina Dos Tejanos,** 4a Calle 12-33, Zona 1 (✆ **502-7765-4360**); and for excellent pizzas and pastas, try either **Restaurante Il Giardino,** 19 Callejón 8-07, Zona 1 (✆ **502/7765-8293**) or **Trattoria La Genovese da Alfredo** 14 Av. A, 3-38, Zona 1 (✆ **502/5915-3231**).

Restaurante Mediterraneo ★★ TAPAS/INTERNATIONAL Tables are spread over several floors, in various nooks and crannies, in this new and hip restaurant inside the Pasaje Enriquez. Most of the menu is made up of a range of tapas, although they aren't strictly traditional Spanish-style tapas. You will find dishes with Greek and French, as well as Spanish influences. Don't miss the eggplant rolls with goat cheese and a sun-dried tomato tapanade. Larger combo plates are also available.

4a Calle 12-33, Zona 1, inside El Pasaje Enriquez. ✆ **502/5515-6724.** Reservations recommended. Tapas Q20–Q75 ($2.65–$10/£1.30–£5). AE, DC, MC, V. Daily 11am–3pm and 5:30–11pm.

Royal Paris ★ FRENCH/INTERNATIONAL This restaurant has the reputation of being the fanciest dining option in town, but the pretense and prices are mellow enough to attract a good share of the local student crowd. Channel the fancy French restaurant by ordering a pork chop in an apple and cream sauce, or go the bistro route for lunch with one of the excellent sandwiches, made on a homemade baguette or whole-wheat bread. Live music is featured here most weekend nights.

14a Av. A 3-06, Zona 1, 2nd floor. ✆ **502/7761-1942.** Reservations recommended. Main courses Q50–Q100 ($6.65–$13/£3.30–£6.50). AE, DC, MC, V. Tues–Sun 11am–3pm and 6–10:30pm; Mon 6–10pm.

XELA AFTER DARK

Xela has a very active nightlife. Many start things off at the very popular **Salon Tecún ★** in the interior passageway of the Enríquez building, fronting the Parque Centro América. The long wooden tables with bench seating fill up most nights with a mix of locals and language students. A better option is **El Balcón de Enríquez ★★**, which is in the same building but has second-floor outdoor seating that overlooks the park below.

Several bars and discos are concentrated within 2 blocks around 14a Avenida A, which is known as Xela's Zona Viva (Live Zone). This is the place to come if you want to bar-hop. Popular dance clubs include **La Parranda,** 6a Calle and 14a Avenida, Zona 1, and **Zona Kokoloko's,** 15a Avenida and 4a Calle.

For a mellower ambience, try **Pool And Beer,** 12a Av. 10-21, Zona 1; **La Fonda del Che,** 15a Av. 7-43, Zona 1; or **El Cuartito,** 13a Av. 7-09, Zona 1. A couple of informal cinemas cater to Xela's student population, showing DVDs on a large flatscreen TV or projected onto a screen. **Blue Angel Video Cafe,** 7a Calle 15-79, Zona 1 (✆ **502/7761-7815**), is the longest running, and features two screening rooms. Films are shown at 8pm and cost Q10 ($1.35/70p). Ask around town, or pick up a copy of the free weekly ***Xela Who*** (www.xelawho.com) to find the current schedule.

A SIDE TRIP: CHICHICASTENANGO

Santo Tomás de Chichicastenango is a small, highland city with perhaps the most impressive—and certainly the most famous—open-air market in all of Guatemala. Although the twice-weekly market and the city have adapted to the flood of tourists, they both maintain a sense of tradition and the indelible mark of Maya culture that stretches back for millennia. The city center is made of narrow, cobblestone streets, and just outside the center, the landscape is one of deep ravines and sparsely populated hillsides. The large main plaza is Chichi's central hub. This is ground zero of the market, and where you'll find the city's main church, and municipal office buildings. Almost all of the hotels, restaurants, banks, shops, and other services can be found within a 4- or 5-block radius of the central plaza.

THE MARKET ★★★ Thursday and Sunday are market days in Chichi, and on these days, the city is a mad orgy of sights, sounds, and smells. Maya craft sellers from across the highlands set up makeshift booths around the central plaza, spilling over on to sidewalks, the church steps, and up various side streets. A broad selection of Guatemalan handicrafts is available, including carved-wood masks and religious figures, ceramic wares, and an immense selection of the country's amazing native textiles. In addition to the craftworks, vendors sell fruits, vegetables, flowers, medicinal herbs, and more. ***Note:*** While a discerning shopper can find quality goods in Chichicastenango's market, much of what is offered is now machine-made and geared toward the mass tourist market. Despite the seeming chaos, there's actually a historical order to the setup, with vendors selling certain products in specific areas that have been designated for as long as anyone can remember. In fact, while tourists might think the entire market is geared toward them, the market is actually the central meeting place for inter-village trade and commerce among the various highland Maya.

Vendors begin arriving in Chichi the afternoon before market day, and set up throughout the evening and into the early morning. The best time to shop is either very early, before the tour buses from Guatemala City and Lake Atitlán begin arriving, or in the afternoon, after everyone's cleared out.

THE IGLESIA DE SANTO TOMÁS ★★ This church was built by Dominican priests more than 450 years ago on top of an ancient Maya worship site. It remains the heart and soul of Chichicastenango and—to this day—is used as much for traditional Maya ceremonial purposes as it is for Catholic Mass. Local Maya can almost always be found on the steps leading up to the church, burning copal incense and candles, and offering prayer. Each of the 18 steps represents one of the months in the Maya calendar. Rather than the expected pews, you'll find makeshift shrines and altars spread out on the floor with pine needles and candles. It was in the church's convent that the oldest known copy of the ancient **Popol Vuh** text was discovered.

The church is on the southeast corner of the main plaza. ***Note:*** Out of respect, the front door of the church is informally reserved for locals and high church officials. Visitors are encouraged to use the side door.

GETTING THERE You best bet for getting to Chichi is with a shuttle company, or as part of an organized tour. All of the tour agencies in Xela, Antigua, Panajachel, and Guatemala City can arrange this. You don't really need a tour guide, and a simple shuttle is probably the best way to go. These run between Q60 and Q210 ($8–$28/£4–£14), depending upon your departure city. Full-day tours cost between Q340 and Q675 ($45–$90/£23–£45), and may include lunch.

8 TIKAL & EL PETEN ★★

548km (340 miles) NE of Guatemala City; 65km (40 miles) N of Flores; 100km (62 miles) NW of the Belize border

Occupying the entire northeastern section of Guatemala, the Petén is Guatemala's largest and least populated province. Most of the Petén is forest—thick tropical rainforest. It is a lush and wild landscape that contains some of Mesoamerica's richest archaeological treasures. The Petén Province is home to perhaps the most impressive and best preserved of the ancient Maya ceremonial cities, **Tikal.** It is also home to numerous other lesser, and less excavated, sites. In addition, the area is a rich and rewarding destination for bird-watchers and ecotourists.

Tikal is the greatest of the surviving Classic Maya cities. It is estimated that Tikal once supported a population of about 100,000 people. Archaeologists have identified over 3,000 structures, and in its heyday, the city probably covered as much as 65 sq. km (25 sq. miles). Tikal is far more extensively excavated than any ruins in Belize, and unlike the grand cities and excavations in Mexico, Tikal rises out of dense jungle. The pyramids here are some of the most perfect examples of ceremonial architecture in the Maya world. Standing atop Temple IV, you are high above the rainforest canopy. The peaks of several temples poke through the dense vegetation. Toucans and parrots fly about, and the loudest noise you'll hear is the guttural call of howler monkeys.

Flores is the unofficial capital of the Petén region of Guatemala. Seen from the air, Flores appears almost perfectly round. This quiet town, with its colonial-style buildings and cobblestone streets, is one of the most fascinating in Guatemala. Though most people spend time here only en route to or from the Tikal ruins, Flores is well worth exploring for a day or two. A walk around the circumference of the island presents a sort of Venetian experience. Buildings come right down to the water's edge, and dugout canoes, kayaks, and motor launches sit at makeshift docks all around the island.

ESSENTIALS

Getting There

BY PLANE **TACA Regional Airline** (✆ **502/2470-8222;** www.taca.com) has two daily flights to **Flores Airport** (**FRS;** ✆ **502/7926-0260** or 7926-0113) from La Aurora International Airport in Guatemala City. Flights depart at 7am and 5:25pm, with return flights at 8:30am and 4:50pm. **TAG Airlines** (✆ **502/2380-9401;** www.tag.com.gt) has one daily flight departing at 6:30am and returning from Flores at 4:30pm. The flight takes around 50 minutes.

The Flores airport is on the road to Tikal, about 2.4km (1½ miles) east of Santa Elena. A taxi from the airport into Santa Elena or Flores should cost you around Q20 ($2.65/£1.30). Collective taxis and minivans to Tikal are usually waiting at the airport (if not, you'll have to head into Santa Elena or Flores first). These charge around Q25 and Q50 ($3.35–$6.65/£1.70–£3.35) per person each way. A private taxi can be hired for Q250 to Q400 ($33–$53/£17–£27).

BY BUS **Autobuses del Norte** (**ADN;** ✆ **502/2251-0610** in Guatemala City, or 7924-8131 in Santa Elena; www.adnautobusesdelnorte.com; Estación Central, 8a Av. 16-41, Zona 1); and **Linea Dorada** (✆ **502/2232-5506** in Guatemala City, or 7926-0070 in Santa Elena; www.tikalmayanworld.com; 16a Calle 10-03, Zona 1) both have regular buses between Guatemala City and Santa Elena/Flores. Fares run between Q180 and Q263 ($24–$35/£12–£18) each way, with a slight discount for purchasing a round-trip fare. The trip on either bus line takes around 8 to 9 hours. If you arrive by bus, you'll have to arrange a taxi, collective taxi, or minivan ride out to Tikal. Linea Dorado also has service to and from Belize City.

BY CAR To drive to Tikal from Guatemala City, you must first drive to Santa Elena. The best and fastest route is via Río Dulce. Take the Carretera al Atlántico (CA-9) out of Guatemala City to La Ruidosa crossroads at Km 245. From here it's 34km (21 miles) north on highway CA-13 to Río Dulce and another 180km (112 miles) from Río Dulce to Santa Elena. From Santa Elena, you'll need to drive 32km (20 miles) to the crossroads at Ixlú (El Cruce), and turn north toward Tikal, which is 65km (40 miles) away. The route and turnoffs are all well-marked, and the drive should take about 8 hours.

Warning: It's strongly advised that you do not drive at night. It's a sad fact that armed groups occasionally set up roadblocks along these isolated, yet frequently trafficked roads. While this is a rare occurrence, it's better to be safe than sorry.

BY ORGANIZED TOUR Organized day trips leave daily for Tikal from Guatemala City and Antigua. Costs for these all-inclusive trips are approximately Q1,875 to Q2,625 ($250–$350/£125–£175) per person including round-trip airfare, ground transportation, park entrance fees, a guide, and lunch. These tours generally leave at around 5am and get back to Guatemala City or Antigua at around 6pm. Budget an additional Q375 to Q1,125 ($50–$150/£25–£75) per person per day for multiday excursions, depending on the level of accommodations chosen. In Guatemala City, call **Maya Vacations** ★ (✆ **502/2426-1400;** www.mayavacations.com); **Clark Tours** (✆ **502/2412-4848;** www.clarktours.com.gt); or **Via Venture** ★★ (✆ **502/7832-2509;** www.viaventure.com).

Getting Around

BY TAXI OR MINIVAN If you don't have a car, the best way to get around this area is by minivan. Minivans from Flores and Santa Elena to Tikal leave roughly every hour between 5am and 10am, and less frequently thereafter. These minivans leave from Tikal for the return trip roughly every hour from noon to 6pm. Every hotel in Flores and Santa Elena can arrange a minivan pickup for you. The trip usually takes an hour and costs Q25 to Q50 ($3.35–$6.65/£1.70–£3.35) per person each way per person, each way. You can buy a round-trip fare at a slight savings; however, this commits you to a specific minivan company, and I've found I prefer paying a little extra to have more flexibility in grabbing my return ride when I'm ready to leave.

A private cab (which is usually a minivan) from Tikal to Santa Elena/Flores will run around Q250 to Q400 ($33–$53/£17–£27) each way. Between Tikal and El Remate, the fare is about Q150 to Q200 ($20–$27/£10–£13). Be sure to bargain, as the first price you are quoted is almost certainly above the going rate and subject to some negotiation.

BY BUS Very inexpensive local bus service connects Flores and Santa Elena to Tikal and several neighboring communities. However, this service is infrequent, slow, and often uncomfortably overcrowded. Linea Dorada (see above) has three daily buses from Santa Elena to Tikal leaving at 5 and 8:30am and 3:30pm. The return buses leave Tikal at 2 and 5pm. Ask at your hotel or around town for current schedules, as they change periodically. The trip takes 2 hours; the one-way fare is Q20 ($2.65/£1.35).

BY CAR There are several local car-rental agencies at the airport. Of these, a good choice is **Tabarini Rent A Car** (© **502/7926-0253;** www.tabarini.com). All rent small jeeps and SUVs. Do get a four-wheel-drive vehicle; even though you may never need the traction or off-road ability, the extra clearance will come in handy. Rates run from Q300 to Q410 ($40–$110/£20–£55) per day.

Orientation

Tikal National Park is located 65km (40 miles) north of the sister towns of Flores and Santa Elena. There is no village or town inside Tikal National Park. There is an entrance booth 18km (11 miles) south of the ruins. After paying your entrance fee and driving in, you will come to the large central parking area and visitor center. This is where you will find the two museums, gift shops, a collection of simple restaurants, and the four hotels mentioned later. The ruins themselves are about a 15- to 20-minute walk through the forest from the trail entrance here.

Flores is a picturesque little town built on an island in the middle of Lake Petén Itzá. A narrow causeway connects Flores to Santa Elena. The name Flores is often used to denote both towns. Since accommodations options are so limited near the ruins, a majority of travelers end up staying in Flores or Santa Elena.

About midway between Flores and Santa Elena, you'll find El Remate, a small village on the eastern shores of Lake Petén Itzá that is a popular spot to stay while visiting Tikal. El Remate is much more tranquil and pristine than Flores or Santa Elena. Currently, a handful of budget lodgings can be found in the tiny village here, while more upscale options are on the lakeshore heading north out of the village.

Visitor Information

There is an information booth run by the Guatemalan Tourist Board, **INGUAT** (© **502/7926-0533;** www.visitguatemala.com) at the Flores airport, and another one in downtown Flores (© **502/5116-3182**) on Avenida Flores, on the north side of the Central

Park. Both can help provide basic maps to the region and ruins, as well as brochures for local hotels and tour agencies.

FAST FACTS There are no banks, ATMs, medical facilities, laundromats, or other major services available at Tikal National Park. There is a small post office, however, for mailing off postcards and letters.

You'll find several banks in downtown Santa Elena. Most have ATMs, and many of these will work with your debit or credit card. There are also a couple of ATMs on the island of Flores. Check with your home bank and the PLUS or Cirrus systems in advance to confirm. All will exchange money. Most of the hotels and restaurants in Flores and Santa Elena will also exchange dollars for quetzales, although they may give you a slightly less favorable rate than you would get at a bank.

The **Flores post office** is on the Avenida Barrios, 1 block south of the Parque Central, or Central Park, which is in front of the church. **Santa Elena's post office** is on Calle 4 and Avenida 7. To contact the **local police,** dial ✆ **502/7926-1365.**

EXPLORING TIKAL

Tikal is one of the largest Maya cities ever uncovered and the most spectacular ruins in Guatemala. The ruins of Tikal are set in the middle of a vast jungle through which you must hike from temple to temple. The many miles of trails through the park provide numerous opportunities to spot toucans and parrots and such wild animals as coatimundis, spider monkeys, howler monkeys, and deer. Together, the ruins and the abundance of wildlife make a trip to Tikal an absolute must for anyone interested in Maya history, bird-watching, or wildlife viewing.

Tikal was a massive ceremonial metropolis. At its height, Tikal may have covered as much as 65 sq. km (25 sq. miles). So far, archaeologists have mapped about 3,000 constructions, 10,000 earlier foundations beneath surviving structures, 250 stone monuments (stelae and altars), and thousands of art objects found in tombs and cached offerings. There is evidence of continuous construction at Tikal from 200 B.C. through the 9th century A.D., with some suggestion of occupation as early as 600 B.C. The Maya reached their zenith in art and architecture during the Classic Period, which began about A.D. 250 and ended abruptly about 900, when for some reason Tikal and all other major Maya centers were abandoned. Most of the visible structures at Tikal date from the Late Classic Period, from 600 to 900.

No one's sure just what role Tikal played in the history of the Maya: Was it mostly a ceremonial center for priests, artisans, and the elite? Or was it a city of industry and commerce as well? In the 16 sq. km (6 sq. miles) of Tikal that have been mapped and excavated, only a few of the buildings were domestic structures; most were temples, palaces, ceremonial platforms, and shrines.

Tikal National Park is open daily from 6am to 6pm. Admission, which must be paid at the entrance gate, is Q150 ($20/£10) per person, per day. If you'd like to stay in the park until 8pm (for sunset and nocturnal wildlife viewing), get your admission ticket stamped at the office behind the Stelae Museum. If you arrive after 3pm, your admission is good for the following day as well. The best times to visit the ruins are in early morning and late afternoon, which are the least crowded and coolest times of day.

Tikal is such an immense site that you really need several days to see it thoroughly. But you can visit many of the greatest temples and palaces in 1 day. To do it properly, as a first-time visitor, you should probably hire a guide. Guides are available at the visitor center and charge around Q150 ($20/£10) for a half-day tour of the ruins. In addition, most hotels and all tour agencies in the region offer guided tours.

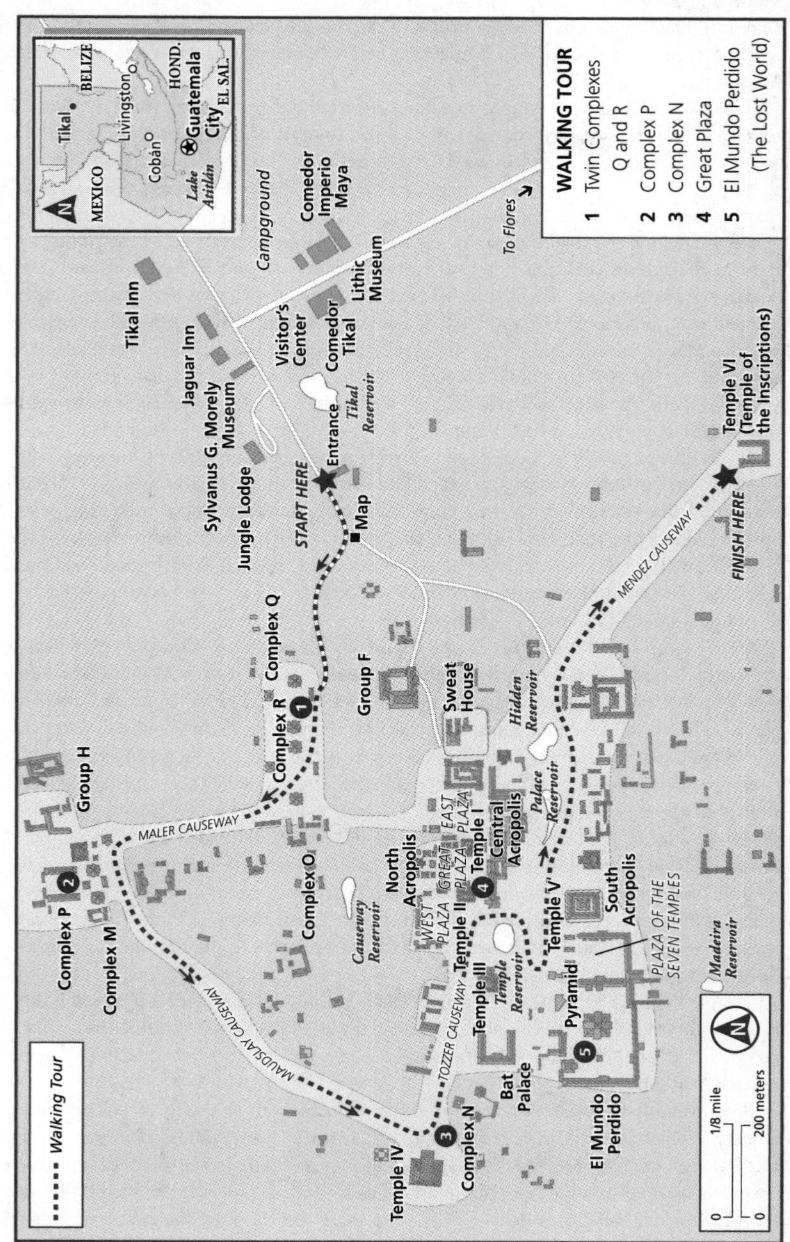
Walking Tour
WALKING TOUR
1 Twin Complexes Q and R
2 Complex P
3 Complex N
4 Great Plaza
5 El Mundo Perdido (The Lost World)
MEXICO
BELIZE
HOND.
EL SAL.
Tikal
Livingston
Cobán
Guatemala City
Lake Atitlán
Tikal Inn
Jaguar Inn
Sylvanus G. Morely Museum
Jungle Lodge
Campground
Comedor Imperio Maya
Visitor's Center
Comedor Tikal
Lithic Museum
To Flores
Entrance
Tikal Reservoir
START HERE
Map
Complex Q
Complex R
Group F
Group H
Sweat House
Hidden Reservoir
MALER CAUSEWAY
Complex P
Complex M
Complex O
Causeway Reservoir
North Acropolis
WEST PLAZA
GREAT PLAZA
EAST PLAZA
Temple I
Temple II
Central Acropolis
Palace Reservoir
Temple V
South Acropolis
PLAZA OF THE SEVEN TEMPLES
Temple III
Temple Reservoir
Pyramid
MAUDSLAY CAUSEWAY
TOZZER CAUSEWAY
Bat Palace
El Mundo Perdido
Temple IV
Complex N
MENDEZ CAUSEWAY
FINISH HERE
Temple VI (Temple of the Inscriptions)
Madeira Reservoir
N
0 1/8 mile
0 200 meters

A Walking Tour

To orient yourself, begin your tour of Tikal at the visitor center and neighboring Stelae Museum. Here you'll find some informative exhibits and relics, as well as an impressive relief map of the site. See "The Museums" below for more information on the Stelae Museum.

A full tour of Tikal will require an extensive amount of walking, as much as 10km (6 miles). The itinerary described here will take you to most of the major temples and plazas, and can be accomplished in about 3 to 4 hours. If your time is really limited, you should follow the signs and head straight to the Great Plaza. If you have the time, consider this route:

Walking along the road that goes west from the entrance area toward the ruins, turn right at the first intersection to get to **twin complexes Q** and **R.** Seven of these twin complexes are known at Tikal, but their exact purpose is still a mystery. Each complex has two pyramids facing east and west; at the north is an unroofed enclosure entered by a vaulted doorway and containing a single stele and altar; at the south is a small palacelike structure. Of the two pyramids here, one has been restored and one has been left as it was found, and the latter will give you an idea of just how overgrown and ensconced in the jungle these structures had become.

At the end of the Twin Complexes is a wide road called the **Maler Causeway.** Turn right (north) onto this causeway to get to **Complex P,** another twin complex, a 15-minute walk. Some restoration has been done at Complex P, but the most interesting points are the replicas of a stele (no. 20) and altar (no. 8) in the north enclosure. Look for the beautiful glyphs next to the carving of a warrior on the stele, all in very good condition. The altar shows a captive bound to a carved-stone altar, his hands tied behind his back—a common scene in carvings at Tikal.

From Complex P, head south on the **Maudslay Causeway** to **Complex N,** which is the site of **Temple IV, the Temple of the Two-Headed Serpent ★★★**. Finished around A.D. 740, Temple IV is the tallest structure in Tikal—64m (212 ft.) from the base of its platform to the top. The first glimpse you get of the temple from the Maudslay Causeway is awesome, most of the temple has not been restored, and all but the temple proper (the enclosure) and its roof comb are covered in foliage. The stairway is occluded by earth and roots, but there is a system of steep stairways (rough-hewed wooden ladders set against the steep sides of the pyramid) to the top of the temple. The view of the setting and layout of Tikal—and all of the Great Plaza—is magnificent. From the platform of the temple, you can see in all directions and get an idea of the extent of the Petén jungle, an ocean of lush greenery. **Temple III (Temple of the Great Priest)** is in the foreground to the east; **temples I** and **II** are farther on at the Great Plaza. To the right of these are the **South Acropolis** and **Temple V.**

Temple IV, and all the other temples at Tikal, are built on this plan: A pyramid is built first, and on top of it is built a platform; the temple proper rests on this platform and is composed of one to three rooms, usually long and narrow and not for habitation but rather for priestly rites.

From Temple IV, walk east along the **Tozzer Causeway** to get to the **Great Plaza,** about a 10-minute walk. Along the way you'll pass the twin-pyramid Complex N, the **Bat Palace,** and Temple III. Take a look at the altar and stele in the complex's northern enclosure—two of the finest monuments at Tikal—and also the altar in front of Temple III, showing the head of a deity resting on a plate. By the way, the crisscross pattern shown here represents a woven mat, a symbol of authority to the Maya.

The Great Plaza ★★★

Entering the Great Plaza from the Tozzer Causeway, you'll be struck by the towering stone structure that is Temple II, seen from the back. It measures 38m (125 ft.) tall now, although it is thought to have been 42m (140 ft.) high when the roof comb was intact. Also called the Temple of the Masks, from a large face carved in the roof comb, the temple dates from about A.D. 700. Walk around this temple to enter the plaza proper.

Directly across from Temple II you'll see Temple I (Temple of the Great Jaguar), perhaps the most striking structure in Tikal. Standing 44m (145 ft.) tall, the temple proper has three narrow rooms with high corbeled vaults (the Maya "arch") and carved wooden lintels made of zapote wood, which is rot-resistant. One of the lintels has been removed for preservation in the Guatemala National Museum of Archaeology and Ethnology in Guatemala City. The whole structure is made of limestone, as are most others at Tikal. It was within this pyramid that one of the richest tombs in Tikal was discovered. Believed to be the tomb of Tikal ruler Hasaw Chan K'awil, when archaeologists uncovered it in 1962, they found the former ruler's skeleton surrounded by some 180 pieces of jade, 90 bone artifacts carved with hieroglyphic inscriptions, numerous pearls, and objects in alabaster and shell. ***Note:*** Tourists can no longer scale temples I or III. However, those in need of serious cardio workouts will get their fill climbing some of the other temples.

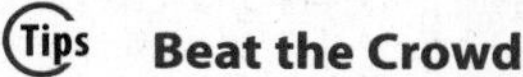

Beat the Crowds

Tikal fills up with tour buses most days, with the hours between 10am and 2pm being the busiest period. I prefer visiting the Great Plaza either before or after the main crowds have left. Feel free to reverse the order of this walking tour if it will help you avoid the masses.

The **North Acropolis** (north side of the Great Plaza) is a maze of structures from various periods covering an area of 8 hectares (21 acres). Standing today 9m (30 ft.) above the limestone bedrock, it contains vestiges of more than a hundred different constructions dating from 200 B.C. to A.D. 800. At the front-center of the acropolis (at the top of the stairs up from the Great Plaza) is a temple numbered **5D-33.** Although much of the 8th-century temple was destroyed during the excavations to get to the Early Classic Period temple (A.D. 300) underneath, it's still a fascinating building. Toward the rear of it is a tunnel leading to the stairway of the **Early Classic** temple, embellished with two 3m-high (10-ft.) plaster polychrome masks of a god—don't miss these.

Directly across the plaza from the North Acropolis is the **Central Acropolis,** which covers about 1.6 hectares (4 acres). It's a maze of courtyards and palaces on several levels, all connected by an intricate system of passageways. Some of the palaces had five floors, connected by exterior stairways, and each floor had as many as nine rooms arranged like a maze.

Before you leave the Great Plaza, be sure to examine some of the 70 beautiful stelae and altars right in the plaza. You can see the full development of Maya art in them, for they date from the Early Classic period right through to the Late Classic period. There are three major stylistic groups: the stelae with wraparound carving on the front and sides with text on the back; those with a figure carved on the front and text in glyphs on the back; and those with a simple carved figure on the front, text in hieroglyphs on the sides, and a plain back. The oldest stele is no. 29 (now in the Tikal Museum—see "The Museums," below), dating from A.D. 292; the most recent is no. 11 in the Great Plaza, dating from A.D. 869.

Moments Sunrise, Sunset

Tikal is a magical and mystical place. Many claim that this magic and mystique is only heightened around sunrise and sunset. Sunsets are easier to catch and a more dependable show. Sunrises tend to be more a case of the sun eventually burning through the morning mist than of any impressive orb emerging. However, afternoons can often be clear, especially during the dry season, allowing for excellent sunset viewing from the tops of the main temples here. If you're staying right at the ruins, your chances are better of catching either or both of these occasions. In fact, visitors staying inside the park are often admitted to Tikal as early as 5am. Aside from this, the most dependable way to catch the sunrise is to sign up with **San Juan Travel** (✆ **502/7926-0042**) for their daily tour leaving Flores at 3:30am. San Juan has special permission to enter the park early, and they promise to get you to the top of Temple IV in plenty of time for Apollo's appearance. The cost is Q60 ($8/£4) per person, and once at Tikal, you can take any of San Juan's regularly scheduled return vans back to Flores.

For do-it-yourselfers, minivans and collective taxis leave Flores and El Remate early enough to get you to the Tikal entrance gate at 6am when it opens. This will generally enable you to get to the top of one of the main temples by 6:30am, which is usually still early enough to catch the sun burning through the mist just over the rainforest canopy. ***Tip:*** For either the sunrise or sunset tour, it's a very good idea to bring along a flashlight.

If you head south from the Temple II, you will come to the area known as **El Mundo Perdido (The Lost World).** This plaza contains the **Great Pyramid,** which stands 34m (114 ft.) high and is the oldest excavated building in Tikal. This pyramid is one of the most popular spots for watching the sunset. If you've timed it right, you might be able to hang out here and watch the show; otherwise, make a mental note to get your bearings and come back later, if possible. Directly east of the Great Pyramid is the **Plaza of the Seven Temples,** which dates to the Late Classic period. Bordering this plaza on the east side is an unexcavated pyramid, and behind this is Temple V. This entire area is known as the **South Acropolis.** You can climb Temple V, but be forewarned, the climb, both up and down a very steep and rather rickety wooden stairway, is somewhat harrowing. The view from above is beautiful. However, the steep pitch of the pyramid's original stairway is almost as scary as the climb.

If you cross through the South Acropolis to the east and then turn north in the general direction of the Great Plaza, you will come to the East Plaza. From here you can walk southeast on the Mendez Causeway to **Temple VI (Temple of the Inscriptions),** which contains a nearly illegible line of hieroglyphics that are the most extensive in Tikal. It's worth coming out this way just for the chance to spot some wild animals, which seem to be fairly common in this remote corner of the park.

Moments Seeing the Forest from the Trees

Just outside the entrance to Tikal National Park is the **Canopy Tour Tikal** (✆ **502/7926-4270;** www.canopytikal.com). A series of treetop platforms are connected by heavy wire cables, so that more adventurous travelers can zip from platform to platform via a harness-and-pulley system. Canopy Tour Tikal actually has two separate zip-line tours to choose from, a somewhat slower tour for wary souls and a faster system for adrenaline junkies. They also have a series of trails and hanging suspension bridges through the thick rainforest here. This attraction is open daily from 7am to 5pm, and the cost is Q225 ($30/£15) per person, including shuttle transportation to or from Tikal or El Remate. For transport to and from Santa Elena or Flores, add on an extra Q35 ($4.65/£2.30).

The Museums

The most formal museum here has been officially christened the **Sylvanus G. Morely Museum,** but is also known as the **Tikal** or **Ceramic Museum.** This museum contains a good collection of pottery, mosaic masks, incense burners, etched bone, and stelae that are chronologically displayed—beginning with Pre-Classic objects on up to Late Classic pieces. Also on exhibit are a number of jade pendants, beads, and earplugs as well as the famous **stele no. 31,** which has all four sides carved. Another fine attraction here is the reconstruction of the tomb of Hasaw Chan K'awil, who was also known as Ah Cacao, or "Lord Chocolate." The museum is by the Jungle Lodge and Jaguar Inn.

The second museum is known as the **Lithic** or **Stelae Museum** and is in the large visitor center, which is on your left as you arrive at the parking area coming from Flores. This spacious display area contains a superb collection of stelae from around the ruins. Just outside the front door of the museum is the scaled relief map (mentioned above) that will give you an excellent perspective on the relationships between the different ruins here at Tikal. Both museums are open daily from 9am to 5pm. A Q20 ($2.65/£1.35) admission will get you into both.

Tip: Only visit the museums if you have extra time, or a very specific interest in either the stelae or ceramic works. The ruins themselves are far more interesting.

OTHER AREA ATTRACTIONS & RUINS

Flores is a wonderful town to explore by walking. The whole island is only about 5 blocks wide in any direction. At the center is a small central park or plaza, anchored by the town's Catholic church. Be sure to take a peek inside to check out the beautiful stained-glass windows. One of the most popular things to do in Flores is take a **tour of the lake ★**. You will be inundated with offers for boat tours. Ask at your hotel or one of the local tour agencies, or talk to the numerous freelancers approaching you on the street. Be sure to inspect the craft beforehand, if possible, and make sure you feel comfortable with its lake-worthiness. Also, make sure your guide is bilingual. These tours last anywhere from 1 to 3 hours, and usually include stops at La Guitarra Island (Guitar Island), which features a picnic and swimming area, as well as at the mostly unexcavated ruins of

Tayasal. Here, be sure to climb **El Mirador ★**, a lakeside pyramid that offers a fabulous view of Flores. Many of these tours also stop at the small **Petencito Zoo** and **ARCAS** (www.arcasguatemala.com), a conservation organization and animal rehabilitation center that has some interpretive trails and displays of rescued animals either in recuperation, or unable to be released. These tours cost between Q75 and Q187 ($10–$25/£5–£13) per person, depending on the length of the tour and the size of your group. Don't be afraid to bargain. Entrance to the zoo is an extra Q20 ($2.65/£1.35).

You can also **explore the lake** on your own in a kayak or canoe. While you can do this out of Flores, I find the lakeshore near El Remate a better place to take out a kayak or canoe. Rates run around Q15 ($2/£1) per hour. To find a worthy craft, ask at your hotel or at one of the local tour agencies. Be careful paddling around the lake; when the winds pick up, especially in the afternoons, it can get quite choppy and challenging.

A host of local tour operators here can arrange any number of tours and activities in the area, as well as guided tours to Tikal and the ruins listed below. The best of these are **Martsam Travel ★★** (**© 866/832-2776** in the U.S. and Canada, or 502/7867-5093 in Guatemala; www.martsam.com) and **San Juan Travel** (**© 502/7926-0042;** sanjuan travel@hotmail.com.gt).

Yaxhá & Other Regional Ruins

Thanks to the publicity bestowed upon this site by the TV show *Survivor: Guatemala,* **Yaxhá ★★** is now one of the prime archaeological sites to visit in Guatemala. In fact, this is the third-largest Maya ceremonial city in Guatemala—behind Tikal and El Mirador. Be sure to climb **Temple 216 ★★★**, located in the East Acropolis. This is the tallest structure here, and provides excellent views of lakes Yaxhá and Sacnab, as well as the surrounding rainforests. The sunsets here rival those in Tikal. Yaxhá is one of the few Maya cities to retain its traditional Maya name, which translates as "green waters." You can combine a visit to Yaxhá with a trip to the ruins of **Topoxté,** which are located on a small island in Lake Yaxhá. This small yet intriguing site is thought to have been a residential city for local elites. However, it was also a fortified city, where Maya warriors put up a valiant defense against Spanish forces. ***Note:*** You'll probably be warned, and see the signs, but just in case, do not swim in Lake Yaxhá, as it is home to a robust population of crocodiles.

Many organized tours here also include a stop at the nearby minor ruins of Nakum, which are currently being excavated. However, this makes for a long day. The turnoff for the 11km (7-mile) dirt road into the site is located about 32km (20 miles) east of Ixlú, or El Cruce. The Q80 ($11/£5.50) admission grants you access to Yaxhá, Topoxté, and Nakum. If you want to stay at Yaxhá, camping is allowed at a well-tended campsite down by the lakeshore.

Another popular site is **El Ceibal ★**, which offers one of the most scenic routes along the way. To reach El Ceibal, you first head the 64km (40 miles) from Flores to Sayaxché, which is a good-size town for El Petén (it even has a few basic hotels). From Sayaxché, you must hire a boat to carry you 18km (11 miles) up the Río de la Pasión. El Ceibal is a Late Classic–era ruin known for having the only circular temple in all of El Petén. There are also several well-preserved stelae arranged around one small temple structure on the central plaza, as well as a ball court. Your best bet for visiting El Ceibal is to book the excursion with one of the tour agencies in Flores or Santa Elena. Full-day trips run around Q447 to Q671 ($60–$90/£30–£45). Overnight trips can also be arranged, combining a visit to El Ceibal to even more obscure Maya sites like Aguateca and Petexbatún. If you want to stay in this area, check out **Chiminos Island Lodge** ★ (✆ **502/2335-3506;** www.chiminosisland.com), which has six rustic yet luxurious cabins in the rainforest on a small island in the waters of the Petexbatún Lagoon.

Finally, truly adventurous travelers can book a multiday jungle trek to **El Mirador** ★★, the largest Maya ceremonial city in Guatemala. Barely excavated, El Mirador features the tallest pyramidal structure in the known Maya world, La Danta, which reaches some 79m (260 ft.) in height. The trip here involves at least 5 days of hiking and jungle camping. **Martsam Travel** ★★ (✆ **866/832-2776** in the U.S. and Canada, or 502/7867-5093 in Guatemala; www.martsam.com) is the best operator to contact for one of these trips.

Spanish Classes

Eco Escuela de Español ★ (✆ **502/5940-1235;** www.ecoescuelaespanol.org) runs a community-based language school program in the small village of San Andrés, on the shore of Lake Petén Itzá. The program costs just $150 (£75) per week, including lodging and three meals daily with a local family, as well as 4 hours of daily class time, usually one-on-one. The setting allows for intensive language instruction, as well as many chances to really interact with the local culture and natural surroundings.

If you want to stick closer to the action in town, check in with the **Dos Mundos Spanish Academy** (✆ **502/5830-2060;** www.flores-spanish.com), which offers a wide range of course and accommodations options.

WHERE TO STAY

Since accommodations in Tikal are limited, most travelers either choose to (or must) overnight in the sister cities of Flores and Santa Elena. Still, this is not necessarily such a bad thing. There's a lot more to do and see in Flores and Santa Elena, and a far wider range of hotels and restaurants to choose from. Still, unless you have more than 2 days to spend exploring the region, I recommend staying near the ruins, as it allows you to enter early and stay late. It also allows you to avoid the Great Plaza and North Acropolis during the peak period of the day, when they are swarmed with day-trippers.

At the Ruins

In addition to the place listed below, the other hotels near the ruins are the **Jaguar Inn** (✆ **502/7926-0002;** www.jaguartikal.com) and **Tikal Inn** (**502/7926-1917;** www.tikalinn.com). Alternately, you can set up a tent on some concrete pads near the parking lot, under an open-air thatch palapa roof. The camping area has shared shower and toilet facilities, and a communal cooking area. The campground charges Q30 to Q45 ($4–$6/£2–£3) per person for camping and use of the facilities. They also rent hammocks, which you can pitch under open-air palapas for Q30 ($4/£2). If you plan on sleeping in a hammock, or even taking an afternoon siesta, you should really try to get a mosquito net that fits over the hammock. Most of the places that rent and sell hammocks in this area have these nets.

Jungle Lodge ★ Also known as Posada de la Selva, this is the biggest and most comfortable hotel right at the park. However, at times there can be a cattle-car feel to the operation. The majority of the rooms, and the best rooms, are housed in duplex bungalows, with high ceilings, white-tile floors, two double beds with mosquito netting, and a ceiling fan. Each has its own little porch with a couple of chairs. The bungalows are connected by stone paths through lush gardens. Two junior suites feature king-size beds, a large Jacuzzi-style tub (but without jets), and private patios in both the front and back of the room. There are 12 older rooms with polished cement floors and shared bathroom facilities. It's hot and steamy here in the jungle, so you'll appreciate the hotel's pool, which is built on a rise and shaped like a Maya pyramid.

Tikal village, Petén. ✆ **502/7861-0447** or 2476-8775. Fax 502/7861-0448. www.junglelodge.guate.com. 50 units (38 with private bathroom). Q1,125 ($150/£75) bungalow; Q300 ($40/£20) double with shared bathroom. MC, V. **Amenities:** Restaurant; bar; laundry service; small outdoor pool; tour desk. *In room:* No phone.

In Flores & Santa Elena

In addition to the places mentioned below, **Hotel Petén** (✆/fax **502/7867-5203;** www.hotelesdepeten.com) in Flores, **Casa Elena** (✆ **502/7926-2235;** www.casaelena.com) in Santa Elena, and **Hotel Isla de Flores** (✆ **502/7926-0614** or 502/2476-8775; www.hotelisladeflores.com) in Flores are all good budget choices.

Hotel Santana ★ This is a great choice if you're looking to snag a lakefront room with a balcony and a view, all at a good price. Most of the rooms here fit the criteria I just mentioned. Still, be sure you get a lake-view room, and not one of the less desirable interior affairs. The rooms are all cool, clean, and fairly spacious, and a cut above the rest of the options on the island in this price range. The open-air dining room is a great place to sit and enjoy the lakeside setting as well. There's a small kidney-shaped pool, with a built-in waterfall and swim-up bar, in a little courtyard to the side.

Calle 30 de Junio, Flores, Petén. ✆/fax **502/7867-5123** or 7867-5421. www.santanapeten.com. 35 units. Q300–Q450 ($40–$60/£20–£30) double. AE, MC, V. **Amenities:** Restaurant; laundry service; outdoor pool. *In room:* A/C, TV.

La Casona del Lago ★★ This is the most luxurious hotel in the Flores area. Located right on the shores of the lake, with excellent views of its waters and picturesque island city, the three-story building is built in an L-shape, around a central pool and Jacuzzi area. Rooms are spacious, with two double beds, white-tile floors, a couple of sitting chairs, and a separate desk area, and they feature a host of modern amenities, including 21-inch televisions. Don't confuse this with **La Casona de la Isla,** which is on Flores, and part of the same small chain of hotels.

1a Calle, Zona 1, Santa Elena, Flores, Petén. ✆/fax **502/7952-8700.** www.hotelesdepeten.com. 32 units. Q645–Q713 ($86–$95/£43–£48) double. Rates higher during peak periods. AE, DC, MC, V. **Amenities:** Restaurant; laundry service; outdoor pool and Jacuzzi. *In room:* A/C, TV, hair dryer, free Wi-Fi.

In El Remate

La Casa de Don David Hotel (✆ **502/5306-2190** or 7928-8469; www.lacasadedondavid.com) is another long-standing popular place in this area, with great service and a friendly vibe.

La Lancha Resort ★★ Owned by Francis Ford Coppola, the main lodge here has a commanding view of the lake and features a soaring, open-air A-frame thatch roof oriented toward the view. Below the lodge is a kidney-shaped pool. A steep trail leads down to the shore of the lake, where you'll find a swimming area and some canoes and kayaks. The rooms are all duplex bungalows. The six "lake-view" units are quite spacious, while the "jungle-view" rooms are more compact. All are tastefully and artistically decorated

ACCOMMODATIONS ■

Casa Elena **13**
Hotel Isla de Flores **7**
Hotel Petén **3**
Hotel Santana **2**
La Casona de la Isla **5**
La Casona del Lago **12**

DINING & NIGHTLIFE ◆

Adictos **11**
Bar Raices **1**
Café Archeologico Yax-há **9**
Capitan Tortuga **4**
La Luna **6**
Las Puertas **8**
Maya Princess **14**
Pizzería Picasso **10**

Flores

Lake Petén Itzá
Calle Unión
Calle Fraternidad
Av. La Libertad
Parque Central
Av. Flores
Calle 10 de Noviembre
Calle 10 de Noviembre
Calle 15 de Septiembre
Calle 30 de Junio
Av. Reforma
Av. Santa Ana
Calle Central
Callejon El Crucero
Calle Centroamérica
Calle Sur
0 100 yds
0 100 m
N

Isla Santa Barbara
FLORES
Lake Petén Itzá
See inset above
SAN BENITO
SANTA ELENA
1a Calle
2a Calle
3a Calle
Parque Central
4a Calle (Calle Principal)
4a Calle A
5a Calle
Calzada Virgilio Rodríguez Macal
3a Av.
4a Av.
5a Av.
6a Av.
7a Av.
8a Av.
Airport
0 1/8 mile
0 1/4 km
N

Flores
Tikal
BELIZE
MEXICO
Livingston
L. Izabal
HOND.
Lake Atitlán
Guatemala City
EL SAL.

Church
Information
Post office

 and very comfortable. All feature a shared wooden veranda, and you can probably figure out the view from the room names.

Lago Petén Itzá, Petén. ✆ **800/746-3743** in the U.S., or ✆/fax 502/7928-8331 in Guatemala. www.lalanchavillage.com. 10 units. Q1,013–Q1,575 ($135–$210/£68–£105) double. Rates lower in the off season, higher during peak periods. AE, MC, V. **Amenities:** Restaurant; bar; bike rental; laundry service; outdoor pool. *In room:* A/C, no phone.

La Mansión del Pájaro Serpiente ★ Finds Set off the main road to Tikal, on a hillside overlooking the lake, this place has both standard and deluxe bungalows, beautiful gardens, and a friendly atmosphere. The bungalows feature beautiful stone and woodworking details, with local textile and crafts filling out the decor. The deluxe rooms feature televisions and air-conditioning. The midsize free-form pool is set amid lush gardens, and almost feels like a natural pond in the jungle. The open-air restaurant has a great view of the lake and specializes in local cuisine. The owners raise peacocks, and there are always several wandering around the grounds here.

El Remate, Petén. ✆/fax **502/7926-8498** or 5702-9434. 11 units. Q330 ($44/£22) double; Q413 ($55/£23) deluxe double. MC, V. **Amenities:** Restaurant; bar; laundry service; outdoor pool. *In room:* No phone.

WHERE TO DINE

Most folks who stay near the ruins take all their meals at their hotel. If you're looking for variety or staying at the campsite, there are several little restaurants *(comedores)* between the main camping area and parking lot and the gate at the beginning of the road to Flores. Within the area of the ruins, you'll find picnic tables beneath shelters and itinerant soft-drink peddlers, but no snack stands. If you want to spend all day at the ruins without having to walk back to the parking area for lunch, take sandwiches. Most of the hotels here and in Flores, as well as the *comedores,* will make you a bag lunch to take into the park.

There are tons of places to eat around Flores and Santa Elena. Most are simple affairs serving local and Mexican cuisine, and geared toward locals and the backpacker crowd. Most of the hotels listed above have decent restaurants, too.

In addition to the places listed below, **Pizzeria Picasso** (✆ **502/7867-5198;** Calle 15 de Septiembre, across from El Tucán) serves pretty good wood-oven pizza and a variety of pastas, while **Café Archeologico Yax-há** (✆ **502/5830-2060;** www.cafeyaxha.com; Calle 15 de Septiembre, across from El Tucán) is a relaxed and welcoming new place that serves local fare, including dishes based on pre-Columbian recipes and ingredients, as well as coffee drinks and fresh fruit smoothies.

Capitán Tortuga ★ INTERNATIONAL This popular restaurant has a long and wide-ranging menu. You can get everything from pizzas to barbecue ribs to vegetarian shish kabobs. They also have a wide range of coffee and espresso drinks, as well as ice creams and freshly baked desserts. The large main dining room sits under a high thatch room. However, I prefer the tables on the small outdoor patio that fronts the lake, or in the second-floor, open-air dining room reached from a stairway out back.

Calle 30 de Junio, next to La Casona de la Isla, Flores. ✆ **502/7867-5089.** Main courses Q30–Q110 ($4–$15/£2–£7.50). MC, V. Daily 11:30am–11pm.

La Luna ★★ Finds INTERNATIONAL This hip little restaurant is the most creative and refined option in Flores. The menu ranges from steak in pepper sauce to lobster tails, with a host of fish and chicken—and even some vegetarian—options in between. There are three separate dining areas, and all are artistically decorated. My favorite room features a faux ceiba tree in the center and a wild sculpture on one wall made of wood and mirrors.

Calle 30 de Junio, across from La Casona de la Isla, Flores. ✆ **502/7926-3346.** Main courses Q40–Q130 ($5.35–$18/£2.70–£9). MC, V. Tues–Sun 11am–11pm.

FLORES & SANTA ELENA AFTER DARK

Most folks simply frequent the bar at their hotel, or stick around after dinner at one of the local restaurants. There are several bars along Calle Sur fronting the lake just over the bridge as you enter Flores. Of these, **Adictos** is one of the liveliest. For a view of the lake and a happening party scene, you can head to **Bar Raices,** at the far western end of Calle Sur. Another good option, near the center of the island, is **Las Puertas,** which plays a mix of house and chill dance tunes in a hip little space, and sometimes features live music; it's at the corner of Calle Centroamérica and Avenida Santa Ana. Finally, if you're in a gambling mood, you can head to the **Maya Princess** (✆ **502/7924-8764**) on 2a Calle 7-00, Zona 1, in Santa Elena. This place has a wide range of electronic gaming machines and nightly bingo, and a swank, Las Vegas–like ambience.

For those staying at one of the hotels out by the ruins, the best nighttime activity is to visit the ruins by moonlight. Those staying here can have their admission ticket validated to allow them to roam the park until 8pm, and in some cases even later, depending on the disposition of the guards. If the moon is waxing, full, or just beyond full, you're in for a real treat (just ask around beforehand about safety issues).

6

El Salvador

by Patrick Gilsenan

El Salvador is like that hot new nightclub no one in town knows about. Yet. It has hundreds of miles of gorgeous Pacific coast to explore, lush national parks to hike, volcanoes to climb, and unique villages to visit. It also offers a population that is among the friendliest and most welcoming you will meet in Central America. And all of this is packed into a country that takes less than a few hours to drive end to end.

What's kept the country such a big secret is that it's been best known in recent times for a bloody civil war that raged from 1980 to 1992 between the nation's working farmers and the government representatives who sought to maintain a power grip on the country. It was an unusually bloody war, often employing tactics of terrorism and torture that left few people unaffected. El Salvador also has a reputation as home to one of the world's most violent street gangs.

Though the war ended 15 years ago and El Salvador has since been among Latin America's more peaceful nations, its history of war and reputation for violence have for years kept many travelers from stopping here. That's changing, however, as the last decade has seen El Salvador quietly reemerge from its turbulent past to become Central America's fastest growing economy. The last 5 years have also seen an explosion in the number and quality of the country's hotels and restaurants.

Don't let the outdated reputation fool you—El Salvador is a great place to explore. Its beaches offer miles of deserted shores and friendly fishing villages, along with some of Central America's best surf spots. Two national parks offer lush semitropical jungle, high cloud forests, waterfalls, rivers, and a plethora of birds and plant life. The capital city of San Salvador offers high-end hotels, restaurants, and nightclubs that would be at home in any of the world's major cities. And the country's small villages offer tiny town squares filled with people whose renowned kindness to one another and visitors is in sharp contrast to the nation's violent but ancient history.

1 REGIONS IN BRIEF

El Salvador is Central America's smallest country—it's roughly the size of Massachusetts—and the most densely populated country in the region, with a population of roughly six million. It's the only Central American country without a Caribbean coast and is bordered by Guatemala to the north, Honduras to the east, and Nicaragua to the south. In addition to the bustling, modern capital of San Salvador, the country comprises dozens of charming rural villages that are starting to cater to tourism, 307km (191 miles) of Pacific coast, and a number of national parks that highlight the country's landscape of steep volcanoes and mountains. The country has distinct rainy and dry seasons and a hot, tropical climate that varies more by altitude than time of year.

SAN SALVADOR & ENVIRONS San Salvador is El Salvador's capital and the second-largest city in Central America. Its 568 sq. km (220 sq. miles) are home to 1.6 million

Tips Small Town Charm

While planning your trip, keep in mind that many of El Salvador's largest cities are far from attractive tourist centers. Though San Salvador offers a level of international luxury you won't find elsewhere in the country, El Salvador's second-tier cities, particularly Sonsonate and San Miguel, offer the hassles of congestion and crime without many modern luxuries. You might stop in both cities to stock up on supplies or catch a long-distance bus, but with better hotels and restaurants usually available just a short trip away, you don't have to base yourself in either place.

residents and the majority of the nation's wealth. Many travelers consider the city to be either an oasis of modern luxury or a gaudy mix of smog and fast food. They're both right. San Salvador does offer many high-end, international restaurants, hotels, and designer shops that would be at home in the world's grandest cities. But Pizza Hut and KFC do seem to be on every corner, bus emissions choke the streets, and all that new luxury collides with the poverty you'll see on the faces of children hustling for change at street lights. It's a city suffering from the growing pains of transformation. But no matter what your opinion of San Salvador is, it is worth a visit for a couple of days. Highlights include a historic downtown containing the nation's iconic buildings, the country's two most important art museums, and hidden gems such as watching the city's lights come alive at dusk from high above in Planes de Los Renderos. Since it's centrally located along El Salvador's two main highways, and most of the country's attractions lie less than a couple of hours away, it can make for a good base city.

WEST & NORTHWEST EL SALVADOR The west's main attractions are the Ruta de las Flores and Parque Nacional El Imposible. The **Ruta de las Flores** is a wonderful 36km (22-mile) drive along a scenic mountain highway winding through thousands of acres of coffee fields and exemplary El Salvadoran villages featuring weekend artisan and food festivals. **Parque Nacional El Imposible** is a huge national park in the far west offering hours of hiking through lush jungles, across streams, and beside picturesque waterfalls. Beside the park is the small village of Tacuba, which serves as a good base camp for park visits. In the northwest, you'll find **Santa Ana,** the second-largest city in the country, with a roster of tourist-friendly colonial sites, and **Parque Montecristo,** a cloud forest preserve that shares a border with Guatemala and Honduras. During rainy season, Montecristo is one of the greenest and most lush environments in the country. The nation's western region also offers the stunning blue waters of **Lago de Coatepeque** and the challenging volcano hikes of **Parque Nacional Los Volcanes.**

NORTH & CENTRAL EL SALVADOR North of San Salvador are the villages of Suchitoto, La Palma, and El Pital. **Suchitoto** is a beautiful mountain village that offers some of the best views and history in the entire country. **La Palma** is another standout town, which is well known as a center of art (particularly for its town murals). And in the far north is **El Pital,** which is the country's highest point at 2,730m (8,975 ft.) above sea level. You can also shop for some of El Salvador's most artistically crafted hammocks in the village of **Concepción de Quezaltepeque,** also known as the City of Hammocks, where nearly the entire town and multiple generations of craftsmen have dedicated themselves to the art of hammock making.

THE COASTS El Salvador's 307km-long (191-mile) Pacific coast is one of the highlights of the country. The coast stretches from the turtle breeding grounds, deserted beaches, and mangrove-filled estuary of **Barra de Santiago,** then goes past some of the region's best diving and Central America's largest pacific reef in **Playa Los Cóbanos** and the unique boutique hotels and great surfing of the **Balsamo Coast,** before finally reaching the wealthy playgrounds of **Costa del Sol** and **Tamarindo.** In between are dozens of small fishing and beach communities to discover.

THE EAST The eastern part of the country is best known for the tragic history of war experienced here (for more on this, see the box on p. 310). In **Perquín,** you'll find a small war museum showcasing the left's efforts during El Salvador's 12-year civil war. In the town of **Mozote** are memorials to the more than 1,000 innocents who were systematically executed over 2 horrific days in December 1981 by members of the El Salvadoran army.

2 THE BEST OF EL SALVADOR IN 1 WEEK

So much to choose from, so little time. El Salvador is a tiny country but it is packed with outdoor and cultural treasures. You could easily spend weeks exploring its attractions. But if you only have 7 days, the below itinerary can offer you a little taste of the country.

This itinerary does not head east simply because the largest number of exemplary villages and natural areas in El Salvador are clustered in the west. But the east offers some excellent attractions, such as Perquín's Museo de la Revolución (p. 313), the historic Mozote monument (p. 314), and the undeveloped and charming Isla de Montecristo (p. 307).

Day ❶: Arrive in San Salvador ★

San Salvador is El Salvador's center of luxury, with the kind of high-end, international restaurants, shopping, and hotels you won't find elsewhere in the country. So take some time to soak up its modern amenities before heading out into El Salvador's more rural areas. Try to arrive in the morning so that you can settle into your hotel and then taxi over to El Centro. In the city center, you can spend a couple of hours viewing El Salvador's iconic **Catedral Metropolitana** ★ (p. 241), **Teatro Nacional** ★ (p. 240), and huge street market **Mercado Central** ★ (where you can perhaps grab lunch; p. 246). Then bus or cab over to the other side of town to spend the afternoon in the Zona Rosa and Colonia San Benito neighborhoods, where you can visit the **Museo de Arte** ★★★ (p. 241) and **Museo Nacional de Antropología Dr. David J. Guzman** ★★ (p. 241). Afterward, stop by the **Mercado Nacional de Artesanias** ★★ (p. 247) or stroll the shops of the **Boulevard del Hipódromo** (p. 246), where you can enjoy a great dinner in one of the area's ethnic restaurants. If you have the energy, continue on to the nightclubs and lounges of the **Multiplaza Mall** (p. 246) or just head back to the hotel to rest up for a trip to Suchitoto the next day.

Day ❷: Suchitoto ★★★

Today, you'll head to Suchitoto (p. 280), 47km (29 miles) north of San Salvador, and one of El Salvador's most charming towns. A much-disputed territory during the civil war, this town has remade itself into a premier cultural destination, with some of El Salvador's best art galleries and boutique hotels, along with a rich history and abundant natural beauty. You can spend the day simply enjoying the vibe, taking in the weekend artisans' market, or going on a daylong history or nature tour.

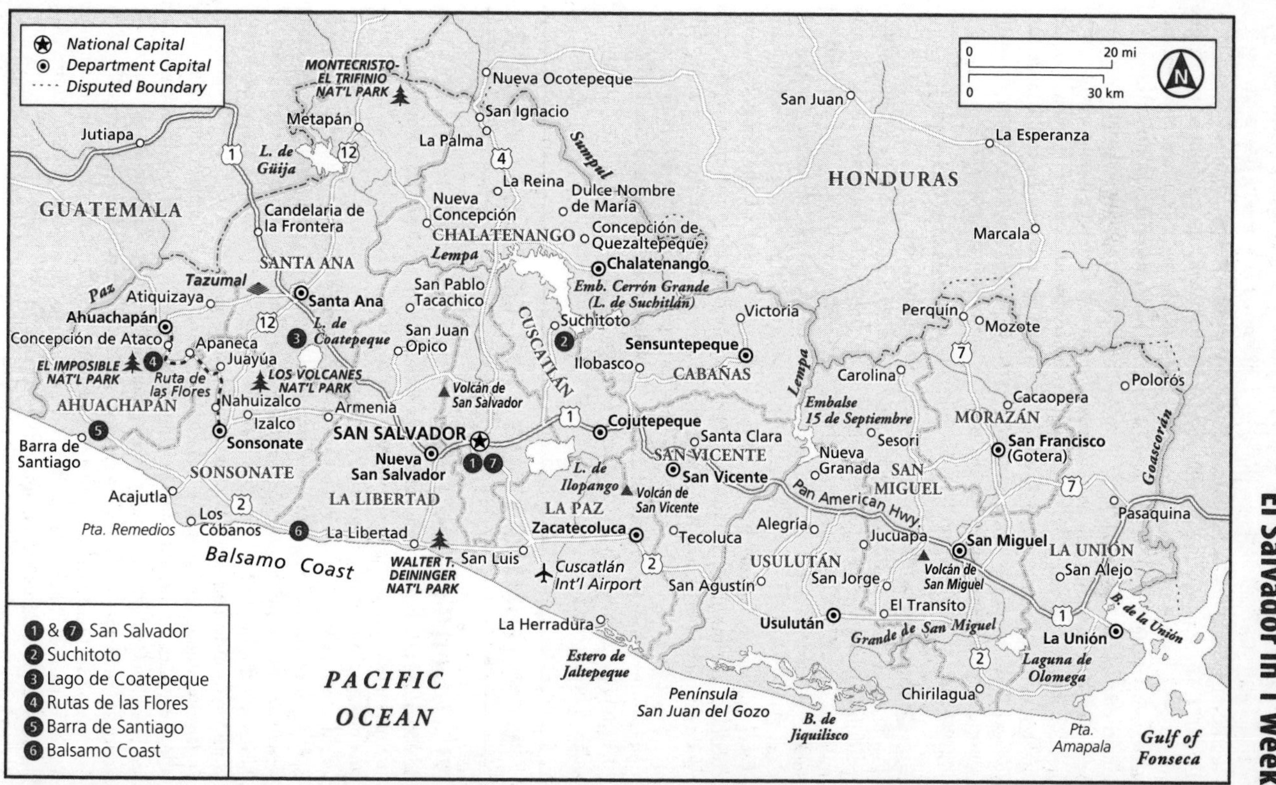

National Capital
Department Capital
Disputed Boundary
0 20 mi
0 30 km
HONDURAS
GUATEMALA
PACIFIC OCEAN
Balsamo Coast
Gulf of Fonseca
SAN SALVADOR
Santa Ana
Sonsonate
Ahuachapán
Chalatenango
Sensuntepeque
Cojutepeque
San Vicente
Zacatecoluca
Usulután
San Miguel
San Francisco (Gotera)
La Unión
Suchitoto
La Libertad
Nueva San Salvador
Concepción de Ataco
Apaneca
Juayúa
Nahuizalco
Izalco
Los Cóbanos
Acajutla
Barra de Santiago
Tazumal
Cuscatlán Int'l Airport
Pan American Hwy.
MONTECRISTO-EL TRIFINIO NAT'L PARK
LOS VOLCANES NAT'L PARK
EL IMPOSIBLE NAT'L PARK
WALTER T. DEININGER NAT'L PARK
L. de Coatepeque
L. de Ilopango
L. de Güija
Emb. Cerrón Grande (L. de Suchitlán)
Embalse 15 de Septiembre
Lempa
Sumpul
Goascorán
1 & 7 San Salvador
2 Suchitoto
3 Lago de Coatepeque
4 Rutas de las Flores
5 Barra de Santiago
6 Balsamo Coast

Day ❸: Lago de Coatepeque ★★

Get up early for the 2½-hour trip due west through Santa Ana or San Salvador to Lago de Coatepeque (p. 262). Coatepeque offers 23 sq. km (9 sq. miles) of pristine, recreational waters in a nearly perfectly round crater lake 740m (2,428 ft.) above sea level. The nation's rich and famous have their mansions along its shores. Each night a spectacular sun sets behind the lush walls of the crater rim, and visitors can spend the day swimming, fishing, riding watercrafts, or soaking in the views.

Day ❹: Rutas de las Flores ★★

The Rutas de las Flores is a collection of beautiful little towns along a 35km (22-mile) stretch of winding mountain road, located about 1½ hours south of Lago de Coatepeque. You can do the route in 1 day if you stop first in **Nahuizalco** (p. 268) to check out the furniture, **Juayúa** (p. 271) to see the black Christ, and **Ataco** ★★★ (p. 272) to see some cool art you won't find elsewhere in El Salvador. End the day in **Tacuba** (p. 275), which offers a number of good hotel choices.

Days ❺ & ❻: Parque Nacional El Imposible ★★ & Barra de Santiago ★★★

Various daylong adventures to **Parque Imposible** (p. 276), a huge, lush national park with one of the country's largest and most diverse wildlife collections and lush, mountainous hiking terrain, are run out of the nearby base camp of Tacuba. The next day, head 1 hour south to **Barra de Santiago** (p. 294) along El Salvador's Balsamo Coast to spend the night.

Day ❼: Balsamo Coast to San Salvador

Barra de Santiago is a tiny fishing village and protected nature area with a mangrove-filled estuary on one side and the Pacific Ocean on the other. You can fish, swim, and surf its deserted beaches, watch giant sea turtles lay their eggs in season, and bird-watch in the estuary. It's a great place to relax before returning home—the airport is an easy 2- to 2½-hour drive past the beautiful beaches and small villages of this coast.

3 PLANNING YOUR TRIP TO EL SALVADOR

VISITOR INFORMATION

El Salvador has a helpful national tourism organization, **CORSATUR,** which features a useful English-language website (**www.corsatur.gov.sv**), a central office in San Salvador, and offices in Suchitoto in the north, Nahuizalco on the Rutas de Las Flores, and Puerto de La Libertad along the Balsamo Coast; see the box "CORSATUR Offices" below for specific info. Alternatively, you can always head to the local city hall, called the Alcaldía, where you'll find the occasional English-speaking employee who can help you out. It's best to do as much research as possible before arriving in El Salvador because most towns don't have tourism offices or English-speaking tourism officials.

If you speak Spanish, one of the country's best sources for localized information is the **Casas de las Culturas,** or Houses of Culture. Nearly every town in El Salvador has a Casa de la Cultura, which serves as a small community center, in addition to dishing out tourist-friendly information. They're not designated tourism offices, so the quality of the information is hit-and-miss, but they're by far your best shot at getting local information in the country's smaller villages. Casas de las Culturas addresses and phone numbers are listed in each section of this chapter where applicable.

CORSATUR Offices

San Salvador: Edificio Carbonel 1, Colonia Roma, Alameda Dr. Manuel Enrique Araujo and Pasaje Carbonel, San Salvador (✆ **503/2243-7835;** www.corsatur.gov.sv; Mon–Fri 8am–5pm). The office offers local and national maps and brochures, and tourism official Claudia Argumedo speaks English.

Puerto La Libertad: Km 34.5 Carretera de Literal, Puerta de La Libertad, La Libertad, El Salvador (✆ **503/2246-1898;** cat.lalibertad@gmail.com; Mon–Fri 8am-5pm, Sat–Sun 8am–4pm). Ask for Dina; she's friendly, patient, and speaks enough English to get you where you need to go.

Nahuizalco: Km 71, Carretera CA-8, Nauizalco, Departmento de Sonsonate (✆ **503/2453-1082;** cat.rutasdelasflores@gmail.com; Mon–Fri 8am–5pm, Sat 8am–4pm). No one in this office speaks English, but they offer some English-speaking hotel and attraction brochures.

Suchitoto: Calle San Martin, Barrio El Centro, Suchitoto, Departmento Custcatlán, El Salvador (✆ **503/2335-1835;** cat.suchitoto@gmail.com; Mon–Fri 8am–5pm, Sat–Sun 8am–4pm). Ask for Manuel Selada.

Other valuable tourism organizations include:

SalvaNatura (33 Av. Sur 640, Colonia Flor Blanca, San Salvador; ✆ **503/2279-1515;** www.salvanatura.org) administers and provides information for Parque Imposible and Parque Nacional Los Volcanes. It's open Monday to Friday from 8am to noon and 2 to 5pm. Staffer Ben Rivera speaks English.

Institute Salvadoreño de Turismo (ISTU; 719 Calle Rubén Darío btw. 9a and 11a Avenida Sur, San Salvador; ✆ **503/2222-8000;** www.istu.gob.sv) provides information about El Salvador's parks and has a great website. It's open Monday to Friday from 7:30am to 3:30pm.

Ministerio de Medio Ambiente y Recursos Naturales (Km 5.5 Carretera a Santa Tecla, Calle and Colonia Las Mercedes, Building MARN No. 2, San Salvador; ✆ **503/2267-6276;** www.marn.gob.sv) is the organization you have to call to enter Parque Montecristo.

Concultura (19 Av. Norte and Calle Guadalupe; ✆ **503/2510-5320;** www.concultura.gob.sv) is the nation's premier arts organization and offers a website with a nationwide arts calendar.

Tour Operators

El Salvador Divers ★ (3a Calle Poniente and 99 Av. Norte 5020, Colonía Escalón, San Salvador; ✆ **503/2264-0961;** www.elsalvadordivers.com) is the country's top scuba certification and tour company, with 3- and 5-day English-language certification courses and dive trips around the country. **Fish El Salvador** (✆ **503/7899-9200;** www.fishelsalvador.com) is a fishing tour company based out of Playa Los Cóbanos. They offer full- and half-day reef and deep sea fishing tours. **Eco Mayan Tours** ★★ (Paseo General Escalón 3658, Colonia Escalón, San Salvador; ✆ **503/2298-2844;** www.ecomayantours.com) is one of the country's largest tour companies, with nationwide tours, travel services, and a helpful

Passing by the Turicentro

Don't let the name "Turicentro" or "Tourist Center" fool you. You'll see signs for these outdated parks near towns, lakes, and mountains around El Salvador but they are nothing special. Though some have pools and small restaurants or *comedores,* they're usually decades-old parks with cement picnic tables and chairs painted in 1970s colors with a few cinder-block cabins. There's nothing necessarily wrong with these places—the Turicentros at Lago Ilopango and Costa del Sol, for instance, are enjoyable enough, provide lake and beach access, and are popular with locals. Just don't expect anything fancy. Turicentros are open daily 8am to 4pm and cost 80¢/40p to enter. They are run by the **Instituto Salvadoreño de Turismo (ISTU;** 719 Calle Rubén Darío btw. 9a and 11a Av. Sur; ✆ **503/2222-8000;** www.istu.gob.sv).

English-language website. **Tour Bus** (4a Calle Poniente 2323, Colonia Flor Blanca, San Salvador; ✆ **503/2260-7544**) can arrange nationwide English-language tours in their unique, high ground clearance minibus—it'll get you places other minibuses can't go.

ENTRY REQUIREMENTS

Residents of the United States, Canada, and the United Kingdom do not need visas and can enter the country at the border with a presentation of a valid passport and the purchase of a $10 (£5) 30-day tourist card. (Visitors can also ask for a 90-day card when entering the country.) Australia and New Zealand residents require tourist visas, which must be arranged in advance and cost $30 (£15).

El Salvador is part of a 2006 border control agreement with Honduras, Guatemala, and Nicaragua, allowing travel between the four countries under one tourist card. The number of days of your tourist card is determined at the first of the four countries entered.

El Salvadoran Embassy Locations

In the U.S.: 2308 California St., NW, Washington, DC 20008 (✆ 202/265-9671; fax 202/232-3763; www.elsalvador.org).

In Canada: 209 Kent St., Ottawa, Ontario, K2P 1Z8 (✆ 613/238-2939; fax 613/238-6940).

In the U.K.: Mayfair House, 8 Dorset Sq., Marylebone, London, NWI 6PU (✆ 0207/224-9800; fax 0207/224-9878).

In Australia: Consulate only: Level three, 499 St. Kilda Rd., Melbourne, VIC 3004 (✆ 03/9867-4400; fax 03/9867-4455; cherrera@rree.gob.sv).

In New Zealand: Consulate only: 1/644 Manukau Rd., Epsom, Auckland 1023 (✆ 09/649-625-4770).

Customs

Visitors to El Salvador can bring in no more than 200 cigarettes or 50 cigars, 2 liters of alcohol, and gifts worth up to $500 (£250). Like most countries, there are heavy restrictions on the import and export of plants, animals, vegetables, and fruit.

MONEY

The unit of currency in El Salvador is the U.S. dollar. The country made the switch from its native colón in 2001 and colones have been phased out since 2004. The U.S. dollar is dispensed in all the normal denominations, but small-town *tiendas* rarely have change for a $20 (£10), so get small bills whenever you can. ATMs, known as *cajeros automaticos*, can be found in all major cities but are hard to come by in rural towns. Even when a smaller town has an ATM, it may not accept your card—stock up on cash when you can.

Bank machines accept most major card networks such as Cirrus, PLUS, Visa, and MasterCard. I've had the best luck with a PLUS card at Scotiabank ATMs. Credit cards are accepted mainly only in the larger hotels, restaurants, and shops. Sometimes you get lucky in the most unexpected places, but generally small shops or restaurants in villages are *solo efectivo* or cash only. Those that accept credit cards usually take American Express, Diners Club, Visa, and MasterCard.

You can just about forget about traveler's checks. Almost no one outside of large San Salvador hotels accepts these anymore. If you feel more comfortable carrying traveler's checks, you can exchange them for currency at most banks or American Express offices (see p. 234 for locations).

The cost of basics in El Salvador varies wildly depending on where you are. A good general rule of thumb puts San Salvador prices largely on par with the United States. You'll spend $6 (£3) or more for long cab rides and $5.50 (£2.75) for most fast food purchases. Outside of San Salvador, however, all costs are considerably lower. A 10- to 15-minute taxi ride in La Palma is $3 (£1.50) and *pupusas* (the national dish) cost 25¢ (15p) each in smaller towns. San Salvador's finer restaurants and hotels—though much more expensive than those in the rest of the country—are also considerably cheaper than comparable places in the United States or the U.K.

WHEN TO GO

PEAK SEASON El Salvador's peak seasons are "Semana Santa" or Holy Week, which precedes Easter Sunday, the month of August, and mid-December through Christmas. Prices during this time can be higher, but not always. Some hotels actually run specials to keep up with the competition; it just depends on how busy the hotel thinks it will be. Either way, you need to book any decent hotel well in advance during these times or you won't get a room.

CLIMATE The country has two distinct seasons in terms of weather. The first is dry season, which runs from November to April. The second is rainy season, which runs from May to October. Since there is little temperature variation between these seasons, the question of which season is best for travel is not a simple one. The short answer would be November, when the rains have stopped but the landscape has not yet dried out. However, both seasons have something to recommend them. In dry season, the country's predominately dirt secondary roads are easier to navigate—some roads are impassible without a four-wheel drive during rainy season—and, well, it's not raining. In rainy season, on the other hand, El Salvador's environment is at its most lush and alive. Rainy season also doesn't necessarily mean all-day downpours: the country's highest elevations do receive daily rain and are often covered in a misty fog, but rainy season in the lower elevations can mean little more than daily afternoon showers.

Temperatures throughout El Salvador vary more according to elevation than season. The beaches and San Salvador can get up into the high 80s°F (low 30s°C) year-round, with even higher heat waves in the summer, while the coldest mountains can fall to near freezing, with averages of 54°F (12°C) to 73°F (23°C) year-round. The coldest month is December and the hottest month is May.

PUBLIC HOLIDAYS Public holidays in El Salvador include New Year's Day (Jan 1), Semana Santa (Holy Thursday through Easter Sunday), Labor Day (May 1), the Festival of El Salvador (Aug 1–6, though the rest of August remains a busy vacation season), Independence Day (Sept 15), Día de la Raza (Oct 12), All Souls Day (Nov 2), and Christmas celebrations (Dec 24, 25, and 31).

HEALTH CONCERNS

COMMON AILMENTS The most common travel ailments in El Salvador are diarrhea and food-born stomach upset. To stay healthy, be sure to drink only bottled water and ice you know to be purified, and stick to established restaurants. Dengue fever, known as "broken bones disease," is also on the rise in El Salvador. There is a low risk of malaria in El Salvador, centered mainly in rural areas of high immigration near the Guatemalan border. See p. 70 in "Planning Your Trip to Central America" for more info on how to prevent and treat common ailments.

VACCINATIONS The only vaccination necessary to enter El Salvador is for yellow fever, which is required only for persons 6 months or older coming from high-risk tropical areas. Those traveling from the U.S. and Europe do not need the vaccination, and the World Health Organization does not recommend it. However, it's a good idea to be up on all your shots, as many diseases that are all but wiped out in other parts of the world still exist in El Salvador. The CDC recommends getting shots for hepatitis A and B, typhoid, measles, rubella, mumps, rabies, and tetanus. It's best to consult a travel clinic 4 weeks prior to travel to check your vaccination history and discuss your itinerary.

GETTING THERE

By Plane

El Salvador's only international airport is Comalapa International Airport or **Cuscatlán International Airport** (**SAL; ✆ 503/2339-9455;** www.cepa.gob.sv/aies/index.php), 44km (27 miles) south of San Salvador. It is a major, 17-gate international hub with daily flights from the United States, Canada, Europe, and South America. **Cuscatlán** also serves as the main hub for primary Central and South American carrier Grupo Taca. The airport serves more than two million passengers per year, and includes numerous rental-car companies, hotel information booths, duty-free shops, and restaurants. All departing international fliers must pay a $32 (£16) departure tax. See p. 236 for more info.

FROM NORTH AMERICA American, Continental, Delta, and Taca offer flights to the United States. **American** flies out of Miami, Los Angeles, and Dallas/Fort Worth. **Continental** flies to and from Houston and Newark. **Delta Airlines** flies out of Atlanta. **Taca Airlines** stops in Chicago, Dallas/Fort Worth, Houston, Los Angeles, Miami, New York and Washington, D.C. TACA, Delta, Continental, and **Northwest** offer flights from Canada to San Salvador, too. See "Appendix: Fast Facts, Toll-Free Numbers & Websites" for airline info.

FROM THE UNITED KINGDOM, AUSTRALIA & NEW ZEALAND There are no direct overseas flights from the U.K., Australia, or New Zealand. You'll need to fly first into the United States—many European flights route out of Miami or Houston to San Salvador.

Tips Older Is Better

Stick to the older buses in El Salvador. You might be tempted to hop on one of the country's newer, more modern-looking buses, but these rides rarely have air-conditioning, they cram just as many people on, and because they have bucket rather than bench seats, you'll have even less room than the older buses. Fortunately, most buses which travel within the country are of the ancient variety. They regularly get fixed up, painted wild colors, decorated with religious symbols, and put back in service. Granted, these buses are packed, hot, bumpy, and stop frequently, but they will get you where you need to go, in style and more comfortably.

By Bus

Central America's major luxury bus carrier, **Tica Bus** (✆ **503/2243-9764;** www.ticabus.com) offers air-conditioned buses from San Salvador to Nicaragua, Honduras, Guatemala, Mexico, Costa Rica, and Panama, ranging from $15 (£7.50) each way to Guatemala and $75 (£38) each way to Panama. Tica arrives into San Salvador's **San Benito Terminal** (Boulevard el Hipódromo, Local #301, Colonia San Benito; ✆ **503/2243-9764**).

The bus company **King Quality** (✆ **503/2271-1361;** www.kingqualityca.com), which also features modern, air-conditioned buses, travels from San Salvador to Guatemalan cities such as Antigua and Guatemala City, as well as San José, Costa Rica. Prices range from $28 (£14) to $62 (£31). King Quality buses arrive into San Salvador's **Puerto Bus Terminal** (Alameda Juan Pablo II at 19a Av. Norte; ✆ **503/2222-2158**).

Finally, the company **Pullmantar** (✆ **503/2243-1300;** www.pullmantur.com) offers $33 (£17) to $49 (£25) trips from Guatemala City to the Hotel Sheraton Presidente in San Salvador (Av. La Revolución, Colonia San Benito; ✆ **800/325-3535**).

By Boat or Ferry

Private charters make the trip from La Unión on the eastern Pacific coast of El Salvador to points in Honduras and Nicaragua; visit **www.corsatur.gov.sv** for details. A ferry cruise journeys about once a month from La Unión to Amapala, Honduras. Check with the navy post in La Unión (✆ **503/2406-0348**) for details.

GETTING AROUND

By Bus

El Salvador is an easy and fun country to see by bus. There are very few places in this small nation that cannot be reached by one of El Salvador's many decades-old, brightly painted, former elementary-school buses. Most city buses are 25¢ to 35¢ (15p–20p) with few, if any, rides within the country costing more than $2 (£1). Salvador's larger cities have dedicated bus depots, but in smaller villages, the buses often come and go directly from the main square. In small towns and along many slow-moving roads, you can also hail buses like you would a taxi by waving your arm.

Buses in El Salvador are also mobile markets and charities. Be prepared for vendors to hop aboard at each stop to sell fruit, bottled water, and *dulces* (candies). You'll likely encounter brightly dressed clowns who solicit for various charities, as well. Though riding a bus in El Salvador is an excellent way to get to know the country's people and culture, don't detour away from the main tourist routes mentioned in this book and avoid nighttime bus travel or you'll risk encountering some safety issues.

By Car

El Salvador is one of the easiest countries in Central America to see by car, since it boasts newly constructed, well-paved, and well-marked highways running the length of the country from east to west and north to south. Hwy. CA-1, also known as the Pan-American Highway or "Carretera Panamericana," is the nation's main artery traveling from the western Guatemalan border through San Salvador to the eastern Honduran border. Hwy. CA-2 runs the same direction along the coast and is intersected by three major north-south highways running the length of the country. Once you get off the main roads, however, things get a little different. The secondary roads are not usually paved. So even in dry season, it's best to rent a truck. In rainy season, I recommend renting a four-wheel-drive as some roads are not passable with regular vehicles.

In terms of safety, do not drive at night in order to minimize your risk of robbery. When visiting larger cities, it's best to leave your car parked in your hotel parking lot and just take buses and cabs; city streets here are often chaotic, filled with people and vendors, and streets are rarely marked. These are not roads you want to drive while reading a map. You should really keep your eyes peeled while driving anywhere in the country: El Salvador's roads are filled with old jalopies moving at half the posted speed, motorcycles puttering along on the shoulder, farmers walking with carts sticking a few feet into the road, and pedestrians just inches from the lane.

See the destination sections below for info on **renting cars** throughout the country.

By Ferry

There is regular ferry service across Lago Suchitlán to Suchitoto (p. 280) and ferries ply the waters around La Unión, but additional ferry service is nonexistent.

By Taxi

Taxis are prevalent in the country's bigger cities and are usually easy to catch around each city's main square—they're safe to hail on the street, except at night, when you should have your hotel call you one. Smaller cities usually don't offer taxis but some feature small moto-taxis which are basically covered, three-wheeled motorcycles. Moto-taxis are often much cheaper than regular taxis—sometimes as little as 25¢ (15p) for a few blocks—and you get the added bonus of wind in your hair.

TIPS ON ACCOMMODATIONS

El Salvador's hotels vary widely in quality, style, and price. San Salvador's larger hotels are mainly multinational chains that follow internationally accepted standards for service and amenities, but most hotels outside the capital are individually owned (which means you'll find some true gems and some real stinkers). There are also a few international and national chain hotels scattered around the country, but generally most small-town hotels are going to be simple, cinder-block or stucco buildings with medium to smallish rooms, minimal decoration, and old furniture. Most are comfortable, with friendly, helpful onsite owners. Just don't expect everything to be shiny and new.

Rates range from more than $125 (£63) for a luxury room in San Salvador to $14 (£7) for a simple, comfortable room in a small mountain town. The bigger the town, the

Telephone Dialing Info at a Glance

The country code for El Salvador is 503, which you use only when dialing from outside the country. Telephone numbers in this chapter include this prefix because most businesses' published phone numbers include the prefix.

To place a call from your home country to El Salvador, dial the international access code (011 in the U.S. and Canada, 0011 in Australia, 0170 in New Zealand, 00 in the U.K.), plus the country code (503), plus the eight-digit phone number.

To place a call within El Salvador, simply dial the eight-digit number beginning with 2 for land lines and 7 for cellphones.

To place a direct international call from El Salvador, dial 00 for international access, plus the country code to the nation you are calling, followed by the area code and local phone number.

higher the price. And an 18% tax, which is included in the prices quoted in this chapter, is applied to all hotel rooms. Rooms aren't necessarily more expensive during Holy Week, Christmas, and early August. Sometimes they are actually cheaper. But they definitely book solid, so make your reservations for these weeks well in advance.

TIPS ON DINING

Outside of the high-end, international restaurants of San Salvador, El Salvadoran dining can get a bit repetitive, with most small-town restaurants offering roughly the same combo of cooked fish, meat, or chicken with rice and salad. Occasionally a restaurant owner throws in an Argentine sausage or a veggie dish. But for the most part, you'll be offered just plainish meat with a starch and greens. There are a few highlights, however. The first is El Salvador's national dish, the *pupusa*. Styles vary but generally *pupusas* are corn tortillas filled with pork and cheese and grilled warm and brown. They're usually served with a side of hot sauce and a tasty *curtido,* which is like a slightly spicy coleslaw, and sell for 25¢ to $1.50 (15p–75p) each. You'll find them everywhere and two to four make a meal. You'll also want to try El Salvador's *refrescos/liquados,* which are a combination of fruit, ice, and water or milk. (My favorite's a banana, milk, and honey concoction.)

If you have a strong stomach, you might want to give one of the country's many *comedores,* which are small, often family-run restaurants, usually with a mom or grandmother in the kitchen serving *pupusas* and a few items based on whatever is available that week. And if you've had your fill of traditional cuisine, a world-class collection of Asian, Brazilian, Italian, Peruvian, and other cuisines is available in San Salvador.

The country's 13% dining tax is normally included in the menu price with an additional 10% tip automatically added to most bills. Check your tab before tipping.

TIPS ON SHOPPING

Like dining, there is a world of difference between shopping in San Salvador and shopping in the rest of the country. San Salvador offers nearly everything you could want or need and is filled with high-end malls and expensive designer shops. But the smaller towns often offer only small *tiendas*—one-room food stores with a few necessities—street markets, and small variety stores.

Weekends tend to see town squares turned into markets offering everything from arts and crafts to cheap calculators. Most El Salvadoran markets also sell traditional artesania—a broad term for El Salvador's various textile, wood, and art crafts, which often take the form of wooden crosses, decorative boxes, or natural wood surfaces painted in the unique style of the country's most famous artist, Fernando Llort (p. 247).

Fast Facts El Salvador

American Express American Express traveler's checks can be exchanged at most banks, but very few businesses in El Salvador accept them. American Express offices are located in San Salvador (Anna's Travel, 3ra Calle Poniente 3737 between 71 and 73 Av. Norte; ✆ 503/2209-8800) or (Servi-Viajes, Paseo General Escalon 3508 No. 4; ✆ 503/2298-6868), in San Miguel (Anna's Travel, 8 Calle Poniente 815, Roosevelt Bario San Filipe, San Miguel; ✆ 503/2661-8282), and in Santa Ana (Anna's Travel, 2 Calle Poniente and 4 Av. Norte No. 4, Santa Ana; ✆ 503/2447-1574).

Business Hours Most banks and Casa de la Cultura community centers are open Monday through Friday 8:30am to 5pm and 8:30am to noon or 1pm on Saturdays. Some banks and Casas de las Culturas have extended Saturday hours. Business offices follow a similar schedule but are closed Saturdays and Sundays. Also note that many national tourist sites such as Tazumal and Joya de Cerén are open Sundays but closed Mondays.

Small-town shops often close for an hour or two around midday and smaller village restaurants close around 6pm. San Salvador's restaurants close between 8pm and 11pm with nightclubs staying open until the wee hours.

Embassies & Consulates The **U.S. Embassy** in San Salvador is located at Urbanización Santa Elena, Antiguo Cuscatlán (✆ 503/2278-4444; http://sansalvador.usembassy.gov). The **Canadian Embassy** can be found at Centro Financiero Gigante, Alameda Roosevelt and 63 Avenida Sur, lobby 2, location 6 (✆ 503/2279-4655). **Australia** has no embassy or consulate, but has an agreement allowing the Canadian embassy to assist Australian citizens. The **United Kingdom** has a consulate at 17 Calle Poniente 320 (✆ 503/2281-5555; gchippendale@gibson.com.sv). The U.K. embassy in Guatemala City, Guatemala (16 Calle 0-55, Zone 10, Edificio Porre Internaciónal, level 11; ✆ 502/2367-5425; www.britishembassy.gov.uk) handles visa and passport issues for residents of the United Kingdom traveling in El Salvador. **New Zealand** does not have a consulate or embassy in El Salvador. Kiwis need to contact the New Zealand embassy in Mexico City (Jamie Balmes 8, 4th floor, Los Morales, Polanco, Mexico, D.F. 11510; ✆ 5255/5283-9460; jorge.arguelles@nzte.govt.nz) for assistance.

Emergencies Emergencies from anywhere in the country can be handled by calling ✆ **911.** Some towns also have local numbers for tourist police, fire, and other agencies. Those numbers are listed below wherever applicable.

Hospitals The nation's premier private hospital is **Hospital de Diagnostico and Emergencias Colonia Escalón** (21a Calle Poniente and 2a Diagnol 429, Urbanización. La Esperanza Paseo del General Escalón, San Salvador; ✆ **503/2506-2000**). If you have a serious medical issue but are not ready or willing to leave the country, this is the place you need to go. Public hospitals, which are not recommended, are scattered throughout the country and can get you patched up well enough for transport home or to San Salvador. A complete list of El Salvador's public hospitals with contact information can be found at www.mspas.gob.sv.

Language Spanish is the official language of El Salvador. Few El Salvadorans outside of San Salvador's hotels speak English, so it's a good idea to learn a few words and to bring a Spanish phrasebook with you.

Maps Maps are exceedingly hard to come by in El Salvador. The main CORSATUR office in San Salvador (p. 236) offers large, colorful, tourism-style country and San Salvador maps. But few small towns offer street maps. Most towns are easy to find off the main highways and are walkable once you arrive.

Newspapers & Magazines *El Diario de Hoy* and *La Prensa* are El Salvador's most readily available newspapers. *El Diario* considers itself to be the country's paper, while *La Prensa* seems to have a more international perspective. Both are written in Spanish. The best English-language magazine you'll find in El Salvador is the Guatemala-based *Revue Magazine,* which offers travel, culture, and business features concerning Central America.

Police Police and other emergency agencies can be reached throughout the country by calling ✆ **911.** A few towns also have designated tourist police offices with additional phone numbers. Those numbers are listed below.

Post Offices & Mail Most towns in El Salvador have post offices marked by a blue sign reading CORREOS. Offices are open Monday through Friday from 8am to 5pm in larger cities and 7am to noon and 2 to 5pm in small towns. To mail a standard letter from El Salvador to the United States costs around 65¢ (35p) and 85¢ (45p) to Europe and Australia. For a list of post office addresses and phone numbers, visit www.gobernacion.gob.sv/eGobierno and click on "Correos de El Salvador."

Safety See the box "Staying Safe" below for info.

Taxes All hotels charge an 18% tax. Restaurants charge 13% on the total cost of the bill, and often sneak in an automatic 10% for service—check your bill carefully to avoid overtipping. See "By Plane" earlier in this chapter for info on the country's airport departure tax.

Telephone & Fax See the box "Telephone Dialing Info at a Glance" above, along with p. 80 in "Planning Your Trip to Central America" for info.

Tipping A 10% tip is automatically added to most restaurant checks, and taxi drivers don't expect a tip. No hard standard exists for bellhops, but $1 (50p) per bag will keep you in their good graces. Also, many tour guides work entirely for tips with a $2 (£1) minimum expected for anytime up to an hour. After that, it's up to you to compensate for exceptional service.

4 SAN SALVADOR ★

San Salvador is a frenetic, modern, international city in which travelers will find examples of the best and the worst of Central America's fastest growing economy. On the plus side, the nation's capital offers one of Central America's most diverse collections of international restaurants. You can sample fusion, Italian, Asian, Brazilian, and other cuisines at restaurants with top-notch service and, at least by North American and European standards, reasonable prices. You can also lay your head on the fluffy pillows of high-end, luxury hotels such a Hilton, Sheraton, and Intercontinental Real and shop at an international collection of designer stores in sparkling new malls such as the Multiplaza and Gran Via. In addition, the city boasts a world-class art museum, a historic center (El Centro), a nearby international airport, and beach resorts within one hour's drive. It's a city with a lot going for it.

On the downside, San Salvador suffers from pollution and heavy traffic and there is a great divide between the rich and the poor here, which means there are some unsafe, crime-ridden neighborhoods. Earthquake damage has taken its toll on older buildings, and the city—which is Central America's second-most populated behind Guatemala City—lacks any grand vistas. Instead of pretty architecture, San Salvador seems to have the highest concentration of fast-food restaurants in the world; Burger Kings, Wendy's, and Pizza Huts are practically on every corner.

If you have limited time in El Salvador, it's best to see San Salvador in 1 or 2 days. That will give you enough time to enjoy its international comforts and to see the main highlights, but leave you ample time to explore the country's small, more charming, towns.

ESSENTIALS

Getting There

BY PLANE El Salvador International Airport, also known as Comalapa or **Cuscatlán International Airport (SAL; ✆ 503/2339-9455;** www.cepa.gob.sv/aies/index.php) is 44km (27 miles) and a roughly 45-minute drive from San Salvador. Cuscatlán International is serviced by major North American carriers such as **American, Delta,** and **Continental** as well as Latin American carriers **Copa** and **Mexicana.** It's also a major hub for Taca airlines with direct flights to major American cities. See "Appendix: Fast Facts, Toll-Free Numbers & Websites" for airline info.

To get to the capital from the airport, take bus no. 138, which costs $1.75 (90p). Alternatively, you can arrange transportation with your hotel or pay $25 (£13) for one of the taxis waiting by the airport exit.

BY BUS You can catch national and international buses at **Terminal de Oriente** (Final de Av. Peralta and Boulevard del Ejército; **✆ 503/2271-4171**) in the east, **Terminal de Occidente** (Boulevard Venezuela, Colonia Roma; **✆ 503/2223-5609**) in the west, and **Terminal del Sur,** also known as Terminal San Marco (Carretera al Aeropuerto; no phone) in the southern part of the city.

You can take **Tica Bus** (**✆ 503/2243-9764;** www.ticabus.com), which is one of Central America's largest and most luxurious carriers with destinations throughout Central America, from the **San Carlos Terminal** (Calle Conception No. 121 at the San Salvador Hotel; **✆ 503/2243-9764**) and **San Benito Terminal** (Boulevard del Hipódromo; **✆ 503/2243-9764**).

Orientation

San Salvador is Central America's largest city in terms of size, sprawling 570 sq. km (220 sq. miles) east from the base of Volcán San Salvador. The three main tourist zones are **El Centro** in the east, and the **Escalón** neighborhood and Boulevard del Hipódromo in **Zona Rosa** in the west. All three neighborhoods are connected by the city's main east-west highway, known as **Alameda Franklin Delano Roosevelt,** east of the **Plaza de Las Américas** and **Paseo General Escalón** west of the plaza. El Centro includes the city's traditional square, national cathedral, and theater and is a crowded, urban area. It's safe during the day, but best not visited at night. Zona Rosa and Escalón are more upscale residential neighborhoods, and offer some of San Salvador's top restaurants, nightclubs, and shops. Adjacent to Zona Rosa to the west, you'll find the Colonia San Benito neighborhood, home to the **Museo Nacional de Antropología Dr. David J. Guzman** and **Museo de Arte.** It's not a good idea to stray too far from these three areas without local knowledge or a guide.

Though most of your travel in San Salvador will be east-west along Roosevelt/Escalón, the city also has a couple of key north-south routes. The main north-south route through the El Centro section is known as Avenida España north of Plaza Barrios and Avenida Cuscatlán south of the Plaza. Avenida Norte, which becomes the Boulevard de Los Heroes, splits the middle of the city; to travel south to the Zona Rosa and Colonia San Benito neighborhoods from the Paseo General Escalón, follow Avenida Manuel E Araujo to Boulevard del Hipódromo.

GETTING AROUND

BY BUS Buses rule the road in San Salvador and are a great way to see the city, since they stop frequently and go just about everywhere. Bus no. 30b is the line you'll most need to remember. The 30b will take you from Metrocentro (Boulevard de Los Héreos and Calle Sisimiles) across town to Zona Rosa and within walking distance of the city's two major museums. Most intercity buses can be taken from in front of the Metrocentro mall. To travel across the city from El Centro, take bus no. 101 to the Plaza de Las Americas, where you can hop on no. 30b.

Most buses cost 25¢ to 35¢ (15p–20p) and run between 5am to 7:30pm daily, with less frequent service on Sundays. The CORSATUR tourist office (see "Visitor Information" below) can provide additional bus route information.

BY TAXI You might want to consider using a cab instead of the bus, depending on how far you're traveling—it costs only about $3 (£1.50) to take a cab many places in the city. Exact fares range depending on your negotiating skills, the driver, and whether or not the cab has a meter. If you speak Spanish, you'll get the best deal by finding a cab without a meter and negotiating a price before getting into the cab. If the taxi has a meter, demand at least an estimate of the cost before agreeing to the trip.

San Salvador has numerous taxicab companies, any of which can be safely hailed on the street during daytime as long as you use a traditional looking taxi (yellow with a little taxi sign on top).

BY CAR Getting around by rental car is a great way to see El Salvador and a horrible way to see San Salvador. The city's roads are packed and not well marked. A wrong turn can also send you into a neighborhood you'd rather not visit or into the midst of a bustling street market. Since taxis are relatively inexpensive and easy to grab, and local buses are cheap and numerous, I recommend leaving your rental at your hotel or renting a car on your way out of the city.

ACCOMMODATIONS ■
Hilton Princess **10**
Hostal Plaza Antigua **20**
Hotel Villa Serena San Benito **11**
Intercontinental Real **25**
Mariscal Hotel & Suites **21**
Quality Hotel Real Aeropuerto **33**
Sheraton Presidente **13**
Suites Las Palmas **9**
Villa Castagnola Hotel **19**

DINING ◆
Alo Nuestro **8**
Fiasca Do Brasil Rodizio & Grill **25**
503 Restaurante and Champagne Lounge **7**
Hunan **1**
Inka Grill **5**
Kalpataru **3**
La Cantata Del Café **17**
Señor Tenedor **4**
Tre Tratelli Pasta Café & Restorante **6**

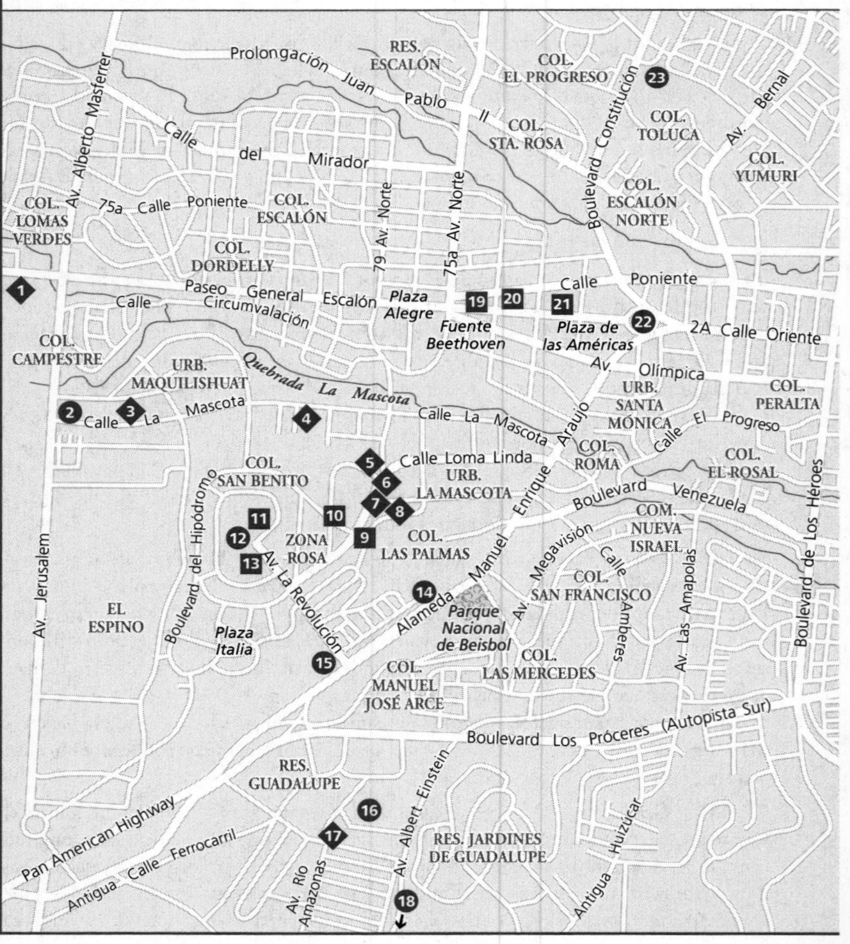

ATTRACTIONS ●

Catedral Metropolitana **27**
Centro Monseñor Romero **16**
El Arbol de Dios **2**
Hospital La Divinia Provedencia **23**
Iglesia El Rosario **29**
Jardin Botanico La Laguna **18**
Los Planes de Renderos **32**
Mercado Ex-Cuartel **30**
Mercado Nacional de Artesanias **14**
Mercado Central **26**
Museo de Arte **12**
Museo Nacional de Antropología Dr. David J. Guzman **15**
Parque Zoológico Nacional **31**
Plaza de Las Américas **22**
Teatro Nacional **28**
Tin Marín Museo de los Ninos **24**

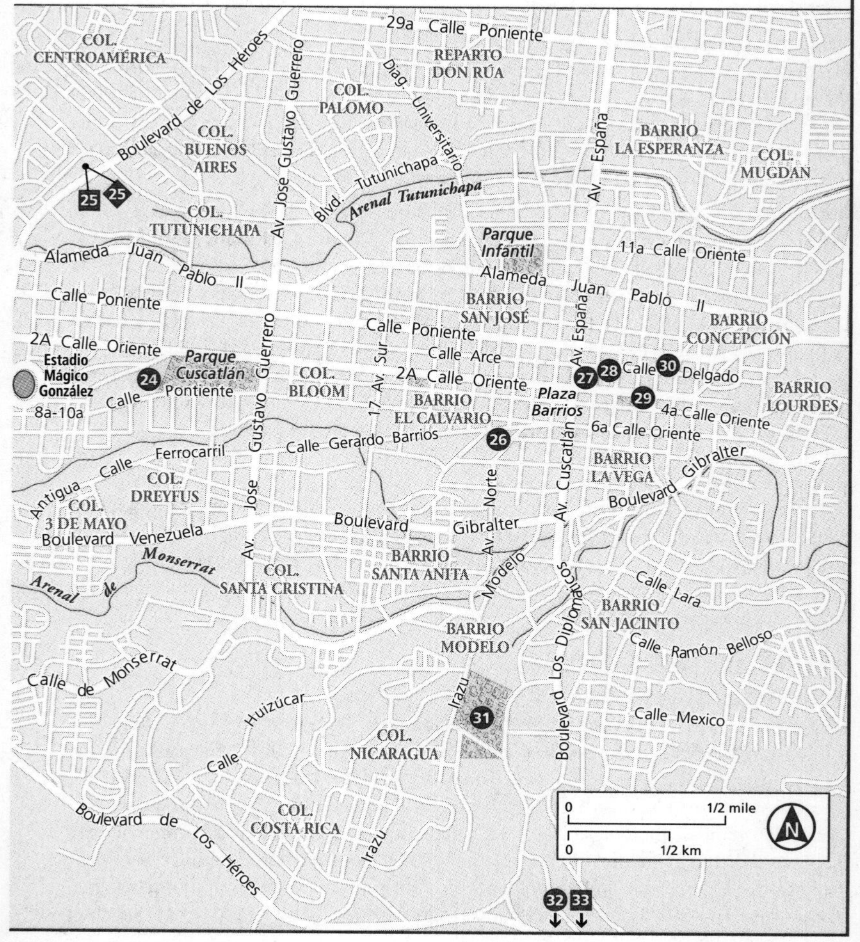

San Salvador offers plenty of local and international rental agencies. **Avis** (✆ 503/2339-9268), **Budget** (airport office ✆ 503/2339-9942; city office ✆ 503/2264-3888), **Hertz** (✆ 503/2339-8004), **Thrifty** (✆ 503/2339-9947), **Alamo** (✆ 503/2367-8000), and **National** (✆ 503/2367-8001) all have airport and downtown San Salvador locations. Locally, **Brothers Rent A Car** (Centro Commercial Feria Rosa bldg. H, local 208, in front of Casa Presidencial; ✆ **503/2218-1856**) offers the best deals. Rates range from $40 to $150 (£20–£75) a day with taxes and insurance.

ON FOOT Both of San Salvador's main tourist centers, El Centro and Zona Rosa, are highly walkable. It's in between those neighborhoods where you'll need transportation. El Centro's attractions are centered around the main square Plaza Barrios, and most of Zona Rosa's sights are along walkable Boulevard del Hipódromo. The city's major museums in the Colonia San Benito neighborhood are also within walking distance of each other.

Visitor Information

San Salvador's national tourism bureau (CORSATUR) office is located at Alameda Dr. Manuel Enrique Araujo, Pasaje and Building Carbonel No. 2, Colonia Roma (✆ **503/2243-7835**), and is open Monday through Friday 8am to noon and 1 to 5pm. The airport also offers a tourism office (✆ **503/2339-9454**) with English-speaking staff that's open Monday through Friday from 7am to 6pm.

FAST FACTS San Salvador offers a plentiful supply of the nation's major banks, and ATMs here accept most common international cards. A **Banco Cuscatlan** (✆ **503/2212-2000**) is in the Galarias Escalón mall along Paseo General Escalón.

Ambulances can be reached directly at ✆ **503/2222-5155** and the fire department is at ✆ **503/2555-7300.** The best medical care can be found at the modern **Hospítal de Diagnóstico Escalón** (99 Av. Norte, Plaza Villavicencio; ✆ **503/2264-4422**).

San Salvador's main **post office** is at 15 Calle Poniente and 19 Av. Norte, El Centro (✆ **503/2555-7600**). Internet access can be found for about $1 (50p) an hour at one of San Salvador's numerous **InfoCentro** (www.infocentros.org.sv) locations.

FESTIVALS

The **Festival of El Salvador** in early August marks a nearly countrywide vacation during which everyone who can heads to their vacation spot of choice. Schools and businesses close so that communities throughout the country can host parades, celebrations, and religious processions honoring Jesus Christ ("El Salvador") as the patron saint of the country. The largest celebrations are here in the nation's capital.

WHAT TO SEE & DO

The Top Attractions

Unfortunately, the big, beautiful **Teatro Nacional** ★ (2 Av. Sur and Calle Delgado 1 block east of Plaza Barrios) has been closed since a damaging 2001 earthquake, though at press time it had a tentative opening date of early 2009. Built between 1911 and 1917, the Teatro Nacional is considered one of Central America's oldest theaters and one of El Salvador's grandest buildings. The French Renaissance structure has 10 large columns across the front and—at least before the earthquake—a grand European interior of high ceilings, big chandeliers, and an opulent, multistory theater. The cultural organization **Concultura** (✆ **503/2221-4380;** www.concultura.gob.sv) can provide current opening date information.

Catedral Metropolitana ★ El Salvador's national cathedral is not as visually stunning as some famous European cathedrals, but it is steeped in El Salvadoran history and offers an example of the nation's adopted artistic style. Historically, the church was the site of deadly massacres prior to the country's civil war and great celebrations after the 1992 peace accords. The church has been damaged and rebuilt three times and is considered a symbol of the nation's rebirth from tragedy. Today the cathedral features a huge mural by El Salvador's most revered living artist, Fernando Llort. As the aesthetics here are somewhat secondary to the history, read up a bit before you go to know what you are looking at.

Av. Cuscatlán and 2a Calle Oriente at Plaza Barrios. No phone. Free admission. Daily 8am–noon and 2–4pm.

Museo de Arte ★★★ The Museo de Arte is one of San Salvador's must-sees. The 2,267-sq.-m (24,400-sq.-ft.) museum includes six rooms of rotating exhibits and a permanent collection that helps newcomers get a sense of the country. One of the highlights is the art exhibited from the 1980-to-1992 civil war period, which clearly but subtly demonstrates the desperation of the time. Immediately in front of the museum is the towering stone mosaic Monument to The Revolution, which depicts a naked man whose outstretched arms are thought to symbolize freedom and liberty. You'll need 1 to 3 hours to explore the museum, and English-language tours are free for parties of 10 or more and $40 (£20) total for parties of 1 to 9. Call or e-mail (educacion@marte.org.sv) 24 hours in advance to schedule an English-language tour.

Final Av. La Revolución, Colonia San Benito. ✆ **503/2243-6099.** www.marte.org.sv. Admission $1.50 (75p) adults, 50¢ (25p) students, free for children 7 and under. Tues–Sun 10am–6pm.

Museo Nacional de Antropología Dr. David J. Guzman ★★ San Salvador's anthropology museum is the city's other must-see, but only if you speak Spanish or can arrange an English-speaking tour. The ancient tools, weapons, pottery, and ceramic artifacts on exhibit here offer an intriguing glimpse into the lives of El Salvador's indigenous community and explain the evolution of agriculture and early trade in the country. However, signs are in Spanish only. Since the museum is only a 10-minute walk from the art museum, it's still worth a quick look if you can't arrange an English tour and are in the area. An English-speaking tour guide is available at the front desk or by calling the number below.

Av. La Revolucíon. Colonia San Benito. ✆ **503/2243-3927.** Admission $3 (£1.50). $5 (£2.50) to bring in camera or video equipment. Tues–Sun 9am–5pm.

Other Attractions

Centro Monseñor Romero ★ This center tells the story and displays the images and personal items of the six Jesuit priests, their housekeeper, and the housekeeper's daughter who were brutally murdered in the university rectory November 16, 1989, in the midst of El Salvador's bloody civil war. The murders made international headlines and demonstrated the war's high level of personal violence. Considering that El Salvador is a country with a complex and occasionally disturbing history, the 30 minutes you'll need to tour this one-room center are worth it to have a broader understanding of the country and its people.

Universidad Centroamericano José Siméon Cañas. ✆ **503/2210-6600,** ext. 422. Free admission. Mon–Fri 8am–noon and 2–6pm; Sat 8–11:30am.

Remembering Monseñor Romero

Monseñor Oscar Arnulfo Romero, commonly referred to as Monseñor Romero, is arguably El Salvador's most revered native son. He was born in 1917 and at age 20, he went to Rome to study at Gregorian University and begin his career in the priesthood. He returned to El Salvador at age 26, and spent the next 20 years as a priest in San Miguel. In 1966, he became secretary of the Episcopal Conference and editor of the archdiocese's newspaper, *Orientación*. In 1975 he was appointed archbishop of the Diocese of Santiago de Maria and was promoted to Archbishop of San Salvador in 1977. Romero was not at first considered to be a revolutionary and his appointment disappointed some of the country's more progressive religious leaders.

Less than a month after his appointment as archbishop, however, Romero was deeply affected by the assassination of his personal friend Rutilio Grande, who had been organizing for the nation's poor. Romero took up Grande's mantle and became an outspoken critic of government repression, injustice, and El Salvador's death squads. He also criticized Jimmy Carter and Pope John Paul II for their governments' support of the El Salvadoran military.

On March 24, 1980, following a sermon in which he was reported to have called on El Salvador's government soldiers to end their repressive tactics, Romero was shot and killed. His funeral in front of the country's national cathedral drew more than a quarter of a million mourners and was itself the site of gunfire and bomb blasts. The chapel where Romero was shot (Calle Toluca, Colonia Miramonte beside Hospital La Divinia Provedencia; ✆ **503/2260-0520**) remains open today with a small plaque marking the tragedy. Across the street, Romero's living quarters have been preserved as a museum with his personal effects and photos of the crime scene and funeral (see above).

El Arbol de Dios Arbol de Dios is the gallery and nonprofit office of El Salvador's most revered living artist, Fernando Llort (see p. 247 for more info), who founded an art movement in a small mountain town in 1972 by teaching locals to use available materials to express their lives. His colorful style of art, which is filled with natural and religious references, has since swept the country and can be found in hundreds of shops and at the National Cathedral. The gallery is small (only a foyer and one room) and requires less than 30 minutes to take in. But if you want to see a few of the original pieces of art that inspired thousands of copies, this is the place. If you're not that into art or Llort, it may not be worth the trip.

Final Calle La Mascota and Av. Masferrer, Colonia Maquilishaut. ✆ **503/2263-9206.** Free admission. Mon–Fri 8am–5pm.

Hospital La Divinia Provedencia ★ It was at the altar of this small hospital chapel in the midst of mass on March 24, 1980, that one of El Salvador's most revered citizens, Monseñor Oscar Arnulfo Romero, was gunned down in front of his parishioners. Today the church remains a working chapel with pictures of Romero and a small plaque marking the place where he was killed. Across the street, Monseñor Romero's living quarters are now a museum displaying his personal items with photos of the crime scene and the thousands who flocked to his funeral in front of the national cathedral. If you're at all interested in the details of El Salvador's civil war, this is worth a visit.

Calle Toluca, Colonia Miramonte. ✆ **503/2260-0520.** Free admission. Mon–Sat 9am–noon and 2–4pm.

Iglesia El Rosario ★★ Finds This is one of the most visually interesting churches in San Salvador, if not the whole country, and well worth the 5-minute walk off the main square. El Rosario's concrete, half-moon, bunker-like appearance is a bit bizarre and unchurchlike from the outside, but inside visitors are greeted by lines of colored light streaming in from abstract stained glass running up the height of its two curved walls. Abstract metal works form the altar and run the length of a third wall. The stations of the cross are represented by spare concrete and metal art pieces and are showcased in a low-ceilinged area, which is lit by natural light filtered through small squares of colored glass.

4a Calle Oriente and 6a Av. Sur. No phone. Free admission. Daily 6:30am–noon and 2–7pm.

Jardín Botánico La Laguna Overrated Unless you're really into plants and flowers, you shouldn't make the trip here. La Laguna is a beautiful and lush 3-hectare (7½-acre) park inside an extinct volcano crater with winding paths through hundreds of species of plants and flowers from around the world. The park, which you can explore in 30 minutes, offers an open-air cafeteria beside a small pond and numerous secluded nooks and crannies to escape the heat. The only problem is that the garden is located in the midst of a busy factory district, so you'll need to dodge trucks and walk through less than savory surroundings to get to the entrance. If La Laguna were in the city center, it would be a real gem, but I can't say it's worth a special trip.

Universidad Centroamericano José Siméon Cañas, Antigua Custcatlán. ✆ **503/2243-2012.** Admission $1 (50p). Tues–Sun 9am–5:30pm.

Parque Zoológico Nacional Kids This leafy 7-hectare (17-acre) zoo south of the city center is a hugely popular weekend spot for San Salvador families. Here you'll find winding, shady paths, and numerous small lagoons inhabited by roughly 400 animals and 125 species including such crowd pleasers as lions, elephants, alligators, and a huge selection of birds.

Final Calle Modelo. ✆ **503/2270-0828.** Admission 60¢ (30p). Wed–Sun 9am–4pm.

Plaza de Las Américas Overrated Plaza de Las Americas is a large, grassy traffic circle in the midst of a busy intersection containing the much photographed "Monumento Salvador del Mundo" or Monument to the Savior of the World. The monument includes a tall, four-sided concrete base with crosses on each side topped with a statue of Christ standing on top of the world. It's fine as statues go, but there's no parking and it's a bit tricky crossing numerous lanes of traffic to reach the circle. So unless you're a photography buff searching for the perfect shot, you might want to just take in the view from a bus window.

Alameda Franklin Delano Roosevelt. No phone. Free admission. Daily 24 hr.

Tin Marín Museo de los Nínos Kids This interactive children's museum and learning center boasts 24 exhibits giving kids fun, hands-on learning in the areas of culture, the environment, health, and technology. Little ones can dress up like doctors in a pretend operating room, put on plays in the theater, walk inside a huge volcano, and learn how to make two child-sized houses more environmentally friendly.

6 and 10 Calle Poniente btw. Parque Cuscatlán and Gimnacio Nacional, Colonia Flor Blanca. ✆ **503/2271-5147.** Admission $2 (£1). Tues–Fri 9am–5pm; Sat–Sun 10am–6pm.

Staying Safe

Traveler safety is a hotly debated topic among travelers and residents in El Salvador. And though everyone has his own take on the subject, the short answer is that El Salvador is a much safer country in which to travel than you probably have heard. However, El Salvador does have its issues and dangers and those should be taken into account. The street gang Mara Salvatrucha, which has members throughout the country, is considered to be among the most violent in the world, and El Salvador has one of the planet's highest homicide rates. Street and bus robberies in bad neighborhoods are also not uncommon—it's foolish to deny these conditions exist. But if you follow a few simple rules, you should have a safe and enjoyable trip.

Among the most important things to consider when traveling in El Salvador is not to stray too far off the travelers' path without knowledge of the area or a guide. Neighborhoods can change quickly and it's often difficult to distinguish between safe and unsafe areas by appearance alone. Some of the leafier, residential neighborhoods immediately outside larger cities are among the most prone to robbery. The main tourist areas of the bigger cities, however, are usually filled with people and are among the most heavily patrolled.

Small-town squares are also usually filled with locals into the evening and are among the safest places you're likely to visit. Don't be spooked by the presence of heavily armed police and private security guarding many of the country's banks, businesses, and tourist areas: El Salvador has a turbulent history and the seemingly ominous presence of armed guards—even in small towns—has simply become part of the culture. Heavy firepower does not mean an area is particularly dangerous.

Avoid traveling between towns or walking away from main squares at night; if you must venture out, always take a cab at night in bigger cities. It's also a good idea not to hike in rural, isolated areas without a guide.

Don't carry or display items of obvious value such as jewelry or expensive cameras; if you don't look like you have anything worth stealing, you're less likely to be robbed. Get in the habit of looping an arm or leg through the strap of your bag when you sit in a restaurant or bus depot, and don't leave bags unattended even for a moment. Simply being aware of what is around you helps: If someplace doesn't feel safe, it probably isn't. Just walk away.

Perhaps the most important safety tip, stressed to me by many El Salvadoran friends and provided as standard advice by government agencies, is to give up your valuables immediately if robbed. El Salvador's criminals are known to turn quickly violent when resisted. So if you're confronted, don't try to reason and don't bargain for your laptop.

Nearby Attractions

Joya de Cerén ★★ While not as visually grand as the nearby Tazumal ruins (p. 260), Joya de Cerén offers one of Central America's best glimpses into the daily lives of the region's Maya ancestors. Discovered in 1976, this UNESCO World Heritage Site comprises the remains of a Maya community frozen in time 1,400 years ago when it was buried beneath the ash of a volcanic eruption. The archaeological park requires about 1 hour to explore and includes a Spanish-language-only museum and the partial remains of the village's buildings, including a shaman's house, a community sauna, and bedrooms with sleeping platforms. Only parts of the buildings remain, so you'll need a little imagination to appreciate what you are seeing. But you won't find ruins anywhere else in the country that are so well preserved, making this definitely worth seeing.

Km 35 Carretera a San Juan Opica. No phone. $3 (£1.50) adults, free for children 4 and under. Tues–Sun 9am–4pm. At press time, the park offered only 1 English-speaking guide; call ahead (✆ **503/2401-5782**) to schedule a tour. Bus: 108 from San Salvador.

Lago Ilopango (Overrated) Ilopango is El Salvador's largest and deepest lake and offers a pleasant afternoon break from the city heat. But unless you are on a prearranged scuba diving trip, Ilopango is overrated as a major attraction. You're better off heading 56km (35 miles) east to Lago de Coatepeque, which has more pristine surroundings, better restaurants, and more activities. But if you just want to get out of the city for a few hours, the 100-sq.-km (40-sq.-mile) Lago Ilopango is an easy 16km (10-mile) drive from the city, and its tourist center, called Parque Acuatico Apulo, offers a handful of inexpensive, gazebo-style restaurants with lake views, a big pool, and $10 (£5) per 30-minute boat tours. You can swim in the lake but the park features only a small, uncomfortable, pebble-filled beach.

Ilopango, which reaches a depth of 250m (820 ft.), is a popular diving spot and El Salvador's top diving tour company. **El Salvador Divers** (✆ **503/2264-0961;** call in advance to arrange a trip) has a lakeside dive facility with dive equipment, boats, and overnight facilities.

Canton Dalores Apulo, Ilopango. ✆ **503/299-5430.** Admission 80¢ (40p). Daily 8am–4pm. Bus: 15.

Los Planes de Renderos ★★ (Finds) Heading up to Los Planes de Renderos to watch the lights of San Salvador come alive on a Sunday night is one of the city's most underrated joys. Planes de Renderos is a small community town about a 20-minute bus ride from San Salvador, with a large overlook offering sweeping views of the city and surrounding mountains. The village also features numerous small shops and *pupusarias*. Though you can venture up to Renderos any night, Sunday is when you'll find El Salvadoran families enjoying a festival-like atmosphere with music, dancers, and street vendors. At dusk, everyone who can fit lines up along Renderos' overlook to watch the lights of San Salvador in the valley below slowly create a sea of lights while the largely unpopulated surrounding mountains fade to black. It's a beautiful sight. A lot of the crowd then heads over to Pupusaria Señor Pico, which is across the street from the overlook and offers tasty snacks and partial views from an upstairs balcony.

Bus: 30 to Planes Los Renderos. Bring extra cash, as the last bus back leaves at 7pm and taxis are $8 (£4).

Parque Archeologío San Andrés If you have time for a third ruin, you'll enjoy your visit here. Otherwise stick to Tazumal and Joya de Cerén. San Andrés is the partially excavated main plaza of a Maya community that was active between A.D. 600 and 900 and ruled over this Valle de Zapotitlán. The site was excavated in 1977 and today consists of a roughly 9m-tall (30-ft.) pyramid—which may have housed royal tombs—and other partially excavated structures. There's also a Spanish-language museum featuring a 1.5×4.5m (5×15-ft.) topographical country map and a large-scale model of the site. San Andrés offers some beautiful long-range views but doesn't stir the imagination like Cerén or offer Tazumal's exemplary architecture. The ruins require less than 30 minutes to explore.

Km 32 Carretera a Santa Ana. ✆ **503/2319-3220** or 2235-9453. Admission $3 (£1.50). Tues–Sun 9am–4pm. Bus: 201 from San Salvador to San Andrés.

Volcán San Salvador Volcán San Salvador is an iconic part of the capital, since it looms over the landscape west of the city. The main volcano complex which peaks at 1,960m (6,430 ft.) was formed after an eruption roughly 70,000 years ago with smaller volcanic activity forming secondary peaks and craters such as Volcán San Salvador's most visited spot, the Boquerón or "big mouth" crater, which is 500m (1,640 ft.) deep and more than 1km (1/2 mile) wide. There have been no violent eruptions on Volcán San Salvador in 800 years but, say experts, even the slightest eruption could have catastrophic effects on the densely populated city. If you decide to explore the complex, don't do so without a guide, as the volcano's proximity to San Salvador makes it a prime robbery area.

Tour companies, such as Eco Mayan Tours (✆ **503/2298-2844**), can arrange transportation and guided tours here.

SHOPPING

San Salvador offers the best upscale shopping in El Salvador, with most high-end shops centered in four large, modern malls (see below). The city's Zona Rosa section along the **Boulevard del Hipódromo** is lined with smaller independent shops and the small **Basilea shopping center** (Boulevard del Hipódromo; ✆ **503/2279-0833**), which features small boutiques and jewelry stores.

San Salvador's largest but least upscale of those malls is **Metrocentro** (Boulevard de Los Héreos and Calle Sisimiles) across the street from the Intercontinental Real Hotel. Metrocentro has a few designer shops, but it's better for basics. More upscale is the **Galerías Escalón** (Paseo General Escalon, No. 3700; ✆ **503/2245-0800**), which is a large mall with designer shops, chic restaurants, and a multiscreen cinema in the midst of the exclusive Escalón residential neighborhood. And about 20 minutes from Metrocentro are the Multiplaza and Gran Via malls. The **Multiplaza Mall** (Calle El Pedregal and Carretera Panamericana a Santa Ana, Antigua Cuscatlán; ✆ **503/2248-9800**) is the city's most upscale mall, with designer shops such as Zara clothing, a multiscreen cinema, and an entire wing offering some of the city's best nightclubs and lounges. About a block from Multiplaza is the **La Gran Via Mall** (Carretera Panamericana a Santa Ana and Calle, Chiltiupan, Antigua Cuscatlán; ✆ **503/2273-8111**), which is smaller than Multiplaza but centered around a large, inviting outdoor courtyard with upscale designer shops, a multiscreen cinema, and restaurants with outdoor seating. If you have time to visit only one of these malls, Gran Via is the best place to eat and people-watch on its central outdoor plaza, Multiplaza has the best nightlife, and Escalón is the place to go for small boutiques.

Markets

Mercado Central (Central Market) ★ Go here if you want to see a decidedly unfiltered and urban El Salvadoran market. This isn't a tourist-centric, hammock-filled pedestrian plaza. The Central Market is a sprawling, seemingly chaotic mercado of blaring horns, shouting vendors, and old women in traditional clothes chopping vegetables in the street and wrangling live chickens. The main attraction at this multiblock indoor and outdoor market is that it is not designed for tourists: It's just *the* place locals go to buy everything from their dinner to electronic gadgets.

Fernando Llort: El Salvador's Preeminent Artist

Fernando Llort, El Salvador's most internationally famous and nationally revered living artist, was born in San Salvador in 1949 and, though he displayed an early talent for art and architecture (Llort obtained a degree in architecture from the University of El Salvador), his signature style only began to emerge in his 20s after Llort relocated to France to study theology. It was during that trip that Llort began to appreciate and identify with his native country, and this would heavily influence the style of art we see today on everything from crosses to clocks on sale in markets around the country.

Upon his return in 1972, Llort moved from San Salvador to the little northern village of La Palma and started an art workshop—"La Semilla de Dios" or "God's Seed"—from which he taught locals how to convey their lives through art. Initially his style included simple shapes and colorful patterns, along with references to El Salvadoran life such as small homes with tile roofs, plants, and animals. Later, as El Salvador's war cast a pall over the country, Llort began to include more religious references in his art. His style of art has since become ubiquitous with El Salvador and has been shown in galleries around the world, including the Museum of Modern Art in New York City, the Vatican, and the White House Museum in Washington, D.C. Perhaps his most famous work currently appears on the front of San Salvador's National Cathedral (p. 241).

Llort left La Palma and returned to San Salvador in 1979 as the talk of war began to escalate. There he founded the gallery and nonprofit "Arbol de Dios," or God's Tree, from which a portion of sales helps foster art appreciation around the country. He remains in San Salvador today with his wife and three children and continues to produce art, working with ceramics, lithographs, and engravings.

6a Calle Oriente btw. Calle del Cementerio and Av. 29 de Agosto, El Centro. (Walk 3 blocks west and 2 blocks south of Plaza Barrios.) No phone. Daily 7:30am–around 6pm.

Mercado Ex-Cuartel Though smaller, calmer, and more tourist-friendly than the nearby Mercado Central, the indoor Mercado Ex-Cuartel is filled with tourist kitsch, the same textile bags you'll see in most Central American markets, and lots and lots of unremarkable women's shoes. There is some original art for sale here along with a smallish collection of interesting decorative boxes and crosses. But if you want a souvenir representative of El Salvador and its artisans, you're better off going to Mercado Nacional de Artesanias or buying in one of El Salvador's small village markets.

8a Av. Sur and Calle Delgado, El Centro. (Walk 1 block north and 3 blocks east of the National Cathedral.) No phone. Free admission. Daily 9am–6pm.

Mercado Nacional de Artesanias ★★ The lack of locals, the paved parking lot, and wave after wave of buses stopping directly in front tells you immediately that this is San Salvador's most touristy marketplace. But despite the lack of local flavor, the quality of the art and crafts is high and the prices aren't bad. The market includes long rows of vendors selling unique hammocks, textiles, ceramics, and decorative crafts from artisans around El Salvador. A midsize textile bag will run you $8 (£4) and a large, well-crafted hammock should cost approximately $26 (£13). You could wait to buy directly from a craftsman in a village market, but you can also buy here knowing the quality is high and the price is surprisingly fair.

Alemeda Dr. Manuel Enrique Araujo, Colonia San Benito. ✆ **503/2224-0747.** Daily 9am–6pm.

WHERE TO STAY

San Salvador is an oasis of international style and service in El Salvador. The Hilton Princess, Sheraton Presidente, and the Intercontinental Real are the most luxurious of the city's international chains and live up to the high standards of those brand names. Local hotel Las Palmas is a newcomer to the luxury scene and my favorite place to stay in town. But all of the hotels listed below are comfortable and have something, be it price, location, or service, to recommend them. The Zona Rosa neighborhood—which includes the Hilton Princess and Las Palmas hotels—is among the city's safest and most tourist-friendly places to stay.

Very Expensive

Hilton Princess ★★ It's a close call, but the Hilton Princess wins the title of San Salvador's most luxurious business hotel. What sets this 11-story chain hotel in the heart of tourist-friendly Zona Rosa apart are its detailed, European castle-style interior and after-work amenities. Although all of San Salvador's high-end business hotels offer what you need to work, the Hilton goes further by easing the stress of commerce with perks such as a huge Jacuzzi and larger-than-average exercise room. From the rich leather and dark woods of Churchill's Bar to the hotel's European murals and statuary, the Hilton also exudes old-world charm and luxury. If your visit is primarily business and you enjoy conducting it in luxury, this is the place to stay.

Av. Magnolias and Boulevard del Hipódromo, Zona Rosa. ✆ **800/321-3232** or 503/2268-4545. Fax 503/2268-4500. www.sansalvador.hilton.com. 204 units. $164–$176 (£82–£88) standard; $223–$235 (£111–£118); executive level. $388 (£169) and up suite. AE, DC, DISC, MC, V. **Amenities:** Restaurant and 2 bars; $14 (£7) airport transfers; concierge; executive level; health club w/Jacuzzi and sauna; 2 floors nonsmoking; outdoor pool; room service. *In room:* A/C, TV, hair dryer, minibar, Wi-Fi.

Intercontinental Real ★ The Intercontinental Real is a high-end, international chain and solid business hotel, but it's a slightly less appealing option overall than the Hilton Princess or the Sheraton. It's located in the city's main commercial district, which though good for business travelers, isn't tourist friendly; the pool and gym are also small and not overly inviting. On the plus side, the Intercontinental is across the street from El Salvador's biggest shopping mall, Metrocentro, and offers the hippest restaurants (p. 261) and lounges of the big three.

Calle Sisimiles and Boulevard de Los Hereos, Colonia Miramonte. ✆ **800/496-7621** or 503/2211-3333. Fax 503/2211-4444. www.ichotelsgroup.com. 234 units. $105–$134 (£53–£67) standard double; $152–$170 (£76–£85) executive double; $413 (£207) and up suite. Rates include continental breakfast. AE, DC, DISC, MC, V. **Amenities:** 3 restaurants; bar; $15 (£7.50) airport transfers; babysitting; concierge; executive level; heath club and spa w/sauna; 181 nonsmoking rooms; small outdoor pool; room service. *In room:* A/C, TV, hair dryer, high-speed Internet, minibar.

Sheraton Presidente ★★ Sheraton Presidente happens to be an excellent high-end business hotel with all the amenities you'll need to get your work done, but it's also a slightly better place to stay than the Hilton Princess for those combining business and pleasure. That's because the Sheraton also offers a huge pool and is a short walk to the city's two major museums and the shop-filled Boulevard del Hipódromo. The outdoor and surprisingly large pool includes a small waterfall to drown out city noise and is next to an outdoor putting green (rare in El Salvador). The interior of this four-story hotel is what you would expect of a high-end chain but nothing more; rooms are of average size with nondescript, corporate decor. The hotel is often near capacity, so book early and request a room on the back side to get pool views and less noise.

Av. La Revolución, Zona Rosa. ✆ **800/325-3535** or 503/2283-4000. Fax 503/2283-4070. www.sheraton.com/sansalvador. 225 units. $164 (£82) standard double; $211 (£106) executive level double; $399 (£200) and up suite. Executive rates include buffet breakfast. AE, DC, DISC, MC, V. **Amenities:** 2 restaurants; bar; $14 (£7) airport transfers; concierge; health club and spa w/sauna; 120 nonsmoking rooms; huge outdoor pool; room service. *In room:* A/C, TV, suites w/kitchens and kitchenettes, hair dryer, minibar, Wi-Fi.

Expensive

Quality Hotel Real Aeropuerto ★ (Kids This Quality Hotel is a bit pricey but much nicer than you would expect of an airport hotel—it's a viable option even if you aren't leaving early in the morning. Just 5 minutes from the Comalapa International Airport and an easy 35-minute drive from downtown, this three-story hotel offers such nonairport touches as an Xbox video game console for the kids, a pool with poolside bar and Jacuzzi, and an upscale restaurant. All the necessary business amenities are also available. The rooms are standard chain size and nondescript, but a few offer pool views. If you want the amenities of the posh city hotels, but the peace and quiet of the suburbs, this is your place.

Km 40.5 Carretera al Aeropuerto, La Paz. ✆ **877/424-6423** or 503/2366-0000. Fax 503/2366-0001. www.qualityinn.com. 149 units. $136–$182 (£68–£91) double. Rates include buffet breakfast. AE, DC, DISC, MC, V. **Amenities:** Restaurant; bar; free airport transfers; babysitting; exercise room; Jacuzzi; 50 nonsmoking rooms; outdoor pool; room service. *In room:* A/C, TV, fridge (in some), hair dryer, minibar (in some), Wi-Fi.

Suites Las Palmas ★★★ (Finds Las Palmas is the best and hippest nonbusiness hotel for the money in the city. Only 2 years old, this modern, seven-story hotel is within walking distance to Zona Rosa's best restaurants and shops, offers big, modern suites with kitchens for the price of other hotels' basic rooms, and boasts unusual designs and amenities throughout. The pool, Jacuzzi, and sleek Asian-fusion restaurant are all set on the rooftop and feature amazing views, as does the exercise room, which includes a wall of glass overlooking the city. The suites are large with king- or queen-size beds, often with kitchens and couches. Suite amenities and prices vary greatly, so pin down what you're getting when making your reservation; request upper floor rooms, which have balconies and views. Though Las Palmas' name doesn't carry the cachet of the international chains in the city, it's every bit as luxurious and a better deal.

Boulevard del Hipódromo, Zona Rosa. ✆ **503/2250-0800.** Fax 503/2250-0888. 47 units. $81–$140 (£41–£70) standard double; $117–$152 (£59–£76) deluxe double; $117–$164 (£58–£82) presidential suite. Some rates include breakfast. AE, DC, DISC, MC, V. **Amenities:** Restaurant; bar; $15 (£7.50) airport transfers; small exercise room; Jacuzzi; 8 nonsmoking rooms; rooftop pool; room service. *In room:* A/C, TV, full kitchens (in some), kitchenettes (in some), Wi-Fi.

Moderate

Hotel Villa Serena San Benito ★★ It's bare bones, but the San Benito is one of the best moderate options in San Salvador. The hotel opened in 2006 and offers huge, sunny suites and rooms, spotless facilities, and, like the nearby Sheraton Presidente, is within walking distance of the city's two major museums and Boulevard del Hipódromo's shopping and restaurant district. The large, airy suites feature big kitchens with modern appliances and separate lounging areas. The staff is also incredibly friendly. On the downside, the hotel doesn't have a pool or restaurant. San Benito is the best choice for those who prefer a great location and a good deal over amenities.

Calle Cicunvalación No. 46, Zona Rosa. ✆ **503/2237-7979.** www.pequenoshoteles.com. 34 units. $62–$73 (£31–£37) double. Rates include continental breakfast. AE, DC, DISC, MC, V. **Amenities:** $23 (£12) airport transfers; nonsmoking rooms available. *In room:* A/C, TV, full kitchens in suites, Wi-Fi.

Mariscal Hotel & Suites The Mariscal is pricier than the other two options in Escalon (see below), but also a bit more upscale. It features 18 big rooms and suites that aren't necessarily any better than the area's other two hotels, but with matching linens and modern furniture sets, it does feel a bit fancier. The one- and two-room suites are large, with couches, dining tables, and well-appointed kitchens. Suites vary in quality, so request a suite with a modern kitchen: Suite no. 1 is the best, with a big bathroom and two televisions. Mariscal is also on a heavily trafficked road, so make sure to request a room farthest from the street when you book.

Paseo General Escalón, No. 3658, Colonia Escolón. ✆ **503/2283-0220.** Fax 503/2223-5889. www.hotelmariscal.com. 18 units. $50–$72 (£25–£36) double; $62–$117 (£31–£59) suite. Rates include continental breakfast. AE, DC, DISC, MC, V. **Amenities:** $20 (£10) airport transfers; all rooms nonsmoking; room service. *In room:* A/C, TV, hair dryer, kitchens (in suites), Wi-Fi.

Inexpensive

Hostal Plaza Antigua ★ Value Plaza Antigua is an excellent, low-priced option in a great location. It isn't going to blow you away with its decor or amenities, but it's in one of San Salvador's nicest neighborhoods, Escalón, and steps from the swanky Galerías Escalón mall. The two-story hotel (which just opened in 2006) is situated around a courtyard with a small pool. Rooms are of average size—all can be viewed on the hotel's website—with nicely tiled bathrooms. Request room no. 5, which is the quietest and catches the afternoon breeze. Given Plaza Antigua's location, it could probably charge more if they decorated a bit.

1a Calle Poniente No. 3844, Colonia Escalón (behind Galerías Escalón). ✆ **503/2223-9900.** Fax 503/2224-5952. www.hostalplazaantigua.com. 15 units. $41–$50 (£21–£25) double. Rates include continental breakfast. AE, DC, DISC, MC, V. **Amenities:** Restaurant; $35 (£18) airport transfer; 3 nonsmoking rooms; small outdoor pool; room service. *In room:* A/C, TV, no phone, Wi-Fi.

Villa Castagnola Hotel Villa Castagnola is another excellent option for comfortable, affordable accommodations in the Escalón neighborhood, though it's about half the size of the Plaza Antigua. With only six rooms, Castagnola is as quiet a hotel as you will find in San Salvador. On-site husband-and-wife managers, Raul and Tatiana Nunes, offer a high level of personal service and will help you arrange area tours. The rooms are also larger than you would expect, and there's a pleasant, upstairs, open-air seating area with great views of Volcán de San Salvador. The best room is no. 1, which has two separate sleeping areas and a big bathroom.

1a Calle Poniente and 73 Av. Norte No. 3807, Colonia Escalón. ✆ **503/2275-4314** or 2275-4315. Fax 503/2211-6482. www.hotelvillacastagnola.com. 6 units. $45–$65 (£23–£33) double. Rates include continental breakfast. AE, DC, DISC, MC, V. **Amenities:** Restaurant; $25 (£13) airport transfers; room service. *In room:* A/C, TV, fridge, Wi-Fi.

WHERE TO DINE

San Salvador offers a world-class array of ethnic restaurants ranging from Asian to Peruvian. And one of the best places to sample those culinary offerings is the Boulevard del Hipódromo in the tourist-friendly Zona Rosa district. This stroll-friendly street on the city's west side offers a cluster of restaurants within just a few blocks. A few trusted Zona

Rosa favorites are listed below, but since the city's restaurant scene is growing rapidly, you might want to take a stroll along the Boulevard to find your own favorite spot.

Expensive

Fiasca Do Brasil Rodizio & Grill ★★ BRAZILIAN It's all about the meat. Fiasca is one of San Salvador's few Rodizio restaurants, which means they keep the *carne* coming. Rodizio is an all-you-can eat Brazilian style of dining in which waiters bring huge skewers of meat or fish to your table and slice the cuts onto your plate. Fiasca specializes in the *picañha* or top rump cut, which many Brazilians consider to be beef's finest. And at Fiasco you don't wait long for your second helping, as the restaurant maintains a ratio of 18 servers to a maximum 92 diners. Opened in October 2007, Fiasca Do Brasil is the principal restaurant of the luxury Intercontinental Real hotel (see above) and offers a unique, high-end dining experience for a reasonable price. As a result, the place is often packed and reservations are required. Ask for one of the raised booths along each wall, which are off the busy main dining floor.

Calle Sisimiles and Boulevard de Los Hereos. ✆ **503/2211-3333.** Reservations required. Rodizio dining $25 (£13). AE, DC, DISC, MC, V. Daily 6am–10:30am, noon–3pm, and 7–11pm.

503 Restaurante and Champagne Lounge ★ SUSHI You can't help but feel a bit hipper than you actually are sitting in this new Zona Rosa restaurant and lounge. Opened in late 2006, the 503 sushi restaurant and lounge offers an ultrachic blazing white interior that extends from the floor, to the walls, to the chairs, to the plates, to the tables. They're all pure white against a wall of windows. But it's the eight-roll sushi plates with unique items such as Icelandic caviar, eel, crab, and salmon mixed with Japanese mayonnaise, avocado, and carrots that are the main attraction. A sophisticated, non-sushi menu, including a delicious chicken breast stuffed with French Camembert cheese in a nut sauce, is also offered. And after 11pm on weekends, 503 transforms into a late-night and early-morning lounge with DJs and a decked-out international crowd. Since Code nightclub (see below) is next door, the custom is to start the night and end the morning at 503.

Boulevard del Hipódromo No. 503, Zona Rosa. ✆ **503/2223-4770.** Reservations recommended weekends. Sushi rolls $6–$12 (£3–£6); main courses $13–$18 (£6.50–£9). AE, DC, DISC, MC, V. Tues–Sat 7pm–3am; Fri–Sat 10am–1pm.

Hunan ★ CHINESE After 10 years in a packed restaurant market, Hunan is still the place to go for Chinese. A bit plain and strip-mall looking from the outside, Hunan's one-room, 250-person seating area is a lesson in Chinese interior design, with intricately carved wooded chairs and embroidered red velvet seats, enormous wall murals, and dozens of porcelain vases with flowers for sale filling up the huge space. But it's Hunan's unique "Pato Peking"–style cuisine, which is a particularly spicy and hearty variety of Chinese cooking, that keeps the diners coming back. Standout dishes include shrimp with tofu in a lobster salsa and duck with black mushrooms and oyster sauce. Hunan's service is also seamless.

Paseo Escalón No. 4999, Colonia Escalón. ✆ **503/2263-9911.** Main courses $18–$26 (£9–£13). AE, DC, DISC, MC, V. Mon–Thurs noon–3pm and 6–10pm; Fri–Sat noon–3pm and 6–11pm; Sun noon–4pm and 6–9pm.

Moderate

Alo Nuestro ★★★ FUSION It's so good, they don't even need to advertise. For almost 10 years, this midsize restaurant has built a quiet, word-of-mouth following as one of the best restaurants in the packed Zona Rosa section of town. What draws the crowds is that Alo Nuestro fuses the best of San Salvador's international dining options into a single restaurant that uses local ingredients. The result is such tasty dishes as crispy sea bass sautéed in asparagus, mushrooms, and sweet corn with a light soy ginger sauce. Another treat is the garlic-spinach stuffed sautéed chicken breast with a blue cheese wine sauce and squash. Unique weekly specials such as sautéed tilapia over *loroco* crepes with basil sauce keep things fresh. The interior is small but spacious, with ample space between the tables, and there's a large romantically lit outdoor deck with a view of the nearby mountains. The restaurant is also surprisingly affordable, with most entrees costing under $20 (£10).

Calle La Reforma No. 225, Zona Rosa. ✆ **503/2223-5116.** Reservations recommended. Main courses $12–$20 (£6–£10). AE, DC, DISC, MC, V. Mon–Thurs noon–2:30pm and 7–10:30pm; Fri noon–2:30pm and 7–11pm; Sat 7–11pm.

Inka Grill ★ PERUVIAN The Inka Grill is a rare taste of the Andes in El Salvador. Dark woods, deep oranges, rich detail, and interesting Inca-inspired art greet diners as they enter this Peruvian oasis a few blocks off the Zona Rosa dining district. The dishes are pure Peruvian, with plates such as the *ronda criolla, chicharrones* or deep-fried rinds of chicken and pig with artichoke hearts, yucca, and sweet potato, or the appetizer of traditional Peruvian *tamales de choclo* (corn tamales) with an onion salsa. Inka Grill is part of a seven-restaurant chain with locations in Costa Rica, Guatemala, the United States, and a second San Salvador location at the Gran Via mall. This spot near Zona Rosa is the better of the two because it is more secluded and tranquil, and offers a more uniquely Peruvian ambience.

79 Av. Sur and Pasaje A, Zona Rosa (a few blocks off Boulevard del Hipódromo). ✆ **503/2230-6060.** Main courses $9.95–$20 (£5–£10). AE, DC, DISC, MC, V. Sun–Wed 2–10pm; Thurs–Sat 2–11pm.

Señor Tenedor ★★ MODERN ITALIAN Ah, romance. Whereas Zona Rosa's Tre Tretelli is a friendly neighborhood Italian, Señor Tenedor is all modern lines and sensual colors. Tenedor is on the first floor of an office building and looks from the outside like the building's cafeteria. But the inside is sleek and date-friendly with booths set beneath sweeping, translucent silk tied with deep red satin. And—here's something you don't find in El Salvador every day—Tenedor features live violin music Tuesday and Friday from 7 to 10pm. Tenador also offers numerous carpaccios, which is a style of modern Italian cooking involving thin slices of beef, fish, or vegetables beneath cheese, olive oil, and other toppers, a unique tobacco-and-rum-flavored steak, and a nice selection of international wines. A sophisticated antipasto lunch buffet is also offered daily. San Salvador has another Tenador location, but this 2-year-old spot is the more secluded and less crowded of the two.

Calle La Mascota No. 533, Colonia Mascota. ✆ **503/2211-8326.** Reservations recommended weekends. Main courses $14–$23 (£7–£12). AE, DC, DISC, MC, V. Mon–Sat 7am–10pm (lunch buffet 11am–3pm).

Tre Tratelli Pasta Café & Restorante ★★ Kids ITALIAN The alluring aroma of Italian herbs, garlic, and tomatoes envelops you the moment you walk into this casual, midpriced Italian restaurant in the heart of Zona Rosa's dining district. The ambience is laid-back but busy, with a semi-open kitchen. The two main dining areas, minimally decorated with Italian advertising art, give off the feel of a friendly neighborhood Italian joint, so the sophisticated menu, fusing Italian cooking with lighter California fare, may surprise you. You'll definitely want to try the *canelone modi de mar,* which is rolled pasta stuffed with fish, shrimp, salmon, zucchini, and red peppers in a cream sauce with mussels and asparagus, or the Mediterranean-style seviche with shrimp, calamari, olive oil,

Spanish Classes in El Salvador

El Salvadorans are famously friendly, patient, and genuinely pleased when visitors attempt to speak their language. But that doesn't mean your high school Spanish isn't painful to listen to. So if you're going to be spending some time here, you might as well brush up on the native tongue. Luckily, numerous short-term, affordable language programs are available throughout the country.

In San Salvador, you'll find the **Mélida Anaya Montes Spanish School**—part of El Salvador's human justice organization Centro de Intercambio y solidaridad (CIS) (Av. Bolivar 103, Colonia Libertad, San Salvador; ✆ **503/2226-5362;** www.cis-elsalvador.org)—which offers one- to four-person classes taught by El Salvadoran teachers, homestays with local families, and a strong emphasis on social justice in El Salvador. Students participate in 4-hour daily classes and can also participate in a program introducing them to El Salvador's political progressive organizations, communities, and political parties. Classes begin on Mondays year-round and cost $223 (£111), plus a $25 (£12) registration fee, per week, including food and lodging. Classes on their own are $100 (£50) per week.

The lakeside hostal **Amacuilco** (Calle Principal, Lago de Coatepeque, Santa Ana; ✆ **503/7822-4051;** amacuilcohostal@hotmail.com) by beautiful Lago de Coatepeque offers a 5-day, 20-hour Spanish course including food, lodging, and kayak rentals for $120 (£60). El Salvador's **SalvaSpan language school** (5a Calle Poniente between 4 and 6 Av. Sur No. 15, Santa Ana; ✆ **503/7051-4171** in El Salvador, or 413/374-0159 in the U.S.) offers language classes at a place of your choosing—for instance, if you want to take 2 days of classes in Suchitoto, 2 days in Playa Sunzal, and 2 days in Ataco, the SalvaSpan teachers can accommodate you. Classes are $175 to $200 (£87–£100) per week for 5 days of 4 hours per day, one-on-one instruction. Homestays can be arranged in San Salvador and Santa Ana for an additional $125 to $150 (£63–£75).

capers, tomato, onions, and garlic. Tre Tratelli's food and service are superior to its midlevel price.

Boulevard del Hipódromo No. 307, Zona Rosa. ✆ **503/2223-0838.** Reservations required for groups larger than 10. Main courses $8–$16 (£4–£8). AE, DC, DISC, MC, V. Daily 11am–11pm.

Inexpensive

Kalpataru ★★ Value VEGETARIAN If you're thinking vegetarian in San Salvador, think Kalpataru. For 22 years, this restaurant and holistic health center has lived up to its printed-on-the-menu mission statement to serve 100% vegetarian in a friendly environment. A few minutes from the city's main restaurant district, Kalpataru is worth the taxi ride for its large selection of $1.30 (65p) vegetarian *pupusas* and tasty but affordable lunch buffet. Kalpataru also offers vegetarian tamales, veggie soups, and veggie pizza. The casual, two-story restaurant includes a meditation center and library with books, CDs, and natural healing products. And Kalpataru is just a 5-minute walk from El Arbol de Dios (p. 242), the gallery of El Salvador's national artist Fernando Llort, which means it's a great place to stop when you need a break from sightseeing.

Calle La Mascota No. 928, Urbanización Maquilishuat. ✆ **503/2263-1204.** Lunch buffet $8.80 (£4.40); main courses $1.30–$5.50 (65p–£2.75). AE, DC, DISC, MC, V. Mon–Sat noon–8pm (lunch buffet noon–3pm); Sat breakfast buffet 7–11am.

La Cantata del Café ★★★ Finds SALVADORAN The vibe is great, the food is better, and the prices are ridiculously low. This little seven-table joint on the corner near the entrance to José Simeón Cañas University doesn't look like much from the outside, but don't let that fool you. A young and friendly staff presides over the artistic space, which boasts local art on the walls, live music in the corner, and a shelf of interesting books to read while sipping one of La Cantata's 30 hot and cold coffee drinks. The laid-back vibe is reason enough to hang out here, but the food—despite the low price—is delicious. Sandwiches, salads, pizza, and pastas all hover around $3 (£1.50). A huge portion of penne pasta with chicken comes piping hot with a rich, spicy sauce, big chunks of chicken, and a side of tasty garlic bread. Add a beer and bottled water and the bill still barely reaches five bucks. La Cantata might be one of the tastiest meals you'll have in San Salvador.

Calle Mediterranio No. 26, Colonia Jardines de Guadalupe (1 block from the entrance to José Simeón Central American University). ✆ **503/2243-9425.** Main courses $2.50–$3.25. (£1.25–£1.65). No credit cards. Mon–Sat 8:30am–8pm.

SAN SALVADOR AFTER DARK

San Salvador offers an excellent array of high-end lounges, dance clubs, and a few laid-back bars. The city's current hot spot is the strip of nightclubs and lounges in the **Multiplaza Mall.** Don't let the word "mall" fool you: On weekends this two-story nightlife strip is packed with San Salvador's stylish young elites. Multiplaza's offerings are modern and upscale, and you'll need to dress your best. **Boulevard del Hipódromo** is San Salvador's other happening nightlife spot, anchored by a major dance club and numerous smaller bars and lounges. Like Multiplaza, you can take a cab to Boulevard del Hipódromo and then barhop by foot the rest of the night. A few independent spots, such as La Luna Casa de Arte, are scattered around the city. But some San Salvador neighborhoods can be dangerous at night, so unless you're with a local, it's best to stick to the better-known spots. Also avoid the "private" clubs suggested by cab drivers.

Theater, Dance & Classical Music

San Salvador's performance art scene lags a bit behind its nightlife, but national and international performances can be found. The most glamorous spot in the country for the performing arts, **Teatro Nacional** (✆ **503/2222-5689**) has been closed since 2001 due to earthquake damage; call for updates. Until it reopens, the best place to see art performances in San Salvador is the **Teatro Presidente** (Final Av. La Revolución; ✆ **503/2243-3407**) located beside the Museo de Arte. The city's downtown **Casa de la Cultura** (Primera Calle Poniente No. 822; ✆ **503/2221-2016**) also has a small space with year-round performances and art exhibits.

The country's premier dance school **La Escuela Nacional de Danza** (1 Calle Poniente No. 1233; ✆ **503/2221-0972**) performs often in the Teatro Presidente and around the country. You can also find a nationwide arts calendar on the website of El Salvador's main arts organization, **Concultura** (✆ **503/2510-5320;** www.concultura.gob.sv).

Dance Clubs

Code ★ Code is less exclusive than Envy, but is the premier nightclub of the Zona Rosa nightlife district. It offers a huge dance floor, a dedicated, 25-and-older section, and great views from an upstairs glass wall and balcony. There's a $10 (£5) cover. Boulevard del Hipódromo, Zona Rosa. ✆ **503/2223-4770.**

Envy ★★ This two-level, flatscreen-TV-filled dance club in the Multiplaza mall is considered San Salvador's most exclusive spot, with three VIP lounges and expensive annual memberships required for El Salvadorans to enter. Foreigners pay $10 (£5) to dance under the stars of a retractable roof and get down to the sounds of an international cadre of DJs. This place has a great vibe and the dance floor is always packed. Multiplaza mall, Calle El Pedregal and Carretera Panamericana a Santa Ana. ✆ **503/2243-2576.**

503 Restaurant and Champagne Lounge ★ In the same building as Code, 503 is a really cool place to wind down the evening. The small, sleek lounge, decorated entirely in white, offers a diverse sushi menu, and is open until the wee hours of the morning on weekends. Boulevard del Hipódromo, Zona Rosa. ✆ **503/2223-4770.**

Stanza 6 ★ Next door to Envy is the much smaller, slightly more chill Stanza 6 lounge. It also has a $10 (£5) cover, DJs, and an exclusive, international club feel. But it's more intimate, with one level and couches for postdance conversations. Multiplaza mall, Calle El Pedregal and Carretera Panamericana a Santa Ana. ✆ **503/2243-7153.**

Live Music & Bars

La Cueva ★★ The tiny La Cueva—or the Cave—is a true bar among Multiplaza's high-end lounges and dance clubs. It's the place you go to have a beer and not worry how you look. It's small, with only a few two-top tables and a four-stool bar inside. But it has lots of outdoor seating, a great vibe, and each weekend features what usually ends up being two guys and a guitar. Multiplaza mall, Calle El Pedregal and Carretera Panamericana. ✆ **503/2243-7155.**

La Luna Casa de Arte ★★★ (Finds) Located off the Boulevard de Los Héreos, about a 10-minute taxi ride from that street's many nightlife spots, La Luna is worth the trip. This popular travelers' spot features live music ranging from 1980s metal to merengue and whatever other unique performances it can scrounge up. It's now well known among *extranjeros* or foreigners, but I've been there a bunch of times and it still somehow feels like a special find. Calle Berlín, Urbinazacíon Buenos Aires off the Boulevard de los Héreos. ✆ **503/2260-2921.**

Zanzibar ★ Zanzibar is a big, fun, open-air bar across the street from Code and overlooking Boulevard del Hipódromo. This is a great place to warm up your night. It's loud, friendly, and unpretentious. Local promoters also often stage DJ and live music events on the adjacent patio. Boulevard del Hipódromo, Zona Rosa. ✆ **503/2279-0833.**

5 SANTA ANA ★

64km (40 miles) W of San Salvador

Though El Salvador's charms aren't normally found in its crowded, hectic cities, Santa Ana's unique Gothic cathedral, ornate theater, and easy access to the country's most significant Maya ruin make it a place worth visiting.

Santa Ana, an easy, 40-minute drive west of San Salvador, is the country's second-largest city, with approximately 275,000 residents. Yet Santa Ana avoids the sprawling nature of San Salvador because most of its attractions are centered around the city's leafy main square, known as Parque Libertad. The city's main in-town attractions are its large, neo-Gothic cathedral and ornate and brightly painted theater. Both are among the county's more architecturally interesting landmarks. The plaza itself also offers a glimpse into old and new El Salvador with young, mohawk-sporting skate punks in stylish clothes mingling with older women in traditional dress.

Perhaps the best reason to visit Santa Anta is that El Salvador's most important Maya ruin, Tazumal, is only a 13km (8-mile) bus ride away. Santa Ana also offers the modern conveniences of bank machines, Internet outlets, and a super grocery store. Though it was once the county's most prosperous town, it now has some unsafe neighborhoods. The tourist-filled main plaza and its immediate surroundings are safe and well patrolled, however.

ESSENTIALS

Getting There

BY BUS From San Salvador, take bus no. 201 to Santa Ana's Metrocentro terminal (at 10a Av. Sur; no phone). The trip takes about 1 hour and 30 minutes and costs $1 to $1.50 (50p–75p).

Buses to and from Metapán (p. 277) leave from Santa Ana's Metrocentro terminal. Bus no. 218 to Tazumal leaves from the corner of 4a Av. Sur and 9a Calle Poniente. Lago de Coatepeque (p. 262) can be reached via bus no. 209 from either the Metrocentro terminal or in front of La Universidad Catolica de Occidente. All these buses leave approximately every 20 minutes, and rates start as low as 35¢ (20p).

BY CAR Simply follow the signs on your 1-hour drive west from San Salvador along the well-paved and well-marked Pan-American Highway, and you'll reach Santa Ana.

Orientation

Santa Ana is a large city but is easily navigated, as most everything you need is immediately on or near Parque Libertad (the center of the city). The main east-west thoroughfare near the central plaza is Calle Libertad Poniente, which becomes Libertad Oriente east of Parque Libertad. And the main north-south route is Avenida Independencia Sur, which becomes Independencia Norte north of the plaza. The character of the surrounding neighborhoods around Parque Libertad can change quickly, especially after dark, so don't wander too far off the main plaza.

Getting Around

BY BUS The only bus you'll likely take while in Santa Ana will be bus no. 51, which runs every 5 minutes from 8am to 10pm daily from the main square to the Metrocentro mall. Keep in mind that the main terminal at 10a Av. Sur is crowded and the buses there often take awhile to depart. Rates within the city run 25¢ (15p).

BY TAXI Taxis are easily found on or near Parque Libertad and cost $4 to $6 (£2–£3) to most parts of Santa Ana. Taxis are not easy to find off the main square, so you'll need to ask your hotel or restaurant to call you a cab in other areas of town; always take a taxi at night, even if it's just for a few blocks.

BY CAR Like San Salvador, it's best to park your car immediately upon arrival. Many of Santa Ana's streets are poorly marked, so it's easy to get lost. And the character of Santa Ana's neighborhoods can change abruptly, so you don't want to take too many wrong turns. Off-street parking is recommended.

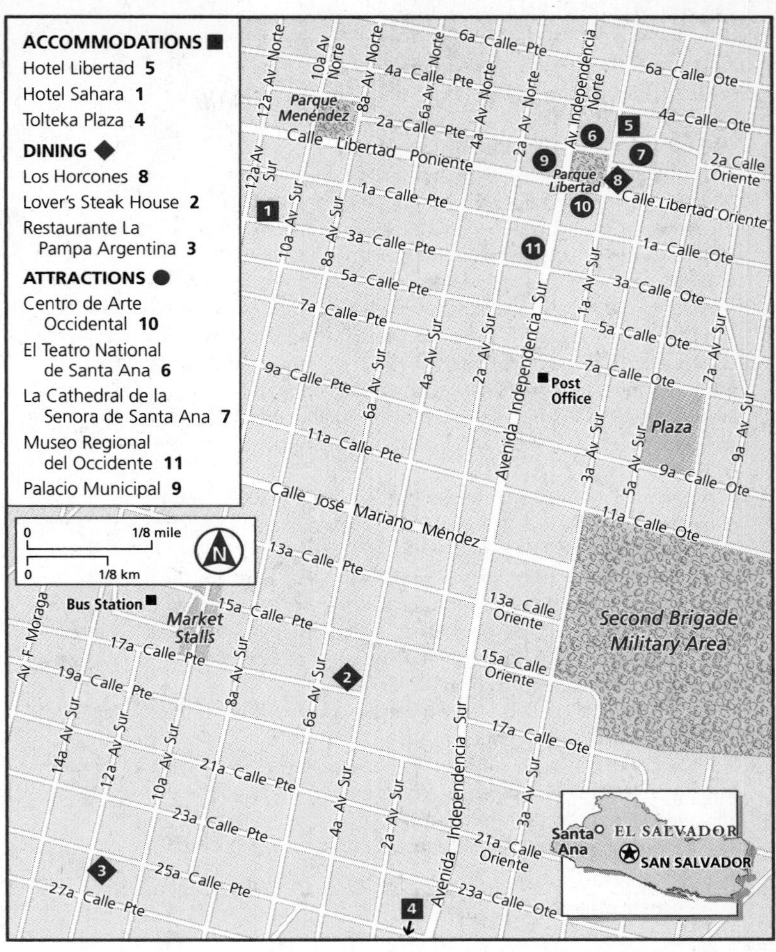

ON FOOT Most everything you'll want to see is right on Parque Libertad or within a couple of blocks of the square. You'll need a taxi to reach a few of the better hotels and restaurants in town, but otherwise you can easily walk from sight to sight.

Visitor Information

Santa Ana does not have a tourist office, so your best source of tourist information will be your hotel staff or an English-language tour guide provided by a company such as **Nahua Tours** (✆ **503/7874-8402**). If you speak Spanish, Santa Ana's **Casa de la Cultura** (2a Calle Poniente; ✆ **503/2447-0084**) can also provide information.

Defining MS-13

Throughout your trip in El Salvador, you'll likely hear the word "Mara" whispered in conversation, as if Maras are boogeymen. And in a way, they are. Mara refers to El Salvador's internationally notorious street gang Mara Salvatrucha or "MS-13." The name has a few meanings, depending on the person telling the story. Some people think the name hails from a combination of the words "Marabunta," which is the name of a fighting ant, and "Trucha," which means "cleverness." Others believe the name is derived from "Mara," meaning gang, and "Salvatrucha," referring to El Salvador's guerrilla fighters.

Whatever the origins of its name may be, MS-13 has transformed itself into one of the world's deadliest gangs, with chapters throughout the United States and Latin America. Mara Salvatrucha was formed in the 1980s in the barrios of Los Angeles by the sons of El Salvadoran immigrants fleeing the country's civil war. The gang is thought to have formed originally as a defense against vicious Los Angeles street gangs already in place. Today, with steady deportations of gang members back to El Salvador, MS-13 maintains a strong presence in the country.

Among MS-13's more notorious crimes were the 2004 slaughter of 28 bus passengers in Honduras and the 2003 killing outside Washington, D.C., of a 17-year-old girl who had agreed to testify against the gang. MS-13 crimes are often identified by their use of machetes to kill or maim their victims. In response to these crimes, El Salvador adopted strict gang-enforcement laws known as "Mano-Dura" or "hard hand," which resulted in hundreds of arrests and prison terms in the early 2000s. Those tactics, however, were later overturned as violations of human rights.

Today, the El Salvadoran government is continuing its efforts to decrease MS-13 influence via less controversial methods, and the majority of the violence has been confined to rival gang members' territories. Other than hearing the name "Maras" whispered in conversation, then, you're unlikely to be affected by this gang during your travels.

For more information about safety in El Salvador, see p. 244.

FAST FACTS Scotiabank is 1 block off the Parque Libertad behind the Municipal Palace at the corner of Calle Libertad and 2a Avenida Norte. The bank has two external ATMs. Internet access can be found at **SGD/Soluciones Graficas Digitales** (Calle Libertad Poniente; ✆ **503/2447-2750**), which is upstairs in a small shopping center on the southeast corner of the square, as well as at the national Internet chain **InfoCentros** (1a Calle Poniente and Av. Jose Matías Delgado; ✆ **503/2447-7750**).

Santa Ana's post office is 4 blocks south of the square at 7a Calle Poniente No. 30, near the corner of 7a Calle Poniente and Avenida Independencia Sur (✆ **503/2441-0084**). The city's main hospital, **Hospital Nacional Regional San Juan de Dios,** is at Final 13 Av. Sur No. 1. (✆ **503/2447-9037**). And an outlet of El Salvador's supercenter grocery store La Dispensa de Don Juan, which offers just about everything you won't find in smaller towns, is on Parque Libertad's southeast corner.

FESTIVALS

If you are in Santa Ana in July, you'll want to check out the "Fiestas Julias" or the July Festival. This month-long celebration involves parades, carnival rides, and music and is also known as Fiesta Patronal, since it honors the city's patron saint.

WHAT TO SEE & DO

Santa Ana's main attractions are its Gothic-style cathedral, old-world-style theater, and the nearby Maya ruins of Tazumal. Many also visit simply to stock up on supplies at the city's modern grocery store before heading north to the Parque Montecristo (p. 277).

Santa Ana's primary in-town attraction, **La Cathedral de la Señora de Santa Ana** (1a Av. Norte, Parque Libertad; ✆ **503/2447-7215;** free admission; Mon–Sat 6:30am–noon and 2–5:30pm, Sun 7am–noon and 2–5:30pm), offers a more elaborate, European, neo-Gothic style than El Salvador's traditional white, Spanish colonial churches. The cathedral, built between 1906 and 1913, features an exterior with lots of old-world-style nooks, crannies, and arches with bell towers on each side. The interior has grand columns and a beautiful marble altar.

El Teatro Nacional de Santa Ana (Parque Libertad; ✆ **503/2447-6268**) is not only one of El Salvador's most attractive buildings, but is also very likely its most lime green. The odd and nearly fluorescent exterior color is the first thing you'll notice about this theater, which opened in 1910 and features a grand balcony overlooking the square. Inside you'll find an ornate, old-world lobby leading to the grand, three-story theater, complete with elaborate molding and ceiling portraits of long-dead artists. Two rows of balconies line the walls and an intricate tile floor fronts that stage. The theater is open Monday to Friday from 8am to noon and 2 to 6pm, as well as Saturdays 8am to noon, with art performances and exhibits held year-round. Call the theater for performance dates and times. Shows cost 50¢ to $3 (25p–£1.50) or you can just take a look inside for a 50¢ (25p) admission fee.

The **Centro de Arte Occidental** (✆ **503/2447-6045**), opposite the Santa Ana theater, was once known to house an art museum, but now primarily offers arts classes to local children. You can poke around the mildly interesting building for free if you ask at the front desk. Two blocks southwest of the square, in the city's old Banco Central de Reserva building, is the **Museo Regional del Occidente** (Av. Independencia Sur No. 8; ✆ **503/2441-1215**) with rotating exhibits covering the natural, social and economic development of the western region, including a permanent, in-depth history of the country's currency. Admission is $1 (50p) and the museum is open Tuesday through Saturday from 9am to noon and 1 to 5pm.

Also on the square is the **Palacio Municipal,** which is Santa Ana's town hall and is usually filled with folks standing in line to do all the things one does at city hall. Though there's not much to see here overall, the palace's courtyard is surprisingly inviting and serves as a respite of peace and quiet from Santa Ana's more hectic main square. You can peek in for free from 8am to noon and 2 to 6pm Monday through Saturday. Another mildly interesting building into which you can peek, depending on your charm and language skills, is the **Casino Santaneco.** This private club across from the national theater features a swank, restored interior that's not open to the public but can be glimpsed if you manage to convince the guy at the front door to let you in.

Outside Santa Ana

Parque Arqueológico Casa Blanca **Overrated** Casa Blanca is a smaller Maya site worth seeing largely because it's a 5-minute taxi ride from Tazumal. Casa Blanca is basically a leafy park with a Spanish-language museum and a winding, 15-minute trail passing a few grassy mounds; one slightly excavated, two-story mound with exposed stone steps; and the park's main attraction, a roughly 9m-tall (30-ft.), partially excavated Maya pyramid. Casa Blanca isn't worth traveling all the way from Santa Ana to see, but as long as you're in the area you might as well stop by.

Km 74.5 on the bypass at the east entrance to Chalchuapa. ✆ **503/2408-4641.** Admission $3 (£1.50) adults. Tues–Sun 9am–4:30pm. Bus: 210 from Santa Ana or 218 from Santa Ana to Tazumal.

Sitio Archeologico Tazumal ★★★ If you had to choose only one ruin to visit in El Salvador, this should be it. Tazumal is the county's most visually interesting and fully excavated set of Maya ruins. Located 13km (8 miles) from Santa Ana, Tazumal, which means "the place where the victims were burned" in the early Quiche language, is the remains of a Maya community that inhabited the area from A.D. 100 to 1200. It's believed that Tazumal functioned as an important trading center, and that much of the site still remains unearthed. Most of the construction here is believed to have taken place from A.D. 400 to 680, and so there are signs of a definite Teotihuacan influence (the Mexican site reached its peak during the same period) in many structures.

On view today are 10 sq. km (6 sq. miles) of ruins, including a fully excavated Maya temple pyramid, ball court, and other structures considered to be classic examples of Maya architecture and similar to those found in other parts of Central America. The park also contains numerous other structures that archaeologists are leaving covered until proper funding and care can be ensured; in addition, officials are currently returning the main pyramid to its natural state via the removal of a ridiculous cement shell that was once thought protective but was later deemed unnecessary. Visitors are no longer allowed to climb any structures here due to damage from the 2001 earthquake.

The site also includes a small museum with a number of artifacts that indicate that this society was in contact with other Central American Maya communities. Though it's much smaller than better known ruins in Guatemala or Honduras, and requires only about 45 minutes to explore, Tazumal's importance to El Salvador's history and its exemplary Maya architecture make it worth the drive. Most tour companies such as the local company **Nahua Tours** (✆ **503/7874-8402**) and the larger **Eco Mayan Tours** (✆ **503/2298-2844;** www.ecomayantours.com) make stops here.

Entrance on Calle Tazumal in Chalchuapa. ✆ **503/2444-0010.** Admission $3 (£1.50) for adults, free for children 4 and under. Tues–Sun 9am–4pm. Bus: 218 from Santa Ana stops 547m (1,794 ft.) from the entrance.

SHOPPING

Though Santa Ana doesn't have any small shops worth mentioning, it does have a large modern shopping mall called **MetroCentro** (✆ **503/2440-6277**). It's on Final Avenida Independencia Sur and is open daily from 9am to 9pm.

WHERE TO STAY

Hotel Libertad ★ Value If you don't need anything fancy, stay here. Hotel Libertad is as bare-bones as it gets. There's no hot water, no Internet, and no restaurant. But it's safe, clean, and just one block off Parque Libertad—which means it's mere minutes away from the cathedral, theater, restaurants, and most of what you'll need in Santa Ana. Because Parque Libertad is Santa Ana's tourist center, the area is also safe and well patrolled by police. Yes, the hotel will not exactly grace the pages of interior design magazines, but it's well maintained and the staff will go out of their way to meet your demands. When booking a room, ask for room no. 15 or 16, both of which are upstairs and farthest away from the lobby.

4a Calle Oriente No. 2, 1 block north of the square (near the corner of Calle Oriente and 1a Av. Norte). ✆ **503/2441-2358.** 12 units. $12–$20 (£6–£10) double. No credit cards. *In room:* Fan, TV, no phone.

Hotel Sahara ★ Overrated Despite its 50-year reputation as Santa Ana's grand hotel, Saraha really isn't that great. Hotel Tolteka Plaza offers more amenities and Hotel Libertad is a lot cheaper. But when you combine location and comfort, Sahara ekes out a victory. It's only 5 blocks from Parque Libertad, offers the convenience of a full-service restaurant and Wi-Fi, and has a pleasant rooftop deck. The rooms are only of average size and the bathrooms even smaller; request room no. 204, which is the biggest overall or room no. 215, which offers the most peace and quiet. The area between the hotel and the main square bustles with a street market during the day but is deserted and can be dangerous at night. Always have the front desk call you a cab after dark.

3a Calle Poniente btw. Av. Sur and Av. José Matías Delgado. ✆ **503/2447-8865.** Fax 503/2447-0456. hotel_sahara@yahoo.com. 30 units. $44–$58 (£22–£29) double. Rates include full breakfast. AE, DC, DISC, MC, V. **Amenities:** Restaurant. *In room:* A/C, TV, Wi-Fi.

Tolteka Plaza ★ Tolteka is Santa Ana's most modern and luxurious hotel option. The rooms are larger than you might expect and the hotel offers a rare-outside-San-Salvador hot water heating system (rather than the usual electronic shower heads). There's also an inviting courtyard pool, Wi-Fi, and a full-service restaurant. The hotel is just a short taxi ride or long walk to the Metrocentro bus terminal, which also means it's about a 10-minute cab ride to Parque Libertad. As part of a national hotel chain, the Tolteka also has a rather corporate feel, with no unique charm and no interesting decor. When booking, try to reserve room no. 101, 106, 201, 219, or 220, as they overlook the pool and are farthest from street noise. The English-speaking staff can arrange tours or a taxi to Parque Libertad.

Av. Independencia Sur. ✆ **503/2487-1000.** Fax 503/2479-0868. www.hoteleselsalvador.com/in-tolteka.htm. 50 units. $59–$71 (£30–£36). AE, DC, DISC, MC, V. **Amenities:** Restaurant; bar; nonsmoking rooms; pool; room service; Wi-Fi in lobby. *In room:* A/C, TV, hair dryer.

WHERE TO DINE

Los Horcones ★ SALVADORAN This laid-back, two-story restaurant and bar is a great place to end the day with a cold beer, comfort food, and a nice view from its upstairs deck overlooking Parque Libertad. The reasonably priced comfort food menu is simple but large, featuring the usual grilled steak, chicken, and fish dishes with salad, rice, and tortillas. You can also find tasty sandwiches and tacos for under $5 (£2.50). Though Los Horcones roughly translates as "the pitchforks," the restaurant's downstairs is inexplicably decorated not with farming furnishings, but with decades-old telephones, a 1970s-era Atari game console, a 1.8m-long (6-ft.) stuffed fish, and a nearly antique DVD player.

1a Av. Norte on Parque Libertad. ✆ **503/2484-7511.** Main courses $5–$11 (£2.50–£5.50). No credit cards. Daily 10:30am–9pm.

Lover's Steak House ★★ Kids STEAK Lover's Steak House is nearly as tasty as its rival La Pampa but with a more casual, family-friendly atmosphere. Bench seating and beer-brand advertising set the laid-back tone of this 16-year-old restaurant. The English and Spanish menu is larger than La Pampa and includes North American comfort food such as chicken wings, hamburgers, and a club sandwich. Portions are also larger, with bigger baked potatoes and lots of vegetables. Since Lover's and La Pampa are about evenly priced and both require a taxi ride, your choice depends on your mood. If you want an upscale, romantic dinner, head to La Pampa. If you have a talkative group, a few kids, or just want a casual vibe, Lover's is the better choice.

4a Av. Sur and 17 Calle Poniente. ✆ **503/2440-5717.** Reservations required for groups of 10 or more. Main courses $9–$22 (£4.50–£11). AE, DC, DISC, MC, V. Sun–Thurs 11am–10pm; Fri–Sat 11am–11pm.

Restaurante La Pampa Argentina ★★★ STEAK/ARGENTINE La Pampa steakhouse is by far Santa Ana's finest restaurant and it serves what is likely to be one of the tastiest steaks you'll have in El Salvador. Opened in summer 2007, the restaurant is styled after and shares a menu with the well-known San Salvador steakhouse of the same name. You'll need a taxi and a few minutes to get here, but it's worth the trip. The modern, hacienda-style interior is elegant but comfortable, with tables far enough apart to allow for quiet conversation. Upstairs seating overlooks the main dining room and includes two, small outdoor terraces. The service is outstanding and on par with that at San Salvador's finest restaurants, with Spanish-speaking waiters able to explain the intricacies of the steaks and cuts. The menu offers 15 steak and sausage options along with fish and chicken dishes, but the specialty of the house is the 224-gram (8-oz.) *entraña,* or skirt-cut steak. Every large steak platter is served with salad, vegetables, potatoes, and a delicious beef consume.

25 Calle Poniente btw. 10a and 12a Av. Sur. ✆ **503/2406-1001.** Reservations recommended. Main courses $9.10–$23 (£4.55–£12). AE, DC, DISC, MC, V. Mon–Thurs 11am–3pm and 6–10pm; Fri–Sun 11:30am–11:30pm.

6 LAGO DE COATEPEQUE ★★

18km (11 miles) S of Santa Ana; 56km (35 miles) W of San Salvador

Lago de Coatepeque, an almost perfectly round crater-lake that is 740m (2,428 ft.) above sea level, makes for one of El Salvador's most beautiful and enjoyable getaways. The lake is a short drive from Santa Ana, which means it's an easy day trip from that town—but it's really worth staying a couple of days here to enjoy all its attractions; the 23-sq.-km (9-sq.-mile) pristine lake is ideal for swimming, fishing, riding watercraft, and simply soaking in beautiful views.

Lago Coatepeque was formed thousands of years ago by the eruption of the nearby ancient volcano, the Coatepeque Caldera. Today, the lake's rich blue waters and lush, tree-filled crater walls serve as a weekend getaway for El Salvador's rich and famous, whose mansions line the shore. Luckily, those rich and famous folks left a roughly 500m (1,640-ft.) section open to the public, which is now filled with restaurants and hotels offering tours, watercraft rentals, and fishing piers. There's little lake access other than through these hotels or restaurants, but most allow single-day use of their piers for a small fee. Perhaps the highlight of any visit here, though, is the sunsets: Each evening, visitors line the hotel piers with cameras ready to capture classic and captivating photos of the sun dipping below the crater walls.

ESSENTIALS

Getting There

BY BUS From Santa Ana (p. 255), take bus no. 209 or 220. From San Salvador (p. 236), take bus no. 201. Tell the driver you want to head to Lago Coatepeque and he'll let you off anywhere you wish along the lake's strip of hotels and restaurants. The ride from Santa Ana takes a little less than 1 hour; the ride takes an hour and a half from San Salvador.

BY CAR From San Salvador, travel west and from Santa Ana travel east along the well-paved Pan-American Highway and follow the well-marked signs to the lake. After reaching the lake area, you'll drive slowly down a winding dirt road along the crater wall to the water. Lago Coatepeque includes only one small section of hotels, so if you get lost, just say, "Los Hoteles?" and locals will point you in the right direction.

Orientation & Getting Around

The majority of Lago Coatepeque's hotels and restaurants are located along a single, approximately 500m (1,640-ft.) stretch of the lake. A dirt road rings the lake and is lined with a nearly unbroken stretch of high, cement walls hiding the lake houses of the nation's wealthy.

The best way to get around this area is by foot; the hotels and restaurants are clustered within walking distance of one another, and some great views can be had by taking a long stroll around the lake. If you are driving, keep in mind that the dirt road around the lake is rocky and best navigated by truck or four-wheel-drive.

You'll need to call a taxi, such as the local company **Taxi Leo** (© **503/2502-2495**) in advance to take you to Santa Ana or the region's other attractions, since taxis can't be hailed on the street.

Visitor Information

Lago Coatepeque doesn't have a visitor center, so your best source of information will be hotel staff or tour companies such as Santa Ana–based, bilingual, **Nahua Tours** (© **503/7874-8402**). The closest **national tourist office** is along the Ruta de las Flores 1km (1/2 mile) east of the town of Nahuizalco (Km 71, Nahuizalco; © **503/2453-1082;** Mon–Fri 8am–5pm and Sat–Sun 8am–4pm). You can also call the national tourist office in San Salvador (© **503/2243-7835**) for info.

There are no bank machines, Internet cafes, or large stores in the area.

WHAT TO SEE & DO

Lago de Coatepeque is primarily a place to lounge by the water, take a swim, or just enjoy the view. For day trippers, the best deal is the $2 (£1) per day fee to use the pier and $4 (£2) per hour kayak rental offered at Hostal Amacuilco (see below). Or stop by Restaurante Las Palmeras (see below), which offers $70 (£35) per hour motorized watercraft rental and 30-minute-to-3-hour lake tours for $25 to $80 (£13–£40).

WHERE TO STAY

Lago de Coatepeque can be a great place to base your exploration of this part of the country, because the archaeological sites of Tazumal, San Andres, and Joya de Cerén, as well as the hiking trails and vistas of Parque Nacional Los Volcanes, are all within 1 hour's drive. Below are your best accommodations options.

Hostal Amacuilco ★ **Value** If you like a laid-back hostel vibe, you'll love Amacuilco. Amacuilco offers nearly everything you'll find at Villa Serena and Torremolinos, only cheaper and with less formality. This small (there are just five rooms), family-friendly hostal sits right on the water and has a lake-view restaurant, a pier, and the most gardenlike setting of all the lake's hotels. Its rooms—including two private rooms every bit as pleasant as those at Torremolinos—are spread among leafy grounds and include a dorm room directly over the water with great views. Amacuilco also offers guests free kayak use and Internet access, as well as a comfortable lounge area with TV. Like most hostals, Amacuilco isn't perfect and could use some paint here and there. But it's cheap, friendly, and offers all the necessities you'll find at the lake's more expensive hotels. A 5-day Spanish course, including food and lodging, is also available for $120 (£60).

Calle Principal. ✆ **503/7822-4051.** amacuilcohostal@hotmail.com. 5 units. $23–$30 (£12–£15) private rooms; $7 (£3.50) per bed in dorm rooms; $4 (£2) camping. No credit cards. **Amenities:** Restaurant; dune buggy rental; Internet (in lobby); free kayak rental; room service. *In room:* A/C (in some), fan.

Hotel Torremolinos Torremolinos is kind of like the resort in the movie *Dirty Dancing*—it has the look and feel of a grand 1950s-era Catskills hotel. Unfortunately, the '50s were a long time ago and, today, this once grand hotel remains charming but very dated. The rooms seem to have been decorated 20 years ago with whatever mismatching items were lying around, the bathrooms aren't attractive, and there's no Internet. On the plus side, the hotel's lakefront property offers cozy gardens, lounge areas with wrought-iron tables and chairs, two pools, and a two-story pier restaurant over the water with nice breezes and great views. Torremolinos is also less expensive than Villa Serena and its restaurant offers the tastiest food on the lake. So if you prefer character over modern amenities and new furniture, Torremolinos is your place.

Calle Principal. ✆ **503/2441-6037.** hoteltorremolinos@gmail.com. 16 units. $32–$47 (£16–£24) 2 to 4 beds per room. Rates include continental breakfast. AE, DC, DISC, MC, V. **Amenities:** Restaurant and bar; canoe, jet ski, and kayak rental; laundry service; nonsmoking rooms; pool. *In room:* A/C, fan, TV (in some), fridge (in some).

Hotel Villa Serena ★ Opened in late 2007, Villa Serena is Lago Coateqeque's most modern and expensive option, so it should be your choice in town if you prefer fancy amenities like Wi-Fi and solar-powered, piping hot showers. The hotel boasts five modern, adequate-sized rooms with sparkling tiled bathrooms, as well as a comfortable seating and hammock area with lake views. There's no restaurant, but breakfast is included and nearby restaurants can deliver. The hotel fills up quickly on weekends, so book in advance; try to ask for room no. 4, which offers the best view. Note that Villa Serena's $25 (£13) per hour kayak rental and $25 (£13) per day charge for non-guests to use the pier are overpriced; nearby Hostal Amacuilco rents kayaks for $4 (£2) per hour and non-guests use its facilities for $2 (£1) per day.

Calle Principal. ✆ **503/2260-7544.** www.hotelvillaserena.com.sv/lcoatepeque. 5 units. $73 (£37) double. Rates include breakfast. AE, DC, MC, V. **Amenities:** Airport transfers ($15); kayak and pedal-boat rental; all rooms nonsmoking; spa. *In room:* A/C, fan.

WHERE TO DINE

Restaurante Barde La Rioja ★★ SALVADORAN This restaurant inside the Hotel Torremolinos (see above) has the best service, food, and ambience on the lake—though the hotel might be a bit dated, its restaurant has definitely kept pace with its grand reputation. Torremolinos offers two large seating areas; you can choose between a main hall with arched columns overlooking the hotel grounds and lake, and a two-story pier sitting high off the water with great views and afternoon breezes. The specialties of the house are the tasty cream of crab soup and lake fish stuffed with shrimp. As with many fine Central American restaurants, diners get a tiny sample appetizer to nibble before the main entrée. Prices are slightly lower than the area's other two large restaurants. The main dining room features live music Sunday afternoons from 1pm to 5pm.

Natural Disasters

El Salvador hasn't had much luck over the last decade when it comes to natural disasters. Perhaps its most well-known such disaster is Hurricane Mitch, which stalled over Central America in October and early November 1998. The hurricane's historic rainfalls caused flooding in El Salvador that killed 374 people and rendered more than 55,000 homeless. The hurricane was also a huge economic setback since it caused major losses to agricultural harvests and road damage due to mudslides, and almost completely destroyed El Salvador's entire eastern region.

Mitch was followed 3 years later by two massive earthquakes on January 13 and February 13, 2001, which measured 7.6 and 6.6 on the Richter scale. The earthquakes and their accompanying landslides damaged thousands of buildings, killed more than 1,000 people, and injured approximately 8,000. Thousands more were left homeless. The country is still recovering from these disasters; for instance, at press time El Salvador's National Theater remained closed due to earthquake damage. Finally, in October 2005, the Volcán de Santa Ana erupted, killing two people and closing the mountain to the public until March 2008. See "A Side Trip to Parque Nacional Los Volcanes" below for more info on this.

Many believe the effects of these natural disasters were made worse by El Salvador's severe deforestation, which is the result of years of exploitive coffee and sugar growing practices and has claimed up to 92% of the country's primary forests. The county's leading environmental groups, **SalvaNatura** (33 Av. Sur 640, Colonia Flor Blanca, San Salvador; ✆ **503/2279-1515;** www.salvanatura.org) and **Ministerio de Medio Ambiente and Recursos Naturales,** Km 5.5 Carretera a Santa Tecla, Calle and Colonia Las Mercedes, Building MARN No. 2, San Salvador; ✆ **503/2267-6276;** www.marn.gob.sv), are now working to implement sustainable agricultural methods. Contact either organization for info on how you can help out.

Calle Principal. ✆ **503/2441-6037.** Main courses \$4.50–\$12 (£2.25–£6); breakfast \$3.50–\$4 (£1.75–£2). AE, DC, DISC, MC, V. Daily 8am–9pm.

Restaurante Las Palmeras (Kids) SALVADORAN Palmeras is a great place to hang out during the day and have a snack or cold beer, but when it's time for dinner, head to the Restaurante Barde La Rioja. This restaurant is the lake's newest and flashiest, featuring dining spaces under a thatched hut and on a bamboo-style pier. You can't go wrong with the chicken sandwich with fries, the garlic shrimp appetizer, or Caesar salad. Though the dinner menu is extensive, with more than 20 fish, beef, and chicken dishes, and the management maintains a family-friendly atmosphere, the entrees are a bit expensive and not as tasty as those at Barde La Rioja.

Calle Principal. ✆ **503/7248-5727.** Main courses \$8–\$20 (£4–£10). AE, DC, MC, V. Daily 7am–9pm.

Restaurante Rancho Alegre SALVADORAN Alegre is Palmeras' older, slightly run-down but less expensive, and every bit as tasty neighbor. The two restaurants have nearly identical fish, beef, and chicken dishes, and are both situated on long piers over the water. But Alegre is not as flashy as Palmeras and its pier has begun to show signs of age. (Renovations were underway at press time.) This appears to be the restaurant of choice for El Salvadorans, though, no doubt because the locals are drawn by the cheap, delicious cuisine. Menu highlights include a delicious $5 (£2.50) Salvadoran breakfast of eggs, beans, cheese, and platano. The restaurant offers rooms for rent as well, but they aren't recommended.

Calle Principal, by Las Palmeras. ✆ **503/2441-6071.** Main courses $6–$15 (£3–£7.50). V. Daily 9am–8pm.

A SIDE TRIP TO PARQUE NACIONAL LOS VOLCANES ★★

Parque Nacional Los Volcanes is the informal name given to the 4,500 hectares (11,110 acres) of private and public lands 8km (5 miles) southwest of Lago de Coatepeque, which are home to the steep and barren Volcán Izalco, the highest volcano in El Salvador, the recently active Volcán de Santa Ana, and the green hills of Cerro Verde.

The park, known officially as Parque Nacional Cerro Verde, is centered around a parking lot near the top of Cerro Verde Mountain, from which visitors set off on challenging, 4-hour round-trip hikes to both Volcán Santa Ana and Volcán de Izalco. An easy 35-minute hike near the summit of Cerro Verde also begins and ends at the parking lot. If you love to hike, this park offers some of the most interesting and convenient treks in the country.

Volcán Santa Ana is the third-highest point in the nation and one of its most active volcanoes; in October 2005 an eruption here killed two people, disrupted numerous villages, and spewed huge volcanic boulders up to a mile away. The eruption closed the volcano to hikers for 3 years, but officials reopened the mountain in March 2008. The 4-hour hike to the 2,381m (7,811-ft.) summit is strenuous, but visitors will be rewarded with stunning views of Lago de Coatepeque. The climb is difficult and you'll need to be in shape, but it's the easier of the park's two major hikes.

Volcán de Izalco is the park's most visually dramatic volcano and challenging climb, requiring a nearly 3-hour scramble up a steep, rocky, and barren moonscape to the 1,952m (6,404-ft.) summit. Izaco is also one of Central America's youngest volcanoes—it formed in 1770 and erupted almost continuously until 1966. The eruptions were said to be so violent that they could be seen be sailors at sea; hence, the volcano was nicknamed the "Lighthouse of the Pacific." Today, the summit is a nearly perfect cone and its spare, blackish landscape stands in sharp contrast to the lushness of the surrounding hills.

Climbing Izalco is only for those in good physical shape. And no matter how physically fit you are, you can't do both climbs in 1 day. All hikes in the park must be led by a guide and guided hikes with a minimum of three people leave the parking lot only once daily at 11am.

Essentials

GETTING THERE & GETTING AROUND From Santa Ana, take bus no. 248, which stops at the park entrance near the parking lot. Buses leave Santa Ana at 8:30am on Tuesday through Thursday and 7:30am Friday through Sunday. They return daily at 3pm. From San Salvador, take a bus directly to Santa Ana (see p. 255 for info) and then follow the directions above, or get off short of Santa Ana in El Congo and ask the driver to direct you to the spot where you can catch the no. 248 bus to the park.

If you're driving from San Salvador, follow Hwy. CA-8 to the exit for El Congo. After exiting, turn right at the gas station. Follow that road until you turn left at the sign for Cerro Verde. The road will dead-end into the Cerro Verde parking lot. From Santa Ana, follow Hwy. CA-1 to the exit for Lake Coatepeque. Almost immediately after exiting, turn left onto Hwy. CA-8. Follow this road until you turn right at the sign for Cerro Verde, after which point the road will dead-end into the park's lot.

VISITOR INFORMATION Park information is available from park administrator **SalvaNatura** (33 Av. Sur 640, Colonia Flor Blanca, San Salvador; ✆ **503/2279-1515;** www.salvanatura.org). The park is open daily 8am to 5pm, but you'll need to arrive before 11am to secure a guide to hike one of the volcanoes; groups meet at the small building in the parking lot that says "Caseta de Guias." Admission is $1 (50p) and the guides work for tips. A small *comedor* serving *pupusas,* roasted chicken, and rice is located in the far corner of the parking lot.

Where to Stay Nearby

Lago de Coatepeque and Santa Ana are both less than 30km (19 miles) away, so you can easily base your trip to Parque Nacional Los Volcanes out of one of those two areas. But, if you want to stay overnight so that you can hike both volcanoes, the best option is nearby Campo Bello, which offers little white igloo-looking cabins, a camping area, and great views of Volcán de Izalco. SalvaNatura (see above) also offers cabins and rooms just off Cerro Verde's parking lot.

Cabañas Campo Bello ★★ (Finds) Located just 20 minutes from the Parque Nacional Los Volcanes, Campo Bello stands out as the most surreal but stunning accommodations choice in the area—seven small, bright white, cement igloos with differently colored, brightly painted doors dot the property, which is backed by a near eye-level view of Volcán de Izalco's rim. Each spare but comfortable igloo features two small bedrooms and a bathroom. Igloo no. 1 offers the best view of the volcano. One-bedroom cabins and tent campsites are also available, and Campo Bello provides tips-only guided tours of both volcanoes from the hotel property.

To get to Campo Bello, veer right at the Campo Bello sign off the main road toward the Cerro Verde parking lot. You'll then need a four-wheel drive during rainy season or a high ground-clearance truck the rest of the year to drive the remaining 15 minutes to the hotel. You can also take the no. 248 bus here; simply tell the driver to let you off at the road for Campo Bello.

At the entrance to Parque Nacional Cerro Verde. ✆ **503/7729-3712** or 2271-0853. Fax 503/2222-1861. www.campobello.com.sv. 14 units. $22 (£11) for 2-person cabins; $35 (£18) for 4-person igloo cabins. No credit cards. **Amenities:** Barbeque pits; volcano tours. *In room:* No phone.

7 RUTA DE LAS FLORES ★★★

Hwy. CA-8, Km 72 to Km 107, starts 68km (42 miles) W of San Salvador

The Ruta de las Flores, or Route of the Flowers, is a collection of five unique mountain villages along a winding, 35km (22-mile) scenic stretch of Hwy. CA-8 in the heart of El Salvador's coffee country. The route is known for the beauty of its flowering coffee plants and unique arts, crafts, and furniture markets, and highlights include the village of Nahuizalco and its hand-crafted furniture; Salcoatitán, with two of the route's more interesting restaurants; and Juayúa, which features the region's largest food and artisan festival as well as a renowned black Christ statue. The route also includes the towns of Apaneca, known for its zip-line canopy tour, and Ataco, which is filled with some of the country's most unique art.

The towns along this route are a few kilometers apart, well marked, and only a short distance off the main highway. The highway itself also offers a few interesting hotels and restaurants. Though all five towns can be seen in one long day or two, you might want to schedule a few days to properly take in the vibe of one of the country's most scenic and culturally unique regions.

ESSENTIALS

Getting There

The first stop on the Ruta de las Flores, Nahuizalco, is 5km (3 miles) from Sonsonate and 68km (42 miles) from San Salvador. To get there from San Salvador, take bus no. 205 to Sonsonate followed by bus no. 249, 23, or 53d. Bus nos. 249 and 23 stop about 1km (1/2 mile) from the center of Nahuizalco but continue into the heart of each of the routes other villages. Bus no. 53d travels only between Sonsonate and Nahuizalco.

Each of the buses mentioned runs daily from roughly 5am to 6pm and costs between 25¢ (15p) and $1 (50p). The 205 bus from San Salvador runs about every 30 minutes, while the local buses come along about every 10 minutes.

It's easy to drive this route: Each of the towns along the way are just a few minutes off main Hwy. CA-8 and are very well marked.

Getting Around

Bus nos. 249 and 23 will take you from just outside Nahuizalco to each of the route's small towns. Once in each town you'll be able to walk to whatever you'd like to see, except for the few hotels and restaurants that are scattered along the main highway. Las Rutas does not offer any taxis, but taxi driver **Israel Rodriguez** (✆ **503/7734-7598**) in Sonsonate can take you from Sonsonate to Las Rutas and from town to town along the route for $15 to $25 (£7.50–£13). Juayúa also offers three-wheeled moto-taxis, which you'll find along the square and which will take you anywhere in Juayúa for less than $1 (50p).

VISITOR INFORMATION

A national tourist office branch (✆ **503/2453-1082**) is at Km 71 on Hwy. CA-8 1km (1/2 mile) east of Nahuizalco. Tourist office staff speak only Spanish, but offer some bilingual pamphlets and brochures about the area. Office hours are Monday to Friday from 8am to 5pm and Saturday and Sunday from 8am to 4pm.

FAST FACTS Make sure you stock up on cash in Juayúa, which is the only town along the Ruta de las Flores with a bank machine. Most vendors and restaurants accept only cash in all five Ruta de las Flores towns. Internet access is available in Juayúa at **Nautilus Cyber** (Calle Merceditas Cáceres and 2a Av. Norte; ✆ **503/2452-2343**) and in Ataco at **Cyber Nautica** (2a Calle Poniente No. 5, Barrio Santa Lucia; ✆ **503/2450-5719**). Small pharmacies are located in Juayúa near the main square.

NAHUIZALCO

Nahuizalco is the first stop on the Ruta de las Flores and offers one of the country's best furniture and wood craft markets. Unlike most El Salvadoran markets, which sell Fernando Llort–inspired arts and crafts (see p. 247 for info), Nahuizalco's market, situated along the town's main road every weekend, is known for its unique wicker and wood

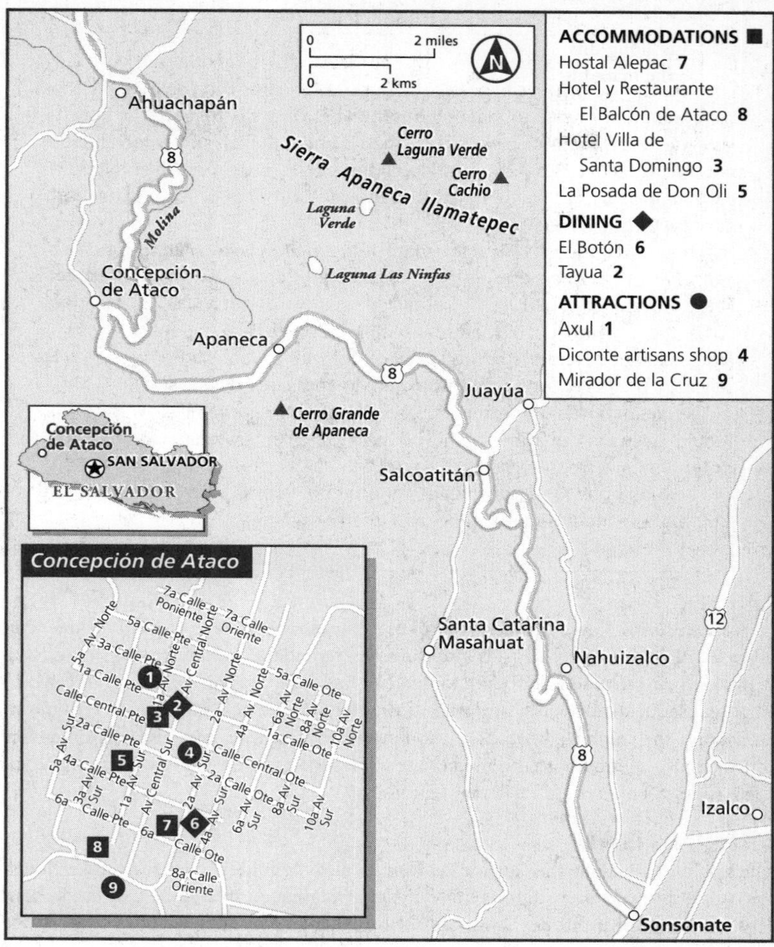

furniture creations. Many of the wares sold at the weekend market can be found during the week in the shops also lining the main road. One of the best of those shops is **Arte y Mueble**, or Art and Furniture (© **503/2453-0125**). The shop's furniture is handcrafted by owner Jose Luis, whose creations are a mix of spare, modern lines and sturdier, dark wood, nature-inspired designs. The store, which can arrange shipping around the world, is open Tuesday through Sunday from 10am to 5pm. Another shop worth checking out is **Artesanias Cassal** (© **503/2453-0939;** open daily from 8am–6pm), which offers interesting wooden masks, jewelry, and art. Finally, about half a block before Nahuizalco's church and square, on the right, is a building with a large, open door, allowing passersby to watch artisans handcraft furniture.

Sonsonate

Sonsonate (65km/40 miles west of San Salvador) is mentioned here only because it is the largest city before the Ruta de las Flores and you'll likely either bus through or catch a connecting bus from here in order to reach the Ruta de las Flores. Sonsonate is not a city you should visit for fun. It's crowded and just not that attractive. But it can be a good place to stock up on cash at the HSBC Bank or groceries at the large La Dispensa de Don Juan grocery store, both right on the main square.

If you find yourself with a few hours here while you're waiting for a bus, Sonsonate does have one redeeming quality—**Parque Acuatico Atecozol.** This is a huge water park located about 10 minutes (about a $5/£2.50 taxi ride) out of the city with lots of shady gardenlike places to relax, a pool-side restaurant, a kids' pool, and the biggest public pool with a water slide I've seen in El Salvador. The park is open daily from 8am to 4pm and admission is 80¢ (40p).

The quaint hotels of the Ruta de las Flores are only a few miles away, so you should really drive on there, but if you have to stay in Sonsonate, try the **Plaza Hotel** (9a Calle Oriente, Barrio El Angel, btw. Av. Nortes 8a and 10a; ✆ **503/2451-6628;** hotelplaza_sonsonate@yahoo.com). Rooms are $35 to $45 (£18–£23), and the hotel features a pool and Internet access.

Nahuizalco is 72km (45 miles) west of San Salvador and is well marked off the main highway. A single main road leads into town and terminates at Nahuizalco's small cathedral and square. The square offers a fountain, a few shady seating spots, and an English-language plaque that lists a short town history. Note that one of Nahuizalco's well-known attractions, the "candlelight market," no longer exists, at least in its old form. Vendors added electric light bulbs to this market a few years ago and now sell mostly family necessities, so it's been rendered unworthy of a visit.

SALCOATITÁN

The second town along the Ruta de las Flores is also the route's smallest village. Though Salcoatitán is pleasant enough, there's no compelling reason to stop here; it takes about 30 seconds to drive through town and Nahuizalco and Juayúa's weekend markets are larger and more interesting. About 2 blocks before Salcoatitán, however, are two of the route's more interesting restaurants, Los Patios and Los Churrascos de Don Rafa.

Los Patios (Calle Principal, 2 blocks east of Salcoatitán; ✆ **503/2401-8590**) is an upscale, modern hacienda-style eatery that opened in October 2007. The restaurant's mountain-view patio overlooks thousands of coffee beans laid out to dry and the machinery used to process them. Los Patios is a bit pricier than other area eateries at roughly $12 (£6) an entree, but the food and ambience are worth the price. The restaurant's owner is also an abstract El Salvadoran sculptor who displays and sells her works from a gallery beside the restaurant.

Immediately across the street, a completely different dining experience can be had at **Los Churrascos de Don Rafa** (✆ **503/2401-8570**). Los Churrascos is an outdoor steakhouse and artisans' shop owned by the colorful local couple Mario Rafeal Burgos and his wife, Anna. Mario, who has a degree in hotel and restaurant management, mans the outdoor grill while chatting with customers in French, Italian, English, and Spanish, while Anna sells her artwork and that of 21 other artisans from a small shop on site. There's no menu, but the standard one-dish offering is a big piece of chargrilled steak, vegetables, and potato or rice, for just $8 (£4). The whole operation is entirely outdoors, so if it's raining, Los Churrascos will be closed.

JUAYUA

Next up is the Ruta de las Flores' largest, most bustling town, offering the region's longest running weekend food and artisan festival as well as mountain and coffee plantation tours. Juayúa is a good place to base your Ruta de las Flores stay, as it is roughly in the middle of the route and boasts hotels, restaurants, and a bank machine in addition to its attractions.

Each Saturday and Sunday here, the large main plaza fills with locals and travelers enjoying daylong live music, dozens of artisan vendors, and a dozen or so food vendors who, for more than a decade, have been frying everything from *pupusas* to chicken tenders. It's a fun, family-friendly atmosphere worth planning your Ruta de las Flores trip around.

Juayúa is perhaps best known for its "Black Christ" statue, which sits above the altar of the **Iglesia de Cristo Negro** cathedral on the main square. Visually, the black Christ looks just like a regular Christ statue painted black. But the concept of the black Christ dates back hundreds of years and is revered throughout Central America via annual black Christ celebrations, including a Juayúa festival each January 6 to January 15. La Iglesia is open daily from 6am to noon and 2 to 6pm, and admission is free.

Guided tours based out of Juayúa take hikers through coffee plantations, past towering waterfalls—including the well known Los Chorros de la Calera—and up to natural hot springs and geysers. Bring a bathing suit, and prepare to get muddy (the mud at the hot springs is supposed to be good for the skin). Tours usually leave early in the morning, range from 5 to 7 hours, and cost $7 to $20 (£3.50–£10). For tour information, visit **Hotel Anáhuac** (1a Calle Poniente and 5a Av. Norte; ✆ **503/2469-2401**). This is Juayúa's best hotel, offering a laid-back, family-friendly, hostal-style environment with six shared and private rooms ranging from $15 (£7.50) for one person to $45 (£23) for four, along with a communal kitchen. The bilingual staff also has lots of information about the route and surrounding areas. A clean, comfortable, and just-off-the-main-square alternative option is **Hotel Y Restaurante El Mirador** (4a Calle Poniente on the left just as you enter town; ✆ **503/2452-2432**). The rooms here are $15 (£7.50) per person, and are basic but comfortable and efficient, with private baths. Perhaps Mirador's best features are its friendly staff and its airy, top-floor, glass-enclosed sitting and dining areas, which have incredible views.

Among the better places to eat in Juayúa is **Restaurante R&R** (2 blocks off the main square at Calle Merceditas Cáceres No. 1–2; ✆ **503/2452-2083**). English-speaking, El Salvadoran chef Carlos Cáceres has created a little Louisiana-style steak house in the midst of the El Salvadoran mountains, and the menu features spicy takes on Tequila, Texas, and New Orleans–style steaks. The Texas steak is amazing. A veggie plate is also available and most items are $3.50 to $10 (£1.75–£5). A little farther from the main square but worth the 10-minute walk from it is **Parque Restaurante La Colina** (Km 82 Carretera a Juayúa; ✆ **503/2452-2916**), which offers excellent—and hard to find—fajitas, along with other Mexican dishes and a host of grilled fish and meat dishes. Most entrees are $4.50 to $9.50 (£2.25–£4.75).

APANECA

Continuing down CA-8 to Km 91, you'll find the small village of Apaneca, which is surrounded by hills of flowering coffee plants and has become best known in the last couple of years for its high-wire, zip-line canopy tour. Information about Apaneca can be found at the local **Casa de la Cultura** (Av. 15 de Abril Sur and Calle Francisco Manendez Oriente, Barrio San Pedro; ✆ **503/2433-0163**).

Apaneca Canopy Tours (Av. 15 de Abril and Calle Central; ✆ **503/2433-0554;** www.apanecanopy.com.sv), which has an office in the center of town, offers 1-hour and 1½-hour zip-line tours, in which participants zip on steel cables hundreds of feet off the ground, over lush forests and a nearby coffee plantation. The company offers 13 cables that are roughly 1,800m (5,906 ft.) above sea level; its longest cable stretches 280m (919 ft.) and the highest is 125m (492 ft.) off the ground. During April and May, or coffee flowering season, thousands of white coffee flowers cover the fields below the tour and in January and February, or harvest season, the flowers are replaced by bright, red berries. All year-round, tour participants can see all the way to Guatemala's active Pacaya Volcano from the highest perch. Also included in the tour is a half-hour walk through a local coffee plantation during which an English-speaking guide explains the elements of the coffee plant and the growing process. The canopy tour even includes some locally grown brew to cap off your experience.

Tours are $30 (£15), and leave from the tour office Tuesday from Sunday at 9:30am, 11:30am, 3pm, and 7pm from June through October and 7 days a week the rest of the year. It's best to make an appointment in advance, but you can also just show up at the times stated above to see if you can get a spot. Off-road **motorcycle and bicycling tours** can also be arranged through Apaneca Canopy Tours.

The best place to stay and eat in town is **Hotel y Restaurante Las Cabañas** (Km 91 Hwy. CA-8, Apaneca; ✆ **503/2433-0500**). This 15-cabin hotel is owned by the same artist owner as Salcoatitlán's Los Patios restaurant (see above) and she has applied the same artistic eye for detail here to create a lush, secluded, garden setting dotted with individual cabins with shady front patios. The cabins themselves are plain, without an overarching design theme, but they are slightly larger than average, comfortable, and cost just $52 (£26) a night. Las Cabañas is immediately on Hwy. CA-8 and just a few blocks walk from the Apaneca town center.

ATACO ★★★

Ataco is my favorite stop along the Ruta de las Flores—it boasts an artistic style and vibe you really won't find elsewhere in the country.

The first thing you may notice about Ataco is the unique, fantastical murals of surreal animals with big eyes and wild hair painted on some of the town's buildings. These whimsical murals set the tone for the town and are the work of young married artists Cristina Pineda and Alvaro Orellana. Their designs, also available on wood, ceramic, and traditional canvas in Ataco's shops, are unlike artwork you'll see anywhere in El Salvador. The couple's main gallery is called **Axul** (1a Calle Poniente and 1a Av. Norte No. 5; ✆ **503/2450-5030**) and is just off the main square. The shop is marked by a fanciful mural on the outside and offers the couple's signature surreal style in various formats. You can chat with Pineda and Orellana and watch other artists at work in the back of the shop daily from 9am to 6pm.

Another of Ataco's attractions is the **Diconte artisans shop** (2 Av. Norte and Calle Central Oriente No. 8; ✆ **503/2450-5030;** ring the doorbell to enter the shop on weekdays), which is part art shop, part textile mill, and part dessert bistro. Diconte offers five rooms of whimsical woodcarvings, paintings, and other crafts in the unique Ataco style as well as a room of colorful textiles made on-site by artisans working five old-style looms. Visitors can watch the textile artisans at work from Diconte's garden-style dessert and coffee shop.

If you want to take a break from art shopping, hike up to the town's **Mirador de la Cruz.** The Mirador is a mountain overlook located a 15-minute hike from the main square. To get there, walk 5 blocks south from the church along 2a Avenida Norte, which becomes 2a Avenida Sur after crossing Calle Central. Continue walking until the road bends to the right. At the bend is a Catholic church, behind which are steps to the overlook. At the end of the steps, turn right, walk through an opening in the fence, and follow the trail to the cross that marks the top of the hill. The hike up to the top is steep but paved, and you'll be rewarded with a great view, some benches to relax on, and a small plaque with information (in English) about Ataco.

Where to Stay & Dine

In addition to the hotels reviewed below, Ataco has two hotels that are open on the weekends only. **Hotel Villa de Santa Domingo** (1 Av. Norte No. 6 in front of the Casa de la Cultura; ✆ **503/2450-5242**) is a good midrange choice offering an 11-room hacienda-style hotel around a main courtyard with a small restaurant and comfortable \$25-to-\$35 (£13–£18) rooms. On Friday and Saturdays only, you can also stay at the well-known, but slightly overrated—they have scaled back operations in recent years and service seems a bit lackluster now—**La Posada de Don Oli** (1a Av. Sur No. 6; ✆ **503/2450-5155**). This half private home and half hotel offers a restaurant and three standard rooms situated around a courtyard, for \$28 (£14). Ask for one of the upstairs rooms with a balcony for the best deal.

One big reason Ataco is my top Ruta de las Flores pick is its unique restaurants. **El Botón** (2a Av. Sur No. 19; ✆ **503/2450-5066**) features a rare-in–El Salvador find of quiche and crepes along with empanadas, coffee, and beer in a whimsical, little French-style button shop/restaurant. **Tayua** (Av. Central Norte No. 31; no phone), which means "for the night" in El Salvador's indigenous Nahautl tongue, offers a small but surprising sandwich, salad, and pasta menu. Standout items include the El Democratico sandwich, with mushrooms and Gruyère cheese on a baguette, and the El Variado—perhaps El Salvador's tastiest sandwich—with black forest ham, salami, and Gouda cheese on a baguette. Salads, pastas, and sandwiches range from \$4 to \$8 (£2–£4). The place has a cool Asian-style decor and is open daily from 10am until customers leave, which is often in the wee hours of the morning on weekends.

Hostal Alepac ★ This little friendly hostal has Ataco's best accommodations. Like many of El Salvador's hostels, it's not fancy. It features two private rooms with nice-size beds, in addition to three dorm rooms with multiple beds, all situated around a private and sunny courtyard and shared bathrooms. But what Alapec lacks in space and amenities it makes up for in community. It's the best place in town to meet other travelers; the young, enthusiastic owner, Alejandro, speaks enough English to provide tourist information and to pass an evening in the courtyard sharing a cold beer or two with his guests. The hostel is also kept spotless by a maid who comes daily, and it offers a full kitchen and dining room, as well as a TV lounge. It's about a 5-minute walk up the hill from the main square and within 2 blocks of El Botón restaurant.

Secunda Av. Sur Final. ✆ **503/2450-5344.** 5 units. \$15–\$20 (£7.50–£10) private room; \$7 (£3.50) dorm bed. No credit cards. **Amenities:** Kitchen; TV lounge. *In room:* No phone.

Hotel y Restaurante El Balcón de Ataco ★ At more than double the price of Hostal Alapec (just a few minutes away), El Balcón is definitely Ataco's luxury option. But the price just might be worth it, as this small six-room hotel is perched on the side of a hill high above town, with room-front balconies offering long-range views of the town and surrounding mountains. The hotel opened in 2007, so the rooms have a modern feel; they're also unusually sunny and offer the convenience of in-room Wi-Fi. There's a full-service restaurant on-site, as well. If you don't want to experience a laid-back hostel vibe and prefer a few more amenities, you should definitely stay here over the Alapec.

8a Calle Oriente and Calle el Naranjito. ✆ **503/2450-5171.** elbalcondeataco@gmail.com. 6 units. $35–$45 (£18–£23). Rates include full breakfast. AE, DC, DISC, MC, V. **Amenities:** Restaurant. *In room:* TV, no phone, Wi-Fi.

AHUACHAPÁN

Like Sonsonate, Ahuachapán (44km/27 miles west of Sonsonate and 16km/10 miles off the route's main CA-8 highway) is technically part of the Ruta de las Flores, but as the busy capital of this department, it is more a place to grab some cash or check your e-mail before heading elsewhere rather than a destination in its own right. Ahuachapán is, however, known for its high level of geothermal activity, and visitors here can tour nearby Los Ausoles, a multiacre gathering of gurgling, steaming pits of superheated mud and water, as well as check out the inside of a nearby power plant that transforms that subterranean heat into electricity. **Eco Mayan Tours** (Paseo General Escalón 3658, Colonia Escalón, San Salvador; ✆ **503/2298-2844;** www.ecomayantours.com) provides tours to the pits—including a chance to roast corn on the cob over them—and a tour of the plant. Tours are $30 (£15) from Ahuachapán or $75 (£38) to and from San Salvador.

Unlike Sonsonate, there are also some sights to see right in town. **Plaza Concordia** (3a Calle Poniente, btw. Av. Menendez and 4a Norte) is the more pleasant of the city's two plazas, which are both just 5 blocks apart on the main street, Avenida Menedez. Concordia Plaza is home to Ahuachapán's plain, main cathedral, **Nuestra Señora La Asunción,** which is known for its interesting stained-glass windows (I don't think they're that spectacular, though). The other main church in town, **Iglesia El Calvario,** is 5 blocks down from the Plaza Concordia on Avenida Menendez, and sports a similarly spartan exterior to the Nuestra Señora.

Most buses arrive and depart town from a crowded section of 10a Calle Oriente, a few minutes moto-taxi ride from Plaza Concordia. A **Scotiabank** is at Avenida Menendez and 4 Calle Poniente, and there's Internet access at **Ciber Café Cetcomp** (2a Av. Sur at 1a Calle Poniente; ✆ **503/2413-3753**).

ALONG CA8 HIGHWAY

The main highway that links the route's little towns also offers a few hotels and restaurants worth considering. The best value, and most beautifully situated, stay along the highway is **El Jardin de Celeste** (Km 94, btw. Apaneca and Ataco; ✆ **503/2433-0277**). This small, 10-cabin hotel and restaurant is set up like a secret garden, with cabins spread among winding, flower-filled paths. The three-to-five-person cabins range from $40 to $63 (£20–£32) and include front porches with hammocks, barbecue grills, and, depending on the cabin, kitchens, dining rooms, and living rooms. Celeste also offers cabins and a coffee shop with cappuccino about a mile east along CA-8, called **Las Flores de Eloisa Lugares Mágicos.**

The highway also offers two luxury options, the **Santa Lucia Hotel and Resort** (Km 86.5 Hwy. CA-8 just outside Apaneca; ✆ **503/24433-0357**) and **Alicante Montaña**

Hotel (Km 93.3 Carretera CA-8 btw. Juayúa and Ataco; ✆ **503/2433-0572**). Santa Lucia is the more luxurious of the two—the 19-room hotel offers a restaurant, pool, children's playground, and tours of a coffee plantation and small nearby archaeological site. Alicante offers a few more amenities than Santa Lucia, with a big Jacuzzi and sauna, exercise room, and massage spa along with an outdoor pool, but it's a bit sterile. Though Alicante has nice views, they've cut down too many trees and it's too close to the highway for the vibe here to be as charming as that at Santa Lucia. Since both hotels cost roughly the same ($71–$80/£36–£40 per night), unless if you really want a sauna, you should stay at the Santa Lucia.

8 TACUBA & PARQUE NACIONAL EL IMPOSIBLE ★★

60km (42 miles) W of Sonsonate; 100km (62 miles) W of San Salvador

Tacuba is a small town in far western El Salvador that hugs the edge of the 3,278-hectare (8,100-acre) Parque Nacional El Imposible and serves as base camp for treks into the park. In addition to boasting great views of the surrounding mountains and volcanoes and a pretty central plaza, Tacuba has enough *tiendas* to keep you stocked up on food and drink and happy after a long day's hike. This area until recently had very few tourists, however, and it's still slowly developing its infrastructure. Currently, there are no banks or ATMs and only two viable lodging options, so plan your accommodations in advance and bring all the cash you'll need.

ESSENTIALS

Getting There & Getting Around

Buses coming to Tacuba from around El Salvador first feed into nearby Ahuachapán, where you can then catch bus no. 264 or one of the many buses with TACUBA written across the top. You'll be dropped off a couple of blocks from Tacuba's town square. From San Salvador to Ahuachapán, take bus no. 202; from Santa Ana to Ahuachapán, take bus no. 210, and from Sonsonate to Ahuachapán, take bus no. 249.

From San Salvador, you can drive the Pan-American Highway (Carretera Panamericana) in the north or CA-8 along the Ruta de las Flores in the south to the town of Ahuachapán. In Ahuachapán, look for Parque Concordia and the white church there, where you'll see a sign directing you onto the road for Tacuba. The drive from Ahuachapán takes about 30 minutes.

Tacuba is a very small town, and most everything is within a short walk of the main square.

Visitor Information

Tacuba does not have a tourist office, so the best source of information is local English-speaking guide **Manolo Gonzales** (✆ **503/2417-4268;** www.imposibletours.com)—he's one of the best guides in the whole region. If you speak Spanish, information is also available at Tacuba's **Casa de la Cultura** (1a Calle Oriente and Av. España, 1 block south of the Alcaldía; ✆ **503/2417-4453**).

FAST FACTS Tacuba has no banks or ATMs, so bring cash. But Tacuba's main street, Avenida Cuscatlán Sur, south of the square, offers a few small tiendas and shops with signs reading CIBER, where there are a few Internet-access computer stations.

EXPLORING PARQUE NACIONAL EL IMPOSIBLE ★★

Parque Imposible is one of El Salvador's most lush and most diverse forests and should be a definite stop for nature lovers. The 3,278-hectare (8,100-acre) park derives its name from its challenging terrain and once-dangerous gorge, which for years claimed the lives of men who traversed the area transporting coffee crops to the south. A bridge was built over the gorge in the 1960s and the forest was declared a national park in 1989. Today, the park is home to more than 400 types of trees, 275 species of birds, and hundreds of species of butterflies. Pumas, wild pigs, and 100 types of mammals, many on the endangered species list, make their home in the park along with more than 50 kinds of reptiles and amphibians. In addition to ample opportunities to spot wildlife, visitors can easily spend days hiking trails through the thick forests, swimming in the natural pools, and jumping off the waterfalls here.

Park admission is $6 (£3) per person. All visitors must first register with park administrator **SalvaNatura** (33 Av. Sur No. 640, Colonia Flor Blanca, San Salvador; ✆ **503/2279-1515;** www.salvanatura.org) to secure a guide and get permission to enter the park. SalvaNatura also offers $10 (£5) per day Spanish-language guides and $40 (£20) day trips from San Salvador including transportation, a Spanish-speaking guide, and entrance fee.

The official park entrance is on the park's south side near the community of San Miguelito. To enter from the south, beginning in Sonsonate, catch bus no. 24-HAS to Cara Sucia. In Cara Sucia, you can catch a $1 (50p) pickup ride the remaining 45 minutes to the park. The pickups leave Cara Sucia at 6:30am, 8am, 10am, 12:30pm, and 2:30pm. They leave the park to return to Cara Sucia at 7am, 9am, 11am, noon, and 2pm. You can also make the drive yourself, but the road is very bumpy and requires a four-wheel-drive or truck with good ground clearance.

Most travelers, however, prefer to enter the park from Tacuba. Since there is no official northern entrance, it's easiest to go with Tacuba's well-known, English-speaking guide Manolo Gonzales. Thirty-something Manolo is the owner of **Imposible tours** (Av. Cuscatlán near Calle 10, Tacuba; ✆ **503/2417-4268;** www.imposibletours.com) and the son of the owners of Hostal de Mama y Papa (see below). Manolo offers 6-to-8-hour day and night tours into the park for $20 (£10) per person including the entrance fee. His most popular tour is an 8-hour waterfall tour, which involves hiking for hours deep into the jungle and jumping from waterfalls ranging from 2 to 12m (6½–39 ft.) in height. On this tour, you'll have to jump or be lowered down the highest waterfall in addition to taking part in hours of rigorous hiking. If you're out of shape or afraid of heights, the tour may not be for you.

Manolo offers an easier $20 (£10) coffee plantation and hot springs tour in which participants witness the entire coffee cultivation process from field to factory, or bean to cup, and then head into the mountains to spend the afternoon soaking in hot springs. There's also a 2-day bicycle tour in which participants are driven to the highest point in the park and ride bicycles down through the jungle all the way to the Pacific Ocean. The rock-bottom $55 (£28) cost includes round-trip transportation from Tacuba, dinner and drinks at the beach, breakfast, lunch, and a kayak tour, along with stops at some towns along the Ruta de las Flores. Other tours include a night animal-watching tour and a tour in which you're driven to the park's highest point before hiking down to a natural swimming pool. Try to call at least 2 days in advance to schedule tours.

WHERE TO STAY

In addition to the below hotel options in Tacuba, Parque Nacional el Imposible offers three campsites for $4 (£2) per night and a hostal, **Hostal El Imposible** (Mariso Sandoval;

✆ **503/2411-5484**) with five, six-person cabins located 800m (2,624 ft.) from the park entrance, for $15 (£7.50) per person.

Hostal de Mama y Papa ★ This small, well-known hostal lives up to its reputation as the place to stay in Tacuba. The setting is lush and gardenlike, with a few hillside rooms offering patios and views. Numerous animals run around the place and there's an actual Mama and Papa tending to the property who'll make you feel right at home. (Mama also runs the hostel's restaurant about 91m [298 ft.] down the road.) As with many of the country's small, independently run hotels, don't expect state-of-the-art rooms or fancy decor. The rooms are average size and the bathrooms are merely functional. But the vibe is friendly and you'll get to hang out with the English-speaking guide Manolo (see "Exploring Parque Nacional El Imposible" above) who lives here. Note that the guest rooms have no locks, but the owners can lock valuables outside.

Av. Cuscatlán near Calle 10. ✆ **503/2417-4268.** 5 units. $6 (£3) per bed in dorms; $15 (£8) per person private rooms. No credit cards. **Amenities:** Restaurant nearby; kitchen. *In room:* Fan upon request, no phone.

Las Cabañas de Tacuba Hotel y Restaurante Las Cabañas is where you should stay if Mama y Papa's is already booked. It's certainly nice enough, but not as handy as a base camp for trips into Parque Imposible; hotel staff will actually tell you to go to Mama y Papa's for any info about the park. Though the property consists of just a few rooms contained in pretty nondescript buildings, the grassy grounds of the hotel are pleasant and there's a big pool (which was being repaired at press time) and open-air restaurant. All the rooms are nothing special in terms of size or ambience, though the newer "cabins" beside the pool are the best value.

1a Calle Poniente, roughly 90m (300 ft.) down the hill from the Alcaldía, Barrio San Nicolas. ✆ **503/2417-4332.** 12 units. $35–$45 (£18–£23) double. Rates include full breakfast. V. **Amenities:** Restaurant; pool. *In room:* Fan, TV.

WHERE TO DINE

El Restaurante de Mamá y Papá ★ Value SALVADORAN This small, laid-back joint half a block or so from the hostel of the same name has no written menu, but Mama has the ingredients to fix you up pretty much whatever comfort food you crave. For lunch or dinner, usually she'll prepare a variety of roasted chicken with french fries or tacos, hamburgers, or hot dogs for around $5 (£2.50). For breakfast, she might cook you a big omelet with whatever veggies are available that day, or a large traditional breakfast of eggs, cream, cheese, beans, and fruit for $6 (£3). Beer is just $1 (50p) and they usually stay open later to accommodate any late-night drinkers.

10a Calle Poniente and Av. Cuscatlán Sur near the Hostal de Mama y Papa. ✆ **503/2417-4268.** Main courses $4–$6 (£2–£3); breakfast $3 (£1.50). No credit cards. Daily 7am–9pm.

9 PARQUE MONTECRISTO & LAGO DE GUIJA

46km (29 miles) N of Santa Ana

Metapán is a medium-size city in El Salvador's far northwest corner that serves as a good base for trips to the beautiful Parque Montecristo cloud forest and to the relatively unexplored but gorgeous Lago de Guija. Though Metapán offers a quaint church and plaza, the primary reason to visit it is so that you can arrange transportation to the park.

ESSENTIALS

GETTING THERE & GETTING AROUND The entrance to Parque Montecristo is approximately 16km (10 miles) and a 40-minute drive north of Metapán. Buses don't run to the park, so to arrange transportation, you'll need to go to the bus depot next door to Hotel San Jose (see "Where to Stay & Dine," below) where you'll find numerous pickup trucks waiting to take you to the park. A 1-day round-trip pickup ride is about $55 (£28).

To get to Lago de Guija from Metapán, take bus no. 235, which leaves about every 10 minutes from the terminal next to the Hotel San Jose (see "Where to Stay & Dine," below). Tell the driver "Lago de Güija" and you'll get off about 5 blocks from the lake, beside a small, bright blue building and a sign reading PLAYA TURISTA with an arrow pointing to a road on the right. Follow that road to the lake.

If you're driving, turn left out of the Hotel San Jose and drive past the bus terminal on your left for about 10 minutes until you see the PLAYA TURISTA sign. Turn right and follow the road to the water. The pickups that take travelers to Parque Monticristo also run the route to the lake for $10 (£5) each way.

VISITOR INFO & FAST FACTS There's a **Scotiabank** (✆ **503/2402-0039**) at Avenida Ignacio Gomez, with a 24-hour ATM. The **Hospital Nacional Metapán Arturo Morales** (✆ **503/2442-0184**) is on Carr Principal, 400m (131 ft.) south of the town's entrance. For Internet access, head to **Ciber Café** (✆ **503/2442-4029**) on 2 Av. Sur.

WHAT TO SEE & DO

Exploring Parque Montecristo

Parque Nacional de Montecristo is a 1,972-hectare (4,874-acre) protected reserve tucked high in El Salvador's mountains, bordering Honduras and Guatemala. (The park's highest point, known as Punto Trifinio, actually extends into Honduras and Guatemala and reaches 2,400m/7,874 ft.) It features some of the country's most lush forests and most diverse flora and fauna, including dozens of orchid species and numerous rare birds like toucans, quetzals, and striped owls. Wild pigs, spider monkeys, coyotes, and other wildlife also inhabit the park but aren't so easily spotted.

The best time to visit the park is right after rainy season when the park is at its most lush. Year-round, though, the region's high humidity and low hanging clouds give the park its mystical cloud forest feel and maintain its perpetually cool, damp environment, which hovers between 42°F and 64°F (6°–18°C). The thick canopy provided by the towering laurel and oak forests also provides the dark cover necessary for an array of orchids, mosses, lichens, and ferns to thrive here. The garden, De Cien Anos, offers Montecristo's best orchid viewing and is an hour's drive (on bumpy, gravel road) from the park entrance. This garden, which is 1,798m (5,900 ft.) above sea level, is open daily from 8am to noon and 1:30pm to 3pm. Montecristo also offers an historic hacienda-style house and a museum with an odd collection of objects ranging from a 3.5m-tall (12-ft.) model of a lookout tower to various animal skulls, along with info about the park's fauna. The museum is open daily from 8am to 3pm.

Los Planes and Montecristo's higher-altitude cloud forests are open November 1 through April 30 from 7am to 3pm daily. Those areas are closed May 1 through October 31 to foster breeding. The rest of the park, including the museum, is open year-round. All visitors must receive prior permission to enter the park from Montecristo's administrative offices at the **Ministerio de Medio Ambiente y Recursos Naturales** (Km 5.5

Carretera a Santa Tecla, Calle and Colonia Las Mercedes, Bldg. MARN No. 2, San Salvador; ✆ **503/2267-6276;** www.marn.gob.sv). Hiking without a guide is prohibited beyond the immediate camping and cabin areas, since the trails are not well marked and it's easy to get lost in the haze of the cloud forest.

The park rents cooking burners, gas stoves, and outdoor barbecue grills for $35 (£18) per night and camping sites for $3 to $6 (£1.50–£3) per night. Dorm beds in an old colonial house near the park entrance with a big, shady front porch are $10 (£5) per night. To reserve a room, call the **Ministerio de Medio Ambiente y Recursos Naturales** (✆ **503/2267-6276**) or the park's main tour guide **Carlos Gutierres Mejiá** (✆ **503/7201-7557**). Carlos speaks only Spanish but can reserve sleeping space, lead guided hikes, or arrange transportation from the park entrance to its higher altitudes.

Exploring Lago de Güija

Also nearby Metapán is the stunningly beautiful Lago de Güija and the marshlands of Lagunas de Metapán. The deep blue Lago de Güija is a 45-sq.-km (17-sq.-mile) lake straddling the El Salvadoran and Guatemalan borders whose shores are lined with largely undeveloped fishing villages and whose waters are dotted with islands where pre-Columbian artifacts were uncovered nearly 85 years ago. The lake's main attractions are its unspoiled beauty and lack of tourist infrastructure. You won't find any info kiosks here. You can just wander the shore until you find a local fisherman who'll take you out on the lake, where you can soak in outstanding views of the surrounding inactive lakeside volcanoes.

If you need to make more concrete plans, call local Spanish-speaking fisherman and tourist boat owner **Pedro San Doval** (✆ **503/2483-9949**) in advance to arrange a tour for about $25 (£13) per hour. **La Perla** (✆ **503/2415-6490**) can set up a boat trip across the border for lunch in a small Guatemalan village for about the same cost.

WHERE TO STAY & DINE

The most convenient place to stay in Metapán if you're heading to Parque Montecristo is **Hotel San Jose** (Carretera Internaciónal 113; ✆ **503/2442-0056**). The hotel is across the street from a small bus terminal and the collection of pickup trucks that take you to the park. It's also within a block of a couple of sandwich shops and next door to the large Supermercado de Todo, where you can stock up on supplies before heading out on any hikes. The 27-room Hotel San Jose is the only high-rise hotel in Metapán, and costs from $35 to $47 (£17–£24) for an average-size room with balcony.

The most enjoyable place to stay in the area, however, is the new **Restaurante y Cabanas La Perla** (Canton Las Piedras, Caserio, Azacualpa; ✆ **503/2415-6490** or 310/880-9782 in the U.S.; www.laperladeazacualpa.com), which is right on Lake Guija, about 20 minutes outside Metapán. This small, four-room hotel, which opened in March 2008, offers gorgeous views of the lake, pedal boats for rent, and a boat that will take you across the lake for lunch in a small Guatemalan village. La Perla features large modern rooms with two queen-size beds for only $35 (£17) per night, a big pool with a poolside bar, and a restaurant with Salvadoran classics and American comfort food ranging from $5 to $7.50 (£2.50–£3.75). The rooms also feature rooftop decks overlooking the water. The hotel provides free round-trip transportation from Metapán with advance reservations. If you don't mind adding 20 minutes to your ride to Montecristo or want to spend a few days on the lake, you should stay here.

10 SUCHITOTO ★★★

47km (29 miles) N of San Salvador

Suchitoto was a volatile and fought-over territory during El Salvador's civil war, and many battles unfolded on the nearby mountain and former guerrilla stronghold of Cerro Guazapa. But Suchitoto has since recovered and remade itself into one of El Salvador's premier scenic and arts destinations. With a mix of international arts, upscale boutique hotels, natural beauty, and famously friendly people, it's now a place where you might plan on coming for a day but end up staying for a week.

This small, walkable town and surrounding area offer camera-ready mountain views, and a charming main square filled on weekends with locals and visitors enjoying the weekly market. The town has also become an international arts center, with the opening of galleries by an array of international owners and the 2000 renovation of Suchitoto's Teatro Las Ruinas, which hosts an annual international arts festival. Over the last few years, some of El Salvador's finest boutique hotels, including the exquisitely designed Los Almendros and Las Puertas on the main square, have made the town a shopping destination, too.

When you consider all the opportunities for day trips, like boat rides on the country's largest man-made lake, **Lago Suchitlán,** and tours to a historic village called **Cinquera,** it becomes obvious that Suchitoto is one of El Salvador's must-go destinations. Since it's centrally located, it's also an excellent spot to base yourself during any extended trip to the country.

ESSENTIALS

Getting There

From San Salvador, take bus no. 129 from Terminal de Oriente (p. 236). Buses leave every 15 minutes, cost 80¢ (40p), and arrive in 1 hour and 45 minutes. Buses stop 1½ blocks from the main square.

If you're driving from San Salvador, follow the Pan-American Highway (Carretera Panamericana) past Lago Ilopango until you see the sign for San Martin. Take the San Martin exit and follow it to the Plaza Central, where you will find signs leading you the remaining 28km (17 miles) to Suchitoto.

Orientation & Getting Around

Most of what you'll want to see in Suchitoto is within a 5-minute walk of the central plaza, known as Parque Centenario. The town is small and walkable, and its streets are quiet and largely traffic free. Avenida 15 de Septiembre runs north-south in front of the plaza and 2A Calle Oriente runs east-west by the plaza, becoming 2a Calle Poniente west of the plaza. Lago Suchitlán is an easy, 30-minute stroll out of town along Avenida 15 de Septiembre but a tough 45-minute climb back.

A ferry also transports cars and people across Lago Suchitlán to the north daily from roughly 7am to 5pm for $7 (£3.50) per car and $2 (£1) per person. To get to the launching area, turn left just before the Turistico Puerto San Juan tourist center and follow the dirt road down to the lake.

Visitor Information

Visitor information is easy to come by in Suchitoto. For the formal scoop, head to the **tourist office** (Av. Francisco Morazán, 2 blocks off the main square; © **503/2335-1782**), which is open daily from 8am to noon and 1pm to 4pm. The office has an English-speaking staff that can offer tips on Suchitoto's attractions and hands out town maps. For a locals' perspective, sit a spell with a cup of coffee on the porch of **Artex Café** (✆ **503/2335-1440**) on the southeast corner of the square. Eventually you'll be joined by an assortment of expats, business owners, and other characters, who come here to use the Internet, enjoy a pastry, or simply pass the time.

The town also has one official English-speaking guide, **Rene Barbón** (✆ **503/7118-1999** or 2335-1679; vistacongasuchi@yahoo.com), who offers excellent outdoor adventure and history tours. Finally, local restaurant owner and English expat **Robert Broz** (✆ **503/2327-2351;** rpbroz@gmail.com) will be more than happy to give you the low-down on town and maybe a ride in his pickup truck around town.

FAST FACTS Suchitoto has only one ATM, which is on the square. Since this ATM doesn't accept all bank cards, it's a good idea to bring all the money you'll need in advance of your stay. Air-conditioned, $1 (50p) per-hour Internet service is available at the **Info-Centros chain** (Calle Francisco Morazán on the main square; ✆ **503/2335-1835**). The **post office** (✆ **503/2304-0104**) is on the other side of the square from InfoCentros, near the corner of Avenida 15 de Septiembre and 2a Calle Oriente.

For health emergencies, you can head to **Hospital Nacional de Suchitoto** (Av. José María Pérez Fernández; ✆ **503/2335-1062**). **Farmacia Santa Lucía** (✆ **503/2335-1063**) is just off the square at Avenida 5 de Noviembre and Francisco Morazán.

WHAT TO SEE & DO

Suchitoto is known as much for its mountain scenery and artsy vibe as for its formal attractions. You can easily spend the morning savoring an Argentine feast prepared by a local sculptor and the afternoon listening to the sounds of thousands of migrating birds on the county's largest man-made lake. You can hike waterfalls and learn of the horrible realities of El Salvador's civil war. Or you can just sit and enjoy the charming square and colorful weekend artisans' market. For some more structured options, though, you may want to consider the following tours.

English-speaking tour guide **Rene Barbón** (✆ **503/2335-1679** or 7118-1999; vistacongasuchi@yahoo.com) offers an array of tours that provide an excellent sense of the region's history and natural beauty. Rene's most popular outing is a 6-hour trip that involves hiking in the 3,921-hectare (9,690-acre) Parque Ecológico de Cinquera and visiting the historic civil war village of Cinquera. The tour also includes a 1½-hour presentation by Cinquera resident Don Pablo, translated by Rene, who gives a firsthand account of the gruesome realities of the civil war. Other tours featured include a 3-hour hike to a nearby waterfall, horseback riding, and nighttime animal-watching tours, as well as a 5-hour flat-water canoe paddling tour. Tours range from $15 to $30 (£7.50–£15).

Eco Tourism La Mora (✆ **503/2323-6874;** www.ecoturismolamora.es.tl) offers Spanish-only hiking and horseback tours to nearby Volcán Guazapa, also known as Cerro Guazapa. This 1,435m (4,707-ft.) mountain is home to 200 plant species and 27 types of birds, as well as many types of butterflies and reptiles. According to some, you can still spot small bomb craters left over from the war here. Two- to 5-hour tours cost $10 to $40 (£5–£20)

You can also take a 2-hour **Historic Building Walking Tour** via the Suchitoto tourist office (Av. Francisco Morazán; ✆ **503/2335-1782**). This tour consists of visits to 32 historic Suchitoto buildings, including the former homes of three presidents and a former convent now serving as an arts center. The tour can be booked with 24 hours notice, and it costs $10 (£5) for 1 to 5 people, and $15 (£7.50) for 5 to 20.

Attractions in Town

In addition the below attractions, be aware that there's a small art museum called the **Casa Museo de Alejandro Cotto** in town, though its hours are so irregular, it can't be considered an official tourist site.

Iglesia Santa Lucia ★ Santa Lucia church is one of El Salvador's premier examples of colonial architecture. Its brilliant white facade, set against a startling green mountain backdrop, is one of the first things visitors see upon arrival into town, and its dark, rich wood interior packs some serious history. The altar is made of elaborately carved wood, and 36 tall wood beams run down the sides of the long, narrow church. Santa Lucia also features numerous life-size statues encased in glass and a small, pen-and-ink drawing of a crying Jesus. It doesn't match the grandeur of Santa Ana's Gothic cathedral (p. 259) but it's one of the country's more beautiful and traditional churches.

Parque Centenario btw. Calle San Marco and 2a Calle Oriente. No phone. Free admission. Daily 8am–noon and 1–6pm.

La Casa del Escultor ★★ The Argentine sculptor Miguel Martino is one of numerous artists who are currently reinventing Suchitoto as an international arts center—but he's the only one who also happens to be a mean cook. In addition to his fine woodworking art, Miguel is well known for his Sunday afternoon Argentine feasts, which take place at his gallery La Casa del Escultor, 2 blocks off the main square. From noon to 4:30pm each Sunday, Miguel prepares huge quantities of Argentine beef and vegetables on a wood-burning grill inside his studio and gallery for the first 30 to 35 people who show up. He then closes the doors and everyone proceeds to drink Argentine wine and talk art or whatever comes up. Plates include five kinds of meats or five types of veggies. Reservations, though not required, are a good idea.

2a Av. Sur, 26-A. ✆ **503/2335-1836.** Free admission. Food $9–$15 (£4.50–£7.50). Gallery hours: Sat–Sun 9am–5pm. Meals: Sun noon–4:30pm.

Los Tercios ★ Even Suchitoto's waterfalls look like art. Los Tercios, a stunning waterfall and small swimming hole located an easy 1.5km (1-mile) stroll out of town, really looks like a piece of modern art, with foot-wide slices of vertical rock jutting out along the face of its 9m (30-ft.) waterfall. The unique shape of the rocks here is thought to have resulted from rapidly cooling ancient magma. Though water only flows over the falls from May to December, Los Tercios is worth a visit year-round, since the unique rock formations are the main attraction. Be prepared to climb down a few rocks to get a good

Moments Art & Culture Festival

If you're anywhere near Suchitoto in February you'll want to stop by the **International Permanent Festival of Art and Culture ★★**. This annual, month-long international performance and art festival was founded by internationally renowned cinematographer and Suchitoto resident Don Alejandro Cotto almost 20 years ago and continues to attract visual and performance artists from around the world. The festival is held each February weekend with free performances in the Teatro Las Ruinas, one of Suchitoto's oldest buildings, which is currently under renovation.

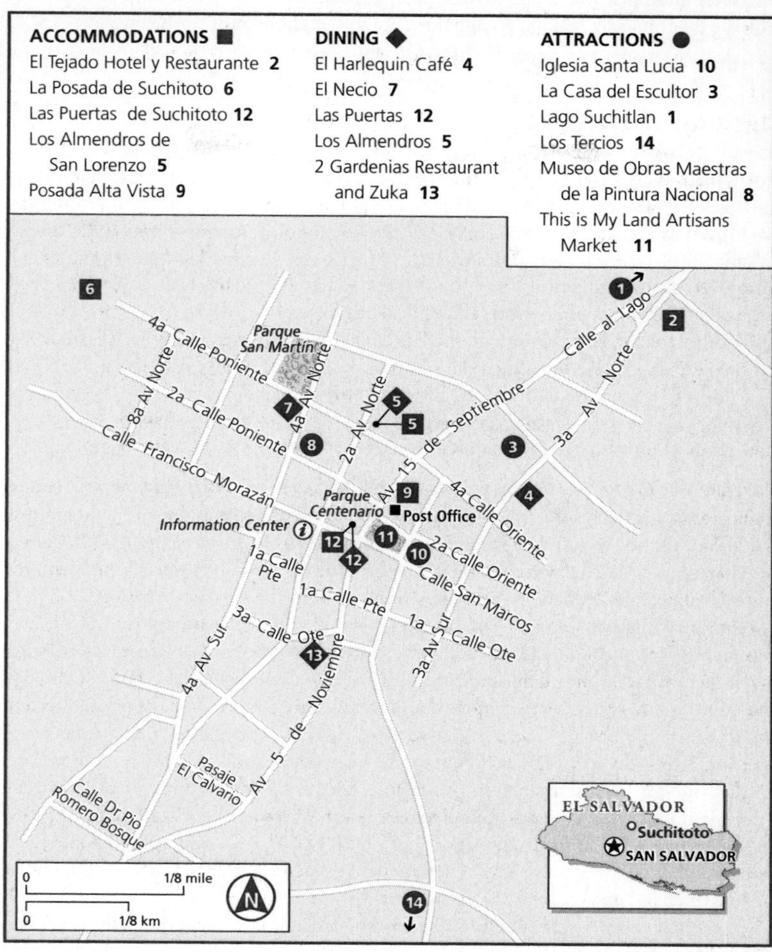

look. Vendors often come here to sell *pupusas* and drinks on the weekends, so refreshments should be on hand after your climb.

1.5km (1 mile) southeast of the main square. Free admission. Walk out of town along Av. 5 de Noviembre and turn left onto Calle a Cinquera just before Noviembre ends. Follow Calle a Cinquera to just past the chain link fence on the left. Turn left through the gate btw. the chain link fence and a small building. Walk straight and look for a path to your right, which will take you to the falls.

Museo de Obras Maestras de la Pintura Nacional The Teatro Las Ruinas (see above) contains this small gallery of El Salvadoran art including 31 abstract, Impressionist, and realist, post-1950 paintings created exclusively by El Salvadoran artists—including Suchitoto's own single-name artist "Chaney" as well as Negra Alvarez and Augusto

Crespin. Also included in the gallery is a traditional Greek-style bust of Suchitoto arts promoter and once world-famous cinematographer Alejandro Cotto. You can visit the gallery year-round by making an appointment at the phone number below.

2 a Calle Poniente and 4a Av. Norte. ✆ **503/2335-1909.** Admission $1.50 (75p). Hours by appointment only.

Outdoor Activities

Lago Suchitlán ★★ Just a short bus ride out of town is the 135-sq.-km (52-sq.-mile), man-made Lago Suchitlán, from where you can take a cooling, scenic boat ride to La Isla de Los Pájaros (Island of the Birds) and listen to the calls of thousands of migrating birds. Lago Suchitlán was created in 1973 when the government dammed Río Lempa to produce electrical power, and now serves as a fishing hole for local communities and a stop-off for migrating birds. Surrounding the lake today are the Puerto San Juan tourist center, a large, open-air restaurant, and stands for craft vendors.

Covered tourist boats are just to the left of the tourist center and offer 45-minute to 1-hour, $25 (£13) lake tours including stops at La Isla de Los Pájaros. Also available are $12 (£6), 30-minute tours that don't include a stop at the island.

Turicentro, Lago Suchitlán. ✆ **503/2335-1957.** Admission 50¢ (25p), 25¢ (15p) children under 7. Daily 7am–7pm. Take the white minibus with Suchitoto written on the side from the center of town.

Parque Ecológio de Cinquera and The Village of Cinquera ★★ Parque Ecológio de Cinquera is a 3,921-hectare (9,690-acre) preserve and forest 1 hour from Suchitoto. It's not as grand as Parque Imposible (p. 276) or Montecristo (p. 277) but it has a small waterfall, a few trails, and is worth a walk in the woods when paired with the historic village of Cinquera located a few minutes from the park entrance.

The tiny village of Cinquera was a stronghold of guerrilla resistance during the civil war and numerous buildings, including the church, have been preserved to show bomb and bullet damage inflicted by government troops. The town square also proudly displays the tail of a downed army helicopter and a mural depicting the history of the war and the image of the brutally executed 15-year-old girl who was the town's first martyr. A separate mural depicts the two ninth-grade boys whose call to arms is said to have sparked the guerrilla resistance in the region. Spanish-language tours of the town are available through **La Asociación de Reconstrucion y Desarrollo Municipal** or ARDM (Main Square 1 block from the Alcaldía; ✆ **503/2389-5732;** ardmcqr@yahoo.es). Or ask around town for Spanish-speaking Cinquera resident Don Pablo, who can provide a unique firsthand and sadly brutal account of the war.

To get here, take bus no. 482 from Suchitoto, which leaves Suchitoto daily at 9:15am and 1:30pm. It returns from Cinquera only once a day at 1pm. The trip takes 1 hour and costs 80¢ (40p).

No phone. Park admission $5 (£2.50). Daily 8am–5pm. Bus: 482.

SHOPPING

Galería de Pascal This small gallery is owned by Pascal Lebailly, a former Paris fashion convention producer and owner of the exquisitely decorated Los Almendros Hotel (p. 285). Lebailly has applied that same sense of fashion and design in choosing the El Salvadoran and Central American art on display and for sale at his gallery. The gallery also includes a small gift shop offering El Salvadoran coffee, ceramics, hammocks, and handbags, among other items. It's open daily from 9am to 7pm. 4a Calle Poniente No. 2b. ✆ **503/2334-1008.**

This is My Land Artisans Market ★★ It's not the biggest or most diverse mercado in El Salvador, but it's definitely one of the most enjoyable. Each Saturday and Sunday, the Association of Artisans and Artists of Suchitoto set up shop on the town square with offerings of El Salvadoran crafts and traditional cuisine. Colorful paintings, textiles and, of course, the Salvadoran food staple, *pupusas,* are in plentiful supply. But the real reason to visit the weekend market is just to enjoy the vibe. There's no better place to watch local families mingle and chat well into the night, listen to local music, and soak in the town's beautiful mountain setting. It's open Friday to Sunday from 9am to 7pm. Parque Centenario. No phone. Free admission.

WHERE TO STAY

Expensive

La Posada de Suchitoto ★ La Posada is a few more blocks off the square than Suchitoto's other high-end hotels, but the pool, lake view, and slightly lower price are worth the 5-minute walk. The 12-room La Posada offers a traditional hacienda-style atmosphere with an attentive staff decked out in colonial garb and a large, lake-view restaurant with tasty, reasonably-priced fare. La Posada is a bit older than the other two pricey hotels, so the rooms and amenities aren't shiny and new. But the colonial character, casual atmosphere, and well-trained staff help balance things out. You'll definitely want to book early to reserve one of the hotel's six lake-view rooms.

Final 4a, Calle Poniente. ✆ **503/2335-1064.** Fax 503/2335-1164. www.laposado.com.sv. 12 units. $62 (£31) lake-view double; $75 (£38) double. Rates include full breakfast. AE, DISC, MC, V. **Amenities:** Restaurant; pool; room service; Wi-Fi in common areas. *In room:* A/C, fan, TV.

Las Puertas de Suchitoto ★★★ Though it's not as luxurious as Los Almendros, you simply can't beat Las Puertas in terms of its view and location. Also renovated within the last few years, Las Puertas is directly on Suchitoto's charming central plaza facing the church. Each of its six large upstairs rooms features custom-designed wood furniture and private balconies, which are perfect places to watch the sun rise over the mountains and light up the towers of Iglesia Santa Lucia. All of the rooms are in single row on the second floor so no room is better than another. The hotel also features a large public balcony overlooking Volcán Quazapa and a tasty restaurant.

2a Av. Norte and Av. 15 de Septiembre. ✆ **503/2393-9200.** www.laspuertassuchitoto.com. 6 units. $77–$95 (£39–£48) double. Rates include full breakfast. AE, DC, DISC, MC, V. **Amenities:** Restaurant; bar; $6.50 per day bike rental; 2 nonsmoking rooms; room service. *In room:* A/C, TV, Wi-Fi.

Los Almendros de San Lorenzo ★★★ This is by far one of the most luxurious, independently owned hotels in El Salvador. Owner and former fashion producer Pascal Lebailly required nearly a year and a half and 30 workers to fully renovate the 200-year-old colonial house that is now his six-room hotel. Each large room is individually decorated in a modern hacienda style with iron bathroom accents and lighting designed specifically for the hotel. A glass-enclosed French restaurant sits above the figure-eight-shaped stone pool and a small, comfortable bar sits beside a central courtyard with fountain. But what makes Los Almendros special is not its size or configuration, but the eye for detail with which Pascal chose the art, furniture, and overall tone. The whole effect is like staying overnight in an interior design show.

4a Calle Poniente, No. 2b. ✆ **503/2335-1200.** www.hotelsalvador.com. 6 units. $85–$120 (£43–£60) double. Rates include full breakfast. AE, DC, DISC, MC, V. **Amenities:** Restaurant; bar; $80 (£40) airport transfers; all rooms nonsmoking; pool. *In room:* A/C, TV.

Moderate

El Tejado Hotel y Restaurante ★★ This is the best moderately priced option in town. Though El Tajado's nine view-less rooms are nothing to e-mail home about, they're comfortable and decently sized, with high ceilings and inviting, hacienda-style tiled front patios. What makes Tejado stand out is the price, which is up to $30 (£15) less than the three higher-end options in town. Tejado also offers a cool, leafy atmosphere, a large open-air restaurant with great lake views, and a big, inviting pool. And since it's only a few blocks off the main square, it's a perfect place for those who adhere to the old "who spends time in their room anyway" style of travel. If you can't get a room, you can still use Tejado's pool for $3.35 (£1.65) a day.

3a Av. Norte No. 58. ✆ **503/2335-1769.** Fax 503/2335-1970. www.eltejadosuchitoto.com. 9 units. $50–$55 (£25–£28) double; $85 (£43) 5-person suite. Rates include full breakfast. AE, DC, DISC, MC, V. **Amenities:** Restaurant; pool; room service; Wi-Fi in common areas. *In room:* A/C, TV, no phone.

Inexpensive

Posada Alta Vista ★ Value It's bare-bones, but affordable, modern, and right off the square. Don't look to Alta Vista for much in terms of amenities, but a clean, comfortable, air-conditioned room with a rooftop deck less than 45m (148 ft.) from the main square for roughly $20 (£10) a night is just about as good a deal as you're going to find. Alta Vista's only downside is that at press time the showers were cold water only. Hotel operators say hot showers are on the way, however. Make sure to request an upstairs front room with a balcony, as those rooms are superior.

Av. 15 de Septiembre, Casa 8, just off Parque Centenario. ✆ **503/2335-1645.** Fax 503/2335-1590. lauriano-melgar@yahoo.com. 8 units. $21 (£11) double. V. **Amenities:** Free coffee in lobby; all rooms nonsmoking. *In room:* A/C, fan, TV, no phone.

WHERE TO DINE

Like El Salvador in general, Suchitoto is a town reinventing itself after a long, difficult history. New restaurants seem to be popping up every year. Listed below are just a few of the established choices, but the main square and side streets also offer a plethora of *comedores* and *pupusarias* that are worth checking out.

El Harlequin Café ★★ Finds Kids SALVADORAN El Harlequin is the kind of funky little place we all hope to find when traveling. Hidden behind a little sign and metal door on a quiet street a couple of blocks off the main square is this romantic hideaway, filled with candlelight, jazzy music, interesting art, and tasty food. The menu is simple but offers a lot to choose from, including comfort food such as a tuna salad, a delicious chicken and rice, and cream soups; there's even a children's menu. Combine the food with the artsy feel and intimate lighting, and El Harlequin stands out as a great place to pass a quiet evening over a bottle of wine.

3a Av. Norte No. 26. ✆ **503/2325-5890.** Main courses $3.50–$8 (£1.75–£4). AE, MC, V, DC. Sun–Mon and Wed–Thurs 10am–10pm; Fri–Sat 10am–midnight.

Las Puertas ★ SALVADORAN Las Puertas offers a mix of first-class service and delicious food at reasonable prices, with prime people-watching views over the plaza. The service is formal and elegant, the chef is imported from San Salvador, and the kitchen is new and high-tech. The result is delicious dishes such as a filling ravioli with shrimp and vegetables. The restaurant's dining room is an open, upscale space with a soaring ceiling and two large windows overlooking the square. Reservations aren't required, but call ahead to ensure outside seating or one of the two window-front tables.

2a Av. Norte and Av. 15 de Septiembre. ✆ **503/2393-9200.** Main courses $11–$13 (£5.50–£7.50). AE, DC, DISC, MC, V. Daily 7am–9pm.

Los Almendros ★★★ FRENCH Eat at least one meal here while you're in town. The food is delicious, the setting is elegant, and the price is a lot lower than you would expect. French owner Pascal Lebailly has employed his well-honed eye for design in creating this casual but upscale, glass-enclosed French restaurant that overlooks Los Almendros romantically lit pool. And with French chef Hérvey Laurent applying his *cordon bleu* skills to delicious dishes such as salmon chargrilled with lime and butter, Los Almendros is likely to serve one of your better meals in El Salvador. The restaurant also takes care to use local ingredients and serves only Salvadoran coffee.

4a Calle Poniente, No. 2b. ✆ **503/2335-1200.** Main courses $5.50–$14 (£2.75–£7). AE, DC, DISC, MC, V. Daily 7:30am–9pm.

SUCHITOTO AFTER DARK

El Necio ★★ Amiable bartenders and posters calling for peace and revolution set the tone for this laid-back, lefty dive joint. In fact, the walls are covered with more than enough images of Che, John Lennon, and a virtual history of leftist icons to keep your mind occupied whenever you're not busy listening to the occasional live music or deep in conversation with one of the friendly locals or travelers who come here to chat over ice-cold Pilsners.

4a Av. Norte, No. 9 (by 4a Calle Poniente). ✆ **503/2335-1964.** Daily 6pm–midnight (or later).

2 Gardenias Restaurant and Zuka Bar ★ This bar/restaurant combo a few blocks from the main square is a great place to sneak away from all the action for a relaxed drink. The food isn't the greatest—the menu offers few surprises with dishes like roasted and grilled meat with a veggie and starch side—but you come here more to drink than to eat. Grab a seat at the big bar, situated in front of wide windows that catch the breeze and the light just right, or on the shady, open-air patio, and get ready to choose from the huge drink menu. There's live music once a month. As a conversation starter, you can try to figure out the theme of the decor, which includes, among other things, numerous papier-mâché female torsos and a classic image of a Parisian cyclist.

3a Calle Poniente, No. 14 (by Av. 5 de Noviembre). ✆ **503/2335-1868.** Main courses $3.50–$6 (£1.75–£3). Mon–Fri 7am–10pm; Sat 10am–midnight; Sun 10am–8pm.

11 CONCEPCION DE QUEZALTEPEQUE

30km (18½ miles) N of Suchitoto; 77km (48 miles) N of San Salvador

Concepción de Quezaltepeque, known as the City of Hammocks, is a tiny village tucked into El Salvador's northern central mountains, where generations of artisans have devoted their lives to making midday naps more enjoyable. Nearly the entire town is involved in hammock production and sales. Some locals weave intricate tapestries that hang from the sides of the hammocks on sale here; others twist individual threads into thin ropes that are eventually crafted into colorful *hamacas* sold in villages around the country.

Quezaltepeque comprises only a few small streets, on which are gathered a group of hammock shops, surrounding a town square, so don't expect to spend more than a couple of hours here. And since you can buy Quezaltepeque-made hammocks around the country, the shopping is not actually the best part of visiting this town. The most enjoyable thing to do here is to chat up a hammock shop owner and ask to see where and how their hammocks are made. With a little charm and a good grasp of Spanish, you might convince someone to, quite literally, show you the ropes. Most craftsmen display their work on weekends, but the best time to ask owners for a behind-the-scenes peek is Tuesday and Wednesday when things aren't so busy.

ESSENTIALS

Getting There & Getting Around

From Suchitoto, take bus no. 129; the trip lasts 1½ hours. From San Salvador, take bus no. 126, which takes about 2 hours and 30 minutes. Both trips will cost you less than $2 (£1).

From San Salvador, drive north out of the city along Hwy. CA-4, from which you will turn west onto Carretera Longitudinal del Norte toward Chalatenango. Follow this road until you turn north toward Chalatenango and spot signs to Quezaltepeque.

Most of Quezaltepeque hammock shops and *comedores* are clustered within a few blocks of the square, so the best way to see the town is on foot.

Visitor Information

There are no hotels, large restaurants, ATMs, or Internet cafes in town, so there isn't much visitor information to be had. But if you speak Spanish, you can stop by the **Casa de la Cultura** (Barrio El Central on the main square; ✆ **503/2331-2242**) to learn more about the town's history. The nearby city of Chalatenango, which you will pass coming and going to Quezaltepeque, offers ATMs, fast-food restaurants, and grocery stores.

WHAT TO SEE & DO

The primary activity here is strolling around looking for deals on hammocks crafted by artisans who have dedicated their lives to the art form. But you'll have an even better time if you can get a peak behind the scenes. I can't guarantee it will happen, but if you call Spanish-speaking hammock artisan **Missal Goldames** (✆ **503/2331-2001**) in advance he might just give you a tour around town. You can also stop by his shop along the main road, 1 block short of the square on the right.

If you don't see any hammocks you like along the main street, ask someone for *otras tiendas de hamaca* and, if you're lucky, they will point you to a friend's house where some are for sale.

WHERE TO STAY & DINE

Quezaltepeque has no hotels and requires only a couple of hours to explore, so there isn't a big reason to stay overnight in the area. If you do, your best option is the new and luxurious Chalate Country Club (see below), 10 minutes outside Quezaltepeque. I don't recommend staying in the nearby city of Chalatenango. It's crowded, unattractive, hard to navigate, and has only three, subpar lodging options that rent rooms by the hour.

Food options in Quezaltepeque are limited to a few, informal *pupusarias* near the hammock shops. If you want a more substantial meal in town, call the restaurant **Teresa de Leon** (1 block off the main street; ✆ **503/2331-2381**) 1 day in advance, as it's only open upon request. You can also head to Chalatenango for fast food or, for the best option in the region, try the restaurant at the Chalate Country Club hotel.

Chalate Country Club ★★ (Finds) (Kids) Chalate is an oasis of luxury that's worth the money if you plan to stay in the area for a few days. Opened in April 2007, this 14-room hotel offers large rooms, modern bathrooms, and grassy and tree-filled private

Volunteer Opportunities in El Salvador

If you enjoy mixing a little humanitarian work in with your volcano hiking and village visiting, El Salvador offers a plethora of volunteer activities from building homes and schools to teaching English. Below are the best options:

Habitat for Humanity (Colonia General Arce, Calle Jorge Domingue 4-H; ✆ **503/2298-3290;** informacion@habitatelsalvador.org.sv) began building earthquake-resistant homes here in 1992 almost immediately after the end of the war and now has six offices and ongoing projects throughout the country. By Habitat estimates, El Salvador—in the wake of Hurricane Mitch and the 2001 earthquake—still remains 630,000 homes short of what's needed. So there's plenty to do, including the construction of completely new communities in Santa Ana and San Vincente. Habitat requires a minimum 5-day commitment and a $45 (£23) per-day fee for room and board, orientation, and transportation. You'll need to register 3 to 6 months in advance of your trip.

If you like working with your hands, you can also check in with **Seeds of Learning** (**SOL;** 585 Fifth St. West, Sonoma, CA 95476; ✆ **707/939-0471**), which builds schools in rural El Salvador. SOL volunteers work literally side by side with local community members to build schools, so volunteers really get to know the people they are helping. SOL, which has been working in El Salvador since 1999, requires a 10-day commitment, and the program costs $1,200 (£600), including lodging at a basic hotel or retreat center, food, transportation, and excursions. Scholarships are available for volunteers under 30 years of age.

English-language skills are also increasingly important to El Salvadorans, and the country has numerous English teaching opportunities. **Global Crossroad** (415 East Airport Freeway, Ste. 365, Irving, TX 75062; ✆ **866/387-7816;** www.globalcrossroad.com) offers 1- to 12-week teaching programs in San Salvador, Sonsonate, and Santa Ana beginning at $899 (£450) for food, housing, and transportation from the airport upon arrival. Volunteers stay with host families and teach primarily children. Global Crossroad also offers short-term volunteer opportunities teaching computer skills, taking care of orphan children, and helping to maintain communities. Travelers willing to make a longer teaching commitment should check out El Salvador–based **Centro de Intercambio y Solidarity** or CIS (Av. Bolivar 103, Colonia Libertad, San Salvador; ✆ **503/2226-5362;** www.cis-elsalvador.org). CIS was formed after the signing of the peace accords to help promote solidarity among the El Salvadoran people and cultural exchange with other countries. Volunteers pay only a $100 (£50) registration fee and $70 (£35) per week for room and board with a local family, and volunteers receive half-price ($50/£25) Spanish classes. A 10-week commitment is required, though. Other CIS volunteer opportunities are available as needs arise.

grounds to explore, two children's pools, and a playground. Parents can lounge by six adult pools or shoot pool on two tables. And the restaurant is a cut above rural El Salvador's normal roasted meat with rice and salad menu. Continental cuisine, such as a tasty chicken breast wrapped in bacon and surf and turf, is $10 to $13 (£5–£6.50). The kids menu ranges from $3.50 to $4.75 (£1.75–£2.40). There's no bus to the hotel, so you'll need to take a $7 (£3.50), 15-minute taxi ride from Quezaltepeque or Chalatenango.

The hotel did not include Wi-Fi at press time, but I was assured it would be installed shortly. The property is also adding a large, upscale housing development, whose owners will be part of a members-only club that will use the property's facilities.

Km 63.5 Carretera a Chalatenango, San Rafael, Chalatenango. © **503/2323-7824.** 14 units. $45 (£23) double. AE, DC, MC, V. **Amenities:** Restaurant; 2 children's pools and playground; health club w/ exercise machines and 2 saunas; 6 outdoor adult pools; room service; tennis courts. *In room:* A/C, TV.

12 LA PALMA & EL PITAL ★

84km (52 miles) N of San Salvador; 50km (31 miles) W of Chalatenango

If you like art, you'll love La Palma. This small mountain town high in the mountains below the Honduran border is the former home of El Salvador's most revered living artist, Fernando Llort, and the birthplace of the art movement he inspired. Today, visitors come from around the world to snap photos of the dozens of Llort-style murals decorating the town's walls and browse its many artisans' shops. Llort moved to La Palma in 1972 and taught the townspeople to create art using available materials to reflect their lives. The resulting art is filled with color, geometric designs, and natural and religious symbols. Llort eventually left La Palma but the artists he inspired continue to create works on display in the galleries and on the buildings along La Palma's two main roads.

Despite its remote location and small size, La Palma has numerous restaurants and a couple of nice hotels. La Palma is also an excellent jumping-off point for hikes up nearby El Pital mountain, which is the highest point in El Salvador and summits on the border with Honduras.

ESSENTIALS

Getting There

BY BUS From Chalatenango, hop on bus no. 125 and ask the driver to let you off at Amayo where you can catch bus no. 119 to the center of La Palma. The trip takes about 1 hour and 15 minutes. You can reach Chalatenango in just over 2 hours from San Salvador on bus no. 125.

BY CAR La Palma is just off Hwy. CA-4, which is the country's main north-south highway. Just drive north a little less than 1 hour from Chaletenango and about 1½ hours from San Salvador and follow the signs. If you reach the Honduran border, you've gone a few miles too far.

Orientation & Getting Around

Like many of El Salvador's rural towns, La Palma is small enough to walk just about everywhere. There are only two main avenues that you can walk end-to-end in about 10 minutes. But if you're feeling lazy, La Palma offers many three-wheeled moto-taxis that will take you anywhere along those two streets for 25¢ (15p). You can also easily catch a $3 (£1.50) moto-taxi that'll take you 10 minutes outside town to the luxurious Entre Pinos resort or small village of San Ignacio.

Visitor Information & Fast Facts

La Palma does not have a tourist information office, but the town sponsors an English-language website, **www.lapalmaelsalvador.com**, which provides a history of the village and general tourist information. There's a **Banco Cuscatlán** (© **503/2305-8331**) with an ATM just off the main square.

What to See & Do

The main thing to do in La Palma is viewing building murals and shopping for arts and crafts in the galleries along the town's two main roads. Keep in mind that the galleries here seem to have a lot of the same style of artwork you'll see in every shop in the country. A trained eye would probably be able to tell the difference, but I couldn't. Though you can pick up a small kitschy souvenir for under $10 (£5), some of the better framed art can be $40 (£20) or more. Since the art is actually fairly expensive, you might just want to bring your camera and take some shots of the beautiful mural art—I consider these to be the best art in town.

Outdoor Activities

La Palma's other attraction is its close proximity to El Salvador's highest point, **El Pital.** El Pital is 30 minutes outside of La Palma, rises 2,730m (8,975 ft.) above sea level, and offers an easy 1½-hour each-way hike to the top up a winding fire road. Only the last 20 minutes get a bit steep, and all along the way are great views. The last stretch to the summit is privately owned, and a family monitors the road. So if two guys come stumbling out of the woods, demanding money, don't sweat it: They own the place. The usual fee is $5 to $8 (£2.50–£4) but you can sometimes get by for half that depending on your charm and guide.

Just before the summit, ask your guide to show you the four-story-high meteor that hit the mountain long before anyone can remember. Risk takers can climb on top of the meteor by walking across a small tree bridging a 12m (40-ft.) drop. At El Pital's summit, you'll find a small, white monument marking the border with Honduras and a radio tower with a guard and vicious-looking dog behind a fence. Like many remote locations in El Salvador, it's not wise to hike up here alone. Your hotel can arrange a guide. To get here by bus, take a moto-taxi from La Palma for $3 (£1.50) to San Ignacio where you will catch the no. 509 bus toward Las Pilas. After about 30 minutes, get off at Río Chiquito and have the driver point you in the right direction.

SHOPPING

Artesanias Kemuel ★ This is the best stand-alone shop in town for Llortian-style arts and crafts. The store offers lots of uniquely painted wood crosses that stand out in a town full of painted wood crosses, and it even sells a rare collection of framed Llort-style works on simple white paper. Artesanias's unique collection might be the result of an inside connection, of course—the store's owner and principal artist, Vitelio Jonathan Contreras, is Llort's nephew by marriage The art pieces and larger crosses cost $25 to $75 (£13–£38). It's open daily from 8am to 6:30pm. Calle Principal, Barrio El Centro. © **503/2305-8501.**

Mercadito Artesanal This market across from the La Estancia Restaurante is a bit smaller than Placita, with just 10 vendors spread around a small courtyard, and it's a bit heavy on the laminated wood art and wood bracelets you'll see in every other mercado in Latin America. But if you look hard, you can find some genuine pieces of interesting, original, locally created art. The market also has a decent amount of women's clothing with simple Llort-esque designs. Textile bags run around $6 (£3) and small, painted decorative chairs run $10 (£5) before haggling. The market also has a small *comedor.* It's open daily from 9am to 7pm. Calle Gerardo Varrios, Barrio El Central, in front of the La Estancia Restaurante. No phone.

Placita Artesanal La Palma ★ Placita is the best market in town to search for original arts and crafts. It's bigger than Mercadito and seems to offer fewer mass-produced items and more locally produced crafts. I spoke with numerous vendors here and they were immediately able to give me the actual names and stories of the artists who produced many of the picture frames, wood boxes, and painted crosses on sale. It's open daily from 8am to 6pm. Barrio El Centro across from La Iglesia Catolica. No phone.

WHERE TO STAY

In addition to the below hotel options, you might consider the **El Pital Highland Hotel** (✆ **503/2222-2009**), which is on the fire road at the start of any hike to El Pital. It offers a restaurant and four-person rooms for $60 (£30), two person rooms for $50 (£25), and $150 (£75) for a two-story, six-person cabin.

Entre Pinos Resort ★★★ Kids This upscale, mountain-lodge-style hotel, which was built in 1998 and is spread over 110 acres, offers comfortable, midsize rooms and enough amenities to keep the family busy for days. Guests can hike or horseback 7km (4 miles) of private dirt roads and trails, play tennis, swim, soak in the big Jacuzzi, and play soccer on a full-size field. Kids tired of all that outdoor activity should like the video arcade. Though the hotel has a remote location up in the mountains, the English-speaking staff can easily arrange tours to the rest of the country, as well as to the Copán ruins in Honduras and El Pital. Entre Pinos is not exactly on par with the corporate megaresorts you'll find in other countries, but it is among El Salvador's best hotels, and serves as a great base for any long El Salvador vacation.

Km 87.5 Carretera Troncal del Norte, San Ignacio. ✆ **503/2335-9312.** Fax 503/2278-2811. www.entrepinosresortandspa.com. 57 units. $111–$120 (£56–£60) double; $130 (£65) 5-person cabins. AE, DC, MC, V. **Amenities:** 3 restaurants; free airport transfers; bikes; health club and spa w/Jacuzzi; 2 pools; 10 nonsmoking rooms; room service; tennis courts; Wi-Fi. *In room:* A/C, fan, TV, fridge, hair dryer.

Hotel La Palma ★★ Value La Palma is the best affordable hotel choice in town. It's rustic and simple but offers a cool, gardenlike setting, a range of room options, great service, and a big restaurant with outdoor seating. The proprietor, Salvador, has owned the place for over 30 years and is happy to use the basic English he's picked up to provide information or arrange trips to El Pital. All of the 32 rooms are simply decorated and of average size but comfortable. Rooms are spread throughout the large, leafy, hillside property, which winds down to a wide, rocky river bed. When you book, request room no. 26. It's the newest room and offers the best view. If that's booked, ask for one of the rooms in the new, white building on the hill.

Barrio El Tránsito, La Palma. ✆ **503/2335-9012.** www.hotelapalma.com.sv. 32 units. $28 (£14) double. No credit cards. **Amenities:** Restaurant; $6 (£3) per day babysitting; room service. *In room:* Wi-Fi, no phone.

Posada de Reyes ★ Finds Just a few miles past Entre Pinos and La Palma is the tiny village of San Ignacio. It's a pleasant, typical El Salvadoran village, with a white church beside a small public square. There's no particular reason to visit, except to catch a bus to El Pital and to stay at the unusually comfortable Posada de Reyes Hotel. This 14-room, three-story hotel was built in 2005 and offers uniquely spectacular views, big rooms, a well-maintained and inviting pool—which is unique among small independently owned El Salvador hotels—and a lush, flower-filled landscape. It looks average from the outside but is modern, spacious, and comfortable on the inside. And at $25 to $35 (£13–£18), it's almost as cheap as Hotel La Palma. Request room no. 15, which has windows on two sides and a balcony. A short moto-taxi ride will get you here from La Palma or you can take bus no. 119.

1 block north of the Alcaldía, Barrio El Centro. ✆ **503/2335-9318.** www.hotelposadadereyes.com. 15 rooms. $25–$35 (£13–£18) double. No credit cards. Pets permitted. **Amenities:** Restaurant; pool; Wi-Fi in lobby. *In room:* A/C, TV, fridge, no phone.

WHERE TO DINE

Del Pueblo Restaurante y Artesanias ★★ Value SALVADORAN If you want protein, this is the place to come. The scent of spicy, simmering beef is the first thing you'll notice as you enter this simple, two-room restaurant, which features one of the town's most interesting abstract murals on its front wall. The specialty of the house is the 170-gram (6-oz.) beef and sausage combo with salad, rice, cheese, and beans; it's delicious. The other items are variations on the same meat, sausage, and chicken theme. Breakfast is a traditional serving of eggs, beans, cheese, and platano. Wine and beer are also available. Locals consider Del Pueblo to be among La Palma's finest restaurants, far more than Restaurante La Estancia (see below).

Calle Principle No. 70, Barrio El Centro. ✆ **503/2305-8504.** Main courses $1.25–$4.95 (65p–£2.50); breakfast $2–$3.25 (£1–£1.65). No credit cards. Daily 7am–8pm.

Restaurante La Estancia Overrated SALVADORAN Since it's continually recommended as one of the best restaurants in town and boasts balcony seating with pretty mountain views, you would think La Estancia would be a big hit. But it's only okay. The dinner menu is not inexpensive by local standards and there's a bit of a feeling of neglect about the place. Still, they have an ample menu that comprises the usual fish, chicken, and meat dishes, with salad and rice sides. And if the food doesn't hold up (on my recent visit, I had an omelet that was way too salty), at least you'll get a table with a view.

Calle Geraldo, Barrios, No. 35 (across from the Mercadito Artesanal). ✆ **503/2335-9049.** Main courses $4–$7 (£2–£3.50). No credit cards. Daily 8am–6:30pm.

Restaurante Los Pinares ★★ LATIN AMERICAN/SALVADORAN Los Pinares, the main restaurant at the Entre Pinos Resort (see above), is definitely worth the few dollars for a moto-taxi ride from La Palma. The restaurant has covered, open-air seating beside an outdoor pool and a large vegetarian, meat, fish, and pasta menu with unique items such as roasted boar and Jalapeña steak. But the best choices might be the mixed salad, which is twice the size and features twice the variety of ingredients as the average El Salvadoran restaurant salad, or the creamy spaghetti with chicken, which has just the right amount of spicy kick. Wine, beer, spirits, and a children's menu are also available. Prices here are two to three times that of the restaurants in La Palma, but the food and service match the added cost.

Km 87.5 Carretera Troncal del Norte, San Ignacio. ✆ **503/2335-9312.** Main courses $9–$23 (£4.50–£12). Breakfast $2–$4.60 (£1–£2.30). AE, DC, MC, V. Mon–Thurs 7am–8pm; Fri–Sun 7am–9pm.

Restaurante y Pupusaria La Palma ★ SALVADORAN It's cheap, tasty, and the portions are huge—perhaps that's why this is *the* place where locals eat in town. Pupusaria La Palma is also one of the seemingly few buildings in town that's not covered in murals (its facade is instead covered in tree trunks). There are actually no decorations at all here, just one room with bench seating and pictures of the entrees on the wall. The menu is as simple as the decor; highlights include items such as roasted and fried shrimp, and chicken served with rice or fries, tortillas, and a salad. The $1.90 (95¢) burritos and tacos are a good bet, but the *hamburgesas* are not too tasty.

Calle Central, across the street from Telecom Internet. ✆ **503/2334-9063.** Main courses $3.75–$6.50 (£1.90–£3.25). No credit cards. Daily 8am–8pm.

13 BARRA DE SANTIAGO ★★★

76km (47 miles) W of La Libertad

Barra de Santiago is bar none one of the most beautiful spots in El Salvador. This protected reserve and tiny fishing village, which is tucked into the southwest corner of the country, features miles of deserted, pristine beaches sitting a few hundred yards from a mangrove-filled estuary teeming with birds. And both are set against a backdrop of the lush hills of Parque Imposible and a wall of volcanoes stretching from Guatemala to Volcán de Izalco in El Salvador's Parque Nacional de Los Volcanes. If you love nature and the sea, Barra de Santiago is one of El Salvador's must-sees.

Barra de Santiago is also one of the country's most active turtle nesting areas, and each August through November visitors can witness giant sea turtles laying eggs along the beach and hundreds of hatched baby turtles making the dangerous journey to the water. Visitors can also paddle or arrange guided tours of the lush mangrove forests and narrow, bird-filled channels, take surfing lessons, or just walk for hours, absorbing the isolated natural beauty.

While here, make sure to take the 15-minute walk along the beach from one of Santiago's two main hotels to the tiny, thatched hut Restaurante Julita, which sits just yards from the confluence of the Pacific Ocean and Santiago's estuary. You can munch on fish caught moments before while viewing the waves of the Pacific on one side and, on the other, the calm waters of the estuary reflecting the line of palm trees and miles of volcanoes that seem to rise from its shores.

Barra de Santiago is a 2-hour drive from San Salvador and offers little infrastructure other than its two beachfront hotels. You'll need to make advanced reservations for both. You'll also want to arrange transportation in the area, as it requires a few twists and turns to get to this undeveloped corner of the country.

ESSENTIALS

Getting There

BY BUS From San Salvador, take a bus to Sonsonate (see p. 270 for info). Then catch bus no. 285, which departs Sonsonate for Barra de Santiago daily at 10am and 4:30pm; it leaves Santiago for Sonsonate daily at 4:30am and noon. The spot where buses arrive and depart is a straight, 5-minute walk from both of Santiago's hotels.

BY CAR From most parts of the country, you can drive here by journeying on CA-12, where you'll head south and then west before turning toward the beach at Km 98.5 (there'll be a sign for Barra de Santiago). From there, it's another 25 to 30 minutes along a bumpy dirt road that will dead-end just before the hotels. It can get a bit tricky, but just stay as close to the beach as possible and you should find your way. You'll need to call your hotel in advance to get info on driving the last few hundred yards along the beach or bay, though.

Orientation & Getting Around

Santiago's two hotels are side by side on the beach and estuary, so you definitely don't need a car to get around (nor are there local buses). A small village with a couple of tiny *tiendas* is about a 10-minute walk or short drive east along the main road from the hotels.

Visitor Information

Both of Santiago's hotels offer small restaurants, but bring everything else you'll need, as the area has no banks, pharmacies, or large stores. There's no official tourist office in town, but the folks at **Capricho Beach House** (see below) can arrange tours in the area and provide info, or you can check with guide **Julio Caesar Aviles** (see below).

WHAT TO SEE & DO

The waves here can occasionally get big with strong rip currents. But most of the time the waves are small enough for beginning surfers or those who just want to go for a swim. Santiago's beaches, unlike others on this coast, are wide, sandy, and uncrowded—you won't have to worry about tangling your lines with anyone else when you're fishing, or bumping into anyone else while surfing. Both hotels listed below can arrange surf lessons and board rental.

You can arrange guided tours of the nearby estuary and mangrove forest with local Spanish-speaking guide **Julio Caesar Aviles** (**© 503/7783-4765**). A 2-hour tour, including a small hike on the protected Isla de Cahete, where small, covered mounds mark the site of protected indigenous artifacts, is $30 (£15) per person. The tour takes you deep into the mangrove channels, where many bird species can be easily spotted. Santiago is also a prime sea turtle nesting area and has been the subject of numerous turtle conservation projects. Each August through November, giant sea turtles lay their eggs on the beach and the tiny hatchlings stumble their way to the water. Both hotels listed below can arrange turtle spotting trips.

WHERE TO STAY

Capricho Beach House ★★ Capricho is a great little five-room hostel right on the beach and steps away from Santiago's protected estuary. It's the more affordable of Santiago's two lodging options and offers four modern, average-size private rooms with shady front patios overlooking the beach. An old cabin with five inexpensive dorm beds and a shared bathroom is also available. Capricho's private rooms are a third the price of the luxury digs next door, comfortable, and more than adequate for a couple of days on the beach. But I don't recommend the dorm beds. They're cheap—only $7 (£3.50) per night—but uncomfortable and unattractive. The hotel has a small, slightly overpriced food menu and all guests are allowed to use the full-service kitchen. If you plan to cook, bring everything you'll need because there are no large grocery stores here. The same owners also run a guesthouse in San Salvador.

Final Calle Principal. **© 503/2260-2481.** www.ximenasguesthouse.com. 5 units. $40 (£20) private room; $7 (£3.50) dorm bed. No credit cards. **Amenities:** Restaurant; $50–$70 (£25–£35) airport and San Salvador transfers; $10 (£5) per day surfboard rental. *In room:* A/C, no phone.

La Coco Tera ★★★ If you have the money, stay here. Coco Tera is one of the more luxurious hotels outside of San Salvador and offers a rare taste of international style in this remote part of the country. This six-room, semi-all-inclusive ecoresort opened in April 2008 and features three modern, two-level cabins each with two huge rooms, luxurious, Asian-inspired bathrooms, and big flatscreen TVs. The hotel property stretches from the bay to the beach and includes a restaurant, bar, and pool dotted with custom-built furniture. The best rooms are the three upstairs units with soaring ceilings, king-size beds, and water-view balconies. The downstairs rooms have two twin beds with pullouts to sleep four. The hotel also offers mangrove, deep sea, and estuary fishing tours as well as activities like water-skiing. Because it's an ecoresort, Coco Tera features solar-powered hot water, brown water recycling, and it even incubates turtle eggs, gathered from illegal vendors around the country, for release into the sea.

Final Calle Principal. © **503/2245-3691.** www.lacocoteraresort.com. 6 units. $117–$190 (£59–£95) upstairs rooms; $95–$145 (£48–£73) downstairs rooms. Package rates vary; see hotel website for exact rates. Rates include 3 meals and nonalcoholic drinks daily. AE, DC, MC, V. **Amenities:** Restaurant; bar; free airport transfers; $875 (£438) full-day deep-sea fishing; $500 (£250) half-day deep-sea fishing; $50 (£25) estuary fishing; free kayak use; pool; $20 (£10) per hour waterskiing; Wi-Fi in common areas. *In room:* AC, TV, no phone.

A DIVING TRIP TO PLAYA LOS CÓBANOS ★

Playa Los Cóbanos is a tiny, not very attractive fishing village about an hour drive east of Barra de Santiago, which lacks any decent hotels and restaurants. The Los Cóbanos area, however, happens to be home to some of the country's best scuba diving, one of El Salvador's only major public golf resorts, and the county's largest all-inclusive resort.

Diving is Cóbanos' main attraction because the town boasts one of Central America's largest reefs and a half-century old shipwreck. Dives are often based out of the popular divers' hotel Los Cóbanos Village Lodge (see below) just a few hundred feet down the beach from the Cóbanos town center. Also just a few kilometers before you reach the town center is the beautiful Las Veraneras Resort (see below) with a new, lush 18-hole public golf course, as well as the huge international, all-inclusive Royal Decameron Salinitas resort (see below).

Essentials

GETTING THERE From Sonsonate, take bus no. 26, which stops directly in Playa Los Cóbanos.

When driving from the east, follow coast highway CA-2 to Hwy. CA-12, where you will turn south toward the ocean and follow the signs to Los Cóbanos. The road dead-ends in the town center 8km (5 miles) after leaving the highway. From Sonsonate, take Hwy. CA-12 and follow the signs.

ORIENTATION & GETTING AROUND The road off the main highway to Playa Los Cóbanos dead-ends into Cóbanos' 2-block long, beachfront town center. The Los Cóbanos Village Lodge is a few hundred feet down the beach; both Decameron and Los Veraneras are within a few minutes' drive.

VISITOR INFORMATION & FAST FACTS As with many of El Salvador's smallest villages, you will need to bring everything you need here since Cóbanos has no banks or large grocery stores. The town center does offer a couple of small but not extraordinary beachfront restaurants. There's no tourist office in town, but the staff at **Las Veranas** and **Los Cóbanos** (see below) can arrange tours and excursions.

What to See & Do

Most tourists come to this area primarily to dive its 161-sq.-km (62-sq.-mile) reef, which teems with tropical fish, moray eels, and occasionally huge green turtles. The summer months (Nov–May) offer the best and, some say, only window of clear visibility to view the region's underwater wildlife. Diving is based largely out of the **Los Cóbanos Village Lodge** near the town center. The lodge has only one full set of diving equipment, so divers will need to make arrangements in advance for additional equipment or contact one of the county's few diving outfitters, such as **El Salvador Divers** (© **503/2264-0961**), which provides English-language certification classes, equipment, and complete dive tours.

Where to Stay & Dine

Sleeping and dining here are confined basically to three area hotels. You'll have to eat where you stay because Cóbanos doesn't offer any restaurants worth recommending and you aren't allowed to eat at Decameron or Veraneras unless you are a guest.

Las Veraneras Resort ★★ (Kids Veraneras is one of El Salvador's most enjoyable and affordable luxury resorts and is home to one of the country's few public golf courses. The resort's biggest draw is its 7,000-yard, 18-hole rolling but open course, which was completed in December 2007. Veraneras also has plenty for nongolfers to do, such as lounging by one of the Veraneras's pools, taking an ocean swim from the sandy beach club, playing tennis, or letting the kids enjoy the large children's play area. The individual, one-story villas are modern and spare but comfortable, with separate living rooms, full kitchens, and shady patios. The resort also features some English-speaking staff and can arrange tours around the country. Veraneras more than delivers on its affordable $59 (£28), two-person with child base rate. Because of all its amenities, Veraneras is a great place to base your El Salvador vacation.

Km 88.5 Carretera a Los Cóbanos. ✆ **503/2420-5000** or 2247-9191. www.lasveraneras.com.sv. 60 units. $59–$159 (£28–£79) villa. AE, DC, DISC, MC, V. **Amenities:** 2 restaurants; 2 snack bars; $30 (£15) airport transfers; bikes; children's play area w/pool; exercise room; golf course; 3 pools; room service; Wi-Fi in common areas. *In room:* A/C, TV, kitchen or kitchenette.

Los Cóbanos Village Lodge ★ Located on the beach just a few hundred feet past the town center, this lodge is an ideal place to base your Los Cóbanos dive vacation. The ocean-view hotel features a couple of two-story, modern thatched-roof *cabañas* with four guest rooms each, a small restaurant, and inviting pool. The rooms are spare but comfortable with room nos. 3 and 4 offering balconies and ocean views. But you don't come to this lodge to stay in your room. You stay here to enjoy the hotel's deep-sea fishing trips, diving tours, and kayak and surfboard rentals. The 5-year-old hotel also has a social conscience—from its opening, it has worked with national and international organizations to preserve Cóbanos's natural resources and improve the lives of the village residents. Unless you prefer all-inclusive resorts (like the Decameron) or are in Los Cóbanos to play golf, (for that, go to Las Veraneras) this lodge is really the only viable option in town.

Caraterra Acajotla. ✆ **503/2420-5248.** www.loscobanos.com. 8 units. $26–$62 (£13-£31) double; extra person $10 (£3). Rates include continental breakfast. AE, DC, MC, V. **Amenities:** Restaurant; Internet in lobby; all rooms nonsmoking; pool; room service; watersports equipment. *In room:* A/C in 2 rooms, fan, TV (in 2 rooms), fridge, no phone.

Royal Decameron Salinitas If you like all-inclusives, you won't be disappointed here. Decameron is El Salvador's largest all-inclusive resort and offers all the grandeur and amenities that a large, multinational chain can offer. Four chlorinated pools and a huge, saltwater pool stretching into the Pacific are scattered around the sprawling, lush property. Rooms, which are large and colorfully decorated, sleep up to four and are located in four multistory buildings with balconies around the property. A cadre of international, all-you-can-eat-and-drink bars and restaurants keep guests full and happy. The generally bilingual staff organizes on-property activities and can arrange tours for an extra charge to El Salvador's Maya ruins, along with windsurfing, scuba diving, and kayaking trips.

Km 79 Carretera a Acaljutla. ✆ **503/2429-9000.** www.decameron.com. 552 units. $118–$158 (£59–£79) double Apr–June; $138–$178 (£69–£89) double Sept–Oct. AE, DC, DISC, MC, V. Rates include all food and drink. **Amenities:** 5 restaurants; 4 bars; $23 (£12) airport transfers; babysitting; exercise room; 5 pools; room service; spa, Jacuzzi, and sauna; free water equipment; Wi-Fi in common areas. *In room:* A/C, TV, fridge.

14 BALSAMO COAST

25km (16 miles) of coast from Puerto La Libertad to Playa Zonte

The Balsamo Coast, the winding 25km (16 miles) of surf, sand, and cliff-side beaches stretching from Puerto La Libertad to just past Playa Zonte, is one of the highlights of El Salvador. Along this strip are some of the country's most beautiful black-sand beaches and traveler-friendly villages. The Balsamo Coast is currently best known, however, for its world-class surfing—the coast is said to be home to the best breaks in all of Central America. The point break in the little village of Playa Sunzal is an excellent place to learn to surf, as the big waves are more than a half a kilometer off the beach with smaller, lesson-friendly waves closer to shore. The Balsamo Coast's other famous break, Punta Roca in La Libertad, is an internationally renowned surf spot best left to the experts.

The Balsamo Coast offers plenty for the nonsurfer to do, as well; hiking, fishing, swimming, and horseback riding are all within reach, and the coast is just a 1-hour drive to the shops, restaurants, and nightclubs of San Salvador.

Beginning in the port city of La Libertad and traveling west, the main villages of the Balsamo Coast are Playa Tunco, Playa Sunzal, and Playa El Zonte. (And in btw. these four towns are signs pointing to smaller oceanfront and fishermen's villages that are waiting to be explored.) **Playa Tunco** is the most developed and interesting of the main villages because it has beachfront restaurants, unique hotels, and Internet cafes, along with a coastline that's great for surfers and swimmers. **Playa Sunzal** is a tiny village about a half-mile farther west, with a famous surf break, a few backpacker surf hostels, and a handful of *pupusarias*. **Playa El Zonte,** the farthest west of the Balsamo Coast's developed villages, is a half-mile stretch of hotels and restaurants fronting a beach that's also a good spot for swimmers and surfers. The region's main town, **La Libertad,** is a crowded, hectic oceanfront city best known for its long fisherman's pier. Other than its Punta Roca surf break and the pier, La Libertad doesn't have much to offer. It also has a reputation for being among the country's most dangerous cities; though it's safe to visit the pier or sightsee in town during daylight hours, there's no reason to stay overnight in La Libertad.

ESSENTIALS

Getting There

BY BUS From San Salvador, take bus no. 102 to Puerto La Libertad. There you'll catch bus no. 192, which travels the length of the Balsamo Coast past Playa El Zonte. Bus no. 80 travels between La Libertad and Playa Sunzal; both bus nos. 192 and 80 will stop wherever you request along the main road. Simply tell the driver which town you'd like to visit and they'll let you off at the right spot. Most towns are a direct 5- to 10-minute walk toward the water from the main road.

BY CAR From San Salvador, follow Hwy. CA-4 for 45 minutes to 1 hour to La Libertad, where you'll turn right at the ocean and follow coastal Hwy. CA-2 west along the Balsamo Coast. Each town is well marked and a short drive off CA-2.

Orientation

The heart of the Balsamo Coast stretches approximately 25km (16 miles) from La Libertad to just past Playa El Zonte along the winding but well-paved coastal Hwy. CA-2.

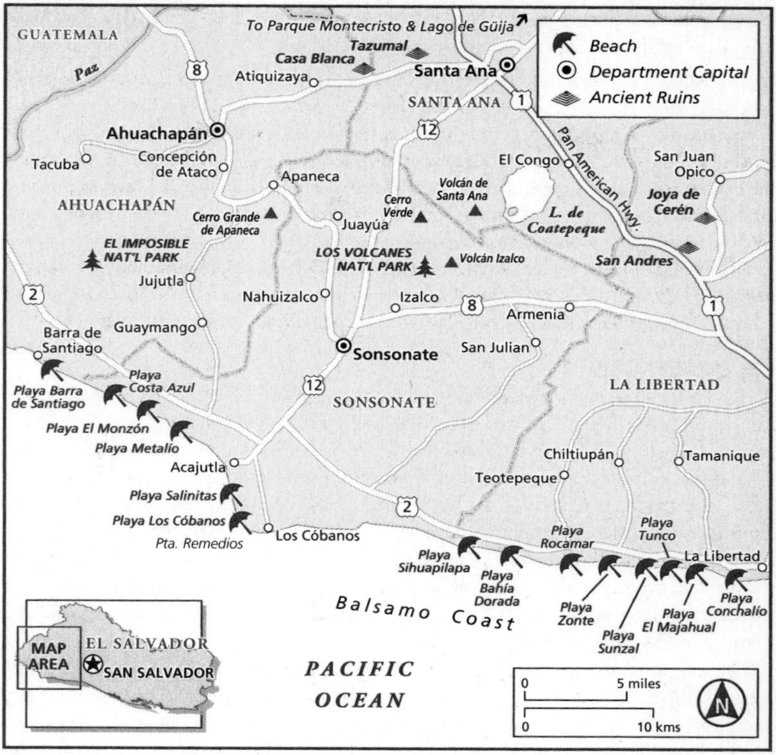

The region is dotted with small fishing villages, rocky and sandy beaches, and cliff-filled alcoves. La Libertad is the largest city here, with ample grocery stores, ATMs, and a post office. Playa Tunco is the second-most developed town, with a number of beachfront hotels, restaurants, surf shops, and Internet cafes.

Getting Around

To get around this coast by bus, simply walk to any spot along the main highway CA-2 and hail one of the many number no. 192 buses that travel in both directions about every 10 minutes; these will drop you off anywhere along the main road.

It's easy to drive around this area on your own: the main road linking all towns, Coastal Hwy. CA-2, is well maintained and the entrances to all the coastal towns are well marked.

The Balsamo Coast also has a number of local taxi drivers who can take you from La Libertad to Playa Sunzal for a negotiable $5 (£2.50) and from La Libertad to Playa Zonte for around $10 (£5). Call **Ricardo** (© **503/7277-3699**) or **Fausto** (© **503/7741-2571**) for a lift.

Visitor Information

The region's national **tourism office** is in Puerto La Libertad (at Km 34.5 Carretera Literal, 90m [300 ft.] from the Shell gas station; ✆ **503/2346-1898**). It's open daily from 8am to 5pm.

FAST FACTS Most of the Balsamo Coast's banks, ATMs, and pharmacies are in La Libertad along 2a Calle Poniente in the center of town. Since La Libertad can be a bit hectic and has a reputation for high crime, it's better to use the ATM and buy your groceries and gas at the large, modern shopping center 1km (1/2 mile) east of town along the coastal road. The shopping center is a 10-minute walk from the La Libertad pier and includes a grocery store and four ATMs that accept a variety of North America bank cards. A Shell gas station is across the street.

La Libertad's **tourist police** can be reached at ✆ **503/2346-1893; ambulance** service can be called at ✆ **503/2335-3049;** and the **fire department** number is ✆ **503/2243-2054.** La Libertad's **post office** is located along 2a Calle Oriente, directly north of the pier.

LA LIBERTAD

Puerto La Libertad is a crowded, hardscrabble, oceanfront city 32km (20 miles) south of San Salvador. Many travelers stop here only briefly to catch buses to the rest of the coast, stock up on supplies, or visit the colorful fisherman's pier. Surfers also flock here from around the world to surf the renowned Punta Roca surf break just outside of town.

La Libertad has a reputation for high crime, but it's perfectly safe to visit the fisherman's pier or stock up on essentials during the day. Since many superior hotels are within a short drive or bus ride, and it's not safe to walk around at night, I don't recommend staying here overnight, though. If you must, the nicest nearby hotel is **Hotel Punta Roca** (4a Calle Poniente and 5a Av. Sur, Puerto La Libertad, La Libertad; ✆ **503/2335-3261**). Rooms are $58 (£29) a night.

The long pier and its nearby market are rightly La Libertad's main attractions. The market's prices vary depending on your negotiating and language skills, but I was recently quoted $3 to $5 (£1.50–£2.50) for half a kilo (1 lb.) of shrimp. You might be able to get a better bargain. Past the market, toward the end of the pier, you can watch as fisherman haul in their morning catch and send it down the pier to market. Just feet from the pier, you can also see local surfers riding the waves and in the distance, the famous surf of the Punta Roca break. The pier is open daily from 6am to 7pm, but nearby, guarded parking is 75¢ (40p) a day.

Banks, ATMs, pharmacies, and grocery stores are on the road just north of the oceanfront; a modern shopping center is 1km (1/2 mile) east along from the pier.

PLAYA TUNCO ★

Playa Tunco, 7.5km (5 miles) west of La Libertad, is the Balsamo coast's most tourist-friendly location and a must stop along this coast. Tourists and El Salvadorans alike flock here on weekends to enjoy the waves, black-sand beaches, laid-back vibe, tasty seafood restaurants, and new and unique hotels. Tunco has something to offer most types of travelers.

Tunco consists of a main road ending on the beach and a side road with beachfront hotels. Numerous small restaurants, hotels, Internet cafes, and a couple of surf shops offering lessons are all tightly packed into this roughly 1km-long (1/2-mile) area. The beach is a long, black-sand beach with large rock formations just offshore. The surf at Tunco and nearby Sunzal can get big, but there's usually a small, near-shore break that can accommodate beginner surfers and swimmers.

Opportunities for outdoor tours abound: for instance, the nearby **Las Olas Beach House** (see below) offers hiking, kayak, surfing, horseback riding, and off-road motorcycle tours. But my favorite activity here is spending evenings on the second-story, thatched-hut deck of Erika's beachfront restaurant (see below), watching the sun go down behind the surfers. That's paradise.

To get here, take bus no. 192 from La Libertad and get off near Km 42 at the main Tunco entrance, which is marked by a large sign advertising the area's many hotels and restaurants. The town center is a 5-minute walk from there.

Where to Stay

One of the great things about Playa Tunco is that it has accommodations to please everyone. The town offers everything from a $3 (£1.50) a night campground that's just 44m (145 ft.) from the ocean to a magical retreat with a sweat lodge and cave bar.

Hotel y Restaurante Tekuaní Kal ★★ Finds This unusual, artistic, Maya-inspired boutique beachfront hotel is worth every penny of its slightly higher rates. Tekuaní Kal, located a few hundred yards off Tunco's main road, is one of the most unique hotels in the country—it's perhaps best known for its large, whimsical, Maya-inspired cement sculptures that are scattered around the gardenlike property. Rounding out the Maya feel is a newly constructed cave bar and a Maya sweat lodge that hosts weekly traditional purification ceremonies led by a local. The property winds down a rocky cliff to the beach and includes a small infinity pool and waterfall. Rooms are of average size with interesting Maya art; room nos. 1 through 4 have the best ocean views. Service is excellent, with a friendly staff and English-speaking on-site owner. The hotel opened in 2007 and its reputation is growing fast, so book early.

Km 42 Carretera Literal. ✆ **503/2389-6388.** 6 units. $70 (£35) double. Rates include breakfast. AE, DC, DISC, MC, V. **Amenities:** Restaurant; small infinity pool and larger swimming pool; room service; sauna. *In room:* A/C, TV, no phone, Wi-Fi.

La Guitara Hotel and Bar ★★ La Guitara is the newest, most modern, low-priced option on the Tunco block and can't be beat for the money. The hotel has nine attached and semiattached cabins with private bathrooms and patios with hammocks. The large grassy property is on the beach and offers a big pool, Ping-Pong and pool tables, and a bar. Tunco offers many low-priced options, but what sets La Guitara apart are its modern, efficient, air-conditioned cabins. Papaya's Lodge (see below) is still the best place in town to meet other travelers, but La Guitara is the place to go if you already have travel companions and want a more tranquil experience and nicer rooms.

Km 42 Carretera Literal. ✆ **503/2389-6398.** 9 units. $30 (£15) double. No credit cards. **Amenities:** Bar; Internet (free in lobby); pool. *In room:* A/C (in 5 rooms), no phone.

Papaya's Lodge ★ Value Papaya's is Tunco's best-known hostel and one of its two best low-cost options. In the middle of the action on Tunco's main street and just a couple hundred yards from the ocean, Papaya's is a laid-back, family-friendly surf hostel with eight rooms, including three with private baths. Payapa's also features a fully stocked kitchen open to guests, a breezy upstairs deck, and a gazebo with hammocks over a small river that runs through the area. Since this is a hostel, don't expect a palace, but know that you'd be hard-pressed to find a more welcoming and well-maintained place to spend a few surf and hammock filled days. The hostel is right beside an Internet cafe and surf shop that offers board rentals and bilingual surf lessons.

Km 42 Carretera Literal. ✆ **503/2389-6231.** www.papayasurfing.com. 8 units. $12–$14 (£6–£12). No credit cards. **Amenities:** Kitchen; surfboard rental. *In room:* Fan, no phone.

Roca Sunzal ★ Kids Roca Sunzal is a good midrange, beachfront option for those who prefer a hotel over a hostel. Immediately across the street from Papaya's Lodge, the 16-room Roca Sunzal offers an open-air, ocean-view restaurant and a central courtyard with a nice-size pool. Roca Sunzal is also one of Tunco's more family-friendly hotels, so there are often lots of kids running around. The rooms are in a two-story, U-shaped building around the pool, so only a few rooms offer beach views. Room no. 13 is the largest of the oceanview rooms, with the best view.

Km 42 Carretera Literal. **503/2389-6126.** Fax 503/2389-6190. www.rocsunzal.com. 16 units. $48–$60 (£24–£30) double Mon–Fri; $58–$70 (£29–£35) double Fri–Sun; $120–$140 (£60–£70) suite. AE, MC, V. **Amenities:** Restaurant; pool; $8–$10 (£4–£5) room service; surfboard rental. *In room:* A/C, fan, TV (in some), kitchen and fridge (in some).

Where to Dine

On the beach at the end of Tunco's main street are two nearly identical restaurants, **Restaurante Erika** (✆ **503/2389-6054**) and **La Bocana Restaurante** (✆ **503/2389-6238**). It's easy to confuse the two, as both offer similar two-story deck seating overlooking the ocean and menus with delicious fish entrees ranging from $7 to $10 (£3.50–£5). The distinguishing factor is that Erika's is more of a locals' joint while La Bocana attracts more tourists. Whichever you choose, aim to grab a seat on one of their decks at sunset, since the views are amazing.

The full-service restaurants at **Tekuaní Kal** (✆ **503/2389-6388**) and **Las Olas** (✆ **503/2411-7553**) also offer great views and fresh seafood entrees, as well as a chance to see these two great hotels without the cost of a room.

Playa Tunco After Dark

Playa Tunco is one of the few small towns in El Salvador to have a nightlife scene, and it's centered around **Roots Campground,** right off the town's main road. Each Saturday, Roots sponsors a live music or DJ party on its huge, grassy, beachfront expanse. The cover charge depends on the event, but it's usually a good time.

PLAYA SUNZAL

Playa Sunzal is a tiny community next door to Tunco (and 9km/5½ miles west of La Libertad), which features a couple of surf hostels, a few *pupusarias* along the main highway, and a rocky point break that's made the village famous among surfers. You can reach Sunzal from the highway or by taking a 10-minute stroll along the beach to the right from Tunco and turning inland at an opening in the retaining wall just before the point break. Follow the path and turn right at your first opportunity. There are a couple of hostels on this path, and *pupusarias* are on the highway ahead and to the left.

Where to Stay & Dine

Las Olas Beach House ★★★ Located 2km (1¼ miles) west of Sunzal's beach, Las Olas has stunningly beautiful cliff-top vistas and is the place to stay in the area if you want an adventurous but upscale vacation. The property has an infinity pool and a huge, saltwater pool at the bottom of the cliff on which it's perched—from here, you get great views of the Sunzal point break and the rocky coast. The sizeable rooms have a Caribbean-Hawaiian surfer vibe, with lots of shells and colorful fabrics used in the decor. But the real attraction is the hotel's adventure offerings. Las Olas' manager and two on-site owners speak English and are adept at taking guests on surfing tours to the best spots in the country, heading up motocross tours through off-road mountain trails, and conducting kayaking, snorkeling, horseback riding, and hiking tours. These folks really know

 **Sink or Swim**

You should swim at your own risk all along the western Pacific coast of El Salvador. There are few if any public lifeguards and most beachfront hotels don't provide them. So if the waves are big, you're not a great swimmer, or it feels like there's too strong a current, you probably shouldn't go in. There are even a number of river mouths meeting the ocean where the current can be particularly overpowering; don't swim in these locations. However, protected Tamarindo area offers the calmest waters in the country and, when the waves are small along Playa Tunco, Playa Sunzal, or Barra de Santiago, you should have no problem. Just keep in mind there is often no one around to save you if you do encounter any issues.

what they're doing and enjoy outdoor experiences as much as their guests. The 3- to 4-hour tours are $25 to $40 (£13–£20).

Las Olas' restaurant is decidedly upscale and includes delicious seafood dishes like mahimahi and a fresh-as-it-comes seafood chowder.

Km 45 Carretera Literal. ✆ **503/2411-7553.** javierlasolas@yahoo.com. 5 units. $70 double with private bathroom; $125 double with shared bathroom. Rates include breakfast. AE, DC, DISC, MC, V. **Amenities:** Restaurant; $35 airport transfers; 2 pools; sports equipment rental w/tours or lessons. *In room:* A/C, no phone.

PLAYA ZONTE

Playa Zonte is a beautiful, approximately 1km (1/2-mile) stretch of sandy and rocky beach a 19km (12 miles) trip west of La Libertad. Many travelers break into Tunco-versus-Zonte camps, with Zonte siders preferring that beach town for its less developed and more laid-back vibe. Surfers like its strong beach break and nonsurfers can enjoy its sandier beaches, depending on the tides.

To get to Playa Zonte, follow coastal highway CA-2 west from La Libertad to approximately Km 53 and look for the La Casa de Frida sign. Turn left there. Coming from the west, look for a sign on your left reading INTERVIDA EL SALVADOR with an image of the earth. Turn right there. The main road into Zonte has two entrances and is like a giant circular driveway leading to the hotel area. So you can take either entrance and get to the same place.

Where to Stay & Dine

Zonte offers a small collection of laid-back beachfront hostels and restaurants. One of the best places to stay in Zonte is the well-known **La Casa de Frida** (Km 53.5 Carretera Literal No. 7, Playa Zonte; ✆ **503/2300-7001**). The many portraits of Mexican artist Frida Kahlo hanging by the entrance confirm that you've found your way to this friendly, three-room hostal. Each room has four beds and it runs $10 (£5) per bed or costs $20 (£10) per person to have the room to yourself. The hostel is right on the beach and its small restaurant is one of the best in town. If Frida's is booked, try the nearby five-room **Olas Permanentes hostal** (Km 53 Carretera Literal, Playa El Zonte; ✆ **503/2300-6422**). This family-friendly and surfer hostal offers private rooms with private bathrooms for $25 (£13) and surfboard rentals for $12 (£6).

In addition to the restaurant at La Casa de Frida, the **Costa Brava Restaurante** (53.5 Carretera Literal, Playa El Zonte, a 5-min. walk west from Frida's; ✆ **503/2302-6068**) offers a big fish and meat menu for $6 to $12 (£3–£6), with oceanview seating.

15 EASTERN PACIFIC COAST

66km (41 miles) SE of San Salvador

Though it's not as developed as the country's western coast, El Salvador's far eastern coast offers a number of attractions. The biggest places to visit here, **Costa del Sol** and **Isla del Montecristo,** are described below, but the region also offers a four-star surfing resort, a unique fishing village, and a sleepy beach town that's great for swimming. Near the town of Playa El Cuco, you'll find the **Las Flores Surf Club,** which is a seven-room, all-inclusive, four-star slice of luxury, with the prices to match. Three- and 4-night, single-occupancy, nonsurfing packages begin at $1,150 (£575) for two or $790 (£395) per person; the surf packages cost a few hundred dollars more. But you get what you pay for—the grounds are set on a beautiful, and private, beach cove; the rooms are enormous and boast a modern, Asian-inspired decor; and the staff caters to your every need. The hotel has been open for about 3 years and each year shuts down for a couple of weeks for upgrades, so make reservations in advance.

Just 2km (1¼ miles) east of the Las Flores Surf Club, you'll find a much different experience in the village of **Playa El Cuco,** which can be reached on bus no. 385 from San Miguel or by driving east along Hwy. CA-2 and following the signs. El Cuco is a medium-size fishing village that also functions as a popular El Salvadoran beach getaway. Swimmers often share the ocean with small boats heading out for the day, and the beach is lined with tables there for drying the fishermen's morning catches, as well as thatched-roof covered restaurants catering to El Salvadorans enjoying the weekend. If you want to step off the normal tourist path for a couple of days, this is a great place to go. El Cuco offers small, nonluxury hotels such as **Hotel Vina del Mar** (Calle al Esterito, 100m/328 ft. off the main square; ✆ **503/2619-9122;** $40/£20 with air-conditioning; $20/£10 without air-conditioning) as well as the more luxurious **Hotel Pacific Paradise** (500m/1,640 ft. before Esterón, Intipucá; ✆ **503/2502-2791**), which has a couple of pools and big, two-bedroom bungalows for $120 (£60) per night.

Farther east, you'll find the calm waters and uncrowded beaches of **Playa Tamarindo.** Tamarindo is nestled into a cove near the end of El Salvador's coast, which makes its ocean waters some of the calmest and best for swimming in the country. The area is also known for quality deep-sea fishing and its inhabited islands 1 hour off the coast. Tamarindo hotels, such as **Hotel Tropico Inn** (La Metaza, Playa El Tamarindo, La Unión; ✆ **503/2649-5082**), aren't cheap at about $75 (£38) a night. But the area is lush, tropical, and you'll likely be the only international traveler around.

COSTA DEL SOL

Costa del Sol's reputation is better than its reality. This stretch of highway southeast of San Salvador, with the Pacific on one side and a beautiful bay on the other, is known as the beach getaway for El Salvador's wealthy elite. If you're invited to one of the locals' large beach houses, no doubt you'll have a blast. But for the average traveler, the region is hard to get a handle on. Huge walls block the beach from the region's homes, and Costa del Sol offers no central area of activity. There's no charming cluster of interesting restaurants or shops, and most visitors usually check into their hotel, hang out on their hotel beach, and eat in their hotel restaurant during their stay.

All that said, Costa del Sol can be an excellent beach day trip, as it's only 25 minutes from the airport and 45 minutes from San Salvador, with public beach access at the local tourist center. Costa del Sol's beaches are also huge, sandier, and, when the waters are calm, better for swimming than the rockier beaches to the west. The area even offers a gorgeous bay with an international cadre of yachts bobbing in its protected waters, where regular folks can rent some watercraft. It's definitely possible to have a great time here, especially is you're looking for a packaged resort experience.

Essentials

Getting There

BY BUS From San Salvador, take bus no. 133 toward Zacatecoluca. Ask to be let off at the road to Costa del Sol. From there, wait for bus no. 19, which will drop you off in front of your hotel along Costa del Sol's main road.

BY CAR From San Salvador, follow Hwy. CA-2 east to Km 43 and look for the detour south toward Costa del Sol. Follow the signs and, as there is no Costa del Sol town center, look for the kilometer markers that match the address of your hotel.

Getting Around

The best way to navigate Costa del Sol is by foot along the beach. You can also catch bus no. 193 anywhere along Costa del Sol's main road, which runs regularly throughout the day.

Visitor Information & Fast Facts

Costa del Sol doesn't have a tourism office, but some hotels have English-speaking front desks, and the tourism office in Puerto La Libertad (Km 34.5 Carretera Literal, 90m/295 ft. from the Shell gas station; ✆ **503/2346-1898**) can provide basic information. It's open daily 8am to 5pm.

This entire region is sorely lacking in tourist services—for hospitals, banks, or Internet access, you'll need to journey back to San Salvador or Puerto La Libertad.

What to See & Do

Boating in the bay and swimming or sunbathing on the beaches are the main attractions here—most people actually just enjoy whatever their hotel has to offer during their visit to the area. But Costa del Sol does have a few places outside of the hotels that are worth checking out, including **Aqua Fun** (Km 75.5 Boulevard; ✆ **503/2305-5294**), a laid-back bar and restaurant on the bay with a big pool, pool table, bay views, and $70 (£35) per hour motorized watercraft rental. It's a good place to take a break from the beach. If you just want to visit for the day, head to Costa del Sol's **Turicentro** (Km 63.5 Boulevard; ✆ **503/2338-2050**). This is one of the country's better tourist centers with beach access, a nice pool, changing rooms, picnic tables, and a restaurant. Admission is 80¢ (40p) and the center is open daily from 7am to 4pm.

Where to Stay

Bahía del Sol Hotel Overrated Bahía del Sol is a reasonably priced and enjoyable enough place to stay, but it's a bit overhyped. It's developed a megaresort reputation because it *is* the place to be if you want to dock your yacht, take a $1,200 (£600) per-day deep-sea fishing excursion, or play blackjack. Its biggest draws are its small casino and marina. But for the average traveler, it's just a slightly-above-average resort, albeit one with some ocean and bayfront rooms and town houses with outdoor Jacuzzis. Most of the rooms, however, are average sized, with nondescript decor, and are situated away from the water and the good views.

Km 78 Boulevard Costa del Sol. ✆ **503/2327-0300** or 2510-7200. www.bahiadelsolelsalvador.com. 55 units. $138–$147 (£69–£74) double; $300 (£150) large suite. Rates include breakfast, lunch, and dinner. AE, DC, DISC, MC, V. **Amenities:** 2 restaurants; 2 bars; deep-sea fishing tours; exercise room; room service; Wi-Fi in lobby and some common areas. *In room:* A/C, TV, full kitchens (in suite).

Comfort Inn ★★ (Kids) Despite its chain hotel status and low-end reputation, the Comfort Inn might be Costa del Sol's best hotel. This six-story, beachfront hotel was built in 2006 with all of the money and technology an international chain can afford—which means everything is newly updated and looks great. All the rooms have balconies with beautiful, long-range Pacific views, and the grounds include two huge pools—one of which is the largest I've seen in El Salvador—a poolside bar, an open-air restaurant, and a wide, sandy beach. The rooms are at least as large as you'll find in other El Salvador hotels and the bathrooms are larger and more modern. Three large suites are also available on the top floor. Room service is a bit slow and a load of laundry is a ridiculous $13 (£6.50), but the decent room rates compensate for this.

Km 75.5 Boulevard Costa del Sol. ✆ **877/424-6423** or 503/2325-7500. www.hoteleselsalvador.com. 63 units. $141 (£71) double; $260 (£130) suite. Rates include 3 meals. AE, DC, DISC, MC, V. **Amenities:** Restaurant; bar; nonsmoking rooms available; 2 pools; room service; Wi-Fi in lobby. *In room:* A/C, TV.

Hotel Pacific Paradise Pacific Paradise is a pleasant but dated, 25-year-old beachfront resort, and it should be your last choice of the three hotels listed here. Its rooms are a distance from the beach and are not exceptionally attractive—think tired, nondescript decor—and are only average sized. The restaurant also rests away from the beach in an odd, glass-enclosed structure offering little in the way of ambience or views. The grounds include a pool surrounded by 1970s-like cement tables with plastic chairs. On the plus side, it's on a big sandy beach, has a grassy interior courtyard, and offers a few two-bedroom, pool-view bungalows. When making reservations, request the presidential suite, one of the bungalows or, at very least, an upstairs room.

Km 75 Boulevard Costa del Sol. ✆ **503/2338-0156.** www.hotelpacificparadise.com. 49 units. $99–$120 (£50–£60) double. Rates include breakfast, lunch, and dinner. AE, DC, DISC, MC, V. **Amenities:** Restaurant; $25 (£13) boat tours of bay; room service; Wi-Fi. *In room:* A/C, TV, no phone.

Where to Dine

Most visitors stick to their hotel restaurants, but Costa del Sol also has two independent restaurants worth trying.

Acajutla Seafood Restaurant ★★ SEAFOOD The seafood is delicious, the scenery is beautiful, and the service is excellent. Acajutla, part of a well-reputed 20-year old seafood chain, is definitely worth leaving your hotel for. Like Mar y Sol, Acajutla is on the bay side of the main road and has great views and bay breezes. But Acajutla surpasses that restaurant with its formal service, its three-page seafood menu, and exquisitely prepared dishes. Among the best is the mixed grilled lobster and crab with butter and garlic sauce. The *sopa de marisco,* or fish soup, is quite hearty, and most of Acajutla's entrees are huge by El Salvador standards. Each entree also begins with a tasty appetizer of tortilla chips in a spicy dip sprinkled with cheese.

Km 73.5 Boulevard Costa del Sol. ✆ **503/2338-0397.** Main courses $12–$18 (£6–£9). AE, DC, MC, V. Daily 8am–10pm.

Mar y Sol ★ (Finds) SALVADORAN Mar y Sol is a comfortable, laid-back, and inexpensive place to have a simple meal, a cold beer, and take in the beautiful view of the bay. The restaurant is located along Costa del Sol's main road and offers a covered, open-air deck with bench seating overlooking the estuary. The one-page, Spanish-only menu is simple, with items like fried or grilled fish, chicken, or steak with rice and salad and cheap empanadas and *pupusas* ($2/£1). But it's the scenery you get for the cost that is Mar y Sol's biggest draw.

Km 75.5 Boulevard Costa del Sol. ✆ **503/2301-8250.** Main courses $4–$10 (£2–£5). No credit cards. Daily 7:30am–7pm.

ISLA DE MONTECRISTO ★★

Isla de Montecristo, 80km (50 miles) southeast of San Salvador, is a gorgeous, largely undeveloped 2.5-sq.-km (1-sq.-mile) island, situated where the large Río Lempa empties into the Pacific. The tiny island is home to acres of fruit trees, a few farming communities, and hundreds of nesting birds. Most visitors come to the island by dugout canoe or small motorboat to spend a couple of days hiking, fishing, or just swinging in a hammock along the river.

The best way to get to the island is to travel to the nearby community of La Pita and catch a boat there across to the island. This 30-minute canoe journey is half the fun of the trip, since you'll spot birds flying low and fish skimming the surface of the water along the way. It takes a bit of effort, especially by bus, to get to La Pita itself, so it's best to call one of the hostels mentioned below to arrange lodging and transportation.

Essentials

Getting There

BY BUS From San Salvador, take bus no. 302 toward Usulután and tell the driver to let you off at San Nicolás Lempa near the Texaco Station. Buses leave from there for the 13km (8-mile) journey to La Pita daily at 5am and 2pm and return at 5:30am and 3pm.

BY CAR Follow Hwy. CA-2 to Km 87 and turn at the Texaco station; then follow the road until it dead-ends in La Pita.

Orientation & Getting Around

Isla de Montecristo is a small, undeveloped island comprising family farms and one tiny town center with two hostels and a restaurant, which serves as the port where visitors arrive and depart. You can walk across the island from the river to the Pacific along unmarked trails in about 30 minutes—there are no buses or taxis on the island.

Visitor Information & Fast Facts

Information about the island and arrangements can be had by calling Montecristo's two hostels (see below) or the local nonprofit **CORDES** (© **503/2235-8262** or 2883-4825; central@telesal.net), which helps local families find work, and can arrange lodging, transportation, and tours.

The island has no shops other than a single tienda, so you'll need to head to San Salvador or Puerto La Libertad for services like banks, hospitals, and Internet access.

What to See & Do

Isla de Montecristo is home to a wide variety of birds, including majestic white egrets which, seemingly on cue, pose for near-perfect photos as they glide low over the calm estuary waters here. Locals can take you on tours in dugout canoes to places where you can spot other bird life, along with the area's unique, 15-centimeter-long (6-in.) jumping fish, which skim along the surface near shore. Or you can simply stroll around the island. Note that the currents on the Pacific side can be strong, so swimming in the ocean is not recommended.

Where to Stay & Dine

The island offers two, thatched-roof hostels with beds and hammocks and one restaurant that will cook you fish and *pupusas*. **Hostal Juan Lobo** (© **503/2634-6387;** no credit cards) has four huts with cement sleeping pads topped by mattresses and a large open-air gazebo with hammocks. Hammocks are $3 (£1.50) a night and two-to-three person cabins are $10 (£5) a night. Much nicer, however, is **Cabanas y Rancho Brisas del Mar** (© **503/2367-2107;** no credit cards) which offers two rustic but comfortable two-bed-plus hammock cabins with patios right on the river for $15 (£7.50) a night. Brisas del Mar also has the island's only open-air, riverside restaurant. Both hostels provide round-trip boat transportation from La Pita for $20 (£10) per person and offer 1-to-2-hour estuary tours for $5 to $10 (£2.50–£5) per person. Prices can often be negotiated down.

Finds **Island Wildlife**

In between Isla de Montecristo and the beaches to its east is the huge island **Bahía de Jiquilisco.** This largely undeveloped inlet offers untouched natural beauty with dozens of mangrove-lined channels to paddle, islands to explore, great views, and beautiful ocean and bay beaches. The bay is also a major stop along the way for 87 types of migratory birds and a nesting ground for sea turtles. It remains one of the coast's most untouched and naturally beautiful areas. The only problems are that the easiest way to get here is by passing through the dangerous and seedy little village of Puerto El Triunfo, and there is little tourism infrastructure immediately around the bay. As a result, Jiquilisco is best explored with a tour company such as **Eco Mayan Tours** (Paseo General Escalón 3658, Colonia Escalón, San Salvador; ✆ **503/2298-2844;** www.ecomayantours.com), which can provide transportation and the equipment necessary to explore the bay.

Back on the mainland in La Pita is **Hostal Lempa Mar** (✆ **503/2310-9901** or 7787-5824; www.lempamar.com; no credit cards), which features small but comfortable, three-person, $15 (£7.50) per night cabins and a riverside restaurant. The hostel will take you to the island for $10 (£5) per person each way.

16 EASTERN EL SALVADOR

Alegría: 49km (30 miles) W of San Migue. Perquín: 53km (33 miles) N of San Miguel. San Miguel: 138km (85 miles) E of San Salvador. San Vicente: 56km (35 miles) E of San Salvador.

Eastern El Salvador might seem less action-packed than the attraction-filled west, but its rural charm and civil-war history make this less visited corner of El Salvador well worth the trip. Highlights include the charming, cool mountainside village of Alegría; the historical town of Perquín, which has the country's most definitive collection of FARC war relics; and the tragic village of Mozote, whose people suffered one of modern Latin America's worst war-time atrocities. Although this is also one of the poorest sections of the country, you'll find the residents of the east to perhaps be the friendliest of your trip.

ALEGRIA ★

Located 1,200m (3,937 ft.) above sea level, high up in coffee country, the charming little town of Alegría offers some of the best views in the nation as well as great hiking trails and a friendly, vibrant community. Late into the evening, the town's small, recently-renovated square teems with multi-generational families chatting with neighbors, kids playing, and teenagers hanging with friends. The small tourism kiosk and the mayor's office, both of which are on the main square, can arrange coffee plantation tours, hikes to a nearby crater lake, and info on the town's more than 150 beautiful flower displays. Situated conveniently between Perquín and San Salvador, Alegría is an easy stop off the main tourist trail.

Understanding El Salvador's Civil War

Exactly how El Salvador's 12-year civil war got started depends on whom you ask. More specifically, it depends on where that person falls on El Salvador's socioeconomic scale. Some on the upper end will tell you the war was caused by senseless terrorism by those who had no right or cause. Some on the lower end of the pay scale see the war as a courageous people's struggle. But, generally speaking, the war began because El Salvador's *campesinos* or peasant farmers got tired of living as, well, campesinos. By the late 1970s, these campesinos had struggled for decades without much forward progress despite occasional and tepid reforms passed by El Salvador's right-wing military government and land-based oligarchy, and calling for war began to seem like the best way to call for change. Add to the mix yet another failed government reform in 1976, the 1980 government assassination of the beloved human rights leader Monseñor Oscar Romero, and the organization in 1980 of four left-wing people's groups into the formidable **Farabundo Martí National Liberation Front (FMLN)** and the stage for war was set. Some had hope that war could be avoided when a group of slightly more moderate government agents took control of the government and nationalized some aspects of the economy in 1979 and 1980. But those moderates didn't go far enough and were themselves soon targets of the country's right-wing military death squads.

The FMLN launched its first major offensive against the El Salvadoran military in 1981 and successfully gained control of areas around Chalatenango and Morazán. The El Salvadoran military's response—with the help of the U.S. government, which spent $7 billion (£3.5 billion) trying to defeat the organization—was fierce and lasting. The war raged on and off for the next 12 years until both sides had had enough. The atrocities of the right, including individual assassinations and the 1981 **Mozote Massacre** (see p. 314 for info), have been well documented since. A peace deal was signed in 1992, most war crimes were legally forgiven, and the FMLN agreed to halt its military operations and become a political party. The FMLN remains a party today, and El Salvador has become not only a peaceful nation but Central America's fastest growing economy. Life among the poor, however, continues to be a struggle.

Essentials

Getting There & Getting Around

From San Miguel, catch any bus toward San Salvador and tell the driver to let you off in Triunfo. There you'll catch a minibus to the city of Santiago de Maria, where you can take one of a steady steam of buses the final 4km (2½ miles) to Alegría. A steady stream of buses also run daily between Alegría and nearby Maria de Santiago, where you can make connections to the rest of the country.

When driving from San Salvador in the west or San Miguel in the east, follow CA-1, also known as the Pan-American Highway (Carretera Panamericana), and get off at the sign for Santiago de Maria. Follow the signs the remaining 4km (2½ miles) to Alegría.

Alegría is a very walkable town; its tourism office, Internet cafe, restaurants, and hotels are all within a few blocks of its town square.

Visitor Information

Tourist information in Spanish is available in a small tourist kiosk just off the main square (no phone; Tues–Sun 8am–4pm).

FAST FACTS Alegría has no banks, ATMs, or post office, but all of these can be found in nearby Santiago de Maria. A pharmacy is located 1 block from the square across from the church. Internet access is available daily from 8am to 9pm for $1 (50p) an hour in a cafe just behind the main tourist kiosk; call ✆ **503/2628-1159** for info. Alegría's tourist police can be reached at ✆ **503/2628-1016** and ambulance service is at ✆ **503/2611-1332.**

What to See & Do

Alegría's main draws are its cool mountain climate, amazing views, and friendly vibe. The town is also known for its dozens of houses with unique flower displays. The mayor's office (in the main square; ✆ **503/2628-1001**) can arrange visits. **Alegría tours** (✆ **503/2611-1497;** www.alegriatours.8m.net) owned by English-speaking Saul Tercios, also offers $15 (£7.50), 2-hour to half-day tours of area coffee farms, a nearby crater lake, and historic sites within Alegría.

Where to Stay

Casa de Huespedes La Palma (Value) This hotel is older and a bit less updated than the Cartagena (see below), but it's comfortable, affordable, and right on the square. The hotel is hidden behind a flower-filled patio, but when you find the front door and ring the bell, you'll be greeted by hotel staff and two very friendly dogs who'll settle you into their comfortable, family-style hotel immediately. The three big rooms here are plain, with almost nothing on the walls, but the rooms are larger than most and, at $10 (£5) per person for a room in the center of town, they're a great deal.

Calle Pedro T Mortiño on the town square. ✆ **503/2628-1012.** 3 units. $20 (£10) double. No credit cards. *In room:* TV.

Vivero y Restaurante Cartagena ★ Cartagena isn't the cheapest property in town, but it's Alegría's best hotel. The hotel is a 10-minute walk from the main square but its flower-filled setting and mountainside views are worth the added trip. The hotel's eight cabins are plain but boast inviting front patios and larger than average sleeping areas. Cabin nos. 3, 4, and 5 are perched on the edge of the mountain and offer amazing views. The cabins fill up in August, December, and around Easter so reserve well in advance during these times. The hotel also has a restaurant and sells plants and locally produced crafts. The walk to the hotel is all downhill but it's a tough hike back up; you can ask the hotel to arrange transportation back to the square.

Final Barrio El Calvario. ✆ **503/2628-2362** or 2628-1131. cral1966@hotmail.com. 8 units. $50–$80 (£25–£40) cabin. No credit cards. **Amenities:** Restaurant. *In room:* No phone.

Where to Dine

La Fonda de Alegría ★ SALVADORAN La Fonda boasts Alegría's largest and most interesting menu. Just down the hill from the square en route to the Cartagena hotel, this restaurant offers a twist on basic Salvadoran cuisine with items such as a 4-ounce steak with Argentine sausage, avocado, and baby onions, and an Argentine sausage plate with refried beans. The English- and Spanish-language menu also features traditional *pupusas,* tacos, and hamburgers. La Fonda doesn't offer much in the way of views, but its open-air seating catches the mountain breezes just right.

 Av. Gólgata. ✆ **503/2628-1010.** Main courses $4.25–$9 (£2.10–£3.50). No credit cards. Daily 9am–9pm.

Restaurante El Portal SALVADORAN Though not as diverse in its offerings as La Fonda, El Portal does offer an ample menu and is right on the square. This 10-table, casual restaurant serves unique items such as Indian-spiced chicken with rice and salad and more traditional fare like steak dishes. It also has two big windows allowing for prime town-square people-watching. But possibly best of all is that El Portal has a working cappuccino machine. In a country with thousands of acres of coffee plants, you'd think there would be cappuccino on every corner. They're actually a rarity, so the frothy blends whipped up here are a real find.

Av. Pedro T Mortiño on the square. ✆ **503/2628-1144.** Main courses $4.50–$9. No credit cards. Daily 9am–9pm.

PERQUIN ★★

Perquín, tucked high in El Salvador's northeast mountains near the Guatemalan border, sheds important light on El Salvador's tragic civil war. This town was the headquarters for the FMLN in this part of the country during the civil war and is today best known for its Museo de la Revolución Salvadoreña, which displays artifacts and tells the story of the revolutionary guerrilla movement's efforts during the war. In addition to this must-see museum, Perquín has a tourist-friendly square, a couple of small artisans' shops, and a cool mountain climate that make it a nice stop.

Essentials

GETTING THERE From San Miguel, take bus no. 332C roughly 53km (33 miles) to Perquín; the bus stops right in the town square. If you're driving from San Miguel, take highway CA-7 for 53km (33 miles) into Perquín.

ORIENTATION Perquín is a small, walkable town with a tiny but attractive village square. Most of what you'll want or need is within a few blocks of the center, and the Museo de la Revolución is a 5-minute walk from the center.

GETTING AROUND Though you can walk to Perquín's attractions, you'll need to arrange a microbus or pickup truck at Perquín's tourist office (Colonia 10 Enero; ✆ **503/2680-4086**) to take you 8km (5 miles) to Mozote. Also, Perquín's best hotel, the Lenca Montana, is 1.5km (1 mile) south of the square.

VISITOR INFORMATION & FAST FACTS Perquín's tourist information office (Colonia 10 Enero; ✆ **503/2680-4086**) is open daily from 8am to 4:40pm. There are no banks or ATMs in Perquín. The **post office** (✆ **503/2675-1054**) is located on the main square opposite the church. Internet is available for $1 (50p) per hour at **Servicomputer** (Calle Principal; ✆ **503/2680-4353**) and a pharmacy is 1 block east of the square across the street from the church.

What to See & Do

El Mirador at Cerro de Perquín Across the street and a 10-minute hike uphill from the Museo de la Revolución (see below) is this lookout point, which is set in an area of the forest that once housed guerrilla camps. There's not much to see here today, since there's nothing obvious remaining from the guerrilla days on the hike. But the Mirador offers a great view and a little exercise.

Be Careful What You Ask For

Most travelers have some awareness of El Salvador's bloody 12-year civil war, which ended with the signing of peace accords in 1992, and are curious to better understand the war and its aftermath. But be careful with that curiosity. El Salvador's civil war was exceedingly violent, often included torture, and took place in a relatively small area. Because of El Salvador's high population density, very few El Salvadorans of a certain age failed to be personally affected by the war. I learned the hard way not to casually ask too many questions about those times. El Salvadorans are renowned for their friendly nature and will tell you about the war if asked. But, almost inevitably their stories will include the loss or torture of a wife, a child, or a father. The war is not a taboo subject, but these are horrific memories that should not be casually unearthed. It's better to ask questions of educators or El Salvadorans you know well.

Av. Los Heroes, Barrio La Paz. No phone. Across the street from the museum. Admission 50¢ (25p). Daily 8am–4pm.

Museo de la Revolución Salvadoreña ★★ This museum is the main reason travelers come to Perquín and for good reason. The small, four-room museum offers illuminating photos and Spanish-language histories of guerrilla martyrs, including those of the war's many female soldiers, and displays civil-war weaponry and equipment along with posters of inspirational slogans used during the war. Big rocket launchers, large chunks of a downed army helicopter, and even an old Ford sedan and Peugeot are displayed. One of the more interesting exhibits is the preserved studio of revolutionary Radio Venceremos. Near the station are the remains of a crater from an army bomb that barely missed its mark. Some museum displays include small English-language explanations and guides are available for a small tip. You shouldn't leave town without having visited this proud piece of the people's history.

Av. Los Heroes, Barrio La Paz. ✆ **503/7942-3721** or 2634-7984. 5-min. walk northwest of the square. Admission $1.20 (60p). Daily 8am–4pm.

Where to Stay & Dine

Within Perquín's town center, you'll find small *comedores* offering *pupusas* and simple roasted chicken or beef. The best are **La Cocina de Mama Toya y Mama Juana** (Carretera a Perquín, a few blocks south of the square; ✆ **503/2680-4045**) and **La Cocina de La Abuela** (Carretera a Perquín, a few blocks south of the square; no phone). Mama Juana is on the left as you enter Perquín and offers the cheapest eats at $2 (£1) for a roasted chicken and rice dinner. Mama Juana's also has some not-so-attractive rooms for $6 (£3) per night. Across the street from Mama Juana's is La Cocina de La Abuela, or "kitchen of the grandmother," which is open Saturdays and Sundays from 7am to 9pm and offers 35¢ (20p) *pupusas* and grilled steak for $4.50 to $7.50 (£2.25–£3.75).

The best restaurant in the area, however, is 1.5km (1 mile) south of town in the **Hotel de Montaña** (Km 205.5 Carretera a Perquín, Morazán; ✆ **503/2680-4046** or 2680-4080). The hotel restaurant has a large, English-language menu with tasty chicken, fish, and meat items from $5.80 to $8.80 (£2.90–£4.40) including a delicious chicken dish with cheese and mushrooms, rice, and salad for $6 (£3). The restaurant also has outdoor seating with great views.

Perquín Lenca Hotel de Montaña ★★ *Finds* Montaña is the best place to stay in the Perquín area. Located 1.5km (1 mile) south of town, this modern, cabin-style hotel sits on a steep mountainside just off the main road and offers modern rooms, a full-service restaurant, and great views. English-speaking hotel owner, informal El Salvador historian, and American native Ronald Brenneman, came to the area to assist refugees during the civil war, fell in love with the country, and decided to stay. The hotel's seven cabins were built in 2000 and the 10 rooms were constructed in 2006. The best deals are the rooms at $30 (£15) per night for two people. The rooms aren't big but have a modern, rustic feel, and are at the top of the mountain with comfortable patios offering high-altitude views. Some of the profits from the hotel go toward funding a grammar school that Brenneman's foundation recently opened in the area.

Km 205.5 Carretera a Perquín. ✆ **503/2680-4046** or 2680-4080. www.perquinlenca.com. 17 units. $50–$110 (£25–£55) cabin; $20–$30 (£10–£20) 2-bed room; $60 (£30) 4-bed room. Rates include full breakfast. AE, DC, DISC, MC, V. **Amenities:** Restaurant; room service. *In room:* Fan, Wi-Fi.

MOZOTE ★★

Mozote is a small village 8km (5 miles) south of Perquín where the El Salvadoran army executed more than 1,000 townspeople on December 11 and 12, 1981. Members of the army rounded up and separated the town's residents into groups of men, women, and children and then executed each group in and around the square and church. The burning of town buildings followed. The massacre is considered one of the worst in modern Latin American history and drew criticism from around the world. The tragedy was recognized by a United Nations truth commission in 1992 after many of the bodies were excavated at the site. Today, the names of the children killed are inscribed in a shrine in the church garden, and the famous Mozote memorial—a metal silhouette of a family holding hands—sits in the town square besides squares of wood inscribed with the names of those who died. Stopping in town to view the memorial here is necessary if you want to fully grasp the tragedy of the country's civil war.

To get to Mozote from Perquín, you'll need to arrange a pickup or microbus with Perquín's tourist office (Colonia 10 Enero; ✆ **503/2680-4086**). If you're driving, turn off the main road south of Perquín at the sign BIENVENIDOS A ARAMBALA. Follow the road for 1.5km (1 mile) and veer right at a fork in the road. Follow it for another 1.5km (1 mile) and turn left at the intersection, then go 2 blocks and turn right at the MONUMENTO EL MOZOTE sign and follow more signs to the town square.

SAN MIGUEL

Founded in 1530 by Spanish settlers, San Miguel is one of the country's oldest major cities and many of its buildings showcase Spanish colonial architecture. But as the country's third-largest city, the town offers neither the sophistication of big-city San Salvador nor the charms of El Salvador's small villages. If you're on a tight schedule, you may not want to go out of your way to stop here, as it doesn't offer anything you can't find in greater supply elsewhere. Since the town does have a large bus terminal with departures around the country, you may very well find yourself at least transferring through here. If you do find yourself in San Miguel with a few hours to kill, rest assured that there are a surprisingly interesting regional museum, a nearby lagoon, a cathedral, and a national theater to tour.

Essentials

GETTING THERE From San Salvador or stops along the Pan-American Highway (Carretera Panamericana), take bus no. 301 approximately 2 hours and 45 minutes west to San Miguel.

If driving from San Salvador, head 2½ hours east along Hwy. CA-1, also known as the Pan-American Highway, and follow the signs.

ORIENTATION & GETTING AROUND The church, national theater, and town's largest grocery store are all on or within a short walk of the main square, which is called **Parque David J. Guzman.** You'll need to take a short $2 (£1) taxi ride to the Museo Regional de Oriente. Taxis are readily available on the main square or can be called from the front desk of your hotel. The only bus you'll need around the city is no. 384, which travels to Laguna de Olemega. San Miguel's large bus terminal (6a Calle Oriente; no phone) has departures to Honduras, San Salvador, and other parts of the country daily.

VISITOR INFORMATION & FAST FACTS San Miguel does not have a tourist office. The city's **Casa de la Cultura** (15 Calle Poniente and 8 Av. Sur; © **503/2661-6582**) provides basic information in Spanish.

Scotiabank and Banco Agricultura, which are 1 block from the square, have ATMs. **ZonaWeb Ciber** (2a Calle Poniente; © **503/2661-8661;** daily 8am–5pm) is half a block south of the cathedral and offers Internet access for 75¢ (40p) per hour. The **post office** (© **503/2661-3709**) is just off the square at 4 Av. Sur.

What to See & Do

San Miguel is not a destination city; there simply isn't a whole lot to see and do here. Among the best options in town are the **Museo Regional de Oriente** (see below) and the **Catedral Nuestra Señora de La Paz** (4a Av. Norte on the main square; no phone; free admission; daily 8am–noon and 2–5pm), which features a soaring, four-story ceiling with large, stained-glass windows lining both walls. A striking, two-story, deep-red curtain hangs behind the 7.5m-tall (25-ft.) altar, and crystal chandeliers hang from the ceiling here. Just behind the cathedral, at 2a Calle Poniente, is the **Teatro Nacional** (no phone; Mon–Sat 8am–4pm; free admission). Inside you'll find a small, but traditional, two-story European performing arts theater that was built between 1903 and 1909. The theater, which offers occasional art shows and sales in the lobby, was renovated in 2003 but still lacks the grandeur of the Santa Ana theater. If you do stop here, head upstairs to the right, where you'll find glass doors with great views of the 2,128m-tall (6,984-ft.) Volcán Chaparrastique, also known as the San Miguel Volcano.

Other than the regional museum, San Miguel's most interesting attraction is **Laguna de Olomega.** Olomega is a small lake, just a 30-minute bus ride from San Miguel, from where you can take a boat ride to tiny Los Cerritos Island for $5 (£2.50) or a 2-hour lake tour for $30 (£15). You'll need to arrange your trips directly with the local fishermen, so I most recommend this trip for those with Spanish-language skills.

Museo Regional de Oriente ★ (Finds) The Museo Regional de Oriente is one of San Miguel's most fascinating attractions and one of the country's newest and most modern museums. The museum opened in November 2007 and offers a rich history of the region's culture and environment through a collection of ceramic, textile, and photo exhibits. At press time, there was an interesting special exhibit explaining the history of the mighty mastodons that once roamed the area. The overall museum is small—only about five rooms—but very well done. The only catch is that the curatorial copy is in Spanish, at least for the moment.

8a Av. Sur and Calle Oriente. ✆ **503/2660-1275.** Admission $1 (50p). Mon–Sat 9am–noon and 1–5pm.

Where to Stay

Comfort Inn ★ As boring as chain hotels can be, San Miguel's Comfort Inn happens to be your best option in town. It has a pool, exercise room, Wi-Fi, small restaurant and bar, and is a short cab ride from the square. It's also across the street from the large, modern Metrocentro Mall. It's a typical, efficient Comfort Inn with typical, efficient Comfort Inn–style rooms. You won't find any surprises here, but in a crowded, sometimes chaotic city like San Miguel, it's nice to have such an oasis of calm efficiency.

Final Alameda Roosevelt and Carratera a La Unión. ✆ **877/424-6423** or 503/2600-0200. Fax 503/2600-0203. www.comfortinn.com. 79 units. $53–$65 (£27–£33) double. Rates include full breakfast. AE, MC, DC, V. **Amenities:** Restaurant; bar; small exercise room; nonsmoking rooms; pool; room service; *In room:* A/C, TV, hair dryer, Wi-Fi.

Hotel Plaza Floresta At roughly $10 (£5) below the other guys, the 28-room Plaza Floresta is San Miguel's best budget option. It's comfortable, but you get what you pay for in terms of size and amenities: The rooms and bathrooms are small, there's no restaurant, and the interior courtyard's pool is tiny. On the upside, Plaza Floresta does offer Wi-Fi, is a quick $2 (£1) taxi ride to the center, and has a nice open-air seating area. The front desk staff is also friendly and helpful. If you're looking to save a few bucks and don't mind missing out on frills, you'll be happy here.

Av. Roosevelt Sur No. 704, Colonia Cuidad Jardin. ✆ **503/2640-1549.** www.hotelplazafloresta.com. 28 units. $31–$47 (£16–£24) double. AE, DC, DISC, MC, V. **Amenities:** Pool. *In room:* AC, TV, Wi-Fi.

Tropico Inn If the Comfort Inn is booked, the Tropico Inn will do. Like the other Tropicos in this national hotel chain, San Miguel's version tries to present itself as a luxury hotel, but doesn't quite get there. You'll be immediately and falsely impressed by the soaring, three-story and recently renovated lobby and the semielegant dining area beside the pool. But the luxury stops as soon as you sign on the dotted line. The hallways are dingy, with low ceilings, the rooms are big but dated, with old tired furniture, and the small pool is crammed in next to a big piece of industrial equipment. Basically everywhere but the lobby looks like it hasn't been touched since the 1970s. Room no. 1 is the biggest, and room nos. 203 and 239 offer the most quiet; most upstairs rooms have balconies overlooking the hotel's interior courtyard.

Av. Roosevelt Sur No. 303. ✆ **503/2661-1800.** www.hotelstropicoinn.com. 99 units. $47–$104 (£24–£52) double. Rates include full breakfast. AE, DC, DISC, MC, V. **Amenities:** Restaurant; pool; room service. *In room:* A/C, TV, Wi-Fi.

Where to Dine

La Pema Restaurante ★ SALVADORAN If you ask a local where to eat, he'll tell you to head to La Pema's. This 35-year-old San Miguel institution is a $3 (£1.50) taxi ride from the main square and isn't much on ambience. (The restaurant is basic, but it includes a huge, airy front dining room with bench seating and a smaller back room where mariachis regularly wander in and play.) Don't be fooled by the large, florescent menu on the wall, however: This place does not serve fast food. Whatever you order here will be good, quality food, especially the *cremas,* which are similar to soup but thicker and filled with dinner-size portions of meat, chicken, or fish. Here, they are served with salad and *pupusas*. La Pema also has a written menu that features their signature $30 (£15) grilled lobster, crab, and shrimp plate, and a smaller $10 (£5) version.

Km 142.5 Carretera a Cuco. ✆ **503/2667-6065.** Main courses $8–$15 (£4–£7.50). AE, DC, MC, V. Daily 10am–5pm. Dancing after 9pm on Fri.

SAN VICENTE

If you're on your way to or from San Salvador, try to take a short detour into San Vicente to have a look at the town's much-photographed clock tower. The five-story white cement tower in the middle of the town square is quite beautiful, with a kind of Dr. Seuss whimsy about it. The tower has been closed and under repair since the 2001 earthquake and, at press time, visitors were prohibited from climbing the structure. But the tower is still worth peeking at if you happen to be driving by. San Vincent's other big attraction, the Iglesia Pilar cathedral, was also damaged by the quake, and at press time was in the midst of a complete renovation.

Essentials

GETTING THERE & GETTING AROUND From San Salvador, you can take bus no. 116 to the center of town. If you're driving, San Vicente is just a few miles off the Pan-American Highway (Carretera Panamericana) and is well marked.

The tower and Iglesia Pilar are on or within walking distance of the square. San Vincent's best hotel, Posada Don Pablito, is about a 10-minute walk from the center.

VISITOR INFORMATION & FAST FACTS San Vicente has no tourist office, but information in Spanish is available at the city's **Casa de la Cultura** (Av. Crescencio Miranda no. 29a, Barrio San Francisco; ✆ **503/2393-1179**). Internet access is also available for 75¢ (40p) per hour at the **Zona Web Ciber Café** (2a Av. Norte no. 3, Barrio San Francisco; ✆ **503/2393-6729**).

What to See & Do

The clock tower and Iglesia El Pilar are the city's two main attractions. But you can also stop by the Casa de la Cultura for information about trips to a nearby hot springs known as Infiernillo and the nearby crater lake of Laguna de Apastapeque.

Where to Stay & Dine

The best place to stay in town is **Posada Don Pablito** (Boulevard Jacinto Castellanos No. 25, Lotificación Vaquerano; ✆ **503/2392-0012;** www.pasadadonpablito.com). This 14-room hotel is a fairly typical independently owned property—think basic but clean and comfortable—but it does have nice-size rooms with air-conditioning and TV, a restaurant, and is the hotel of choice for organizations such as USAID and Habitat for Humanity. Rooms are $23 to $59 (£12–£30) a night. You might also be tempted to stay at the Central Park Hotel on the square. Don't be; it's not very nice.

The most recommended restaurant in town is **Casa Blanca** (2a Calle Oriente, Barrio Santuario; ✆ **503/2393-0549**). Though this place has been around for 20 years and nearly everyone in town will point you straight here, Casa Blanca was a bit of a letdown on my last visit. The ambience is better than the food. Cool sculptures hang on the walls and birds even fly about inside the space, but its handful of meat, chicken, and fish dishes, while fine, don't impress. Main courses are $4 to $12 (£2–£6).

7

Honduras

by Nicholas Gill

Honduras has been unjustly overshadowed by its neighbors for decades. For some time, divers have passed over Honduras to go to Belize, nature and beach lovers have traveled to Costa Rica, and culture and history buffs have headed to Guatemala and Mexico. This is beginning to change, though, as more and more tourists are coming to realize that all of these attractions can be found in Honduras, and that, even though large crowds and overdevelopment threaten other Central American countries, Honduras is still practically untouched, with more cloud forests and unexplored tracts of wilderness than anywhere in the region.

Much of it may still be taken up by banana cultivation, but few other countries in the world today can lay claim to such obvious natural beauty. About the size of Tennessee, Honduras is home to 20 national parks, a couple of biosphere reserves, and nearly 100 other protected ecological areas. The cultural diversity here is nothing to laugh at either. The country has almost eight million people, mostly *mestizos* (mixed descendants of the Spanish and Ameri-Indians), as well as another 10% divided among eight main indigenous groups: the Lencas, the Chortís, the Tolupan, the Garífunas, the Miskitos, the Pech, the Tawahkas, and the Bay Islanders.

Adventure has been woven into the very fabric of this country over the past 400 years. Christopher Columbus set foot on the Bay Islands and the North Shore on his fourth and final voyage to the Americas in 1502, but that may be the most boring tale. Consider also that the country's history involves pirates raiding gold from Spanish ships and hiding the booty in caves on the Bay Islands, archaeologists searching for Maya ruins and crystal skulls, and a North American named William Walker launching a raid on the country with his own small army. Throw in conquistadors, indigenous warriors, multinational fruit corporations, whale sharks, and indigenous land rights and you have one of the most exciting environments on the planet.

Until recently, Honduras's tourist infrastructure has been limited, but things are slowly coming together. Visitors can now expect more variety, better hotels, and a far greater range of wild and wonderful tours and attractions than has ever existed here before. Cruise landings on the Bay Islands are expected to explode in the next decade as the ports are expanded. Luxury ecolodges near La Ceiba can now compete with anywhere else in Central America, and beach resorts are set to turn Tela Bay into the next Cancun. The Maya ruins of Copán are luring more and more visitors from countries to the north. Even La Mosquitia, traditionally one of the least accessible and unorganized places in the Americas, is turning to community-based tours and excelling at them.

1 THE REGIONS IN BRIEF

Covering 111,369 sq. km (43,000 sq. miles), Honduras is the second-largest country in Central America (Nicaragua is the largest) and the only one without volcanoes. It borders the Caribbean Sea, Pacific Ocean, Guatemala, Nicaragua, and El Salvador and is only a short ferry ride from Belize. Like points on a compass, the country can be divided into four major geographical sections: the lush forests and coastline to the north, the impenetrable jungles of La Mosquitia to the east, the mountains and pine forests of the western and central parts of the country, and the dry, dusty south. Forty percent of Honduras is made up of rainforests, while the coasts comprise nearly 966km (600 miles) of beaches.

THE SOUTH The country's 100km (62-mile) Pacific coast separates Honduras from El Salvador in the west and Nicaragua in the east, and marks the western boundary of the southern region, which extends up to the sprawling capital of **Tegucigalpa** (called Tegus by locals). Tegucigalpa is the cultural center of the country and home to several excellent museums, great restaurants and markets, and a smattering of luxury hotels. Just outside town, you will find small craft villages and one of the best national parks in the country, the **Parque Nacional La Tigra.**

THE WEST Mountains, cowboys, Maya ancestors, ancient ruins, cloud forests, Catholic festivals, and the largest lake in the country all join together to create western Honduras, one of the most diverse regions of the country. From the economic hub of the country, **San Pedro Sula,** you'll move southward across the fertile Sula valley to the Maya ruins of **Copán,** passing the bird-watching hot spot of **Lago de Yojoa,** the one-time capital of Central America, **Gracias,** the cigar and coffee center of **Santa Rosa de Copán,** and the colonial town of **Comayagua.**

THE NORTH COAST The north coast is an ecodream of lush tropical forests, 805km (500 miles) of empty white-sand beaches, fruit farms, and enough adrenaline-pumping sports to keep you busy for months. Near La Ceiba, the country's official capital of ecotourism, you'll find the **Cuero y Salado Wildlife Refuge,** raging white water on the **Río Cangrejal,** the waterfalls and hiking trails of **Pico Bonito National Park,** and easy access to the Bay Islands and the Cayos Cochinos. **Tela,** with even more natural attractions, like the Lancetilla Botanical Garden and Los Micos Lagoon, is set to become the site of a major beach project that could soon drastically change this laid-back banana town. Elsewhere in the region, you'll find friendly Garífuna villages and the once happening beachfront and Spanish fort in **Trujillo.**

THE BAY ISLANDS Stilted island houses, turquoise water, Garífuna settlements, and some of the best diving on earth make the Bay Islands one of the leading attractions in the country. While you'll find a growing number of cruise ports and luxury resorts on **Roatán** and a number of hostels and cheap restaurants on the backpacker paradise that is **Utila,** these two islands still retain their laid-back charm. The least visited of the three Bay Islands, **Guanaja,** is practically untouched.

LA MOSQUITIA This largest tract of wilderness in Central America is often called a mini-Amazon. The region is as wild as they come and is made up of indigenous tribes, rarely visited biological reserves, and tiny coastal communities where electricity is a rare luxury. Tour groups are increasingly exploring the **Río Platáno Biosphere Reserve** via rafting trips, though they are facing competition from new community-based ecotourism projects to the reserve.

2 THE BEST OF HONDURAS IN 1 WEEK

This itinerary will take you to the major attractions in the country, from the Maya ruins of Copán, to the mangroves and tropical forests of the North Coast, to the turquoise waters of the Bay Islands. It covers a little bit of everything. If you are less concerned about beaches and diving, opt to change your time in the Bay Islands for a quick fly in and out trip to La Mosquitia, or to spend more time exploring the Copán Ruínas area. Alternatively, you may be content to spend your entire trip lying on the beach or diving in Roatán or Utila, rather than heading inland at all. (Though San Pedro Sula is the country's largest international airport, it's possible to take an international flight directly to Tegucigalpa, Roatán, or La Ceiba, too).

Days 1 & 2: Arrive in San Pedro Sula and Head to Copán ★★★

Upon landing in San Pedro Sula, head directly to the town of **Copán Ruínas** ★★★ (p. 356) and spend your first day exploring the town. The next morning, wake up early to tour the Maya ruins of Copán before the crowds arrive, along with **Las Sepulturas** ★ (p. 360). Have lunch at **Hacienda San Lucas** ★★★ (p. 363)—or save it for dinner—and then take the afternoon and evening to explore the markets, **Museo Regional de Arqueología Maya** ★ (p. 362), or bars in town.

Days 3 & 4 From Santa Rosa de Copán to Tela ★★

From Copán, travel away from the border and into the mountains to check out the **Flor de Copán cigar factory** ★★ (p. 367) in Santa Rosa de Copán, stopping at the Maya ruins of **El Puente** ★ (p. 356) on the way. Then travel **La Ruta Lenca** ★★ (p. 373), stopping in small villages and exploring colonial churches, before settling into your hotel in **Gracias** (p. 369), the capital of the department of Lempira.

Wake up early the next morning for your best chance at seeing the elusive resplendent quetzal and other wildlife during your hike through **Parque Nacional Montaña de Celaque** ★★★ (p. 373). Afterward, head to **Tela** on the coast to check into the **Hotel Telamar** ★★★ (p. 378), once the home of United Fruit executives and now a five-star resort.

Days 5 & 6: See More Attractions Around Tela or Journey to La Ceiba ★

Wake up early to check out Jardín Botánico **Lancetilla** ★★ (p. 377), the world's second-largest botanical garden, or to take a boat tour in Parque Nacional Jeanette Kawas or **Punta Sal** ★★★ (p. 377), where you can spot howler monkeys, jaguars, and hundreds of species of birds.

Alternatively, head a few hours up the coast to **La Ceiba,** perhaps to check into the **Lodge at Pico Bonito** ★★★ (p. 389) in Pico Bonito National Park. You can easily spend 2 days here hiking, rafting, or on zip-line tours. Day-trip options abound, too, including snorkeling **Cayos Cochinos** ★★★ (p. 392), one of the most unspoiled coral reefs in the country, or visiting the Garífuna village of **Chachauate** ★ (p. 392).

Days 7 & 8: The Bay Islands ★★★

From La Ceiba, catch a ferry or plane for a short trip to Roatán, the most developed of the Bay Islands. Here you can explore West End Beach and dive on the world's second-largest barrier reef. In addition, you can head to **Anthony's Key** ★★ (p. 406) to swim with dolphins, take part in zip-line canopy tours in **Gumbalimba Park** ★ (p. 407), or visit the Garífuna communities on the east end of the island.

On day 8, transfer to the San Pedro Sula airport to make your flight out of the country.

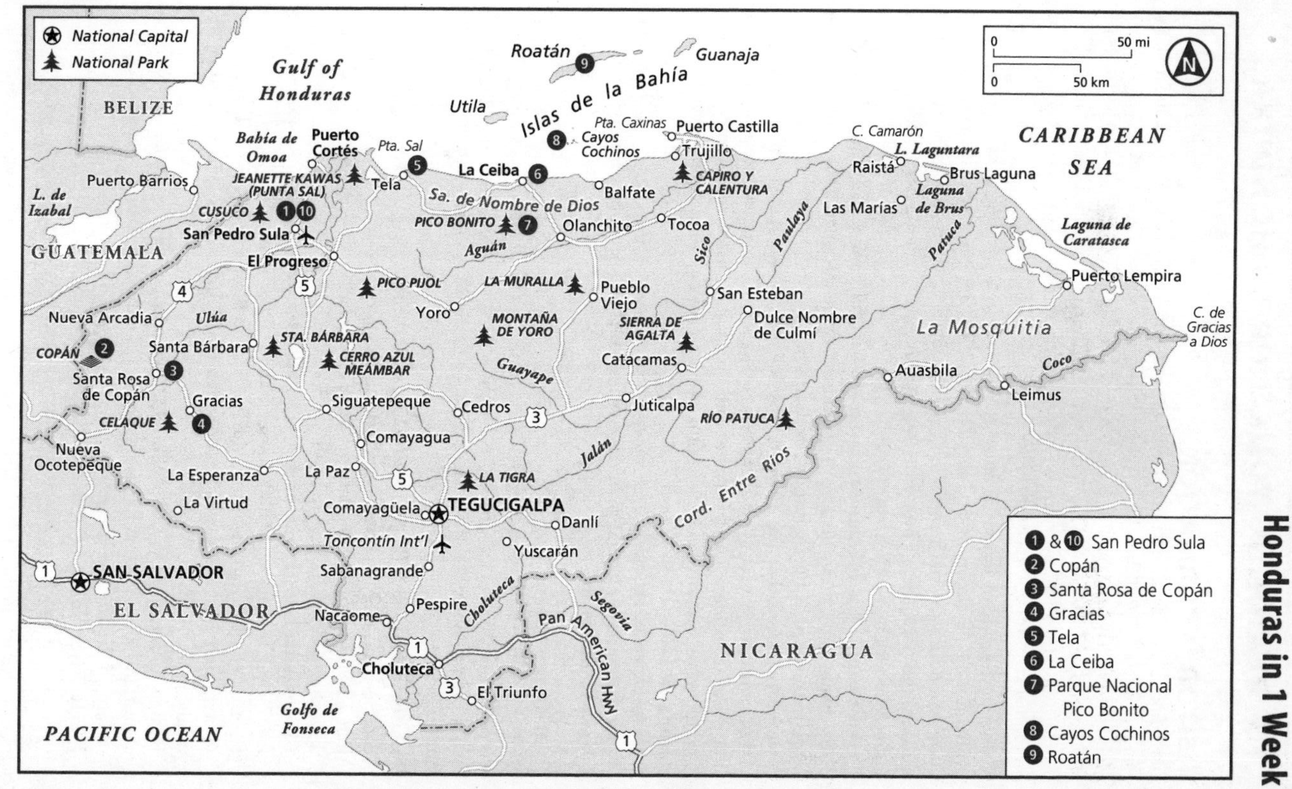
National Capital
National Park
0 50 mi
0 50 km
N
Gulf of Honduras
BELIZE
Roatán
Guanaja
Utila
Islas de la Bahía
Pta. Caxinas
Cayos Cochinos
Puerto Castilla
Trujillo
C. Camarón
L. Laguntara
CARIBBEAN SEA
Bahía de Omoa
Puerto Cortés
Pta. Sal
La Ceiba
Raistá
Brus Laguna
Laguna de Brus
L. de Izabal
Puerto Barrios
JEANETTE KAWAS (PUNTA SAL)
Tela
Sa. de Nombre de Dios
Balfate
CAPIRO Y CALENTURA
Las Marías
CUSUCO
San Pedro Sula
PICO BONITO
Olanchito
Tocoa
Paulaya
Laguna de Caratasca
GUATEMALA
El Progreso
Aguán
Sico
Patuca
PICO PIJOL
LA MURALLA
Pueblo Viejo
San Esteban
Puerto Lempira
Nueva Arcadia
Ulúa
Yoro
MONTAÑA DE YORO
SIERRA DE AGALTA
Dulce Nombre de Culmí
La Mosquitia
C. de Gracias a Dios
COPÁN
Santa Bárbara
STA. BÁRBARA
CERRO AZUL MEÁMBAR
Catacamas
Guayape
Auasbila
Coco
Santa Rosa de Copán
Gracias
Siguatepeque
Cedros
Juticalpa
Leimus
CELAQUE
RÍO PATUCA
Comayagua
Jalán
Nueva Ocotepeque
La Esperanza
La Paz
LA TIGRA
Cord. Entre Ríos
La Virtud
Comayagüela
TEGUCIGALPA
Danlí
Toncontín Int'l
Yuscarán
SAN SALVADOR
Sabanagrande
EL SALVADOR
Pespire
Choluteca
Nacaome
Segovia
Pan American Hwy
NICARAGUA
El Triunfo
Golfo de Fonseca
PACIFIC OCEAN
1 & 10 San Pedro Sula
2 Copán
3 Santa Rosa de Copán
4 Gracias
5 Tela
6 La Ceiba
7 Parque Nacional Pico Bonito
8 Cayos Cochinos
9 Roatán

3 PLANNING YOUR TRIP TO HONDURAS

VISITOR INFORMATION

You'll find a municipal or regional tourism office in nearly every city throughout the country, often in small booths in central parks and squares; these are generally open Monday to Friday from 8am to 4pm, often with a 1-hour break at noon. The **Instituto Hondureño de Turismo (IHT),** or the National Tourism Institute, does not have offices abroad, but promotes the country through their website: www.letsgohonduras.com. Additional websites of interest include:

- **www.bayislandsvoice.com**: A monthly newsmagazine covering the history, art, culture, dining, development, and social issues of Roatán, Utila, and Guanaja.
- **www.hondurasthisweek.com**: This English-language newspaper passed out in tourist towns and big cities all over Honduras has an online edition with weekly features, videos, podcasts, weather reports, and news.
- **www.hondurastips.honduras.com**: An excellent full online and print guidebook to the major tourism destinations in Honduras, with information and maps that are updated seasonally by the Institute of Tourism.
- **www.larutamoskitia.com**: The definitive site for exploring La Mosquitia. Questions about when to go, how to get there, what to do, and what you will see are all answered in detail. The site is run by a nonprofit community-based tour agency that offers multiday tours throughout the region and arranges day tours from individual communities.
- **www.sidewalkmystic.com**: An independent online planning guide to Honduras, with descriptions of highlights, travelogues, hotel and restaurant listings, and other how-to information.

Tour Operators

While many international tour operators run tours to Honduras, they are almost always contracted out through local operators such as those mentioned below. Booking directly will save you a bundle. Most are based in La Ceiba, but have offices in other parts of the country as well.

- **Garífuna Tours ★★** (✆ **504/440-3252;** www.garifunatours.com) is one of the most complete and well respected operations in the country. While they specialize in day-long adventure trips to the national parks along the North Coast near La Ceiba and Tela, they also run package tours to the Bay Islands, La Mosquitia, and Copán.
- **La Mosquitia Eco Adventures ★★** (✆ **504/414-5798;** www.lamoskitiaecoaventuras.com) is run by internationally known naturalist Jorge Salaverri. They offer everything from 10- to 14-day rafting trips in the Río Plátano Biosphere Reserve and explorations in even more remote parts of La Mosquitia to day hikes in national parks along the north coast.
- **Roatán Charters ★** (✆ **800/282-8932;** www.roatan.com) is a one-stop shop for almost any tour, regional flight, or hotel in Honduras or Belize, though they focus mostly on the Bay Islands.
- **Jungle River Tours** (✆ **504/440-1268;** www.jungleriverlodge.com) is a budget operator that focuses on adventure activities such as rafting, kayaking, and hiking in select destinations along the north coast.

Telephone Dialing Info at a Glance

The country code for Honduras is 504, which you use only when dialing from outside the country. Telephone numbers in this chapter include this prefix because most businesses' published phone numbers include the prefix.

- To place a call from your home country to Honduras: Dial the international access code (011 in the U.S. and Canada, 0011 in Australia, 0170 in New Zealand, 00 in the U.K.) plus the country code (504), followed by the number in Honduras. For example, a call from the United States to Tegucigalpa would be 011+504+000+0000.
- To place a call within Honduras: All you have to do is dial the number, as area codes are nonexistent.
- To place a direct international call from Honduras: Dial 193 for an international operator. Dial the country code of the destination you are calling, plus the area code and the local number.

- **La Ruta Mosquitia** ★★★ (✆ **504/406-6782;** www.larutamoskitia.com) is a grassroots tourism initiative that arranges a wide variety of day tours and guided 4- to 9-day excursions with cultural groups in La Mosquitia.

ENTRY REQUIREMENTS

Citizens of the United States, Canada, Great Britain, South Africa, New Zealand, and Australia require valid passports to enter Honduras as tourists. Citizens of any of these countries conducting business or enrolled in formal educational programs in Honduras also require visas. Tourist cards, distributed on arriving international flights or at border crossings, are good for stays of up to 90 days. Keep a copy of your tourist card for presentation upon departure from Honduras. (If you lose it, you'll have to pay a small fine.) You can extend your visa, once, for another 90 days at any immigration office for $20 (£10).

Honduras is part of a 2006 border control agreement with El Salvador, Guatemala, and Nicaragua allowing travel between the four countries under one tourist card. The number of days of your tourist card is determined at the first of the four countries entered.

Honduran Embassy Locations

In the U.S.: 3007 Tilden St., NW, Ste. 4M, Washington, DC 20008 (✆ **202/966-7702;** www.hondurasemb.org).

In Canada: 151 Slater St., Ste. 805, Ottawa, ON, K1P-5H3 (✆ **613/233-8900;** www.embassyhonduras.ca).

In the U.K.: 115 Gloucester Place, London, W1U 6JT (✆ **020/7486-4880;** honduras.embassy-uk.co.uk).

In Australia: Level 7, 19-31 Pitt St., Sydney NSW 2000, P.O. Box H6, Australia Square NSW 2000 (✆ **02/9247-1730**).

CUSTOMS

Any travel-related merchandise brought into Honduras, such as personal effects or clothing, is not taxed. Visitors entering Honduras may also bring in no more than 400 cigarettes, 500 grams of pipe tobacco, or 50 cigars, and 2.5 liters of alcoholic beverages per adult.

MONEY

The unit of currency in Honduras is the **lempira.** The value of the lempira has held steady around the current exchange rate of about 19 lempira to the U.S. dollar (or 38 lempira to the British pound), which is the rate used for prices listed in this book. Bills come in denominations of 1, 2, 5, 10, 20, 50, 100, 200, and 500. There are no lempira coins. ***Note:*** American dollars are commonly accepted in the Bay Islands, particularly at hotels—as a result, some reviews in that section only list rates using American and British currencies.

Dollars, pounds, and euros can be exchanged in banks, many hotels, as well with unofficial street money-changers found in parks, airports, and border crossings. ATMs are the most common way to exchange money, and most cities here have multiple banks with ATMs, many of them operating 24 hours. **BAC, Unibanc,** and **Banco Atlantida** are the most reliable and are compatible with a variety of networks, including Cirrus, PLUS, Visa, and MasterCard. Honduran banks do not usually charge a fee to use their ATMs, but your own institution might charge you for foreign purchases or withdrawals, so check before you go. You'll find ATMs in banks, grocery stores, gas stations, and pharmacies.

Traveler's checks are becoming less and less common, yet are still used occasionally and can be exchanged at most banks in the country, though a 2% fee is often charged. Visa and MasterCard are widely accepted throughout Honduras, and American Express and Diners Club are becoming increasingly more common, although 12% surcharges are normal.

WHEN TO GO

PEAK SEASON High tourist season in Honduras is during national holidays and the dry season, running roughly from January to June. Rain can occur anytime during the year, and flooding in the highlands can completely shut down roads and transportation at any time. For the Bay Islands, you should book well in advance during Semana Santa (Easter week) and Christmas/New Year's. The best months for spotting whale sharks are March and April, when rates also tend to go up. In La Mosquitia, the drier months (Feb–May and Aug–Nov) are easiest for travel; it stays nicer year-round in the Bay Islands.

CLIMATE Honduras lies completely within the Tropics. Temperatures range from hot and humid on the Caribbean coast (75.2°–93.2°F/24°–34°C), to mild and even cool in highland areas (60.8°–68°F/16°–20°C), to hot and dry along the southern Pacific coast (82.4°–89.6°F/28°–32°C). Seasonally, temperatures don't vary drastically and the change mostly relates to elevation. The amount of precipitation does vary, though. May to November is typically considered the rainy season for the interior, while September to January brings the rains for the North Coast, Bay Islands, and La Mosquitia. Hurricane season runs from August to November, although most, not all, hurricanes are a minor inconvenience.

PUBLIC HOLIDAYS Honduras's national holidays are New Year's Day (Jan 1), Maundy Thursday (Mar 20), Good Friday (Mar 21), Americas Day (Apr 14), Labor Day/May Day (May 1), Independence Day (Sept 15), Morazán Day (Oct 3), Christopher Columbus Day (Oct 12), Army Day (Oct 21), and Christmas Day (Dec 25).

Spas & Wellness Centers in Honduras

Honduras still has a long way to go in terms of attracting wellness travelers, especially compared to neighbors such as Costa Rica. Still, there are decent wellness retreats in a few parts of the country and some promising new projects on the horizon. The mountains in the west, once the land of the Mayas, are the center of spiritual and wellness tourism in the country. **Hacienda San Lucas** near Copán (p. 363) often holds comprehensive yoga and spiritual cleansing retreats led by internationally renowned names in the field, while the Gracias area is becoming more and more known for its hot springs. On the **Bay Islands,** several resorts have spas, though the range of treatments and services offered is nowhere near those featured in nearby Caribbean island resorts. Several new spas are in the works in this part of the country, however, including a chic **Nikki Beach** project set to open in the fall of 2010.

HEALTH CONCERNS

COMMON AILMENTS Few visitors to Honduras experience anything other than run-of-the-mill traveler's diarrhea in reaction to unfamiliar foods and any microorganisms in them, although outbreaks of cholera and hepatitis have occurred in recent years. Honduras's tap water should be avoided. Mosquito borne illnesses such as **malaria** and **dengue fever** do occur in Honduras, especially during the rainy season, when mosquitoes are most prevalent. See p. 70 in "Planning Your Trip to Central America" for more info.

VACCINATIONS Hepatitis A, polio, tetanus, smallpox, and typhoid shots are recommended (but not required) for visitors planning to be in contact with local residents on an extended basis. A hepatitis B shot is suggested as well, but not required. Malaria and yellow fever are extremely rare, yet if you intend on visiting extremely remote areas in La Mosquitia, you may want to discuss with your doctor your options for prevention.

GETTING THERE

By Plane

Honduras has four international airports, in San Pedro Sula (p. 341), Tegucigalpa (p. 330), Roatán (p. 400), and La Ceiba (p. 381).

FROM NORTH AMERICA There are nonstop flights and connections from the United States and Canada to every international airport, although the most frequent flights land in San Pedro Sula's **Ramón Villeda Morales International Airport (SAP)** and Tegucigalpa's **Toncontín International Airport (TGU).** The major carriers are **American, Continental, Delta, TACA,** and **Spirit.** There are daily nonstop flights from Miami, Atlanta, Houston, Ft. Lauderdale, and Newark (seasonally) to San Pedro Sula and/or Tegucigalpa. There are also nonstop flights to Roatán (Bay Islands) on Thursdays, Saturdays and/or Sundays with Continental (Houston), Delta (Atlanta) and TACA (Miami and Houston). See "Appendix: Fast Facts, Toll-Free Numbers & Websites" for airline phone numbers and websites.

Atlantic Airlines (**© 504/440-2343;** www.atlanticairlinesint.com) has sporadic service from Roatán, La Ceiba, and San Pedro Sula to Belize, Managua, and Grand Cayman.

FROM EUROPE There are no direct flights between the U.K. or Europe to Honduras. Delta, Continental, and American Airlines fly between Europe and Honduras through transfer points in the United States.

FROM AUSTRALIA & NEW ZEALAND From Australia and New Zealand, your best bet for getting to Honduras is by connecting in a North American gateway such as Los Angeles or Houston, and then taking any of the airlines listed under "From North America" above.

By Cruise Ship

Getting to Honduras by cruise ship is becoming increasingly popular. At present, the only cruise ship dock is at Coxen Hole in Roatán, which serves **Carnival** (✆ **888/227-6482;** www.carnival.com), **Royal Caribbean** (✆ **866/562-7625;** www.royalcaribbean.com), **Princess** (✆ **800/774-6237;** www.princesscruises.com), and **Norwegian** (✆ **866/234-7350;** www.ncl.com) cruise lines. In the summer of 2009, a new Carnival Cruise terminal will open in Roatán, greatly increasing the frequency of cruise ship stops at the port.

By Ferry

From Puerto Cortés, 64km (40 miles) north of San Pedro Sula, there is ferry service to Placencia, Belize with the **D-Express** (✆ **504/991-0778**) on Mondays at 10am, returning Fridays at 9:30am. The trip takes 4 hours and costs L950 ($50/£25).

By Bus

Bus travel to and from other Central American countries is quite common with long-term travelers, but it might be too slow going if you're visiting the region for a short time. The most popular bus operator in the region is **Tica Bus** (16a Calle and Av. 5; ✆ **504/220-0579;** www.ticabus.com), which has daily departures from Tegucigalpa to San Salvador (6½ hr. away), Managua (7–8 hr. away), and Guatemala City (14 hr. away) that continue as far as Mexico and Panama. **Hedman Alas** (13a Calle and Av. 11; ✆ **504/237-7143;** www.hedmanalas.com) offers daily service from Copán to Antigua and Guatemala City. There are many less direct routes to the El Salvador, Guatemala, and Nicaragua borders via slow, crowded chicken buses that rarely cost more than a dollar or two. If you are on a budget or just traveling a short distance, these aren't a bad choice, but if you have less time, stick to a reputable, express company—prices anywhere in the region rarely top L95 ($5/£2.50) per hour of travel.

GETTING AROUND

Apart from the coasts and between San Pedro and the capital of Teguigalpa, highways and paved roads in the country are severely lacking, even to national parks and tourist attractions. In and around La Mosquitia and to/from the Bay Islands, transportation by water or air is your only option for getting around.

By Plane

While the country's regional air carriers are more expensive than transportation by road or ferry, they are still relatively reasonably priced and can shave a day or two off your total travel times within Honduras. The country has three domestic airlines: the regional TACA airline **Isleña** (✆ **504/441-3190;** www.flyislena.com), **Atlantic Airlines** (✆ **504/440-2343;** www.atlanticairlinesint.com), and **Aerolíneas Sosa** (✆ **504/443-2519;** aerososa@psinet.hn). Each has regular flights to/from major destinations in the country including San Pedro Sula, Tegucigalpa, La Ceiba, Roatán, Guanaja, Utila, Puerto Lempira, and Brus Laguna. **Sami Airlines** (✆ **504/442-2565** in La Ceiba, or 433-8031 in Brus

Laguna) has charter flights in four-person planes to La Ceiba and destinations in La Mosquitia such as Ahuas, Palacios, Belen, Brus Laguna, and Puerto Lempira. **Bay Island Airways** (✆ **504/946-5665** in the U.S., or 933-6077 in Roatán; www.bayislandairways.com) offers transport around the Bay Islands via small seaplanes. See the destination sections below for more info.

By Ferry

There is regular ferry service from the north coast of Honduras to the Bay Islands. The **Galaxy Wave** (✆ **504/445-1795**) travels daily from La Ceiba to Roatán at 9:30am and 4:30pm, and from Roatán and La Ceiba at 7:30am and 2pm for a cost of L500 ($26/£13). The **Utila Princess** (✆ **504/425-3390**) travels daily between La Ceiba and Utila at 9:30am and 4pm, and from Utila to La Ceiba at 6:20am and 2pm for a cost of L400 ($21/£11). **Island Tours** (✆ **504/434-3421**) has a less frequent service from Trujillo to Guanaja on Sundays and Thursdays at 4pm, and from Guanaja to Trujillo on Mondays and Fridays at 9am for a cost of L750 ($40/£20).

By Bus

There are literally hundreds of bus companies in Honduras, most operating out of dirt lots and only offering travel to nearby destinations. Routes between major cities often have the fastest service and are a cheap and easy way to get from place to place. Buses to more offbeat destinations are usually slower and more crowded. There are two luxury bus companies popular with foreign travelers that travel to major cities: **Hedman Alas** (✆ **504/237-7143;** www.hedman-alas.com) has frequent service between San Pedro Sula, Tegucigalpa, Tela, La Ceiba, and Copán. **Viana Clase de Oro** (✆ **504/225-6584**) has five first-class buses journeying daily between Tegucigalpa and San Pedro Sula that continue on to La Ceiba. You can expect to pay roughly L38 to L76 ($2–$4/£1–£2) per hour of bus travel on a luxury service. For local buses, you might pay a 10th of that.

By Car

Car and motorcycle rentals are readily available at most major airports from multinational companies such as Avis, Payless, Hertz, and Budget, as well as local companies. (See "Appendix: Fast Facts, Toll-Free Numbers & Websites" for info.) The highways along the North Coast, between San Pedro Sula and Tegucigalpa, and between San Pedro Sula and Copán, are the best in the country. Elsewhere roads are partially paved or unpaved and are frequently flooded or impassable during the rainy season.

By Taxi

In Tegucigalpa and some of the country's other major destinations or cities, taxis are supposed to have and use meters, although this isn't always the case. In more rural areas, taxis almost never have meters. See "By Taxi" under the specific towns below for more info.

TIPS ON ACCOMMODATIONS

Accommodations in Honduras range from full-scale resort complexes and luxury hotels aimed at business travelers to small guesthouses, bed-and-breakfasts, and rooms rented out of someone's house. Price ranges listed in hotel write-ups reflect low to high season, though apart from the Bay Islands, most hotels do not have high season rates.

High tourist season in Honduras is during national holidays and the dry season, running roughly from January to June, depending on what part of the country you're visiting. There is a 4% tourism tax added to all hotel rates, in addition to the 12% standard tax.

TIPS ON DINING

Let's speak bluntly: Honduras is not known for its cuisine. It does not have the creative culinary background and diverse regional plates that Latin American countries like Mexico or Peru have. Yet, if you look around and even go off the beaten track a bit there are some absolute gems. The national dish of Honduras is the *plato tipico,* an array of beef, plantains, beans, marinated cabbage, sour cream, and tortillas. *Anafres,* a refried black bean and cheese fondue served in a clay pot accompanied by tortilla chips, is the favorite appetizer in the country. Like tacos in Mexico or *pupusas* in El Salvador, the *baleada*—a folded wheat flour tortilla filled with beans, crumbled cheese and sour cream, and sometimes beef, chicken, or pork—is a snack food found everywhere in the country. In the highlands, *chuletas de cerdo,* or pork chops, are on most restaurant menus, as are steaks and other beef dishes. On the north coast and the Bay Islands, Garífuna restaurants, or *champas,* which are thatched-roof wooden shacks often on stilts, are well known for their *tapado,* a seafood stew made with sweet potatoes, malanga, yucca, and plantains. Other popular stews are made with coconut milk and served with cassava bread.

A 10% service fee is often tacked onto bills at high-end restaurants; otherwise, it's customary to leave a 10% tip.

TIPS ON SHOPPING

While large air-conditioned shopping malls with international chains can be found in large cities like San Pedro Sula and Tegucigalpa, the best shopping for souvenirs in Honduras is often found on the street or in small artisan markets. Common items from the **western** and **southern** parts of the country include cigars, coffee, woven baskets, jade jewelry, leather goods, Lenca pottery, embroidery, and woodcarvings. **Copán** is the unrivaled center for arts and craft shopping, with a dozen small markets and many more small shops and street vendors. The **Guamilito Market** in San Pedro Sula has items from all over the country, as do the artisan shops in **Valle de Angeles.** On the **Bay Islands,** Garífuna paintings and textiles, woodcarvings, woven straw baskets, hats, wind chimes, and carved coconuts can be found in small souvenir shops in Utila and Roatán. When cruise ships are docked at Coxen Hole, there are usually small stands selling handicrafts from around the country, though prices tend to be high. In **La Mosquitia,** woodcarvings, textiles, and jewelry can be purchased, in most cases directly, from villagers.

Fast Facts Honduras

American Express American Express is represented in Honduras by **BAC** in Tegucigalpa at Boulevard Suyapa, Fte. (✆ **800/327-1267**). The office is open Monday to Friday from 9am to 4pm and Saturday 9am to noon.

Business Hours Banks are open Monday to Friday from 8:30am to 4:30pm, and on Saturday from 9am to noon. General business hours are Monday through Friday from 9am to 5pm, although most restaurants and shops stay open to at least 8pm and are open daily.

Doctors Many doctors in Honduras, especially in San Pedro Sula and Tegucigalpa, speak basic English. For a list of English-speaking doctors, call your embassy.

Embassies & Consulates The **U.S. Embassy** is in Tegucigalpa, at Avenida La Paz (✆ **504/236-9320;** www.honduras.usembassy.gov). The **Canadian Embassy** in Tegucigalpa is at Edif. Finaciero Banexpo Local #3, Col Payaqui, Boulevar San Juan Bosco (✆ **504/232-4551;** www.embassyhonduras.ca). The **British Consulate** can be found in Tegucigalpa at Colonia Reforms 2402 (✆ **504/237-6577;** reforma@cascomark.com). There are no Australian or New Zealand embassies or consulates in Honduras.

Emergencies For a police emergency, call ✆ **199.** For fire, call ✆ **198.** To call an ambulance, dial ✆ **195.**

Hospitals The best hospitals and medical centers in Honduras are in San Pedro Sula and Tegucigalpa, and for any serious treatment it would be preferable to transfer to either city. The cost of medicine and treatment can be expensive, but most hospitals and pharmacies accept credit cards.

The best hospital in Tegucigalpa is the **Honduras Medical Center** on Avenida Juan Lindo (✆ **504/216-1201**); in San Pedro, try **Hospital Centro Médico Betesda** at 11a Avenida NO and 11a Calle NO (✆ **504/516-0900**).

Language Spanish is the main language in Honduras, but most people on the Bay Islands speak English. The Native languages of Lenca, Miskito, and Garífuna are also spoken in some regions.

Post Offices & Mail Honduras has no stamp-vending machines or post boxes, so you'll have to head to the post office to send a postcard, or ask your hotel if they can do it for you. A letter sent via regular mail to the U.S. will arrive in 5 to 10 days; the cost, at press time, is L30 ($1.50/75p) for a letter and L20 ($1/50p) for a postcard. Most post offices are open Monday to Friday from 8am to 5pm, and Saturday 8am to noon. DHL and FedEx have offices in major cities such as Tegucigalpa, San Pedro Sula, and La Ceiba.

Safety San Pedro Sula, La Ceiba, and especially Tegucigalpa have crime problems similar to most other major Latin American cities. Most crime involves petty theft, although violent crime is not unheard of. Visitors should take measures against being pickpocketed, especially in crowded areas and at night, and they should not leave valuables in a parked vehicle due to frequent break-ins.

Taxes Honduras levies a steep 12% **sales tax,** called ISV (Impuesto de Servicios), on all goods and services except medicine. There is a 4% tourism tax added to all hotel rates, tours, and car rentals additional to the 12% ISV, although small hotels and community-based tour operators may not add the tax, especially if you can pay in cash. Many high-end hotels and restaurants also add a 10% service charge, which is meant to take care of tipping.

There is an international departure tax of approximately $34 (£17), payable in cash only in U.S. dollars or Honduran lempiras, from any of the country's international airports. The departure tax on all domestic flights is approximately $1.50 (75p), and is also payable only in U.S. dollars or Honduran lempiras.

Telephone See the box "Telephone Dialing Info at a Glance" earlier in this chapter, along with p. 80 in "Planning Your Trip to Central America" for info.

Tipping Diners should leave a 10% to 15% tip in restaurants, although some high-end restaurants automatically include gratuity. In hotels, tipping is left to the guest's discretion. There's no need to tip taxi drivers.

4 TEGUCIGALPA

241km (150 miles) S of San Pedro Sula; 86km (53 miles) S of Comayagua

Many travelers would rather not try to pronounce the name of the capital of Honduras, let alone visit it. (By the way, it's pronounced "Te-*goo*-si-*gal*-pa"). Whatever horror stories you have heard about Central American capitals, don't take them too seriously, though. While it isn't a favorite tourist destination like Copán, La Ceiba, or the Bay Islands, Tegus, as Hondurans call it, is actually a fairly pleasant place if you can get past the smog. True to its name, which means "silver mountain" in the indigenous language of Nahuatl, the city sits snugly in a valley at about 1,000m (3,000 ft.), sheltering it from the sweltering heat that plagues San Pedro Sula and La Ceiba. There are several great museums and churches within the colonial center, a great clump of cloud forest nearby, and the largest cathedral in the country, along with a revered pilgrimage site, is only minutes from the center.

The city was founded on September 29, 1578, but it wasn't until 1880 that the capital was moved here from Comayagua by President Marco Aurelio Soto. In 1938 the city of Comayagüela was incorporated into Tegucigalpa and nearly doubled the size, which today stands at over one million inhabitants. The city is no longer the economic center of the country (that honor now belongs to San Pedro) but, as the capital and largest city in Honduras, it's still an important area for commerce and politics.

ESSENTIALS

Getting There

BY PLANE Although most international travelers fly into the larger and more modern San Pedro Sula Airport, Tegucigalpa's **Tocontín International Airport** (**TGU; © 504/234-2402**) does have a few international routes. **American Airlines** (**© 504/220-7585**), **Continental Airlines** (**© 504/550-7124**), and **TACA** (**© 504/221-6495**) all land here from North American destinations.

Regional airlines serving the capital are: **Isleña Airlines** (**© 504/236-8778;** www.flyislena.com), **Aerolíneas Sosa** (**© 504/443-2519**), and **Atlantic Airlines** (**© 504/440-2343;** www. atlanticairlinesint.com). There are no direct flights to the Bay Islands or La Mosquitia, but there are easy connections in La Ceiba.

Tocontín has just one ATM, a craft shop, a call center, and a small cafe, but little else. The airport is 6km (4 miles) south of the center on the highway to Choluteca. A taxi to downtown will be about L190 to L230 ($10–$12/£5–£6). Alternatively, you can catch a northbound bus or collective taxi to the center of town for L20 ($1/50p) right outside the main airport gates—just listen for the touts shouting "Te-goose."

BY BUS **Hedman Alas** (13a Calle and Av. 11; **© 504/237-7143;** www.hedmanalas.com) has luxury service four times a day to San Pedro Sula (4 hr. away; L535/$28/£14), where connections can then be made to Copán, Tela, or La Ceiba. **Viana Clase de Oro** (Blvd. FFAA at the ESSO station; **© 504/225-6584;** L600/$32/£16) has five first-class buses daily to San Pedro Sula that continue onto La Ceiba from 6:30am to 6pm.

Other options for getting to San Pedro include the operator **Saenz** (Centro Commercial Perisur; **© 504/233-4229;** L456/$24/£12), which has regular and first-class, nonstop service six times a day to the capital, along with **El Rey Express** (Banco Central; **© 504/237-8561;** www.reyexpress.net; L418/$22/£11), which stops in Comayagua as well as San Pedro. For La Ceiba (7 hr. away), try the operator **Cristina** (**© 504/441-2028;** L475/$25/£13), which has five daily departures between 5:30am and 3:30pm.

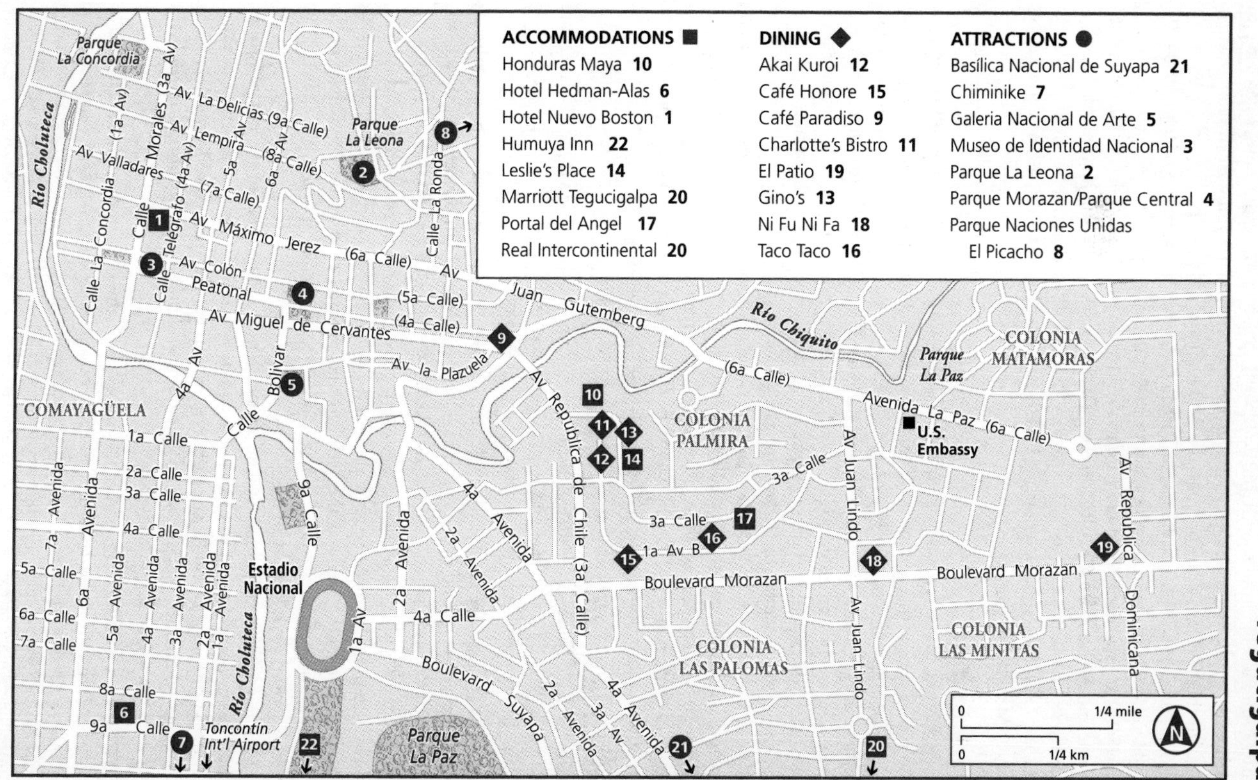
ACCOMMODATIONS ■
Honduras Maya 10
Hotel Hedman-Alas 6
Hotel Nuevo Boston 1
Humuya Inn 22
Leslie's Place 14
Marriott Tegucigalpa 20
Portal del Angel 17
Real Intercontinental 20
DINING ◆
Akai Kuroi 12
Café Honore 15
Café Paradiso 9
Charlotte's Bistro 11
El Patio 19
Gino's 13
Ni Fu Ni Fa 18
Taco Taco 16
ATTRACTIONS ●
Basílica Nacional de Suyapa 21
Chiminike 7
Galeria Nacional de Arte 5
Museo de Identidad Nacional 3
Parque La Leona 2
Parque Morazan/Parque Central 4
Parque Naciones Unidas
El Picacho 8
Parque La Concordia
Río Choluteca
Av La Delicias (9a Calle)
Av Lempira (8a Calle)
Av Valladares
(7a Calle)
Calle Morales (3a Av)
Calle La Concordia (1a Av)
Calle Telégrafo (4a Av)
Av Máximo Jerez (6a Calle)
Av Colón (5a Calle)
Peatonal
Av Miguel de Cervantes (4a Calle)
Parque La Leona
Calle La Ronda
Av Juan Gutemberg
Río Chiquito
Av la Plazuela
Bolivar
COMAYAGÜELA
Calle
1a Calle
2a Calle
3a Calle
4a Calle
5a Calle
6a Calle
7a Calle
8a Calle
9a Calle
9a Calle
7a Avenida
6a Avenida
5a Avenida
4a Avenida
3a Avenida
2a Avenida
1a Avenida
Estadio Nacional
Toncontín Int'l Airport
1a Av
2a Avenida
4a Calle
Boulevard Suyapa
Parque La Paz
4a Avenida
2a Avenida
3a Av
Av Republica de Chile (3a Calle)
COLONIA PALMIRA
COLONIA LAS PALOMAS
3a Calle
1a Av B
Boulevard Morazan
Av Juan Lindo
Parque La Paz
COLONIA MATAMORAS
(6a Calle)
Avenida La Paz (6a Calle)
U.S. Embassy
Av Republica Dominicana
COLONIA LAS MINITAS
0 1/4 mile
0 1/4 km
N

Travelers crossing the El Salvador and Nicaragua borders have several options. To get to El Amatillo (3½ hr. away; L140/$7/£3.50), on the El Salvador border you have to catch one of the buses leaving from the Mercado Mayoreo, southwest of Comayagüela on the highway to Olancho. For the Nicaraguan border at El Paraiso (2 hr. away; L120/$6/£3) via Danli, try **Discua Litena** (Mercado Jacaleapa; ✆ **504/230-0470**), which leaves every hour from 6:30am to 7:30pm.

If you're traveling elsewhere in Central America, your best choice is **Tica Bus** (16a Calle and Av. 5; ✆ **504/220-0579;** www.ticabus.com), a company that has daily departures to San Salvador (6½ hr. away; L950/$50/£25), Managua (7–8 hr. away; L1,045/$55/£28), and Guatemala City (14 hr. away; L1,140/$60/£30) and journeys as far as Mexico and Panama.

Orientation

Tegus is one of the few colonial cities in Central America that does not follow a typical Spanish layout with a grid of streets surrounding a central square, mostly because of the uneven surface of the city. The colonial center of the city is more of a narrow strip on a central grid of about 7×20 blocks, and there are several squares—the largest is Parque Morazán, or the Parque Central. The city's pedestrian-only street, Calle Peatonal, leads west from this square and other main streets and avenues run into or parallel to it. Most of the city's museums, churches, and artisan shops can be found within 6 blocks of Parque Central, too. The commercial center of the city and where you will find the best hotels, restaurants, and shops is **Colonia Palmira,** on the north side of the fast-food lined Boulevard Morazán. West of the Río Choluteca, a river that divides the city, and southwest of the center is the neighborhood of **Comayagüela,** where most of the city's bus terminals can be found; this is a poorer, less safe part of town.

Getting Around

ON FOOT Much of Tegucigalpa can be explored on foot. The colonial center and Colonia Palmira are all safe and secure during the day, though you should stick to taxi cabs during the night and never travel alone, just to be sure.

BY TAXI Taxis are cheap, plentiful, and far safer for getting between neighborhoods than walking or taking the city's public buses. Traveling within the center is usually less than L40 ($2/£1) via cab. You can also take *colectivo* taxis for about half the price.

BY BUS Most city buses run from the south or west and journey through Comayagüela before heading north and east out of the city. You'll probably use the no. 21 Tiloarque–La Sosa bus, which has stops at the Mercado Mayoreo and throughout downtown, or the no. 32, which stops at the National University, the most. It'll cost only about L10 (50¢/25p) to get anywhere in town.

Although Tegucigalpa doesn't have a main bus terminal, most of the bus companies have terminals within a few blocks of each other in the Comayagüela section of town. Because this neighborhood isn't safe, use caution getting there and do not leave your baggage unattended. In fact, you might want to simply take cabs instead of busing it around town, because of safety issues.

BY CAR Tegucigalpa is right on one of the best highways in the country, CA 5, which ends 241km (150 miles) away in San Pedro Sula, passing Lago de Yojoa, Siguatepe, and Comayagua en route. CA 5 also heads south to Choluteca, where you can connect with CA 1, or the Pan-American Highway (Carretera Panamericana), which runs to El Salvador, Nicaragua, and beyond.

The CA 11-A road to Copán is a jaw-dropping route through the mountains, which is windy, mostly unpaved, and sometimes impassable due to rain. Many drivers prefer to head back toward San Pedro Sula and catch highway CA 4.

If you're heading to the north coast, you have two options: one is to go back to San Pedro Sula, and the other is an unpredictable route through the wild Olancho region that is prone to highway robberies and poor roads. Most choose the prior.

Car-rental agencies are located both at the airport and in town. Companies include **Avis** (Edificio Marinakys at Blvd. Suyapa; ✆ **504/239-5712;** www.avis.com), **Payless** (Edificio Saenz at Blvd. Europea; ✆ **504/245-7054;** www.paylesscarrental.net), and **Hertz** (Centro Comercio Villa Real; ✆ **504/235-8582;** www.hertz.com).

Visitor Information

The **Instituto Hondureño de Turismo** (Av. Cruz and Calle Mexico; ✆ **504/220-1600;** www.letsgohonduras.com) has friendly English-speaking staff who can provide general information and give you a copy of their excellent bilingual guide, *Honduras Tips.* It's open Monday to Friday from 7:30am to 4:30pm.

FAST FACTS Most banks and ATMs are either downtown or along Boulevard Morazán, as well as the malls. **BAC** (Blvd. Morazán and Av. Cruz) exchanges traveler's checks and has a 24-hour ATM, as does **Banco Atlántida** on Parque Central. There's an official currency exchange booth at the airport; less official operations are on Calle Peatonal and in the Parque Morazán.

Honduras Medical Center (Av. Juan Lindo; ✆ **504/216-1201**), one of the country's top hospitals, is open 24 hours, as is **Clinica Viera** (across from the Alcadia; ✆ **504/237-3156**).

Hondutel, 1 block off Parque Central at Av. Colón and Calle El Telégrafo, offers international calls, although you can find cheap call service at any of the cybercafes in the colonial center.

Most hotels have some sort of laundry service, though independent operators will do it for far cheaper. One to try is **Super Jet** (Av. Juan Gutenberg before it turns into Av. La Paz), which has same-day service for L30 ($1.50/75p) per kilo.

The main **police** office is at 5a Av. and Avenida Lempira; police can be reached by dialing ✆ **504/779-0476** or 199.

The downtown **post office** is at Avenida Barahona and Calle El Telégrafo. There is also a **DHL** (✆ **504/220-1800**) and **Mailboxes, Etc.** (✆ **504/232-3184**) on Boulevard Morazán.

Safety note: Tegucigalpa as a whole is not a safe city. Parts, such as the center of town and Boulevard Morazán, are fine for strolling during the day, but don't flash any valuables like jewelry, cameras, or iPods. In other areas, especially in Comayagüela and around the bus terminals, walk with extreme caution and try to avoid walking alone. At night, always take taxis wherever you go.

FESTIVALS

The Virgen of Suyapa, a 6-centimeter-tall (2-in.) cedar statue of the Virgin Mary, is one of the holiest Catholic relics in Honduras and Central America. Every February 3 and the week surrounding that date is **La Feria de la Virgen de Suyupa,** a time for celebration of the iconic statue throughout Tegucigalpa and the whole country. The processions and festivities in Tegucigalpa center around the Basílica de Suyapa.

Attractions in Town

Parque Morazán or **Parque Central ★★** is the epicenter of all activity in the city's colonial center, and most museums and churches can be found within a few blocks of it. In addition to the park's attractions that are listed below, it's worth seeing the baroque **Cathedral,** on the eastern edge of the park, which was built between 1765 and 1782 and honors Saint Michael (San Miguel) the Archangel, Tegucigalpa's patron saint. **Iglesia de Nuestra Señora de los Dolores,** a few blocks northwest of the park, was built in 1732, and features an attractive selection of religious art such as reliefs of the Stations of the Cross, along with a carved altar. The big plaza fronting the church is often packed with artisan stalls and food vendors. Other churches such as **Parroquia San Francisco,** the oldest church in the city (it was built in 1592), and **Iglesia la Merced** beside the Galeria Nacional de Arte, are worth a look when they're open (hours vary).

Chiminike ★★ (Kids Opened in 2003, this fun, funky children's museum is all about interactivity. Exhibits like a grocery store and construction site have been secretly designed to get kids to learn about the world without them knowing it. Shhh! Most fun is the room dedicated to El Cuerpo Humano, or the human body room, where there's a giant Operator game, a crawl through intestinal tract, and the chance to make fart noises. Also in the museum is a giant volcano that produces "lava," a bubble room, a VW Beetle that encourages finger-paint graffiti, and a room tilted at a 22-degree angle.

Blvd. Fuerzas Armadas de Honduras, 7km (4¼ miles) south of the center. ✆ **504/291-0339.** www.chiminike.com. Admission L50 ($2.50/£1.25). Tues–Fri 9am–noon and 2–5pm; Sat–Sun 10am–1pm and 2–5pm.

Galeria Nacional de Arte ★★ The most important art museum in the country, the Galeria Nacional de Arte is housed beside Iglesia la Merced in a building that dates from 1694, and that in its past lives was a convent and home to the Universidad Nacional. The well-planned exhibits, labeled in both English and Spanish, are displayed chronologically according to when they were created. The exhibits begin with rock art and petroglyphs from pre-Maya civilizations, and then move into stone and ceramic art from the Mayas and other indigenous groups. The colonial period is widely represented with oil paintings, gold and silver objects, sculptures, and religious art. The modern era has hundreds of excellent pieces from internationally known Honduran painters like Pablo Zelaya Sierra and José Antonio Velásquez.

Plaza de la Merced. ✆ **504/237-9884.** Admission L50 ($2.50/£1.25). Mon–Sat 9am–4pm; Sun 9am–1pm.

Museo de Identidad Nacional ★★ This absolutely brilliant new museum opened in 2006 in the former Palace of Ministries. It features some surprisingly big-name art exhibitions from around Latin America and also displays the history of the country from its Pre-Columbian beginnings to modern times via charts, photos, documents, scale models, art, and intriguing artifacts like the femur and tibia of a giant sloth. Their latest addition is *Virtual Copán,* an animated film showing four times a day, that takes you through a virtual tour of the Maya ruins and explains how they were built. It's a great introduction to the ruins if you haven't been there already.

Av. Baranhona and Calle El Telégrafo. ✆ **504/238-7412.** www.min.hn. Admission L50 ($2.50/£1.25). Tues–Sat 9am–5pm; Sun 10am–4pm.

Parque Naciones Unidas El Picacho (Kids This new park about 6km (4 miles) from the center of town is home to the huge concrete statue of Christ, *Cristo del Picacho,* that watches over the city. The main reason to come to this park is for the views of the capital and the surrounding mountains. But there's also a small zoo with animals from around the country like monkeys, snakes, macaws, and iguanas, as well as a taxidermy collection that, in my opinion, is located too close to the living creatures. Buses here leave from behind Iglesia Los Dolores (see above).

Entrance 5km (3 miles) north of downtown. Admission L20 ($1/50p). Daily 8am–5pm.

Attractions Outside Town

This serene, 18th-century Spanish mining town of **Santa Lucia,** about 30 minutes outside Tegucigalpa, is a favorite weekend retreat for the residents of Tegucigalpa. There are small artisan shops, outdoor cafes, an 18th-century church with Spanish oil paintings, and a few nice lodges, including the **Hotel Santa Lucía Resort** (✆ **504/779-0540;** www.santaluciaresort.com.hn). Doubles range from L475 to L950 ($25–$50/£13–£25). To get here from Tegucigalpa, take any San Juancito–bound bus and ask to be let off at the turnoff from town, 2km (1¼ miles) from the actual center.

The colonial mountain village of **Valle de Angeles** ★ is 22km (14 miles) east of Tegucigalpa, just 8km (5 miles) past Santa Lucía. Though it's nearly empty during the week, it's packed full during the weekends with day-trippers from Tegucigalpa. It's far more touristy than Santa Lucía, but in a good way. The town has been virtually restored to its 16th-century glory. Many of the streets are pedestrian-only and are lined with *artesenía* shops that sell goods from all over the country like woodcarvings, wicker baskets, hand-carved furniture, paintings, Lenca pottery, dolls, and even a leather factory and outlet. Items cost quite a bit less than in Tegucigalpa. From Tegucigalpa (45 min. away) you can catch a bus from the corner of Avenida Próceres and Avenida República Dominicana.

The **Basílica Nacional de Suyapa** ★★ (no phone; www.virgendesuyapa.hn) is the largest cathedral in the country, but is perhaps better known for being the discovery site of a tiny cedar statue of the Virgin Mary. This statue, discovered in 1747, is famous throughout Honduras for its healing powers. The Virgin has long been the patron saint of the country and in 1982 was even named by papal decree as the patron saint of all of Central America. The permanent home of the statue is actually the nearby Iglesia de Suyapa, but the statue is brought to this Gothic cathedral, which was built in 1954, for special events like the Feria de la Virgen de Suyapa. The cathedral's grounds are open to visitors every day, but the basilica itself is open only during Mass and holidays. You can take a taxi to Suyapa, 7km (4¼ miles) south of the center on Blvd. Suyapa, from Parque La Merced; a standard taxi should cost about L55 to L95 ($3–$5/£1.50–£2.50).

Outdoor Activities

Tegucigalpa is far from a major golfing destination, but it does have a small, 9-hole course, considered one of the best in the country. The **Villa Elena Country Club** (✆ **504/224-0400;** www.villaelenacountry.com) is 9km (6 miles) north of the capital on the road to San Pedro Sula, and in a new residential and ecological reserve area. On the premises are a Mexican restaurant, a bar, and tennis courts.

For the best views of the city, hike up the steep twisting **Parque La Leona** of Barrio Buenos Aires, which features a small, grassy area with benches, a playground, and a small cafe. There are a few interesting colonial mansions bordering the park, though all are private residences. If you want to save your strength, you can take a taxi there and walk back down to the center. (Just avoid doing so after dark.)

SHOPPING

If you can't make it out to **Valle de Angeles** for souvenir shopping (p. 335), which offers wares for quite a bit cheaper than in the city, head to any of the artisan stalls by the Iglesia Los Dolores and along Avenida Miguel de Cervantes, just before the bridge to Colonia Palmira. Or check out **Megaplaza Mall,** on Avenida Juan Pablo II near the Marriott Hotel, which has all the chain shops and restaurants that you would expect in a big North American mall.

WHERE TO STAY

Very Expensive

Honduras Maya ★ Standing proudly on the top of the hill in what could be considered the best location in Colonia Palmira, the 10-story Honduras Maya hotel and convention center is a favorite of both business travelers and tourists. Much of the hotel has been renovated in the past few years, which has definitely helped revive it. Don't worry, though; the Maya designs on the boxy facade are still there. The rooms, comparable to the Marriott and Real Intercontinental, have all been given a face-lift as well. Corner rooms have windows on two sides and thus the best views, which on clear days at sundown show the city in a beautiful glow. There are several terraces with restaurants and bars, as well as a few shops and an attached casino, the best in the capital. On weekends, the hotel often hosts weddings and private parties and may fill up with people milling about with cocktails.

3a Calle and Av. Republica de Chile, Colonia Palmira. ✆ **504/280-5000.** www.hotelhondurasmaya.com. 163 units. L2,470 ($130/£65) double. Rates include breakfast. AE, MC, V. **Amenities:** 2 restaurants; bar; casino; exercise rooms; pool; tennis courts. *In room:* A/C, TV, minibar, Wi-Fi.

Marriott Tegucigalpa Kids While it's a small step down from the Real Intercontinental next door, the Tegucigalpa Marriott—formerly the Crown Plaza—is more or less exactly what you would expect from the international chain: It's big, with lots of facilities, a nice pool that will please any family, a few good restaurants, and a great complimentary breakfast buffet, but otherwise it's nothing you haven't seen before. Like the Real Intercontinental, it is out of the way of the center and most attractions, unless chain restaurants and an air-conditioned mall are on your itinerary.

Av. Roble, beside Multiplaza Mall. ✆ **504/232-0033.** Fax 504/235-7700. www.marriott.com. 153 units. L3,020 ($159/£80) double; L3,500 ($184/£92) executive room. Rates include breakfast. AE, DC, MC, V. **Amenities:** Restaurant; bar; fitness center; pool; spa. *In room:* A/C, TV, hair dryer, minibar, Wi-Fi (additional charge).

Portal del Angel ★★★ Some laughed when the idea of a luxurious boutique hotel in Tegucigalpa was being floated around, but Portal del Angel has been up and running for a decade now. Why? Because it has style. It's both hip and elegant at the same time. Marble pillars and wrought-iron balconies are paired with tropical plants and floors say tropical opulence in every way. Rooms are better yet, with lots of space, good lighting from large windows, parquet and caoba floors, and locally made hand-carved chests and furniture. The bar closes at 10pm, but that's late enough for a fine Honduran cigar and glass from their decent wine list. It's in the Zona Viva neighborhood, within a block from a handful of the city's top restaurants and bars.

Av. República del Perú 2115, Colonia Palmira. ✆ **504/**239-6538. www.portaldelangel.com. 23 units. L2,470 ($130/£65) double; L3,800 ($200/£100) suite. MC, V. **Amenities:** Restaurant; bar; pool; shuttle service. *In room:* A/C, TV.

Real Intercontinental ★★★ The guiding principle behind this hotel, the top hotel in the city, is to make guests feel like they aren't even in Tegucigalpa. Upon entering the property, you are transported to a world of marble floors and pillars, vaulted ceilings, Moorish arches, shaded lounges, and tropical plants in all the right places. Rooms, remodeled in 2005, now have flatscreen TVs, clock radios with MP3 connections, and an earthy decor, punctuated by some tasteful jungle-themed art. Executive suites have computers with flatscreen monitors, cordless phones, fax machines, and a VCR. The biggest downside to the hotel, especially if you are here to sightsee, is that you are isolated well away from the center, albeit in an up-and-coming area with chain restaurants and a mall.

Av. Roble, next to Multiplaza Mall. ✆ **504/290-2700.** Fax 504/231-2828. www.ichotelsgroup.com. 157 units. L2,565 ($135/£68) double; L5,130 ($270/£135) suite. AE, DC, MC, V. **Amenities:** Restaurant; bar; fitness center; pool. *In room:* A/C, TV, hair dryer, minibar, Wi-Fi (additional charge).

Expensive

Humuya Inn ★★ Finds First-rate service and a well-maintained property are what make this surprisingly under-recognized hotel great. Rooms and common areas are painted brightly and have high wood-beam ceilings and tile floors. Indigenous art is sprinkled throughout, lending the hotel a personal touch that some of the larger and more expensive chain hotels in town lack. Rooms are clean and decently sized, and have the same amenities of hotels that charge twice the price. The only potential drawback is that the hotel is in a residential area, about 10 minutes from the city center; in my opinion, this is actually a plus, since it helps keep your stay quiet.

Colonia Humuya 1150. ✆ **504/239-2206.** Fax 504/239-5099. www.humuyainn.com. 12 units. L1,140 ($60/£30) double; L1,710 ($90/£45) suite. MC, V. **Amenities:** Restaurant; laundry service. *In room:* A/C, TV, fridge (suites only), hair dryer, Wi-Fi.

Moderate

Leslie's Place ★ What's that tiny bed-and-breakfast doing tucked in between the Honduras Maya and other high-rise hotels on top of the hill in Colonia Palmira? It's serving as a welcome change, that's what. This bright-yellow private home–turned inn is one of the better budget places to stay in the area. Though they're not as impressive as those at the nearby, much more expensive, resorts, rooms are spacious and breezy, with tile floors and matching wood furniture. There's a pleasant breakfast and lunch area beside the property's garden.

Calzada San Martin 452, Colonia Palmira. ✆ **504/220-5325.** Fax 504/220-7492. www.dormir.com. 20 units. L1,254 ($66/£33) double with fan; L1,450 ($76/£38) double with A/C. Rates include breakfast. MC, V. **Amenities:** Restaurant. *In room:* A/C, fan, TV, Wi-Fi.

Inexpensive

Hotel Hedman-Alas While the location in the somewhat unsafe neighborhood of Comayagüela isn't great for a long-term stay, this hotel is a good choice if you just want a place to crash for a night or two, or you have an early bus to catch. It's run by the best bus line in Honduras, and their Tegucigalpa terminal is just a few blocks away. Rooms are secure, clean, and have TVs. There are certainly better, more attractive rooms to be found in the city, but not at this price.

4a Av. btw. calles 8a and 9a, Comayagüela. ✆ **504/237-9333.** www.hedmanalas.com. 19 units. L380 ($20/£10) double. Rates include breakfast. No credit cards. *In room:* A/C, TV.

Hotel Nuevo Boston One of the few acceptable budget places to stay in the city center, the American-owned Nuevo Boston is just a few steps from the Iglesia Los Dolores (p. 334).

The rooms surround two small courtyards and are pretty basic; there aren't even TVs. Rooms facing the street are bigger and have balconies. Reliable hot water and clean private bathrooms are available, though, which is about all you can hope for in this price range.

Maximo Jeréz 321, center of town. ✆ **504/237-9411.** 6 units. L340 ($18/£9) double. No credit cards. *In room:* Fan.

WHERE TO DINE

Expensive

Akai Kuroi ★ JAPANESE This trendy, new Japanese and sushi restaurant, in Colonia Palmira and not far from the Honduras Maya, may be pricey, but it's for a good reason. The rolls, sashimi, and teppanyaki are all beautifully prepared and the service is outstanding. Since this is one of the city's more decidedly upscale dining spots, on most evenings you'll find a group of beautiful young people drinking and sharing a sushi boat here.

Av. Republica de Peru beside Hotel San Martín, Colonia Palmira. ✆ **504/208-4435.** Main courses L190–L475 ($10–$25/£5–£13). AE, MC, V. Mon–Sat noon–11pm; Sun noon–7pm.

Charlotte's Bistro ★ INTERNATIONAL Though Charlotte's is situated across the street from the Villa Real shopping plaza and is very much in the center of Tegucigalpa, blink and you might think you stumbled into a Parisian cafe. The restaurant, tucked into a leafy colonial house, is one of the more romantic options in town and more elegant than nearby trendier restaurants, like Akai Kuroi. The food is eclectic, ranging from French and Italian to Thai, Indian, and Honduran. There's also a coffee bar selling cakes and pastries, where you can stop by for a snack or to linger after your meal.

3a Calle and Av. Republica de Chile, Colonia Palmira. ✆ **504/238-1803.** Main courses L130–L265 ($7–$14/£3.50–£7). MC, V. Mon–Wed noon–10pm; Thurs–Sat noon–11pm.

El Patio ★★ HONDURAN In operation for 3 decades, El Patio is legendary in the capital for its Honduran cuisine. The rustic atmosphere, complete with a brick patio and open grill, seems to have struck a chord with the populace and has attracted everyone from priests, presidents, and famous Honduran musicians. Grilled meats and chicken are the specialty and are all served with french fries, plantains, or onion rings. There's also a large pinchos menu, consisting of small meat plates with kabobs of chicken, beef, pork, shrimp, or chorizo all prepared in a dozen different ways.

Near the end of Blvd. Morazán, Colonia Palmira. ✆ **504/221-4141.** Main courses L150–L265 ($8–$14/£4–£7). MC, V. Daily 11am–11pm.

Ni Fu Ni Fa ARGENTINE This Argentine-style steakhouse is one of the current it spots in Colonia Palmira. Thick slabs of beef—mostly high-quality imported cuts, including multi-person combination platters with chorizo, pork, ribs, and steak—are the modus operandi here. There's also a nice salad bar, full bar, and selection of Argentine wine. A second location recently opened in the Barrio Los Andes section of San Pedro.

Mall El Dorado at Blvd. Morazán, Colonia Palmira. ✆ **504/221-2056.** Main courses L130–L340 ($7–$18/£3.50–£9). AE, MC, V. Daily 11am–11pm.

Moderate

Café Honore ★ DELI Café Honore, a small airy eatery with just a handful of tables situated on a busy restaurant strip in Colonia Palmira, is best known for gourmet sandwiches that most locals only dream of being able to eat daily. Only high-quality meats and cheeses, which are sold on the deli side of the restaurant, and freshly baked breads are used. There's also a nice array of soups, including tasty corn chowder, a global wine list, and Putomayo music collections often playing.

Av. Republica de Argentina 1941, Colonia Palmira. © **504/239-7566.** Main courses L75–L150 ($4–$8/£2–£4). MC, V. Daily noon–10pm.

Gino's ★ Kids ITALIAN Owned by the Honorary Consul General to Belize, Gino's is one of the few decent Italian offerings in Tegucigalpa. Expect nothing less than homemade sauces, pastas, and rosemary and sea-salt-scented focaccia. Simple recipes and fresh ingredients are the key to first-rate Italian food, and Gino's has shown that it can compete with the best of them. Finish your meal with a cappuccino and tiramisu, both of which make this casual and family-friendly little place worth the trip.

Av. Republica de Peru beside Hotel San Martín, Colonia Palmira. © **504/238-1464.** Main courses L70–L140 ($6–$12/£3–£6). MC, V. Mon–Fri 11am–6pm (Wed until 9pm); Sat 11am–3pm.

Taco Taco Value MEXICAN Taco Taco is just a block from Boulevard Morazán, not far from many of the town's best dining choices. Yet it has maintained its backyard barbecue feel, with a handful of umbrella-covered plastic tables set upon the dirt front yard and the small interior dining room. The menu comprises authentic Mexican snack foods like tacos, flautas, and chalupas, all served with several homemade hot sauces. The beer and margaritas are all incredibly cheap, so many in for a long night start out here before moving to a more posh spot nearby. Don't confuse this restaurant with a similarly named Mexican restaurant, Taco Loco, on Boulevard Morazán.

Av. Republica de Peru, Colonia Palmira. © **504/239-7131.** Main courses L75–L150 ($4–$8/£2–£4). No credit cards. Daily noon–10pm.

Inexpensive

On the patio in front of Iglesia Los Dolores (p. 334), as well as other locations around the city center, there are food stalls set up selling some of the tastiest dishes in the capital for the cheapest prices. You'll find Honduran baleadas, Salvadoran *pupusas,* grilled chicken and beef kabobs, and the occasional intestine. As always with street food, try to stick to the cleaner stalls and the ones the locals are going to. Credit cards aren't accepted, and most meals cost between L10 and L60 (50¢–$3/25p–£1.50).

Café Paradiso ★★ CAFE This is a true cafe in every sense of the word. Not only is it a perfect place for coffee, tea, and snacks like ham and cheese croissants, but it serves as a hub of local art and culture. In addition to boasting a small bookstore and free Wi-Fi, the cafe shows indie movies every Tuesday, hosts poetry readings on Thursdays, and features acoustic music acts on the weekends. Located in an aged colonial building with wrought-iron windows, the Paradiso also has more Spanish flair than most other places in the center. For anyone who's antiestablishment or looking to tune into the local art scene, it's paradise.

Av. Miguel Paz Barahona 1351, center of town. © **504/237-0337.** Main courses L55–L110 ($3–$6/£1.50–£3). No credit cards. Mon–Sat 10am–10pm.

TEGULCIGAPA AFTER DARK

The most elegant way to spend an evening in the capital is to head to a highbrow performance downtown at the spectacular Teatro Nacional Manuel Bonilla (Av. Barahona at Parque Herrera; © **504/222-4366**), modeled after the Plaza Athenée in Paris. On select nights throughout the year you will find opera, dance, and concerts featuring some of the best performers in the country. You can ask at the box office or check the local newspapers for dates and prices.

There are several casinos in Tegucigalpa hotels, though the only one that's any good is the **Casino Royale** at the Honduras Maya (p. 336). They have table games like Blackjack, roulette, and baccarat, as well as a small section of slot machines. Bring an ID to get in and don't even think about wearing shorts—it's a dressy nightlife spot.

Most of the city's bars and clubs are located in Colonia Palmira along Blvd. Morazán, and most have covers of about L100 ($5/£2.50). **O-bar** (Blvd. Morazán and Av. Juan Lindo), a sleek bar and lounge attracting a mix of 20- and 30-somethings, has a small dance floor accentuated by lasers and black lights. If you bring your hotel room key, you have a much better chance of getting in. **Bamboo ★** (Blvd. Morazán at the last stoplight) is the most exclusive bar in Tegucigalpa, and inside it you'll find any number of young, beautiful things and the guys trying to pick them up. This is the most gay-friendly bar in town. If you are staying at one of the more upscale hotels, ask your concierge to put you on the guest list. Also, don't count out **Sabor Cubana** (Av. República de Argentina 1933) in Colonia Palmira for salsa dancing.

For a pub atmosphere, try **Salt & Pepper** (Calle Castaño Sur; ✆ **504/235-7738**). If you'd like to catch a movie, the best theater is the **Cinemark** (✆ **504/231-2044;** www.cinemarkca.com) at the Multiplaza Mall on Avenida Juan Pablo II.

A SIDE TRIP TO PARQUE NACIONAL LA TIGRA ★

This 238-sq.-km (148-sq.-mile) cloud forest park, the first protected area in the country, is located, amazingly, only 22km (16 miles) from Tegucigalpa. Named a national park in 1982, La Tigra had been nearly destroyed by loggers and the El Rosario Mining Company until the government stepped in, although much of what is left is secondary growth. Remnants of mine shafts and buildings can still be found in the park, although they should be avoided in most instances.

Most who visit the park are after one thing: birds. More than 350 species have been identified in the park, which is second in the country to Lago de Yojoa. Rare species such as the resplendent quetzal, wine-throated hummingbird, and the rufous browned wren, are seen by a lucky few, as are mammals such as pumas, agoutis, and armadillos. Plant life includes pine forests, bromeliads, orchids, ferns, lichens, and mushrooms.

There are eight good hiking trails through the park, as well as two entrances. At the first entrance, at Jutiapa, there's a small **visitor center** (✆ **504/238-6269;** www.amitigra.org) with a few cabins and a small new ecolodge with rooms for rent for L475 ($25/£13) per person. Most hiking trails begin from this first entrance; these trails are used by the majority of tourists and are in good condition. The **Sendero Principal,** the main route through the park that extends 6km (4 miles) from one end to the other, follows what was once the main road for the miners, and has been allowed to deteriorate into a more natural state. Almost all other trails branch off from this one, including the **Sendero la Cascada,** a trail that reaches a small waterfall (it's best visited Oct–Feb, when the water is more visible) after 2km (1.25 miles). It connects to the **Sendero la Mina,** or the mine trail, several kilometers from the other end of the park. **Sendero las Plancitos,** an 8km (5-mile) loop from the Sendero Principal, is the longest, toughest, and least used trail in the park and your best chance at spotting wildlife.

The second entrance, at the western end of the park, is located at the **El Rosario Mining Company headquarters** 3km (1¾ miles) above the town of San Juancito. There's a small ecolodge, **Cabaña Mirador El Rosario** (✆ **504/987-5835**) run by a German couple not far from the entrance. A double runs L475 ($25/£13). Camping is not allowed in the park, but there is a small campground (L100/$5/£2.50 per person) near the Jutiapa entrance with fire pits and toilets.

Unless you are going with a tour company or have your own car, access to the park is not exactly easy. To get to Jutiapa by bus, you need to catch an El Hatillo–bound bus (the trip takes 1½ hr., and buses run daily every 45 min. beginning at 6am), from the Dippsa station, at Avenida Jeréz and Avenida Plazuela. Let the driver know you are going to the park and he'll drop you about 2km (1¼ miles) from the entrance at Los Planes, the closest you can get. For the western entrance, take a San Juancito–bound bus (the trip takes 1½ hr., and buses leave daily at 3pm) from Mercado San Pablo. From San Juancito, you must walk or hitch a ride the 3km (1¾ miles) uphill to El Rosario.

Grayline Tours (www.graylinemundomaya.com) runs 6-hour tours from Tegucigalpa on a regular basis and includes lunch and a guided hike on a short trail from Jutiapa. The cost is $90 (£45). **Amitigra** (✆ **504/232-6771;** www.amitigra.org), a nonprofit ecological foundation in Tegucigalpa, controls access to the park and can make arrangements for staying overnight in the visitor center.

The park is open daily from 8am to 5pm. Admission is L190 ($10/£5) per adult, and L95 ($5/£2.50) per child.

5 WESTERN HONDURAS

The western part of Honduras is a land far removed from the country's beach mind-set—it's a place where cowboys share the streets with cars and where orchids grow amid plentiful pine forests. For many, this is the real Honduras, and it technically also includes the must-see ruins of Copán; Santa Rosa de Copán, one of the centers of the country's cigar production; and Gracias, Central America's first capital and the gateway to the cloud forests of Parque Nacional Montaña de Celaque—all of which are covered separately below.

Your first foray into the West will most often be the pulsating capital of San Pedro Sula. While it lies in the corner of the region, you almost always have to come through this vibrant, cluttered city to get anywhere here. As you travel farther away from San Pedro Sula, the population thins out substantially, the mountains grow taller, and the fog and mist thicken. Even deeper into the mountains are numerous Lenca villages such as La Campa, which have remained practically unchanged for centuries.

SAN PEDRO SULA

San Pedro Sula, the loud, brash, economic transportation hub of Honduras (241km/150 miles north of Tegucigalpa) often serves to introduce visitors to the western part of the country, if not the country as a whole, although many high-tail it out of here almost immediately after arriving. There is little of interest to passing tourists other than a few good hotels, westernized malls, North American chain restaurants, a handful of good markets, a couple of museums, and some upscale clubs. The chaotic, sometimes dangerous center lacks much charm and the city's wealthy cling to the suburbs on the surrounding hillsides.

The city was founded on June 27, 1536, by Don Pedro de Alvarado and was originally named Villa de San Pedro de Puerto Caballos, although it was quickly renamed San Pedro "Sula," from the Usula word that means "Valley of Birds." The town was intended to be a point of transfer of goods from Nicaragua, El Salvador, and Guatemala onto the coast at Puerto Cortés. However, persistent pirate attacks nearly destroyed that mission, and the town was practically deserted by the 19th century. It remained a rural backwater until the 1920s when the United Fruit Company set up shop here to expand their banana plantations; the population subsequently exploded from about 10,000 to 100,000 in just a few years. Much of the country's industry and exportation still revolves around the city, which is the second largest in the country after Tegucigalpa. The population today is just over 500,000.

Essentials

Getting There

BY PLANE Ramón Villeda Morales International Airport, sometimes just called **San Pedro Sula International Airport (SAP;** no phone), sits 15km (9 miles) east of the city on the road to La Ceiba. It is the country's busiest airport and offers the most international connections. Continental, American Airlines, Delta, TACA, and Spirit fly here directly from points in the U.S. such as Miami, Houston, Atlanta, New York, Los Angeles, and Fort Lauderdale. Regional airlines serving San Pedro include **Isleña Airlines** (✆ **504/552-8322;** www.flyislena.com), **Aerolíneas Sosa** (✆ **504/550-6545**), and **Atlantic Airlines** (✆ **504/557-8088;** www.atlanticairlinesint.com); these airlines fly to Tegucigalpa, La Ceiba, Roatán, and other Central American destinations such as San Salvador, San Jose, Guatemala City, and Managua.

A taxi from the airport to the center of town should run about L190 to L230 ($10–$12/£5–£6). There's also a **Hedman-Alas** (✆ **504/553-1361;** www.hedmanalas.com) bus terminal at the airport, with buses that run three times a day to La Ceiba or six times a day to Copán or Tegucigalpa.

BY CAR All roads lead to San Pedro. It is the transportation hub of the country and almost always a necessary point of transfer between any two long-distance points. The best highway in the country and one of the best in all of Central America—CA 5—traverses the distance between San Pedro Sula and Tegucigalpa and passes through Lago de Yojoa, Siguatepe, and Comayagua along the way. It can be extremely crowded (semi trucks use this road to haul goods from one coast to the other) and accidents can sometimes drag traffic to a screeching halt, yet if things move smoothly you can make the 241km (150-mile) trip between the coasts in under 4 hours on this road.

If you're coming to San Pedro Sula from Tela, La Ceiba, or elsewhere on the North Coast, take **CA 13.** If you're driving here from Copán, you have a pretty much straight shot on highway **11** to the town of La Entrada, from where you will continue on **CA 4** to downtown.

Most major North American car-rental agencies, such as **Avis** (✆ **504/668-3164;** www.avis.com), **Budget** (✆ **504/668-3179;** www.budget.com.hn), **Hertz** (✆ **504/668-3156;** www.hertz.com), and **Thrifty** (✆ **504/668-3154;** www.thrifty.com) have a counter at the San Pedro airport, as well as an office in town.

BY BUS The city's new station, the **Terminal Metropolitana de Autobuses** is 5km (3 miles) south of town, on CA 5 toward Tegucigalpa. **Hedman Alas** (7 and 8 Av., 3 Calle NO; ✆ **504/553-1361;** www.hedmanalas.com) is the best bus line in Honduras and the most useful for tourists who are sticking to the country's main destinations. It has mostly nonstop, first-class service several times per day to the San Pedro airport (20 min. away), Tela (1½ hr. away), La Ceiba (3 hr. away), Trujillo (6 hr. away), Copán Ruínas (3 hr. away),

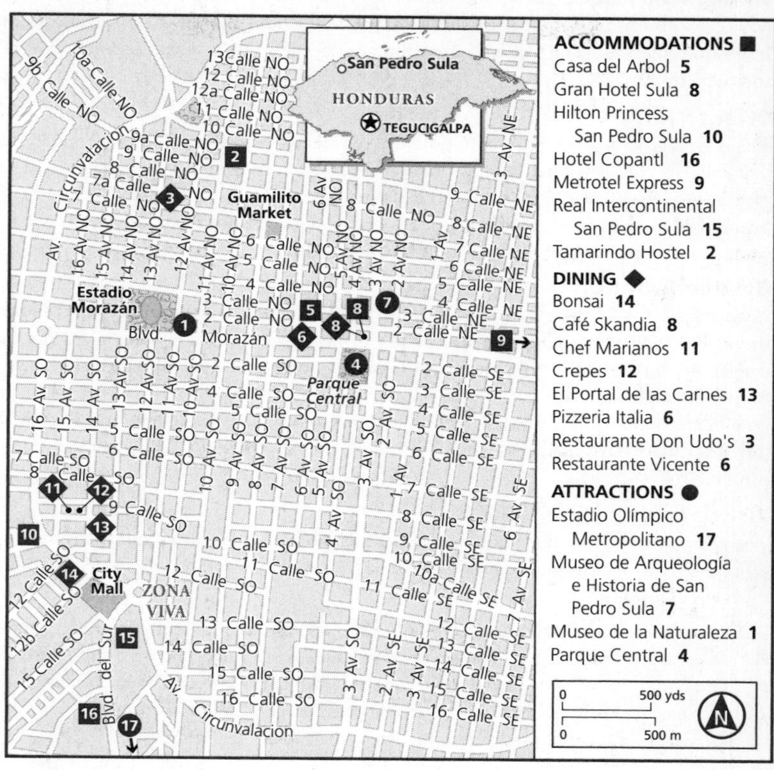

Comayagua ($3^1/_2$ hr. away), and Tegucigalpa ($4^1/_2$ hr. away). The company also offers connecting service in Copán to Guatemala City and Antigua, Guatemala.

Other companies that travel from San Pedro Sula to Tegucigalpa include **Saenz** (✆ **504/553-4969**), which has regular and first class, nonstop service six times a day to the capital, **El Rey Express** (✆ **504/550-8950;** www.reyexpress.net), and **Viana** (Av. Circunvalación; ✆ **504/556-9261**), which offers Clase Oro/Gold Class service to Tegucigalpa, as well as La Ceiba.

To reach Gracias, try **Gracianos** (✆ **504/656-1403**) at the main terminal, which has departures until 2pm for the $4^1/_2$-hour ride that passes through Santa Rosa de Copán and La Entrada. To reach Tela, try **Tela Express** (9 Av. 9 and 10 Calle; ✆ **504/550-8355**) with five daily departures. If you're heading to La Ceiba and Trujillo, check out **Cotuc** (✆ **504/520-1597**), which has five daily trips from the main terminal.

To reach Managua or Guatemala City, your best choice is **TICA** (✆ **504/556-5149**), which runs buses daily at 5am from the main terminal. Buses first stop in Tegucigalpa before heading out of the country.

BY FERRY Puerto Cortés, located 64km (40 miles) north of San Pedro Sula, is one of the largest and most advanced ports in Central America. From this port, there is ferry service to Placencia, Belize, with the **D-Express** (© **504/991-0778**) on Mondays at 10am from the Muelle de Cabotaje, returning Fridays at 9:30am. The ride takes 4 hours, and costs L950 ($50/£25).

Orientation

The dividing marker for San Pedro Sula is **Avenida Circunvalación,** a large boulevard that encircles the downtown area, with Parque Central at its center. Many amenities, like gas stations, restaurants, and malls, can be found radiating off this avenue. The center of town is laid out in a standard grid divided by four quadrants: northeast, southeast, northwest, and southwest. Avenues lead from north to south and streets from east to west.

Getting Around

Apart from a few of the major hotels, almost every site of interest to the typical traveler sits within the circular Circunvalación and can be reached on foot. Some areas can be dangerous, through, and robberies have occurred, so it is best to take taxis, especially during the night.

While the confusing, crowded, and often dangerous public bus system here is of little use to travelers, taxis are cheap and plentiful. A ride anywhere in the center will rarely run over L35 ($2/£1).

Visitor Information

There's no official visitor center in San Pedro Sula, but you can check out the private tour office **Servicios Culturales y Turisticos** (Calle 4a btw. Av. 3a and 4a; © **504/552-4048**) for maps and information.

FAST FACTS **Banco Atlántida** (© **504/558-1580**) on Parque Central exchanges traveler's checks, gives cash advances on credit cards, and has an ATM. There are also ATMs in every mall, most of the large hotels, some gas stations, and scattered about downtown in 24-hour booths. There's a black-market currency exchange at Parque Central, but rates are no different from the money-changers in storefronts and at the airport.

You can contact your embassy for a list of doctors in San Pedro or try **Centro Médico Betesda** (Av. 11a NO and Calle 11a NO; © **504/516-0900**), which is open daily 24 hours for emergencies and has consultations from 9 to 11am and 3 to 6pm.

Within a few blocks of Parque Central, there are literally a dozen small Internet cafes charging less than L20 ($1/50p) per hour that also have net phones for international calls and software for downloading digital photos. Alternatively, try the local telephone company **Hondutel,** at Avenida 4a SO and 4a Calle SO, where you can make long-distance calls for a few lempira a minute. There's also a cybercafe at the airport, but prices there are four times as expensive.

There are dozens of small *lavanderias* that will wash, dry, and fold your clothes in a day for about L60 ($3/£1.50) per load. For fast service, head to **Astroclean** (Av. 14a SO and Circunvalación), just across from the City Mall.

The **Tourist Police** (Av. 12a NO and Calle 1a; © **504/550-3472**) take calls daily, for 24 hours.

The post office is at Avenida 3a SO and Calle 9a SO Correos. You can send packages from here, but a safer and more efficient way is through **DHL** (Circunvalación at Brigada No. 105; © **504/550-1000**) or **FedEx** (Calle 17 and Av. 10 SO No. 56).

What to See & Do

Parque Central (Central Park) is the heart of San Pedro and is located smack in the middle of town at 1 Calle and 3 Avenida. Most of the city's attractions, as well as restaurants and shops, are clustered around this park. Though the park lacks the charm of colonial centers in Tegucigalpa and Comayagua, it's still the most identifiable landmark (apart from the giant Coca-Cola sign on one of the hillsides) and most popular meeting place in the city. The **San Pedro Sula Cathedral,** at the 3 Avenida side of the park, was only built in 1949, and doesn't have the history or elegance of some of the country's better known churches; nevertheless it is worth a peek (it's only open during Mass) in this attraction-starved city.

Museo de Arqueología e Historia de San Pedro Sula (Museum of Anthropology and History of San Pedro Sula) ★ Only a few blocks from Central Park, this must-see museum walks you through the history of the Sula Valley and Honduras from pre-Columbian times, during colonial rule, and into the modern era. Most of the artifacts, which have labels in English and Spanish, were found in the area. There's a small bookstore and handicraft shop inside with a fine array of hard-to-find books on the Mayas, Honduran history, and handmade crafts from indigenous tribes.

3a Av. and 4a Calle NO. ✆ **504/557-1496.** Admission L40 ($2/£1). Mon–Sat 9am–4pm; Sun 9am–3pm.

Museo de la Naturaleza (The Nature Museum) This regional natural history museum details the plant and wildlife of the Sula Valley and the rest of the country through the art of taxidermy, bones, diagrams, and extensive charts and labels. It's worth a look if you have a particular interest in biology or have time to kill in San Pedro, but otherwise is skippable.

Calle 1 and Av. 12a NO. ✆ **504/557-6598.** Admission L20 ($1/50p). Mon–Sat 8am–noon and 1–4pm.

Parque Nacional El Cusuco

While it is difficult to reach and not nearly as majestic as Parque Nacional Celaque (p. 373), **El Cusuco ★★** is well worth the time and effort if you're in the San Pedro Sula area for a few days. Set in the Merendón Mountain Range—45km (28 miles) away—the park is dominated by lush, unspoiled cloud forest and some of the most diverse avian life of any national park in the country. If you arrive early, you have the chance to spot quetzals (they're easiest to spot Apr–June), toucans, parrots, and even a few mammals. There are two trails from the visitor center, Quetzal and Las Minas, that take no more than a few hours to explore. You can usually hire a guide from the visitor center for L90 ($5/£2.50).

If you don't have a car, the next best way to get here is by a guided tour. One recommended tour operator to try is **Garífuna Tours** (p. 322). Admission is L285 ($15/£7.50), and the park is open daily from 8am to 4:30pm.

Your best option for staying overnight here is in one of the cabins in Buenos Aires run by **Fundación Ecologista HR Pastor** (Av. 12a NO and Calle 1a; ✆ **504/557-6598**). Cabins run L230 ($12/£6) per person and must be reserved in advance.

Sports & Outdoor Activities

Soccer is undoubtedly the most popular past time in Honduras, and San Pedro's **Estadio Olímpico Metropolitano** (5km/3 miles southeast of the center; no phone) is one of the top venues in the country for a match. Occasionally national team games are held at the stadium but you will most likely have to settle for one of the league games featuring either of the local teams: Motagua and Real España. You can buy tickets right at the doors and games rarely sell out; tickets range from L100 to L500 ($5–$25/£2.50–£13).

Shopping

The sprawling **Guamilito Market** ★ between 8 and 9 Avenida and 6 and 7 Calles NO has products from around the country, as well as El Salvador and Guatemala, which fill up literally hundreds of small stalls. You'll find everything from hammocks, T-shirts, and pottery to cigars, Maya figurines, jewelry, coffee, and Garífuna coconut carvings. Expect to bargain and never accept your first price. Of special note is the small section of women that make tortillas not far from the food stalls—even if you don't buy anything, the market is worth a visit to see these women at work. The market is open daily from 10am to 5pm.

For high-quality handcrafted leather handbags and purses, try **Danilo's** (Av. 18 SO and Calle 9; ✆ **504/552-0656;** www.danilos.com). **Maymo Art Gallery** (2 Calle SO and 7 Av. No. 24; ✆ **504/553-0318**) exhibits and sells paintings from numerous Honduran artists, such as Benigno Gomez, Roque Zelaya, and Maury Flores.

The best malls in Honduras can be found in San Pedro. **City Mall** (Circunvalación and Carr; no phone), opened in late 2005, is home to more than 200 shops, a Cinemark movie theater, seven banks, and almost 30 restaurants.

Where to Stay

Very Expensive

Hilton Princess San Pedro Sula ★ Although the Hilton is 2km (1¼ miles) from the city center, it's just a banana's toss away from the Zona Viva and its nearby malls. The boxy yet elegant Republican-style building has all the amenities you would expect from a Hilton: a small sofa and seating area, 250-thread-count sheets, Crabtree and Evelyn soaps, and HBO. There's also a decent but overpriced restaurant, an English pub, and a resortlike pool area that could easily fit in on any Caribbean beach. It's a small step down from the Real Intercontinental in overall quality, but not by much.

10 Calle and Av. Circunvalación SO. ✆ **504/556-9600.** Fax 504/556-9595. www.sanpedrosula.hilton.com. 124 units. L2,870 ($151/£76) double; L3,820 ($201/£101) suite. AE, DC, MC, V. **Amenities:** Restaurant; bar; pool. *In room:* A/C, TV, hair dryer, minibar, Wi-Fi.

Hotel Copantl (Kids) The Hotel Copantl, the largest hotel in San Pedro Sula, is comparable to the Honduras Maya in Tegucigalpa in a number of ways. It's just outside the center, attracts loads of business travelers, and its large, upscale complex features restaurants, bars, a handful of tennis courts, and an Olympic-size swimming pool. Tile floors, floral bedspreads, and heavy wood furniture don't add much character to the rooms, but are exactly what you would expect for this type of hotel. Additionally, the Copantl is home to the only major casino in the city and its proximity to the Multi Plaza Mall and Zona Viva is a big plus, especially for kids and teens.

Blvd. del Sur. ✆ **504/556-7108.** www.copantl.com. 190 units. L2,470 ($130/£65) double; L2,660 ($140/£70) suite. AE, MC, V. **Amenities:** Restaurant; bar; casino; fitness center; pool; tennis court. *In room:* A/C, TV, minibar, Wi-Fi.

Real Intercontinental San Pedro Sula ★★ The best thing about this hotel is that it doesn't feel like it's in the city. The tropical plant–lined driveway and posh marble entryway give the impression of a resort atmosphere that is only further encouraged by the umbrellas, chaise longues, turquoise pool, and waiters strolling around with rum-based drinks with little umbrellas sticking out of them. The rooms and services are what you would expect from a Real Intercontinental: bright, luxurious, comfortable, clean, and modern. Most of the hotel was remodeled in 2007, so for the time being, it still has a leg up on the nearby Hilton Princess. They missed out on adding some local touches like local art, however, except in the beautiful Vertigo bar.

Colonia Hernandez and Blvd. de Sur. ✆ **504/ 545-2500.** Fax 504/545-2527. 142 standard rooms and 7 suites. L2,641 ($139/£70) double, L7,200 ($378/£189) suite. AE, DC, MC, V. **Amenities:** Restaurant; bar; pool. *In room:* A/C, TV, hair dryer, minibar, Wi-Fi.

Expensive

Casa del Arbol ★ (Finds) From the moment you walk into this boutique hotel, you'll feel like you've set foot in a cozy hospital—the cleanliness is that noticeable. The rooms and bathrooms are borderline spitshine-clean, but otherwise standard with grayish walls, tile floors, and patterned bedspreads. There's also a small desk and a teeny-weeny balcony that you can barely plant two feet on. The hotel is built around a big leafy tree, which gives it somewhat of a tropical vibe and adds some character that every other hotel in the city misses. It's not on the best street in town, so try and taxi in and out.

6 Av. btw. 2 and 3 Calle NO. ✆ **504/504-1616.** Fax 504/557-1725. www.hotelcasadelarbol.com. 13 units. L1,500 ($80/£40) double. Rates include breakfast. AE, MC, V. **Amenities:** Restaurant; bar. *In room:* A/C, TV.

Gran Hotel Sula While the lack of significant renovations has caused the Gran Hotel to become not as grand as it once was, its rooms are decently sized and its amenities are almost comparable to the Hilton or Real Intercontinental, including new flatscreen TVs that were added in 2008. Many of the rooms have balconies overlooking neighboring Parque Central; the lower levels can get a bit noisy, so opt for one of the higher levels or a room in the back facing the pool. Their 24-hour Skandia coffee shop/diner and Granada restaurant (with an excellent Sun brunch) make it hard to leave the hotel, but if you do, almost everything is just a few steps away.

Parque Central. ✆ **504/552-9999.** www.hotelsula.hn. 117 units. L1,520 ($80/£40) double; L2,000 ($105/£53) suite. AE, MC, V. **Amenities:** Restaurant; bar; coffee shop; gym; pool. *In room:* TV, kitchenette and fridge in suite, Wi-Fi.

Moderate

Metrotel Express ★ Formerly the Microtel Inn and Suites, this hotel is all about location. If you plan to head out to the Bay Islands or elsewhere in the country and not spend much time in town, this is a midrange oasis of calm and convenience by the airport. The rooms are reminiscent of a North American cookie-cutter chain hotel like a Days Inn, yet haven't been worn in. Larson's restaurant, their American diner, isn't half bad; it serves all-day breakfast and is a much better option than the fast food over at the airport. Nice bonuses include a little pool area and helpful staff who can arrange trips to Lago de Yojoa or Tela.

Km 4 Blvd. al Aeropuerto. ✆ **504/559-0300.** Fax 504/559-0303. www.hotelhonduras.com. 60 units. L1,140 ($60/£30) double. Rates include breakfast. AE, MC, V. **Amenities:** Restaurant; bar; business center w/high-speed Internet; pool. *In room:* TV, Wi-Fi.

Inexpensive

Tamarindo Hostel ★ The Tamarindo is the unequivocal home of the San Pedro backpacker scene. Accommodations are divided between dorm-style rooms and private rooms, all with their own bathroom and hot water showers. Funky painted walls with Honduran art, graffiti, tapestries, and whatever else fits with Tamarindo's eclectic and cool vibe keep the decor interesting. There are loads of extras like a community room with a TV and DVD collection, two terraces with hammocks, free use of the kitchen, and even a small pool.

9 Calle NO and 11 Av. No. 1015, Barrio Los Andes. ✆ **504/557-0123.** www.tamarindohostelcom. 3 dorm rooms and 3 private rooms. $11 (£7) per person dorm; $40 (£20) private room. MC, V. **Amenities:** Pool. *In room:* A/C, Wi-Fi.

Where to Dine

Expensive

Bonsai JAPANESE The two-level, air-conditioned Bonsai, a couple of blocks from the Hilton, is the premier sushi and sashimi bar in town. The large menu spans tempura, yakitori rolls, sashimi, and sampler plates. If you're there with a few people, try the Titanic Sushi boat, which can easily feed four. There's a full bar stocking international liquor and wine.

Calle 14a, above the Hilton. ✆ **504/552-9445.** Main courses L150–L380 ($8–$20/£4–£10). AE, MC, V. Daily noon–3:30pm and 5:30–11pm.

El Portal de las Carnes STEAK It's safe to say that El Portal de las Carnes is the best Uruguayan steakhouse in Honduras. That may sound like an understatement, but several of them are actually spread around the country. Brochettes, ribs, sirloin, filet mignon, and national and imported beef of every other sort are paired with seviches and seafood. This upscale yet rustic eatery is popular among the business crowd.

10 Calle and 15 Av., Barrio Suyapa. ✆ **504/552-6137.** www.relportal.com. Main courses L152–L300 ($8–$16/£4–£8). AE, MC, V. Mon–Sat 11:30am–2pm and 5–10pm.

Restaurante Don Udo's ★ INTERNATIONAL This often crowded Dutch-owned restaurant has been a staple on San Pedro's restaurant scene for decades, and they recently opened a restaurant and hotel in Copán Ruínas. The colonial ambience at this first location attracts San Pedro's upper crust, who come for a decent variety of international dishes like pastas, steaks, seafood, and sandwiches. Their set lunch menus, usually three courses, are a great value. They have one of the more rounded wine lists in San Pedro with bottles from Argentina, Chile, and Italy. Their outdoor patio occasionally has live music.

13 Av. NO and 7a Calle NO. ✆ **504/553-3106.** Reservations recommended. Main courses L170–L420 ($9–$22/£4.50–£11). AE, MC, V. Mon–Sat 11:30am–2pm and 6–11pm; Sun 10am–2pm.

Moderate

Chef Marianos ★★ Finds HONDURAN On a gastronomic level, Chef Marianos is perhaps the most important restaurant in San Pedro. Their specialty is high quality—yet excellent value—Honduran coastal and Garífuna specialties like conch seviche, grilled and steamed fish platters, and *tapado* (a seafood stew). Every table is set with a side of delicious coconut bread. The often packed restaurant is situated in a cheery, converted house in the Zona Viva neighborhood.

9a Calle SO and 15a Av. SO, Zona Viva. ✆ **504/552-5492.** Main courses L114–L230 ($6–$12/£3–£6). MC, V. Daily 11am–10pm.

Pizzeria Italia PIZZA Adjacent to and run by the same owners of Restaurante Vicente (see below), Pizzeria Italia is the oldest pizzeria in town and it's as classic a rustic pizzeria joint as they come, with just a few rickety tables in the dining area. The pies beat those dished out at the North American pizzeria chains that dominate the city, hands down.

Av. 7 and Calle 1 NO. ✆ **504/550-7094.** Main courses L75–L200 ($4–$10/£2–£5). MC, V. Daily 11am–10pm.

Restaurante Vicente ★★ ITALIAN This restaurant has been open since 1962 and so, as with the owners' other restaurant, Pizzeria Italia, it's definitely an institution of sorts in town. It's more formal than the pizzeria, and doles out standard Italian fare such as pastas, risottos, calzones, and wine—it's a menu that has changed very little through the years, and it probably never will, since folks keep coming back.

Av. 7 and Calle 1 NO. ✆ **504/552-1335.** Main courses L90–L275 ($5–$14/£2.50–£7). MC, V. Daily 11am–10pm.

Inexpensive

Café Skandia INTERNATIONAL This 24-hour cafe and diner is the most reliable restaurant nearby Parque Central. Located in the Gran Hotel Sula (p. 347), it serves hearty Honduran breakfasts, *baleadas,* and roast chicken as well as North American items like burgers, onion rings, milkshakes, and even apple pie a la mode.

1a Calle NO at Parque Central. ✆ **504/552-9999.** Main courses L55–L150 ($3–$8/£1.50–£4). MC, V. Daily 24 hr.

Crepes ★★ INTERNATIONAL/COLOMBIAN Modeled after a similar Colombian chain, Crepes serves sweet and savory crepes filled with anything you can imagine. The restaurant also serves *arepas* (a cornmeal patty stuffed with cheese or veggies), burgers, steaks, homemade soups, and even charcoal steaks that make for a sweet diversion from typical Honduran or North American fare. The vibe is fast and casual, but the space avoids feeling too much like a chain restaurant.

7 Calle and 19 Av., Barrio Río de Piedras. ✆ **504/553-5797.** Main courses L75–L190 ($4–$10/£2–£5). AE, MC, V. Daily 11:30am–10pm.

San Pedro Sula After Dark

While the consensus has always been that La Ceiba has the best nightlife in Honduras, San Pedro isn't far behind and it's catching up fast. Along the Circunvalación and in the Zona Viva, at avenidas 15a and 16a SO between calles 7a and 11a SO, are the majority of the city's many bars, lounges, and clubs. To start the night off right, head to **Beer Bar** (third floor of the City Mall; ✆ **504/580-1343**) where you can find a vast assortment of beers, both bottle and tap, from across Latin America, Europe, and the U.S.

Two of the best late-night clubs in town are **Confetti's Disco** (Circunvalación and 7a Av. NO; ✆ **504/557-3033**) and **Kawamas Bay** (Circunvalación and 10a Av. NO; no phone). If you like DJs blasting loud house, techno, salsa, and crowds of hard-partying hip 20-somethings, and can dance until dawn, then these two places (just a block apart) are your best bet. Covers vary depending on the night, but usually range from L60 to L120 ($3–$6/£1.50–£3).

If slinging back gin and tonics and playing roulette or blackjack are more your thing, check out **Casino Copan** in Hotel Copantl (p. 346).

LAGO DE YOJOA ★

Although it is right on CA 5 between the big tourist sites of San Pedro Sula and Tegucigalpa, few travelers do more than see this breathtaking lake from their bus window. Covering 89 sq. km (55 sq. miles), at 700m (2,200 ft.) above sea level, and surrounded by misty pine-covered mountains, coffee fincas, and two national parks, this is the largest natural lake in the country and is one of Central America's most overlooked natural attractions. Birders have long come to the Yojoa, though, because nearly 400 species have been identified on the lake and on its shores. If you left your binoculars and avian identification charts at home, there are still plenty of ways to enjoy the setting, from renting a rowboat, to hiking in either of the two cloud forests, touring a Lenca archaeological site, or sampling beers in the country's first microbrewery.

Essentials

GETTING THERE & GETTING AROUND You'll need to have your own car to explore the more remote corners of the lake, as there aren't taxis in town. The country's major highway, CA 5, runs between San Pedro Sula and Tegucigalpa and passes right beside the eastern edge of the lake and the town of La Guama, from where you can easily take Hwy. 54 to the north and Peña Blanca. You can also get to/from San Pedro directly via the windy Hwy. 54, though this takes a bit longer at about 2 hours.

Any Tegucigalpa bound bus that's coming from San Pedro will let you off at La Guama and vice versa; the ride from San Pedro Sula takes 3 hours. Minibuses (L10/50¢/25p) regularly ply the route between here and La Guama and Peña Blanca, as do taxis, which cost around L20 ($1/50p).

ORIENTATION CA 5 parallels the eastern edge of the lake, where most restaurants and hotels can be found, as well as the small town of La Guama and Parque Nacional Cerro Azul Meámbar. On the north side of the lake, you will find the town of Peña Blanca, which is a more secluded place to base yourself, as well as the Parque Eco-Archeological de Los Naranjos. On the western side of the lake is Parque Nacional Montaña de Santa Barbara.

VISITOR INFORMATION Most of the parks in this area are self-guided, so you can easily hire locals to guide you at any of the entrances. The **D&D Brewery** (✆ **504/994-9719;** www.dd-brewery.com) runs a variety of organized tours in the region, though.

What to See & Do

Parque Eco-Archeological de Los Naranjos ★ This small Lenca site on the northern edge of the lake is a far better eco park than an archaeological one. Just a few mounds and piles of stones can be found at the site, which dates back to approximately 700 B.C. More exciting are the 6km (3³/₄ miles) of stone paths and dirt trails that weave through much of the complex, including a hanging bridge. This is one of the best spots for bird-watching around the lake, and there's even a small tower for birders near the mounds. A small museum and visitor center with information on finds at the site and general background of the Lencas graces the entrance and parking area. To get here from La Guama or Peña Blanca, you can catch a minibus to El Jaral on Hwy. 54, which should drop you off on the main drag, if not right at the park.

3km from the town of Peña Blanca, El Jaral. ✆ **504/650-0004.** Admission L100 ($5/£2.50). Daily 8am–4pm.

Parque Nacional Cerro Azul Meámbar ★★ The majestically misty mountains along the eastern side of the lake make up this 478-sq.-km (297-sq.-mile) park. The base of the park comprises coffee plantations and tropical forests, which turn to pine forest

Volunteer Opportunities in Parque Nacional Cerro Azul Meámbar

The Christian NGO Proyecto Aldea Global/Project Global Village (✆ **504/239-8400;** www.paghonduras.org) has been in charge of managing Parque Nacional Cerro Azul Meámbar since 1992. Conserving the natural environment, providing sustainable development for the rural communities that live in the buffer zone around Cerro Azul, and helping to jump-start ecotourism projects are just part of the work they do in and around the park. Groups and individuals are encouraged to contact the nonprofit organization if interested in lending a helping hand to one of their numerous projects in the area.

that then turn to cloud forests as the mountain climbs to a height of 2,047m (6,714 ft.). The park is a significant supplier of water to the surrounding communities and contributes more than 70% of the water to Lago de Yojoa. The isolation of the park means that wildlife here is flourishing. Several hundred bird species including keel-billed toucans and resplendent quetzals, as well as more than 50 species of mammals, such as peccaries, tapirs, monkeys, pumas, and jaguars, can be found inside the park. Plus there are loads of orchids, an elfin forest, and a handful of waterfalls.

From the visitor center near Los Pinos, there's access to three main hiking trails, ranging from 1 to 8km (.5–5 miles) in length. There are several other trails into the park from surrounding communities as well.

Like many of the cloud forests in Honduras, this one is nearly impossible to reach, even though it has six entrances. Public transportation to the park is nonexistent and you definitely need a 4WD to go on your own. The main entrance is at the town of Los Pinos. To get to there, take the marked turnoff at La Guama from CA 5 and continue up the steep, bumpy road for about 15 minutes until you reach Santa Elena and then follow the signs until you reach Los Pinos and the visitor center. There are a few rustic cabins (L135/$7/£3.50) for rent if you prefer to stay the night.

Turnoff at La Guama for Los Pinos. ✆ **504/239-8392.** www.paghonduras.org/panacam. Admission L20 ($1/50p). Daily 8am–6pm.

Parque Nacional Montaña de Santa Barbara This cloud forest park on the western side of Lago de Yojoa is dominated by the second-highest peak in the country, Santa Barbara, sometimes called El Maroncho. The mountain is as pristine as they come and visitors here are rewarded with some of the biggest biodiversity in the country. Orchids, more than 400 species of birds like trogons, toucans, and woodpeckers, as well as butterflies, fungi, spider monkeys, anteaters, and jaguars, can all be spotted. There is no infrastructure in the park whatsoever, but there are a few unmarked trails that can reach the 2,744m (9,000-ft.) summit, over about a 2 or 3 days' walk. You can ask around for a guide in the villages of El Playón, Los Andes, or San Luis Planes, which border the park, for approximately L200 ($11/£5.50) per day. The park can be reached by catching a bus from Peña Blanca to any of the towns that border it, though it's most easily seen on a guided tour.

Free admission. For information, try the Santa Barbara tourist office at ✆ **504/643-2338.**

Pulhapanazak Falls ★★ Pulhapanazak is the awe-inspiring waterfall that adorns tourist brochures and posters when you land at pretty much every airport in Honduras.

The 43m-high (26-mile) waterfall on the Río Amapa crashes down to a rocky base and radiates a heavy mist from the moist tropical air. Occasionally you can catch a glimpse of a scarlet macaw or toucan in the trees around the falls.

There's a pretty park with a cafeteria and picnic tables above the falls, as well as a few swimming holes. Guides, usually local kids that hang around outside the park, can take you in a small cave behind the waterfall for a small tip. It's a slippery and often muddy path down to the base, so be extra careful.

It's easiest to reach Pulhapanazak on a guided tour, since getting here by bus is time-consuming and complicated. (By public transportation you must catch a San Pedro headed bus from Peña Blanca and then, after about 10km/6 miles, get off at San Buenaventura. From here you must catch a taxi westward 45 min. or so up a bumpy dirt road to the entrance.)

Admission L20 ($1/50p). Daily 6am–6pm.

Outdoor Activities

Bass fishing, which once attracted fishermen here from around the world until the stocks were severely depleted, is slowly making a comeback in the lake; there are lots of opportunities to sail here, too. **Honduyate Marina** (right on CA 5; ✆ **504/608-3726**), is the best operator to use for getting out on the water. They rent out sailboats and fishing boats, and even give tours on an old ferry. Another option is to head to the **D&D Brewery** (see below) and rent a rowboat for about L55 ($3/£1.50) per day.

Hummingbirds, orioles, motmots, cuckoos, tanagers, oropendolas, toucans, and even the occasional resplendent quetzal are among the nearly 400 birds that have been recorded around the lake. An expert guide from **D&D Brewery** (✆ **504/994-9719**) can arrange day trips to the best birding spots, at a charge of L225 ($12/£6) per person.

Where to Stay

D&D Bed and Breakfast ★★ Run by American expat and bluegrass musician Robert Dale, who also runs the attached D&D microbrewery, this quirky little compound is set on one of the most beautiful areas of the lake. The easygoing setup and service gives the impression that you're staying at a friend's house, which is a good thing. Standard rooms in the lodge are quite plain and a bit cramped—they just barely fit a bed and bathroom—but the overall value is good for the price. The cabins, one of which has a Jacuzzi, are much more spacious, newer, and have small porches with hammocks. D&D can also arrange bird-watching and tours in the national parks, and hook you up with a rowboat for exploring the lake.

3.7km (2¼ miles) past Peña Blanca, El Mochito. ✆ **504/994-9719.** www.dd-brewery.com. 4 standard rooms and 5 cabins. L230 ($12/£6) double; L500 ($26/£13) cabin. Rates include breakfast. No credit cards. **Amenities:** Restaurant; bar; laundry service; pool. *In room:* Fan.

La Posada del Lago Right on CA 5, this upscale yacht club, which is also known as the Honduyate, is by far the fanciest place to sleep on the lake. All of the enormous rooms are bright and clean, and come with little extras like DVD players and sitting areas; most important, all rooms boast amazing lakeside views. The property also has a few small cabins nearby, which are older and far more rustic. The lodge and Chalet de Lago restaurant are a favorite of wealthy vacationing Hondurans and locals alike—this is very much the lake's social hub.

Km 161 of Hwy. CA 5. ✆ **504/608-3726.** www.honduyatemarina.com. 5 rooms and 4 cabins. L1,690 ($89/£45) double; L2,090 ($110/£55) suite; L285 ($15/£7.50) cabin. Rates include breakfast. AE, MC, V. **Amenities:** Restaurant; bar; boat charters; pool. *In room:* A/C, fan, TV/DVD, Wi-Fi.

Where to Dine

In addition to the below recommended restaurant, a string of maybe 30 or so seafood restaurants rest along highway CA 5 on the edge of the lake. All are open-air eateries serving more or less the exact same menu. You get to pick your fish, usually tilapia, and the preparation such as *frito* (fried) or *a la plancha* (grilled). It's served whole (with the head and fins), and accompanied by lime and fried plantain chips. Main courses run L75 to L150 ($4–$8/£2–£4), and the restaurants are generally open daily 10am to 8pm.

D&D Brewery ★★★ INTERNATIONAL When American expat Robert Dale discovered he couldn't get a decent pint in Honduras, he decided to brew his own. Thus the D&D Brewery became the first and only microbrewery in the country. Using hops imported from Stowmarket in England, the tiny brewery pumps out stouts, ales, lagers, and even mango beers, as well as their own sodas flavored with mango, apricot, and raspberry. Locally picked blueberries are used to make blueberry soda and the restaurant's famous blueberry pancakes. The rest of the menu is a mix of American and Honduran staples like omelets, fresh soups, burgers, and *anafres* (black bean and cheese fondue, served with chips). Dale occasionally will bust out his guitar and supply bluegrass music to accompany your meal.

3¾ km (2¼ miles) past Peña Blanca. ✆ **504/994-9719.** www.dd-brewery.com. Main courses L76–L152 ($4–$8/£2–£4). No credit cards. Daily 10am–8pm.

COMAYAGUA

For more than 3 centuries Comayagu, which is 71km (45 miles) south of Lago de Yojoa, was the capital of Honduras, until it was moved to Tegucigalpa in 1880. The city was founded in 1537 by the Spanish explorer Alonso de Cáceres and it has, without a doubt, the strongest colonial history in the country. Traces of the city's prominent past can still be seen in the architecture of the palaces, churches, and squares—all slowly being restored—in the city center. For much of the year, the town is empty, only seeing a trickling of tourists, but during Semana Santa (Holy Week), the city comes alive for the most passionate religious celebration in the country.

Essentials

GETTING THERE & GETTING AROUND Comayagua is just a few blocks northeast of the highway, CA 5, which runs between Tegucigalpa (1½ hr. away) and San Pedro Sula (3½ hr. away). **El Rey Express** (✆ **504/237-8561;** www.reyexpress.net) runs hourly to both San Pedro and Tegucigalpa. **Transportes Rivera** (1a Av. SO and 2a Calle SO; ✆ **504/772-1208**) runs to San Pedro hourly from 5am to 4pm. To get to Lago de Yojoa, get on any San Pedro–bound bus and ask to be let off at the lake. Buses stop and can be picked up at the Texaco gas station toward the turnoff to the highway.

Anywhere in Comayagua can be reached on foot. The town follows a standard grid, surrounding the Parque Central. Nearly all churches, museums, and restaurants can be found within a few blocks of this square.

VISITOR INFORMATION In the Parque Central, there's a small **Tourist Center** (✆ **504/772-2080;** www.comayagua.hn) with maps and brochures.

Banco Atlántida (1a Calle NO and 2a Calle NO) will exchange traveler's checks and has an ATM. To make long-distance calls, head to **Hondutel** (1a Av. NE and Calle 5a NO). Internet cafes are scattered all around the center.

Moments Semana Santa

Semana Santa (Holy Week) ★★★ is a huge deal in Comayagua. From Palm Sunday to Easter Sunday, the city is flooded with tourists, pilgrims, day-trippers, and everyone else who wants to experience the most passionate religious celebration in Honduras. Processions and festivities occur every day in and around Comayagua's colonial churches and plazas. Good Friday is for many the most important day of this week; it's also when you will see *alfombras,* colorful sawdust carpets, laid out to be trampled on during the solemn Via Crucis Procession, in which a volunteer carries a cross on his back through the streets beginning at 10:30am. If you plan on staying in the city during Semana Santa, be sure to book your hotel as much as 6 months in advance.

What to See & Do

At press time, the entire colonial center of town was undergoing a major renovation funded by the Spanish Cooperation Agency that was expected to last several years. In addition to the attractions reviewed in full below, you might stop to at least check out the exterior of the colonial churches **Nuestra Señora de la Caridad** (7a Calle NO and 3a Av. NO) and **Iglesia y Convento de San Francisco** (Av. 1a NE and 7a Calle NO) by the Parque Central. Though the **Caxa Real** (1a Av. NE and 6a Calle NO, near Plaza de San Francisco), the country's first tax collection house, has been more or less destroyed by fires and earthquakes over the years, you can stop by to see its stone facade.

Catedral de Santa María ★★ The towering white cathedral on the north end of Parque Central, also known as La Iglesia de la Inmaculada Concepción, is considered by many to be the most beautiful cathedral in all of Honduras. Construction began on it in the late 17th century and was completed on December 8, 1711. Four of the original 16 hand-carved wood and gold-plated altars still survive. The clock in the church tower is one of the oldest in the world and the oldest in the Americas. Built around 1100 for the Alhambra in Granada, the clock was given to the town as a gift from King Phillip III and originally was placed in the Iglesia La Merced before being moved here. The church is undergoing an extensive renovation and it is closed to the public for the next several years.

Southeast corner of Parque Central. Call for admission prices and hours once it's reopened.

Iglesia La Merced Just 4 blocks south of Catedral de Santa María and fronting a small plaza of its own, Iglesia La Merced is the oldest church in Comayagua and one of the oldest in Central America. It was built in 1550, though an earthquake in 1774 destroyed one of the belfries and caused extensive damages. Inside are several paintings that date from the 16th century.

1a Av. NE and 1 Calle NO. Free admission. Daily 7am–8pm.

Museo Colonial de Arte Religioso This museum is located within a building that dates back to 1558 and was home to the first university in Central America. The collection derives from Comayagua's colonial churches, which were once virtual storehouses of valuable art. You'll see chalices, sculptures, paintings, and historical documents such as Honduran general Francisco Morazán's marriage certificate.

Av. 2a de Julio and 3a Calle NO. ✆ **504/772-0169.** Admission L40 ($2/£1). Mon–Sat 9am–noon and 2–4:30pm.

Museo Regional de Arqueología Formerly a presidential mansion and the site of the National Congress of Honduras, this newly renovated museum surrounding a grassy courtyard is home to probably the most comprehensive collection of Lenca artifacts. Most pieces on display are from archaeological sites within the valley and region surrounding Comayagua. Artifacts include textiles, pottery, stone carving, tools for grinding corn, and even petroglpyhs; a few small rooms are also devoted to exhibits on national Honduran culture. There's a small craft store in the back of the museum.

6a Calle NO and Av. 20 de Julio. ✆ **504/772-0386.** Admission L20 ($1/50p). Tues–Sun 8am–4:30pm.

Where to Stay

Hotel Casa Grande ★★ Finds This small bed-and-breakfast, hidden away on an unassuming street a few blocks from the square, is one of the most atmospheric hotels in western Honduras. Chances are that when the city of Comayagua finishes its renovation and more tourists start arriving here, you'll hear much more about this colonial building cum bed-and-breakfast. Stone and *azulejo* tile walls and lots of tropical plants augment the lobby and halls, while wood floors and hand-carved wood furniture give the rooms a splash of personality.

7a NO. Abajo, Comayagua. ✆ **504/772-0772.** Fax 504/772-0441. www.casagrande-hotel.com. 10 units. L1,102 ($58/£29) double. Rates include breakfast. MC, V. **Amenities:** High-speed Internet in lobby; laundry service. *In room:* A/C, fan, TV.

Hotel Santa Maria Right on the highway, this modern hotel lacks the charms of the cozy Hotel Casa Grande, but in regard to comfort and amenities, nothing compares to it in Comayagua. Rooms are clean, and have the look and amenities of a Holiday Inn. There are conference facilities and well-manicured gardens, but the best reason to stay here is the big, refreshing swimming pool.

Km 82 on CA 5. ✆ **504/772-7672.** Fax 504/772-7719. 28 units. L1,560 ($82/£41) double. MC, V. **Amenities:** Restaurant; bar; pool. *In room:* A/C, TV, Wi-Fi.

Where to Dine

Cactus Restaurant MEXICAN Right on a busy corner across from Iglesia La Merced, this Mexican restaurant is a welcome new addition to the Comayagua dining scene. Standard Mexican fare like tacos and nachos, plus a few beef and shrimp plates, taste great and are all cheap. Tables are either indoors with air-conditioning or on their outdoor patio, and both are graced by Mexican decor and music.

Parque La Merced. No phone. Main courses L55–L150 ($3–$8/£1.50–£5). MC, V. Wed–Mon 11am–10pm.

Casa Castillo INTERNATIONAL Set in the renovated colonial Libertad Hotel on the south side of Parque Central, this restaurant's atmosphere is a better reason to come here than the food, which is mediocre at best. Pastas, steaks, pork chops, sausage, and a few seafood dishes may come as a pleasant surprise if you are sick of Honduran foods, but otherwise you should go elsewhere. The cheap, heaping breakfasts here are a better bet than lunch or dinner, though.

Parque Central. ✆ **504/772-3528.** Main courses L130–L280 ($7–$15/£3.50–£7.50). MC, V. Tues–Sun 11am–9pm.

Villa Real ★ HONDURAN/INTERNATIONAL Just behind the cathedral, this elegant restaurant makes good use of its colonial structure and flower-filled courtyard. Various rooms are filled with period furniture and art, which you are more than welcome to explore before

La Entrada & the Ruins of El Puente

If you're planning on exploring western Honduras, you'll likely be stopping at La Entrada at one point. This town serves as a junction of CA 4 and CA 11, so it is lined with buses that lead to Copán (2 hr. away), San Pedro Sula (1½ hr. away), Santa Rosa (1½ hr. away), and lesser known villages in the region.

La Entrada is a dusty, uninteresting town that would serve as nothing more than a transport hub if it weren't for the Maya ruins of **El Puente** ★, which are just 10km (7½ miles) away. This is the second-most important archaeological park in all of Honduras after Copán, although you wouldn't know it by the number of visitors. Unless your visit parallels that of a tour bus, you'll likely have the entire site to yourself. The majority of the buildings on the site, opened in 1994, date from the Late Classic Period between the 6th and 9th centuries. Of the more than 200 buildings found in the park, only 9 have been excavated. The centerpiece is a medium-size pyramid set on a wide grassy plaza that's lined with a few other buildings that have been cleared from the encroaching jungle. There's a small visitor center and museum at the entrance, about 1km (½ mile) from the ruins.

To get to the El Puente archaeological site, you will need to hire a taxi, which costs L230 ($12/£6) round-trip from La Entrada. Admission is L55 ($3/£1.50) and the park is open daily from 8am to 4pm. Or you can go on a guided tour, through Hotel El San Carlos (see below).

You can easily visit El Puente as a day trip, but if you'd like to stay overnight, **Hotel El San Carlos** (junction of CA 4 and CA 11; ✆ **504/661-2228;** www.hotelelsancarlos.com; L600/$33/£17 double) is the only decent place to stay in the area. Just a few meters from the junction, this 45-unit hotel actually isn't half bad. There's a pool where you can listen to the squawks of their two macaws, clean rooms with cable TV, and a restaurant that happens to be the best in town.

or after your meal. Hearty Honduran *tipicos*—steak, rice, beans, tortillas, white cheese, and avocado—are standard fare here, as are *chuletas de cerdo* (pork chops) and grilled seafood.

Behind the cathedral, Parque Central. ✆ **504/772-0101.** Main courses L100–L250 ($5–$17/£2.50–£8.50). MC, V. Daily 11am–11pm.

6 COPAN RUINAS ★★★ & COPAN TOWN ★★

64km (40 miles) W of La Entrada; 12km (7 miles) S of the Guatemalan border

Not far from the Guatemalan border lies Copán, one of the most spectacular Maya ceremonial cities of Mesoamerica. The town, 1km (½ mile) from the archaeological site, is a small picturesque city with rough cobblestone streets and a buzzing central plaza that's the heart and soul of the place. It is reminiscent of a more compact version of Cusco, Peru, although tourism is growing here at an equally impressive rate. For example, in the

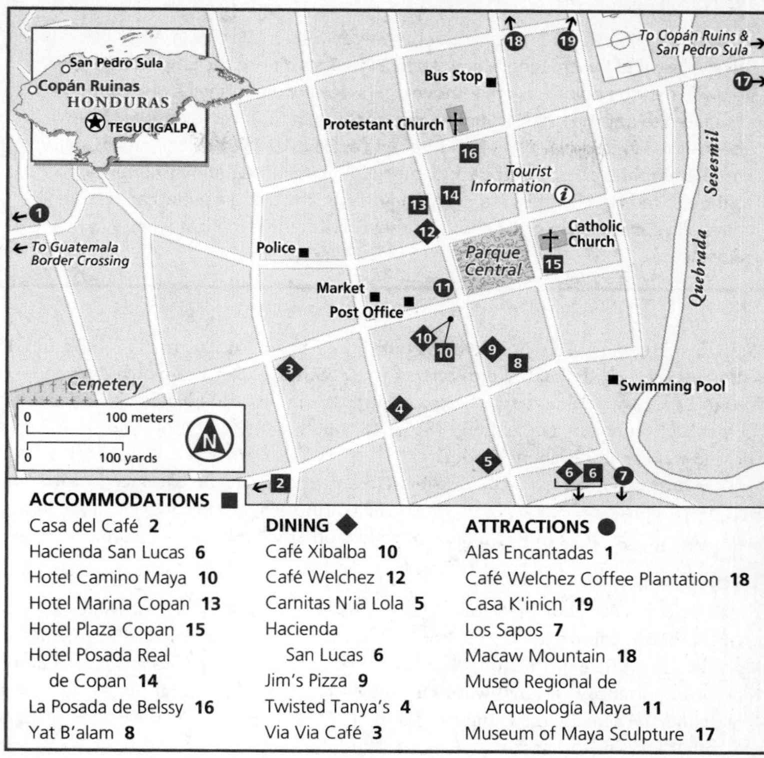

1970s, there were just a couple of small hotels mostly visited by archaeologists. Now there are more than 70. Copán is surrounded by beautiful forests with waterfalls, hot springs, and excellent bird-watching and adventure tourism possibilities.

ESSENTIALS

Getting There

BY CAR If you're driving to Copán from San Pedro Sula, you have a pretty much straight shot on **CA 4** to La Entrada, where you can continue on **highway 11** to Copán, a 2½-hour drive.

To get to and from Tegucigalpa is much trickier. From Copán, there is a beautiful route through the mountains to Gracias from La Entrada on **CA 11-A,** but the road is windy, mostly unpaved, and sometimes impassable due to rain. Many drivers prefer to head back toward San Pedro Sula and catch **Hwy. 20** or **CA 5** south for the 3½-hour drive to the capital.

From the Guatemalan border at El Florido, it's just a 12km (7-mile) drive to Copán Ruínas.

Tips Crossing the Border

Crossing the border at El Florido on your way to Guatemala City or Antigua is relatively easy and the crossing is now open 24 hours a day, so the long waits and crowds that the point was once known for have now diminished significantly. Be prepared to pay the L20 ($1/50p) departure tax (although some travelers have been asked for more) leaving Honduras and a L25 ($1.30/65p) fee to enter Guatemala. Both sides accept lempira and quetzals, Guatemala's national currency, although money-changers are everywhere. If you're driving a rental car, be sure to have all your papers in order and clear the trip with the rental-car agency in advance.

BY BUS **Hedman Alas** (✆ **504/651-4037** in Copán Ruínas, or 651-4037 in San Pedro Sula; www.hedmanalas.com) offers five daily trips to San Pedro Sula with connections to La Ceiba, Tela, and Tegucigalpa. They also run buses to Guatemala City daily at 1:30pm and 6pm. The fare is L665 ($35/£18) one-way, L1,140 ($60/£30) round-trip. The one-way trip takes about 5 hours.

Local buses also run from the dirt lot across the bridge at the entrance to town and head to La Entrada, 2 hours away, where riders can then transfer to a bus for Gracias, Santa Rosa de Copán, San Pedro Sula, or several other villages in the region.

Orientation

It may be confusing, but the actual Maya ruins here are called Copán, while the little town is officially known as Copán Ruínas. Most folks refer to it generically as Copán or make the appropriate distinction when necessary. The town is very compact, and everything of importance is located within a 4-block radius of the central plaza. No official street names are actually used, and directions are given in relation to the central plaza or some other known landmark.

Getting Around

You can easily walk anywhere in Copán Ruínas, including from town to the archaeological site. However, if you need a taxi, they are plentiful and inexpensive. Most of the taxis are small motor taxis or tuk tuks, which circulate around town and gather on the north and south sides of the central plaza. If you can't find one, call **Cooperativo Multicomer** (✆ **504/651-4054**) or **Lulo** (✆ **504/961-7823**). A taxi ride between town and the archaeological site should cost L20 to L40 ($1–$2/50p–£1) per person.

Visitor Information & Fast Facts

Banco Atlántida and **BAC** both front the central plaza and are fast and safe places to exchange money or use an ATM. To contact the local **police,** dial ✆ **504/651-4060.** The **post office** (✆ **504/651-4447**) is just west of the Copán Museum. There are a half-dozen or so Internet cafes around town; most charge around L20 to L40 ($1–$2/50p–£1) per hour. For medical emergencies, ask your hotel, or call Dr. Boqui at the **Clínica Handal** (✆ **504/651-4408**). **Hondutel,** half a block south of the central plaza, is the best place for international phone calls.

WHAT TO SEE & DO

Copán ★★★

Copán is one of the grandest and most magnificently preserved of all Maya ceremonial cities. Surrounded by thick jungle and set beside the gentle Copán River, the ruins are famous for their raw stone-carved hieroglyphics, massive stelae, and the impressive Hieroglyphic Stairway. Your visit here should include the extensive archaeological ruins, recently excavated tunnels, and Museum of Maya Sculpture.

The current area around Copán has been inhabited since at least 1400 B.C., and some of the earlier discoveries here show Olmec influences. The Great Sun Lord Quetzal Macaw, who ruled from A.D. 426 to 435, was the first of 16 consecutive kings who saw the rise and fall of this Classic Maya city. Some of Copán's great kings included Smoke Jaguar, 18 Rabbit, and Smoke Shell. The history of these kings is meticulously carved into the stones at the ruins.

Copán was famously "discovered" in 1839 and bought for just $50 by the adventurer John L. Stephens, who documented the story in his wonderful book, *Incidents of Travel in Central America, Chiapas and Yucatán* (1841). The book is beautifully illustrated by Stephens's companion Frederick Catherwood.

Visitor Information

The entrance to the Copán archaeological site is located along a well-marked highway about a half-mile from the town of Copán Ruínas. The visitor center and ticket booth are at one end of the parking lot; the Museum of Maya Sculpture is at the other. The Copán Guides Association has a booth at the entrance to the parking area. Here, you can hire a bilingual guide for a 2-hour tour of the site, which includes the Sepulturas, for L950 ($50/£25), no matter the size of your group. These guides are extremely knowledgeable, and are highly recommended to hire for your first visit. They aren't necessary to tour the museum, as the signs are in English, or the tunnels, which are so short that the guide isn't necessarily of much value.

Admission to the archaeological site, which includes the main Copán ruins and the Sepulturas, is L285 ($15/£7.50). Admission does not include a guide. Visits to the tunnels and Museum of Maya Sculpture are extra.

Museum of Maya Sculpture ★★

Considering that the ruins get more and more crowded as the day goes on, I recommend that you visit the new Museum of Maya Sculpture after seeing the ruins. The museum is located across from the entrance to the archaeological park, a few hundred yards from the small visitor center where you pay your entrance fee. This large, two-story structure was built to protect some of Copán's more impressive pieces from the elements. Inside you'll see beautifully displayed and well-documented examples of a broad range of stone carvings and hieroglyphics. At the center of the museum is a full-scale replica of the Rosalia Temple, which lies well-preserved inside the core of Temple 16 (which you'll see later at the ruins). The museum also contains the reconstructed original facade of one of the site's ball courts. Admission to the museum is L95 ($5/£2.50).

The Ruins ★★★

The ruins are at the end of a relatively short path from the museum exit. I recommend starting at the western plaza of Temple 16. As you face Temple 16, the Acropolis will be to your left. A trail and steps lead around the back, where you can enjoy a view over the Copán River to the surrounding mountains. Follow the path to the Patio of the Jaguars, where you'll find the entrances to the Rosalia and Jaguar tunnels. Continue on over the top of the Acropolis and the Temple of Inscriptions, and then down into the Great Plaza, where Copán's greatest hieroglyphic treasures were found.

The Temple of Inscriptions anchors the south end of the Great Plaza. To its east is the Hieroglyphic Stairway. This stairway, built by King Smoke Shell, rises up some 64 steps, each of which is carved or faced with hieroglyphs, telling the history of Copán's kings and their line of succession. To those literate in the language, the stairs once read as a giant book. Today, many of the carved stairs have fallen or faded, but enough remain to give a sense of the scale of this amazing achievement. The stairway is currently under cover, which makes it difficult to see. The lighting is poor, especially on cloudy days, but the trade-off in terms of preservation makes this necessary.

At the foot of the Hieroglyphic Stairway, and all around the Great Plaza, are examples of Copán's carved stelae. Many of these are carved on all four sides with detailed depictions of rulers, animals, and mythic beasts, as well as glyphs that tell their stories. Some of the stelae are originals, while others are replicas.

Las Sepulturas ★

Located about 2km (1½ miles) from the Great Plaza, Las Sepulturas is believed to have been a major residential neighborhood reserved for Copán's elite. The site gives you a sense of what the day-to-day living arrangements of an upper-crust Maya may have been like. Las Sepulturas was once connected to the Great Plaza by a broad, well-worn causeway (which has been identified by NASA with digital satellite imaging), but today it's reached via a gentle path through lush forests with excellent bird- and animal-watching opportunities.

The Rosalia & Jaguar Tunnels ★

Opened to the public in 1999, these two tunnels give visitors a firsthand look at the historical layering technique of the Maya builders, who would construct subsequent temples around and over existing ones, no matter how beautiful and intricate the original. Entrance to the two tunnels is an extra L190 ($10/£5) above the general admission, though these are well-lit modern excavations and not tunnels left by the ancient Maya, so it's a tossup whether or not it's really worth the extra money. However, the tunnels are fascinating and do give you a further sense of the massive scale of the archaeological undertaking.

Attractions in & Around Town

Alas Encantadas This is a small butterfly garden and breeding project with loads of winged creatures, exhibits illustrating the various stages of metamorphosis, and a botanical garden with more than 200 species of orchids.

300m (984 ft.) outside of town on the road to the Guatemalan border. ✆ **504/651-4133.** Admission L100 ($5/£2.50) for adults, L35 ($1.85/95p) for children. Daily 8am–4:30pm.

Café Welchez Coffee Plantation ★★ Finca Santa Isabel is where the Café Welchez brand shade-grown coffee is produced. The tour, which leaves by bus from Copán, begins in the mountain nursery and takes you through the entire processing method with the occasional chance to spot birds and butterflies in the surrounding rainforest.

Outside Copán. ✆ **504/651-4200.** www.cafehonduras.com. Tours are given daily with Yaragua Tours (✆ **504/651-4147;** www.yaragua.com) and cost L475 ($25/£13) per person, including transportation.

Casa K'inich (Kids) The Casa K'inich, or the Maya Children's Museum, has interactive and educational exhibits that teach kids (and adults) how to count and add in different

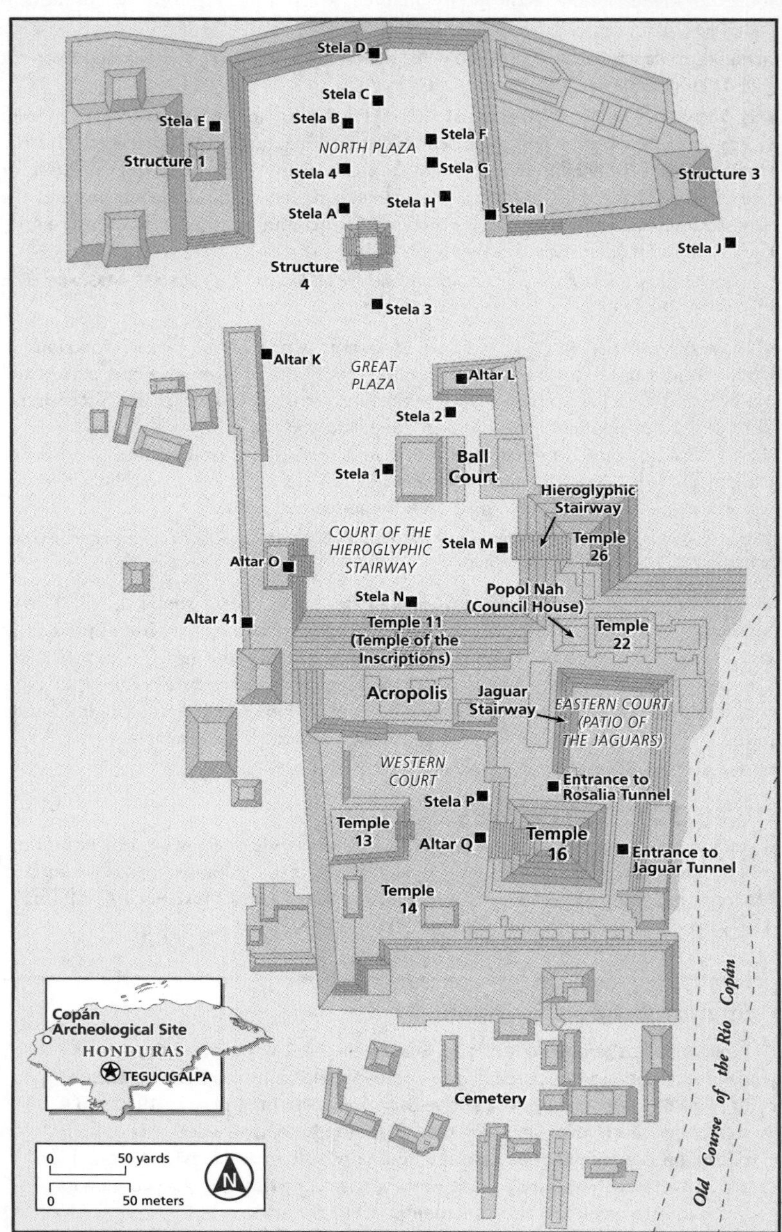
Stela D
Stela C
Stela B
Stela E
NORTH PLAZA
Stela F
Structure 1
Stela G
Stela 4
Structure 3
Stela H
Stela A
Stela I
Stela J
Structure 4
Stela 3
Altar K
GREAT PLAZA
Altar L
Stela 2
Ball Court
Stela 1
Hieroglyphic Stairway
COURT OF THE HIEROGLYPHIC STAIRWAY
Stela M
Temple 26
Altar O
Popol Nah (Council House)
Stela N
Temple 22
Altar 41
Temple 11 (Temple of the Inscriptions)
Acropolis
Jaguar Stairway
EASTERN COURT (PATIO OF THE JAGUARS)
WESTERN COURT
Entrance to Rosalia Tunnel
Stela P
Temple 13
Altar Q
Temple 16
Entrance to Jaguar Tunnel
Temple 14
Copán Archeological Site
HONDURAS
TEGUCIGALPA
Cemetery
Old Course of the Río Copán
0
50 yards
0
50 meters
N

Mayan dialects and how to play the ancient ballgame of the Maya. The museum is located in the rear of the public library building, which fronts the north side of the central plaza.

North side of Parque Central. ✆ **504/651-4105.** www.asociacioncopan.org. Free admission. Mon–Sat 8am–noon and 1–4pm.

Los Sapos The small ceremonial site of Los Sapos, located across the river from Copán, is believed to be tied to ancient Maya birthing and fertility practices. This is a very small and minimally excavated site. You can see some stone carvings of *sapos,* or frogs, and the carved figure of a pregnant woman. In addition, the site features the exposed foundations of a few large structures. Several tour agencies in town offer horseback riding tours that include a visit here.

5km (3 miles) from Copán Ruínas, on the grounds of Hacienda San Lucas. ✆ **504/651-4495.** Admission L40 ($2/£1). Daily 9am–5pm.

Macaw Mountain ★ Kids Macaw Mountain is one of the newer attractions in Copán Ruínas and features an extensive collection of tropical birds, primarily parrots and macaws, and some local raptors. The way the birds are displayed makes this place special. (The enclosures are quite large and well done, and you can even walk through some of them.) This attraction is spread out over a lush setting of a tropical forest and coffee plantation, with a beautiful river and well-designed trails. There's an excellent riverside restaurant and a separate coffee shop with home-roasted beans.

4.8km (3 miles) west of the central plaza up a dirt road. ✆ **504/651-4245.** www.macawmountain.com. Admission L200 ($10/£5). Daily 9am–5pm.

Museo Regional de Arqueología Maya ★ Also known simply as the Copán Museum, this museum holds a small collection of pottery and artifacts from the ruins, as well as a series of interpretive and explanatory displays. Perhaps the most interesting exhibit here is the complete burial niche of an ancient Copán scribe. If you're going to the ruins and the museum there, there's no need to visit this place. However, if you're hanging around town, it will only take you about 30 to 45 minutes to tour all the exhibits.

West side of Parque Central. No phone. Admission L40 ($2/£1). Daily 9am–5pm.

OUTDOOR ACTIVITIES

If you want to do some bird-watching, take a horseback ride, soak in a nearby hot spring, explore some caves, or tube on the Copán River, contact a local tour agency such as **McTours** (✆ **504/651-4453;** www.mctours-honduras.com), **Yaragua** (✆ **504/651-4147;** www.yaragua.com), or **Xukpi** (✆ **504/651-4435**).

Spanish Schools in Copán

While it isn't as popular as Antigua, Guatemala, a few hours away, Copán has a decent offering for those seeking to improve their Spanish skills. **Ixbalanque** (✆ **504/651-4432;** www.ixbalanque.com) has been running since 1990 and is one of the best known language schools in Honduras. One week with 20 hours of one-on-one classes, meals, accommodations with a local family, and one tour are $210 (£105). **Guacamaya** (www.guacamaya.com) has a similar program for $225 (£113) a week and also can arrange volunteer work.

SHOPPING

The streets of Copán Ruínas are brimming with simple souvenir shops selling T-shirts, jade carvings, hammocks, masks, cigars, and Guatemalan crafts and textiles. There are several good markets scattered within a couple of blocks of the square with independent vendors that haul their crafts in from the surrounding villages. The best are **Pabellon Maya** (✆ **504/643-2833**) beside the ATM on the plaza and **Casa del Sol** ★ (✆ **504/651-3559**) just off the plaza.

La Casa de Todo, 1 block downhill from the Banco de Occidente corner of the central plaza (✆ **504/651-4185**), is an excellent gift shop with unique local crafts, a coffee shop, an Internet cafe, and a simple restaurant serving Guatemalan fare; they even have a couple of rooms for overnight stays and laundry services. **Casa del Jade** (no phone; www.casavillamil.com) 1 block north of the plaza, is part of a Guatemalan chain that sells a wide variety of jewelry and collectibles that contain the Maya's preferred stone.

WHERE TO STAY

Expensive

Hacienda San Lucas ★★★ **Finds** This is my favorite hotel in the area, set on a hillside across the river from and overlooking the Copán archaeological site. The rustic elegance of the rooms is a throwback to its former life as a farm and ranch, as are the high wood-beam and plank ceilings. The large rooms each are outfitted with two queen-size beds, a large shared veranda with hammocks, and a beautiful stone shower. The hotel restaurant has excellent meals, and they have recently built a yoga platform overlooking the river and ruins. The hotel abuts the Los Sapos ruins, and has several excellent hiking trails on its grounds. Sunsets are taken on a long lawn off of the main lodge building.

5km (3 miles) south of Copán Ruínas on the road to Los Sapos ruins. ✆ **504/651-4495** or 651-4495. www.haciendasanlucas.com. 8 units. L615 ($85/£43) double. Rates include full breakfast. AE, MC, V. **Amenities:** Restaurant; bar; yoga studio.

Hotel Marina Copan ★★ The best hotel in Copán Ruínas proper spans an entire city block facing the central plaza. The rooms are all tastefully decorated and come with large TVs, while the suites have tons of space and other nice touches, such as a Jacuzzi, a kitchenette, and a view. My favorite is no. 331, a third-floor corner suite with a large balcony and a great view of town. Many of the standard rooms come with a balcony, so it's worth requesting one when you make a reservation. There's a pool in the center of the hotel and plenty of areas to relax among plants and fountains.

Parque Central. ✆ **877/893-9131** in the U.S. and Canada, or 504/651-4070 in Copán Ruínas. Fax 504/651-4477. www.hotelmarinacopan.com. 52 units. L615 ($85/£43) double; L2,280–L4,750 ($120–$250/£60–£125) suite. Rates lower in the off season, higher during peak periods. AE, MC, V. **Amenities:** Restaurant; bar; small gym w/sauna; laundry service; midsize pool; room service. *In room:* A/C, TV, Wi-Fi.

Hotel Posada Real de Copan ★★ What it lacks in proximity to the center it makes up for via its one-of-a-kind views—the Posada Real, the largest hotel in the area, overlooks the Maya ruins of Copán. This hotel, more than any other in Western Honduras, is a resort. The vast property, etched out of the dense jungle, surrounds a central courtyard that houses a pool. The rooms are a bit on the plain side, with reddish tile floors, gold or orange walls, wood furniture, and little else in the way of decor. The hotel is a hit with conferences, weddings, meetings, conventions, and most other large events.

1km (1/2 mile) from town near the archaeological site. ✆ **504/651-4480.** Fax 504/651-4497. www.posadarealdecopan.com. 80 units. AE, MC, V. L1,615 ($85/£43) double. **Amenities:** Restaurant; bar; helipad; laundry service; pool; shuttle service. *In room:* A/C, fan, TV.

Moderate

Casa del Café ★ This house-turned-bed-and-breakfast, located a few blocks outside the center of town, has a good view of the Copán valley and the mountains of neighboring Guatemala. The rooms are all cheery, bright, and comfortable. Those occupying the higher ground are a little older and smaller, but they have the aforementioned view from their shared veranda. The newer rooms have exposed beam ceilings and beautiful mosaic tile sinks, with a veranda that lets out onto a small garden. The owners are extremely knowledgeable about the area, and they also rent out a few fully equipped apartments nearby.

1 block south and 4 blocks west of the central plaza. ✆ **504/651-4620.** Fax 504/651-4623. www.casadecafecopan.com. 10 units. L855 ($45/£27) double. Rates include full breakfast. AE, MC, V. **Amenities:** Laundry service. *In room:* No phone.

Hotel Camino Maya (Kids) The Camino Maya occupies prime corner space on the central plaza, and so it competes with the Hotel Plaza Copan for the title of best-located moderate hotel. The lower level is home to the lobby and the Xibalba bar, run by Twisted Tanya's (see below), and Elisa's restaurant, while the second level holds the guest rooms. These rooms aren't terrible, but the floral bedspreads, tacky wallpaper and curtains, and mismatching wood and metal furniture could use a makeover. The hotel beats the Plaza Copan in extras, though. As space in the center of Copán is limited, the hotel's recreation area, with two pools, extensive gardens, hammocks strung from trees, two restaurants, and short trails, is a huge plus of staying here. Nonguests can use this recreation area, just 4 blocks from the main hotel, for L40 ($2/£1) a day.

Southeast corner of Parque Central. ✆ **504/651-4518.** Fax 504/651-4517. www.caminomayahotel.com. 23 units. L1,178 ($62/£31) double. Rates include breakfast. MC, V. **Amenities:** Restaurant; bar; pool. *In room:* A/C, fan, TV, fridge.

Hotel Plaza Copan This hotel has a good location on the corner of the central plaza with a good deal to boot. All of the rooms are spacious and feature red-tiled floors and high ceilings. Number 213 comes with a king-size bed and a private corner balcony overlooking the central plaza. There's a small pool in the central courtyard and a popular restaurant. The hotel also has a helpful tour desk.

Parque Central. ✆ **504/651-4508.** Fax 504/651-4039. www.plazacopanhotel.com. 20 units. L1,045 ($55/£28) double. Rates lower in the off season, higher during peak periods. AE, MC, V. **Amenities:** Restaurant; bar; laundry service; small pool. *In room:* A/C, TV.

Yat B'alam ★★ (Value) Opened in late 2007, this absolutely charming independent hotel is one of the best values in western Honduras. I'm hesitant to call it a boutique hotel for fear that the price will go up; it's currently an absolute steal. If it were located in Antigua, just a few hours across the border, it would cost three times as much. The ground floor is laid out like a cobblestone colonial street lined with craft shops and a cafe. There are just a handful of rooms, all on the second level with tiled floors, dark-wood contemporary furniture, and deep red decor. The triples have particularly high ceilings, and rooms near the street have the best views. Common areas with couches are sprinkled throughout, and boast good views, as well.

Calle la Independencia. ✆ **504/651-4338.** Fax 504/651-3517. www.yatbalam.com. 6 units. L1,235 ($65/£33) double. MC, V. **Amenities:** Cafe; laundry service. *In room:* A/C, fan, TV, fridge, Wi-Fi.

Inexpensive

La Posada de Belssy If you need a clean, no-frills room but have outgrown sleeping in backpacker dorms, cross your fingers that La Posada de Belssy isn't full. They have a cool rooftop lounge that's always full of other travelers chatting about their Central American exploits, but few other amenities.

1 block north of the plaza. ✆ **504/651-4680.** 8 units. L390 ($20/£10) double. No credit cards. *In room:* TV, fan.

WHERE TO DINE

Expensive

Hacienda San Lucas ★★★ INTERNATIONAL/HONDURAN The in-house restaurant at this lovely hotel is probably the best restaurant in Copán, and certainly the most atmospheric. Meals are served in an open-air patio in front of the old hacienda building. The five-course candlelit dinners are one of the finest culinary experiences in Honduras today, with the choice of main courses including the house specialty of fire-roasted chicken with *adobo* sauce, a mole based on the herbs, spices, and nuts used by the ancient Maya of this area. Lunches are a bit more casual and range from homemade tamales to a salad-and-sandwich combination. The dinner hours listed below are for seatings; you can then stay and enjoy the meal, which often takes around 2 hours. A taxi here from town should run you L50 to L75 ($2.60–$3.90/£1.30–£1.95) each way.

5km (3 miles) south of Copán Ruínas on the road to Los Sapos ruins. ✆ **504/651-4495.** www.haciendasanlucas.com. Reservations necessary. Lunch L135–L285 ($9–$15/£4.50–£7.50); prix-fixe dinner L475 ($25/£13). AE, MC, V. Daily 8:30am–3pm and 7–8:30pm.

Twisted Tanya's ★★ INTERNATIONAL Part upscale fusion restaurant and part itinerant party central, this place mixes together elegance and extravagance in equal doses. The lovely open-air, second-floor corner dining room has white muslin curtains and fancy table settings. Their theory is "If it is in the market, it's on the menu," and the white-board menu changes daily, and may include anything from homemade curries with coconut rice to salmon in a Jack Daniel's glaze. There are always a couple of vegetarian items to choose from. Twisted Tanya's offers a L285 ($15/£7.50) prix-fixe menu of soup or salad, entree, and dessert. An early-bird backpacker special will get you soup, pasta, and dessert for just L114 ($6/£3). The desserts here are all homemade, decadent, and deservedly renowned. Their popular two-for-one happy hour is from 4 to 6pm.

1 block south and 1 block west of the central plaza. ✆ **504/651-4182.** www.twistedtanya.com. Reservations recommended. Main courses L115–L285 ($6–$15/£3–£7.50). AE, MC, V. Mon–Sat 2–10pm.

Moderate

Carnitas N'ia Lola ★★ (Kids) HONDURAN Grilled and barbecued meats are the specialty of this two-level restaurant literally on the edge of town. Nia's is one of the most consistently popular restaurants in Copán, partly because of the delicious food and partly because of the waitresses who carry drinks and dishes from the kitchen on their heads. Brochettes, typical dishes, tacos, and steaks are all good. *Anafre,* a bean fondue eaten with tortilla chips, is served in place of bread. Happy hour is from 6:30 to 8:30pm.

2 blocks south of the central plaza. ✆ **504/651-4196.** Main courses L120–L300 ($6–$15/£3–£7.50). MC, V. Daily 7am–10pm.

Via Via Café INTERNATIONAL/VEGETARIAN I find the food at this popular spot a bit disappointing, but you can't beat it as a meeting place for locals and tourists alike. There are a few tables on a small, streetside porch, and more in a lush open-air interior courtyard. While there are some chicken dishes on the menu, this place really caters to vegetarians. One of the best dishes here is the *capela,* a homemade carrot-and-pesto lasagna. There are a host of other options, including Thai curries, Indian *pakoras,* and hearty sandwiches, baleadas, and veggie burgers. This place is actually part of an extensive international chain that caters specifically to itinerant backpackers.

1½ blocks west of the central plaza. ✆ **504/651-4652.** www.viaviacafe.com. Main courses L70–L90 ($3.50–$4.50/£1.75–£2.25). MC, V. Daily 7am–10pm.

Inexpensive

Café Welchez INTERNATIONAL Café Welchez's setting at the corner of the central plaza gives this small-room cafe one of the best views in town. While it is a bit pricey compared with Copán's other restaurants, the food is decent, especially for a light meal, and it's a nice, quiet place to rest your feet and read a book. Try their *ticucos a la crema,* a corn tamale with red beans slathered in a creamy sauce. Quiche, sandwiches, locally grown coffees, ice coffees and drinks, and coconut flan round out the menu.

Central plaza. ✆ **504/651-4070.** Main courses L60–L200 ($3–$10/£1.50–£5). MC, V. Daily 7am–10pm.

Jim's Pizza ★ (Kids) INTERNATIONAL This expat and tourist hangout, sometimes called Pizza Copan, is the best place for a pie in Copán. Period. You'll also find a small selection of subs, grilled chicken, and steaks. Their big-screen TV is usually fronted by sports fans who can't miss a game while on vacation.

1 block south of the plaza. No phone. Main courses L95–L190 ($6–$10/£3–£5). MC, V. Daily 2–10pm.

COPÁN RUÍNAS AFTER DARK

Copán Ruínas is a relatively quiet town. Aside from the hotel and restaurant bars (of which Twisted Tanya's is always a good call), the most happening spot seems to be **Café Xibalba** (inside the Camino Maya hotel; ✆ **504/651-4182**). In addition, you might try the **Tunkul Bar** (1½ blocks west of the central plaza; ✆ **504/651-4410**), or head to the **Via Via Café** (see above) for a more relaxed vibe. **Wine Barcito** (Calle Independencia 1 block south of Parque Central; no phone), in a tiny room beside the Pabellon Maya souvenir shop, is tops for wine. **Papa Chango's** (down the hill from the center and near the Hedman-Alas bus station; no phone), is the only real spot for a very late night, as a noise ordinance in the center forces restaurants and bars in Copán to close by midnight.

7 SANTA ROSA DE COPAN

45km (28 miles) to Gracias; 110km (68 miles) to Copán

Santa Rosa is the commercial and administrative hub of western Honduras and, though it isn't overflowing with tourist sights, it makes a good base for exploring elsewhere in the department of Lempira. The town has long been known for growing high-quality tobacco, and this crop has played an important part in the town's history. The La Real Factoria del Tabaco was established here by the Spanish in 1765, and it led to considerable wealth for the city. Today the city still boasts a number of pretty, azulejo-covered colonial buildings that were built by the Spanish, and tobacco remains an important part of the economy.

ESSENTIALS

Getting There

BY BUS The city's bus terminal sits in a lot on the main road about 1.5km (¾ mile) from the center. Direct buses make the 3-hour trip to San Pedro Sula about four times per day; tickets cost L80 ($4/£2). To get to Copán Ruínas, you can take either a 3-hour direct bus (L40/$2/£1) or transfer after 1½ hours to La Entrada (L20/$1/50p) for a Copán bus (L20/$1/50p). Buses also make the 1¼-hour trip to Gracias (L30/$1.50/75p) and the 2½-hour trip to the Guatemalan border at Aguas Caliente (L75/$3.75/£1.90). All buses leave when they're full, not according to a set schedule.

BY CAR From San Pedro Sula, take CA 4 to La Entrada and head south on CA 11-A; the trip takes about 2½ hours. To drive to/from Copán, you must also go through La Entrada, and transfer to Hwy. 11.

Orientation

There are two sections of Santa Rosa. The first is the colonial core of the city, which centers around the top of a hill that includes Parque Central and the Centro Historico. The other lines the highway about 1km (½ mile) from the center, and is where you'll find the bus terminal, the cigar factory, and many poorly constructed residences.

Getting Around

Most of Santa Rosa can be seen on foot. The center radiates out only a few blocks in each direction from the square. It's easier to take a taxi, but you can also walk to the highway, bus terminal, and factories in about 20 minutes.

Taxis can shuttle you between the center and the highway for L15 to L20 (75¢–$1/40p–50p).

Visitor Information

The tourist office (✆ **504/662-2234**) is in a round building smack in the middle of Parque Central and doubles as a cybercafe. It's open Monday to Saturday from 8am to noon and 1:30 to 6pm. You can contact the tour company **Lenca Land Trails** (✆ **504/662-1128**), to arrange tours into nearby Lenca villages and to other destinations across the region.

Banco Atlántida (south side of Parque Central) has a 24-hour ATM and will exchange traveler's checks.

FESTIVALS

While it isn't as large as the **Semana Santa (Holy Week)** celebrations in Comayagua, the 7 days before Easter are still quite a spectacle in Santa Rosa de Copán. Six traditional processions reenact the Easter story and begin on Holy Thursday.

WHAT TO SEE & DO

Beneficio Maya One of Santa Rosa's main coffee producers is located in this small factory just down the street from the Flor de Copán Cigar Factory. The famous Café Copan brand of coffee, mostly exported to Europe, is processed here, while the beans are grown on the hills outside of town. Although it may say so on most tourist brochures and guidebooks, there is no official tour here, but if you ask nicely they will show you around. Products can't be bought on-site, but can easily be purchased in shops in town. 6 blocks from the bus terminal, Barrio Miraflores. ✆ **504/662-1665.** www.cafecopan.com. Free admission. Mon–Sat 10am–noon and 1–5pm.

Flor de Copán Cigar Factory ★★ Just entering this building is intoxicating—the scent of tobacco is in the air right as you enter the premises. During your tour of this factory, you'll get a fascinating look into a full-fledged, working Honduras factory. Highlights include peeks at warehouses full of drying tobacco leaves, as well as rooms of workers deveining the leaves, shaping the tobacco, rolling the cigars, and finally packing the final product for export.

4 blocks east of the bus terminal, Barrio Miraflores. ✆ **504/662-0111.** L40 ($2/£1). Daily 10am–2pm.

SHOPPING

Although you can't buy cigars at the Flor de Copán cigar factory, you can purchase them from the distributor **Tabacos Hondureños S.A.** ★★ (Centanario 168; ✆ **504/662-0111**), which has a small shop right in town a block from the park. Several large humidors stock a wide selection of cigar boxes from the Santa Rosa de Copán factory, which produces a variety of labels. Prices are significantly cheaper than they are outside of the country. A few handicrafts and regional products can also be found here and in the small shops around Parque Central.

WHERE TO STAY

Moderate

Casa Real ★ While it lacks the colonial style of Hotel Elvir and is a bit more out-of-the-way from the center, the more modern Casa Real has by far the best setup in Santa Rosa. Their grassy courtyard is centered around a pleasant open-air restaurant, Casa Romero, and a pool area that seems straight out of a Roatán resort. The rooms are, sadly, much plainer than the beautiful property, with clean tile floors, but shoddy furnishings and decor. The price is good for what you get, but this hotel has the potential to be so much more—all it needs is an interior decorator.

Calle 2a and 3a NO. ✆ **504/662-0801.** Fax 504/662-0802. www.hotelcasarealsrc.com. 50 units. $52 (£26) double with A/C; $40 (£20) double without A/C. MC, V. **Amenities:** Restaurant; bar; fitness center; pool. *In room:* A/C (in some), fan, TV.

Hotel Elvir ★ This hotel has been open since 1955, but you wouldn't guess it, since it's undergone several renovations and remodels. The standard rooms are spacious but a bit boring and bland; the two suites are considerably nicer, larger, and have Jacuzzis. Still, the services are the best in the city and the facilities—including a rooftop pool with great views and a delightful open-air colonial courtyard—are first-rate. Best of all, the hotel is right in the heart of town, and hotel owner Max Elvir, one of the staunchest promoters of tourism in western Honduras, is on hand to give you sightseeing tips and to arrange tours.

Centanario and Av. 3a NO. ✆ **504/662-0103.** www.hotelelvir.com. 43 units. $45 (£23) double; $110 (£55) suite. Rates include breakfast. AE, MC, V. **Amenities:** Restaurant; bar; fitness center; high-speed Internet in lobby; pool. *In room:* A/C, TV.

Inexpensive

Hotel VIP Copán Don't be fooled by the name—the VIP is in no way a place for VIPs. The hotel sits on a crowded and noisy street, a block from the park, and a limo probably couldn't even get here if it tried. The standard rooms lack windows and air-conditioning, and are a bit smaller than the suites and borderline dingy. The suites are much better. They are new, clean, full of natural light, and some look out onto the small but nice pool area. Overall, the hotel isn't terrible, as long as you don't expect the royal facilities that the name implies. If the Elvir and the Casa Real are full or a bit out of your budget, you won't find a better hotel in town.

Calle 1a and 3a NE. ✆ **504/662-0265.** hotelcopan@latinmail.com. 34 units. $25 (£13) double; $40 (£20) suite. MC, V. **Amenities:** Restaurant; bar; pool. *In room:* A/C (in some), fan, TV.

WHERE TO DINE

Flamingo's ★★ INTERNATIONAL Flamingo's is the classiest restaurant in Santa Rosa and where the tobacco bigwigs dine when they're in town. The menu is mostly international, with a few coastal Honduran staples like conch soup and *pescado al ajillo* (fish in garlic sauce). Grilled meats, pastas, and salads are also served. There's a full bar and even a small wine list, perhaps the only wine list in the cowboy-friendly department of Lempira.

Av. 1a SE. ✆ **504/662-0654.** Main courses L95–L285 ($5–$15/£2.50–£7.50). AE, MC, V. Wed–Mon 11am–11pm.

Pizza Pizza ★ (Kids) PIZZA Owned by an American expat and his Honduran wife, Pizza Pizza is a favorite stop for everyone from budget travelers to expats to locals. It's in the courtyard of a small colonial building about 5 blocks south of Parque Central. Hand-tossed dough, homemade sauces, and a brick oven make this the best pizzeria in town—out of a total of three. The menu features a few pastas and sandwiches too. Plus it's a cybercafe and there's a decent book exchange.

Centenario and 5a NE. ✆ **504/662-1104.** Main courses L76–L152 ($4–$8/£2–£4). No credit cards. Thurs–Tues noon–10pm.

Ten Nepel ★ CAFE This tiny cafe and coffee shop directly beside Hotel Elvir is good for java, juice, or a quick snack. There are just a couple of tables in an elegant setting, and highlights on the menu include the granitas, espresso, and bagels.

Centanario and Av. 3a NO. ✆ **504/662-3238.** L10–L40 (50¢–$2/25p–£1). No credit cards. Daily 8am–6pm.

8 GRACIAS

45km (28 miles) to Santa Rosa de Copán; 155km (96 miles) to Copán

You wouldn't know it just by looking at it, but this sleepy town was once the Spanish capital of Central America. After its founding in 1536, it was named Gracias a Dios, after founder Captain Juan de Chavez, a Spanish conquistador, spent many long days combing the mountains for flat land: "Gracias a Dios que hemos hallado tierra llana" ("thank God that we found flat land") were reportedly the first words out of his mouth when he found the town. In 1544, Gracias became home to the Spanish Royal courthouse and was given jurisdiction over a territory that covered the vast area between Mexico and Panama, but that didn't last long. Four years later, the court moved to Antigua, Guatemala, and little else was ever heard about Gracias for many years.

Having been overshadowed by nearby Copán (and Antigua) for far too long, Gracias is now preparing to make a statement. Hotels are expanding, tours to nearby Lenca villages are drawing press, its hot springs are becoming more developed, and the number of visitors to the national park here, Parque Nacional Celaque, is growing every year. For now, though, cowboy hats are still the favorite accessory, the dusty old square remains the town's main hangout, and for many throughout the region, the word "Gracias" still means "thank you."

ESSENTIALS

Getting There

BY BUS The bus terminal is a dusty lot across the street from the market. Direct buses make the 5-hour drive from San Pedro Sula about five times per day; the ride costs L100 ($5/£2.50). To get here from Copán Ruínas, you must first take a 2-hour bus ride to La Entrada

National Hero: Lempira

Honduras's currency, the lempira, was named after the Lencan warrior of the same name. In the early 1530s, as the Spanish conquistadors invaded Honduras for the first time, this warrior led an uprising that is still remembered to this day and revered across the country. After the Spanish settled in Gracias a Dios and began to move freely across the region, Lenca attacks on small parties of conquistadors became common. The Spanish invited the native chiefs of the region to a meeting and, upon showing up, all were hanged. However, one didn't show.

Lempira, which means "man of the mountain" in Lenca, gathered a large group of warriors at a fort at Peñol de Cerquín near Erandique, even convincing rival tribes to join them. They began raiding Spanish settlements, which prompted the Spanish to gather their own forces to retaliate. With all their might, they attacked Peñol de Cerquín for 6 months but could not take the fort. This resulted in Captain Alonso de Cáceres initiating a peace accord. From here the details get murky depending on whose history lesson you accept. Spanish historian Antonio de Herrera has described a scene where Lempira, upon calling for nothing less than a Spanish withdrawal from the region, was shot and killed by a Spanish soldier. Other accounts have a soldier, Rodrigo Ruíz, fighting Lempira to the death or Lempira escaping wounded, only to be later beheaded by the Spanish on his sickbed at Piedra Parada. Regardless how Lempira died, the Lencas or other tribes never put forth significant resistance against the Spanish again.

(L40/$2/£1) and then transfer to a Copán bus for another 2-hour ride. Buses head to a few other nearby destinations too.

BY CAR From San Pedro Sula (4 hr. away) or Copán (3 hr. away), take CA 4 to La Entrada, and then head south on CA 11-A until hitting Gracias.

Orientation & Getting Around

Gracias comprises a small grid of streets that sits on a dash of flat land in the most mountainous part of Honduras, at the foot of the pine-covered Montaña de Celaque. Roads leading to the city are only partially paved, which is why getting there often requires going through San Pedro Sula, even if you're coming from Tegucigalpa.

Apart from its surrounding sites, most of the attractions in Gracias can be seen on foot. The colonial core of the city is concentrated around a small grid of streets less than 10 blocks long.

To get to Celaque or to the hot springs, you will need to take a taxi, which can be found near the market or the park. Alternatively, you can visit on a guided tour; see "Parque Nacional Montaña de Celaque" below for info.

Visitor Information

The **tourist office** is in a small kiosk in the middle of the park. It's open Monday to Friday from 8am to noon and 2 to 5pm, as well as Saturday from 8 to 11:30am.

FAST FACTS Gracias itself lacks an ATM, but **Banco de Occidente** at the Parque Central will exchange currency and traveler's checks. There are a few small cybercafes around the park and most are quite slow. For international phone calls, head to **Hondutel,** 1 block from the park, beside the post office.

WHAT TO SEE & DO

The **Parque Central,** a small tree-filled square surrounded by colonial buildings, is the most active spot in town, which isn't saying much. **La Iglesia de San Marcos,** on the southern side of the park, was built in the late 1800s. Beside it you can find the remnants of the **Audiencia de los Confines,** now the home of the parish priest. One block to the north is **Las Mercedes,** the most attractive of the three colonial churches in the city. The facade dates from 1610.

Balneario Aguas Termales ★ Kids After a day of hiking the steep hills of Celaque, there's nowhere better to turn than this naturally steamy pool of thermal water. The Balneario hot springs complex sits hidden on a hill submerged in pine woods outside of town. There are several pools ranging from 33°C to 36°C (92°F–96°F), which attract a steady stream of tourists and locals. It's most crowded on nights and weekends, and particularly family friendly (there are even changing rooms here, a rarity in the country). There's a small cafe and bar near the pools. You can buy oranges, which are believed to give skin a healthy glow, from any of the vendors working the site.

6.5km (4 miles) south of Gracias. Admission L30 ($1.50/75p). Daily 8am–8pm.

Casa Galeano & Jardin Botanico ★ Once the home of a wealthy colonial family, this restored colonial house from the 1840s has quickly become one of the best museums in western Honduras outside of Copán. Colonial artifacts, models of villages, old photographs, murals, and pre-Columbian tools are paired with a brilliant folk-art collection of masks and other items created by the region's indigenous cultures. There are rotating art exhibitions as well, mostly from unknown regional artists. In the rear of the building is a botanical garden. The collection of plants here, originally begun by the Galeanos, is one of the oldest botanical gardens in Central America. It's quite small, but the assortment of native species is good.

In front of Iglesia San Marcos. Admission L30 ($1.50/75p). Daily 9am–6pm.

El Fuerte de San Cristóbal This small fort, perched atop a hill just a short walk from the Parque Central above Hotel Guancascos, boasts the best views of Gracias. Apart from the tomb of one-time Honduras (1841–42) and El Salvador (1847–52) president Juan Lindo and a few Spanish cannons there is little of cultural interest here, however. The fort was renovated in late 2007.

4 blocks west of Parque Central, above Hotel Guancascos. Free admission. Daily 8am–4pm.

Shopping

Aside from the gift shops at Guancascos and Posada de Don Juan, there's no better place in town to shop than **Lorendiana** (Calle Principal, 2 blocks south of the Mercado Municipal; ✆ **504/656-1058**). By browsing the wares on sale at this one-room co-op, you'll get a real feel for the bounty of Lempira's forests. You'll find rows and rows of jars of preserves, hot sauces, dulce de leche, candy, dried fruit, tortillas, and handicrafts, all at good prices.

WHERE TO STAY

Guancascos ★ What sets this hotel apart from others in Gracias is the view. Since it's located on an old coffee farm on the hillside below San Cristóbal Fort, guests can see the city's entire grid of streets, colonial churches, and terra-cotta roof tiles from the porch chairs of the top-level rooms. All rooms have wood floors, simple furniture, and regional accents like handicrafts and paintings. The Dutch owner makes sure the gardens are full of flowering shrubs and trees, which attract a loyal following of hummingbirds and butterflies, and is a wealth of information on the area—the owner can easily set up guided tours to Parque Nacional Celanque. The open-air restaurant here (also with great views of the city) doubles as a common area.

Below Fuerte de San Cristóbal. ✆ **504/656-1219.** www.guancascos.com. 11 units. $25 (£13) double. MC, V. **Amenities:** Restaurant; high-speed Internet in lobby. *In room:* TV.

Hotel Finca El Capitan While it doesn't have the colonial vibe that the places in the center of town have, Finca El Capitan does take advantage of its surrounding lush foliage. The rustic ranch-style buildings here, topped with clay-tiled roofs, all have porches with hammocks and rocking chairs that face the central gardens, gazebos, stone paths, and swimming pool. No room is the same, and the size of each differs slightly, though the quality is uniform throughout. The furniture and bedspreads are worn and the furniture basic. The hotel has the same feel and attracts a similar crowd as the Villas del Agua Caliente, particularly Hondurans on family reunions or those on business retreats.

Beside Iglesia Santa Lucia. ✆ **504/656-1659.** www.hotelfincaelcapitan.galeon.com. 14 units. $30 (£15) double. No credit cards. **Amenities:** Restaurant; bar; high-speed Internet in business center. *In room:* A/C, fan, TV, fridge (in some).

Posada de Don Juan ★★ Value There is no hotel in Gracias better prepared to handle the onslaught of tourists who are expected to descend on Gracias in the not too distant future. In addition to building their own private hot spring facilities on the road to Santa Rosa, the hotel doubled in size in 2008, by adding suites and a pool, and expanding its restaurant dramatically. Any remaining construction is limited to an annex of the hotel, so guests won't notice the noise. The hotel's 25 rooms have bright walls with wood-beamed ceilings and tile floors, and surround a cobblestone courtyard that doubles as a parking lot. The linens are clean, the bathrooms modern, and for the price, the amenities are outstanding.

1 block from the park. ✆ **504/656-1020.** www.posadadedonjuan.com. 25 units. $30 (£15) double. AE, MC, V. **Amenities:** Restaurant; bar. *In room:* A/C, fan, TV, Wi-Fi.

Villas del Agua Caliente Kids This series of rustic cabins is strewn on a hillside a few hundred feet from Balneario Aguas Termales (see above). It's a bit isolated, so if you don't have a car, getting in and out can be problematic. Some of the bungalows have several bedrooms and could sleep a decent-size family, while others are smaller, yet still spacious. Simple handmade wood furniture, Lenca decor, and wall hangings define the otherwise bland rooms.

At Balneario Aguas Termales. ✆ **504/608-5370.** 16 units. L300 ($16/£8) double. Rates include breakfast. No credit cards. **Amenities:** Restaurant; bar. *In room:* TV, fan.

WHERE TO DINE

Cafeteria la Posada ★ HONDURAN Although this hotel restaurant is expanding to become the largest restaurant in town, until construction is completed, it remains just a small two-room eatery with just a few tables and bar. They make a mean *chuleta de cerdo* (pork chop) with plantains, but the seafood dishes, burgers and sandwiches, and full Honduran breakfasts are also quite good.

Inside Posada de Don Juan. ✆ **504/656-1020.** www.posadadedonjuan.com. Main courses L76–L228 ($4–$12/£2–£6). AE, MC, V. Daily 6:30am–9pm.

El Gran Caudillo HONDURAN Adjoining the Hotel San Francisco, El Gran Caudillo is a one-room bar and restaurant with some of the best *comida típica* and international dishes in the city. *Anafre,* a bean-and-cheese fondue that's occasionally made with sausage, is great here, especially accompanied by one of their cheap drinks. Fajitas, tacos, steaks, and burgers round out the menu.

Center of town. ✆ **504/656-1559.** Main courses L76–L228 ($4–$12/£2–£6). MC, V. Daily noon–10pm.

Guancascos ★ INTERNATIONAL/HONDURAN The food is only part of the allure of this restaurant in the Guancascos hotel (see above)—the elevated view is the main attraction. The on-site small gift shop, which stocks helpful information on sites and activities in the area, means the restaurant serves as something of a visitor center, too. The good food ranges from local staples like *baleadas* and Honduran breakfasts to German-style artisan breads and fresh juices.

Below Fuerte de San Cristóbal. ✆ **504/656-1219.** www.guancascos.com. Main courses L57–L190 ($3–$10/£1.50–£5). MC, V. Daily 7am–10pm.

SIDE TRIPS FROM GRACIAS

La Ruta Lenca ★★

La Ruta Lenca, or the Lenca Route, is a grass-roots tourism initiative to help bring tourism revenue to the small villages near Gracias and give tourists insight into a little-known indigenous group, the Lencas. The circuit passes through the mountain villages of La Campa, Belen Gualcho, San Manuel de Colohete, San Sebastián, Corquín, and Mohaga, among others that surround Gracias. The string of rural towns that dot this part of the country feature adobe houses, corn and bean fields, the occasional museum and colonial church, and beautiful mountain views. The Lenca are derived from Chibcha-speaking Indians who came from Colombia and Venezuela more than 3,000 years ago. They number around 100,000 in Honduras and 40,000 or so in El Salvador, and are known throughout the country for their earthenware pottery; many Lenca towns have small craft cooperatives. The best times to visit any Lenca villages are during Sunday markets and *Guancascos,* annual gatherings between two villages to celebrate peace.

The association of guides **Colosuco-Celaque** (✆ **504/656-0627**), based in Gracias and Santa Rosa, offer tours for L200 to L300 ($10–$15/£5–£7.50) per group of one to five Lenca villages and the opportunity to combine trips with activities such as viewing colonial architecture, mountain biking, hiking, bird-watching, and horseback riding.

Parque Nacional Montaña de Celaque ★★★

Meaning "box of water" in the Lenca dialect, Celaque is one of the largest tracts of cloud forest remaining in Central America and one of the most unspoiled national parks in the country. Its 11 rivers supply villages as far away as El Salvador with fresh water. Nearly 50 species of mammals, several hundred species of birds, and a few dozen reptiles have been identified in the park. Celaque's pine forests hide rare wildlife such as resplendent quetzals, ocelots, jaguars, monkeys, and pumas, but consider yourself lucky to catch a glimpse of just one of these, as the dense mist and fog often obscures views.

The only way to see the park is by hiking a pretty steep ascent, and the often wet and muddy trails along the way make it difficult for older travelers and those who aren't physically fit. From the visitor center, on the Gracias side there is one main trail leading uphill that branches off into several other trails. (A few well-placed signs and ribbons mark where the trails break off.) The shortest trail takes about 2 to 3 hours, and lets you off at a small outlook where the Santa Lucia waterfall can be seen from afar. A more difficult hike is the 2,383m (7,816-ft.) climb up Cerro El Gallo, which winds for about 3 or 4 hours through spider monkey stamping grounds before reaching the top. Hardest of all is a hike to the top of Cerro de las Minas, the tallest peak in Honduras at 2,849m (9,344 ft.); it requires at least 2 days.

There are a few small campsites on the El Gallo and Las Minas trails and you can also bunk at the **visitor center** (no phone, at the forest's edge by Río Arcagual) for L50 ($2.50/£1.25).

The park is easily reached by car from Gracias, which is 9km (6 miles) away, although tours often leave from Santa Rosa and other towns that surround the park. From Gracias, you can also take a moto-taxi for about L100 ($5/£2.50) to the end of the road, which is a 30-minute or so walk to the visitor center.

Guides are not required, but recommended. Walter Murcia, who runs **Puma Trail Tours** (✆ **504/656-1113;** waltermurcia@hotmail.com), is the most respected guide in the area. Other guides can be arranged in Gracias at **Guancascos** (see above) or through **Colosuco-Celaque** (see above). It's best to arrange a guide a few days in advance. Admission to the park is L50 ($2.50/£1.25).

9 THE NORTH COAST ★

Everywhere you look in the north coast region of Honduras, the tourism infrastructure is thriving and playing off of the region's healthy cultural and environmental diversity. Garífuna villages and *mestizo* cities live side by side a growing number of American retiree communities, and ecotourism is on the verge of a major eruption—swanky new jungle lodges are being erected on former chocolate plantations and hiking trails are carving their way through national parks like Pico Bonito. Zip-line tours are now as common as *pan de coco,* kayaking and canoe tours can be had in every mangrove forested lagoon, and serious birders are descending upon the region like migrating herons. Up and down the coast, major beach projects are also in the works; the most significant could possibly turn Tela Bay into the next Cancun.

Though it seems like the north coast is finally getting its moment in the spotlight, this part of the country is steeped in history. Spanish explorers and conquistadors first entered the country here, and colonial-era forts still guard the coast from would-be pirate attacks. The Garífuna, an ethnic group descended from Carib Indians and West African slaves, arrived along this coast at the end of the 18th century. And the presence of Dole and Chiquita here made this town an important part of the country's history as a banana republic.

TELA ★★

By 2010, you probably won't be able to recognize Tela, a beachside town 87km (54 miles) east of San Pedro Sula. A major government tourism initiative, with help from the World Bank, is sure to turn Tela Bay into one of the most important beach destinations in

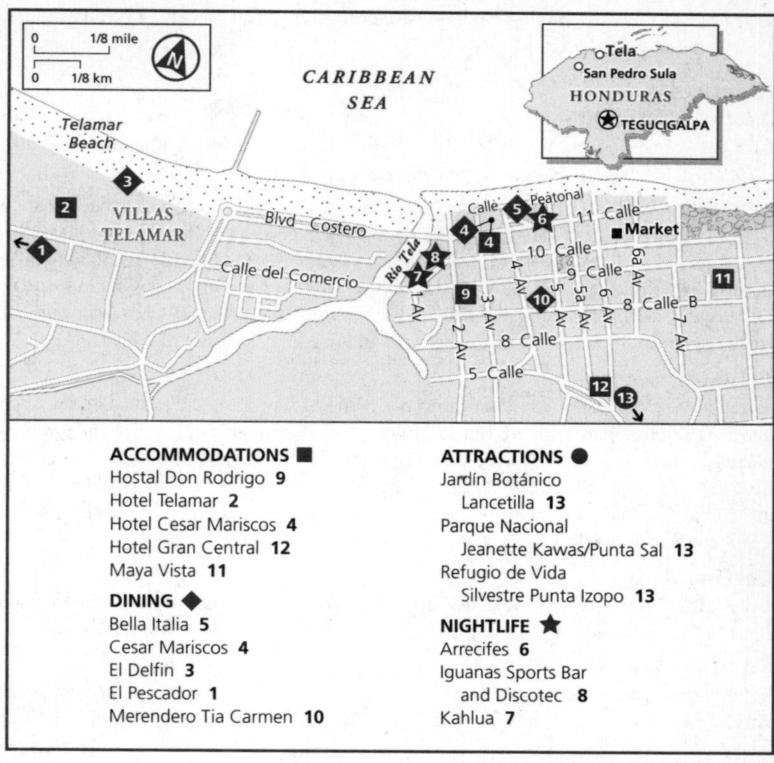

Central America. Rumors have it that within a couple of years there will be several four- and five-star megaresorts, an 18-hole designer golf course, and a marina operating in the area. Controversy has been swirling around the project, though, as opposition groups are claiming that a Cancun-like resort would completely wipe out the already fragile ecosystem at the city's Laguna de los Micos and do little for the Garífuna communities there. These groups may have run out of luck, though. Ground has already been broken for one of the resorts, roads are now being expanded, and 20 new bilingual tourist police have already been trained and hired.

The conquistador Cristobal de Olid founded this city on May 3, 1524, the day of the Holy Cross, and gave it the name Triunfo de la Cruz. The abbreviation of the name, T. de la +, would eventually lead to the shortened name of Tela. In the early 1800s, the Garífunas began to arrive here from Roatán and set up communities all over Tela Bay, many of which are still around to this day. Toward the end of the century, the municipality began to form around the banana plantations of the Tela Railroad Company, a subsidiary of the United Fruit Company, which owned the Chiquita brand. The company monopolized city politics, until moving their offices to La Lima in 1976.

Today, as tourism has taken a firm hold of the city, its days as a banana republic are a thing of the past. While the skeletal remains of the Tela Railroad and United Fruit offices are gathering dust, the employee homes have been turned into one of the country's finest resorts, the Hotel Telamar.

Essentials

Getting There

BY CAR Tela sits directly on CA 13 halfway between San Pedro Sula and La Ceiba, each a little more than an hour away depending on traffic.

BY BUS Any bus headed between La Ceiba and San Pedro Sula will make a stop at Tela. For San Pedro, try **Tela Express** (2a Av. NE just past the train tracks; ✆ **504/550-8355**) with five daily departures making the 1½-hour trip for L60 ($3/£1.50). If you're heading to La Ceiba or Trujillo, catch a **Cotuc bus** (at the Dippsa gas station on the highway; ✆ **504/441-2199**) or head to the minibus terminal at 9a Calle NE. The bus to La Ceiba is L40 ($2/£1) and the bus to Trujillo is L120 ($6/£3).

Orientation

The city of Tela sits on the southernmost point of Tela Bay; Parque Nacional Punta Izopa and Parque Nacional Jeannette Kawas/Punta Sal flank each side of the city and are connected by unpaved roads that are sometimes impassable when it rains. The city center, Tela Vieja, is quite compact, with a small grid of streets hugging the coast. The Río Tela splits the town into two, with Tela Vieja on the east and Tela Nueva—home of the Villas Telamar and the old Tela Railroad buildings—on the west bank.

Getting Around

ON FOOT Anywhere in the actual city of Tela can be reached on foot, but to reach most of the surrounding attractions, you will need some form of motorized transport.

BY CAR Your own car is the best method of transport if you wish to explore the national parks and coast on your own. There are no car-rental agencies in Tela, so you'll have to head to the airports in La Ceiba (p. 381) or San Pedro Sula (p. 341).

BY TAXI Taxis are best for getting to Lancetilla, the surrounding beaches, and Garífuna villages along the coast, but most drivers won't make the long trips to the national parks. A ride in town should cost no more than L20 ($1/50p).

BY BUS Minibuses and pickups ply the highway and coastal roads, though they are infrequent. Most cost only L10 (50¢/25p).

Visitor Information

For tourist information, try the **Tela Chamber of Commerce** (www.telahonduras.com) or **PROLANSATE** (Edificio Kwawas at Calle del Comercio; ✆ **504/448-2042;** www.prolansate.org), which has brochures, maps, and information regarding the national parks in the area.

FAST FACTS All amenities can be found in Tela Vieja. The most convenient bank, **Banco Atlantida** (4a Av. NE and 9a Calle NE), has an ATM and exchanges traveler's checks. You can make international calls at **Hondutel** (4a Av. NE and 7a Calle NE) or at most of the Internet cafes near Parque Central. The **Tourist Police** (✆ **504/448-0253;** daily 24 hr.) can be found at 11a Calle NE and 4a Avenida NE.

What to See & Do

Moving west from Tela along the coast, you will encounter the Garífuna communities of Triunfo de la Cruz, Tornabé, San Juan, La Ensenada, Río Tinto, and lastly Miami. The farther you get from Tela, the more traditional the villages become. **Miami ★★★**, which sits on a small sandbar between the ocean and the Los Micos lagoon in **Parque Nacional Jeanette Kawas/Punta Sal,** is the most interesting visit. Literally unchanged for 200 years, the village is completely comprised of thatched huts without electricity or running water. Local boatmen can paddle you out on dugout canoes or take you out on motorized boats into the lagoon. Once reaching the town, you can lounge on the empty white-sand beach there or munch on fresh seafood from the informal restaurants the locals set up for tourists.

You can get to Miami with your own car, but the village is more commonly visited on tours to the national park with **Garífuna Tours** (✆ **504/448-2904;** www.garifunatours.com) or **Caribe Expeditions** (✆ **504/448-2083;** www.caribeexpeditions.com). The standard L55 ($3/£1.50) park admission fee applies to entering the village.

Jardín Botánico Lancetilla ★★ Lancetilla, the second-largest tropical botanical garden in the world, was established in 1926 by American botanist William Popenoe, who was hired by United Fruit to research varieties of bananas and figure out how to best treat diseases found in the plantations. Popenoe was a curious fellow, though, and quickly began to import plants and fruits from around the world to Lancetilla, including the African Palm, which has long been one of the most important cash crops in the country. United Fruit continued Popenoe's work for years after he left. The Honduran government, which took control in 1974, continues the research today at the garden.

Botany is not the only science of interest in the park. Ornithology is a big deal here, too. Nearly 400 species of birds have been recorded in Lancetilla, as well as numerous butterflies and reptiles. Bird tours leave at dawn in the hopes of spotting trogons, tanagers, orioles, motmots, and toucans, among others. Call Lancetilla a few days ahead of time to arrange a tour, for L300 ($16/£8) per group.

There's a small cafeteria and a few basic cabins with air-conditioning and private bathrooms near the visitor center, but they're occasionally filled with researchers. They run L380 ($20/£10) per night.

5km (3 miles) north of Tela. ✆ **504/448-1740.** www.lancetilla.org. Admission L115 ($6/£3). Daily 7:30am–3pm.

Parque Nacional Jeanette Kawas/Punta Sal ★★★ Parque Nacional Punta Sal was renamed after the Honduran activist and president of Prolansate, Jeanette Kawas Fernández, who was killed after establishing the park amid controversy from business groups who claimed the land. Few will argue, though, about the amazing biodiversity in the 782-sq.-km (484-sq.-mile) park. Wildlife found here includes marine turtles, dolphins, manatees, caimans, migratory birds (which are easiest to spot Nov–Feb), ocelots, peccaries, monkeys, and many others.

On the western end of the Bay of Tela, the park is divided into two parts: the lagoon and the peninsula. Acting as a barrier for Tela Bay from the *nortes,* strong winds that blow in the winter months, the peninsula is made up of a triple threat of postcard-perfect beaches, pristine coral reefs, and lush green jungle—dolphins and howler monkeys are regularly seen during the snorkel tours here. Micos Lagoon is separated by a small sandbar from the ocean. Surrounding it are numerous canals that weave through mangrove forests where hundreds of bird and animal species can be seen.

Nearly every tour operator in Tela, including **Garífuna Tours** (✆ **504/448-2904;** www.garifunatours.com) and **Caribe Expeditions** (✆ **504/448-2083;** www.caribeexpeditions.com) leads almost-daily tours to either the peninsula or the lagoon. You can also hire a boat in Miami, though prices are similar and will not include transportation from Tela.

West End of Tela Bay, Miami. No phone. Admission L55 ($3/£1.50); tours L475–L570 ($25–$30/£13–£15) per person depending on group size. Daily 8am–6pm.

Refugio de Vida Silvestre Punta Izopo ★ Twelve kilometers (19 miles) from Tela on the eastern end of Tela bay, Punta Izopa has a similar ecosystem to Jeanette Kawas, yet is far less visited. Here the Platáno and Hicaque rivers empty into the ocean in a maze of canals and lagoons sheltered by mangroves. The diverse bionetwork harbors caimans, manatees, turtles, monkeys, and a long list of avian life. The reserve is best explored by kayak. **Garífuna Tours** (✆ **504/448-2904;** www.garifunatours.com) and most other Tela tour operators regularly lead trips here using top kayaks. The cost is about L475 to L570 ($25–$30/£13–£15) per person. You can also recruit boatmen in Triunfo de la Cruz (just west of the park), though you will need to get a group together to make it worthwhile.

Outdoor Attractions

A dozen kilometers (7½ miles) or so of white-sand beaches backed by lazy palm trees stretch around Tela Bay. The best beach in the city proper is in front of the Hotel Telamar (below), west of the Río Tela, which is open to the public and has beach chairs and umbrellas for rent (L25/$1.25/65p). In Tela Vieja, the beachside boardwalk has a few restaurants, bars, and craft vendors, though the beach is often dirty and unsafe to leave your valuables. Better beaches can be found outside the city, though, in the Garífuna villages like Tornabé and Miami.

Shopping

There are a few souvenir shops scattered around Tela Vieja. The best is **Casa del Sol,** a chain that is right in the Hotel Cesar Mariscos (see below). For jewelry and crafts, try the vendors that line up on the boardwalk and also near the El Delfin restaurant and the beach at the Villas Telamar.

Where to Stay

Expensive

Hotel Telamar ★★★ (Kids) The Telamar is easily one of the best, most unique accommodations in the country today and exactly the kind of place that is going to set Tela apart from places like Cancun, Mexico, and the Papagayo peninsula in Costa Rica in the years to come. This one-time gated community of houses for the executives of the Tela Railroad Company has been renovated to become a full scale village-style resort. Guest accommodations are in either the neighborhood of pastel-colored one- to four-bedroom stilted villas or the new main buildings. Rooms in the newer, more modern hotel section face the ocean or the pool, while the remodeled villas face either the ocean or the gardens. Kids will delight in their 90m-long (300-ft.) swimming pool with a slide, along with the bridges, children's

Spanish Classes Around Tela

The **Mango C@fe** (✆ **504/448-0338;** www.mangocafe.net) has the only Spanish school in town with 20 hours of one-on-one introductory classes per week for L2,166 ($114/£57). Intermediate and advanced classes, as well as discounts at the affiliated **Hotel Mango** (Av. Panama and the Río Tela; ✆ **504/448-0338**) are also available.

play area, and a second, smaller pool. Even when the lineup of megaresorts opens in this region in 2010, it will be hard to match the history and character here.

1km (1/2 mile) west of town, Tela Nueva. ✆ **504/269-4414.** Fax 504/448-2984. www.hoteltelamar.com. 210 units. From $90 (£45) double; from $220 (£110) villa. AE, MC, V. **Amenities:** Restaurants; bars; golf course; pool; tennis court. *In room:* A/C, TV, hair dryer, kitchen (in villa), Wi-Fi.

Moderate

Hostal Don Rodrigo ★ Value This recently renovated century-old building, not far from the Puente Vieja in downtown Tela, is one of the best deals in the city. If it wasn't so cheap, you could say it's a boutique hotel. Fine-looking exposed brick walls give the singles, doubles, and triples here a refined look and feel. Handmade wood furniture and decor comprised of local art and handicrafts lend the hotel a uniquely Tela-ized feel, as do the open-air wrap around hallways surrounding the three-level building that affords decent views of the old city. The hotel runs a small tour company in the lobby with trips to the national parks and biking and kayaking excursions.

1/2 block from the Puente Viejo on Calle del Comercio, Tela Vieja. ✆ **504/448-0303.** www.hostaldonrodrigo.com. 14 units. L812 ($43/£22) double; additional beds are L100 ($5.20/£2.60). MC, V. *In room:* A/C, TV, fan, no phone.

Hotel Cesar Mariscos A small step up from the nearby Hotel Sherwood, this hotel is right next door on the Tela beachfront. It's owned by Caribe Expeditions, a tour operator that runs trips to Punta Sal, and was built in 1996 above the well-known restaurant of the same name. Cheery rooms with tile floors and lots of light look out onto their small infinity pool and the beach. Opt for the rooms with private balconies. The property also has one five-person apartment with a small kitchen.

Calle Peatonal and Av. Uruguay. ✆ **504/448-2083.** www.hotelcesarmariscos.com. 20 units. L1,215 ($64/£32) double. Rates include continental breakfast. Apartment L2,090 ($110/£55). MC, V. **Amenities:** Restaurant; bar; pool. *In room:* A/C, TV.

Inexpensive

Hotel Gran Central ★★ Finds This completely restored building, just 2 blocks from Parque Central, is easily one of the best architectural transformations on the North Coast. What was once a dilapidated building now has a decidedly tropical urban feel with high ceilings, black-and-white tiled floors, and potted plants sitting everywhere. Rooms have wood shutters, palm trees painted on the walls, high ceilings, and private terraces. If they replaced the worn furniture—especially the couches—with more modern pieces, they could quadruple the rate. It reminds me of the chic boutique hotels in renovated colonial buildings that are all the rage in Cartagena, Colombia.

Av. Honduras. ✆ **504/448-1099.** www.hotelgrancentral.com. 8 units. L665 ($35/£18) double; L1,330 ($70/£35) apt. AE, DC, MC, V. **Amenities:** Restaurant; bar. *In room:* A/C, TV, fan.

Maya Vista ★★ Maya Vista's French Canadian owners have created a tiny paradise of sorts in the city proper, just a block from the Río Hiland where it meets with the Caribbean. Quiet and relaxing, with tall leafy trees that are woven through the design of the whole building, the property is suggestive of a treehouse. A rooftop lookout tower and several thatched roof terraces with hammocks allow for expansive views all the way to Punta Izopo. Rooms with one to three beds are decorated with murals of Maya designs and beach themes; I recommend opting for one of the slightly more expensive rooms with balconies. The owners will create meal and accommodations packages on request.

8a Calle NE and 9a Av. NE. ✆ **504/448-1497.** www.mayavista.com. 9 units. L475–L1,045 ($25–$55/£13–£28) double. AE, MC, V. **Amenities:** Restaurant; bar. *In room:* A/C, TV, fridge (in some).

Where to Dine

Expensive

El Delfin ★ INTERNATIONAL This thatched-roof beach palapa in front of the Telamar supplies the beach chairs and sometimes the music for the cleanest and most prime piece of sand in Tela. During the day it's mostly filled with hungry beachgoers who come for sandwiches, burgers, grilled seafood, and shrimp every which way. Toward sundown, the bar heats up and margaritas, mojitos, and cuba libres can be spotted at every table. There's occasionally live music.

1km (1/2 mile) west of town, Tela Nueva. ✆ **504/269-4414.** Main courses L115–L270 ($6–$14/£3–£7). MC, V. Daily 7am–11pm.

Moderate

Cesar Mariscos ★★ SEAFOOD All activity on Tela's small beachfront boardwalk, including children selling *pan de coco,* revolves around this restaurant, which is widely considered the best in town. Tables are set in the indoor dining room, under the boardwalk canopy, or under the umbrellas on the sidewalk. While they have beef on the menu, seafood is the specialty here. The shrimp in garlic sauce is one of the best on the north coast, while the grilled fish, lobster, and seafood stew all taste equally as sweet.

Calle Peatonal and Av. Uruguay. ✆ **504/448-2083.** Main courses L95–L305 ($5–$16/£2.50–£8). MC, V. Daily 7am–10pm.

El Pescador ★ Finds SEAFOOD This lively Garífuna restaurant relies on the catches of neighborhood fishermen down the coast from the city in the village of San Juan. It's just a small shack on the beach with plastic chairs and tables and a sandy concrete floor. Seafood specialties like grilled shrimp, fish, lobster, and *tapado,* a Garífuna seafood stew with fish, coconut, and cassava, are all on the menu.

2km (1¼ miles) west of town, San Juan. ✆ **504/448-1073.** Main courses L95–L190 ($5–$10/£2.50–£5). No credit cards. Wed–Mon 9am–7pm.

Inexpensive

Bella Italia Kids ITALIAN Run by Italian expats that spent many years in Santa Rosa de Copán managing a similar restaurant, this is the best of several pizzerias in town. Right on sidewalk tables facing the beach, the restaurant offers a full range of pastas, pizzas, and calzones that any child or adult will appreciate.

4a Av. NE and Calle Peatonal. ✆ **504/448-1055.** Main courses L75–L190 ($4–$10/£2–£5). No credit cards. Daily noon–8pm.

Merendero Tia Carmen HONDURAN This small, informal eatery is the best spot for typical Honduran dishes, especially their delicious *baleadas,* a tortilla stuffed with beans, cheese, and anything else you have your heart set on. There are also tacos, *liquados,* fresh fruit juices, and coffee.

Calle 8 and Av. 4. No phone. Main courses L38–L95 ($2–$5/£1–£2.50). No credit cards. Daily 7am–8pm.

Tela After Dark

The sidewalk tables at **Arrecifes** (no phone) on the boardwalk just past Cesar Mariscos attract an upscale young crowd who come for cheap mixed drinks and beer. The bar at **El Delfin restaurant** (see above) gets busy on the weekends when there is occasionally live music; the Hotel Telamar property also boasts a small bar and disco that is usually filled with upper-crust locals and hotel guests. A smattering of discos are situated in town, but all are a bit seedy. The most popular are **Iguanas Sports Bar and Discotec** (10a Calle NE and 2a Av. NE; no phone) and **Kahlua** (10a Calle NE and 2a Av. NE; no phone), each next door to the other in the Zona Viva. Covers on Fridays and Saturdays are L100 ($5/£2.50).

LA CEIBA ★

La Ceiba, the third-largest city in Honduras and the capital of the department of Atlántida, is named after a huge Ceiba tree on the coast that was once a community meeting place. Recently, the city (97km/60 miles east of Tela) has become known as the country's ecotourism headquarters. The city itself, only established a little more than 100 years ago, is sort of thrown together and dirty, its beaches are polluted, and it doesn't hold much of interest to passing tourists. It works best as a base to explore the countless remarkable attractions that are within a short drive, such as Class 4 white-water rapids, hiking trails through several stunning national parks, a wildlife refuge with caimans and manatees, vast empty beaches, sprawling pineapple plantations, and much more. Let's not leave out that the city is the jumping-off point for the Bay Islands, by both ferry and plane, and the Cayos Cochinos. Whether you like the gritty town or not, you must come through La Ceiba if you want to experience the finest natural wonders in Honduras.

Essentials

Getting There

BY PLANE La Ceiba's **Golosón International Airport (LCE; © 504/443-3925)** is 12km (8 miles) west of the city on the road to Tela. The only international airlines that land at the airport are **TACA** (**© 504/441-3191**), **Skyservice** (seasonal to Toronto; **© 800/701-9448**), and **Atlantic Airlines** (**© 504/440-2347;** www.atlanticairlinesint.com), which serves the Bay Islands, Managua, Grand Cayman, and Belize City. If you are flying to/from the Bay Islands, you can try domestic airlines such as **Isleña** (**© 504/441-3354;** www.flyislena.com), and **Aerolineas Sosa** (**© 504/443-1399**), as all offer daily flights. There are ATMs, a few small shops and snack bars, and money-exchange services, an Internet cafe, and car-rental counters in the terminal. A 10- to 15-minute taxi ride from Golosón International to the center of town should cost about L115 ($6/£3).

BY BOAT From La Ceiba, there are two high-speed ferries that run twice a day to Roatán and Utila from the Muelle de Cabotaje, 5km (3 miles) east of La Ceiba. For Roatán, the ***Galaxy Wave*** (**© 504/443-463;** Safeways_Galaxy@yahoo.com) departs La Ceiba at 9:30am and 4:30pm, returning at 7am and 2pm from the terminal at Dixon's Cove. The one-way price is L420 ($22/£11) and the ferry has room for 360 people, air-conditioning, a sun deck, and a small snack shop.

The ***Utila Princess II*** (**© 504/425-3390**) makes the hour-long trip back and forth between the Municipal Pier Utila. The ship, which is about one-third the size of the *Galaxy Wave,* departs La Ceiba at 9:30am and 4pm, returning at 6:20am and 2pm. The price is L373 ($20/£10) each way.

Yachts from around the Caribbean commonly stop in La Ceiba and occasionally will take on passengers for a fee or in exchange for work. If you are looking for a ride or need a place to anchor, the **Lagoon Marina** (**© 504/440-0614;** www.lagoonmarinalaceiba.com) is your best bet. There are 25 slips for boats up to 36m (120 ft.) in length, as well as a nice pool area, bar, and apartments for rent by the month L14,250 ($750/£325).

BY BUS Two luxury bus companies, Hedman Alas and Viana Express, have their own terminals in town. **Hedman Alas' terminal** (**© 504/441-2199;** www.hedmanalas.com) is on the main highway east of town toward Trujillo, beside the Supermercado Ceibeño #4. Their four daily buses (5:15am–5:30pm) make the 1½-hour trip to Tela before making the

3½-hour trip to San Pedro Sula, where connections can be made to Copán and Tegucigalpa. **Viana** (✆ **504/441-2330**), whose terminal is just west of the main bus terminal near the Esso gas station, has similar service.

All other bus companies operate out of the **Main terminal** (Mercado San Jose, Blvd. 15 de Septiembre) about 2km (1¼ miles) west of the center. **Diana** (✆ **504/441-6460**) has nine daily departures for San Pedro Sula between 6am and 5:30pm. For the 7-hour ride to Tegucigalpa, **Cristina** (✆ **504/441-2028**) has five daily departures between 5:30am and 3:30pm. For the 3-hour trip to Trujillo, try **Cotuc** (✆ **504/441-2199**), which runs throughout the day from 8am to 6pm.

BY CAR La Ceiba straddles CA 13 on the north coast about halfway between San Pedro Sula and Trujillo. There aren't as many big car-rental companies in the city as there are in San Pedro or Tegucigalpa, but there are a few. Apart from **Avis** (CA 13 at La Ceiba; ✆ **504/441-2802;** www.avis.com.hn), most rental companies have counters at the airport, including local companies **Advance** (✆ **504/441-1105;** www.advancerentacar.com) and **Ace** (✆ **504/441-2929;** www.acerentacar.com).

Orientation

The city of La Ceiba is sandwiched between the imposing green mountains of Pico Bonito National Park and the Caribbean Sea. Much of the town straddles the highway, CA 13, although urban sprawl is heading in every direction. A handful of estuaries split the town into several sections, with the center surrounding the wide, shady Parque Central. Two main avenues, San Isidro and 14 de Julio, run parallel to the beach. The mostly Garífuna neighborhood, Barrio La Isla, to the northeast of the park along the beach, is where you will find the Zona Viva, quite a few hotels, restaurants, and tour operators.

Getting Around

Almost everything of interest within the city sits within a 10-block radius of the Parque Central, so getting around on two legs is easy. But buses are a cheap and useful way to get around to outlying areas. You can easily flag down any of the frequent buses on the main highway, going in the direction you are headed, either toward Tela or Trujillo, for less than L20 ($1/50p) for short distances.

A taxi anywhere in the center should run no more than L40 ($2/£1), while trips to the airport or the ferry terminal are about three or four times more.

Visitor Information

There's a **visitor center** (✆ **504/440-1562**) on the first floor of the Banco de Occidente building on Parque Central; it's open Monday to Friday from 8am to 4pm. There's another office (✆ **504/440-3044**) at Avenida San Isidro and 8a Calle with more brochures and maps.

FAST FACTS **Banco Atlantida** (Av. San Isidro and 6a Calle) and **BAC** (Av. San Isidro and 5a Calle) in the center of town have 24-hour ATMs and will exchange traveler's checks. Both have second locations at the Megaplaza Mall.

The hospital **Eurohonduras** (1a Calle and the beach; ✆ **504/443-0244**) is open 24 hours. To reach the police, call ✆ **504/441-0860,** daily 24 hours.

Lavamatic Ceibeño, in Barrio La Isla at Av. Pedro Nufio and Calle 6, has coin-operated machines and drop-off service, for L55 ($3/£1.50) per 10 pounds. It's open daily from 7:30am to 9pm.

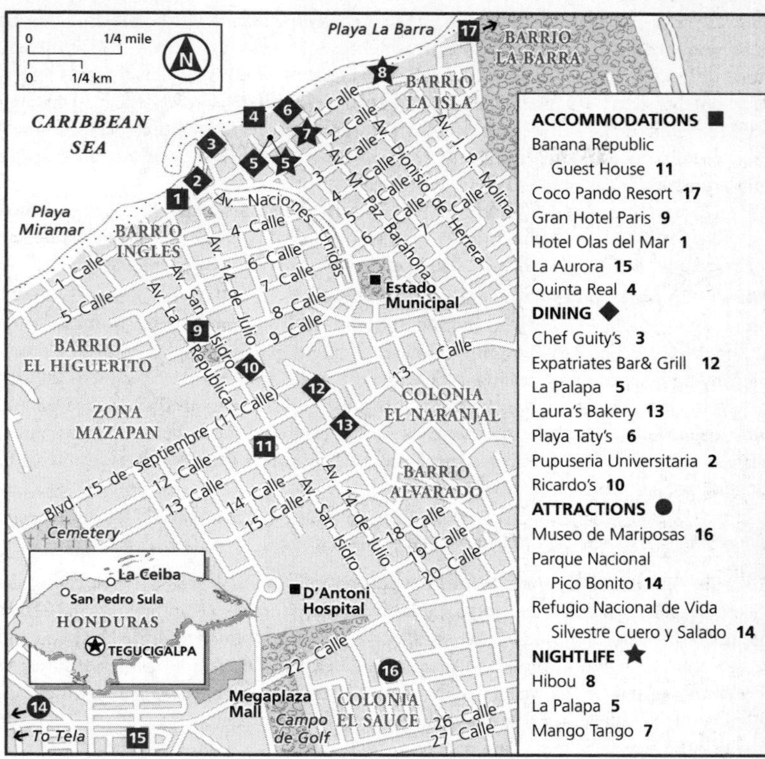

There are a four or five Internet cafes within 2 blocks of the park with high-speed service for less than L30 ($1.60/80p) per hour. They also provide cheap international calls. **Hondutel** (Av. Rosa and 6a Calle) offers local and international calls.

The **post office** is at Avenida Morazán and 14a Calle.

Festivals

More than 200,000 visitors from around Honduras and Central America descend upon La Ceiba during **La Feria San Isidro,** or Carnaval week, which takes place every May and culminates on the third Saturday of the month. While the celebration of the city's patron saint, San Isidro, is the motive, the festival has far less of a religious theme than that in Comayagua. Here it's more of a big party where live music, dancing, parades, an endless lineup of food and T-shirt vendors, and endless intoxication takes place each night in a different part of town. The last night of the festival is the most intense, with horses, floats, and costumed dancers parading down Avenida San Isidro. It's not as organized as carnival in Rio or in Mardi Gras, but a spectacle to behold nevertheless. Reserve hotel rooms months in advance during this time of year.

What to See & Do

In addition to the below attractions, there are several Garífuna communities within a short drive of the city that make for a quick and inexpensive trip. The most interesting is **Sambo Creek,** 21km (13 miles) east, which is a peaceful retreat from the grime and noise of La Ceiba. Some travelers even prefer to base themselves here, as it boasts several nice hotels, such as **Hotel Canadien** (© **504/440-2099;** www.hotelcanadien.com; $35/£18 double), as well as a clean beach and several excellent traditional Garífuna seafood restaurants. Boatmen can even arrange trips to the Cayos Cochinos if you get a group together.

Garífuna Tours (© **504/440-3252;** www.garifunatours.com) or **Omega Tours** (© **504/440-0334;** www.omegatours.info) are two good operators in the area, who can set you up with trips to Garífuna villages and to the below attractions.

Museo de Mariposas (Kids) This private 93-sq.-m (1,000-sq.-ft) museum exhibits more than 14,000 butterflies, moths, and insects from more than 100 countries, although more than 9,000 are from Honduras. Highlights include blue-tipped damselflies, flying cockroaches, walking sticks, and black tarantula wasps. Specimens are displayed in glass cases that cover the walls, and guided tours point out the largest, smallest, most colorful, heaviest, and most unusual. Other exhibits include butterfly traps, information posters, night collecting setups, and a 25-minute video on insects (available in English or Spanish).

Casa G-12, 3 blocks south of Hotel La Quinta, Colonia El Sauce. © **504/442-2874.** www.hondurasbutterfly.com. Admission L50 ($3/£1.50). Mon–Sat 8am–5pm.

Refugio Nacional de Vida Silvestre Cuero y Salado ★★★ Three rivers, the Cuero, Salado, and San Juan, feed this massive estuary that is one of the most important natural reserves in Honduras. Since wildlife is abundant, with just a little luck, you will see a decent selection of birds and mammals. There are almost 200 species of birds on record in the reserve, as well as sloths, ocelots, jaguars, otters, howler and white face monkeys, iguanas, caimans, and the elusive West Indian manatee.

Since the reserve is nearly impossible to find on your own, even if you're a seasoned guidebook writer, the best way to explore the canals and mangrove forests is by boat from the visitor center in Salado Barra. Two-hour motorboat tours leave regularly from this visitor center, although some longer tours, on which you have a much better chance of encountering manatees, are also available. Going with a tour operator such as **Garífuna Tours** (see above) or **Omega Tours** (see above) is a much easier way to see the park and far cheaper in most instances; it usually costs L760 to L950 ($40–$50/£20–£25). If you are going on your own, you will have to fork over money for admission plus the entire cost for the boat and guide, rather than splitting it.

Considering wildlife-watching is best done at dawn, you might want to stay the night at the visitor center's dorm lodging, which runs L135 ($7/£3.50), or pitch a tent (L55/$3/£1.50) on the premises of the park. There's a small cafeteria by the visitor center.

30km (19 miles) west of La Ceiba. © **504/443-0329.** Rail journey L190 ($10/£5). Admission L189 ($10/£5), guide L125 ($7/£3.50), and 2-hr. boat tour L275 ($14/£7). Daily 6:30am–6pm.

Parque Nacional Pico Bonito ★★★ Named after a jagged green 2,436m (7,990-ft.) mountain just south of La Ceiba, Pico Bonito national park is central to La Ceiba's eco-future. Outside of boasting one of the top nature lodges in the world, the more than 100,000-hectare (24,700-acre) park ranges in altitude from sea level to more than 2,000m (6,500 ft.), which results in seven different ecosystems and an extremely high level of biodiversity. While much of the park is off-limits and remains unexplored, there are large tracts of nearly virgin rainforest, cloud forest, waterfalls, rivers, and crystalline pools to explore. Bird life includes more than 400 bird species such as toucans, trogons, motmots, and hummingbirds, while mammals spotted here include jaguars, ocelots, tapirs, pumas, deer, and white faced and spider monkeys, as well as hundreds of species of reptiles, amphibians, and butterflies.

There are several entrances into Pico Bonito and a few different ways to see the park; fortunately, access is getting easier. The most common entry point is through **Pico Bonito Lodge.** It used to be that you had to be a guest to access their trails; however, guided tours ($30/£15 per person) for nonguests have recently been established that include lunch at the lodge. Their private trails have the best infrastructure and contain several bird-watching towers, well-marked stone paths, and a swimming hole on the Coloradito River. You must make reservations in advance with the lodge.

In the town of El Pino, 19km (12 miles) west of La Ceiba, next door to the lodge and just past the Quebrada Seca Bridge, there is another entrance, which most tour operators in La Ceiba use. Here you will find the 2.5km (1.5-mile) **Zacate River Trail,** which passes a few nice swimming holes and ends at the Cascada Zacate. The **El Pino Tourist Committee** (**© 504/386-9878**) arranges guided hikes on the trail for $26 (£13) per person including the $6 (£3) park admission fee. Alternatively, just hop on any Tela or San Pedro Sula–bound bus and ask to be let off at El Pino.

Recently, a trail has opened on the eastern border of the park, on the Río Cangrejal side, at Km 8.8 on the La Ceiba–Yaruca highway near the town of **Las Mangas.** A Yaruca-bound bus will let you off here, or a taxi should be about L250 to L285 ($13–$15/£6.50–£7.50). This entrance is more commonly used by tour operators leading white-water rafting tours on the river, but is increasingly being used by hikers as well. There is just one main trail that shouldn't take more than 2 to 3 hours each way. It begins with a hanging bridge over the river and extends to the 60m (197-ft.) Cascada El Bejuco, as well as a couple of smaller waterfalls.

The nonprofit community organization **Guaruma** (**© 504/406-6782;** www.guaruma.org) has two different guided hikes in the park, led by trained young locals: the 2-hour (L60/$3/£1.50 per person) **Guarama trail** and the 4-hour (L120/$6/£3 per person) **La Muralla trail.** Reservations should be made a few days in advance. **Jungle River Tours** (**© 504/440-1268;** www.jungleriverlodge.com) also runs guided hikes here that include a free night at their Jungle River Lodge (see "Where to Stay," below).

Outdoor Activities

Beaches

The beaches in La Ceiba city are polluted and possibly even dangerous to your health and physical well-being. If you must, try the beach in front of Quinta Real (see below), which is the most manicured, although the water is still putrid. A much better beach is Playa de Perú, 2km (1¼ miles) east of the Muelle de Cabotaje.

Canopy Tours

There are now two zip-line canopy tours near La Ceiba, in which participants are strapped to a long metal line and propelled by gravity at high speeds from platform to platform over the jungle. The tours are the closest the average person can get to swinging on a vine like Tarzan through the jungle. **Jungle River Tours** (**© 504/440-1268;** www.jungleriverlodge.com) offers a tour that runs over the Río Cangrejal in Pico Bonito National Park. The exhilarating 2½- to 3-hour excursion unfolds over a total of eight

Spanish Classes in La Ceiba

La Ceiba is home to a handful of language schools, most offering 20 hours of classwork a week, homestays with local families (optional), workbooks, some organized activities, and three daily meals. Two recommended schools are **AmeriSpan** (✆ **215/751-1100;** www.amerispan.com; $270/£135 per week) and the **Central American School** (✆ **504/440-1707;** www.ca-spanish.com; $150/£75 per week).

high wires, the longest being 198m (660 ft.). The trip costs L665 ($35/£18) and includes a free night at the Jungle River Lodge, but not transport—that runs an additional L38 to L152 ($2–$8/£1–£4).

A second canopy tour has been established in **Sambo Creek,** 21km (13 miles) east of La Ceiba on the road to Trujillo; look for the signs along the highway. The zip lines are about a 30-minute horseback ride through thick rainforest from the tour office. The 13 different cables end at a small waterfall and swimming hole fed by thermal springs. Departures are at 9am and 2pm. This tour is operated by **Turaser** (✆ **504/429-0509;** www.hondurasroatantravel.com) out of the Palma Real Resort; it costs $45 (£23).

Horseback Riding

While horseback riding is more common in the mountains of the western half of Honduras, tours are increasing in popularity along the north coast. **Omega Tours** (✆ **504/440-0334;** www.omegatours.info) has several different rides. Day trips include a ride along the beach (6 hr.) near the Río Bonito and another ride (4–8 hr.) on a dry riverbed in the buffer zone of Pico Bonito National Park, leading to the village of La Colorada, to a Petroglyph rock, and/or the small Maya ruins of Chibcha. All trips, which range from L760 to L1,425 ($40–$75/£20–£38) include a free night in their lodge. They also offer multiple day trips on the Río Sico and to the Río Blanca Valley.

White-Water Rafting & Kayaking ★★

The Río Cangrejal, cutting its way right through Pico Bonito National Park, offers some of the best white-water rafting and kayaking anywhere in Central America. Plus it is only 45 minutes from La Ceiba. The river is populated by Class 2 to 5 rapids, which pass through lush green forests, beside waterfalls, and over sometimes into massive granite boulders. Trips begin with a short hike to the drop-in site and last 2½ to 7 hours, depending on the sections of the river you sign up for.

Nearly every tour operator in La Ceiba does some kind of rafting or kayaking trip on the Río Cangrejal, as well as on the Río San Juan toward Tela. Prices are significantly cheaper than a rafting trip in North America or Europe, ranging from L665 to L1,140 ($35–$60/£18–£30). **Jungle River Tours** (✆ **504/440-1268;** www.jungleriverlodge.com) and **Omega Tours** (✆ **504/440-0334;** www.omegatours.info) throw in free nights in their lodges (see "Where to Stay," below) with their tour, while **Garífuna Tours** (✆ **504/440-3252;** www.garifunatours.com) offers package deals that combine rafting trips with other activities around La Ceiba. All trips with these operators include lunch, transport to/from La Ceiba, experienced guides, and quality safety equipment.

Shopping

The best place for a wide selection of handicrafts, including Garífuna dolls, Lenca pottery, tribal textiles and jewelry, and other assorted items from around the region and country, is the **Rain Forest Souvenir shop** (Av. La Bastilla; ✆ **504/443-2917**). Alternatively, **Souvenir El Buen Amigo** (✆ **504/414-5504**) has a variety of handicrafts and regional items at its two locations, beside Expatriates Restaurant in Barrio El Iman and on Avenida 14 de Julio, downtown. **Piq' Art Gallery** (Av. Morazán beside Farmacia Kielsa; ✆ **504/440-4041;** www.piqartgallery.com) sells paintings from Honduran artists as well as assorted crafts and furniture. They just opened a small cafe and plan on turning it into a B&B, too.

The new **Mall Megaplaza,** at Avenida Morazán and 22a Calle (no phone), is home to North American chain stores, fast-food restaurants, a movie theater, an Internet cafe, and a few banks. Visiting this mall makes for a completely un-Honduran experience, but there is air-conditioning. It's open daily from 10am to 9pm.

Even if you don't buy anything, it's worth the effort to just walk through La Ceiba's main rambling **street market** ★ to check out the mouthwatering fruits and vegetables on display. If you look hard enough, you'll find a *baleada* stand or two. For stuff like CDs, DVDs, shoes, sunglasses, beach towels, or crafts, look no further. The market is on 6a Calle and Avenida 14 de Julio, and is open Monday to Saturday from 6am to 5pm, and Sunday from 6am to noon. It costs L10 to L50 (50¢–$2.50/25p–£1.25) to enter the market grounds.

Where to Stay

Expensive

Quinta Real ★★ (Kids) Quinta Real is a resort in the heart of the city fronting the beach. If you're looking for a true beach resort, forget it. The beach here is polluted and filthy, although they at least try to give the impression of cleanliness. It's best to stick by their glitzy, yet kid-friendly, pool area where you can still look out onto the ocean. Don't get this hotel confused with the Palma Real, which is 22km (14 miles) to the east. Unlike that quiet oasis, this hotel is carved out of the otherwise rough-and-tumble Zona Viva, and surrounded by raucous bars and restaurants. It manages to be an oasis of sorts, however, by keeping clean, modern, and exclusive. Tiled floors, light wood furniture, and your average beach decor fill out the clean, modern rooms. Suites feature an extra sitting room. It's not the Ritz, but it's the classiest thing in La Ceiba proper.

Av. 15 de Sept. and Av. Victor Hugo, Zona Viva. ✆ **504/440-3311.** Fax 504/440-3315. www.quintarealhotel.com. 81 units. $82 (£41) double; $180 (£90) suite. AE, MC, V. **Amenities:** Restaurant; bar; laundry service; pool. *In room:* TV, hair dryer, Wi-Fi.

Moderate

Coco Pando Resort ★ (Value) At a few miles west of La Ceiba and halfway to the airport, this small hotel, which attracts a mostly international crowd, feels more out-of-the-way than it actually is. If you don't have a car or intend to move around a lot, staying here might be an issue, though they do offer free pickups and drop-offs. Pine wood walls and tile floors make the large rooms lean toward the rustic; however, they do have everything you could ask for, like a minifridge, air-conditioning, and purified water dispensers. Their Iguana Bar and Restaurant in a beachfront *champa* is one of the better dining options in the area. All-inclusive packages are available as well.

5km (3 miles) west of La Ceiba on the road to the airport. ✆ **504/9969-9663.** www.cocopando.com. 7 units. L950 ($50/£25) double high season; L665 ($35/£18) double low season. MC, V. **Amenities:** Restaurant; bar; high-speed Internet in lobby. *In room:* A/C, fan, TV, fridge.

Gran Hotel Paris While most hotels on a town's main square can publicize their good location, that's not necessarily the case for the Gran Hotel Paris, which is situated on Parque Central. La Ceiba's main square is noisy, crowded, dirty, and hard to get around because of the steady traffic circling it. You may want to opt for one of the better hotels along the beach or outside of town if you're looking for quiet. If you want to be right in the action, though (a big plus during the Feria de San Isidro), look no further than this hotel. Plain, uninteresting rooms, with standard amenities like TVs, call to mind those at chains like the Motel 6, but all rooms have at least been remodeled recently. Rooms in the front overlook the square, while the ones in back look onto the leafy courtyard and the surprisingly pleasant pool.

North side of Parque Centra, Barrio El Higuerito. ✆ **504/440-1414.** hotelparis@psinet.hn. 63 units. L840 ($44/£22) double. MC, V. **Amenities:** Restaurant; bar; pool. *In room:* A/C, TV.

La Aurora The big square glass La Aurora is right on the highway not far from hordes of fast-food chains and gas stations, which makes it especially convenient if you intend on exploring destinations outside the city. Little differentiates the hotel from a standard Holiday Inn just off a highway exit in the United States. It even smells the same, down to the chlorine from the pool that wafts through the halls. Rooms are bland, but the beds are comfortable, the floors clean, and there's even a small couch in most.

Carretera La Ceiba-Tela. ✆ **504/440-2060.** 45 units. L880 ($46/£23) double. MC, V. **Amenities:** Jacuzzi, pool. *In room:* A/C, TV, minibar, Wi-Fi.

Inexpensive

Banana Republic Guest House This small guesthouse is owned and operated by Jungle River Tours and set in a restored house on a downtown La Ceiba side street. There's a mix of rooms with private and shared bathroom and two dorms that sleep five or six. All have high ceilings, wood floors, and are clean, but otherwise simple. There are lots of common areas with hammocks and gardens where you can chat with other travelers who probably just got back from one of the day tours run out of this spot.

Av. La Republica and Calle 12, Barrio Solares Nuevo. ✆ **504/440-1268.** Fax 504/440-1268. www.jungleriverlodge.com. 6 units. L85 ($4.50/£2.25) dorm; L230 ($12/£6) double; L180 ($9.50/£4.75) double without bathroom. AE, MC, V. **Amenities:** Restaurant; bar; high-speed Internet in lobby; kitchen; laundry service. *In room:* Fan.

Hotel Olas del Mar ★ (Finds This beachfront hotel in the center, just across the bridge to the Zona Viva, is one of the most overlooked in the city and left out of most guidebooks. It's hard to see why. The rooms are basic but clean, the outside hallways have a few nice lounge areas, and the view is the same as from the Quinta Real. The beds are a bit stiff and the rooms are bare-bones plain, but compared to similarly priced hotels in the area, it's a steal. Did I mention they have a nice big sun deck facing the beach that's a nice place to kick off your sandals and relax?

Av. 14 de Julio and 1 Calle, Zona Viva. ✆ **504/440-1857.** Fax 504/443-3681. www.hotelolasdelmar.com. 19 units. L600 ($32/£16) double. MC, V. **Amenities:** Restaurant; karaoke bar. *In room:* A/C, TV.

Hotels Outside La Ceiba

Very Expensive

Las Cascadas ★★ Las Cascadas is far more chic and luxurious than the lodge at Pico Bonito, yet it doesn't feel pretentious at all. Located beside a waterfall and several small creeks that run into the Río Cangrejal, it couldn't have a more dramatic setting. The two suites and two cabins are all constructed of polished river stone, wood, and thatched roofs and all include screened-in porches overlooking the waterfall, stone showers, and a queen-size mahogany canopy bed and one or two single beds. The suites are attached to the lodge, while the cabins are separate. The Bejuco cabin adds a Bali-style outdoor shower, while the River House adds a kitchen. All rooms are all-inclusive, which includes beer and wine. ***Note:*** This lodge does not allow young children as guests.

Km 8.8 Carretera La Ceiba-Yaruca. ✆ **877/271-6407** in the U.S., or 504/9805-2200. www.lascascadas lodge.com. 4 units. $310 (£155) double. Rates include meals, drinks, and airport transfers. AE, MC, V. **Amenities:** Restaurant; bar; entertainment room; gift shop; high-speed Internet in lobby; Jacuzzi; satellite phone; pool. *In room:* A/C, fan, hair dryer.

The Lodge at Pico Bonito ★★★ *Moments* When you first arrive at Pico Bonito, you'll be greeted by a tuxedoed staff member who'll hand off a tropical drink with a little umbrella. It only gets better from there. The Lodge at Pico Bonito is the only luxury ecolodge in all of Honduras, and the luxury shows: The 21 posh cabins here are adorned with Hemmingway-esque rattan furniture and wood floors, small porches dissected by lazy hammocks, and chic, modern bathrooms decorated with Mexican tiles. The cabins are connected to the main lodge via a raised wooden walkway that runs through cacao and coffee trees. Pico Bonito purposely lacks cable TV and Wi-Fi, but does have quieter amenities rarely found in ecolodges, such as warm showers, in-room massage services, and gourmet dining in its insanely overpriced yet still amazing Mesoamerican-themed restaurant.

The lodge is set at the foot of 2,400m (8,000-ft.) Pico Bonito, and boasts a 98,800-hectare (247,000-acre) area of pristine cloud and rainforest, which is home to crocodiles, spider monkeys, tapirs, and jaguars. Two hundred acres of the property are the buffer area of Pico Bonito National Park. A private butterfly sanctuary and serpentarium are on the grounds, and the lodge runs a number of guided hiking and other adventure tours.

La Ceiba, Atlantida, CP 31101. ✆ **888/428-0221** or 504/440-0388. www.picobonito.com. 21 units. $180 (£90) standard cabin; $255 (£176) superior cabin. AE, MC, V. **Amenities:** Restaurant; bar; butterfly farm and serpentarium; high-speed Internet in lobby; pool. *In room:* A/C, fan.

Expensive

Palma Real Beach Resort ★ The Palma Real, the only true beach resort on La Ceiba's Caribbean coast, is 22km (14 miles) east of the city on the road to Trujillo just past Sambo Creek. This sprawling residential and entertainment complex is on a beautiful stretch of sand, seemingly in the middle of nowhere, and has a massive pool that stretches across almost the entire property. The facilities, which are also used by the residents of the 150 villas in the complex, include a small water park (the Water Jungle, with a wave pool, lazy river, and a few slides), Hola Ola Theater (with nightly shows and live music), the Caña Brava Restaurant (with buffet meals), several a la carte restaurants, and the Guiffitti Disco. The rooms at the resort are exactly what you would expect, nothing more, and nothing less: clean tile floors, clunky wood furniture, and unadventurous bedspreads and decor. Packaged deals attract plenty of Canadians, Hondurans, and El Salvadorans.

Km 20 Carretera La Ceiba-Trujillo. ✆ **504/429-0501.** Fax 504/429-0505. www.grupopalmareal.com. 160 units. AE, MC, V. $160 (£80) double. **Amenities:** Restaurant; bar; disco/theater; pool; tennis courts. *In room:* A/C, TV, hair dryer, safe, Wi-Fi.

Inexpensive

Jungle River Lodge This small lodge beside the Río Cangrejal in Pico Bonito National Park is owned by Jungle River Tours and is most often used in conjunction with one of their tours, usually for free. The lodge itself is constructed of all natural materials and completely submerged in the jungle. Rooms, which are a mix of dorms and some doubles with and without bathrooms, are smallish and basic, but for the price and the convenience, they can't be beat.

Km 8.8 Carretera La Ceiba-Yaruca. ✆ **504/440-1268.** Fax 504/440-1268. www.jungleriverlodge.com. 7 units. L180 ($9.50/£4.75) dorm; L330 ($18/£9) double without bathroom; L455 ($24/£12) double with bathroom. AE, MC, V. **Amenities:** Restaurant; bar. *In room:* Fan.

Where to Dine

Moderate

Expatriates Bar & Grill ★ CONTINENTAL As you can probably guess by the name, Expatriates is a big time hangout for the English-speaking crowd in La Ceiba. Their charcoal grill pumps out goodies similar to those at any respectable North American grill like steaks, fish, shrimp, and chicken breasts. Spicy chicken wings, nachos, and even vegetarian dishes are a welcome retreat for homesick snowbirds. The *chuletas* (pork chops) are served with beans and rice and are mouthwatering. Flatscreen TVs offer the best access in La Ceiba to any North American sporting event. A decent selection of Honduran cigars, a full bar, plenty of tropical cocktails, and free Wi-Fi are added bonuses.

Calle 12, Colonia El Naranjal. ✆ **504/440-1131.** Main courses L95–L265 ($5–$14/£2.50–£7). MC, V. Mon–Fri 3:30–11:30pm; Sat–Sun 11am–late.

La Palapa INTERNATIONAL This rambunctious palapa directly behind the Quinta Real (p. 387) is one of the most happening spots in town for food and drinks. It's better known for drinking than eating, though they have a fairly large menu and the place isn't nearly as grimy as some other restaurants in town. The food is modeled after a Mexican grill, and is heavy on lots of finger foods as well as platters of chorizo and grilled meat, steaks, tacos, nachos, fish, and pasta. Service tends to be slow. There are DJs or live music on the weekends.

Calle 1, by Hotel Quinta Real, Zona Viva. ✆ **504/443-3844.** Main courses L95–L300 ($5–$15/£2.50–£7.50). MC, V. Daily 11am–late.

Playa Taty's ★★ INTERNATIONAL This rustic beachfront *champa* in the Zona Viva dishes up some of the surprisingly highest quality, most eclectic menu items around. There's a variety of steaks and seafood combo platters served with salad and garlic mashed potatoes, plus sandwiches, jambalaya, shrimp étouffée, and coconut shrimp. The grilled grouper with lime cream is delicious on its own, but enters heavenly territory when paired with a piña colada or glass of sangria.

On the beachfront, 1 block east of Hotel Quinta Real, Zona Viva. ✆ **504/440-1314.** Main courses L165–L300 ($8.75–$16/£4.40–£8). MC, V. Wed–Sat 11am–11pm; Sun 11am–8pm.

Ricardo's ★★ INTERNATIONAL Well known throughout the North Coast, Ricardo's has been attracting fruit company execs, wealthy Hondurans, politicians, and everyone else who would like a touch of class with their meal for years. As the framed awards hanging from the walls will make sure you know, this spot has even been named the best restaurant in Central America on several occasions. Start your meal with what is the best salad bar in La Ceiba. For an entree, you can choose among great pasta and soup dishes, along with beef filet and grilled or steamed fish in a number of hearty, citrusy, or spicy sauces. For dessert, sink your taste buds into a *pastel de tres leches,* or three-milk cake. Dining is either in the air-conditioned dining room or on the outdoor patio, both of which have an equally formal atmosphere.

Av. 14 de Julio and Calle 10a, Zona Mazpan. ✆ **504/443-0468.** Main courses L133–L342 ($7–$18/£3.50–£9). AE, MC, V. Mon–Sat 11am–1:30pm and 5:30–10pm.

Inexpensive

Chef Guity's ★ HONDURAN Hidden away on a shady piece of beach in the Zona Viva, sandwiched between the bridge and the Quinta Real, this *champa,* a traditional elevated thatched beach hut, is renowned for its Garífuna seafood specialties. Views and breezes from the ocean add to the pleasure of dining at this rustic two-level restaurant, though it is the food that sets it apart. The seviche (raw seafood marinated in lime juice), makes for a good choice of appetizer. Grilled kingfish, seafood stews, *caracols* (snails), steaks, and chicken round out the entree options, all of which attract a loyal following of mostly locals.

On the beachfront, west of the Quinta Real, Zona Viva. No phone. Main courses L75–L190 ($4–$10/£2–£5). No credit cards. Mon–Sat 11am–10pm.

Laura's Bakery (Kids) CAFE/BAKERY The always-fresh selection of preservative-free baked goods at Laura's easily make it top in a long line of La Ceiba bake shops. Their subs and sandwiches, both on fresh French baguettes, are good for a meal, while sugary snacks like pies, pastries, muffins, biscotti, and cookies make for good pick-me-ups any time of the day. The sweet cinnamon rolls are great with a mug of java.

Calle 13a, Colonia El Naranjal. ✆ **504/443-1494.** Main courses L40–L100 ($2–$5/£1–£2.50). No credit cards. Mon–Fri 6am–7:30pm; Sun 7am–5pm.

Pupuseria Universitaria SALVADORAN *Pupusas* are the Salvadoran equivalent of the Honduras *baleada.* Both are simple snack foods that use more or less the same ingredients. The bigger-than-normal *pupusas* here are filled with either *chicharrón* (fried pork) and cheese or just plain cheese, wrapped in a doughy corn tortilla, and served with hot sauce. Other classic Salvadoran items are on the menu as well. On weekends the tables fill up with a preclub crowd that comes here to snack and drink.

1a Calle and Av. 14 de Julio, Zona Viva. ✆ **504/440-1070.** Main courses L50–L150 ($2.50–$7.50/£1.25–£3.75). No credit cards. Daily 11am–9pm.

La Ceiba After Dark

La Ceiba is known for its nightlife, though standards rise and fall. Most clubs are open from Wednesday or Thursday through Saturday from the afternoon until the early morning, and covers are generally L100 ($5/£2.50). The most upscale place in town, and your best chance at encountering another tourist, is **Hibou ★★** (✆ **504/440-1700**), a multipart club on the beach at Avenida Bonilla. The indoor part is a full-on disco with a raised dance floor, several bars, and DJs blasting the latest Top 40 reggaeton and rock tracks, while the outdoor section is a more atmospheric, thatched-roof beach bar with

Volunteer Opportunities in Northern Honduras

The North Coast of Honduras, centering around La Ceiba, is one of the most active volunteering centers in Central America. Dozens of organizations have offices in the city and help arrange projects for anyone willing to lend a helping hand. Two standouts are **Guarama** (✆ **504/406-6782;** www.guaruma.org), a Honduras-based nonprofit that helps promote environmental awareness and conservation in the Río Cangrejal watershed on the eastern edge of Pico Bonito National Park, and **Children of the Light** (✆ **504/3304-1414;** www.thechildrenofthelight.org), a Christian organization that has built a school and has organized other community outreach projects for street children in the region.

occasional live music. **La Palapa** (✆ **504/443-3844**), behind the Quinta Real, is popular with visitors and upscale Hondurans who want to eat and drink with a group of friends, but don't want to stand in a crowded disco. There's occasionally live music.

There are a cluster of discos and grungy multi-level bars in the Zona Viva on Calle 1a, like **Mango Tango** (no phone), that can be good for a drink or two, though the crowd varies depending on the night. Others, like Two Chicas or Ledee2, are more of a gamble. While many travelers do stop into both clubs, they can be quite dangerous; I recommend sticking with the more upscale clubs.

CAYOS COCHINOS ★★★

When skies are clear, you can see the Cayos Cochinos, or Hog Islands, off the north coast of Honduras—that's how close to the mainland they are. Thirty kilometers (19 miles) northeast of La Ceiba, these two small islands, 13 coral cayes, and few tiny sandbars—almost all privately owned—are as close to paradise as one could imagine. The two main islands, Cayo Menor and Cayo Mayor/Grande, are home to just one luxury ecoresort, a few private homes, a research station, and one small Garífuna community. That's it. If isolation is what you want, then look no further. The vibe here is highly similar to the laid-back San Blas Islands off the coast of Panama.

The coral reefs surrounding the islands are some of the most undisturbed on the Meso-American Barrier Reef System and were designated as a Marine Protected Area in 1993 and a Marine Natural Monument in 2003. No commercial fishing is allowed in the 489-sq.-km (304-sq.-mile) reserve, and rules are strictly enforced, which has allowed the reefs and the fish that live on it to flourish. Wildlife on the land—which is also protected—includes pink boa constrictors, iguanas, sea turtles, and tropical birds, among other amphibians and reptiles. Legend has it that the Hog Islands were so named because pirates left hogs there for a convenient food supply during their travels.

Essentials

Getting There & Getting Around

The Cayos Cochinos can only be reached by boat, most often via a day trip from La Ceiba. The trip takes approximately 1 to 1½ hours, depending on the tide. The easiest way to get there is either by staying at the one hotel, the Plantation Beach Resort, that provides transportation or by visiting on a tour with **Garífuna Tours** (✆ **504/440-3252;** www.garifunatours.com) in La Ceiba, which runs almost daily snorkel tours to the cayes, including a stop for lunch at Chachauate. This tour runs $34 (£17).

It is also possible to reach the cayes from the towns of Sambo Creek and Nueva Armenia by hiring a local boatman or fisherman, but you must get a small group together to make it affordable. Dive boats frequently come on day trips from Roatán, while yachts from around the Caribbean moor here as well.

There is a L190 ($10/£5) fee (L95/$5/£2.50 when you come with a tour operator) upon entering the Cayos Cochinos, to be paid at the Fundación Cayos Cochinos research station on Cayo Menor.

What to See & Do

Tiny **Chachauate Cay ★** is home to the only permanent settlement in the Cayos Cochinos. The Garífuna village has no running water or electricity and the only bathrooms are in communal outhouses. The thatched houses are home to just a few dozen families that eke out a living from fishing and tourism. There are a couple of small eateries serving fried fish and plantains, plus a few craft stands that are set up informally when a tour boat arrives. Locals rent out their homes to visitors for around L100 ($5/£2.50) per night.

Outdoor Activities

The mountainous **Cayo Grande** is home to several good **hiking trails** through the lush jungle, beginning right at Plantation Beach resort and running to the highest points of the island—from where on a clear day you can see miles in every direction. At the highest point, 140m (459 ft.), there is a small lighthouse.

The turquoise waters and unspoiled coral reef around the Cayos Cochinos are an ideal spot for underwater exploring, so much so that many prefer diving and snorkeling here to the Bay Islands. There are more than 60 dive sites scattered around the reserve, and many others that have yet to be named. Within the walls, drifts, small wrecks, and sea mounds, you'll find sponges, grunts, sea fans, sea whips, grouper, lobsters, sea urchins, and parrotfish. Less common are manta rays, bottlenose dolphins, whale sharks, and hawksbill turtles. Most dive resorts in the Bay Islands will lead day trips here, but the only dive operation based in the Cayos Cochinos is at the Plantation Beach Resort (see below).

Where to Stay

Plantation Beach Resort ★★★ Located on Cochino Menor, this upscale resort is as removed from the modern world as a beach resort can get and still manage to be comfortable. Electricity is the biggest amenity, and that's a good thing—there's nothing to distract you from soaking in the beautiful surroundings. The lodge—set on 4 hectares (10 acres) of virgin forest—was built of stone and mahogany native to the tiny island. Rooms vary in size, but the quality is roughly the same throughout, with tile or wood floors punctuating a rustic yet cozy setup. Plantation has one of the better dive operations in the country and offers PADI certification courses. Transportation to the resort is not included with a stay, but the hotel will arrange pickup from San Pedro Sula or La Ceiba. Their small restaurant is *the* hangout in town for visiting yachties who moor near the hotel.

Cochino Menor. ✆ **866/751-0147.** www.plantationbeachresort.com. 12 units. $100 (£50) double; $750 (£375) all-inclusive weekly fee, including diving; $650 (£325) all-inclusive weekly fee without diving. V. **Amenities:** Restaurant; bar; watersports equipment. *In room:* Fan.

TRUJILLO

The coastal city of Trujillo, long a beach retreat for the people of San Pedro Sula and Tegucigalpa, still has yet to fully recover from the 1998 devastation of Hurricane Mitch.

Volunteer Opportunities in the Cayos Cochinos

Research and volunteering opportunities in the Cayos Cochinos are run in conjunction with the **Honduras Coral Reef Fund** (✆ **504/442-2670;** www.cayos cochinos.org). The organization leads all scientific research on the islands, which includes surveying the reef, protecting sea turtle nesting sites, collecting data on the pink boas, and establishing ecotourism projects on Chachauate, among other tasks. There are basic accommodations at the HCRF Marine Research Center on Cayo Menor. Bookings and 12-day scheduled programs are run through Biosphere Expeditions (www.biosphere-expeditions.org); you must have a PADI open-water certification for some programs.

It's not that the place is a mess, but rather that tourists just haven't been flocking here. The beaches are now in good shape and the airport has been repaired, but there aren't any flights. Trujillo seems to have completely missed the rampant progress going on in places like La Ceiba, 165km (102 miles) east, but that might change: The first rumbles of development have begun west of the city, yet at the rate things are going, any significant change is still a way off.

Trujillo has born witness to many of the most significant events in Central American history. On August 14, 1502, Christopher Columbus set foot on the American mainland here for the first time on his fourth and final voyage. The first Catholic Mass on the continent soon followed. In 1860 the North American William Walker, after having previously taken over Nicaragua with a small army and a failed attempt to invade Costa Rica, conquered the fort of Trujillo. After 5 days of fighting with British and Honduran forces, however, Walker surrendered and was executed by Honduran authorities. In the early 1800s, Trujillo was one of the first places on the mainland where Garífuna settlers—after they were dumped on Roatán by the British—began to build communities. The Garífuna influence is still strong along the coast of Trujillo Bay to this day.

Essentials

Getting There

BY CAR CA 13, which begins at El Progresso outside of San Pedro Sula, runs parallel to the coast all the way to Trujillo, first stopping in Tela and La Ceiba. Two more scenic roads run through the interior of the country through Olancho, highways 39 and 23, but neither is well paved and both are often impassable during heavy rain.

BY BUS The terminal for **Cotuc** (✆ **504/444-2181**) buses is in Barrio Critsales, although they also stop at the Texaco gas station toward the entrance to town, about 1km (1/2 mile) from the center. Cotuc buses travel daily to La Ceiba (3 hr. away), Tela (4 1/2 hr. away), and San Pedro Sula (6 hr. away). Cotraipbal also runs buses to these destinations, which depart from the terminal next to the Texaco station, almost every other hour.

BY BOAT While it isn't one of the high-speed super ferries that operate between Roatán, Utila, and La Ceiba, the **Bimini Breeze** does get you back and forth between Trujillo and Guanaja, eventually. The ferry leaves Trujillo on Tuesdays and Sundays at 4pm and returns on Mondays and Fridays at 9am. You can buy tickets directly on the boat for L650 ($34/£17), or call ✆ **504/987-0875** for reservations.

Trujillo is also the departure point for boats down the Mosquito Coast, which leave only sporadically from the Muele de Cabotaje. Boats run to Brus Laguna at least once a week, usually leaving in the afternoon and arriving in the morning. The fee is L250 ($15/£7.50).

Orientation

The colonial center of Trujillo is built on a hill beside the town's fort, high up from the bay, and surrounded by green mountains. A few roads lead down to the beach below the center, where there is a string of seafood shacks and the Garífuna neighborhood of Cristales. A single dirt road runs west along the coastline to the Garífuna communities of Santa Fe and Guadalupe. The unused airport, 1km (1/2 mile) away from Trujillo's center, is on the eastbound road outside of town. Puerto Castillo, Trujillo's deepwater port, is 8km (6 miles) east across the bay.

Getting Around

Trujillo's center is easily navigable by foot, even when you factor in having to walk up and down the hill to the beach below. The bus terminal and many of the town's hotels will need to be reached by taxi, however. Local buses run sporadically to Santa Fe to the west, leaving from the old cemetery. More frequent buses head east to Puerto Castillo from the Texaco terminal.

Visitor Information

For tourist information, see **The Trujillo Honduras Pages** (www.trujillohonduras.com). **Banco Atlantida** on the Parque Central has a 24-hour ATM and will exchange traveler's checks. Internet access can be found at a number of small shops near the park or at **Casa Kiwi** (see "Where to Stay," below). You can make long-distance phone calls at **Hondutel,** 1 block south of the park.

What to See & Do

Cementerio Viejo ★ Now that the weeds have been pulled and the site is renovated, the gates of this old cemetery in the center of town have officially been unlocked and opened to the public. Many of the graves are more than 300 years old. The most significant is the grave of William Walker, the American adventurer who launched several invasions of Central American nations and was shot by a firing squad in Trujillo in 1860. His grim end is noted on his epitaph with the word "fusilado."

6 blocks southeast of Parque Central. No phone. Free admission. Daily dawn–dusk.

Fortaleza de Santa Barbara ★ Imposing its iron fist from its elevated point in the center of town is the Fortaleza de Santa Barbara, a Spanish colonial fortress that was erected to help defend Trujillo Bay from pirate attacks. The 17th-century fort, which was renovated in 2005, was reportedly much bigger centuries ago and extended all the way down to the beachfront. Today you will find a vast outline of stone walls with moss growing through the cracks and a couple of small buildings. A row of iron cannons point out toward the water below and, if you've drunk plenty of *guifitty* (a Garífuna moonshine), incoming buccaneers. There is a small museum within the fortress with a collection of colonial items, muskets, pirate relics, naval memorabilia, and Garífuna masks.

Northeast corner of Parque Central. No phone. Admission L95 ($5/£2.50). Daily 8am–noon and 1–4pm.

Museo Rufino Galan This idiosyncratic little museum is closer to a junk heap than an official museum. The barely standing wood building, a few blocks from the square, is filled with piles of pre-Columbian artifacts, alleged pirate relics, books, chests, farm equipment, old tools, and anything else that is good at collecting dust. There's even a pet spider monkey tied up outside. You may have to ask around for the owner, as the museum doesn't follow any set hours.

Calle 18 de Mayo and Río Cristales. No phone. Admission L50 ($2.50/£1.25). Hours vary.

Parque Nacional Capiro y Calentura The 1,235m (4,052-ft.) mountain that stands proudly behind the center of Trujillo is the setting for this 4,500-hectare (11,115-acre) national park. There is very little infrastructure to the park and hikers rarely come this way. Those that do are rewarded with vibrant bird life, including macaws, the occasional howler monkey, and several distinct zones of tropical forest. The entrance to the park is via a dirt path south of town, and the park office is staffed on rare occasions. It takes about 3 hours to reach the top of the peak, where there is a small radar station. For the best bird-watching, it is best to set out before dawn.

3km (2 miles) south of Parque Central. Admission L60 ($3.50/£1.75). Daily 8am–4pm.

Spanish Classes in Trujillo

Certified teachers at **Bravo Spanish School** (✆ **504/434-4635;** www.bravospanishschool.com) teach beginner, intermediate, and advanced classes beginning every Monday. Their standard program includes 20 hours of air-conditioned classes, a workbook, a 7-day homestay with a local family, and three daily meals for $220 (£110).

Refugio de Vida Silvestre Guaimoreto Similar to Cuero y Salado and the Laguna de los Micos on the north coast, Guaymoreto, 5km (3 miles) east of Trujillo, is a large lagoon surrounded by mangrove forest, intersected with canals, and home to abundant wildlife. Migratory birds flock here from November to February. Due to the lack of tourists in Trujillo, there aren't any tour operators that arrange trips here anymore; therefore, you must go to the lagoon and negotiate with a local fishermen for a canoe or boat ride (roughly $15/£7.50 per 2 hr.). **Casa Kiwi** (✆ **504/434-3050;** www.casakiwi.com) sometimes will arrange trips here as well.

5km (3 miles) east of Trujillo. ✆ **504/434-4294.** Free admission.

Outdoor Activities

The main reason most visitors trek all the way out to Trujillo is for its **beaches.** Wide golden sands, gentle breezes, very few waves, and even fewer beachgoers make the beaches here seem like deserted islands. The best places to enjoy the sun are in front of the *chambas* below the fort, where you can borrow a beach chair, or near the airport and the Hotel Christopher Columbus (see "Where to Stay," below). Emptier beaches can be found hidden below the road in the small coves that stretch for 19km (12 miles) to the west of town.

To the west of Trujillo, down a potholed dirt road, is a string of Garífuna fishing villages. All are home to a few thatched seafood shacks, a basic *hospedaje* or two, *punta* music flowing through the air, and serene beaches with rarely a soul in sight. **Santa Fe,** 12km (8 miles) from Trujillo, is my favorite stop because of its legendary **Comedor Caballero ★★** (no phone), aka Pete's Place, a traditional Garífuna restaurant on the beach with some of the best seafood on the North Coast. A bit farther and even more difficult to reach are the villages and beaches of **San Antonio** and **Guadeloupe.** Buses leave from the Cementerio Viejo in the center of town to these villages several times per day.

Shopping

Small artisan shops can be found around Parque Central and toward the beach. The best is **Artesma Garífuna** (✆ **504/434-3583**) in Barrio Cristales, which sells beach gear, coconut carvings, drums, and an array of little knickknacks.

Where to Stay

Moderate

Hotel Christopher Columbus ★ Kids The Hotel Christopher Columbus surely has seen better days. It was once billed as one of the top hotels on the north coast, but then Hurricane Mitch scared off all the customers. Now it is simply starving for guests. They keep the lime green paint fresh, but the place is practically always empty and it's beginning to show its age. Rooms are very outdated, almost to the point of being cool again—they call to mind a 1950s-style roadside motel, with retro furniture and even spots of Astroturf on the terrace. Still, the full-scale resort, on one of the best stretches of beach in town, is a decent stay, and the surprisingly friendly and upbeat staff help you overlook any failings. Added family-friendly bonuses are that the pool area isn't bad, and that they have a small dock, kayaks, and snorkel equipment for guests to use.

1km (1/2 mile) east of Parque Central, beside the airport. ✆ **504/434-4966.** Fax 504/434-4971. 52 units. L1,200 ($63/£32) double. AE, MC, V. **Amenities:** Restaurant; bar; tennis courts; watersports equipment. *In room:* A/C, TV.

Tranquility Bay (Value) Tranquility Bay's five small seaside cabins are tucked away down a forested hill near the beach, a few miles west of town. Each cabin has a terra-cotta roof, a small porch with a couple of chairs, walls decked out in cheery yellow paint, and a few splashes of Honduran decor. Though the cabins aren't luxurious, they are clean and a decent overall value. There's a nice big inviting pool close to the beach, and they have a small creek that runs through the property. If you don't have your own transport, access to town can be an issue.

3km (1 3/4 miles) west of town. ✆ **504/928-2095.** www.tranquilitybayhonduras.com. 5 units. L855 ($45/£23) double. No credit cards. **Amenities:** Restaurant; bar. *In room:* Fan.

Inexpensive

Casa Kiwi ★★ (Finds) Six kilometers (3 3/4 miles) east of Trujillo on the road to Puerto Castilla, a New Zealand woman has set up Casa Kiwi, Trujillo's best backpacker hangout. The quickly expanding compound is right on a quiet stretch of beach with little other civilization around. The rooms, all available at bargain prices, are in your choice of dorms, private rooms, or cabins. While the dorms are clean and the cabins are more private, the middle rooms are the best overall value. Apart from Casa Kiwi's stand-alone bar and restaurant, there's loads of little extras like a pool table and bike and snorkeling rentals. This place also hosts the occasional weekend bonfire party, and arranges tours.

6km (3 3/4 miles) from Trujillo on the road to Puerto Castilla. ✆ **504/434-3050.** www.casakiwi.com. L500 ($26/£13) *cabaña;* L150 ($8/£4) double; L70 ($4/£2) dorm. No credit cards. **Amenities:** Restaurant; bar; Internet cafe; pool table. *In room:* A/C (in *cabañas*), fan.

La Quinta Bay Hotel If you tried to get any closer to the airport, you'd be on the runway. The La Quinta, which has no relation to the U.S. chain of the same name, is right on the side of the airport across from Hotel Christopher Columbus and the beach. If planes were still running, staying here might be a rather noisy endeavor, but for now it's quite convenient and quiet. The rooms are simple yet clean and more modern than those at the Columbus. There is no restaurant on-site, so you're stuck with the facilities on the beach or will have to catch a cab into the center.

1km (1/2 mile) east of Parque Central, beside the airport. ✆ **504/434-4732.** 25 units. L500 ($26/£13) double. MC, V. *In room:* A/C, TV.

Where to Dine

Mambo CUBAN The food at Mambo, one of the more upscale restaurants in town, is slanted toward Cuban grub, with a few local favorites thrown in, too. The beans and rice, grilled fish, sandwiches, pastries, and coffee are all good choices. On weekends there is sometimes live music and dancing, which can attract a crowd of area expats.

3a Calle. No phone. Main courses L75–L200 ($4–$10/£2–£5). No credit cards. Mon–Fri 11am–8pm; open later on weekends.

Merendero del Centro HONDURAN This bustling little *tipico* restaurant is good for quick and simple but filling Honduran breakfasts of beans, corn tortillas, eggs, and

ham. They're best known for their *baleadas* and dirt-cheap lunch specials, though. Plastic tables and kids running around add some authenticity, if nothing else.
3a Calle. No phone. Main courses L55–L110 ($3–$6/£1.50–£3). No credit cards. Daily 6am–8pm.

Playa Dorado ★★ Kids HONDURAN Of the several *champas* on the beach below the fort (any of which are the most atmospheric places to eat in town), Playa Dorado is the best. The owners will let you pick your fish, priced by size, and choose how you want it prepared. Their *camarones al ajillo,* shrimp sautéed with garlic and lime and served with a big plate of french fries, has my mouth watering even as I type. There are a few beef items on the menu, but considering that you are on the beach, I'd stick with seafood.
On the beachfront below the fort. No phone. Main courses L75–L225 ($4–$12/£2–£6). No credit cards. Daily 11am–9pm.

Trujillo After Dark

Rogue's Gallery, sometimes called Jerry's, in the concrete, tin-roofed building near the beach *champas,* is good for a sunset cocktail or beer. There are a couple of decent beachfront bars beside the Hotel Christopher Columbus, such as the **Bahia Bar** and **Gringo Restaurant & Bar,** but on my last visit, only the Bahia was open. **Truxillo Disco,** at the edge of a bluff facing the sea, is the most popular disco in town. Don't show up before 10pm or you'll be alone. There's no cover.

10 THE BAY ISLANDS ★★★

Las Islas de la Bahía, or the Bay Islands, are best known for their clear Caribbean waters and their pristine coral reef—the second largest in the world. The three main islands of Roatán, Utila, and Guanaja, along with Barbareta and 60 or so other tiny cayes, have long been one of the major dive destinations in the world. Although they are no longer the cheapest places in the world to get dive certification, prices remain considerably cheaper than anywhere else in the Caribbean and package deals for divers are vast. All-inclusive tours that include lodging, food, dives, airfare, and anything else you can throw in can be had for any visitor seeking a deal.

The cultural makeup of the islands has been a tumultuous one. The first pre-Columbian settlers were likely related to the Pech Indians on the mainland and a few small archaeological sites are still scattered among the surrounding hills. Christopher Columbus is believed to be the first European to find the islands, when he anchored in Guanaja in July 1502. In the following decades, Spanish ships came to take native slaves and set up *encomiendas,* where, in exchange for Christianization, the indigenous people were forced to pay tribute and labor to the Spanish Crown. As the Spanish began to loot the New World of its gold and transport the riches across the Caribbean back to Spain, the islands became a hide-out for French and English raiding boats. Pirates such as Henry Morgan and John Coxen began to frequent the islands for the next 2 centuries, although they left little trace. War broke out between England and Spain in 1739, and the British took control of the islands and set up forts at Port Royal in Roatán. They were returned to Spain in the treaty of Aix-la-Chapelle in 1748, taken back by the British during another war in 1779, and then left uninhabited after Spanish attacks in 1782. In 1797, a few thousand Garífuna, descendants of Carib Indians and African slaves from the Cayman Islands, were dumped at Punta Gorda in Roatán by the British and many settled there while others headed for the mainland. In the 1830s, a new wave of white and black

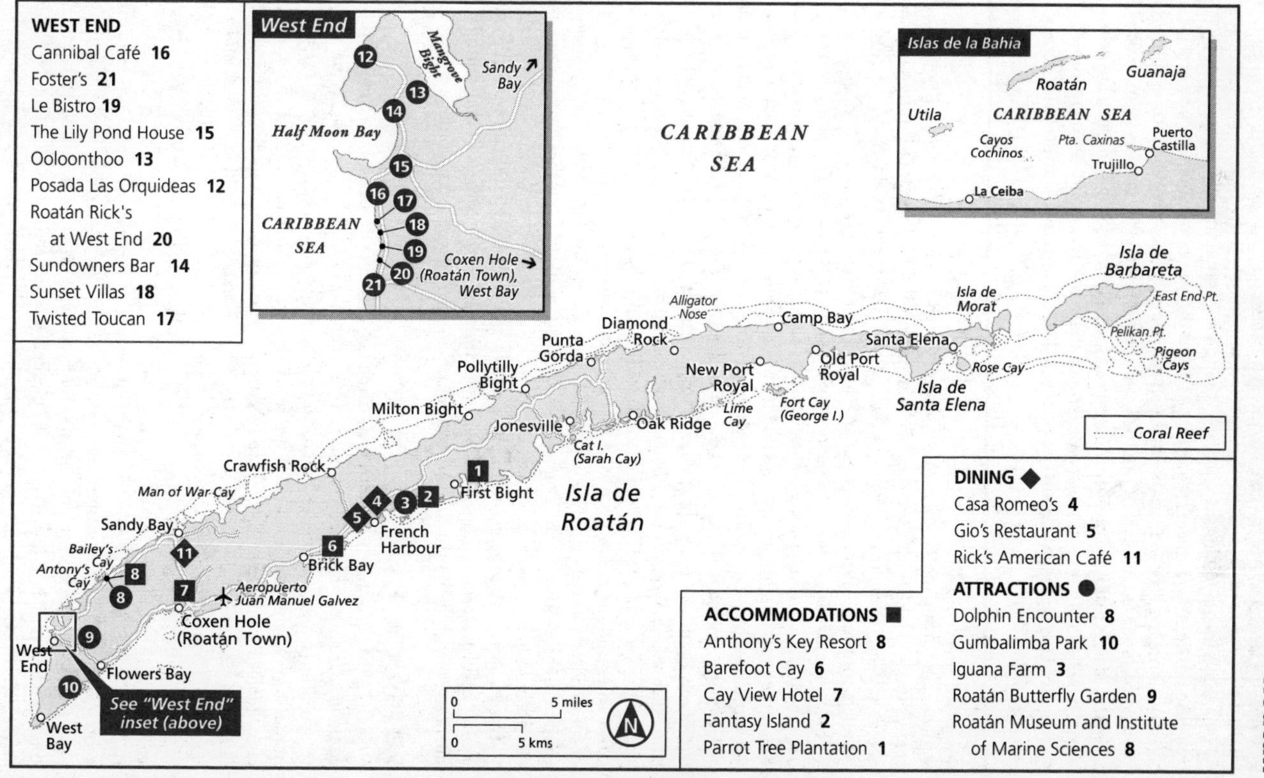
WEST END
Cannibal Café 16
Foster's 21
Le Bistro 19
The Lily Pond House 15
Ooloonthoo 13
Posada Las Orquideas 12
Roatán Rick's at West End 20
Sundowners Bar 14
Sunset Villas 18
Twisted Toucan 17
West End
Mangrove Bight
Sandy Bay
Half Moon Bay
CARIBBEAN SEA
Coxen Hole (Roatán Town), West Bay
CARIBBEAN SEA
Islas de la Bahia
Roatán
Guanaja
Utila
CARIBBEAN SEA
Cayos Cochinos
Pta. Caxinas
Puerto Castilla
Trujillo
La Ceiba
Isla de Barbareta
East End Pt.
Isla de Morat
Pelikan Pt.
Pigeon Cays
Alligator Nose
Diamond Rock
Camp Bay
Punta Gorda
Santa Elena
Pollytilly Bight
New Port Royal
Old Port Royal
Rose Cay
Isla de Santa Elena
Milton Bight
Lime Cay
Fort Cay (George I.)
Jonesville
Oak Ridge
Cat I. (Sarah Cay)
Coral Reef
Crawfish Rock
Man of War Cay
First Bight
Isla de Roatán
Sandy Bay
French Harbour
Bailey's Cay
Antony's Cay
Brick Bay
Aeropuerto Juan Manuel Galvez
Coxen Hole (Roatán Town)
West End
Flowers Bay
See "West End" inset (above)
West Bay
0 5 miles
0 5 kms
N
DINING
Casa Romeo's 4
Gio's Restaurant 5
Rick's American Café 11
ATTRACTIONS
Dolphin Encounter 8
Gumbalimba Park 10
Iguana Farm 3
Roatán Butterfly Garden 9
Roatán Museum and Institute of Marine Sciences 8
ACCOMMODATIONS
Anthony's Key Resort 8
Barefoot Cay 6
Cay View Hotel 7
Fantasy Island 2
Parrot Tree Plantation 1

Tips — Ouch! Watch Out for Sand Flies

One thing the Bay Islands do not lack is sand flies, sometimes called no-see-ums. These pesky little gnatlike creatures, one-third the size of mosquitoes, bite and leave annoying little red bumps that you cannot help but itch. While some of the major resorts send their staff out to rake the sand, which kills sand fly eggs, much of the islands just have to deal with them, especially on Utila, where they are particularly fierce. There is no best repellent for these nasty buggers. Some recommend Cactus Juice Sun Cream or Coconut Oil, while others feel just regular bug spray works best.

settlers came from the Caymans and set up the main towns that remain population centers today. The British government claimed control over the islands during this time, and although Honduran sovereignty of the islands was recognized in 1859, many of the islanders continued to see themselves as a part of the British Empire.

Today, the Bay Islands are at a major turning point in their history. Fishing, which has been the lifeblood of the islanders for several centuries, is quickly being replaced by tourism as the most important trade. Luxury home developments targeting North Americans are creeping onto every island and slews of Latino workers from the mainland are attracted by the high standards of living and available work, while the native Afro-Caribbean population is getting pushed to the fringes of the islands. Entire chunks of land, such as the West End of Roatán, are being snapped up by developers, and hotels and resorts are replacing the islands' once traditional stilted wood houses. The influx of cruise ships on Roatán has already added adventure parks and tour buses, and there's talk of more ports and bigger ships, but for the time being, the Bay Islands are still serene Caribbean hide-outs, where English just happens to be the mother tongue and the American dollar is the main currency.

High season is almost year-round here and it can be especially difficult to find rooms during holiday weeks. Things get a bit slower from January to February and during the hurricane season in September and November, and prices will drop significantly.

ROATÁN ★★

Roatán, 29km (18 miles) east of Utila, is the largest, most developed, and most visited of the Bay Islands. The real estate market has been hot in recent years, but is now closer to spewing lava as once quiet beach communities become full-scale resorts or second homes for North Americans, who are flocking here like barracudas and snapping up every inch of available land. The cruise season is also expanding rapidly—Royal Caribbean and Carnival cruises alone are investing a combined $80 million in increasing the capacity. When a cruise ship is docked at Coxen Hole, look out: The island will be crawling with craft markets and tour buses, and the best beaches like West Bay become crowded with families of sun worshipers.

Much of the new development is on the west side of the island, where tourism is concentrated, while Garífuna communities dominate the eastern half. But if you look in the right places, you can still see the Bay Islands of yesteryear. Many of the island's hills remain undeveloped enough to be covered in Tropical Oak, Evergreen Palms, and Gumbo Limbo trees, and just one (partly paved, partly potholed) road runs the length of the island.

Diving and snorkeling remain the most popular activities on the island, but other options are expanding rapidly. Now you can also zip-line across the jungle-clad hills, take a submarine hundreds of feet into the ocean, or take an aerial real-estate tour.

Essentials

Getting There

BY PLANE While most tourists come from La Ceiba via ferry or flight, an increasing number of international travelers are flying directly into Roatán's Juan Manuel Gálvez International Airport, sometimes called simply **Roatán International Airport (RTB; © 504/445-1088)**. It's 3km (1³/₄ miles) from Coxen Hole on the highway to French Harbour. Continental, Delta, American Airlines, and Taca fly here directly between points in the U.S. such as Houston, Newark, Atlanta, and Miami. See p. 707 in the appendix for airline phone numbers and websites.

If you are flying to/from La Ceiba, you are limited to domestic airlines. **Atlantic Airlines** (**© 504/445-1179;** www.atlanticairlinesint.com), **Isleña** (**© 504/445-1918;** www.flyislena.com) and **Aerolineas Sosa** (**© 504/445-1154**) all offer daily flights. **Bay Island Airways** (**© 504/946-5665** in the U.S., or 933-6077; www.bayislandairways.com) offers interisland transport via small seaplanes from the West End.

Most tourists will take a taxi from the airport, which should run under L40 ($20/£10) to anywhere on the island. If you walk out of the airport to the highway, you can also catch one of the frequent buses that run during the day. They run L20 to L40 ($1–$2/50p–£1) per person.

BY FERRY Roatán's super ferry, the ***Galaxy Wave*** (**© 504/445-1798** or 443-4630; Safeways_Galaxy@yahoo.com), zooms passengers from the ferry terminal at Dixon's Cove in Roatán to La Ceiba at 7am and 2pm, and returns at 9:30am and 4:30pm. The price is L420 ($22/£11) each way, and the ferry has room for 360 people and offers air-conditioned rooms, a sun deck, and a small snack shop. It looks like a monster compared to Utila's small ferry and is much more stable; however, folks with weak stomachs might end up feeling sick by the time they step off the ship, particularly during the choppier afternoon trips. From the ferry terminal, you can catch a taxi, rent a car, or catch a bus simply by walking out to the main road.

BY CRUISE SHIP At last check, Norwegian, Premier, and Sun Cruises make port calls at Coxen Hole on Tuesday, Wednesday, and Thursdays, while Radisson, Wind Star, Commodore, and Regal also make port calls on a less frequent basis.

Orientation

Roatán sits 56km (35 miles) from La Ceiba on the North Coast of Honduras, and smack-dab in between Utila and Guanaja. The 64km-long (40-mile) and no more than 4km-wide (2¹/₂-mile) island has a mountainous center that is covered in lush, green jungle. One main highway zigzags from one end of the island to the other, hitting every major settlement along the way. Coxen Hole, in the center of the island, is home to the majority of the population and is the transportation hub of Roatán.

Getting Around

BY BUS During daylight hours, buses and minibuses ply back and forth from one end of the island to the other on Roatán's one main road for a fare of L20 to L40 ($1–$2/50p–£1) per person depending on how far you travel. Most buses will only travel east or west from Coxen Hole to one end of the island.

BY CAR With a decent highway that runs much of the length of the island, driving in Roatán is a pleasant way to explore the island and reach some of the more remote sites. Several rental-car agencies have stands at the airport, including **Caribbean Rent a Car** (✆ **504/455-6950;** www.caribbeanroatan.com) and **Avis** (✆ **504/445-1568;** www.avis.com.hn). Prices range from about L855 to L152 ($45–$80/£23–£40) per day.

BY TAXI Taxi stands are located in every major tourist center and waiting taxis sit outside most of the island's largest resorts. Prices are relatively high compared with the mainland. A ride from the airport or Coxen Hole to the West End will run about L200 ($10/£5) per person. After 6pm, when the buses stop running, fares go up. Colectivo taxis, which pick up other passengers, are a cheaper option.

BY WATER TAXI Water taxi service runs daily from 9am to 9pm and is a convenient way to get between West End and West Bay. Just flag down a passing boat at any dock and one should stop. The fare is L30 ($1.50/75p) during the day and L38 ($2/£1) in the evening.

BY SCOOTER You can rent motorized scooters at stands across the island. **Captain Van's Rentals** (✆ **504/403-8751;** www.captainvans.com) on the West End, and West Bay is the most popular and accessible operator for visitors. The cost is about L741 ($39/£20) per day.

Visitor Information

The **Roatán Marine Park Office** (Half Moon Bay, West End; ✆ **504/445-4206;** www.roatanmarinepark.com) has dive maps, some equipment, and information on saving the reef and natural sites in the Bay Islands. You can also buy a L190 ($10/£5) Roatán dive tag/bracelet here.

Almost every hotel on the island has a **dive center** or can give you special rates with one. Dive packages and certification courses attract a majority of travelers to Roatán, where rates are some of the lowest in the world, at less than $40 (£20) per dive.

FAST FACTS Most of the large hotels, such as the Mayan Princess (p. 411), have ATMs, and there are a few stand-alones scattered about in the West End and elsewhere. All other banks can be found in Coxen Hole or French Harbour. You can exchange traveler's checks at **BANFAA,** located in the airport.

You can find cybercafes and calling centers scattered about the major tourist centers, but these computers tend to be slow. Most hotels now have Wi-Fi or a computer with Internet access for guests to use.

The majority of hospitals can be found in Coxen Hole, although many travelers prefer the small **Anthony's Key Medical Clinic** (✆ **504/445-1003**) in Sandy Bay.

Coxen Hole

Coxen Hole, the largest city and capital of the department of the Bay Islands, isn't the idyllic beach paradise that you might expect to find in Roatán. It's more of a, well, hole. Whether you like it or not, though, chances are you are going to pass through the city, which is home to the airport and the ferry and cruise terminal, and functions as a transportation hub for buses and taxis. Apart from a few small hotels and restaurants, there isn't much in the way of tourist amenities—you're probably better off basing yourself in another part of Roatán.

One of the highlights of visiting this part of Roatán is **Yaba Ding Ding** (Bonilla Building on the waterfront; no phone; www.yabadingding.com), which is one of the best craft shops in all of Honduras. Named after the local slang for pre-Columbian artifacts, the store stocks excellent Lenca pottery, straw baskets and weavings from the highlands, Garífuna art, and more. It's open Monday to Saturday from 9am to 5pm.

Where to Stay

Cay View Hotel Of the handful of small, budget, crumbling hotels that sit near the water by the ferry dock at Coxen Hole, the Cay View is probably the best. With 19 rooms, it's certainly the largest. Rooms aren't pretty and are quite worn, but there's air-conditioning, cable TV, and a decent Honduran restaurant and bar overlooking the water. It's a handy spot to keep in mind only if you arrive to the island too late to drive to a different part of Roatán, and just want a cheap place to stay for a night.

Oceanfront, Coxen Hole. ✆ **504/445-0269.** 19 units. $25 (£13) double. No credit cards. **Amenities:** Restaurant; bar. *In room:* A/C, TV.

French Harbour

French Harbour was once better known as the home of one of the largest fishing fleets in the Western Caribbean, but is quickly becoming engulfed by the onslaught of tourism and residential developments aimed at foreigners. While the compact town and port hold most of the town's population, the area as a whole is more spread out and self-contained than the West End and West Bay. Most of the hotels are fairly isolated and have their own private beaches, dive centers, and restaurants, so most visitors find little reason to leave their individual compounds or venture into town.

For scuba diving here, try **Coco View Resort** (✆ **504/911-7371;** www.cocoviewresort.com) or **Fantasy Island Resort** (✆ **504/455-7499;** www.fantasyislandresort.com).

What to See & Do

Iguana Farm ★ Kids Several thousand iguanas inhabit this property in French Key, just east of French Harbour, toward Fantasy Island. There are four different species on the farm, all native to the Bay Islands, and they are absolutely everywhere. Watch when you walk, as these things will literally fall out of the trees and bushes. There's also a small pool with sea turtles and tropical fish. The place is pretty basic overall, but well worth a look.

French Key, just east of French Harbour. ✆ **504/975-7442.** Admission L100 ($5/£2.50). Daily 8am–3:30pm.

Where to Stay

Barefoot Cay ★ Kids A small walk-on barge regularly travels the 328m (100 ft.) back and forth from the main island and the 1.6-hectare (4-acre) island of Barefoot Cay, a newish resort area on the south shore of Roatán. Apart from the marina, which attracts yachties from around the Caribbean, the property has just four bungalows, two with two bedrooms and two with one bedroom. The spacious buildings have full kitchens and patios, as well as Balinese showers, which are partially open-air. The pool area—with its adjacent two-level *cabaña*—is the social center of the property and a decent place to grab a meal or drink, or to soak in a 360-degree view of the cay. On the waterfront, there's an 863m-long (260-ft.) dock and a thatched-roof palapa with a lowered platform, which grants easy access for kayakers who want to circle the cay or snorkelers who want to explore the reef that's just offshore.

Btw. French Harbour and Brick Bay. ✆ **504/455-6235.** Fax 504/455-6304. www.barefootcay.com. 4 units. $185 (£93) double. MC, V. **Amenities:** Restaurant; bar; pool; spa services; watersports equipment. *In room:* A/C, fan, TV/DVD, fridge, kitchen, Wi-Fi.

Fantasy Island This 8.4-hectare (21-acre) island is one of Roatán's original megaresort complexes and is still one of the largest hotels on the island. Even without Mr. Roarke and

Top Scuba Diving Sites in Roatán

Roatán is nothing less than a diving paradise. There are more than 130 dive sites scattered around the island and, in just 1 day of diving, you can experience the full range of dives from coral reefs, canyons, and walls to wrecks and tunnels. The waters are crystal clear, and the reef, part of the second-largest barrier reef in the world, runs just offshore. Many of the best dive sites are literally right off the dock or within a 5-minute boat ride. Following is a list of the best dive sites:

- **Mary's Place ★★★**: Mary's Place near Sarah Cay is one of the most legendary dive sites around the island. Here you crawl through volcanic tunnels, crevices, and canyons around a reef plateau that has vertical walls that drop as much as 36m (120 ft.). You'll encounter black groupers, feather black coral, gorgonians, large bearded fire worms, and barrel sponges.
- **Four Sponges ★**: This dive site in Sandy Bay is one of the most complete, and is the best for beginning divers. The site is defined by its different levels of reef that range from 3 to 36m (10–120 ft.), allowing for the opportunity to encounter a wide range of sea life, like electric-blue chromis, barracuda, toadfish, yellow jawfish, scorpianfish, and sponges.
- ***Prince Albert* Wreck:** Since it sank back in 1985 near the Coco View Resort, the 50m (165-ft.) ship *Prince Albert* has attracted more soft coral growth than any other wreck on the island. There's also a sunken DC-3 plane that you can explore nearby.
- **Calvin's Crack:** This Jonesville dive site is defined by the huge—Calvin must have been a big guy—crevice ranging from 98 to 262m (30–80 ft.) in depth that runs through the reef. Brain, leaf, and black coral, sponges, gorgonians, rainbow parrotfish, fan leaf algae, and the occasional sea horse can often be sighted along the walls of the crevice.
- **Spooky Channel ★★**: The Spooky Channel (sometimes called Wayne's Place), on the northwest shore near Sandy Bay, is well, spooky. The floor, ranging from 66 to 295m (20–90 ft.), is lined with sea whips and crabs, and cleaner shrimp crawl about on the abundant coral formations.
- ***El Aguila* Wreck:** *El Aguila* is a 656m (200-ft.) cargo ship that sank in 1997 by Anthony's Key Resort and was later split in three by Hurricane Mitch. It sits 328m (100 ft.) below the surface of Sandy Bay. Green Moray and garden eels can be found in varying spots around the wreck, as are large grouper, blue parrotfish, glassy sweepers, nudibranches, and anemones.

Tattoo there to oversee operations, the complex has grown to include an impressive array of attractions like a pool, several bars and restaurants, numerous lounges, a private dock, a major dive operation with a handful of boats and certification courses, and a huge crescent-shaped beach that sits right in front of the hotel. The rooms, which are set back from the beach in two-level structures, have basic beach decor, wood floors, wicker furniture, and plain bedspreads; each room also has a beachfront balcony. They are nothing fancy, but casual and friendly, which could describe the general feel of the entire property.

French Harbour. ✆ **504/455-7499.** www.fantasyislandresort.com. 109 units. $125 (£63) per person. Rates include 3 daily meals and diving. MC, V. **Amenities:** Restaurant; bar; pool; tennis and basketball courts; watersports equipment. *In room:* A/C, TV, fan, fridge.

Parrot Tree Plantation This sprawling, 67-hectare (168-acre) gated community is already turning heads all over the Caribbean, although it is far from complete. Right now visitors can stay in rooms, villas, and condos, and visit the Sante Spa. More houses and a 150-room luxury hotel are in the works, though it could be a few years before completion. The rooms available differ drastically in size and style, although all are bright, new, and clean and can be rented by the day, week, or month. The turquoise waters are home to a small marina with moorings for up to 20 berths; beachside, there is a vast collection of constructions from a pool, a few shops, and a coffeehouse. Plans include adding up to five restaurants, a fitness center, a yacht club, and numerous other goodies that should give you little reason to leave the resort.

East of French Harbour. ✆ **504/3320-7177.** www.parrottreeplantation.com. $95 (£48) per night in the Sante Spa; $1,800 (£900) a month for the Casa Playa. MC, V. **Amenities:** Restaurant; pool; spa. *In room:* A/C, fan, high-speed Internet, kitchen (in some).

Where to Dine

Casa Romeo's ITALIAN Romeo's, set in the hotel of the same name, has been a Honduras institution since 1976, and many of the recipes have been passed down since the 1940s from Romeo's father Don Di, who owned the famous Maxim's in La Ceiba and later the Buccaneer Inn on Roatán. The menu ranges from Italian standards like *penne alla carbonara* to thick cuts of beef and seafood that are prepared every which way from *fra diavolo* (in spicy tomato sauce) to breaded and grilled. My favorite item is the conch chowder. The restaurant is on the edge of the harbor and makes good use of the view.

Main St. ✆ **504/455-5854.** Main courses L152–L285 ($8–$15/£4–£7.50). AE, MC, V. Mon–Sat 10am–2:30pm and 5–10pm.

Gio's Restaurant ★ SEAFOOD Few dare to utter the name Gio's without mentioning king crab, and for good reason: People have been flocking to this restaurant since it opened several decades ago for its special king crab *al ajillo* (in garlic sauce). Other seafood dishes and even steaks are finely executed and cater to finicky international tourists. There are two separate dining rooms; one is open air on the dock, while the other sits inside with the air-conditioning blasting. All seats have inviting views of the harbor, and make for ideal spots for relaxing with a drink in your hand for the rest of the day.

Under the El Faro Inn, Main St. ✆ **504/455-5214.** Main courses L190 ($10–$20/£5–£10). MC, V. Mon–Sat 10am–2pm and 5–10pm.

Sandy Bay

Sandy Bay is a tranquil town on the north coast that has become a popular stop on many cruise ship tours, which come to experience the cultural highlights of the islands. Standout attractions here include the Roatán Museum and Institute of Marine Sciences, and a dolphin encounter. Note that, while the beaches in the reserve are stunning and surrounded by some of the most dramatic coral formations in Roatán, the beaches in town are murky and scruffy.

For scuba diving and snorkeling, try Sandy Bay's most popular resort, **Anthony's Key Resort** (see "Where to Stay" below).

What to See & Do

Dolphin Encounter ★★★ Kids On Bailey's Key, which is part of Anthony's Key Resort, the famous Bottlenose Dolphin encounter program offers visitors the rare chance to interact with these wonderful creatures. Open-water dives, snorkel programs, and beach encounters are the most common option, and allow for physical interaction with dolphins. More involved are the training programs where you can work with the training staff at the Roatán Institute for Marine Sciences in 1- or 2-day sessions. There's also a dolphin show every day except Wednesday at 4pm.

Kids can get in on the dolphin action, too: Every summer Anthony's Key Resort and the Institute of Marine Sciences offer **Dolphin Scuba camps** ($850/£425 per camper) where children can learn about dolphins and even swim and interact with them. They get to practice their scuba diving and snorkeling, as well as learn about the ecosystem and cultures of Roatán. Think of it as an exotic summer camp.

Bailey's Key, Roatán Institute for Marine Sciences, Sandy Bay. ✆ **504/445-3008.** L100 ($5/£2.50) admission for the dolphin show, L2,128 ($112/£56) for a nonguest dolphin dive.

Roatán Museum and Institute of Marine Sciences ★★ The Institute of Marine Sciences is the island's main scientific research center and so is host to technical lectures and serious research, but it's also a place where tourists can learn about the ecology of the Bay Islands through captivating exhibits. Displays feature fish, reptiles, birds, plants, and other examples of island life, and there are exhibits on the history and culture of the area. The facility is part of the 13-sq.-km (5-sq.-mile) Sandy Bay marine reserve.

Roatán Institute for Marine Sciences, Sandy Bay. ✆ **504/445-3008.** Admission L100 ($5/£2.50). Daily 8am–5pm.

Where to Stay

Anthony's Key Resort ★★ For 4 decades, Anthony's Key Resort has been one of the leading dive and leisure destinations in the Bay Islands. If you are looking for a hotel that will completely transport you to another world, this is it. The vast complex is submerged in mangrove and palm forests and is reminiscent of an island village where frequent water taxis shuffle you back and forth from place to place. The property is set partly on two small cayes and partly on the north shore of the island near Sandy Bay. There are 56 single-unit wooden bungalows, 10 of them on the hill on the main island, with the rest on the key. Bailey's Key, just west of the main key, is home to the best beach on the property and a Dolphin Encounter lagoon. Also on the grounds are the Institute of Marine Sciences and Roatán Museum, which guests can enjoy for free.

Anthony's Key Resort, Sandy Bay. ✆ **954/929-0090.** www.anthonyskey.com. 56 units. From $479 (£240) per person for a 4-night dive package with 3 daily meals and activities. MC, V. **Amenities:** Restaurant; bar; museum; laundry service; pool; watersports equipment. *In room:* A/C (in some), fan.

Where to Dine

Rick's American Café CONTINENTAL You won't find Humphrey Bogart at this Rick's, just a cool island atmosphere and good food. Rick's has one of the best Continental menus on the island, which explains how it has survived all these years of hurricanes and downtimes. They have what could be the best baby back ribs in Central America, as well angus beef burgers, sashimi, steaks, oysters, and lobster, among other dishes. There are nice views of the treetops and the water, especially at sunset when the decent wine and cocktail list and Honduran humidor gets its best use. There's occasionally live music and special events during American sporting events. It's a popular spot for weddings, too.

South side of the main road, Sandy Bay. ✆ **504/445-3123.** Main courses L133–L380 ($7–$20/£3.50–£10). MC, V. Tues–Sun 5pm–late.

Moments **Roatán Festival**

Garífuna Day on April 12 marks the date of the arrival of the Garífuna on Roatán in 1797, and celebrations are held all along the north coast of the country and the Bay Islands. Hundreds of thousands of people revel in the streets, march in parades, and party on the beaches for much of the night, so get ready to party if you're in town on this date.

West End

West End, so-called because it is on the west end of Roatán, is the tourist center of the island and is home to the most hotels, restaurants, bars, dive shops, tour operators, and general tourist amenities. From the highway, the town hugs the road and the beach in both directions for just a mile or two. The town itself is quite small and has a sort of thrown-together feel to it, since buildings are scattered about with no apparent order. Prices tend to be cheaper here than in the West Bay, thus attracting plenty of backpackers and die-hard divers, although it is still more upscale than anywhere on Utila.

Essentials

GETTING THERE & GETTING AROUND The West End can be reached by bus from Coxen Hole for L40 ($2/£1), by a water taxi for L30 to L38 ($1.50/75p) from West Bay, or by a regular taxi from anywhere on the island. There is a taxi stand near the entrance to the highway where a few cabs (which charge L200/$10/£5 to Coxen Hole) are usually waiting.

VISITOR INFORMATION If you want to explore the island for a day or two, a great option is to rent a mountain bike, scooter, or motorcycle. **Captain Van's** (✆ **504/403-8751;** www.captainvans.com) has locations in both the West End, on Main Street near the Baptist Church, and the West Bay Mall. Prices begin at L171 ($9/£4.50) per day for a bike and L741 ($39/£20) per day for a scooter.

What to See & Do

Gumbalimba Park ★ Kids Gumbalimba is a good place to come if you have just 1 day in Roatán and want to experience as much as you can, which is why the place is often packed when a cruise ship is in town. It's kind of a one-stop adventure shop. There's a zip-line section, a large stretch of beach with clear kayaks, SNUBA, snorkel gear, and a pool, and even a small cave with cheesy replica pirates and exhibits that describe their historical relationship with the Bay Islands. Their main attraction, though, is their nature trail that runs through an area of very dense jungle and is filled with rare tropical plants and flowers native to the region, as well as a hanging rope bridge over a small lake, cages of macaws and other parrots, and a small island that's home to a few monkeys.

On the West Bay Rd. btw. West End and West Bay. ✆ **504/445-1033.** www.gumbalimbapark.com. Admission L323 ($17/£8.50); L1,045 ($55/£28) for park admission and zip-line package. Daily 9am–4pm.

Roatán Butterfly Garden Try to spare a few hours for a visit to Roatán's butterfly garden. Tours are self-guided through the 278-sq.-m (3,000-sq.-ft.) walk-through enclosure, and they give you a small chart to identify the 30 or so rare butterfly species and tropical plants. Separate from the butterflies are a few cages of birds native to Honduras such as aracaris and toucans.

Near the entrance to the highway, West End. ✆ **504/445-4481.** www.roatanbutterfly.com. Admission L100 ($5/£2.50). Sun–Fri 9am–5pm.

West End beaches are smallish and not nearly as nice as those in the West Bay (just a quick water-ferry ride away), but there are a few spots where the water is just as clear as anywhere on the island. Half Moon Beach is probably the best option. For scuba diving and snorkeling, try **Coconut Tree Divers** (✆ **504/445-4081;** www.coconuttreedivers.com); **Reef Gliders** (✆ **504/403-8243;** www.reefgliders.com); or **Native Sons** (✆ **504/445-4003;** www.nativesonsroatan.com).

If you don't dive, snorkel, or even swim but still want to experience the undersea world of the Bay Islands you have a few options. The **Roatán Institute of Deep Sea Exploration** (no phone; www.stanleysubmarines.com) offers 3,280 to 6,560m (1,000–2,000 ft.) dives and shark dives inside the safety of a submarine. The small vehicles have room for just one pilot and two passengers. **Underwater Paradise** (✆ **504/445-6465**) has semi-submarine glass-bottom boat tours three times day from the Half Moon Bay Resort for L380 adults or L190 children ($20–$10/£10–£5), and the **Coral Explorer** (✆ **504/455-5379**) has a similar tour from West Bay.

For another unique perspective on the island, **Bay Island Airways** (✆ **504/946-5665** in the U.S., or 933-6077; www.bayislandairways.com) offers a variety of ways to view the island from the air. They have aerial real estate tours (L6,840/$360/£180 per hour for two), trips to the Pigeon Keys (L9,880/$520/£260 for a 3-hr. tour for two), and simple sightseeing and photography tours (L2,280/$120/£60 for a 15-min. flight for two).

The waters surrounding Roatán are full of Pelagic species like tuna, wahoo, mahimahi, blue and white marlin, shark, and king mackerel. **Early Bird Fishing Charters** (✆ **504/445-3019;** www.earlybirdfishingcharters.com), a member of the conservation-minded Fisherman's Association of Roatán, leads frequent excursions from the West End to waters all around the island. Prices begin at L7,600 ($400/£200) for a half-day tour with one to four people.

Shopping

All shops in Roatán are on Main Street in the West End, but most are little stores selling a mishmash of things. One standout store is **Wave Gallery** (✆ **504/445-4303**), in a bright yellow house on the beach, which is worth a browse for its paintings, jewelry, and crafts made by Honduran artists.

Where to Stay

The Lily Pond House ★★ (Finds This charming little house, just off the main road near Half Moon Bay, is inundated with lush garden and trees, making it just as attractive for the birds and butterflies as those who are looking for something completely different from the typical dive resorts that make up many of the accommodations in Roatán. The honeymoon suite is the largest of the four rooms, although all rooms don't really differ that much in size or amenities. All are quite spacious, with wood floors and canopy beds. Plus they have private entrances, en suite bathrooms, and porches, so you can keep your privacy. They also hold yoga classes on the rooftop garden three times a week.

Half Moon Bay, West End. ✆ **504/403-8204.** www.lilypondguesthouse.com. 4 units. $95 (£48) double. No credit cards. **Amenities:** Breakfast room; airport transfers; laundry service. *In room:* A/C, TV w/DVD, fridge, Wi-Fi.

Posada Las Orquideas (Value Posada Las Orquideas sits in front of Mangrove Bight, where there isn't a beach, but there is a dock and a wharf with beach chairs, and the town beaches are just a 10-minute walk away. The three-level building opened in April 2006 and the rooms still seem new with their shiny wood floors and wicker furniture. There's a nice balcony in every room with a table and hammock where you can watch the boats pass by in the water below. The Posada is an overall good value.

To the right from the highway, West End. ✆ **504/445-4387.** www.posadalasorquideas.com. 18 units. From $70 (£35) double low season and $80 (£40) double high season (July–Sept; Dec–Apr). A/C is an additional $15 (£7.50). AE, MC, V. **Amenities:** High-speed Internet (free in lobby); kayaks. *In room:* A/C, fridge, kitchen (in some).

Sunset Villas ★ Sunset is the most luxurious place to stay by West End standards and has the most beautiful pool area in town. Rooms are rented from the hotel or the one- or two-bedroom condos in the villas that make up the property. The large condos are the better value, particularly if you are sharing a two-bedroom. The living rooms sport a typical Floridian-like decor, with tiled floors and wicker furniture, while the bedrooms are a bit more elegant. Flatscreen TVs and large patios or balconies are added bonuses. The biggest downside of the property is that the rooms lack any decent views of the ocean, but all villas do look out on the large pool area.

Their restaurant is in the Buccaneer, which sits toward the beach directly in front of the property, just a couple of minutes' walk away.

To the left from the highway, West End. ✆ **504/445-4100.** www.roatanhotels.com. 29 units. From $90 (£45) hotel room; $158 (£79) condo room. MC, V. **Amenities:** Restaurant; bar; dive center; high-speed Internet (free, in lobby); pool; laundry service. *In room:* A/C, fan, TV, kitchens (in condos).

Where to Dine

Cannibal Café ★ Kids MEXICAN This wildly popular restaurant and bar in front of the Sea Breeze Inn is always a great choice for a snack or drink. It's set in a rustic wooden shack, and serves the sorts of standard Americanized Mexican fare like burritos and nachos that appeal to hungry divers. Get a margarita to wash your meal down and you'll fit right in at this party spot.

Main St., West End. ✆ **504/445-4026.** L76–L152 ($4–$8/£2–£4). No credit cards. Mon–Sat 10:30am–10pm.

Foster's ★ INTERNATIONAL Foster's is in a stilted house in the middle of the ocean connected to the shore by a few-hundred-foot dock. You literally can't get a better sea view from here, which is why this is the spot in town for a sunset meal or drink. Burgers, chicken wings, coconut shrimp, seafood, and steaks make up most of the menu. It can get boisterous on weekend nights, when there is either a DJ or live band.

On a dock over the water off of Main St., West End. ✆ **503/403-8005.** Fax 503/403-8789. www.fostersroatan.com. Main courses L133–L380 ($7–$20/£3.50–£10). AE, MC, V. Mon–Sat 10:30am–midnight.

Le Bistro ASIAN This Southeast Asian–inspired restaurant is one of the more adventurous in the West End. Much of the menu is comprised of Vietnamese treats like *acras* (fritters), egg rolls, spring rolls, and wontons that come served with your choice of fillings such as shrimp, grouper, pork, chicken, or vegetables. They also have beef hot pots, *Mixao* (chicken and shrimp over noodles in a ginger sauce), and combo platters. The restaurant itself is quite rustic; wedged between a bust dive shop and another store, it seems as if it was directly imported from a Saigon market stall.

Main St., West End. ✆ **504/403-8854.** Main courses L114–L209 ($6–$11/£3–£5.50). No credit cards. Daily 6–9pm.

Ooloonthoo ★★ INDIAN Ooloonthoo is probably the best restaurant in Roatán. Canadian chef Paul James and his Indian wife have done such a good job of giving this restaurant an authentic Indian coastal feel, you might just think you're in Goa while dining here. The decor is simple, with little touches like background Indian music, silk saris draped across the ceiling, and banana leaves strewn on the tables all adding to the am-I-still-in-Honduras ambience. Curries made from scratch dominate the menu, such as the Rogan Josh or pork vindaloo, while other highlights include Tandoori Cornish game hen and *murgh masala,* a mild northern Indian chicken dish.

To the right from the highway to Half Moon Bay, West End. ✆ **504/403-8866.** www.ooloonthoo.com. L95–L380 ($5–$20/£2.50–£10). MC, V. May–Nov Mon–Fri 6–9pm; Dec–Apr Sun–Fri 6–9pm.

Roatán Rick's at West End INTERNATIONAL Think of a traditional American grill and give it a little bit of island style in a rustic atmosphere. That's Roatán Rick's. They have steaks, burgers, pasta, sports on TV, and a nightly happy hour from 4 to 6pm. There's even curry and lobster on the menu.

Main St., West End. ✆ **504/403-8237.** Main courses L114–L266 ($6–$14/£3–£7). MC, V. Mon–Sat 10:30am–10pm.

West End After Dark

Sundowners Bar ★ This thatched-roof beach bar is one of the West End's main hangouts. Its prime spot on one of the best sections of beach in town draws lots of walk-ups, as do the specials on beer, mixed drinks, and the 4-to-7pm happy hour. Try the Monkey Lala, a frozen blend of Kahlúa, ice cream, coconut, and vodka.

Main St., West End. ✆ **504/445-4158.**

Twisted Toucan This British-owned and -operated bar is one the favorite nightspots and hangouts in the West End. Pretty much everyone ends up here late nights because of the cheap drinks and raucous crowd. There's a daily 4-to-7pm happy hour.

Main St., West End. No phone. www.twistedtoucanroatan.com.

West Bay

About 2km (1¼ miles) southwest of the West End sits a 1.5km (1-mile) stretch of powdery white sand, set against the mellow tides of a perfectly turquoise sea. This is West Bay, the finest beach in all of Honduras and one of the top beaches in all of the Caribbean. If your idea of a good vacation is to lounge around in the sand and sun with a continuous rotation of tropical drinks being brought your way, look no further. The focus here is less on diving—although diving is still a big deal—than general beachgoing activity. When you decide to move from your palm-fringed slumber, you can ride jet skis, take a boat tour, or browse the souvenir stands sprinkled across the beach. If you want to snorkel, you can rent gear almost anywhere and walk a few feet into the water to spot all sorts of colorful fish swimming around a good tract of coral reef.

Almost the entire beach is chockablock full of hotels and condos, the majority of which have no more than a few dozen rooms. Although the town is currently lacking in other tourist amenities like restaurants, that's changing—West Bay has so many new tourist projects in the works that it sometimes feels more like a construction site than a resort area. When a cruise ship is in town, the place can get downright crowded, but for much of the week, West Bay is still an idyllic beach resort.

What to See & Do

The 1.5km (1-mile) West Bay Beach ★★★ is the main attraction here and one of the region's best beaches. The water resembles an aquarium of sorts, since you can see right down to the bottom and watch brightly colored marine life pass you by. Many of the resorts have beach chairs and umbrellas set up in the sand, although you may need to pay a fee and get a wrist band to use them. Apart from snorkeling, you can rent Wave Runners or go parasailing, ride a paddle boat, or water-ski.

For scuba diving and snorkeling, try **Bananarama** (✆ **504/445-5005;** www.bananarama dive.com) or **Octopus Dive School** ★ (✆ **504/403-8071;** www.octopusdiveschool.com).

Where to Stay

Bananarama (Kids) You probably won't find anything this comfortable in this price range in West Bay. Apart from the two-bedroom beachfront King House that's available for rent and includes a full kitchen, none of the rooms at Bananarama are what you would call luxurious, but all are cozy in a rustic way. Rooms vary in size and quality, but all are brightly colored and have a decent selection of amenities. Bananarama doesn't have a pool, but it does sit on a nice stretch of beach and they have an ample selection of beach chairs for guests. Stays also include breakfast at their restaurant, the Thirsty Turtle Bar and Grill, and use of kayaks. Their PADI five-star Gold Palm dive center, which offers a full range of certification courses and packages, is one of the best known on the island, and a good percentage of the guests here make use of it.

West Bay, Roatán. ✆ **504/445-5005.** www.bananaramadive.com. 21 units. From $75 (£38) double; $570 (£285) for a 7-night dive package per person. No credit cards. **Amenities:** Restaurant; bar; watersports equipment. *In room:* A/C, fan, TV, fridge, microwave.

Infinity Bay Spa & Resort ★ Though it's currently less glamorous than the Mayan Princess, this condo/resort complex is undergoing a major revamp that should soon make it a more luxurious option. Studios, one-, two-, and three-bedroom condos are set in three-level villas facing the pool or West Bay beach. All rooms are very modern with stainless-steel appliances, flatscreen TVs, tiled floors, and contemporary furniture and decor. Apart from the condo section, much of the resort was under construction on my last visit. A full spa and health club, as well as other amenities, were being erected in Phase 2 of the property, which should open sometime in early 2009. As of last check, the highlights are their long dock that extends far into the water, poolside bar, and beachfront restaurant.

West Bay, Roatán. ✆ **504/445-5016.** Fax 504/445-5062. www.infinitybay.com. 145 units. $125 (£63) oceanview studio in the low season; $150 (£75) the rest of the year. 2-bedrooms start at $240 (£120); 3-bedrooms at $375 (£188). MC, V. **Amenities:** Restaurant; bar; airport transfers. *In room:* A/C, fan, TV, full kitchens (in nonstudios), Wi-Fi.

Mayan Princess ★★ (Kids) The Mayan Princess is the most luxurious resort in Roatán and one of the top accommodations in all of Honduras. The posh units are privately owned and rented out through the hotel management. The one-bedroom and two-bedroom condos still feel like the tile has just been laid and the wicker furniture never sat in. They have full kitchens, a dining area, living rooms, and a patio or balcony that faces the ocean or sprawling pool area that runs almost the length of the complex and is bordered by tropical gardens that are interwoven with waterfalls and walkways. The oceanfront side of the property is the best in the West Bay because of the primo beach chairs and umbrellas and the good bit of shade that covers their beach bar and restaurant, one of the best all-around dining options in the West Bay.

West Bay, Roatán. ✆ **504/445-5050.** Fax 504/445-5065. www.mayanprincess.com. 60 units. From $165 (£83) for a poolside room on weekdays and $189 (£95) on weekends. MC, V. **Amenities:** Restaurant; bar; laundry service; pool; watersports equipment; Wi-Fi. *In room:* A/C, fan, TV, kitchen.

Pizzeria Il Pomodoro/Buffalo Steakhouse INTERNATIONAL These are actually two restaurants near the Paradise Beach Club, which share the same kitchen and are only separated by a partial wall. Regardless of which restaurant you dine in, you can order from both menus. The pizzeria menu offers pastas, lasagnas, and wood-fired pizzas, while the steakhouse offers beef imported from the U.S. in the form of T-bones, rib-eyes, and New York strips. To make things more complicated, they have an attached gelateria, Angelo's, which serves dessert. Since the West Bay has few other dining options that aren't overpriced resort restaurants, the multifaceted talents of this über restaurant come as a relief.

Paradise Beach Club, West Bay. © **505/403-8066.** Main courses L133–L342 ($7–$18/£3.50–£9). AE, MC, V. Daily noon–midnight.

West Bay After Dark

Bar Pirata On clear days you can see the entire island and the coast of the mainland from this thatched roof bar on the road to the West End. The beer is cold, the cocktails strong, and they occasionally have Sunday barbecues. This is West Bay's local hangout, and expats as well as locals are loyal customers.

On the road to West End. © **504/425-3988.** www.lapiratabar.com. No credit cards. Daily 5pm–late.

De La Vina Wine Bar The only real wine bar in the Bay Islands is located in the West Bay Mall, and it attracts an older and more sophisticated crowd than other spots in the Bay Islands. There are just a few tables in the interior dining area (which boasts air-conditioning) and a handful of sidewalk tables. In addition to a nice list of mostly South American wines, cheese and cigars are on hand; they occasionally host wine classes.

West Bay Mall, West Bay. © **504/445-5044.** www.roatanwinebar.com. MC, V. Daily 4–10pm (closing hours vary).

UTILA ★★

Utila has only one main settlement, called East Harbour, or simply Utila town. Although it is the smallest of the three main Bay Islands and the nearest to the mainland (at 29km/18 miles west of Roatán), Utila is still the wildest and most untouched. Islanders, many of them the descendants of pirates and Garífunas from the Caymans, are eager to casually chat with anyone about the weather or local news. Some may even tell you that Captain Morgan's lost booty from his raid on Panama in 1671 is still hidden in the surrounding hills.

Apart from a few chic dive resorts, almost the entire population of Utila is clustered together along one stretch of coast, while nearly the other 80% or so is made up of mangroves and wetlands. Many have called this island a backpacker paradise because of the cheap accommodations, restaurants, the bar scene that rages well into the night almost every night, and the sandy bottom rates for dive certification—once considered the lowest in the world. It is far less polished than nearby Roatán, but beach resorts are slowly starting to carve their way out of the mangroves outside of town. Even the certification costs are roughly on par with Roatán these days. Chances are that it is going to be a good while before a dirt-cheap dorm bed in a rickety old house goes out of style in Utila, though.

Essentials

Getting There

BY PLANE Two small airlines make the 20-minute trip between Utila and La Ceiba, with connections to Tegucigalpa and San Pedro Sula. **Aerolineas Sosa** (© **504/443-2519**) makes the trip twice a day Monday to Saturday and three times on Sundays. **Atlantic Airlines** (© **504/425-3364;** www.atlanticairlinesint.com) has flights to/from

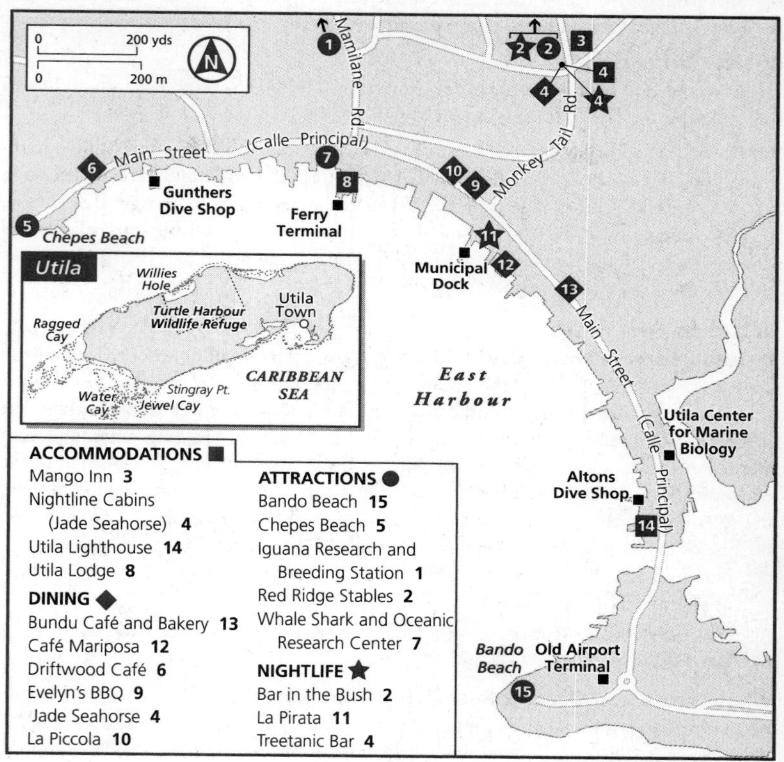

La Ceiba on Monday, Wednesday, Friday, and Saturday. Occasionally they have flights on Saturdays direct to Roatán. Taxis, which cost L40 to L60 ($2–$3/£1–£1.50 per person) await flights for the 10-minute trip to town.

BY FERRY The ***Utila Princess II*** (**© 504/425-3390**) makes the hour-long trip back and forth between the Municipal pier Utila and the Muelle de Cabotaje dock in La Ceiba. The ferry departs Utila daily at 6:20am and 2pm, and returns to La Ceiba at 9:30am and 4pm. Ticket booths are located on both piers. The price is L373 ($20/£10) each way.

Orientation & Getting Around

The crescent-shaped East Harbour on the eastern end of Utila is where 90% of the population of the island lives. The Municipal Pier marks the center of town; Main Street, the main road on the island, runs perpendicular about 1km (1/2 mile) in each direction. To the left is Sandy Bay and to the right is a small peninsula that ends at the bridge that connects to Bando Beach. With a few exceptions, almost all hotels and tourist amenities can be found within 1km (1/2 mile) of the pier. Another road, Cola de Mico or Monkey Tail Road, branches off Main Street up over Pumpkin Hill, eventually leading to the airport and the north side of the island.

There are just a few cars on Utila, let alone taxis. Considering almost everywhere is within walking distance or reached over water, the only time you will really need a taxi or a car is to get back and forth from the airport.

Visitor Information

Head to the **Bay Island Conservation Society** (✆ **504/425-3260**) for info and maps on Utila and the Bay Islands. It's open Monday to Friday from 7am to 7pm.

FAST FACTS There are two banks in East Harbour, both conveniently within a hummingbird's flight of the pier. **Banco BGA** (✆ **504/425-4117**) and **Banco Atlantida** (✆ **504/425-3374**) exchange traveler's checks and have an ATM. **Mango Tree House,** on Main Street just to the left from the pier, is the island's most reliable Internet cafe and can also make international phone calls. **Hondutel,** beside the Bay Island College of Diving, also makes international calls.

What to See & Do

Iguana Research and Breeding Station (Kids) The small nonprofit German-run station is a learning center for those interested in not only iguanas, but also the tortoises, snakes, frogs, spiders, fish, and other animal life found on the Bay Islands. Many live species can be found in aquariums, terrariums, and outdoor breeding cages; and your admission includes a brief tour where kids can walk into—if they dare—some of the enclosures. This is one of the few places in the world where you can catch a glimpse of the spiny tail or swamp iguana, a species endemic to Utila and in danger of extinction because of the islanders' love of eating them and the destruction of the mangroves. Longer tours to the Bat Caves, Pumpkin Hill, and the mangrove forests are also available, as well as volunteering opportunities.

Follow Mamilane road until you see the signs for the turnoff. ✆ **504/425-3946.** www.utila-iguana.de. Admission L40 ($2/£1). Mon, Wed, and Fri 2–5pm.

Whale Shark and Oceanic Research Center ★★ The whale shark, the largest fish in the world, is frequently seen in Utilan waters, and the island is a hot spot for whale shark research. This small organization is focused on protecting these creatures and the coral reefs by collecting data with the help of divers and operators, educating the public, and hosting and participating in major studies. The good news for visitors to Utila is that they have a full line of courses and tours. Their 4-hour whale shark encounter and research trips include a short background lecture on whale shark ecology, the use of snorkel gear, and the possibility of seeing whale sharks up close in the water. They also offer PADI specialty courses such as AWARE fish ID and Coral Reef Conservation courses and underwater photography. Volunteers are often needed to help with whale shark research and development of the program.

Main St., in front of the Bay Islands College of Diving. ✆ **504/425-3760.** www.wsorc.com. Free admission. Daily 8am–7pm.

Outdoor Activities

HORSEBACK RIDING Located on the road to the airport, **Red Ridge Stables** (✆ **504/390-4812**) offers horseback riding treks to the inner jungle, Pumpkin Hill Beach, the freshwater caves, and to other destinations on the island that aren't submerged completely in swamp and mangroves. Trips run L665 ($35/£18) for a 2-hour ride.

KAYAKING A few hotels and several shops in town, including **Utila Water Sports** (✆ **504/425-3264;** www.utilawatersports.com) and the bar at Bando Beach (see below), rent kayaks to explore the channels, lagoons, and the mangroves around the island.

Sun Jam Festival

For 1 weekend night every August, partygoers from around Honduras descend upon the tiny 1.2-hectare (3-acre) island Water Cay off Utila for the raucous Sun Jam festival. Local fishermen wait at Utila's pier to transport attendees to the decade-old festival, where top DJs from around the region pump electronic music to a lively and often intoxicated crowd. The crowd is limited to 1,500, so buy your tickets (which cost L760/$40/£20) a few weeks in advance. For info, visit www.sunjamutila.com

SNORKELING & SCUBA DIVING ★★ With prices hovering around L4,750 ($250/£125) for a PADI 4-day Open Water Certification, it is no wonder that scuba divers from around the world descend on this small island. Almost any certification or course can be taken on the island from a number of dive shops. There are roughly 90 permanent mooring buoys around the island, giving access to the reefs, wrecks, walls, and tunnels that frequently line the pages of top diving magazines. The most frequent whale shark sightings tend to be in March and April.

The dive shops on Utila are second to none in Honduras. On Main Street in East Harbour, dive instructors seem to outnumber people five to one. Competition is fierce and the operators can be catty at times, but standards tend to be relatively high. Some operators to try include: **Alton's Dive Center** (**© 504/425-3704;** www.diveinutila.com); **Bay Islands College of Diving ★** (**© 504/425-3291;** www.dive-utila.com); **Captain Morgan's Dive Shop** (**© 504/425-3349;** www.divingutila.com); **Deep Blue Divers** (**© 504/425-3211;** www.deepblueutila.com); **Utila Dive Center ★** (**© 504/425-3350;** www.utiladivecenter.com); and **Utila Water Sports** (**© 504/425-3264;** www.utilawatersports.com).

SWIMMING While Utila isn't known for its beaches like other places in Honduras, it does have a few decent options for sunbathers and swimmers. There are several good beaches within walking distance of town. **Bando Beach** (**© 504/425-3137**), just past the bridge from the Point, is privately owned and you must pay a small admission (L40/$2/£1) to get in. Occasionally they host Full Moon Parties that attract top DJs from the region. There's a small beach bar that also rents snorkel gear and kayaks. **Chepes Beach** to the west of Sandy Bay is the main public beach. They are constantly at work at improving the infrastructure by adding sand and facilities.

The small, uninhabited **Water Cay** is similar to many of the beaches you'll find in the Cayos Cochinos: It's made of a cluster of palm trees circled by a white sandy beach and turquoise water. Charters and dive trips often stop here for lunch or weekend barbecues and parties. The first weekend of August, it is host to the largest party in Utila, the Sun Jam festival (see above).

Where to Stay

Expensive

Deep Blue ★ This award-winning PADI Resort is, like all other upscale accommodations in Utila, west of Sandy Bay and only reached by boat. The 10 deluxe rooms, all in one main building, are clean and contemporary without being overly posh. They have hardwood floors, handmade wood furniture, pleasant blue bedspreads and curtains, and

Top Five Scuba Diving Sites in Utila

- **CJ's Drop Off:** Near Turtle Harbour on the north side of the island, these dramatic coral cliffs sink about 5m (15 ft.) to 100m (328 ft.)—one of the biggest vertical drops in the entire Caribbean. The walls are teeming with sea life. There's a chance to see stingrays, moray eels, and hawksbill turtles.
- ***Halliburton:*** Sunk by divers, for divers. This large wreck, submerged under 30m (100 ft.) of water, is covered in brightly colored sponges and coral, including fireworms found on the deck. Moray eels are often seen around the hull of the ship, while groupers and barracudas can be seen all around it.
- **Stingray Point ★**: Two reef walls sprinkled with canyons and topped by a coral garden come together at this site on the western end of the island. Spotted eagle rays and stingrays can often be found in the sandy channels here. Large sea fans and soft coral plumes are particularly copious in the area.
- **The Maze:** This north side site is defined by the wide canyon and a significant wall drop (40m/130 ft.). Elkhorn coral and star coral are matched in beauty by the variety of plant life such as sea fans and rope sponges. The famous Willy's Hole, filled with glassy sweepers, is also found here.
- **Black Hills ★★**: Black Hills, a large seamount with steep drop-offs, is about 1.5km (1 mile) off the south shore of Utila and home to a vibrant array of sea life such as hawksbill turtles, queen angelfish, thousands of blue and yellowtail wrasse, horseeye jacks, sea horses, and spadefish. Sea fans, whips, and gorgonians and other sea plants litter the site.

feature art provided by Gunter Kordovsky, who runs Gunter's Driftwood gallery in town. Deep Blue, which has three great dive sites just off its shores, has long been one of the most respected dive operators on the island and many of the guests here take advantage of all-inclusive dive packages. The resort is also heavily involved in the study of whale sharks, through their Whale Shark and Oceanic Research Project (see above for info).

West of Sandy Bay. ✆ **504/425-2015.** Fax 504/425-3211. www.deepblueutila.com. 10 units. 1-week dive packages from $1,200 (£600) in high season. Rate includes dives and 3 daily meals. MC, V. **Amenities:** Restaurant; bar; Internet in lobby; watersports equipment. *In room:* A/C, fan, fridge, Wi-Fi.

Utopia Village ★ Utopia Village is a type of accommodations that's somewhat new to Utila—a stylish, boutique resort. It was created by a group of seven friends from the U.S., Canada, and the U.K. who have combined their individual talents to create the first truly upscale boutique hotel on the island. Rooms are in one of two buildings and adorned with hardwood floors, contemporary furniture, and a decor that swings between Caribbean and Balinese. The overall feel of the beachfront property is hip and a tad New Age, but they don't go overboard and the result is more than pleasant. The resort was still very much a work in progress on my last visit, however—the pool was still in the works and they were still perfecting their staff. One downside, or upside, of staying here is that the resort is a few miles from town and you can only get back and forth by a 20-minute boat ride.

On the western end of the island. ✆ **504/3344-9387.** www.utopiautila.com. 19 units. Diving, fishing, and spa packages such as $1,399 (£700) for a 7-night dive package during the shoulder season. Minimum 4-night stay required. MC, V. **Amenities:** Bar; dive center; Internet in lobby; meditation/yoga garden; movie lounge; pool table; spa. *In room:* A/C, fan, fridge, Wi-Fi.

Moderate

Nightline Cabins (Jade Seahorse) ★★ Finds If Peter Pan came to Utila, this is where the boy wonder would stay. The Nightline Cabins at the Jade Seahorse are some of the most unique accommodations in all of Honduras or Central America for that matter. Every inch of the property is covered in some sort of whimsical decor or piece of art, mostly from flea market purchases in LA and markets in Central America. Each room is a wonderland of design, utilizing bright colors and mosaics and uncharacteristic layouts. All bathrooms have quirky details like curved glass walls and seashell soap trays. At night, the leafy trees and walkways that punctuate the property are lit up quite prettily, guiding guests to the on-site Jade Seahorse restaurant (see "Where to Dine" below) and Treetanic Bar (see "Utila Nightlife" below).

Calle Cola de Mico. ✆ **504/425-3270.** www.jadeseahorse.com. 6 units. $72 (£31) double. MC, V. **Amenities:** Restaurant; bar. *In room:* A/C, Wi-Fi.

Utila Lodge ★★ Sometimes just called the Lodge, this small hotel spread out on stilts over East Harbour has been a staple on the Utila dive scene for a few decades. The worn cabins, built entirely of island pine, are situated completely over the water and all have screened-in porches where you can relax in a hammock and watch the sun sink into the harbor. Accommodations are not luxurious by any means, but are clean and comfortable, and have all the modern amenities that the high-end resorts on the west end of the island do. At the end of their huge dock (in fact, the entire resort is a dock of sorts) there's a Jacuzzi, which is a perfect place to end the day after a few dives. Many that stay here come in conjunction with the associated Bay Islands College of Diving that sits next door. As a result, the lodge offers facilities to the entire dive community of Utila, including a 24-hour trauma center equipped with the island's only hyperbaric recompression chamber.

West of the Municipal pier. ✆ **504/425-3143.** www.utilalodge.com. 8 units. $149 (£75) double July–Jan; $179 (£90) double Feb–June. 7-night dive packages start at $899 (£450) per person, including 3 daily meals, dives and equipment, airport transfers, and a bottle of wine. MC, V. **Amenities:** Restaurant; bar; Jacuzzi; pool table; watersports equipment. *In room:* A/C, fan, cable TV, Wi-Fi.

Inexpensive

Mango Inn ★★ Value Kids In the budget-to-midrange category, the Mango Inn, tucked away on a busy corner on Cola de Mico road, is without question the best option on the island. There are a variety of rooms spread around the leafy property, many of them facing the large pool area. The deluxe cabins were built in 2003 and have high ceilings, huge tiled showers, a small sitting room, and porch, while the less expensive rooms all have similar amenities but are slightly smaller and older. Last but far from least, the huge Mango Cottage, next door to the hotel, comes with a full kitchen and family room, screened veranda, two bedrooms, and fresh modern decor. Dive packages with two daily dives begin at $609 (£305) and are available via the Utila dive center, which has the same owners.

Calle Cola de Mico. ✆ **504/425-3335.** Fax 504/425-3327. www.mango-inn.com. 16 units. $39 (£19) double June–Dec, $43 (£22) Jan–May; $83–$91 (£42–£46) deluxe cabins; $115–$126 (£58–£63) Mango Cottage. MC, V. **Amenities:** Restaurant; bar; pool. *In room:* A/C, fan, TV, fridge (in some).

Utila Lighthouse Utila Lighthouse is a traditional style two-level Bay Island stilted house set over the water, on a quiet corner of town near the bridge to Bando Beach. Built in 2006 by a local family, the hotel still feels untouched and the shiny wood floors and the flowered bed linens haven't seen much wear. The Lighthouse has a very simple, clean island style and the entire building is surrounded by a wraparound patio with ample seating and great views of the harbor and lagoon. There is little in the way of resort amenities, but all the dive centers, restaurants, and shops of East Harbour are within a short walk of the property.

About 10 min. to the right from the Municipal pier just before the bridge. ✆ **504/425-3164.** www.utilalighthouse.com. 12 units. $50 (£25) double per night; $295 (£148) per week. No credit cards. *In room:* A/C, fan, TV, fridge, kitchenette, microwave, Wi-Fi.

Where to Dine

Moderate

Café Mariposa INTERNATIONAL This eye-catching yellow restaurant is the first thing you'll see when you arrive at the Municipal pier. Because of its elevated position, sticking out onto the harbor, there's probably not a better view of the water than from here. The menu is pricier than most of the restaurants in town—which isn't saying much—but it's well worth the minor splurge for a decent meal. There's an eclectic menu of salads, grilled dishes, and seafood. Fridays are gourmet pizza night, while Saturday is all-you-can-eat tacos. Happy hour is from 5 to 7pm, just in time for sunset, and there's free Wi-Fi daily.

East of the Municipal pier. ✆ **504/425-2979.** Main courses L95–L190 ($5–$10/£2.50–£5). No credit cards. Wed–Sat 5–10pm; Sun 9am–noon.

Evelyn's BBQ ★ INTERNATIONAL From the slow, chatty waiters to the almost excessive Bob Marley and Jamaica memorabilia on the walls, this place exudes a definite island vibe. The barbecue dishes, mostly made on the streetside charcoal grill, like blackened mahimahi, grilled shrimp, and steaks, are well worth the price. When it rains, this creaky wooden building's streetside porch is the best place to watch the parade of tourists running through the mud, trying not to get wet.

West of the Municipal pier by Monkey Tail Rd. No phone. Main courses L95–L228 ($5–$12/£2.50–£6). MC, V. Daily noon–10pm.

La Piccola ITALIAN Sometimes called Kate's Italian restaurant, La Piccola is an Italian restaurant that's actually run by Italians, and without question, it is the most elegant restaurant offering on Utila. Dining rooms are set around a candlelight patio and a leafy garden. Impressively, this restaurant suits any budget. They offer cheaper dishes aimed at budget travelers—a must on this island—like spaghetti and pesto, along with less backpackerish dishes like filet mignon. There's even a decent wine list with bottles from South America and Europe.

West of the Municipal pier, on Calle Principal. ✆ **504/425-3746.** Main courses L95–L285 ($5–$15/£2.50–£7.50). No credit cards. Wed–Sun 5–10pm.

Inexpensive

Bundu Café and Bakery INTERNATIONAL/BREAKFAST Open for breakfast, lunch, and dinner, the Bundu is a top choice for hungry divers looking for a carboliscious meal. Crepes, banana pancakes, and omelets are top breakfast items, while half-pound burgers, chicken salad and avocado wraps, and pizzas make up the lunch and dinner menus. A big plus is the huge book exchange here, the largest on the island, as well as the free Wi-Fi and full bar.

East of the Municipal pier, on Calle Principal. ✆ **504/425-3557.** Main courses L57–L114 ($3–$6/£1.50–£3). No credit cards. Thurs–Mon 6am–10pm.

Driftwood Café ★★ INTERNATIONAL This restaurant reaching over the water in Sandy Bay claims home-style Texas cooking as their line of attack, but the menu is actually more eclectic and well rounded. Beer battered fish and chips, barbecue ribs and chicken, T-Bone steaks, and one hell of a fish stick are all on offer. Sundays mean smoked brisket, along with a daylong happy hour. To start the night off right, try their Chilled Monkey Balls, a potent shot made with homemade Kahlúa.

Calle Principal, east of Chepes Beach, Sandy Bay. ✆ **504/425-3366.** Main courses L76–L190 ($4–$10/£2–£5). No credit cards. Daily 8am–9:30pm.

Jade Seahorse ★ CARIBBEAN/INTERNATIONAL This restaurant, set on the ground floor of the Nightline Cabins (see above), looks like your grandfather's tool shed after eating peyote. In keeping with the whimsical theme of the hotel, the restaurant is cluttered with woodcarvings, mosaics, ship wreckage, and whatever else can be hung on a wood beam. Thankfully, the food is not as off-the-wall, but dishes like their West Indian vegetarian chili or any of the seafood entrees slathered in coconut, citrus, or other creative sauces *are* delicious.

Calle Cola de Mico. ✆ **504/425-3270.** www.jadeseahorse.com. Main courses L95–L171 ($5–$9/£2.50–£4.50). No credit cards. Daily 6–10pm.

Utila After Dark

Bar in the Bush On Wednesdays and Fridays, when everywhere else in town closes, the party moves up Cola de Mico road to this late night bar. It's the closest thing to a discothèque on Utila. On any given night, you'll see DJs spinning the latest reggaeton and dance tracks to an already toasted crowd. Just west of Calle Cola de Mico. No phone.

La Pirata This rooftop bar just beside the Municipal Pier is on the third floor, so you will have to hike up the stairs to get there. For a sunset drink or a nightcap after a big diving day, it's a good choice and worth the trip, though. Broussard Plaza. ✆ **504/425-3114.**

Treetanic Bar ★ This bar, fashioned after a shipwreck and set high in a cluster of mango trees at the Jade Seahorse (see above), easily makes for the most surreal setting in town. The nightly happy hour at 5 to 6pm has a loyal following of dive instructors and expats. Calle Cola de Mico. ✆ **504/425-3270.** www.jadeseahorse.com.

GUANAJA ★

It's a funny little place, Guanaja. In many ways, it's the forgotten Bay Island. Christopher Columbus landed here on July 30, 1502, during his fourth and final voyage to the Americas, but he didn't stay long. Over the next few centuries the island became a favorite pirate hide-out and was visited by everyone from Henry Morgan and Blackbeard to the Barbarossa brothers. Today, most locals base themselves around the small key Bonacca Cay, while the main island remains practically untouched. The islanders, an amalgamation of culture if there ever was one, jump back and forth between Caribbean English and Spanish, and everyone seems to be related in some way.

Time is told in hurricanes by the roughly 10,000 or so residents. In 1998, Hurricane Mitch's 483kmph (300-mph) winds blew over the island's once dominant pine trees and knocked many of the stilted houses right off their stilts. Especially hard hit was Mangrove Bight, on the eastern end of the island, which was virtually wiped off the map. A decade later, while nearby Roatán and Utila are experiencing rampant development, Guanaja has seen very little. Hotels and restaurants close on a frequent basis, but then are bought by someone else and reopened. It's a constant cycle. There is frequent talk of large luxury resorts opening here, but so far little action. Some development is occurring on the West

End, mostly because North Americans and wealthy Hondurans are building vacation homes there, but for now Guanaja remains one of the most unspoiled islands in the Caribbean.

Essentials

Getting There

BY PLANE Guanaja's airstrip sits in the middle of the main island, across from Bonacca, beside a mangrove lined canal. This is one of the most no-frills airports you will ever see, down to the baggage claim area, which is on the docks—bags are unloaded via rolling carts that come right from the plane. Once you have your luggage you will need a boat transfer to your hotel (which should be able to arrange a boat for you), or a water taxi to Bonacca (which wait for arriving planes).

Three airlines make the 30-minute trip on an almost daily basis between Guanaja and La Ceiba, with connections to Tegucigalpa and San Pedro Sula. **Isleña** (© **504/441-3190;** www.flyislena.com) has daily flights from La Ceiba at 9:50am and returning at 10:30am. **Aerolineas Sosa** (© **504/453-4359**) makes the trip daily at 10am and 4pm. **Atlantic Airlines** (© **504/453-4211;** www.atlanticairlinesint.com) has flights Monday through Friday from La Ceiba at 7am and a second flight on Wednesdays at 4pm. Passengers can buy tickets at any of the airline offices on Bonacca, right near the taxi dock. (You can't buy a ticket at Guanaja's airport.)

Charter flights are also available to/from Roatán and Utila, although these are quite expensive and you will need to arrange these well in advance. Keep in mind that all planes that land in Guanaja are small, averaging just 15 to 20 seats, so luggage restrictions often apply.

BY FERRY Unlike Roatán and Utila, Guanaja lacks regular ferry service from the mainland. In 2007 a very slow, no-frills ferry service on the *Bimini Breeze* began between Trujillo and Guanaja, running twice a week. It's used mainly by locals, and it leaves from Trujillo on Tuesdays and Sundays at 4pm and from Guanaja on Mondays and Fridays at 9am. You can buy tickets directly on the boat for L650 ($34/£17), or call © **504/987-0875** for reservations.

Occasionally you can ask around on the docks of La Ceiba, Trujillo, and ports along the Mosquito Coast for transport to Guanaja via freighters, although expect to wait around for up to a few weeks.

Orientation

Guanaja lies approximately 70km (43 miles) from the North Coast of Honduras and just 12km (7 miles) east of Roatán. It is the tallest of the Bay Islands and is almost completely covered by hills. The western tip is cut off from the rest of the island by a small canal, "the Cut," running just beside the airport. Bonacca town, the center of nearly all services and the most populated part of the island, isn't actually on the main island, but is off a small cay hanging just off the South coast. There are no roads on the island except one small stretch that runs for just a few kilometers between the settlements of Savannah and Mangrove Bights, on the eastern end of the island.

Getting Around

BY WATER TAXI Even though regular water taxi service prices are quite high, because of the cost of fuel here, water taxis are one of the best ways to get around the island. Standard prices are listed at the airport and on the ferry dock at Bonacca town. You can generally flag down a taxi while waiting on any dock.

BY FERRY There is one regular ferry service from Bonacca to Savannah Bight on the *Sava,* which runs back and forth several times a day. This is by far the cheapest way to get around the island at about L20 ($1/50p) each way.

Visitor Information

Most hotels will give tours of Bonacca, but you can just as easily visit on your own. Locals, including New York–raised **Hundo Sanders,** give informal tours of the town for a small fee. You'll have to ask around town for info, as Hundo doesn't work out of a formal tour center.

FAST FACTS Apart from the occasional shop that sells basic supplies, almost all facilities of any kind can be found in Bonacca town. The town's only cybercafe is on the main street turning left from the ferry dock, as is the bank **Banco Atlántida** (© **504/453-4262**), which exchanges currency and traveler's checks, and several small pharmacies. For phone service, make a right from the docks to the **Hondutel** office (© **504/455-1389**).

What to See & Do

Bonacca town ★★★, a short ride from the main island, is the most populous part of Guanaja and one of the most unique communities in the Bay Islands and the entire Caribbean. It's also known as Bonacca Cay and by locals as, simply, the Cay. Though the vibe here remains refreshingly laid-back, there's a desire to clean up and begin attracting more tourists to what many call jokingly the "Venice of Honduras." (In late 2007, Bonacca was completing one of the first municipal projects in years—adding plumbing.)

The population in Bonacca primarily comprises immigrants from the Cayman Islands that settled here in the 1830s, with a growing number of Latinos from the mainland and a scattering of expats. Apart from the many stilted pastel houses that branch out all across the water and line the canals, there are three small guesthouses, a couple of churches, and a handful of shops and tiny restaurants. The town is divided into small clusters with silly nicknames like firetown, honkytown, funkytown, and Vietnam. But perhaps because of its overall small size, Bonacca is an extremely tightly knit—and gossipy—place. If you're walking from one end to the other, someone on the other end will likely have already heard about you by the time you arrive.

Outdoor Activities

FISHING Bonefishing is a popular activity in Guanaja and can be done just offshore all around the island. A world record for largest bonefish was set here not long ago. Every hotel can offer a trip. Deep-Sea charters frequently troll for marlin, tuna, wahoo, mahi-mahi, mackerel, and barracuda. **Coral Bay** (© **866/266-7974;** www.coralbay.ca.) has bonefishing, fly-fishing, and deep-sea charters around the island for around $250 (£125) for a half-day charter.

HIKING Being the most mountainous of the Bay Islands does have its advantages. Several kilometers of hiking trails can be found crisscrossing the tiny island, mostly from the northern side. The **Big Gully Waterfall** is a short hike from Michael's Rock on the north side of the island, through fields of avocado, coco plums, and banana trees. The falls have a small pool at the bottom, but it isn't very deep unless there's a good rain the day before. From the falls you can continue to the highest point on the island at 408m (1,362 ft.). Between the settlements of Mangrove and Savannah Bights, on the eastern end of the island, there's a small pre-Columbian ruin, one of the very few on the Bay Islands. Signs pointing it out are nonexistent, though, so you'll have to simply keep a lookout for it or ask a local where it is.

Top Scuba Diving Sites in Guanaja

- **Mestizo Reef:** The life-size statue of Christopher Columbus at this site was erected in 2006 in honor of the 500-year anniversary of Columbus discovering Guanaja. There's also a statue of Lenca hero Lempira, Spanish cannons, vases, and 16th-century relics.
- **Vertigo:** The drastic drop-off—from 11m (35 ft.) to almost 48m (160 ft.)—on this section of the barrier wall is teeming with life. Black and white crinoids can be spotted here, along with deepwater gorgonians, barrel sponges, grouper, and trumpetfish.
- ***Don Enrique* Wreck:** This classic Guanaja dive centers on a sunken shrimp boat at about 27m (90 ft.) of water, although the mast stands upward to about 15m (50 ft.) below the surface. Lots of colorful fish circle the site and spotted eagle rays are frequently seen.
- ***Jado Trader* Wreck:** This is one of Guanaja's most visited sites and one of the most talked about wrecks in the Caribbean. The sunken freighter sits in 33m (110 ft.) of water on a sandy shelf beside a barrier wall. It's a deep descent, even for advanced divers, but the rewards—morays, grouper, yellowtail, and the occasional hammerhead shark—are well worth it.

SCUBA DIVING ★★ As with everywhere else in the Bay Islands, tourism in Guanaja is oriented toward diving. Every resort on Guanaja has dive masters and boats and offers packages for divers by the week and sometimes month. The reef here isn't affected by the island runoff like in Utila and Roatán, but some damage has occurred from pollution from Bonacca and Savannah Bight. Still, Guanaja's reef is in pretty good shape and sees very few divers compared with the other islands. Every resort on the island has its own dive outfit and offers accommodations and dive packages. Diving without a room is generally more expensive and costs about L760 to L950 ($40–$50/£20–£25). Both **Nautilus** (✆ **952/953-4124;** www.usdivetravel.com) and **Coral Bay** (✆ **866/266-7974;** www.coralbay.ca) offer dive packages and dives without accommodations.

SWIMMING If Caribbean crowds turn you off but you still want crystal-clear water and coral reefs, Guanaja is the place for you. Miles of sandy white beaches backdropped by untouched lush green hills are the island's specialty. The best beaches are at the northern side of the island near **Michael's Rock** or at the **West End** near the West Peak resort. Smaller strips of sand can be found elsewhere, including on the cayes that are sprinkled off the southern coast out from Savannah Bight.

Where to Stay

Expensive

Dunbar Villa and Nautilus Resort ★★ Few hotels can lay claim to a setting so dramatic—this chic white house literally sits on Dunbar's Rock, a picturesque location off Sandy Bay that also happens to have caused much controversy. (City officials sold this rock, a local landmark, to the hotel developer and were literally chased off Bonacca Cay as a result.) The property itself resembles something better suited for the island of Capri or a

Dalí painting than the Caribbean backwater. There are seven rooms with air-conditioning at Nautilus, which has the same owner and can be reached via free skiffs at any time, and four guest rooms at the Dunbar Villa. Apart from the small deck that leads to the dock and a small garden, you are mostly limited to the inside of the hotel (which boasts an honor bar and dining room) and a few balconies. Rooms at the Dunbar Villa are clean, but fairly sparse and basic with wood furniture, tile floors, and fans. Nautilus has similar rooms and amenities and has direct access to a wide stretch of white sandy beach.

Sandy Bay, Guanaja. ✆ **952/953-4124.** www.usdivetravel.com. 11 units. $1,197 (£598) per person, per week double at either hotel. Rates include dives and meals. MC, V. **Amenities:** Dining room; laundry service. *In room:* A/C (in some), no phone.

Moderate

Coral Bay Dive Resort ★ New owners recently remodeled this small collection of seaside-facing cabins on the hillside directly across from Bonacca Cay. It's set back on a corner of the main island between the airport and Sandy Bay, tucked away among stilted houses and empty green hills. The private stretch of beach here is matched by a small waterfall and trickling stream that runs throughout the property and provides an elegant soundtrack for sleep. The 12 large and airy wood cabins are clean and cozy, with satellite TVs, modern tiled bathrooms, and electric showers. There's a dive master on-site and they have a decent kayak to use if desired. Seven-night packages (running about $1,008/£504) include island tours, hikes, sunset cruise, diving, bone and deep-sea fishing, horseback riding, and a day trip to Bonacca.

South side of the main island. ✆ **866/266-7974.** www.coralbay.ca. 12 units. Cabins $160 (£80) a night for divers and $144 (£72) for nondivers during high season and holidays. Rates include 3 daily meals and airport transfers. MC, V. **Amenities:** Bar; dining room; pool. *In room:* A/C (in some), satellite TV, fridge.

The End of the World Resort This small resort sits on a 5km (3-mile) stretch of beach overlooking Michael's Rock on the northwestern side of the island. It's not far from the Island House and a short hike from Guanaja's best waterfall, but the property still manages to feel like it's at the ends of the earth. The five wood *cabañas*—all with private bathrooms, hot water, fans, island-style decor, and ocean views—are parked up on the hillside and surrounded by lush foliage. This is one of the up-and-coming dive hotels on the island and it has the only scuba certification program. A range of tours are available, from fishing, to kayaking, to bar-hopping excursions, to general island sightseeing. The two-story tropical beach bar/clubhouse attracts quite a few locals and is one of the better hangouts on Guanaja.

Michael's Rock, Guanaja. ✆ **504/402-3016.** Fax 305/768-0246. www.guanaja.com. 5 units. $120 (£60) double. 7-day dive packages available for $950 (£475) per person. No credit cards. **Amenities:** Restaurant; bar. *In room:* No phone.

Island House This small wooden hotel on the northwestern side of the island is owned and operated by Bo Bush, a local islander descended from English pirates, and his family. Bush has a wealth of knowledge about the island and even gives informal barhops and tours of Bonacca. The property has one main house and two small guesthouses, all set into the pine-covered hillside. Rooms have Spanish tile floors, simple wooden furniture, and balconies, as well as fans and satellite TV. There's good snorkeling and diving right off the beach and you're free to use the hotel's kayaks to paddle around nearby Michael's Rock. The dock bar is a good gathering place for the few locals that live on this side of the island.

Michael's Rock, Guanaja. ✆ **504/991-0913.** Fax 504/453-4146. www.bosislandhouse.com. 5 units. $70 (£35) double. Rates include 3 meals, welcome cocktail, and airport transfers. 7-day dive packages from $650 (£325). MC, V. **Amenities:** Restaurant; bar; high-speed Internet (free in lobby). *In room:* Satellite TV.

Inexpensive

Airport Hillton No, not that Hilton: You won't find Paris and Nikki here, but the Airport Hillton does have the sort of charm that you could only find in Guanaja. The small three-room hotel, constructed in classic Bay Island style, sits in the isolated bay fronting the island's airport. The rooms aren't posh by any means, but have private bathrooms, hot water, fans, and satellite TV. It's run by American Captain Al, who has lived on the islands for decades, and his son Andy. The Hillton also has an oceanfront bar and restaurant, and Captain Al operates the Thirst and Last Stop Bar/snack stand at the airport. If you need to charter a boat he can help you out as well.

By the Guanaja Airport. ✆ **504/453-4469.** 3 units. $50 (£25) double. No credit cards. **Amenities:** Restaurant; bar. *In room:* Satellite TV, no phone.

Hotel Miller There are three small guesthouses on Guanaja and other informal rooms for rent, but Hotel Miller is by far the best and the only one that actually attempts to appear like a working hotel. The two-story house sits smack-dab in the middle of Bonacca town, a few minutes from the taxi dock. For the Bay Islands, the place is far from idyllic—it resembles Grandma's house with its lace curtains and collection of beat-up Victorian furniture, rooms are dingy and worn, there's no ocean view, and not much light comes in from the small windows. Still, the place is clean and the price is the best you will find anywhere in Guanaja. For those on extremely tight budgets, ask about the even cheaper rooms without TV or air-conditioning.

Bonacca town, Guanaja. ✆ **504/453-4527.** Fax 504/453-4202. 29 units. $32 double (£16). No credit cards. **Amenities:** Dining room; Internet; laundry service. *In room:* A/C (in some), satellite TV, no phone.

Where to Dine

Crazy Parrot Bar CONTINENTAL Although it's sometimes closed for long stretches of time, this great bar, sitting on a small peninsula in Sandy Bay, is one of the best island-style bars and restaurants in Guanaja. It boasts a classic Floridian style with mosaic tiles, a small sand football pitch, pool, foosball table, and art from a local artist Ian Fisher. Food is standard island fare like fresh fish, fried chicken, lobster fritters, fish soup, jerked chicken, and barbecue. There's karaoke on most nights.

Sandy Bay, Guanaja. No phone. Main courses L115–L350 ($6–$18/£3–£9). No credit cards. Tues–Sun noon–10pm (hours vary).

Graham's Place ★ SEAFOOD On a small cay a short taxi ride away from Bonacca or Savannah Bight, Graham's Place is by far the most attractive restaurant in Guanaja, primarily because of its sweeping views of the main island, and it's also a major party location. The menu at the thatched-roof, open-air restaurant is defined by whatever's fresh in the cooler, usually fish that was caught that day. It also features sandwiches, chicken, and meat dishes, along with a long list of tropical drinks and beers. The dock area where the restaurant resides functions as an aquarium of sorts, since there's a small pen keeping the tropical fish, stingrays, and sea turtles—bought so they wouldn't be eaten by the locals—from swimming away. The owner, Graham, who hails from the Cayman Islands, also has a few apartments for rent in the area.

Graham's Cay, Guanaja. ✆ **305/407-1568.** www.grahamsplacehonduras.com. Main courses L135–L300 ($7–$15/£3.50–£7.50). No credit cards. Daily 7am–10pm.

Mexi Treats MEXICAN The only Mexican or remotely Latin place on Guanaja is this favorite of hungry divers, who often stop here to refuel with lunch, and other tourists staying on the island. It's the only true fast-food joint in the area, with a menu of *chilaquiles,* *baleadas,* nachos, burritos, and burgers. It's a bit of a dive, but for a cheap, hearty meal (and for fast food that doesn't seem mass produced), it's your best choice.

Bonacca. ✆ **504/453-4170.** Main courses L55–L110 ($3–$6/£1.50–£3). No credit cards. Mon–Fri 8am–1:30pm and 6–9:30pm; Sat–Sun 6am–10pm.

11 LA MOSQUITIA

La Mosquitia is the largest tract of virgin tropical rainforest in Central America and the Northern Hemisphere; it's a mini-Amazon of sorts. While it covers the entire northeastern part of the country, the region is only sparsely populated with villages of indigenous groups like the Pech, Tawahka, Garífuna, and Miskitos, as well as mainland Mestizos. The region has five distinct natural zones: the Río Plátano Biosphere Reserve, the Tawahka Anthropological Reserve, the Patuca National Park, the Cruta Caratasca Wildlife Refuge, and the Rus Rus Biological Reserve. Many of the zones are practically untouched and packed with rare wildlife of every imaginable sort. Yet there is not a luxury ecolodge in sight. Apart from a few ingenious tour companies, the region is almost unexplored and just waiting for a tourist boom. If you are looking for an adventure or a place well off the beaten path, you've got it.

This region was inhabited as far back as 1000 B.C. by Chibcha-speaking Indians who migrated here from South America, which over time divided into separate indigenous groups such as the Pechs and Tawahka. Christopher Columbus, the first European to visit, stopped briefly on his fourth voyage in 1502. Spanish missionaries were the first to explore the region, though it took them nearly a century of rebellion from the tribes to establish any sort of permanent settlement. (It didn't help that pirates frequently raided Spanish ships laden with riches from South America, which deterred further settlements.) Government control over the region has been loose at best; it wasn't until the 1950s that any sort of formal governance began to take shape here, but at times lawlessness still reigns supreme, simply because the region is too big and sparse to properly control.

ESSENTIALS

Getting There

BY PLANE All commercial flights to La Mosquitia originate in La Ceiba. **Aerolineas Sosa** (✆ **504/445-1154**) flies to Brus Laguna three times per week, leaving at 10am and returning at 11am. Sosa also flies to Puerto Lempira from Monday to Friday at 8am, returning at 11am. Flights are often canceled due to weather and lack of passengers. **Sami Airlines** (✆ **504/442-2565** in La Ceiba, or 433-8031 in Brus Laguna) occasionally flies from La Ceiba to Brus Laguna or Belen. The runway at Palacios, which was once the main access point in the region, is currently closed due to lack of repair. From each airstrip you should have no problem walking to town.

BY BOAT Along the North Coast of Honduras, irregular boat service links the coast of La Mosquitia to the rest of the country. The docks at **Puerto Castilla** are the best place to get word of the next boat, which generally leave at least once per week. Don't expect a luxury cruise, though; these are cargo ships with absolutely no facilities for travelers. You are pretty much stuck to sleeping on the deck in the open air and providing your own food.

BY BUS It is possible to make it to La Mosquitia by bus, although if your plan is to go during the rainy season (Oct–Jan) don't expect this to work. From **Tocoa,** just south of Trujillo, you can catch a pickup truck, or *paila,* to Batalla leaving from the Municipal

Market daily between 7 and 11am. The ride is 4 to 5 hours and costs L400 ($21/£11). In Batalla, there will be boats waiting to take you the additional 1- to 2-hour journey to Palacios, Raista, and Belen for roughly L150 ($8/£4).

Getting Around

BY BOAT Traveling independently in La Mosquitia isn't cheap or easy—it's much easier to get around here with a tour operator. Though options are still extremely limited and you should always expect to wait around a few days here and there, your best method of independent transport is by water. Along the coast you can almost always find a boat to take you from one community to the next. Often the locals expect tourists to hire a local boatman for a private boat and will stay mum on information on when the next boat leaves. Since regular schedules aren't posted, you just have to cross your fingers and hope you speak to the right person. There is direct boat service, priced per boat, between most major destinations, as follows: Palacios to Raista/Belen (L800/$42/£21; 1½ hr.), Raista/Belen (L3,000/$158/£79; 5 hr.), Raista/Belen (L1,500/$79/£39, 2 hr.), and Brus Laguna to Las Marias (L3,500/$184/£92; 6 hr.). If your Spanish is good, you can also ask around at the docks for colectivo boats, which are considerably cheaper.

BY PLANE **Sami Airlines** (✆ **504/442-2565** in La Ceiba, or 433-8031 in Brus Laguna) can get you from one town to the next via four-person planes. They have offices in Ahuas, Palacios, Belen, Brus Laguna, and Puerto Lempira.

Tour Operators

If you have a limited amount of time or a set schedule for traveling in La Mosquitia, a trip with a tour operator is your only choice. Most have several tours available that will combine multiday rafting trips down the Río Plátano or Río Patuca, visits to indigenous villages, wildlife-watching, hiking, and stays at private campgrounds and lodges. They make use of planes and have arrangements with local transportation organizations to make sure your trip moves smoothly. Trips can last anywhere from 3 days to several weeks. Some operators to try include:

- **La Ruta Moskitia** ★★ (✆ **504/443-1276;** www.larutamoskitia.com), a 100% community-owned and -operated tourism initiative, offers both day trips from Raista, Belen, and Brus Laguna, as well as multiday tours through the region that have been applauded by the international media. Both land- and air-based tours are available. They list upcoming tours that you can join on their website (thus reducing the price by being in a group) and offer tips to help plan an independent adventure.
- **La Mosquitia EcoAdventures** ★ (✆ **504/440-2124;** www.lamoskitiaecoaventuras.com) has 8- to 12-day rafting expeditions on the Tawahka Asangni Biosphere Reserve and custom bird-watching tours throughout La Mosquitia.
- **Omega Tours** (✆ **504/440-0334;** www.omegatours.info) has a wide variety of tours from La Ceiba to La Mosquitia, including 8- to 12-day trips on the Río Patuca, a 13-day trip on the Río Plátano, and many shorter trips to see Petroglyphs and isolated villages.

WHAT TO SEE & DO

Reserva de la Biosfera del Río Plátano ★★★

This is simply one of the most astounding natural reserves in the entire world. The Río Plátano Biosphere Reserve, named a UNESCO World Heritage Site in 1980, is home to more than 525,000 hectares (1.3 million acres) of wetlands, beaches, pine savannas, tropical forests, and rivers. Here indigenous communities of the Pech and Miskito live much the way they have for hundreds of years. The reserve is home to some of the highest levels of biodiversity anywhere in the world, and nearly 400 species of birds have been recorded here, including great green and scarlet macaws, harpy eagles, jabirus, toucans, kingfishers, the aplomado falcon, and numerous migratory species. The lagoons and rivers are home to manatees, southern river otters, caimans, and several rare species of sea turtles. On land, you'll find Baird's tapirs, jaguars, giant anteaters, spider monkeys, white-tailed deer, and white-lipped peccaries, among others. While extensive tourism infrastructure is lacking here and there isn't even a visitor center or admission fee, community-based ecotourism programs are steadily growing.

It's easiest to visit the reserve via guided tour. The best time to visit is during the dry season, which runs from February to May and from August to November.

Reserva de la Biosfera del Tawahka Asangni ★★

This isolated reserve, created in 1999, is one of the last remaining homes of the highly threatened Tawahka indigenous group, who number under 1,000 and live in only a handful of communities here. The reserve sits beside the border with Nicaragua, Olancho, and the Río Plátano Biosphere Reserve. Access is limited to flights from Brus Laguna to the villages of Wampusirpi and Ahuas or the 7- or 10-day rafting expeditions down the Río Patuca from Juticalpa.

La Mosquitia Villages

While the tourist infrastructure is slowly improving in La Mosquitia, it is still in many cases practically nonexistent. Phones are rare, which makes hotel reservations almost impossible. Transportation between each village, while the distances are relatively short, can take a day of waiting until a boat or plane fills up.

Most of La Mosquitia's towns are within the confines of the Río Plátano Biosphere Reserve or a short distance from it, so getting around here by tour (see "Tour Operators" above for info) is much easier than doing self-guided tours. Most visitors, unless on a multiday tour, will base themselves in Las Marías, Raista, Belén, or Brus Laguna and take day tours from there. Apart from Puerto Lempira, which is on the far corner of La Mosquitia and best reached by plane, all towns are within a 30-minute to 6-hour boat ride from one another. When entering the region by land, nearly all visitors make the trip from west to east, so the villages below are listed in that order.

Palacios

While it no longer has a landing strip, the Mosquitia town of Palacios is often a stop for many who choose to travel overland in the region. The town can sometimes be unsafe, though. Drug runners coming from South America often hang out here, and the city is becoming increasingly known for lawlessness. There are a few basic hotels such as **La Moskitia** (**© 504/978-7397**), with doubles for L330 ($18/£9), and several basic *comedores* here.

Plaplaya

This Garífuna village at the western edge of the Laguna de Ibans and the Caribbean is best known for creating the **Sea Turtle Conservation Project,** which protects the green, loggerhead, and leatherback turtles that nest on the nearby beaches every year. Tours for the beaches depart during the evenings from February to September to help spot egg-laying turtles and nests. The Sea Turtle project is run by locals with the help of NGO Rare Conservation (www.rareconservation.org) and the nonprofit tour operator La Ruta

Moskitia (www.larutamoskitia.com). There are just a few very basic accommodations in family homes in Plaplaya, and no real tourist hotels.

Raista-Belén ★★

These two connected Miskito towns sit on a thin strip of land between the Laguna de Ibas and the Caribbean. There are numerous tours you can take from here, and there are a few small ecolodges, such as the **Pawanka Beach Cabins** (no phone; L190/$10/£5 per person) and **Raista Ecolodge** (no phone; L190/$10/£5 per person). Neither has phones, so your only hope is to turn up with your fingers crossed and hope they have a room. On the extremely rare occasion that these hotels are booked, there are a number of other small guesthouses or rooms in family homes that you can certainly get a room in.

From either of these towns, you can hire boatmen to take you to explore the nearby wildlife-infested creeks of Parú, Ilbila, and Banaka, where there are good opportunities to spot birds and monkeys.

Las Marías ★

Las Marías is a Pech community on the Río Plátano in the highlands of the rainforest and the community farthest into the Biosphere Reserve from the coast. It's reached by motor boat from Palacios and Brus Laguna. The village has organized a small ecotourism operation with a variety of tours. Here you can organize a hike (3 days) to Pico Dama, the largest mountain in the region, or head 5 hours on a dugout canoe *(pipante),* to the Walpaulbansirpe petroglyphs.

Brus Laguna

With telephone service and electricity daily from 5 to 10pm, Brus Laguna is one of the more progressive towns in La Mosquitia. For many visitors, the town is their entry point and base in the region. From here you can reach Raista-Belen, Palacios, Las Marias, and the Río Plátano Biosphere Reserve by regular boat service. There are several small hotels in town, the best being **Hotel La Estancia** (✆ **504/433-8043**), with doubles for L300 ($16/£8).

Fishing for snook, tarpon, and grouper is so good in the lagoon here that fishermen from around the world pay visits. Tours can also be arranged in town to visit the English fort on Cannon Island, the Great Pine Savannah, the Yamari Savannah Cabanas, and the Río Plátano Biosphere Reserve.

Puerto Lempira

While from a tourism perspective little is going on in Puerto Lempira, which is on the far eastern border near Nicaragua, it does have the best facilities in the region. Among its good hotels is **Hotel Yu Baiwan** (Calle Principal, a half-block from the pier; ✆ **504/898-7653**), which has doubles for L450 ($24/£12). There are also restaurants, Internet access, 24-hour electricity, and the only bank in La Moskitia (though it doesn't have an ATM). The capital of the Gracias a Dios department sits on the Laguna de Catarasca, the largest lagoon on the coast, and is connected by road to Nicaragua.

8

Nicaragua

by Charlie O'Malley

The view from your hammock can vary wildly in Nicaragua. It may be of a lush jungle island, a turquoise Caribbean shore, a green sandy lagoon with a volcano in the background, or a beautiful colonial archway with intricate Spanish tiles. Whatever it is, you're guaranteed one constant: peace and tranquillity in what is Central America's largest and safest country. It is hard to believe that Nicaragua's recent history has been one of war, rebellion, earthquakes, volcanic eruptions, and devastating hurricanes. This country is so fully on the mend and experiencing an energetic and colorful renaissance, that it couldn't be more primed to be discovered by travelers.

This land of poetry and poverty, murals and martyrs, is located on the lower elbow joint of the Central American isthmus. Honduras borders it to the north and Costa Rica to the south. Its landscape varies greatly from the volcanic lowlands along the Pacific to the impenetrable swampland of its Caribbean coast, with misty mountain highlands in between. It is dominated by two large lakes that are in turn dominated by volcanic peaks towering above the waterline. It is a land of coffee, tobacco, and banana plantations. Despite being the second-poorest nation in the Western Hemisphere, its people are proud, educated, and passionate about literature and art. It is the birthplace of Rubén Darío—a giant of Spanish poetry—and the location of a vibrant art scene based around the primitive paintings of the Solentiname Archipelago.

If you're after fun and adventure, you can surf the rum-and-sunshine town of San Juan del Sur or hike the jungle paradise of Miraflor nature reserve; or choose between visiting the misty mountain retreats of the Northern Highlands versus the white, deserted beaches of the Caribbean Corn Islands. But people are not just coming here to kick back but also to give back. The country has a profusion of volunteering opportunities, from helping street kids in Granada to rehabilitating wildlife on Ometepe Island. Wherever and however you decide to visit the country, know that Nicaragua's fascinating history and character will surely make an impression on you—as will those glorious views from your hammock.

1 THE REGIONS IN BRIEF

The vast majority of Nicaraguans live and work in the **Pacific Lowlands** on the west coast of the country, and this is where you will undoubtedly be spending much of your time. In this part of the country, lofty volcanoes tower along hot dusty plains that run from the northern highlands and around two major lakes as far as the Pacific coastline and Costa Rica. At its center is the strange, elusive capital city of **Managua** on the shore of Lago Xolotlán, also known as Lago de Managua. Technically, the Northwest, Granada, and Masaya, and the Southwest all fall within this larger region, but I've divided up this chapter according to these three smaller subregions.

THE NORTHWEST The university city of **León** oozes history with its countless churches and museums and the largest cathedral in Central America. Here you can surf dark Pacific shores or darker volcanic slopes. The fertile volcanic soil and two distinct seasons here means this low-lying area is the country's most agriculturally productive region, though much of it is also dry jungle bush.

GRANADA & MASAYA León's colonial rival **Granada** is on the great, dominating lake of Cocibolca, also known as Lago de Nicaragua. The old merchant city is an architectural marvel and easily the most beautiful spot in Nicaragua. It is also close to many of Nicaragua's best attractions, such as the handicraft Mecca **Masaya** and the satellite artisan villages known as **Pueblos Blancas. Volcán Masaya** is the most accessible and frightening field of craters and red-hot lava, while **Volcán Mombacho** boasts great hiking. The huge crater lake **Laguna de Apoyo** is a refreshing dip and peaceful shore-side retreat.

THE SOUTHWEST Nicaragua's southwestern shore is littered with numerous beach towns, the most interesting of which is **San Juan del Sur,** close to the Costa Rican border. This colorful clapboard village lies amid a string of beautiful beaches offering great surfing, fishing, and lounging. To the south is **Reserva La Flor,** the scene of spectacular nighttime turtle hatching.

LAGO DE NICARAGUA The wide, expansive Lago de Nicaragua is surrounded by volcanic peaks and is home to hundreds of islands, including the cone-shaped twin peaks of **Isla de Ometepe,** a serene jungle island with excellent trekking, horse riding, and beaches. Farther south is the rainbow-colored artists' colony **Archipelago de Solentiname.** Lake Nicaragua is also the only freshwater lake to hold shark. The Río San Juan connects it to the Caribbean, and the lake's eastern shore is tantalizingly close to the Pacific coast. The truly adventurous can take the pirate route from here down the jungle river of San Juan to the old Spanish fort of **El Castillo.**

THE CARIBBEAN The Caribbean coast and its huge interior cover half of Nicaragua, and this region comprises the widest lowland plain in Central America. It is also the most sparsely populated part of Nicaragua and in many ways seems like a different country. It's far from hospitable, especially to the north. Swampy, tropical rainforest is punctuated by lagoons, deltas, and muddy river mouths. Though it may not be as hot as the western side of the country, it is very wet and humid.

Twenty-three rivers run from the central highlands as far as the Atlantic coast. The Río Coco in the north is the longest and forms part of the Honduran border. The Río San Juan to the south forms the boundary with Costa Rica and makes for an epic journey from **Lago Nicaragua.** The people are different, too, a rattle bag of indigenous tribes (predominantly Miskito) mixed with Afro-Caribbeans and descendants of English buccaneers. They speak both Spanish and patois English and predominantly live off fishing, along with a little lumbering and tourism.

The most important towns are the rusty ports of **Bluefields** and **Puertas Cabezas.** The former is becoming important from a tourism point of view. The gritty town of Bluefields can only be reached by river or air but is the gateway to the beautiful **Pearl Lagoon** and the sandy, desert islands of the **Pearl Cays.** It is also the jumping-off point to reach two Nicaraguan jewels—the **Corn Islands,** 80km (50 miles) off the coast and surrounded by perfect white beaches and coral reef amid turquoise waters.

THE NORTH-CENTRAL REGION North of Lago Xolotlan (Lago Managua), the ground gradually rises into the steep mountain highlands of Northern Nicaragua, pushing as far as the country's highest mountain, the 2,438m-high (7,996-ft.) **Pico Mogotón**

at the Honduran border. Here the temperature is cooler and the landscape picturesque. River valleys run through pine-covered hills and cloud forests of hardwood. Waterfalls, orchids, and numerous birds vie for your attention in important nature reserves such as **Miraflor.** This region is also very fertile in parts and agriculturally important, producing Nicaragua's black gold, coffee, as well as tobacco and livestock. Apanás Dam here is an important source of electricity for the entire country.

In the far north, you'll find numerous small towns in a rugged interior—the two most important are **Estelí** and **Matagalpa.** This is cowboy country, home to a tough and resilient people who can be hospitable and aloof at the same time, but are always fascinating. It is one of the least visited parts of the country but offers excellent trekking and nature watching, as well as lodgings in lush mountain retreats and fair-trade coffee plantations.

2 THE BEST OF NICARAGUA IN 1 WEEK

It might appear small, but Nicaragua has lots to see and do. It is impossible to visit everywhere in the country in 1 week, especially when you experience the country's awful bumpy roads and decrepit public transport system. And you probably won't want to leave most towns after just a bit of time spent there—with the possible exception of Managua. Below is a sweeping tour of the country that leaves out some amazing places, such as León and the Northern Highlands. You might very well want to expand your trip by another week so as to see these parts of the country. In order to do this itinerary, you'll also have to get around on private transport shuttles or taxis. If you are on a tight budget and plan on using public transport, you'll need to allot more time for getting around the country.

Days ❶ & ❷: Arrive in Managua & Head to Granada ★★★

After flying into Managua, don't hang around the capital too long. It has its hidden charms, but more beautiful places beckon, like the radiant colonial city of **Granada,** 2 hours south. Head there immediately, and settle into the **Hotel Plaza Colon** ★★★ (p. 479) to relax and perhaps sip a rum on the rocks from the gigantic balcony overlooking the colorful plaza. The next morning, catch a horse and carriage ride through the city's enchanting cobbled streets and down to the lake shore, where you can take a short boat tour of **Las Isletas** archipelago (see p. 483 for tips on how to see the islands in a less touristy manner).

Days ❸ & ❹: Tour Isla de Ometepe ★★ & Arrive in San Juan del Sur ★

Arrange a tour company to pick you up at your hotel and take you to the small town of **San Jorge,** where you can catch a boat across to the twin peak jungle island of **Ometepe.** You won't have time to climb its volcanic peaks, but a 4WD will take you on a coastal tour of this island of howler monkeys, pre-Columbian carved stones, and mud-bathing farm animals.

Arrive back in San Jorge in the early evening to be transferred to the beach town of **San Juan del Sur.** Stay at the lovely villa known as **La Posada Azul** ★★ (p. 498) and eat in the garden of **El Colibri** ★★ (p. 500). The following day, catch a water taxi up the coast to some beautiful, secluded beaches or, depending on the time of year, take a night excursion to watch the spectacular turtle hatching in **Playa La Flor** ★ (p. 497).

Days ❺ & ❻: The Corn Islands ★★

Catch a taxi back to Managua for the midday flight to these Caribbean treasure islands. Soak up the sunset on bleach-white **Picnic Beach** ★★★ before retiring to a rustic restaurant on stilts amid turquoise waters called **Anastasia's on the Sea** ★ (p. 522). Stay at the very

comfortable **Casa Canada** ★★ (p. 520) and enjoy its gorgeous pool before snorkeling the pink coral beach of **Sally Peaches** (p. 519).

Day 7: Managua

Head back to Managua, and give the capital a second look if you have time to do so before your flight. Take a tour of its ghost-downtown, the **Zona Monumental.** Visit the tomb of poet Rubén Darío and peer into the majestic ruins of the city's old cathedral. Have time for dinner? Enjoy deep-fried shrimp at the fondue restaurant **Urbahn** ★ (p. 455) and shop for some last-minute gifts of rum and cigars in the shopping mall below.

3 PLANNING YOUR TRIP TO NICARAGUA

VISITOR INFORMATION

The **Instituto Nicaraguense de Turismo,** or INTUR, has offices in all the country's main cities, though some are better than others and only a few have English-speaking staff. The ministry's two websites **www.intur.gob.ni** and **www.visitanicaragua.com** are written entirely in Spanish, with very limited information, but they boast some gorgeous images. INTUR's main office is in the Hotel Crowne Plaza in Managua (1c Sur; ✆ **505/254-5191**). They also have an office across the road, 1 block west of the Plaza Inter Mall (✆ **505/222-6610**). In both you will find a pretty good selection of maps and guides.

For other travel-related info, try the following websites:

- **www.nicaragua.com**: This is a slick, well-presented site with very good English-language articles and overviews of all the main regions. It is, however, limited regarding hotel information, since it primarily functions as a booking service.
- **www.vianica.com**: This is an excellent website with information on the entire country—it goes further than most travel sites by giving out actual phone numbers and websites of hotels and restaurants.
- **www.nicaliving.com**: Nicaliving is a website by and about expats living in Nicaragua. Though the information can be a little hit-and-miss, it's worth checking out for its blogs, to see what the issues of the day are.
- **www.marena.gob.ni**: This is a government website listing all the national parks and protected areas within the country. It is entirely in Spanish.

Tour Operators

You might also contact the below travel agencies that specialize in trips to Nicaragua:

- **Tours Nicaragua ★★**, El Sol #110, Colonial Los Robles, Managua (✆ **505/252-4035;** www.toursnicaragua.com), specializes in private tours with highly qualified guides. Itineraries are custom-designed and can include nature trips to the Solentiname Archipelago, adventure tours on Ometepe Island, or beach holidays on the Pacific coast.
- **Nicaragua Adventures ★**, on the corner beside the Spanish Consulate, Granada (✆ **505/883-7161;** www.nica-adventures.com), run 1-day to 5-day package tours, including one called "3 Seas" that whisks you from the Caribbean Corn Islands to Lago de Nicaragua to the Pacific coast.
- **Vapues Tours,** on the northern side of Iglesia El Laborio, León (✆ **505/606-2276;** www.vapues.com), is a more conventional tour company that organizes a variety of group excursions, including day tours to Volcán Mombacho and city tours of León and Managua.
- **Explore Nicaragua Tours,** 30m (98 ft.) west of Iglesia Las Palmas, Managua (✆ **505/250-1534;** www.explorenicaraguatours.com.ni.com), is a clearinghouse for tours all over the country, including coffee farms in Matagalapa. They also arrange flights, car rentals, and hotel reservations.

ENTRY REQUIREMENTS

Citizens of the United States, Canada, Australia and New Zealand, and the European Union require just a passport to enter Nicaragua and may stay for up to 90 days. The passport must be valid for at least 6 months after the date of entry. Visas can be extended at the Office of Immigration in Managua for $12 (£6) a month. The office, called the **Dirección General de Migración y Extranjería** (✆ **505/244-3989**), is located 2½ blocks north of the Tenderi stoplights.

Nicaragua is part of a 2006 border control agreement with Honduras, Guatemala, and El Salvador, allowing travel between the four countries under one tourist card. The number of days of your tourist card is determined at the first of the four countries entered.

When leaving Nicaragua, you must pay a C665 ($35/£18) airport tax, which must be paid in cash in either U.S. dollars or Nicaraguan córdobas. (This is sometimes included in the price of your airline ticket.) There is also a tourist entry fee of C95 ($5/£2.50) that must be paid upon arrival into the country.

Nicaraguan Embassy-Consulate Locations

For countries not listed below, consult www.ni.embassyinformation.com.

In the U.S. and Canada: 1627 New Hampshire Ave., NW, Washington, DC 20009 (✆ **202/939-6531;** fax 202/939-6532).

In the U.K.: 36 Upper Brooke St., London W1Y 1PE (✆ **171 409 2593;** fax 171 409 2536; www.nicaragua.embassyhomepage.com).

In New Zealand: 50 Clonbern Rd., Remuera (✆ **64/9/373-7599;** fax 64/9/373-7646; c.tremewan@auckland.ac.nz).

CUSTOMS

There is a C133 ($7/£3.50) entrance fee for all tourists. In theory, you may also be asked for an onward ticket and proof of sufficient funds, but this rarely happens. There is a tax on all electronic, alcohol and other luxury goods that are not obviously personal objects (things still in their box, for example).

MONEY

The official Nicaraguan currency is the **córdoba** (it is sometimes referred to as a peso). It is made up of 100 **centavos.** Money is denominated in notes of 10, 20, 50, 100, and 500 córdobas. Coins are made of 1 and 5 córdobas and 50 centavos. At press time, the exchange rate was 19 córdobas to the American dollar and 38 to the British pound. It's often difficult to find change for 100-córdoba notes and next to impossible to change the princely sum that is a 500-córdoba note (a bank is your best bet for doing so).

Telephone Dialing Info at a Glance

The country code for Nicaragua is 505, which you use only when dialing from outside the country. Telephone numbers include this prefix because most businesses' published phone numbers include the prefix.

- **To place a call from your home country to Nicaragua:** Dial the international access code (011 in the U.S., 0011 in Australia, 0170 in New Zealand, 00 in the U.K.) plus the country code (505), the city or region's area code, and the local number.
- **To make long-distance calls within Nicaragua:** Dial a 0 before the seven-digit number.
- **To place an international call from Nicaragua:** Add 00 before the country code.
- Dial ✆ **113** for **directory assistance.** Dial ✆ **110** for **long-distance assistance.** Dial ✆ **116** to make **collect calls** to the U.S., U.K., Australia, and Canada. Dial ✆ **118** for **police** help, dial ✆ **115 06 120** to report a fire, and ✆ **128** for the Red Cross.

Córdobas are virtually useless outside Nicaragua and should be changed before you leave. Prices in this chapter are quoted in córdobas with the symbol C, American dollars with the symbol $, and the British pound with the symbol £. Because of high inflation and volatile exchange rates, prices quoted here may vary greatly in accuracy.

Sales tax in Nicaragua is known as IGV (Impuesto General de Valor) and allows for an extra charge of 15% on all goods. Always check menus and price lists to see if it's included in the quoted price.

CURRENCY EXCHANGE U.S. dollars are widely accepted in Nicaragua and can be used to pay taxis, hotels, restaurants, and stores. Do keep some córdobas on hand because you might run into spots where you'll need them, however. You can convert your currency in hotels, at *casas de cambio* (money-exchange houses), at some banks, and at Managua International Airport. It is difficult to change traveler's checks outside the capital; see p. 445 for locations of currency exchange houses there.

ATMS ATMs are becoming increasingly available, even in far-flung places like the Corn Islands. There are plenty in the main cities, such as Managua, Granada, León, and Rivas (try gas stations and shopping malls). Don't bet on finding any off the beaten path. Typically, ATMs are connected to **Cirrus** (✆ **800/424-7787**) or **PLUS** (✆ **800/843-7587**) networks. Many ATMs also accept Visa and MasterCard.

CREDIT CARDS If you choose to use plastic, Visa, American Express, MasterCard, and Diners Club are the commonly accepted cards. Credit cards are accepted at most hotels and restaurants except the very cheapest ones. You cannot use credit cards in taxis or at most attractions (museums, parks, and so on).

WHEN TO GO

PEAK SEASON The tourist season runs from December to April, culminating in Easter celebrations (early Apr).

CLIMATE Like most of Central America, Nicaragua's climate is tropical and the year is split between summer (Dec–Apr) and winter (May–Nov), though the temperature is consistent throughout the year, ranging from 55°F (12°C) to 70°F (28°C). The main seasonal difference involves rainfall; the rainy season falls between May and October, with hurricanes buffeting the coast in September and October. Generally speaking, the Caribbean side of the country receives a lot more rainfall than the Pacific side. Altitude is also a factor with the weather—the highlands have a more springlike climate compared to the hotter and more humid lowlands and coastal areas.

PUBLIC HOLIDAYS Public holidays include New Year's Day (Jan 1); Easter Week (Thurs, Fri, Sat before Easter Sunday), Labor Day (May 1), and Christmas Day (Dec 25). Liberation Day (July 19) celebrates victory over the Somoza regime, while the Battle of San Jacinto (Sept 14) rejoices the ending of William Walker's tyranny in 1856. Independence Day (Sept 15) is followed by Día de los Muertos (Nov 2), or the Day of the Dead, which is the Latin American version of All Souls' Day. Feast of the Immaculate Conception (Dec 8) is also known as La Purisma.

HEALTH CONCERNS

Contaminated water and food, as well as mosquitoes, are the usual sources of discomfort in Nicaragua. Always be careful about what you eat and insist on bottled water. As for those pesky mosquitoes, a good anti-repellent with DEET should be enough to see off bugs that bear unwanted gifts such as dengue fever and malaria. Go to www.cdc.gov for

Spas & Wellness Centers in Nicaragua

Paticia Cuadra, a half-block west of Iglesia San Juan, Masaya (✆ **505/278-3224**), offers acupuncture and reflexology treatment and specializes in Reiki Tibetan chakra for less than C190 ($10/£5) an hour. **Luna Bella Day Spa,** 1 block south and half a block east of El Colibri restaurant (p. 500), San Juan del Sur (✆ **505/803-8196;** www.lunabella.org), offers relaxing 1-hour massages that cost C760 ($40/£20). See p. 500 for more info. **Cecalli ★**, 1km (1/2 mile) south of Estelí (✆ **505/713-4048;** cecalli@ibw.com.ni), is a nature museum, herb garden, and clinic that administers acupuncture and massage therapy among other holistic practices. See p. 531 for info.

more specific info on malaria hot spots (relegated to rural areas in Nicaragua), and also see p. 56 in "Planning Your Trip to Central America" for info.

GETTING THERE

By Plane

Augusto C Sandino International Airport (**MGA;** ✆ **505/233-1624;** www.eaai.com.ni), is 11km (7 miles) east of Managua and is the country's main airport. Here you'll find direct flights from Miami, Houston, Dallas, Mexico City, San Salvador, Panama City, and San José. **American Airlines** (✆ **800/433-7300** in the U.S., or 505/255-9090 in Managua; www.aa.com) flies twice a day from Miami. **Continental Airlines** (✆ **505/278-7033** in Managua; www.continental.com) operates one evening flight from Houston. **Delta** (✆ **505/254-8130** in Managua; www.delta.com) has a daily flight to Atlanta. **Spirit Airlines** (✆ **505/233-2884** in Managua; www.spiritair.com) operates a daily flight to Fort Lauderdale.

Copa (✆ **505/267-0045** in Managua; www.copaaircom) has connections all over Central America, particularly Guatemala, Panama, San José, and San Salvador. **Aeroméxico** (✆ **800/226-0294** in the U.S., or 505/266-6997 in Managua; www.aeromexico.com) flies four times a week to Mexico City. **TACA** (✆ **505/266-3136** in Managua; www.taca.com) operates flights from Miami, Panama, and San Salvador. **Iberia** (✆ **800/772-4642;** www.iberia.com) flies once a day to Miami with onward connections to Europe.

By Bus

There are a handful of established international bus companies that trundle up and down the Central American isthmus. All have separate stations and offices in Barrio Martha Quezada in Managua and some have offices in León, Rivas, and Granada where you can also alight. **Tica Bus,** 2 blocks east of the Antiguo Cine Doradao (✆ **505/222-6094** or 222-3031; www.ticabus.com), is the best known operator, with intercity routes going as far as Mexico City. The bus from Honduras leaves Tegucigalpa daily at 9:15am, takes 8 hours, and costs C570 ($30/£15). The bus from San José in Costa Rica leaves daily at 3am, takes 7 hours, and costs C266 ($14/£7). They also operate a route from San Salvador, leaving from the Hotel San Carlos at 3am and arriving in Managua 9 hours later. The cost is C475 ($25/£13).

King Quality/Cruceros del Golfo, opposite Tica Bus (✆ **505/228-1454;** www.kingqualitycg.com) has a reputation for being more comfortable, and provides meals. Their service from Honduras leaves at 6am and 2pm and costs C684 ($36/£18). The Costa Rica service leaves San José at 3pm, takes 8 hours, and costs C703 ($37/£19). The bus from San Salvador leaves at 3:30am, 5:30am, and 11:30am. It takes 12 hours and costs C836 ($44/£22).

Trans Nica, 300m (984 ft.) north of Rotonda Metrocentro and 50m (164 ft.) east (✆ **505/277-2104** or 270-3133), services El Salvador, Costa Rica, and Honduras. Their bus from Costa Rica departs from San Juan at 4:30am, 5:30am, and 9am. It takes 9 hours and costs C190 ($10/£5). **Central Line,** next to King Quality (✆ **505/254-5431**), goes south to San José in Costa Rica. The service leaves Costa Rica at 4:30am and takes 9 hours. The cost is C285 ($15/£7.50). For departure times from Managua, see "Getting There" in the Managua section on p. 442.

For those on a strict budget, who are in no hurry and don't mind the discomfort of jumping off and changing buses at the border, getting around by a chicken bus (see "Getting Around" below for info), is another option. The two main crossings on the Honduran border are Guasale and El Espino. These buses arrive and depart in Managua at **Mercado Israel Lewites,** also known as **Boer** (✆ **505/265-2152**) and **Mercado Mayoreo** (✆ **505/233-4729**). The main crossing into Costa Rica is Peñas Blancas. Buses arrive and depart from **Mercado Roberto Huembes** (no phone). It is very important that you get two stamps—an exit and entrance stamp—from the corresponding immigration office on either side, or you may have problems entering or leaving at the border.

By Cruise Ship/Ferry

San Juan del Sur is now a well-established stop off for luxury cruise liners plying the Caribbean and Pacific coast via the Panama Canal. Two reputable companies that make this trip are Miami-based **Seabourn Cruise Line** (www.seabourn.com) and California-based **Princess Cruises** (www.princess.com).

GETTING AROUND

It's hard to pinpoint the most difficult part about getting around in Nicaragua, as getting around the country is very often taxing. Decrepit roads and a chaotic public transport system mean you may have to plump for an expensive taxi or shuttle ride between cities if you don't fancy taking a chicken bus. Fortunately everything is relatively close and the only real epic journeys are if you want to explore the interior highlands or get to the Caribbean by land and sea.

By Plane

At the end of Managua's airport terminal, there is a tiny departure lounge that accommodates Nicaragua's two domestic airline operators. **La Costeña** (✆ **505/263-2142;** www.flylacostena.com) and **Atlantic Airlines** (✆ **505/222-5787;** www.atlanticairlines.com.ni) provide "puddle jumper" propeller planes that carry people and packages to Puerto Cabezas, San Carlos, Bluefields, and the Corn Islands. For more information, see the destination sections throughout this chapter.

By Bus

Have you ever wondered where those old yellow school buses go after being decommissioned from carrying North American children? They go south. The potholed roads of Nicaragua are full of trundling **"chicken buses"** or old school buses, which riders (some of whom *do* carry livestock) can hop on and hop off of at multiple destinations, making for a very slow ride.

The country also has small express vans that are faster than chicken buses, but—since they still allow as many folks as possible to pile on along the way—can get very crowded and uncomfortable on long journeys.

Some better-quality bus companies do exist, but in general traveling by bus is a colorful yet exhausting and sometimes intimidating business. For exact arrival and departure points in each city, and for the names of bus companies, check "Getting There" and "Getting Around" info in each town detailed below.

By Taxi & Shuttle Bus

Taking taxis or shuttle buses is an increasingly popular way of getting around the country. Small, private companies, usually connected to a travel agency or hotel, will pick you up at your airport or hotel and transfer you to your next destination. It is particularly popular for those traveling between the main tourist destinations—Granada, San Juan del Sur, Managua, and León. The price depends on whether you are lucky enough to have somebody else sharing the ride, but will never be less than C570 ($30/£15) between destinations. Two reputable companies are **Tierra Tour** (© **505/315-4278;** www.tierratour.com) and **Paxeos** (© **505/552-8291;** www.paxeos.com). See "By Taxi" under "Managua" later in this chapter for info on taking taxis within the city.

By Car

Nicaragua used to be described as a country of oxen and Mercedes Benz, but now it is more like a country of old school buses and SUVs. In general, the roads are very bad and you will be doing yourself a big favor if you spring for a four-wheel-drive. One good thing about driving here is that there is very little traffic. The Northern Highlands is the most beautiful area for touring by car.

Car rentals are generally cheap, but it is wise to shop around. Make sure you get unlimited mileage or are aware of the charge per kilometer if you go over. A car costs C288 ($15/£7.50) to C1,727 ($90/£45) per day, and more if you require a 4WD. The best known company is **Hertz** (© **505/266-8400** in the Intercontinental Hotel, or 222-2320 in the airport; www.hertz.com). **Lugo Rent-a-Car** (© **505/266-4477**) and **Dorado Rent-a-Car** (© **505/278-1825**) are both located at Rotonda El Dorado in Managua. **Alamo** has a desk in the international airport (© **505/277-4477;** www.alamonicaragua.com) and offices in Granada and San Juan del Sur. **Budget,** 1 block south of Estatua Montaya (© **505/255-9000;** www.budget.com.ni) and **Avis,** 1/2 block south of Estatua Montaya (© **505/268-1838;** www.avis.com.ni) are two other good options. Note that many towns (such as Masaya) lack rental car outlets, so if you are intent on touring the country by car, it is probably best that you do so from Managua or Granada.

TIPS ON ACCOMMODATIONS

Hotels in Nicaragua are improving all the time, but lower your expectations the farther you get away from the capital or tourist centers like Granada and San Juan del Sur. Even in increasingly popular destinations like the Corn Islands and Isla de Ometepe, luxury hotels are still in short supply. In general, though, the country does offer great variety in terms of accommodations, from all exclusive resorts on the Pacific coast to authentic Spanish colonial houses in Granada. The Northern Highlands and the lake islands offer rustic working farms with lots of personality but little in modern amenities. Most prices for hotels below are quoted in U.S. and British currency only, since most don't quote their rates in córdobas.

TIPS ON DINING

Nicaragua isn't exactly a culinary destination, but Managua has the best choices regarding restaurants, with Granada coming a distant second. León and San Juan del Sur are beginning to get some very good high-end eateries, as well. In general, buffet-style restaurants, called *comedores,* are very popular, as are street grills *(fritangas)* on the side of the road. Every town has a Mercado Municipal, with ultra-cheap food stalls. Corn, rice, and beans dominate most menus but you'll also come across an incredible amount of seafood, especially lobster and shrimp.

In Nicaragua, prices on menus in most restaurants exclude a 15% tax and a 10% service charge. These are automatically added to your bill at the end.

TIPS ON SHOPPING

Nicaragua is handicraft heaven. Masaya, 29km (18 miles) south of Managua, is the center of the handicraft scene in the country. Here you'll find everything from cotton hammocks, woodcarvings, rocking chairs, textile arts, leatherwork, and ceramics. The Monimbó neighborhood in Masaya is famous for leatherwork, woodwork, embroidery, and toys. Every town and city has a central market where you will find similar goods, as well. The Solentiname Islands are famous for primitive art and Managua has many art galleries that display such work.

Fast Facts Nicaragua

American Express **American Express** is located at the Viajes Atlántida office, 1 block east of Rotonda El Gueguense, Managua (✆ **505/266-4050**). It is open Monday to Friday from 9am to 5pm.

Business Hours Banks are generally open weekdays from 8:30am to 4pm and some are open on Saturday mornings. Shopping hours are weekdays from 8am to midday and 2 to 5pm and Saturday 8am to noon. Shopping centers are open daily from 10am to 8pm.

Embassies All embassies are in Managua, as follows: **United States,** Carr Sur Km 4.5 (✆ **505/266-6012,** or 266-6038 after hours); **Canada,** De los Pipitos, Calle Nogal No. 25, Bolonia (✆ **505/268-0433** or 268-3323), and the **United Kingdom,** on Carretera Masaya, Los Robles (✆ **505/278-0014** or 278-0887). **Australia** and **New Zealand** do not have an embassy or consulate in Nicaragua.

Emergencies The following emergency numbers are valid throughout Nicaragua. For an ambulance, call ✆ **128;** in case of fire, call ✆ **115;** for police assistance, call ✆ **118.**

Hospitals The best hospital in Managua is the **Hospital Bautista,** 1km (½ mile) east of the Intercontinental Hotel (✆ **505/249-7070** or 249-7277); some staff members are English-speaking.

Language Nicaragua's official language is Spanish, but a form of creole English is also frequently used along the Caribbean coast and the Corn Islands.

Maps It is hard to produce reliable maps of towns and cities that have no street names yet, but Intur makes a good effort at it. *Guía Mananic* is one good country map that can be purchased at most bookstores in the country.

Newspapers & Magazines Major local papers are *El Nuevo Diario* (center-left), and *La Prensa* (conservative). *La Tribuna* is the country's main business paper and *El Mercurio* is the most popular tabloid.

Post Offices & Mail Post offices are generally open Monday through Friday from 8am to 6pm and Saturday from 8am to 1pm. Airmail postage for a letter weighing 7 ounces or less from Nicaragua to North America is 60¢ (30p) and $1 (50p) to Europe. Mail takes on average between 7 and 10 days to get to the U.S. and Europe.

Safety Isolated parts of Northern Nicaragua (ex Contra country) are still considered lawless, such as northern Jinotega province and remote parts of Matagalpa and Nueva Guinea. In the more populated southern parts and poorer areas of Managua, crime is reportedly on the increase, but it's by no means as bad as other Central America countries. Travelers should be especially alert to pickpockets and purse snatching on the streets and on buses. Always keep your belongings in sight while dining or drinking and expect street kids to ask for money or food. A different safety concern, but worth noting, is the strong Pacific currents and lack of coast guards. Be aware of this while enjoying the beach.

Taxes Nicaragua's value-added tax (IGV) is 15% and is generally added on after the bill, especially when eating in the finer restaurants. If you're ever unsure about a price, ask if the bill includes *el impuesto* (the tax). See "Entry Requirements" earlier in this chapter for info on the airport departure tax.

Telephone & Fax Public phones take either phone cards (sold at kiosks on the street) or coins. Local calls cost 20 centavos or about 5¢/2.50p to start, and charge more the longer you talk. ENITEL is the name of the biggest phone company, though it is still often referred to as TELCOR. You will find an ENITEL office in all major cities and towns. There are telephone booths on many corners, but you may have difficulty finding one that accepts change (it's easier to find ones that work with calling cards).

See "Telephone Dialing Info at a Glance," earlier in this chapter, along with p. 434 in "Planning Your Trip to Central America" for more info.

Tipping A 10% tip is expected at cafes and restaurants. This is often added to the bill automatically, even though the waiter/waitress may never see it. If you are worried your tip is not getting into the right hands, give a little extra to the waiter directly. You are not obliged to pay the automatic tip if the service was bad.

4 MANAGUA

Managua looks like a bomb hit it. The city is a scattered, disheveled, and disorganized urban sprawl where everything is spread out and there is no center. The truth is a bomb *did* hit it, in the form of a massive earthquake in 1972. It flattened the city center, and planners decided it was pointless to rebuild on such a shifting tectonic nightmare again.

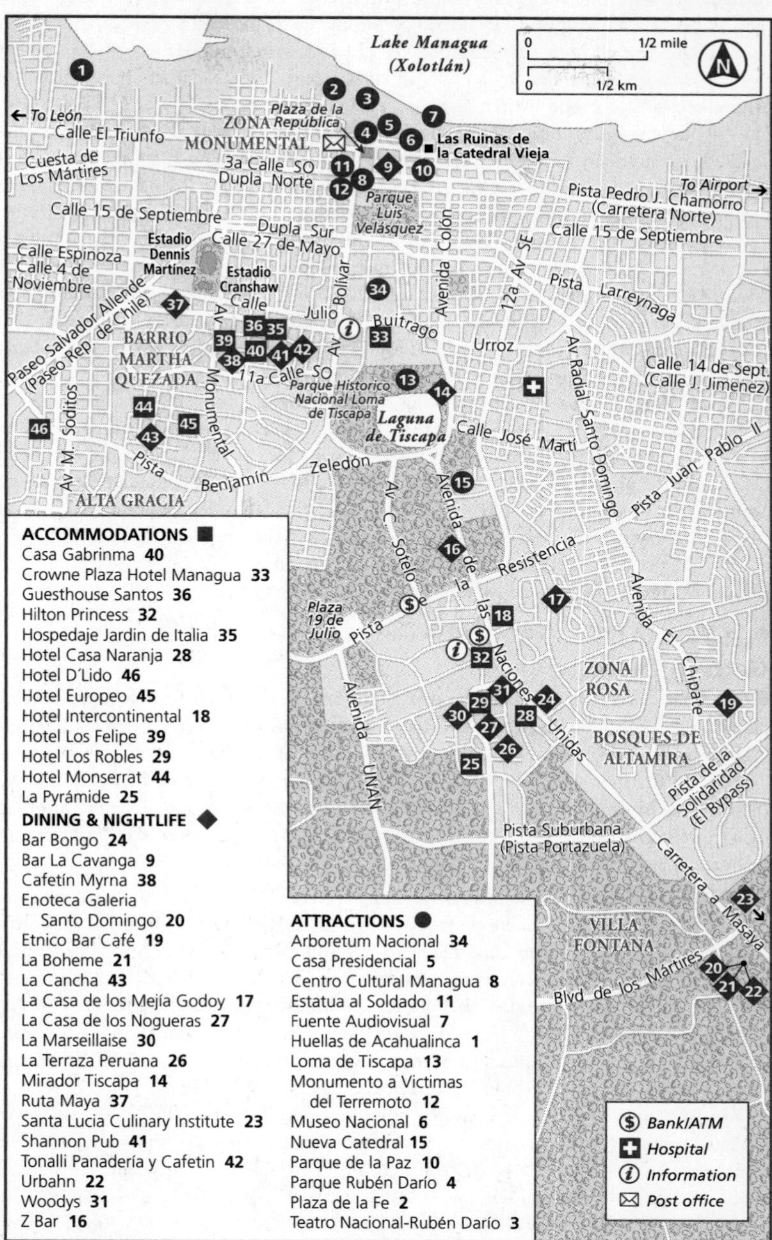
Lake Managua
(Xolotlán)
0 1/2 mile
0 1/2 km
N
← To León
Calle El Triunfo
Cuesta de Los Mártires
Plaza de la República
ZONA MONUMENTAL
Las Ruinas de la Catedral Vieja
3a Calle SO
Dupla Norte
Parque Luis Velásquez
To Airport →
Pista Pedro J. Chamorro (Carretera Norte)
Calle 15 de Septiembre
Dupla Sur
Calle 27 de Mayo
Estadio Dennis Martínez
Estadio Cranshaw
Calle Espinoza
Calle 4 de Noviembre
Av. Bolívar
Avenida Colón
12a Av SE
Pista Larreynaga
Calle Julio Buitrago
Urroz
Paseo Salvador Allende (Paseo Rep. de Chile)
BARRIO MARTHA QUEZADA
11a Calle SO
Av. Monumental
Parque Historico Nacional Loma de Tiscapa
Laguna de Tiscapa
Calle 14 de Sept. (Calle J. Jimenez)
Av. Radial Santo Domingo
Calle José Martí
Av. M. Soditos
Pista Benjamín Zeledón
ALTA GRACIA
Pista Juan Pablo II
Av. C. Sotelo
Avenida de las Naciones Unidas
Pista de la Resistencia
Plaza 19 de Julio
Avenida El Chipate
ZONA ROSA
BOSQUES DE ALTAMIRA
Avenida UNAN
Pista de la Solidaridad (El Bypass)
Pista Suburbana (Pista Portazuela)
Carretera a Masaya
VILLA FONTANA
Blvd de los Mártires
ACCOMMODATIONS
Casa Gabrinma 40
Crowne Plaza Hotel Managua 33
Guesthouse Santos 36
Hilton Princess 32
Hospedaje Jardin de Italia 35
Hotel Casa Naranja 28
Hotel D´Lido 46
Hotel Europeo 45
Hotel Intercontinental 18
Hotel Los Felipe 39
Hotel Los Robles 29
Hotel Monserrat 44
La Pyrámide 25
DINING & NIGHTLIFE
Bar Bongo 24
Bar La Cavanga 9
Cafetín Myrna 38
Enoteca Galeria Santo Domingo 20
Etnico Bar Café 19
La Boheme 21
La Cancha 43
La Casa de los Mejía Godoy 17
La Casa de los Nogueras 27
La Marseillaise 30
La Terraza Peruana 26
Mirador Tiscapa 14
Ruta Maya 37
Santa Lucia Culinary Institute 23
Shannon Pub 41
Tonalli Panadería y Cafetin 42
Urbahn 22
Woodys 31
Z Bar 16
ATTRACTIONS
Arboretum Nacional 34
Casa Presidencial 5
Centro Cultural Managua 8
Estatua al Soldado 11
Fuente Audiovisual 7
Huellas de Acahualinca 1
Loma de Tiscapa 13
Monumento a Victimas del Terremoto 12
Museo Nacional 6
Nueva Catedral 15
Parque de la Paz 10
Parque Rubén Darío 4
Plaza de la Fe 2
Teatro Nacional-Rubén Darío 3
Bank/ATM
Hospital
Information
Post office

The result is a ghost-downtown surrounded by dispersed, anonymous neighborhoods, pockmarked with craters and crisscrossed with streets that lack character as much as they lack names. It is a frustrating, bewildering place and easily the least accessible, the hardest to negotiate, the toughest to discover capital city in Central America.

If the city seems like one big accident, that is precisely because it is. Originally it had always been just a proud little indigenous fishing village on the shores of Lago Xolotlán—proud enough to beat off the somewhat surprised and vengeful Spanish. But the small village suddenly found itself the country's capital when León and Granada reached a compromise to end their vicious 19th-century rivalry and chose Managua. With hindsight they might have chosen differently. A devastating earthquake in 1931 caused havoc, as did a fire several years later. The city experienced a brief boom in the fifties and sixties and was one of the region's most advanced metropolises. That all changed on December 23, 1972, when another earthquake hit, and 8 sq. km (5 sq. miles) were flattened and 10,000 killed. Revolution followed and the city was bombed by its own leaders. The rich elite fled to Miami and the city stagnated under the Sandinistas. It is only in recent years that Managua has finally begun to emerge from the rubble.

Today, Managua is a city of sprawling markets, chaotic bus terminals, tacky theme bars, and boisterous dance clubs. Once you figure out how to negotiate and get around this strange city of 1.5 million souls, you'll see it has a lot to offer. Despite the chaos and heat, it is, after all, the cultural, political, economic, and academic engine of the country. You also can't avoid Managua, as all international flights land here. Whether you stay or not it is up to you. Stay long enough and you can dance on volcanic rims, eat in tropical courtyards, listen to poetic folklore, experience a vibrant art scene, peek into crumbling cathedrals and, ultimately, understand Nicaragua all the more.

ESSENTIALS

Getting There

BY PLANE See "Getting There," on p. 436, for info on arriving into the country by plane. The small, modern **Augusto C Sandino International Airport (MGA; © 505/233-1624;** www.eaai.com.ni), is 11km (7 miles) east of Managua. An airport taxi costs C380 ($20/£10) into the city center, though you can save some money by walking across the roadway in front and hailing an ordinary city cab. Always negotiate before jumping in. Frequent city-bound buses pass in front but again you must cross the busy street to hail one, as none enter the airport grounds.

BY INTERNATIONAL BUS Managua has no central bus station, and each international bus company has its own departure points in Barrio Martha Quezada. **Tica Bus,** 2 blocks east of the Antiguo Cine Doradao (**© 505/222-6094** or 222-3031; www.ticabus.com), has the most intercity routes and goes as far as Mexico City. The bus to Honduras leaves for Tegucigalpa daily at 5am, takes 8 hours, and costs C570 ($30/£15). The bus to San José in Costa Rica leaves daily at 6am and 7am and noon, takes 9 hours, and costs C266 ($14/£7). Tica Bus also operates a route to San Salvador, leaving at 5am and arriving in San Salvador 12 hours later. The cost is C551 ($29/£15).

King Quality/Cruceros del Golfo, opposite Tica Bus (**© 505/228-1454;** www.kingqualitycg.com) has a reputation for being more comfortable, and provides meals. The Honduras bus departs daily at 3:30am and 11:30am, takes 8 hours, and costs C684 ($36/£18). The bus to San José in Costa Rica leaves daily at 1:30am, takes 9 hours, and costs C703 ($37/£19). They also operate a route to El Salvador, leaving at 3:30am, 5:30am and 11:30am and arriving in San Salvador 12 hours later. The cost is C836 ($44/£22).

Trans Nica, 483km (300 miles) north of Rotonda Metrocentro (© **505/277-2104**), services El Salvador and Costa Rica. Their bus to Costa Rica departs at 5:30am, 7am and 10am. It takes 9 hours and costs C192 ($10/£5). A luxury bus leaves at midday and costs C384 ($20/£10). The San Salvador bus leaves at 5am and costs C480 ($25/£13), taking 12 hours. **Central Line,** next to King Quality (© **505/254-5431**) goes south to San José in Costa Rica, leaving at 4:30am and costing C285 ($15/£7.50). For departure times to Managua from Honduras, Costa Rica, and El Salvador see "Getting There" on p. 436.

BY DOMESTIC BUS To travel from Managua to other Nicaraguan cities, you must first get your head around the several stations and markets and meeting points that dot each city, each serving as a transport hub for a particular direction.

Mercado Roberto Huembes (no phone) serves the south, primarily Masaya, Granada, Rivas, San Juan del Sur, and the Cost Rican border. It is in the southeast of the city, on Pista Portezuelo, halfway between Rotonda Centroamérica and Semaforos de Rubenia. A taxi to this terminal should not cost more than C114 ($6/£3). Huembes is the biggest and busiest terminal in the city. Make sure you get off at the bus stop side of the market, known as *parada de los buses.* Be aware that you will be swamped by touts as soon as you get out of your taxi, and it is normal for them to grab your stuff and run to whatever bus they want to put you on. Always check that the one you get put on truly is the next one leaving or the *expreso* by asking around.

Buses to the north and east depart from **Mercado Mayoreo** (© **505/233-4729**) in the far eastern fringes of the city, on Avenida de Circunvalacion Mercado Mayor. Here you can get buses to Estelí, Matagalpa, Jinotega, and San Carlos. A taxi to the market should not cost more than C152 ($8/£4) from the city center, or you can take the urban bus *Ruta 102* from Barrio Martha Quezada. **Expresos del Norte** (© **505/233-4729**) is one of the better companies with a punctual schedule and good-condition *expreso* buses that service the northern part of the country.

Mercado Israel Lewites (© **505/265-2152**), sometimes referred to as El Boer, takes you west and northwest to León, Chinandega, and the Honduran border. This chaotic place is located in the western outskirts of the city on Avenida Heroes de Batahola, 1km (1/2 mile) south of the American embassy. A taxi to the market should not cost more than C95 ($5/£2.50) from the city center.

The **UCA** is the city's biggest university and also a convenient spot to jump on an express minibus or microbus to Masaya and Granada. It is located 1 block from the Rotonda Metro Centro. Microbuses depart when full (every 20 min. or so), from 6am to 9pm.

Orientation

Managua is less a city and more a collection of bland neighborhoods bundled together. Be prepared to get lost and confused. No matter where you choose to stay in Managua, you will also have to jump in a taxi to properly see the highlights, as it is so spread out.

The former downtown area hugs the southern shore of Lake Xolotlan and is now known as the **Zona Monumental.** It sits beside the lakefront in the northwest quadrant of the city. Directly south is the city's hilltop Laguna Tiscapa, and between it is the area with the famous La Pyramide hotel and the Plaza Shopping Mall. To the east is the budget hotel neighborhood known as **Barrio Martha Quezada.** South of the Laguna Tiscapa is the area known as the **Microcentro,** with its five-star hotels and nightlife district—known as the **Zona Rosa.** Managua's best and safest market, Mercado Roberto Huembes, lies 2km (1 1/4 miles) east of the Microcentro. The city's more upscale neighborhoods are known as **Los Robles, Altamira, Bolonia,** and **San Juan.**

The Pan-American Highway (Carretera Panamericana) crosses Managua in a horseshoe shape and is known as Carretera Masaya on its southeast approach and Carretera Norte in the northeast.

STREET MAPS If you plan on hanging around this city, you are going to need a good map. The government organization **INETER** (© **505/249-2746;** www.ineter.gob.ni) produces the best street map of Managua (it's the best city map of Nicaragua, for that matter). Maps can be purchased at their main office opposite the Hospital Metrópoli Xolotlán and cost C75 ($4/£2). The tourism board **Intur** (© **505/222-3333;** www.intur.gob.ni) also provides free maps but these seem to only feature the establishments that are advertised; see "Visitor Information" below for locations.

Getting Around

BY BUS Though Managua's *urbano* bus system is cheap and frequent, it has a woeful reputation for pickpockets and robberies, and well-dressed foreigners are said to be especially targeted. In general, if you stick to the city center and take buses during daylight hours, though, you should be okay. The buses can also get very overcrowded during rush hour as they are the only form of public city transport. Buses come along every 10 minutes and charge a fare of C4 (25¢/15p).

You can only alight at designated bus stops. Following are the most convenient routes. **Urbano 109** travels from Plaza de la República to Mercado Roberto Huembes, passing by Plaza Inter. **Urbano 110** goes from Mercado Israel Lewites (Boer) to Mercado Mayoreo, passing La UCA, Metrocentro, Rotonda de Centroamérica, Mercado Huembes, and Mercado Iván Montenegro. **Urbano 116** starts at the Montoya statue and passes Plaza Inter and Mercado Oriental before ending at Rotonda Bello Horizonte. **Urbano 118** goes from Parque Las Piedrecitas to Mercado Mayoreo, passing Mercado Israel Lewites (Bóer), Rotonda El Gueguense, Plaza Inter, and Mercado Oriental. **Urbano 119** goes from Lindavista to Mercado Huembes, passing Rotonda El Gueguense and la UCA.

BY TAXI Don't panic—cabs will honk at you before you even see them. Even occupancy won't stop them from stopping, and strangers often share taxis (this is a dangerous practice at night). Taxis are not metered, so it is imperative that you agree on a price before boarding and make sure you determine whatever amount is quoted is per person or group. Fares go up 50% after dark. Because of Managua's puzzling address system, you will find yourself overdepending on drivers to get you around. Always try and have the address of your hotel in Spanish. Most hotels will recommend their own favored taxi companies, but many may charge a premium rate.

BY CAR Driving in Managua is like getting lost in a huge bowl of noodle soup—the streets are that messy and intertwined. That said, traffic is pretty light and the roads in the city center are in fairly good condition. Just be warned, even the most advanced GPS system will still get you lost. You should only get a car in this city if you intend on living here or plan a tour of the country. See p. 707 for car-rental agency info.

ON FOOT Unless you are a marathon walker, do not mind the heat, and are in absolutely no rush, don't plan on getting around Managua on foot. This city is frustrating for walkers as it is so spread out; in addition, the streets lack charm and even worse, names. What may hurt the most are the frequent missing manhole covers. If you do insist on getting by on foot, keep your eyes peeled or you might risk serious injury.

Where the Streets Have No Name: Getting Around in Managua

Managua is a city that has no street names nor numbers, that uses as reference points landmarks that don't exist anymore, and that insists on using a unit of measurement (the *vara*) not recognized anywhere else. The city also doesn't even use the fundamental cardinal points north, east, or west. To make it worse, some places have two names (which is perhaps better than having none at all). It is a wonder people get anywhere!

And yet somehow they do. Once you master the old indigenous-colonial positioning system, you can appreciate its convoluted logic. Here are some tips on how to "address" the problem and stop yourself or your taxi driver from driving around in circles and going up the bend.

Landmarks are all-important, whether one exists or not. Most addresses start with a well-known building, roundabout, or monument, followed by how many blocks or *varas* in whatever direction. (A *vara* is an old Spanish unit of measurement that equals .8m.)

North is *al lago* (toward the lake). East is *arriba* (referring to the rising sun). West is *abajo* (referring to the setting sun) and the South is *al sur*. A typical example of an address using these terms looks like this: Donde fue la Vicky, 4c al lago, 30 vrs arriba. This translates as "From where Vicky was, 4 blocks north and 20 varas east."

Other important words to remember are *cuadra* (block, often abbreviated as "c") *al frente* (in front of) and *contiguo a* (beside). *Casa esquinera* means the corner house.

The above rules apply to most Nicaraguan cities and towns, with slight differences such as in Granada where "al lago" means east. Because of its size, Managua is definitely the most difficult and cryptic town to get around, though.

Visitor Information

Intur has its main city office 1 block south and 1 block west of the **Intercontinental Hotel** (✆ **505/222-3333;** www.intur.gob.ni). It is open from 8am to 12:30pm and 1:30 to 5pm. There's also an office at the airport (✆ **505/263-3176**), which is open daily from 7am to 7pm.

FAST FACTS ATMs are outside most banks, in malls and service stations, and at the airport. Most banks will also change dollars to córdobas. There are bank branches all over the city, in particular around Plaza España (also known as Rotonda El Gueguense), along with casual street changers (known as coyotes). **Banpro,** Edificio Malaga, Plaza España (✆ **505/266-0069**) and **Bancentro** (✆ **505/268-5013**) are two conveniently located banks.

Exchange all traveler's checks in Managua if you can, as there are very few places outside the city that will change these checks. There's an **American Express** 1 block east of

 Rotonda El Gueguense (✆ **505/266-4050**). **Multicambios,** half a block east of Rotonda El Gueguense (✆ **505/266-8407**), also changes traveler's checks.

The grandly titled main post office, **Palacio de Correos** (✆ **505/222-2048;** www.correos.com.ni), is 2 blocks west of the Plaza de la Republica in the former Enitel building. Here you'll also find an excellent philatelist store.

Farmacia 24 Horas, 150m (492 ft.) east of Rotonda Bello Horizonte (✆ **505/240-06233**), is good for any late-night pharmacy emergencies. **Farmacia 5 Estrellas,** 3½ blocks north of Semafor El Colonial (✆ **505/248-8026**), is an option closer to the center.

Hospital Vivian Pellas, Carretera Masaya Km 9.7 (✆ **505/255-6900;** www.hospitalvivianpellas) is the city's most modern (it was built in 2004) and best-equipped hospital. **Hospital Bautista,** 2 blocks south of Casa RMA, Barrio Largaespada (✆ **505/249-7070**), also has a good reputation.

The main headquarters of the **Policia Nacional** (✆ **505/277-4130**) are situated in the Edificio Faustino Ruiz, Plaza del Sol. For **emergencies,** dial ✆ **118.**

Most hotels and hostels will arrange laundry service for a price. **Dryclean USA** (✆ **505/270-1107**) has branches all over the city. One is close to Plaza Bolonia, behind Santa Fe Steakhouse. Another is at Carretera Masaya Km 3.5.

Internet cafes are dotted all around the city, but if you have trouble locating one, just head to any of the malls that dot the city. **iMac Center,** 1 block east and ½ block south of the Semáforo UCA (✆ **505/270-5918**), offers cheap Internet at $1.50 (75p) an hour. It is open daily from 8am to 8pm. **Cyber City,** in front of UCA (✆ **505/604-7416**), is another good place, as is the modern and comfortable **Cyber,** on the ground floor of Plaza Inter. They charge $2 (£1) an hour and are open daily 10am to 10pm.

If you find yourself needing a restroom while in the Zona Monumental, head to the Centro Cultural Managua. There are public bathrooms on the second floor.

WHAT TO SEE & DO

Downtown

Even the most ramshackle cities have a dynamic downtown area. However, Managua is different. Unfortunately the city's center **(Zona Monumental)** was destroyed by a powerful earthquake in 1972 and the whole area has been left largely untouched and put aside, as its name implies, for monuments of the past and the occasional government building. It is a dilapidated, decrepit zone with many poor squatters and empty buildings. Yet it is worth an early-morning stroll around to see what remains and to learn the stories behind each building. At night it is best avoided. Its center is the **Plaza de la Revolución,** otherwise known as the Plaza de la Republica, depending on your political point of view. The most interesting thing to see here is **Las Ruinas de la Catedral Vieja,** a half-block east of the plaza—it's a poetic testament to the tragic history of Nicaragua. Completed in 1929, this cathedral survived several earthquakes until the big one in 1972 made it too dangerous to enter. Much of it still stands, and you can peer into its shell-like structure and spy beautiful frescoes and statues.

Palacio Nacional de la Cultura is just south of the old cathedral and was once the National Congress. It was here that Sandinista rebels instigated a hostage siege in 1978 that ended with the release of political prisoners. Now it is the beautifully restored site of the **Museo Nacional** (✆ **505/222-2905**). The museum has an extensive collection of pre-Columbian pottery and statues, and is situated in the same building as the National

Library. There is a marvelous revolutionary mural above the main staircase that leads up to the library. The museum is open from 8am to 5pm daily. Admission is C40 ($2/£1).

The **Casa Presidencial** sits opposite the Palacio Nacional. Completed in 1999, this president's office created a controversy as loud as its colors because of its exorbitant cost. Just south of the plaza is the **Centro Cultural Managua** (**© 505/222-5291**). This used to be Managua's main hotel, the Gran Hotel, until the 1972 earthquake literally toppled the top floors. Now all that remains are two stories of exhibition rooms and concert halls. Opening hours are from 9am to 4:30pm Monday to Saturday, with later openings for shows. Murals decorate the entire building and an arts-and-crafts fair is held here the first Saturday of every month. The building is free to enter, though there may be an admission price for any special exhibitions and performances.

On the lakeside of the Plaza de La Republica, in **Parque Rubén Darío,** you'll find a stark white statue dedicated to Nicaragua's greatest poet, Rubén Darío. Continue your literary-themed walk by next strolling through **Plaza de la Cultura República de Guatemala.** This is dedicated to the Guatemalan writer and 1967 Nobel winner Miguel Angel Asturias Rosales. His book *El Presidente* is one Latin America's greatest portraits of a tyrant.

The **Teatro Nacional Rubén Darío ★** (**© 505/266-3630;** www.tnrubendario.gob.ni) was built in 1969 and is one of the few buildings to survive the 1972 earthquake. It's a beautiful structure and the cultural heart of Managua. The 1,200-capacity auditorium here hosts plays, dance performances, and even the occasional fashion show. There is also an exhibition space upstairs in what is known as the Chandelier Room (after a set of chandeliers donated by the Spanish government). Performances can be sporadic, but its daytime opening hours are from Monday to Friday from 10am to 6pm and Saturday to Sunday from 10am to 3pm. It is where Nicaragua's great come to rub shoulders but don't let that turn you off. Tickets are very affordable. The theater is 1 block north of the Plaza de la Republica, in front of the **Malecon,** Managua's lakeside promenade, which features food stalls and great views of the breezy Lake Xolotlán in the distance. (Note that the water is unsuitable for bathing, however.)

Just west of the theater is **Plaza de la Fe (Faith Plaza),** ex-president Alemán's concrete homage to Pope John Paul II. That president was later discovered to have stolen from the state's coffers, but perhaps he thought his papal extravagance might buy him a place in heaven anyway. Alemán was also responsible for building the dancing fountain known as the **Fuente Audiovisual,** just south of Teatro Rubén Darío. Water here jumps to the sweeping tunes of Strauss and *cumbia,* and it is actually impressive—when it's working properly. Unfortunately, it diverted badly needed money from the Hurricane Mitch reconstruction fund. You can catch the sound-and-light show at the fountain every evening from 6 to 7pm and 9 to 10pm, though go in a taxi and do not hang around, as this particular area is not safe at night.

Three blocks south on Avenida Bolivar is the **Estatua al Soldado,** otherwise known as *El Guerrillero sin Nombre* (the Unknown Guerrilla). This is a large, muscular paramilitary statue, with a pickax in one hand and an AK-47 in another. It is an important city landmark, but 3 blocks east you'll find something a little more conciliatory and bipartisan. The **Parque de la Paz ★** is a lighthouse growing out of a buried mound of weapons and tanks—a symbolic proclamation by ex-president Violeta Chamorro that the Contra war was over. The nearby shantytown and general poverty are reminders that this country has some problems to solve yet.

One final, poignant statue to see downtown is the **Monumento a Victimas del Terremoto,** a memorial to those who died in the earthquake of 1972. It is located in front of the **Cancilleria,** where the Iglesia de San Antonio used to stand. If you want a simple explanation about why this city is so fragmented and just plain ugly, see this portrait of a man standing amid the wreckage of his home, and read its moving poem by Pedro Rafael Gutierrez called "Requiem for a Dead City."

Sights Outside Zona Monumental

Arboretum Nacional (Kids) In this small, sunny forest, you'll find a collection of 200 of Nicaragua's native flora. More popular with visiting schoolchildren than tourists, the arboretum is worth a visit for anyone craving greenery in this ungreen city. Still, it must be said, some plants look better than others. It is especially worth visiting in March when Nicaragua's national flower, the *sacuanoche,* comes into fragrant bloom. The red flower of the national tree, the *malinche,* blossoms here from May through August.

Av. Bolivar, Barrio Martha Quezada. ✆ **505/222-2558.** Admission C5 (25¢/15p). Mon–Fri 8am–5pm.

Huellas de Acahualinca ★ Situated 2km (1¼ miles) north of the Telcor building on the way to the lake, this remarkable site displays 6,000-year-old footprints of men, women and children forming a line along what is suspected to have been a riverbed. The question is; were they fleeing a volcanic eruption or just going for a swim? One thing is for sure, it is perhaps one of the oldest pieces of evidence of human activity in Central America. The site now has a simple museum showcasing the footprints.

It is best to catch a taxi here and ask the driver to wait to take you home, as the area is isolated and a little dangerous. A two-way taxi ride should not cost more than C152 ($8/£4). The more adventurous can dress down and catch bus no. 112 in front of Plaza de la Republica or 102 on Calle Colon in Barrio Martha Quezada.

Acahualinca, El Cauce. ✆ **505/266-5774.** Admission C38 ($2/£1). Mon–Fri 8am–5pm.

Loma de Tiscapa A statue of Sandino stands on this high point behind the Intercontinental Hotel (p. 450). Also known as Parque Historico, the Loma de Tiscapa was once the site of Somoza's presidential palace and it now offers a blustery view of the city and the Tilcapa volcanic lagoon. The lake itself is now polluted but you can do a canopy tour across it to the crater if you are feeling really courageous (and don't mind risking drowning in sewer water). The zip-line platform from which you launch yourself is open Monday to Saturday from 8am to 4:30pm and costs 190C ($10/£5). Other historical sites in the area include Las Masmorras, a notorious Somoza jail now closed to the public, and the old site of the American Embassy, destroyed in the 1972 earthquake.

Western end of Calle José Martí, 1km (½ mile) north of Nueva Catedral. No phone.

Nueva Catedral From the outside, this church looks like it was designed by a vengeful atheist architect. Inside, the atmosphere is a little more serene and Zen-like, but it's still hard to figure out whether you are in a Soviet nuclear reactor or Islamic prison. Commissioned by Catholic philanthropist and Domino's Pizza founder Tom Monaghan, the building's one abiding characteristic is the multitude of onion-shaped domes that make up the roof. Described by one visitor as "the worst church in the world," it has a disquieting feel, not improved by its isolated location alongside squatter shacks and a barbed-wire perimeter fence. The end effect is so bad, it's almost good.

South of Tiscapa, on the Carretera Masaya. ✆ **505/278-4232.** Free admission. Mass is celebrated here Tues–Sat at noon and 6pm and Sun 11am–6pm.

Fun Facts **Martínez National Baseball Stadium**

Managua's landmark baseball arena, **Estadio Dennis Martínez,** has changed names more times than one can remember and been knocked about by more than one earthquake. Nicaraguans still come out in droves to pursue their national obsession of baseball, however, and to cheer on the home team of Boer. The stadium is located in the city center, 2 blocks north of Barrio Martha Quezada. Admission is 40C ($2/£1).

SHOPPING

Markets

Mercado Roberto Huembes ★, both a market and a significant transit stop for the city's chicken buses and intercity expresses, is chaotic, colorful, and overwhelming. It is also the most tourist-friendly and accessible of all the big markets in Managua. You'll find everything from fruit to hubcaps here. Its arts and crafts stalls are just as good as anything you'll get in Masaya, and it's also a great place to find local music CDs. The market is open daily from 7:30am to 5pm, and is located 4km (2½ miles) southeast of the Zona Monumental on Pista Portezuelo.

There are other major markets dotted around the city's suburbs, most notably **Israel Lewites** (also known as Boer) where you can catch an express bus to Rivas and San Juan del Sur. It is 3km (1¾ miles) southwest of the Zona Monumental on Avenida Heroes de Batahola and sells everything from cheap toys to fresh fruit. It is open daily from roughly dawn to dusk. One market to avoid is the sprawling **Mercado Oriental,** 2km (1¼ miles) east of Plaza de la Revolución. It's part flea market and crime black spot; you should only go to this sprawling hive of commerce and thievery if you are looking for trouble.

Much more civilized is **Mama Delfina,** 1 block north of Enitel Villa Fontana (✆ **505/267-8288**). Here you'll find a pleasant minimarket of gorgeous handicrafts from all over the country and a coffee shop upstairs where you can cool off and rest. It is open daily from 8am to 7pm.

Malls

Okay, perhaps visiting a shopping mall is not an authentic Latin American experience, but believe it or not the mall is here to stay and Nicas have taken to the indoor, air-conditioned nightmare as heartily as the world in general has. Some of Managua's best restaurants are situated in or beside a mall, and many of the city's malls differ in size, quality, and authenticity. So allow yourself the guilty pleasure if you need to, and run those last-minute errands under one roof. Just be careful which mall you choose. **Metrocentro,** in front of rotonda Rubén Darío (✆ **505/271-9450;** www.gruporoble.com), is the usual gamut of designer labels and screaming babies and is best avoided unless you have a penchant for giving your money to rich multinationals while in a poor country that needs it more.

Plaza Inter, in front of Hotel Crowne Plaza, Managua (✆ **505/222-2613;** www.plazaintermall.com.ni), is a little more down-to-earth, but still filled with lots of foreign stores and goods. The **Centro Comercial de Managua,** Colonia Centroamérica, in front of Colegio Salvador Mendieta (✆ **505/277-3762**), is an open selection of fashion stores, bookshops, banks, Internet cafes, and one post office. It is 1 block north of the National Cathedral. My favorite mall, however, is **Galerias Santa Domingo** (✆ **505/276-5080**), an upmarket collection of stores and open-air restaurants, which is a 10-minute taxi ride southeast of the city center.

Art Galleries

Managua has an exciting art scene, with a forte for producing colorful primitivist paintings that the whole country is famed for. Many of the city's galleries act as meeting points and venues for the city's musicians, artists, writers, and intellectuals. One such place is **Códice ★**, 1 block south and 2 blocks east of the Hotel Colon (✆ **505/267-2635**), with a relaxing patio cafe next to a courtyard and gallery rooms exhibiting paintings and sculptures. It is open Monday to Saturday from 9am to 7pm. **Galeria Solentiname,** 600m (197 ft.) south of the UNAN in Barrio Edgard Munguía Transfer (✆ **505/277-0939**), is operated by artist Doña Elena Pineda and specializes in art from the colorful archipelago. Part of a family of artists, Elena can help set you out with trips to the islands. The gallery is open Monday to Saturday from 9am to 5pm.

Galeria Casa de los Tres Mundos ★, 2½ blocks north of the restaurant La Marseillaise, Los Robles (✆ **505/552-4176**), is the Managua base of poet, sculptor, and priest Ernesto Cardenal and showcases work from the Solentiname Islands. It is also the headquarters of the Nicaragua's writers' association and holds a library and bookstore. It is open Monday to Friday from 10:30am to 1:30pm. **Galería Praxis,** 1 block west and 1 block north of the Optica Nicaraguense, Colonia (✆ **505/266-3563**), exhibits paintings, sculptures, and sketches and has a pleasant cafe. **Galería Añil,** 1 block west and 8m (26 ft.) south of Canal 2 TV, Bolonia (✆ **505/266-5445**), features avant-garde work by Nicaraguan and Latin American artists. It is open Monday to Friday from 2 until 7pm.

El Aguila, Carretera Sur Km 6, in front of Farm 22-24 (✆ **505/265-0524**), is the house and workshop of one of Nicaragua's most famous artists, Hugo Palma. It's open Monday to Saturday from 9am to 5:30pm, but call ahead to ask about visiting. **Galería Epikentro,** 7 blocks north and 2½ blocks west of Rotunda El Gueguense (✆ **505/266-2200**), holds frequent book readings and shows a mix of contemporary and primitivist art. It's open Monday to Friday from 9am to 6pm. **Galería Pléyades.** Centro BAC, 2nd floor, Carretera Masaya Km 4 (✆ **505/274-4114**), exhibits a broad range of Nicaraguan art. It's open Monday to Friday from 9am to 6pm.

WHERE TO STAY

Lodgings of varying quality are spread all over the city, and what zone you choose to stay in will have a big effect on your first and lasting impressions of Managua. The Microcentro is a concrete jungle, but it's where the best five-star accommodations can be found. On the opposite end of the scale, Barrio Martha Quezada is where all the budget hotels and hostels are clustered. With its handful of Internet cafes and bars, the whole zone has earned the name Gringolandia, but I find it to be rather abandoned and uninviting in general, especially at night. It is relatively safe, though the barrio to the east has a reputation for being dangerous; if you are careful, you will be fine. In my experience the more upscale leafy suburbs like Los Robles, Altamira, and Bolonia have some of the nicest hotels and restaurants.

Very Expensive

Hotel Intercontinental ★★ If you want five-star convenience in the center of the city, the Intercontinental is hard to beat. First opened in 2000 and refurbished in 2006, this hotel makes a good first impression with its lobby, a large, attractive space with brick domed ceilings, cream-colored pillars, and fine art on the wide corridor walls. The decor throughout is equally muted and modern. Rooms are expansive and soundproof, with king-size beds, flatscreen TVs, wide and accommodating safes, and an all-important coffeemaker that'll give you a pick-me-up before you start pounding the streets. The medium-size bathrooms have good shower heads and mirrored wardrobes. The mostly business clientele enjoy the on-site international restaurant and the mall that's conveniently across the street. It is one of the few places you can buy the export-only El Padron cigars; ask at the back bar. My only complaint is that the hotel charges a high commission for any currency exchange transactions.

South of Metrocentro Mall on Carretera Masaya, Microcentro. ✆ **800/444-0022** in the U.S., or 505/278-4545. Fax 505/278-6300. www.ichotelsgroup.com. 164 units. From $161 (£81) double; from $345 (£173) suite. Airport shuttle for C96 ($5/£2.50) one-way. AE, DC, MC, V. **Amenities:** Cocktail lounge and restaurant; concierge; health and fitness center; laundry service; outdoor pool; room service. *In room:* A/C, cable TV, hair dryer, minibar.

Expensive

Hilton Princess A short, sun-blasted stroll from the Intercontinental, the Hilton Princess is a smaller, more claustrophobic version of its more expansive neighbor. The style could best be described as mock classical, with its wood paneling and marble floors somewhat betrayed by low ceilings, garish carpets, and piped-in elevator music. Nevertheless, everything is clean and immaculate and the rooms are big, gorgeous, and very comfortable. The huge beds lie bathed in lots of light, with a small business desk in dark polished wood and a handy coffeemaker and ironing board tucked away in the wardrobe. The bathrooms come in that ubiquitous cream color that all top hotels seem to prefer, with a wash basin that's separate from the small bathtub and shower. Overall you could do worse for a stopover in Managua, and the hotel is popular with a business clientele and the diplomatic corps. The hotel's restaurant is open to the public, as is a small gentleman's-style club bar called the Clancy. Staff members are very efficient and quick to resolve the occasional mishap.

2 blocks from Intercontinental Hotel on Carretera Masaya, Microcentro. ✆ **505/255-5777.** Fax 505/270-5710. www.managua.hilton.com. 107 units. From $104–$189 (£52—£95) double. AE, DC, MC, V. **Amenities:** Bistro and bar; concierge; fitness room; laundry/valet service; pool; room service. *In room:* A/C, cable TV, hair dryer, Internet, minibar.

Hotel Casa Naranja ★ Finds Casa Naranja has character *and* comfort. This boutique hotel is hidden behind lots of greenery on a quiet residential street close to the commercial district. The decor is warm, inviting, and very tropical. Attractive terra-cotta tiles go nicely with genuine antique furniture, all set around a gorgeous colorful garden. The rooms are a good size, with feather-stuffed mattresses and lots of light. There are rooms for the allergy prone and some are even wheelchair accessible—a novelty in Nicaragua. All in all you could not do much better, if chain hotels are not your style but you still like your luxuries.

Km 4.5 Carretera Masaya, Microcentro. ✆ **305/396-2214** in the U.S., or 505/277-3403. www.hotelcasanaranja.com. 9 units. From $90 (£45) double; from $105 (£53) suite. Rates include breakfast. Airport pickup available. AE, DC, MC, V. **Amenities:** Room service; bar; concierge; laundry and dry cleaning. *In room:* A/C, cable TV, hair dryer, Wi-Fi.

Hotel Los Robles Though Casa Naranja seems to pay a little bit more attention to detail, Los Robles comes a close second in the boutique, expensive hotel category. Attractive ironwork and heavy, dark-wood antiques adorn this colonial house with a hacienda-style front. All this leads to a beautiful leafy garden with splashes of colored flowers and a trickling fountain. The rooms are big and airy, with hand-crocheted bedspreads. The bathrooms are more than adequate with an all-important high-pressure hot shower. Lake Managua is only several blocks away and it's a short stroll to some of Managua's best restaurants and bars. All in all, staying in Los Robles should feel like staying in the house of a rich, elusive aunt, one who happens to also do a great breakfast buffet.

30m (98 ft.) south of Restaurante La Marseillaise, Los Robles. ✆ **505/267-3008.** Fax 505/270-1074. www.hotellosrobles.com. 14 units. From $95 (£48) double. AE, DC, MC, V. **Amenities:** Breakfast room; business center w/Wi-Fi; concierge; laundry and dry cleaning; room service. *In room:* Cable TV, cellphone free of charge, hair dryer.

Moderate

Best Western Las Mercedes Technically, you can walk across the street from the airport to this hotel, though you might kill yourself in the process, as it's a busy road. The rooms are somewhat simple and identical but perfectly adequate. The hotel's main attraction is a nice pool with loungers surrounded by a tropical garden of palm trees and plants. Because of its location, the Best Western makes a good stopover if you don't plan on hanging around Managua or a good first port of call if you want to rest and freshen up before you venture farther into the city. Despite its conventional feel, the hotel has made forward-thinking efforts regarding renewable energy, such as heating water using solar panels. That said, that hot water can be a little unreliable and in general the hotel could be a little cleaner.

In front of Aeropuerto Internacional de Managua, Km 10.5 Carretera Norte. ✆ **800/528-1234** in the U.S., or 505/255-9910. www.lasmercedes.com.ni. 184 units. $65 (£33) double. Free transfers to and from airport. AE, DC, MC, V. **Amenities:** Bar and restaurant; business center; gym; laundry and dry-cleaning services; 2 swimming pools; room service; Wi-Fi. *In room:* A/C, cable TV, hair dryer.

Crowne Plaza Hotel Managua ★★ This is one of Managua's most famous hotels and a prominent city landmark—like La Pyramide (see below), it's shaped like a giant pyramid. Howard Hughes turned it into his home in the '70s when he had plans to transform the Corn Islands into the new Las Vegas. The earthquake soon put a stop to that, and his plane was the first one out of Managua after the disaster struck. Formerly known as the Intercontinental, the Crowne Plaza has had an extreme makeover and is very different from the basic hotel that journalists used to hunker down in to cover the war. Now you'll find luxurious rooms with lots of light, color, and spacious bathrooms. The large outdoor pool is possibly one of the best in the city.

Octavo Call Suroeste 101, Barrio Martha Quezada. ✆ **505/228-3530.** www.ichotelsgroup.com. 60 units. From $104 (£52) standard double; from $148 (£74) suite. Airport shuttle available. AE, DC, MC, V. **Amenities:** Restaurant, concierge; gym; laundry and dry cleaning; outdoor pool; spa. *In room:* Cable TV, high-speed Internet, minibar.

Hotel D'Lido (Value) Located on a quiet residential street, Hotel D'Lido doesn't particularly stand out from the other suburban homes in this quiet neighborhood. Its rooms are simple but spacious, though the furniture could do with a revamp and the bedspreads are a little too bright for my taste. Nevertheless, D'Lido is a reliable hotel that has been operating since the 1970s. It's also a good budget option, especially when you consider the inviting pool out back along with the thatched roof veranda and courtyard. It's a 15-minute drive from the center of town.

Carretera Sur Km 3 (2½ blocks south of Centro Toyota Autonica), Altagracia. ✆ **505/266-8965.** www.hoteldlido.com. 32 units. From $35 (£18) double; from $45 (£23) triple; from $55 (£28) quadruple. Rates include breakfast. Airport pickup for an extra fee. AE, DC, MC, V. **Amenities:** Pool. *In room:* Cable TV, Internet and computer stations (in some rooms).

Hotel Europeo Value Kids This is a pleasant, good-value hotel set on a suburban street that's a 5-minute taxi ride from the micro center. Tidy, elegant rooms overlook a tropical courtyard with a nice pool and open-air restaurant serving delicious lobster. Bathrooms are small with an enclosed shower and somewhat noisy air extractors. Despite nice touches like art hanging on the walls and attractive wooden ceilings, the decor could stand a little sprucing up. Still, it makes for a relaxing stay and serves as a great escape when you tire of touring the city.

60m (197 ft.) west of Canal 2, Bolonia. © **505/268-2130.** Fax 505/268-5999. www.hoteleuropeo.com.ni. 35 units. From $63 (£32) double; from $74 (£37) triple. Rates include breakfast. AE, MC, V. **Amenities:** Bar and grill; laundry service; pool. *In room:* A/C, cable TV, high-speed Internet, safe.

Hotel Montserrat Contemporary meets colonial with a Nicaraguan twist is how I'd best describe Hotel Montserrat. Open since 1990, it is family run and very much retains a homey feel, with nice pastel-colored walls and local crafts scattered around. The building, however, is new, so you can enjoy its old-world aesthetic with all the modern advantages. There are times things don't go as smoothly as they should—on my last visit, there was no hot water sporadically, for example—but in general this is a comfortable hotel in a nice residential zone close to the city center. There is a relaxing restaurant serving an eclectic mix of Thai, Middle Eastern, and Nicaraguan cuisine on-site, too.

1 block west and half a block north of Optica Vision, Bolonia. © **866/978-6260** in the U.S., or 505/266-5060. www.hotelmontserrat.com. 15 units. From $50 (£25) double; from $65 (£33) triple. Rates include breakfast. Airport transfer $20 (£10). AE, MC, V. **Amenities:** Bar/restaurant; laundry service. *In room:* A/C, cable TV, fridge, Wi-Fi.

La Pyramide ★ Managua seems to have a monopoly on pyramid-shaped hotels, and La Pyramide, located in a residential area that is close to shops and bars, is a smaller, more downscale rival to the Crowne Plaza. This particular pyramid-shaped boutique building is decked out in orange clad tiles and blue window frames and was built with the idea of creating "a home on the road." Every suite is named after a Pharaoh. The German owner is very much focused on the comfort of mind, body, and spirit. The queen-size beds in each room certainly look after your body. The restaurant is perfect for the diet conscious with an emphasis on health foods and an extensive veggie menu.

1 block south, 1 block east and a further 2½ blocks south of Gimnasio Hércules, San Juan. © **505/278-0687.** www.lapyramidehotel.com. 8 units. From $45 (£23) standard double; from $60 (£30) suite. Airport shuttle available. AE, DC, MC, V. **Amenities:** Restaurant; laundry and dry cleaning. *In room:* Cable TV, high-speed Internet, minibar.

Inexpensive

Barrio Martha Quezada is the central district where all the backpackers and budget travelers go. Here you'll find a cluster of hostels and *hospedajes* where quality varies wildly. Below are some of the best, but it must be said that if you really want to enjoy Managua you should spend a bit more and stay in one of the nicer districts like Bolonia and Los Robles. One advantage Barrio Martha Quezada has is that there are a handful of Internet cafes and bars, and international bus companies such as Tica Bus pass through here.

In addition to the two hotels below, also try **Casa Gabrinma,** 1 block south and half a block east of Ticabus (© **505/222-6650**); though it might not look like much from the outside, once you get inside, it improves with a nice inner courtyard and five basic but clean rooms. Rates start at $10 (£5). **Hospedaje Jardín de Italia,** 1 block north of Shannon Pub (© **505/222-7967**) is another good choice, with clean rooms and private bathrooms. Rates start at $20 (£10).

Guesthouse Santos This is the *mochileros* (backpackers) favorite place to bunk down for a couple of days and exchange war stories. A large funky courtyard is surrounded by multicolored rooms, some of which have private bathrooms. Try and get a piece of mattress upstairs as there is more of a breeze up there. Though everything could use a good scrub, the many folks who stay here don't seem to care—this is the best place in town to meet others traveling around Central America.

1 block north and 1½ blocks west of Tica Bus, Barrio Martha Quezada. ✆ **505/222-3713.** 12 units (including 2 large dorms). From $6 (£3) dorm; from $14–$17 (£7–£8.50) double; from $24 (£12) triple. AE, DC, MC, V. **Amenities:** Bar and restaurant; laundry facilities; music library; pool table; TV room. *In room:* Fan, high-speed Internet, no phone.

Hotel Los Felipe This is the best budget hotel in the Martha Quezada area. The small rooms have low beds and garish bedcovers, but are quiet, bright, and simply furnished. Some have tiny private bathrooms. There is a swimming pool set in a leafy courtyard with a palm-thatched dining area. The restaurant offers good Nicaraguan fare. Some rooms are quite crammed with bunk beds that hold four people. Others are more private and all have a psychedelic color system that extends out onto the white railed street entrance, which sports a blue wall and funky wooden sign.

1½ blocks west of Tica Bus, Barrio Martha Quezada. ✆ **505/222-6501.** www.hotellosfelipe.com.ni. 28 units. From $15 (£7.50) double with fan; $25 (£13) double with A/C. AE, MC, V. **Amenities:** Internet kiosk; minigym; laundry service; pool. *In room:* A/C (in some), fan, cable TV.

WHERE TO DINE

Don't let the city's shabby appearance fool you. When it comes to food, Managua offers everything. If you are finally beginning to tire of *gallo pinto,* the capital offers many restaurants that serve much more than just rice and beans. You will find Asian, French, and Italian eateries dotted around the city but mostly in the better off neighborhoods or the shopping malls. This is the only place in the country you'll get fondue, Peruvian, or sushi. For the more budget conscious there is no shortage of street outlets and roadside grills (called *fritangas*), especially in the Martha Quezada area and the Rotonda Bello Horizonte. Trendy restaurants open and close all the time or just change addresses, so don't be afraid to ask a local where to go for the latest gourmet spots.

Expensive

Intermezzo del Bosque NICARAGUAN The location could not be better, on a forested hillside overlooking the city and lake. Wrought-iron furniture sits on a circular platform with a breathtaking view. Behind this platform is a large wooden dome-shaped dining area that calls to mind an indigenous village hall. The menu comprises well-presented seafood and grilled meat dishes. The lobster, set on a bed of pasta shells with white sauce, is particularly good. There is live music, with traditional costume and dance performances on weekends. It might get a little too touristy, but you won't care when you take in the view—this place manages to make Managua look beautiful, which is no small achievement.

5km (3 miles) south of Colegio Centroamérica. ✆ **505/271-1428.** www.intermezzodelbosque.com. Main courses C384 ($20/£10). AE, DC, MC, V. Tues–Fri 5–11pm; Sat–Sun 12:30–11pm.

La Boheme MEDITERRANEAN/FUSION This restaurant is located in the upscale mall known as Galerias Santo Domingo. Its decor, however, is very much Old World, with stone granite walls and arched galleries. Everything is beautifully lit by wall candles and back lights, lending a romantic vibe. There is a large circular alcove in the corner and more conventional seating up front. Some dishes are works of art that border on kitsch, such as the chicken and potato purée in the shape of a chick. (This nevertheless tastes delicious.) The wine list is particularly good, with labels from all over the world, including France and Italy.

Galerías Santo Domingo, Módulo 3B, Zona Viva. ✆ **505/276-5288.** Main courses C250 ($13/£6.50). AE, DC, MC, V. Daily noon–midnight.

La Casa de los Nogueras ★ MEDITERRANEAN This restaurant kept popping up when I asked around in town for recommended restaurants, and I was not disappointed when I ate here. La Casa de los Nogueras exudes class and the Mediterranean-style food matches the decor in exquisite taste and presentation. The restaurant is set in an authentic colonial-style villa on a residential street and is decorated with ornate religious paintings, hanging beneath high ceilings and set amid antique furniture. Try the delicious breaded cutlets on a bed of corn purée with mint sauce.

Av. Principal No. 17, Los Robles. ✆ **505/278-2506.** Main courses C384 ($20/£10). AE, DC, MC, V. Daily noon–3pm and 7–10pm.

La Marseillaise FRENCH/INTERNATIONAL La Marseillaise is a culinary institution in Managua and was one of the first restaurants to offer gourmet cuisine since before the war. The building itself is a work of art, with a beautifully manicured lawn and sculpted hedge leading to an arched door and villa-style house. Inside, pieces of fine art adorn the walls, as Nicaragua's beautiful people dine on delicious filets of fish and meat in rich sauces. The desserts are alone worth a visit. The restaurant is situated on a suburban street in Los Robles—just spot all the sparkling SUVs parked outside and you'll know you have arrived.

Calle Principal, #4 (4 blocks north of Enitel Villa Fontana), Los Robles. ✆ **505/227-0224.** AE, DC, MC, V. Main courses C500 ($15/£7.50). Daily noon–3pm and 6–10pm.

Urbahn ★ *Finds* *Kids* FONDUE Its location in an upscale shopping mall may not bode well for those looking for unique atmosphere, but on any given Saturday evening, this place is alive with hungry, middle-class Nicaraguans who come here to savor delicious morsels dipped in bubbling sauces. Alcohol-powered burners are placed in the middle of each table, until the oil is spitting hot and begging to be dipped with meat, shrimp, chicken, sausage, or bacon—you name it. Meat fondue is the specialty, but they also do cheese and chocolate, as well as conventional salads and pasta. Even if you're not hungry, it's fun to come here and attempt to "cook"—kids should get a special kick out of dipping their food. The restaurant has a well-appointed interior but all the action is outside on the pleasant, open-air terrace, which is shared with other restaurants. The wine list is decent and includes good Australian Shiraz and Argentine whites.

Galerías Santo Domingo, Local 41-D, Zona Viva. ✆ **505/276-5342.** AE, DC, MC, V. Main courses C192 ($10/£5). Daily 8pm–midnight.

Moderate

La Terraza Peruana ★ *Finds* PERUVIAN If you want real seviche washed down with real pisco sour, La Terraza is the place to go. This is a laid-back restaurant with a great ambience, too. Small stone picnic tables sit within a tropical veranda covered in terra-cotta tiles, in the center of which is a trickling fountain. The staff are prompt and serve with a smile. In addition to seviche, the menu offers kabobs, beef stew, pasta, and fish, and a small bar serves cocktails. Try the olive oil—it was the best I had in Nicaragua.

80m (263 ft.) north of the Pasteleria Sampson, Microcentro. ✆ **505/278-0031.** Main courses C150 ($8/£4). AE, DC, MC, V. Daily noon–11pm.

Cooking Classes in Managua

Santa Lucia Culinary Institute (✆ **505/276-2652;** www.culinariosantalucia.com), which happens to be one of the finest restaurants in town, also conducts cookery classes with internationally qualified chefs. Classes cost C285 ($15/£7.50) a session, a good deal considering you get to eat what you cook.

Santa Lucia Culinary Institute ★★ NICARAGUAN/INTERNATIONAL When William Gutierrez arrived in the United States, he had only $20 in his pocket and a fine taste in coffee. He eventually set up the Santa Lucia coffee brand and became famous among the finest Washington restaurant chefs as the man who brought good coffee to the American palate. It was while showing those same chefs around his coffee plantation in Nicaragua that they came up with the idea of setting up an institute to train young Nicaraguans in the culinary arts. The result is this impeccable school and restaurant. The dining area includes a spacious patio with white canvas covering a wooden framed roof. Inside, conical steel lamps hang over slick, diner-style seating. Combined with the red walls and stylish furniture, this gives the venue a classy and modern style. On the menu, you'll find a great variety of international and local dishes, such as smoked salmon carpaccio, tortilla soup, and lobster cooked in lemon and wine. See "Cooking Classes in Managua" above for info on the classes here.

At the entrance to the Las Colinas neighborhood. ✆ **505/276-2651.** www.culinariosantalucia.com. Main courses C250 ($13/£6.50). AE, DC, MC, V. Daily noon–3pm and 6–11pm.

Inexpensive

La Cancha, Bolonia Plaza España 4c al Oe 3c al N 1/2c al E (✆ **505/268-0641**), is a famous hole-in-the-wall restaurant, popular with Sandinistas. It makes for a lively lunch spot with its simple decor and menu items like charcoal grilled Argentine beef. No liquor is allowed, strictly wine. Main courses start at C150 ($8/£4). From Plaza España in Bolonia, it is 4 blocks west, then 3 blocks north, then a half-block east. **Cafetín Myrna,** 1 block west of Ticabus, Martha Quezada (✆ **505/222-7913**), serves spectacular breakfasts, complete with juices and pancakes. It is open 6am until lunchtime daily. Breakfast starts at C150 ($8/£4).

Tonalli Panadería y Cafetin (Moments) BAKERY The bright mural outside this bakery, which displays the female gender symbol intertwined with pre-Columbian motifs, gives away that Tonalli is something more than just a shop dispensing delicious bread and pastry. In addition to being a great place to stop for a hearty breakfast or strong afternoon coffee, Tonalli is also a woman's cooperative and is active in promoting health and social issues. The cafe is set in a simple orange cottage with terra-cotta tiling, and boasts a lovely garden courtyard with seating.

2 1/2 blocks from Cine Cabrera, Barrio Martha Quezada. ✆ **505/222-2678.** Breakfast starts at C150 ($8/£4). AE, DC, MC, V. Mon–Fri 7am–7pm; Sat 7am–3pm.

MANAGUA AFTER DARK

The capital is undoubtedly the best place in the country if you're a night owl, want to catch some live music, or show off your dancing skills. You'll find drinking holes all over the city, but it is best to stick to certain areas that are safer. **Zona Rosa** is the disco strip.

It stretches along the Carretera Masaya from the new cathedral to the Rotunda Centroamérica and beyond. Here you'll find an ever-changing string of pubs, clubs, and restaurants that come and go with alarming frequency. You'll also find a cluster of bars in front of the Hotel Crown Plaza. Another popular nightlife spot is the **Zona Viva,** around the Galerias Santo Domingo shopping mall. For up-to-date listings on what's going on around town, check *Esta Semana,* an entertainment listings supplement in the newspaper *El Nuevo Diario,* or go to the website www.bacanalnica.com.

Live Music

Look hard enough and you'll find live music performances all over the city. I've listed the best and most established venues below, but if mariachis light your fire, you should also go for a stroll around the **Rotonda Bello Horizonte.** This busy roundabout, surrounded by fast food restaurants and cheap eateries, is very much a local hangout, and is the favored circuit for groups of baritone mariachis and wandering troubadours doing their thing *con gusto*. Bars like the **Shannon pub** (see below) also stage the occasional live mariachi performance.

Bar La Cavanga ★ Finds Perhaps the only place in the eerie Zona Monumental where you can get a stiff drink and some spontaneous live music, Bar La Cavanga is a 1950s-style bar resurrected from the ruins of the old Gran Hotel. Next door is the Centro Cultural but it's here that you'll get some real culture in the form of jazz and folk music. It is all very atmospheric and has lots of character, down to the pictures of old Managua on the walls. If you step upstairs you'll see the wreckage of the old hotel and realize why it is called La Cavanga, or the Heartbreak. Near the Centro Cultural Managua. ✆ **505/228-1098.** Admission C150 ($8/£4).

La Casa de los Mejía Godoy ★★ Moments There's no better way to immerse yourself in the heart of Nicaraguan culture than by taking a seat at the Casa de los Mejía Godoy, the city's most famous live music venue. Here you'll find the renowned musical brothers Enrique and Carlos Mejía Godoy performing what has become the soundtrack to the country's revolution and the heartbeat of a culture that revels in songs and storytelling. Both brothers hail from the misty northern hills of the country but it is Carlos who brings to the city the *campesinos'* take on waltz, polka, and mazurka, using his accordion, guitar, and lyrics to create songs fueled by love, gossip, and nature. His most famous song, *Nicaragua Nicaraguita,* is the country's national anthem in all but name.

Carlos' brother Luis Enrique provides the flip side of Nicaraguan music, the energizing Latin beats of salsa and merengue that blare from every bar and car. Yet he too is an important chronicler of Nicaraguan everyday life. Both brothers have been active Sandinistas from the very beginning—not that politics ever gets in the way of their performances. Both are accomplished, charismatic showmen who move the crowd to tears and laughter with famous songs interspersed with anecdotes and jokes. Carlos often performs on Thursday and Saturday, and his brother on Friday. Reservations are recommended and tickets cost approximately C285 ($15/£7.50). There is a music and book store and a cafe on the premises, so it may be worth stopping by here even if you can't make a performance. 2 blocks south of the Plaza del Sol Shell station, Los Robles. ✆ **505/270-4928.** www.mejiagodoy.org. Tickets $8–$15 (£3–£14).

Mirador Tiscapa There are not many music venues in the world perched atop a volcano rim. Mirador Tiscapa is an open-air restaurant overlooking the Tiscapa crater lake with a large dance floor offering live performances of salsa, merengue, and rumba on Saturday nights. Out back is a smaller dance floor with disco beats for a younger crowd. Bo Largaespada Paseo Tiscapa, Managua. ✆ **505/222-3452.** Admission C150 ($8/£4).

Ruta Maya ★ Here you'll find an open-air courtyard with a marquee that comes alive with crowds dancing to live performances. The music is eclectic, with everything from reggae to salsa and acoustic shows being played. Ruta Maya is melting pot for all that is happening in Managua regarding music and culture, and generally draws an older, more discerning clientele. 150m (492 ft.) east of Estatua de Montoya, Managua. ✆ **505/268-0698.** Cover C190 ($10/£5).

The Bar Scene

Lo and behold, **Shannon Pub ★★** (50m/164 ft. from Hospedaje El Bambú, Barrio Martha Quezada; no phone) is an Irish pub right in Nicaragua that's actually owned and run by an Irishman. Ironically, the Irish owner has forsaken the plastic paddy look and the bar's decor is more Nicaraguan than mock Hibernian, save for the green bar and occasional Irish-tinged poster. Popular with both locals and travelers, this bar sells the occasional can of Guinness and there's a dartboard for anybody who fancies a game of bull's-eye—that's if you can keep your eyes off the particularly good-looking waitresses and waiters long enough to play. The owner, Don Miguel (that's Michael in Dublin), is a good source for local info and the most happening nightspots.

Bar Bongó (✆ **505/277-4375**) is one of the livelier spots in the Zona Rosa district, with Cuban food and live music on weekends. It is 3 blocks south of the Metrocenter. **Enoteca Galerías Santo Domingo** (✆ **505/276-5113**) is a busy wine bar in the shopping mall of the same name that attracts a well-polished clientele, especially on weekends. **Etnico Bar Café,** Planes de Altamira (✆ **505/270-6164**), is a moodily lit bar with some world music going on in the background. **Woodys,** 40m (131 ft.) south of Hotel Seminole (✆ **505/278-2751**), is a popular "after office" drinks place with a pavement terrace. They specialize in chicken wings and *chichilados* (a spicy beer version of a bloody mary). **Z-Bar,** Antiguo Rest Los Gauchos (✆ **505/278-1735**), has an open-air bar with a dance floor churning out good old-fashioned rock 'n' roll.

Nightclubs

El Chaman in the Metrocentro Mall (✆ **505/278-6111**) is a young and popular dance club with the most ridiculous American Indian–themed decor. Yet it has been around for quite a while now and keeps packing visitors and locals into its smoke-filled corridors to listen to rock and techno. The cover charge is C190 ($10/£5). **El Quetzal ★**, Rotonda Centroamérica, in front of Registros Publicos (✆ **505/277-0890**), is an old school salsa and *cumbia* dance hall. You'll be the only tourist there but that's fine, as long as you can shimmy like the rest of the mixed, raucous crowd. The cover charge is C190 ($10/£5).

XS, Zona Rosa (✆ **505/277-3086**), is your typical glittery nightclub with mirrors to admire yourself in (and others) and punch the air to techno. The cover charge is C190 ($10/£5). It is located in front of T.G.I. Friday's on Carretera Masaya. **Hipa Hipa ★**, Plaza Coconut Grove (✆ **505/278-2812**), attracts a wealthy and trendy college-age crowd that take to its three boisterous dance floors to groove to salsa, merengue, and techno. It's famed for attracting *fresas,* or strawberries, as Managua's *It girls* are affectionately known. The cover charge is C190 ($10/£5). The doormen are notoriously selective, so dress up and pout. **O.M.,** Carretra Masaya, across from T.G.I. Friday's (no phone), is where to go if you like being treated like a rock star and charged accordingly. The cover charge is C190 ($10/£5).

Island Taste ★★, 2 blocks east of Siemens, Km 6, Carretera Norte (no phone), is a lot more down-to-earth and a famous hangout for Caribbean exiles in the capital. The friendly crowd gets down to proper roots style Caribbean tunes. **Moods,** Zona Viva, Galerías Santo Domingo (✆ **505/276-5276**), is "the place" at the moment (though its moment will have likely passed by the time you read this). Here disco, house, and electro are played in a somewhat sterile but boisterous disco-bar. The cover charge is C190 ($10/£5). **Club Hollywood,** Zona Rosa, Edificio Delta (✆ **505/267-0263**), is arguably Managua's most exclusive nightclub, so dress sharp. The cover charge is C190 ($10/£5).

A SIDE TRIP TO POCHOMIL BEACH

Pochomil is a pleasant Pacific beach that is a 90-minute drive from the city and popular with weekenders. The sand is dark with seashells and the sea waves are large and relentless. The lone fishermen standing in the water casting nets add to the local, laid-back feel. The beach's "center" is a basic, down-at-the-heel strip of anonymous restaurants selling seafood, soda, and beer. Accommodations options are somewhat limited and the beach is virtually deserted on weekdays except during Easter celebrations. It's the most convenient escape from the scorching capital and your quickest route to a hammock if you have just arrived or are just about to leave the country. Note that there is a perennial problem with telephone service in the village.

WHERE TO STAY

Altamar Altamar is a definite downgrade compared to its more luxurious cousin Vistamar farther up the beach (see below). Here you'll find very basic rooms in a rickety building, which are crudely decorated but homey in a beach-bum kind of way. Wooden parrots hang from a roof of dirty terra-cotta tiles, and stained floors and moldy walls go hand and hand with a pretty patio, which has a great view of the bay and a shaded veranda with a pool table and makeshift bar. This is definitely a backpacker-class spot, but with lots of character, some lovely staff, and plenty of space. Its location could not be better (or worse) amid all the weekend action.

Pochomil Beach. ✆ **505/407-9975** or 601-2727. 12 units. From $40 (£20) double. No credit cards. **Amenities:** Restaurant and bar; pool. *In room:* A/C, cable TV.

Hotel Ticomo Mar This is a large, crumbling compound with little character but lots of space. The rooms are huge and hold two double beds and expansive kitchenettes. The wide, featureless courtyard sports hammocks, some palm trees, and a tired looking kiddy pool. It faces the beach but has little charm or color. "Adequate" is an adequate description. The Ticomo Mar is popular with families from the capital.

4 blocks south of Casa de Gobierno and 1 block toward the beach. ✆ **505/269-6299.** 28 units. $45 (£15) private room with bathroom. No credit cards. **Amenities:** Kitchen; TV room. *In room:* Fan.

Vistamar ★ (Moments) (Kids) This hotel has the best and most luxurious accommodations on the beach. Pink clapboard chalets are surrounded by a circle of palm trees and a white picket fence; at the center are two inviting, kidney-shaped pools and a small bar thatched with palm fronds and adorned with flowers. The bungalows are split into two good-size rooms with large fans overhead and tiled floors leading to a floor-length window facing the beach. This opens out onto a sunset veranda with rocking chairs and hammocks. The overall mood is light and beachlike, with ceramic lamps and delightful shell-inlaid tile work in the smallish bathrooms. Everything is immaculate and well maintained. The hotel is close to the main beach, but you may be happy to stay put and simply enjoy the decent but somewhat expensive restaurant or the small spa, which offers "hot rock" treatments. Most staff members are friendly and attentive (the one exception being the front desk staffers, who could be a bit livelier).

Pochomil Beach. ✆ **505/265-0431.** Fax 505/265-8099. www.vistamarhotel.com. 43 units. From $85 (£43) double. AE, DC, MC, V. **Amenities:** Restaurant and bar; babysitting service; dance classes; Internet in lobby; kids' club; pool. *In room:* A/C, cable TV.

5 LEON ★ & THE NORTHWEST

100km (62 miles) NW of Managua

Granada might have all the style, but León has all the substance. This historic university city may not be as unblemished and beautiful as its southern rival, but its history of rebellion and political radicalism, coupled with a vibrant and enthusiastic populace, means it wears its wounds with pride and makes for a fascinating visit. Those wounds come in the form of bullet-scarred buildings and an ancient abandoned colonial city called *León Viejo.* Its pride comes in the form of countless churches, museums, and the largest cathedral in Central America, along with narrow cobbled streets that lead to tiny parks and provocative murals. León is very much a city with character and with a story to tell. Perhaps that's why León is the birthplace of Nicaragua's greatest hero, the poet Rubén Darío, and is the center of an exciting art scene.

Today, it may be the dusty, hot capital of the northwest, but León was once the capital of the nation. It lost its title in 1852, but has been at the forefront of Nicaraguan politics ever since and was a focal point during the Sandinista revolution. The Somoza regime met rebellion with bombings and persecution and at one stage torched the central market. A failed uprising in 1978 was the beginning of the end for the dictatorship, and the city was liberated soon after. Every sultry corner seems to have a story. If you are going to do one guided city tour in Nicaragua, you should do so in León.

León is finally opening up to visitors with new hotels that can match the best in Granada. It is a city you may intend on just passing through, but will doubtless end up lingering in longer than you intended. It also makes a great base for seeing the northwest region of the country. Within striking distance are the dark sandy strands of Poneloya and las Peñitas beaches, as well as the wildlife reserve of Isla Juan Venado, which offers a mangrove sanctuary for nesting turtles. Ten smoking volcanoes stand in line like sentries from Lago Managua to the Gulf of Fonseca. They stand over the swelteringly hot lowlands of which historic León, the thriving agro-city Chinandega, and the coastal port Corinto are the most important towns. Those volcanoes may appear ominous, but they provide rich soil—making the area an agricultural powerhouse and the most populated part of the country. Nevertheless, this northwest region is poor and still recovering from the catastrophic consequences of Hurricane Mitch, which washed away every bridge north of Managua. If you come to hike the area's many volcanoes, walk or surf its dark Pacific strands, watch turtles nesting, or simply indulge yourself in León, the cradle of the revolution, you will be helping to play an important part in the burgeoning tourism industry here.

ESSENTIALS

Getting There

BY BUS León's **bus station,** 6a Calle NE (✆ **505/311-3909**) is 1km (1/2 mile) northeast of the center. Managua is 75 minutes away by microbus and a ride from there costs

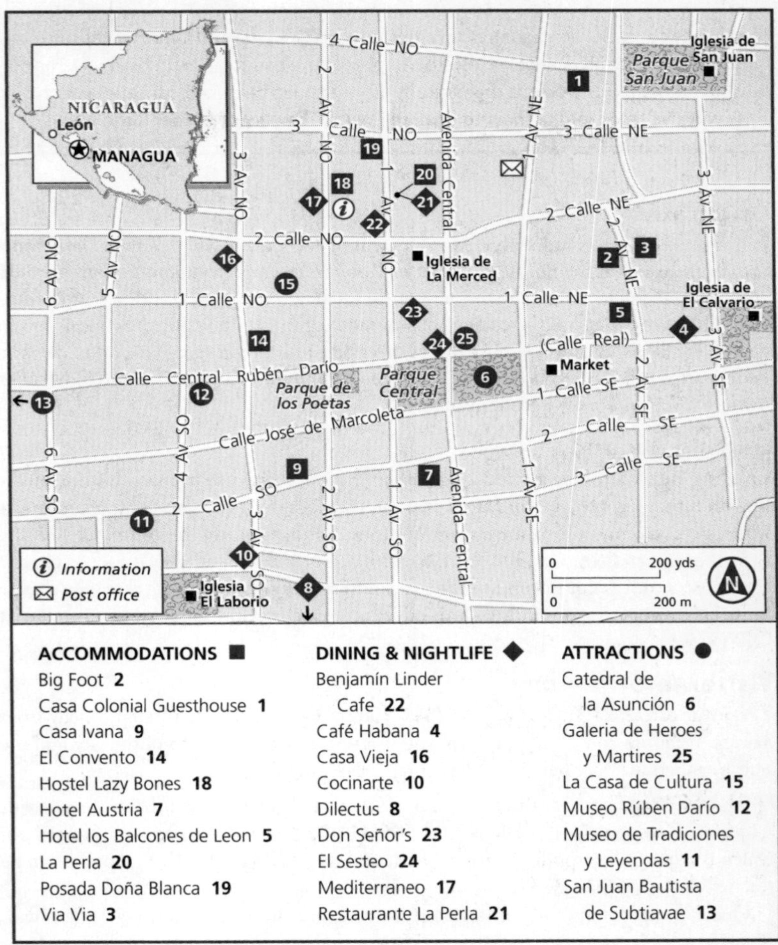

C23 ($1.20/60p); buses depart a few times daily. Estelí is 3½ hours away and a ride there costs C81 ($4.20/£2.10); there are two buses a day at 5am and 3pm. Chinandega is a half-hour away and the ride there takes 1½ hours by ordinary bus and 45 minutes by microbus. There are also connections to Corinto (1½ hr.) and Matagalpa (3 hr.).

BY TAXI-SHUTTLE **Tierra Tour,** 1½ blocks north of Iglesia La Merced (© **505/315-4278;** www.tierratour.com), organizes transfers to Managua and farther afield. Their shuttle service leaves daily for Granada at 4pm. Price depends on the size of your group, but their schedules are flexible and they can drop you off right at your hotel.

Tips Driving Advice

It's easy to reach Nicaragua's main cities, such as Granada and León, by car since these cities are all relatively close to or right off the country's main highway. The state of the roads worsens dramatically as you go farther afield, however, which is why I've listed info on how to drive to only the smaller or farther flung towns.

Orientation

León's street system is numerical. Avenida Central and Calle Central Rubén Darío junction form an axis at the northeast corner of Parque Central. Streets going north or south are called calles and ascend numerically, as do avenidas that go west and east of Avenida Central System. Generally speaking, this numbering system is ignored by locals; when giving directions, they will almost always describe a location in terms of landmarks. The main market called Mercado Central is situated behind the cathedral. The old indigenous town of Subtiava is now a western suburb.

Getting Around

León is good for strolling around—it's perhaps easiest to discover its many historic buildings on foot. To get to outlying areas, you can take local buses or *ruleteros* (pickup trucks with canvas covers), which leave from Mercado Central and the bus terminal (see "By Bus" above). Fares cost C6 (30¢/15p). Note that the roads around the city are in terrible condition, and it is not uncommon to see children filling potholes with dirt in exchange for coins from passing motorists. Taxis are easy to catch on any corner and fares start at C40 ($2/£1).

Visitor Information

The **Intur office,** 2a Av. NO (✆ **505/311-3682**), is open Monday through Friday from 8am to 12:30pm and 2 to 5pm. Here you can find an excellent map of the city and the staff members are very helpful, though they speak little English.

FAST FACTS There are three ATMs 1 block east of the cathedral; banks to try with ATMs are **Credomatic,** 1a Calle NE (✆ **505/311-7247;** www.bac.net), and **Bancentro,** which is 20m (66 ft.) south of Parque La Merced (✆ **505/311-0911**). The police can be reached at ✆ **505/311-3137.**

One efficient Internet outlet is **Compuservice,** in front of Policlinica la Fraternidad. It is fast, reliable, and open Monday to Saturday from 8am to 9:30pm and Sunday from 9am to 6pm. **Club en Conexion,** 3 blocks north and a half-block east of the Cathedral, offers Internet access, along with air-conditioning, and is open Monday to Friday from 7:30am to 9:30pm and Saturday 7:30am to 7pm.

Go to **Farmacia Lopez,** Calle Rubén Darío (✆ **505/311-3163**) for any pharmacy needs. The area's largest hospital is **Hospital San Vicente** (✆ **505/311-6900**), past the bus station.

The main post office, **Correos de Nicaragua** (✆ **505/311-2102**), is 3 blocks north of the cathedral. You'll find public phones outside the Enitel office on the northwest corner of the Parque Central.

Clean Express, 4 blocks north of the cathedral (✆ **505/438-8393**), offers 1-hour laundry service. It's open Monday to Saturday from 7am to 7pm.

Tour Operators

Vapues, on the north side of Iglesia El Laborio (✆ **505/895-9157;** www.vapues.com), is one of the city's main tour operators, organizing everything from flights to hotel reservations. **Tierra Tour,** 1½ blocks north of Iglesia La Merced (✆ **505/315-4278;** www.vapues.com), organizes tours of the area and transfers to Managua and farther afield. **Surf Tours Nicaragua** (✆ **505/440-4123;** www.surftoursnicaragua.com) specializes in surfing tours of the north Pacific coast and offers 7-day packages with accommodations included.

Quetzaltrekkers ★, 1½ blocks east of Iglesia La Recollecion (✆ **505/311-6695;** www.quetzaltrekkers.com) is an agency with a difference. It is run by volunteers and all profits go to helping street kids in León. They conduct volcanic hiking tours to Momotombo and Cerro Negro, among others.

Julio Tours ★, a half-block north of the cathedral (✆ **505/311-1927** or 625-4467; juliotours2000@yahoo.es), is operated by Julio Pineda, an excellent English-speaking city guide who specializes in historical and cultural tours of the city.

What to See & Do

León was originally founded in 1524 by Francisco Hernández de Córdoba in the foothills of Volcán Momotombo. The volcano proved to be a volatile neighbor, and after a series of earthquakes and an eventual eruption in 1610, the Spanish were forced to move

Festivals in León

Día de la Purísima Concepción takes place on December 7 and is known for *Griteria* (shouting), a type of religious trick or treat. Groups of people walk around, shouting up at any households that display a shrine and declaring their happiness over Mary's conception. Next it's sweets and treats all around. The following day is the Dia de la Concepción de Maria, when the whole country goes parade crazy.

Semana Santa (Easter, late Mar or early Apr) is a big occasion in Nicaragua, and León is particularly famous for its colorful celebrations. As well as the usual religious parades and street parties with lots of food and drink, artists lay out elaborate pictures on the ground using colored sawdust. The usually religious depictions are beautiful but unfortunately get swept away at the end of the festival. Semana Santa is also a week where everybody heads for the beaches of Poneloya and Las Peñitas for some rum and sunshine.

La Griteria Chiquita is a variation on the more famous *Griteria* in December and a holiday that's unique to León. It happens on August 14, the anniversary of a 1947 eruption from nearby Cerro Negro that threatened to destroy the city. A local priest initiated a "shouting" and stopped the volcano in its tracks, and this is now celebrated with parades and other festivities.

Día de la Virgen de Merced celebrations start on September 23rd, when revelers run through the street dressed up as one big spitting bull. The next day is a little more sedate, as the town people parade sans costume through the streets in honor of the city's saint.

30km (19 miles) east and reestablish the city where it now stands. The old city lay lost and covered in ash until it was rediscovered in 1967. Excavations have revealed a fascinating site, including the headless corpse of Hernández de Córdoba beside the remains of his executioner Pedrarias Dávila. The founding Spaniard was punished for insubordination. **León Viejo,** a neat collection of brick walls and pillar stumps, is now a UNESCO World Heritage Site, with spectacular views from the surrounding hills. It makes for a great 1-day tour and can be organized by most travel agencies in León city. If you would prefer to go there independently, catch a bus to La Paz Centro 3km (1¾ miles) east of the city. There you catch another bus to Puerto Momotombo 15km (9 miles) away. Be aware that the last bus returns from the ruins at 3pm. On-site there is a small **Visitor Center** (✆ **505/886-2087**) and local English-speaking guides will take you around for a small fee. The ruins are open daily from 8am to 5pm.

Major Attractions

Cathedral de la Asunción ★★★ The Catedral de la Asunción, which took 100 years to build and is easily the biggest church in Central America, is a must-see when visiting the city and it dominates the town center. Three architectural styles grace its magnificent proportions—colonial, neoclassical, and baroque. Rumors swirl around the question of why such a huge majestic church was built in such a small city. Some think that the original architectural plans were swapped accidentally for the plans of Lima Cathedral. Others believe that the local clergy secretly elaborated on the plans after a much smaller version was approved by Spain. Whatever its origins, it was a huge undertaking. The original bishop who started the project was replaced by seven others before the cathedral finally held its first Mass in 1747.

Underground tunnels once linked the cathedral to the eight most important churches in the city, a cunning plan to thwart pirates. The original building was destroyed by rampaging Englishman William Dampier in 1685 and one statue of a black Christ still bears the hack wounds of a pirate's sword. Those same tunnels were appropriated by the city authorities in the last century and are now part of the city's sewage system.

The cathedral is now home to some masterpieces of Spanish colonial art and acts as a kind of pantheon to some of Nicaragua's most national famous figures. Here you'll find the Tomb of Rubén Darío, guarded by a weeping lion. You will also find other important figures such as Alfonso Cortes, Salomon de la Selva, and Miguel Larreynaga. At the cathedral's center is a beautiful, Spanish-style courtyard known as the Patio de Principes. The cathedral's domed roof holds the bell La Libertad that announced to the world the independence of Central America from the Spanish empire. Be sure to inquire at Intur for a tour of the church's atmospheric, Gothic roof. With its lichen-stained cupolas and buttresses, it's a great photo opportunity, and of course there is a good view of the surrounding city and countryside from there, too.

Central Plaza. ✆ **505/311-0717.** Admission C38 ($2/£1). Mon–Sat 8am–noon and 2–4pm.

Galeria de Héroes y Mártires This is a homegrown photographic exhibition celebrating León's fallen revolutionary figures. It celebrates those who stood and fell against the Somoza regime, and is run by the mothers of such martyrs. There's a small craft shop on-site if you feel like buying a revolutionary souvenir. Ask for the curator Madre Cony to show you around.

1a Calle NE. No phone. Suggested admission C19 ($1/50p). Mon–Fri 8am–5pm; Sat 8am–noon.

La Casa de Cultura ★ This quaint, colonial building with an imposing wooden balcony is a hive of activity regarding culture and education. There is a rotating art exhibition of local and international artists, often with a biting social commentary. Here you can also take dance, music, and art classes and there is always a chessboard available to challenge the local Kasparov. See the "Spanish Classes in León" box below for info on language classes and homestay immersions here.

1a Calle NE. ✆ **505/311-21166.** Free admission but varying fees for classes. Mon–Fri 8am–noon and 2–6pm.

Museo de Tradiciones y Leyendas (Kids) This is one of León's quirkiest and most interesting museums, housing a collection of handcrafted figurines that celebrates Nicaragua's rich heritage of legends and characters. Its founder, Señora Toruña, has re-created such colorful folk figures as the Pig Witch and the Golden Crab. Kids should particularly enjoy this museum.

2a Calle SO. ✆ **505/311-2886.** Admission C7 (35¢/20p). Mon–Sat 8am–noon and 2–5pm (hours vary).

Museo Rubén Darío Born in 1867, Darío is Latin America's greatest poet and a pioneer of 19th-century modernism. Here you can visit his childhood home—a neat and simple adobe-style house. There are copies of the Paris magazine he produced as well as correspondence when he was ambassador to Argentina and Spain. You'll also find a collection of original copies of his books, poetry that inspired the Nicaraguan people with words such as "If one's nation is small, one makes it large through dreams."

Calle Central, 3 blocks west of plaza. ✆ **505/311-2388.** Free admission, but donations are welcome. Tues–Fri 8:30am–noon and 2–5pm; Sat 9am–noon.

San Juan Bautista de Subtiavae ★ Located 1km (1/2 mile) west of the central plaza in the old indigenous quarter of Subtavia is León's oldest intact church. Restored in the 1990s, it is remarkable for the gorgeous sun icon that's carved into its ceiling. The clergy placed such an unusual pagan symbol in a Catholic church to attract an initially reluctant local audience. The arched timber roof held up by stout wooden pillars and the intricate filigreed altar is a testament to the amazing skill of the indigenous craftsmen.

13 Av. SO. No phone. Free admission. Mon–Sat 8am–3pm.

Other Sights

León has countless churches and plazas to explore, as well as buildings and murals of historical significance. **Iglesia de la Recoleccion,** 1a Av NE, is a gorgeous church of carved stone representing vines around a pillared facade. The baroque construction has a well-preserved and imposing bell tower. **Iglesia de El Calvario** is on a small hill overlooking Calle Central Rubén Darío. Its twin red-brick bell towers guard a neoclassical facade, and inside you'll find two marvelous statues of the Good Thief and the Bad Thief. Colorful panels depict biblical scenes while slim wooden columns hold decorative motifs.

Spanish Classes in León

La Casa de Cultura, 1a Calle NE (✆ **505/429-0848;** escleon@ibw.com.ni), offers a variety of Spanish classes and homestays. **Metropolitana Spanish School,** half a block west of Iglesia El Calvario (✆ **505/311-1235;** www.metropolitana-ss.com), organizes one-on-one classes and immersion courses.

La Iglesia y Convento de San Francisco, located in front of the Museo Rubén Darío (see above) has two gorgeous altars, and a pretty, tree shaded courtyard to the side.

One and a half blocks from the city's main cathedral is **Iglesia La Merced.** This was constructed in 1762 by the Mercederian order and has fine examples of baroque and neoclassical design. It faces a small park and has an attractive bell tower, with nice views below. **Iglesia San Juan,** 3a Av SE, is located in an old atmospheric part of town amid small adobe houses. This charming church was built in 1625. If you continue farther north, 1 block from its east side, you'll come across León's old abandoned train station.

Every Saturday, the tidy and open **Parque Central ★**, on the northern side of 1 Calle SE, holds a community fiesta called Tertulia Leonesa involving live music with lots of food and drink. It starts in the afternoon and goes on until midnight. Lots of worthwhile attractions radiate from around this park. **Colegio La Asuncion,** 1a Calle SO, was the first theological college in Nicaragua. **Palacio Episcopal,** 1a Calle SE, is an attractive colonial building, as is the **Colegio de San Ramón,** 1a Calle SE. The **Mausoleo de los Héroes y Mártires** is within a small plaza bordered by a fascinating mural detailing the revolution. **Casa de Obrero,** 2a Av. NO, is the place where poet Rigoberto López Pérez assassinated the dictator Anastasio Somoza Garcia while dressed as a waiter. There is a plaque outside the house celebrating the event as the "beginning of the end." You can take another trip down revolutionary lane at the **Old Jail,** 4a Calle SO, which was the site of a significant skirmish between rebels and the national guard. It is now a remembrance garden.

Moments Volcano Hopping from León

The **Maribio Volcanoes** are within striking distance from León. They afford several 1-day excursions of vigorous mountain climbing rewarded with spectacular views. **Momotombo** is one of the most challenging (and can also be visited in 1 day from Managua). Rising 1,280m (4,198 ft.) in a perfect cone shape, its upper half is made up of loose shale, which makes it hard to conquer. The volcano has erupted 14 times in the past 500 years, and the geothermal plant on its slopes provides a quarter of Nicaragua's electricity. It takes 8 hours up and down and is best done with a local tour company, though you can get there independently by hiking beyond the ruins of León Viejo and going north along the highway. Here you enter through the power plant, but access is often denied.

Cerro Negro is a more popular volcano hike and a little easier. That is not to say it is less exciting. This 675m-high (2,214-ft.) volcano may not look as impressive as its sister cones, but it is one of the most active in the country and constantly belches noxious fumes. It takes 3 hours to go up and down, but go early to avoid the midday heat, as there is absolutely no shade. The slopes are increasingly popular for a spot of volcano board surfing on the way down, which is great fun. Any of León's tour operators can arrange this, but make sure you get proper protective gear. To get there independently you must jump on a bus and go east to the town of Lechecuago. Here you will find a poorly maintained trail that takes you to the top.

Note: Neither of these volcano hikes are a walk in the park, especially when the wind is up. Bring plenty of water, and be prepared for a workout.

OUTDOOR ACTIVITIES

KAYAKING The nature reserve **Isla Juan Venado ★★** is an intriguing stretch of mangrove swamp with abundant wildlife. It makes for a perfect spot of paddling. The reserve is situated 30 minutes west near the beach town of Las Peñitas. Beach hostel **Barca de Oro** (✆ **505/031-7275;** www.barcadeoro.com) rents out kayaks and surfboards.

SURFING The nearby coast is not as famous for surfing as farther south but there are plenty of big waves to catch. **Surf Tours Nicaragua** (✆ **505/440-4123;** www.surftoursnicaragua.com) specializes in surfing tours of the north Pacific coast and offers 7-day packages with accommodations included.

TREKKING The nearby volcanoes Momotombo and Cerro Negro (see the "Volcano Hopping from León" box above for details) are the most popular trekking excursions. **Quetzaltrekkers,** 1 1/2 blocks east of Iglesia La Recollecion (✆ **505/311-6695;** www.quetzaltrekkers.com), specializes in treks to both places, as does **Big Foot** (✆ **505/636-7041**).

SHOPPING

León is not a shopping-oriented city, and handicrafts stores are thin on the ground. Because of its university, though, there are many bookstores—with Sandinista-themed books often dominating the bookshelves. **Libreria Don Quijote,** 2 blocks west of the plaza, is one of the city's better known shops. The **Ben Linder Café,** 2 blocks north of Parque Central (✆ **505/311-0548**), has a small gift store offering organic coffee, soapstone, and local art. For fruits and vegetables, as well as clothes, go to the **central market** right behind the Cathedral; it opens at 7am and closes at 8pm.

WHERE TO STAY

Accommodations in León are improving all the time and there are plenty of places to choose from in the city center, many with atmospheric courtyards and relaxing hammocks. All hotels listed below are within waking distance of the central plaza and cathedral.

Expensive

El Convento ★ This luxury hotel certainly lives up to its name—it was actually reconstructed from the ruins of a convent established in 1639. Its low, cream-colored colonial walls are next to a church, so you may feel like you're entering a religious order when you arrive. There is nothing monastic about its interior, however. It has one of the most elaborate courtyards of any hotel in the country—it's immense, with sculpted hedges encircling a beautiful fountain. A blue-pillared gallery surrounds the central patio, leading to sumptuous rooms with polished tile floors, king-size beds, and antique furniture. The ballroom, an immense space with elegant chandeliers, and the art gallery, which boasts an expansive lobby, high raftered ceilings, and baroque woodcarvings, are both worth peeking into. Overall, this hotel is atmospheric and very seductive, though nearby La Perla trumps it in terms of customer service.

3 Av. NO, by Iglesia San Francisco. ✆ **505/311-7053.** Fax 505/311-7067. www.hotelelconvento.com.ni. 32 units. From $87 (£44) double; from $110 (£55) triple; from $115 (£58) suite. Rates include breakfast. AE, DC, MC, V. **Amenities:** Restaurant; coffee shop; laundry service; room service. *In room:* A/C, cable TV, Internet.

La Perla ★★ Elegant and spacious, La Perla is a jewel of a property. This large, colonial mansion has been restored with great attention to detail by its two American owners. Its glittering white facade leads to a palatial interior of high ceilings and contemporary Nicaraguan art. In addition to a spectacular central courtyard, there is a smaller courtyard farther back, with an immaculate blue-tiled pool. Rooms vary in size; the presidential suite is definitely the biggest, with sweeping dimensions, a giant, half-poster bed, a grandiose wardrobe with elaborate woodcarvings, and huge double doors that open out onto two small street balconies. The standard rooms are much more compact and less impressive but still impeccably decorated, with soft carpets and flatscreen TVs. At the front of the hotel is one of León's best restaurants, while the Canal Bar makes for a good stop for a drink. The staff is bilingual and super friendly.

1 Av. NO, 1 block north of Iglesia la Merced. ✆ **505/311-3125.** Fax 505/311-2279. www.laperlaleon.com. 15 units. From $105 (£53) double; from $125 (£63) suite; from $150 (£75) presidential suite. Rates include breakfast. AE, MC, V. **Amenities:** Restaurant and bar; pool. *In room:* A/C, cable TV, minibar, Wi-Fi.

Moderate

Hotel Austria (Kids) This is a modern, medium-size hotel that somewhat lacks character but has a good location and decent service. The rooms are large and some have balconies that overlook an attractive courtyard with a lawn. The decor is modern with pine or wicker furniture and loud scarlet and green bedcovers. The rooms could do with a little more light, but the bathrooms are large and well maintained. In general it is a clean establishment, and family friendly. Use of the Internet is an extra charge.

2 Calle SO, 1 block SW of the cathedral. ✆ **505/311-1206.** Fax 505/311-1368. www.hotelaustria.com.ni. 35 units. From $57 (£29) double; from $68 (£34) triple. AE, MC, V. **Amenities:** Restaurant; high-speed Internet in lobby; laundry service. *In room:* A/C, cable TV.

Hotel Los Balcones de León (Value) Los Balcones has a delightful, lived-in, colonial feel. A lush courtyard with lots of flowerpots, plants, and ornaments leads to a handsome wooden stairway and big communal balcony with colorful seating. (Be warned that the balcony can be rather noisy, as it overlooks a busy street.) The rooms vary greatly but the best are upstairs and have inviting wrought-iron bed frames resting on varnished floorboards. The rooms downstairs are not as nice and lack good light; all rooms come with medium-size, well-equipped bathrooms.

Corner of 1 Calle NE and 2 Av. NE. ✆ **505/311-0250.** Fax 505/311-0233. www.hotelbalcones.com. 20 units. From $55 (£28) double; from $71 (£36) triple; from $77 (£38) quadruple. Rates include breakfast. AE, DC, MC, V. Airport transfer available. **Amenities:** Restaurant and bar; Internet in lobby; laundry service; 24-hr. reception. *In room:* A/C, cable TV.

Posada Doña Blanca This roomy bed-and-breakfast is set in an old town house with modern touches. The courtyard is large and lush with a spacious veranda of polished tiles and dark-wood rocking chairs. Rooms (including bathrooms) vary in size from small to super big and some are a little dark, with disappointingly low ceilings. Ask for room no. 4 as it has much more space and a high ceiling. Everything is immaculate; the furniture is a mix of antique or modern replica. This family-run establishment has friendly staff and a great location just down the street from La Perla (see above).

3 Calle NO, 1 block north of Iglesia La Merced. ✆ **505/311-2521.** www.posadadonablanca.com.com. 6 units. From $68 (£34) double. AE, DC, MC, V. **Amenities:** Internet in lobby; laundry service. *In room:* A/C, TV.

Inexpensive

In addition to the spots below, another hostel in León making a name for itself is **Big Foot** (✆ **505/636-7041**). Australian and Dutch owned, it has established itself as the expert on volcano surfing on the nearby Cerro Negro. This is a fun excursion but physically exerting, especially if the wind is up. The hostel is located a half-block from the Servicio Guardian, in front of Via Via hostel (see below).

If hostels are not your style, but you're watching your córdobas, try **Casa Ivana** (✆ **505/311-4423**). This budget hotel has a good location beside the Teatro Municipal and provides clean and basic rooms set around a pretty courtyard with wicker chairs. Doubles cost $10 (£5).

Casa Colonial Guesthouse (Value) Charming, welcoming, and very cozy, this lovely old villa with a lush, narrow courtyard, filled with flowers and wandering turtles, leads to small but comfortable rooms of cream-colored walls and arched wooden doors. Some have spectacular four-poster beds. Everything is clean and immaculate, including the bathrooms. It makes for a great hangout; there's even a TV in the covered patio for those who like their *telenovelas.* This is undoubtedly one of the best budget options in the city, with a nice relaxing atmosphere and friendly owner.

4 Calle NO, 1/2 block west of Parque San Juan. ✆ **505/311-2279.** 10 units. $15 (£7.50) double. Breakfast $2 (£1) extra. AE, MC, V. **Amenities:** Breakfast room; TV room. *In room:* No phone.

Hostel Lazy Bones This huge open-air backpacker's hostel seems to have struck a nice balance between privacy and gregariousness with 11 stable-style private rooms, three of which have their own bathroom, and two big cavernous dorms. These all run the length of a very long courtyard, which functions as part lawn, part bar, part pool, and part pool hall, and is decorated with the usual funky motifs that are the rage in hostels the world over. In this case, decor comes in the form of a big colorful mural overlooking hammocks, sofas, and wicker chairs. The entire building has high ceilings and is partially shaded by a clunky terra-cotta tile rooftop. There is free Internet, free coffee, and even free 10-minute phone calls to the folks back home. But for a hostel, it is quite expensive (breakfast is extra and frankly not worth it) and it was half empty when I was there—which is maybe not a bad thing.

2 Av. NO, 2 1/2 blocks from the Parque de los Poetas. ✆ **505/311-3472.** www.lazybonesleon.com. 13 units. From $7 (£3.50) dorm; from $20 (£10) double with shared bathroom; from $25 (£13) double with private bathroom. AE, DC, MC, V. **Amenities:** Bar; laundry; pool. *In room:* No phone.

Via Via Part hostel, part cafe, and part meeting point, Via Via is a backpacker's favorite, with dorms and three private rooms facing a lush courtyard. The rooms have recently been decorated and now come with fans and mosquito nets. The courtyard has a lovely atmosphere, particularly in the evenings and on weekends when there's live music. An in-house travel agency provides interesting tours such as art workshops and cooking classes with locals. The inexpensive restaurant offers hearty meals including decent vegetarian options. Via Via is part of a global network of hostels and cafes and a great place to hook up with fellow travelers if you're traveling alone.

2 Av. NE, 50m (164 ft.) south of the Servicio Agrícola Gurdián. ✆ **505/311-6142.** www.viaviacafe.com. 1 dorm with 14 beds and 3 private rooms. From $3 (£1.50) dorm; from $8 (£4) double; from $12 (£6) triple. AE, MC, V. **Amenities:** Restaurant; laundry service. *In room:* Fan, no phone.

WHERE TO DINE

Down-to-earth León has equally down-to-earth food. Because of its sizeable student population, most restaurants serve *comida tipica,* cheap traditional fare, as well as ubiquitous burgers and pizzas. It might be some time before the city's restaurants earn culinary accolades, yet slowly but surely, gourmet centers are beginning to pop up. Wherever you go, you'll usually get character in the form of high ceilings, tiled floors, and a courtyard.

Expensive

Restaurante La Perla ★★ INTERNATIONAL/NICARAGUAN Here you'll find perhaps the finest dining in all of León. Part of La Perla hotel, this restaurant's elegant white facade and tall enchanting ceilings are enough to give you an appetite for Nicaraguan and international cuisine. Paintings by some of the country's greatest artists hang on the walls and the large salon is framed by handsome mahogany doors and large windows overlooking the front courtyard and street. On the menu you'll find Caesar salad, filet mignon, and fresh crab picked on the same day from the nearby Poneloya beach. The pâté platter is delicious, as is the smoked salmon. The restaurant has one of the finest wine lists in the country. The gracious owners Mark and Tim are often on hand to share a joke or story and are excellent hosts. You can finish the evening with a coffee with beans grown by the owners on the side of a volcano or a cocktail in the adjoining Canal Bar. Eating here makes for a very memorable experience.

1 Av. NO, 1½ blocks north of Iglesia la Merced. ✆ **505/311-3125.** www.laperlaleon.com. Main courses C342–C570 ($18–$30/£9–£15). AE, DC, MC, V. Daily noon–3pm and 7–11pm.

Moderate

In addition to the restaurants reviewed below, **Casa Vieja,** 1½ blocks north of Iglesia San Francisco (✆ **505/311-3701**), attracts a mixed crowd and has a laid-back, bohemian feel. It also has an attractive bar that serves pub grub; a snack here should not cost more than C152 ($8/£4). **Café Habana,** on Calle Central and Rubén Darío (no phone), is a small bar and restaurant run by a Cuban expat. It has a friendly atmosphere and serves great steak and mojitos. A main course should cost no more than C190 ($10/£5). Note that service can be slow.

Cocinarte VEGETARIAN/CAFE Fancy some falafel? Cocinarte is a handsome little eatery with a sister restaurant in Managua. Here you can try their delicious pasta al pesto or just drop by for a steaming cup of organic coffee. The decor is tasteful and there are themed evenings such as romantic Fridays and Jazzy Sundays.

3 Av. SO, to the north of Iglesia el Laborío. ✆ **505/315-4099.** Main courses C190–C285 ($10–$15/£5–£7.50). No credit cards. Tues–Sun noon–11pm.

Mediterraneo ★ Finds INTERNATIONAL This is a colorful, relaxing restaurant with bossa nova humming in the background and well-dressed waiters running between well-heeled diners. Though there's an interior dining area, of course, the courtyard is where the action is. At night, it is an elegant sight with its black-and-white tiled floor, backlit palm fronds, and vibrant artwork on the sunflower-yellow walls. The menu is extensive, offering everything from beef stroganoff to pizza (they even do delivery) to pasta. There are some delicious complimentary tomato and garlic tapas to get the ball rolling. The service could be a little bit more prompt, but it is fast by Nicaraguan standards. There is a nice small bar out front if you get impatient and fancy an aperitif or want to try a French or Italian wine from the wine list.

2 Av. NO, 1 block north of La Casa de Cultura. ✆ **505/895-9392.** Reservations recommended on weekends. Main courses C190–C285 ($10–$15/£5–£7.50). No credit cards. Tues–Sun noon–11pm.

Inexpensive

Benjamin Linder Cafe ★ CAFE Set on a noisy street corner with big, open doorways and chessboard tiles, this humble establishment is named after an American volunteer killed by the Contras (see "The Life & Times of Benjamin Linder" box below) A colorful mural of the modern American hero is displayed on the back wall and photos adorn the wall. The crumbling town house has a rough-and-tumble feel, but you'll quickly forget that as you sip one of their great cappuccinos or hot chocolates. The menu includes tapas and breakfast (with a rarity in Nicaragua—oatmeal) is served all day. There is a small gift display with ceramic handicrafts and home-produced coffee, and the restaurant adjoins a popular Internet cafe. A portion of all proceeds here go toward supporting a local charity for children with disabilities.

2 Calle NO, 2 blocks north of Parque Central. ✆ **505/311-0548.** Main courses C95 ($5/£2.50). No credit cards. Daily 8:30am–4:30pm.

El Sesteo CAFE This large, airy corner cafe sits on the main plaza with huge doorways looking out onto all the action passing by. Big fans whirl high up in the ceilings and old photos of León's movers and shakers adorn the walls, while people sit at large wooden tables set on old-fashioned tiles. The establishment oozes history; you can tell that some of the clientele, with faces as worn as the old leather seating, are just bursting to tell a story. The menu is nothing special, offering meat and seafood in hearty portions. It is a good stop for a *liquado* and sandwich, though if you fancy something different, try the *chancho con yucca* (fried pork with yucca and cabbage).

Corner of Av. Central and Parque Central. ✆ **505/311-5327.** Main courses C152–C190 ($8–$10/£3–£5). No credit cards. Daily 7am–10pm.

The Life & Times of Benjamin Linder

Benjamin Linder was a young engineering graduate from California who moved to Nicaragua in the early 1980s. An accomplished juggler and unicyclist, Linder was inspired by the 1979 Sandinista revolution and, like hundreds of other *internacionalistas,* wished to contribute toward helping the country's poor. He moved to the Northern Highlands and helped out in community projects such as vaccination drives. It was there that he put his skills as a juggler to good use. He dressed as a clown and with his unicycle encouraged families to visit the local clinic for measles jabs. He also began work on a small hydroelectric dam with the aim of bringing light to the village of San José de Bocay. While working there, the 27-year-old was ambushed and killed by Contra rebels, along with two Nicaraguan companions.

His death in 1987 made world headlines. It came amid an intense debate in the United States over the government's support of counterrevolutionary rebels. The Contras were trained and funded by a Reagan administration that feared that the Sandinista government was a communist threat in Central America. Linder's death shone light on a conflict that had killed 30,000 Nicaraguans. It contributed to Congress finally withdrawing support a year later.

Linder is now revered in Nicaragua and celebrated in countless murals as a juggling ambassador. You can visit the Benjamin Linder Café in León and see one such mural celebrating his life. He is held up by many as an American who made a positive contribution, and his efforts have now been duplicated by countless Americans doing good works in Nicaragua, whether they are Peace Corps volunteers or hotel owners funding public libraries (see the box "Volunteering Opportunities in Nicaragua" on p. 484). Benjamin Linder's grave can be visited in the Northern city of Matagalpa. Hundreds of mourners attended his funeral and he had a most poignant guard of honor—a line of children dressed as clowns.

LEÓN AFTER DARK

Don Señor's (© **505/311-1212**), is a disco, restaurant, and bar that gets a healthy mix of students and expats. It is open from Tuesday to Saturday and can be just as lively on a weeknight as a Saturday night. It is located in front of Parque La Merced. **Dilectus** (© **505/311-5439**) is León's version of a supper club, with lots of space and style. It is located on the outskirts on the road to Managua. Thursday is mariachi night. Live music can be caught on weekends at **Via Via** and **Benjamin Linder Cafe;** see "Where to Dine" above for details.

A SIDE TRIP TO PONELOYA & LAS PEÑITAS BEACHES

Twenty kilometers (13 miles) west of León, down one of the worst potholed roads I have ever experienced, are two beautiful beaches known as Poneloya and Las Peñitas. Popular with Leoneses escaping the city heat during the weekend, these dark-sand beaches are deserted on weekdays, though they're growing increasingly popular with surfers. ***Beware:*** The dark waves here are big and the currents strong. There is no lifeguard and drownings are frequent, especially during the high season (Easter week).

Essentials

Buses leave every half-hour from the Mercadito Subtiava, 12 blocks west of the city center; jump on any of the urban buses that ring the city and they will eventually pass by the market. Incredibly, the big old school buses to the beach are sometimes faster than taxis, as the latter drive incredibly slowly in order to avoid the Swiss-cheese-like road's potholes. The last bus returns to the city at 6:40pm and costs C20 ($1/50p).

Where to Stay on the Beach

The best hotels are on the southern strand of Las Peñitas; highlights are listed below.

Barca de Oro Barca de Oro won't win any architectural awards, but its location is perfect, as it is pitched right on the beach at the northern end of Isla Juan Venado, the mangrove and lagoon reserve famous for its turtle nesting. This hostel, which is set in a simple building held up by red-brick pillars and white concrete trellis, is popular with backpackers and surfers. The decor is basic, with plastic seating and multicolored tablecloths everywhere, but you get a mosquito net with your bed and incredible sunset views. Kayaks and surfboards are available for rent, and the English-speaking owners are proactive when it comes to organizing tours exploring the reserve.

Las Peñitas. © **505/317-0275.** www.barcadeoro.com. 23 units. $30 (£15) double. No credit cards. **Amenities:** Restaurant; bar. *In room:* No phone.

Hotel Suyapa Beach Opened in 1995, this three-story bright yellow hotel is modern, clean, and family run. There is an open-walled seafood restaurant out front on the beach and a pleasant pool area with sun loungers in the hotel garden. The rooms are simple and medium-size with spotless bathrooms. The small, modern lobby has colorful wicker chairs but is somewhat lacking in ambience and decoration.

Las Peñitas. © **505/885-8345.** www.suyapabeach.com. 22 units. $35 (£18) double. Rates include buffet breakfast. AE, DC, MC, V. **Amenities:** Restaurant; bar; pool. *In room:* A/C, TV, hair dryer, minibar.

OTHER SIDE TRIPS AROUND LEÓN

Los Hervideros de San Jacinto

Hervidero means "hotbed," and that description is no exaggeration when it comes to this ragged patch of land, 25km (16 miles) north of León. Los Hervideros de San Jacinto is basically a field of boiling mud, with steam rising from thermal vents and hiding the nearby peak of Volcán Telica. The bubbling muck is literally too hot to dip your hand into, though apparently it's very good for your skin complexion once it has cooled down. There are absolutely no tourist facilities here (though there is talk of the inevitable luxury hotel) and the site itself is not pretty, but it is fascinating. The mud patch is close to the town of San Jacinto and is a good 1-day excursion from the city. **Quetzaltrekkers** (© **505/311-6695;** www.quetzaltrekkers.com) and **Big Foot** (© **505/636-7041**) will help you organize an excursion there or you can just take a taxi or bus to the town of San Jacinto (take the Estelí or San Isidro service). The entrance has a large arched gateway where you'll find street vendors and guides.

Isla Juan Venado Wildlife Reserve ★

Have you ever wanted to see a mangrove warbler? Perhaps that's not on everybody's list of things to see, but this small yellow bird can only be found in mangrove swamps, and such a place exists on the Pacific coast west of León, just south of Las Peñitas. Isla Juan Venado is a 21-sq.-km (13-sq.-mile) wetland reserve that you can explore by boat or kayak. Here you'll find pelicans and herons stepping over crocodiles, iguanas, and caimans in a labyrinth of channels and waterways. This is also an important turtle nesting site, where thousands of turtles hatch at night. Tours can be arranged with operators in the city (p. 463) or you can go independently and hire a boat in Las Peñitas village. There is an entrance fee of C38 ($2/£1).

6 GRANADA ★★★ & THE MASAYA REGION

50km (31 miles) S of Managua; 150km (93 miles) SE of León

The Mexican poet Francisco de Icaza once said, "There is nothing sadder than being a blind man in Granada" and his words ring true for anyone visiting the magical town that is Granada. It's a living, breathing museum to the opulence of the old Spanish Empire. Among its highlights are a luminous cathedral, which stands in front of one of the country's most vibrant squares, and its pretty cobbled streets, which run down to the dark shores of Lake Cocibocha (also known as Lago de Nicaragua). Granada is a delightful surprise in contrast to the mediocre shabbiness of Managua; history clings to every chunky terra-cotta tile that drapes this town's multicolored one-story cottages and town houses.

Granada's perfectly preserved beauty is all the more surprising considering its tumultuous history of violence and plunder. Back in the 16th and 17th centuries, the city was pillaged by pirates and buccaneers and completely razed by the despot William Walker. The American filibusterer went so far as to plant a sign in its smoldering ruins declaring; "Here was Granada." The words and the man soon died but the city lived on. Founded in 1524 by Francisco Fernandez de Córdoba, it is Nicaragua's oldest city and sits at the foot of the Volcán Mombacho. Its access to the Caribbean via the Río San Juan allowed it to become a rich city of Spanish merchants and landowners. It is and was the conservative bastion of Nicaragua and was capital of the country several times as it pursued a sometimes vicious tug of war for control with the more liberal Léon in the north.

Today Granada is a prosperous, conservative city, benefiting greatly from a surge in tourism and property development. Tourists have replaced pirates and the only rumpus these days is caused by the squawking flock of jackdaws that swarm through the trees in its central plaza. Though more and more foreigners are deciding to stay and Granada has a sizeable expat community, you can tell this beautiful city will never lose its proud Nicaraguan roots. It has some of the country's best hotels and restaurants and is an ideal base to explore the rest of the country. Nearby are the finger of islands Las Isletas, the handicrafts center Masaya, and the towns of Pueblos Blancos, as well as outdoorsy excursions to places like Volcán Mombachoand Laguna de Apoyo.

ESSENTIALS

Getting There

BY BUS Buses leave Managua from in front of the university campus UCA (2 blocks west of the Metrocenter) daily every 15 minutes, starting at 5:50am and ending at 8pm. You can also catch a regular Granada-bound bus from Mercado R Huembes in Managua, starting at 5:25am and terminating at 9:30pm. There are several bus terminals in Granada, depending on where you are going or where you are coming from. **COGRAN** (✆ **505/552-2954**), is 1½ blocks south of the plaza's southwest corner and is used by *expresos* on route to Managua. The trip takes 1 hour and costs C12 (65¢/35p). Buses leave every 20 minutes, starting at 5:45am and ending at 8pm. On weekends the service ends at 7pm and service ends at 6pm on Saturday and Sunday. **Parque Sandino** is another departure point. It is on the north side of the city close to the old railway station. All buses pass by the entrance road to Masaya.

The southbound bus to Rivas from Granada leaves from the **Shell Palmira,** on the south side of the city, beside the Palé superstore. The trip takes 2 hours and costs C25 ($1.30/65p). The first departure is at 5:45am and the last at 3:10pm. If you want a direct bus to Masaya you must go to the bus stop behind **Palé,** although most Managua-bound buses will drop you off close to the town.

International bus companies have their own individual dropping off and departure points, all along Avenida Arrellano on the west side of the city. **TicaBus** (✆ **505/552-4301**) is a half-block south of the old hospital. The Panama-bound bus leaves at 7am but it is advisable to get there at 6:15am. **TransNica** (✆ **505/552-6619**) is 3 blocks south of the old hospital, on the corner of Calle Xalteva. There are three departures for Costa Rica, at 6:30am, 8am, and 11am (but arrive early to get a seat). The ride takes 7 hours and costs C160 ($8 /£4)

BY SHUTTLE/TAXI **Paxeos,** beside the cathedral on the southeast corner of Parque Colon (✆ **505/552-8291;** www.paxeos.com), organizes private and shared transfers to and from Managua airport and other locations such as San Jorge (where you catch the ferry to Isla de Ometepe). The trip to Managua costs between C570 ($30/£15) and C860 ($40/£20) depending on group size.

BY BOAT The small port is located at the east end of Calle La Calzada. Here boats leave on Monday and Thursday for the 4-hour trip (C80/$4.20/£2.10) to Alta Gracia on Isla de Ometepe (a faster ferry leaves from nearby San Jorge). The boat continues onto San Carlos, stopping at Morrito and San Miguelito on the northern shore of Lago de Nicaragua. The entire trip takes 14 hours and costs C230 ($12/£6), returning on Tuesdays and Fridays. There are no cabins or sleeping accommodations on the boat, and it can be quite uncomfortable, especially if there are rough seas and many people.

You can also get to Ometepe from **Granada** on a 4-hour voyage that leaves twice a week. The ***Mozorola*** (✆ **505/552-8764**) leaves every Wednesday and Saturday at 11am and docks at Altagracia on the island. It returns every Tuesday and Friday at 11am. The fare is C20 ($1.05/55p)

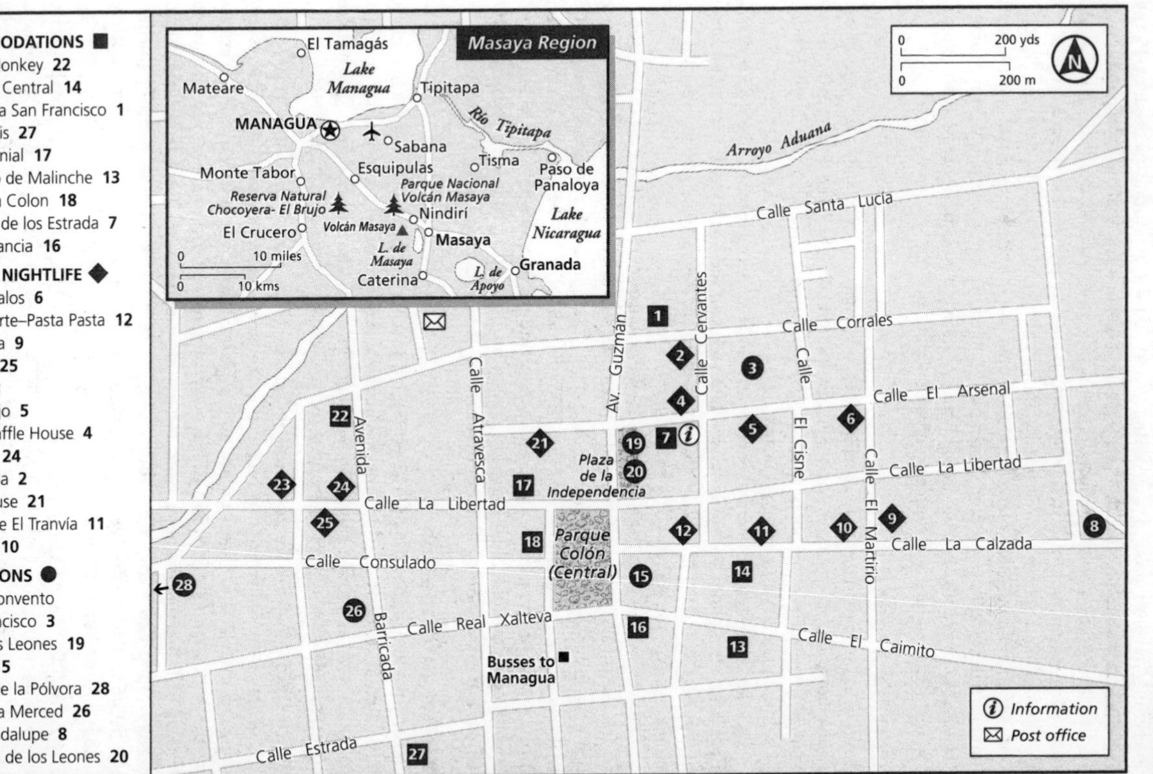
ACCOMMODATIONS
Bearded Monkey 22
Hospedaje Central 14
Hostal Casa San Francisco 1
Hostel Oasis 27
Hotel Colonial 17
Hotel Patio de Malinche 13
Hotel Plaza Colon 18
La Casona de los Estrada 7
La Gran Francia 16
DINING & NIGHTLIFE
Café Chavalos 6
Café DecArte–Pasta Pasta 12
Café Melba 9
Café Nuit 25
El Club 23
El Tercer Ojo 5
Kathy's Waffle House 4
La Fabrica 24
La Hacienda 2
Mimi's House 21
Restaurante El Tranvía 11
Zoom Bar 10
ATTRACTIONS
Antiguo Convento San Francisco 3
Casa de los Leones 19
Catedral 15
Fortaleza de la Pólvora 28
Iglesia de la Merced 26
Iglesia Guadalupe 8
La Plazuela de los Leones 20
Masaya Region
El Tamagás
Lake Managua
Mateare
Tipitapa
Río Tipitapa
MANAGUA
Sabana
Tisma
Paso de Panaloya
Monte Tabor
Esquipulas
Parque Nacional Volcán Masaya
Reserva Natural Chocoyera- El Brujo
Nindirí
Lake Nicaragua
El Crucero
Volcán Masaya
Masaya
L. de Masaya
Granada
Caterina
L. de Apoyo
0 10 miles
0 10 kms
0 200 yds
0 200 m
N
Arroyo Aduana
Calle Santa Lucía
Calle Corrales
Calle Cervantes
Calle El Cisne
Calle El Arsenal
Calle La Libertad
Calle El Martirio
Calle La Calzada
Calle El Caimito
Av. Guzmán
Calle Atravesca
Avenida Barricada
Calle Consulado
Calle Real Xalteva
Calle Estrada
Plaza de la Independencia
Parque Colón (Central)
Busses to Managua
Information
Post office

Orientation

Everything revolves around the central plaza (known as Parque Central or Parque Colón), and the sunlit cathedral that overlooks it will be your first and lasting impression of the city. The best hotels are located around the lively tree-lined plaza. Calle Calzada runs along the northern side of the cathedral in an easterly direction toward the lake and the dock. This street is partially pedestrianized and where you'll find many of the city's best restaurants and cafes, along with some hotels. Calle Atravesada is a narrow, busy commercial street, running north and south, 1 block west of the plaza. Volcán Mombacho rises to the south and the easterly lake has a scruffy waterfront and departure point for Las Isletas, known as Complejo Turístico Cocibolca.

Getting Around

You can easily explore central Granada on foot, though you may want to jump on one of the horse and carriages at the main plaza in order to feel like royalty as you trot through the streets. A half-hour ride should cost no more than C95 ($5/£2.50); always agree on a price before getting on board.

Bicycles are for rent at **Bearded Monkey,** Calle 14 de Septiembre (© **505/552-4028**), **Bicicleteria** (no phone), a half-block south of the park, and **De Tour,** 150m (492 ft.) east of the Alcaldía (© **505/552-0155;** www.detour-nicaragua.com). A bike for the day should not cost more than C190 ($10/£5).

Taxis can be found on the southern side of the square. Fares start at C30 ($1.50/75p).

You don't really need a car to explore Granada itself, but having one will help if you're planning excursions in the surrounding area. Car rentals cost approximately C768 ($40/£20) a day. **Alamo** (© **505/552-2877**) has an office in the Hotel Colonial, 20m (66 ft.) west of the plaza's northwest corner. **Budget** (© **505/552-2323;** budgetgr@hotmail.com) is at the Shell Guapinol station on the road to Managua. **Avis** (© **505/467-4780;** reservations@avis.com.ni) is on Calle La Calzada in the city center.

Visitor Information

Intur, Calle El Arsenal (© **505/552-6858**), is 1 block from the cathedral and a half-block behind the Casa de Leones. It is open Monday to Friday from 8am to midday and 2 to 5pm. Here you will find a good map detailing all the city's historic buildings. The website **www.granada.com.ni** gives an excellent pictorial display of the city but little else.

TOUR OPERATORS **Vapues Tours,** in the blue house next to the cathedral (© **505/552-8291;** www.vapues.com) is one of the city's main agencies, and it organizes everything from transfers to flights to local tours. **Tierra Tour,** Calle la Calzada, 2 blocks east of the cathedral (© **505/552-8723;** www.tierratour.com), organizes excursions to Masaya and Ometepe Island, as well as kayaking excursions on Lago de Nicaragua and canopy tours. **Eco Expedition Tours,** Calle la Calzada, 3½ blocks east of cathedral (© **505/552-8103**) organizes regular boat tours of Las Isletas that cost approximately C285 ($15/£7.50) and can also arrange transfers.

FAST FACTS An ATM can be found at the Esso garage on the main road and at Lacayo supermarket on Calle Real Xalteva. ATMs are also at **Banpro,** Calle Atravesada, in front of Teatro González (© **505/552-2723**) and **Bancentro,** farther down Calle Atravesada (© **505/552-6555**). **Banco de América Central** on the plaza changes traveler's checks and gives cash advances on Visa and MasterCard with no commission. You will also find many street money-changers in this area.

Internet access costs approximately $1.30 (65p) per hour and there are plenty of cafes dotted around the city. Try **Café E-mail** on Avenida Guzman near Parque Central. It is open daily from 7am to 10pm. **Inter Café** on Calle la Libertad, also near Parque Central, is open from 8am to 9pm Mondays to Saturdays.

In case of an emergency, call ✆ **505/552-2977** for the police, or ✆ **552-2711** for an ambulance.

The main **post office** is on Calle Atravesada opposite Cine Karawala.

Piscis Laundry Service, Calle El Martiro and Avenida Libertad (✆ **505/552-8239**) will pick up and deliver to your hotel. **Mapache,** Calle la Calzada and El Cisne (✆ **505/611-3501**) also picks up and delivers laundry, as well as tailoring.

WHAT TO SEE & DO

A visit to **Antiguo Convento San Francisco** ★★★ (✆ **505/552-5535**) should be at the top of your sightseeing list. This navy blue structure was first built in 1529 and destroyed by pirate Henry Morgan in 1679 and again by William Walker in 1856 during his notorious sacking of the city. It has risen from the ashes several times and acted as a barracks, university, and now a fully restored museum. As well as being a beautiful building in its own right, with countless galleries and courtyards, it houses a remarkable collection of pre-Columbian statues with zoomorphic forms of birds and jaguars found on Zapatera Island. The museum is 2 blocks north and 1 block east of the main cathedral. It is open Monday to Friday from 8:30am to 5:30pm and Saturday to Sunday from 9am to 4pm. Admission is C38 ($2/£1).

Nearby is the **Casa de los Leones,** Calle Guzman and El Arsenal (✆ **505/552-6437;** free admission), a historic building with a neoclassical facade. It is now a cultural space, housing exhibition rooms, a library, bookshop, cafe, and concert hall. It's open daily 7am to 6pm and is situated on the majestic, pillar-lined walkway that's called **La Plazuela de los Leones.** This walkway runs along the northeastern corner of the city's epicenter—**Parque Colon** (also known as Parque Central) ★—a lively central square that's crammed with stalls, food vendors, musicians, and circling horse and carriages that carry tourists around the city. The city square holds the city's main landmark, the magnificent, luminous orange **Catedral** on Calle Guzman and La Calzada. Despite the stunning exterior, the church's interior is quite simple and somewhat disappointing; it was built in the 20th century on the ruins of a previous church. It is open daily from 7am to 8pm. Admission is free.

If you cross the park and walk east on Calle Real Xalteva for 2 blocks, you'll come across the **Iglesia de La Merced** ★★, Real Xalteva and 14 de Septiembre. This is considered Granada's most beautiful church, and its baroque facade and intricate interiors have inspired poets for centuries, while withstanding a tumultuous history of pirate attacks and civil war skirmishes. The bell tower offers great views of the city but is often not open (ask the caretaker, if you can find him). The church has irregular opening hours but it is always best to go early. Admission is free.

Six blocks farther west on Calle Xaletva, is the **Fortaleza de la Pólvora,** a fort built in 1748 to guard munitions and ward off pirates. Its medieval structure was used as a jail during the Somoza dictatorship. It is now a military museum and makes for an interesting visit—you can even climb one of its five small towers. It has no fixed opening hours, but you should gain entrance if you arrive during daylight hours.

On the eastern side of the city, 4 blocks from the Parque Colon on Calle la Calzada, is the dark and atmospheric **Iglesia Guadalupe.** Calle la Calzada continues east to the

Spanish Classes in Granada

Nicaragua Mia, Calle El Caimito, 3½ blocks east of Parque Colon (✆ **505/552-8193**), is a women's cooperative offering individual Spanish classes. **Ave Nicaraguita,** Calle El Arsenal, 5 blocks east of Parque Colon (✆ **505/552-8538;** www.avenicaraguita.com), is worth checking out for group classes; they also offer classes in Managua.

gray shores of **Lago Cocibolca.** Here you'll find Granada's version of a waterfront walk, known as **Complejo Turístico Cocibolca.** Though the lake provides some magnificent panoramic views, the shore is sadly neglected and litter-strewn. You'll pass it on the way to the departure point for tour boats going to Las Isletas.

OUTDOOR ACTIVITIES

CANOPY TOURING The slopes of **Reserva Natural Volcán Bombacho** offer some spectacular opportunities to glide through the jungle. **Canopy Tours Mombacho** (✆ **261/267-8256**) has a 16-platform course that's located close to the park entrance. **Hacienda Cutirre** has a spectacular 17-platform canopy system on the eastern face of the volcano. Trips there can be arranged through **Mombotour** (✆ **261/552-4548;** www.mombotour.com).

HIKING **Reserva Natural Volcán Bombacho** has some of the best-maintained trails in the country. Numerous travel operators offer 1-day excursions here or you can take a short bus ride to the park entrance. It is possible to hike from the city to the huge crater lake, **Laguna de Apoyo** (p. 486), a popular watering hole holding abundant wildlife within its rim. **Volcán Masaya National Park** (p. 490) offers a jaw-dropping look into the gates of hell and is possible to see in a day excursion from the city.

HORSEBACK RIDING **Blue Mountain** (✆ **505/552-5323;** www.bluemountainnicaragua.com) is a ranch outside the city where you can also lodge and do wildlife excursions. Rates start at C760 ($40/£20).

KAYAKING **Laguna de Apoyo** has several launching pads for those who fancy some paddle time. You can rent kayaks from lakeside lodgings **San Simian Eco Resort** (✆ **505/813-6866**) or the **Monkey Hut** (✆ **505/887-3546**). More interesting to explore are the chain of islands called Las Isletas in Lago de Nicaragua. Here there are some bird-filled waterways and an interesting island fort called El Fortin.

SHOPPING

The **Mercado Municipal** is a busy, sprawling hive of activity 1 block south of the central plaza. Here you'll find everything from soap to sombreros. It is open daily from 6am to 6pm. **Galeria Istmo,** Calle Atravesada, in front of Bancentro (✆ **505/552-4678;** www.galeriaistmo.com), offers the best in Nicaraguan art and design. **Casa Natal,** 1½ blocks east of Calle El Caimito (no phone), sells handicrafts from all over Nicaragua, including woodcarvings from Solentiname and black ceramics from Jinotega. **Casa de Antiguedades,** 1 block north of Calle Arsenal (✆ **505/874-2034;** haroldsandino@hotmail.com) is a treasure-trove of antiques and is great for a morning browse.

Granada has the best selection of colonial-style hotels in all of Nicaragua. Even the most humble *hospedaje* will have an atmospheric courtyard and gallery with rocking chairs beneath arched pillars. That said, the rooms themselves may strike you as small, with claustrophobic bathrooms and dangerously steep stairs, especially if you have had one *cerveza* too many late at night.

Expensive

Hotel Patio de Malinche Value Kids This hotel's attractive but humble entrance belies a magnificent colonial complex with two lush courtyards, one with a spectacular pool. A tastefully decorated two-story building of whitewashed walls and arched wooden doorways surrounds the main courtyard. This courtyard leads to large, airy rooms done up in muted tones with the occasional splash of color, such as a scarlet bedspread or hand-woven tablecloth. Rocking chairs and hammocks are placed in strategic locations throughout the hotel, making for an abundance of great places to rest. It might lack the artful details of other historic hotels in the city but the Patio de Malinche has a bright, welcoming atmosphere that makes up for it.

Calle El Caimito, by Calle El Cisne. ✆ **505/552-2235.** www.patiodelmalinche.com. 15 units. From $64 (£32) double; from $76 (£38) triple. Rates include breakfast. AE, DC, MC, V. Airport pickup $35 (£18). **Amenities:** Bar; laundry service; pool; Wi-Fi. *In room:* A/C, cable TV, Internet.

Hotel Plaza Colon ★★★ Moments This is a magnificent hotel in every sense. The one abiding memory I have of this beautiful hotel is sipping rum on its wide, polished balcony, while overlooking the boisterous plaza, filled with tourists and vendors working to the rhythm of merengue. The sumptuous decor hits the right balance between colonial authenticity and the modern traveler's expectations. Rooms have modern amenities like cable TV, but also come with grand built-in wardrobes and luxurious king-size beds. Exquisite tiled floors lead to a majestic inner balcony that runs around a glorious courtyard and pool. Everything is lustrous and elegant and the service is prompt and reliable. Make sure to get the staff to adjust the air-conditioning to silent mode and be prepared for a dawn chorus of jackdaws singing outside. Below, adjoining the genteel lobby, is an excellent wine store.

Calle Consulado, by Parque Colon. ✆ **505/552-8489.** Fax 505/552-8505. www.hotelplazacolon.com. 27 units. From $99 (£50) double; from $179 (£90) suite. Rates include breakfast. AE, DC, MC, V. **Amenities:** Wine bar; Internet (in lobby); pool. *In room:* A/C, cable TV, minibar.

La Gran Francia Staying at la Gran Francia feels like residing in a museum, albeit, a beautiful, well-located, and courtly museum. Impeccably done religious paintings hang on the walls and a wooden monk greets you at the bottom of the stairs. The Spanish-tiled steps lead to an upper gallery surrounding a long courtyard with a small blue pool below. The rooms are grand in every sense. An ample, inviting bed is surrounded by considerable space, punctuated with stout furniture and a small balcony overlooking a busy side street. In the nice-size bathrooms, original ironwork faucets hang over hand-painted wash basins displaying old-fashioned street scenes. My only criticism of this place is that the staff is very much like the sculptures that grace the hotel's nooks and crannies—wooden and unresponsive. Across the street is the hotel's restaurant, which boasts a mellow, inviting bar where guests can enjoy a free welcome drink after checking in.

Southeast corner of Parque Central and Calle El Caimito. ✆ **505/552-6000.** Fax 505/552-6001. www.lagranfrancia.com. 21 units. From $110 (£55) double; from $125 (£63) triple; from $120 (£60) suite. Rates include breakfast. AE, MC, V. **Amenities:** Restaurant and bar; laundry service; pool; room service. *In room:* A/C, cable TV, Internet, minibar.

Moderate

Hostal Casa San Francisco Located on a quiet side street, this agreeable little hotel has a sidewalk bar and restaurant out front, and a miniature courtyard out back. The main walkway through the property leads to a small pool and on the right a picturesque building with delightful, tastefully decorated rooms. Large fans hang over four-poster beds and the charming bathrooms have a colorful tiled partition separating the shower. The San Francisco is compact, attractive, and well maintained, with lots of character. It makes for a quiet, snug hideaway with a heavy dose of colonial splendor.

207 Calle Corrales, by the Antiguo Convento San Francisco. ✆ **505/552-8235.** www.csf-hotel-granada.com. 9 units. From $45 (£23) standard; from $55 (£28) king/twin. Rates include breakfast. 5% discount for cash. AE, DC, MC, V. **Amenities:** Restaurant; small pool; room service. *In room:* A/C, cable TV, Wi-Fi.

Hotel Colonial ★ (Finds) As you approach this midsize hotel and note its attractive, navy blue facade and row of international flags, you might think it is just another conventional four-star lodging. Yes, it is conventional, but it's conventional done Granada style. The reception area is a spectacle of green walls and Corinthian pillars holding up an intricate ceiling of classic moldings. Curling balustrades of marble are graced with giant Grecian urns holding potted plants. The courtyard, with a pool and mosaic-covered island bar, is just as lavish a spectacle. The hotel's rainbow-hued colors run into the rooms themselves, which are big with beautiful four-poster beds and polished floors. The suites have giant corner Jacuzzis tucked beneath green tiled archways. It is all rather over-the-top but refreshingly different for anyone used to the muted gray and beige tones that seem to plague the modern chain hotel. This hotel has character, and friendly, professional bilingual staff.

Calle La Libertad, 25m (82 ft.) west of Parque Central. ✆ **505/552-7581.** Fax 505/552-7299. www.hotelcolonialgranada.com. 37 units. From $70 (£35) double. AE, DC, MC, V. **Amenities:** Restaurant; pool. *In room:* A/C, cable TV, Wi-Fi.

La Casona de los Estrada ★ A stay at the boutique La Casona de Estrada ensures that you'll have a classic Granada experience. You'll feel like you are one of the old aristocracy as you walk through its wide entrance hall, graced with a huge gilded mirror, and into the large open courtyard, which is alive with plants and flowers. The rooms are handsome and boast high wooden ceilings and large tiled floors, though some are much bigger than others—ask what is available at check in. The bathrooms are smallish but spotless and everything is well maintained. This place manages to make you feel like you're staying at an enormous palace when actually there are only six rooms, some of which overlook the garden and one of which has its own private courtyard. La Casona has the added advantage of a friendly, attentive staff.

Calle El Arsenal, by the Antiguo Convento San Francisco. ✆ **505/552-7393.** www.casonalosestrada.com. 6 units. From $50 (£25) double. Rates include breakfast. Airport transfers available. AE, DC, MC, V. **Amenities:** Bar; room service. *In room:* A/C, cable TV.

Inexpensive

In addition to the places reviewed below, **Hospedaje Central** (✆ **505/552-9500**) is a popular backpacker hangout with over 80 beds and a lively social scene. It is not the prettiest property in town, nor the cleanest, but it offers bargain bunk beds for less than C114 ($6/£3) a head and a street cafe. Private rooms are also available. Its large, rambling building is located 1½ blocks east of the central plaza, on Calle Calzada.

Bearded Monkey The Bearded Monkey has positioned itself as the most popular and funky *mochilero* (backpacker) hangout in Granada. With its huge bulletin board, free movie screenings, book exchange, music library, and copious number of hammocks, it's a backpacker paradise. The cafe bar acts as good meeting point, with a dartboard to help break the ice and bikes to rent if you wish to explore more than just the hostel's large courtyard of palm trees. The old colonial building holds both dorms and private rooms, some of which have no windows. A mosquito net will definitely come in handy here, as will bug spray. The owners also operate the Monkey Hut in Laguna de Apoyo (p. 487).

Av. 14 de Septembre and Costado. ✆ **505/552-4028.** www.thebeardedmonkey.com. 10 units (including 3 large dorms). From $6 (£3) dorm; from $14–$17 (£7–£8.50) double; from $24 (£12) triple; from $22–$36 (£11–£18) suite. Transport shuttle $1 (50p) one-way. AE, DC, MC, V. **Amenities:** Bar and restaurant; high-speed Internet in lobby; laundry facilities; pool table; TV room. *In room:* No phone.

Hostel Oasis ★ Value This hostel has nary a multicolored barn door or funky mosaic-tiled bathroom in sight. The Oasis breaks the mold by instead offering the sort of stylish facilities you'd expect in a more expensive bed-and-breakfast, except here guests sleep in dorms and can use the kitchen. Its main asset is its great pool, which is in a back courtyard surrounded by stone-clad columns holding up a gallery of balconies and doorways. There is also a very pleasant garden courtyard with sun loungers. The dorms are basic but not too claustrophobic, though the bunk beds might be too short for some lankier readers. The private rooms are small and functional but all the furniture matches, the TV works, and everything is immaculate. Opened in 2002, the Oasis is for the more discerning *mochilero* who wants a little luxury without paying too high a price.

Calle Estrada and Av. Barricada. ✆ **505/552-8006.** www.nicaraguahostel.com. 19 units. From $6 (£3) dorm; from $10 (£5) private room. AE, DC, MC, V. **Amenities:** Cafe; high-speed Internet in lobby; laundry service; pool. *In room:* A/C (extra charge), fan, cable TV (extra charge).

WHERE TO DINE

Granada has its fair share of sidewalk cafes, but be aware that on the more popular streets, you will get harassed by persistent panhandlers if you sit outside. Most restaurants are located on the pedestrian street Calle La Calzada or 2 blocks north of it, close to Antiguo Convento San Francisco.

Expensive

El Tercer Ojo ★ FUSION El Tercer Ojo is an exotic haven of Far Eastern delight. The interior is a visual feast, with purple silk cushions and curtains and a golden Buddha watching from the liquor shelf. A small bar with Yves Saint Laurent prints leads to a pleasant, colorful courtyard adorned with artwork and face masks. The menu is extensive and includes Asian staples such as Thai chicken and shrimp with Vietnamese curry. There are a variety of tapas, shish kabobs, and fish dishes like mussels sautéed in wine sauce. Speaking of wine, this laid-back and intimate restaurant has a pretty good international list with offerings from Argentina, Italy, Spain, France, and Chile.

Calle El Arsenal, on the corner of Antiquo Convento San Francisco. ✆ **505/552-6451.** Main courses C200 ($10/£5). AE, DC, MC, V. Daily 11am–11pm.

Restaurante El Tranvía ★★ INTERNATIONAL/SEAFOOD This old-fashioned restaurant is tucked inside the roomy Hotel Dario. Its large white salon, with giant doors looking out onto Calle La Calzada and old black-and-white photos on the wall, makes for an elegant and cool (six big fans hum overhead) setting. The menu is very much concentrated on seafood, with lobster from the Corn Islands featured strongly. The shrimp *al Diablo* is a spicy mix of shrimp with pepper, tomatoes, and ginger. It also comes in a curry sauce or a sauce of scotch and mushrooms mixed with coconut milk.

The wine list is decent, with average wines hailing from lots of countries. The dining experience here is definitely romantic—you may get serenaded by some wandering musicians during your meal. The waiters are dressed formally but wear a smile.

Calle La Calzada (150m/492 ft.) northeast from the cathedral. ✆ **505/552-3400.** www.hoteldario.com/tranviaeng.htm. Main courses C285–C380 ($15–$20/£7.50–£10). AE, DC, MC, V. Daily noon–10pm.

Moderate

Café DecArte–Pasta Pasta CAFE/ITALIAN Now here is a concept that will hopefully catch on elsewhere in the country. During the day, this establishment takes on the guise of a casual coffee shop called DecArte, offering excellent tuna and curry sandwiches and Thai peanut salad. Chill-out music plays in the background and people enjoy the small, modern courtyard and local art on the walls. It then closes during the late afternoon only to resurrect itself as a nocturnal Italian restaurant, called Pasta Pasta, complete with red checkered tablecloths, wine bottle baskets, and opera music in the background. Both restaurants are excellent.

Calle La Calzada, 1 block east of the cathedral. ✆ **505/552-6461.** Main courses C114–C190 ($6–$10/£3–£5) at both restaurants. AE, DC, MC, V. Daily 11am–4pm for Café DecArte and daily 5–10pm for Pasta Pasta.

Café Melba VEGETARIAN Set in a simple colonial building with a pretty courtyard, Café Melba offers up spectacular breakfasts like potato pancakes in a unpretentious environment. Later in the day, items like homemade veggie burgers and black beans are dished out, to be washed down with fresh juice. Run by Californian expat Talia, the kitchen offers other vegan-style dishes, along with tapas. The restaurant also hosts movie nights on Wednesdays and karaoke on Saturdays.

In addition to managing this restaurant, Talia runs a volunteer movie production company that trains local girls in movie production. She always needs volunteers; for more information, go to www.cinegranada.org.

Calle El Martiro, 1/2 block from La Calzada. ✆ **505/552-0261.** Main courses C114–C190 ($6–$10/£3–£5). No credit cards. Tues–Sun 8am–2pm and 5–11pm.

Inexpensive

Café Chavalos *Finds* NICARAGUAN Set up by the energetic American Donna Tabor, Café Chavalos takes street kids off the street and into the kitchen, by training them as chefs and waiters. The restaurant is large and somewhat cavernous but nicely decorated with uplifting slogans, shell patterns, and wrought-iron furniture. Though the menu here is a little on the short side, Donna is such a great host (she's always on hand to make sure everything runs smoothly) that eating here makes for a wonderful experience—plus, by eating here, you'll be helping to give local kids a future.

Calle La Calzada, by the Iglesia Guadalupe. ✆ **505/552-2178.** Main courses C114–C190 ($6–$10/£3–£5). AE, DC, MC, V. Daily 6am–10pm.

Kathy's Waffle House CAFE Kathy's seems to be the breakfast spot for foreigners in Granada, though the occasional local drops by to enjoy menu items like massive round Belgian waffles in a variety of delicious sauces. French toast and full egg breakfasts are also on the menu, as well as very decent milkshakes and smoothies. Diners sit on an elevated patio in front of the beautiful Convento San Francisco—it's a perfect spot to start your day and plot out your itinerary.

Calle El Arsenal, 1/2 block west of the Antiguo Convento San Francisco. No phone. Snacks C95 ($5/£2.50). AE, MC, V. Daily 7am–2pm.

Mimi's House ★ CAFE This has to be the prettiest Internet cafe in all of Nicaragua. Checkerboard floor tiles lead through a colorful space to a back courtyard decorated with plants, trees, fairy lights, and butterfly-shaped candleholders on the wall. Inside there is seating with tables as well as a line of computers and a phone booth. It's a very charming cafe, and a great place to recharge and catch up on e-mails.

Calle El Arsenal, 1½ blocks west of Antiguo Convento San Francisco. ✆ **505/552-5770.** Main courses C114–C190 ($6–$10/£3–£5). No credit cards. Daily 8am–10pm.

GRANADA AFTER DARK

The more upscale bars and nightclubs in town are located west of the central plaza, while the more down-at-heel local joints can be found on the lakeshore close to the Complejo Turistico. **Café Nuit ★**, half a block west of the Piedra Bocona, Calle La Libertad (✆ **505/552-7376**), is one of Granada's liveliest nightspots and a great opportunity to shake off any reservations and swing your hips to live salsa and merengue. A long walkway of palm plants leads to an attractive courtyard adorned with ivy and fountains and stone circular seating. There is a corner bar at the back dispensing cold beers and cocktails and a kitchen to the side serving tapas and canapés. The band plays every night and often doubles up as bouncers if the crowd of locals and foreigners get a little too excited. It is open daily except Tuesdays from 7pm to 1am. On Fridays and Saturdays there is a cover charge of C$20 ($1/50p). **El Club,** Calle La Libertad and Avenida Barricada Granada (✆ **505/552-7376;** www.elclub-nicaragua.com), is young, trendy, and cool. A well-appointed disco bar up front leads to a designer style courtyard of pebbled walkways, backlit palm trees, and purposely worn furniture. Over the bar hangs a series of clocks giving global times with a political twist, one for Napoleon, another for Gandhi, and so on. This new establishment does not get going until really late and there is also an adjoining hotel of the same name for revelers who like their bed to be close to the dance floor.

Zoom Bar, La Calzada, 3 blocks from Parque Colon (✆ **505/643-5855;** www.zoom bar.biz), claims to be Granada's only real pub and is a good place to go for huge burgers and sports. Not far away, facing El Convento San Francisco, is a pleasant watering hole called **La Hacienda** (✆ **505/552-5108**). Opened in 2007, it has a nice front terrace and attractive bar, which is good for day or evening drinking. There is live music every Friday night. **La Fabrica** (no phone) is a well known venue that draws a great crowd looking for cocktails and rock. It is located 1½ blocks from the plaza's northwest corner.

For more down-at-the-heel discos, you need to go to the Complejo Turistico Cocibolca, near the waterfront. Here there is a strip of bars and nightclubs, the best of which are **Pantera** (no phone) and **Cesars** (✆ **505/552-7241**). Be warned however, this part of town at night is for the young, adventurous, and even foolish. If you do fancy seeing this part of town, make sure you get a taxi back as the walk into the city is through a notoriously crime-ridden spot.

SIDE TRIPS FROM GRANADA

Las Isletas

Trailing away from Granada's southern waterfront is the 365-island archipelago known as Las Isletas, formed by a volcanic eruption from nearby Mombacho over 10,000 years ago. These tiny jungle islands are hosts to mini-monkey sanctuaries, humble *campesino* huts and lavish mansions, and attractions like an island cemetery and an old Spanish fort called **Fortín San Pablo.** It is a popular 1-day excursion, so boats leave frequently from the southern end of the **Complejo Turístico Cocibolca** (p. 476). You can go there independently by taking a taxi or walking a half-hour south along the shore of the Centro

Volunteering Opportunities in Nicaragua

Nicaragua has always attracted an unconventional tourist, starting with the pirates and Californian gold prospectors who came here centuries ago. A new breed of visitor appeared after the Sandinista revolution—thousands of *internacionalistas* intent on joining the great leap forward and helping the country's poor and impoverished (the less than committed were wittily referred to as Sandalistas). Those idealists have now morphed into ordinary people doing amazing things, and Nicaragua is now officially a hot spot for volunteering opportunities in Central America. Below is a list of the more established volunteer organizations offered in the country, but just scratch the surface, and you'll find many more. If you are serious about taking up a good cause, you need to commit considerable time (at least a month) and have basic Spanish skills to get the most from your experience.

GRANADA

Building New Hope is a Pittsburgh-based nonprofit organization that runs a learning center for underprivileged kids, among many other projects in Granada. The volunteer organizer is Donna Tabor and she can be contacted through their website www.buildingnewhope.org. Tax deductible donations are also welcome.

Hogar Madre Albertina is a girls' orphanage that sorely needs money and volunteers. Desperate to get rid of an old laptop? You can donate yours here, as well as donate your time by teaching a word processing class. The orphanage is located 2 blocks north of Colegio Padre Misieri, and you can call ✆ **505/552-7661** for info.

La Esperanza Granada (✆ **505/552-7044;** www.la-esperanza-granada.org) helps educate locals in rural areas as well as offers badly needed healthcare. They provide cheap accommodations and can organize homestays if you're looking for total cultural and language immersion. Their office is located in Hospedaje Central, 1½ blocks east of the central plaza.

Cineastas de Granada was started by Californian Thalia Drori with the aim of teaching teenage girls the craft of filmmaking. Workshops involve writing, producing, cinematography, sound, and editing. Teachers and equipment are required. Tax-deductible donations can be made through the Building New Hope organization. Thalia can be contacted at her vegetarian restaurant Café Melba or via the website www.cinegranada.org

SAN JUAN DEL SUR

San Juan del Sur Biblioteca Movil (janem101@aol.com) is sponsored by the Hester J. Hodgdon Libraries for All Program. Teachers and donations are required as well as Spanish books, which can be sent to the library's U.S. depository at 1716 del Norte Blvd., Loveland, CO 80538, or directly dropped off.

The **Newton-San Juan del Sur Sister City Project** is a Massachusetts-based nonprofit organization that sends teams of doctors, dentists, and builders to

San Juan. Visit their website www.newtonsanjuan.org or contact their local representative Rosa Elena Bello at rosaebel@ibw.com.ni.

The **Pangea Partnership** (www.pangeapartnership.org) offers "meaningful travel" in the form of sustainable development projects and workshops. They specialize in straw bale construction and require volunteers who are not afraid to get their hands dirty.

Fundación A. Jean Brugger (www.piedrasyolas.com/brugger_eng.htm) focuses on children's educational needs, offering uniforms, school supplies, and scholarships to students from poor backgrounds.

MATAGALPA

Habitat for Humanity (**✆ 505/772-6121;** www.habitatnicaragua.org.ni) is a Christian organization that builds decent housing for the poor, in an effort to "change Nicaragua house by house." They have projects all over the country, including León and Bluefields. Their Matagalpa branch is located 2 blocks east of the Deportiva Brigadista.

Centro Girasol (**✆ 505/772-6030**) is a community center that can hook you up with different organizations that require volunteers such as indigenous rights campaigners **Movimento Comunal** and **Comunidad Indígena.** Their offices are located in the yellow building at the bridge, as you enter the city from Managua.

OMETEPE

Nuestro Pequeños Hermanos operates an orphanage in San Lázaro that offers volunteer programs on the island and in other parts of Central America. Visit their website at www.nphamigos.org for info.

La Suerte Biological Teaching Station (www.lasuerte.org) is dedicated to protecting tropical rainforests and wildlife. They offer teaching opportunities to students and professors and accommodate educational groups with the goal of "bridging the Americas."

Bainbridge-Ometepe Sisters Island Association (www.bosia.org) does countless good works on the island, including promoting fair trade coffee, creating schools, scholarships, and water systems.

MANAGUA

Si a la Vida (www.asalv.org) works with troubled kids and opens up their opportunities through education, sports, and art. They seek volunteers with experience in healthcare, construction, and agriculture. They also operate a retreat on Ometepe Island.

Casa Ben Linder (www.casabenlinder.org) is a meetinghouse and resource center devoted to helping alleviate poverty.

Turistico until you reach a building with small pontoons and boats that leave as soon as they fill up. Or take a tour with any of the travel operators in the city center (p. 476).

I found the islands to be a disappointment. Every rock seemed to be sporting a real estate sign and the motorboats scared away all wildlife. The quality of restaurants in the touristy parts of the islands left a lot to be desired, too. The true way to enjoy the islands is to avoid the herd and go farther out in a kayak or private boat. Aquatic birds such as egrets, herons, and cranes can be spotted in the early morning or evening. A separate archipelago, known as **Isla Zapatera,** lies 2 hours away from Granada and is famous for its pre-Columbian stone carvings (a spectacular collection of which can be seen in the Convento San Francisco; see p. 477).

Reserva Natural Volcán Mombacho ★★

Look south from your hotel balcony and you'll see a mountain with a wide, blunted summit. Look closer and you'll realize that the summit is in fact the jagged crater of a huge volcano that blew its top 10,000 years ago. Volcán Mombacho is still active, though it has been 500 years since its last significant eruption knocked its side wall out and drained its lake, sweeping away an Indian village in the process. Hidden in its high, dark cloud forest are red-eyed frogs, howler monkeys, and orchids. Its lower slopes have given way to coffee plantations and ranches but its upper reaches are now a protected reserve, with some of the best maintained nature trails in the country. One such trail is called **Sendero el Crater,** a 2-hour track around the volcano's 1,345m-high (4,411 ft.) rim, during which you'll have ample chances to take in the forest-lined interior and its numerous mammals, birds, and types of flora. During this hike, you will also pass fascinating *fumaroles*—ground vents blasting out hot sulfurous air. **Sendero la Puma** is a more arduous trek, as it is twice as long and involves climbing to some look out points with fantastic views. It takes 3 hours to complete.

The reserve is managed by a NGO called **Fundación Cocibolca** (**© 261/552-5858;** fcocibol@ibw.com.ni) and is open from Tuesday to Sunday, though Tuesday and Wednesday are normally reserved for organized groups. Admission is C190 ($10/£5). The most convenient way to visit the reserve is through the numerous travel operators in town that offer 1-day excursions; see p. 476 for info. If you wish to go there independently, jump on a Rivas or Nandaime bus and alight at Empalme el Guanacaste. It is then a half-hour walk uphill to the park entrance. Once you pay the entrance fee, an old army truck leaves every 2 hours to take you up to the foundation's Biological Station 6km (3¾ miles) away. Here they offer mountain-lodge-style accommodations for those who wish to spend the night on the side of an active volcano. If you have your own transport (4WD only) there is an extra charge of C285 ($15/£7.50) per vehicle to enter the reserve.

In addition to great hiking, the slopes of Mombacho offer some spectacular canopy runs. **Canopy Tours Mombacho** (**© 261/267-8256**) is located close to the reserve entrance. This 16-platform course is 1,700m (5,576 ft.) long and many tour operators include it in their 1-day tour of the reserve. There is also a spectacular 17-platform canopy system at **Hacienda Cutirre** on the eastern face of the volcano. This is a little more difficult to access and best arranged with travel operators and canopy specialists **Mombotour** (**© 261/552-4548;** www.mombotour.com).

Laguna de Apoyo

Directly west of Granada is a huge, pristine volcano lake known as Laguna de Apoyo. This dark blue body of water is 200m (656 ft.) deep and set in a lush, forest-covered circular valley with nature trails, small villages, and the occasional ministerial mansion. The crater is alive with animals, including white-face monkeys, butterflies, toucans, and hummingbirds. The Volcán Apoyo is very much dormant, though it is known to tremor occasionally and the lake holds some underwater thermal vents. Because of the lake's isolated habitat, it contains several unique species of fish.

Getting There

It's a 20-minute drive from Granada to Laguna de Apoyo and a C285 ($15/£7.50) taxi ride is the most convenient way of getting there. Alternatively, you can arrange the trip via the hostel **Bearded Monkey** (see earlier in this chapter) or its sister lodge the **Monkey Hut** (see below). Don't think about driving on your own: Once you get off the highway from Granada, the road is a beautifully brick-paved lane—an anomaly in a country with such bad roads. But the perfect paving stops after just a few minutes, and the rest of the way makes for very difficult driving.

Another way of getting to the lake is to simply walk from Granada. A dirt road from the city cemetery's northeast corner heads west until you reach a crossroads just below the crater's lip. You must then turn right and cross a field to get a view of the lake. The trek takes approximately 3 hours there and back.

Where to Stay

There are several hotels and lodges along the lakeshore, many with wooden piers for swimmers and kayakers. Below are the best.

The Monkey Hut The Monkey Hut is the sister lodge to the Bearded Monkey in Granada but has a lot more class. This property's wide, terraced garden, filled with comfy sun loungers, leads down to the shore. Guests stay in a handsome wooden cottage, which has a handful of private rooms and dorm beds to choose from. It makes for a nice, peaceful getaway, with homey qualities like a shared kitchen and basketball court. There is a wooden pier to dive off or set sail from in kayaks or tire tubes.

Laguna de Apoyo, 100m (328 ft.) from bottom of hill. ✆ **505/887-3546.** www.thebeardedmonkey.com/monkeyhut.htm. 15 units. From US$10 dorm; $23–$25 (£12–£13) double; from $45–$70 (£23–£35) la *cabaña* (2–4 persons). AE, DC, MC, V. **Amenities:** Bar; communal kitchen; barbecue; watersports equipment. *In room:* No phone.

Norome Villas ★ Kids Narrow white pillars hold up palm-fronded roofs in this self-contained, large resort that is easily the most luxurious lodging on the lake. Nicely tiled floors lead to orange, Caribbean-style villas. There is a gorgeous pool and spectacular lakeside restaurant and bar. Though this place is known to book big, package-tour-oriented groups, it is quite a classy act and there is lots of space to escape to, including forest trails and a spa. The complex sits snugly by the lakeside and some of the villas require a stiff climb upward. It is also open to day visitors.

Eastern shore of Laguna de Apoyo. ✆ **505/883-9093.** www.noromevillas.com. 142 units. From $65 (£33) standard; from $75 (£38) studio; from $84 (£42) 1-bed villa; from $129 (£65) 2-bed villa; from $159 (£79) 3-bed villa. AE, MC, V. **Amenities:** Restaurant and bar; Internet in lobby; pool; spa. *In room:* A/C, TV, hair dryer, kitchen area.

San Simian Eco Resort This place, consisting of five ecohuts that descend toward the lake, is perfect for those who want isolation and perhaps a good swim, while staying someplace that's sustainable. The accommodations themselves are basic but comfortable. Rooms are situated in palm-roofed cottages, and are small with a circular, open-air bathroom (plan on cold showers). There is an herb garden below the restaurant and hammocks around the bar. Though some little annoyances exist, like dragging doors and clasps that don't quite catch, what's more important is that the view is spectacular and there's an abundance of outdoor activities on hand, including kayaks, a small catamaran, and floaters to rent from their mini dock.

1km (1/2 mile) past Norome resort. ✆ **505/813-6866.** www.sansimian.com. 5 units. From $50 (£25) double. AE, MC, V. **Amenities:** Restaurant; bar; watersports equipment. *In room:* Fan.

7 MASAYA

89km (55 miles) from Granada

Welcome to Masaya—Nicaragua's capital of shopping. In a country that is a treasure-trove of quality handicrafts, Masaya is the industrious nucleus, churning out an endless array of tempting souvenirs such as intricate pottery, handsome woodcarvings, sturdy leather goods, and beautiful hand-woven hammocks. This restless city of 100,000 creative souls is spread along a hot plain and up a gentle slope to the Masaya crater lake, with the smoldering Volcán Masaya in the distance. Though it was first explored by the Spanish in the 16th century, the city was not founded until 1819. It has a fiery history of rebellion and resistance to whoever tried to impose their will, be it a volcano, filibusterer, American marine, or dictator. What was left of the city's colonial heritage was shattered by a series of earthquakes in 2000, yet it retains a colorful and vibrant character.

Most visitors experience Masaya as a 1-day shopping trip from the capital or Granada and many never venture beyond the Gothic, palm-lined walls of Masaya's block-size Old Market (Mercado Viejo). That's a pity, as the city has more to offer than what you can stuff in your suitcase. In addition to its beautiful waterfront promenade and an old fort, the nearby Volcán Masaya is the most accessible active crater in the country and the most terrifying and exciting to visit. In the surrounding tabletop mountains are a string of villages known as the Pueblos Blancos, each with their own niche in hand-honed craftsmanship. Masaya is also famous for throwing a good street party, with festivals running throughout the year featuring such colorful participants as 3.6m-tall (12-ft.) women on stilts, costumed dogs, and "headless" priests. Arrive at the right time, in fact, and you might never want to leave the party.

Spanish Classes near Masaya

Mariposa Eco Hotel & Spanish School (✆ **505/418-4638;** www.mariposaspanishschool.com) is situated in the hills between Masaya and Managua and offers a farmhouselike atmosphere with plain, comfortable rooms and Spanish classes. Efficiently run by its English owner Paulette, the program offers a unique mix of wholesome country living and language classes.

Most everything about this place is ecofriendly. The restaurant serves organic food, there's an organic garden, and even the private bathrooms have organic shampoo and soap. The lodge is quite difficult to find, so be sure to arrange a transfer from either Masaya or Managua.

ESSENTIALS

Getting There

BY BUS From Managua, take any southbound bus from the Mercado Huembes. You'll be dropped off at Masaya's **Mercado Municipal,** on the western side of the city. The journey takes 1 hour and costs C20 ($1/50p). Another departure point in Managua is the **UCA** (p. 443), from where microbuses leave every 20 minutes, dropping passengers off at **Parque San Miguel,** 1 block east of the Mercado Viejo. The ride is 45 minutes and costs C20 ($1/50p).

From Granada take any Managua-bound bus from **COGRAN,** 1½ blocks southwest of the plaza, or one of the Masaya expresos that leave from behind the **Palé Supermarket.** The journey takes 45 minutes and costs C20 ($1/50p), and passengers are dropped off at Masaya's Mercado Municipal. The Mercado is also the main departure point when you are leaving Masaya.

BY TAXI/SHUTTLE **Paxeos,** beside the cathedral in Granada (✆ **505/552-8291;** www.paxeos.com), can organize private and shared transfers to and from Masaya. The trip to Granada costs between C570 ($30/£15) and C860 ($40/£20), depending on group size.

Getting Around

A car is not necessary in the city but definitely worthwhile if you want to explore the surrounding area. **Budget** (✆ **505/522-5788**) has an office at Km 28, Carretera Masaya. **Hotel Ivania's** (p. 491) is the only place in town that rents out cars. Alternatively, you might hire a taxi for the day so you can sit back, relax, and not get lost. A car and driver for the day in this area should cost approximately C1,100 ($60/£30).

Visitor Information

Intur (✆ **505/522-7615**) is inside the Mercado Viejo and offers good maps and information regarding workshops in the surrounding area. It is open Monday to Friday from 8am to 12:30pm and 1:30 to 5pm, and on Saturday from 8am to 12:30pm.

FAST FACTS There are plenty of ATMs conveniently located within the Mercado Viejo (Old Market). **Banpro** (✆ **505/522-7366**), is on the southwestern corner of the market, as is **Bancentro** (✆ **505/522-4337**). **Banco de América Central** changes traveler's checks and is located 1 block north of the market. You will also find many street money-changers in this area.

There are several Internet cafes on the south side of the park. **Cablenet Café** is opposite the Hotel Regis and is open daily from 8am to 10pm, except Sundays when it closes at 3pm. The main **hospital** (✆ **505/522-2778**) is on the main road to Granada. The city's **police station** (✆ **505/522-4222**) is a half-block north of the old market. A post office is inside the Mercado Viejo, as is a DHL counter.

WHAT TO SEE & DO

Attractions in Masaya

Mercado Nacionál de Artesanía ★★, also known as the Mercado Viejo, is the biggest attraction in town. This entire block is a hive of stalls and cultural activity and is easily the showcase market for the country's thriving handicrafts industry. Built in 1891, it was destroyed during the revolution and restored in 1997. It is easy to stay several hours within its stone walls and browse the many stalls selling everything from cotton hammocks to colorful art. Here you'll also find conventional stores, cafes, ATMs, and the tourist office. The market is located 1 block east of the central plaza, also known as Parque 17 de Octubre. It's open daily from 8am to 7pm.

Museo y Galería Héroes y Mártires (inside the town hall, Alcaldía, 1 1/2 blocks north of the central park; no phone) is a small museum dedicated to those who fought the Somoza regime. Among its exhibits of photos and guns is an unexploded napalm bomb. The museum is open Monday to Friday from 8am to 5pm. Admission is free but donations are welcome. **El Malecón** ★ is the breezy city promenade 6 blocks west of the central plaza. It sits high above the waterline but affords great views and has several cafes to take a break in. This waterfront comes alive with people whenever there is a game at the nearby baseball stadium. It's a great place to visit while atop one of the many horse and carriages that trundle through the city streets.

The **Catedral de la Asunción** (on the main plaza; no phone) is also worth a visit. Damaged by the 2000 earthquake, the early-19th-century baroque church is undergoing restoration but can still be entered during services; admission is free. **Iglesia de San Jeronimo** (5 blocks north of the central plaza; no phone) is a plainer church but affords a great view of the city from its bell tower. Admission is 50¢/25p.

Attractions Outside Masaya

Coyotepe Fort (Moments) Coyotepe fort held political prisoners and was used by the National Guard to mortar bomb the city during the 1980s revolution. It was also the location of the heroic last stand by national hero Benjamín Zeledón against U.S marines in 1912. Now it is a quieter place, with helpful boy scouts conducting visits of the facility and its unwelcoming dungeons. Whitewashed battlements and squat, yellow-domed towers overlook the city and lakes and afford a pleasant visit that belies this structure's dark history. The fort is a 1km (1/2-mile) hike north of the old train station but I recommend taking a taxi, as it is a fairly hard stroll.

Carretera Masaya Km 1. No phone. C19 ($1/50p). Daily 8am–5pm.

Volcán Masaya National Park ★★★ Volcán Masaya is not a normal cone-shaped volcano but rather a low, gaping wound of smoking craters and glowing lava. The whole effect is so frightening that the Spanish took to calling this volcano the "gates of hell" and the local Chorotegas tribe christened it the "mountain that burns" and made human sacrifices there in the hope that doing so might avert more eruptions. It is easily the most accessible live volcano in Nicaragua, because a road leads directly to its chasm. This park is also an unforgettable experience. It is at once intriguing and terrifying, especially when you learn that in 2000, it hurled a large boulder that destroyed a nearby car in the parking lot. In the same lot today, the attendants advise you to park facing downhill so as to make a quick getaway—very reassuring.

The park consists of several volcanoes and craters and is easy to explore, with a system of hiking trails, many of which can be done independently. The self-guided trail Sendero los Coyotes is a 6km (3.75-mile) walk from the visitor center and runs through lava pits to a lake. The Santiago Crater is home to a curious species of parakeets that seem immune to the pit's noxious fumes; the crater is best viewed from the parking lot at the edge. El Comalito is a small, smoking hillock and Tzinancanostoc a series of lava tunnels. Both can only be visited with a guide along the Coyote trek. On some treks you may have to change direction because of the fumes, and you'll need to get a gas mask to see the lava holes up close. Most travel operators offer 1-day excursions to the park from Managua, Granada, or Masaya. To get there independently, you must travel 6km (3 3/4 miles) north of Masaya on the main highway.

A visitor center, where you can get a good map and brochure of the site, and nature museum are 2km (1¼ miles) from the main entrance. Make sure to buy your tour tickets at the visitor center before you rendezvous with your guide at the crater.

Carretera Masaya Km 6. ✆ **505/552-5415.** Daily 9am–4:45pm. Admission C77 ($4/£2).

SHOPPING

Any shopping excursion in Masaya should include a stop at the Mercado Viejo (see "What to See & Do" above) but there are other shopping outlets around the city that cry out for your attention, too. **Mercado Municipal Ernesto Fernández** is a bigger, more chaotic, and somewhat crammed market with cheap restaurants and butcher stalls as well as a good selection of handicrafts and leather ware. Goods are also slightly cheaper than at the Mercado Viejo. The market is adjacent to the main bus terminal and a few blocks from the Mercado Viejo. It is open daily from 8am to 7pm.

You'll find hammocks everywhere in Masaya, but if you'd prefer to see their place of origin, check out the ***fabricas de hamacas*** (hammock workshops) located in Barrio San Juan, 2 blocks east of the Malecon and 1 block north of the Old Hospital. One good stand alone hammock shop to try is **Los Tapices de Luis,** a store specializing in hammocks and wall hangings.

Museo Galería Motivación Sevilla, half a block west of Calle Central, just before Iglesia San Jeronimo (✆ **505/860-4466**), is an art gallery and gift store specializing in primitivist paintings. **Guitarras Zepeda** ★, 200m (656 ft.) west of the Unión Fenosa (✆ **505/883-0260;** guitarraszepeda@yahoo.com), is one of the most respected guitar workshops in the country. The owner Sergio will show you how they craft beautiful mahogany and pearl inlaid instruments. Note that he has very few guitars for sale off-the-shelf, so you must order most guitars 2 weeks in advance. Prices range from C1,900 to C5,700 ($100–$300/£50–£150).

If you want to see more arts and crafts workshops in the city, walk 1km (½ mile) south of the central plaza to the indigenous barrio of **Monimbó.** Here you'll find a thriving cottage industry of shoemakers, basket weavers, saddle makers, and woodcarvers. Ask in the central tourist office for information or just knock on some doors when you get there. If that still does not satisfy your urge to spend, go farther afield to the workshops of the Pueblos Blancos (see "A Side Trip to Pueblos Blancos," below).

WHERE TO STAY & DINE

Considering its many attractions and exhaustive shopping possibilities, Masaya should have more and better hotels. Unfortunately, the town is very much a 1-day excursion on most people's itineraries, with people preferring to stay in Granada or Managua instead. Thus, there's a dearth of decent inns.

Hotel Ivania's, 3½ blocks from the Iglesia El Calvario (✆ **505/522-5825;** www.hotelivanias.com), is one of the town's better establishments, with unusually helpful, attentive staff (a rare thing in Nicaragua), as well as a convenient town center location and a restaurant. The decor is dated and slightly idiosyncratic—the hotel's facade is an attractive pink color with stone carved window frames, but inside it gets rather dark and garish. The rooms are small and the bathrooms smaller but the hotel does have an all-important backup generator. Rates start at $55 (£28) for a double.

Hotel Maderas Inn, half a block east of Iglesia San Jeronimo (✆ **505/522-5825**), is a small family-run property that's tucked inside a modern yellow house. It has a good location and a friendly staff. The decor is plain, except for the hammocks on the roof terrace—they're a great place to relax. Doubles start at $21 (£11).

Moments Festivals in Masaya

The Masaya calendar is so chock-full of parades and street parties, you have to wonder how the locals ever get around to weaving the hammocks or making the rocking chairs they're so famous for selling. The city's festivals are a rich mix of indigenous, religious, and colonial customs and all the parties here are very much a family affair, with each household bringing its own particular flavor to the celebrations. Below is a month-by-month listing of the best festivals.

January: Drums, whistles, and chanting reverberate around the streets of Masaya during the **Festival of San Sebastian,** particularly in the barrio of Monimbó. Sticks clatter as a battle is staged before the eventual reconciliation, when crowds shout "Viva San Sebastian!" Though Masaya's celebrations are good, the town of Diriamba (30km/19 miles southwest of Masaya) is generally recognized as throwing the most colorful and authentic San Sebastian parade in the country, with a lively mix of pagan satire and colonial pomp. The festival takes place on January 19, 20, and 21.

February: Every dog gets its day during the 3 weeks before Easter Sunday. Locals spill out onto the city streets with their pets dolled up in elaborate costumes for the **Festival of San Lázaro.** They are giving thanks to the patron saint of pets for keeping their little loved ones in good health. The canine fashion parade gathers first at the Santa Maria Magdalena church on Plaza Monimbo and then parades from there.

March/April: The whole country goes crazy for Easter, and Masaya is no different during Semana Santa celebrations.

May: The Santiago crater in Volcán Masaya National Park burst into life in 1852 and threatened to engulf the city until it was stopped in its tracks by **La Señora de la Asunción.** This miracle is celebrated on May 20, by people swamping the streets and exchanging crosses made from platted palm leaves.

A SIDE TRIP TO THE PUEBLOS BLANCOS ★

A scattering of isolated "white villages," or Pueblos Blancos, sits in the hills south of Masaya, and make for a perfect 1-day excursion by car or bus from Masaya, as well as from Managua or Granada. These villages got their name from their simple Spanish-style churches and occasional white *casitas,* with colorful doors and windows. Each individual town is known for producing a signature handicraft, be it ceramic wind chimes or bamboo furniture, so shopping is the main draw here.

Any trip to the Pueblos Blancos should start with a journey up the **Catarina Mirador,** a spectacular lookout point on the rim of Laguna de Apoyo crater lake. Here you can make believe you can see all of Nicaragua, with Granada and Masaya at your feet and the twin peaks of Ometepe Island in the distance on Lago de Nicaragua. The town itself is famous for its basket making and lush, tropical nurseries. The mirador is behind the village church

June: During the month of June, the Pueblo Blancos of San Juan de Oriente, Diriá, and Diriomo throw the most bizarre processions as part of the build-up to the fiestas patronales, with dancing warriors reenacting battles by beating each other over the head with bulls' penises. Another village, called Masatepe, has a much more civilized horse parade on the first Sunday of the month.

September: September 20 is the kickoff for the **Fiestas Patronales** (patron saint celebrations), or weekend parties in different neighborhoods that carry on until December. Mock battles take place as well as folkloric dance routines. Boisterous groups go from door to door in costumes, shimmying to cheerful and uplifting *marimba* music.

October: The fantastical Masayan creature called the *chancha bruja* (witch pig) comes to life during the **Fiesta de los Aguisotes** (Bad Omen Festival), as well as other folkloric ghouls such as the *arre chavalo* (headless priest). During **Fiesta de Toro Venado,** Masayans take on the guise of public figures and ridicule them through song, dance, and processions. Both parties take place on the last weekend of October, on Friday and Sunday respectively.

November: During the **Folkloric Festival,** Masaya celebrates its handicrafts heritage, with artisanal stalls appearing all around the city. The festival takes place the last week of November.

December: The **Procesión de San Jerónimo** is the big one, the final blow out of the Fiestas Patronales (Christmas celebrations). On the first Sunday of the month, Saint Jerónimo (the city's patron saint) is paraded through streets that are crammed with flower bearers and dancers. Traditional stomping routines are also performed. Early on Christmas Day, all the town's children enthusiastically spill out onto the street with pots, pans, and fireworks—anything that makes noise—calling everybody to church to celebrate Christ's birth.

and can be easily approached on foot; if you are driving, you'll have to pay an admission of C20 ($1/50p).

Catarina Mirador was apparently the favored hangout of the military leader Augusto C. Sandino, and it's where he dreamed about and plotted Nicaragua's liberation. He was born in the nearby village of **Niquinohomo,** 3.2km (2 miles) away, where a grand bronze statue now stands in his honor. Close to the northwest corner of the town plaza is Sandino's childhood home, which is now a small museum and library. The town also has a charming little colonial church called **Parroquia Santa Ana** that is reputedly 320 years old. Both the museum and church have erratic opening hours, but if you ask around you should eventually find somebody with info and a key.

Several miles east and southeast is the colorful village of **San Juan de Oriente.** Pottery is the specialty here and if you ask at any store they should allow you to take a look at their backyard workshops with kilns. Continue south and you'll reach the twin villages of **Diriá** and **Diriomo,** which face each other on the highway. Diriá has a good hilltop view and some trails from here lead down to the shore of Laguna de Apoyo. Diriomo is famous for its black magic and *brujas* (witches) who will read your fortune, or at least give you the right directions back to Masaya.

To visit **Masatape,** you must double back and follow the road northwest. This sleepy village is the country's rocking chair capital and is highly regarded for its excellent mahogany and wicker carpentry. Stop for a late lunch at **Mi Teruño Masatepino** (✆ **505/887-4949**), a charming open-air eatery just south of the town on the highway close to Pio XII. Continue west and you'll reach the largest of the Pueblos Blancos, **San Marcos,** a thriving university town with a pretty town plaza.

To return to Masaya, you can take the northern road through la Concepción or backtrack east to Catarina. (This is also the road to Granada and Managua.) Though it's easiest to see the pueblos by rental car, frequent buses do shuttle around the region, albeit at a slow pace, and do not pass through every town. Buses leave daily from Mercado Municipal in Masaya, Mercado Huembes in Managua, and 1 block south of Granada's market. Expreso buses pass through the Pueblos Blancos every 40 minutes Monday through Friday, but less so on weekends. The Intur office in Masaya (p. 489) offers good maps of the region.

8 SAN JUAN DEL SUR ★ & THE SOUTHWEST

138km (85 miles) S of Managua; 96km (60 miles) S of Granada; 215km (133 miles) S of Léon

San Juan del Sur used to be a sleepy little Pacific coast hamlet, until it was discovered by backpackers and surfers as the perfect spot to hang a hammock and enjoy a rum-colored sunset. It is now Nicaragua's top Pacific coast destination for foreign visitors and its pioneering blond-haired wave riders have gradually given way to silver-haired property seekers. Retirement homes are beginning to dot the surrounding hillsides and upscale hotels are appearing along the coast. There is now even the occasional cruise liner idling in the bay.

Fortunately, development here is happening at a not-too-fast pace and San Juan has not lost the laid-back charm that attracted travelers here in the first place. The area is perfect for beach wandering, leisure sailing, deep-sea fishing, and scuba diving. And the town still comes alive for holidays, particularly for its delightful religious flotilla on July 16. The lunar cycles between September and April see a beach party of a different kind—the mass hatching of turtles and their spectacular but treacherous rush to the sea. This takes place just south of the town and has to be one of Nicaragua's most amazing sights.

ESSENTIALS

Getting There

BY TAXI/SHUTTLE The safest, fastest and most convenient way to get to San Juan del Sur is via a shuttle service that picks you up at your hotel. **Adelante Express** (✆ **505/850-6070;** www.sanjuanvan.com) arranges taxis or vans to Managua, with rates that run from C760 to C570 ($30–$40/£15–£20) depending on group size. **Mundo Tel,** 1½ blocks from San Juan market (✆ **505/568-2573**), also arranges taxi transfers to and from Managua and Granada.

BY BUS Buses leave from **Mercado R Huembes** in Managua at 10:30am, 4pm, and 5:30pm (3 hr.; C58 ($3/£1.50) but it's a long, bumpy ride, with lots of stops. The 4pm

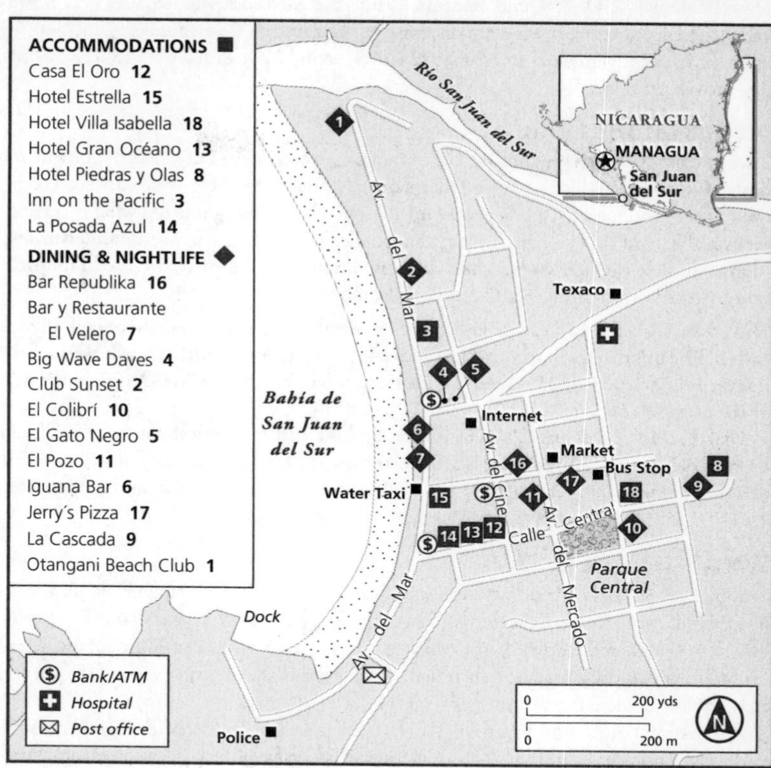

is the "Expresso" in name only. Buses going to Managua directly leave from the **San Juan del Sur market** (at calles Central and Market) at 5am and 6am daily. There are buses to Rivas every 45 minutes (1 hr.; $1/50p) between 5am and 5:30pm, where you then catch a connection to Managua and elsewhere. **Central Line S.A,** half a block west of the market (✆ **505/568-2573**), has direct buses to Managua at 10am, going to the Antiguo Cine Cabrera, on Avenida 27 Mayo.

Orientation & Getting Around

San Juan del Sur is small and easy to explore by foot. Beaches farther north and south can be accessed by boat, taxi, or shuttle bus. **Rana Tours** (✆ **505/0877-9255**) operates a daily water taxi to Maderas beach at 11am, returning at 5pm. They have a beach kiosk in front of the Hotel Estrella from which the boat departs. A round-trip costs C190 ($10/£5).

Hostel **Casa Oro,** 1 block west of the plaza (✆ **505/458-2415**), organizes beach shuttles three times a day to Majagual and Maderas beach at 10am, 12:30pm, and 4pm. The cost is C361 ($5/£2.50) round-trip.

Taxis are easy to catch on any street corner, but always negotiate the price before jumping in.

Alamo (✆ **505/277-1117**) has an office in front of the restaurant El Velero in the Hotel Colonial. **Bike & Quad Rentals,** beside the Mercado Municipal (✆ **505/568-2439**), does exactly what they say on the sign. **Elizabeth's Guesthouse,** 75m (246 ft.) east of Mercado Municipal (✆ **505/822-7075**), rents bicycles for C95 ($5/£2.50) per day, as well as rooms.

Visitor Information

Plans are afoot to open a tourism office in San Juan del Sur, but for the moment the hostel **Casa Oro,** 1 block west of the plaza (✆ **505/458-2415;** www.casaeloro.com), does a very good job of keeping people up-to-date with what is going on, what excursions are available, and the ever-changing bus timetable. The website **www.sanjuandelsur.org.ni** gives limited listings; **www.vianica.com** is a more comprehensive site, with information such as hotel addresses and telephone numbers.

FAST FACTS You can exchange money or withdraw cash at **Bancentro,** half a block east of El Timon restaurant (✆ **505/568-2449**), or at **Procredit,** 1 block west of the market (✆ **505/853-3433**). Traveler's checks can be changed at **Casa Oro,** 1 block west of the plaza (✆ **505/458-2415**).

Dial ✆ **118** for police, ✆ **115** for fire, and ✆ **128** for an ambulance. The closest hospital is in Rivas, though there is a clinic known as **Centro de Salud** that will take care of minor ailments. It is 20m (1,312 ft.) southwest of the Texaco station and is open from 7am to 8pm Monday to Saturday and 8am to noon on Sunday.

WHAT TO SEE & DO

San Juan del Sur has little of historical significance to see except the town's old clapboard houses and its simple wooden church, Parroquia San Juan, on the main plaza. The **Lighthouse,** a 1-hour trek south of the town, is also worth a visit. You must follow a trail behind the town dock until you turn right. This site has a spectacular view of the sea and coast. Below it there is a pelican nesting area.

San Juan del Sur's other main attractions are the beaches and sea, though it must be said, this is not the Caribbean. Contradicting what many property developer brochures may show you, the water is not turquoise clear and the beaches here are not dazzling white and lined with endless palm trees. There are lots of water activities to be had, though; see below for info.

OUTDOOR ACTIVITIES

BEACHES Surfers first put this once sleepy village on the map, and it's the string of beaches north and south of the town that continue to attract the most visitors. The town's beach is itself slightly disappointing, as the sand is dark and there is no privacy, except sometimes at the northern end. Neither is it suitable for surfing, as there is usually just a gentle swell. If you want big waves and paradise-like isolation, you will have to venture farther up or down the coast. Facilities for all these beaches are in general limited to a few beach bum campsites and shore-side kiosks, so be sure to pack some food and refreshments for the day.

Playa Marsella and **Playa Madera** ★ are 30 minutes north by water taxi or car. Here you'll find lovely, breezy beaches with big waves and some good snorkeling opportunities. **Bahía Majagual** is a beautiful cove a little farther to the north. **Playa Remanso** is the first beach to the south. It has a long shore, which is ideal for exploring and rock hopping. Continue walking south for 30 minutes and you'll reach two lovely beaches called

Playa Tamarindo and **Playa Hermosa. Playa Coco** (18km/11 miles south of the town), is the best regarding facilities, with a restaurant and several cabins to rent.

Eighteen kilometers (11 miles) south of San Juan del Sur is one of Nicaragua's most fascinating beaches—and that's not because of its breaks or palm trees. **Playa La Flor ★** is a 1.6km (1-mile) stretch of wildlife preserve and scene of nighttime *arribades,* or mass turtle hatchings. Twenty thousand olive ridley turtles nest on the beach every year, and 45 days later, their offspring hatch and break for the water. This happens from July to February, though the best time to see the nesting happen is in August or September. Always go with a reputable guide and be aware of turtle-watching etiquette, like not using the flash on your camera. **Hostel Casa Oro,** 1 block west of the plaza (✆ **505/458-2415**), organizes excellent nighttime excursions, including a brief pre-tour video explaining the phenomenon and how to act responsibly while witnessing an unforgettable sight.

CANOPY TOURING **Da Flying Frog** (✆ **505/611-6214;** tiguacal@ibw.com.ni) specializes in an epic 3.2km (2-mile) canopy ride through the forest. Trekking and horseback riding are also available. The tour entrance is on a ranch a small distance from the town on the Chocolata Road.

DIVING **Scuba Shack** (✆ **505/480-1931;** www.scubashack-nicaragua.com) is a PADI-registered company located on the coastal street, 1 block north of the Inn on the Pacific (see below). It is open Thursday to Tuesday from 8am to 5pm. They offer everything from open water to dive master courses, starting at C4,750 ($250/£125). They also have an outlet in the Piedras y Olas hotel.

FISHING ★ The coast offers excellent sea fishing, with marlin, yellow tuna, sail fish, and snapper all available to catch. The best time of the year to fish is April to November. **Superfly** (✆ **505/884-8444;** www.superflynica.com) is one of the better established fishing outfits in town, operating catch-and-release tours. They also organize snorkeling and scuba diving excursions and relaxing sunset cruises in their minifleet of three boats.

SAILING ★ San Juan del Sur's surrounding coastland makes the perfect playground for an afternoon on a yacht. **Aida Sailing Tours** (✆ **505/568-2287**) offers 1-day and half-day tours in its yacht. Prices start at C570 ($30/£15) per person**. Hotel Piedras y Olas** (✆ **505/568-2110**) also organizes similar excursions.

SURFING It was surfers who first put San Juan del Sur on most travelers' radars, and you will still find many boarders testing the waves on the beaches north and south of the town. **Dale Dagger's Surf Nicaragua,** 1 block inland from the Mercado Municipal (✆ **505/568-2492;** www.nicasurf.com), is one of the better established surfing outfitters, offering excursions and weeklong packages. It's best to write or call in advance to assure your spot.

WHERE TO STAY

Every rickety town house in San Juan del Sur seems to have a HOSPEDAJE sign, indicating the resident family has some rooms available for budget travelers. The town's more-upscale hotels are located on the outskirts or at the northern end of the beach. If you like your creature comforts, make sure to inquire that the hotel has its own generator, as power cuts are frequent and no electricity often means no water.

Expensive

Hotel Piedras y Olas Overrated Kids This gleaming, garden hotel dominates the town's main hillside. Brick steps and white walls rise through the property's gardens and

Morgan's Rock Hacienda & Eco Lodge

San Juan del Sur has attracted its fair share of luxury accommodations in recent years but none have created quite the same buzz as **Morgan's Rock Hacienda and Eco Lodge ★★** (✆ **506/223-26449,** Costa Rica office; www.morgansrock.com). Eighteen kilometers (11 miles) north of the town, with its own private beach, you'll find a cluster of luxury bungalows, assessed by a 100m (328-ft.) suspension bridge over a tropical gorge. Architecturally stunning and with superb attention to detail, the lodge combines both luxury and environmentally friendly accommodations. Rates start at $241 (£120) for a double in the high season.

palm trees, passing its large restaurant La Cascada to the left, before continuing upward to a complex of guest rooms, villalike cottages, and private homes. The style is big and clunky, with uneven walls and glass tiles adorning open kitchens and expansive bedrooms. These are rooms designed for giants and they're a bit over-the-top, with a cold, cavernous feel. Farther up, there are a series of pools and one restaurant, all set in lush gardens that are open to the public. The view from the gardens is fantastic. Beware of a 50% cancellation fee if you cancel within 7 days of your stay.

Calle Central, 1½ blocks east of Parque Central. ✆ **505/568-2110.** www.piedrasyolas.com. From $125 (£63) double; from $145 (£73) cabin (sleeps 4); from $155 (£78) casita (sleeps 4); from $190 (£95) townhouse casa (sleeps 4); from $190 (£95) casa (sleeps 6). Rates include breakfast. AE, DC, MC, V. **Amenities:** Bar and restaurant; Internet in lobby; laundry service; pool. *In room:* A/C, cable TV, kitchenette.

Inn on the Pacific Its cream-colored, mock Spanish facade is a touch tacky, but you can't beat this hotel for its beachfront location and comfortable, huge rooms, five of which have large kitchenettes. The lobby is small, dark, and uninviting, but get past that, and you'll find that generally everything is clean and well maintained. Each room has a flatscreen TV and individual sofa, and the bathrooms are large if dimly lit. Spacious balconies offer good views of the bay, though they do overlook a busy street that can be noisy.

Av. Costera, 150m (492 ft.) north of Restaurante El Timón. ✆ **505/880-8120.** Fax 505/568-2439. www.innonthepacific.net. 7 units. From $92 (£46) twin; from $103 (£52) single suite (sleeps 2); from $126 (£63) penthouse (sleeps 2); from $126 (£63) double suite (sleeps 4). Rates include breakfast. AE, DC, MC, V. **Amenities:** Pool; 24-hr. security. *In room:* A/C, TV, Internet, kitchenette.

La Posada Azul ★★ This is probably the most delightful boutique hotel in town, and it boasts an authentic charm and decor that makes you feel like you've stepped back in time. High ceilings grace neat wooden interiors and an old-world living room. Wicker wardrobes match wicker headboards in the generously sized rooms. The bathrooms are small but bright and cheerful. The veranda is spectacular; long and wide, it runs the length of the house alongside a lovely flower garden with a fountain and small pool out back. This atmospheric villa was built in 1910 but completely refurbished in December 2007, and everything is now immaculate and new.

Calle Central, 2½ blocks west of Parque Central. ✆ **505/568-2524.** www.laposadaazul.com. 7 units. From $115 (£58) twin; from $135 (£68) double. Rates include breakfast. AE, DC, MC, V. **Amenities:** Pool; TV room; Wi-Fi. *In room:* A/C.

Moderate

Hotel Gran Oceano *Value* The Hotel Gran Oceano is a good budget option without being too budgety in appearance. It's tucked away in a beautiful mansion-style building in the town center. The highlight here is the attractive central courtyard of brown pillars and garden plants, and the inviting front patio with rocking chairs and beautiful ceramic tile work. However, the standard rooms are not so grand—everything is quite small, including the beds, wardrobes, and bathrooms. Still, rooms are colorful and appealing, and they come at a great price. There are some larger rooms available for more money, as well.

Calle Central, 2½ blocks west of Parque Central. ✆ **505/568-2219.** www.hotelgranoceano.com.ni. 23 units. From $46 (£23) double; from $60 (£30) triple. Rates include breakfast. AE, MC, V. **Amenities:** Pool. *In room:* A/C, cable TV.

Hotel Villa Isabella *Finds* This hotel is situated in a handsome house in a leafy area directly behind the town's church. The rooms are generously sized, with two double beds, neat wooden furniture, gleaming white walls, and large ceiling fans; bathrooms are large and pristine. There are apartment-style rooms out back and a medium-size pool. The reception area is large and welcoming, and the adjoining dining room offers great American-style breakfasts that change daily. A generator ensures that there's constant electricity. The American owner Mike is a fount of information regarding the area; he also rents storage space next door.

Calle Central, on the northeast corner of Parque Central. ✆ **505/568-2568.** Isabella@ibw.com.ni. 15 units. From $90 (£45) double. Rates include breakfast. AE, DC, MC, V. **Amenities:** Pool; Internet in lobby. *In room:* A/C, TV.

Inexpensive

Casa el Oro ★ Casa el Oro has that colorful, tumbledown feel that's popular with backpacker hostels the world over. This hostel, the best in town, also serves as San Juan del Sur's unofficial tourism office, dispensing info on everything from bus timetables to Spanish classes. You can change traveler's checks, swap books, and organize beach shuttles and turtle nesting excursions through the proactive owners. They even have a copy of every available restaurant menu for guests to peruse through before deciding where to dine. A set of tidy dorms are arranged around a courtyard with an open-air kitchen. There are some private rooms, too, which are small and basic (with shared bathrooms) but comfy.

Calle Central, 1 block west of the plaza. ✆ **505/568-2415.** www.casaeloro.com. 10 units (7 dorms). From $20 (£10) double. AE, DC, MC, V. **Amenities:** Restaurant/bar; TV room. *In room:* Fan, no phone.

Hotel Estrella This is as ramshackle as you can get. The Estrella is a crumbling corner building facing the beach and claims to be the oldest hotel in San Juan, since it's been in operation since 1929. It's certainly seen better days, but if you're on a tight budget and wanting to avoid hostels, looking for a slice of real Nicaragua, and don't mind its derelict decor, this is the place for you. Creaking stairs rise above a small patio out back, leading to some very basic rooms, which have shared bathrooms. Nonetheless, it has character and atmosphere, along with friendly owners.

Calle Costera, 2 blocks west of the market. ✆ **505/568-2210.** hotelestrella1929@hotmail.com. 10 units. From $20 (£10) double. No credit cards. **Amenities:** Restaurant. *In room:* Fan.

WHERE TO DINE

In addition to the more formal restaurants reviewed below, you might want to check out one of the many identical thatched roof restaurants that line the beachfront here. They all serve excellent shrimp and lobster dishes ranging from C285 ($15/£7.50) to C380

Massaging Out the Kinks in San Juan del Sur

Luna Bella Day Spa (© **505/803-8196;** www.lunabella.org) is run by Luna, a Hawaiian-trained masseuse who has transferred her skills from Hollywood to San Juan del Sur. She offers relaxing 1-hour massages that cost C760 ($40/£20), as well as facials and pedicures. The spa is located 1 block south and half a block east of El Colibri restaurant (see below). Services are by appointment only.

($20/£10). The **Mercado Municipal ★** has a small, cluttered food hall that offers great value chicken and rice dishes for less than C76 ($4/£2) a portion. **Jerry's Pizza,** in front of the Mercado Municipal (© **505/804-6640**), dishes out American-style breakfast for C152 ($8/£4).

Expensive

El Colibri ★★ Moments INTERNATIONAL This restaurant is as enchanting as its name implies—*el colibri* is Spanish for hummingbird. Set within a funky, colored clapboard house with a large veranda overlooking a lovely garden, the building itself is a piece of art put together from recycled materials by its Anglo-Irish owner Mary O'Hanlon and her Italian husband. Mosaic-framed mirrors hang between stained-glass lamps and African face masks. Elephant woodcuts are illuminated by candelabras and there are delightful touches like small colored stones that hold down the place mats, lest the sea breeze carry them away. The menu could best be described as adventurous and organic. Hummus dip complements beef kabobs and the filet mignon comes in a sauce made with bacon and vodka cream. The homemade pâté is a revelation, made from chicken, bacon, and sherry. Check the chalkboard for the best on offer, as the menu is very much seasonal. Laid-back music adds to the overall relaxing atmosphere.

On the east side of Parque Central, 1 block south of Hotel Villa Isabella. © **505/863-8612.** Reservations recommended. Main courses C150 ($8/£4). AE, MC, V. Daily 6–11pm.

El Pozo ★★ Finds MODERN AMERICAN Californians Christian and Claire opened this gourmet restaurant in August 2007 with the intention of bringing some contemporary American-style cuisine to a town that lacks stylish restaurants. They've succeeded with this small, modern bistro, which has a minimalist design, with an open kitchen at the back, hardwood furniture, and a cane ceiling. The menu includes dishes like a refreshing watermelon salad and a delicious tamarind pork chop.

El Pozo is also a good stop off point for a late-night cocktail. The small, inviting bar up front serves the best martinis in town. The wine list is unusually good, with French champagne and Italian wines among others.

Av. del Mercado, 10m (33 ft.) south of the market. © **505/806-5708.** Main courses C150–C245 ($8–$13/£4–£6.50). AE, DC, MC, V. Thurs–Mon 6pm–1am.

La Cascada ★ INTERNATIONAL La Cascada is very much like the hotel Piedras y Olas it belongs to—it's big, impressive, and somewhat over-the-top. The large, open space is the size of a movie set and doubtless will be used some day in a tropical Hollywood blockbuster. The top here is in fact a grandiose thatched roof that encompasses a curved bar, spacious dining area, and terrace with a wide-screen view of the bay. There is a pool up front if you fancy a dip between courses. The menu is an imaginative mix of

Cajun sausage soup and almond stir-fry with the usual delicious mix of lobster and shrimp thrown in. The staff is very friendly and speaks English.

Calle Central, 1½ blocks east of Parque Central. ✆ **505/568-2110.** Main courses C150–C270 ($8–$14/£4–£7). AE, DC, MC, V. Daily 6:30am–11pm.

Moderate

Bar y Restaurante El Velero CUBAN/SEAFOOD This Cuban restaurant, situated in a thatched-roof building with an open view of the bay, is typical of the many restaurants that line the beach in town. It is a little down-at-the-heel but has a nice atmosphere and is the perfect spot for a beer at sunset. Simple lobster and shrimp dishes dominate the menu, and there is a small bar at the back offering beer and rum. The owner José (el Capitán) is often in attendance

Av. del Mar, 70m (230 ft.) north of the Hotel Estrella. ✆ **505/568-2473.** elvelerocontigo@hotmail.com. Main courses C120–C200 ($6–$10/£3–£5). AE, MC, V. Daily 9am–9pm.

Big Wave Daves (Kids) CONTINENTAL The decor at Big Wave Daves could best be described as "roadhouse meets beach hut"—this rambling but inviting restaurant is inside a yellow wooden shack, with a thatched roof out back. The menu offers comfort food like hamburgers, pasta, and shrimp, making this a good bet for children looking for familiar food. There is occasional live music and the bar comes alive at night with both expats and locals looking for just what it says on the door: "Cold beer served with a smile." There's even a small book exchange here.

½ block east of Bancentro. ✆ **505/568-2151.** www.bigwavedaves.net. Main courses C90–C150 ($5–$8/£2.50–£4). No credit cards. Daily 7am–2am.

Inexpensive

El Gato Negro ★★ (Finds) CAFE El Gato Negro is the perfect place to while away some hours reading a good book and enjoying great freshly roasted coffee and bagels. This warm, inviting cafe has a long bar, leading to a giant coffee bean grinder, and attention-getting red walls that are adorned with local photos and paintings. But what really catches your attention here is the extensive book collection, which runs around half the room. Here you'll find everything from literary novels to airport page-turners to a valuable collection of Nicaraguan history books. ***Be warned, however:*** Books must be purchased before you can collapse on one of the many sofas and start perusing. There is also a small garden out back if you want to work on your tan while you read. The average paperback costs approximately $15 (£7.50).

1 block east of Timon, next to Big Wave Daves. ✆ **505/809-1108.** www.elgatonegronica.com. Main courses C90–C150 ($5–$8/£2.50–£4). AE, DC, MC, V. Daily 7am–3pm.

SAN JUAN DEL SUR AFTER DARK

Like any beach town, San Juan del Sur has its fair share of reveling vacationers enjoying rum and doing research into whether they prefer Victoria or Toña beer. Yet, the town's nightlife is pretty sedate and civilized, with just a few bars along the beachfront and two all-night discos. **Iguana Bar** ★, half a block north of El Velero restaurant (✆ **505/568-2085**), attracts a lively young crowd of locals and visitors. It is on the beachfront and has a bar upstairs and downstairs. **Bar Republika** (no phone) is a small street bar located a half-block west of the Mercado Municipal. **Club Sunset,** in a green clapboard house on the waterfront (no phone), opens up to all-night dancers Fridays and Saturdays. It has outside seating if the mixture of salsa and reggaeton blaring inside gets to be a little too much. There is a cover charge of C50 ($2.50/£1.25). **Otangani Beach Club** (no phone) is a rough-and-ready roadhouse-style disco at the northern end of the waterfront. The cover charge is C50 ($2.50/£1.25).

A SIDE TRIP TO RIVAS

The bustling, yet laid-back market town of Rivas is southern Nicaragua's main city and capital of the province. Though it's not a tourist destination in its own right, this town of 45,000 people serves as a connecting crossroad to travelers from the north who are going south to Costa Rica, west to San Juan del Sur, or east to the nearby small port of San Jorge, to catch the ferry to Isla de Ometepe. Not many people hang around long enough to savor Rivas's old-world charm, but it is worth taking an afternoon to stroll through its colorful plaza and see the surrounding historic buildings if you connect through it.

This town of mango trees and chattering parakeets has a rich history. It's perhaps best known as the site of William Walker's Waterloo, for the marauding filibusterer was defeated at the Battle of Rivas here in what proved to be the beginning of his end. Some Rivenses, as the locals are known, actually claim to be direct descendants of Walker to this day. Rivas is also the birthplace of Violetta Chamorro, the 1990s-era president who did much to reunite the war-torn country. And Rivas was a major stop on Cornelius Vanderbilt's stagecoach express to the Pacific during the Californian gold rush. In addition to serving as a key transportation hub, it is now the center of a thriving agricultural hinterland producing corn, rice, beans, sugar cane, and tobacco.

Essentials

GETTING THERE & GETTING AROUND Buses to Rivas from San Juan del Sur leave every 30 minutes from the bus stop next to the municipal market. Rivas' **bus terminal** (✆ **505/453-4333**) is 10 blocks west of the Pan-American Highway, next to the market. Buses leave for San Juan del Sur every 45 minutes. The journey time is 1 hour and costs C20 ($1/50p).The first bus leaves at 6am and the last at 6pm.

Buses depart for Managua every 25 minutes from 4:30am to 6pm. The ride from here to Managua takes 3 hours and costs C40 ($2/£1). Buses leave for Granada every 45 minutes, and the trip takes 2 hours and costs C30 ($1.50/75p).

You can catch a taxi to San Juan del Sur from the town center of Rivas. It should not cost more than C40 ($2/£1) per person. Shared taxis also go to San Juan del Sur and cost approximately C190 ($10/£5), or less if you have to share.

VISITOR INFORMATION Exchange money or withdraw cash at **Bancentro,** a half-block east of Iglesia San Francisco (✆ **505/563-0001**), or at **Banpro,** in front of Parque Central (✆ **505/563-3323**).

The **post office,** northwest of the park, provides a fax service, as does **ENITEL,** 1 block west of the park; it's open daily from 7am to 9:40pm. There are a cluster of Internet cafes northwest and west of the park.

Farmacia Rivas, 2 blocks east of park (✆ **505/563-4292**), is a well-stocked drugstore, as is **Clinica Maria Unmaculada.** Both are open Monday to Friday from 8am to 4:30pm and Saturday from 8am to midday.

What to See & Do

Iglesia Parroquial de San Pedro, 1 block east of central plaza, is a beautiful, but worn-down cathedral with dark stains over its white walls and gilded ledges, along with two very impressive bell towers. It was built in the 18th century and has an interesting mix of architecture styles, with a colonial facade up front and a dome at the rear bearing a colorful fresco that depicts Catholicism conducting a sea battle with secularism and communism, and, of course, triumphing. Mass is held here every evening at 6pm. Open hours are daily 7 to 11am and 5 to 8pm. Admission is free. Another interesting church to see is the **Iglesia de San Francisco,** 4 blocks west of the Parque Central. Beneath it lies a secret tunnel that runs to the city's plaza. The church is open daily from 7 to 11:30am and 5:30 to 8pm. Admission is free.

The town's museum, the **Museo de Historia y Antropologia** (3 blocks north of the Iglesia de San Francisco; ✆ **505/563-3708**), has an interesting collection of pre-Columbian artifacts. The building itself is beautiful, with a low tiled roof and grassy courtyard. It is a former plantation house that played an important role during the Battle of Rivas, during which William Walker briefly took hold of it. It also has an early published poem by the poet Rubén Darío. The museum is open daily 9am to noon and 2 until 5pm. Admission is C19 ($1/50p).

Biblioteca Pública de Rivas is the local library and the town's oldest building, with the bullet wounds to prove it. It is open Monday to Friday from 9am to 1pm and 3 to 7pm. **Rivas Cemetery** is a great place to catch a sunset and wander among some ornate graves of important national figures. It's a pleasant stroll southeast of the town.

Where to Stay

Rivas is not exactly on the "best hotels in the world" circuit, which is not surprising considering that most people opt to base themselves in one of the beachfront paradise hotels in San Juan del Sur or colonial resorts in Granada. Nevertheless, if you do find yourself looking for an inn, you could do worse than stay at the **Hotel Cacique Nicarao** (✆ **505/564-3234**). Located 1 block west of the park, it is a modern hotel with comfortable rooms. Doubles start at $55 (£27) and include TV and air-conditioning. The **Hospedaje Hilmor** (✆ **505/776-7826**) is a big drop in standards but has a central location and clean rooms. Prices start at $10 (£5).

Where to Dine

Hotel Cacique Nicarao (✆ **505/564-3234**) has the best restaurant in town. The only other decent options are **Chop Suey** (✆ **505/563-3235**) on the southwest corner of the park and **Pizza Hot** opposite the Iglesia San Pedro. **Café Estilo Libre** is situated north of the Texaco station and has a pleasant outdoor area.

9 LAGO DE NICARAGUA & ISLA DE OMETEPE ★★

125km (75 miles) SW of Managua; 2km (1¼ miles) E of San Jorge

The twin peaks of the Concepción and Maderas volcanoes rise out of Lago de Nicaragua, forming a muddy jungle island that sustains 35,000 people, countless birdlife, cattle, and howler monkeys. Fireflies dance beneath banana trees as people on old buses, bikes, horses, and even oxen negotiate the rutted roads and countless trails. Rocks carved into zoomorphic figures and pre-Columbian petroglyphs dot the landscape of tropical forest and patchwork fields. The rich, volcanic soil provides abundant crops of bananas, maize, coffee, avocados, and beef, most of which is crammed on the boats that ply the waterway between the island and the mainland port of San Jorge, 1 hour to the west.

The island here, known as Isla de Ometepe, is sacred ground. Legend has it that the Nahuatl tribe fled the Aztecs and went southward in search of a mythical region with two mountains in a lake. There is reason to believe, through the countless artifacts that litter the island, that Nicaragua's pre-Columbian heritage began on the island. In many ways, the islanders remain a people apart from the rest of the country. The turmoil and violence that wracked the mainland for centuries in general bypassed the island, famously referred to by folk singer Luis Enrique Mejia Godoy as "an oasis of peace." The only real drama on the island occurs from beneath the ground. In fact, Ometepe used to be two islands before eruptions and lava flow formed the isthmus Istián that now connects both volcanoes. Volcán Concepción is still very much alive, hurling rocks and spewing lava four times in the last century. The last thunderous occasion was in 1957, when the islanders showed their fierce independence and resolutely refused to leave after they were ordered by the government to evacuate.

Their reluctance to leave is understandable. The island is an idyllic adventure spot, a rural retreat, and a hiker's paradise. For many visitors, the peaks beckon to be climbed, but be warned: It is a hard slog and can only be done with a guide. Others prefer just to wander the volcanoes' lower reaches, bathe on the island's dark beaches, cool off in some spring water pools and waterfalls, or explore the island's many coves and lagoons by foot or kayak.

ESSENTIALS

Getting There

BY BOAT **San Jorge** port just outside Rivas is the main departure point to reach the island. The car/passenger *Ferry Ometepe* (© **505/459-4284** in Moyogalpa) departs at 10:30am, 2:30pm, and 5:30pm. The fare is C40 ($2/£1) per person and C570 ($30/£15) per vehicle, and the crossing takes approximately an hour. Vehicle owners should always call well in advance to book (at least 3 days) and again the day before. Try and get to the dockside office an hour before departure to get your tickets and ensure a spot. The ferry often leaves as soon as it fills up and before the appointed hour. The ferry returns to the mainland from Moyogalpa at 6:45am, 12:30pm, and 4pm.

A handful of other boats cross to Moyogalpa, leaving at 9am, 9:30am, 11:30am, 12:30pm, 1:30pm, 3:30pm, and 4:30pm. The fare is C30 ($1.60/80p) and, as on the ferry, the passengers are a colorful mix of locals toting cattle and fruit and whatever else they can get on board. The water can be choppy; it's best to go early in the morning or late in the evening for the smoothest sailing. The smaller boats return to San Jorge from Moyogalpa at 5:30am, 6am, 6:30am, 7am, 11am, 11:30am, and 1:30pm.

You can also get to Ometepe from Granada on a 4-hour voyage that leaves twice a week. The ***Mozorola*** (© **505/552-8764**) leaves every Wednesday and Saturday at 11am and docks at Altagracia on the island. It returns every Tuesday and Friday at 11am. The fare is C80 ($4/£2). A ferry called the ***EPN*** leaves Granada every Monday and Thursday at 3pm, stopping in Altagracia before continuing south to San Miguelito and San Carlos. It returns through Altagracia every Tuesday and Friday at 11pm. Be aware, however, that if the sea is rough, the ferry may skip its stop at Altagracia altogether.

Getting Around

ON FOOT The island is a hiker's paradise, with numerous trails, but beware that some of the paths can be rough going and it is very easy to get lost. You will certainly need a guide for any treks up to the volcanoes.

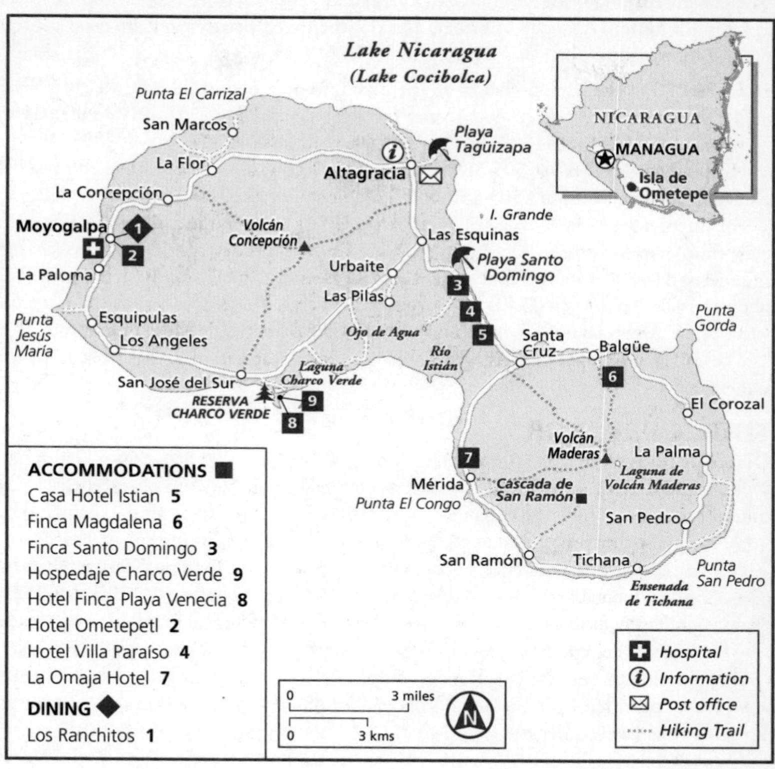

BY CAR/TAXI If you want to travel around the island independently, you'll have to get a 4WD. **Hotel Ometepetl** rents old Toyotas and Suzukis for approximately C760 ($40/£20) for 12 hours. Taxis are plentiful and drivers will swarm you as soon as you step off the boat, as will touts selling rooms and tours.

A pickup taxi from the port to Santo Domingo beach should cost approximately C342 ($18/£9). Two reliable taxi services are **Marvin Arcia** (✆ **505/459-4114**) and **Rommel Gómez** (✆ **505/459-4112**).

BY BUS Old school buses lumber around the island at hourly intervals between Moyogalpa and Altagracia, and they usually travel in a counterclockwise direction. The fare for these buses is C6 (30¢/15p). All buses leave directly from Moyogalpa dock. The journey between both towns takes 1 hour and, from Altagracia to Balgue, it takes another hour. There are less frequent services to outlying towns like San Ramon and Merida. The bus service on Sunday is much reduced and even sometimes nonexistent. Be warned, these bus journeys can be slow and uncomfortable and, if you are traveling across the isthmus, it can seem to take forever.

Visitor Information

There is an **Intur** (no phone) office in the plaza of Altagracia. It is open from 9am to 1pm and 3 to 5pm Monday to Friday. Most of the hotels listed below are good sources of local information, too.

FAST FACTS There are no banks on the island, so be sure to stuff your wallet in Rivas before boarding the boat. You can cash traveler's checks at the **Hotel Ometepetl** in Moyogalpa (✆ **505/569-4278**) for a hefty 10% commission.

Hospital Moyogalpa (✆ **505/569-4247**) is 3 blocks east of the plaza. Altagracia also has a small **Centro de Salud** (✆ **505/552-6089**) on the southeast corner of the town plaza.

For Internet access in Moyogalpa, go to **Arcia Cyber Café** on the main street. It is open daily from 8am to 9pm. In Altagracia, the **Casa Rural,** on the south side of the plaza, has Internet service, as does the craft store **Tienda Fashion,** 1 block south of the park. For phone service, head to **ENITEL** in Moyogalpa, which is 1½ blocks east of the principal street or the **Altagracia** office, which is in front of the plaza beside Museo Ometepe.

There is a **post office** in Altagracia, on the corner of the plaza beside the Museo Ometepe.

TOUR OPERATORS

Ometepe Tours ★, in front of the ferry dock in San Jorge (✆ **505/563-4779** in San Jorge, or **569-4242** in Moyogalpa; www.ometepetours.com.ni), run an excellent 1-day tour of the island, which leaves San Jorge at 9:30am and arrives back on the mainland by 5pm. They also arrange multiday package stays with hotels and transport included.

On the island, you'll find several options regarding tours. **Bernan Gómez** (✆ **505/836-8360**) is a reputable guide, as is the company **Exploring Ometepe** (✆ **505/895-5521;** exploringometepe@hotmail.com). They also organize horse riding and rent out motorbikes. Also check out **Ometepe Ecotours** (✆ **505/569-4244;** hugonava@ibw.com.ni).

If you decide to trek to the volcanoes, make sure you get a reputable guide (known as a *baqueano*) outfitted with a radio and first aid kit. Guide quality and prices can vary, so ask around before you decide.

WHAT TO SEE & DO

Moyogalpa on the western side of the island is a small and quiet town with a sloping main street. The town fountain is a model of the island—water spouts from its "volcanoes," though it has not worked for years. Moyogalpa is the main port that services the island and is a hive of activity when the boats come in. Its pretty, hilltop church is at the top of the main street. It has a white facade and attractive wooden doorways and affords a beautiful view from the bell tower. The town museum **Sala Arqueoligica** (✆ **505/569-4225;** admission C19/$1/50p), 1 block west of the plaza, functions half as an artifact display and half as a handicraft store—it sells local handicrafts and displays pre-Columbian pieces found by the owner. Both the museum and the shop are open Monday to Friday from 9am to 6pm.

Altagracia is the second-biggest town on the island and a prettier place than Moyogalpa. Its central plaza, known as Parque Central, is a large patch of grass with a shop and playground. The area is famous for its vampire bats, but don't worry, they only target chickens and other small animals. This is where the boats from Granada dock, at a port 3km (1¾ miles) north of the town. **El Museo Ometepe** (1 block from the park; no phone) has some interesting ceramic artifacts found on the island. It is open daily from 9am to 5pm. Admission is C20 ($1/50p). **Playa Taguizapa** is a pleasant beach that's a 30-minute walk east of the plaza.

Five kilometers (3 miles) south of Moyogalpa is the long, sandy peninsula of **Punta Jesús Maria,** a tranquil beach that offers the opportunity of beer with a sunset. A cab from Moyogalpa should not cost more than C190 ($10/£5) each way. Ten kilometers (6¼ miles) east on the islands' underbelly is **Reserva Charco Verde ★**. Here the jungle rolls down on a black volcanic beach and monkeys howl from the treetops. It is excellent for some bird-watching or kayaking around the bay or through its green lagoon. Be prepared to get your feet wet, as the wooden walkway has collapsed. Some nearby hospedajes offer boat trips and horse riding excursions. There's a voluntary admission fee of C19 ($1/50p). From the reserve, you can hike through to an isolated cove called **El Tesoro del Pirata ★**. The two volcanoes stand on either side of this serene and peaceful beach.

However, if it is a real beach you want, you must go to **Playa Santo Domingo.** This 4km (2½-mile) stretch of dark sand, with a green jungle backdrop, connects both islands along the Isthmus Istián. The beach can appear a little tatty in parts but in general is very nice and one of the few in the world that can boast a volcano at either end. It's also where the island's best accommodations are located and a great spot for bathing in the shallow waters—the gray-green waters are choppy yet warm and inviting, and there are thatched parasols if the heat gets to be too much. A 30-minute walk up a dirt track beside Villa Paraiso is a bathing complex called **Ojo del Agua ★**, a series of rock-lined pools fed by a natural spring and surrounded by tall trees. It can get a little crowded, but it's great fun dangling from the swing ropes and watching suicidal divers jump from crazy heights here. The entrance fee is C19 ($1/50p).

Cascada San Ramón is a spectacular 50m (164-ft.) waterfall on the southern slopes of Volcán Madera. To get there you must go to the small town of San Ramón, 4km (2½ miles) south of Merida. It's a 3-hour hike from there to the falls, but well worth it.

OUTDOOR ACTIVITIES

BIKING Volcanic mountains in the area equal lots of slopes, so the island offers some thrilling rides—it is perfect for mountain biking. You can rent bikes from many of the hospedajes on the island, including Hotel Hacienda Merida. **Comercial Arcia,** 2 blocks south of Moyogalpa church, also rents bikes, at a rate of C19 ($1/50p) an hour.

The east coast of Maderas makes for a particularly good and challenging spin, and along the way, you can stop to see the cave paintings in Tichana and petroglyphs near Corazal. Make sure to get a good bike, as it is tough terrain.

HIKING ★ Besides notching a volcanic peak or two into your belt (see "Climbing Ometepe's Volcanos," below), the island provides ample opportunities to go for a wander, trip upon ancient pre-Columbian relics, and admire the stunning sunsets. Just pick a path, but remember that much of what you walk upon is private property and, though the islanders in general have no problem with you traipsing across their lands, you should always ask for permission first. Most hotels and lodges have their own set of circuits and interesting things to see close by, one example being the petroglyphs of Finca Magdalena (p. 509).

HORSEBACK RIDING In many ways, horseback riding is the best way to get around this muddy, steep terrain. Indeed I'm surprised no independent operator is offering rides yet. Ask at your hotel for what they offer regarding saddleback riding.

KAYAKING ★ Reserva Charco Verde is a good spot for paddling. You can rent kayaks to take out there at the nearby **Hospedaje Charcoe Verde** (✆ **505/887-9302**). Another great splash is along the coast north of Merida and up the **river Istián.** It can be tough going if you have the wind against you but once you get on the river, it makes it all

Climbing Ometepe's Volcanoes

You don't often get the opportunity to stand beside a lake within a volcano but you can do so in Isla de Ometepe, Nicaragua. However, such bragging rights don't come easy. **Volcán Maderas** may be the smaller of the two volcanoes surrounding Isla de Ometepe (at 1,394m/4,572 ft.) and the most frequently hiked, but it is not easy going. Getting there involves an all-day hike up a steep incline, passing coffee plantations and the occasional pre-Columbian carved stone along the way, and down into its inner rim. This last part requires ropes, so it is imperative that you go with a reputable, fully equipped guide. People who attempt the volcanoes alone can end up lost, injured, or dead. There are two ways of approaching the peak, either through the grounds of Finca Magdalena near Balgue (they will charge a small fee if you are not a guest; p. 509) or from the other side at Merida. Hotel Hacienda Merida (p. 507) arranges excursions in which trekkers descend at Finca Magdalena and are transported back to the hotel.

Volcán Concepción is the big one—a perfectly formed cone 1,610m (5,280 ft.) high. It is a long and arduous 10 hours up and down and a different experience from Maderas in the sense that you walk on a live volcano that could erupt at any time. The last time it rattled its bowels was in 1957 and it has done so four times in the past 100 years. Do the math; it is due for another eruption soon. A thick jungle forest of monkeys and birds gives way to rocks and shale the higher you go here. A stiff wind helps or hinders you along until suddenly the hot sulfurous belch blasts upward from the crater as you reach the rim. This is what forms the almost permanent cloud that clings to the peak. If you are lucky and come on a clear day, you'll be rewarded with the sight of the volcano's chilling stony interior and spectacular views of the island—you'll want to linger and take in its otherworldly atmosphere. La Sabana is the best place to start your climb to Concepción. You can also approach the volcano from a trail behind Altagracia. Again, you must go with a guide, even if you just want to explore the lower reaches, as it is very easy to get lost.

worthwhile. Another less challenging kayak trip is to **Isla el Congo** south of Merida. Ask at your hotel about kayak rentals for the river Istián and Isla el Congo.

WHERE TO STAY

There are no true luxury hotels on the island. What you get instead are charming, down-to-earth, rustic lodges with slow but friendly service. Moyogalpa has the best concentration of budget options, but my advice is to get out of that town and stay on the island, where there are plenty more places at reasonable rates.

Moderate

Finca Santo Domingo This large blue bungalow-style hotel is a little rough around the edges but is surrounded by gorgeous green foliage and boasts roll-out-of-bed access to the beach. It has very basic rooms and you might get some nighttime intruders in the form of snakes and ants. Be prepared for cold-water showers only, and few amenities other than a restaurant and Internet service.

Playa Santo Domingo. ✆ **505/694-1594.** 15 units. From $21 (£12) double; from $33 (£17) triple; from $35 (£18) cabin (sleeps 2); from $41 (£21) cabin (sleeps 3). AE, MC, V. **Amenities:** Restaurant; bike rental; Internet in lobby. *In room:* Fan or A/C.

Hotel Villa Paraíso ★ You might have to line up behind a herd of cows on the muddy dirt track leading up to this quite isolated hotel, but the view from your patio hammock will make it all the more worthwhile. Often cited as the best hotel on the island, the Paraiso offers attractive stone and wood cabins perched on a cliff with Volcán Maderas to the right. The rooms are good sized, though the two beds are small and low and surface areas could be cleaner. Each comes with a private, rustic bathroom. The restaurant is a mite tacky, with wine barrels set into a concrete bar and a stone mosaic overhead, and service is slow. Still, it offers delicious fresh fish platters, among other dishes.

Playa Santo Domingo. ✆ **505/563-4675.** 25 units. From $46 (£23) double; from $63 (£32) suite; from $52 (£26) quadruple. AE, DC, MC, V. **Amenities:** Restaurant; Internet in lobby; pool. *In room:* A/C, TV.

La Omaja Hotel (Kids) Set on a steep hill with great views of Concepción, La Omaja offers somewhat spartan cabins set amid a lush garden of green carpet lawn, shrubs, and palm trees. The rooms are nice and big, accommodating two good-size double beds. The decor could stand a bit of sprucing up and the furniture is merely functional, with deck chairs serving as sitting chairs. Only the deluxe and family cabins have private bathrooms. There are no screens on any of the windows, so bring bug repellent.

Merida. ✆ **505/885-1124.** www.laomaja.com. 6 units. From $35 (£17) deluxe cabin (sleeps 4); from $25 (£13) family cabin (sleeps 5). $5 (£2.50) per person shared cabin. AE, DC, MC, V. **Amenities:** Restaurant; Internet in lobby; laundry service. *In room:* A/C, fan (in shared cabin), TV.

Inexpensive

The colorful, two-story **Casa Hotel Istian** (✆ **505/868-8682**) is quite the find, as it is close to Playo Domingo and has its own private beach. The property is pretty basic but attractive, with large open balconies and lots of hammocks. Rooms are large and clean and come with or without a private bathroom. Rates are a bargain, since they start at $6 (£3). **Hotel Finca Playa Venecia** (✆ **505/887-0191**) has simple cabins with an excellent location close to the green lagoon of Charco Verde. There is a nice lounge area with hammocks, set in what can best be described as a pastoral paradise. The restaurant is decent and the owner rents out bikes and horses to explore the area further. Cabin prices start at $20 (£10).

Finca Magdalena (Finds) (Kids) What Finca Magdalena lacks in luxury it makes up for in community spirit and pure heart. It's actually the confiscated property of rich landowners who found themselves on the wrong side during the revolution. It is now a coffee cooperative of 24 families who offer dorm-style accommodations in a huge barnlike hacienda, along with some cottages for those who'd like a little more privacy. There are some wardrobe-size double rooms in the main building. Be prepared for cold showers and communal meals, but also lots of character and a chance to sample a simple farming lifestyle.

The plantation's coffee and honey are available for purchase, and it provides easy access to sites like the Volcán Madera and petroglyphs scattered around the wild garden grounds. The finca is quite a long haul from Moyogalpa, taking 2 hours on the bus, followed by a 2km (1¼-mile) walk uphill.

Balgue. ✆ **505/880-2041.** www.fincamagdalena.com. 21 units. From $30 (£15) cabin; $8 (£4) double; $4 (£2) dorm. No credit cards. **Amenities:** Restaurant; communal kitchen. *In room:* Fan, no phone.

Hospedaje Charco Verde This hotel is conveniently located right beside the lagoon reserve and offers handsome wooden cabins with lots of light and space. It has a more rural setting than Hotel Ometepetl and is accordingly more rustic. The beds are big and the furniture comfortable, with a nice veranda and hammock. The owners have a farm nearby and they also rent out kayaks and horses. From here you can arrange short boat trips to Isla de Quiste or just along the shoreline. There is also a restaurant and bar on the premises that is open to the public.

Charco Verde. ✆ **505/887-9302.** www.charcoverde.com.ni. 8 units. From $35–$45 (£17–£23) double. AE, MC, V. **Amenities:** Restaurant; bike rental. *In room:* Fan or A/C.

Hotel Ometepetl This hotel is one of the better established on the island and boasts a convenient location in the center of Moyogalpa. It has an attractive courtyard, with an effusion of plant life, a large pool, and nice lounging areas with giant hammocks. Chunky wooden furniture sits on tiled floors that lead to pleasant-size rooms with private bathrooms. The open-air restaurant has lots of light and white tablecloths on the tables. Service can be mixed, however, and the air-conditioning problematic. The hotel also offers jeep rentals and is the only place on the island that accepts traveler's checks.

Moyogalpa, 50m (164 ft.) uphill from port. ✆ **505/569-4276.** 13 units. From $18 (£9) double; from $25 (£13) triple; from $35 (£16) quad. AE, DC, MC, V. **Amenities:** Pool. *In room:* Fan or A/C.

WHERE TO DINE

All the better hotels in town have restaurants, so you should not have to wander too far for a meal. **Restaurant Villa Paraiso,** in the Hotel Villa Paraiso (✆ **505/563-4675**), is one of the best hotel restaurants. It serves international fare and is open daily from 7am to 9pm, serving breakfast, lunch, and dinner. Main courses start at C200 ($10/£5). **Restaurante Charco Verde** ★, in the Hospedaje Charco Verde (✆ **505/887-9302**), is another pleasant hotel restaurant offering a wide variety of food, such as pasta, steak, and giant filet of fish. The dining area is set under a large wooden roof with open walls. It is open daily from 7am to 8pm. Meals start at C180 ($9.50/£4.50). Finally, you may want to try **Restaurante Ometepetl** (✆ **505/569-4132**) in the hotel of the same name. It has a pleasant open front dining area and serves Nicaraguan staples. It's open daily from 6am to 10pm. Meals start at C150 ($8/£4).

For a stand-alone restaurant in Moyogalpa, try **Los Ranchitos,** 4 blocks uphill from the dock and half a block south (✆ **505/569-4112**), which offers inexpensive fare in an open-air setting. It is popular with both locals and visitors and the menu includes everything from pizza to fish in huge portions. It is open daily from 7am to 9pm. The restaurant also offers a taxi service for those who have gorged on too much fried plantain and cannot walk home. Main courses start at C95 ($5/£2.50).

A SIDE TRIP TO ARCHIPELAGO DE SOLENTINAME

The Solentiname Archipelago is a scattering of 36 islands in the southern corner of Lago Nicaragua. Geographically it is an isolated, tropical backwater, but historically and culturally it is the nucleus of Nicaragua's world-famous primitive art movement and a hotbed of liberation theology. That's due mainly to poet and priest Ernesto Cardenal, who came here in the late '60s and encouraged ordinary islanders to pick up a paint brush and paint what they saw. The result was astounding—vibrant renditions in oil and balsa wood of the islands' nature and people. Complete families became artists and by the early '70s TV crews were coming to make documentaries about the phenomenon. Only 750 people live on the islands today but they act as hosts to hundreds of tourists every year who come to paint, observe, or study the region's rich natural wonders.

Essentials

Getting There

BY PLANE & BOAT Getting to Solentiname is not easy and is particularly grueling if you are on a budget. The fastest but more expensive way is to catch a plane from Managua to the uninteresting river town of San Carlos, and then to catch the 2-hour boat ride to the dock in Mancarrón. **La Costeña** (✆ **505/263-1228** in Managua, or 583-0271 in San Carlos) operates a daily "puddle jumper" flight. It leaves Managua at 9am daily except Fridays and Sundays when it leaves at midday. It departs from San Carlos daily at 10am, except Fridays and Sundays when it leaves at 1pm. The journey takes 50 minutes and costs approximately C2,660 ($140/£70) round-trip. Flights should be booked well in advance and reconfirmed.

The scheduled boat from San Carlos leaves on Saturdays and Tuesdays at 1pm, returning on Mondays and Thursdays. The cost is C95 ($5/£2.50). Private boats can be arranged but expect to pay C2,280 ($120/£60) one way. You can arrange this directly with a dockside boat owner *(panguero)* or book in advance through **Intur** in San Carlos, opposite Clínica San Lucas (✆ **505/583-0301** or 583-0363) or **Armando Ortiz's Viajes Turisticos,** by the Western Union (✆ **505/583-0039**).

BY BOAT A ferry called the *EPN* leaves Granada every Monday and Thursday at 3pm, stopping in Altagracia on Isla de Ometepe before continuing south to San Miguelito and San Carlos. It arrives in San Carlos at 6am the next day. It is wise to get to the ticket office 2 hours before departure. First-class seats cost C228 ($12/£6) and are on the upstairs deck, which is air-conditioned. Second class is on the lower deck, without air-conditioning, and costs C152 ($8/£4). The ferry returns through Altagracia every Tuesday and Friday at 3pm. Be aware, however, that if the sea is rough it may skip its stop at Altagracia altogether.

BY BUS The bus trip to San Carlos is a 300km (196-mile) epic journey and a supreme test of endurance. The road is in a terrible condition for much of the way and the bus ride is a bone-shaking one and travels at a snail's pace. This is purely for people on a strict budget with lots of time on their hands. Buses leave from Managua's Mayoreo Market at 8am and 11:45am. The fare is C190 ($10/£5). During bad weather, the road closes completely. From San Carlos you then catch the boat to the islands (see "By Plane & Boat," above).

Getting Around

Only two of the 36 islands have tourist facilities. They are **Isla Mancarrón** and **Isla Elvis Chavarría** (also known as Isla San Fernando). Isla Mancarroncito and Isla Donald Guevara (also known as Isla la Venada) are the only two other populated islands. *Collectivo* water taxis run twice a week between these islands, though you can of course charter your own *panga,* at a price—in general gas is much more expensive in this part of the country. There is a definite advantage to organizing a packaged trip with a tour company, including transport, accommodations, and a guide. Independent travelers will need to allot lots of time and adopt a flexible attitude to getting around.

Visitor Information

There is no tourist information office on the islands but lodge owners such as Maria Guevara at **Albergue Celentiname** (✆ **505/276-1910**) are more than happy to help with any queries. Another excellent source of info is **Doña Maria Amelia Gross** (✆ **505/583-0271**), who runs the La Costeña office in San Carlos. The **San Carlos Intur office,** in front of the Clinica San Lucas (✆ **505/583-0301** or 583-0363), has brochures and can help arrange transport. It's open Monday to Saturday from 10am to 6pm.

Tour Operators & Travel Agencies

MUSAS (El Museo Archipiélago de Solentiname), organizes 4-day tours of the archipelago, including accommodations and transportation from San Carlos. They can be contacted through ACRA in San Carlos (✆ **505/583-0095**) or in Managua (✆ **505/249-6176;** musasni@yahoo.com). Prices depend on group size but expect to pay at least C5,700 ($300/£150) for a 4-day tour.

The operator **Galería Solentiname,** Colonia Centro America, 3 blocks south of Iglesia Fatima, Managua (✆ **505/252-6262** or 277-0939; gsolentiname@amnet.com.ni), can organize package tours; it's owned by the same family that operates Don Julio Lodge on La Isla Elvis Chavarria. **Solentiname Tours,** Apartado Postal 1388, Managua (✆ **505/265-2716;** www.solentinametours.com), offers countrywide tours including several days on the islands and down the Río San Juan. **Tours Nicaragua** (✆ **505/252-4063;** www.toursnicaragua.com) also offers packages on both islands.

What to See & Do

Solentiname will require you to switch frequencies and slow right down. There is not much to do here, though there's lots to see and admire. **Mancarrón** is the main island. Only 200 people live on its 20 sq. km (13 sq. miles) of lush green vegetation, with the 260m-high (853-ft.) Cerro Las Cuevas dominating the waterline. Close to the dock there are a collection of houses and the interesting **Iglesia Solentiname ★** designed by Ernesto Cardenal. This tiny adobe building is probably the most colorful and quirky church you'll see in Nicaragua, with playful images set on its white walls and a simple altar with pre-Columbian patterns. It was here that Erenesto Cardenal began his project in the 1960s to bring art to the islands. Close by is the **APDS** complex. This is the local development association and here they have a display room holding books, art, and artifacts about the islands, including info on its artists and Ernesto Cardenal.

La Isla Elvis Chavarria is named after a young martyr killed during the revolution. Also known as San Fernando, it is the archipelago's second-biggest island and has a sizeable community with a school and health clinic. **El Museo Archipiélago de Solentiname** or MUSA (no phone), is a museum, art gallery, library, information point, medicine garden, and arboretum. Just follow the butterflies and hummingbirds up the garden path behind the village and you'll find it. The museum is open daily from 7am to noon and 2 to 5pm. Admission is C19 ($1/50p).

La Cueva del Duende is an underwater cave of mythological importance to the islanders. They believed that it was the path to the other side and marked on the walls are representations of the dead. It is only accessible in the dry season (Mar and April). **Mancarroncito** is one of the archipelago's wilder, untouched islands with a 100m-high (328-ft.) peak shrouded in thick green jungle. **Zapote** is a bird sanctuary with a colony of 20,000 birds—it gets noisy here, especially during the dry season. **El Padre** is just as noisy, because of its boisterous howler monkey community.

Where to Stay

There are many families on both **Isla Mancarrón** and **Isla Elvis Chavarría** that open their doors to strangers and rent rooms in a homestay fashion. Look around for signs posted outside these houses. Bear in mind that, wherever you choose to stay will also be where you will eat, as the islands have no dining scene.

Moderate

Hotel Mancarrón These are by far the plushest accommodations you'll get on the archipelago. The property, made up of homes with red roof tiles and white adobe walls, sits up in a 3-hectare (7½-acre) site that is bordered by forest and lakes. Rooms are simple, spacious, and overlook the dock. A large dining room with a bar is on-site. All water is heated by solar energy, though there is also a backup generator. The hotel organizes excursions to local artists' workshops and will arrange art lessons for those who want to capture the island's colors. Note that there are ongoing issues over ownership that may affect the hotel's future.

Isla Mancarrón. ✆ **505/583-9015** or 883-6122. 12 units. From $35 (£18) double; from $45 (£23) triple; $50 (£25) quadruple. AE, DC, MC, V. **Amenities:** Restaurant/bar; TV room. *In room:* Fan.

Inexpensive

Albergue Celentiname Located on the western edge of La Elvis, this family-run lodge has been in operation since 1984 and provides eight rustic cabins with shared bathrooms. It has a waterfront setting and great views of the islands, volcanoes, and the Cost Rican border. The cabins are basic and a little dark, but are clean and come with an all-important hammock and small porch. There's an attractive restaurant on the grounds. The hospitality of the hosts is what really makes this place memorable, however. Doña María Guevara and her family are all painters and are enthusiastic in sharing the delights of the island. You also can't beat the lodge when it comes to providing an ultimate jungle experience—you'll be surrounded by a cacophony of wildlife sounds at most times.

Isla San Fernando. ✆ **505/276-1910** or 893-1977. 8 units. $60 (£30) double. AE, DC, MC, V. **Amenities:** Restaurant. *In room:* Fan, no phone.

A TRIP DOWN THE RÍO SAN JUAN TO EL CASTILLO

San Carlos is a hot, fetid port town straight out of a Graham Greene novel. It is the sort of place you only stay in if waiting for something—usually the next boat to the Solentiname Archipelago or the next plane to Managua. If you find yourself trapped in this grubby little place, the two best hotels are **Hotel Carelys** (✆ **505/583-0389**) and **Cabinas Leyko** (✆ **505/583-0354**). Very basic rooms at both range from C380 ($20/£10) to C950 ($50/£25).

San Carlos is at the mouth of the **Río San Juan** and the departure point for a pleasant river journey 70km (43 miles) downriver to the old historical fort town of **El Castillo.** The truly adventurous can continue another 140km (87 miles) to the lonely Caribbean port town of **San Juan del Norte.** Boats to El Castillo depart at 8am midday and 3pm daily and cost C100 ($5/£2.50) and return to San Carlos at 5am, 7am, and 2pm. The journey takes 3 hours and affords beautiful views of the wide river and its green, tree-lined banks. Birdlife is abundant, with large flocks of egrets and cormorants swirling overhead. Look out for the occasional kingfisher and the large silver fish called a tarpon, which slips through the water like a dolphin. You might think you have reached the end of the world on this boat trip, but believe it or not, thousands of people once traveled up this river when it was the popular Vanderbilt route to California during the gold rush. Some old abandoned steamboats can be seen farther downstream past El Castillo. This river journey is interrupted by several stops to pick up and drop off people at small settlements on the way to the fort. The occasional boat even pulls up to sell food and drinks.

Montecristo River Lodge

Several miles before El Castillo is a rustic resort set on a lush green slope. You cannot miss it, as its name, **Montecristo** (✆ **505/583-0197;** www.montecristoriver.com), is spelled out in huge white letters along the riverbank and a long thatched walkway leads up to its series of huts and cabins. Originally a simple fishing lodge, Montecristo now practices sustainable tourism, by offering eco-friendly accommodations set in a wildlife refuge with hiking trails. The hotel also organizes river excursions on their small fleet of boats.

Once in El Castillo, you'll find the dark-stained stone remains of the Spanish fort **El Castillo de la Inmaculada Concepción de Maria ★**, which reminded me of a Maya temple. It's a relic of just how important the river was as a gateway between Europe and Central America. The Spanish built several forts along the river to deter marauding pirates bent on raiding prosperous Granada. El Castillo was the biggest, and was constructed between 1602 and 1625. The fort is situated on a river bend and sits high over the village, with excellent views downriver. In its heyday it had 32 cannons trained on any strangers coming this way and was a formidable obstacle. It was the scene of many skirmishes and sieges, with the British briefly taking it in 1780. It now holds an interesting museum and library, which charge a single entrance fee of C19 ($1/50p). It is open daily from 10am to 4pm.

The village of El Castillo itself hugs the riverbank and is home to 1,500 souls. If you should decide to stay, the best hotel is **Hotel Albergue El Castillo** (✆ **505/892-0174**). Rooms with shared bathrooms start at C285 ($15/£7.50).

10 THE CARIBBEAN ★★

Don't let its reputation fool you. Nicaragua's Caribbean coast is not entirely the whirlpool of turquoise postcard images you may have heard about or seen. Most of this steaming 520km (322 ft.) of Atlantic coast is a dense and inhospitable plain of tropical forest—impenetrable and very wet. Its spotty weather is one of the reasons La Costa is a world apart from the rest of Nicaragua; the Spanish never actually got around to conquering it and it was a British, Protestant protectorate for many years until it was joined in name only with its Spanish neighbor in 1894. Its rich history of Miskito Indian culture and pirate heritage means its people are more like West Indians than Nicaraguans and they generally speak a lilting form of English creole rather than Spanish.

The Caribbean still remains very much isolated from the rest of Nicaragua, and its main town, Bluefields, is only accessible by sea or air. Little tourist infrastructure, be it visitor centers or shopping spots, exists here. Yet there are signs that the coast is opening up. The Corn Islands, 80km (50 miles) off the coast, are particularly becoming more popular, as they do actually offer a postcard-perfect white-beach paradise.

BLUEFIELDS

440km (272 miles) SE of Managua; 465km (288 miles) SE of Granada

In Bluefields, a gritty but colorful port town of 50,000, the Caribbean collides with Latin America. The end result is a languid and slightly edgy place, which perhaps is in keeping with the fact that the town was named after a pirate (a Dutch marauder called Blewfeldt). It was a thriving 19th-century town, living off timber, bananas, and God (in the form of Moravian missionaries whose neat little churches dot the region). The 20th century saw a decline in the region's fortunes, compounded by a confrontational attitude by the Managua government.

Today, a heady ethnic mix of Miskito Indian, *mestizo,* Spanish, and West Indian locals call the town home. Bluefields is also an important port with a murky bay and murkier crime image. This image is somewhat unfounded, though the area is becoming famous for abandoned bales of cocaine rolling up on its coast (known as white lobster) and the social problems such a phenomenon causes. Many people choose to skip the town on their way to the Corn Islands, but if you do decide to linger, you'll find some of the best nightclubs and party spots in Nicaragua as well as access to incredible coastal wildlife and landscapes such as the Pearl Lagoon and the tropical archipelago known as the Pearl Cays.

Essentials

Getting There

BY PLANE **Bluefields Airport** (**BEF;** no phone) is a tiny, modern terminal 3km (1¾ miles) south of the town. There are always taxis outside when a plane arrives. **La Costeña** (✆ **505/263-1228** in Managua, or 572-2500 in Bluefields) operates daily services between Managua and Bluefields with an onward journey to the Corn Islands. **Atlantic Airlines** (✆ **505/222-5787** in Managua, or 572-1299 in Bluefields; www.atlantic airlines.com.ni) does the same. Both have small, turbo-powered airplanes that are not for the fainthearted.

BY BUS & BOAT **Transportes Vargas Peña** (✆ **505/280-4561**) offers a bus-boat package from Managua, leaving Mercado Iván Montenegro at 9pm daily. The journey takes from 12 to 15 hours and is not pleasant, as the road is very bad. **Transportes Aguilar** (✆ **505/248-3005**) offers a similar service, leaving from Mayoreo at 9pm. Both trips cost roughly C350 ($18/£9) one-way.

The river town of Rama is the boat departure point from the mainland to Bluefields. A large boat leaves every Tuesday and Saturday at 11am and takes 5 hours. The cost is C95 ($5/£2.50). Faster *pangas* run daily at 6am, which take 2 hours. The cost is C190 ($10/£5).

Getting Around

Taxis cost less than C19 ($1/50p) for most trips within the town and there are plenty of buses that trundle around the town. The fare is C5 (25¢/15p). To go farther afield you'll need a boat or *panga* (open motor boat). **Jipe,** Mercado Municipal (✆ **505/572-1871**), is a water taxi company that provides private excursions to the area's surrounding attractions. *Pangas* leave for el Bluff and Pearl Lagoon from the town pier and cost between C19 and C57 ($1–$3/50p–£1.50). The last boats return at 4pm.

Visitor Information

There is an **Intur office** half a block south of the park (✆ **505/572-1111**); it's open Monday to Friday from 9am to 4:30pm. **CIDCA** (no phone), a research and local history organization, is 50m (164 ft.) north of the police station and offers good information on the area. It's open Monday to Friday from 8am to 5:30pm. A good website to check is **www.bluefieldspulse.com**; it offers events listings and local news.

What to See & Do

Bluefields itself has no bathing beaches. Much of the area was destroyed by Hurricane Joan in 1988, after which the port was moved across the bay at El Bluff. You can reach

El Bluff, where giant fishing boats and tankers are docked amid fish-packing factories, on boats that run daily across the bay. It's an ugly but interesting harbor scene. Bluefields' most interesting building is the shore-side **Moravian Church.** Rebuilt after the hurricane; it was first constructed in 1848, and now sports a red roof and neat wooden paneling reminiscent of Caribbean buildings. It is in front of the Municipal Dock and is open for morning and evening services at 8am and 6pm.

Where to Stay

The best places to stay in Bluefields are north of the town pier. I recommend spending a little extra on accommodations here, as some of the budget options are the sort of places that are rented by the hour.

Oasis Hotel Casino ★, 150m (492 ft.) from the bay (✆ **505/572-0665;** www.oasiscasinohotel.com), is one of the better moderately priced hotels in town, with large rooms and suites. Beds are big and comfortable and the rooms come with air-conditioning and cable TV. Doubles start at $60 (£30). **Hotel Bluefields Bay** (✆ **505/572-0120;** tiairene@ibw.com.ni), 2 blocks north of the Municipal Dock, is a well-appointed B&B by the shoreline. Rooms start at $28 (£14). **Hotel South Atlantic II,** west of the municipal market (✆ **505/572-1022**), is another good option. Rooms start at $35 (£17) and have air-conditioning and TV.

For inexpensive rooms, **Hotel Caribbean Dream,** 20m (66 ft.) south of the Municipal Market (✆ **505/572-0107**), has a nice blue-and-white veranda facing the main street. Rooms start at $20 (£10) and come with air-conditioning and private bathrooms. Alternatively, try **Mini Hotel Central,** dockside by the Municipal market (✆ **505/572-2372**), which is well run and has friendly owners. Rooms start at $25 (£13).

Where to Dine

Fresh seafood is the order of the day here, and shrimp and lobster are featured prominently on every menu. I recommend taking advantage of the relatively cheap prices and trying something more unusual like yellowfin and snapper cooked with vegetables and coconut curry. While in town, you should also try coco bread, a popular puffed loaf of bread, as well as hot coconut buns. Most formal restaurants in town open for lunch and close at 10pm daily.

Manglares Restaurant ★, in the Hotel Bluefields Bay (✆ **505/572-0107**), has the best seaside dining in the area, along with a nice location on a dock over the bay. Main courses start at C180 ($9.50/£4.25). Another seafood restaurant with a great view is **El Flotante,** 4 blocks south of the church. Main courses start at C200 ($11/£5.50). **La Loma Rancho** is set on a hill overlooking the town and has a pleasant open-air dining area. Main courses start at C180 ($9.50/£4.25). If you like your meals formal and elegant, go to **Chez Marcel** (✆ **505/572-2347**), where they do exquisite lunches and dinners. Main courses start at C250 ($13/£6.50).

The restaurant within the **Hotel South Atlantic II** (✆ **505/572-1022**) serves excellent seafood and meat dishes that won't bust your budget. Main courses start at C120 ($6.30/£3.15). Another good hotel restaurant within the same price range is the **Mini-Hotel Central** (✆ **505/572-2372**).

Bluefields After Dark

This so-called "Jamaica of Nicaragua" certainly comes alive at night and the locals have no inhibitions when it comes to getting down. Bluefields lives and breathes music, and the bars and clubs here play an eclectic mix, to say the least. One minute you might be

Attractions Around Bluefields

Greenfields Nature Reserve is a private nature reserve that offers excellent jungle excursions and canoeing trips in the surrounding pristine wilderness. It can be seen in a 1-day trip from Bluefields that costs approximately $15 (£7.50). Contact ✆ **505/268-1897** or visit www.greenfields.com.ni for info.

Pearl Lagoon is a small, peaceful village an hour away from Bluefields by boat and is a lovely, relaxing antidote to the shabbiness of that town. Pearl Lagoon has a beautiful church, and a variety of lodgings are springing up here regularly. It is often used as a base to explore the paradise-like archipelago known as the **Pearl Cays ★★**. *Pangas* leave for Pearl Lagoon each day regularly (as soon as they fill up) but it advisable to go to the dock in Bluefields as early as possible. The trip itself is beautiful, since it takes you up the Río Escondido and through a maze of streams and waterways, filled with wildlife. The fare costs C100 ($5/£2.50) one-way.

grinding to Daddy Yankee and next weeping into your beer to Tammy Wynette. Whatever you do, make sure you get a taxi to and from the venues listed below, for safety reasons.

Four Brothers, 6 blocks south of the park in Barrio Puntafria, is a popular roadhouse disco that gets a good mix of people. It is open Thursday to Sunday and the party here goes on all night. **Fresh Point ★** is a similar roadhouse disco, but with a slightly livelier scene. It is 2km (1¼ miles) north of the city and has a pleasant outdoor area with palm trees and tables. Saturday night is the best night here. **La Loma Rancho** (see "Where to Dine," above), is a restaurant that converts into a happening party spot on Thursday through Sunday, with great views overlooking the city. **Cima Club,** 1 block west of Moravian Church on Avenida Cabezas, is a more laid-back joint, with salsa and Latin beats and a little karaoke, as well as open-air seating.

CORN ISLANDS ★★★

The Corn Islands, consisting of 6-sq.-km-long (3¾-sq.-mile) Big Corn and 1.5-sq.-km (1-sq.-mile) Little Corn, are two kernels of Caribbean paradise located 83km (52 miles) east of the Nicaraguan coast and are perhaps my favorite part of Nicaragua. The islands' luminous coastal bays and shores are ideal for diving, snorkeling, fishing, or simply sunning. And how could you *not* be happy on islands with names like Coconut Point, Sally Peaches, and Jokeman Bank?

Though the islanders, many of whom have surnames like Morgan and Dixon that call to mind the pirates and adventurers who landed here years ago, are traditionally dependent on fishing and coconut growing for a living, tourism is quickly becoming another prominent economic force here. I sincerely hope that this increasing tourism unfolds in a sustainable manner, for these are two true treasure islands, with some of the best beaches I have ever wandered upon. The laid-back vibe also lends itself to some great parties: during Easter, the otherwise deserted beaches get packed with revelers, as they do for the Crab Soup Festival in late August, a traditional festival celebrating slave emancipation.

There is very little happening here in terms of nightlife, however. Unlike nearby Bluefields, the only thing to do here after dark is stroll along the beach or have a drink in your hotel—so don't come expecting to party.

Essentials

Getting There

BY PLANE **Corn Island Airport** (**RNI;** no phone) is served by two small airlines that make connections to Bluefields and Managua. **La Costeña** (✆ **505/575-5131**) and **Atlantic Airlines** (✆ **505/270-5355**) both depart from Managua at 6:30am and 2pm daily and leave the island at 8am and 3pm. The journey takes 1½ hours; arrive at least 30 minutes before departure and always reconfirm your outward flight on arrival. Expect to fly in small, antiquated propeller-powered planes.

The airport is 2km (1¼ miles) from Brig Bay. There are always several taxi drivers waiting at the tiny airport when each plane arrives. The fare is C15 (75¢/40p) per person no matter where you go, though you may be charged a little extra for luggage.

BY BOAT Three boats depart from Bluefields on different days. A 5-hour express called *Río Escondido* departs at 9am every Wednesday, returning at 9am on a Tuesday. The cost is C100 ($5.20/£2.65). A ferry called *St Nikolas* (✆ **505/695-3344**) leaves on Fridays at 9am and takes 7 hours. It returns on Sundays at midday. The cost one-way is C100 ($5.20/£2.65). The *Captain D* (✆ **505/850-2767**) leaves on Tuesdays at 9am and takes 7 hours, returning on Fridays at midday. The cost one-way is C150 ($7.90/£3.85). All boats dock at Brig Bay, Big Corn Island's main port.

A *panga* leaves daily from the Great Corn Island dock at 10am and 4pm to Little Corn. The journey takes 25 minutes and costs 120C ($6.30/£3.15) one-way. The boat leaves from Little Corn dock to return to Big Corn at 7am and 2pm daily.

Getting Around

A taxi costs C15 (80¢/40p) per person to travel anywhere on the island and C21 ($1.05/55p) after 10pm or if you have a lot of luggage. There is a small minibus that circles the island at a cost of C5 (30¢/15p). Perhaps the most fun way to get around is to hire one of the many golf carts that cost C190 ($10/£5) per hour. Contact **Arenas Beach Hotel** (✆ **505/456-2220**) to do so.

Orientation

The bigger island here, **Big Corn,** has the most facilities and even a 12km (7½-mile) ring road that circles the island, frequented by the occasional car, taxi, and golf cart. This is where you'll find the island's main port Brig Bay, and the only airport. Generally, the best beaches in Big Corn are to the southwest, as it is more sheltered than the eastern side, though the reverse happens in November. The north end has the best spots for snorkeling.

Little Corn is as close as you'll get to a deserted island without being left completely forlorn. It's wilder and more untamed than its bigger brother and draws a sturdier traveler who can withstand the 30km (19-mile) boat ride here. There are no cars and the only concrete path is near the dock; the rest is beach trails and dirt paths. How long it will stay like this remains to be seen but if you have a primitive streak and enjoy being surrounded on all sides by coral reef and mango trees, Little Corn is for you.

Visitor Information

FAST FACTS **Banpro,** on the road to Hotel Puertas del Sol, Brig Bay (✆ **505/575-5107**), is the only bank on the island. Though the islands' only ATM was installed here in 2008, it's best to bring plenty of cash to the island in case you can't get to the bank.

With a Visa credit card, you can take out money at Banpro and the airport. Money transfers can be arranged at the **Western Union** outlet (✆ **505/575-5074**) beside the Caribbean Depot, close to the dock.

Corn Island Hospital (✆ **505/575-5236**) is behind Nautilus and is open every day, all day. For an English-speaking doctor, call Dr. David Somarriba (✆ **505/575-5184**) or for a dentist, call ✆ **505/575-5236. Pharmacy Monica** (✆ **505/575-5251**) is in front of government house in the center of the island. It is open Monday to Saturday from 8am to 6pm and Sunday from 8am to noon. **Pharmacy Guadelupe** (✆ **505/575-5217**) is farther east and is open Monday to Saturday from 7am to 9pm.

Most of the better hotels on the island should have Internet service. **Cyber Café,** near Nautilus, charges C40 ($2.10/£1.05) per hour. The **Western Union** outlet (see above) also provides Internet and fax services.

For emergencies, dial ✆ **101.** For other matters, call ✆ **505/575-5201.**

What to See & Do

The first thing you should do is head straight for the beaches, the best of which is **Picnic Beach ★★★**, located in the south bay of Big Corn. This is a long white strand beach, with gentle turquoise waters and not a soul in sight (for now anyway). Another beautiful Big Corn beach is **Sally Peaches** on the northeastern side of the island. Here you have shallow pools and pink coral sand. It is unsuitable for swimming (because of rocks) but makes for great photo opportunities from the hill here, **Mount Pleasant,** upon which you'll find a small watchtower. The watchtower can be accessed by a path in front of Nicos Bar.

Outdoor Activities

Spotted tiger rays, black tip sharks, stingrays, spider crabs, parrot fish, angel fish, barracuda, and triggerfish; they are all out there in the pristine waters waiting for you to drop in and say hello. **Nautilus Dive,** north of Brig Bay (✆ **505/575-5077;** www.divebigcorn.com) is the most established dive operator on the island. It offers everything from open water to advanced courses and allows guests to explore the island's three coral reefs or a volcanic pinnacle known as **Blowing Rock.** Fun dives start at C855 ($45/£22) and a 3-day open-water course costs C5,225 ($275/£138). Nautilus Dive also offers snorkeling tours and glass-bottom boat excursions over reefs and shipwrecks for those who don't want to get their feet wet. The outfit's German and Guatemalan owners Regina and José have recently branched out and opened a gift store and restaurant by the same name, close to the dive shop.

Anastasias on the Sea, North Shore (✆ **505/575-5001;** www.cornislandparadise.com), is a hotel, restaurant, marine park, and fishing outfitter. You can rent snorkeling equipment through them for C10 (50¢/25p) or kayaks for C15 (80¢/40p) at their amazingly beautiful location, or go on a full-day sport or fly-fishing excursion, which can cost between C2,850 ($150/£75) and C7,600 ($400/£200). **Blue Runner Charter,** Southend (✆ **505/820-2809**), is run by true blue local fisherman Alwin Taylor and offers sea tours and fishing trips.

Where to Stay in Big Corn

Thankfully, the island has not been overrun with concrete and gated hotels—yet. There are plans to develop conventional resorts here in the next few years, but on a small enough scale for the island's fragile ecosystem to sustain them. Time can only tell if that will happen. For the moment, most of the accommodations options on the island are limited to two-star basics with a few memorable exceptions. It is wise to stay in a hotel that has an adjoining restaurant and make sure the hotel has its own electric generator. Otherwise, when the lights go out, you'll have to be happy with a hammock and a glass of rum. Since tourism is a relatively new phenomenon in this area, be warned that service can be slow wherever you go.

Expensive

Arenas Beach Hotel ★ Kids Situated on what must be one of the most spectacular beaches in the world (Picnic Beach), the Arenas is a spacious hotel and cabin complex that opened in 2006. Don't let the exterior colors or decor turn you off. Bright orange and blue walls topped with white lattice arches might not be to everybody's taste, but they hide a collection of spacious rooms with great views and a large veranda. The bungalows have a little more style and character with their pine walls and stained glass lamps. The hotel has no pool but you'll understand why when you step out front onto the amazing white beach—it renders a chlorinated swim obsolete. The hotel also has a very good if expensive restaurant and is family-friendly, with a number of rooms that comfortably fit up to six people.

Picnic Beach. ✆ **505/456-2220.** www.arenasbeachhotel.com. 22 units. From $75 (£38) double; from $105 (£53) triple; from $100 (£50) quad. Rates include breakfast. MC, V. **Amenities:** Restaurant and bar; laundry service; room service. *In room:* A/C, TV, Wi-Fi.

Casa Canada ★★ This chunk of ocean-side paradise is easily the most beautiful and well-appointed hotel on the island. The row of cottage-style rooms might look unassuming from the island roadway, but on the other side they face a nicely tiled pool and long rock shore of palm trees and small patches of lawn. Rooms are large with every type of modern amenity, including a coffeemaker, small kitchenette, and blessedly silent air conditioner. The beds are big and comfortable and the bathrooms are medium-size and immaculate. The rooms are lined along a beachfront garden, which features a resident monkey and iguana for entertainment. The hotel's restaurant provides excellent seafood and hearty breakfasts.

Canadian owner Larry is a perfect, gregarious host and the staff is equipped to set up many organized tours. Though the Casa Canada's particular slice of actual sandy beach is very small, since this whole island is one big beach, that should not be a problem. The only possible annoyance is the sound of crashing waves a few feet from your doorway—but I think that's an asset.

South End. ✆ **505/644-0925.** www.casa-canada.com. 21 units. From $85 (£43) double. AE, MC, V. **Amenities:** Bar and restaurant; Internet; infinity pool. *In room:* A/C, TV/DVD, minibar.

Paraiso Club This cluster of palm-fringed cabins stands in private grounds a stone's throw from the beach. They look exotic and inviting from the outside but are somewhat disappointing on the inside—cramped, with low ceilings and very basic bathrooms. The beds are also hard and the decor could do with renovating. The Paraiso Club is a step down from Casa Canada and attracts a younger, hardier clientele. Its main attraction is its two friendly Dutch owners and a lively restaurant bar with excellent food. Access to the hotel is down an unpaved road close to Brig Bay.

Brig Bay. ✆ **505/575-5111.** www.paraisoclub.com. 15 units. From $60 (£30) double; from $85 (£43) triple; from $100 (£50) quadruple. Rates include breakfast. MC, V. Free airport transfer. **Amenities:** Restaurant and bar; laundry service; room service. *In room:* A/C, TV, Wi-Fi.

Moderate

Hotel Morgan Value This roadside complex of timber and pink plaster cottages is a little worn and tired but a good value. The small, low beds complement the old-fashioned laminated furniture, and the bland bathrooms are medium-size and clean. The purple rocking chair out front adds a touch of color to the drab decor, and, though rooms don't have views, there is a pretty decent seafood restaurant in the main building, with a good view of the sea.

North End, beside Victoria beer warehouse. ✆ **505/575-5052.** 10 units. From $35 (£18) twin. AE, DC, MC, V. **Amenities:** Restaurant. *In room:* A/C or fan, TV, fridge.

Martha's Bed and Breakfast From a distance, this place appears fantastic. A beach entrance leads to a bridge over a lagoon of inky black water, after which you can follow a flowered pathway through a lawn of palm trees until a plantation-style mansion appears, replete with a veranda and wicker rocking chairs. So far, so good. Up close, though, the property's garish red railings smack of bad taste, and the rooms themselves are a little disappointing. They are medium-size with an overpowering smell of disinfectant; flowered quilts cover low, small beds and the open wardrobes are oddly placed in the bathrooms. Though it's not perfect, Martha's B&B, owned by the English-speaking Martha (of course), does have an ideal location, right in front of Picnic Beach.

South West Bay. ✆ **505/835-5930.** 8 units. From $50 (£25) double; from $55 (£28) triple. Rates include breakfast. All-inclusive packages available. No credit cards. **Amenities:** Dining area. *In room:* A/C, TV.

Inexpensive

Anastasia's on the Sea ★ Anastasia's is shabby, but in an absolutely charming way. This budget hotel practically sits on its beach's turquoise waters, which are perfect for snorkeling amid exotic fish and psychedelic-colored shells. The hotel consists of a long, wide corridor with marine-themed murals and badly done tile mosaics. Blue doors on either side lead to fair-size rooms that have a musty odor and two double beds. The service is lousy but the staff endearing. What can I say? I loved it. You may hate it. The hotel also offers kayak and fishing rod rental, and has a good restaurant (reviewed in the "Where to Dine" section below).

North End. ✆ **505/937-0016.** www.cornislandparadise.com. 17 units. From $29 (£15) double. No credit cards. **Amenities:** Restaurant. *In room:* Fan or A/C, TV.

Where to Stay in Little Corn

Sunshine Hotel ★, a 3-minute walk from the pier, 50m (164 ft.) north of the Fresh Lobster Company (✆ **505/405-9422;** www.sunshinehotellittlecornisland.com), is a bright yellow establishment with clean and tidy rooms. The owner, Glynis, is famous for her cooking, especially her excellent breakfasts. Prices start at $45 (£23) per room. **Hotel Los Delfines** (north of Jokeman Bank; ✆ **505/820-2241;** www.hotellosdelfines.com.ni) comprises two charming Caribbean-style bungalows of white wooden pillars and green picket balustrades surrounding verandas and balconies. Its location is central, close to where most of the villagers live and the nearby dock. Its 17 well-appointed rooms start at $35 (£18), though kids 11 and under stay for free. **Dereks Place,** Georges Cay (✆ **505/419-0600;** www.deresplacelittlecorn.com), offers basic, but romantic "treehouse"–style huts on a green lawn overlooking the shore on the northern tip of the island. Prices start at $25 (£13) per room.

Where to Dine

In Big Corn

In addition to the restaurants reviewed below, all hotels listed above have in-house restaurants where you can dine. Lobster and shrimp appear on nearly every menu. The former is causing some controversy, as overfishing and unsafe conditions for poorly paid lobster divers is compelling many people to say it's unethical to eat it anymore. What you should definitely try, however, is the popular local dish *run down,* a delicious mix of vegetables, coconut milk, and seafood, which is so called because it brings you back to life if you feel a little "run down."

Anastasia's on the Sea ★ SEAFOOD Anastasia's restaurant is very much like its hotel—crumbling apart and absolutely charming. A long wooden dock leads to a wide rickety building on stilts set amid brilliant turquoise water. It looks like it was all put together by driftwood and one good gust of wind will take it all away. Beautiful servers dish up fresh fish such as yellowtail and kingfish, but they do so slowly. Plan on arriving at least an hour before you feel even a twinge of hunger, as service is that slow. There are worse places to wait, though—the restaurant is surrounded on all sides by water and there's a veranda facing the horizon with inviting hammocks. At night, the restaurant shifts somewhat into a country music roadhouse—a beer-swilling, honky-tonking, foot-tapping Caribbean paradise.

North End. ✆ **505/937-0016.** www.cornislandparadise.com. Main courses C114–C170 ($6–$9/£3–£4.50). No credit cards. Daily 7am–10pm.

Nautilus Eat & Art (Kids) INTERNATIONAL This rickety, old wooden restaurant is laden with psychedelic artwork that exudes a marine theme. Life buoys, shells, and fishing nets hang as decorations alongside local paintings on the veranda. The food is wholesome and comes in huge portions, with standout items being the delicious callaloo soup, curry, and mounds of steaming shrimp cooked in lemon juice and tequila. Pizza is featured prominently on the menu and is available for delivery—a rarity in the country. Overall, I had a disappointing dining experience here on my last visit, when few fellow diners were present. But I can imagine that with a crowd or family, it's a great place to pass an evening. There is frequently a live duo of musicians playing country-and-western music, Corn Island style.

Brig Bay. ✆ **505/451-7216.** Main courses C114–C171 ($6–$9/£3–£4.50). No credit cards. Daily 8am–10pm.

In Little Corn

Stand-alone restaurants are far and few between in Little Corn. The best places to eat are attached to the hotels listed under "Where to Stay," above, though there are two notable exceptions: **Bridget's First Stop Comedor** (no phone) just north of the dock is popular with locals, who come to eat its home-cooked shrimp and lobster, and **Elsa's** (no phone) on the eastern side of the island is a beachside restaurant that does hearty grilled dishes.

11 NORTH-CENTRAL NICARAGUA

Deep, fertile valleys drift upward into misty skies, hiding humble homesteads, dark forests, manicured fields, and tumbling waterfalls. North-central Nicaragua is mysterious, charming, and relatively unknown. It is also very chilly. Here the lush landscape of the highlands makes for a cool, refreshing climate that'll come as a welcome relief if you've just arrived from the hot coast.

Though this is cowboy country today—a land of hardy farmers with easy smiles and humble hospitality—the region hasn't always been so peaceful. This tough, beautiful land was a war zone for much of the 20th century. It was here that the legendary liberal General Sandino battled American marines, part of a war for power with the U.S. in which the mountain town of Ocotal won the honor of being the first city in history to be air raided in 1931. After an American-backed president came to power in 1937, things were relatively calm here until the rise of the Contras in the 1980s wreaked havoc. A 1990s peace treaty allowed farmers to once again work their fields of tobacco, coffee, and vegetables without a rifle slung over their shoulders. Then complete disaster struck in the form of Hurricane Mitch in 1998. The devastating storm most affected the north of the country, wiping away entire towns.

Fortunately, this part of Nicaragua is calm again, and the only clouds on the horizon are those real ones that roll down the mountain and envelope you. The north has truly proved itself to be an enduring beauty. Commerce has returned in the form of abundant harvests and swarming street vendors. Ecotourists are attracted by trekking in the pristine jungle. Agro-tourism is booming in the form of coffee cooperative and tobacco plantation tours.

 Whether its custom-made cowboy boots in the town of Estelí, or isolated rural retreats near the town of Matagalpa, this part of Nicaragua cannot fail to attract and enchant you.

MATAGALPA

130km (81 miles) N of Managua; 230km (143 miles) N of León

Enjoy a cup of the finest coffee in the world while admiring this beautiful valley city and its surrounding green hills. The "Pearl of the North" has steep hilly streets and clean mountain air and is settled by 80,000 Norteños who occupy themselves mostly with cattle or coffee beans. Though it's not the tidiest of towns, it nevertheless has a rural charm and is comfortably nestled along a narrow, unassuming stream called the Río Grande de Matagalpa—actually Nicaragua's second-longest river, which flows the whole way to the Caribbean.

Matagalpa was first settled by the Nahuatl Indians, and though the Spanish introduced cattle in the 17th century and the Germans introduced coffee in the 19th, they both originally came here looking for gold. While gold wasn't discovered, the city became a coffee boomtown and important economic center for the country. Such fortune has waned a bit since the drop in the price of beans. This town is also the birthplace of the greatest Sandinista, Carlos Fonseca, and the resting place of the much-loved juggling volunteer Benjamin Linder. In addition to boasting great shops selling local black ceramics and coffee farms primed for visitors, Matagalpa makes a good base for nearby treks in the beautiful tropical forest; it's also the last stop before the famous Selva Negra Mountain Resort.

Essentials

GETTING THERE Matagalpa's main bus station **COTRAN Sur,** 1km (1/2 mile) west of Parque Darío (© **505/782-3809**), services routes from Estelí, Jinotega, León, Masaya, and Managua. The Managua buses depart every hour from Mercado Mayoreo in the capital, take 2 1/2 hours, and cost C75 ($4/£2).

Small *collectivos* also travel every 30 minutes between Matagalpa and Managua, starting at 5am and ending at 6pm. There are two services daily from León bus station to Matagalpa. They depart at 5am and 3pm, take 3 hours, and cost C50 ($2.60/£1.30). The reverse service goes to León at 6am and 3pm.

There is a smaller bus station called **COTRAN de Guanaco** (no phone) in the north of the city that serves towns farther in the interior such as San Ramón and Río Blanca. The roads to such places are sometimes impassable in the rainy season, however.

ORIENTATION The heart of the city stretches along the eastern bank of the river and its epicenter lies between two plazas, **Parque Morazán** and **Parque Rubén Darío,** the former of which is alive with people walking, talking, selling, or just admiring the plaza's many trees and birds. Incredibly, there are only two streets with names in the entire city, Avenida José Benito Escobar and Avenida Central Don Bartolomé Martinez.

GETTING AROUND If your legs are up for it, try to walk everywhere in the city proper—the city's steep streets open up its secret charms. Taxis within the town cost C10 (50¢/25p) and there are regular city buses that crisscross the town for C3 (15¢/10p).

The surrounding area has some of the most scenic roads in all of Nicaragua, especially the curving valley road to Jinotega. I recommend renting a car so that you can pull into neighboring coffee plantations and stop to explore beautiful cedar, pine, and hardwood forests. **Budget** (© **505/772-3041;** www.budget.com.ni) has an outlet at La Virgen Shell Station on the southern outskirts of the town. **Autos Economicos de Nicaragua** (© **505/772-2445**) is half a block west of the park on its northern side; **Rent a Car Simo** (© **505/772-6290**) is 1 block west and half a block south of the Banco Mercantil, and **Simo's Rent a Car** (✆ **505/772-6260**) is on the corner of El Progresso. Rates for all agencies start at C665 ($35/£17) per day.

Visitor Information

Intur, 1 block north of Parque Rubén Darío (✆ **505/612-7060**), has a friendly, enthusiastic staff. It's open Monday to Friday from 8am to noon and 1:30 to 5pm. For hiking maps, go to **Centro Girasol,** 2 blocks south and 1 block west of COTRAN (✆ **505/772-6030**).

Matagalpa Tours, half a block east of Banpro (✆ **505/772-0108;** www.matagalpa tours.com), is the trekking expert for the area. They also conduct tours of the coffee farms and arrange overnight stays in nearby ecolodges.

Drop into the excellent **Centro Girasol,** 2 blocks south and 1 block west of COTRAN (✆ **505/772-6030**), for information concerning horseback riding in the area.

FAST FACTS Most of the city's banks are situated on the southeast corner of Parque Morazán. **Banpro** is 1 block south of Parque Morazon on Avenida Bartolomé Martinez (✆ **505/772-2574**). There is an ATM at **BAC** (✆ **505/772-5905**), a half-block east of the southeast corner of Parque Morazán. Casual money-changers operate on all corners in this area, as well. Money transfers can be arranged at the **Western Union outlet** (✆ **505/778-0069**) a half-block north of the Alcaldia.

Internet outlets are throughout the city, but **CyberCafé Downtown** has the best location, a half-block west of the southwest corner of the Parque Darío. It's open daily from 8:30am to 8pm. All outlets charge approximately C40 ($2.10/£1.05) an hour. Cheap international calls can be made from most Internet cafes. Public phones are in the post office and a number of card-based booths are dotted around town. The main **ENITEL office** is 1 block east of Parque Morazán. It's open daily from 7am to 9pm.

Matagalpa Hospital (✆ **505/772-2081**) is north of the city on the road to San Ramón. **Pharmacy Matagalpa** (✆ **505/772-7280**) is in front of the restaurant Pescamar. It's open Monday to Saturday from 8am to 6pm and Sunday 8am to noon.

For emergencies, dial **101.** For other matters, call ✆ **505/772-3870.** The fire brigade can be called at ✆ **505/772-3167.**

The main post office, **Correos de Nicaragua Matagalpa** (✆ **505/772-4317**), is 1 block south and 1 block west of Parque Morazán's southeastern corner.

Shopping

This area is famous for its black ceramics and you'll find numerous outlets selling such pottery. **Ceramica Negra,** next to Parque Darío Ruben (✆ **505/772-2464**), specializes in this type of ceramic as does **La Casa de la Carámica Negra,** 2 blocks east of Parque Morazá on the northern side (✆ **505/772-3349**). **Centro Girasol,** in the yellow corner building past the first bridge (✆ **505/772-6030**), has a crafts store and food store with local organic produce.

Moments **Mark Your Calendar**

If you're in town on or around September 24, get ready to put on your cowboy hat and join the town's annual party. Festivities on this date include a farmer's fair, bullfights, parades, and traditional dancing on the city's principal streets. The party gets going a week beforehand with the local fire brigade parading a statue of the **Virgen de la Merced** through the city streets. It culminates in a grand show of horsemanship on the city streets on the 25th.

What to See & Do

In Town

La Iglesia de Molaguina, 2 blocks east and 2 blocks north of Parque Darío (no phone), is a beautiful, simple church. It is popular with locals and has a curious history in the sense that nobody can remember when exactly it was built. East of the city, in the local cemetery, you'll find the final resting place of **Benjamin Linder,** an American volunteer killed during the war (see the box on p. 471). His simple gravestone reflects his passion for juggling and unicycling.

Casa Cuna Carlos Fonseca This tiny adobe building is the birthplace of Carlos Fonseca, founder of the FSLN and martyr of the revolution. As a result, he is Matagalpa's most famous son. The building exhibits artifacts from the *commandant's* life, such as his typewriter, uniforms, and other memorabilia.

1 block east of Parque Darío's south side. ✆ **505/772-3665.** Free admission. Mon–Fri 8am–noon and 2–5pm.

El Templo de San José de Laborio One of the earliest church sites in the city, El Templo is historically significant, as it was used as base by the indigenous tribes during an uprising in 1881. The current baroque-style church was built in 1917 but rests on the foundations of ruins that date from 1751.

Parque Darío. No phone. Free admission. Daily 5–8pm.

La Cathedral de San Pedro Undoubtedly Matagalpa's most imposing building, the city cathedral seems like many Nicaraguan churches—completely out of proportion to the size and importance of the city. Built in 1874, this third-largest church in all of Nicaragua has a brilliant white exterior and a huge, cavernous nave guarded by two massive bell towers. It is decorated in a simple baroque style with some beautiful woodcarving and paintings inside. Though the church dominates the entire city skyline, it's best viewed from the city's northern hillside.

North side of Parque Morazán. No phone. Free admission. Daily 5–8pm.

Coffee Cooperatives Around Matagalpa

While you're in the area, you should definitely try to take a tour of some coffee cooperatives—it's a great opportunity to break the tourist bubble and meet real Nicaraguans in their natural environments. A coffee tour called **La Ruta del Café** brings you to the often humble, rustic farms owned by the region's small coffee producers. You will learn the coffee process and be taught why the fair trade concept is so important to these small, struggling producers. You can even choose to stay in a family farmhouse and join in the harvest, which runs from December to February.

Contact **CECOCAFEN,** 2 blocks east of Banco Uno (✆ **505/772-6353;** turismo@cecocafen.com), for info. This umbrella organization of coffee cooperatives will organize tastings, day trips, and overnight stays. **Finca Esperanza Verde★★** (see below) is one of the better known coffee-farm lodges, and it's been lauded for its responsible tourism. It is 30km (19 miles) from Matagalpa, close to the town of San Ramón.

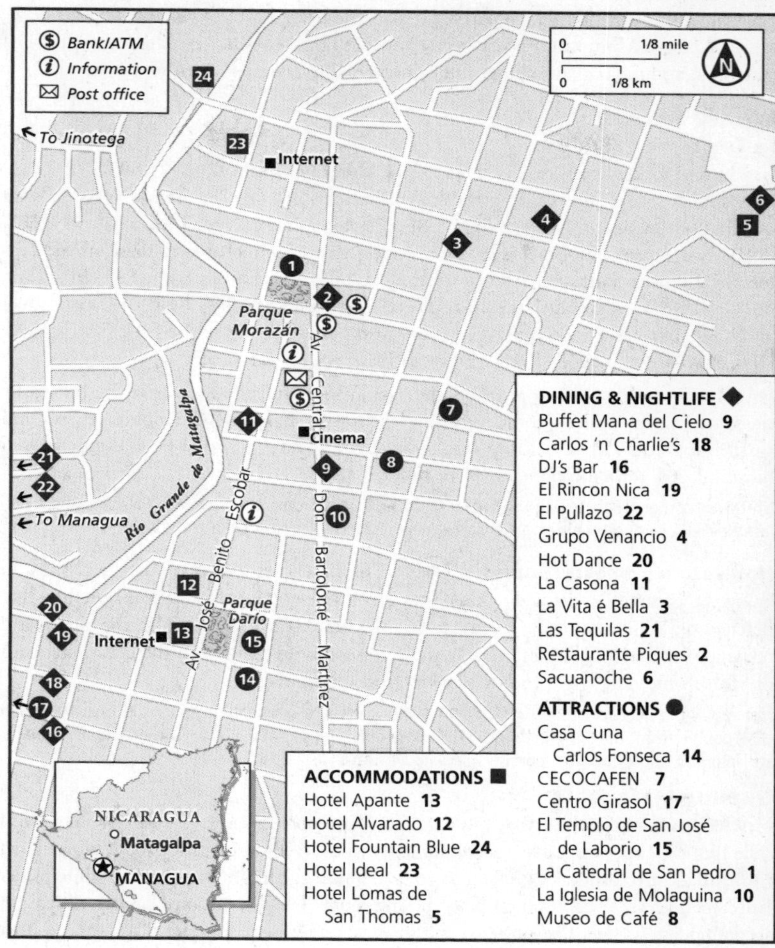

Museo de Cafe More a local history museum than an homage to coffee, this building displays murals and photographs and a small selection of indigenous artifacts. You can buy a bag of local coffee here, and it is good meeting point to hook up with other travelers in the area.

On Main St., 2 blocks east of the mayor's office. ✆ **505/772-4608.** Free admission. Mon–Fri 8am–noon and 2–5pm.

Around Matagalpa

Cerro Apante is a 1,442m-high (4,729-ft.) hill that dominates the town from its southeastern location. It makes for a good half-day hike, and has splendid views at the top. Start at the northeastern corner of Parque Darío and walk southeast down Calle Principal.

You'll eventually begin to leave the city, walking through the neighborhood of Apante. (If you get lost, just ask for "el cerro.") The actual summit is off-limits, but if you follow the ridgeline north you'll find a footpath that takes you back down to the town another way.

Selva Negra Mountain Resort (see below) has trails that offer excellent wildlife, bird-watching, and monkey-watching. The famous nature reserve is open to day visitors.

Where to Stay

In Town

In addition to the hotels reviewed below, the **Hotel Fountain Blue** (✆ **505/772-2733**) is small, laid-back, and comfortable and makes for a relaxing stay. It is 1½ blocks west of Salomón Lopez and rooms start at $20 (£10) for a double. **Hotel Ideal** (✆ **505/772-2483**) is a decent city hotel with some rooms that are much better than others. It is located 2 blocks north and 1 block west of the cathedral. Rates start at $25 (£13) for a double, with breakfast included. The **Hotel Apante** (✆ **505/772-6890**) is very small and basic, but has a good central location on the western side of the park. The upstairs terrace boasts good views. Rates start at $15 (£7.50) for a double.

Hotel Alvarado This is probably the best quality budget option in town, owned by the same French-speaking couple who own the town's pharmacy. The rooms are basic and small but come with a balcony overlooking a busy street, and the mountain view is beautiful. Ask for a top floor room for the best views.

Northwest corner of Parque Darío. ✆ **505/772-2830.** 8 units. From $10 (£5) double. Rates include breakfast. No credit cards. **Amenities:** Dining area. *In room:* TV.

Hotel Lomas de San Thomas ★ Kids This hotel's restaurant is worth a visit just to enjoy the panoramic views. The San Tomas is a yellow, modern-colonial style building perched on a hill east of the town and has the best accommodations in the city. It is a relaxing place, with light, airy rooms and terra-cotta tile floors with the occasional dash of Spanish tile. The larger rooms here are great for families.

Just east of the Guanaca school. ✆ **505/772-4201.** www.hotellomassnthomas.com. 25 units. From $45 (£23) double; from $60 (£30) triple; from $70 (£35) family (sleeps 4). AE, DC, MC, V. **Amenities:** Restaurant/bar; Internet; laundry service; room service. *In room:* Cable TV.

Outside Matagalpa

Finca Esperanza Verde ★★ Finds This "farm of green hope" is a pioneer in responsible tourism and sustainable agriculture. Here you'll find cabins and a lodge surrounded by organic coffee plantations, cloud forest, waterfalls, and a butterfly farm. A white picket fence encloses an open, timber-framed dining room. The green-roofed cabins, which can accommodate six, are solar-powered and the drinking water comes from a natural spring. The buildings are constructed from handmade brick and other local materials. The lodge is a leading light on the Ruta del Café, and sets up tours to that route's coffee plantations during harvest time from November to February. The farm itself is a nature reserve with hundreds of species of birds and butterflies and, of course, orchids. There is also a campsite with a roofed picnic area set amid a coffee and banana grove.

Yucul Rd., 18km (11 miles) east of San Ramón. ✆ **505/772-5003.** www.fincaesperanzaverde.org. 6 units. $12 (£6) dorm; from $45 (£23) cabin for 2. Rates include breakfast. No credit cards. **Amenities:** Restaurant. *In room:* Fan, no phone.

Hotel Fuente Pura Do not be surprised if you catch a monkey swinging past the window of your room while watching the beautiful sunset here. This hotel is set at the perimeter of El Arenal Nature Reserve and is surrounded by deep forest and lush coffee plantations. The restaurant is especially fitted with large windows, so you can take advantage of the stunning panoramic views. The rooms are large, modern, and somewhat low-key, with mismatched furniture and plastic garden chairs. There is lots of light and everything is sparkling clean.

Km 142 (half-hour drive from Matagalpa on the road to Jinotega). ✆ **505/876-5081.** 8 units. From $20 (£10) double. Rates include breakfast and dinner. No credit cards. **Amenities:** Dining area. *In room:* TV, DVD player.

Selva Negra Mountain Resort ★★ An old battle tank marks the entrance to this legendary hotel. The Bavarian-style wooden cabins betray its German ownership ("selva negra" means black forest). They are set around a pond in what is a working coffee farm called La Hammonia. Here you can tour the farm, horseback ride, hike, or simply enjoy the peacefulness of this mountain cloud forest retreat. It has excellent wildlife-watching and there is even a stone chapel for those true romantics who wish to get married amid all this nature. The owners are very friendly and also operate a youth hostel on the grounds. The wood frame and brick and glass-fronted cabins come with porches and private bathrooms and are fairly basic but homey. The farm is also open to day visitors. It's a 20-minute drive from Matagalpa on the scenic road to Jinotega.

Km 140 Carretera, Matagalpa-Jinotega. ✆ **505/612-3883.** www.selvanegra.com. 34 units. From $30 (£15) dorm; from $50–$125 (£25–£63) bungalow; from $100–$150 (£50–£75) chalet. AE, DC, MC, V. **Amenities:** Restaurant. *In room:* No phone.

Where to Dine

Some of the best restaurants are located outside the city. In fact, if you are staying in any of the finca lodges listed above, you can experience fresh, organic food right where it is grown. **Sacuanoche** (✆ **505/772-4201;** www.hotellomassnthomas.com) is part of Hotel Lomas de San Tomas (see "Where to Stay" above) and serves an eclectic menu such as fajitas, steaks, and shrimp dishes. The spacious restaurant has lots of natural light and a great view over the valley. **La Vita é Bella,** Colonia Lainez (✆ **505/772-5476;** vitabell@ibw.com.ni), is a rare find—a genuine Italian restaurant in the heart of cowboy country. The menu is very much vegetarian-friendly, with a little chicken Marsala thrown in for die-hard carnivores. They even serve genuine Italian vodka. This pleasant restaurant is open for lunch and dinner. The restaurant is located on a narrow high street 2 blocks east and 2 blocks north of the cathedral.

El Pullazo, on the highway to Managua, is humble in appearance but big at heart. The menu is genuine Nicaraguan, with great beef dishes, *guirila* pancakes, and *cuajada* cheese. It must be one of the few places with a fish tank in the Northern Highlands. The popular **Buffet Mana del Cielo** (✆ **505/772-5686**) offers huge buffet-style meals where the choice of Nicaraguan food will make your mouth water. The restaurant is 1½ blocks south of Banco Uno and is open daily from 7am to 9pm. **Restaurante Piques** (✆ **505/772-2723**) is a laid-back Mexican restaurant, half a block east of the BAC bank, close to Parque Morazán. It is open daily from 10am to midnight.

The down-to-earth **El Disparate de Potter** (✆ **505/621-3420**) makes for a perfect lunch stop while touring the beautiful Matagalpa–Jinotega road. The name refers to a rocky outcrop that was blasted apart by an English landowner while building a road to his coffee farm in the 1920s. The roadside restaurant is popular with locals and serves standard Nicaraguan fare, in a space with a great view. (There's even a viewing platform nearby.) The restaurant is open daily from 8:30am to 8pm.

Matagalpa After Dark

Grupo Venancia ★, 3 blocks north and 4 blocks east of Parque Morazán (✆ **505/772-3562**), is an excellent cultural space that was started by a volunteer woman's group with the idea of creating a venue for music, dance, and the arts in general. It has a low-key atmosphere with an open-air bar offering live performances and movie screenings. It attracts a good mix of Matagalpa's well-heeled culture vultures and a bohemian crowd, especially on Saturdays. If you have some time on your hands, they are always looking for volunteers to help out as they also organize workshops, publish books, and have a radio show.

Parque Darío ★ is the venue for festivals called Noches Matagalpinas every last weekend of the month—expect live music, food stands, and a very festive atmosphere.

In general, locals here are fond of scuffing their cowboy boots to ranchera, merengue, and reggaeton. Saturdays nights are the liveliest, with roadhouse discos like **Las Tequilas,** 3km (1³/₄ miles) out on the Managua highway, coming alive with revelers. **DJ's Bar** goes all week with an open-air bar offering pub grub and hammocks. It is located 2¹/₂ blocks west of Parque Darío. **Carlos 'n Charlie's,** 2 blocks south of the market, dishes out Latin beats on Thursdays, Fridays, and Saturdays and attracts an upscale, cosmopolitan crowd.

Other good nightlife spots, all located in the area 3 blocks west of Parque Darío, toward the market, are **Hot Dance,** which attracts a younger crowd, **La Casona,** which is the best place in town on Friday nights, and **El Rincon Nica,** a popular beer stop with live music on Fridays.

ESTELÍ

Estelí is sometimes called the "Diamond of the Segovias." Such a sobriquet might be a little exaggerated, but Estelí *is* set on a broad flat valley, surrounded by peaceful rural villages, and is a glorious sight in the sun. Its elegant cathedral and shady plaza make for a very pleasant stroll, and you can easily spend a day or two here taking in its revolutionary murals, shopping for excellent handicrafts, and perhaps visiting one of the cigar factories or coffee farms in the area.

A staunch Sandinista stronghold, Estelí was heavily bombed by the Somoza regime during the worst years of the revolution, adding credence to its other, less appealing, nickname—the "River of Blood." Hurricane Mitch left its mark too—the usually dry Río Estelí became a massive torrent that gorged its way through the city's hinterland, taking people and houses with it. Thankfully, the town has now settled back into a peaceful farming lifestyle. It's currently a city of 110,000 and an important agricultural center for tobacco, wheat, cattle, and cheese. It's also the closest town to the spectacular Miraflor Nature Reserve, the waterfall Salto Estanzuela, and the Tisey reserve, and is the biggest Nicaraguan city before the Honduran border.

Essentials

Getting There

BY BUS The city's market bus station is known as **COTRAN Sur,** 15 blocks south of Parque Central (**✆ 505/713-6162**), and it serves major cities such as Managua, León, and Matagalpa. There are hourly buses for the capital that take 3 hours and cost C60 ($3.15/£1.60). The last bus for Estelí from Managua is at 5:45pm. Matagalpa-bound buses leave from Estelí every 30 minutes, with the last bus leaving at 4:20pm. This trip takes 2 hours and costs C38 ($2/£1). There are only two services a day between León and Estelí. These buses leave León at 6:30am and 3pm and Estelí at 6:45 and 3:10pm. The journey takes 3 hours and costs C60 ($3.15/£1.60).

There are also numerous microbuses that serve these routes regularly.

BY CAR To drive from Managua, you must take the airport road east to Tipitapa and then go north via Sebaco. The road then forks with Matagalpa northeast and Estelí northwest. **Budget Rent a Car** (**✆ 505/713-2584;** esteli@budeget.com.ni) is located

20m (66 ft.) south of the Monumento Centenario on the Panamericana. **Dollar Rent A Car** (✆ **505/713-3060**) is on the Panamericana at Km 1140.

Orientation & Getting Around

The city center is tucked between the Río Estelí and the Pan-American Highway and is easily explored by foot. The commercial heart is based around the intersecting streets of Calle Transversal and Avenida Principal (also know as Avenida Central). There is a street numbering system based around this axis, but it is typically ignored. Most everything is a few blocks from the Plaza or Texaco station.

Visitor Information

There's a small **Intur,** behind the Hospital Viejo (✆ **505/713-6799**), but it's short on maps and flyers. It is open Monday to Friday from 7am to 2pm. Many of the city's Spanish schools are good sources of information concerning where to go in the area, as well. **Agencia de Viajes Aries** (✆ **505/713-3369**) is a conventional agency offering transport bookings and tours of the area. It is located 1 block west and half a block south of the ENITEL building on Avenida Principal.

FAST FACTS There are three banks situated on the corner 1 block west and 1 block south of the plaza, one of which is **Bancentro,** 2½ blocks south of the plaza on Avenida Principal (✆ **505/713-6549**). There is an ATM located at **Texaco Starmart,** 5 blocks north of the soccer stadium. Money-changers operate along Avenida Principal. Money transfers can be arranged at the **Western Union** outlet (✆ **505/713-5046**), which is 60m (197 ft.) south of the store Super Las Segovias. **Hotel El Mesón,** 1 block north of the plaza (✆ **505/713-2655**), is one of the few places that will change traveler's checks.

A number of Internet cafes are situated north of the plaza. All charge approximately C38 ($2/£1) an hour and are open all day every day. You might try **@Gnica,** which is 1 block south of the southwest corner of the plaza. The main **ENITEL** office is 1 block east of the post office (✆ **505/713-2222**). It's open Monday to Friday from 8am to 8pm and Saturday 8am to 5pm.

El Hospital Regional de Estelí (✆ **505/713-6300**) is south of the city on the road to Managua. **Pharmacia Corea,** 1 block north of the market (✆ **505/713-2609**), offers mail services and money transfers in addition to stocking pharmaceutical goods.

In case of emergencies, dial ✆ **101.** For other matters, call the police station at ✆ **505/713-2615.**

The main post office, **Correos de Nicaragua Estelí,** is at the junction with Calle Transversal and Avenida Central.

Herbal Heaven

Cecalli ★ (✆ **505/713-4048;** cecalli@ibw.com.ni), which means "family" in Nahuatl, is a nature museum and nursery that has earned a reputation as the herbal medicine center of Nicaragua. The farm is 1km (½ mile) south of Estelí, next to La Casita Café, and has an herb garden and clinic that administers acupuncture and massage therapy among other holistic practices. This pioneering organization is taking advantage of a population that still retains traditional medicinal knowledge. These old cures are often cheaper than more conventional pharmaceuticals. The organization also has a small store in the town center on Avenida Central, 1½ blocks north of plaza.

Shopping

If you're after leather cowboy boots, you need to stop by Estelí. All around avenues 1a N.O. and Avenida Central you'll find stores selling quality leather goods in the form of belts, hats, saddles, and of course footwear for the discerning *vaquero.* Most shops will carefully measure your feet and rustle up a custom-made pair of boots in less than a week, for around C1,140 ($60/£30).

Artesanía La Esquina, 1 block north of the cathedral (© **505/713-2229**), and **Artesanía Nicaraguense,** 1 block south of the cathedral (© **505/713-4456**), have a good selection of local soapstone pieces and Ducualí pottery as well as general Nicaraguan handicrafts. **Guitarras y Requintas el Arte,** beside INISER (© **505/713-7555**), sells beautifully crafted guitars and mandolins.

What to See & Do

In addition to the below attractions, check out the **Museo de Historia y Arqeuología** (© **505/713-3753**), which houses a small, mildly interesting collection of pre-Columbian artifacts. It is in the same building as the Casa de Cultura and is open 9am to midday except Wednesdays and weekends. You might also want to see **Empresa Nica Cigars,** next to COTRAN Sur (© **505/713-2230**), which is a cigar factory that allows tours of the premises and a chance to buy a *puro* (cigar).

Iglesia de San Francisco This grand, cream-colored church with its neoclassical facade and elegant twin bell towers stands in front of the town's bustling central plaza (Parque Central). The church has been rebuilt several times, each time getting bigger and more sophisticated. It began as a simple adobe structure in 1823 and was revamped with a baroque facade in 1889. Architecturally, it is the most interesting building in the city.

Parque Central. No phone. Free admission. Daily 5–8pm.

La Galeria de Héroes y Mártires This simple but touching one-room museum is a tribute to the many young men and women who died in Estelí's darkest days—when it was an urban battleground between the Sandinistas and the National Guard. Curated by 300 women who lost their children in the war, the museum exhibits old photos, weaponry, uniforms, and personal items of the fallen. The building itself used to be a Somoza jailhouse, and you'll often find mothers of the martyrs in attendance to give their personal stories of those awful times. You can ask to see other memorabilia that are not on permanent display.

1/2 block south of the church. © **505/713-3753.** Mon–Sat 9am–4pm.

La Casa de Cultura This is Estelí's cultural nucleus, with activities such as dance performances, art classes, and music instruction taking place every week. The spacious lobby holds regular exhibitions by local artists and there are live events most weekends. A pleasant open-air cafe is out back, serving vegetarian fare and fresh juices. You can't miss the building, as it is completely covered in colorful murals.

Av. Central and Calle Transversal. No phone. Free admission. Mon–Fri 9am–noon and 2–5pm.

Attractions Around Estelí

One of the best area hiking excursions is to the lush green and picturesque **Estanzuela Falls,** a 20m (66-ft.) cascade with a pool that's perfect for swimming and cooling off in. You must take the road to the hamlet of Estanzuela just south of the city (turn right after the hospital) to get to the path. It is only an hour-long walk, but take food and water, as there are no stores after the highway junction. **Reserva Tisey** nature reserve is worth visiting just to climb its hill and enjoy its spectacular view. On a clear day, the Pacific

Reserva Natural Miraflor

Miraflor means "flower view," and the 206-sq.-km (127-sq.-mile) patch of pristine nature that is **Reserva Natural Miraflor ★★** certainly lives up to its name. It has one of the largest colonies of orchids in the world, with 300 species blooming amid begonias and moss-draped oak trees. Tall pine trees hide toucans and parakeets while armadillos and skunks scurry across the forest floor. Howler moneys jump from branch to branch while sloths just do their thing and hang out. There are over 200 bird species and numerous butterflies all sharing this diverse habitat of tropical savanna, jet black marshy swamp, dry bush, and a cloud forest that peaks at 1,484m (4,868 ft.).

Five thousand people are also scattered across the reserve, some of whom offer homestays where you can sit on a simple, rickety veranda and enjoy the view while sipping homegrown chamomile tea or coffee. You can trek or horseback ride to hilltop lookout points, ancient caves, prehistoric mounds, and pre-Columbian settlements. La Chorrera is one of the more ambitious hikes, the destination being a spectacular 60m-high (197-ft.) waterfall.

The reserve is very much a local initiative, operated and preserved by the community that lives here with little or no government help. They are pioneers in sustainable farming, organic agriculture, fair trade produce, and of course, ecotourism. The reserve's facilities are rustic and unassuming. There is little or no electricity, nor piped water. This is no five-star jungle hideaway but nature in all its raw glory—as such, it's perfect for birders, horseback riders, artists, and orchid lovers. It is possible to visit the reserve in 1 day, but to truly appreciate it, it's wise to stick around, stay with a family for a few days, and explore it further.

UCA, 2 blocks north and 1 block west of the Esso station in Estelí (✆ **505/713-2971;** www.miraflor.org), is one of the main cooperatives that oversee the reserve. They can help with excursions and homestays. The office is open Monday to Friday from 8am to 12:30pm and 2 to 5pm. **Posada La Soñada** (✆ **505/713-6333** in Estelí) is a well-established lodge that's very basic but comfortable, with a large porch stuffed with hammocks and rocking chairs. The owner, Doña Corina, is famous for her vegetarian cooking. **Finca Lindos Ojos** (✆ **505/713-4041** in Estelí) has 14 comfortable rooms that start at $50 (£25) for a double. The lodge is an organic coffee farm with solar-powered lighting, and is operated by a German couple. They also offer tours in the area.

Miraflor is a 45-minute, bone-shaking ride from Estelí in a colorful school bus. There are four buses a day. The earliest leaves from COTRAN Sur at 6am. The rest leave from COTRAN Norte at noon, 2:15pm, and 3:40pm. The UCA (see above) can also help with transport.

lowlands and a line of volcanic peaks as far away as Lake Managua sweep before you. The reserve itself is made up of organic farms and jungle treks. You can go horseback riding or stay at the **Eco Posada Tisey** (✆ **505/713-6213**), an organic farm that offers simple rooms for $20 (£10) and dorm beds for $10 (£5). It is 8km (5 miles) southwest of the city, a little beyond Salto Estanzuela on the same road.

Where to Stay

Expensive

Hotel Cualitlan Swiss-style chalets of light-varnished wood are set around a lush courtyard, and rocking chairs sit on a small porch facing a tropical garden full of flowers, including orchids. The rooms themselves are a little cramped and the bathrooms are basic, but this is definitely one of the better-quality small hotels in the area. Its main attractions are the lush gardens and peaceful surroundings. The restaurant has a creative menu and is set beneath a tree canopy.

2 blocks south and 4 blocks east of COTRAN Sur. ✆ **505/713-2446.** cuallitlan@zonaxp.com. 6 units. From $30–$40 (£15–£20). AE, MC, V. **Amenities:** Dining area. *In room:* Fan, TV.

Hotel Los Arcos ★ Hotel Los Arcos is an excellent nonprofit endeavor that meets the needs of tourists while helping the local community. *Familias Unidas* has been training young people since 1997 and their students played a large part in building this hotel. The hotel's beautiful colonial building is a delightful rainbow of colors such as bright pink walls and orange backdrops, crowned with blue arches and yellow railings, all surrounding a floral courtyard. The large rooms have simple, monastic furnishings and, though the bathrooms are small, they have pretty colored tiles and glass bricks. Don't be hard on the staff, as they are actually in training! The hotel also has a pleasant cafe bar called Vuela Vuela.

1 block north of the cathedral. ✆ **505/713-3830.** www.familiasunidas.org/introduction.htm. 18 units. From $40 (£20) double; from $50 (£25) triple; from $60 (£30) quadruple. AE, MC, V. **Amenities:** Restaurant/bar. *In room:* Fan, TV.

Moderate

Hotel El Mesón, 1 block north of the cathedral (✆ **505/713-2655**), is small, quiet, and centrally located. Chairs sit on a small porch and the rooms are clean, if a little bare. All have fans and a private bathroom and some come with air-conditioning. There is also a restaurant and covered courtyard. Rates start at $20 (£10) for a double. The hotel also offers a car rental service and organized tours. It is one of the few places you can cash traveler's checks in town as well.

Hotel Nicarao, on Avenida Principal, just south of the plaza (✆ **505/713-2490**), is small and cozy. Comfortable rooms surround a pleasant courtyard where many guests hang out and exchange travel stories. It has a nice laid-back atmosphere and very friendly owners. Doubles start at $20 (£10).

Inexpensive

Hotel Miraflor, 20m (66 ft.) north of the signal lights at Parque Central (✆ **505/713-2003**), is a popular and clean place to meet fellow travelers. The friendly owner also runs a restaurant next door. Be warned, if you want an early night, the noise of gabby travelers here might drive you crazy. Rates start at $15 (£7.50) for a double with a private bathroom. **Hotel Estelí,** a half-block north of Super las Segovias (✆ **505/713-2902**), is an excellent budget choice with 13 nicely furnished rooms, all with a private bathroom and TV. Doubles start at $15 (£7.50).

Where to Dine

Expensive

Café Bar Vuela Vuela ★, in the Hotel los Arcos (✆ **505/713-3830**), is set in tropical gardens and is one of Estelí's best restaurants, serving a mix of tasty meat and seafood dishes. The best thing about dining at Vuela Vuela is that it's a good cause, though—the Familias Unidas NGO trains young people in the culinary arts here. **La Casita ★★** (✆ **505/713-4917**) is part farmhouse restaurant, part coffeehouse, and is located just

Spanish Language Schools in Estelí

The Internationalists may have come and gone, but they left behind a large selection of Spanish schools. Estelí is a great place to stop and brush up on your Spanish because it has a number of good schools. **Asociación de Madres de Héroes** (© **505/713-3753;** emayorga70@yahoo.com) is a good place to start. It is located in the Galería de Héroes y Mártires listed earlier in this chapter. **Cenac Spanish School** (© **505/713-2025**) offers homestays and intensive courses. It is located on the Panamericano, close to Calle 7a SE.

outside the city near the new hospital (opposite La Barranca). Its Scottish owner David Thomson is an expert in natural resource management and puts his knowledge to good use via this beautiful farm. Diners can enjoy great coffee, fresh bread, cheeses, and yogurts in a garden by a beautiful stream, with relaxing music playing in the background. Meals start at C100 ($5/£2.50). Also on sale are local crafts and herbal medicines. It's a unique place and definitely worth the short taxi ride.

Moderate

Juventus Centro Cultural, 2 blocks west of the plaza's southwest corner (no phone), is situated on a hill overlooking the river with great views. This open-air coffeehouse has a pleasant courtyard serving delicious sandwiches and milkshakes. A snack should not cost more than C90 ($4.50/£2.25). **El Rincon Pinareño,** 1 block south of the park (no phone), is a popular Cuban restaurant that also sells cigars. Main courses start at C140 ($7/£3.50). **La Gran Via,** 20m (66 ft.) south of the bank corner, beside the post office (© **505/713-5465**), is a Chinese restaurant with a lovely garden patio. The decor is nothing special, but who cares, when the chop suey comes in such huge portions? Main courses cost approximately C120 ($6/£3).

Inexpensive

Cafetin El Recanto, 1 block south and half a block east of the post office (© **505/713-2578**), is *the* place to go for breakfast in Estelí. The *gallo pinto* is tasty and substantial and comes with fried eggs. Most important, service is prompt and prices are reasonable. A hearty breakfast should not cost more than C60 ($3/£1.50). Have you had enough of chicken and beans yet? **Comedor Popular la Soya,** 2½ blocks south of the park on the Avenida Central (no phone), cannot fail to offer something different, as its menu is completely devoted to soy. Main courses are C80 ($4.20/£2.10).

After Dark in Estelí

Put together Cuba and Nicaragua and you get revolution, music, rum, and cigars—and all can be found in abundance at **Rincon Legal,** beside the Super-Mercado Las Segovia (© **505/713-2887**). Owner Frankie Legal had Cuban and Nicaraguan culture in mind when he opened this colorful bar that attracts a bohemian and international crowd. **Discotheque Tabú** (© **505/713-2961**) is the best place to go to dance Norteño style. It is popular with both locals and expats, and has a ladies' night on Thursdays. It's 1 block south of the Texaco station beside the Pepsi warehouse. **El Rancho de Pancho** (© **505/713-2569**) is several miles north of the city on the Pan-American Highway and is particularly popular on Saturday nights. **Centro Recreativo Las Segovias,** on the southern side of the main plaza (© **505/713-2970**), is a lively place, with a younger crowd that comes to dance to disco on Saturday nights.

9

Costa Rica

by Eliot Greenspan

"¡Pura Vida!" (Pure Life!) is Costa Rica's unofficial national slogan, and in many ways it defines the country. You'll hear it exclaimed, proclaimed, and simply stated by Ticos from all walks of life, from children to octogenarians. It can be used as a cheer after your favorite soccer team scores a goal, or as a descriptive response when someone asks you, "How are you? (¿Como estas?)" It is symbolic of the easy-going and gentle nature of this country's people, politics, and personality.

Costa Rica is the most popular and trendy tourist spot in Central America. To cope with the popularity and demand, the country has undergone massive development over the past 10 years, with the principal tourist towns busting at the seams with hotels, restaurants and bars, and large luxury resorts springing up along its long Pacific coast.

Despite this boom, Costa Rica remains rich in natural wonders and biodiversity, where you can still find yourself far from the maddening crowds. The country boasts a wealth of unsullied beaches that stretch for miles, small lodgings that haven't attracted hordes of tourists, jungle rivers for rafting and kayaking, and spectacular cloud and rainforests with ample opportunities for bird-watching, hiking, and wildlife viewing.

With no armed forces, Costa Rica is sometimes called the "Switzerland of Central America," and has historically been an oasis of tranquillity in a region that has been troubled by civil war and armed conflict for centuries.

1 THE REGIONS IN BRIEF

Bordered by Nicaragua in the north and Panama in the southeast, Costa Rica is only slightly larger than Vermont and New Hampshire combined. Much of the country is mountainous, with three major ranges running northwest to southeast. Among these mountains are several volcanic peaks, some of which are still active. Between the mountain ranges are fertile valleys. With the exception of the dry Guanacaste region, much of Costa Rica's coastal area is hot and humid and covered with dense rainforests.

SAN JOSÉ & THE CENTRAL VALLEY The Central Valley is characterized by rolling green hills that rise to heights between 900 and 1,200m (2,952–3,936 ft.) above sea level. It's Costa Rica's primary agricultural region, with coffee farms making up the majority of landholdings. The country's earliest settlements were in this area, and today the Central Valley (which includes San José) is densely populated, crisscrossed by decent roads, and dotted with small towns. Surrounding the Central Valley are high mountains, among which are four volcanic peaks. Two of these, **Poás** and **Irazú,** are still active and have caused extensive damage during cycles of activity in the past 2 centuries.

GUANACASTE The northwestern corner of the country near the Nicaraguan border is the site of Costa Rica's sunniest and most popular **beaches.** There are literally scores of popular beach destinations, towns, and resorts along this long stretch of coastline. Guanacaste is experiencing quite a bit of development. Condos, hotels, luxury resorts, and golf courses are going in at a steady pace. That's not to say you'll be towel-to-towel with thousands of strangers. On the contrary, you can still find long stretches of deserted sands. More and more travelers to Costa Rica are flying directly into and out of Liberia, and bypassing San José and most of the rest of the country. In addition to beaches, Guanacaste boasts semiactive volcanoes, several lakes, and one of the last remnants of tropical dry forest left in Central America.

PUNTARENAS & THE NICOYA PENINSULA Just south of Guanacaste lies the Nicoya peninsula. Similar to Guanacaste in many ways, the Nicoya peninsula is nonetheless somewhat more inaccessible, and thus much less developed and crowded. However, this is starting to change. The neighboring beaches of **Malpaís** and **Santa Teresa** are perhaps the fastest growing hot spots anywhere along the Costa Rican coast. While similar in terms of geography, climate, and ecosystems, as you head south from Guanacaste, everything begins to get more humid and moist. The forests are taller and more lush than those found in Guanacaste. The Nicoya peninsula itself juts out to form the Golfo de Nicoya (Nicoya Gulf), a large, protected body of water.

THE NORTHERN ZONE This inland region lies to the north of San José and includes rainforests, cloud forests, hot springs, the country's two most active volcanoes (**Arenal** and **Rincón de la Vieja**), **Braulio Carrillo National Park,** and numerous remote lodges. Because this is one of the few regions of Costa Rica without any beaches, it primarily attracts people interested in nature and active sports. The **Monteverde Cloud Forest,** perhaps Costa Rica's most internationally recognized attraction, is a top draw in this region.

THE CENTRAL PACIFIC COAST Because it's the most easily accessible coastline in Costa Rica, the central Pacific coast boasts the greatest number of beach resorts and hotels. **Manuel Antonio,** a popular coastal national park as well as the resort area that surrounds it, is the prime destination on this stretch of coast. The beaches here are backed by heavily forested hills and mountains. This region is actually home to the highest peak in Costa Rica—**Mount Chirripó.**

THE SOUTHERN ZONE This hot, humid region remains one of Costa Rica's most remote and undeveloped. It is characterized by dense rainforests and rugged coastlines. Much of the area is protected in **Corcovado** and **La Amistad** national parks. There is a wealth of wonderful nature lodges spread around the shores of the **Golfo Dulce** and along the **Osa Peninsula.** If you like your ecotourism authentic and challenging, you'll like the southern zone.

THE CARIBBEAN COAST Most of the Caribbean coast is a wide, steamy lowland laced with rivers and blanketed with rainforests and banana plantations. The culture here is predominantly Afro-Caribbean, with many residents speaking an English or Caribbean patois. The northern section of this coast is accessible only by boat or small plane and is the site of **Tortuguero National Park,** which is known for its nesting sea turtles and riverboat trips. The towns of **Cahuita, Puerto Viejo,** and **Manzanillo,** on the southern half of the Caribbean coast, are increasingly popular destinations. The coastline here boasts many beautiful beaches and, as yet, few large hotels.

2 THE BEST OF COSTA RICA IN 1 WEEK

The timing is tight, but this itinerary packs a lot into a weeklong vacation. This route takes you to a trifecta of Costa Rica's primary tourist attractions: Arenal Volcano, Monteverde, and Manuel Antonio. You can explore and enjoy tropical nature, take in some beach time, and experience a few high-adrenaline adventures to boot.

Day ❶: Arrive & Settle into San José

Arrive and get settled in **San José.** If your flight gets in early enough and you have time, head downtown and tour the **Museos del Banco Central de Costa Rica (Gold Museum)** ★★ (p. 566).

Head over to the **Teatro Nacional (National Theater;** p. 572). If anything is playing that night, buy tickets for the show. For a delicious dinner, I recommend **Grano de Oro Restaurant** ★★ (p. 568), which is an elegant restaurant with seating in and around an open-air central courtyard in a beautiful downtown hotel.

Day ❷: Hot Rocks

Rent a car and head to the Arenal National Park to see **Arenal Volcano** ★★. Settle into your hotel and spend the afternoon at the **Tabacón Grand Spa Thermal Resort** ★★★ (p. 606) working out the kinks from the road. In the evening either sign up for a volcano-watching tour or take one on your own by driving the road to **Arenal National Park** and finding a quiet spot to pull over and wait for the sparks to fly.

Day ❸: Adventures Around Arenal, Ending Up in Monteverde ★★

Spend the morning doing something adventurous around Arenal National Park. Your options range from white-water rafting to mountain biking to horseback riding and then hiking to the Río Fortuna Waterfall. My favorite is the **canyoning** adventure offered by **Pure Trek Canyoning** ★★ (p. 606). Allow at least 4 hours of daylight to drive around **Lake Arenal** to **Monteverde.** Once you get to Monteverde, settle into your hotel and head for a drink and dinner at **Sofia** ★★ (p. 601).

Day ❹: Monteverde Cloud Forest Reserve ★★★

Wake up early and take a guided tour of the **Monteverde Biological Cloud Forest Reserve** (p. 595). Be sure to stop in at the **Hummingbird Gallery** ★ (p. 598) next door to the entrance after your tour. There's great shopping, and the scores of brilliant hummingbirds buzzing around your head are always fascinating. Spend the afternoon visiting several of the area's attractions, which might include any combination of the following: the **Butterfly Garden** ★, **Orchid Garden** ★, **Monteverde Serpentarium, Frog Pond of Monteverde,** and the **Bat Jungle** (p. 598).

Day ❺: From the Treetops to the Coast

Use the morning to take one of the **zip-line canopy tours** here. I recommend **Selvatura Park** ★★ (p. 596), which has a wonderful canopy tour, as well as other interesting exhibits. Be sure to schedule the tour early enough so that you can hit the road by noon for your drive to **Manuel Antonio National Park** ★★ (p. 612). Settle into your hotel and head for a **sunset drink** at one of the several roadside restaurants with spectacular views over the rainforest to the sea. You can drop off your car at any point now and just rely on taxis and tours.

Day ❻: Manuel Antonio

In the morning take a boat tour of the **Damas Island estuary** (p. 617) with Jorge Cruz, and then reward yourself for all the hard touring so far with an afternoon lazing

Costa Rica in 1 Week

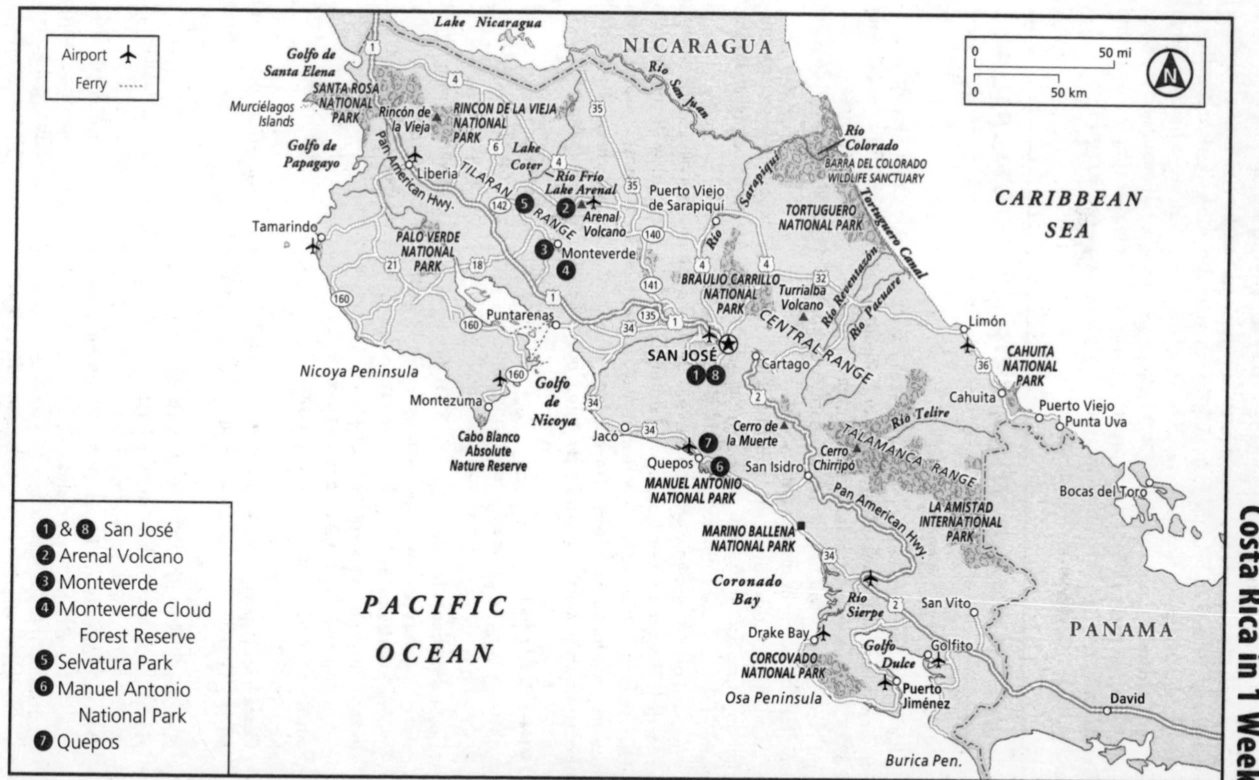

on one of the beautiful beaches inside Manuel Antonio National Park. If you just can't lie still, be sure to hike the loop trail through the rainforest here and around **Punta Catedral** (Cathedral Point) ★★ (p. 616). Make reservations at the **Sunspot Bar & Grill** ★★ (p. 621) for an elegant and intimate final dinner in Costa Rica.

Day 7: Saying Adiós

Fly back to **San José** in time to connect with your departing flight home. If you have extra time, feel free to head back into Manuel Antonio National Park, do some souvenir shopping, or simply laze around your hotel pool. You've earned it.

3 PLANNING YOUR TRIP TO COSTA RICA

VISITOR INFORMATION

In the United States or Canada, you can get basic information on Costa Rica by contacting the **Costa Rican Tourist Board (ICT,** or Instituto Costarricense de Turismo) (✆ **866/2678-2742;** www.visitcostarica.com). Travelers from the United Kingdom, Australia, and New Zealand will have to rely primarily on this website because the ICT does not have toll-free access in these countries.

In addition to this official site, you'll be able to find a wealth of Web-based information on Costa Rica with a few clicks of your mouse. In fact you'll be better off surfing, as the ICT site is rather limited and clunky.

You can pick up a map when you arrive at the ICT's information desk at the airport, or at their downtown San José offices (although the map included with this book is generally better). Perhaps the best map to have is the waterproof country map of Costa Rica put out by **International Travel Maps** (www.itmb.com), which can be ordered direct from their website or any major online bookseller, like Amazon.com.

Tour Operators

If you're looking for some help organizing your trip, there are a host of Costa Rican–based and specialized tour operators. Here is a list of some of my favorites:

- **Costa Rica Expeditions** ★★ (✆ **2257-0766;** www.costaricaexpeditions.com) offers everything from 10-day tours covering the entire country to shorter trips to all of the major destinations in Costa Rica. All excursions include transportation, meals, and lodging. Its tours are some of the most expensive in the country, but it is the most consistently reliable outfitter and its customer service is excellent. If you want to go out on your own, Costa Rica Expeditions can supply you with just transportation from place to place.
- **Costa Rica Experts** (✆ **800/827-9046** or 773/935-1009; www.costaricaexperts.com) offers a large menu of a la carte and scheduled departures, as well as day trips and adventure packages.
- **Horizontes** ★★ (✆ **2222-2022;** www.horizontes.com) offers a wide range of individual, group, and package tours, including those geared toward active and adventure travelers. The company generally hires responsible and knowledgeable guides.
- **Overseas Adventure Travel** ★★ (✆ **800/493-6824;** www.oattravel.com) offers good-value natural-history and "soft adventure" itineraries with optional add-on excursions. Tours are limited to 16 people and are guided by naturalists. All accommodations are in small hotels, lodges, or tent camps.

Telephone Dialing Info at a Glance

In March 2008, Costa Rica changed all of its phone numbers from seven to eight digits. The change involved adding a "2" to the beginning of all existing land line numbers, and an "8" to all existing cellphone numbers. All of the phone numbers listed in this book are the current eight-digit number. However, if you come across an old seven-digit number (on a billboard or brochure, for example): old cellphone numbers began with either a "3" or an "8." All other numbers were land lines. Toll-free and emergency numbers were not affected.

- **To place a call from your home country to Costa Rica:** Dial the international access code (011 in the U.S. and Canada, 0011 in Australia, 0170 in New Zealand, 00 in the U.K.), followed by the eight-digit local number. For example, a call from the U.S. to Costa Rica would be 011+502+XXXXX+XXX.
- **To place a call within Costa Rica:** There are no regional, city or area codes inside Costa Rica. Simply dial the eight-digit number.
- **To place a direct international call from Costa Rica:** Dial the international access code (00), plus the country code of the place you are dialing, plus the area code and the local number.
- **To reach an international operator,** dial ✆ 116. Major long-distance company access codes are as follows: **AT&T** ✆ 0800/011-4114; **Bell Canada** ✆ 0800/015-1161; **British Telecom** ✆ 0800/044-1044; **MCI** ✆ 0800/012-2222; **Sprint** ✆ 0800/013-0123.

ENTRY REQUIREMENTS

Citizens of the United States, Canada, Great Britain, and most European nations may visit Costa Rica for a maximum of 90 days. No visa is necessary, but you must have a valid passport, which you should carry with you at all times while you're in Costa Rica. Citizens of Australia, Ireland, and New Zealand can enter the country without a visa and stay for 30 days, although once in the country, visitors can apply for an extension.

If you overstay your visa or entry stamp, you will have to pay around $45 (£22) for an exit visa. If you need to get an exit visa, a travel agent in San José can usually obtain one for a small fee and save you the hassle of dealing with Immigration. If you want to stay longer than the validity of your entry stamp or visa, the easiest thing to do is cross the border into Panama or Nicaragua for 72 hours and then reenter Costa Rica on a new entry stamp or visa. However, be careful: Periodically the Costa Rican government has cracked down on "perpetual tourists"; if it notices a pattern of exits and entries designed simply to support an extended stay, it might deny you reentry.

Costa Rican Embassy Locations

In the U.S.: 2114 S St. NW, Washington, DC 20008 (✆ **202/234-2945;** www.costarica-embassy.org for consulate locations around the country).

In Canada: 325 Dalhousie St., Ste. 407, Ottawa, Ontario K1N 5TA (✆ **613/562-2855**).

In the U.K.: 14 Lancaster Gate, London, England W2 3LH (© **020/7706-8844**). There are no Costa Rican embassies in Australia or New Zealand, but you could try contacting the honorary consul in Sydney, Australia, at Level 11, De La Sala House, 30 Clarence St., Sydney NSW 2000 (© **02/9261-1177**).

CUSTOMS

Visitors entering Costa Rica are officially entitled to bring in 500 grams of tobacco, 5 liters of liquor, and $500 (£250) in merchandise. Cameras, computers, and electronic equipment for personal use are permitted duty-free. Customs officials in Costa Rica seldom check tourists' luggage.

MONEY

The unit of currency in Costa Rica is the **colón.** In July 2008, there were approximately 515 colones to the American dollar. To check the very latest exchange rates before you leave home, point your browser to **www.xe.com/ucc**.

The colón is divided into 100 **céntimos.** Currently, two types of coins are in circulation. The older and larger nickel-alloy coins come in denominations of 10, 25, and 50 céntimos and 1, 2, 5, 10, and 20 colones; however, because of their evaporating value, you will probably never see or have to handle céntimos, or anything lower than a 5-colón coin. In 1997 the government introduced gold-hued 5-, 10-, 25-, 50-, 100-, and 500-colón coins. They are smaller and heavier than the older coins, and while the plan was to have them eventually phase out the other currency, this hasn't happened yet.

There are paper notes in denominations of 1,000, 2,000, 5,000, and 10,000 colones. You might hear people refer to a *rojo* or *tucán,* which are slang terms for the 1,000- and 5,000-colón bills, respectively. One-hundred-colón denominations are called *tejas,* so *cinco tejas* is 500 colones. The 2,000 and 10,000 bills are relatively new, and I've yet to encounter a slang equivalent. Because of the unstable nature of the colón, rates in this chapter are only listed in U.S. dollars and U.K. pounds (at a two-to-one ratio).

CHANGING MONEY You can change money at all banks in Costa Rica. However, be forewarned that service at state banks can be slow and tedious. The principal state banks are **Banco Nacional** and **Banco de Costa Rica.** You're almost always better off finding a private bank. Luckily, there are hosts of private banks around San José, and in most major tourist destinations.

Since banks handle money exchanges, there are very, very few exchange houses in Costa Rica. One major exception to this is the **Global Exchange** office at the airport. They exchange at more than 10% below the official exchange rate.

Hotels will often exchange money and cash traveler's checks as well; there usually isn't much of a line, but they might shave a few colones off the exchange rate. Be very careful about exchanging money on the streets; it's extremely risky. In addition to forged bills and short counts, street money-changers frequently work in teams that can leave you holding neither colones nor dollars.

ATMS ATMs are ubiquitous in Costa Rica. You'll even find them in some pretty remote areas such as Puerto Viejo and Puerto Jiménez. It's probably a good idea to change your PIN to a four-digit PIN. While many ATMs in Costa Rica will accept five- and six-digit PINs, some will only accept four-digit PINs.

CREDIT CARDS MasterCard and Visa are accepted most everywhere in Costa Rica. American Express and Diners Club are less common, but still widely accepted. To report lost or stolen credit cards, you can try the local numbers listed here, or call collect to the United States.

In Costa Rica, **Visa's** emergency number is ✆ **0800/011-0030. American Express** cardholders and traveler's check holders should call ✆ **0800/012-3211. MasterCard** holders should call ✆ **0800/011-0184.** For other credit cards, or for a local representative of the above companies, call **Credomatic** at ✆ **2295-9898.**

WHEN TO GO

PEAK SEASON & CLIMATE Costa Rica's high season for tourism runs from late November to late April, which coincides almost perfectly with the chill of winter in the United States, Canada, and Great Britain. The high season is also the dry season. If you want some unadulterated time on a tropical beach and a little less rain during your rainforest experience, this is the time to come. During this period (and especially around the Christmas holiday), the tourism industry operates at full tilt—prices are higher, attractions are more crowded, and reservations need to be made in advance.

Local tourism operators often call the tropical rainy season (May through mid-Nov) the "green season." The adjective is appropriate. At this time of year, even brown and barren Guanacaste province becomes lush and verdant. I personally love traveling around Costa Rica during the rainy season (but then again, I'm not trying to flee winter in Chicago). It's easy to find or at least negotiate reduced rates, there are far fewer fellow travelers, and the rain is often limited to a few hours each afternoon (although you can occasionally get socked in for a week at a time). ***A drawback:*** Some of the country's rugged roads become downright impassable without four-wheel-drive during the rainy season.

Costa Rica is a tropical country and has distinct wet and dry seasons. However, some regions are rainy all year, and others are very dry and sunny for most of the year. Temperatures vary primarily with elevations, not with seasons: On the coasts it's hot all year; in the mountains it can be cool at night any time of year. Frost is common at the highest elevations (3,000–3,600m/9,840–11,808 ft.).

The **rainy season** (or "green season") runs from May to mid-November. Costa Ricans call this wet time of year their winter. The **dry season,** considered summer by Costa Ricans, runs from mid-November to April. In Guanacaste, the dry northwestern province, the dry season lasts several weeks longer than in other places. Even in the rainy season, days often start sunny, with rain falling in the afternoon and evening. On the Caribbean coast, especially south of Limón, you can count on rain year-round, although this area gets less rain in September and October than the rest of the country.

In general, the best time of year to visit weather-wise is in December and January, when everything is still green from the rains, but the sky is clear.

PUBLIC HOLIDAYS Official holidays in Costa Rica include **January 1** (New Year's Day), **March 19** (St. Joseph's Day), Thursday and Friday of Holy Week, **April 11** (Juan Santamaría's Day), **May 1** (Labor Day), **June 29** (St. Peter and St. Paul Day), **July 25** (annexation of the province of Guanacaste), **August 2** (Virgin of Los Angeles's Day), **August 15** (Mother's Day), **September 15** (Independence Day), **October 12** (Discovery of America/Día de la Raza), **December 8** (Immaculate Conception of the Virgin Mary), **December 24** and **25** (Christmas), and **December 31** (New Year's Eve).

HEALTH CONCERNS

In order to stay healthy during your trip in Costa Rica, know your physical limits, and don't overexert yourself in the ocean, on hikes, or in athletic activities. Respect the tropical sun and protect yourself from it. See p. 56 in "Planning Your Trip to Central America" more info on treating and avoiding illness.

COMMON AILMENTS Your chance of contracting any serious tropical disease in Costa Rica is slim, especially if you stick to the beaches or traditional spots for visitors. However, malaria, dengue fever, and leptospirosis all exist in Costa Rica, so it's a good idea to know what they are; see "Health" in "Planning Your Trip to Central America" for more info.

Although **malaria** is rarely found in urban areas, it's still a problem in remote wooded regions and along the Caribbean coast. Of greater concern is **dengue fever,** which has had periodic outbreaks in Latin America since the mid-1990s. It seems to be most common in lowland urban areas, and Puntarenas, Liberia, and Limón have been the worst-hit cities in Costa Rica.

Even though the water in San José and most popular destinations in Costa Rica is generally safe, and even though you've been careful to buy bottled water, order *frescos en leche* (fruit shakes made with milk rather than with water), and drink your soft drink warm (without ice cubes—which are made from water, after all), you still might encounter some intestinal difficulties.

VACCINATIONS No shots or inoculations are required to enter Costa Rica. The exception to this is for those who have recently been traveling in a country or region known to have yellow fever. In this case, proof of a yellow fever vaccination is required.

GETTING THERE

BY PLANE It takes between 3 and 7 hours to fly to Costa Rica from most U.S. cities. Most international flights still land in San José's **Juan Santamaría International Airport (SJO;** see p. 550). However, more and more direct international flights are touching down in Liberia's **Daniel Oduber International Airport (LIR;** see p. 580). Liberia is the gateway to the beaches of the Guanacaste region and the Nicoya Peninsula, and a direct flight here eliminates the need for a separate commuter flight in a small aircraft or roughly 5 hours in a car or bus. If you are planning to spend all, or most, of your vacation time in the Guanacaste region, you'll want to fly in and out of Liberia. However, San José is a much more convenient gateway if you are planning to head to Manuel Antonio, the Central Pacific coast, the Caribbean coast, or the Southern zone.

Numerous airlines fly into Costa Rica. Be warned that the smaller Latin American carriers tend to make several stops (sometimes unscheduled) en route to San José, thus increasing flying time.

From North America, **Air Canada, American Airlines, Continental, Delta, Frontier, TACA, Mexicana, Spirit Airlines,** and **US Airways** all have regular direct flights to Costa Rica.

From Europe, **Iberia** has established routes to San José, some direct and others with one connection. Alternately, you can fly to any major U.S. hub city and make connections to one of the airlines mentioned above.

See "Appendix: Fast Facts, Toll-Free Numbers & Websites" for phone numbers and websites for these airlines.

BY BUS Bus service to Costa Rica runs regularly from both Panama City, Panama, and Managua, Nicaragua. If at all possible, it's worth the splurge for a deluxe or express bus. In terms of travel time and convenience, it's always better to get a direct bus rather than one that stops along the way—and you've got a better chance of getting a working restroom in a direct/express or deluxe bus. Some even have television sets showing video movies.

There are several bus lines with regular daily departures connecting the major capital cities of Central America. **Transnica** (✆ **2223-4242**) and **Tica Bus Company** (✆ **2221-0006;** www.ticabus.com) both connect Costa Rica and Nicaragua. **Panaline** (✆ **2256-8721;** www.panalinecr.com) and Tica Bus both have daily service between Costa Rica and Panama. Tica Bus in fact has buses running from Mexico all the way down to Panama. From Managua, it's 9 hours and 450km (279 miles) to San José, and the one-way fare is around $20 to $35 (£10–£18). From Panama City, it's a 16-hour, 900km (558-mile) trip. The one-way fare is around $25 to $40 (£13–£20) one-way.

Whenever you're traveling by bus through Central America, try to keep a watchful eye on your belongings, especially at rest and border stops, whether they're in an overhead bin or stored below decks in a luggage compartment.

GETTING AROUND

It's pretty easy to get around Costa Rica, and your options range from rental cars and commuter flights, to public buses and regularly scheduled tourist shuttles.

BY PLANE Flying is one of the best ways to get around Costa Rica. Because the country is quite small, flights are short and not too expensive. The domestic airlines of Costa Rica are Sansa and Nature Air. **Sansa** (✆ **877/767-2672** in the U.S. and Canada, or 2290-4100 in Costa Rica; www.flysansa.com) operates from a separate terminal at San José's Juan Santamaría International Airport (p. 550), and offers a free shuttle bus from its downtown San José office to the airport.

Nature Air (✆ **800/235-9272** in the U.S. and Canada, or 2299-6000; www.natureair.com) operates from **Tobías Bolaños International Airport** in Pavas, 6.4km (4 miles) from San José. The ride from downtown to Pavas takes about 10 minutes, and a metered taxi fare should cost $10 and $20 (£5–£10). The ride from the airport to downtown is a different story: Most taxis refuse to use their meter, and the standard fee is set at double the metered rate.

BY BUS This is by far the most economical way to get around Costa Rica. Buses are inexpensive and relatively well maintained, and they go nearly everywhere. There are two types: **Local buses** are the cheapest and slowest; they stop frequently and are generally a bit dilapidated. **Express buses** run between San José and most beach towns and major cities; these tend to be newer units and more comfortable, although very few are so new or modern as to have bathroom facilities, and they sometimes operate only on weekends and holidays.

Two companies run regular, fixed-schedule departures in passenger vans and small buses to most of the major tourist destinations in the country. **Gray Line** (✆ **2220-2126;** www.graylinecostarica.com) and **Interbus** (✆ **2283-5573;** www.interbusonline.com) are two private shuttle bus companies with a host of departures leaving San José each morning and heading or connecting to most of the major tourist destinations in the country. There are return trips to San José every day from these destinations and a variety of interconnecting routes. Fares run between $25 and $45 (£13–£23) depending upon the destination.

Beware: Both of these companies offer pickup and drop-off at a wide range of hotels. This means that if you are the first picked up or last dropped off, you might have to sit through a long period of subsequent stops before finally hitting the road or reaching your destination. Moreover, I've heard some horror stories about both lines, concerning missed or severely delayed connections.

BY CAR Renting a car in Costa Rica is no idle proposition. The roads are riddled with potholes, most rural intersections are unmarked, and, for some reason, sitting behind the wheel of a car seems to turn peaceful Ticos into homicidal maniacs. But unless you want to see the country from the window of a bus (inconvenient) or pay exorbitant amounts for private transfers (expensive), renting a car is still your best option for independent exploring. Four-wheel-drives are particularly useful in the rainy season (May to mid-Nov) and for navigating the bumpy, poorly paved roads year-round.

The following companies have desks at both international airports, and in some cases at major destinations around the country: **Alamo** (✆ **800/462-5266** in the U.S., or 2242-7733 in Costa Rica; www.alamocostarica.com), **Adobe Rent A Car** (✆ **800/769-8422** in the U.S., or 2442-2422 in Costa Rica; www.adobecar.com), **Avis** (✆ **800/331-1212** in the U.S., or 2293-2222 in Costa Rica; www.avis.com), **Budget** (✆ **800/527-0700** in the U.S., or 2255-4750 in Costa Rica; www.budget.co.cr), **Dollar** (✆ **800/800-4000** in the U.S., or 2443-2950 in Costa Rica; www.dollarcostarica.com), **Hertz** (✆ **800/654-3001** in the U.S., or 2443-2422 in Costa Rica; www.hertz.com), **National Car Rental** (✆ **877/862-8227** in the U.S., or 2290-2422 in Costa Rica; www.natcar.com), **Payless Rent A Car** (✆ **800/729-5377** in the U.S., or 2257-0026 in Costa Rica; www.payless carrental.com), **Thrifty** (✆ **800/847-4389** in the U.S., or 2257-3434 in Costa Rica; www.thrifty.com), and **Toyota Rent A Car** (✆ **2441-1411** in Costa Rica; www.toyota rent.com).

Because many roads are poorly maintained, I recommend that you rent a 4WD. All of the agencies listed above rent four-wheel-drive vehicles. While you may never use the four-wheel-drive, the added clearance will definitely come in handy. Rates run between $45 and $150 (£23–£75) per day, with unlimited mileage and insurance, depending upon the type of vehicle you rent.

BY TAXI In San José and some of the other major destinations or cities, taxis are supposed to have and use meters, although this isn't always the case. In more rural areas, taxis almost never have meters. **Tipping** taxi drivers is not common, nor expected.

TIPS ON ACCOMMODATIONS

When the Costa Rican tourist boom began in the late 1980s, hotels popped up like mushrooms after a heavy rain. By the 1990s the country's first true megaresorts opened, more followed, and still more are under construction or in the planning phase. Except during the few busiest weeks of the year, there's a relative glut of rooms in Costa Rica. Most hotels are small to midsize, and the best ones fill up fast most of the year. Still, in broader terms, the glut of rooms is good news for travelers and bargain hunters. Less popular hotels that want to survive are being forced to reduce their rates and provide better service.

Rates given in this chapter do not include the 16.3% room taxes, unless otherwise specified. These taxes will add considerably to the cost of your room.

TIPS ON DINING

Simply put, Costa Rican cuisine is less than memorable. San José remains the unquestioned gastronomic capital of the country, and here you can find many of the cuisines of the world served at moderate prices. However, the major beach destinations of Tamarindo, Manuel Antonio, and the Papagayo Peninsula are starting to catch up.

Costa Rica is a major producer and exporter of beef; consequently, the country has plenty of steakhouses. Unfortunately, quantity doesn't mean quality. Unless you go to one of the better restaurants or steakhouses, you will probably be served tough steaks, cut thin. Still, all is not lost. With the increase in international tourism, local chefs have created "nouvelle Costa Rican cuisine," updating timeworn recipes and using traditional ingredients in creative ways.

If you're looking for cheap eats, you'll find them in little restaurants known as ***sodas,*** which are the equivalent of diners in the United States. At a *soda,* you'll have lots of choices: rice and beans with steak, rice and beans with fish, rice and beans with chicken, or, for vegetarians, rice and beans. You get the picture. Rice and beans are standard Tico fare and are served at all three daily meals. Also, although plenty of seafood is available throughout the country, at *sodas,* it's all too often served fried.

Keep in mind that there is an additional 13% sales tax, as well as a 10% service charge. By law, Costa Rican restaurants must show their prices with the 13% sales tax figured in. However, this is often not the case. In addition, Ticos rarely tip, but that doesn't mean that you shouldn't. If the service was particularly good and attentive, you should probably leave a little extra.

TIPS ON SHOPPING

Serious shoppers will be disappointed in Costa Rica. Aside from coffee and hand-painted wooden oxcarts, there isn't much that's distinctly Costa Rican. To compensate for its own relative lack of goods, Costa Rican gift shops do a brisk business selling crafts and clothes imported from Guatemala, Panama, and Ecuador.

Notable exceptions to the generally meager crafts offerings include the fine wooden creations of **Barry Biesanz ★★** (**© 2289-4337;** www.biesanz.com). His work is sold in many of the finer gift shops around and at his own shop, but beware: Biesanz's work is often imitated, so make sure that what you buy is the real deal (he generally burns his signature into the bottom of the piece). **Lil Mena** is a Costa Rican artist who specializes in working with and painting on handmade papers and rough fibers. You'll find her work in a number of shops around the country.

Joe to Go

Two words of advice: Buy coffee. Lots of it.

Coffee is the best shopping deal in all of Costa Rica. One pound of coffee sells for around $3 to $6 (£1.50–£3). It makes a great gift and truly is a local product.

Café Britt is the big name in Costa Rican coffee. These folks have the largest export business in the country, and, although high-priced, its blends are very dependable. Café Britt is widely available at gift shops around the country, and at the souvenir concessions at both international airports. My favorites, however, are the coffees roasted and packaged in Manuel Antonio and Monteverde, by **Café Milagro** and **Café Monteverde,** respectively. If you visit either of these places, definitely pick up their beans.

The best place to buy coffee is in any supermarket. (Why pay more at a gift shop?) If you buy prepackaged coffee in a supermarket, the whole beans will be marked either *grano* or *grano entero* (for whole bean), or *molido* (for ground). If you opt for ground, be sure the package is marked puro; otherwise, it will likely be mixed with a good amount of sugar, the way Ticos like it.

You might also run across **carved masks** made by the indigenous Boruca people of southern Costa Rica. These full-size balsa-wood masks come in a variety of styles, both painted and unpainted, and run anywhere from $15 to $80 (£7.50–£40), depending on the quality of workmanship. **Cecilia "Pefi" Figueres ★★** makes practical ceramic wares that are lively and fun. Look for her brightly colored abstract and figurative bowls, pitchers, coffee mugs, and more at some of the better gift shops around the city.

Fast Facts Costa Rica

American Express American Express Travel Services is represented in Costa Rica by **ASV Olympia,** Oficentro La Sabana, Sabana Sur, in San José (✆ **242-8585**), which can issue traveler's checks and replacement cards and provide other standard services. To report lost or stolen Amex traveler's checks within Costa Rica, call the number above or ✆ **257-0155,** or call collect to ✆ **313/271-7887** in the United States.

Business Hours Banks are usually open Monday through Friday from 9am to 4pm, although many have begun to offer extended hours. Offices are open Monday through Friday from 8am to 5pm (many close for 1 hr. at lunch). Stores are generally open Monday through Saturday from 9am to 6pm (many close for 1 hr. at lunch). Stores in modern malls generally stay open until 8 or 9pm and don't close for lunch. Most bars are open until 1 or 2am, although some go later.

Doctors Contact your embassy for information on doctors in Costa Rica, or see "Hospitals," below.

Embassies & Consulates The following are all located in San José: **United States Embassy,** in front of Centro Commercial, on the road to Pavas (✆ **2519-2000,** or 2220-3127 after hours in case of emergency); **Canadian Consulate,** Oficentro Ejecutivo La Sabana, Edificio 5 (✆ **2242-4400**); and **British Embassy,** Paseo Colón between calles 38 and 40 (✆ **2258-2025**). There are no Australian or New Zealand embassies in Costa Rica.

Emergencies In case of any emergency, dial ✆ **911** (which should have an English-speaking operator); for an ambulance, call ✆ **128;** and to report a fire, call ✆ **118.** If 911 doesn't work, you can contact the police at ✆ **2222-1365** or 2221-5337, and hopefully they can find someone who speaks English.

Hospitals In San José try Clínica Bíblica (Av. 14 btw. calles Central and 1), which offers emergency services to foreign visitors at reasonable prices (✆ **522-1000;** www.clinicabiblica.com), or the **Hospital CIMA** (✆ **2208-1000;** www.hospitalsanjose.net), located in Escazú on the Próspero Fernández Highway, which connects San José and the western suburb of Santa Ana and has the most modern facilities in the country. For hospitals in other cities, see the "Fast Facts" for each individual city.

Language Spanish is the official language of Costa Rica. However, in most tourist areas, you'll be surprised by how well Costa Ricans speak English.

Newspapers & Magazines There are six Spanish-language dailies in Costa Rica and one English-language weekly, the *Tico Times.* In addition, you can get *Time, Newsweek,* and several U.S. newspapers at some hotel gift shops and a few of the bookstores in San José. If you understand Spanish, *La Nación* is the paper you'll want. Its "Viva" and "Tiempo Libre" sections list what's going on in the world of music, theater, dance, and more.

Police Dial ✆ **911** or 2222-1365 for the police. They should have someone available who speaks English.

Post Offices & Mail At press time, it cost 155 colones (30¢/15p) to mail a letter to the United States, and 180 colones (35¢/15p) to Europe. You can get stamps at a post office and at some gift shops in large hotels. Most post offices are open Monday through Friday from 8am to 5:30pm, and Saturday from 7:30am to noon.

Given the Costa Rican postal service's track record, I recommend paying an extra 600 colones ($1.20/60p) to have anything of any value certified. Better yet, use an international courier service or wait until you get home to post it. **DHL,** on Paseo Colón between calles 30 and 32 (✆ **2209-0000;** www.dhl.com); **EMS Courier,** with desks at the principal metropolitan post offices (✆ **800/900-2000,** or 2202-2900); **FedEx,** which is based in Heredia but will arrange pickup anywhere in the San José metropolitan area (✆ **800/463-3339;** www.fedex.com); and **United Parcel Service,** in Pavas (✆ **2290-2828;** www.ups.com), all operate in Costa Rica. ***Note:*** Despite what you may be told, packages sent overnight to U.S. addresses tend to take 3 to 4 days.

If you're sending mail *to* Costa Rica, it generally takes between 10 and 14 days to reach San José, although it can take as much as a month to get to the more remote corners of the country. Never send cash, checks, or valuables through the Costa Rican mail system.

Safety Although most of Costa Rica is safe, petty crime and robberies committed against tourists are endemic. San José is known for its pickpockets, so never carry a wallet in your back pocket. A woman should keep a tight grip on her purse (keep it tucked under your arm). Thieves also target gold chains, cameras and video cameras, cellphones, prominent jewelry, and nice sunglasses. Be sure not to leave valuables unsecured in your hotel room. Given the high rate of stolen passports in Costa Rica, mostly as collateral damage in a typical pickpocketing or room robbery, it is recommended that, whenever possible, you leave your passport in a hotel safe, and travel with a photocopy of the pertinent pages. Don't park a car on the street in Costa Rica, especially in San José; plenty of public parking lots are available.

Rental cars generally stick out and are easily spotted by thieves. Don't leave anything of value in a car parked on the street, not even for a moment. Be wary of solicitous strangers who stop to help you change a tire or take you to a service station. Although most are truly good Samaritans, there have been reports of thieves preying on roadside breakdowns. There have actually been numerous cases of scammers deliberately puncturing tires at a stoplight or parking area and then following the victim until they pull over to change the suddenly flat tire.

Public intercity buses are also frequent targets of stealthy thieves. Finally, single women should use common sense and take precaution, especially after dark. I don't recommend that single women walk alone anywhere at night, especially on seemingly deserted beaches, or dark uncrowded streets.

Taxes All hotels charge 16.3% tax. Restaurants charge 13% tax and also add on a 10% service charge, for a total of 23% more on your bill.

There is a $26 (£13) departure tax for all visitors leaving by air. This tax must be purchased prior to check-in. There are desks at the main terminal of all international airports where you can pay this tax. Some local travel agencies and hotels offer to purchase the departure tax in advance, as a convenience for tourists. You must give them authorization, as well as your passport number, and pay a small service fee.

Telephone & Fax For tips on making calls, see "Telephone Dialing Info at a Glance" on p. 541, as well as p. 56 in "Planning Your Trip to Central America."

Tipping Tipping is not necessary in restaurants, where a 10% service charge is always added to your bill (along with a 13% tax). If service was particularly good, you can leave a little at your own discretion, but it's not mandatory. Porters and bellhops get around 50¢ (25p) per bag. You don't need to tip a taxi driver unless the service has been superior; a tip is not usually expected.

4 SAN JOSE & THE CENTRAL VALLEY

To most, San José seems little more than a chaotic jumble of cars, buses, buildings, and people. The central downtown section of San José exists in a near-constant state of gridlock. Antiquated buses spewing diesel fumes and a lack of emission controls have created a brown cloud over the city's sky. Sidewalks are poorly maintained and claustrophobic, and street crime is a serious problem. Most visitors quickly seek the sanctuary of their hotel room and the first chance to escape the city.

Still, things have been improving in recent years. Mayor Johnny Araya has led ambitious and controversial campaigns to rid the narrow sidewalks of impromptu and illegal vendors, to reduce the clutter of billboards and overhead signs, and to bury a good share of the city's electrical and phone cables. Moreover, San José is the country's only major metropolitan city, with varied and active restaurant and nightlife scenes, several museums and galleries worth visiting, and a steady stream of theater, concerts, and other cultural events that you won't find elsewhere in the country.

At 1,125m (3,690 ft.) above sea level, San José enjoys springlike temperatures year-round. This climate, along with the beautiful views of lush green mountainsides, can make San José a pleasant city to visit. And if that isn't enough for you, you'll find that it's extremely easy to get out into the countryside. Within an hour or two, you can climb a volcano, go white-water rafting, hike through a cloud forest, and stroll through a butterfly garden—among many other activities.

ESSENTIALS

Getting There

BY PLANE **Juan Santamaría International Airport** (**SJO;** ✆ **2437-2626** for 24-hr. airport information) is located near the city of Alajuela, about 20 minutes from downtown San José. A taxi into town costs between $12 and $18 (£6–£9), and a bus is only 75¢ (40p). The Alajuela–San José buses run frequently and will drop you off anywhere along Paseo Colón or at a station near the Parque de la Merced (downtown, btw. calles 12 and 14 and avs. 2 and 4). There are two separate lines: **Tuasa** (✆ **2442-6900**) buses are red; **Station Wagon** (✆ **8388-9263**) buses are beige/yellow. At the airport you'll find the bus stop directly in front of the main terminal, beyond the parking structure. Be sure to ask whether the bus is going to San José, or you could end up in Alajuela.

The airport here is in the midst of a major renovation and expansion, a process that has been plagued by work stoppages, delays, and bickering between the government and international company in charge of the work. Despite the major remodeling, chaos and confusion continue to greet arriving passengers the second they step out of the terminal. You must abandon the luggage carts just before exiting the building and then face a gauntlet of aggressive taxi drivers and people offering to carry your bags. Fortunately, the official airport taxi service has a booth inside the terminal after you clear Customs. The entire airport renovation and expansion should be completed sometime in mid-2009.

In terms of taxis, you should stick with the official airport taxi service, **Taxis Unidos Aeropuerto** (**© 2221-6865**), which operates a fleet of orange vans and sedans, charging fixed prices according to your destination. Despite the fact that Taxis Unidos has an official monopoly at the airport, you will usually find a handful of regular cabs (in traditional red sedans) and "pirate" cabs, freelance drivers using their own vehicles. You could use either of these latter options, and they tend to charge a dollar or two less, but I recommend using the official service for safety and standardized prices. Keep a very watchful eye on your bags: Thieves have historically preyed on newly arrived passengers and their luggage. You should tip porters about 50¢ (25p) per bag.

You have several options for **exchanging money** when you arrive at the airport. There's an ATM in the baggage claim area, which is connected to both the PLUS and Cirrus networks. There's also a **Global Exchange** money exchange booth just as you clear Customs and Immigration. It's open whenever there are arriving flights; however, these folks exchange at more than 10% below the official rate. There's a branch of the **Banco de San José** inside the main terminal, on the second floor across from the airline check-in counters, as well as a couple more ATMs up there.

Tip: There's really no pressing need to exchange money the minute you arrive. Taxis Unidos accepts U.S. dollars. You can wait until after you settle into your hotel, and see if the hotel will give you a good rate of exchange, or use one of the many downtown banks or ATMs.

BY BUS If you're coming to San José by bus, where you disembark depends on where you're coming from. (The different bus companies have their offices, and thus their drop-off points, all over downtown San José. When you buy your ticket, ask where you'll be let off.) Buses arriving from Panama pass first through Cartago and San Pedro before letting passengers off in downtown San José; buses arriving from Nicaragua generally enter the city on the west end of town, on Paseo Colón. If you're staying here, you can ask to be let off before the final stop.

Orientation

Downtown San José is laid out on a grid. *Avenidas* (avenues) run east and west, while *calles* (streets) run north and south. The center of the city is at **Avenida Central** and **Calle Central.** To the north of Avenida Central, the avenidas have odd numbers beginning with Avenida 1; to the south, they have even numbers beginning with Avenida 2. Likewise, calles to the east of Calle Central have odd numbers, and those to the west have even numbers. The main downtown artery is **Avenida 2,** which merges with Avenida Central on either side of the downtown area. West of downtown, Avenida Central becomes **Paseo Colón,** which ends at Parque La Sabana and feeds into the highway to Alajuela, the airport, Guanacaste, and the Pacific coast. East of downtown, Avenida

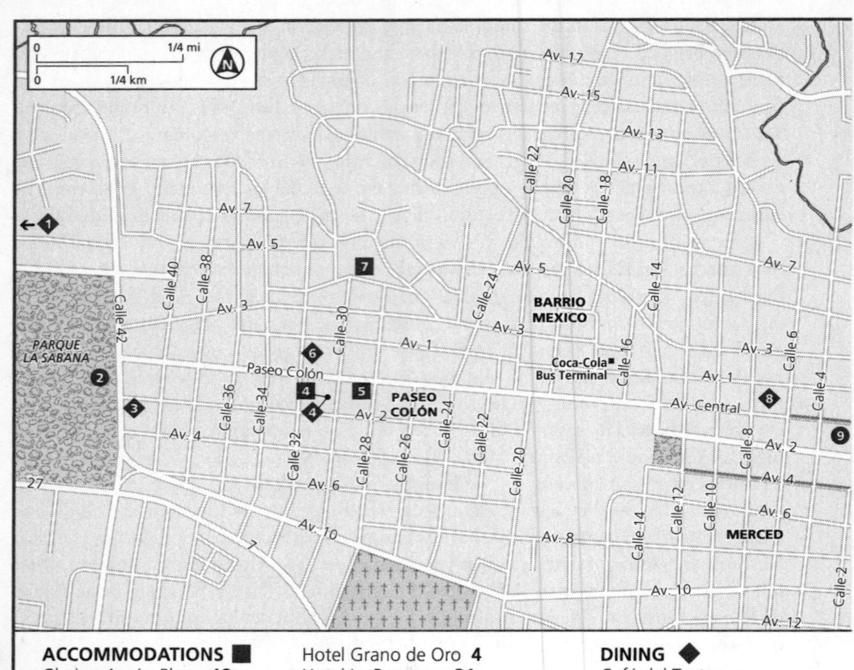

ACCOMMODATIONS ■
Clarion Amón Plaza **18**
Costa Rica Backpackers **30**
Gran Hotel Costa Rica **11**
Hotel Aranjuez **32**
Hotel Britannia **19**
Hotel Cacts **7**
Hotel Doña Ines **27**
Hotel Don Carlos **22**
Hotel Grano de Oro **4**
Hotel Le Bergerac **31**
Hotel Rosa del Paseo **5**
Hotel Santo Tomas **20**
Kap's Place **33**
Pension de la Cuesta **24**
Radisson Europa Hotel **16**
Sleep Inn **25**
Tranquilo Backpacker's **21**

DINING ◆
Café del Teatro Nacional **13**
Café Mundo **17**
Cafeteria 1830 **11**
Grano de Oro Restaurant **4**
Machu Picchu **6**

Central leads to San Pedro and then to Cartago and the Pan-American Highway (Carretera Panamericana) heading south. **Calle 3** takes you out of town to the north, onto the Guápiles Highway that leads to the Caribbean coast.

Getting Around

BY TAXI Although taxis in San José have meters *(marías),* the drivers sometimes refuse to use them, particularly with foreigners, so you'll occasionally have to negotiate the price. Always try to get them to use the meter first (say "ponga la maría, por favor"). The official rate at press time is around 90¢ (45p) for the first kilometer (1/2 mile) and around 70¢ (35p) for each additional kilometer. If you have a rough idea of how far it is to your destination, you can estimate how much it should cost from these figures. After 10pm taxis are legally allowed to add a 20% surcharge. Some of the meters are programmed to include the extra charge automatically, but be careful: Some drivers will use the evening

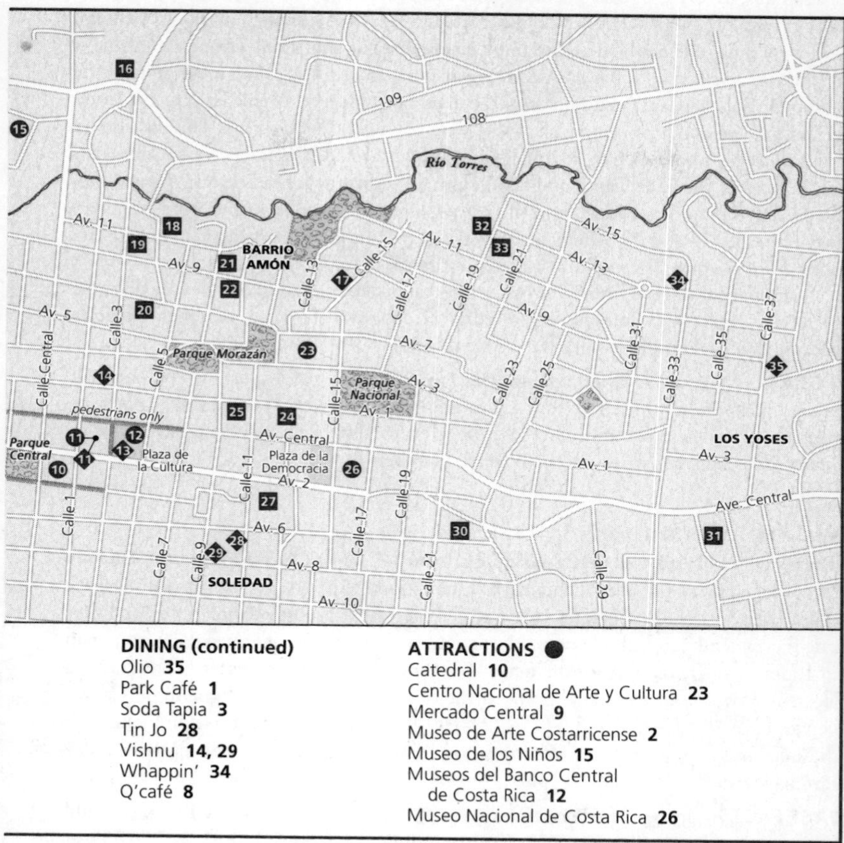

setting during the daytime or (at night) to charge an extra 20% on top of the higher meter setting.

Depending on your location, the time of day, and the weather (rain places taxis at a premium), it's relatively easy to hail a cab downtown. You'll always find taxis in front of the Teatro Nacional and around the Parque Central at Avenida Central and Calle Central. Taxis in front of hotels and the El Pueblo tourist complex usually charge more than others, although this is technically illegal. Most hotels will gladly call you a cab, either for a downtown excursion or for a trip back out to the airport. You can also get a cab by calling **Coopetaxi** (**© 2235-9966**), **Coopetico** (**© 2224-7979**), or **Coopeguaria** (**© 2226-1366**). **Cinco Estrellas Taxi** (**© 2228-3159**) is another company that is based in Escazú but services the entire metropolitan area and airport, and claims to always have an English-speaking operator on call.

BY BUS Bus transportation around San José is cheap—the fare is usually somewhere around 10¢ to 45¢ (5p–25p)—although the Alajuela/San José buses that run in from the airport cost 75¢ (40p). The most important buses are those running east along Avenida 2 and west along Avenida 3. The **Sabana/Cementerio** bus runs from Parque La Sabana to downtown and is one of the most convenient buses to use. You'll find a bus stop for the outbound Sabana/Cementerio bus near the main post office on Avenida 3 near the corner of Calle 2, and another one on Calle 11 between avenidas Central and 1. This bus also has stops all along Avenida 2. **San Pedro** buses leave from Avenida Central between calles 9 and 11, in front of the Cine Capri, and take you out of downtown heading east. **Escazú-** and **Santa Ana**–bound buses leave from the Coca-Cola bus station, as well as from Avenida 1 between calles 24 and 28. Alternatively, you can pick up both the Escazú and Santa Ana buses from the busy bus stop on Calle 42, just north of Gimnasio Nacional.

Board buses from the front. The bus drivers can make change, although they don't like to receive large bills. Be especially mindful of your wallet, purse, or other valuables, because pickpockets often work the crowded buses.

BY CAR Most major car-rental agencies have offices at the airport. If not, they will usually pick you up or deliver your car to any San José hotel. If you decide to pick up your rental car in downtown San José, be prepared for some very congested, chaotic streets. See "Appendix: Fast Facts, Toll-Free Numbers & Websites" for car-rental agency info.

Visitor Information

There's an **Instituto Costarricense de Turismo (ICT; ✆ 2443-1535;** www.visitcosta rica.com) desk at the Juan Santamaría International Airport, located in the baggage claims area, just before Customs. You can pick up maps and browse brochures, and they might even lend you a phone to make or confirm a reservation. It's open daily from 9am to 10pm. If you're looking for the **main ICT visitor information center** in San José, it's located below the Plaza de la Cultura, at the entrance to the Gold Museum, on Calle 5 between avenidas Central and 2 (**✆ 2222-1090**). The people here are helpful, although the information they have to offer is rather limited. This office is also open Monday through Saturday from 9am to 5pm.

FAST FACTS In case of an **emergency,** call **✆ 911.** You can reach the **Red Cross** and request an **ambulance** at **✆ 2233-7033;** for **police assistance** call **✆ 2222-1365** or 2295-3643.

Clínica Bíblica, Avenida 14 between calles Central and 1 (**✆ 2522-1000;** www. clinicabiblica.com), is a large, modern hospital, conveniently located close to downtown and with several English-speaking doctors. The **Hospital CIMA** (**✆ 2208-1000;** www. hospitalsanjose.net), located in Escazú on the Próspero Fernández Highway, which connects San José and the western suburb of Santa Ana, has the most contemporary and best facilities in the country.

American Express Travel Services is represented in Costa Rica by **ASV Olympia,** Oficentro La Sabana, Sabana Sur (**✆ 2242-8585;** www.asvolympia.com), which can issue traveler's checks and replacement cards and provide other standard services.

Internet cafes can be found all over San José. Rates run between 50¢ and $2 per hour (25p–£1). Many hotels have their own Internet cafe or allow guests to send and receive e-mail. And many have added wireless access, either for free or a small charge. You can also try **Racsa,** Avenida 5 and Calle 1 (**✆ 2287-0087;** www.racsa.co.cr), the state Internet monopoly, which sells prepaid cards in 5-, 10-, and 15-hour denominations for connecting your laptop to the Web via a local phone call. Some knowledge of configuring your computer's dial-up connection is necessary, and you'll want to factor in the phone call charge if calling from a hotel. Most Internet cafes have access to Skype, Net2Phone, or some other VoIp service which allows you to make international calls at a reasonable price.

The main post office *(correo)* is on Calle 2 between avenidas 1 and 3 (© **800/900-2000** toll-free in Costa Rica, or 2202-2900; www.correos.go.cr).

WHAT TO SEE & DO

Most visitors to Costa Rica try to get out of the city as fast as possible so they can spend more time on the beach or off in the rainforests. But there are a few attractions in San José to keep you busy. Some of the best and most modern museums in Central America are here, with a wealth of fascinating pre-Columbian artifacts.

ORGANIZED TOURS There really isn't much reason to take a tour of San José. It's so compact that you can easily visit all the major sights on your own, as described below. However, if you want to take a city tour, which will run you between $15 and $40 (£7.50–£20), here are some companies you can use: **Horizontes Travel ★★**, Calle 32 between avenidas 3 and 5 (© **2222-2022;** www.horizontes.com); and **Swiss Travel Service** (© **2282-4898;** www.swisstravelcr.com). These same companies also offer a complete range of day trips out of San José. Almost all of the major hotels have tour desks, and most of the smaller hotels will also help arrange tours and day trips.

One interesting alternative to the standard tour bus based city tours is the **Tico Walks** (© **2283-8281;** www.ticowalks.com), a guided 2½-hour walking tour of the downtown center that takes in many of the city's top architectural sites and urban attractions. The tour runs every Tuesday, Thursday, Saturday, and Sunday at 10am, and costs $10 (£5) per person. Private tours are also available.

The Top Attractions

In addition to the attractions listed below, you might consider a quick stop at San José's main **cathedral.** The church and its interior are largely unspectacular. However, you'll see a pretty garden, as well as a massive marble statue of Pope Juan Pablo II, with a woman and child, carved by celebrated Costa Rican sculptor Jorge Jiménez Deredia. Deredia also has a work at the Vatican. The cathedral is located at the corner of Avenida 2 and Calle central.

The **Museo Nacional de Costa Rica ★** (© **2257-1433;** www.museocostarica.go.cr) is an important historical museum located on Calle 17, between avenidas Central and 2, on the Plaza de la Democracia. You might also want to visit the **Centro Nacional de Arte y Cultura (National Center of Art and Culture)** (© **2257-7202;** www.madc.ac.cr), a full city block complex that houses the offices of the Cultural Ministry, several performing-arts centers, and the Museum of Contemporary Art and Design. This place is located on Calle 13 between avenidas 3 and 5.

Museo de Arte Costarricense (Costa Rican Art Museum) ★★ This small museum at the end of Paseo Colón in Parque La Sabana was formerly the country's principal airport terminal. Today it houses a collection of works in all mediums by Costa Rica's most celebrated artists. On display are some exceptionally beautiful pieces in a wide range of styles. In addition to the permanent collection of sculptures, paintings, and prints, there are regular temporary exhibits. Be sure to check out the outdoor sculpture garden. So far, the collection is small, but it does include at least one representative work each by José Sancho, Jorge Jiménez Deredia, Max Jiménez, and Francisco Zuñiga. You can easily spend an hour or two at this museum—more if you take a stroll through the neighboring park.

Calle 42 and Paseo Colón, Parque La Sabana Este. ✆ **2222-7155.** www.musarco.go.cr. Admission $5 (£2.50) adults, $3 (£1.50) students with valid ID, free for children and seniors, free for everyone Sun. Tues–Fri 9am–5pm; Sat–Sun 10am–4pm.

Museo de Los Niños (Children's Museum) Kids A former barracks and then a prison, this museum houses an extensive collection of exhibits designed to edify and entertain children of all ages. Experience a simulated earthquake or make music by dancing across the floor. Many exhibits encourage hands-on play. If you're traveling with children, you'll definitely want to come here. The museum sometimes features limited shows of "serious" art and is also the home of the National Auditorium. You can spend anywhere from 1 to 4 hours here, depending on how long your children linger at each exhibit. Be careful, though: The museum is large and spread out; it's easy to lose track of a family member or friend.

Calle 4 and Av. 9. ✆ **2258-4929.** www.museocr.com. Admission $2 (£1) adults, $1.20 (60p) students and children 17 and under. Tues–Fri 8am–4:30pm; Sat–Sun 10am–5pm.

Museos del Banco Central de Costa Rica (Gold Museum) ★★ Directly beneath the Plaza de la Cultura, this unusual underground museum houses one of the largest collections of pre-Columbian gold in the Americas. On display are more than 20,000 troy ounces of gold in more than 2,000 objects. The sheer number of small pieces can be overwhelming and seem redundant, but the unusual display cases and complex lighting systems show off every piece to its utmost. This complex also includes a gallery for temporary art exhibits, separate numismatic and philatelic museums (coins and stamps, for us regular folks), a modest gift shop, and a branch of the Costa Rican Tourist Institute's info center. Plan to spend an hour or two here.

Calle 5, btw. avs. Central and 2, underneath the Plaza de la Cultura. ✆ **2243-4202.** www.museosdelbancocentral.org. Admission $6 (£3) adults, $4 (£2) students, 80¢ (40p) children 11 and under. Daily 9:30am–5pm.

Outside San José

A host of excellent attractions and adventures await visitors just outside of San José. The following are some of my favorites:

Café Britt Farm ★ Although bananas are the main export of Costa Rica, most people are far more interested in the country's second-most-important export crop: coffee. Café Britt is one of the leading brands here, and the company has put together an interesting tour and stage production at its farm, which is 20 minutes outside of San José. Here, you'll see how coffee is grown and visit the roasting and processing plant to learn how a coffee "cherry" is turned into a delicious roasted bean. Tasting sessions are offered for visitors to experience the different qualities of coffee. There is also a restaurant and store where you can buy coffee and coffee-related gift items. The entire tour, including transportation, takes about 3 to 4 hours. Allow some extra time and an extra $10 (£5) for a visit to their nearby working plantation and mill. You can even strap on a basket and go out coffee picking during harvest time. The folks here offer several full-day options that combine a visit to the Britt Farm with a stop at Poás Volcano, a nearby Butterfly Farm, or the Rain Forest Aerial Tram Caribbean. They've also begun offering mountain-bike tours in the Heredia hills above their farm, ending with lunch or refreshments at their restaurant.

North of Heredia on the road to Barva. ✆ **2277-1600.** www.coffeetour.com. Admission $20 (£10) adults, $16 (£8) children 6–11; $37 (£19) adults and $33 (£17) children, including transportation from downtown San José and a coffee drink; add $15 (£7.50) for full buffet lunch. 3 tours daily: 9 and 11am, and 3pm during the high season; reduced schedule in the off season. Store and restaurant daily 8:30am–5pm year-round.

INBio Park ★★ Kids Run by the National Biodiversity Institute (Instituto Nacional de Biodiversidad, or INBio). This place is part museum, part educational center, and part nature park. In addition to watching a 15-minute informational video, visitors can tour two large pavilions explaining Costa Rica's biodiversity and natural wonders, and hike on trails that re-create the ecosystems of a tropical rainforest, dry forest, and premontane forest. A 2-hour guided hike is included in the entrance fee, and self-guided-tour booklets are also available. There's a good-size butterfly garden, as well as a Plexiglas viewing window into the small lagoon. One of my favorite attractions here is the series of animal sculptures donated by one of Costa Rica's premiere artists, José Sancho. There's a simple cafeteria-style restaurant for lunch, as well as a coffee shop and gift shop. You can easily spend 2 to 3 hours here.

400m (1,312 ft./4 blocks) north and 250m (820 ft./2½ blocks) west of the Shell station in Santo Domingo de Heredia. ✆ **2507-8107.** www.inbio.ac.cr. Admission $23 (£12) adults, $13 (£6.50) children 12 and under. Daily 8am–6pm (admission closes at 4pm). INBio Park can arrange round-trip transportation from downtown for $18 (£9) per person.

La Paz Waterfall Gardens ★★ Kids The original attraction here is a series of trails through primary and secondary forests alongside the La Paz River, with lookouts over a series of powerful falls, including the namesake La Paz Fall. In addition to an orchid garden and a hummingbird garden, you must visit their huge butterfly garden, which is easily the largest in Costa Rica. A small serpentarium, featuring a mix of venomous and nonvenomous native snakes, and several terrariums containing various frogs and lizards, are also parts of the attraction. There's even a man-made trout pond where you can cast for trout, or just take a swim with them. While the admission fee is a little steep, everything is wonderfully done and the trails and waterfalls are beautiful. A buffet lunch at the large cafeteria-style restaurant costs an extra $12 (£6) for adults, or $6 (£3) for kids. This is a good stop after a morning visit to the Poás Volcano. Plan to spend 2 to 4 hours here.

6km (3¾ miles) north of Varablanca on the road to San Miguel. ✆ **2225-0643.** www.waterfallgardens.com. Admission $32 (£16) adults, $20 (£10) children and students with valid ID. Daily 8:30am–5:30pm. Take a Puerto Viejo de Sarapiquí bus from Calle 12 and Av. 9 (make sure it passes through Varablanca and La Virgen), and ask to be let off at the entrance. Buses are infrequent, and coordinating your return can be difficult, so it's best to come in a rental car or arrange transport.

OUTDOOR & WELLNESS ACTIVITIES

Due to the chaos and pollution, you'll probably want to get out of the city before undertaking anything too strenuous. But if you want to brave the elements, there are a few outdoor activities in and around San José.

Parque La Sabana (at the western end of Paseo Colón), formerly San José's international airport, is the city's center for active sports and recreation. Here you'll find everything from jogging trails, soccer fields, and a few public tennis courts to the National Stadium. All the facilities are free and open to the public. Families gather for picnics, people fly kites, and there's even an outdoor sculpture garden. If you really want to experience the local culture, try getting into a pickup soccer game here. However, be careful in this park, especially at dusk or after dark, when it becomes a favorite haunt for youth gangs and muggers.

BIRD-WATCHING Serious birders will certainly want to head out of San José, but it is still possible to see quite a few species in the metropolitan area. Two of the best spots for urban bird-watching are the campus at the **University of Costa Rica,** in the eastern suburb of San Pedro, and **Parque del Este ★**, located a little farther east on the road to San Ramón de Tres Ríos. You'll see a mix of urban species, and if you're lucky, you might spy a couple of hummingbirds or even a blue-crowned motmot. To get to the university campus, take any San Pedro bus from Avenida Central between calles 9 and 11. To get to Parque del Este, take the San Ramón/Parque del Este bus from Calle 9 between avenidas Central and 1. To hook up with fellow birders, e-mail the **Birding Club of Costa Rica ★★** (**✆ 2282-5365;** costaricabirding@hotmail.com), which frequently organizes expeditions around the Central Valley and beyond.

GOLF & TENNIS If you want to play tennis or golf in San José, your options are limited. If you're looking for a real local experience on some rough concrete courts, you can take a racket and some balls down to **Parque La Sabana.** However, the best facilities for visiting golfers and tennis players are found at **Parque Valle del Sol ★** (**✆ 2282-9222;** www.vallesol.com), in the western suburb of Santa Ana. The 18-hole course here is open to the general public. Greens fees are $90 (£45) per golfer per day, including the cart and unlimited playing both on the course and driving range. The tennis courts here cost around $8 (£4) per hour. Reservations are essential. The golf course at the Cariari Country Club is not open to the general public.

JOGGING Try **Parque La Sabana,** mentioned above, or head to **Parque del Este,** which is east of town in the foothills above San Pedro. Take the San Ramón/Parque del Este bus from Calle 9 between avenidas Central and 1. It's never a good idea to jog at night, on busy streets, or alone. Women should be particularly careful about jogging alone. And remember, Tico drivers are not accustomed to sport joggers on residential streets, so don't expect drivers to give you much berth.

SOCCER (FÚTBOL) Ticos take their *fútbol* seriously. Costa Rican professional soccer is some of the best in Central America, and the national team, or *Sele (selección nacional),* qualified for the World Cup in 2002 and 2006, although they made early exits both times. The soccer season runs from September to June, with the finals spread out over several weeks in late June and early July.

You don't need to buy tickets in advance. Tickets generally run between $2 and $15 (£1–£7.50). It's worth paying a little extra for *sombra numerado* (reserved seats in the shade). This will protect you from both the sun and the more rowdy aficionados. Costa Rican soccer fans take the sport seriously, and several violent incidents, both inside and outside the stadiums, have marred the sport in recent years, so be careful. Other options include *sombra* (general admission in the shade), *palco* and *palco numerado* (general admission and reserved mezzanine), and *sol general* (general admission in full sun).

The main San José team is Saprissa (affectionately called El Monstruo, or "The Monster"). **Saprissa's stadium** is in Tibás (take any Tibás bus from Calle 2 and Av. 5). Games are often held on Sunday at 11am, but occasionally they are scheduled for Saturday afternoon or Wednesday evening. Check the local newspapers for game times and locations.

SPAS & WORKOUT FACILITIES Most of the higher-end hotels have some sort of pool and exercise facilities. You'll find the best of these at the **Marriott Costa Rica Hotel** (p. 565) and **Crowne Plaza Corobicí** (Autopista General Cañas, Sabana Norte; **✆ 800/227-6963;** www.crowneplaza.com). If you're looking for a good, serious workout, I

Taking In the Arts

Art lovers should check out Molly Keeler's 1-day **Art Tour★** (© **8359-5571** or 2288-0896; www.costaricaarttour.com), which includes scheduled visits to the studios and personal shops of prominent local artists working in a wide range of mediums.

recommend the **Multispa ★** (© **2231-5542**), located in the Tryp Corobicí. Even if you're not a guest at the hotel, you can use the facilities here and join in any class for $15 (£7.50) per day. Multispa has five other locations around the Central Valley.

SHOPPING

THE SHOPPING SCENE San José's central shopping corridor is bounded by avenidas 1 and 2, from about Calle 14 in the west to Calle 13 in the east. For several blocks west of the Plaza de la Cultura, **Avenida Central** is a pedestrian-only street mall where you'll find store after store of inexpensive clothes for men, women, and children. Depending on the mood of the police that day, you might find a lot of street vendors as well. Some shops close for lunch, while others remain open (it's just the luck of the draw for shoppers).

MARKETS There are several markets near downtown, but by far the largest is the **Mercado Central,** located between avenidas Central and 1 and calles 6 and 8. Although this maze of stalls is primarily a food market, inside you'll find all manner of vendors, including a few selling Costa Rican souvenirs, crude leather goods, and musical instruments. Be especially careful about your wallet or purse and any prominent jewelry because very skilled pickpockets frequent this area. All the streets surrounding the Mercado Central are jammed with produce vendors selling from small carts or loading and unloading trucks. Your best bet is to visit on Sunday or on weekdays; Saturday is particularly busy.

There is also a daily street market on the west side of the **Plaza de la Democracia.** Here you'll find two long rows of outdoor stalls selling T-shirts, Guatemalan and Ecuadorian handicrafts and clothing, small ceramic *ocarinas* (a small musical wind instrument), and handmade jewelry. The atmosphere here is much more open than at the Mercado Central. You might be able to bargain prices down a little bit, but bargaining is not a traditional part of the vendor culture here, so you'll have to work hard to save a few dollars.

Finally, two other similar options downtown include **La Casona,** Calle Central between avenidas Central and 1 (© **2222-7999**), a three-story warren of crafts and souvenir shops; and **El Pueblo,** a tourism complex built in the style of a mock colonial-era village, with a wide range of restaurants, gift shops, art galleries, bars, and discos.

MODERN MALLS With globalization and modernization taking hold in Costa Rica, much of the local shopping scene has shifted to large megamalls. Modern multilevel affairs with cineplexes, food courts, and international brand-name stores are becoming more ubiquitous. Although they lack the charm of small shops found around San José, they are a reasonable option for one-stop shopping; most contain at least one or two local galleries and crafts shops, along with a large supermarket, which is always the best place to stock up on local coffee, hot sauces, liquors, and other nonperishable foodstuffs.

Boutique Annemarie Occupying two floors at the Hotel Don Carlos, this shop has an amazing array of wood products, leather goods, papier-mâché figurines, paintings, books, cards, posters, and jewelry. You'll see most of this stuff at the other shops, but not in such quantities or in such a relaxed and pressure-free environment. At the Hotel Don Carlos, Calle 9, btw. avs. 7 and 9. ✆ **2221-6063.**

Galería Amón ★ Located in a stylish old house in the historic Barrio Amón district, this gallery features contemporary artists from Central and South America. Feature exhibits are mixed with a regularly rotating collection of works from a stable of artists. The spaces are ample and well-lit, giving this place almost a museum-like feel. No. 937 Calle 7 btw. avs. 7 and 9. ✆ **2223-9725.** www.amon937.com.

Galería 11–12 ★★★ This outstanding gallery deals mainly in high-end Costa Rican art, from neoclassical painters such as Teodorico Quirós to modern masters such as Francisco Amighetti and Paco Zuñiga, to current stars such as Rafa Fernández, Rodolfo Stanley, Fernando Carballo, and Fabio Herrera. Plaza Itzkatzu, off the Prospero Fernández Hwy., Escazú. ✆ **2288-1975.** www.galeria11-12.com.

Galería Namu ★★★ This shop has some very high-quality arts and crafts, specializing in truly high-end indigenous works, including excellent Boruca and Huetar carved masks and "primitive" paintings. It also carries a good selection of more modern arts and craft pieces, including the ceramic work of Cecilia "Pefi" Figueres. This place organizes tours to visit various indigenous tribes and artisans as well. Av. 7 btw. calles 5 and 7. ✆ **2256-3412.** www.galerianamu.com.

Orinoco Arts & Crafts Gallery ★★ With a stellar and varied collection from Costa Rica and around Latin America, particularly Venezuela and Guatemala, this shop has some of the best high-quality arts and craft pieces you'll find in the country. The selection ranges from paintings and sculptures, to baskets, woodcarvings, textiles, and ceramic works. Plaza Itzkatzu, off the Prospero Fernández Hwy., Escazú. ✆ **2288-2949.** www.orinocoarts.com.

WHERE TO STAY

In San José, your hotel choices range from expensive luxury resorts to budget pensions charging only a few dollars a night. However, these two extremes are the exceptions, not the norm. The vast number of accommodations, and the best deals, are in the $90-to-$160 (£45–£80) price range. Within this relatively moderate bracket, you'll find restored homes that have been turned into small hotels and bed-and-breakfasts, modern hotels with pools and exercise rooms, and older downtown business hotels.

While, in general, there are plenty of rooms to go around in San José, the small boutique hotels and better-run establishments (including those recommended here) are often booked well in advance during the high season.

CHOOSING WHERE TO STAY **Downtown hotels** are convenient to museums, restaurants, and shopping, but they can be noisy. Many people are also bothered by the exhaust fumes that permeate downtown streets. Moreover, because the streets of downtown are not especially safe, particularly at night, you should plan on taking taxis whether you stay downtown or in a nearby neighborhood or suburb. **Barrio Amón** is the downtown neighborhood with the most character and remnants of colonial architecture. If you want clean air and a peaceful night's sleep, consider staying out in the suburbs. **Escazú** and **Santa Ana** are both quiet yet modern suburbs, and many of the hotels there have great views. Heading east from downtown, **Los Yoses** is fairly close to the center of the action yet is still quiet. If you've rented a car, make sure your hotel provides secure parking or you'll have to find (and pay for) a nearby lot. If you plan to take some day tours, you can just as easily arrange these from a hotel situated outside the downtown area.

If you're heading out to Guanacaste, the central Pacific, or the northern zone, you might consider a hotel or bed-and-breakfast either near or beyond the airport. Sure, you give up proximity to downtown, but you can cut as much as an hour off your travel time to any of these destinations.

Downtown San José/Barrio Amón

Expensive

In addition to the place listed below, you might also check out the **Radisson Europa Hotel** (✆ **888/201-1718** in the U.S., or 2257-3257; www.radisson.com).

Clarion Amón Plaza ★ Located on the north edge of the historic Barrio Amón neighborhood, this hotel is a pretty dependable business-class option. There's nothing particularly distinctive about the property or rooms here; however, in terms of service, location, and price, this hotel gets my nod over the nearby Holiday Inn. I recommend paying the extra $30 (£15) for the executive-floor rooms, which get you free happy hour food and drinks, a separate lounge area, and more recently upgraded and furnished rooms. While the food is merely average, the ambience of their little outdoor, sidewalk cafe, El Cafetal de la Luz, is delightful. There's also a swank casino on-site. You can often do better than the rates listed below if you book through www.choicehotels.com.

Av. 11 and Calle 3 bis (A.P. 4192-1000), San José. ✆ **877/424-6423** in the U.S. and Canada, or 2523-4600 in Costa Rica. Fax 2523-4614. www.hotelamonplaza.com. 87 units. $130–$160 (£65–£80) double; $220 (£110) suite. AE, DC, MC, V. Free parking. **Amenities:** Restaurant; bar; lounge; babysitting; casino; small exercise room; Jacuzzi; laundry service; nonsmoking rooms; sauna. *In room:* A/C, TV, hair dryer, free Wi-Fi.

Moderate

In addition to the hotels listed below, the **Sleep Inn** (✆ **2222-0101;** www.choicehotels.com; Av. 3 btw. calles 9 and 11) is a modern, American-style chain hotel in the heart of downtown. The **Hotel Britannia** (✆ **800/263-2618** in the U.S.; www.hotelbritanniacostarica.com; Calle 3 and Av. 11) is the most elegant of the many small hotels in downtown that have been created from restored old houses. **Hotel Doña Inés** (✆ **2222-7443;** www.donaines.com) on Calle 11 between avenidas 2 and 6, and **Hotel Santo Tomás** (✆ **877/446-0658** in the U.S., or 2255-0448 in Costa Rica; www.hotelsantotomas.com) on Avenida 7, between calles 3 and 5, are two little boutique hotels that are also good options.

Gran Hotel Costa Rica The Gran Hotel Costa Rica has arguably the best location of any downtown hotel (bordering the Teatro Nacional and the Plaza de la Cultura), and a major remodeling has finally brought the rooms and amenities almost up to snuff. Most of the rooms here are fairly large, and they sport fresh carpets, paint, and furnishings. However, they still feel a bit spartan and dated, and hot water seems to be on seriously short supply. Although it's set in a half-block from busy Avenida 2, some find the street noise a problem here. The Cafeteria 1830, reviewed separately below, is perhaps the hotel's greatest attribute. It's memorable not so much for its food as for its atmosphere—it's an open-air patio that overlooks the National Theater, street musicians, and all the activity of the Plaza de la Cultura.

 Av. 2, btw. calles 1 and 3, San José. ✆ **800/949-0592** in the U.S., or 2221-4000. Fax 2221-3501. www.grandhotelcostarica.com. 104 units. $81–$97 (£41–£49) double; $135–$179 (£66–£90) suite. Rates include breakfast buffet. AE, DC, MC, V. Free parking. **Amenities:** 2 restaurants; bar; small casino; small gym; laundry service; room service. *In room:* TV, minibar, free Wi-Fi.

Hotel Don Carlos ★★ Finds If you're looking for a small downtown hotel that is unmistakably Costa Rican and hints at the days of the planters and coffee barons, this former president's mansion is the place for you. Inside you'll find a slew of art and craft works and archaeological reproductions, as well as orchids, ferns, palms, and parrots. The rooms are distinct and vary greatly in size, so be specific when you reserve, or ask if it's possible to see a few when you check in. Breakfast is served in an outdoor orchid garden and atrium. The gift shop here is one of the largest in the country, and guests get unlimited free local calls, one free international call, and free Internet access with the hotel's computer or Wi-Fi network.

779 Calle 9, btw. avs. 7 and 9, San José. ✆ **2221-6707.** Fax 2258-1152. www.doncarloshotel.com. 33 units. $75–$95 (£38–£48) double. Rates include continental breakfast. AE, MC, V. Free parking. **Amenities:** Restaurant; bar; Jacuzzi; laundry service; room service. *In room:* TV, hair dryer, free Wi-Fi.

Inexpensive

In addition to the places listed below, **Kap's Place** (✆ **2221-1169;** www.kapsplace.com), located across from the Hotel Aranjuez on Calle 19 between avenidas 11 and 13, is another good choice, while real budget hounds might want to try either **Tranquilo Backpackers** (✆ **2222-2493;** www.tranquilobackpackers.com), on Calle 7 between avenidas 9 and 11, **Pensión de la Cuesta** (✆ **2256-7946;** www.pensiondelacuesta.com), at 1332 Cuesta de Núñez, Av. 1 between calles 11 and 15, or **Costa Rica Backpackers** (✆ **2221-6191;** www.costaricabackpackers.com), on Avenida 6 between calles 21 and 23.

Hotel Aranjuez Value This is probably the best and deservedly most popular budget option close to downtown. Located on a quiet and safe street in the Barrio Amón neighborhood, this hotel is made up of five contiguous houses. All rooms are simple and clean, and some are a little dark. Rooms and bathrooms vary greatly in size, so ask when reserving, or try to see a few rooms when you arrive. The nicest features here, aside from the convivial hostel-like atmosphere, are the lush and shady gardens; the hanging orchids, bromeliads, and ferns decorating the hallways and nooks; and the numerous open lounge areas furnished with chairs, tables, and couches—great for lazing around and sharing travel tales with your fellow guests. The hotel has a couple of computers, as well as a free Wi-Fi network, and provides free local calling.

Calle 19, btw. avs. 11 and 13 (A.P. 457-2070), San José. ✆ **877/898-8663** in the U.S., or 2256-1825. Fax 2223-3528. www.hotelaranjuez.com. 36 units, 6 with shared bathroom. $25 (£13) double with shared bathroom; $40–$47 (£20–£24) double with private bathroom. Rates include breakfast buffet. V. Free parking. **Amenities:** Restaurant; bar; several lounge areas; laundry service. *In room:* TV, free Wi-Fi.

La Sabana/Paseo Colón

Moderate

If the following option is full, **Hotel Rosa del Paseo** (✆ **2257-3225;** www.rosadelpaseo.com) offers similar charms, but not quite as elegantly.

Hotel Grano de Oro ★★ Finds San José boasts dozens of old homes that have been converted into hotels, but the Grano de Oro tops them all in terms of design, comfort, ambience, and service. The hotel offers a variety of room types to fit a range of budgets and tastes. I favor the patio rooms, which have French doors opening onto private patios. For additional luxuries, you can stay in one of the suites, which have whirlpool tubs. If you don't grab a suite, you still have access to the hotel's two rooftop Jacuzzis. The hotel's restaurant serves excellent international cuisine and some of the best desserts in the city. The owners of this hotel, Eldon and Lori Cooke, are the prime movers behind a noble shelter for young, unwed mothers, Casa Luz.

Calle 30, no. 251, btw. avs. 2 and 4, 150m (492 ft./1½ blocks) south of Paseo Colón, San José (mailing address: SJO 36, P.O. Box 025216, Miami, FL 33102). ✆ **2255-3322.** Fax 2221-2782. www.hotelgranodeoro.com. 40 units. $105–$140 (£53–£70) double; $160–$275 (£80–£138) suite. AE, MC, V. Free parking. **Amenities:** Restaurant; bar, lounge; concierge; 2 rooftop Jacuzzis; laundry service; all rooms nonsmoking; room service. *In room:* TV, minibar, safe, free Wi-Fi.

Inexpensive

Hotel Cacts (Finds) Housed in an attractive, tropical contemporary home on a business and residential street, this is one of the more interesting and unusual budget hotels in San José. The seemingly constantly expanding complex is a maze of rooms and hallways on several levels. Rooms vary considerably in size. The deluxe rooms here come with televisions and telephones, whereas the standard rooms lack both of these amenities. The newest additions are a small pool and separate Jacuzzi, in a lush garden patio. The staff here is very helpful, and the hotel will receive mail and faxes, change money, and store baggage for guests.

Av. 3 bis, no. 2845, btw. calles 28 and 30 (A.P. 379-1005), San José. ✆ **2221-2928** or 2221-6546. Fax 2221-8616. www.hotelcacts.com. 26 units. $45–$60 (£23–£30) double. Rates include breakfast buffet. MC, V. Free parking. **Amenities:** Lounge; Jacuzzi; laundry service; all rooms nonsmoking; small outdoor pool; free Wi-Fi. *In room:* No phone in some rooms.

San Pedro/Los Yoses

Moderate

In addition to the places listed below, the **Hotel Boutique Jade** (✆ **2224-2455;** www.hotelboutiquejade.com) is a modern business-class hotel with an excellent restaurant, while the **Hotel 1492 Jade y Oro** (✆ **2256-5913;** www.hotel1492.com) is another good option in a converted home, bedecked in interesting artwork.

Hôtel Le Bergerac ★★ The Hotel Le Bergerac offers up spacious and comfortable accommodations, personal service, and gourmet meals. Le Bergerac is composed of three houses with courtyard gardens in between. Almost all the rooms are fairly large, and each is a little different. I favor those with private patio gardens. In the evenings candlelight and classical music set a relaxing and romantic mood. The hotel's long-standing L'Ile de France restaurant serves exquisite French and Continental dinners for guests and the public by reservation only.

Calle 35 no. 50 (A.P. 1107-1002), San José. ✆ **2234-7850.** Fax 2225-9103. www.bergerachotel.com. 26 units. $85–$140 (£43–£70) double. Rates include full breakfast. AE, DC, MC, V. Free parking. **Amenities:** Restaurant; lounge; concierge; laundry service. *In room:* TV, hair dryer.

Escazú & Santa Ana

Located about 15 minutes west of San José and about the same distance from the international airport, these affluent suburbs have experienced rapid growth in recent years, as the metropolitan area continues its urban sprawl. Both Escazú and Santa Ana are popular with the Costa Rican professional class and North American retirees and expatriates, and quite a few hotels have sprung up to cater to their needs. It's relatively easy to commute between Escazú or Santa Ana and downtown via bus or taxi.

The **Real InterContinental San José** (✆ **2208-2100;** www.gruporeal.com) is a large, upscale resort hotel just off the highway, adjacent to a major shopping mall. The **Hotel**

 Milvia (✆ **2225-4543;** www.hotelmilvia.com) is an offbeat, little hotel with bright and airy rooms.

Expensive

Alta Hotel ★★ This small boutique hotel is infused with old-world charm. Curves and high arches abound. My favorite touch is the winding interior alleyway that snakes down from the reception through the hotel. Most of the rooms here have wonderful views of the Central Valley from private balconies; the others have pleasant garden patios. The rooms are up to contemporary resort standards, although some have slightly cramped bathrooms. The suites are considerably larger, each with a separate sitting room, as well as large Jacuzzi-style tubs in spacious bathrooms. The master suite has a steam bath as well. The hotel's La Luz restaurant (p. 570) is one of the more elegant and creative dining spots in the Central Valley.

Alto de las Palomas, old road to Santa Ana. ✆ **888/388-2582** in the U.S. and Canada, or 2282-4160. Fax 2282-4162. www.thealtahotel.com. 23 units. $167 (£84) double; $197 (£99) junior suite; $390 (£195) master suite; $820 (£410) penthouse. Rates include continental breakfast and round-trip airport transfers. AE, DC, MC, V. Free parking. **Amenities:** Restaurant; bar; concierge; exercise room; Jacuzzi; laundry service; midsize pool; room service; sauna. *In room:* A/C, TV, hair dryer, minibar, free Wi-Fi.

Moderate

In addition to the hotels listed below, the **Courtyard San José** (✆ **888/236-2427** in the U.S. and Canada, or 2208-3000; www.marriott.com) and **Quality Hotel Santa Ana** (✆ **877/424-6423** in the U.S. and Canada, or 2204-6700; www.choicehotels.com) are both modern business-class hotels a few miles from each other, right on the western Próspero Fernández Highway connecting Santa Ana and Escazú with San José. **Casa de las Tías** (✆ **2289-5517;** www.hotels.co.cr/casatias.html) is a quaint, family-run hotel in downtown Escazú.

Hotel Casa Alegre Finds Housed in a converted home on a residential side street just a couple of blocks from Santa Ana's central square and church, this hotel offers spacious, comfortable rooms. The decor leans heavily on Southwest American artwork and design touches, combined with Guatemalan textiles and locally made heavy wooden furniture. My favorite rooms are the upstairs units. A midsize outdoor pool that's good for lap swimming takes up much of the backyard, but there's a shady lounge area out back as well.

Santa Ana. ✆/fax **2203-7467.** www.hotelcasaalegre.com. 8 units. $65–$79 (£33–£40) double. Rates include full breakfast. AE, MC, V. **Amenities:** Laundry service. *In room:* TV, free Wi-Fi.

Heredia & Alajuela (Airport Area)

Alajuela and Heredia, two colonial-era cities that lie much closer to the airport than San José, are two great places to find small, distinct, and charming hotels. If you plan to get yourself to a remote beach or rainforest lodge as quickly as possible and to use San José and the Central Valley purely as a transportation hub, or if you just detest urban clutter, noise, and pollution, you might choose one of the hotels listed below.

Very Expensive

In addition to the places listed below, the **Doubletree Cariari by Hilton** (✆ **800/222-8733** in the U.S. and Canada, or 2239-0022; www.cariarisanjose.doubletree.com) is a modern resort hotel near the airport, while, **Xandari Resort & Spa ★★** (✆ **866/363-3212** in the U.S., or 2443-2020 in Costa Rica; www.xandari.com) and **Vista del Valle Plantation Inn ★★** (✆ **2450-0800** or ✆/fax 2451-1165; www.vistadelvalle.com) are two more luxury boutique hotels worth considering.

Finca Rosa Blanca Country Inn ★★★ Finds Finca Rosa Blanca is an eclectic architectural confection set amid the lush, green hillsides of a coffee plantation. Square corners seem to have been prohibited in the design of this beautiful home. There are turrets and curving walls of glass, and arched windows. Everywhere the glow of polished hardwood blends with white stucco walls and brightly painted murals. Inside, original artwork abounds, and each room is decidedly unique. The views are fabulous. If breathtaking bathrooms are your idea of the ultimate luxury, consider splurging on the master suite, which has a stone waterfall that cascades into a tub in front of a huge picture window. Still, all of the suites and villas have the same sense of eclectic luxury, with beautiful tile work, and creative design touches at every turn. Each comes with a private Jacuzzi tub.

Santa Bárbara de Heredia (mailing address: SJO 3475, P.O. Box 25369, Miami, FL 33102). ✆ **2269-9392.** Fax 2269-9555. www.fincarosablanca.com. 13 units. $270–$425 (£135–£213) double. Rates include breakfast. AE, MC, V. Free parking. **Amenities:** Restaurant; bar; lounge; babysitting; concierge; small exercise room; Jacuzzi; laundry service; all rooms nonsmoking; small free-form pool set in the hillside; full-service spa; room service. *In room:* Minibar, free Wi-Fi .

Marriott Costa Rica Hotel ★★ For my money, the Marriott is the best large luxury resort hotel in the San José area. Amenities are plentiful, and service here is excellent. The hotel is designed in a mixed colonial style, with hand-painted Mexican tiles, antique red-clay roof tiles, weathered columns, and heavy wooden doors, lintels, and trim. The centerpiece is a large open-air interior patio that somewhat replicates Old Havana's Plaza de Armas. All rooms are plush and well appointed, although the bathrooms seem slightly small for this price. The large lobby-level bar features daily piano music and weekend jazz nights, with both indoor and patio seating.

San Antonio de Belén (A.P. 502-4005). ✆ **888/236-2427** in the U.S. and Canada, or 2298-0844 in Costa Rica. Fax 2298-0033. www.marriott.com. 299 units. $249 (£125) double; $299 (£150) executive level; $550 (£275) master suite; $1,000 (£500) presidential suite. Rates lower in off season. AE, DC, MC, V. Free valet parking. **Amenities:** 3 restaurants; bar; lounge; free airport shuttle; babysitting; concierge; golf driving range; health club; Jacuzzi; laundry service; nonsmoking rooms; 2 pools; room service; sauna; 3 tennis courts; Wi-Fi. *In room:* A/C, TV, hair dryer, Internet, minibar.

Peace Lodge ★★ Finds Located alongside the popular La Paz Waterfall Gardens, the rooms here just might be some of the most impressive in the country—and the bathrooms in the deluxe units easily earn that distinction. The rooms are large and feature sparkling wood floors and trim, handcrafted four-poster beds, beautiful stone fireplaces, intricately sculpted steel light fixtures, and a host of other creative touches and details. Every room has a private balcony fitted with a mosaic-tiled Jacuzzi. The deluxe bathrooms come with a second oversize Jacuzzi set under a skylight in the middle of an immense room that features a full interior wall planted with ferns, orchids, and bromeliads and fed by a functioning waterfall system. Guests here have full access to all the tours and attractions of the La Paz Waterfall Gardens (p. 557) during normal operating hours and beyond.

6km (3¾ miles) north of Varablanca on the road to San Miguel. ✆ **954/727-3997** in the U.S., or 2482-2720 or 2225-0643 in Costa Rica. www.waterfallgardens.com. 17 units. $245–$305 (£123–£153) double; $395 (£198) villa. Rates include breakfast and entrance to La Paz Waterfall Gardens. Rates lower in off season; higher during peak weeks. AE, MC, V. **Amenities:** Restaurant; bar; Jacuzzi; laundry service; 2 outdoor swimming pools; free Wi-Fi. *In room:* A/C, TV, minibar.

Moderate

In addition to the places listed below, **Viña Romantica** (✆ **2430-7621;** www.vinaromantica.com) is a cozy new bed-and-breakfast in the hills just above Alajuela, which is earning strong praise for its amiable hosts and excellent restaurant. **Pura Vida Hotel** (✆ **2441-1157;** www.puravidahotel.com) and **Orquídeas Inn** (✆ **2433-7128;** www.orquideasinn.com) are popular Alajuela options convenient to the airport as well.

However, if you want to be right next to the airport, check out the **Hampton Inn & Suites** (✆ **800/426-7866** in the U.S., or 2436-0000 in Costa Rica; www.hamptoninn.com).

Hotel Bougainvillea ★ Value The Hotel Bougainvillea is an excellent choice—a great value if you're looking for a hotel in a quiet residential neighborhood not far from downtown. It offers most of the amenities of the more expensive resort hotels around the Central Valley, but it charges considerably less. The views across the valley from this hillside location are wonderful, and the gardens are beautifully designed and well tended. Rooms are carpeted and have small triangular balconies oriented to the views. These folks offer free wireless Internet connections throughout most of the hotel.

In Santo Tomás de Santo Domingo de Heredia, 100m (328 ft./1 block) west of the Escuela de Santo Tomás (A.P. 69-2120), San José. ✆ **2244-1414.** Fax 2244-1313. www.hb.co.cr. 81 units. $100–$115 (£50–£58) double; $123–$135 (£61–£68) suite. Rates include hourly downtown shuttle bus. AE, DC, MC, V. Free parking. **Amenities:** Restaurant; bar; babysitting; Jacuzzi; laundry service; nonsmoking rooms; midsize pool in attractive garden; sauna; room service; 2 lighted tennis courts; free Wi-Fi. *In room:* TV, hair dryer, free Wi-Fi.

WHERE TO DINE

Downtown San José

Moderate

Café Mundo ★ Finds INTERNATIONAL This place combines contemporary cuisine with an ambience of casual elegance. Wood tables and Art Deco wrought-iron chairs are spread spaciously around several rooms and open-air verandas in this former colonial mansion. The appetizers include vegetable tempura, crab cakes, and chicken satay alongside more traditional Tico standards such as *patacones* (fried plantain chips) and fried yuca. There's a long list of pastas and pizzas, as well as more substantial main courses. There are nightly specials and delicious desserts. One room here boasts colorful wall murals by Costa Rican artist Miguel Cassafont. This place is almost always filled with a broad mix of San José's gay, bohemian, theater, arts, and university crowds.

Calle 15 and Av. 9, 200m (656 ft./2 blocks) east and 100m (328 ft./1 block) north of the INS bldg. ✆ **2222-6190.** Reservations recommended. Main courses $5.50–$18 (£2.75–£9). AE, MC, V. Mon–Thurs 11am–11pm; Fri 11am–midnight; Sat 5pm–midnight.

Cafeteria 1830 INTERNATIONAL With veranda and patio seating directly fronting the Plaza de la Cultura, this is one of the best spots for a casual bite and some good people-watching. A wrought-iron railing, white columns, and arches create an old-world atmosphere; on the plaza in front of the cafe, a marimba band performs and vendors sell handicrafts. The menu is basic and the food is respectable, if unspectacular, but there isn't a better place downtown to bask in the tropical sunshine while you read the paper over breakfast or have a light lunch, and it's a great place to come before or after a show at the Teatro Nacional.

At the Gran Hotel Costa Rica, Av. 2, btw. calles 1 and 3, San José. ✆ **2221-4011.** Sandwiches $5.50–$8 (£2.75–£4.50); main courses $7–$35 (£3.50–£17). AE, DC, MC, V. Daily 24 hr.

Tin Jo ★★ Finds CHINESE/PAN-ASIAN San José has hundreds of Chinese restaurants, but most simply serve up tired takes on chop suey, chow mein, and fried rice. In contrast, Tin Jo has a wide and varied menu, with an assortment of Cantonese and Szechuan staples, as well as a range of Thai, Japanese, and Malaysian dishes, and even

Moments: Only in the Central Valley: Dining Under the Stars on a Mountain's Edge

Although there are myriad unique experiences to be had in Costa Rica, one of my favorites is dining on the side of a volcano with the lights of San José shimmering below. These restaurants, called *miradores,* are a resourceful response to the city's topography. Because San José is set in a broad valley surrounded on all sides by volcanic mountains, people who live in these mountainous areas have no place to go but up—so they do, building roadside cafes vertically up the sides of the volcanoes.

The food at most of these establishments is not spectacular, but the views often are, particularly at night, when the wide valley sparkles in a wash of lights. While the town of **Aserri,** 10km (6¼ miles) south of downtown San José, is the king of miradores, there are also miradores in the hills above Escazú and in San Ramón de Tres Ríos and Heredia. The most popular is **Le Monestère** (**© 2289-4404;** closed Sun), an elegant converted church serving somewhat overrated French and Belgian cuisine in a spectacular setting above the hills of Escazú. I recommend coming here just for the less formal **La Cava Grill,** which often features live music, mostly folk-pop but sometimes jazz. I also like **Mirador Tiquicia** (**© 2289-5839**), which occupies several rooms in a sprawling old Costa Rican home and has live folkloric dance shows on Thursday.

some Indian food. Dishes not to miss include the salt-and-pepper shrimp, beef teriyaki, and Thai curries. For dessert, try the sticky rice with mango, or banana tempura. The waiters here are some of the most attentive in Costa Rica. The decor features artwork and textiles from across Asia. Tin Jo is also a great option for vegetarians, and even vegans.

Calle 11, btw. avs. 6 and 8. **© 2221-7605** or 2257-3622. Main courses $8–$22 (£4–£11). AE, MC, V. Mon–Sat 11:30am–3pm and 5:30–10pm (Fri–Sat kitchen open 'til 11pm); Sun 11:30am–10pm.

Inexpensive

In addition to the places listed below, the **Q'Café** (**© 2221-0707**) is a delightful little European-style cafe with a pretty perch above the busy corner of Avenida Central and Calle 2. Try to grab a seat overlooking the action on the street below. Vegetarians might want to head to one of several **Vishnu** (**© 2256-6063**) restaurants located around downtown and the central valley.

Café del Teatro Nacional ★ CONTINENTAL/COFFEEHOUSE Even if there's no show on during your visit, you can enjoy a light meal, sandwich, dessert, or a cup of coffee here, while soaking up the neoclassical atmosphere. The theater was built in the 1890s from the designs of European architects, and the Art Nouveau chandeliers, ceiling murals, and marble floors and tables are pure Parisian. There are also plenty of desserts and a wide range of coffee drinks. On sunny days, there's outdoor seating at wrought-iron tables on the side of the theater. In addition to the regular hours of operation listed below, the cafe is open until 8pm any evening that there is a performance in the theater.

In the Teatro Nacional, Av. 2 btw. calles 3 and 5. **© 2221-1329.** Sandwiches $3–$7 (£1.50–£3.50); main courses $5–$12 (£2.50–£6). AE, MC, V. Mon–Sat 9am–4:30pm.

Expensive

Grano de Oro Restaurant ★★ Finds CONTINENTAL This elegant restaurant is set around a lovely interior courtyard of the Hotel Grano de Oro (p. 562). The atmosphere here is intimate, relaxed, and refined, all at the same time. The menu features a wide range of meat and fish dishes. The *lomito piemontes* is two medallions of filet mignon stuffed with Gorgonzola cheese in a sherry sauce, while the *pernil de conejo* is a rabbit thigh stuffed with a mushroom pâté and served with a Dijon mustard sauce. If you opt for fish, I recommend the macadamia-encrusted corvina, which is served with a light and tangy orange sauce. Be sure to save room for the "Grano de Oro pie," a decadent dessert with various layers of chocolate and coffee mousses and creams. This place has a good wine list, including a range of options by the glass.

Calle 30, no. 251, btw. avs. 2 and 4, 150m (492 ft./1½ blocks) south of Paseo Colón. © **2255-3322.** Reservations recommended. Main courses $8.50–$30 (£4.25–£15). AE, MC, V. Daily 6am–10pm.

Park Café ★★★ Finds FUSION Having opened and run a Michelin two-star restaurant in London and another one-star joint in Cannes, Richard Neat now finds himself turning out his impressive fusion cuisine in an intimate space spread around the interior patio courtyard of a stately old downtown mansion, which also doubles as an antique and imported furniture store. The menu changes regularly but might feature some roasted scallops with ricotta tortellini in a pumpkin jus, or some expertly grilled quail on a vegetable purée bed, topped with the poached quail egg. Presentations are artfully done, and often served in such a way as to encourage sharing. The well-thought-out and fairly priced wine list is a perfect complement to the cuisine.

Sabana Norte, 1 block north of Rostipollos. © **2290-6324.** Reservations recommended. Main courses $12–$25 (£6–£13). V. Tues–Sat noon–2pm and 7–9:30pm.

Moderate

For good Peruvian fare, head to the ever popular **Machu Picchu** (© **2222-7384**), on Calle 32, between avenidas 1 and 3. These folks have a sister restaurant over in San Pedro (© **2283-3679**), and another in Santa Ana (© **2203-7657**), set on a hillside with a great view over the valley below.

El Chicote ★ COSTA RICAN/STEAK This is one of San José's most venerable and popular steakhouses. The large room is divided by half-walls planted with tropical flora and a bevy of hanging ferns. There are heavy wooden beams and plenty of varnished-wood accents all around. True meat aficionados should order the imported rib-eye or 1½-pound T-bone. There's an extensive selection of fish and poultry dishes as well. Everything comes with a choice of baked or mashed potatoes, black beans, and fresh tortillas. The wine list features a broad range of Italian, Spanish, French, and California wines.

Av. Las Américas, 400m (1,312 ft./4 blocks) west of the ICE bldg., Sabana Norte. © **2232-0936** or 2232-3777. Reservations recommended. Main courses $8–$22 (£4–£11). AE, MC, V. Mon–Fri 11am–3pm and 6–11pm; Sat–Sun 11am–11pm.

Inexpensive

Soda Tapia COSTA RICAN The food is unspectacular, dependable, and quite inexpensive at this very popular local diner. There's seating inside the brightly lit dining room, as well as on the sidewalk-style patio fronting the parking area. Dour but efficient waitstaff take the order you mark down on your combination menu/bill. This is a great place for late-night eats or for before or after a visit to Parque La Sabana or Museo de

Arte Costarricense. These folks also have another site in a small strip mall in Santa Ana (© **2203-7174**).

Calle 42 and Av. 2, across from the Museo de Arte Costarricense. © **2222-6734.** Sandwiches $2–$4 (£1–£2); main dishes $4–$8 (£2–£4). MC, V. Sun–Thurs 6am–2am; Fri–Sat 24 hr.

San Pedro/Los Yoses

In addition to the restaurants listed below, local and visiting vegetarians swear by the little **Comida Para Sentir Restaurante Vegetariano San Pedro** (© **2224-1163**), located 125m (410 ft./1¼ blocks) north of the San Pedro Church. Despite the massive size and popularity of the nearby **Il Pomodoro,** I prefer **Pane E Vino** (© **2280-2869**), an excellent pasta-and-pizza joint on the eastern edge of San Pedro.

If you want to try an excellent Argentine-style steakhouse, head to **Donde Carlos** (© **2225-0819**) in Los Yoses. Finally, if you're hankering for sushi, try **Ichiban** ★ (© **2253-8012**) in San Pedro, or **Matsuri** ★ (© **2280-5522**), a little farther east in Curridabat.

Moderate

Olio ★ Value MEDITERRANEAN The exposed brick walls, dark-wood wainscoting, and stained-glass lamps imbue this place with character and romance. Couples might want to grab a table in a quiet nook, while groups tend to dominate the large main room or crowd the bar. There are even a few outdoor tables on a narrow sidewalk beside some train tracks, and nonsmokers might want these, as the main bar and dining areas are often tightly packed and smoke-filled. The extensive tapas menu features traditional Spanish fare, as well as bruschetta, antipasti, and a Greek *mezza* plate. You can also get a range of larger main dishes and pastas. The midsize wine list features very reasonably priced wines from Italy, France, Spain, Germany, Chile, Greece, and even Bulgaria.

Barrio California, 200m (656 ft./2 blocks) north of Bagelman's. © **2281-0541.** Main courses $5–$14 (£2.50–£7). AE, DC, MC, V. Mon–Fri 11:30am–1am; Sat 4pm–midnight.

Inexpensive

Whappin' Finds COSTA RICAN/CARIBBEAN You don't have to go to Limón or Cahuita to get good home-cooked Caribbean food. In addition to *rondon,* a coconut milk–based stew or soup, you can also get classic rice and beans cooked in coconut milk, as well as a range of fish and chicken dishes from the coastal region. I like the whole red snapper covered in a spicy sauce of sautéed onions. Everything is very simple, and prices are quite reasonable. After a dinner of fresh fish, with rice, beans, and *patacones,* the only letdown is that the beach is some 4 hours away.

Barrio Escalante, 200m (656 ft./2 blocks) east of El Farolito. © **2283-1480.** Main courses $8–$12 (£4–£6). AE, MC, V. Mon–Sat 11:30am–2:30pm and 6–10pm.

Escazu & Santa Ana

These two suburbs on the western side of town have the most vibrant restaurant scene in San José. Although there's high turnover and sudden closings, this remains a good area to check out for a variety of dining experiences. In addition to the places mentioned below, **Il Panino** ★ (© **2228-3126**) is an upscale sandwich shop and cafe, in the Centro Comercial El Paco. Located just outside of Santa Ana, **Essentia** ★ (© **2203-7503**) is another excellent fusion restaurant. **Barbecue Los Anonos,** 6 blocks west of the Los Anonos bridge in San Rafael de Escazú, next to the Sarretto Market (© **2228-0180**), is *the* place to come if you're craving a 16-ounce T-bone on the west side of town.

Finally, a good one-stop option to consider is the Plaza Itskatzu shopping center located just off the highway and sharing a parking lot with the Courtyard San José. Here you'll find a wide variety of moderately priced restaurant options, including **Tutti Li** (✆ **2289-8768**), a good Italian restaurant and pizzeria; **Chancay** (✆ **2289-6964**), which serves Peruvian and Peruvian/Chinese cuisine; **La Guagua** (✆ **2288-5112**), serving up tasty Cuban food; **Las Tapas de Manuel** ★ (✆ **2288-5700**), a Spanish-style tapas restaurant; and franchise outlets of both **Hooters** (✆ **2289-3498**) and **Outback Steakhouse** (✆ **2288-0511**).

Expensive

Bacchus ★★★ *Finds* ITALIAN My favorite Italian restaurant in San José, this place is housed in a historic home that is over a century old. You'd never know it following a massive restoration and remodel. Nevertheless, this place somehow seamlessly blends the old with the new in an elegant atmosphere. The best tables are on the covered back patio, where you can watch the open kitchen and wood-burning pizza oven in action. The menu features a range of antipasti, pastas, pizzas, and main dishes. Everything is perfectly prepared and beautifully presented. The desserts are also excellent, and the wine list is extensive and fairly priced.

Downtown Santa Ana. ✆ **2282-5441.** Reservations required. Main courses $8–$24 (£4–£12). AE, MC, V. Tues–Sat noon–3pm and 6–11pm; Sun noon–9pm.

La Luz ★★ CALIFORNIA/FUSION La Luz was one of the first fusion restaurants in Costa Rica, and it continues to serves up some of the better prepared and more adventurous food in Costa Rica. I keep coming back for the fiery garlic prawns, which are sautéed in ancho chili oil and sage and served over a roasted-garlic potato mash. The whole thing is served with a garnish of fried leeks and a tequila-lime butter and cilantro-oil sauce. I also enjoy the passion-fruit-glazed duck breast. On top of an extensive menu, there are nightly specials and a wide selection of inventive appetizers and desserts. The glass-walled dining room is one of the most elegant in town, with a view of the city lights. La Luz is also open for breakfast and lunch.

In the Alta Hotel (p. 564), on the old road to Santa Ana. ✆ **2282-4160.** Reservations recommended. Main courses $14–$21 (£7–£11). AE, DC, MC, V. Daily 6:30am–10pm.

SAN JOSÉ AFTER DARK

Catering to a mix of tourists, college students, and just generally party-loving Ticos, San José has a host of options to meet the nocturnal needs of visitors and locals alike. You'll find plenty of interesting clubs and bars, a wide range of theaters, and some very lively discos and dance salons.

To find out what's going on in San José while you're in town, pick up a copy of the ***Tico Times*** (English) or ***La Nación*** (Spanish). The former is a good place to find out where local expatriates are hanging out; the latter's "Viva" and "Tiempo Libre" sections have extensive listings of discos, movie theaters, and live music.

BARS & PUBS There seems to be something for every taste here. Lounge lizards will be happy in most hotel bars in the downtown area, while students and the young at heart will have no problem mixing in at the livelier spots around town.

The funky 2-block stretch of **San Pedro** ★★ just south of the University of Costa Rica has been dubbed La Calle de Amargura, or the "Street of Bitterness," and it's the heart and soul of the college and youth scene. Bars and cafes are mixed in with bookstores and copy shops. After dark the streets are packed with teens, punks, students, and professors barhopping and just hanging around. You can walk the strip until someplace strikes your fancy—you don't need a travel guide to find **Omar Khayyam** (✆ **2253-8455**),

A One-Stop Shop

A good place to sample a range of San José's nightlife is in **El Pueblo,** a shopping, dining, and entertainment complex done up like an old Spanish village. It's just across the river to the north of town. The best way to get there is by taxi; all the drivers know El Pueblo well. Within the alleyways that wind through El Pueblo are a dozen or more bars, clubs, and discos—there's even an indoor soccer playing field. **Fiesta Latina** (✆ **2222-8782**), **Twister** (✆ **2222-5746**), and **Friends** (✆ **2233-5283**) are happening party spots. Across the street, **Copacabana** (✆ **2233-5516**) is a popular dance spot. For a mellower option, inside El Pueblo, try **Café Art Boruca** (✆ **2221-3615**).

Marrakech Pool & Pizza (✆ **253-2049**), **Mosaikos** (✆ **2280-9541**), **Tavarua Surf & Skate Bar** (✆ **2225-7249**), **Terra U** (✆ **2225-4261**), or **Caccio's** (✆ **2224-3261**), which lie at the heart of this district—or you can try one of the places listed below. ***Note:*** La Calle de Amargura attracts a certain unsavory element. Use caution here. Try to visit with a group, and don't carry large amounts of cash or wear flashy jewelry.

Other good options include **Café Expresivo** (✆ **2224-1202;** 4 blocks east of the Santa Teresita Church, Barrio Escalante), **El Observatorio** ★ (✆ **2223-0725;** Calle 23 btw. avs. Central and 1), and **El Cuartel de la Boca del Monte** ★★ (✆ **2221-0327;** Av. 1 btw. calles 21 and 23; 50m/164 ft./½ block west of the Cine Magaly). The latter is a local institution and packed to the gills most nights from Wednesday through Saturday.

Finally, if you want a taste of old San José, check out **Chelles** ★ (✆ **2221-1369;** Av. Central and Calle 9), a bare-bones 24-hour joint in the heart of downtown.

DANCE CLUBS You'll find plenty of places to hit the dance floor in San José. Salsa and merengue are the main beats that move people here, and many of the dance clubs feature live music on the weekends. You'll find a pretty limited selection, though, if you're looking to catch some small-club jazz, rock, or blues.

To mix with locals, head either to **Castro's** ★ (✆ **2256-8789;** Av. 13 and Calle 22, Barrio Mexico), which has several dance and lounge areas spread over several floors, or **El Tobogán** ★★ (✆ **2223-8920;** 200m/656 ft./2 blocks north and 100m/328 ft./1 block east of the La República main office, off the Guápiles Hwy.) where the dance floor seems to be as big as a football field.

For a more contemporary, and younger scene, try **Utopia** (✆ **2221-6655;** Radial San Antonio de Belén-Santa Ana) or **Vértigo** (✆ **2257-8424;** Edificio Colón, Paseo Colón).

Most of the places listed above charge a nominal cover; sometimes it includes a drink or two.

LIVE MUSIC The daily "Viva" and Friday's "Tiempo Libre" sections of *La Nación* newspaper have weekly performance schedules.

Perhaps the most dependable club to catch live music is the **Jazz Café** ★ (✆ **2253-8933;** www.jazzcafecostarica.com) in San Pedro, or its sister club **Jazz Café Escazú,** just off the highway between San José and Escazú.

Visiting artists stop in Costa Rica on a regular basis. Recent concerts have featured hard rockers Smashing Pumpkins and Iron Maiden, pop phenom the Black Eyed Peas, Brazilian maestro Caetano Veloso, reggaeton giant Daddy Yankee, and Mexican singing sensations Ricky Martin and Chayanne. Many of these performances take place in San

 José's two historic theaters, the **Teatro Nacional** (see below) and the **Teatro Melico Salazar,** Avenida 2 between calles Central and 2 (© **2221-4952**), as well as at the **Auditorio Nacional** (see below). Really large shows are usually held at soccer stadiums or large, natural amphitheaters.

PERFORMING ARTS Theater is very popular in Costa Rica, and downtown San José is studded with small theaters. However, tastes tend toward the burlesque, and the crowd pleasers are almost always simplistic sexual comedies. The **National Theater Company** is an exception, tackling works from Lope de Vega to Lorca to Mamet. Similarly, the small independent group **Abya Yala** also puts on several cutting-edge avant-garde shows each year. Almost all of the theater offerings are in Spanish, although the **Little Theater Group** (www.littletheatregroup.org) is a long-standing amateur group that periodically stages works in English. Finally, **Britt Expresivo** (© **2277-1600;** www.brittexpresivo.com) has been staging regular works ranging from original pieces to Shakespeare to Beckett, in both English and Spanish, at the small theater up at Café Britt (p. 556) in the hills above Heredia. Check the *Tico Times* to see if anything is running during your stay.

The **National Symphony Orchestra** is respectable by regional standards, although its repertoire tends to be rather conservative. Symphony season runs March through November, with concerts roughly every other weekend at the **Teatro Nacional,** Avenida 2 between calles 3 and 5 (© **2221-5341;** www.teatronacional.go.cr), and the **Auditorio Nacional** (© **2256-5876**) at the Museo de Los Niños (p. 566). Tickets cost between $3 and $25 (£1.50–£13) and can be purchased at the box office.

Costa Rica's cultural panorama changes drastically every November when the country hosts large arts festivals. In odd-numbered years, **El Festival Nacional de las Artes** reigns supreme, featuring purely local talent. In even-numbered years, the month-long fete is **El Festival Internacional de las Artes,** with a nightly smorgasbord of dance, theater, music, and monologue from around the world. Most nights of the festival offer between 4 and 10 shows. Many are free, and the most expensive ticket is usually around $5 (£2.50). For exact dates and details, you can contact the Ministry of Youth, Culture, and Sports (© **2255-3188;** www.mcjdcr.go.cr), although you might have trouble getting any information if you don't speak Spanish.

SIDE TRIPS & ADVENTURE TOURS FROM SAN JOSÉ

San José makes an excellent base for exploring the beautiful Central Valley and the surrounding mountains. For first-time visitors, the best way to make the most of these excursions is usually to take a guided tour, but if you rent a car, you'll have greater independence. Some day trips also can be done by public bus.

A number of companies offer a wide variety of primarily nature-related day tours out of San José. The most reputable include **Costa Rica Expeditions ★★** (© **2257-0766;** www.costaricaexpeditions.com), **Costa Rica Sun Tours ★** (© **2296-7757;** www.crsuntours.com), **Horizontes Tours ★★** (© **2222-2022;** www.horizontes.com), and **Swiss Travel Service** (© **2282-4898;** www.swisstravelcr.com).

Before signing on for a tour of any sort, find out how many fellow travelers will be accompanying you, how much time will be spent in transit and eating lunch, and how much time will actually be spent doing the primary activity. I've had complaints about tours that were rushed, that spent too much time in a bus or on secondary activities, or that had a cattle-car, assembly-line feel to them. The tours below are arranged by type of activity. In addition to these, you'll find tours that combine two or three different activities or destinations.

BUNGEE JUMPING There's nothing unique about bungee jumping in Costa Rica, but the site here is quite beautiful. If you've always had the bug, **Tropical Bungee** (**© 2248-2212;** www.bungee.co.cr) will let you jump off an 80m (262-ft.) bridge for $65 (£33); two jumps cost $95 (£48). Transportation is provided free from San José twice daily. These folks also offer paragliding tours.

CANOPY TOURS & AERIAL TRAMS Getting off the ground and up into the treetops is extremely popular in Costa Rican tourism, and there are scores of such tours around the country. You have several options relatively close to San José, and one actually in the city center.

The quickest and easiest way to experience a zip-line canopy tour from San José is to head to the La Sabana park and take the **Urban Canopy Tour** (**© 2215-2544**). Given that this tour is set on a relatively flat patch of city park, it is neither as extensive nor as exciting as the other options listed in this section. Still, the tour has eight zip-line cables, with the longest being some 200m (650 ft.) long. The tour costs $20 (£10).

Another option is the **Rain Forest Aerial Tram Caribbean ★** (**© 2257-5961;** www.rainforesttram.com), built on a private reserve bordering Braulio Carrillo National Park. The tramway takes visitors on a 90-minute ride through the treetops, where they have the chance to glimpse the complex web of life that makes these forests unique. These folks also have a butterfly garden, serpentarium, and frog collection, as well as their own zip-line canopy tour. There are well-groomed trails through the rainforest and a restaurant on-site, so a trip here can easily take up a full day. The cost for a full-day tour, including both the aerial tram and canopy tour, all the park's other attractions, and transportation from San José and either breakfast or lunch, is $105 (£53). For walk-ins, the entrance fee is $55 (£28); students and anyone 17 and under pay $28 (£14). Because this is a popular tour for groups, I highly recommend that you get an advance reservation in the high season and, if possible, a ticket; otherwise you could wait a long time for your tram ride or even be shut out.

DAY CRUISES Several companies offer cruises to lovely Tortuga Island in the Gulf of Nicoya. These full-day tours generally entail an early departure for the 2½-hour chartered bus ride to Puntarenas, where you board your vessel for a 1½-hour cruise to Tortuga Island. Then you get several hours on the uninhabited island, where you can swim, lie on the beach, play volleyball, or try a canopy tour, followed by the return journey.

The original and most dependable company running these trips is **Calypso Tours ★** (**© 2256-2727;** www.calypsotours.com). The tour costs $99 (£50) per person and includes round-trip transportation from San José, a basic continental breakfast during the bus ride to the boat, all drinks on the cruise, and an excellent buffet lunch on the beach at the island. The Calypso Tours main vessel is a massive motor-powered catamaran. A second runs a separate tour to a private nature reserve at **Punta Coral ★**. The beach is much nicer at Tortuga Island, but the tour to Punta Coral is much more intimate, and the restaurant, hiking, and kayaking are all superior here.

HIKING Most of the tour agencies listed above offer 1-day guided hikes to a variety of destinations. In general, I recommend taking guided hikes to really see and learn about the local flora and fauna.

MOUNTAIN BIKING The best bicycle riding is well outside of San José—on dirt roads where you're not likely to be run off the highway by a semi, or run head-on into someone coming around a blind curve in the wrong lane. Several companies run a variety of 1-day and multiday tours out of San José. Several of these tours are entirely or primarily

Holy Smoke! Choosing the Volcano Trip That's Right for You

Poás, Irazú, and Arenal volcanoes are three of Costa Rica's most popular destinations, and the first two are easy day trips from San José (see below). Although numerous companies offer day trips to Arenal, I don't recommend them because there's at least 3½ hours of travel time in each direction. You usually arrive when the volcano is hidden by clouds and leave before the night's darkness shows off its glowing eruptions. For more information on Arenal Volcano, see p. 601.

Tour companies offering trips to Poás and Irazú include **Costa Rica Expeditions**★★ (✆ **2257-0766**), **Horizontes**★★ (✆ **2222-2022**), and **Swiss Travel Service** (✆ **2282-4898**). Prices range from $30 to $50 (£15–£25) for a half-day trip, and from $50 to $110 (£25–£55) for a full-day trip.

The 3,378m (11,080-ft.) **Irazú Volcano**★ (✆ **2551-9398**) is historically one of Costa Rica's more active volcanoes, although it's relatively quiet these days. It last erupted on March 19, 1963, the day that President John F. Kennedy arrived in Costa Rica. There's a good paved road right to the rim of the crater, where a desolate expanse of gray sand nurtures few plants and the air smells of sulfur. The landscape here is often compared to that of the moon. There are magnificent views of the fertile Meseta Central and Orosi Valley as you drive up from Cartago, and if you're very lucky, you might be able to see both the Pacific Ocean and the Caribbean Sea. Clouds usually descend by noon, so get here as early in the day as possible.

A short trail leads to the rim of the volcano's two craters, their walls a maze of eroded gullies feeding onto the flat floor far below. Dress in layers; this might be the Tropics, but it can be cold up at the top if the sun's not out. The park restaurant, at an elevation of 3,022m (9,912 ft.), with walls of windows looking out over the valley far below, claims to be the highest restaurant in Central America. Admission is $10 (£5).

If you don't want an organized tour, buses leave for Irazú Volcano daily at 8am from Avenida 2 between calles 1 and 3 (across the street from the entrance to the Gran Hotel Costa Rica). The fare is $7 (£3.50) round-trip, with

descents. **Costa Rica Biking Adventure** (✆ **2225-6591;** www.bikingincostarica.com) offers a variety of mountain-biking tours using high-end bikes and gear. A 1-day trip costs between $80 and $160 (£40–£80) per person.

A new and unique option is to take a **Railbike Tour** (✆ **8303-3300;** www.railbike.com). This tour involves a mountain bike rigged to a contraption that fits over railroad tracks. Taking advantage of some abandoned rail routes, this tour takes a scenic trip through the countryside outside of San José. The full-day tour costs $75 (£38) and includes all equipment, plus a light breakfast and full lunch.

RAFTING, KAYAKING & RIVER TRIPS Cascading down Costa Rica's mountain ranges are dozens of tumultuous rivers, several of which are very popular for white-water rafting and kayaking. If I had to choose just one day trip out of San José, it would be a the bus leaving the volcano at 12:30pm. This company is particularly fickle; to make sure that the buses are running, call © **2530-1064,** although that might not help much, since they often don't answer their phone, and speak Spanish only. If you're driving, head northeast out of Cartago toward San Rafael, and then continue driving uphill toward the volcano, passing the turnoffs for Cot and Tierra Blanca en route.

Poás Volcano ★★ (© **2482-2424**) is 37km (23 miles) from San José on narrow roads that wind through a landscape of fertile farms and dark forests. As at Irazú, there's a paved road right to the top, although you'll have to hike in about 1km (1/2 mile) to reach the crater. The volcano stands 2,640m (8,659 ft.) tall and is located within a national park, which preserves not only the volcano but also dense stands of virgin forest. Poás's crater, said to be the second largest in the world, is more than a mile across. Geysers in the crater sometimes spew steam and muddy water 180m (590 ft.) into the air, making this the largest geyser in the world. There's an information center where you can see a slide show about the volcano, and there are well-groomed and marked hiking trails through the cloud forest that rings the crater. About 15 minutes from the parking area, along a forest trail, is an overlook onto beautiful Botos Lake, which has formed in one of the volcano's extinct craters.

Be prepared when you come to Poás: This volcano is often enveloped in dense clouds. If you want to see the crater, it's best to come early and during the dry season. Moreover, it can get cool up here, especially when the sun isn't shining, so dress appropriately. Admission to the national park is $10 (£5).

In case you don't want to go on a tour, there's a daily bus (© **2442-6900** or 222-5325) from Avenida 2 between calles 12 and 14 that leaves at 8am and returns at 2pm. The fare is $5 (£2.50) round-trip. The bus is often crowded, so arrive early. If you're driving, head for Alajuela and continue on the main road through town and follow signs for Fraijanes. Just beyond Fraijanes you will connect with the road between San Pedro de Poás and Poasito; turn right toward Poasito and continue to the rim of the volcano.

white-water rafting trip. For between $75 and $110 (£38–£55), you can spend a day rafting through lush tropical forests; multiday trips are also available. Some of the most reliable rafting companies are **Aventuras Naturales ★** (© **800/514-0411** in the U.S., or 2225-3939), **Exploradores Outdoors ★** (© **2222-6262**), and **Ríos Tropicales ★** (© **2233-6455**). These companies all ply a number of rivers of varying difficulties, including the popular Pacuare and Reventazón rivers.

The Sarapiquí River is also a popular waterway for day trips out of San José. **Ecoscapes Highlights Tour** (© **2297-0664;** www.ecoscapetours.com) runs a jampacked trip here that combines a stop at the La Paz waterfall, a visit to a banana plantation, a rainforest hike, and a boat ride on the river for $83 (£42) per person, including round-trip transportation, breakfast, and lunch.

Perhaps the best-known river tours are those that go up to **Tortuguero National Park ★★**. It's possible to do this tour as a day trip out of San José, but it's a long, tiring, and expensive day. You're much better off doing it as a 1- or 2-night trip.

Cartago & the Orosi Valley

These two regions southeast of San José can easily be combined into a day trip. You might also squeeze in a visit to the Irazú Volcano (see box above, for details).

Cartago

Located 24km (15 miles) southeast of San José, **Cartago ★** is the former capital of Costa Rica. Founded in 1563, it was Costa Rica's first city—and was, in fact, its *only* city for almost 150 years. Irazú Volcano rises up from the edge of town, and although it's quiet these days, it has not always been so peaceful. Earthquakes have damaged Cartago repeatedly over the years, so today few of the old colonial buildings are left standing. In the center of the city, a public park winds through the ruins of a large church that was destroyed in 1910 before it could be finished. Construction was abandoned after the quake, and today the ruins sit at the heart of a neatly manicured park, with quiet paths and plenty of benches. The ruins themselves are closed off, but the park itself is lovely.

Cartago's most famous building is the **Basílica de Nuestra Señora de los Angeles (Basilica of Our Lady of the Angels) ★**, which is dedicated to the patron saint of Costa Rica and stands on the east side of town. Within the walls of this Byzantine-style church is a shrine containing the tiny carved figure of **La Negrita,** the Black Virgin, which is nearly lost amid its ornate altar. Legend has it that La Negrita first revealed herself on this site to a peasant girl in 1635. Miraculous healing powers have been attributed to La Negrita, and, over the years, a parade of pilgrims have come to the shrine seeking cures for their illnesses and difficulties. August 2 is her patron saint's day. Each year, on this date, tens of thousands of Costa Ricans and foreign pilgrims walk to Cartago from San José and elsewhere in the country in devotion to this powerful statue. The walls of the shrine are covered with a fascinating array of tiny silver images left as thanks for cures affected by La Negrita. Amid the plethora of diminutive silver arms and legs, there are also hands, feet, hearts, lungs, kidneys, eyes, torsos, breasts, and—peculiarly—guns, trucks, beds, and planes. There are even dozens of sports trophies that I assume were left as thanks for helping teams win big games. Outside the church, vendors sell a wide selection of these trinkets, as well as little candle replicas of La Negrita.

More than 1km (1/2 mile) east of Cartago, on the road to Paraíso, you'll find **Lankester Gardens ★** (**© 2552-3247**), a beautiful botanical garden known for its orchid collection.

GETTING THERE **Lumaca** buses (**© 2537-0347**) for Cartago leave San José every 3 to 5 minutes between 5am and 9pm, with slightly less frequent service until midnight, from Calle 3 and Avenida 2. You can also pick up one en route at any of the little covered bus stops along Avenida Central in Los Yoses and San Pedro. The length of the trip is 45 minutes; the fare is about 60¢ (30p).

Orosi Valley

The Orosi Valley, southeast of Cartago and visible from the top of Irazú on a clear day, is generally considered one of the most beautiful valleys in Costa Rica. The Reventazón River meanders through this steep-sided valley until it collects in the lake formed by the Cachí Dam. There are scenic overlooks near the town of Orosi, which is at the head of the valley, and in Ujarrás, which is on the banks of the lake. Near **Ujarrás** are the ruins of Costa Rica's oldest church (built in 1693), whose tranquil gardens are a great place to sit and gaze at the surrounding mountains. In the town of Orosi itself, there is yet another colonial church and convent, built in 1743. A small museum here displays religious artifacts. Near the town of Cachí, you'll find **La Casa del Soñador** (**© 2577-1983**), the home and gallery of the late sculptor Macedonio Quesada and his sons, who carry on the family tradition.

From the Orosi Valley, it's a quick shot to the entrance to the **Tapantí National Park ★** (**© 2552-4823**), where you'll find some gentle and beautiful hiking trails, as well as riverside picnic areas. The park is open daily from 8am to 4pm; admission is $10 (£5).

If you're interested in staying out here, check out the charming little **Orosi Lodge** (**© 2533-3578;** www.orosilodge.com), which is right next to some simple hot spring pools.

GETTING THERE If you're driving, take the road to Paraíso from Cartago, head toward Ujarrás, continue around the lake, and then pass through Cachí and on to Orosi. From Orosi, the road leads back to Paraíso. It is difficult to explore this whole area by public bus because this is not a densely populated region and connections are often infrequent or unreliable. However, there are regular buses from Cartago to the town of Orosi. These buses run roughly every half-hour and leave the main bus terminal in Cartago. The trip takes 30 minutes, and the fare is 60¢ (30p).

Heredia & Sarchi

Located northwest of San José, you can combine visits to Heredia and Sarchi into a long day trip (if you have a car), perhaps in conjunction with a visit to Poás Volcano and/or the Waterfall Gardens. The scenery here is rich and verdant, and the small towns and scattered farming communities are truly representative of Costa Rica's agricultural heartland and *campesino* tradition. This is a great area to explore on your own in a rental car, if you don't mind getting lost a bit (roads are narrow, winding, and poorly marked). If you're relying on buses, you'll be able to visit any of the towns listed below, but probably just one or two per day.

The road to Heredia turns north off the highway from San José to the airport. If you're going to Sarchí, take the highway west toward Puntarenas. Turn north to Grecia and then west to Sarchí. There'll be plenty of signs.

Heredia

Set on the flanks of the impressive Barva Volcano, this city was founded in 1706. Heredia is affectionately known as "the City of Flowers." A colonial church inaugurated in 1763 stands in the central park. The stone facade leaves no questions as to the age of the church, but the altar inside is decorated with neon stars and a crescent moon surrounding a statue of the Virgin Mary. In the middle of the palm-shaded park is a music temple, and across the street, beside several tile-roofed municipal buildings, is the tower of an old Spanish fort. Of all the cities in the Meseta Central, Heredia has the most colonial feel to it. Heredia is also the site of the **National Autonomous University,** so you'll find some nice coffee shops and bookstores near the school.

Surrounding Heredia is an intricate maze of picturesque villages and towns, including Santa Bárbara, Santo Domingo, Barva, and San Joaquín de Flores. San Isidro de Heredia has a lovely, large church with an ornate facade. However, the biggest attraction up here is the **INBio Park ★★** (**© 2507-8107;** p. 557). Located on 5 hectares (12 acres) in Santo Domingo de Heredia, this place is part museum, part educational center, and part nature park. This is also where you'll find the **Café Britt Farm ★** (**© 2277-1600;** p. 556). Anyone with an interest in medicinal herbs should plan a visit to the **Ark Herb Farm** (**© 8846-2694** or 2269-4847; www.arkherbfarm.com). These folks offer guided tours of their gardens, which feature more than 300 types of medicinal plants. The tour costs $12 (£6) per person, and includes a light snack and refreshments. Reservations are required.

If you make your way to San Pedro de Barva de Heredia, stop in at **La Lluna de Valencia ★★** (✆ **2269-6665**), a delightful rustic Spanish restaurant with amazing paella, delicious sangria, and a very amiable host.

GETTING THERE Buses leave for Heredia every 5 minutes between 5am and 11pm from Calle 1 between avenidas 7 and 9, or from Avenida 2 between calles 12 and 14. Bus fare is 45¢ (25p).

Sarchí ★

Sarchí is Costa Rica's main artisan town. The colorfully painted miniature **oxcarts** that you see all over the country are made here. Oxcarts such as these were once used to haul coffee beans to market. Today, although you might occasionally see oxcarts in use, most are purely decorative. However, they remain a well-known symbol of Costa Rica. In addition to miniature oxcarts, many carved wooden souvenirs are made here with rare hardwoods from the nation's forests. There are dozens of shops in town, and all have similar prices. Perhaps your best one-stop shop in Sarchí is the large and long-standing **Chaverri Oxcart Factory ★** (✆ **2454-4411**), which is right in the center of things, but it never hurts to shop around and visit several of the stores.

Aside from handicrafts, there are other reasons to visit Sarchí. Built between 1950 and 1958, the town's main **church ★** is painted pink with aquamarine trim and looks strangely like a child's birthday cake.

My favorite attraction in Sarchí is the **Else Kientzler Botanical Garden ★★** (✆ **2454-2070**) which features an extensive collection of several thousand types of plants, flowers, and trees.

While there are no noteworthy accommodations in Sarchí itself, the plush **El Silencio Lodge & Spa ★** (✆ **2291-3044;** www.elsilenciolodge.com) is located about a 35-minute drive away in a beautiful mountain setting.

GETTING THERE **Tuan** (✆ **2258-2004**) buses leave San José about five times throughout the day for Sarchí from Calle 18 between avenidas 5 and 7. The fare is $1.20 (60p). Alternatively, you can take any Grecia bus from this same station. In Grecia they connect with the Alajuela-Sarchí buses, leaving every 30 minutes from Calle 8 between avenidas Central and 1 in Alajuela.

5 GUANACASTE & THE NICOYA PENINSULA ★★

Liberia: 217km (135 miles) NW of San José, 132km (82 miles) NW of Puntarenas; Playa Hermosa/Papagayo: 258km (160 miles) NW of San José, 40km (25 miles) SW of Liberia; Playa del Coco: 253km (157 miles) NW of San José, 35km (22 miles) W of Liberia; Tamarindo: 295km (183 miles) NW of San José, 73km (45 miles) SW of Liberia

With a long, beautiful and varied shoreline, **Guanacaste** well deserves its designation as Costa Rica's "Gold Coast." Occupying the northwest corner of the country, Guanacaste is the driest and most consistently sunny region in Costa Rica. Not surprisingly, it is home to many of the country's most popular beaches and resorts.

Guanacaste province is named after the tall and broad shady trees that still shelter the herds of cattle that roam the dusty inland savanna here. In addition to the beaches,

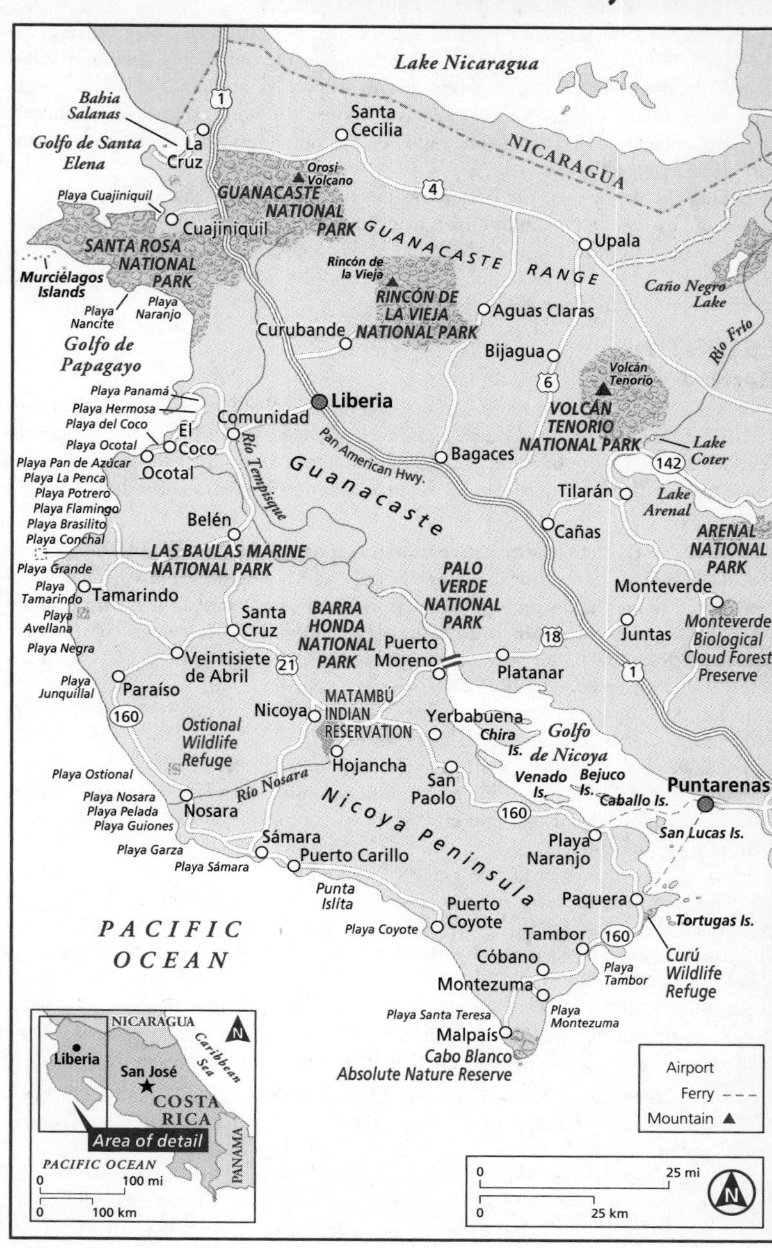
Lake Nicaragua
NICARAGUA
Bahia Salanas
Golfo de Santa Elena
La Cruz
Santa Cecilia
Orosi Volcano
GUANACASTE NATIONAL PARK
GUANACASTE RANGE
Playa Cuajiniquil
Cuajiniquil
SANTA ROSA NATIONAL PARK
Murciélagos Islands
Playa Nancite
Playa Naranjo
Rincón de la Vieja
RINCÓN DE LA VIEJA NATIONAL PARK
Upala
Caño Negro Lake
Río Frío
Aguas Claras
Bijagua
Volcán Tenorio
VOLCÁN TENORIO NATIONAL PARK
Golfo de Papagayo
Curubande
Liberia
Playa Panamá
Playa Hermosa
Playa del Coco
Playa Ocotal
El Coco
Comunidad
Playa Pan de Azúcar
Playa La Penca
Playa Potrero
Playa Flamingo
Playa Brasilito
Playa Conchal
Ocotal
Río Tempisque
Pan American Hwy.
Guanacaste
Bagaces
Lake Coter
Tilarán
Lake Arenal
ARENAL NATIONAL PARK
Cañas
Belén
LAS BAULAS MARINE NATIONAL PARK
Playa Grande
Playa Tamarindo
Tamarindo
Playa Avellana
Playa Negra
PALO VERDE NATIONAL PARK
Monteverde
Monteverde Biological Cloud Forest Preserve
Juntas
Santa Cruz
BARRA HONDA NATIONAL PARK
Puerto Moreno
Platanar
Veintisiete de Abril
Playa Junquillal
Paraíso
Nicoya
MATAMBÚ INDIAN RESERVATION
Yerbabuena
Chira Is.
Golfo de Nicoya
Ostional Wildlife Refuge
Hojancha
Playa Ostional
Río Nosara
San Paolo
Venado Is.
Bejuco Is.
Caballo Is.
Puntarenas
Playa Nosara
Playa Pelada
Playa Guiones
Nosara
Nicoya Peninsula
San Lucas Is.
Playa Garza
Playa Sámara
Sámara
Puerto Carillo
Playa Naranjo
Punta Islíta
Paquera
Tortugas Is.
PACIFIC OCEAN
Playa Coyote
Puerto Coyote
Tambor
Cóbano
Playa Tambor
Curú Wildlife Refuge
Montezuma
Playa Santa Teresa
Playa Montezuma
Malpaís
Cabo Blanco Absolute Nature Reserve
Airport
Ferry
Mountain
0 25 mi
0 25 km
N
NICARAGUA
Caribbean Sea
Liberia
San José
COSTA RICA
PANAMA
Area of detail
PACIFIC OCEAN
0 100 mi
0 100 km
1
4
6
142
18
21
160
1

resorts, and cattle ranches, Guanacaste has several active volcanoes and one of the last remnants of tropical dry forest left in Central America.

The beaches and resorts of the southern **Nicoya peninsula** are more isolated, less developed, and just a bit wilder than those found to the north on Guanacaste's Gold Coast. The two main beach destinations in this area are Montezuma and Malpaís. Both offer miles of uncrowded beaches and lush forests all around. Montezuma features a couple of gorgeous waterfalls to visit, while Malpaís is becoming one of the country's top surf destinations.

During the dry season, the hillsides in Guanacaste and the Nicoya Peninsula turn brown and barren. Dust from dirt roads blankets the trees in many areas, and the scenery seems far from tropical. On the other hand, if you happen to visit this area in the rainy season, the hillsides are a beautiful, rich green, and the sun usually shines all morning, giving way to an afternoon shower—just in time for a nice siesta.

ESSENTIALS

Getting There

Whether you fly directly to Liberia, or take a commuter flight from San José, the fastest and easiest way to get to Guanacaste and the Nicoya Peninsula is by air. If you want the freedom and flexibility of a car, you can always rent one in Guanacaste. However, if you're touring the country by car, or want to save money, you can also drive or take a bus.

BY AIR The **Daniel Oduber International Airport (LIR; © 2668-1010)** in Liberia is a small, modern international airport that receives a steady stream of scheduled commercial and charter flights throughout the year. Major commercial airlines with regularly scheduled service include: **American Airlines** (**© 800/433-7300;** www.aa.com); **Continental** (**© 800/231-0856;** www.continental.com); **Delta** (**800/241-4141;** www.delta.com); and **US Airways** (**© 800/622-1015;** www.usairways.com)

In addition, numerous commercial charter flights arrive from various North American and European cities throughout the high season.

There are small commuter airstrips in Tamarindo, Nosara, Punta Islita, and Tambor. If you're going to Tamarindo or Playa Grande, and coming from San José, flying into and out of Tamarindo is your best option. If you're going to Montezuma or Malpaís, you'll want to fly into Tambor.

Most of the beaches in Guanacaste are between a 25- and 55-minute drive from the Liberia airport. If you're going to Playa Hermosa, Playa Ocotal, or the Papagayo Peninsula, you're best off flying into Liberia. Playa Flamingo, Playa Brasilito, Playa Conchal, and Sugar Beach are slightly closer to Tamarindo, but the differences are almost negligible.

Sansa (**© 877/767-2672** in the U.S. and Canada, or 2290-4100 in Costa Rica; www.flysansa.com) and **Nature Air** (**© 800/235-9272** in the U.S. and Canada, or 2299-6000; www.natureair.com) have regular daily flights to all the airstrips in this area.

BY BUS **Gray Line** (**© 2220-2126;** www.graylinecostarica.com) and **Interbus** (**© 2283-5573;** www.interbusonline.com) both have daily shuttle service to all the beaches mentioned in this chapter. Fares run between $34 and $40 (£17–£20).

You can also take inexpensive Costa Rican bus lines to many Guanacaste beaches. Tickets cost between $4.50 and $8 (£2.25–£4), and the trips take between 5 and 6 hours. You can buy tickets on the bus or just prior to departing at the station. In most cases, getting a confirmed ticket in advance is very hard and usually unnecessary.

The following is a listing of the schedules, terminal locations, and contact information of the major bus companies servicing the major beach destinations of Guanacaste.

- **Playa del Coco: Pulmitan** buses (✆ **2222-1650**) leave San José for Playa del Coco at 8am and 2 and 4pm daily from Calle 24 between avenidas 5 and 7.
- **Playa Hermosa and Playa Panamá:** A **Tralapa** express bus (✆ **2221-7202**) leaves San José daily at 3pm from Calle 20 and Avenida 3, stopping first at Playa Hermosa and then at Playa Panamá.
- **Playa Brasilito, Playa Flamingo, and Playa Potrero: Tralapa** express buses (✆ **2221-7202** in San José, or 2654-4203 in Flamingo) leave San José daily at 8 and 10:30am and 3pm from Calle 20 between avenidas 3 and 5, stopping at playas Brasilito, Flamingo, and Potrero, in that order.
- **Tamarindo: Tracopa-Alfaro** express buses (✆ **2222-2160**) leave San José daily for Tamarindo at 8:30 and 11:30am and 3:30pm, departing from Calle 14 between avenidas 3 and 5. **Tralapa** (✆ **2221-7202**) also has one daily direct bus to Tamarindo leaving at 4pm from their main terminal at Calle 20 between avenidas 3 and 5.
- **Montezuma: Transportes Rodríguez Hermanos** (✆ **2642-0219**) runs three daily direct buses between San José and Montezuma. The buses leave from the Coca-Cola bus terminal at Calle 12 and Avenida 5 at 7:30 and 11:30am and 3:30pm.

BY CAR Driving to Guanacaste from San José is a relatively easy and straight shot, with only two major routes.

If you're going to any of the more northern beaches, take the Pan-American Highway (Carretera Panamericana) west from San José, and follow the signs for Nicaragua and the Guanacaste beaches. Turn left at the major crossroads at the entrance to Liberia. This intersection is very well marked, and will point you toward Santa Cruz and the various Guanacaste beaches. The turnoffs for all the subsequent beaches are also well marked. Driving to Liberia from San José takes approximately 3½ to 4 hours. From Liberia, it's another 25 to 55 minutes to most of the beaches in this area.

If you're going to Tamarindo, Playa Conchal, or Playa Brasilito, the most direct route is by way of the La Amistad bridge over the Tempisque River. Take the Pan-American Highway west from San José. Forty-seven kilometers (29 miles) past the turnoff for Puntarenas, you'll see signs for the turnoff to the bridge. After crossing the river, follow the signs for Nicoya and Santa Cruz. Continue north out of Santa Cruz until just before the village of Belén, where you'll find the well-marked turnoff for the various beach towns. In another 20km (12 miles), you'll hit the village of Huacas. Take the left fork for Playa Tamarindo, and head straight for the road to Playa Flamingo, Playa Brasilito, Playa Conchal, and Sugar Beach.

To drive to Montezuma and Malpaís, take the Pan-American Highway from San José to Puntarenas and catch the ferry to Paquera. Ferries to Paquera leave Puntarenas roughly every 2 to 3 hours between 5am and 8:30pm. The trip takes 1½ hours, and the fare is around \$9 to \$12 (£4.50–£6) per car; \$1 to \$2 (50p–£1) per adult, and 70¢ to \$1 (35p–50p) for children. From Paquera it's about another 45 minutes to Montezuma, and an hour to Malpaís.

Orientation

The Guanacaste and the Nicoya Peninsula occupy the bulk of Costa Rica's northwestern landmass, from the Nicaraguan border down to the Gulf of Nicoya. For tourists, most of the region's appeal lies with its miles and miles of beautiful beaches. The capital of Guanacaste is the city of Liberia, where you'll find the Daniel Oduber International

Airport. The city itself holds little appeal for most tourists. In fact, although much of the landmass here is inland, the only major non-coastal attraction is the Rincón de la Vieja volcano and the surrounding Rincón de la Vieja National Park.

Getting Around

The best way to get around Guanacaste is by taxi or rental car, or as part of an organized tour. For information on the many available tour options, ask at your hotel, or see below.

BY TAXI Taxis are available at the airport and in all the major beach towns. Any hotel in the area can call you a taxi. Rates range from $3 to $6 (£1.50–£3) for short rides, to $20 to $45 (£10–£23) for longer jaunts between more-distant towns and destinations.

BY CAR If you're looking to rent a car after arriving in the region, **Adobe** (✆ 2667-0608), **Alamo** (✆ 2668-1111), **Avis** (✆ 2668-1138), **Budget** (✆ 2668-1118), **Dollar** (✆ 2668-1061), **Economy** (✆ 2666-2816), **Hertz** (✆ 2668-1048), **Payless** (✆ 2667-0511), **Sol** (✆ 2666-2222), **Thrifty** (✆ 2665-0787), and **Toyota** (✆ 2668-1212) all have local offices at the Liberia airport, and in some cases in various destination beaches.

BY BUS Public buses are not a practical means for most tourists to get around Guanacaste. Although regular local buses connect most of the major beach towns and destinations with Liberia, you'll find virtually no connections among the different beach towns and destinations.

Visitor Information

A small information kiosk will greet you at the Liberia airport, but invariably your best bet for information will be your hotel front desk, concierge, or tour desk. Tour desks are available at almost every hotel in the region, as well as tour offices in most major beach towns.

FAST FACTS If you need to contact the **police,** dial ✆ **911,** and for an **ambulance** dial ✆ **128.** The Liberia Hospital (✆ **2666-0011**) is the best hospital in the area. A smaller hospital lies in the city of Santa Cruz. Most of the beach towns have some sort of health clinic. If you're in Montezuma or Malpaís, the closest major hospital is the Monseñor Sanabria Hospital in Puntarenas (✆ **2663-0033**), although there are several doctors and a local clinic (✆ **2642-0208**) in Cóbano.

Banks and ATMs are in Playa del Coco, Playa Hermosa, Playa Flamingo, Tamarindo, and Malpaís. In Montezuma you'll have to head 1.6km (1 mile) or so up the hill to Cóbano. You'll find easy access to the Web and plenty of Internet cafes in all of the major beach towns and destinations of this region.

INTRODUCING THE BEACHES & ATTRACTIONS

The beaches of Guanacaste and the Nicoya Peninsula come in various shapes and sizes. Some are protected and calm, while others feature strong surf. Some are quite developed, while others are home to just a few hotels and small resorts.

Here's a quick rundown of the principal beach destinations, running (more or less) from north to south.

PAPAGAYO PENINSULA The turnoff for this long narrow peninsula is the first you'll hit heading west from the Liberia airport. The peninsula features several stunning and often deserted beaches, including **Playa Nacascolo,** which is inside the property of the Four Seasons Resort—but all beaches in Costa Rica are public, so you cannot be denied entry. Almost all the beaches here are very well protected, with little or no wave action.

PLAYA HERMOSA & PLAYA PANAMA Surrounded by steep forested hills, **Playa Hermosa** is a curving gray-sand beach that is long and wide and rarely crowded. It's also relatively protected and is consistently one of the region's calmest beaches for swimming. Fringing the beach is a swath of trees that stays surprisingly green right through the dry season. The shade provided by these trees, along with the calm protected waters, is a big part of the beach's appeal.

Beyond Playa Hermosa, you'll find the still underdeveloped **Playa Panamá** and, farther on, the calm waters of **Bahía Culebra,** a large protected bay dotted with small, semiprivate patches of beach and ringed with mostly intact dry forest. After years of neglect and abuse, Playa Panamá has been cleaned up and cars and camping have been severely restricted, making this a beautiful beach once again.

PLAYA DEL COCO & PLAYA OCOTAL **Playa del Coco** was one of the first beaches in Guanacaste to be developed, and it has long been a popular destination with middle-class Ticos and weekend revelers from San José. It's also a prime scuba-diving spot. The beach, which has grayish-brown sand, is quite wide at low tide and almost nonexistent at high tide. In between high and low tides, it's just right.

Playa Ocotal is a tiny pocket cove featuring a small salt-and-pepper beach bordered by high bluffs. It's quite beautiful. When the water is calm, you'll find good snorkeling around some rocky islands close to shore. You'll see a fair amount of residential development here, as well as a couple of small hotels and resorts.

PLAYAS CONCHAL, BRASILITO & FLAMINGO Playa Conchal is the first in a string of beaches stretching north along this coast. For decades this was the semiprivate haunt of a few beach cognoscenti. The unique beach here is made up primarily of soft crushed shells *(conchas).* Nearly every place you could walk, turn, or lay down your towel used to be shell-collectors' heaven. Unfortunately, as Conchal has developed and its popularity spread, unscrupulous builders have brought in dump trucks to haul away the namesake seashells for landscaping and construction, and the impact is noticeable.

Just beyond Playa Conchal to the north, you'll come to **Playa Brasilito,** a tiny beach town and one of the few real villages in the area. The soccer field is in the center of the village, and around its edges you'll find a couple of little *pulperías* (general stores). Playa Brasilito is popular both with Ticos and budget travelers from abroad. **Playa Flamingo** is located on a long spit of land that forms part of Potrero Bay. The beach here is a beautiful stretch of white sand. For my money, Playa Flamingo has perhaps the prettiest stretch of sand up here, and the town is starting to boom again, after years laying seemingly dormant.

If you continue along the road from Brasilito without taking the turn for Playa Flamingo, you'll soon come to **Playa Potrero.** The sand here is a hard-packed brownish gray, but the beach is long, deserted, and quite calm for swimming. You can see the hotels of Playa Flamingo across the bay. Drive a little farther north, and you'll find the still undeveloped **Playa La Penca** and, finally, **Playa Pan de Azúcar,** a beautiful little salt-and-pepper beach with one lone small resort hotel backing it, Hotel Sugar Beach.

PLAYA GRANDE & TAMARINDO **Playa Grande** is a long, isolated, and sparsely developed stretch of beach with strong surf. It's very popular with surfers, which can make the beach unsuitable for swimming at times. Playa Grande is one of the principal nesting sites for the giant leatherback turtle, the largest turtle in the world. I almost hate to mention places to stay in Playa Grande because the steady influx of tourists and development could doom this beach as a turtle-nesting site.

Tamarindo is a bustling boomtown and one of the most popular beaches on the Gold Coast. Tamarindo boasts a mixture of hotels in a variety of sizes and price ranges and an eclectic array of restaurants, as well as several seemingly out-of-place modern strip malls.

Ongoing development continues to spread up the hills inland from the beach and south beyond to **Playa Langosta.** The beach itself is a long, wide swath of white sand that curves gently from one rocky headland to another. Behind the beach are low, dry hills that can be a dreary brown in the dry season but that instantly turn green with the first brief showers of the rainy season. Fishing boats bob at their moorings at the south end of the beach, and brown pelicans fish just outside the breakers.

PLAYA MONTEZUMA & MALPAÍS **Montezuma ★★** enjoys near-legendary status among backpackers, UFO seekers, hippie expatriates, and European budget travelers. Although it still maintains its alternative vibe, Montezuma is steadily maturing, and has grown to become a great destination for all manner of travelers looking for a quiet beach retreat surrounded by some stunning scenery. After all, the natural beauty, miles of almost abandoned beaches, rich wildlife, and jungle waterfalls first made Montezuma famous, and they continue to make this one of my favorite beach towns in Costa Rica.

Malpaís translates as "badlands," and while that moniker may have fit at one time, it's no longer very appropriate. The beach here is a long, wide expanse of light sand dotted with rocky outcroppings. Sure, it can get rough, but the surfers love it. The road out here from Cóbano used to be even rougher than the surf, but it's gradually being tamed. This place is one of Costa Rica's most rapidly developing hot spots, and hotels and restaurants are opening up at a steady pace. Still, it will take some time before this area becomes overly crowded. Although Malpaís is frequently used to name all the beaches in the area, the popular Playa Carmen and Santa Teresa are the real names of the two budding beaches just to the north.

WHAT TO SEE & DO

Nearly all the hotels and resorts in Guanacaste have a tour desk or can help you arrange a variety of popular day tours and activities. Prices range from $35 to $120 (£18–£60) per person, depending on the length of the tour and the activity or activities involved.

Exploring the Region

RINCÓN DE LA VIEJA NATIONAL PARK ★★ This national park begins on the flanks of the **Rincón de la Vieja volcano** and includes the volcano's active crater. Fumaroles, geysers, and hot pools can all be observed here. In addition to hot springs and mud pots, you can explore waterfalls, a lake, and volcanic craters. The bird-watching is excellent, and the views across the pasturelands to the Pacific Ocean are stunning.

Several excellent trails run inside the Rincón de la Vieja National Park. More-energetic hikers can tackle the 8km (5 miles) up to **the summit** and explore the several craters and beautiful lakes up here. On a clear day, you'll be rewarded with a fabulous view of the plains of Guanacaste and the Pacific Ocean below. The easiest hiking is the gentle **Las Pailas loop.** This 3km (1.75-mile) trail is just off the Las Espuelas Park entrance and passes by several bubbling mud pots and steaming fumaroles. This trail crosses a river, so you'll have to either take off your shoes or get them wet. The whole loop takes around 2 hours.

My favorite hike here is to the **Blue Lake** and **La Cangrejo waterfall.** This 5km (3-mile) trail passes through several different life zones, including dry forest, transitional moist forest, and open savanna. A variety of birds and mammals are commonly sighted.

Pack a lunch; at the end of your 2-hour hike in, you can picnic at the aptly named Blue Lake, where a 30m (98-ft.) waterfall empties into the small pond with crystal-blue hues that are amazing.

CABO BLANCO ABSOLUTE NATURE RESERVE As beautiful as the beaches around Montezuma are, the beaches at **Cabo Blanco Absolute Nature Reserve ★★**, 11km (6¾ miles) south of the village, are even more stunning. Located at the southernmost tip of the Nicoya Peninsula, Cabo Blanco is a national park that preserves a nesting site for brown pelicans, magnificent frigate birds, and brown boobies. The beaches are backed by lush tropical forest that is home to howler monkeys. You can hike through the preserve's lush forest right down to the deserted, pristine beach, which is 4km (2½ miles) away. Or you can take a shorter 2km (1¼-mile) loop trail through the primary forest here. This is Costa Rica's oldest official bioreserve and was set up thanks to the pioneering efforts of conservationists Karen Mogensen and Nicholas Wessberg. Admission is $10 (£5); the reserve is closed on Monday and Tuesday.

Shuttle buses head from Montezuma to Cabo Blanco roughly every 2 hours beginning at 8am, and then turn around and bring folks from Cabo Blanco to Montezuma; the last one leaves Cabo Blanco around 5pm. The fare is $2 (£1) each way. These shuttles often don't run during the off season. Alternatively, you can share a taxi: The fare is around $15 to $20 (£7.50–£10) per taxi, which can hold four or five passengers.

Outdoor & Wellness Activities

There's a host of adventure, sport, and outdoor activities to keep you busy here, from surfing and sailing, to horseback riding and hiking. There are several golf courses in the area, as well as various zip-line canopy tours. Again, your hotel tour desk and local tour agencies will be your best bet for seeing what's available near you.

CANOPY TOURS If you want to try one of the zip-line canopy tours, your best option in this area is the **Canyon Tour** operation at **Hacienda Guachipelin** (see below). This tour has a little bit of everything, with treetop platforms as well as cables crisscrossing a deep mountain canyon, some suspended bridges, a couple of pendulum swings, and two rappels.

However, if you don't want to head that far afield, there are a couple of other options near some of the beach towns mentioned above: **Cartagena Canopy Tour** (**© 2675-0801**) just outside of Tamarindo; **Witch's Rock Canopy Tour** (**© 2667-0661**) out on the Papagayo peninsula; and **Waterfall Canopy Tour ★** (**© 8823-6111** or 2642-0808), over and beside the main waterfall in Montezuma.

FISHING The waters off Guanacaste's coast are teaming with fish and world-class sportfishing opportunities. Anglers can land marlin and sailfish, as well as tuna, dorado, roosterfish, and more.

A half-day of fishing, with boat, captain, food, and tackle, should cost between $200 and $600 (£100–£300) for two to four passengers; a full day should run between $400 and $1,600 (£200–£800). The wide range in prices reflects a wide range in the size of the boats, equipment, and distance traveled.

Although fishing is good all year, the peak season for billfish is between mid-April and August.

A host of boats and captains dot the Guanacaste coast. Some of the better operators include: **Capullo Sportfishing** (**© 2653-0048;** www.capullo.com) in Tamarindo; **Oso Viejo** (**© 8827-5533;** www.flamingobeachcr.com) in Playa Flamingo; and **Tranquilamar** (**©**/fax **2670-0400** or 8814-0994; www.tranquilamar.com) in Playa del Coco.

GOLFING Golf is just beginning to take off in Costa Rica, but you'll find some of the country's best courses in Guanacaste.

The **Paradisus Playa Conchal ★★** (✆ **2654-4123**) is home to an excellent golf course featuring a few wonderful views of the ocean. This Robert Trent Jones–designed resort course is open to the walk-in public from neighboring hotels and resorts. It costs $180 (£90) in greens fees for as many rounds as you can squeeze into 1 day, including a cart. If you tee off after 1pm, it's $120 (£60).

South of Tamarindo, **Hacienda Pinilla ★★** (✆ **2680-7000;** www.haciendapinilla.com) is a beautiful 18-hole links-style course. The course is currently accepting golfers staying at hotels around the area, with advance reservations. Greens fees run around $165 (£83) for 18 holes, including a cart.

Located about (10km) outside Playa del Coco, the new **Papagayo golf & Country Club** (✆ **2697-1313;** www.papagayo-golf.com) offers a full 18-hole course, with a pro shop, driving range, and rental equipment. It costs $80 (£40) in greens fees, including a cart.

Finally, the most impressive course in the country is the Arnold Palmer–designed course at the **Four Seasons Resort ★★★** (✆ **800/819-5053** in the U.S., or 2696-0000 in Costa Rica; www.fourseasons.com). This stunning course features ocean views from 15 of its 18 holes. However, the course is only open to hotel guests.

HORSEBACK RIDING In addition to a trot down one of the beaches in the area, there's plenty of stunning scenery in the hillsides, forests, and farmlands around Guanacaste, making for a pleasant horseback ride.

Be careful; many of the folks offering horseback riding in this area, especially those plying the beaches themselves, are using poorly trained and poorly kept animals. Be sure you feel comfortable with the condition and training of your mount.

If your hotel tour desk can't arrange this for you, the following companies are all reputable, with good horses: **Casagua Horses** (✆ **2653-8041**); **Brasilito Excursions** (✆ **2654-4237**); **Flamingo Equestrian Center** (✆ **2654-4089**); **Finca Los Caballos** (✆ **2642-0124;** www.naturelodge.net).

SAILING The winds off Costa Rica's Pacific coast are somewhat fickle and can often be slight to nonexistent. However, from December through March, they can be quite strong, with impressive gusts. Still, plenty of sailing options abound if you want to head to sea here.

A host of different boats take out day charters ranging from a few hours to a full day. Many include some food and drinks, as well as a break or two for some swimming or snorkeling. Some will take you to a deserted beach, and others let you throw a line overboard for fishing.

Rates run around $35 to $50 (£18–£25) per person for a few hours or a sunset cruise, and $60 to $120 (£30–£60) per person for longer outings.

If your hotel can't line up a sail for you, here are a few good boats to check out: ***Blue Dolphin*** (✆ **2653-0446;** www.sailbluedolphin.com), a 12m (40-ft.) catamaran based in Tamarindo; ***Samonique III*** (✆ **8388-7870;** www.costarica-sailing.com), a 16m (52-ft.) ketch sailing out of Playa Flamingo; and ***Don Bosco*** (✆ **2670-0181**), a 20m (65-ft.) ketch also based in Playa Flamingo.

SCUBA DIVING Some of Costa Rica's best diving can be had around the offshore islands and underwater rock formations of Guanacaste. Most hotel and tour desks can arrange a dive trip for you. Many also offer certification courses or shorter resort courses, the latter of which will get you some basic instruction and a controlled dive in the shortest amount of time.

One-Stop Adventure Shop

Hacienda Guachipelin (✆ **2666-8075;** www.guachipelin.com) offers a range of adventure tour options, including horseback riding, hiking, white-water river inner-tubing, a waterfall canyoning and rappel tour, and a more traditional zip-line canopy tour. The most popular is the hacienda's **1-Day Adventure pass** ★★, which allows you to choose as many of the hotel's different tour options as you want and fit them into one adventure-packed day. The price for this is $80 (£40), including lunch.

Almost all of the beach hotels and resorts of Guanacaste offer day trips here, or you can book directly with the lodge, including transportation. ***Be forewarned:*** There's a bit of a cattle-car feel to the whole operation, with busloads of day-trippers coming in from the beach. Also, I have found the inner-tube adventure to be extremely dangerous and somewhat carelessly run, especially during or just after the rainy season.

While here, you can take advantage of the hot spring pools, and hot mud pools at the hacienda's **Simbiosis Spa** (✆ **2666-8075;** www.simbiosis-spa.com). A $15 (£7.50) entrance fee gets you a stint in a sauna, self-application of the hot volcanic mud, and free run of the pools. ***Be forewarned:*** The pools are better described as warm, not hot, mud pools, and mud is the operative word here. A wide range of massages, mud wraps, facials, and other treatments are available at very reasonable prices.

A two-tank dive should run between $70 and $130 (£35–£65) per person, depending primarily on the distance traveled to the dive sites.

If you don't set up your dive trip through your hotel, several very reputable dive operations are in the area. The best of these are: **Diving Safaris de Costa Rica** ★ (✆ **2672-1259;** www.costaricadiving.net), in Playa Hermosa; **Rich Coast Diving** (✆ **800/434-8464** in the U.S. and Canada, or 2670-0176 in Costa Rica; www.richcoastdiving.com), in Playa del Coco; and **Resort Divers** (✆ **2672-0106;** www.resortdivers-cr.com), which has set up shop at several of the hotels in this area.

SURFING The Guanacaste coast is home to some of Costa Rica's best and most consistent surf breaks. Whether you're already a pro or you're looking to get your feet wet, you'll find beaches and breaks that are just right for you.

For beginners, Tamarindo and Malpaís are your best bets, with consistent shore breaks, and numerous surf shops renting boards and giving lessons.

More-experienced surfers will want to explore the coast more, looking for lesser known and more remote breaks. While not secrets, these include Playa Grande, Play Negra, and Playa Avellanas. For a more remote spot, try booking a boat out of Playas del Coco to take you to Witch's Rock or Ollies Point, inside the Santa Rosa National Park.

WHERE TO STAY IN GUANACASTE & THE NICOYA PENINSULA

Very Expensive

In addition to the places below, you might consider **Ylang Ylang Beach Resort** ★★ (✆ **2642-0636;** www.ylangylangresort.com) in Montezuma; **Hotel & Villas Cala**

 Luna ★★ (✆ **800/503-5202** in the U.S. and Canada; www.calaluna.com) in Playa Langosta; or the **Hilton Papagayo Resort** ★★ (✆ **800/445-8667** in the U.S. and Canada; www.hilton.com) in Playa Panamá.

Flor Blanca Resort ★★★ Finds This lush and plush hotel is hands down the most luxurious option on the Nicoya Peninsula and one of the top boutique hotels in the country. The individual villas are huge, with a vast central living area opening onto a spacious veranda. The furnishings, decorations, and architecture boast a mix of Latin American and Asian influences. Most overlook lush gardens, and about half have views through to the sea. Every unit features a large open-air bathroom with a garden shower and teardrop-shape tub set amid flowering tropical foliage. There's a modern, full-service spa, and complimentary yoga, kickboxing, and cardio workout classes are regularly offered. The beautiful free-form pool is on two levels, with a sculpted waterfall connecting them and a shady Indonesian-style gazebo off to one side for lounging around in.

Playa Santa Teresa, Cóbano, Puntarenas. ✆ **2640-0232.** Fax 2640-0226. www.florblanca.com. 11 units. \$675–\$850 (£335–£425) double; \$975–\$1,250 (£488–£625) 2-bedroom villa for 4; \$950 (£475) "honeymoon house." Rates lower during off season; higher during peak weeks. Transfer to and from Tambor airstrip is included. AE, DC, MC, V. No children 13 and under. **Amenities:** Restaurant; bar; bike rental; small open-air gym; laundry service; pool; room service; spa; watersports-equipment rental. *In room:* A/C, kitchenette, free Wi-Fi.

Four Seasons Resort Costa Rica ★★★ Kids Set on a narrow spit of land between two white-sand beaches, this is the most luxurious and impressive large-scale resort in Costa Rica. The architecture is stunning, with most buildings featuring flowing roof designs and other touches imitating the forms of turtles, armadillos, and butterflies. The rooms on the third and fourth floors have the best views and are priced accordingly. The others have either garden views or partial ocean views. Each has a large private balcony with a sofa, a table and a couple of chairs. On the rocky hill at the very end of the peninsula are the resort's suites and villas. The resort also features the Four Seasons' renowned service (including family-friendly amenities such as kid-size bathrobes and childproof rooms), one of the best-equipped full-service spas in the country, and a truly spectacular golf course.

Papagayo Peninsula, Guanacaste. ✆ **800/819-5053** in the U.S., or 2696-0000. Fax 2696-0500. www.fourseasons.com/costarica. 153 units. \$735–\$950 (£368–£475) double; \$1,670–\$10,000 (£835–£5,000) suite and villa. Children stay free in parent's room. AE, DC, DISC, MC, V. **Amenities:** 4 restaurants; 2 bars; lounge; babysitting; children's programs; concierge; championship 18-hole golf course; laundry service; nonsmoking rooms; 3 free-form pools; room service; modern, full-service spa; 2 tennis courts; watersports equipment. *In room:* A/C, TV/DVD, hair dryer, Wi-Fi.

Expensive

Other good options in this category include **Villa Alegre** (✆ **2653-0270;** www.villaalegrecostarica.com) in Playa Langosta; **El Ocotal Beach Resort** (✆ **877/862-6825** in the U.S. and Canada; www.ocotalresort.com) in Ocotal; and **Milarepa** (✆ **2640-0023;** www.milarepahotel.com) in Malpaís.

Hotel Capitán Suizo ★★ Kids This well-appointed beachfront hotel sits on the quiet southern end of Tamarindo. The rooms are housed in a series of two-story buildings. The lower rooms have air-conditioning and private patios; the upper units have plenty of cross ventilation, ceiling fans, and cozy balconies. In effect, all the rooms are suites, with separate sitting/living room areas. The spacious bungalows are spread around the shady grounds; these all come with a tub in the bathroom and an inviting outdoor shower among the trees. The hotel's free-form pool is very pretty, with tall shade trees all around. The shallow end slopes in gradually, imitating a beach, and there's also a separate children's pool. Perhaps the greatest attribute here is that it's just steps from one of the calmer and more isolated sections of Playa Tamarindo, making it a good family pick.

Playa Tamarindo, Guanacaste. ✆ **2653-0353** or 2653-0075. Fax 2653-0292. www.hotelcapitansuizo.com. 22 units, 8 bungalows. $175–$195 (£88–£98) double; $235–$275 (£118–£138) bungalow; $360 (£180) suite. Rates include breakfast buffet. Rates lower in off season; higher during peak periods. AE, MC, V. **Amenities:** Restaurant; bar; babysitting; small exercise room; laundry service; midsize pool and children's pool. *In room:* Fridge.

Sueño del Mar ★ Finds Located on Playa Langosta, Sueño del Mar has charming touches: four-poster beds made from driftwood; African dolls on the windowsills; Kokopeli candleholders; and open-air showers with sculpted angelfish, hand-painted tiles, and lush tropical plants. Fabrics are from Bali and Guatemala. Somehow all of this works well together, and the requisite chairs, hammocks, and lounges nestled under shade trees right on the beach add the crowning touch. The honeymoon suite is a spacious second-floor room, with wraparound screened-in windows, a delightful open-air bathtub and shower, and an ocean view. The beach right out front is rocky and a bit rough, but it does reveal some nice, quiet tidal pools at low tide; it's one of the better sunset-viewing spots in Costa Rica.

Playa Langosta, Guanacaste. ✆/fax **2653-0284.** www.sueno-del-mar.com. 4 units, 2 casitas. $195 (£98) double; $220–$295 (£110–£148) suite or casita. Rates include full breakfast. Rates lower in off season; higher during peak periods. No children 11 and under. MC, V. **Amenities:** Laundry service; small pool; free use of snorkel equipment and boogie boards; free Wi-Fi. *In room:* A/C, hair dryer.

Moderate

In addition to the hotels listed below, you could also look into **El Velero Hotel** (✆ **2672-1017;** www.costaricahotel.net) and **Villa del Sueño Hotel** ★ (✆ **800/378-8599** in the U.S. and Canada; www.villadelsueno.com) in Playa Hermosa; **Hotel Villa Casa Blanca** (✆ **2670-0518;** www.hotelvillacasablanca.com) in Ocotal; **Hotel Sugar Beach** ★★ (✆ **2654-4242;** www.sugar-beach.com) in Playa Pan de Azúcar; and **Trópico Latino Lodge** ★ (✆ **2640-0062;** www.hoteltropicolatino.com) in Santa Teresa.

Hotel Playa Hermosa Bosque del Mar ★ Finds Tucked away under shady trees, this sprawling beachfront spread has an enviable location on the southern end of Playa Hermosa. The cool and cozy rooms have tile floors, air-conditioning, and contemporary furniture and fixtures. The suites are larger and come with two queen-size beds, a mini-fridge, and a coffeemaker. The pretty free-form pool sits in a shady spot under several tall trees, with a broad deck area and separate unheated Jacuzzi beside it.

Playa Hermosa, Guanacaste. ✆ **2672-0046.** Fax 2672-0019. www.hotelplayahermosa.com. 32 units. $85–$145 (£43–£73) double. Rates lower in off season; higher during peak periods. MC, V. Turn left at the 1st road into Playa Hermosa; the hotel's white archway gate is about 1km (1/2 mile) down this dirt road. **Amenities:** Restaurant; bar; Jacuzzi; laundry service; outdoor pool. *In room:* A/C, TV, free Wi-Fi.

Hotel Pasatiempo A long-standing and highly dependable option, this hotel is set back from the beach 200m (656 ft.) in a grove of shady trees. Most rooms are housed in duplex buildings, but each has its own private patio with a hammock or chairs. The two suites are very comfortable and well equipped. Each room bears the name of a different beach, and the bedroom walls feature hand-painted murals. A small yet very inviting pool sits in the center of the complex. The popular restaurant here also has a pool table, a nightly happy hour, cable TV with live sporting events, good snacks, and occasional live music.

 Playa Tamarindo, Santa Cruz, Guanacaste. © **2653-0096.** Fax 2653-0275. www.hotelpasatiempo.com. 17 units. $99–$129 (£50–£65) double. Rates lower in off season; higher during peak periods. AE, MC, V. **Amenities:** Restaurant; bar; laundry service; midsize pool; free Wi-Fi. *In room:* A/C, no phone.

Inexpensive

In addition to the places below, **Hostal La Botella de Leche** (© **2653-0189;** www.labotelladeleche.com), **Malpaís Surf Camp & Resort** (© **2640-0031;** www.malpaissurfcamp.com), and **Tsunami Backpackers** (© **2653-0956**) are all popular Tamarindo budget options, and the latter also allows camping. While in Brasilito, I recommend **Hotel Brasilito** (© **2654-4237;** www.brasilito.com).

Amor de Mar ★ Value This hotel has an idyllic setting overlooking the ocean. With its wide expanse of neatly trimmed grass sloping down to the sea, tide pools (one of which is as big as a small swimming pool), and hammocks slung from the mango trees, this is the perfect place for anyone who wants to do some serious relaxing. The rooms are housed in a beautifully appointed two-story building, which abounds in varnished hardwoods. Although simply appointed, most rooms have plenty of space and receive lots of sunlight. Five have air-conditioning. My favorite room is no. 5, which now has exclusive access to a long second-floor balcony with a superb ocean view.

Montezuma (A.P. 22, Cóbano de Puntarenas). ©/fax **2642-0262.** www.amordemar.com. 11 units, 9 with private bathroom. $45–$55 (£23–£28) double with shared bathroom; $70–$90 (£35–£45) double with private bathroom; $170 (£85) house. Rates lower in off season. V. **Amenities:** Restaurant; laundry service. *In room:* No phone.

Cabinas Zully Mar The Zully Mar has long been a favorite of budget travelers, although they've definitely upgraded their rooms and upped their prices over the years. The best rooms here are in a two-story white-stucco building with a wide, curving staircase on the outside. They have air-conditioning, tile floors, long verandas or balconies, overhead or standing fans, large bathrooms, and doors that are hand-carved with pre-Columbian motifs. The less expensive rooms are smaller and darker and just have ceiling fans. There is a small free-form pool that's refreshing if you don't want to walk across the street to the beach. This place is set on the busiest intersection in Tamarindo, smack-dab in the center of things, and noise can be a problem at times.

Playa Tamarindo, Guanacaste. ©/fax **2653-0140.** Fax 2653-0028. www.zullymar.com. 25 units. $46–$79 (£23–£40) double. Rates higher during peak periods. AE, MC, V. **Amenities:** Restaurant; laundry service; small pool. *In room:* Minifridge, no phone.

WHERE TO DINE

In most of the beach destinations in this region, your best dining option is to find a simple, and sanitary, restaurant close to the water serving basic Tico fare and fresh seafood. Of the restaurants in this vein, I especially like **Camarón Dorado** (© **2654-4028**) in Brasilito.

Very Expensive

In addition to the places listed below, **Nectar** (© **2640-0232**), at the Flor Blanca Hotel in Santa Teresa, is another top choice in this category, with a beautiful open-air beachfront dining area and a superb fusion menu.

La Laguna del Cocodrilo Bistro ★★★ FUSION This small open-air restaurant has impressed me every time I've eaten here. Beautiful presentations and creative use of ingredients are the norm. The menu changes regularly, but the chefs always focus on using the freshest and best ingredients available. Be sure to save room for dessert, as they are always excellent. One of the best ways to go here is to simply opt for the nightly tasting menu, which will feature anywhere from five to seven courses, including dessert. The restaurant has a good wine list, and they keep their bottles properly cool, to compensate for the often unforgiving Guanacaste heat.

On the main road, toward the north end of Tamarindo. © **2653-3897.** Reservations recommended. Main courses $14–$26 (£7–£13). MC, V. Mon–Sat 7:30am–9pm.

Mar y Sol ★★ Finds CONTINENTAL/SEAFOOD Catalan chef Alain Taulere has prepared food for regular folk and royalty. For visitors to his hilltop restaurant in Flamingo Beach, he offers a small, well-executed selection of fresh seafood and meats. The ambience is casually formal, with the open-air main dining room dimly lit by old-fashioned lampposts and covered by a thatched roof. Along with a surf-and-turf combo featuring filet mignon and either lobster tails or jumbo shrimp, menu highlights include rich and creamy lobster bisque, and a hearty bouillabaisse. I enjoyed the tender duck served with passion fruit–cognac sauce. Call in advance for free transportation from and back to your hotel.

Playa Flamingo. © **2654-4151.** Reservations recommended for dinner in high season. Main courses $14–$32 (£7–£16). AE, DC, MC, V. Nov–Apr daily 10am–3:30pm and 5–10pm; May–Aug daily 2–10pm. Closed Sept–Oct.

Moderate

In addition to the places mentioned below, in Montezuma, be sure to stop in at **El Sano Banano Village Cafe ★** (**© 2642-0944**) for their excellent vegetarian and seafood fare, and nightly movies. While in Tamarindo, check out what's shaking at **Dragonfly Bar & Grill ★★** (**© 2653-1506**), which has a creative fusion menu and huge servings, or, **Café de Playa** (**© 2670-1621**), which is the hippest place in town, with a broad fusion menu and chill Euro-chic ambience.

Ginger ★★ INTERNATIONAL/TAPAS In this creative and architecturally stylish restaurant, the food is an eclectic mix of modern takes on wide-ranging international fare, all served as tapas, meant to be shared while sampling some of the many cocktails and wines served here. Still, it's easy to make a full meal. Order the house special ginger-glazed chicken wings, along with some spring rolls, and a plate of fresh mahimahi marinated in vodka and Asian spices. There are also more traditional Mediterranean and Spanish-style tapas, as well as delicious desserts.

On the main road, Playa Hermosa. © **2672-0041.** Tapas $4–$8 (£2–£4). AE, MC, V. Tues–Sun 11:30am–10pm.

Playa de los Artistas ★★★ Finds ITALIAN/MEDITERRANEAN This open-air restaurant fronts the beach. There are only a few tables, so be sure to reserve. If you don't get a seat and you feel hearty, try the low wooden table surrounded by tatami mats on the sand. Meals are served in large classy and creative plates, or in broad wooden bowls set on ceramic-ringed coasters or on large wooden planks lined with banana leaves. The menu changes nightly but always features several fish and seafood dishes. The fresh grouper in a black-pepper sauce is phenomenal, as is the moscardini polenta, a tasty appetizer of polenta pieces topped with grilled calamari tentacles and pecorino cheese. The outdoor brick oven and grill turns out consistently spectacular grilled fish and seafood.

Across from Hotel Los Mangos. © **2642-0920.** Reservations recommended. Main courses $6.50–$14 (£3.25–£7). No credit cards. Mon–Sat noon–4pm and 5:30–9:30pm.

Inexpensive

Marie's COSTA RICAN/SEAFOOD With large, new digs, this long-standing local standby is still a great place for a quick bite or a leisurely sit-down meal. The menu has grown steadily over the years, although the best option here is always some simply prepared fresh fish, chicken, or meat. Check the blackboard for the daily specials, which usually highlight the freshest catch, such as mahimahi *(dorado),* marlin, and red snapper. You'll also find such Tico favorites as *casados* (rice-and-bean dish), rotisserie chicken and seviche, as well as burritos and quesadillas.

Playa Flamingo. ✆ **2654-4136.** Reservations recommended for dinner during the high season. Sandwiches $4–$8 (£2–£4); main courses $6.50–$21 (£3.25–£11). V. Daily 6:30am–10pm.

Soda Piedra Mar (Finds) COSTA RICAN/SEAFOOD This simple open-air restaurant is set on a rocky outcropping just steps away from the sea. The place is little more than a zinc-roofed shack that seems as if a stiff breeze would quickly level it. There are only a few tables here under the low roof; weather permitting, more tables are set in the sand under the sun or stars. The fare is simple, but the fish is guaranteed fresh, the portions are hearty, and the setting and sunsets are wonderful.

On the beach in Malpaís. ✆ **2640-0069.** Main courses $3–$15 (£1.50–£7.50). No credit cards. Daily 8am–8pm.

GUANACASTE & THE NICOYA PENINSULA AFTER DARK

Nightlife varies from beach town to beach town. Tamarindo and Playa del Coco are probably the two rocking-est towns, while Flamingo, Brasilito, and Playa Hermosa are pretty quiet in comparison.

Some of my favorite bars in the area include the **Lizard Lounge** ★ and **Zouk Santana** ★ in Playa del Coco; **La Barra** ★ and **Rey Sol** in Tamarindo; and **Chico's Bar** in Montezuma.

For those looking for some gaming, there are two casinos in Tamarindo: the **Jazz Casino,** across from the El Diriá hotel, and the casino at the **Barceló Playa Langosta** resort; as well as one in Playa del Coco at the **Coco Bay Hotel & Casino,** in the heart of town, and another in Playa Flamingo at **Amberes,** just up the hill off the beach at Amberes.

6 MONTEVERDE ★★

167km (104 miles) NW of San José; 82km (51 miles) NW of Puntarenas

Monteverde translates as "green mountain," and that's exactly what you'll find at the end of the steep and windy rutted dirt road that leads here. Next to Manuel Antonio, this is Costa Rica's most internationally recognized ecotourism destination. The fame, rapid growth, and accompanying traffic have led some to dub it the Monteverde Crowd Forest. Nevertheless, the reserve itself and the extensive network of private reserves around it are incredibly rich in biodiversity, and a well-organized infrastructure helps guarantee a rewarding experience for both first-time and experienced ecoadventurers.

The village of Monteverde was founded in 1951 by Quakers from the United States who wanted to leave behind a constant fear of war as well as an obligation to support continued militarism through paying U.S. taxes. They chose Costa Rica primarily

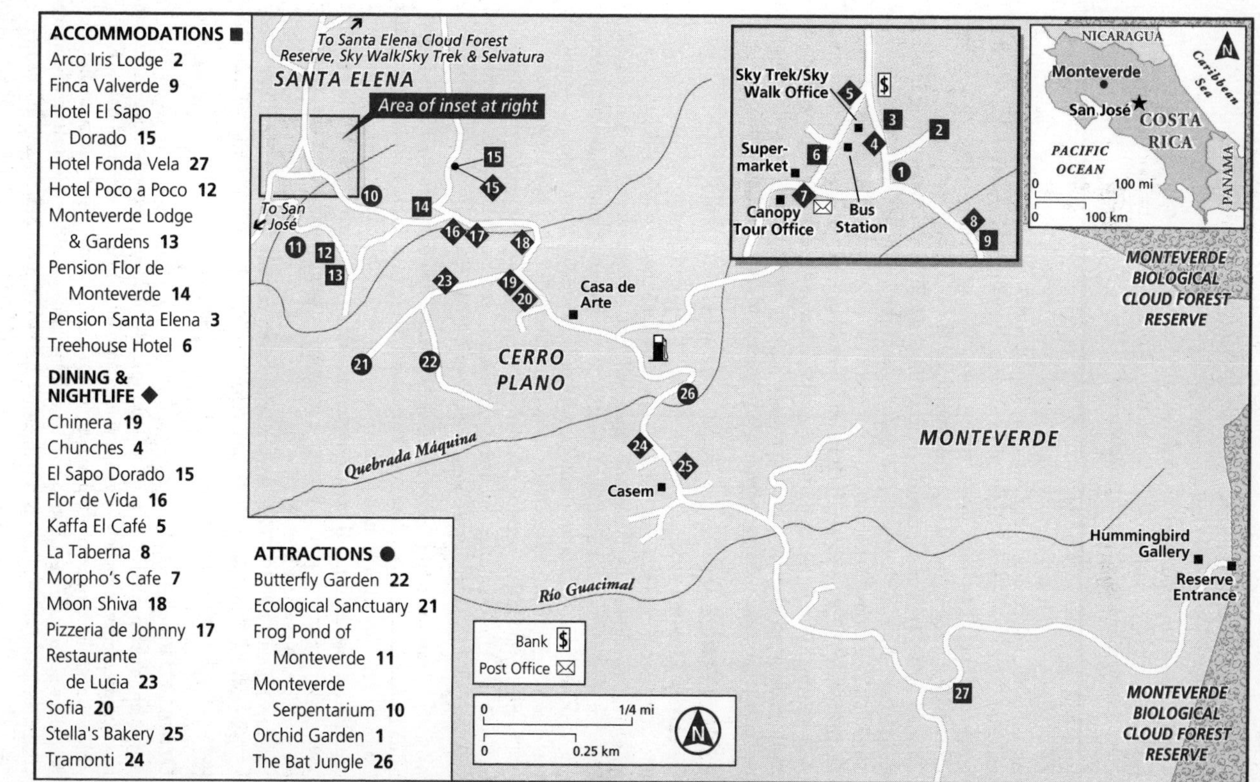
ACCOMMODATIONS ■
Arco Iris Lodge 2
Finca Valverde 9
Hotel El Sapo Dorado 15
Hotel Fonda Vela 27
Hotel Poco a Poco 12
Monteverde Lodge & Gardens 13
Pension Flor de Monteverde 14
Pension Santa Elena 3
Treehouse Hotel 6
DINING & NIGHTLIFE ◆
Chimera 19
Chunches 4
El Sapo Dorado 15
Flor de Vida 16
Kaffa El Café 5
La Taberna 8
Morpho's Cafe 7
Moon Shiva 18
Pizzeria de Johnny 17
Restaurante de Lucia 23
Sofia 20
Stella's Bakery 25
Tramonti 24
ATTRACTIONS ●
Butterfly Garden 22
Ecological Sanctuary 21
Frog Pond of Monteverde 11
Monteverde Serpentarium 10
Orchid Garden 1
The Bat Jungle 26
To Santa Elena Cloud Forest Reserve, Sky Walk/Sky Trek & Selvatura
SANTA ELENA
Area of inset at right
To San José
CERRO PLANO
Casa de Arte
Casem
Quebrada Máquina
Río Guacimal
MONTEVERDE
Hummingbird Gallery
Reserve Entrance
MONTEVERDE BIOLOGICAL CLOUD FOREST RESERVE
MONTEVERDE BIOLOGICAL CLOUD FOREST RESERVE
Sky Trek/Sky Walk Office
Super-market
Canopy Tour Office
Bus Station
Bank
Post Office
0 1/4 mi
0 0.25 km
N
NICARAGUA
Monteverde
San José
COSTA RICA
Caribbean Sea
PACIFIC OCEAN
PANAMA
0 100 mi
0 100 km

Today's Forecast: Misty & Cool

Make sure you understand that the climatic conditions that make Monteverde such a biological hot spot can leave many tourists feeling chilled to the bone. More than a few visitors are unprepared for a cool, windy, and wet stay in the middle of their tropical vacation, and can find Monteverde a bit inhospitable, especially from August through November.

because it had no standing army. Although Monteverde's founders came here to farm the land, they wisely recognized the need to preserve the rare cloud forest that covered the mountain slopes above their fields, and to that end they dedicated the largest adjacent tract of cloud forest as the Monteverde Biological Cloud Forest Reserve.

Cloud forests are a mountaintop phenomenon. Moist, warm air sweeping in off the ocean is forced upward by mountain slopes, and as this moist air rises, it cools, forming clouds. This constant level of moisture has given rise to an incredible diversity of innovative life forms and a forest in which nearly every square inch of space has some sort of plant growing. Within the cloud forest, the branches of huge trees are draped with epiphytic plants: orchids, ferns, and bromeliads. This intense botanic competition has created an almost equally diverse population of insects, birds, and other wildlife.

ESSENTIALS

Getting There

BY CAR From San José, take the Pan-American Highway north. About 20km (12 miles) past the turnoff for Puntarenas, there will be a marked turnoff for Sardinal, Santa Elena, and Monteverde. From this turnoff, the road is paved almost as far as the tiny town of Guacimal. From here it's another 20km (12 miles) to Santa Elena. It should take you a little over 2 hours to reach the turnoff and another 1 hour or so from there.

The final going is slow because the roads into Santa Elena are rough, unpaved dirt and gravel affairs. However, once you arrive, the roads in and around Santa Elena are paved, including all the way to Cerro Plano, and about halfway to the Cloud Forest Preserve.

BY BUS **Transmonteverde** express buses (✆ **2222-3854** in San José, or 2645-5159 in Santa Elena) leave San José daily at 6:30am and 2:30pm from Calle 12 between avenidas 7 and 9. The trip takes around 4 hours; the fare is $4.20 (£2.10). Buses arrive at and depart from Santa Elena. If you're staying at one of the hotels or lodges toward the reserve, you'll want to arrange pickup if possible, or take a taxi or local bus. Departing buses follow the same schedule.

Gray Line (✆ **2220-2126;** www.graylinecostarica.com) and **Interbus** (✆ **2283-5573;** www.interbusonline.com) both also have daily buses to Monteverde, with connections to most other major destinations in the country. The fare is around $35 (£18).

Orientation

As you approach Santa Elena, take the right fork in the road if you're heading directly to Monteverde. If you continue straight, you'll come into the little village of **Santa Elena,** which has a bus stop, a health clinic, a bank, a general store, a laundromat, and a few simple restaurants, budget hotels, souvenir shops, and tour offices. **Monteverde,** on the other hand, is not a village in the traditional sense of the word. There's no center of town—only dirt lanes leading off from the main road to various farms. This main road has signs for all the hotels and restaurants mentioned here, and it dead-ends at the reserve entrance.

Getting Around

Various buses run daily between the town of Santa Elena and the Monteverde Biological Cloud Forest Reserve. The first bus leaves Santa Elena for the reserve at 6am and the last bus from the reserve leaves there at 4pm. Fare is $1.50 (75p). There's also periodic van transportation between the town of Santa Elena and the Santa Elena Cloud Forest Reserve. Ask around town and you should be able to find the current schedule and book a ride for around $2 (£1) per person. A **taxi** (**✆ 2645-6969** or 2645-6666) between Santa Elena and either the Monteverde Reserve or the Santa Elena Cloud Forest Reserve costs around $8 to $10 (£4–£5) for up to four people. Count on paying between $4 and $10 (£2–£5) for the ride from Santa Elena to your lodge in Monteverde.

Visitor Information & Fast Facts

The telephone number for the **local clinic** is **✆ 2645-5076;** for the **Red Cross, ✆ 2645-6128;** and for the **local police, ✆ 911** or 2645-6248. There's a 24-hour gas station located about halfway between the town of Santa Elena and the Monteverde Biological Cloud Forest Reserve. The **Farmacia Monteverde** (**✆ 2645-7110**) is right downtown. There's a **Banco Nacional** (**✆ 2645-5610**) in downtown Santa Elena and **Coopemex** (**✆ 2645-6948**) on the road out to Santa Elena, near Finca Valverde; both have 24-hour ATMs.

WHAT TO SEE & DO

The **Monteverde Biological Cloud Forest Reserve ★★★** (**✆ 2645-5122;** www.cct.or.cr) is one of the most developed and well-maintained natural attractions in Costa Rica. The trails are clearly marked, regularly traveled, and generally gentle in terms of ascents and descents. The cloud forest here is lush and largely untouched. Still, keep in mind that most of the birds and mammals are rare, elusive, and nocturnal. Moreover, to all but the most trained of eyes, those thousands of exotic ferns, orchids, and bromeliads tend to blend into one large mass of indistinguishable green. However, with a guide hired through your hotel, or on one of the reserve's official guided 2- to 3-hour hikes, you can see and learn far more than you could on your own. At $15 (£7.50) per person, the reserve's tours might seem like a splurge, especially after you pay the entrance fee, but I strongly recommend that you go with a guide.

Perhaps the most famous resident of the cloud forests of Costa Rica is the quetzal, a robin-size bird with iridescent green wings and a ruby-red breast, which has become extremely rare due to habitat destruction. The male quetzal also has two long tail feathers

Tips **Alternative Transport**

You can travel between Monteverde and La Fortuna by boat and taxi, or on a combination boat, horseback, and taxi trip. See "Boats, Horses & Taxis" on p. 604 for details. Any of the trips described there can be done in the reverse direction departing from Monteverde.

Seeing the Forest for the Trees, Bromeliads, Monkeys, Hummingbirds . . .

Because the entrance fee to Monteverde is valid for a full day, I recommend taking an early morning walk with a guide and then heading off on your own either directly after that hike or after lunch.

that can reach nearly .6m (2 ft.) in length, making it one of the most spectacular birds on earth. The best time to see quetzals is early morning to midmorning, and the best months are February through April (mating season).

ADMISSION, HOURS & TOURS The reserve is open daily from 7am to 4pm, and the entrance fee is $15 (£7.50) for adults and $7.50 (£3.75) for students and children. Because only 160 people are allowed into the reserve at any one time, you might be forced to wait for a while. Most hotels can reserve a guided walk and entrance to the reserve for the following day for you, or you can get tickets in advance directly at the reserve entrance.

Some of the trails can be very muddy, depending on the season, so ask about current conditions. If the mud is heavy, you can rent rubber boots at the reserve entrance for $2 (£1) per day. They might make your hike much more pleasant. Night tours of the reserve leave every evening at 7:15pm. The cost is $15 (£7.50), including admission to the reserve, a 2-hour hike, and, most important, a guide with a high-powered searchlight. For an extra $2 (£1), they'll throw in round-trip transportation to and from your area hotel.

Active Adventures Outside the Reserve

CANOPY TOURS & MORE There's a glut of canopy tours in the Monteverde area, but I can only recommend those mentioned below. Anybody in average physical condition can do any of the adventure tours in Monteverde, but they're not for the fainthearted or acrophobic. Beware of touts on the streets of Monteverde, who make a small commission and frequently try to steer tourists to the operator paying the highest percentage.

One of the most complete attractions in the area is **Selvatura Park ★★** (**© 2645-5929**; www.selvatura.com). Located close to the Santa Elena Cloud Forest Reserve, this place is the best one-stop shop for various adventures and attractions in the area. In addition to an extensive canopy tour, with 15 cables connecting 18 platforms, they also have a network of trails and suspended bridges, a huge butterfly garden, a hummingbird garden, a snake exhibit, and a wonderful insect display and museum. Prices vary depending upon how much you want to see and do. Individually, the canopy tour costs $40 (£20); the walkways and bridges, $20 (£10); the snake and reptile exhibit, $12 (£6); and the butterfly garden and the insect museum, $10 (£5) each. Packages to combine the various exhibits are available, although it's definitely confusing, and somewhat annoying, to pick the perfect package. For $108 (£54), you get the run of the entire joint, all the tours, lunch, and round-trip transportation from your Monteverde hotel.

Another popular option is offered by the folks at **Sky Trek ★★** (**© 2645-5238;** www.skytrek.com), a growing complex of aerial adventures and hiking trails. This is one of the more extensive canopy tours in the country, with two very long cables to cross.

The longest of these is some 770m (2,525 ft.) long, high above the forest floor. There are no rappel descents here, and you brake using the pulley system for friction. This tour costs $44 (£22).

One of the oldest canopy tours in the country is run by the **Original Canopy Tour** ★ (✆ **2645-5243;** www.canopytour.com), which has an office right in the center of Santa Elena. This is one of the more interesting canopy tours in Costa Rica because the initial ascent is made by climbing up the hollowed-out interior of a giant strangler fig. The 2- to 2½-hour tours run three times daily and cost $45 (£23) for adults, $35 (£18) for students, and $25 (£13) for children 11 and under.

BIRD-WATCHING & HIKING You can also find ample bird-watching and hiking opportunities outside the reserve boundaries. Avoid the crowds at Monteverde by heading 5km (3 miles) north from the village of Santa Elena to the **Santa Elena Cloud Forest Reserve** ★★ (✆ **2645-5390;** www.reservasantaelena.org). This 310-hectare (765-acre) reserve has a maximum elevation of 1,680m (5,510 ft.), making it the highest cloud forest in the Monteverde area. There are 13km (8 miles) of hiking trails, as well as an information center. Because it borders the Monteverde Reserve, a similar richness of flora and fauna is found here, although quetzals are not nearly as common. The $12 (£6) entry fee at this reserve goes directly to support local schools. The reserve is open daily from 7am to 4pm. Three-hour guided tours are available for $15 (£7.50) per person, not including the entrance fee. A night tour ($15/£7.50) is also offered each evening at 7pm.

Sky Walk ★ (✆ **2645-5238;** www.skytrek.com) is a network of forest paths and suspension bridges that provides visitors with a view previously reserved for birds, monkeys, and the much more adventurous traveler. The bridges reach 39m (128 ft.) above the ground at their highest point, so acrophobia could be an issue. The Sky Walk and its sister attraction, **Sky Trek** (see above), are located 3.5km (2¼ miles) outside of the town of Santa Elena. The Sky Walk is open daily from 7am to 4pm; admission is $17 (£8.50). For an extra $10 (£5), a knowledgeable guide will point out the diverse flora and fauna on the walk. For $50 (£25) per person, you can do the Sky Trek canopy tour and then walk the trails and bridges of the Sky Walk. Reservations are recommended for the Sky Trek.

Finally, you can walk the trails and grounds of the **Ecological Sanctuary** (✆ **2645-5869;** www.ecologicalsanctuary.com), a wildlife refuge and private reserve located down the Cerro Plano road. This place has four main trails through a variety of ecosystems, and wildlife viewing is often quite good here. There are a couple of pretty waterfalls off the trails. Open daily from 6:30am to 7pm; admission is $9 (£4.50) for self-guided hiking on the trails; $24 (£12) during the day for a 2-hour guided tour; and $15 (£7.50) for the 1½-hour guided night tour that leaves at 5:30pm.

HORSEBACK RIDING There's excellent terrain for horseback riding all around Monteverde. **Meg's Riding Stables** (✆ **2645-5560**), **La Estrella Stables** (✆ **2645-5075**), **Palomina Horse Tours** (✆ **2645-5479**), and **Sabine's Smiling Horses** (✆ **2645-6894;** www.smilinghorses.com) are the more established operators, offering guided rides for around $10 to $15 (£5–£7.50) per hour.

Other Attractions in & Around Monteverde

It seems as if Monteverde has an exhibit or attraction dedicated to almost every type of tropical fauna. It's a pet peeve of mine, but I really wish these folks would band together and offer some sort of general pass. However, as it stands, you'll have to shell out for each individual attraction.

Butterflies abound here, and the **Butterfly Garden** ★ (✆ **2645-5512**), located near the Pensión Monteverde Inn, displays many of Costa Rica's most beautiful species. Besides the hundreds of preserved and mounted butterflies, there are a garden and a greenhouse where you can watch live butterflies. Admission is $9 (£4.50) for adults and $7 (£3.50) for students and children, including a guided tour. The best time to visit is between 9:30am and 1pm, when the butterflies are most active.

If your taste runs toward the slithery, you can check out the **Monteverde Serpentarium** (✆ **2645-5238;** www.snaketour.com), on the road to the reserve. It's open daily from 8am to 8:30pm and charges $8 (£4) for admission. The **Frog Pond of Monteverde** ★ (✆ **2645-6320;** www.ranario.com), a couple of hundred meters north of the Monteverde Lodge, is probably a better bet. The $10 (£5) entrance gets you a 45-minute guided tour, and your ticket is good for 2 days. A variety of amphibian species populates a series of glass terrariums. In addition, these folks have also added a butterfly garden. This place is open daily from 9am to 8:30pm. I especially recommend that you stop by at least once after dark, when the tree frogs are active.

The **Bat Jungle** (✆ **2645-6566**) is an in-depth look into the world life and habits of these odd flying mammals. A visit here includes several different types of exhibits, from skeletal remains, to a large enclosure where you get to see various live species in action—the enclosure and room are kept dark, and the bats have had their biological clocks tricked to be active in the daytime. The Bat Jungle is open daily from 9:30am to 8:30pm. Admission is $10 (£5). In addition to a good gift shop and separate coffee shop, where they make homemade chocolate, these folks also have a small interpretive museum focusing on the history of the Quaker community here. Admission to this museum is $5 (£2.50)

If you've had your fill of birds, snakes, bugs, butterflies, and bats, you might want to stop at the **Orchid Garden** ★ (✆ **2645-5308;** www.monteverdeorchidgarden.com), in Santa Elena across from the Pension El Tucano. This botanical garden boasts more than 425 species of orchids. The tour is fascinating, especially the fact that you need (and are given) a magnifying glass to see some of the flowers in bloom. Admission is $7 (£3.50) for adults and $5 (£2.50) for students. It's open daily from 8am to 5pm.

Almost all of the area hotels can arrange a wide variety of other tours and activities, including guided night tours of the cloud forest and night trips to the Arenal Volcano (a tedious 4-hr. ride, each way).

SHOPPING

The best-stocked gift shop in Monteverde is the **Hummingbird Gallery** ★ (✆ **2645-5030**). You'll find the gallery just outside the reserve entrance. Hanging from trees around it are several hummingbird feeders that attract more than seven species of these tiny birds. At any given moment, there might be several dozen hummingbirds buzzing and chattering around the building and your head.

Another good option is **CASEM** (✆ **2645-5190**), located on the right side of the main road, just across from Stella's Bakery. This crafts cooperative sells embroidered clothing, T-shirts, posters, and postcards with photos of the local flora and fauna, Boruca weavings, locally grown and roasted coffee, and many other items to remind you of your visit to Monteverde.

Over the years, Monteverde has developed a nice little community of artists. Around town you'll see paintings by local artists such as Paul Smith and Meg Wallace, whose works are displayed at the Fonda Vela Hotel and Stella's Bakery, respectively. You might also check out **Casa de Arte** ★ (✆ **2645-5275**), which has a mix of arts and crafts in many mediums and is just off the main road to the reserve, as well as **Flor de Vida** (✆ **2645-6328**), which has some unique custom-made jewelry and clothing.

WHERE TO STAY

When choosing a place to stay in Monteverde, be sure to check whether the rates include a meal plan. In the past almost all the lodges included three meals a day in their prices, but this practice is waning. Check before you assume anything.

Expensive

Hotel El Sapo Dorado ★★ Located on a steep hill between Santa Elena and the reserve, El Sapo Dorado offers some of the more charming and comfortable accommodations in Monteverde. The spacious cabins are built of hardwoods both inside and out and are surrounded by a grassy lawn. Big windows let in lots of light, and high ceilings keep the rooms cool during the day. Some of the cabins have fireplaces, a welcome feature on chilly nights and during the peak parts of the rainy season. A remodeling in 2008 has left most cabins updated, with larger, more modern bathrooms, and more lively decor. My favorite rooms are the sunset suites, which have private terraces with views to the Gulf of Nicoya and wonderful sunsets.

Monteverde (A.P. 9-5655), Puntarenas. ✆ **2645-5010.** Fax 2645-5180. www.sapodorado.com. 30 units. $122 (£61) double. Rates include breakfast and taxes. Lower rates in the off season. MC, V. **Amenities:** Restaurant; bar; laundry service; free Wi-Fi. *In room:* Hair dryer.

Moderate

In addition to the hotels listed below, **Finca Valverde** (✆ **2645-5157;** www.monteverde.co.cr), **Hotel Fonda Vela** (✆ **2645-5125;** www.fondavela.com), and **Hotel Poco A Poco** (✆ **2645-6000;** www.hotelpocoapoco.com) are other good options in this price range.

Arco Iris Lodge ★ Value This is my favorite hotel right in Santa Elena and an excellent value to boot. The rooms are spread out in a variety of separate buildings, including several individual cabins. All have wood or tile floors and plenty of wood accents. My favorite is the "honeymoon cabin," which has a Jacuzzi tub and its own private balcony with a forest view and good bird-watching, although room nos. 16 and 17 are other good choices, also with their own small private balconies. Although they don't serve lunch or dinner, breakfast is offered in a spacious and airy dining and lounge building, where refreshments are available throughout the day and evening.

Monteverde (A.P. 003-5655), Puntarenas. ✆ **2645-5067.** Fax 2645-5022. www.arcoirislodge.com. 19 units. $75 (£38) double; $180 (£90) honeymoon cabin. AE, MC, V. **Amenities:** Lounge; laundry service. *In room:* No phone.

Monteverde Lodge & Gardens ★★ Kids This was one of the first ecolodges in Monteverde, and it remains one of the most popular. Rooms are large and comfortable, and thanks to ongoing upkeep and remodeling, are some of the best in town. Most feature angled walls of glass with chairs and a table placed so that avid bird-watchers can do a bit of birding without leaving their rooms. The gardens and secondary forest surrounding the lodge have some gentle groomed trails and are home to quite a few species of birds. Perhaps the lodge's most popular attraction is the large hot tub in a big atrium garden just off the lobby.

Monteverde (mailing address: SJO 235, P.O. Box 25216, Miami, FL 33102-5216). ✆ **2257-0766** reservations office in San José, or 2645-5057 at the lodge. Fax 2257-1665. www.monteverdelodge.com. 28 units. $95 (£48) double. Rates slightly lower in off season; higher during peak periods. AE, MC, V. **Amenities:** Restaurant; bar; Jacuzzi; laundry service. *In room:* Safe.

Inexpensive

In addition to the hotel listed below, there are quite a few *pensiones* and backpacker specials in Santa Elena and spread out along the road to the reserve. The best of these are **Pensión Santa Elena** (✆ **2645-5051;** www.pensionsantaelena.com) and **Pensión Flor de Monteverde** (✆ **2645-5758;** www.pensionflordemonteverde.com).

Finally, it is possible to stay right at the **Monteverde Biological Cloud Forest Reserve** (✆ **2645-5122;** www.cct.or.cr). A bunk bed, shared bathroom, and three meals per day here run $40 (£20) per person. For an extra $10 (£5) you can actually get a room with a private bathroom. Admission to the reserve is included in the price.

Treehouse Hotel Housed in Santa Elena's first, and only, high-rise building, this hotel offers clean and spacious rooms in the center of town. Taking up the third—and highest—floor of this building, the rooms vary in size and the number of beds they feature. The best rooms come with small balconies overlooking the town, although these are also susceptible to street noise, particularly early in the morning and on weekend nights. All rooms feature bright-white tile floors, colorful bedspreads, and sparse furnishings. Although the building is modern, it is built around a massive old fig tree, hence the hotel's name.

Santa Elena, Puntarenas. ✆ **2645-7475** or 8389-2573. 7 units. $45 (£23) double. MC, V. **Amenities:** Restaurant; laundry service. *In room:* TV, hair dryer, no phone, safe.

WHERE TO DINE

Most lodges in Monteverde have their own dining rooms, and these are the most convenient places to eat, especially if you don't have a car. Because most visitors want to get an early start, they usually grab a quick breakfast at their hotel. It's also common for people to have their lodge pack them a bag lunch to take with them to the reserve, although there's a decent little *soda* at the reserve entrance.

In addition to the places listed below, you can get good pizzas and pastas at **Tramonti** (✆ **2645-6120**) and **Pizzeria de Johnny** (✆ **2645-5066**), both located out along the road to the reserve. In Santa Elena, **Morpho's Café** (✆ **2645-5607**) serves excellent and inexpensive fare in a lively ambience. Also, the restaurant at the **Hotel Poco a Poco** (✆ **2645-6000**) gets good marks with a wide range of international dishes. A popular choice for lunch is **Stella's Bakery** (✆ **2645-5560**), across the road from the CASEM gift shop. The restaurant is bright and inviting, with lots of varnished woodwork, as well as a few outdoor tables. Two long-standing and deservedly popular local eateries are **Restaurante de Lucía** (✆ **2645-5337**), which specializes in grilled meat and fish, and **El Sapo Dorado** (✆ **2645-5010**), located at its namesake hotel, which serves varied and creative international fare. Finally, **Chimera** (✆ **2645-6081**) is a new, upscale tapas restaurant, owned and run by the folks behind **Sofia** (see below).

Flor de Vida INTERNATIONAL/VEGETARIAN With large new digs, this longstanding local favorite continues to serve up some of the best and healthiest fare to be found in Monteverde. Large picture windows line two walls here, and there's a small lounge area in one corner, with books, magazines, and board games. When it's cold and windy out, I like to start off with a bowl of their pumpkin-almond soup. For lunch, their veggie burger with roasted potatoes is hard to beat, and for dinner I tend to favor the Thai fish curry. In addition to the regular menu, there are always daily specials.

On the road btw. Santa Elena and the reserve, on your right. ✆ **2645-6823.** Reservations recommended during high season. Main courses $8–$13 (£4–£6.50). MC, V. Daily 7am–10pm.

Tips **Take a Break**

If all of the activities in Monteverde have worn you out, stop in at the **Kaffa El Café** (✆ **2645-6335**), a downtown coffee shop, or **Chunches** (✆ **2645-5147**), a bookstore with a small coffee shop and espresso bar that also doubles as a laundromat.

Sofia ★★ Finds COSTA RICAN/FUSION This restaurant serves top-notch eclectic cuisine in a beautiful setting. Start everything off with a mango-ginger mojito and then try one of their colorful and abundant salads. Main courses range from seafood *chimichangas* to chicken breast served in a guava reduction. The tenderloin comes with a chipotle butter sauce, or in a roasted red pepper and cashew sauce, either way served over a bed of mashed sweet potato. The best seats here are close to the large arched picture windows overlooking the neighboring forest and gardens.

Cerro Plano, just past the turnoff to the Butterfly Farm, on your left. ✆ **2645-7017.** Reservations recommended during high season. Main courses $11–$16 (£5.50–£8). AE, DC, DISC, MC, V. Daily 11:30am–9:30pm.

MONTEVERDE AFTER DARK

The most popular after-dark activities in Monteverde are night hikes in one of the reserves and a natural-history slide show (see "Other Attractions in & Around Monteverde," earlier in this chapter). However, if you want a taste of the local party scene, head to **La Taberna** ★, which is just outside of downtown Santa Elena before the Serpentarium. This place attracts a mix of locals and tourists, cranks its music loud, and often gets people dancing. Alternatively, **Flor de Vida, Kaffa El Café,** and **Moon Shiva** sometimes feature live music, theater, or open-mic jam sessions. **El Sapo Dorado** has been hosting live dance bands from San José most Monday evenings.

You'll also want to check to see if there's any live music or another performance going on at the **Monteverde Amphitheater,** a beautiful open-air performance space, located up a steep driveway up from Stella's Bakery, next to Bromelia's.

7 THE ARENAL VOLCANO & ENVIRONS ★★

140km (87 miles) NW of San José; 61km (38 miles) E of Tilarán

I've visited scores of times, and I never tire of watching red lava rocks tumble down the flanks of **Arenal Volcano,** and listening in awe to its deep rumbling. If you've never experienced them firsthand, the sights and sounds of an active volcano are awe-inspiring. Arenal is one of the world's most regularly active volcanoes. In July 1968, the volcano, which had lain dormant for hundreds of years, surprised everybody by erupting with sudden violence. The nearby village of Tabacón was destroyed, and nearly 80 of its inhabitants were killed. Since that eruption, 1,607m (5,271-ft.) Arenal has been Costa Rica's most active volcano. Frequent powerful explosions send cascades of red-hot lava rocks down the volcano's steep slopes. During the day these lava flows smoke and rumble. If you are lucky enough to be here on a clear and active night—not necessarily a guaranteed occurrence—you'll see the night sky turned red by lava spewing from Arenal's crater.

Lying at the eastern foot of this natural spectacle is the tiny farming community of **La Fortuna.** This town has become a magnet for volcano-watchers, adventure tourists, and assorted travelers from around the world. A host of budget and moderately priced hotels are in and near La Fortuna, and from here you can arrange night tours to the best volcano-viewing spots, which are 17km (11 miles) away on the western slope, on the road to and beyond the Tabacón Grand Spa Thermal Resort.

ESSENTIALS

Getting There

BY PLANE **Nature Air** (✆ **800/235-9272** in the U.S. and Canada, or 2299-6000; www.natureair.com) and **Sansa** (✆ **877/767-2672** in the U.S. and Canada, or 2290-4100 in Costa Rica; www.flysansa.com) both have daily flights to **Arenal/La Fortuna** airport (**FON;** no phone) from San José. In addition, Nature Air has flights to and from Tamarindo, while Sansa connects Arenal/La Fortuna with flights to Liberia.

BY CAR There are several routes to La Fortuna from San José. The most popular is to head north on the Pan-American Highway and then exit at Naranjo, continuing north through Zarcero to Ciudad Quesada. From Ciudad Quesada, one route goes through Jabillos, while the other goes through Muelle. The former route is better marked, slightly shorter, and generally better maintained, but the severe weather and heavy traffic quickly take their toll, and the roads up here can be notoriously bad for long stretches. This route offers wonderful views of the San Carlos valley as you come down from Ciudad Quesada, and Zarcero, with its topiary gardens and quaint church, makes a good place to stop, stretch your legs, and snap a few photos.

You can also stay on the Pan-American Highway until San Ramón (north of Naranjo) and then exit, and head north through La Tigra. This route is also very scenic and passes through areas of cloud forest. The travel time on any of the above routes is between 2½ and 3½ hours.

BY BUS **Buses** (✆ **2255-0567**) leave San José for La Fortuna roughly every 2 hours between 6am and 5:30pm from the **Atlántico del Norte** bus station at Avenida 9 and Calle 12. The trip lasts 4 hours; the fare is $3.40 (£1.70). The bus you take might be labeled TILARAN. Make sure it passes through Ciudad Quesada. If so, it passes through La Fortuna; if not, you'll end up in Tilarán via the Pan-American Highway, passing through the Guanacaste town of Cañas, a long way from La Fortuna.

Alternatively, you can take a bus from the same station to Ciudad Quesada and transfer there to another bus to La Fortuna. These buses depart roughly every 30 minutes between 5am and 7:30pm. The fare for the 2½-hour trip is $2.80 (£1.40). Local buses between Ciudad Quesada and La Fortuna run regularly through the day, although the schedule changes frequently, depending on demand. The trip lasts 1 hour; the fare is $1.50 (75p).

Buses depart La Fortuna for San José roughly every 2 hours between 5am and 5:30pm; in some instances, you might have to transfer in Ciudad Quesada. From there, you can catch one of the frequent buses to San José.

Gray Line (✆ **2220-2126;** www.graylinecostarica.com) and **Interbus** (✆ **2283-5573;** www.interbusonline.com) both have two daily buses to La Fortuna from San José. Both companies also run routes from La Fortuna with connections to most other major destinations in Costa Rica.

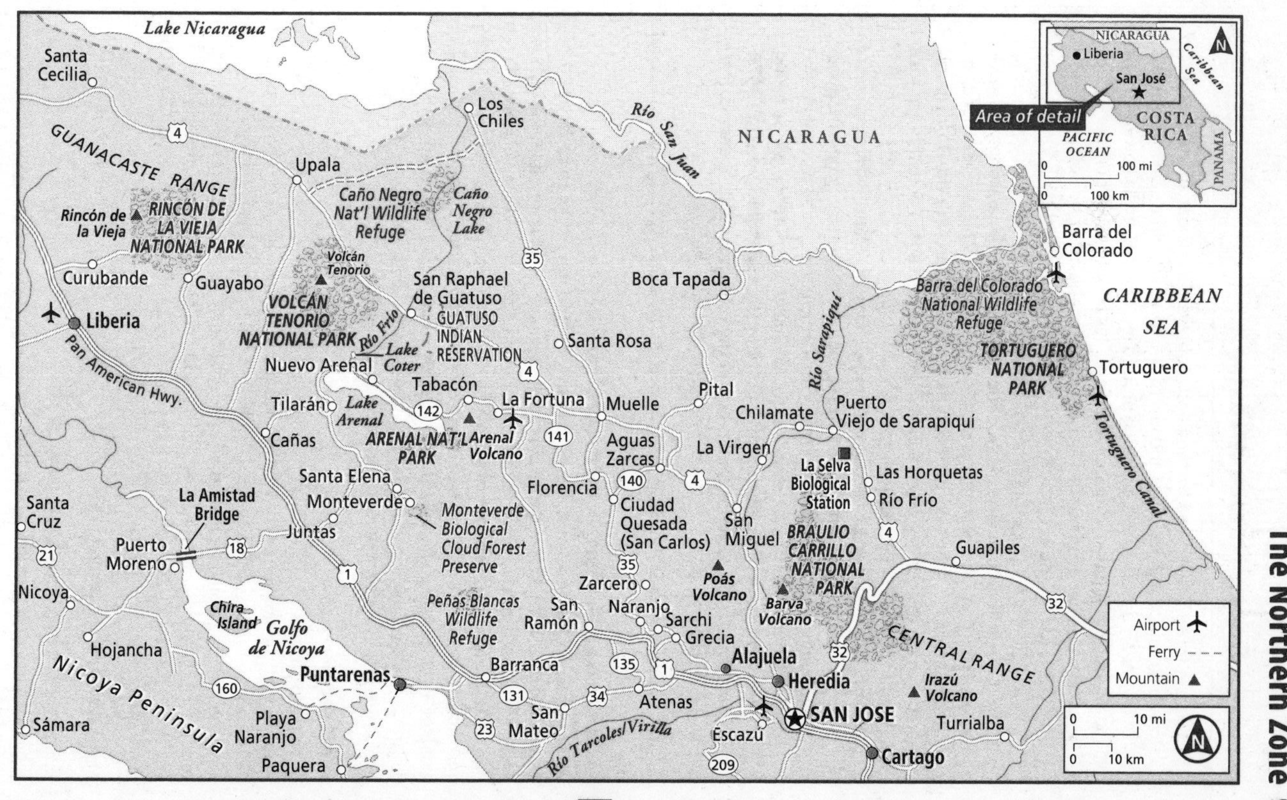
NICARAGUA
Liberia
San José
COSTA RICA
PACIFIC OCEAN
Caribbean Sea
PANAMA
100 mi
100 km
Area of detail
Lake Nicaragua
Santa Cecilia
Los Chiles
Río San Juan
NICARAGUA
GUANACASTE RANGE
Upala
Caño Negro Nat'l Wildlife Refuge
Caño Negro Lake
Rincón de la Vieja
RINCÓN DE LA VIEJA NATIONAL PARK
Volcán Tenorio
Curubande
Guayabo
San Raphael de Guatuso
Boca Tapada
Barra del Colorado
Barra del Colorado National Wildlife Refuge
CARIBBEAN SEA
Liberia
VOLCÁN TENORIO NATIONAL PARK
Río Frío
GUATUSO INDIAN RESERVATION
Lake Coter
Santa Rosa
Río Sarapiquí
TORTUGUERO NATIONAL PARK
Tortuguero
Pan American Hwy.
Nuevo Arenal
Tabacón
Tilarán
Lake Arenal
La Fortuna
Muelle
Pital
Chilamate
Puerto Viejo de Sarapiquí
Tortuguero Canal
Cañas
ARENAL NAT'L PARK
Arenal Volcano
Aguas Zarcas
La Virgen
La Selva Biological Station
Las Horquetas
Río Frío
Santa Elena
Monteverde
Florencia
Ciudad Quesada (San Carlos)
San Miguel
Santa Cruz
La Amistad Bridge
Juntas
Monteverde Biological Cloud Forest Preserve
BRAULIO CARRILLO NATIONAL PARK
Guapiles
Puerto Moreno
Poás Volcano
Zarcero
Barva Volcano
Nicoya
Chira Island
Golfo de Nicoya
Peñas Blancas Wildlife Refuge
San Ramón
Naranjo
Sarchí
Grecia
Airport
Ferry
Mountain
Hojancha
CENTRAL RANGE
Alajuela
Heredia
Irazú Volcano
Nicoya Peninsula
Puntarenas
Barranca
Atenas
SAN JOSE
Turrialba
Sámara
Playa Naranjo
San Mateo
Río Tarcoles/Virilla
Escazú
Cartago
Paquera
10 mi
10 km
4
35
142
141
140
18
21
1
35
32
135
160
131
34
23
209

Boats, Horses & Taxis

You can travel between La Fortuna and Monteverde by boat and taxi, or on a combination boat, horseback, and taxi trip. A 10- to 20-minute boat ride across Lake Arenal cuts out hours of driving around its shores. From La Fortuna to the put-in point is about a 25-minute taxi ride. It's about a 1½-hour four-wheel-drive taxi ride between the Río Chiquito dock on the other side of Lake Arenal and Santa Elena. These trips can be arranged in either direction for between $25 and $45 (£13–£23) per person, all-inclusive.

You can also add on a horseback ride on the Santa Elena/Monteverde side of the lake. There are several routes and rides offered. The steepest heads up the mountains and through the forest to the town of San Gerardo, which is only a 30-minute car ride from Santa Elena. With the horseback ride, this trip runs around $50 to $70 (£25–£35) per person.

Warning: The riding is often rainy, muddy, and steep. Many find it much more arduous than awe-inspiring. Moreover, I've received numerous complaints about the condition of the trails and the treatment of the horses, so be very careful and demanding before signing on for this trip. Find out what route you will be taking, as well as the condition of the horses if possible. **Desafío Expeditions** (✆ **2479-9464;** www.desafiocostarica.com) is one of the more reputable operators. They will even drive your car around for you while you take the scenic route.

Orientation & Visitor Information

As you enter La Fortuna, you'll see the massive volcano directly in front of you. La Fortuna is only a few streets wide, with almost all the hotels, restaurants, and shops clustered along the main road that leads out of town toward Tabacón and the volcano. There are several information and tour-booking offices and Internet cafes, as well as a couple of pharmacies, general stores, and laundromats on the streets that surround the small central park that fronts the Catholic church. There's a **Banco de Costa Rica** as you enter La Fortuna, just over the Río Burío bridge, and a **Banco Nacional** in the center of town, across the park from the church. Both have ATMs.

Getting Around

If you don't have a car, you'll need to either take a cab or go on an organized tour if you want to visit the hot springs or view the volcano eruption. There are tons of taxis in La Fortuna (you can flag one down practically anywhere), and there is always a line of them ready and waiting along the main road beside the central park. A taxi between La Fortuna and Tabacón should cost around $6 (£3). Another alternative is to rent a car when you get here. **Alamo** (✆ **2479-9090;** www.alamocostarica.com) and **Poás** (✆ **2479-8027;** www.carentals.com) both have offices in La Fortuna.

WHAT TO SEE & DO

Experiencing the Volcano ★★

The first thing you should know is that Arenal Volcano borders a region of cloud forests and rainforests, and the volcano's cone is often socked in by clouds and fog. Many people come to Arenal and never get to see the exposed cone. Moreover, the volcano does go through periods when it is relatively quiet.

The second thing you should know is that you can't climb Arenal Volcano—it's not safe due to the constant activity. Several foolish people who have ignored this warning have lost their lives, and others have been severely injured.

Still, waiting for and watching Arenal's regular eruptions is the main activity in La Fortuna and is best done at night when the orange lava glows against the starry sky. Although it's possible simply to look up from the middle of town and see Arenal erupting, the view is best from the north and west sides of the volcano along the road to Tabacón and toward the national park entrance. If you have a car, you can drive along this road, but if you've arrived by bus, you will need to take a taxi or tour.

Arenal National Park constitutes an area of more than 2,880 hectares (7,114 acres), which includes the viewing and parking areas closest to the volcano. The park is open daily from 8am to 10pm and charges $10 (£5) admission per person. The trails through forest and over old lava flows inside the park are gorgeous and fun. However, at night the view from inside the park is no better than on the roads just outside it.

Every hotel in town and several tour offices offer night tours to the volcano. (They don't actually enter the park; they stop on the road that runs btw. the park entrance and the Arenal Observatory Lodge.) Often these volcano-viewing tours include a stop at one of the local hot springs, and the price varies accordingly.

Note: Although it's counterintuitive, the rainy season is often a better time to see the exposed cone of Arenal Volcano, especially at night. I don't know why this is, but I've had excellent volcano-viewing sessions at various points during the rainy season; during the dry season the volcano can often be socked in solid for days at a time. The bottom line is that catching a glimpse of the volcano's cone is never a sure thing.

Other Adventurous Pursuits in the Area

Aside from the impressive volcanic activity, the area around Arenal Volcano is packed with other natural wonders.

ATV **Fourtrax Adventures** (✆ **2479-8444;** www.fourtraxadventure.com) offers a 3-hour adventure through the forests and farmlands around La Fortuna. The tour includes a stop at a jungle swimming hole, as well as a visit to a butterfly farm. You get good views of the volcano, as well as the La Fortuna Waterfall. The cost is $75 (£38) per ATV. A second rider on the same ATV costs $30 (£15).

CANOPY TOURS & CANYONING There are numerous ways to get up into the forest canopy here. Perhaps the simplest way is to hike the trails and bridges of **Arenal Hanging Bridges** (✆ **2290-0469;** www.hangingbridges.com). Located just over the Lake Arenal dam, this attraction is a complex of gentle trails and suspension bridges through a beautiful tract of primary forest. It's open daily from 7:30am to 4:30pm; admission is $22 (£11).

Another option is the **Sky Tram ★★** (✆ **2479-9944;** www.skytrek.com), an open gondola-style ride that begins near the shores of Lake Arenal and rises up, providing excellent views of the lake and volcano. From here you can hike their series of trails and suspended bridges. In the end you can hike down, take the gondola, or strap on a harness and ride their zip-line canopy tour down to the bottom. The zip-line tour here features several very long and very fast sections, with some impressive views of the lake and volcano. The cost is $66 (£33) for the combined tram ride up and zip-line down tour. It's $55 (£28) to ride the tram round-trip.

Taking a Soothing Soak in Hot Springs

Arenal Volcano has bestowed a terrific fringe benefit on the area around it: several naturally heated thermal springs.

Located at the site of the former village that was destroyed by the 1968 eruption, **Tabacón Grand Spa Thermal Resort** ★★★ (✆ **2519-1900;** www.tabacon.com) is the most extensive, luxurious, and expensive spot to soak your tired bones. A series of variously sized pools, fed by natural springs, are spread out among lush gardens. At the center is a large, warm, spring-fed swimming pool with a slide, a swim-up bar, and a perfect view of the volcano. One of the stronger streams flows over a sculpted waterfall, with a rock ledge underneath that provides a perfect place to sit and receive a free hydraulic shoulder massage. The resort also has an excellent spa on the grounds offering professional massages, mud masks, and other treatments, as well as yoga classes (appointments required.) The spa here even has several permanent sweat lodges, based on a Native American traditional design. A full-service restaurant, garden grill, and a couple of bars are available for those seeking sustenance.

Entrance fees are $70 (£35) for adults and $35 (£17) for children 11 and under. These rates include either a buffet lunch or dinner, and are good for a full day. After 6pm, you can enter for $45 (£23) not including any meals. The hot springs are open daily from noon to 10pm (spa treatments can actually be scheduled as early as 8am, and hotel guests can enter at 10am). The pools are busiest between 2pm and 6pm. Management enforces a policy of limiting visitors, so reservations (which can be made online or by phone) are recommended.

Baldi Hot Springs (✆ **2479-9651**), next to the Volcano Look Disco, are the first hot springs you'll come to as you drive from La Fortuna toward Tabacón. This place has grown substantially over the years, with many different pools, slides, and bars and restaurants spread around the expansive grounds. However, I find this place far less attractive than either of the other two options mentioned here. There's much more of a party vibe at Baldi, with loud music often blaring at some of the swim-up bars. Admission is $30 (£15).

Just across the street from Baldi Termae is the unmarked entrance of my current favorite local hot spring, **Eco Termales** ★★ (✆ **2479-8484**). Smaller and more intimate than Tabacón, this series of pools set amid lush forest and gardens is almost as picturesque and luxurious, although there are far fewer pools, the spa services are much less extensive, and there is no view of the volcano. Reservations are absolutely necessary here, and total admissions are limited so that it is never crowded. Admission is $24 (£12).

If you'd like a bigger rush than the canopy tours offer, you could go "canyoning" with **Pure Trek Canyoning** ★★ (✆ **866/569-5723** in the U.S. and Canada, or 2461-2110; www.puretrekcostarica.com) and **Desafío Expeditions** ★★ (✆ **2479-9464;** www.desafiocostarica.com); both offer canyoning adventures. This adventure sport is a mix of hiking through and alongside a jungle river, punctuated with periodic rappels through and alongside the faces of rushing waterfalls. Pure Trek's trip is probably better for first-timers and families with kids, while Desafío's tour is just a bit more rugged and adventurous. Pure Trek charges $90 (£45), while Desafío charges $85 (£43). Both of these companies offer various full-day excursions, mixing canyoning with other adventure tours.

Finally, you can also take a bungee jump in La Fortuna at **Arenal Bungee** (© **2479-7440;** arenalbungee.com). The bungee jump here is a 40m (130-ft.) fall from a steel tower constructed on the outskirts of downtown La Fortuna. You can try a water landing, as well as a "rocket launch," which is kind of the equivalent of becoming a human sling shot. Jumps, falls, and rocket shots cost $39 (£20). This attraction is open 9:30am to 9:30pm daily, so you can even partake in the fun after dark.

HIKING & HORSEBACK RIDING Horseback riding is a popular activity in this area, and there are scores of good rides on dirt back roads and through open fields and dense rainforest. Volcano and lake views come with the terrain on most rides. Horseback trips to the Río Fortuna waterfall are perhaps the most popular tours sold, but remember, the horse will get you only to the entrance; from there, you'll have to hike a bit. A horseback ride to the falls should cost between $20 and $45 (£10–£23), including the entrance fee.

One popular and strenuous hike is to **Cerro Chato,** a dormant volcanic cone on the flank of Arenal. There's a pretty little lake up here. **Desafío Expeditions ★** (© **2479-9464;** www.desafiocostarica.com) leads a 4- to 5-hour hike for $65 (£33), including lunch.

Aventuras Arenal (© **2479-9133;** www.arenaladventures.com), **Desafío Expeditions ★★** (© **2479-9464;** www.desafiocostarica.com), and **Sunset Tours** (© **2479-9800;** www.sunsettourcr.com) are the main tour operators. In addition to the above tours, each of these companies offers most of the tours listed in this section, as well as fishing trips and sightseeing excursions on the lake, and transfers to other destinations around Costa Rica.

RÍO FORTUNA FALLS Leading the list of side attractions in the area is the impressive **Río Fortuna Waterfall ★** (© **2479-8360**), about 5.5km ($3^1/_2$ miles) outside of town in a lush jungle setting. You can drive or hike to just within viewing distance. When you get to the entrance to the lookout, you'll have to pay a $6 (£3) entrance fee to actually check out the falls. It's another 15- to 20-minute hike down a steep trail to the pool formed by the waterfall. You can swim, but stay away from the turbulent water at the base of the falls—several people have drowned here. Instead, check out and enjoy the calm pool just around the bend, or join the locals at the popular swimming hole under the bridge on the paved road, just after the turnoff for the road up to the falls. Open daily from 8am to 4pm.

MOUNTAIN BIKING This region is very well suited for mountain biking. Rides range in difficulty from moderate to extremely challenging. You can combine a day on a mountain bike with a visit to one or more of the more popular attractions here. **Bike Arenal ★** (© **866/465-4114** in the U.S. and Canada, or 2479-9454; www.bikearenal.com) is the only dedicated operator in the field, with an excellent collection of top-notch bikes and equipment and a wide range of tour possibilities.

WHITE-WATER RAFTING & CANOEING For adventurous tours of the area, check out **Desafío Expeditions ★★** (© **2479-9464;** www.desafiocostarica.com) or **Wave Expeditions ★★** (© **2479-7262;** www.waveexpeditions.com). Both companies offer daily raft rides of Class 1 to 2, 3, and 4 to 5 on different sections of the Toro, Peñas Blancas, and Sarapiquí rivers. A half-day float trip on a nearby river costs around $45 (£23) per person; a full day of rafting on some rougher water costs $70 to $90 (£35–£45) per person, depending on what section of what river you ride. Both companies also offer mountain biking and most of the standard local guided trips. If you want a wet and personal ride, try Desafío's tour in inflatable kayaks, or "duckies," down the pristine Arenal River.

Side Trips from La Fortuna

La Fortuna is a great place from which to make a day trip to the **Caño Negro National Wildlife Refuge** ★. This vast network of marshes and rivers (particularly the Río Frío) is 100km (62 miles) north of La Fortuna near the town of Los Chiles. This refuge is best known for its amazing abundance of bird life, including roseate spoonbills, jabiru storks, herons, and egrets, but you can also see caimans and crocodiles. Bird-watchers should not miss this refuge, although keep in mind that the main lake dries up in the dry season (mid-Apr to Nov), which reduces the number of wading birds. Full-day tours to Caño Negro average between $45 and $60 (£23–£30) per person. However, most of the tours run out of La Fortuna that are billed as Caño Negro never really enter the refuge but instead ply sections of the nearby Río Frio, which features similar wildlife and ecosystems.

You can also visit the **Venado Caverns,** a 45-minute drive away. In addition to plenty of stalactites, stalagmites, and other limestone formations, you'll see bats and cave fish. Tours here cost around $45 (£23). All of the tour agencies and hotel tour desks can arrange or directly offer trips to Caño Negro and Venado Caverns.

SHOPPING

La Fortuna is chock-full of souvenir shops selling standard tourist fare. However, you'll find one of my favorite craft shops here. As you leave the town of La Fortuna toward Tabacón, keep your eye on the right-hand side of the road. When you see a massive collection of wood sculptures and a building reading **Original Grand Gallery** (no phone), slow down and pull over. This local artisan and his family produce works in a variety of styles and sizes. They specialize in faces, many of them larger than a typical home's front door. You can also find a host of animal figures, ranging in style from purely representational to rather abstract.

WHERE TO STAY

While La Fortuna is the major gateway town to Arenal Volcano, for my money, the best places to stay are located on the road between La Fortuna and the National Park.

Very Expensive

In addition to the hotels reviewed below, other good upscale choices include **Arenal Kioro** ★★ (© **888/866-5027** in the U.S. and Canada, or 2461-1700; www.hotelarenalkioro.com) and **Lost Iguana Resort** (© **2267-6148;** www.lostiguanaresort.com).

Tabacón Grand Spa Thermal Resort ★★★ This is the most-established, extensive, and popular resort in the Arenal area—and for good reason. Many rooms have excellent, direct views of the volcano. Rooms on the upper floors of the 300-block building have the best vistas. Still, a number of rooms have obstructed, or no, views. My advice: Book a "Standard Superior," which will come with a view that is definitely worth the $30 (£15) splurge over the straight "Standard."

All rooms are large, with heavy, dark-stained wooden furniture. Most come with a private terrace or balcony with a table and a couple of chairs. Nine of the rooms are truly accessible to travelers with disabilities. Guests enjoy privileges at the spectacular hot-springs complex and spa across the street (see "Taking a Soothing Soak in Hot Springs" on p. 606), including slightly extended hours. When you consider the included entrance fee to the hot springs, the rates here are actually rather reasonable.

On the main road btw. La Fortuna and Lake Arenal, Tabacón (P.O. Box 181-1007, Centro Colón, San José). © **877/277-8291** in the U.S. and Canada, or 2519-1900 reservations in San José, or 2460-2020 at the resort. Fax 2519-1940. www.tabacon.com. 114 units. \$230–\$330 (£115–£165) double; \$340–\$370 (£170–£185) suite. Rates higher during peak periods. AE, DC, MC, V. **Amenities:** 2 restaurants; 2 bars; exercise room; Jacuzzi; laundry service; large pool w/swim-up bar; extensive hot springs and spa facilities. *In room:* A/C, TV, hair dryer, Wi-Fi.

Expensive

Magic Mountain Hotel ★★ It was just a matter of time till luxury found its way to La Fortuna. Located just on the outskirts of town—as you head toward Tabacón—this three-story hotel has large and luxurious rooms, with plenty of perks. All come with a private balcony facing the volcano. The junior suites are even bigger, with a separate sitting area, large shower with rainwater shower head, and private volcano view in-room Jacuzzi. I like no. 506, which is an end unit, with spectacular views. There's a spa and large free-form pool, with two separate outdoor Jacuzzis and separate children's pool, as well as the town's only sports bar.

La Fortuna, San Carlos. © **2479-7246.** Fax 2479-7248. www.hotelmagicmountain.com. 46 units. \$145 (£73) double; \$300 (£150) suite. Rates lower in the off season. Rates include buffet breakfast. AE, MC, V. **Amenities:** Restaurant; bar; 2 Jacuzzis; laundry service; outdoor pool; spa. *In room:* A/C, TV, hair dryer, minibar, free Wi-Fi.

Moderate

Other good options in this price range include **Montaña de Fuego Inn ★** (© **2460-1220;** www.montanafuegohotel.com) and **Volcano Lodge** (© **866/208-9819** in the U.S. and Canada, or 2460-6080; www.volcanolodge.com), on the road between town and Tabacón; and **Hotel La Fortuna** (© **2479-9197;** www.fortunainn.com) and **Hotel San Bosco** (© **2479-9050;** www.arenal-volcano.com) in the town of La Fortuna proper.

In addition to the places mentioned above and below, there has been ongoing construction along the entire length of the road between La Fortuna and Tabacón over the past years. If you have a car and some time, you might want to stop and check out any new or interesting hotels or cabins that strike your fancy along the way.

Arenal Observatory Lodge ★★ This place is very close to the volcano and built on a high ridge, with a spectacular view of the cone. The best rooms here are the junior suites and villas. Still, the "Smithsonian" rooms feature massive picture windows, with a direct view of the volcano. This is one of the better nature lodges for travelers with disabilities: Five rooms are truly equipped for wheelchair access, and a paved path extends almost 1km (1/2 mile) into the rainforest. When you're not hiking or on a tour, you can hang by the volcano-view swimming pool and Jacuzzi.

To get here, head to the national park entrance, stay on the dirt road past the entrance, and follow the signs to the Observatory Lodge. A four-wheel-drive vehicle used to be required for the 9km (5 1/2-mile) dirt road up to the lodge, but two bridges now eliminate the need to ford any major rivers, and a traditional sedan will *usually* make it even in the rainy season.

On the flanks of Arenal Volcano (A.P. 13411-1000, San José). © **2290-7011** reservations number in San José, or 2479-1070 at the lodge. Fax 2290-8427. www.arenalobservatorylodge.com. 42 units. \$70 (£35) La Casona double; \$93 (£47) standard double; \$122 (£61) Smithsonian; \$140 (£70) junior suite. Rates include breakfast buffet. Rates lower in off season. AE, MC, V. **Amenities:** Restaurant; bar; Jacuzzi; laundry service; pool. *In room:* No phone.

Inexpensive

Most of the budget lodgings in this area are found in the town of La Fortuna. **Cabinas Los Guayabos** (✆/fax **2460-6644**) and **Cabinas Palo Verde** (✆ **2460-9791**) are two good, economical options, with views and locations that rival some of the more expensive lodgings listed above.

In addition to the place listed below, backpackers should check out **Arenal Backpackers Resort** (✆ **2479-7000;** www.arenalbackpackers.com), which bills itself as a five-star hostel. It has both shared-bathroom dorm rooms, and more upscale private rooms, but even backpackers get to enjoy the large pool, Wi-Fi, and volcano views.

Hotel Las Colinas Like the Hotel La Fortuna (above), this long-standing downtown hotel was torn down and rebuilt. Today, Las Colinas sits as the centerpiece to a new little minimall, with some shops and a small spa. The rooms run the range from simple budget accommodations to spiffy junior suites with a private volcano-view balcony and Jacuzzi. The budget rooms come with televisions, but lack the other amenities found in the rest of the rooms. The best feature of the new hotel is its ample rooftop terrace where breakfasts are served. All of the water here is solar heated.

La Fortuna (A.P. 06), San Carlos. ✆ **2479-9305.** Fax 2479-9160. www.lascolinasarenal.com. 19 units. $42 (£21) budget room double; $55–$60 (£23–30) double; $70 (£35) junior suite. Rates include breakfast and taxes. Rates lower in off season. MC, V (5% surcharge). **Amenities:** Restaurant; free Wi-Fi. *In room:* A/C, TV, fridge.

WHERE TO DINE

Dining in La Fortuna is nowhere near as spectacular as volcano viewing, although, given the area's popularity, there's no lack of options. The favorite meeting places in town are the **El Jardín Restaurant** (✆ **2479-9360**) and **Lava Rocks** (✆ **2479-8039**); both are on the main road, right in the center of La Fortuna. Other choices include **La Choza de Laurel** (✆ **2479-9231**), **Rancho La Cascada** (✆ **2479-9145**), and **Restaurante Nene's** (✆ **2479-9192**). For good pizza and Italian cuisine, try either the new **Anch'io** (✆ **8350-4040**) near the heart of town, or **El Vagabundo** ★ (✆ **2479-9565**), just on the outskirts.

For some fine and fancy dining, you can try **Los Tucanes** ★★ (✆ **2460-2020**) restaurant at the Tabacón Grand Spa resort.

Don Rufino COSTA RICAN/INTERNATIONAL Set on a busy corner in the heart of town, this restaurant is easily the best—and the busiest—option right in La Fortuna. The front wall and bar area open on to the street and are often filled both with local tour guides and tourists. Try the *pollo al estilo de la abuela* (Grandma's chicken), which is baked and served wrapped in banana leaves, or one of the excellent cuts of meat. It's a good choice for breakfast, and the bar stays open most nights until 2am.

Downtown La Fortuna. ✆ **2479-9997.** Main courses $5–$28 (£2.50–£14). Reservations recommended during the high season. AE, MC, V. Daily 7am–11pm.

El Novillo del Arenal ★ *Finds* STEAK/COSTA RICAN This place is the definition of "nothing fancy." In fact, it's just some lawn furniture (tables and chairs) set on a concrete slab underneath a high, open zinc roof. Still, it has garnered a well-deserved reputation as the best steakhouse in the area. The steaks are big and tender and well prepared. The chicken and fish dishes are huge as well and also nicely done. Meals come with garlic bread, fries, and some slaw. If the night is clear, you can get a good view of any volcanic activity from the parking lot here.

On the road to Tabacón, 10km (6¼ miles) outside of La Fortuna. ✆ **2479-1910.** Reservations recommended. Main courses $5.50–$12 (£2.25–£6). MC, V. Daily 10am–10pm.

Volunteer & Learning Opportunities in Costa Rica

Below are some institutions and organizations that are working on ecology and sustainable development projects in Costa Rica.

Asociación de Voluntarios para el Servicio en las Areas Protegidas (ASVO) ★ (✆ **2258-4430;** www.asvocr.org) organizes volunteers to work in Costa Rican national parks. A 2-week minimum commitment is required, as is a basic ability to converse in Spanish. Housing is provided at a basic ranger station, and there is a $15 (£7.50) daily fee to cover food, which is basic Tico fare.

Caribbean Conservation Corporation (✆ **800/676-2018** in the U.S., or 2278-6058; www.cccturtle.org) is a nonprofit organization dedicated to sea turtle research, protection, and advocacy. Their main operation in Costa Rica is headquartered in Tortuguero, where volunteers can aid in various scientific studies, as well as nightly patrols of the beach during nesting seasons to prevent poaching.

Costa Rica Rainforest Outward Bound School (✆ **800/676-2018** in the U.S., or 2278-6058; www.crrobs.org) is the local branch of this well-respected international adventure-based outdoor-education organization. Courses range from 2 weeks to a full semester, and offerings include surfing, kayaking, tree climbing, and learning Spanish.

Eco Teach (✆ **800/626-8992** in the U.S.; www.ecoteach.com) works primarily in facilitating educational trips for high school and college student groups. Trips focus on Costa Rican ecology and culture. Costs run around $1,445 to $1,595 (£723–£798) per person for a 10-day trip, including lodging, meals, classes, and travel within the country. Airfare to Costa Rica is extra.

The **Institute for Central American Development Studies** ★ (✆ **2225-0508;** www.icads.org) offers internship and research opportunities in the areas of environment, agriculture, human rights, and women's studies. An intensive Spanish-language program can be combined with work-study or volunteer opportunities.

The **Monteverde Institute** (✆ **2645-5053;** www.mvinstitute.org) offers study programs in Monteverde and also has a volunteer center that helps in placement and training of volunteers.

Lava Lounge ★ *Finds* INTERNATIONAL This downtown La Fortuna open-air restaurant combines a very simple setting, with a sleek and somewhat eclectic menu. Healthy and hearty sandwiches, wraps, and salads are the main offerings here. You can get a traditional burger, or one made with fresh grilled tuna. For more substantial fare, there's traditional Costa Rican *arroz con pollo,* and a *casado,* built around a thick pork chop. You can also get several different pasta dishes, and every evening there are dinner specials, which may include some coconut-battered shrimp with a mango salsa, or a prime sirloin steak in a green-pepper or red-wine sauce.

 Downtown La Fortuna, on the main road. ✆ **2479-7365.** Reservations not necessary. Main courses $6–$10 (£3–£5). AE, MC, V. Daily noon–midnight.

LA FORTUNA AFTER DARK

La Fortuna's biggest after-dark attraction is the volcano, but the **Volcano Look Disco** on the road to Tabacón is trying to compete. If you get bored of the eruptions and seismic rumbling, head here for heavy dance beats and mirrored disco balls. In town the folks at Luigi's Hotel have opened a midsize **casino** next door to their hotel and restaurant, while the open-to-the-street bar at **Don Rufino** is a popular spot for a drink. Finally, there's a cozy sports bar, with a pool table and flatscreen televisions on the second floor at the **Hotel Magic Mountain.**

8 MANUEL ANTONIO ★★

140km (87 miles) SW of San José; 69km (43 miles) S of Playa de Jacó

Manuel Antonio was Costa Rica's first major ecotourist destination and it is still one of its best. The views from the hills overlooking Manuel Antonio are spectacular, the beaches (especially those inside the national park) are idyllic, and its jungles are crawling with howler, white-faced, and squirrel monkeys, among other forms of exotic wildlife. The downside is that you'll have to pay more to see it, and you'll have to share it with more fellow travelers. Moreover, development here is threatening to destroy what makes this place so special. What was once a smattering of small hotels tucked into the forested hillside has become a long string of lodgings along the 7km (4 1/3 miles) of road between Quepos and the national park entrance. Hotel roofs now regularly break the tree line, and there seems to be no control over zoning and unchecked ongoing construction. A jumble of snack shacks, souvenir stands, and makeshift parking lots line the beach road just outside the park, making the entrance road look more like a shanty than a national park.

Still, this remains a beautiful destination, with a wide range of attractions and activities. Gazing down on the blue Pacific from high on the hillsides of Manuel Antonio, it's almost impossible to hold back a gasp of delight. Offshore, rocky islands dot the vast expanse of blue, and in the foreground, the rich, deep green of the rainforest sweeps down to the water. It's this superb view that keeps people transfixed on decks, patios, and balconies throughout the area.

Those views that are so bewitching also have their own set of drawbacks. If you want a great view, you aren't going to be staying on the beach—in fact, you probably won't be able to walk to the beach. This means that you'll be driving back and forth, taking taxis, or riding the public bus.

If you're traveling on a budget or are mainly interested in sportfishing, you might end up staying in the nearby town of **Quepos,** which was once a quiet banana port; the land to the north was used by Chiquita to grow its bananas. Quepos currently features a wide variety of restaurants, souvenir and crafts shops, and lively bars. Moreover, it stands to see even more improvement when the new Marina Pez Vela project is completed in early 2009. Located right near the center of town, this complex will feature a modern 270-slip marina, a 100-room hotel, shops, and condo units.

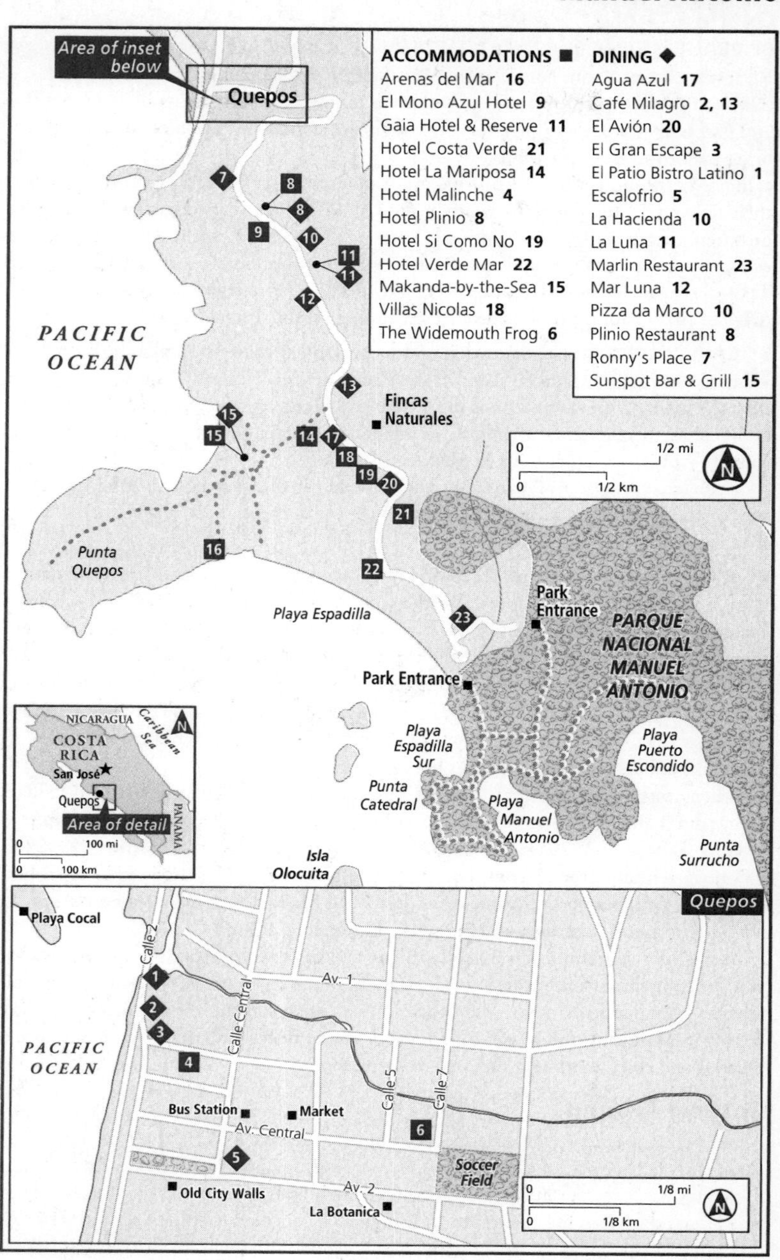

Area of inset below
Quepos
ACCOMMODATIONS
Arenas del Mar 16
El Mono Azul Hotel 9
Gaia Hotel & Reserve 11
Hotel Costa Verde 21
Hotel La Mariposa 14
Hotel Malinche 4
Hotel Plinio 8
Hotel Si Como No 19
Hotel Verde Mar 22
Makanda-by-the-Sea 15
Villas Nicolas 18
The Widemouth Frog 6
DINING
Agua Azul 17
Café Milagro 2, 13
El Avión 20
El Gran Escape 3
El Patio Bistro Latino 1
Escalofrio 5
La Hacienda 10
La Luna 11
Marlin Restaurant 23
Mar Luna 12
Pizza da Marco 10
Plinio Restaurant 8
Ronny's Place 7
Sunspot Bar & Grill 15
PACIFIC OCEAN
Fincas Naturales
0 1/2 mi
0 1/2 km
Punta Quepos
Playa Espadilla
Park Entrance
PARQUE NACIONAL MANUEL ANTONIO
Park Entrance
Playa Espadilla Sur
Punta Catedral
Playa Manuel Antonio
Playa Puerto Escondido
Punta Surrucho
Isla Olocuita
NICARAGUA
Caribbean Sea
COSTA RICA
San José
Quepos
Area of detail
PANAMA
0 100 mi
0 100 km
Quepos
Playa Cocal
Calle 2
Av. 1
Calle Central
PACIFIC OCEAN
Calle 5
Calle 7
Bus Station
Market
Av. Central
Soccer Field
Old City Walls
Av. 2
La Botanica
0 1/8 mi
0 1/8 km

Getting There

BY PLANE **Sansa** (✆ **877/767-2672** in the U.S. and Canada, or 2290-4100 in Costa Rica; www.flysansa.com) and **Nature Air** (✆ **800/235-9272** in the U.S. and Canada, or 2299-6000; www.natureair.com) both have a number of daily flights between San José and Quepos, and both airlines also offer flights or connections to most of the country's other major tourist destinations.

Both Sansa and Nature Air provide minivan airport-transfer service coordinated with their arriving flights. The service costs around $5 (£2.50) per person each way, depending on where exactly your hotel is located. Speak to your airline's agent when you arrive to confirm your return flight and coordinate a pickup at your hotel for that day if necessary. Taxis also meet incoming flights as well. Expect to be charged between $8 and $12 (£4–£6) per car for up to four people, depending on the distance to your hotel.

BY CAR From San José, the easiest and most popular route is to take the narrow and winding old highway, which turns off the Pan-American Highway just west of Alajuela near the town of Atenas and joins the Costanera Highway near Orotina. Just follow the many signs to hotels in either Jacó or Manuel Antonio. When you reach Jacó, it's a straight shot and another hour to Manuel Antonio.

If you're coming from Guanacaste or any point north, take the Pan-American Highway to the Puntarenas turnoff and head south on the Costanera Highway, the coastal road to Jacó.

BY BUS **Express buses** (✆ **2223-5567**) to Manuel Antonio leave San José daily at 6am, noon, and 6 and 7:30pm from the Coca-Cola bus terminal at Calle 16 between avenidas 1 and 3. Trip duration is 3½ hours; the fare is $5.50 (£2.75). These buses go all the way to the park entrance and will drop you off at any of the hotels along the way.

Regular buses (✆ **2223-5567**) to Quepos leave San José daily at 7 and 10am and 2 and 4pm. Trip duration is 4½ hours; the fare is $4.40 (£2.20). These buses stop in Quepos. From here, if you're staying at one of the hotels on the road to Manuel Antonio, you must take a local bus or taxi to your hotel.

When you're ready to depart, express buses to San José leave daily at 6 and 9:30am, noon, and 3 and 5pm. Local buses to San José leave at 5 and 8am and 2 and 4pm.

Gray Line (✆ **2220-2126;** www.graylinecostarica.com) and **Interbus** (✆ **2283-5573;** www.interbusonline.com) both have two buses daily. The fare is $35 (£18). Both companies will pick you up at most San José– and Manuel Antonio–area hotels and also offer connections to various other popular destinations around Costa Rica.

In the busy winter months, tickets sell out well in advance, especially on weekends; if you can, purchase your ticket several days in advance. However, you must buy your Quepos-bound tickets in San José and your San José return tickets in Quepos. If you're staying in Manuel Antonio, you can buy your return ticket for a direct bus in advance in Quepos and then wait along the road to be picked up.

Getting Around

A taxi between Quepos and Manuel Antonio (or any hotel along the road toward the park) costs between $3 and $6 (£1.50–£3), depending upon the distance. At night or if the taxi must leave the main road (for hotels such as La Mariposa, Parador, Makanda, and Arenas del Mar), the charge is a little higher. If you need to call a taxi, dial ✆ **2777-3080** or 2777-0425. Taxis are supposed to use meters, although this isn't always the case.

If your taxi doesn't have a meter, or the driver won't use it, try to negotiate in advance. Ask your hotel desk what a specific ride should cost, and use that as your guide.

The bus between Quepos and Manuel Antonio takes 15 minutes each way and runs roughly every half-hour from 6am to 7pm daily, with one late bus leaving Quepos at 10pm and returning from Manuel Antonio at 10:30pm. The buses, which leave from the main bus terminal in Quepos, near the market, go all the way to the national park entrance before turning around and returning. You can flag down these buses from any point on the side of the road. The fare is 30¢ (15p).

You can also rent a car from **Adobe** (**© 2777-4242**), **Alamo** (**© 2777-3344**), **Economy** (**© 2777-5260**), **Hertz** (**© 2777-3365**), **National** (**© 2777-0368**), or **Payless Rent-a-Car** (**© 2777-0115**) for around $50 (£25) a day. All have offices in downtown Quepos, but with advance notice, someone will meet you at the airport with your car for no extra charge.

If you rent a car, never leave anything of value in it unless you intend to stay within sight of the car at all times. Car break-ins are common here. There are a couple of parking lots just outside the park entrance that cost around $3 (£1.50) for the entire day. You should definitely keep your car in one of these while exploring the park or soaking up sun on the beach. And although these lots do offer a modicum of protection and safety, you should still not leave anything of value exposed in the car.

Visitor Information

There's no real tourism information office in Quepos or Manuel Antonio. Your best source of information will be your hotel desk. The various tour operators around town are also a good bet.

FAST FACTS The telephone number of the **Quepos Hospital** is **© 2777-0922.** In the event of an emergency, you can also call the **Cruz Roja** (**Red Cross; © 2777-0116**). For the **local police,** call **© 2777-1511** or 2777-2117.

Several major Costa Rican banks have branches and ATMs in downtown Quepos. The **post office** (**© 2777-1471**) is located in downtown Quepos. There are several pharmacies in Quepos, as well as a pharmacy at the hospital, and another close to the park entrance.

There's an ample array of **Internet cafes** around Quepos and along the road to Manuel Antonio, and many hotels have them as well. There are also a half-dozen or so laundromats and laundry services in town.

WHAT TO SEE & DO

Exploring the National Park

One of the most popular national parks in the country, Manuel Antonio is also one of the smallest, covering fewer than 680 hectares (1,680 acres). Its several nearly perfect small beaches are connected by trails that meander through the rainforest. The mountains surrounding the beaches quickly rise as you head inland from the water; however, the park was created to preserve not its beautiful beaches but its forests, home to endangered squirrel monkeys, three-toed sloths, purple-and-orange crabs, and hundreds of other species of birds, mammals, and plants. A guide is not essential here, but unless you're experienced in rainforest hiking, you'll see and learn a lot more with one. A 2- or 3-hour guided hike should cost between $25 and $45 (£13–£23) per person. Almost any of the hotels in town can help you set up a tour of the park. If you decide to explore the park on your own, a basic map is usually available at the park entrance for $1 (50p).

ENTRY POINT, FEES & REGULATIONS The park (✆ **2777-5185**) is closed on Monday but is open Tuesday through Sunday from 8am to 4pm year-round. You'll find the park entrance at **Playa Espadilla,** the beach at the end of the road from Quepos. To reach the park station, you must cross a small, sometimes polluted stream that's little more than ankle-deep at low tide but that can be knee- or even waist-deep at high tide. It's even reputed to be home to a crocodile or two. For years there has been talk of building a bridge over this stream; in the meantime you'll have to either wade it or pay a boatman a small voluntary tip for the very quick crossing. Just over the stream, you'll find the small ranger station. The Parks Service allows only 600 visitors to enter each day, which could mean that you won't get in if you arrive in midafternoon during the high season. Admission is $10 (£5).

THE BEACHES **Playa Espadilla Sur** (as opposed to Playa Espadilla, which is just outside the park; see "Hitting the Water," below) is the first beach within the actual park boundaries. It's usually the least-crowded and one of the best places to find a quiet shade tree to plant yourself under. However, if there's any surf, this is also the roughest beach in the park. **Playa Manuel Antonio,** which is the most popular beach inside the park, is a short, deep crescent of white sand backed by lush rainforest. The water here is sometimes clear enough to offer good snorkeling along the rocks at either end, and it's usually fairly calm. At low tide Playa Manuel Antonio shows a very interesting relic: a circular stone turtle trap left by its pre-Columbian residents. From Playa Manuel Antonio, there's another slightly longer trail to **Puerto Escondido,** where a blowhole sends up plumes of spray at high tide.

THE HIKING TRAILS From either Playa Espadilla Sur or Playa Manuel Antonio, you can take a circular hike around a high promontory bluff. The farthest point on this hike, which takes about 25 minutes round-trip, is **Punta Catedral ★★**, where the view is spectacular. The trail is a little steep in places, but anybody in average shape can do it. I have done it in sturdy sandals, but you might want to wear good hiking shoes. This is a good place to spot monkeys, although you're more likely to see a white-faced monkey than a rare squirrel monkey. Another good place to see monkeys is the **trail inland** from Playa Manuel Antonio.

Finally, there's a trail that leads first to Puerto Escondido (see above) and **Punta Surrucho,** where there are some sea caves. Be careful when hiking beyond Puerto Escondido: What seems like easy beach hiking at low tide becomes treacherous to impassable at high tide. Don't get trapped.

Hitting the Water

BEACHES OUTSIDE THE PARK **Playa Espadilla,** the gray-sand beach just outside the park boundary, is often perfect for board surfing and bodysurfing. At times it's a bit rough for casual swimming, but with no entrance fee, it's the most popular beach with locals and visiting Ticos. A full-day rental of a beach umbrella and two chaise longues costs around $10 (£5). (These are not available inside the park.) This beach is actually a great spot to learn how to surf. There are also open-air shops renting surfboards and boogie boards along the road fronting this beach. If you want a lesson, check in with the **Manuel Antonio Surf School** (✆ **2777-4842;** www.masurfschool.com), which has a roadside kiosk on the road to Manuel Antonio.

BOATING, KAYAKING, RAFTING & SPORTFISHING TOURS **Adventure Manuel Antonio** (✆ **2777-1084;** www.adventuremanuelantonio.com) and **Iguana Tours** (✆ **2777-2052;** www.iguanatours.com) are the most established and dependable tour operators in the area; both offer river rafting, sea kayaking, mangrove tours, and guided hikes. Depending on rainfall and demand, they will run either the Naranjo or Savegre rivers. I very much prefer the **Savegre River ★★** for its stunning scenery.

Another of my favorite tours in the area is a mangrove tour of the Damas Island estuary. These trips generally include lunch, a stop on Damas Island, and roughly 3 to 4 hours of cruising the waterways. You'll see loads of wildlife. The cost is usually around $60 to $70 (£30–£35).

Among the other boating options around Quepos/Manuel Antonio are excursions in search of dolphins and sunset cruises. **Iguana Tours** (see above) and **Planet Dolphin** (✆/fax **2777-1647;** www.planetdolphin.com) offer these tours. Most tours include a snorkel break and, if lucky, dolphin sightings.

Quepos is one of Costa Rica's billfish centers, and sailfish, marlin, and tuna are all common in these waters. If you're into sportfishing, try hooking up with **Blue Fin Sportfishing** (✆ **2777-0000;** www.bluefinsportfishing.com), **Blue Water** (✆ **800/807-1585** in the U.S. and Canada, or 2777-4841; www.sportfishingincostarica.com), or **High Tec Sportfishing** (✆ **2777-3465;** www.hightecsportfishing.com). A full day of fishing should cost between $400 and $1,800 (£200–£900), depending on the size of the boat, distance traveled, tackle provided, and amenities.

SCUBA DIVING & SNORKELING **Manuel Antonio Scuba Divers** (✆ **2777-3483;** www.manuelantoniodivers.com) and **Oceans Unlimited ★** (✆ **2777-3171;** www.oceansunlimitedcr.com) offer both scuba diving and snorkel outings, as well as certification and resort courses. Because of river runoff and often less than stellar visibility close to Quepos, the best trips involve some travel time. However, **Isla del Caño** is only about a 90-minute ride (each way). This is one of the best dive sites in Costa Rica, and I highly recommend it.

Other Activities in the Area

ATV If you want to try riding a four-wheel ATV (all-terrain vehicle), check in with **Fourtrax Adventures** (✆ **2777-1829;** www.fourtraxadventure.com). Their principal tour is a 3-hour adventure through African palm plantations, rural towns, and secondary forest to a jungle waterfall, where you stop for a dip. Either breakfast or lunch is served, depending on the timing. Cost is $95 (£48) per ATV. A second rider on the same ATV costs $30 (£15).

BUTTERFLY GARDEN **Fincas Naturales/The Nature Farm Reserve ★** (✆ **2777-1043;** www.butterflygardens.co.cr) is just across from (and run by) Hotel Sí Como No (p. 619). A lovely bi-level **butterfly garden ★** is the centerpiece attraction here, but there is also a private reserve and a small network of well-groomed trails through the forest. A 1-hour guided tour of the butterfly garden costs $15 (£7.50) per person, or $35 (£18) when combined with a 1-hour guided hike through the forest. This is also a good place to do a night tour ($30/£15).

CANOPY ADVENTURES There are several canopy tours in the area. The most adventurous is offered by **Canopy Safari ★** (✆ **2777-0100;** www.canopysafari.com), which features 21 treetop platforms connected by a series of cables and suspension bridges. Adventurers use a harness-and-pulley system to "zip" between platforms, using a leather-gloved hand as their only brake. The **Titi Canopy Tour** (✆ **2777-3130;** www.titicanopytours.com) is a similar but mellower setup. A canopy tour should run you between $50 and $70 (£25–£35) per person.

HORSEBACK RIDING If you want to do some horseback riding, contact **Stable Equus** (✆ **2777-0001**), which charges $35 (£18) for a 2-hour ride in Manuel Antonio. This stable treats its animals more humanely than other stables in the immediate Manuel Antonio area and is also concerned with keeping horse droppings off the beaches. Back in the hills, **Brisas del Nara** ★ (✆ **2779-1235;** www.horsebacktour.com) offers full- and half-day horseback excursions that pass through both primary and secondary forest and feature a swimming stop at a jungle waterfall. A full-day tour, including breakfast and lunch, costs $65 (£33) per person; and $50 (£25) for a half-day tour, with less time on the horse.

SPAS & WELLNESS CENTERS There are quite a few massage therapists around Manuel Antonio and a couple of day spas. The best of these are **Raindrop Spa** (✆ **2777-2880;** www.raindropspa.com), **Spa Uno** ★ (✆ **2777-2607;** www.spauno.com), and **Serenity Spa** ★ at the Hotel Sí Como No (p. 619). A wide range of treatments, wraps, and facials are available at all of the above.

SHOPPING

If you're looking for souvenirs, you'll find plenty of beach towels, beachwear, and handmade jewelry in a variety of small shops in Quepos and at impromptu stalls down near the national park. If you're looking for higher-end gifts, check out **L'Aventura Boutique** (✆ **2777-1019**), on Avenida Central in Quepos. The Hotel Sí Como No's **Regálame** (www.regalameart.com) gift shop is also pretty well stocked. Look for handmade batik and tie-dye clothing at **Guacamole** (✆ **2777-2071**) in the Plaza Yara shopping center.

One of my favorite hangouts has always been **Café Milagro** ★★ (✆ **2777-1707;** www.cafemilagro.com), a homey coffeehouse and gift shop with two locations in the area. You'll find local art for sale on the walls and a good selection of Cuban cigars and international newspapers, too. The original storefront, just over the bridge on your left as you enter Quepos, is now expanded, and there's another branch on the main road to Manuel Antonio right across from the turnoff for Hotel La Mariposa.

WHERE TO STAY

Take care when choosing your accommodations in Quepos/Manuel Antonio. There are very few true beachfront hotels here. In fact, most of the nicer hotels here are 1km (1/2 mile) or so away from the beach, high on the hill overlooking the ocean.

Very Expensive

In addition to the places listed below, **Gaia Hotel & Reserve** ★★ (✆ **800/226-2515** in the U.S.; www.gaiahr.com), **Hotel La Mariposa** ★ (✆ **800/549-0157** in the U.S.; www.lamariposa.com) and **Makanda by the Sea** ★★ (✆ **888/625-2632** in the U.S.; www.makanda.com) are also all good choices.

If you're coming for an extended stay with your family or a large group, look into **Escape Villas** ★★ (✆ **877/533-8988** in the U.S., or 2777-5258 in Costa Rica; www.villascostarica.com), which rents a broad selection of very large and luxurious private villas with all the amenities and some of the best views in Manuel Antonio.

Arenas del Mar ★★★ *Finds* Finally, Manuel Antonio has a hotel that combines the best of all worlds—direct beach access, a rainforest setting, fabulous views, and luxurious accommodations. Designed and built by the folks behind Finca Rosa Blanca (p. 565), this place is deeply committed to sustainability. Not all rooms have ocean views, so be sure to specify if you want one. All feature tasteful decor, cool yellow tile floors, and plenty of wood and tile accents. Most have outdoor Jacuzzi tubs on their private balconies. The restaurant, lobby, and main pool are set on the highest point of land here, and several spots have fabulous views of Manuel Antonio's Punta Catedral.

Manuel Antonio. ✆/fax **2777-2777.** www.arenasdelmar.com. 38 units. $220 (£110) double; $360 (£180) suite; $580 (£290) 2-bedroom apt. Rates lower in off season; higher during peak periods. Rates include full breakfast. AE, MC, V. **Amenities:** Restaurant; bar; snack bar; babysitting; concierge; laundry service; 2 small outdoor pools; room service; spa. *In room:* A/C, TV, minibar, free Wi-Fi.

Expensive

Hotel Sí Como No ★★ Finds Kids This long-standing favorite is a lively, upscale, midsize resort that blends in with and respects the rainforests and natural wonders of Manuel Antonio. This is a place equally suited to families traveling with children and to couples looking for a romantic getaway. The standard rooms are quite acceptable, but it's worth the splurge for a superior or deluxe room or a suite. Most of these are on the top floors of the two- to three-story villas, with spectacular treetop views out over the forest and onto the Pacific. These units all have a bedroom with an adjoining living-room area, a private balcony, and either a kitchenette or a wet bar. There are a series of deluxe suites with lots of space and large garden bathrooms, some of which have private Jacuzzis.

Manuel Antonio (mailing address: Mail Stop SJO 297, P.O. Box 02558216, Miami, FL 33102). ✆ **2777-0777.** Fax 2777-1093. www.sicomono.com. 60 units. $190–$240 (£95–£120) double; $275–$310 (£138–£155) suite. Rates include breakfast buffet. Rates lower in off season. Extra person $30 (£15). Children 5 and under stay free in parent's room. AE, MC, V. **Amenities:** 2 restaurants; 2 bars; babysitting; free beach shuttle; concierge; 2 Jacuzzis; laundry service; 2 midsize pools, including 1 w/small water slide; modest spa; free Wi-Fi. *In room:* A/C, hair dryer, minibar.

Moderate

In addition to the hotels mentioned below, **El Mono Azul Hotel** (✆ **800/381-3578** in the U.S. and Canada; www.monoazul.com), **Hotel Costa Verde** (✆ **866/854-7958** in the U.S. and Canada; www.costaverde.com), and **Hotel Plinio** (✆ **2777-0055;** www.hotelplinio.com) are other good options in this category.

Hotel Verde Mar ★ Value This place offers excellent proximity to the national park and the beach. From your room it's just a short walk to the beach (Playa Espadilla) via a raised wooden walkway. All the rooms here have plenty of space, nice wrought-iron queen-size beds, tile floors, a desk and chair, a fan, and a small porch. All but two of the rooms come with a basic kitchenette. Some of the larger rooms even have two queen-size beds. There's a small pool here, for when the surf is too rough.

Manuel Antonio (A.P. 348-6350), Quepos. ✆ **877/872-0459** in the U.S. and Canada, or 2777-1805 in Costa Rica. Fax 2777-1311. www.verdemar.com. 24 units. $90–$100 (£45–£50) double; $105–$120 (£53–£60) suite. Rates lower in off season. AE, MC, V. **Amenities:** Small pool. *In room:* A/C, kitchenette, no phone.

Villas Nicolás ★★ Value These large villas offer a lot of bang for your buck. Built as terraced units up a steep hill in deep forest, they give you the feeling that you're in the jungle. Most are quite spacious and well appointed, with wood floors, throw rugs, and comfortable bathrooms; some rooms even have separate living rooms and full kitchenettes, which make longer stays comfortable. My favorite features, though, are the balconies, which come with sitting chairs and a hammock. Some of these balconies are massive and have incredible views. In fact, the rooms highest up the hill have views that I'd be willing to pay a lot more for, and a few of them even have air-conditioning.

 Manuel Antonio (A.P. 236, Quepos). ✆ **2777-0481.** Fax 2777-0451. www.villasnicolas.com. 20 units. $115–$165 (£58–£83) double. Weekly, monthly, and off season (May–Nov) rates available. AE, MC, V. **Amenities:** Laundry service; small pool. *In room:* A/C (in some units), fridge.

Inexpensive

In addition to the place listed below, the **Widemouth Frog** (✆ **2777-2798;** www.widemouthfrog.org) is a hostel option in downtown Quepos, which even has its own swimming pool.

Hotel Malinche A good choice for budget travelers, the Hotel Malinche has consistently been my top choice in this category right in Quepos. The standard rooms are small but have hardwood or tile floors and clean bathrooms. Some of those on the second floor even have small private balconies that open on to a small interior courtyard. The more expensive rooms are larger and have air-conditioning, TVs, and carpets.

Half-block west of downtown bus terminal, Quepos. ✆ **2777-1833.** Fax 2777-0093. hotelmalinche@racsa.co.cr. 24 units. $25–$55 (£13–£23) double. AE, MC, V. *In room:* No phone.

WHERE TO DINE

For the cheapest meals around, try a simple *soda* in Quepos, or head to one of the open-air joints on the beach road before the national park entrance. Of these, **Marlin Restaurant** (✆ **2777-1134**), right in front of Playa Espadilla, and **Mar Luna** (✆ **2777-5107**), on the main road just beyond Hotel La Colina, are your best bets. For simple pasta, pizzas, and Italian gelato, head to **Escalofrío** (✆ **2777-0833;** downtown Quepos) or **Pizza de Marco** (✆ **2777-9400;** in the Plaza Yara shopping center). In addition to the places listed below, another good option, on the outskirts of Quepos, is **Mi Lugar,** or **"Ronny's Place"** (✆ **2777-5120;** www.ronnysplace.com).

For a taste of the high life, head to the **La Luna** at Gaia Hotel & Reserve for their sunset tapas menu. The views are great and the creative tapas are reasonably priced.

Other good and worthwhile options include **Agua Azul** (✆ **2777-5082**), **El Avión** (✆ **2777-3378**), **La Hacienda** (✆ **2777-3473**), and **Plinio Restaurant** (✆ **2777-0055**), all located along the road between Quepos and the National Park.

El Gran Escape ★★ SEAFOOD This Quepos landmark is consistently one of the most popular restaurants in the area. The fish is fresh and expertly prepared, portions are huge, and the prices are reasonable. If that's not enough of a recommendation, the atmosphere is lively, the locals seem to keep coming back, and the service is darn good for a beach town in Costa Rica. If you venture away from the fish, the menu features hearty steaks, giant burgers, and a wide assortment of delicious appetizers, including fresh tuna sashimi. Breakfasts here are also excellent.

On the main road into Quepos, on your left just after the bridge. ✆ **2777-0395.** Reservations recommended in high season. Main courses $5–$24 (£2.50–£12). V. Daily 7am–11pm.

El Patio Bistro Latino ★★ NUEVO LATINO/FUSION This small bistro-style restaurant is an outgrowth of the popular coffeehouse and roasting company Café Milagro. The same attention to detail and focus on quality carries over here. By day you can get a wide range of coffee drinks and specialties, as well as full breakfasts, fresh-baked sweets, and a variety of salads, sandwiches, and light lunch dishes. By night, things get more interesting and this humble little spot serves up some of the best food in Manuel Antonio. Their regularly changing menu features inventive main dishes that take advantage of local ingredients and various regional culinary traditions.

Manuel Antonio. ✆ **2777-4982.** Reservations recommended. Main courses $6–$19 (£3–£9.50). AE, MC, V. Daily 6am–10pm.

Sunspot Bar & Grill ★★ Finds INTERNATIONAL Dining by candlelight under a purple canvas tent at one of the few poolside tables here is one of the most romantic dining experiences to be had in Manuel Antonio. The food's some of the best in town as well. The menu changes regularly but features prime meats and poultry and fresh fish, excellently prepared. The rack of lamb might get a light jalapeño-mint or mango chutney, and the chicken breast might be stuffed with feta cheese, kalamata olives, and roasted red peppers and topped with a blackberry sauce. There are nightly specials and a good selection of salads, appetizers, and desserts.

At Makanda by the Sea (p. 618). ✆ **2777-0442.** Reservations recommended. Main courses $10–$25 (£5–£13). V. Daily 11am–10pm.

MANUEL ANTONIO AFTER DARK

The bars at the **Barba Roja** restaurant and the **Hotel Sí Como No** are good places to hang out and meet people in the evenings. For shooting pool, I head to the **Billfish Sportbar & Grill** at the Byblos Resort. For tapas and local *bocas,* try **Salsipuedes,** which translates as "get out if you can." If you want to find some live music, **Bambu Jam** ★ and **Dos Locos** are your best bets. In downtown Quepos, **Mar y Blues, Sargento Garcia's, Wacky Wanda's,** and the **Fish Head Bar** at El Gran Escape are all popular hangouts.

For real late-night action, the local favorite appears to be **Arco Iris,** which is located just before the bridge heading into town.

If you enjoy gaming tables, the **Hotel Kamuk** in Quepos and the **Byblos Resort** on the road to Manuel Antonio both have small casinos and will even foot your cab bill if you try your luck and lay down your money.

9 THE SOUTHERN ZONE

Golfito: 87km (54 miles) S of Palmar Norte, 337km (209 miles) S of San José; Drake Bay: 145km (90 miles) S of San José, 32km (20 miles) SW of Palmar; Puerto Jiménez: 35km (22 miles) W of Golfito by water (90km/56 miles by road), 85km (53 miles) S of Palmar Norte

Costa Rica's southern zone is an area of rugged beauty, with vast expanses of virgin lowland rainforest and few cities, towns, or settlements. Lushly forested mountains tumble into the sea, streams still run clear and clean, scarlet macaws squawk raucously in the treetops, and dolphins frolic in the **Golfo Dulce.** The **Osa Peninsula** is the most popular attraction in this region and one of the premier ecotourism destinations in the world. It's home to **Corcovado National Park** ★★★, the largest single expanse of lowland tropical rainforest in Central America, and its sister, **Piedras Blancas National Park** ★★. Scattered around the edges of these national parks and along the shores of the Golfo Dulce are some of the country's finest nature lodges. These lodges, in general, offer comfortable to nearly luxurious accommodations, attentive service, knowledgeable guides, and a wide range of activities and tours, all close to the area's many natural wonders.

The best of these nature lodges are located around Drake Bay, Puerto Jimenez, and along the shores of the Golfo Dulce, or "Sweet Gulf." Despite being the largest and most important city in Costa Rica's southern zone, Golfito, in and of itself, is neither a popular nor a particularly inviting tourist destination. However, Golfito is still a major sportfishing center and a popular gateway to some of the lodges along the Golfo Dulce, as well as the isolated beach towns of Playa Zancudo and Pavones, farther south.

Although most of the lodges listed below are quite cozy, and some are even spectacular, remember, none of these nature lodges have in-room televisions, telephones, or air-conditioning. Although this region is noted for its hot and steamy weather, most of these nature lodges are built with cool tile or wood floors and plenty of shade and ventilation. I never find it uncomfortable, and hordes of satisfied visitors seem to agree. However, if you are particularly sensitive to the heat, or particularly fond of air-conditioning, be sure to book a hotel with in-room air-conditioning.

ESSENTIALS

Getting There

BY PLANE Most travelers fly to the southern zone. **Sansa** (© **877/767-2672** in the U.S. and Canada, or 2290-4100 in Costa Rica; www.flysansa.com) and **Nature Air** (© **800/235-9272** in the U.S. and Canada, or 2299-6000; www.natureair.com) both have daily flights to Drake Bay, Golfito, and Puerto Jiménez. All of the lodges listed below will work with you to coordinate your transportation to their remote locations.

BY CAR Take the Pan-American Highway east out of San José (through San Pedro and Cartago) and continue south on this road. In about 3 hours, you'll reach San Isidro de El General. Although you can continue on the Pan-American Highway all the way south, it is currently faster, smoother, and safer to turn off in San Isidro and head to Dominical, picking up the Southern Highway or Costanera Sur in Dominical. From here it's a fast and smooth shot down to Palmar Norte, where you meet up again with the Pan-American Highway. When you get to Río Claro, you'll notice a couple of gas stations and quite a bit of activity. Turn right here and follow the signs to Golfito. If you end up at the Panama border, you've missed the turnoff by about 32km (20 miles). The complete drive takes about 6 hours.

If you're heading to Puerto Jiménez, take the turnoff for La Palma, Rincón, and Puerto Jiménez. This road is paved at first, but at Rincón it turns to gravel. The last 35km (22 miles) are slow and rough, and, if it's the rainy season (mid-Apr to Nov), it'll be too muddy for anything but a four-wheel-drive vehicle.

BY BUS Express buses to Golfito leave San José daily at 7am and 3pm from the **Tracopa** station on the Plaza Viquez at Calle 5 between avenidas 18 and 20 (© **2221-4214**). The trip takes 7½ hours; the fare is $6 (£3). Buses depart Golfito for San José daily at 5am and 1:30pm from the bus station near the municipal dock.

A **Transportes Blanco-Lobo** express bus (© **2257-4121**) leaves San José for Puerto Jiménez daily at noon from Calle 12 between avenidas 7 and 9. The trip takes 8 hours; the fare is $7 (£3.50). Buses depart Puerto Jiménez for San José daily at 5am.

BY BOAT There are speedboats working as boat taxis between Puerto Jiménez and Golfito. The fare is $5 (£2.50), and the ride takes a little under 30 minutes. These boats leave five or six times throughout the day, beginning at around 5am and finishing up at around 5pm. Ask around town, or at the docks for current schedules.

There is also a daily passenger launch. This slower boat takes 1½ hours, and the fare is $3 (£1.50). The ferry leaves the public dock in Golfito at 6am for Puerto Jiménez. The return trip to Golfito leaves Puerto Jiménez's municipal dock at 11:30am.

It's also possible to charter a water taxi in Golfito for the trip across to Puerto Jiménez. You'll have to pay between $40 and $80 (£20–£40) for an entire launch, some of which can carry up to 12 people.

Getting Around

Most of the lodges listed in this section are very isolated. All will work with you to coordinate your transportation to and from the destination, as well as during your stay.

Visitor Information & Fast Facts

You'll find banks and ATMs in Golfito and Puerto Jiménez, but neither in Drake Bay. Hospital Golfito (✆ **2775-1001**) is the only hospital in the region, although there are several doctors and a local clinic (✆ **2735-5029**) in Puerto Jiménez.

WHAT TO SEE & DO

All lodges in the area also offer a host of half- and full-day tours and activities, including hikes in Corcovado National Park, horseback rides, and sportfishing. In some cases, tours are included in your room rate or package; in others, they must be bought a la carte. Other options include mountain biking and sea kayaking. Most of these tours run between $60 and $120 (£30–£60), depending on the activity, with scuba diving ($90–$135/£45–£66 for a two-tank dive) and sportfishing ($450–$1,400/£225–£700, depending on the size of the boat and other amenities) costing a bit more.

Exploring Corcovado National Park ★★★

Exploring Corcovado National Park is not something to be undertaken lightly, but neither is it the expedition that some people make it out to be. The weather is the biggest obstacle to overnight backpacking trips through the park. Within a couple of hours of Puerto Jiménez (by 4WD vehicle) are several entrances to the park; however, there are no roads in the park, so once you reach any of the entrances, you'll have to start hiking. The heat and humidity are often quite extreme, and frequent rainstorms can make trails fairly muddy. If you choose the alternative—hiking on the beach—you'll have to plan your hiking around the tides when often there is no beach at all and some rivers are impassable.

Because of its size and remoteness, Corcovado National Park is best explored over several days; however, it is possible to enter and hike a bit of it for day trips. The best way to do this is to book a tour with your lodge (see "Where to Stay & Dine," below).

GETTING THERE & ENTRY POINTS The park has four primary entrances, which are really just ranger stations reached by rough dirt roads. When you've reached them, you'll have to strap on a backpack and hike. Perhaps the easiest one to reach from Puerto Jiménez is **La Leona ranger station,** just outside the town of Carate. From Carate, it's a 3km (1¾-mile) hike to La Leona. To travel there by "public transportation," pick up one of the collective buses (actually, a 4WD pickup truck with a tarpaulin cover and slat seats in the back) that leave Puerto Jiménez for Carate daily at 6am and 1:30pm, returning at 9am and 4pm. Remember, these "buses" are very informal and change their schedules regularly to meet demand or avoid bad weather, so always ask in town. One-way fare is around $8 (£4). A small fleet of these pickups leaves just south of the new bus terminal, and will stop to pick up anyone who flags them down along the way. Your other option is to hire a private taxi, which will charge approximately $70 to $80 (£35–£40) each way to or from Carate.

Trail Distances in Corcovado National Park

It's 14km (8½ miles) from La Leona to Sirena. From Sirena to San Pedrillo, it's 23km (14 miles) along the beach. From San Pedrillo, it's 20km (13 miles) to Drake Bay. It's 19km (12 miles) between Sirena and Los Patos.

You can also travel to **El Tigre,** about 14km (8¾ miles) by dirt road from Puerto Jiménez, where there's another ranger station. But note that trails from El Tigre go only a short distance into the park.

The third entrance is in **Los Patos,** which is reached from the town of La Palma, northwest of Puerto Jiménez. From here, there's a 19km (12-mile) trail through the center of the park to **Sirena,** a ranger station and research facility (see "Beach Treks & Rainforest Hikes," below). Sirena has a landing strip that is used by charter flights.

The northern entrance to the park is **San Pedrillo,** which you can reach by hiking from Sirena or by taking a boat from Drake Bay or Sierpe (see "Beach Treks & Rainforest Hikes," below). It's 14km (8¾ miles) from Drake Bay.

If you're not into hiking in the heat, you can charter a plane in Puerto Jiménez to take you to Carate or Sirena. A five-passenger plane should cost around $200 to $400 (£100–£200) one-way, depending on your destination. Contact **Alfa Romeo Air Charters** (✆ **2735-5353** or 2735-5112; www.alfaromeoair.com) for details.

FEES & REGULATIONS Park admission is $10 (£5) per person per day. Only the Sirena station is equipped with dormitory-style lodgings and a simple *soda,* but the others have basic campsites and toilet facilities. All must be reserved in advance by contacting the **ACOSA** (Area de Conservación de Osa) in Puerto Jiménez (✆ **2735-5036;** fax 2735-5276; pncorcovado@hotmail.com). For a good overview of the park and logistics, check out **www.corcovado.org**. Its offices are adjacent to the airstrip. Only a limited number of people are allowed to camp at each ranger station, so make your reservations well in advance.

BEACH TREKS & RAINFOREST HIKES The park has quite a few good hiking trails. Two of the better-known ones are the beach routes, starting at either the La Leona or San Pedrillo ranger stations. None of the hikes is easy, but the forest route from the Los Patos ranger station to Sirena, although long, is less taxing than either of the beach treks, which can be completed only when the tide is low. The route between the Los Patos/Sirena hike is 19km (12 miles) through beautiful rainforest.

Sirena is a fascinating destination. As a research facility and ranger station, it's frequented primarily by scientists studying the rainforest. One of the longest hikes, from San Pedrillo to Sirena, can be done only during the dry season. Between any two stations, the hiking is arduous and takes all day, so it's best to rest for a day or so between hikes if possible.

Remember, this is quite a wild area. Never hike alone, and take all the standard precautions for hiking in the rainforest. In addition, be especially careful about swimming in any isolated rivers or river mouths because most rivers in Corcovado are home to crocodiles.

WHERE TO STAY & DINE IN THE PARK: CAMPSITES, CABINS & CANTINAS Reservations are essential at the various ranger stations if you plan to eat or sleep inside the park (see "Fees & Regulations," above). **Sirena** has a modern research facility with dormitory-style accommodations for 28 persons, as well as a campground, *soda,* and landing strip for charter flights. There is also camping at the **La Leona, Los Patos,** and **San Pedrillo** ranger stations. Every ranger station has potable water, but it's advisable to pack in your own; whatever you do, don't drink stream water. Campsites in the park are $4 (£2) per person per night. A dorm bed at the Sirena station will run you $12 (£6)—you must bring your own sheets, and a mosquito net is highly recommended—and meals here are another $35 (£18) per day. Everything must be reserved in advance.

Around Puerto Jimenez

Kayaking trips around the estuary and up into the mangroves and out into the gulf are popular. Contact **Escondido Trex** ★ (✆ **2735-5210;** www.escondidotrex.com). There are daily paddles through the mangroves, as well as sunset trips where you can sometimes see dolphins. These folks also do guided rainforest hikes and can have you rappelling down the face of a jungle waterfall. More adventurous multiday kayak and camping trips are also available, in price and comfort ranges from budget to luxury (staying at various lodges around the Golfo Dulce and Matapalo).

For a real adventure, check in with **Psycho Tours** ★★ (✆ **8353-8619;** www.psychotours.com). These folks run a variety of adventure tours, but their signature combo trip features a free climb up (with a safety rope attached) the roots and trunks of a 60m-tall (200-ft.) strangler fig. You can climb as high as your ability allows, but most try to reach a natural platform at around 18m (60 ft.), where you take a leap of faith into space and are belayed down by your guide. This is preceded by an informative hike through primary rainforest, often wading through a small river, and followed by a couple of rappels down jungle waterfalls, the highest of which is around 30m (100 ft.). You can do either one of the above adventures separately, but I recommend the 5- to 6-hour combo tour, which costs $110 (£55).

If you want to learn to surf, contact **Mike's Surf School** ★ (✆ **8382-7796**), which is run by Mike Hennessy, and located near some excellent learning waves on Pan Dulce beach.

Around Drake Bay

One of the most popular excursions from Drake Bay is a trip out to **Isla del Caño** and the **Caño Island Biological Reserve** ★★ for a bit of exploring and snorkeling or scuba diving. The island is located about 19km (12 miles) offshore from Drake Bay and was once home to a pre-Columbian culture about which little is known. A trip to the island will include a visit to an ancient cemetery, and you'll also be able to see some of the stone spheres believed to have been carved by this area's ancient inhabitants. Few animals or birds live on the island, but the coral reefs just offshore teem with life and are the main reason most people come here. This is one of Costa Rica's prime **scuba spots** ★★. Visibility is often quite good, and there's even easily accessible snorkeling from the beach. All of the Drake Bay lodges offer trips to Isla del Caño.

One of the most interesting tour options in Drake Bay is a 2-hour **night tour** ★★ (✆ **8382-1619;** www.thenighttour.com; $35/£18 per person) offered by Tracie Stice, who is affectionately known as the "Bug Lady." Equipped with flashlights, participants get a bug's-eye view of the forest at night. You might see reflections of some larger forest dwellers, but most of the tour is a fascinating exploration of the nocturnal insect and arachnid world. Consider yourself lucky if she finds the burrow of a trapdoor spider or large tarantula.

In addition to the places listed below, the following lodges are all excellent options: **El Remanso ★★** (✆ **2735-5569;** www.elremanso.com); **Lapa Ríos ★★** (✆ **2735-5130;** www.laparios.com); **Corcovado Lodge Tent Camp ★** (✆ **800/886-2609** in the U.S. and Canada; www.corcovadolodge.com); **Playa Nicuesa Rainforest Lodge ★★** (✆ **866/504-8116** in the U.S.; www.nicuesalodge.com); **Hotel Jinetes de Osa** (✆ **866/553-7073** in the U.S. and Canada; www.drakebayhotel.com).

Bosque del Cabo Rainforest Lodge ★★★ *Finds* This secluded jungle lodge is a fabulous ecolodge. The individual cabins are all spacious and beautifully furnished, and have wooden decks or verandas to catch the ocean views. The Congo cabin is my choice for its spectacular view of the sunrise from your bed. All cabins have indoor bathrooms, while tiled showers are set outdoors amid flowering heliconia and ginger. About half of the units also have outdoor bathtubs.

There's a trail down to a secluded beach that has some tide pools and ocean-carved caves. Another trail leads to a jungle waterfall, and several others wind through the rainforests of the lodge's 260-hectare (650-acre) private reserve. The wildlife viewing here is excellent. If you're too lazy to hike down to the beach, there's a beautiful pool by the main lodge. Other attractions include a canopy platform 36m (118 ft.) up a Manu tree, reached along a 90m (295-ft.) zip line, as well as a bird- and wildlife-watching rancho set beside a little lake on the edge of their tropical gardens and surrounded by forest.

Osa Peninsula (mailing address: Interlink 528, P.O. Box 02-5635, Miami, FL 33102). ✆/fax **2735-5206** or 8389-2846. www.bosquedelcabo.com. 10 units. $350–$390 (£175–£195) double. Rates include 3 meals daily and taxes. $25 (£13) round-trip transportation from Puerto Jiménez. MC, V. **Amenities:** Restaurant; bar; laundry service; midsize pool; surfboard rental. *In room:* No phone.

Drake Bay Wilderness Resort ★ This is one of the best-located lodges at Drake Bay. It backs onto the Río Agujitas and fronts the Pacific. The rooms here are less fancy than those at some of the other lodges listed here, but they are clean and comfortable, with ceiling fans, small verandas, good mattresses on the beds, and private bathrooms. The best room here is a pretty deluxe honeymoon suite on a little hill toward the rear of the property, with a great view of the bay. There are also five budget cabins that share bathroom and shower facilities.

Because it's on a rocky spit, there isn't a good swimming beach on-site, but there's a saltwater pool in front of the bay, and, depending on the tide, you can bathe in a beautiful small tide pool formed by the rocks.

Drake Bay (A.P. 13710-1000, San José). ✆ **561/762-1763** in the U.S., or ✆/fax 2770-8012 in Costa Rica. www.drakebay.com. 25 units. $90 (£45) per person per day with shared bathroom; $130–$160 (£65–£80) per person per day standard and deluxe. Rates include all meals and taxes. Rates lower in off season. AE, MC, V. **Amenities:** Restaurant; bar; free use of canoes and kayaks; free same-day laundry service; small saltwater pool; free Wi-Fi. *In room:* Hair dryer, no phone.

La Paloma Lodge ★★★ *Finds* Set on a steep hill overlooking the Pacific, with Isla del Caño in the distance, the luxurious individual bungalows at La Paloma offer expansive ocean views that, combined with the attentive and amiable service, make this my top choice in Drake Bay. All of the bungalows feature private verandas, and are set among lush foliage facing the Pacific. The large two-story Sunset Ranchos are the choice rooms here, with fabulous panoramic views. The standard rooms, which are located in a row in one long building, are smaller and less private than the cabins, but they're still quite attractive and have good views from their hammock-equipped balcony. The beach is about a 7-minute hike down a winding jungle path, and the lodge also offers scuba certification courses.

Drake Bay (mailing address: A.P. 97-4005, San Antonio de Belén). ✆ **2293-7502** or ✆/fax 2239-0954. www.lapalomalodge.com. 11 units. $1,100–$1,400 (£550–£700) per person for 4 days/3 nights with 2 tours; $1,245–$1,620 (£623–£810) per person for 5 days/4 nights with 2 tours. Rates are based on double occupancy and include round-trip transportation from San José, all meals, park fees, indicated tours, and taxes. Rates slightly lower in off season. AE, MC, V. **Amenities:** Restaurant; bar; laundry service; small tile pool w/spectacular view; free Wi-Fi around the main lodge. *In room:* Minibar, no phone.

10 CARIBBEAN COAST BEACHES: CAHUITA & PUERTO VIEJO

213km (132 miles) E of San José, 55km (34 miles) S of Limón; Cahuita: 200km (124 miles) E of San José, 42km (26 miles) S of Limón, 13km (8 miles) N of Puerto Viejo; Tortuguero: 250km (155 miles) NE of San José, 79km (49 miles) N of Limón

Costa Rica's Caribbean coast can seem a world apart from the rest of the country. The pace is slower, the food is spicier, the tropical heat is more palpable, and the rhythmic lilt of patois and reggae music fills the air. Much of this coast was settled by Afro-Caribbean fishermen and laborers who came to this region in the mid-1800s to work on the railroad and banana plantations here. Today the population is still in large part made up of English-speaking blacks, whose culture and language set them apart from other Costa Ricans.

This remains one of Costa Rica's least discovered and explored regions. More than half of the coastline here is still inaccessible except by boat or small plane. Aside from the jungle canals, rainforests, and turtles of **Tortuguero National Park** (which is covered separately on p. 632), two small and atmospheric beach towns, **Cahuita** and **Puerto Viejo,** are the main attractions here. Cahuita is the quieter of the two, with a small and pretty national park backing its beaches and coral reefs, while Puerto Viejo is much more lively, with a strong surfer culture. Both boast some of the prettiest stretches of beach in the country.

ESSENTIALS

Getting There

BY BUS **MEPE** express buses (✆ **2257-8129**) to Cahuita and Puerto Viejo leave San José daily at 6 and 10am, noon, and 2 and 4pm from the Caribbean terminal (Gran Terminal del Caribe) on Calle Central, 1 block north of Avenida 11. The trip takes about 4 hours to Cahuita, and an extra half-hour all the way to Puerto Viejo. Buses leave Puerto Viejo for San José daily at 7:30, 9, and 11am, and 4pm, stopping in Cahuita about a half-hour later.

Gray Line (✆ **2220-2126;** www.graylinecostarica.com) and **Interbus** (✆ **2283-5573;** www.interbusonline.com) also each have a daily bus from San José to both Cahuita and Puerto Viejo.

BY CAR The Guápiles Highway heads north out of San José on Calle 3 before turning east and passing close to Barva Volcano and through the rainforests of Braulio Carrillo National Park en route to Limón. The drive takes about 2½ hours and is quite beautiful. As you enter Limón, about 5 blocks before the busiest section of downtown, watch for a paved road to the right, just before the railroad tracks. Take this road south to Cahuita and Puerto Viejo. Alternatively, there's a turnoff with signs for Sixaola and La Bomba several miles before Limón. This winding shortcut skirts the city and puts you on the coastal road several miles south of town. From Limón it's roughly another 30 minutes to Cahuita, and 45 minutes to Puerto Viejo.

Getting Around

Both Cahuita and Puerto Viejo are tiny little towns, and you can easily walk anywhere in the "downtown" section of each. To get to hotels and destinations a little farther afield you'll find taxis in both towns. You're best bet is to ask your hotel to call you one, or call **René** (© **2755-0243**) or **Wayne** (© **2755-0078**) in Cahuita, or **Bull** (© **2750-0112** or 8836-8219) or **Delroy** (© **2750-0132**) in Puerto Viejo.

Visitor Information

Your hotel and the small local tourist agencies will be your best sources of information, especially in Cahuita. In Puerto Viejo, you can stop in at the **Asociación Talamanqueña de Ecoturismo y Conservación ★★ (ATEC; Talamancan Association of Ecotourism and Conservation; © 2750-0398** or ©/fax 2750-0191; www.ateccr.org), across the street from the Soda Tamara, a local nonprofit that runs excellent tours, has an Internet cafe, and serves as the de facto information center for the town.

FAST FACTS **Tony Facio Hospital** (© **2758-0580**) located just outside of downtown Limón, is the closest hospital. There's no bank or ATM in Cahuita, but you'll find both in Puerto Viejo, as well as several in Limón. To contact the police in Cahuita, dial © **2755-0217;** in Puerto Viejo, dial © **2750-0230.**

There are Internet cafes and small laundromats in both towns.

WHAT TO SEE & DO

Cahuita National Park ★★

Cahuita National Park features a long, beautiful curve of white sand backed by dense lowland rainforest. Although the soft white sand, lush coastal forest, and picture-perfect palm lines are a tremendous draw, the park was actually created to preserve the 240-hectare (787-acre) **coral reef** just offshore. The reef contains 35 species of coral and provides a haven for hundreds of brightly colored tropical fish.

The trail behind the beach stretches a little more than 6.4km (4 miles) to the southern end of the park at **Puerto Vargas,** where you'll find the park headquarters and a basic campground. It's a flat walk, but a rewarding one because there's good wildlife viewing and easy access to the beach. The grunting sounds you hear off in the distance are the calls of howler monkeys, which can be heard from more than a mile away.

The **in-town entrance** to the park is just over a footbridge at the end of the village's main street. It has bathroom facilities, changing rooms, and storage lockers. This is the best place to enter if you're just interested in spending the day on the beach and maybe taking a little hike in the bordering forest. The official park entrance is at **Puerto Vargas.** This is where you should come if you plan to camp at the park or if you don't feel up to hiking a couple of hours to reach the best snorkeling spots. The road to Puerto Vargas is approximately 5km (3 miles) south of Cahuita on the left.

Officially, **admission** is $10 (£5) per person per day, but this is collected only at the Puerto Vargas entrance. You can enter the park from the town of Cahuita for free or with a voluntary contribution. The park is open from dawn to dusk for day visitors.

The Manzanillo-Gandoca Wildlife Refuge ★★

The Manzanillo-Gandoca Wildlife Refuge, 15km (9 1/3 miles) south of Puerto Viejo, encompasses the tiny village of Manzanillo, and extends all the way to the Panamanian border. Manatees, crocodiles, and more than 350 species of birds live within the boundaries of the reserve. The reserve also includes the coral reef offshore—when the seas are calm, this is the best **snorkeling** and **diving** spot on this entire coast. No admission fee is charged. If you want to explore the refuge, you can easily find the single, well-maintained trail by walking along the beach just south of town until you have to wade across a small river. On the other side, you'll pick up the trail head.

Otherwise, you can ask around the village for local guides or check out **Aquamor** ★ (✆ **2759-9012**), a kayak and dive operation located on the one main road in town. These folks rent kayaks. Depending on tides and sea conditions, this is a great way to explore the mangroves and estuaries, visit several nearby beaches, and even snorkel or dive the nearby coral reef.

Buses run sporadically throughout the day between Puerto Viejo and Manzanillo. You could also hire a cab for around $6 (£3) to Punta Uva or $10 (£5) to Manzanillo. Alternatively, it's about 1 1/2 hours each way by bicycle, with only two relatively small hills to contend with. It's also possible to walk along the beach all the way from Puerto Viejo to Manzanillo, with just a couple of short and well-worn detours inland around rocky points. However, I recommend you catch a ride down to Manzanillo and save your walking energies for the trails and beaches inside the refuge.

CULTURAL & ADVENTURE TOURS A host of local tour agencies offer a range of tour and adventure options, including snorkeling trips, jungle tours, white-water rafting trips, bird-watching outings, zip-line canopy adventures, and tours to the Bribri reservation. Rates run from $20 to $110 (£10–£55) depending upon the activity, group size, and length of the tour.

In Cahuita, I recommend **Cahuita Tours and Adventure Center** (✆ **2755-0000;** www.cahuitatours.com). While in Puerto Viejo, you should check in with the **Asociación Talamanqueña de Ecoturismo y Conservación** (**ATEC; Talamancan Association of Ecotourism and Conservation;** ✆ **2750-0398** or ✆/fax 2750-0191; www.ateccr.org), **Puerto Viejo Tours & Rentals** (✆ **2750-0411**), and **Terraventuras** (✆ **2750-0750;** www.terraventuras.com).

Several operators and makeshift roadside stands in both towns offer bicycles, scooters, boogie boards, surfboards, and snorkel gear for rent. Shop around and compare prices and the quality of the equipment before settling on any one.

SURFING Surfers will want to head to Puerto Viejo. Just offshore from the tiny village park is a shallow reef where powerful storm-generated waves sometimes reach 6m (20 ft.). **Salsa Brava,** as it's known, is the prime surf break on the Caribbean coast. Even when the waves are small, this spot is recommended only for very experienced surfers because of the danger of the reef. Other popular beach breaks are south of town on Playa Cocles. If you're interested in surf lessons or want to rent a board, check in with **Aventuras Bravas** (✆ **8849-7600**).

WILDLIFE VIEWING UP CLOSE & PERSONAL Bird-watchers and sloth lovers should head 9km (5 1/2 miles) north of Cahuita to **Aviarios del Caribe and the Buttercup Sloth Rescue Center** ★ (✆/fax **2750-0775;** www.slothrescue.org). The folks here run a sloth rehabilitation project and also offer guided canoe tours through the surrounding estuary and river system. More than 330 species of birds have been spotted here. The

3½-hour canoe tour costs $30 (£15) per person and leaves at 6am and 3pm. There's also a 1¼-hour canoe tour combination that includes a visit to the sloth rehabilitation center and a self-guided hike on its trails for $20 (£10) per person.

NOT YOUR EVERYDAY GARDENS There are several interesting botanical, butterfly, and multipurpose gardens in this area. On the main highway, just north of the main entrance to Cahuita, is the **Mariposario Cahuita** (© **2755-0361**), a large, informative butterfly farm attraction that charges $8 (£4) and is open daily from 8:30am to 3:30pm. It's best to come in the early morning on a sunny day, when the butterflies are most active.

In Puerto Viejo, be sure to visit the **Finca La Isla Botanical Gardens ★** (© **2750-0046** or 8886-8530), 200m (656 ft.) inland from the Black Sand Beach. You'll see medicinal, commercial, and just plain wild flowering plants, fruits, herbs, trees, and bushes. Visitors get to gorge on whatever is ripe at the moment. Entrance to the garden or loop trail is $5 (£2.50) per person, or $10 (£5) with the guided tour.

Cacao Trails ★ (© **2756-8186;** www.cacaotrails.com) is a one-stop attraction featuring botanical gardens, a small serpentarium, an open-air museum demonstrating the tools and techniques of cacao cultivation and processing, and a series of trails. There's also a large open-air restaurant, and a swimming pool for cooling off. You can also take canoe rides on the bordering Carbon River, and even watch sea turtles lay their eggs during the nesting season. Admission to the attraction is $25 (£13), including a guided tour. A full-day tour, including lunch and a canoe trip, as well as the guided tour, costs $47 (£24). During turtle nesting season, they do night tours to watch sea turtles lay their eggs.

WHERE TO STAY

In Cahuita

In addition to the places listed below, **Magellan Inn** (©/fax **2755-0035;** www.magellan inn.com) and **Alby Lodge** (©/fax **2755-0031;** www.albylodge.com) are both excellent, intimate, long-standing local options.

El Encanto Bed and Breakfast ★★ (Value) The individual bungalows at this little bed-and-breakfast are set in from the road on spacious and well-kept grounds. The bungalows themselves are also spacious and have attractive touches such as wooden bed frames, arched windows, Mexican-tile floors, Guatemalan bedspreads, and framed Panamanian molas hanging on the walls. There is a separate two-story, three-bedroom, two-bathroom house with a full kitchen at the rear of the grounds, as well as a deluxe room. Breakfasts are served in the small open dining room surrounded by lush gardens. Nice extra touches here include a small kidney-shaped pool, a wood-floored meditation hall, a covered garden gazebo, and an open-air massage room.

Cahuita (A.P. 7302-7), Limón (just outside of town on the road to Playa Negra). © **2755-0113.** Fax 2755-0432. www.elencantobedandbreakfast.com. 7 units. $65–$85 (£33–£43) double. Rates include full breakfast. Rates slightly lower in off season; higher during peak weeks. MC, V. **Amenities:** Small pool. *In room:* No phone.

In & Around Puerto Viejo

There are tons of lodging options in and around Puerto Viejo. **Banana Azul Guest House** (© **2750-2035** or 8351-4582; www.bananaazul.com) is an economical option just north of town on Black Sand Beach, while down south of town you might also consider **Cariblue Bungalows** (© **2750-0035;** www.cariblue.com) or **Playa Chiquita Lodge** (© **2750-0062;** www.playachiquitalodge.com).

For some serious luxury, check out the **Tree House Lodge ★★★** (**✆ 2750-0706;** www.costaricatreehouse.com) whose four individual houses are architectural and artistic marvels.

Cabinas Casa Verde ★★ Value This is my favorite hotel right in Puerto Viejo town, regardless of price. A quiet sense of tropical tranquillity pervades this place. Most of the rooms are large, with high ceilings, tile floors, private bathrooms, and a private veranda. The rooms with shared bathrooms are housed in a raised building with a wide, covered breezeway between the rooms. There are also two fully equipped apartments available in a neighboring duplex. Everything is very well maintained, and even the shared bathrooms are kept immaculate. The hotel features a good-size outdoor pool with waterfall, and a separate outdoor massage hut. There is also a small but well-stocked gift shop and a poison-dart-frog garden. Even though it's an in-town choice, there's great bird-watching all around the grounds.

A.P. 37-7304, Puerto Viejo, Limón. ✆ **2750-0015.** Fax 2750-0047. www.cabinascasaverde.com. 17 units, 9 with private bathroom. $40–$50 (£20–£25) double with shared bathroom; $70 (£35) double with private bathroom. Rates include taxes. Rates slightly lower in off season; higher during peak weeks. Discounts offered for cash payments. AE, MC, V. **Amenities:** Bicycle rental; pool; tour desk. *In room:* No phone.

La Costa de Papito ★ Value This small collection of individual and duplex cabins is located just across from Playa Cocles, about 1.6km (1 mile) south of Puerto Viejo. The wooden bungalows come with one or two double beds, artfully tiled bathrooms, and an inviting private porch with a table and chairs and either a hammock or a swing chair. There's also a larger two-bedroom unit. The Pure Jungle Spa, located on the premises here, is an excellent little day spa.

Playa Cocles, Puerto Viejo, Limón. ✆/fax **2750-0080** or 2750-0704. www.lacostadepapito.com. 13 units. $54–$74 (£27–£37) double. Rates lower in off season. AE, DISC, MC, V. **Amenities:** Restaurant; bar; bicycle rental; laundry service; small spa. *In room:* No phone.

WHERE TO DINE

In Cahuita

In addition to the place listed below, I recommend **Cha Cha Cha ★** (**✆ 8394-4153**) for its excellent seafood and inspired fusion cuisine, and **Sobre Las Olas** (**✆ 2755-0109**) for its fabulous setting and view.

Restaurant Edith Finds CREOLE/SEAFOOD This place is a local institution, and deservedly so. If you want a taste of the local cuisine in a homey, sit-down environment, this is the place. The menu is long, with lots of local seafood dishes and creole combinations such as yuca in coconut milk with meat or vegetables. It's often crowded, so don't be bashful about sitting down with total strangers at any of the big tables. Hours can be erratic; it sometimes closes without warning, and service can be painfully slow.

By the police station, Cahuita. ✆ **2755-0248.** Reservations not accepted. Main courses $5–$20 (£2.50–£10). No credit cards. Mon–Sat 11am–10pm; Sun 4–9pm.

In & Around Puerto Viejo

To really sample the local cuisine, you need to look up a few local women. Ask around for **Miss Dolly, Miss Sam, Miss Isma,** and **Miss Irma,** who all serve sit-down meals in their modest little *sodas* in downtown Puerto Viejo.

El Loco Natural (**✆ 2750-0263**) offers creative and spicy international fare and often features live music.

La Pecora Nera ★★★ Finds ITALIAN This open-air joint on the jungle's edge has a deserved reputation as the finest Italian restaurant in the region, if not the country. Owner Ilario Giannoni is a whirlwind of enthusiasm and activity, switching hats all night long from maitre d' to chef to waiter to busboy in an entertaining blur. Sure, he's got some help, including his grandmother, who makes gnocchi, but it seems like he's doing it single-handedly. The menu has a broad selection of pizzas and pastas, but your best bet is to just ask Ilario what's fresh and special for that day, and to trust his instincts and inventions.

50m (164 ft.) inland from a well-marked turnoff on the main road south just beyond the soccer field in Cocles. ✆ **2750-0490.** Reservations recommended. Main courses $7–$28 (£3.50–£14). AE, MC, V. Tues–Sun 5:30–11pm.

Soda Tamara Value COSTA RICAN This little local joint has an attractive setting for such an economical place. The painted picket fence in front gives the restaurant a homey feel. The menu features standard fish, chicken, and meat entrees, served with a hefty helping of Caribbean-style rice and beans. You can also get *patacones* (fried chips made out of plantains) and a wide selection of fresh-fruit juices. At the counter inside, you'll find homemade cocoa candies and unsweetened cocoa biscuits made by several women in town. They're definitely worth a try.

On the main road. ✆ **2750-0148.** Main courses $4–$15 (£2–£7.50). AE, MC, V. Daily 11am–11pm.

Cahuita & Puerto Viejo After Dark

As I said before, Cahuita is the quieter of the two towns. Here folks tend to gather in the evenings at either **Coco's Bar** ★, a classic Caribbean watering hole, or the **National Park Restaurant,** which has a popular bar and disco on most nights during the high season and on weekends during the off season.

Down in Puerto Viejo there are two main dance spots, **Johnny's Place** ★ and **Stanford's.** Both have small dance floors with ground-shaking reggae, dub, and rap rhythms blaring. One of the more popular places in town is **Hot Rocks,** a large dirt lot with some canvas catering tents over its bar and part of the table area. This place has a huge screen upon which several late-run movies are projected each night. For a more sophisticated ambience, try the downtown **Baba Yaga,** or the ocean-side **E-Z Times.** Finally, for a more local scene, check out **Bar Maritza's,** which really seems to go off on Sunday nights.

Heading just south out of town, the **Cut Back** is a popular spot with backpackers and bohemians, with a solid after-hours scene.

11 JUNGLE CANALS & TURTLE NESTING IN TORTUGUERO ★

Sometimes dubbed "the Venice of Costa Rica," Tortuguero is a remote village connected to the rest of mainland Costa Rica by a series of rivers and canals. This aquatic highway is lined almost entirely with a dense tropical rainforest that is home to howler and spider monkeys, three-toed sloths, toucans, and great green macaws. A trip through the canals is nothing like touring around Venice in a gondola, but it is a lot like cruising the Amazon basin—on a much smaller scale.

"Tortuguero" comes from the Spanish name for the giant sea turtles *(tortugas)* that nest on the beaches of this region every year from early March to mid-October. The chance to see this nesting attracts many people to this remote region, but just as many come to explore the intricate network of jungle canals and view the wildlife that live here.

ESSENTIALS

Getting There

There are no roads into Tortuguero. The only way to get here is by boat or small plane. Flying to Tortuguero is convenient if you don't have much time, but a boat trip through the canals and rivers of this region is often the highlight of any visit to Tortuguero. However, be forewarned: Although this trip can be stunning and exciting, it can also be long, tiring, and uncomfortable. You'll first have to ride by bus or minivan from San José; then it's 2 to 3 hours on the water, usually on hard wooden benches or plastic seats.

All of the lodges listed in this section offer transportation along with their lodging and tour packages. The transportation can be either by air or boat, or a mixture of the two (one-way by air, one-way by water).

Budget travelers can do it on their own, with a mix of public buses and private water taxis. If you want info on the current state of this method, check out the site www.tortuguerovillage.com, which has detailed directions about how to get to Tortuguero by a variety of routes.

Orientation

Tortuguero is one of the most remote locations in Costa Rica. There are no roads into this area and no cars in the village, so all transportation is by boat or foot. Most of the lodges are spread out over several kilometers to the north of the village of Tortuguero on either side of the main canal; the small airstrip is at the north end of the beachside spit of land.

Tortuguero Village is a tiny collection of houses connected by footpaths. The village is spread out on a thin spit of land, bordered on one side by the Caribbean Sea and on the other by the main canal. At most points, it's less than 300m (984 ft.) wide. If you stay at a hotel on the ocean side of the canal, you'll be able to walk into and explore the village at your leisure; if you're across the canal, you'll be dependent on the lodge's boat transportation. However, some of the lodges across the canal have their own network of jungle trails that might appeal to naturalists.

Visitor Information

There is an **information center** (✆ **8833-0827**) in town in front of the Catholic church. This is a good place for independent travelers looking to arrange local tours and onward travel.

FAST FACTS There are no banks, ATMs, or currency-exchange houses in Tortuguero, so be sure to bring sufficient cash in colones to cover any expenses and incidental charges. The local hotels and shops generally charge a hefty commission to exchange dollars. You'll find a dependable Internet cafe at **La Casona** (✆ **2709-8092**), a small restaurant and budget hotel in the heart of the village.

EXPLORING THE NATIONAL PARK

Four different species of sea turtles nest in Tortuguero National Park: the green turtle, the hawksbill, the loggerhead, and the giant leatherback. The prime nesting period is from **July to mid-October** (Aug and Sept are peak months). The park's beaches are excellent places to watch sea turtles nest, especially at night. Appealingly long and deserted as they are, the beaches are not great for swimming. The surf is usually very rough, and the river mouths have a nasty habit of attracting sharks that feed on the turtle hatchlings and many fish that live here.

Green turtles are perhaps the most common turtle found in Tortuguero, so you're more likely to see one of them than any other species if you visit during the prime nesting season. The **giant leatherback** is perhaps the most spectacular sea turtle to watch laying eggs. The largest of all turtle species, the leatherback can grow to 2m (6½ ft.) long and weigh well over 1,000 pounds. It nests from early March to mid-April, predominantly in the southern part of the park.

You can explore the park's rainforest, either by foot or by boat, and look for some of the incredible varieties of wildlife that live here: jaguars, anteaters, howler monkeys, collared and white-lipped peccaries, some 350 species of birds, and countless butterflies, among others. Boat tours are far and away the most popular way to visit this park, although one frequently very muddy trail starts at the park entrance and runs for about 2km (1¼ miles) through the coastal rainforest and along the beach.

ENTRY POINT, FEES & REGULATIONS The Tortuguero National Park entrance and ranger station are at the south end of Tortuguero Village. Admission to the park is $10 (£5). However, most people visit Tortuguero as part of a package tour. Be sure to confirm whether the park entrance is included in the price. Moreover, only certain canals and trails leaving from the park station are actually within the park. Many hotels and private guides take their tours to a series of canals that border the park and are similar in terms of flora and fauna but don't require a park entrance. When the turtles are nesting, you will have to arrange a night tour in advance with either your hotel or one of the private guides working in town. These guided tours generally run between $10 and $15 (£5–£7.50).

ORGANIZED TOURS In addition to the lodges mentioned below, tour companies in San José, as well as those in Cahuita and Puerto Viejo, offer 2-day/1-night excursions to Tortuguero, including transportation, all meals, and limited tours around the region. Prices for these trips range between $90 and $200 (£45–£100) per person, and—depending on price—guests are lodged either in one of the basic hotels in Tortuguero Village or one of the nicer lodges listed below. Reputable companies offering these excursions include the **Learning Trips** (✆ **800/723-2674** in the U.S. and Canada, or 2258-2293 in Costa Rica; www.costa-rica.us) and **Caño Blanco Marina** (✆ **2256-9444**). Alternately, you could go with **Fran and Modesto Watson** ★ (✆ **2226-0986**; www.tortuguerocanals.com), who are pioneering guides in this region and operate their own boat; they offer a range of overnight and multiday packages, with lodging options at most of the major lodges here.

EXPLORING THE VILLAGE

The most popular—in fact, the only—attraction in town is the small **Caribbean Conservation Corporation's Visitors' Center and Museum** ★ (✆ **2709-8091**; www.cccturtle.org). The museum has information and exhibits on a whole range of native flora and fauna, but its primary focus is on the life and natural history of the sea turtles. Most visits to the museum include a short, informative video on the turtles. There's a small gift shop here, and all proceeds go toward conservation and turtle protection. The museum is open Monday through Saturday from 10am to noon and 2 to 5:30pm, and Sunday from 2 to 5pm. There's a $1 (50p) admission charge, but more generous donations are encouraged.

Aside from the above museum, it's always fun and interesting to simply walk the paths and sidewalk of this tiny village.

WHERE TO STAY & DINE

A number of nature lodges are in and around Tortuguero. All offer a variety of multiday packages, including meals, transportation, and tours. My favorites are **Manatus Hotel ★★** (✆ **2239-4854;** www.manatushotel.com), **Laguna Lodge ★** (✆ **2272-4943;** www.lagunatortuguero.com), and **Tortuga Lodge** (✆ **800/886-2609;** www.tortugalodge.com). Budget travelers should check out **Casa Marbella** (✆/fax **2709-8011;** http://casamarbella.tripod.com).

10

Panama

By Jisel Perilla

Panama is a country that's undergoing a reinvention. Though it existed off the radar of international travelers and investors for many years, those days are coming to an end at remarkable speed. Now that the dust has long settled after the infamous Noriega era, political stability has taken hold and offered hope for the country's future. In fact, Panama celebrated its one-millionth international visitor last year, quite impressive for a tiny country of just over three million. It seems that every day, a new retirement community breaks ground, a new restaurant opens its doors, or a new beachside luxury resort is in the works here.

Rapidly emerging from under Costa Rica's shadow, Panama has a geography similar to that of its neighbor to the north—pristine rainforest, gorgeous beaches, picturesque mountain villages, wildlife galore, and, as an added bonus, a thriving, cosmopolitan city often compared to Miami. However, and this is the best part, Panama is still a relatively cheap country.

Panama claims a history rich with Spanish conquistadores and colonists, pirates, gold miners and adventurers, canal engineering, international trade, and mass immigration from countries as close as Jamaica and as far away as China. The pastiche of European and African cultures blended with the country's seven indigenous groups has had a tangible effect on Panama's architecture, cuisine, language, and folklore.

Given Panama's compact size and diversity, visitors here can take part in wildly different experiences without having to travel very far. The growing expat and retirement community, as well as the large number of Chinese, Colombian, and Venezuelan immigrants, make Panama a fascinating country to visit, and—as people from all over are discovering—an ideal place to live.

1 THE REGIONS IN BRIEF

Panama, an S-shaped **isthmus** that measures little more than 77,700 sq. km (30,000 sq. miles), is just slightly smaller than South Carolina—yet there is a huge diversity of landscapes and microclimates within this tiny nation. Costa Rica borders Panama to the west, Colombia to the east; and, in what can be vexing to the traveler with no sense of direction, the Pacific Ocean to the south and the Caribbean Sea to the north. Because Panama City faces southeast, travelers are presented with the uncommon view of the sun rising over the Pacific. At its narrowest point, Panama measures just 50km (31 miles) wide.

Besides the isthmus, Panama is made up of than 1,500 **islands,** many of them uninhabited and cloaked in thick vegetation. These islands are grouped into four regions. In the Caribbean Sea there are the Bocas del Toro and San Blas archipelagos; in the Pacific Ocean, Las Perlas Archipelago in the Gulf of Panama, and Coiba Island and its accompanying tiny islands in the Gulf of Chiriquí.

Panama is home to two **mountain ranges,** the Serranía del Darién in the east, and the Cordillera Central in the west, the latter of which is home to the highest peak in the country, the dormant Volcán Barú, at 3,475m (11,400 ft.). This is the only place in Panama where you are likely to experience brisk temperatures—the rest of the country averages 75°F to 85°F (24°C–29°C) year-round.

Panama is a centralized nation, with about a third of its population of three million living in Panama City; in comparison, the population of the second-largest city, Colón, is just under 200,000 residents. The country is divided into nine *provincias,* or provinces, three provincial-level indigenous territories called *comarcas,* and two subprovincial *comarcas.* See the map on p. 639 for a visual guide to the regions outlined here.

PANAMA CITY, THE CANAL & SURROUNDINGS Beyond the urban streets of Panama City, the Canal Zone is characterized by a species-rich, dense tropical rainforest, hundreds of rivers, mangrove swamps, the Pacific Ocean coastline, and Las Perlas Archipelago in the Gulf of Panama. Thanks to the Panama Canal and its reliance on the local watershed, the rainforest in this area is protected as a series of national parks and reserves (Chagres, Soberanía, Sherman, and Camino de Cruces, for example).

CENTRAL PANAMA Considered the country's cultural heartland, this area covers the Coclé Province and the Azuero Peninsula. In Coclé, city dwellers flock to popular El Valle de Antón, a verdant mountain hideaway located in the crater of an extinct volcano (1,173m/3,850 ft. at its highest peak). The Pacific coast southwest of the city is another popular weekend getaway for its beaches and a few all-inclusive resorts. Farther southwest, the Azuero Peninsula has been largely deforested, but it is still a popular destination for its traditional festivals, handicrafts, and Spanish villages whose architecture dates back to the medieval era.

BOCAS DEL TORO ARCHIPELAGO Bocas del Toro is in the northwest corner of the country, near the border with Costa Rica, and it's one of the more popular and easily accessed Caribbean destinations. This region is characterized by an eclectic mix of indigenous groups, Spanish descendants, Afro-Caribbeans, and, more recently, American expats, as well as a funky, laid-back Caribbean vibe. Visitors come to scuba dive, snorkel, go boating, see wildlife, or just soak in the bohemian vibe of Bocas Town, the capital city, or some of the area's more remote, protected islands.

THE WESTERN HIGHLANDS & GULF OF CHIRIQU The Western Highlands is a veritable paradise of fertile peaks and valleys, crystal-clear rivers, mild temperatures, and fresh air. The region is undergoing a palpable growth spurt as hundreds of North Americans continue to buy second and retirement homes here, so expect to hear a lot of English. The region centers around the skirt of Volcán Barú, a dormant volcano capped by a moist cloud forest. Farther south are the humid lowlands, the capital city David, and the wondrous coast and islands of the Gulf of Chiriquí. Also here is Isla Coiba National Park, one of the most diverse and pristine islands for scuba diving and snorkeling in the world.

THE DARIÉN The easternmost region of Panama is known as the Darién Province, a swath of impenetrable rainforest and swampland that is undeveloped, save for a handful of tiny villages and indigenous settlements. The interior of the Darién can be reached only by foot, boat, or small plane—and herein lies its allure for adventure travelers. Within the province lies the Darién National Park, most of it inaccessible except for the Cana Research Station, an area revered by birders worldwide for the abundance of endemic and "show-bird" species such as macaws and harpy eagles, the largest predator in the world. Along the Pacific shore is the famous Tropic Star Lodge, but otherwise, lodging in the Darién is in rustic shelters and tents.

THE COMARCA KUNA YALA (THE SAN BLAS ARCHIPELAGO) Though commonly referred to as the San Blas Archipelago, this semiautonomous region, or *comarca,* is named for the Kuna Yala, perhaps Panama's most well-known indigenous group. The Kuna are recognized for their tightly knit culture, colorful clothing, and handicrafts such as *mola* tapestries. More than 300 lovely, palm-studded islands in turquoise Caribbean waters make up the archipelago in what is truly an unspoiled paradise.

2 THE BEST OF PANAMA IN 1 WEEK

Given Panama's compact size, and the short flights that quickly connect you to other destinations, travelers can pack a lot into a week here—but the timing is tight. This itinerary includes a 2-day visit to Bocas del Toro, but you might opt instead to spend 2 nights in Boca Chica, near David, and to visit Isla Coiba the first day (a long day trip, but worth it), then head out to the Gulf of Chiriquí National Marine Park the next day for sportfishing or lounging on the beach of an uninhabited island.

Day 1: Getting to Know Panama City

Arrive and get settled in **Panama City★★**. If your flight arrives early, visit **Panama Viejo★★★** (p. 655) to get your historical bearings, then head across town for a walking tour of **Casco Viejo ★★★**. Travelers with little time will want to head straight to Casco Viejo, where they can dine on Panamanian food at **S'cena★★★** (p. 668) or **Manolo Caracol★★** (p. 668).

Day 2: Getting Deep in the Jungle

One of Panama's top parks for birding, hiking, and just immersing yourself in the earthy, steamy environs of thick rainforest is only 45 minutes from Panama City: **Soberanía National Park★★★** (p. 676). Leave early and bring your binoculars to view hundreds of birds on a walk or mountain-bike ride along **Pipeline Road★★**; join a **jungle cruise** to see monkeys, crocodiles, and transiting ships on the Panama Canal; ride a dugout canoe up the Chagres River to visit an **Emberá village** (p. 678). In the afternoon, pay a visit to the country's star attraction, the **Panama Canal ★★★**, at the **Miraflores Locks ★★★** (p. 673), where you can have lunch and tour their visitor center. Head back to Panama City and cool off with a stroll or bike ride along the **Amador Causeway★★** (p. 659).

Days 3 & 4: To the Highlands

Fly to **David** and grab a taxi or rent a car for the 45-minute drive to **Boquete ★★★**. Settle into your hotel and spend the afternoon getting to know the town on foot or by bike, visiting the town's public gardens and other sights. Another option is to dive into an adventurous afternoon activity such as a canopy ride on the **Boquete Tree Trek** (p. 686) or a low-key booked visit to the coffee farm **Café Kotowa★★** (p. 687). The following day, spend the day **rafting** (p. 679) on a Class 2 to Class 5 river. You can also book a bird-watching tour that includes **Finca Lérida ★★★** (p. 687) and **Volcán Barú National Park★** (p. 685).

Days 5 & 6: From the Highlands to the Lowlands

Catch an early morning flight from David to **Bocas del Toro ★**, and settle in to a

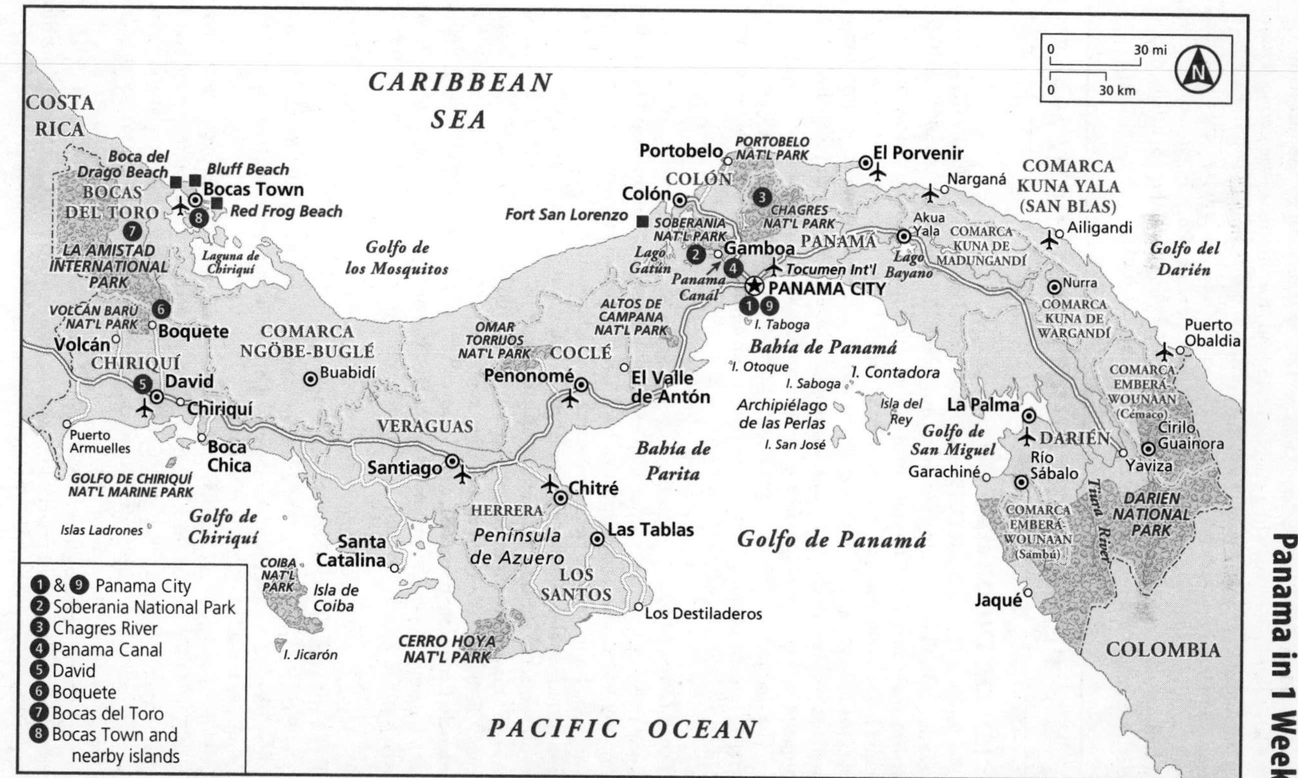
CARIBBEAN
SEA
PACIFIC OCEAN
0
30 mi
0
30 km
N
COSTA
RICA
COLOMBIA
Boca del
Drago Beach
Bluff Beach
Bocas Town
Red Frog Beach
BOCAS
DEL TORO
LA AMISTAD
INTERNATIONAL
PARK
Laguna de
Chiriquí
Golfo de
los Mosquitos
VOLCÁN BARÚ
NAT'L PARK
Boquete
Volcán
CHIRIQUÍ
David
Chiriquí
Puerto
Armuelles
Boca
Chica
GOLFO DE CHIRIQUÍ
NAT'L MARINE PARK
Islas Ladrones
Golfo de
Chiriquí
COMARCA
NGÖBE-BUGLÉ
Buabidí
VERAGUAS
Santiago
Santa
Catalina
COIBA
NAT'L
PARK
Isla de
Coiba
I. Jicarón
CERRO HOYA
NAT'L PARK
HERRERA
Península
de Azuero
Chitré
Las Tablas
LOS
SANTOS
Los Destiladeros
OMAR
TORRIJOS
NAT'L PARK
COCLÉ
Penonomé
El Valle
de Antón
ALTOS DE
CAMPANA
NAT'L PARK
Bahía de
Parita
Fort San Lorenzo
Portobelo
PORTOBELO
NAT'L PARK
COLÓN
Colón
CHAGRES
NAT'L PARK
SOBERANIA
NAT'L PARK
Lago
Gatún
Gamboa
Panama
Canál
PANAMÁ
Tocumen Int'l
PANAMA CITY
I. Taboga
Bahía de Panamá
I. Otoque
I. Saboga
I. Contadora
Archipiélago
de las Perlas
I. San José
Isla del
Rey
Golfo de Panamá
El Porvenir
Narganá
COMARCA
KUNA YALA
(SAN BLAS)
Ailigandi
Akua
Yala
COMARCA
KUNA DE
MADUNGANDÍ
Lago
Bayano
Nurra
COMARCA
KUNA DE
WARGANDÍ
Golfo del
Darién
Puerto
Obaldia
COMARCA
EMBERÁ-
WOUNAAN
(Cémaco)
Cirilo
Guainora
Yaviza
La Palma
Golfo de
San Miguel
DARIÉN
Río
Sábalo
Garachiné
COMARCA
EMBERÁ-
WOUNAAN
(Sambú)
Tiura River
DARIEN
NATIONAL
PARK
Jaqué
1 & 9 Panama City
2 Soberania National Park
3 Chagres River
4 Panama Canal
5 David
6 Boquete
7 Bocas del Toro
8 Bocas Town and
nearby islands

hotel in **Bocas Town** ★, on Isla Colón. Preplan an afternoon tour with your hotel or an outfitter to visit **Swan's Cay** and **Boca del Drago** beach ★★ (p. 696) and rent a bicycle and pedal out to **Bluff Beach,** or take another hop over to **Isla Bastimentos** ★★★ (p. 697).

Day ❼: Leaving Bocas del Toro
Spend the morning wandering around town and soaking up the Caribbean vibe, architecture, and culture. There are quite a few **souvenir shops** in Bocas where you can pick up gifts before your flight back to Panama City.

3 PLANNING YOUR TRIP TO PANAMA

VISITOR INFORMATION

The **Panama Tourist Board,** known as the Autoridad de Turismo Panama (ATP), has a website and toll-free number for North Americans and Canadians (✆ **800/231-0568;** www.visitpanama.com); English-language brochures are available. The website offers more information than can be gotten from any ATP representative on the phone, and also has links to other helpful sites. Make sure to check out **www.panamainfo.com** as well; it's probably the best travel site currently available on Panama and they also publish a quarterly magazine with tourist, real estate, and restaurant information.

The magazines ***9°80*** (www.panama980.com), **Focus** (www.focuspanama.com) and ***Hello Panama*** are other bilingual quarterly or biannual travel/tourist publications available at most hotels and restaurants.

Tour Operators

Local travel agencies are another good source of information. **Ancon Expeditions** ★★ (✆ **269-9415;** www.anconexpeditions.com) is the foremost tour operator in Panama, with a full-time staff of degreed naturalists and bird-watching experts, a handful of remote lodges, and offerings of day excursions and preset and custom-planned journeys to all corners of Panama. **Adventures in Panama** ★ (✆ **315/849-5144** in the U.S., or 236-5814; www.adventuresinpanama.com), whose slogan is "No Tours, Just Adventures," is the operator to go to for active sports such as kayaking, mountain biking, and rock climbing around Panama, and day adventures around Panama City. The best bird-watching operator in the country is **Advantage Panama** (www.advantagepanama.com), which offers general day and half-day adventure tours in addition to bird-watching excursions.

ENTRY REQUIREMENTS

The Terrorism Prevention Act of 2004 now requires U.S. citizens traveling to Panama to present a valid passport. (Previously, only a driver's license and copy of your birth certificate were needed to enter Panama.)

Citizens of the United States, Canada, Great Britain, and most European nations may visit Panama for a maximum of 90 days. No visa is necessary, but you must have a valid passport and a $5 (£2.50) tourist card, paid when entering by land or at the airline counter before your departure. Carry your passport and tourist card, or better yet, a photocopy, with you at all times.

Important: Travelers must be able to demonstrate proof of sufficient funds if requested, and they must present an onward or return ticket. Panama charges a departure tax of $20 (£10) at the airport (it may already be included in your ticket).

Panamanian Embassy Locations

In the U.S.: 2862 McGill Terrace NW, Washington, DC 20008. © **202/483-1407;** info@embassyofpanama.org.

In Canada: 130 Albert St., Ste. 300 K1P 5G4 Ottawa, ON. © **613/236-7177;** info@panama-embassy.ca.

In the U.K.: 40 Hertford St., London W1Y 7TG. © **44171/409-2255.**

CUSTOMS

Visitors to Panama may bring with them personal items such as jewelry, and professional equipment including cameras, computers, and electronics, as well as fishing and diving gear for personal use—all of which are permitted duty-free. Customs officials in Panama seldom check arriving tourists' luggage.

MONEY

The unit of currency in Panama is the U.S. dollar, but the Panamanian balboa, which is pegged to the dollar at a 1:1 ratio, also circulates in denominations of 5¢, 10¢, 25¢, and 50¢ coins. (U.S. coins are in circulation as well.) Balboa coins are sized similarly to their U.S. counterparts, and travelers will have no trouble identifying their value.

Exchanging Money

Travelers with pounds or euros may exchange money at **Banco Nacional,** which has branches in the airport and across the nation. To save time, you may want to convert your money into dollars before arriving in Panama.

ATMs

The easiest and best way to get cash in Panama is from an ATM, available throughout Panama in banks and supermarkets, and identifiable by a red SISTEMA CLAVE sign with a white key. ATMs, called *cajeros automáticos,* can be found in larger towns only, so if you're visiting out-of-the-way destinations such as an offshore island, plan to bring extra cash. To find ATM locations in Panama, check out www.sclave.com/english.html.

Note that some ATMs in Panama limit withdrawals to $200 (£100) per day, others to $500 (£250).

Credit Cards

Credit cards are widely accepted in Panama City, and most chain hotels, resorts, and B&Bs, moderate-to-upscale restaurants, malls, as well as most travel agencies, take MasterCard and Visa. American Express and Discover are becoming increasingly more popular. Diners Club is not widely accepted. In rural areas and smaller towns, make sure to bring enough cash, as few businesses are likely to take credit cards.

In the event of a lost or stolen card, **Visa**'s emergency number is © **800/847-2911** toll-free in the U.S., or call 410/902-8022 collect from Panama. **American Express** cardholders and traveler's check holders should call © **207-1100** in Panama, or its 24-hour service in the United States at 800/111-0006. **MasterCard** holders should call © **800/307-7309,** or make a collect call to 636/722-7111.

Traveler's Checks

Traveler's checks are readily accepted at major hotels, but less so at budget hotels and many restaurants. In fact, beyond major hotels and banks, businesses in Panama seem reluctant to accept traveler's checks. Instead of bringing traveler's checks, use an ATM for cash if you can; bring traveler's checks only as a backup in the event of a lost or stolen card.

WHEN TO GO

PEAK SEASON The best time to visit Panama is during the **dry season** between mid-December and mid-April. Keep in mind that this is also the most expensive time to visit Panama, and hotels jack their rates by up to 50%. Destinations such as the Chiriquí Highlands, el Valle de Anton, and Bocas del Toro see more rain than the rest of the country, though mornings are usually bright and sunny. If you are unable to visit during the dry season, keep in mind that the early months (Apr–July) are characterized by sudden, heavy thunderstorms in the afternoon that are short in duration, and can happen every few days. Often, the skies are sunny in the morning or afternoon.

For up-to-date information on weather in Panama, go to **www.panama-maps.com** or **www.accuweather.com**.

CLIMATE Panama lies between 7 degrees and 9 degrees above the Equator, which places it firmly within the Tropics. Accordingly, average year-round temperatures are a balmy 75°F to 85°F (24°C–29°C), varying only with altitude. The average temperature in the Chiriquí Highlands, for example, is 60°F (16°C), and is the only area in Panama where you will likely feel cold.

Humidity is always high in Panama, and rainfall varies noticeably between the Pacific and Caribbean sides of the country, with some areas in the Caribbean receiving almost twice the yearly rainfall of Panama City. The Chiriquí Highlands experiences a variety of microclimates that can change drastically, sometimes even within a few miles. In Boquete, high winds and a peculiar misting rain called *bajareque* are common from mid-December to mid-February; January sees the occasional thunderstorm, and March to May are the sunniest months.

PUBLIC HOLIDAYS Like any respectable Latin American country, Panama has many religious and non-religious holidays. Most are celebrated on Mondays to allow for 3-day weekends. Official holidays in Panama include January 1 (New Year's Day), January 9 (Martyr's Day), Good Friday, Easter Sunday, May 1 (Labor Day), August 15 (Founding of Old Panama—observed in Panama City only), October 12 (Hispanic Day), November 2 (All Souls' Day), November 3 (Independence Day), November 4 (Flag Day), November 5 (Colón Day—observed in the city of Colón only), November 10 (First Call for Independence), November 28 (Independence from Spain), December 8 (Mother's Day), and December 25 (Christmas Day).

HEALTH CONCERNS

Travelers have a low risk of contracting a tropical disease while in Panama. Cases of **malaria** are not common and mostly afflict rural citizens who live in remote areas, such as Ngöbe-Buglé Indian tribes in Bocas del Toro, the Darién, and the San Blas Archipelago. More common than malaria is **dengue fever,** an infectious disease caused by an arbovirus transmitted by daytime mosquitoes. **Hepatitis A** can occur in impoverished areas with poor sanitation, but visitors can and should get vaccinated at home. See "Health" in "Planning Your Trip to Central America" for more info.

Panama is also home to many ticks and sand flies, as well as poisonous snakes such as the pit viper, the fer-de-lance, and the patoca, but bites are rare, and can easily be avoided by wearing long pants or good boots while hiking.

Telephone Dialing Info at a Glance

Panama has a seven-digit phone numbering system, and there are no city or area codes. The country code for Panama is 507, which you use only when dialing from outside the country. Cellphones are prefixed by 6; in this book, telephone numbers include this prefix because most businesses' published phone numbers include the prefix.

- **For directory assistance:** For a number within Panama, dial ✆ **102.** For assistance with finding an international number, dial ✆ **106** for an operator who can connect you with international directory assistance.
- **For operator assistance:** If you need operator assistance when making a call, dial ✆ **106.** For an international operator in the U.S., dial ✆ **109** (AT&T), **108** (MCI), or **115** (Sprint).
- **To call Panama from outside the country:** First dial the international access code—**011** from the U.S.; **00** from the U.K., Ireland, or New Zealand; or **0011** from Australia. Then dial the country code **(507)** followed by the number.
- **To make international calls from within Panama:** First dial **00** and then the country code (U.S. or Canada 1, U.K. 44, Ireland 353, Australia 61, and New Zealand 64). Next dial the area code and number. For example, if you want to call the British Embassy in Washington, D.C., dial ✆ **00-1-202-588-7800.**
- **Toll-free numbers:** In Panama, numbers beginning with 800 are toll-free, but calling an "800" number in the States from Panama is not toll-free. In fact, it costs the same as an overseas call.

More common illnesses that affect tourists are TD, or **traveler's diarrhea,** caused by microbes in food and water, and sunstroke. See p. 70 in "Planning Your Trip to Central America" for info on how to prevent and treat these illnesses.

GETTING THERE

By Plane

All international flights land at the newly expanded **Tocumen International Airport (PTY; ✆ 238-2600)**. Air Panama flights from Costa Rica to Panama City land at the Marcos A. Gelabert Airport, which is more commonly referred to as **Albrook Airport (PAC; ✆ 315-0241)**. There is also direct service from San José, Costa Rica, to the **Aeropuerto Enrique Malek** in David (**DAV; ✆ 316/9000;** www.flyairpanama.com) and to the Bocas del Toro airport. Taca Airlines (see below) has service from Costa Rica, arriving at Tocumen.

The following airlines serve Panama City from the United States, using the gateway cities listed. **American Airlines** has two daily flights from Miami; Copa Airlines has two daily flights from Miami, and one daily flight from Orlando, New York, and Los Angeles. **Delta Airlines** offers one daily flight from Atlanta; Taca has one daily flight from all major U.S. hubs, but with a stopover in El Salvador or Costa Rica. Mexicana offers daily flights from Miami, Dallas, and Los Angeles; however, they connect with Copa Air in Mexico City, so you're better off with a direct flight with Copa. From Canada, flights to Panama City are available through American Airlines, with a connection in Miami. See "Appendix: Fast Facts, Toll-Free Numbers & Websites" for airline info.

From London, **Iberia** (✆ **0870/609-0500** in the U.K., or 227-3966 in Panama; www.iberia.com) has daily flights to Panama City that connect in either Madrid or Costa Rica; **American Airlines** and **British Airways** have daily flights that connect in Miami; **Continental Airlines** has daily flights that connect in Orlando or Houston; **Delta** has a daily flight that connects in Atlanta.

From Australia, **Qantas** (✆ **9691-3636;** www.qantasair.com) has daily flights in conjunction with Copa Air from Sydney, connecting in Honolulu or Los Angeles; **Air New Zealand** (✆ **507-264-8756** in New Zealand; www.airnewzealand.com) also works in conjunction with Copa Air with one daily flight from Auckland, connecting in Los Angeles.

By Bus

Buses from Costa Rica arrive in cities throughout Panama, and all major carriers have their final stop in Panama City. Remember, if you're crossing into Panama from Costa Rica by bus or car, you'll have to go through Customs, which can take up to 2 hours, and you'll have to buy a $10 (£5) visitor stamp for your passport. There are no buses between Colombia and Panama.

Two companies offer service to and from Costa Rica: **Tica Bus** (✆ **314-6385;** www.ticabus.com) and **Panaline** (✆ **227-8648**). Both companies have large, air-conditioned coaches. Tica Bus leaves for San José at 11am, Panaline leaves at 12:30pm; the cost is $50 (£25) round-trip.

By Boat

These mainstream cruise lines offer trips to Panama from the States, some of which include stops elsewhere in Central America: **Celebrity Cruises** (✆ 800/647-2251; www.celebritycruises.com); **Disney Cruise Line** (✆ 800/951-3532; www.disneycruise.com); **Holland America** (✆ 877/724-5425; www.hollandamerica.com); **Norwegian Cruise Lines** (✆ 800/327-7030; www.ncl.com); **Oceania Cruises** (✆ 800/531-2300; www.oceaniacruises.com); **Orient Lines** (✆ 800/333-7300; www.orientlines.com); **Princess Cruises** (✆ 800/774-6237; www.princess.com); and **Royal Caribbean** (✆ 866/562-7625; www.rccl.com).

GETTING AROUND

By Plane

Air travel is a safe and quick way to get around Panama. Because of rising fuel costs, however, note that prices are rapidly increasing. **Aero Perlas** (✆ **315-7500;** www.aeroperlas.com) and **Air Panama** (✆ **316-9000;** www.flyairpanama.com) are Panama's two air carriers, servicing major destinations in the country. More-remote destinations in Panama can be reached by scheduled or charter flights aboard a small plane, which touches down on a dirt airstrip. Airlines charge a 5% tax on all flights. See "Getting Around" in the separate sections below for more info.

By Car

Driving in Panama allows you the most flexibility and costs about the same as in the U.S. Because gas is a little more expensive, this isn't the cheapest option, but it allows you to visit outlying attractions for less money than the cost of a private tour. The biggest headaches for drivers are poorly maintained side roads and lack of signage. If you're planning on traveling along country or secondary roads, or during wet, muddy conditions, consider a 4WD vehicle with high clearance, and book ahead since these vehicles sell out fast.

Among the agencies operating in Panama are: **Avis** (© 800/230-4898 in the U.S., or 278-9444; www.avis.com); **Budget** (© 800/527-0700 in the U.S., or 263-8777; www.budgetpanama.com); **Hertz** (© 800/654-3131 in the U.S., or 260-2111; www.hertz.com); **National** (© 800/227-7368 in the U.S., or 265-2222; www.nationalpanama.com); **Payless** (© 800/582-7432 in the U.S., or 222-1881; www.payless.com.pa); **Thrifty** (© 800/847-4389 in the U.S., or 264-2613; www.thrifty.com). Renting a car usually costs $40 to $80 (£20–£40) a day. **Thrifty** rents significantly cheaper 4WD vehicles than any other rental company in Panama.

By Bus

Bus travel is the cheapest form of transportation in Panama, and service is available to all distant corners of the country. Buses are not large coaches but rather "maxivans" that seat around 10 to 25 people, so expect a reasonable level of comfort but nothing as fancy as reclining seats. All buses that head to the interior leave from Panama City's Albrook Terminal, which is about a $2 (£1) taxi ride from downtown. Buses to major towns such as David or Valle de Anton leave more or less on the hour or half-hour throughout the day. Excepting buses headed to Costa Rica, bus service operates on a first-come, first-served basis.

It's not necessary to reserve your tickets ahead of time unless you are traveling on a holiday weekend or during December or Easter week, but be sure to arrive at the terminal at least 45 minutes ahead of time.

By Taxi

Some taxis work directly for a hotel, and rip off guests by charging up to three times the going fare, and they're not going to budge when you contest the fare. These are the taxis that await guests directly at the front door. Simply walk out to the street and flag a taxi down for cheaper fare. In Panama City, David, Colón, and Boquete, taxis can be hailed off the street relatively easily, though calling ahead will only cost you $1 or $2 (50p–£1) more. This is an especially good option in Colón, where it's not particularly smart to walk around too much. In small towns and more remote destinations, you'll probably have to have your hotel or restaurant call a taxi for you.

TIPS ON ACCOMMODATIONS

High season in Panama is the dry season, roughly between mid-December and mid-April. While hotels in Panama City keep their rates consistent throughout the year, hotels in popular tourist destinations such as Bocas del Toro and the Chiriquí Highlands increase their prices by as much as 30% to 50% during the dry season. Price ranges listed in hotel reviews reflect a range encompassing low and high season; for example, $50 to $75 (£25–£38) for a double would mean $50 (£25) from May to November and $75 (£38) from December to April. Precise start and end dates for high season may vary from hotel to hotel. Keep in mind that some hotels, particularly in beach areas such as Bocas del Toro or other remote areas, may close entirely during rainy season, so always call ahead to verify that your hotel will be open.

TIPS ON DINING

Panama is a melting pot of cultures and ethnic groups, and the dining scene here reflects this, especially in Panama City. International restaurants such as Italian, Swiss, Chinese, Middle Eastern, and creative, fusion-style eateries please more sophisticated palates and are plentiful. There are a lot of solid choices for cheap dining, too, and the usual fast-food chains abound.

In general, **Panamanian food** is tasty, but a lot of it is fried—especially breakfast items like empanadas, *hojaldras* (fried bread), and tortillas. Outside of major cities and tourist destinations, travelers will find mostly traditional Panamanian food that is heavy on seafood—primarily *pargo* (red snapper), *corvina* (sea bass), *langostina* (jumbo shrimp), calamari, and *pulpo* (octopus). Though Panamanian fare is quite good, there isn't much diversity, and meat and seafood are always paired with the ubiquitous coconut rice and beans, a small cabbage salad, and *patacones* (fried green plantains).

For inexpensive dining, Panama has dinerlike ***cafeterías*** that serve a set meal called ***comida corriente,*** which consists of an appetizer or soup, main course, and usually a beverage; these generally cost from $3 to $5 (£1.50–£2.50). ***Panaderías*** are bakeries and a good bet for a modest breakfast of a pastry and coffee; some even have tables.

Tipping is a customary 10% of the total bill. ***Note:*** Avoid overtipping and check the breakdown of charges on your bill, because many restaurants automatically charge a 10% service fee as a tip. The tax on restaurant bills is 5%.

TIPS ON SHOPPING

Shoppers will feel quite at home in Panama. Handicrafts are relatively cheap and easy to find. Most destinations, even small towns, will have at least one store selling handicrafts, and weekend markets are often the most colorful and exciting way to get your hands on traditional Panamanian arts, though don't forget to bargain!

There are modern shopping malls in Panama City on par with those found in the U.S. Outside major cities however, clothing and jewelry shopping is limited to small shops, and quality isn't exceptional. Though Colón's free trade zone is famous all over Latin America for its "deals and steals," the reality is that, unless you're shopping in bulk, you're not going to get any great deals here, and the hassle of getting to Colón simply isn't worth the trip.

Despite the name, Panama hats did not originate in Panama but in Ecuador, and were traditionally made by the Ecuadorian indigenous group from the Manabí Province using fibers from the *toquilla* palm. The hat was first popularized by Ferdinand de Lesseps during the French canal effort, and later during the canal building by the U.S., when thousands were imported from Ecuador and given to workers for protection from the blistering tropical sun. Hence, the name "Panama hat" stuck. Really, you'd have the best luck ordering a high-quality hat over the Internet from a reputable importer, though you'll find a range of hats in Panama City at the stands at Plaza Cinco de Mayo, as well as a limited selection at the YMCA Handicrafts Market in Balboa.

Fast Facts Panama

American Express American Express Travel Services has an office on Avenida Balboa (✆ **207-1100,** or for 24-hr. service in the United States, 800/111-0006). This office issues traveler's checks and replacement cards, along with other standard services. To report lost or stolen traveler's checks within Panama, call the numbers above, or try ✆ **207-1111.**

Business Hours Hours for service-oriented businesses in Panama are generally 8am to 1:30pm and 3 to 5pm on weekdays, and 8am to noon on Saturdays. Shops open at 9 or 10am and close at 6 or 7pm; shopping malls close around 8pm. Grocery stores are open 24 hours or 8am to 8pm.

Drugstores Called *farmacias* in Spanish, drugstores are plentiful in Panama City. For 24-hour service, visit a branch of **El Rey supermarket,** the most central of which is on Vía España in Panama City.

Embassies & Consulates The **United States Embassy** is located at Avenida Balboa and Calle 38 Este (✆ 207-7030). The **Canadian Embassy** is at World Trade Center, first floor (✆ 264-9731). The **British Embassy** is at Calle 53 Este and Nicanor de Obarrio (✆ 269-0866). **Australia** and **New Zealand** do not have an embassy or consulate in Panama; however, the British Embassy can provide consular assistance to citizens of those countries.

Emergencies For fire, dial ✆ **103;** for an ambulance, dial **Seguro Social** at ✆ **229-1133,** or contact **Cruz Roja** at ✆ **228-2187.**

Hospitals Many Panamanian doctors receive their medical degrees in the U.S., and therefore many speak English. The best hospitals in Panama City are **Centro Medico Paitilla,** at Calle 53 and Avenida Balboa (✆ **265-8800**); **Clínica Hospital San Fernando,** at Vía España (✆ **227-4733**), **Hospital Nacional,** at Avenida Cuba between calles 38 and 39 (✆ **207-8100** or 207-8102), and **Hospital Punta Pacífica,** at Calle 53 in Bellavista (✆ **204-8000**). Punta Pacífica is the newest and most advanced hospital in the country and is affiliated with the Johns Hopkins hospital.

Language Spanish is the official language in Panama, though English is widely spoken in the tourism industry, and many hotel owners are native English-speakers themselves. Panama's seven indigenous groups speak their own languages in their communities, and in some isolated areas indigenous groups do not speak Spanish fluently. On the Caribbean coast, creoles speak a patois called Guari-Guari or Wari-Wari, a mix of English, Spanish, and Ngöbe-Buglé.

Laundromats Hotel laundry services are very expensive. Laundry (both coin-operated and serviced) and dry-cleaning businesses can be found throughout Panama City; in smaller towns, there is at least one laundromat available.

Maps ATP's information desk at the Tocumen Airport offers a general map of Panama City, but the best available is **Mapi,** produced by bookstore El Hombre de la Mancha and available at their stores or at the Gran Morrison stores (see "Bookstores," on p. 662). This map is also available at gift shops in major hotels. The tourism publication ***Focus*** has a fold-out map that is accurate but does not show all street names; this publication can be found at hotels and other tourism-oriented shops and restaurants.

Newspapers & Magazines Panama's principal daily newspaper is *La Prensa;* the five other dailies include *La Panamá América, Crítica Libre, El Universal,* and *La Estrella. La Prensa* publishes a weekend guide supplement on Thursdays, and is the best paper for event listings. The English-language *Panama News,* once available in print, is available online at www.thepanamanews.com. *The Panama Visitor* is in Spanish and English and is a free, bimonthly publication for tourists. You can find copies of the *Miami Herald* in English at supermarkets and at the Gran Morrison chain. ***Hello Panama, Focus, 980,*** and ***The Panama Planner*** are quarterly or bi-annual magazine publications available at many hotels and tourist sites.

Police For police, dial ✆ **104** or **316-0080.**

Post Offices & Mail Panama has no stamp vending machines or post boxes, so you'll have to head to the post office to send a postcard, or ask your hotel if they can do it for you. A letter sent regular mail to the U.S. will arrive in 5 to 10 days; the cost, at press time, is 35¢ for a letter and 25¢ for a postcard. For quick service, send a package via a courier; see "Fast Facts" under "Panama City," below.

Safety Panama is one of the safest countries in Latin America. As in any large city, you'll want to keep a close watch on your personal belongings in Panama City and disperse your cash and credit cards on your person. You should avoid certain neighborhoods, such as El Chorrillo, San Miguelito, and Casco Viejo at night, but otherwise you're unlikely to face any serious problems. The U.S. Department of Homeland Security states that kidnappings and murders have occurred in the Darién Province near the border with Colombia, but all Darién destinations in this chapter are safe. In destinations like Bocas del Toro and the Kuna Yala Islands, where tourism is quickly increasing, robbery is becoming somewhat of an issue, but as long as you keep your guard up, you shouldn't encounter any problems. Panama law requires that foreigners carry their passport with them at all times, but play it safe and carry a photocopy of only the opening pages and entrance stamp or tourist card.

Smoking In 2007, Panama banned smoking in all public buildings. That means that guests cannot technically smoke in any hotel guest room or on the premises, and have to go outside to do so. (Nonsmoking rooms are not noted in hotel reviews below because of the across-the-board policy.) This rule is more flexible outside of Panama City, and you may be able to get away with smoking on your hotel terrace, but technically, it is not allowed.

Taxes All hotels charge 10% tax. Restaurants charge 5% on the total cost of the bill, and often sneak in an automatic 10% for service—check your bill carefully to avoid overtipping. See "Entry Requirements" earlier in this chapter for info on the airport departure tax.

Telephones The cheapest way to phone in Panama is to use a prepaid phone card, available in kiosks, supermarkets, and pharmacies in quantities of $5 (£2.50), $10 (£5), and $20 (£10)—however, these cards have a life span of 15 to 30 days. **ClaroCOM** has the best rates with 5¢ (2.50p) per minute for national and international calls to the U.S. and the U.K., and 35¢ (15p) per minute to cellular phones. Cable and wireless **Telechip** cards are less of a value at 15¢ (10p) per minute for national calls and 25¢ (10p) per minute for international calls. The cards have an access phone number and a scratch-off code, as well as bilingual service. Remember that hotels charge a connection fee even if the connection number is a toll-free number.

Also see p. 80 in "Planning Your Trip to Central America" and the "Telephone Dialing Info at a Glance" box earlier in this chapter for info.

Tipping Tipping in Panama at restaurants is 10% (on top of tax; see "Taxes," above). Taxi drivers do not expect tips, but you might consider it if you've rented a taxi for the day. Porters and bellhops should be tipped $2 to $5 (£1–£2.50) depending on the caliber of the hotel.

Useful Phone Numbers **U.S. Dept. of State Travel Advisory:** © 202/647-5225 (staffed 24 hr.); **U.S. Passport Agency:** © 202/647-0518; **U.S. Centers for Disease Control International Traveler's Hot Line:** © 404/332-4559.

4 PANAMA CITY ★★

Long overshadowed by the Panama Canal and with a reputation as a hub for drug-running, Panama City is not only reinventing itself as the thriving commercial and financial hub of the Americas, it is asserting itself as a burgeoning tourist destination. Panama City (commonly referred to simply as "Panama") is one of those rare Central American capitals that has it all: a high standard of living, a seemingly endless supply of investment from abroad, a surplus of natural beauty, and a rich cultural brew of ethnicities and religions. There is a sizeable expat presence in the city, as well as a growing Asian community, both of which continue to change the face of Panama City. It has been called the new Hong Kong and Miami—a sleek and modern city proud of its rôle as host to the world.

Signs of Panama City's reinvention are everywhere. The Amador Causeway, formerly a U.S. military base, is ground zero for several multimillion-dollar condominium and commercial-center developments, such as the new Biodiversity Museum designed by famed architect Frank Gehry. The run-down 19th-century buildings of Casco Viejo have been revitalized with private and public funds and declared a World Heritage Site by UNESCO. Along the coast, swiftly rising skyscrapers, spurred by an irresistible 20-year tax exemption, portend a megalopolis in the making: By 2009, 5 of the 10 tallest buildings in Latin America will be here in Panama City, including the tallest, at 104 floors. Even the dirty Panama Bay is undergoing a $360-million cleanup.

But Panama City's visitors need not venture far from their air-conditioned hotels to immerse themselves in the wild tropical jungle that is characteristic of this region. Even the city's Metropolitan Park is the protected home of more than 200 species of birds, mammals, and reptiles. Dozens of remarkable destinations outside the city limits can be reached in less than 2 hours, meaning travelers can spend the day exploring but head back to the city and be well fed and rested for the next day's adventure.

ESSENTIALS

Getting There

BY PLANE All international flights, except those from Costa Rica, land at the newly expanded **Tocumen International Airport (PTY; © 238-2700)**, 21km (13 miles) from Panama City. Flights from Costa Rica to Panama City land at Albrook Airport (see below), and there is direct service from San José to David and Bocas del Toro airports. **Air Panama** (**© 315-0439;** www.flyairpanama.com) has service from San José, Costa Rica to Isla Colón, on Monday, Wednesday, and Friday at 10am; service from Bocas del Toro to San José leaves at 8:35am. **Nature Air,** a Costa Rican airline that is represented in Panama by **Bocas Air Adventures** (**© 656-0460** in Panama, or 800/235-9272 in the

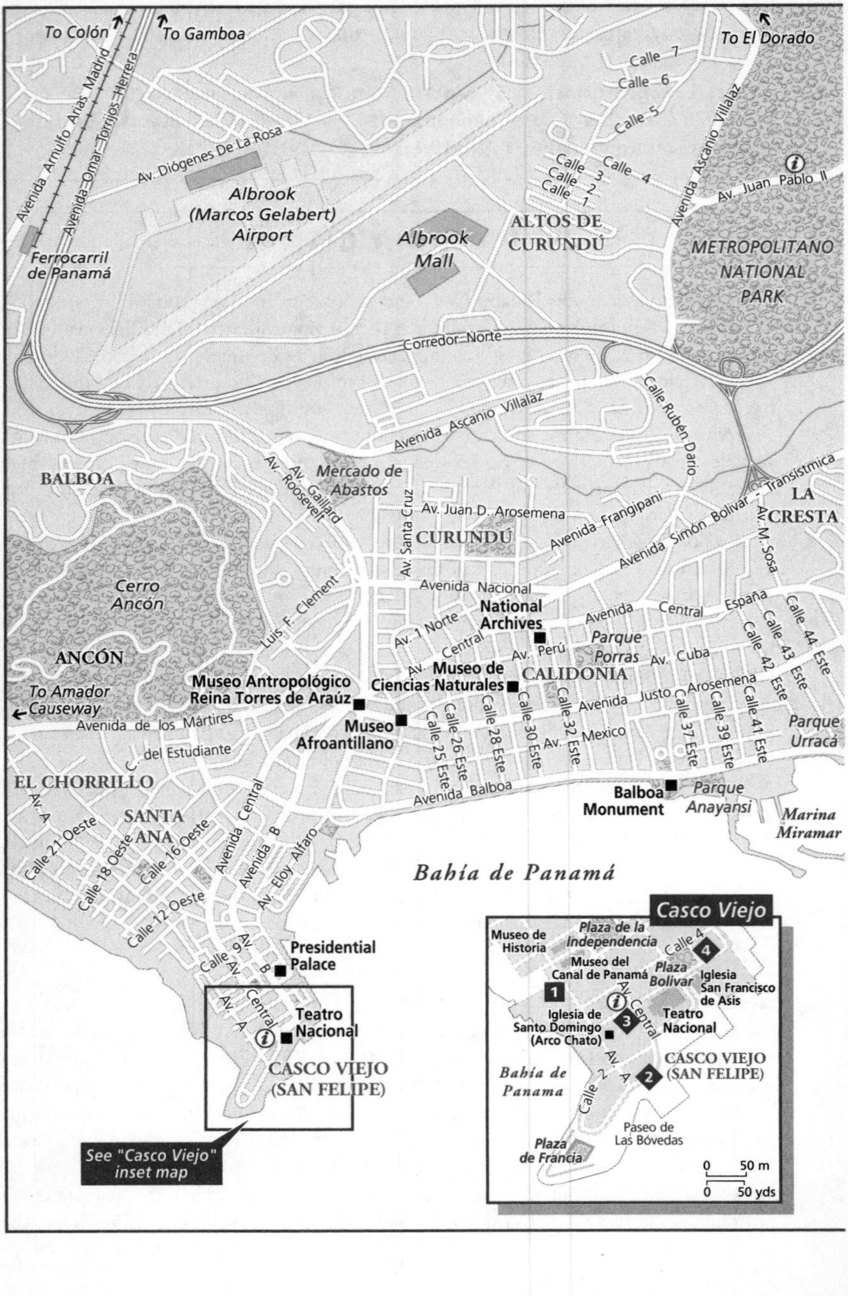

To Colón
To Gamboa
To El Dorado
Avenida Arnulfo Arias Madrid
Avenida Omar Torrijos Herrera
Av. Diógenes De La Rosa
Albrook (Marcos Gelabert) Airport
Ferrocarril de Panamá
Albrook Mall
ALTOS DE CURUNDÚ
Calle 7
Calle 6
Calle 5
Calle 4
Calle 3
Calle 2
Calle 1
Avenida Ascanio Villalaz
Av. Juan Pablo II
METROPOLITANO NATIONAL PARK
Corredor Norte
Calle Rubén Darío
BALBOA
Mercado de Abastos
Av. Gaillard
Av. Roosevelt
Av. Santa Cruz
Av. Juan D. Arosemena
CURUNDÚ
Avenida Frangipani
Avenida Simón Bolívar - Transístmica
LA CRESTA
Av. M. Sosa
Cerro Ancón
ANCÓN
Luis F. Clement
Avenida Nacional
National Archives
Av. 1 Norte
Av. Central
Avenida Central España
Av. Perú
Parque Porras
Av. Cuba
CALIDONIA
Museo de Ciencias Naturales
Museo Antropológico Reina Torres de Araúz
To Amador Causeway
Avenida de los Mártires
Museo Afroantillano
C. del Estudiante
Calle 25 Este
Calle 26 Este
Calle 28 Este
Calle 30 Este
Calle 32 Este
Avenida Justo Arosemena
Av. Mexico
Calle 37 Este
Calle 39 Este
Calle 41 Este
Calle 42 Este
Calle 43 Este
Calle 44 Este
Parque Urracá
EL CHORRILLO
Av. A
Avenida Balboa
Balboa Monument
Parque Anayansi
Marina Miramar
SANTA ANA
Calle 21 Oeste
Calle 18 Oeste
Calle 16 Oeste
Avenida Central
Avenida B
Av. Eloy Alfaro
Calle 12 Oeste
Bahía de Panamá
Calle 9
Av. B
Av. Central
Av. A
Presidential Palace
Teatro Nacional
CASCO VIEJO (SAN FELIPE)
See "Casco Viejo" inset map

Casco Viejo
Museo de Historia
Plaza de la Independencia
Calle 4
Museo del Canal de Panamá
Plaza Bolívar
Iglesia San Francisco de Asis
Av. Central
Iglesia de Santo Domingo (Arco Chato)
Teatro Nacional
Bahía de Panama
Av. A
Calle 2
CASCO VIEJO (SAN FELIPE)
Paseo de Las Bóvedas
Plaza de Francia
0 50 m
0 50 yds

ACCOMMODATIONS ■
The Bristol Panama **9**
Hotel la Casa de Carmen **14**
Hotel Milan **16**
Radisson Decapolis Hotel **11**
The Canal House **1**
The Panama Marriott Hotel **12**
Veneto Hotel & Casino **17**

DINING ◆
Ego **4**
El Trapiche **13**
Eurasia **5**
Fusion **11**
Las Barandas **9**
Madame Chang **8**
Manolo Caracol **3**
Market **7**
Napoli **15**
Palms **6**
S'cena **2**
Ten Bistro **10**

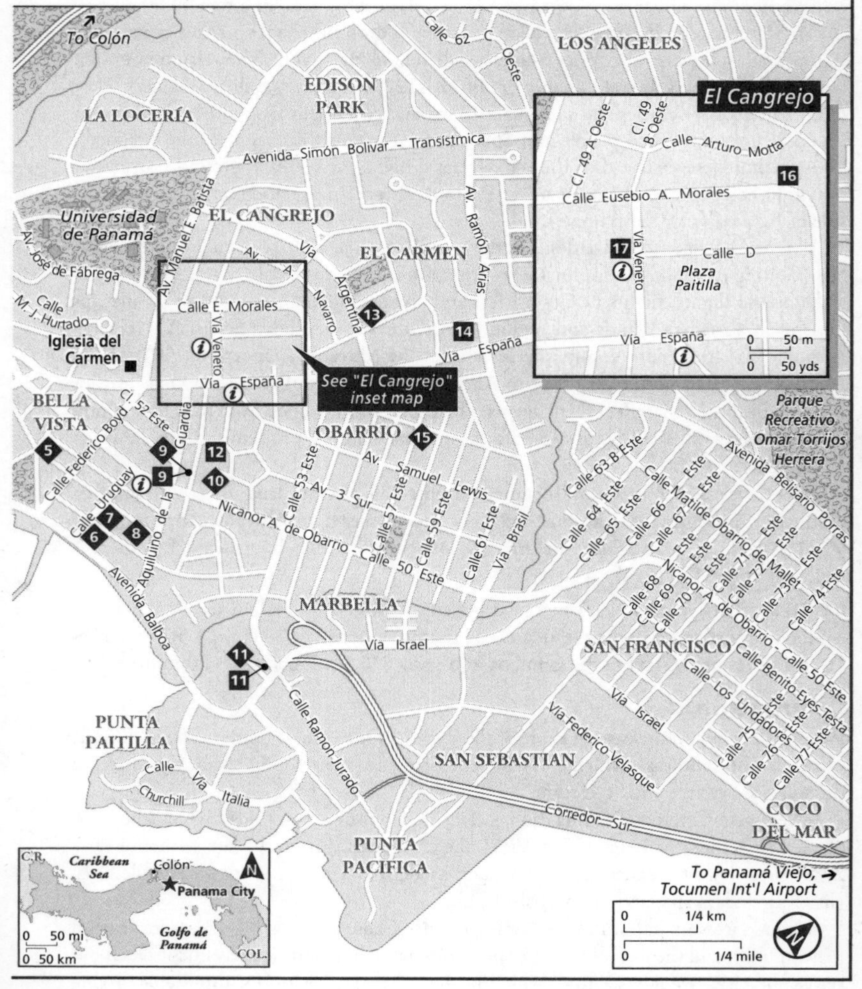

PANAMA 10 PANAMA CITY

 U.S.; www.natureair.com) has one flight to Bocas from San José (with connections from Quepos, Liberia, and Puerto Jiménez) on Tuesday, Thursday, and Saturday, leaving at 8am and returning from Bocas at 10:30am.

There are **ATP visitors' kiosks** inside Tocumen's arrival terminal (one in baggage claim and another through the Customs gate), with information about Panama City and some brochures; it's recommended, though, that travelers research accommodations and make reservations before their arrival because hotels are often booked.

The unit of currency in Panama is the U.S. dollar, so for those coming from the United States, there is no need to exchange money. Pounds and euros can be exchanged at the **Banco Nacional** (**© 238-4161;** Mon–Fri 8am–5pm and Sat 10am–3pm) in the arrival terminal; this bank also has ATMs in the airport terminal.

A licensed taxi to Panama City costs $25 (£13), plus toll fees for a total of about $30 (£15). Many hotels offer free scheduled pickup and drop-off service, or you can arrange transportation for a cheaper price—inquire when booking at your hotel. Another option for taxis is with **Easy Travel Panama** (**© 6617-4122;** www.easytravelpanama.net). They offer high-quality vehicles and bilingual drivers, and cost about the same as regular taxis ($40/£20 for one or two people and $50/£25 for three or four people, tolls included), but you must reserve ahead of time. Easy Travel offers personalized ground transportation anywhere; contact them for prices for long-distance destinations (the beaches outside of Panama City, for example).

All rental-car agencies have desks in the arrival terminal and are open 24 hours a day. See "Getting Around," below, for more information.

Domestic flights, flights to Costa Rica, and charter flights to the 150 or so airstrips located on Panama's islands and remote jungle areas leave from **Marcos A. Gelabert Airport,** which is more commonly referred to as **Albrook Airport** (**© 501-9271**). Albrook is located northwest of Cerro Ancón (Ancón Hill) off Avenida Omar Torrijos Herrera, near the canal. Rental-car agencies here are generally open from 8am to 6:30pm. Each company offers a key drop-box for customers who need to return a vehicle when rental desks aren't open.

Tip: Travelers who arrive at Tocumen Airport and plan to head directly to another destination in Panama via a domestic flight must transfer to **Albrook Airport** (**PAC; © 315-0241**), about a 45-minute drive (or longer during rush hour) from Tocumen. A taxi costs about $30 (£15).

BY BUS If arriving by bus, you'll be dropped off at the Albrook bus terminal near the Albrook airport and shopping center. A taxi to town costs $2 to $3 (£1–£1.50) and takes 10 to 15 minutes. A taxi to the Gamboa area costs $20 (£10) and takes 30 minutes.

Orientation

Panama City lies on the eastern shore of the Panama Canal and is bordered by the Pacific Ocean to the southeast, which can disorient first-time visitors unaccustomed to seeing the sun rise over the Pacific Ocean.

In very general terms, Panama can be divided into **four areas:** Old Panama (the ruins of the first settlement here); Casco Viejo, the city center during the late 19th and early 20th centuries; the former Canal Zone; and modern Panama, with its wide boulevards, glittering skyscrapers, and impoverished slums.

At the southwest end of the city lie the Amador Causeway, Casco Viejo, Cerro Ancón (Ancón Hill), and the former Canal Zone. From here, three principal avenues branch out across the city. Avenida Central, which begins in Casco Viejo as a thriving shopping center hawking cheap, imported goods, changes its name to Avenida Central España as it passes through Calidonia, and then becomes Vía España as it runs through the commercial area and financial district of El Cangrejo. Avenida Balboa extends the length of the coast, then forks into Vía Israel, later called Cincuentenario as it heads out to Old Panama. Corredor Sur, a fast-moving toll expressway, connects the city with Tocumen Airport. Avenida Simón Bolivar (also known as Av. 2da. Norte Transístmica) heads north to Colón; however, a new toll expressway, called the Corredor Norte, provides a faster route to Colón, eventually connecting with the Transístmica around Chilibre.

Getting Around

BY TAXI Taxis are inexpensive, safe, and plentiful—except when it is raining during rush hour and it seems that every worker heading to, or leaving, work is trying to flag one down. Quite often, a taxi will stop for another passenger if he or she is headed in your general direction, but the driver will usually deliver you to your destination first. Taxis charge $1.25 to $2 (65p–£1) for most destinations within Panama City, but confirm the price beforehand as the "zones" that taxi drivers use for price reference are vague. Taxis from the city center to the Amador Causeway will run you about $5 (£2.50). Unscrupulous drivers may try to charge you more, especially to and from the Amador Causeway.

ON FOOT Panama City is not easy to navigate on foot because of its interweaving streets, streets that are not signed, and lack of recognizable landmarks for visitors. Also, many neighborhoods aren't within walking distance of each other. To get around without a fuss, take a cab.

On the other hand, the best (really only) way to see **Casco Viejo** is on foot so that you can savor the neighborhood's colonial architecture, visit a museum, and stop for lunch. Avenida Balboa has a long seafront walkway that starts near Punta Paitilla and ends at the Mercado de Marisco (the fish market). The Calzada de Amador (Amador Causeway) was designed for walking, jogging, and bicycling, with some 6.5km (4 miles) of landscaped pedestrian trails.

BY BUS You'll feel more comfortable getting around Panama City by taxi than by bus. There are no printed bus routes on the city's buses, but the name of the bus's destination should appear on a sign in the front window. Panama City is supposedly overhauling its public transportation system, as the city's famous "Red Devils" are replaced by a modern fleet of coaches, but these plans have been in the works for years without any visible progress. Red Devils are retired U.S. school buses that drivers individualize with electric graffiti art, flashing lights, and other knickknacks, and they are driven until the wheels fall off. Though emblematic of the funky, vibrant culture that makes Panama what it is, Red Devils are often in the news for crashing and other unsafe practices, and "devil" drivers are notorious for their reckless driving. The fee for taking one is just 25¢ (15p), though.

BY CAR You won't need or want a rental car while visiting just Panama City, considering how economical taxis are. Pay attention to every sign on the road because some road signs are small and easy to miss; other times there is no "official" sign for a turnoff, but a couple of commercial signs with the town name, giving you only a vague idea of where you are. Travelers who have a basic command of Spanish and who can ask for directions will have the easiest time. Bring a good map and ask the rental agency exactly how to get to your destination.

If you do decide to rent a car, there are car-rental kiosks for most major car-rental agencies at both the Tocumen and Albrook airports (car-rental agencies at Tocumen are open 24 hr.; Albrook rental agencies are open 8am–6:30pm), and each agency has a few locations in town. If you are renting a car to visit outlying areas such as the canal, Portobelo, or the Panamanian interior, have your rental agency show you, in detail, the quickest and most efficient route to your destination.

VISITOR INFORMATION

The **Autoridad de Turismo Panama**'s (**ATP;** ✆ **526-7000** or 526-7100; www.visitpanama.com) main office is on Calle Samuel Lewis on the first floor of Edificio Central, across from the Camosa. Although it's open to the public, it does not have a proper information center. ATP has two other visitor centers; one is located at Vía España and Ricardo Arias (✆ **269-8011**); in Old Panama on Vía Cincuentenario (✆ **226-4419**), and another is in Casco Viejo at Avenida Central and Calle 3 (✆ **211-3365**).

FAST FACTS **American Express Travel Services** has an office on Calle 50 and Calle 59 (✆ **269-2971,** or 800/528-4800 for 24-hr. service in the U.S.). This office provides traveler's checks and replacement cards, along with other standard services. To report lost or stolen traveler's checks within Panama, call the numbers above, or try ✆ **1/336-393-1111,** American Express's international collect-call service.

Drugstores are plentiful in Panama City. For 24-hour service, visit a branch of **El Rey** supermarket, the most central of which is on Vía España (✆ **223-1243**). Another reliable pharmacy is **Farmacias Arrocha** (✆ **360-4000**), with locations at Vía España in front of El Panama Hotel, Vía Argentina, and Punta Paitilla.

For fire, dial ✆ **103;** for an ambulance, dial **Seguro Social** at ✆ **502-2532,** or **Cruz Roja** at ✆ **228-2187.** Dial ✆ **104** or 316-0080 for the police.

Many international courier and express-mail services have offices in Panama City, including **UPS** (✆ **269-9222**) in Obarrio (near El Cangrejo) at Calle 53 E in the Edificio Torre Swiss Bank; **FedEx** (✆ **800-1122**) on Calle 3 in Costa del Oeste; **Mail Boxes Etc.,** a one-stop service with locations on Avenida Balboa in Paitilla in the Marisol Building, no. 1, next to McDonald's (✆ **264-7038**), on Vía España, next to Niko's Café in the Financial District (✆ **214-4620**), and in the Multiplaza Mall (✆ **302-4162**).

The best hospitals in Panama City are **Centro Médico Paitilla,** at Calle 53 and Avenida Balboa (✆ **265-8800**); **Clínica Hospital San Fernando,** at Avenida Central España (✆ **305-6300**); **Hospital Nacional,** at Avenida Cuba between Calle 38 and Calle 39 (✆ **207-8100** or 207-8102); and **Hospital Punta Pacífica,** at Calle 53 in Bella Vista (✆ **204-8000**). Punta Pacífica is the newest and most advanced hospital in the country and is affiliated with Johns Hopkins University.

The best Internet cafe in town is **ClaroCOM,** at Avenida Eusebio A. Morales and Avenida Vía Veneto (✆ **200-0015;** Mon–Sat 8am–10:30pm and Sun 9am–8:30pm), with **free wireless** service if you have a laptop, no matter how long you need to be connected, as well as plentiful computers. Or try **Esc@pate Internet cafe,** on Vía Argentina close to Avenida España (✆ **263-0616**). There are plenty of Internet cafes all over the city center and el Dorado, all charging about $1 to $1.50 (50p–75p) per hour.

Lavandería Diamond Dry Cleaners Plus (✆ **213-2216;** closed Sun) is at Calle J in El Cangrejo. **Lavandería Flash** (✆ **213-8092**) is at Vía Argentina. **SU-PERC-KLIN** is in Bella Vista next to Supermercado Riba-Smith (✆ **225-7869**), and in El Cangrejo in front of the Einstein statue at Calle F and Calle L-1 (✆ **223-5666**).

A Safety Note for Panama City

As Latin American cities go, Panama City is very safe for foreign travelers, especially those who stay out of unsavory neighborhoods such as Calidonia, Curundú, El Chorrillo, Santa Ana, and Chinatown. As in any major urban area, use common sense when it comes to safekeeping valuables—for example, don't put your wallet in your back pocket. Also consider taking money out of ATMs during the day to avoid stepping out from a brightly lit ATM into darkness.

Postal service is scarce in Panama City; your best bet is to ask your hotel to mail something for you, or try Mail Boxes Etc. (see above). The central post office (Correos y Telégrafos) is open Monday to Friday 8am to 4pm and Saturday 8am to 1pm, and is located on Avenida Central in front of the Mercado de Mariscos (✆ **212-7680**).

WHAT TO SEE & DO

Few cities in the Americas can compete with Panama City when it comes to things to see and do. Some travelers spend their entire visit in and around Panama City, touring sights such as the historical ruins of Panama Viejo, walking the enchanting streets of Casco Viejo, visiting Metropolitan Park, or strolling along the Amador Causeway. Visitors can also head outside the city limits for day excursions such as boating in the canal, birdwatching and trekking in Soberanía National Park (p. 676), and visiting Emberá Indian villages (p. 678).

It is recommended that travelers book a city tour; transportation is included, and the experience is enriched by interpretative background provided by a bilingual guide. Half-day city tours include a morning visit to Old Panama and Casco Viejo; full-day tours head to the Miraflores Locks at the canal in the afternoon. **Panama Tour Bus** ✆ **264-4466;** www.PanamaTourBus.com) offers a bilingual hop-on, hop-off tour that picks you up at your hotel—or the hotel closest to you—with stops at the Panama Canal, Albrook Shopping Mall, the Amador Causeway, and Casco Viejo. Tours cost $30 (£15). There's no need to buy tickets ahead of time; just call ahead to find out what time they'll be picking passengers up at your hotel. **Ancon Expeditions** (✆ **269-9415;** www.anconexpeditions.com), **Gloria Mendez Tours** (✆ **263-6555;** www.viajesgloriamendez.com), **Panama Travel Experts** (✆ **265-5323;** www.panamatravelexperts.com, and **Pesantez Tours** (✆ **263-8771;** www.pesantez-tours.com), also offer full- and half-day tours of Panama City and the surrounding area.

Panama Viejo ★★★

Panama Viejo, or Old Panama, comprises the ruins of the oldest capital in the Americas. The ruin site covers 23 hectares (57 acres) on the city's eastern edge, where visitors will find crumbling buildings sprinkled about and connected by paths with interpretive signs in both Spanish and English. The good view from this part of the city sweeps east to the Casco Viejo peninsula, and beyond Panama Viejo's significance as a culturally unique attraction it is also a pleasant park and recreation area that provides visitors with a chance to get out and stretch their legs. Some people come here for a sunrise jog along Panama Viejo's path, which hugs the seafront.

This is the best-funded archaeological site in all of Panama and, accordingly, you'll find here a superb **Panama Viejo Visitors' Center & Museum** ★★★ (✆ **226-8915;**

Tues–Sun 9am–5pm; $6/£3 adults, $5/£2.50 seniors, and $3/£1.50 students; entrance fee includes admission to both the museum and the Cathedral Tower ruin site). The two-story museum offers a thorough historical account, but is the right size so as not to overwhelm visitors with too much information (exhibits are in English and Spanish). There are handsomely displayed pre-Columbian artifacts dating from 700 to 500 years before the Spanish arrival, a model of the city in its 17th-century heyday, interactive video displays of what archaeologists imagine the buildings' interiors to have looked like, and colonial furnishings, clothing, pottery, and more.

The site's most important relic, the **Torre de la Catedral (Cathedral Tower),** is now complete, with a steel interior staircase that visitors can climb for the first time in over 335 years; at the top are expansive city views. The tower is too fragile to bear the weight of a replica of the old bell that rang out across the city during colonial times, so a speaker, which chimes at 6:30am, 12:30pm, and 6:30pm, has been installed. ***Tip:*** Visit the tower in the afternoon, when the morning tour buses have gone. Otherwise, you might find yourself waiting up to 20 minutes to enter. There are Spanish-speaking guides who offer free tours of the tower. If you skip the museum, the cost to get in the area around the tower is $4 (£2) for adults, $3 (£1.50) for seniors, and $2 (£1) for students; it's open Tuesday to Sunday, 8:30am to 6pm. The cathedral is a good 15-minute walk from the museum.

One of the city's best **handicrafts markets** is at Panama Viejo, and has recently been relocated to the visitor center (no phone; call the visitor center for information; daily 8am–5 or 6pm). ***Note:*** Even though the Cathedral Tower and museum are closed on Monday, you can still visit the ruins and walking paths.

Casco Viejo ★★★

Casco Viejo, the Old Quarter, is also referred to as Casco Antiguo or by its original and formal name, San Felipe. No trip to Panama City would be complete without a visit to this quintessentially charming neighborhood, with its narrow streets; its turn-of-the-19th-century Spanish-, Italian-, and French-influenced architecture; its bougainvillea-filled plazas, and its breezy promenade that juts out into the sea. Visitors often compare Casco Viejo to Havana or Cartagena. The neighborhood's historical importance and antique beauty spurred UNESCO, in 1997, to declare it a World Heritage Site. Because Casco Viejo provides such an ideal place to wander around and lose yourself in the antique splendor of the city streets, you should really take a walking tour of this area. Following are the main points of interest, and you can really begin and end wherever it suits you.

Of particular interest in Casco Viejo are the **Catedral Metropolitana** and the Museo del Canal Interoceánico (see the "Other Museums in Panama City" box below) on the south side of the Plaza de Independencia. Plaza Bolivar is home to the **Palacio de Bolivar,** now the offices of the Ministry of Foreign Relations, as well as the totally restored UNESCO designated **Salón Bolivar** (**© 228-9594;** Tues–Sat 9am–4pm, Sun 1–5pm; $1/50p adults, 25¢/15p children) site of the famous 1826 congress organized by Bolivar to discuss the unification of Colombia, Mexico, and Central America. Also, don't forget to check out the **Iglesia y convento de San Francisco de Asis.** Built between 1905 and 1908, on the grounds of the old Concepción Monastery, the lovely **Teatro Nacional** hosts theater and classical-music and ballet performances. The cost to enter and poke around is $1 (50p) per person. It's open Monday to Friday from 8am to 4pm and sometimes on weekends (but with no set schedule).

The **Plaza de Francia (French Plaza)** is a historically important site and a delightful place to stroll around. When you head down Calle 1a, the road turns into an inviting and lovely walkway called **Paseo Esteban Huertas,** which is partially covered by pretty bougainvillea. You're walking atop *las bóvedas,* or "the vaults," which originally functioned as a Spanish dungeon and later as a jail, storehouse, and offices. Continue along the walkway and down to the French Plaza.

Only ruins remain of **Iglesia de Santo Domingo,** built in 1678, but the victim of several fires including one in 1781, from which time it was never rebuilt. The church kept its fame, however, through the building's unusual supporting arch made of stone, which survived the fire. The arch, called Arco Chato, was unusual in that it was long and not very arching, seemingly defying gravity. Next to the ruin site is the **Museo de Arte Religioso Colonial** (p. 659).

Casa Góngora, a house built in 1760 by a wealthy merchant, was renovated with city funds, and much of its original woodwork, including ceiling beams, has been maintained. The Casa is also now home to the **Casa de la Cultura y del Artista Panameño** (✆ **212-0388**), a cultural center for local artists, with occasional live jazz music, folkloric presentations, fashion shows, and changing art exhibitions.

Your last stop is at the most famous of Casco Viejo's churches, the **Iglesia de San José,** and its baroque golden altar. The story goes that when pirate Henry Morgan raided Old Panama, a priest had the altar painted black to hide it; from a block east on Avenida A, turn left on Calle 7 and walk 1 block to reach it.

Safety note: Generally speaking, the peninsula of Casco Viejo, starting at Calle 11 Este and heading east and away from the Santa Ana neighborhood, is safe. There are two principal entryways into Casco Viejo but both pass through poor ghettos, so always take a **taxi** to get here. Taxis for a trip out of Casco Viejo can usually be found around the Plaza de la Independencia, or if you are dining here, have the restaurant call one for you.

Cerro Ancon ★★

This conspicuous forested hill that rises 198m (650 ft.) above the city is another "reverted" property from the canal days that is now open to the public. The hill is bordered in the north by Heights and Culebra streets, and avenidas Arías and de los Mártires in the south. At the entrance to the office of the environmental organization ANCON, at Calle Quarry Heights, a winding, pedestrian-only road provides for a brisk uphill walk to a **lookout point ★★★**, with 360-degree views of the city center, Casco Viejo, and the canal. The hill is home to tiny Geoffrey's tamarins, *ñeques* (agoutis), and migratory birds. Cerro Ancón is currently the focus of a controversial proposal by developers who want to raze the hilltop for a restaurant and parking lots, and install a cable car to transport visitors. Stiff resistance—even the mayor has jumped into the fray, voicing his disapproval—means this is not likely to happen anytime soon, if ever. **Mi Pueblito** (entrance at Cerro Ancon from Av. de los Martires; ✆ **228-9785;** $2/£1 adults, free for kids 11 and under; Tues–Sun 9am–6pm), is a kitschy mock village depicting different Panamanian cultures; it's really only worth a visit if you won't be traveling outside Panama City. The **Panama Canal Murals** are located inside the Canal Administration building (no phone; free admission), located high on a grassy slope of Cerro de Ancon. Aside from the murals, the building is worth a visit for its glass cupola.

Other Museums in Panama City

Museums across Panama are underfunded and poorly staffed, and the story in the capital isn't any different just because it's a metropolitan city. Recently, there have been some improvements, like the reopening of the **Araúz Anthropology Museum** (✆ **262-8338**) which moved to a far better location in the Albrook neighborhood and updated its previously lackluster exhibitions a few years ago. Still, most museums in Panama City are worth visiting only if you happen to already be in the neighborhood.

The **Museo Afroantillano** ★ (✆ **501-4130;** Calle 24 Oeste and Av. Justo Arosemana; Tues–Sat 8:30am–3:30pm; admission $1/50p) is a small museum housed in the 1910-era Iglesia de la Misión Cristiana. The Museo Afroantillano (Afro-Antillian Museum) pays tribute to the more than 30,000 West Indians who represented 85% of all foreign laborers during the building of the canal. Within the museum are reconstructed examples of their poor living quarters, and there are old photos and other antiques from the early 1900s. The neighborhood here is awfully sketchy, so take a cab directly to and from here.

The **Museo Antropológico Reina Torres de Araúz** (✆ **232-7485;** Los Llanos de Corundu, by the Parque Natural Metropolitano; Mon–Fri 9am–4pm; free admission at press time) is Panama's best anthropology museum, with more than 15,000 pre-Columbian pieces, including artifacts from the Barriles tribe, the earliest residents of Panama until 700 B.C. At press time, the museum was still in the process of opening at its new home at the Museo Tucán, which is a far prettier location on the edge of the Metropolitan Park. By the time you read this, the museum will—fingers crossed—be open and will feature a fresh design and extra funding. Considering that it's the pet project of the president's wife, Vivian, this might not be too far-fetched a wish.

Parque Natural Metropolitano ★★★

The Metropolitan Park is the only protected tropical forest within the city limits of a major urban area in the Americas. In other words, take one 5- to 10-minute taxi ride and you can delve into the earthy environs of thick jungle with a surprising array of fauna, more than 200 species of birds, and 40 species of mammals. The park is overseen by the Smithsonian Tropical Research Institute, which carries out scientific studies here, and by the city, which maintains an administration center with maps, educational exhibits, and a bookstore. If you're planning to visit any regional national parks such as Soberanía, skip this attraction; if your visit to the country is limited to Panama City, this park is a must-see.

Three short trails give visitors a chance to get out and stretch their legs. **Los Momótides** trail is the shortest (30 min.) and therefore the most appropriate trail for young children and visitors in a hurry. It begins at the administration center, but you must cross busy Avenida Juan Pablo II, so be careful. **Mono Tití Road** heads up to Cedro Hill and a lookout point with sweeping views of the city; alert hikers occasionally catch sight of Geoffrey's tamarins, a pint-size primate, along this trail. The most difficult trail, and the longest at 2 hours round-trip, is **Cienequita Trail,** which begins just up the road from the center. It is possible to connect with Mono Tití Road after reaching the lookout point.

Museo de Arte Contemporáneo ★ (✆ **262-8012;** www.macpanama.org; Av. de los Martires at Calle San Blas; Tues–Sun 9am–5pm; admission $1/50p), the city's Contemporary Art Museum, has improved over the years, but it is still erratic when it comes to the quality of temporary exhibitions. Their permanent collection features a selection of mostly watercolor and oil paintings by well-known and up-and-coming Panamanians and other Latin Americans.

Museo de Arte Religioso Colonial ★ (✆ **501-4127;** Av. A at Calle 3a, Casco Viejo; Tues–Sat 8am–4pm, Sun 1–5pm; admission $1/50p) exhibits a small but vivid collection of 220 religious art pieces and is housed in the old Santo Domingo convent, famous for the Arco Chato. The religious pieces are the last vestiges from the height of colonial baroque art in the Americas.

The **Museo del Canal Interoceánico de Panamá ★★★** (✆ **228-6231;** www.sinfo.net/pcmuseum; Av. Central at Plaza Independencia; Tues–Sun 9am–5pm; admission $2/£1) is the best museum in Panama City and an obligatory stop for every traveler. The museum is a study of the Panama isthmus—from pre-Columbian times, to the arrival of the Spanish, to the French and the American canal-building efforts, through the present day. Historical documents here include the 1977 Carter-Torrijos treaty that turned over control of the canal to Panama in 2000, multimedia and interactive exhibits, mock-household exhibits of everyday life during the history of the canal, a register of the U.S. Senate votes approving the canal, and a floor of old coins and stamps, including the famous Nicaragua stamp with an erupting volcano that was sent to senators to sway them from choosing that country to build a canal.

The park is open daily from 6am to 6pm; the visitor center is open Monday to Friday 7am to 5:30pm and Saturday 8am to 1pm. Adult entrance is $2 (£1) per person. English tours are $5 (£2.50) per person with a reservation made at least 24 hours in advance; call ✆ **232-5516** or 232-5552 or visit www.parquemetropolitano.org. There are also trail maps available for a small fee.

Calzada de Amador (Amador Causeway) ★★

The Amador Causeway is a series of three small islands—Naos, Perico, and Flamenco—connected by a road and pedestrian walkway that projects out into the Panama Bay, offering spectacular views of the glittering city skyline and a consistent breeze. The islands, once the haunt of pirates, were connected in the early 1900s with rock and dirt excavated from the Culebra Cut in the Panama Canal to form a breakwater for a protective harbor for ships waiting to enter the canal, and to prevent the buildup of sediment. Later, the United States militarized the promontory and fortified it with an ordinance for protection during the two world wars. The causeway remained off-limits to Panamanians until 1999, when the canal handover opened this prime spot of real estate, much to the delight of walkers, joggers, bike riders, and diners. There is nothing like jogging or walking along the causeway early in the morning with the sun rising over the Pacific and casting its pastel hues on the glittering high-rises of downtown Panama City. The causeway is packed on Sundays.

Large-scale, multimillion-dollar real-estate projects are on the horizon for the causeway, including a grand hotel, a casino, condo development, and new marinas. By any measure, Panamanians are most excited about the opening of the new **Bridge of Life Biodiversity Museum,** designed by renowned architect Frank Gehry (who is married to a Panamanian), which features high-concept exhibitions about the relationship between nature and man. Check the website, **www.biomuseopanama.org**, for more information. The museum wasn't quite ready at press time, but should be opening up to the public soon. For now, the **Punta Culebra Marine Exhibition Center** ★★ (✆ **212-8793;** Isla Naos; Tues–Fri 1–6pm, Sun 10am–6pm; admission $1/50p) is one of the Causeway's most popular attractions, and features a number of interesting exhibitions and displays. It's a good place to visit if you're traveling with kids. Within the center's grounds are a "touching pool" that allows kids to handle and closely examine aquatic life such as sea cucumbers, sea urchins, and starfish; an aquarium with tropical fish and a comparison between coral reefs of the Pacific and Atlantic; and an information center with videos.

OUTDOOR, SPECTATOR SPORT & WELLNESS ACTIVITIES

Soccer never cast its spell over Panama as it has with the rest of Latin America—here baseball is king, yet stadium crowds and big-league games are not common. Games are mostly by national and local teams vying for regional championships. For spectator sports, check out the horse races (below) for a lively show and lots of colorful Panamanian characters. Walking and bicycling are best on the Amador Causeway, especially early in the morning with the sunrise.

BIRD-WATCHING Serious birders will want to visit renowned sites such as Pipeline Road (p. 676). Within the city limits, **Metropolitan Park** (p. 658) is a fine spot for glimpsing some of the more than 200 species found here. Check the Panama Audubon Society's website, **www.panamaaudobon.org**, for upcoming field trips to the park and other destinations around the city.

HORSE RACING The **Hipódromo Presidente Remón** (✆ **217-6060;** www.hipodromo.com) inaugurated more than a half-century ago, is a prestigious venue and a fun place to spend an afternoon. Races are held on Thursdays, Saturdays, Sundays, and holidays. To get here, take a taxi to Vía José Agustín Arango, on the way out to the airport. The Hipódromo can be reached via the Corredor Sur or by following Vía España until it turns into Vía Arango.

SPAS & WORKOUT FACILITIES Nearly every moderate to high-end hotel has a fitness center, and major hotels have full-service spas, which are the best in the city. Especially noteworthy are the spas at the **Veneto, Decapolis Radisson,** and **Marriott.** These hotels allow you to book a session even if you're not lodging there.

SHOPPING

You'll hear a lot of talk about duty-free shopping in Panama City, but it's exaggerated. Really, the only place you can duty-free shop is at the plethora of stores at the Tocumen Airport. Shopping complexes such as the **Flamingo Center** on the Amador Causeway limit duty-free purchases to cruisers landing at their port. Even the duty-free zone in Colón is overrated, as most wholesalers do not sell to independent travelers. The major shopping malls here offer excellent quality and national and international brands, though prices are comparable to those in the United States. A principal shopping avenue is **Vía España,** where both high- and low-end shops vie for business, as well as grocery stores and pharmacies. Designer stores are located around Calle 53 in Marbella and in the nearby World Trade Center's Centro de Comercio. Also try Plaza Paitilla in the Paitilla neighborhood. You'll find electronics shops around Vía Estronga, in the Financial District.

Shopping Malls

Multiplaza Pacific (✆ **302-5380**) offers the most in terms of selection and quality, yet it is the most expensive in town. Colombian-owned **Multicentro** (✆ **208-2500**), conveniently located across from the Radisson on Avenida Balboa, has a number of Latin-diva-style boutiques; there's also a cinema and a casino. **Albrook Mall** (✆ **303-6333**) is an air-conditioned shrine to low-cost outlet shopping, but you'll have to do a lot of digging around to find a gem. Because it is next to the bus terminal, it is busy with families who arrive from the interior of Panama, ready to shop. There is a cinema at Albrook Mall, too.

Markets

The **Mercado de Mariscos** ★★★, on Avenida Balboa and Calle 15 Este, is distribution headquarters for fresh seafood pulled from the Pacific and Caribbean. It's a vibrant market with lots of action as fishmongers shout while they deftly fillet corvina, tuna, octopus, and more.

Molas, the reversed appliqué panels made by Kuna Indian women, rank high on the list of popularity for souvenirs and gifts, either sewn onto a beach bag, as a shirt, or sold individually for you to frame or stitch onto anything you'd like (pillowcases are an ideally sized canvas). Other popular handicrafts, such as *tagua* nuts or vegetable ivory carved into tiny figurines, Ngöbe-Buglé dresses, and Emberá Indian baskets and masks, can be found at the following markets. These markets do not have phones, and all are open daily within the general hours of 8 or 9am to 5 or 6pm (until about 2pm Sun). The **Mercado Nacional de Artesanías** ★★★, in Panama Viejo next to the visitor center, is expansive and sells handicrafts from around the country. In Balboa, on Avenida Arnulfo Arias Madrid and Amador, is a small **YMCA Handicrafts Market** ★, with mostly Kuna and Emberá indigenous arts and crafts, and clothing. A little farther east and up Avenida Arnulfo Arias Madrid is the **Kuna Cooperative** ★★, featuring Kuna handicrafts.

The new **Flamenco Shopping Plaza** is on the Amador Causeway (✆ **314-0908;** hours are variable but generally noon–11pm; www.fuerteamador.com). It caters predominantly to cruisers docking here, but shops are open to the general public (except the duty-free shop). The Plaza is a high-end, one-stop shopping area for souvenirs, jewelry, and upscale handicrafts. Come prepared: Visit their website and print out their discount coupons worth a savings of 10% to 15%, depending on the store.

Art Galleries

Galería Bernheim, at Calle 50 and Calle Alquilino in the Financial District (✆ **223-0012**), has a lengthy roster of paintings and other artwork for sale, as well as antique maps and delicately carved *tagua* nuts. **Imagen Galería de Arte,** located at Calle 50 and Calle 77 (✆ **226-2649**), displays mostly paintings and sculpture by local artists, and offers professional framing. As the name states, **Arts & Antiques** (✆ **264-8121**) sells antiques and art antiques representing Spanish colonial, Art Deco, Victorian, and other epochs. The store is located in the Balboa Plaza on Avenida Balboa at Calle Anastacio Ruiz.

Bookstores

Exedra Books, on the corner of Vía Brasil and Vía España (✆ **264-4252;** www.exedra books.com; Mon–Fri 10am–8pm and Sat 10am–7pm), is the city's top resource for English-language books. The Smithsonian's small but excellent **Corotu Bookstore,** at the Earl S. Tupper Research and Conference Center on Avenida Roosevelt in Ancón (✆ **212-8000;** www.stri.org; Mon–Fri 10am–4:30pm) offers a comprehensive collection of books about Panama's flora, fauna, history, and culture, including large-format photo books, maps, and gifts. **El Hombre de la Mancha** (✆ **263-6218;** www.bookshombredela mancha.com) is a bookstore cafe with a small selection of English-language fiction and the best Panama City map in town. They have locations in the Multiplaza, Multicentro, Albrook Mall, and the Centro Comercial Camino de Crucez Boulevar El Dorado; or try Calle 52 at Avenida Federico Boyd (✆ **263-6218**). The **Gran Morrison** chain (Vía España at Calle 51 Este, ✆ **269-2211;** Punta Paitilla, ✆ **264-5266**), has a limited English-language book section and a variety of U.S. magazines such as *People* and *Time.*

Jewelry

During the centuries before the arrival of the Spanish, indigenous groups produced decorative gold pieces called *huacas,* which they buried with the dead to protect their souls in the afterlife. The word comes from the Incas, meaning something that is revered, such as an ancestor or a god. Spurred by the theft of *huacas* from the national anthropology museum, an American living in Panama during the 1970s set up **Reprosa** (at Av. Samuel Lewis; ✆ **269-0457;** daily 9am–6pm) which makes elaborate and stunning jewelry casts using the "lost wax" process of the ancient indigenous groups. If you're searching for a one-of-a-kind, luxury gift for someone special, come here. Reprosa has several more demure collections that include orchids, treasures from the sea, and so forth.

Reprosa also offers a popular factory tour to demonstrate the casting and assembly process. The factory can be found just off the Costa del Este exit near Panama Vieja, and just after turning left on the first street next to the Felipe Motta shop. English-language tours cost $10 (£5) per person and must be booked at least 1 day in advance; call Monica at ✆ **271-0033.**

Outdoor Gear & Clothing

It's best to buy your outdoor gear and equipment before your trip—there isn't a wide selection of outdoor products in Panama. The chain store **Outdoors** (✆ **302-4828** or 208-2647) represents the brands Columbia and Caterpillar, and their stores carry clothing and footwear, sleeping bags, and accessories for biking, fishing, bird-watching, and other adventure sports. Outdoors has stores in the Multicentro, Multiplaza, and a low-cost outlet store in the Albrook Mall. **Sportline** at Albrook Mall (see above) also sells outdoor gear and equipment.

WHERE TO STAY

The best chain hotels are located in **El Cangrejo** and the **Area Bancaria. Casco Viejo** is home to lovingly renovated antique homes for rent by the night or week. Elsewhere in the city, particularly in the **Marbella/Coastal,** on the slope of leafy **Cerro Ancon,** and near the **Amador Causeway,** there are many excellent, often smaller lodging options. Outside el Cangrejo or the Area Bancaria taxis can cost up to $5 (£2.50) to the city center. For a clean and basic budget option near the Amador Causeway, be sure to check out **Hostal Amador Familiar** (Calle Akee Casa 1519; ✆ **314-1251** or 6747-6229; www.

hostalfamiliaramador.com; $13/£6.50 bed, $35/£18 double no air-conditioning, $40/£20 double with air-conditioning).

El Cangrejo/Area Bancaria (Financial District)

Very Expensive

The Bristol Panama ★★★ This boutique hotel is an excellent choice for business travelers and those seeking quiet, centrally located accommodations. The decor, uncharacteristic of tropical Panama City, is done in conservative, richly textured hues with mahogany furnishings—it's very English in style. Guest rooms have carpeted floors, divine beds featuring deluxe bedding (fluffy down comforters and pillows), and double-paned windows that allow for a good night's sleep. Luxury bathrooms with spacious Italian-marble countertops, potted orchids, and a big bathtub add even more comfort to the guest rooms. The on-site restaurant **Las Barandas** is one of the best in town.

Aquilino de la Guardia at Obarrio. ✆ **265-7844.** www.thebristol.com. 56 units. $335 (£168) double; $450 (£225) junior suite. AE, DC, MC, V. **Amenities:** Restaurant; bar; piano bar; complimentary butler; concierge; fitness center; laundry service; room service. *In room:* A/C, TV, DVD and VHS player, CD player, hair dryer, minibar, Wi-Fi (at an additional cost).

The Panama Marriott Hotel ★★★ The Panama Marriott is the overall best big-scale hotel in the city. Their high-tech fitness center is enormous, and the spa is extensive and reasonably priced. There are amenities galore and the staff provides courteous, helpful service. The guest rooms are spacious and attractive; standard doubles have a couch and large bathroom. Executive rooms are higher up and nearly identical to standard rooms, but come with upgraded amenities such as a private lounge on the 19th floor with a dynamite view. The Marriott also has a casino, opened in 2005, for a little gaming action and disco nightlife, but one big word of caution: Rooms that end in even numbers suffer from the pounding of DJ music and partying on weekends.

Calle 52 at Ricardo Arias. ✆ **210-9100,** or 800/228-9290 toll-free in the U.S. and Canada. www.marriott.com/PTYPA. 295 units. $170 (£85) double; $205 (£103) executive. AE, DC, MC, V. **Amenities:** Restaurant; deli; sports bar; babysitting; casino; concierge; laundry and dry-cleaning service; outdoor pool; room service; spa and 24-hr. fitness center w/whirlpool, steam room, and sauna. *In room:* A/C, TV, hair dryer, minibar.

Expensive

Radisson Decapolis Hotel ★★★ Think glass and steel, a sleek martini-and-sushi bar, stark decoration, and hallways filled with a rainbow of ambient light. Bright, spacious guest rooms (with walk-in closets and big bathrooms) are mostly white with wood-grain paneling and touches of whimsical lime, orange, and leopard print. Large, blown-up photos hanging on the walls portray Panama's various ethnic groups; some of these photos, of seminude Emberá Indian women, have bothered certain buttoned-up types—but this is not a hotel that appeals to that sort of traveler, anyway. On weekends, there is a throbbing party atmosphere in the lobby-level lounge and fourth-floor pool, which draws the young glitterati of Panama City.

Av. Balboa at the Multicentro Mall. ✆ **215-5000,** or 888/201-1718 in the U.S. www.radisson.com. 240 units. $286 (£143) double standard; $308 (£154) executive double; $341 (£171) executive suite. AE, MC, V. **Amenities:** Restaurant; martini/sushi bar and pub-style bar; babysitting; concierge; fitness center; coin-operated laundry; room service; full-service spa. *In room:* A/C, TV, CD player, hair dryer, Internet, minibar, safe.

Veneto Hotel & Casino ★★ The Veneto likens itself to a Las Vegas–style hotel/casino, and from the garish exterior it's easy to see why—but step inside the wide, low-slung lobby and enter a hotel with a lot of style. The rooms here are all business, with conservative furniture and cool tones of blue; the beds are ultra-comfortable with crisp linens, duvets, and orthopedic mattresses, and there are luxurious marble-inlaid bathrooms. The Veneto bills itself as a five-star hotel, but everywhere there are slight defects—some hardly noticeable, others hard to miss. The bathroom has poor lighting, and there's no cable TV. On the other hand, the pool here hints at resort glamour, and their spa is one of the most complete in Panama, plus the service is courteous and accommodating. Some doubles are an odd rectangular shape and feel a little claustrophobic; they vary in size so you might want to ask to see more than one.

Av. Eusebio A. Morales at Vía Veneto. ✆ **340-8888,** or 877/531-2034 in the U.S. www.vwgrand.com. 301 units. $100 (£50) double; $170 (£85) junior suite. AE, DC, MC, V. **Amenities:** 3 restaurants; pool bar and 24-hr. sports bar; babysitting; concierge; laundry service; outdoor pool; room service; state-of-the-art spa and fitness center w/whirlpool, steam, and sauna. *In room:* A/C, TV, Internet, minibar.

Inexpensive

Hostal La Casa de Carmen ★ Finds Tucked away on a residential street 1 block from Vía España, this eight-room guesthouse is a delightful find for budget travelers seeking a homey atmosphere and personalized attention. The Casa de Carmen is in a converted home and therefore rooms vary in size (and price); one room has bunk beds for backpack travelers, and another is an apartment with kitchen facilities for longer-term renters. Other rooms are doubles with private or shared bathrooms. A perk here is the tranquil, plant-filled backyard patio, with lounge chairs, hammocks, and a small dining area for the free continental breakfast. Casa de Carmen is infused with color and art, and even the rooms are themed "Lilac," "Brown," "Green," and so on, but they are no-frills rooms—adequately comfortable but not deluxe.

Calle 1a between Vía Porras and Vía Brasil, El Carmen. ✆ **263-4366.** www.lacasadecarmen.net. Doubles average $30 (£15). No credit cards. **Amenities:** Self-service kitchen; free Internet; self-service laundry; TV room. *In room:* A/C, no phone.

Hotel Milan ★ Value This is a no-frills hotel, but it's relatively new and everything is fresh and works properly. For the price, you'd have a hard time finding a better deal when looking for a downtown hotel close to restaurants and shops. Rooms are plain and only suites come with a minifridge, but the frilly bedspreads and aqua-blue guest-room walls add a touch of character. The "suite" is a large double with a whirlpool tub (situated incongruously in a room behind a small bar), and not worth the extra cash. The lighting in guest rooms is awfully dim, so order a proper nightstand lamp from the front desk. Economic doubles are slightly smaller versions of doubles. A 55-room expansion is planned for the end of 2009, a result of the hotel's popularity. There is usually a 25%-to-50% discount going on, so be sure to ask. Service is a bit slow, but the hotel is safe, clean, and a good lodging option if you're just looking for a place to sleep and ambience and service aren't high on your list of priorities.

Av. Eusebio A. Morales 31. ✆ **263-6130.** hotelmilan@cwpanama.net. 53 units. $60–$70 (£30–£35) economy double; $90 (£45) suite. AE, MC, V. **Amenities:** Restaurant/bar; 24-hr. Internet connection in lobby; laundry service; room service. *In room:* A/C, TV, fridge (in suite), Internet service in all new rooms (late 2009).

Cerro Ancon/Balboa

Expensive

Country Inn & Suites—Panama Canal ★ Kids Located near the Amador Causeway and fronting the ocean, this hotel is worth considering if you have kids, seek quiet accommodations, and/or want plenty of space to walk, jog, or ride a bike. Room service is provided by an adjoining T.G.I. Friday's, so if you're looking for a "Panamanian" experience, or if you want to feel the pulse of the city, this is not your place. The hotel has a view that sweeps from the Bridge of the Americas to the Causeway, overlooking bobbing sailboats and ships awaiting the canal crossing. The decor is country-style and guest rooms look like any cookie-cutter hotel room, but with tile flooring. They all have terraces and kitchenettes, though, and there is an irresistible outdoor pool and a 3.2km (2-mile) walkway along the coast. Insist on an oceanview room—it only costs $15 (£8) more, and the sparkling nighttime view of the bridge is the unique perk of this hotel.

Av. Amador at Av. Pelícano, Balboa. ✆ **211-4501,** or 800/456-4000 in the U.S. www.panamacanalcountry.com/amador. 98 units. $130 (£65) deluxe standard; $160 (£80) junior suite; $195 (£98) master suite. AE, MC, V. **Amenities:** Restaurant; bar; bike rental; children's play area; gym; laundry service; outdoor pool; tennis courts; spa. *In room:* A/C, TV, fridge, free Wi-Fi.

Moderate

La Estancia ★★ Value Located on the forested slope of Cerro Ancón in a renovated 1960s Canal Zone home, La Estancia is a quiet refuge from the hustle and bustle of Panama City. You're likely to see plenty of birds, sloths, and even monkeys from one of the hotel's many balconies as you read the morning paper. The B&B has spotless, bright accommodations and personalized service that includes an on-site, reputable travel agency. Doubles are either en suite, or have a bathroom just outside the door. (Choose the latter—the bathroom is for your use only, and these rooms have terraces.) The two suites are enormous, and have sleek kitchens and long outdoor terraces. The intimacy of La Estancia encourages socializing among guests—those seeking absolute privacy will be happiest in a suite or a second-floor room, which has its own common area.

Quarry Heights, Cerro Ancón. ✆ **314-1417.** www.bedandbreakfastpanama.com. 10 units. $45 (£23) double; $75 (£38) suite. MC, V. **Amenities:** Snack bar; Internet access (Wi-Fi); self-service laundry. *In room:* Hair dryer (upon request).

Casco Viejo

Casco Viejo offers travelers lovingly restored apartments that can be rented nightly or weekly by **Arco Properties,** Calle 2A Oeste, Galería San Felipe (✆ **211-2548;** www.arcoproperties.com). Rental properties are on a space-available basis (most owners live outside Panama City and visit for short periods during the year), and they feature daily maid service but limited parking. The cost for a one- to two-bedroom apartment ranges, per night, from $100 to $200 (£50–£100) May to November, and $150 to $250 (£75–£125) December to April. Check out the Arco Properties website for photos (some rentals are fancier than others), or e-mail for availability at Clara@arcoproperties.com. Remember, Casco Viejo can be a bit sketchy at night, so be sure to take a taxi to and from your hotel.

Another option, **Los Cuatro Tulipanes ★★★** (✆ **211-0877;** www.loscuatrotulipanes.com) offers four apartments housed in fully restored mansions and buildings scattered throughout Casco Viejo, and is a top-notch option in the old quarter for those seeking a memorable lodging experience.

For the most unforgettable lodging experience in this part of town, consider the **Canal House ★★** (✆ **228-1907;** www.canalhousepanama.com). Each room here is different from the next, but all are elegant, with tactful, tropical decor; orthopedic beds; and expensive, stylish furniture. The best room is the expansive downstairs Mira Flores Suite, which feels more like an apartment than a hotel room, complete with separate sleeping, living, and work areas. Daniel Craig stayed in this room during the filming of *Casino*

Royale. The two upstairs bedrooms, the Gatun and San Miguel rooms, are comfortable, tactfully decorated, and attractive, but a bit dim. Perhaps the best thing about the Canal House is the service—whether you want complete privacy or a more hands-on experience, the staff will accommodate your needs. Rooms run between $135 and $300 (£68–£150).

WHERE TO DINE

Like any port city worth its salt, Panama City has a gastronomic scene influenced by a melting pot of immigrants from around the world, and by its regional neighbors Colombia, Mexico, and Peru. Foodies will be overjoyed by what's on offer in this metropolitan city: Chinese food ranked by gourmets as the some of the best on this side of the Pacific, fine European cuisine, Middle Eastern eateries, Argentine steakhouses, English-style pubs, and, of course, Panamanian restaurants influenced by Afro-Caribbeans, indigenous groups, and Spanish descendants.

The Hotel Deville's trendy **Ten Bistro** (Calle 50 at Beatriz M. de Cabal; ✆ **206-3100**) serves contemporary, French-influenced food where each main course costs—you guessed it—$10 (£5). The Decapolis Radisson's **Fusion** restaurant (Av. Balboa at the Multicentro Mall; ✆ **215-5000**) and its hip sushi lounge is the trendiest see-and-be-seen venue in town for dining. For live dinner shows, head to **Las Tinajas ★★★** (✆ **269-3840;** Calle 51) or **Al Tambor de la Alegría ★★** (✆ **314-3380;** Brisas de Amador), both of which serve up tasty Panamanian fare and feature live folkloric dancing. Though very touristy, the shows are entertaining.

For cheap Panamanian food, you can't beat the 24-hour chain **Niko's Café,** which, in addition to basic sandwiches, serves 100 snacks and items, such as a tamale or fried egg, for less than 90¢ (45p) each. Niko's can be found at Vía España and Calle Gerardo Ortega (Calle 51B Este, near the Continental Hotel), at the Albrook Bus Terminal, or on Calle 50 (Nicanor Obarrio). The **Mercado de Mariscos** restaurant, above the seafood market (p. 661) in Calidonia, serves delicious seafood fare and is a popular lunchtime spot. There are also many hole in the walls and cafeterias that serve what's called ***comida corriente,*** a cheap daily special that might include a beverage. American fast-food chains, such as Dunkin' Donuts, Bennigan's, McDonald's, T.G.I. Friday's, and Subway, are everywhere.

GROCERY & SPECIALITY STORES The supermarket chain **El Rey** is Panama's largest, and most branches are open 24 hours a day. The most convenient location is on Vía España, near El Panama Hotel; there is another in the Albrook area, on Avenida Omar Torrijos on the way to Gamboa. Another option is El Rey or Super 99. The premier wine store in town is **Felipe Motta,** in Marbella on Calle 53 (✆ **302-5555**), which is perhaps the largest such store in Central America, and has reasonable prices. For organic groceries and health products, try **Orgánica** in Marbella, at the Plaza Paitilla mall on Ramón H. Jurado (✆ **215-2400;** Mon–Fri 10am–5pm) or **Super Gourmet** (✆ **212-3487;** info@supergourmetcasco.com) behind the Canal Museum in the Casco Viejo neighborhood (Av. A and 6th St.) which offers many organic and healthy choices as a well as a deli serving tasty sandwiches and lunch options.

Bella Vista/Area Bancaria/El Cangrejo

Expensive

Eurasia ★★★ FUSION One of Panama City's tonier restaurants, Eurasia is the only restaurant in Central America to receive a five-diamond rating from the American Academy of Hospitality. The ambience is elegant, with papaya-colored walls, lavish art, heavy

Spanish ironwork, and checkered marble floors, and there is a slightly more casual dining area near the bar. Waiters in starched white shirts and shiny cummerbunds provide some of the best service in all of Panama, and you'll feel more like you're dining in a beautifully decorated Spanish-style mansion than an urban restaurant. Eurasia revamps its menu every 12 to 18 months, but you can expect to find classics such as prawns in tamarind and coconut sauce or grilled chateaubriand Indochine with petite potatoes and fine herbs.

Calle 48, Bella Vista. ✆ **264-7859.** eurasia_restaurant@hotmail.com. Reservations recommended for dinner. Main courses $7–$29 (£3.50–£15). AE, MC, V. Mon–Fri noon–3pm and 7–10:30pm; Sat 7–11pm.

Palms ★★★ Finds FUSION Palms is an avant-garde and tropical-chic homage to great style and innovative cuisine. The menu is divided into "collections," as in the appetizer "collection" and the dessert "collection," displayed on a kitschy menu. I love their clam chowder with smoked pork, the tuna tartar, pumpkin ravioli with sage butter, and sautéed prawns with a garlic-and-corn risotto. Grilled steaks and fresh fish are also offered. Their simple crème brûleé and chocolate pecan tart with coffee sauce satisfies your sweet tooth without being overwhelming. The atmosphere is relaxed, but it's a good idea to dress smartly nonetheless.

Calle 48 and Calle Uruguay. ✆ **265-7256.** palmsrestaurant@cableonda.net. Reservations accepted. Main courses $12–$20 (£6–£10). AE, MC, V. Mon–Fri noon–3pm and 6:30–11pm; Sat 6:30–11pm.

Moderate

Madame Chang ★★★ CHINESE Some of the best Chinese food found outside China is here in Panama, and Madame Chang is where you come to savor it. Few restaurants serve a more delectable Peking duck, but other tasty menu items include jumbo shrimp *a la sal,* gingery San Blas crab, prawn rolls, and clams in black-bean sauce—really, everything on the menu is worth recommending, so you'll have to go with whatever seems appealing. The elegant ambience is more smart-casual than button-up conservative, and the cuisine blends traditional recipes from all Chinese provinces, but with a contemporary touch. Madame Chang also shakes up killer martinis.

Av. 5A and Calle Uruguay. ✆ **269-1313.** Reservations recommended. Main courses $8–$22 (£4–£11). AE, MC, V. Daily noon–3pm and 6–11pm.

Market ★★★ STEAK Market has made a place for itself as *the* place to dine in the city, filling up for breakfast, lunch, and dinner almost every day. Though a relative newcomer to the Panama City dining scene, Market already has a respectable following, including Panama's vice president, who has a permanent table booked for Sunday brunch. Essentially, this is an upmarket burger joint with an ingredients-based menu. Try the tasty pork chops, grown locally by Chiriquí highlands farmers, or the popular "sliders," miniature, delicious hamburgers. The restaurant is divided into two distinct areas: the main room is reminiscent of an upscale market deli (hence the name) boasting a sleek bar, contemporary decor, and a cool cement floor. The second floor, known as the zebra room, is airy and fresh, and perfect for those looking for a bit more privacy.

Corner of Calle Urugay and Calle 47. ✆ **264-9401.** www.marketpanama.com. Reservations recommended. Main courses $5.75–$45 (£2.90–£23). AE, DC, MC, V. Mon–Fri 7:30am–midnight; Sat–Sun 11:30am–midnight.

Inexpensive

Napoli Kids ITALIAN This causal, Italian eatery in the Obarrio neighborhood is over 20 years old. It's always bustling and is a longtime favorite with Panamanian families. The place lacks ambience and feels a bit like a cafeteria, but the smartly dressed staff is polite and helpful, and parents won't have to worry that their children are disturbing other diners, as it can get pretty loud here. Dishes are tasty and hearty, particularly the spaghetti *al pescatore* and the many pizza selections. The tiramisu is also good, and there's a decent selection of Italian and international wines.

Calle 57 Obarrio. ✆ **263-8800.** napoli@liberty-tech.net. Main courses $5–$11 (£2.50–£5.50). AE, MC, V. Tues–Sun 11am–11pm.

El Trapiche ★★ PANAMANIAN Ask anyone in Panama City where to savor great Panamanian food, and chances are the first place they'll recommend is El Trapiche. There's nothing palatial about it, but you can cool off in the air-conditioned dining room or people-watch from the outdoor sidewalk cafe. Newcomers to Panama should not miss the house specialty, the "Panamanian Fiesta" combination plate, which offers a taste of eight different local dishes. This is also where you'll want to try the hefty Panamanian breakfast—order tasajo entomatado (beef jerky) with eggs and fried-bread hojaldras. Main courses, such as broiled sea bass or smoked pork chops with rice, beans, and fried plantains, are hearty and satisfy big appetites. Their fresh fruit juice blends are refreshing on a hot day.

Vía Argentina at Av. 2a B Norte. ✆ **269-4353.** Main courses $3–$11 (£1.50–£5.50). AE, MC, V. Sun–Thurs 7am–11pm; Fri–Sat 7am–midnight.

Casco Viejo

Expensive

Manolo Caracol ★★ INTERNATIONAL This artistic eatery may not appeal to every diner, but I say give it a try. Manolo, the Spanish chef, professes "cooking with love," and his adventurous and creative daily menu embraces fresh, in-season products he finds every morning in the local market. (He's the only chef in town who personally trolls the fish market seeking the best and most exotic seafood.) There's no ordering here: Customers pay $15 (£7.50) for lunch and $20 (£10) for dinner (drinks excluded), and sit back and wait for a vibrantly composed parade of up to 12 courses to be slowly ushered to their table. A day's menu might include sole carpaccio, green mango seviche, pork loin with pineapple, and gingery prawns. Meals range from delicious to mediocre, depending on the menu and who's cooking, and service can be regular to shabby, accounting for the mixed reviews among customers.

Calle 3 at Av. Central Sur (in front of the National Theater). ✆ **228-4640** or 228-9479. www.manolocaracol.net. Reservations recommended for dinner. Fixed-price lunch $15 (£7.50), per person, drinks additional. AE, MC, V. Mon–Sat noon–3pm and 7–10:30pm.

S'cena ★★★ INTERNATIONAL This sexy, sophisticated jazz club/upscale restaurant is the perfect spot for an all-in-one night out. The jazz club, Platea, is on the first floor, the restaurant on the second. The bar in Platea is a good place to start or end a meal, and they serve appetizers for less-hungry patrons. Upstairs, S'cena is casually elegant and exudes a New York vibe via its white table linens and exposed brick walls. The cuisine is very good and Mediterranean influenced, crafted by a talented young chef on loan from Spain. The meal begins with a complimentary *amuse-bouche,* a tiny appetizer to pique the taste buds. Follow it with shellfish sautéed in Pernod or octopus caramelized in white wine. Main courses include fish and meat dishes, and a few pasta highlights such as "Grandmother's Catalan Cannellonis."

In front of old Club Union. ✆ **228-4011.** Reservations recommended. Main courses $9–$18 (£4.50–£9). AE, MC, V. Tues–Sun noon–4pm and 7:30–11pm. Bar open until 1am on weekends.

Moderate

Ego ★ TAPAS Ego is a cosmopolitan bar/cafe, on a quiet corner of Plaza Bolívar, specializing in tapas. Make a meal out of hot chili seviche; a salad of arugula, fig, and Camembert cheese; and cilantro beef skewers. Nicely mixed cocktails, a long swooshing bar, and outdoor seating are a few of Ergo's perks. (There's air-conditioned seating indoors.) Large, cold pitchers of sangria are also a treat.

Calle Antonio J. de Sucre, on the corner of Plaza Bolívar. ✆ **262-2045.** Tapas $4–$8.50 (£2–£4.25). AE, DC, MC, V. Mon–Sat 5–11:30pm.

Amador Causeway

Expensive

Bucanero ★ SEAFOOD Of all the restaurants in the Flamenco shopping area, Bucanero, with its kitschy maritime decor, serves the best food. The restaurant is seriously overpriced, but the portions are hearty and the cuisine is a step above that of its neighbors. There are meats on the menu (including *parrilladas,* or barbecue meat platters), but the specialty is seafood. Start with a tangy seviche, and then have the stuffed sea bass, a rich Parmesan-cheese crab gratin, or jumbo shrimp in a vodka sauce. There are shared platters for groups. Dining is on a breezy veranda overlooking a parking lot and the Flamenco Shopping Plaza. Live jazz is featured on Wednesday, and salsa music on Thursday and Friday.

Flamenco Shopping area (end of the Amador Causeway). ✆ **314-1774.** Reservations accepted. Main courses $14–$26 (£7–£13). AE, MC, V. Daily 11:30am–midnight.

Moderate

Mi Ranchito ★ PANAMANIAN This is certainly not the best Panamanian food in the city (El Trapiche and Tinajas fill that bill), but nevertheless the great view of the Panama City skyline and the almost constant cool breeze that blows through accounts for its crazy popularity among tourists and Panamanians alike. The restaurant is open-air and under a massive thatched-roof *bohio* on Isla Naos, near the Smithsonian Museum. You'll find typical Panamanian dishes here such as grilled meat, prawns, sea bass, and snapper served in a garlic or tomato-and-onion sauce and paired with coconut rice and fried plantains. Stick with the fresh fish and shellfish dishes, and an ice-cold beer. After lunch, you can rent a bike next door and go burn off all those calories.

Isla Naos. ✆ **228-4909.** Reservations not accepted. Main courses $7–$10 (£3.50–£5). MC, V. Mon–Sat 9:30am–12:30am; Sun 9:30am–11pm.

PANAMA CITY AFTER DARK

Nightspots are concentrated in four neighborhoods: Bella Vista (also called Calle Uruguay), the Amador Causeway, Marbella (Calle 53 Este), and Casco Viejo, but underground dance clubs pop up across town like mushrooms, and can be best found by asking your concierge or checking out the weekend supplement in Thursday's ***La Prensa*** newspaper. *La Prensa* also has a daily section called Vivir + which lists nightly events, but in Spanish only. Also check out the calendar at **www.thepanamanews.com**.

The Performing Arts

Theater, Ballet & Classical Music

Theater tickets can be purchased by calling the theater directly, or you can buy tickets at **Blockbuster** locations and at the bookstore **El Hombre de la Mancha** or **Exedra Books** (see "Bookstores" on p. 662). All theater productions are in Spanish, with the exception of the **Ancón Theater Guild** (**✆ 212-0060;** www.tga-panama.com; admission by roughly $10/£5 donation). The well-respected guild has been around for more than 50 years.

Classical music productions, plays, and ballet take place at Panama City's turn-of-the-20th-century **National Theater,** on Avenida B in Casco Viejo, but shows are infrequent. The best Spanish-language theater productions can be found at **Teatro la Quadra,** on Calle D in El Cangrejo (**✆ 214-3695;** www.teatroquadra.com; tickets average $10/£5). **Teatro ABA** at Avenida Simon Bolívar (Transístmica), near Avenida de los Periodistas in front of the Riba Smith supermarket (**✆ 260-6316;** tickets cost an average of $5/£2.50), produces half its own shows and rents out its 200-person theater to independent groups; productions are mostly comedies, dramas, and well-established plays. Check www.prensa.com for theater listings here. **Teatro en Círculo,** on Avenida 6C Norte at Vía Brasil (**✆ 261-5375**), is an esteemed playhouse with original Panamanian productions and classic international productions. The historic **Teatro Anita Villalaz** (**✆ 211-4020;** tickets average $10/£5), on Plaza Francia in Casco Viejo, is administered by the National Cultural Institute (INAC); the intimate theater is home to folkloric productions, concerts, and plays, some of which are produced by the University of Panama students.

The Club & Music Scene

The nightclubs listed below open at 10pm but don't really get going until midnight or later; during the first hours of operation, however, nightclubs typically offer drink specials. Ladies' night specials are a bargain for women, giving them free drinks and entry. Otherwise, expect to pay between $7 and $10 (£3.50–£5) for a cover charge, more if there is live music. Nightclub partyers tend to dress smart for the occasion, so don your slinkiest or sharpest outfit or risk being refused entry (or just feeling out of place). For folkloric presentations in a less-trendy environment, try **Las Tinajas★★★** or **Al Tambor a la Alegría.** Large stadium bands play at the **Figali Convention Center,** on the Amador Causeway (**✆ 314-1414**), or at the **Atlapa Convention Center,** on the east side of town (**✆ 226-7000**). For schedules, call or check *La Prensa*'s weekend supplement.

Bar Platea★ (**✆ 228-4011**) is a sophisticated bar/club located on the ground floor of a colonial town house in Casco Viejo. The club shares the building with its partner S'cena restaurant. Platea is cozy and classy, and appeals to an older crowd more so than the city's other clubs. **Liquid,** Calle 50 at Calle Jose de la Cruz, in front of the World Trade Center, Marbella (**✆ 265-3210**), is cool, chic, and laid-back, catering to a well-heeled crowd, but without the velvet-rope attitude of big-city clubs. Liquid is the place to go for dancing, featuring one of the largest dance floors in the city. The music here ranges from thumping beats to rock. **Moods** (**✆ 263-4923;** Calle 48 and Calle Uruguay, Bella Vista) caters to an older crowd (late 20s to 40s), who sweat to primarily reggae and Latin music—on Saturdays, the reggae is often live. If you arrive late, expect to wait and be given the once-over by bouncers. **Next★★**, Avenida Balboa, Marbella (**✆ 265-8746**), is the biggest dance club in Panama—some say in all of Central America—and it's everything you'd expect in a full-scale, throbbing *discoteca:* spacious dance floor, electronic house music, and a full bar and lounge. Thursday is "crossover" night with more musical variety. The *discoteca* offers drink specials until midnight. **Oz Bar and Lounge,** Calle 53 Este, Marbella (**✆ 265-2805**), draws Panama City's elite 20-somethings for its chic decor, live DJ music (mostly house and chill-out), and popular Tuesday karaoke nights. Friday from 9 to 11pm is ladies' night, with free shots, and Saturday "Cocktail" Night means women get free sangria until midnight.

Bars

Office workers spill into bars after work for their 5-to-7pm happy hours; the best deals, however, are at bars that cater to late-night revelers: To reel people in before the late crowd, these bars offer happy hours from 10pm to midnight, and even 100% free drinks (usually for women).

The Amador Causeway is an up-and-coming nightlife spot, with new bars and restaurants opening monthly. As a nightspot, the area tends to draw groups of friends, and an upscale, older crowd. The **Wine Bar** (see below) cut the ribbon on their new locale in 2006, with the same offerings as their El Cangrejo location, but with a better view (located at the Brisas del Amador area). At the end of the Causeway, within the Flamenco Shopping Plaza, are a handful of bars, dance spots, and live-music venues such as **Traffic Island,** with Latin music and cocktails, and a windswept veranda with city views; also try **Bar Baviera,** the **Ancla Sport Bar,** or **Karnak.** These nightspots are all next to each other in an American-style minimall—you could head here and stroll around until you find something to your liking. Closer to the city and the Figali Convention Center is **Las Pencas,** with live music on weekends and folkloric presentations every Wednesday at 8pm. **Bennigan's Irish Grill** at the end of the Amador Causeway is also a well-known nighttime hot spot with Panamanians and foreigners alike.

Decapolis Radisson Sushi Bar & Martini Lounge ★★, Avenida Balboa at the Multicentro Mall, on the lobby level of the Decapolis Hotel (✆ **215-5000**), is *the* place to see and be seen on Friday and Saturday nights. **El Pavo Real,** Calle 51 and Calle 50, around the corner from the Marriott (✆ **262-2448**), is a traditional British pub with pints of lager and Guinness, pub grub, dartboards and pool, and lots of dark wood. It's a local hangout for the English-speaking expat crowd in Panama, so expect to run into a lot of foreigners here. The **Istmo Brew Pub,** Avenida Eusebio A. Morales and Via Veneto (✆ **265-5077**), was Panama City's first brewpub and it has a wide-ranging following—the crowd here varies from night to night (foreign residents, Panamanians, tourists). Opened in 2005, the pleasant, wood-hewn pub has outdoor seating on picnic tables and a limited menu of simple meat dishes and sandwiches. **Wine Bar,** Avenida Eusebio A. Morales, next to the Las Vegas Suites (✆ **225-0914**), caters to wine lovers, by serving more than 200 varieties from Europe, Chile, and California. The mood picks up during their live music sets, which are usually one-man acts.

The Gay & Lesbian Scene

Panama is a mostly Catholic country and although the gay and lesbian scene here is not underground, it is discreet. There are a couple of clubs in the city that operate without much fanfare, and attacks, raids, harassment, and so on are thankfully not very common. For a calendar of gay and lesbian events, check out **www.farraurbana.com**. There are few, if any, venues or events directed at the lesbian-only scene, yet lesbians are welcome at gay venues. Clubs are open at 10pm Wednesday through Sunday; weeknight cover charges are around $3 to $5 (£1.50–£2.50), $8 to $10 (£4–£5) on weekends. Early arrivals can take advantage of happy-hour drink specials (sometimes free drinks).

The most established gay clubs are **BLG,** at Calle 49 and Calle Uruguay (✆ **265-1624**), with dancing to top DJ music Thursday to Saturday, and other special events like Gay Pride Nights on weekdays; and **Lips** (no phone) at Avenida Manuel Espinoza Batista, next to Café Duran, with nightly drag shows on weeknights and dancing on Fridays and Saturdays. The largest gay dance club, Box, is now called **Glam: The Club**

Spas in Panama

There are no "destination" spas in Panama, but most resorts and a couple of upscale hotels have a top-of-the-line spa, or at the very least provide services such as massage, a gym, a sauna, and sometimes a steam room. I don't foresee a huge boom in this market in Panama, in spite of its rapid growth worldwide, but a few hotel owners are slowly catching on to this hot trend. Below are the best spas for hotels that are listed in this chapter.

Decapolis Radisson ★★ (✆ **215-5000;** www.radisson.com), a sleek, trendy hotel, has the Aqua Spa, the top spa in Panama City in terms of service and hip decor, and you don't have to be a guest to book an appointment. They offer a full range of treatments and a stylish salon for one-stop makeovers.

Veneto Hotel & Casino ★★ (✆ **340-8888;** www.venetocasino.com) has a building facade that screams Las Vegas, but inside it's as elegant as can be, and their Bamboo Sea Spa & Gym is a calm oasis that opens out onto a rooftop swimming pool. This is the spa with the widest range of treatments (Vichy-style), including hot stone massage, mud baths, aromatherapy, hydrotherapy and facials, and more.

Panamonte Inn & Spa ★ (✆ **720-1324;** www.panamonteinnandspa.com) is the place to go in Boquete to be pampered. It's a country-cozy-style spa and is very complete, with shiatsu, Swedish and sports massage, a sauna and steam room, skin and spa treatments using Natura Bisse products, body scrubs, and mud treatments. Their facials are especially noteworthy.

(✆ **265-1624**), and focus has shifted to nightly drag shows, concerts, fashion shows, and more, followed by late-night dancing until dawn (the best nights are Fri–Sat). To get here, you need a taxi; the club is at Tumba Muerto (in the Urb. Industrial La Esperanza neighborhood) on Vía Ricardo J. Alfaro. **Punta G,** at Calle D in El Cangrejo (next to Ginza Teppanyaki; ✆ **265-1624**), has barmen clad in spandex, DJ music, and a dance floor.

Casinos

Gambling is legal in Panama, and virtually every major hotel in the city has an adjoining casino. You'll find slot machines, video poker, gaming tables, sports betting, and special shows and parties. The hottest casino at the moment is at the **Veneto Hotel & Casino** (✆ **340-8081**). The Veneto has a sophisticated gaming area and often hosts over-the-top parties such as E! Entertainment's *Wild On.* There is a sushi bar here, too. **El Panama Hotel** (✆ **215-9440**) has one of the newer centrally located casinos, which offers cheap drink specials for women. The **Sheraton Hotel and Convention Center** (✆ **305-5100**) has a large, elegant casino, but its out-of-the-way location means it's really only visited by guests. The bar here, though, is popular with young Panamanians.

5 THE PANAMA CANAL & THE CANAL ZONE ★★★

77km (48 miles) long from Panama City to Colón

The construction of the Panama Canal was one of the grandest engineering feats in the history of the world, an epic tale of ingenuity and courage that was marked by episodes of tragedy. When it was finally completed in 1914, the canal cut travel distances by more than half for ships that previously had to round South America's Cape. Today, the canal is one of the most traveled waterways, annually handling around 13,000 ships that represent 5% of global trade.

Though the history of the canal dates back to the 16th century, when Vasco Núñez de Balboa discovered that Panama was just a narrow strip of land separating the Caribbean from the Pacific, the first real attempt to construct a canal was begun by the French in 1880, led by Ferdinand de Lesseps, the charismatic architect of the Suez Canal. The Gallic endeavor failed miserably, however, as few had anticipated the enormous challenge presented by the Panamanian jungle, with its mucky swamps, torrential downpours, landslides, floods, and, most debilitating of all, mosquito-borne diseases such as malaria and yellow fever. In the end, more than 20,000 perished.

In 1903, the United States bought out the French and backed Panama in its secession from Colombia in exchange for control of the Canal Zone. For the next 10 years, the U.S., having essentially eradicated tropical disease, pulled off what seemed impossible in terms of engineering: It carved out a 14km (9-mile) path through the Continental Divide and constructed an elevated canal system and a series of locks to lift ships from sea level up to 26m (85 ft.) at Lake Gatún. The lake, created after construction crews dammed the Chagres River near the Gatún Locks, was at the time the largest man-made lake in the world.

In 1977, U.S. President Jimmy Carter and President Omar Torrijos of Panama signed a treaty that would relinquish control of the canal to the Panamanians on December 31, 1999. It was a controversial move because most Americans did not believe that Panama was up to the task—but those concerns have proved to be unfounded. As an autonomous corporation, the Panama Canal Authority has reduced safety problems and improved maintenance and productivity to the point where the canal basically runs itself.

It takes between 8 and 10 hours to transit the entire canal. There are three locks, the **Miraflores, Pedro Miguel,** and **Gatún,** whose maximum size is 320m (1,050 ft.) in length and 34m (110 ft.) in width. Ships built to fit through these locks are referred to as **Panamax** ships, which set the size standard until the 1990s, with the building of post-Panamax ships (mostly oil tankers) that are up to 49m (160 ft.) wide. The Panama Canal Authority, seeking to avoid becoming obsolete, is constructing two multibillion-dollar three-chamber locks to increase traffic and allow for wider ships. A national referendum in 2006 approved this expensive canal overhaul, and engineers are already hard at work toward making it happen.

SEEING THE PANAMA CANAL IN ACTION

Miraflores Locks ★★★

The best land-based platform from which to see the Panama Canal at work is at **Miraflores Visitors Center** ★★ (© **276-8325;** www.pancanal.com), located about a 15-minute drive from the heart of the city. The center is an absorbing attraction for both kids and adults, with four floors of exhibitions and interactive displays—and a theater—providing information about the canal's history and its impact on world trade, plus explanations of how the region's natural environment is crucial to the function of the canal. Ships can also be viewed from an observation deck. In fact, it's probably Panama's best museum. ***Tip:*** You'll have better luck catching sight of enormous Panamax ships in the afternoon around 2 or 3pm.

The center is open daily from 9am to 5pm (the ticket office closes at 4pm). Admission to the center's exhibitions and observation terrace is $8 (£4) adults, $5 (£2.50) children and students with ID, and free for children 4 and under; it costs $5 (£2.50) for adults, and $3 (£1.50) for children to visit only the restaurant and gift shop.

Perhaps the best thing about visiting here is the **Miraflores Visitors Center Restaurant** ★★★ (daily 11am–11pm; main courses $7–$20/£3.50–£10), where you can dine while watching colossal ships transit the locks just a hundred feet away. Lunch is the most popular time to eat, so arrive early or make a reservation for then; whenever you dine, try to get a table as close to the railing as possible. At night, the locks are well lit and provide clear views of the ships. The food is not bad either, but what you're really here for is the one-of-a-kind view.

GETTING THERE City tours of Panama City (p. 640) usually include 2-hour stop at Miraflores, or you can take a taxi for $25 to $30 (£13–£15) round-trip for a 45-minute to 1-hour visit. Agree on a price with the driver beforehand.

Transiting the Panama Canal ★★★

Visitors to Panama who are not part of a long-haul cruise can still transit the canal by boat on a journey from Panama City to Colón, or they can do a partial transit from Gamboa to the Pacific or vice versa.

Panama Marine Adventures (**© 226-8917;** www.pmatours.net) offers partial canal transit with a shuttle leaving from the Flamenco Resort and Marina on the Amador Causeway at 10am and going to their *Pacific Queen,* docked at Gamboa. Trips leave every Saturday year-round, and every Thursday and Friday from January to April. The company offers full transit of the canal one Saturday every month (check the website for dates) leaving at 7:30am, first passing through the Miraflores locks and finishing at the Gatún Locks; the company provides transportation by vehicle back to Panama City. Partial transit costs $115 (£58) for adults and $65 for kids 11 and under; full transit costs $165 (£83) for adults and $75 (£38) for kids 12 and under. The price includes all transportation, a bilingual guide, and lunch and soft drinks. The *Pacific Queen* has a capacity of 300 passengers.

Canal & Bay Tours (**© 209-2009** or 209-2010; www.canalandbaytours.com) is a pioneer in canal tourism, offering transit aboard one of two boats, the refurbished *Isla Morada,* a wooden boat with a capacity of 100 guests, or the *Fantasía del Mar,* a steel boat with a capacity of 500 passengers. The company offers full-day transit of the canal the first Saturday of every month for $165 (£83) adults, $75 (£38) children 11 and under; and partial transit every Saturday for $115 (£58) adults, $60 (£30) children 11 and under. Canal & Bay has full transit and partial transit (you pick) the third Tuesday of every month from January to April. Tours leave at 7:30am from the Flamenco Marina, docking in Gamboa or Gatún, depending on the tour. They also offer Saturday evening **"Rumba in the Bay"** tours of the Bay of Panama, leaving at 9:30pm from their pier, with live music and an open bar.

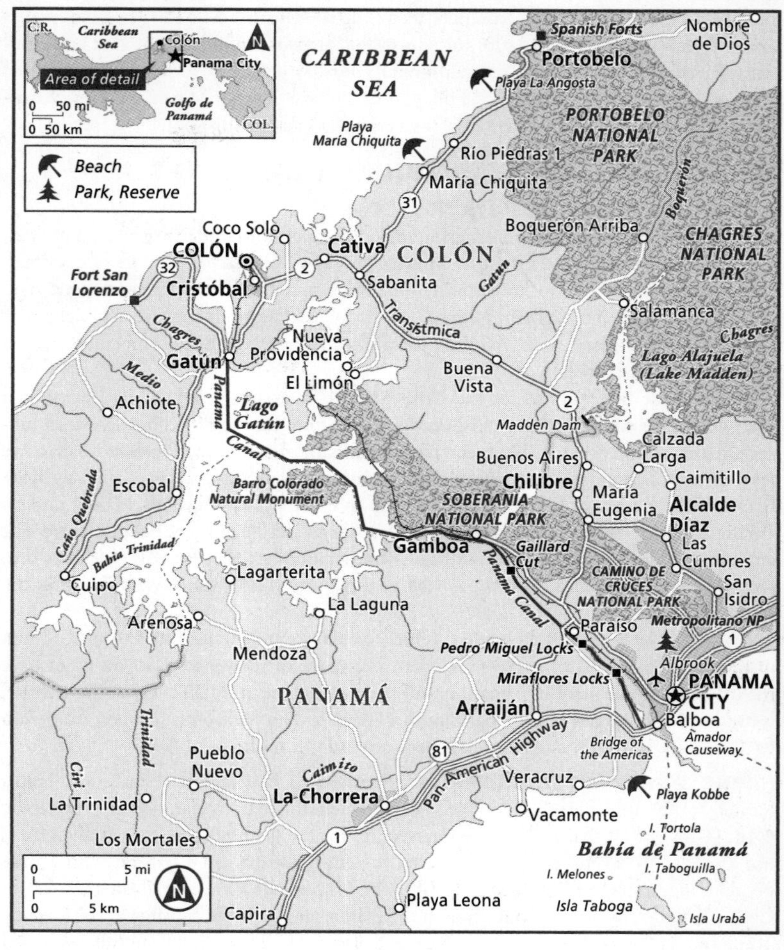

Panama Yacht Tours (✆ **263-5044;** www.panamayachtours.com) owns six yachts ranging from 18 to 37m (58–122 ft.) for 1 to 100 people, with prices starting at $3,500 (£1,750), not including food, beverages, and dock fees. Clearly, this is an expensive option, best for groups seeking to escape the "cattle call" sort of trip. Private transits leave early from Gamboa and transit southbound, arriving at the Flamenco Marina at 4:30pm; the other leaves from Pier 19 in Balboa at 7:30am for the northbound journey to Gamboa (travelers return to Panama City via land). Private transits require at least a week to 2 weeks' advance notice. They also offer fixed departure tours similar to the ones above, costing $115 (£58) for adults and $65 (£33) for kids for partial transit and $165 (£83) and $75 (£38) for full transit, plus 5% tax.

Ancon Expeditions (✆ **269-9415;** www.anconexpeditions.com) also offers full and partial transits of the canal. Ancon provides early morning hotel pickup to the Port of Balboa, where you'll board a passenger ferry. Partial transits cost $150 (£75) for adults and full transits cost $199 (£100) for adults. Full transits are offered the first and third Saturday of every month with one additional Thursday departure in January, and partial transits depart every Thursday and Friday from January through March and every Saturday year-round. After transiting, a bus will take you back to your hotel.

MORE HIGHLIGHTS AROUND PANAMA CITY

Soberanía National Park ★★★

Wildlife from North and South America, including migratory birds, meets here in Soberanía, creating a hyper-diverse natural wonderland. The park has 105 species of mammals and a staggering number of bird species—525 at last count. There are jaguars, yes, and collared peccaries and night monkeys, too, but you're more likely to catch sight of a coatimundi, three-toed sloth, or diminutive tamarin monkey. Bring binoculars even if you're not an avid birder.

There are several ways to see the park. ANAM, the park ranger service, has several excellent hiking trails for day excursions that range from easy to difficult; there are a full-scale resort, a birder's ecolodge, a recreational park and zoo, and the Pipeline Road, a site revered for its abundant diversity of birds. Soberanía National Park is open daily from 6am to 5pm, and costs $3 (£1.50) per person to enter (it's free for kids 11 and under). Paying is tricky; they ask that you stop at the ranger station to pay because there isn't anyone to collect money at the trail head—but it's unlikely that every visitor does this. Play it safe, though, and stop to pay; the pass permits you to use any trails within the space of a day.

The park can be accessed by rental vehicle or taxi from Panama City (40 min. away), or by joining a tour. If you take a taxi, plan a time for the driver to pick you up or have the driver wait. For more information, call the park's office at ✆ **232-4192;** the website, www.anam.gob.pa, has limited park info in Spanish. The park office is open from 7am to 7pm daily, but if no one is inside, check around out back.

HIKING & BIRD-WATCHING TRAILS **Sendero El Plantación (Plantation Trail),** located at the turnoff for the Canopy Tower lodge on the road to Gamboa, is a moderate, 6.4m (4-mile) trail that ends at the intersection for the Camino de Cruces trail. This is not a loop trail, so hikers will either need to return via the same trail or, with a little preplanning, arrange to be dropped off at the Camino de Cruces trail on the road to Colón, hike northwest and connect with the Plantation Trail, and finish near the Canopy Tower, or vice versa (see Camino de Cruces, below). The Plantation Trail follows a road built in the 1910s by La Cascadas Plantation, the largest in the old Canal Zone during that period, producing cacao, coffee, and rubber. Alert hikers will spot remnants of these crops, especially the cacao plant. This trail is popular with bird-watchers, but mammals such as tamarins are frequently seen, too.

Continuing on the road to Gamboa, and to the right, is the trail head for **Sendero Charco (Pond Trail),** an ultraeasy, 20-minute loop that follows the Sardinilla River. The trail gives even the most reluctant walkers a brilliant opportunity to immerse themselves in thick tropical rainforest.

A little more than a mile past the bridge and turnoff to Gamboa Resort is **Camino de Oleoducto,** better known as **Pipeline Road ★★**, the celebrity trail for bird-watching in Panama, renowned worldwide as a record-setting site for 24-hour bird counts. Bird-watching starts at the crack of dawn, when the avian world is at its busiest, so try to make it here at least before 9am, if not earlier. In spite of the name, the Pipeline Road is not drivable. More than half the bird-watchers who visit here walk only a mile or so, but if you like to hike or mountain bike (see below), push on because the chances of spotting rare birds and wildlife increase the farther you go. To get here by vehicle, pass the Gamboa Resort turnoff, and continue until you reach a fork. Turn left here onto a gravel road and continue until you see the Pipeline Road sign.

Soberanía's other prime attraction is historic **Camino de Cruces (Las Cruces Trail).** Before the railway and the canal existed, the only path from the Caribbean to the Pacific was the Chagres River to what's now called Venta de Cruces, followed by a treacherous walk along Las Cruces Trail. The Spanish used this route during the 16th century to transport looted treasure to the Caribbean and onward to Spain. In some areas, the cobblestone remains of the trail still exist or have been restored, and can be seen even if you walk just 10 or 20 minutes from the picnic area and trail head off Madden Road. The trail is moderate to difficult, and is about 9.7km (6 miles) to its terminus at Venta de Cruces. From here, a local boat can pick you up and drop you off at the Gamboa resort, but you'll need a guide (a tour or your hotel can arrange this for you). Backpackers can camp along the trail, but must pay a $5/£2.50 fee at the park ranger station beforehand. If this trail really piques your interest, check out Ancon Expeditions' 8-day "Camino Real Tour," which gives travelers a taste of what it was like to cross the isthmus by foot during the Gold Rush era, and includes tent lodging in the rainforest and at an Emberá Indian village.

The second alternative is to hike the trail and turn into the Plantation Trail, which finishes near Canopy Tower and the road to Gamboa. This hike takes around 5 hours to complete and is a moderately difficult trek. To get to the trail head, continue straight at the fork in the road to Gamboa on what's known as Madden Road (but not signed as such). The road presents a lovely drive through the park along a road flanked with towering rainforest canopy. About 6km (3¾ miles) past the fork there are covered picnic tables and the trail head.

Lago Gatun

Engineers understood that the only feasible way to build the Panama Canal was to employ a system of locks to lift ships up and over higher altitudes on the isthmus, and central to this was the creation of Gatún Lake. The lake flooded roughly 425 sq. km (164 sq. miles), an area slightly larger than Detroit, creating islands out of hilltops and submerging entire forests and villages.

The thick rainforest that cloaks the shoreline provides water for Gatún Lake, which in turn provides water for the canal locks, and therefore the Canal Authority is keen to keep deforestation at bay. This is good news for ecotravelers—wildlife sightings are common. Ships traverse 38km (24 miles) across the lake from the Gatún Locks to the Gaillard Cut, and travelers can take part in this experience with a partial canal transit (see "Transiting the Panama Canal," above), join a jungle cruise on the lake, or even go fishing on the lake. Getting out on the lake provides a more intimate view of the canal than a visit to the Miraflores Locks does.

JUNGLE CRUISES ★★★ Half-day jungle cruises in Lake Gatún are mini-adventures that are as fun for kids as for adults, and they are dependable ways to catch sight of monkeys such as white-faced capuchins, howler monkeys, and Geoffrey's tamarins up-close and in their natural habitat. Expect also to see sloths, crocodiles, caimans, turtles, and even *capybaras,* the world's largest rodent. The boat ride also allows passengers to get unusually close to monster tankers and ships transiting the canal. The **Gamboa Resort** offers a jungle cruise as part of their in-house excursions; others leave from the Gamboa pier and provide land transportation to and from Panama City. Guides provide passengers with an entertaining account of the history of the canal, the mechanisms that operate the canal, and fun anecdotes, while ducking in and out of island passageways searching for birds and wildlife. **Ancon Expeditions** (p. 640) has the best guides and service, not to mention the most experience in the area. Their Panama Canal Boat Rainforest Adventure leaves early from Panama City and returns in the late afternoon; the cost is $110 (£55) adults and $65 (£33) kids 12 and under, which includes lunch and all transportation. **Advantage Panama** (p. 640) also offers a rainforest land and water tour including a stroll through Soberanía National Park before boarding their aquatic vessel. The tour lasts about 6 hours, includes drinks and snacks, and costs $87 (£44).

Jungle Land Explorers, part of Panama City Tours (✆ **260-8205;** www.Gatún explorer.com), offers an interesting motorboat tour of Gatún Lake and a stop at their anchored, double-decker ***Gatún Explorer*** houseboat, where guests have lunch and kick back in the middle of the jungle; kayaking and fishing are also options. They have a library with educational videos and books, too. The tour leaves from La Represa dock on the west side of the canal; however, round-trip transportation from Panama City is included, leaving at 8am and returning at 4:30pm. Note that the *Gatún Explorer* works with cruise ship excursionists, and therefore they offer their jungle cruise on **Sundays** only, whereas Ancon can usually plan something any day of the week.

FISHING ★★★ I give this activity three stars because in Gatún Lake you're guaranteed a fish—or your money back. The lake is packed with peacock bass, and all you need to do is just casually throw a line in and you'll easily snag one, sometimes within minutes. **Cahill's Fishing** (✆ **315-1905** or 6678-2653; www.panamacanalfishing.com) has a 5.5m (18-ft.) Fun Deck with a 115-horsepower motor, live bait box, and fishing rods, and he charges $395 (£198) a day for two people plus $20 (£10) for each additional angler. The price includes snacks and beer. They recently began offering ocean boats for inshore fishing.

Río Chagres & Embera Villages

The Chagres River flows from the San Blas Cordillera down into Gatún Lake near Gamboa—on the other side of the lake, the river is blocked by the Gatún Dam, which created its namesake lake. Travelers visit this river for two reasons: cultural tours of Emberá Indian villages, or intermediate-level white-water rafting. Along the way, the jungle-draped riverbanks teem with birds, animals, and fluttering butterflies, providing an exciting sense of adventure without having to invest a lot of time or money.

EMBERA INDIANS VILLAGE TOUR ★★ Emberá Indians are native to the Darién Province, but many groups have resettled here on the banks of the Chagres River. For the most part, they continue to live life much as they have for centuries, traveling by dugout canoe, wearing nothing more than a skirt or sheath, and sleeping under thatched-roof huts. To earn income, the Emberá villages Parara Puru, Emberá Puru, and Emberá Drua, which are close to the mouth of the Chagres River, have opened to tourism, allowing visitors to share in their culture and see how they live. For a few bucks, you can have an Emberá hand paint a traditional "tattoo" with *jagua* vegetable dye on a part of your body (kids love this), but keep in mind that it takes 10 to 14 days for the stain to go away! Part of the tour includes a typical Emberá lunch and watching a folkloric dance show; like most folkloric shows, these are demonstrations of rituals long gone, but the music and dancing are still entertaining. Bring your swimsuit because tours include a walk to a cascade for a dip in cool water. All Panamanian tour operators offer this Emberá trip, though prices vary. **Ancon Expeditions** charges $130 (£65) for this half-day trip.

RAFTING ★★ The tour company **Aventuras Panama** (✆ **260-0044;** www.aventuras panama.com) specializes in what it calls the "Chagres Challenge," with a hiking and rafting trip down the Class 2 and 3 river. It's a long float but technically not difficult, and it starts early, leaving Panama City at 5am by 4WD and going to the village San Cristóbal. From here you hike for more than an hour to the put-in site on the Chagres. The rafting portion lasts about 5 hours, but included in that along the way is a picnic lunch on the river. Travelers pass by Emberá villages but do not spend much time there. Expect to arrive back in Panama City around 7pm. The cost is $165 (£83) per person, and includes transportation, breakfast, and lunch, and all equipment. You must be between the ages of 12 and 70 to participate. They also offer many other kayaking and rafting tours all over Panama.

Summit Gardens Park & Zoo ★★

This zoo has a wonderful display of "showcase" wildlife, including tapirs, white-faced capuchins and spider monkeys, ocelots, a jaguar, puma, collared peccaries, and more, some of which have been rescued from unscrupulous wildlife poachers (the young tapir "Lucia" was saved during a sting operation that nabbed two Panamanians trying to sell her on the Internet). But without a doubt, the **harpy eagle** takes center stage here—it even has its own interpretive center. The harpy is Panama's national bird and the largest eagle in the world, about half the size of an average human—it really is worth a visit just to see the size of this regal bird.

Summit began as a botanical garden in 1923, created by the U.S. in an effort to reproduce and distribute tropical plants from around the world. It is now home to the world's leading collection of palms, among other exotic species. Because Panama City has few green spaces for a picnic or a chance to let the kids run free, Summit is popular with families on weekends. The grassy picnic area and park are free, or you can pay $8 (£4) for a covered eating area and barbecue pit. The zoo costs $1 (50p) for adults and teens, kids 12 and under get in free, and it's open daily from 9am to 5pm. Call ✆ **232-4854** for more information, or check out their site at www.summitpanama.org.

Where to Stay & Dine

Canopy Tower ★★ Moments Canopy Tower is an ex-U.S.-military radar station that has been converted into a fantasy lodge for bird-watchers—something like a cross between a stylish B&B and a scientific research center. There is a 360-degree observation deck that provides stunning views and a platform for observing the 200-plus species of birds and a comfy social lounge with wraparound windows that are flush with the trees. The best room here is the Blue Cotinga Suite, one of two "suites," which are really large doubles with a hammock and private bathroom. Doubles on the second floor are comfortably spaced; however, the pie-slice single rooms are tiny and noisy in the morning (starting at 5:30am), and they do not have curtains. Bird-watchers are the majority of guests here, so it's early to bed and up at sunrise. Single rooms have shared bathrooms.

Road to Gamboa. ✆ **264-5720** or 6687-0291. www.canopytower.com. $105–$195 (£53–£98) per person double; $152–$220 (£76–£110) per person suite. Call about special packages. Rates include meals, but not tours. AE, MC, V. **Amenities:** Restaurant; bar.

Volunteer & Study Programs in Panama

The following are a few institutions and nonprofit groups that work on sustainable development or other environmental or social projects in Panama.

Global Vision International (✆ **800/776-0188;** www.earthwatch.org) is a U.K.-based organization that provides support and services to charities, NGOs, and governmental agencies for conservation and humanitarian projects. In Panama, they offer a 2-week volunteer program at two turtle-nesting sites in Bocas del Toro. Volunteers tag, measure, and monitor turtles—and pay $1,525 to do so, sleeping in rustic huts. The program runs from March to mid-June.

Habitat for Humanity International (✆ **202/628-9171** in the U.S., or 263-3035; www.habitat.org) is a nonprofit, nondenominational Christian volunteer organization that builds homes around the world for needy people. Habitat began two housing projects in 2003 in Panama at Altos de la Colina and Chilibre. They accept volunteer workers; however, volunteers are expected to pay for all living costs including food and housing, as well as the flight to Panama.

Summit Garden & Zoo (✆ **232-4850;** www.summitpanama.org) has volunteer programs working in animal care or environmental education, as well as in their botanical garden, providing opportunities to learn about Panamanian flora and fauna and conservation issues, pick up new skills, and generally help the park through its renovation that began in 2006.

Gamboa Rainforest Resort ★★ Kids Sprawled along the shore of the Chagres River in Soberanía National Park, the Gamboa Rainforest Resort is an ideal destination for families with kids, given the resort's jungle boat cruises, aerial tram ride through the rainforest, and minizoo of reptile, butterfly, and marine species exhibits. Every amenity under the tropical sun is offered here, such as a full-service spa, guided tours, and several restaurants. Very spacious double rooms have garden or river views (with private balconies) and a pleasant yet anonymous chainlike decor; attractive suites have Indonesian furniture and large living areas. The bathrooms are elegant and spacious.

Gamboa. ✆ **314-5000,** or 877/800-1690 in the U.S. www.gamboaresort.com. 107 units. $175–$250 (£88–£125) double with garden view; $195–$285 (£98–£143) double with river view; $290–$350 (£145–£175) junior suite; $150–$215 (£125–£108) 1-bedroom apartment. AE, MC, V. **Amenities:** 3 restaurants; 2 bars; bicycle rental; concierge; laundry service; outdoor pool; room service; spa and fitness center; tennis courts; watersports equipment. *In room:* A/C, TV, minibar, hair dryer.

6 BOQUETE ★★★

40km (25 miles) from David; 473km (293 miles) from Panama City

Boquete is located in a steep-walled, green, and flower-filled valley on the flank of the Barú Volcano and at the shore of the Caldera River. Despite Boquete's somewhat utilitarian downtown made of cheap, concrete-poured buildings, the town on the whole oozes

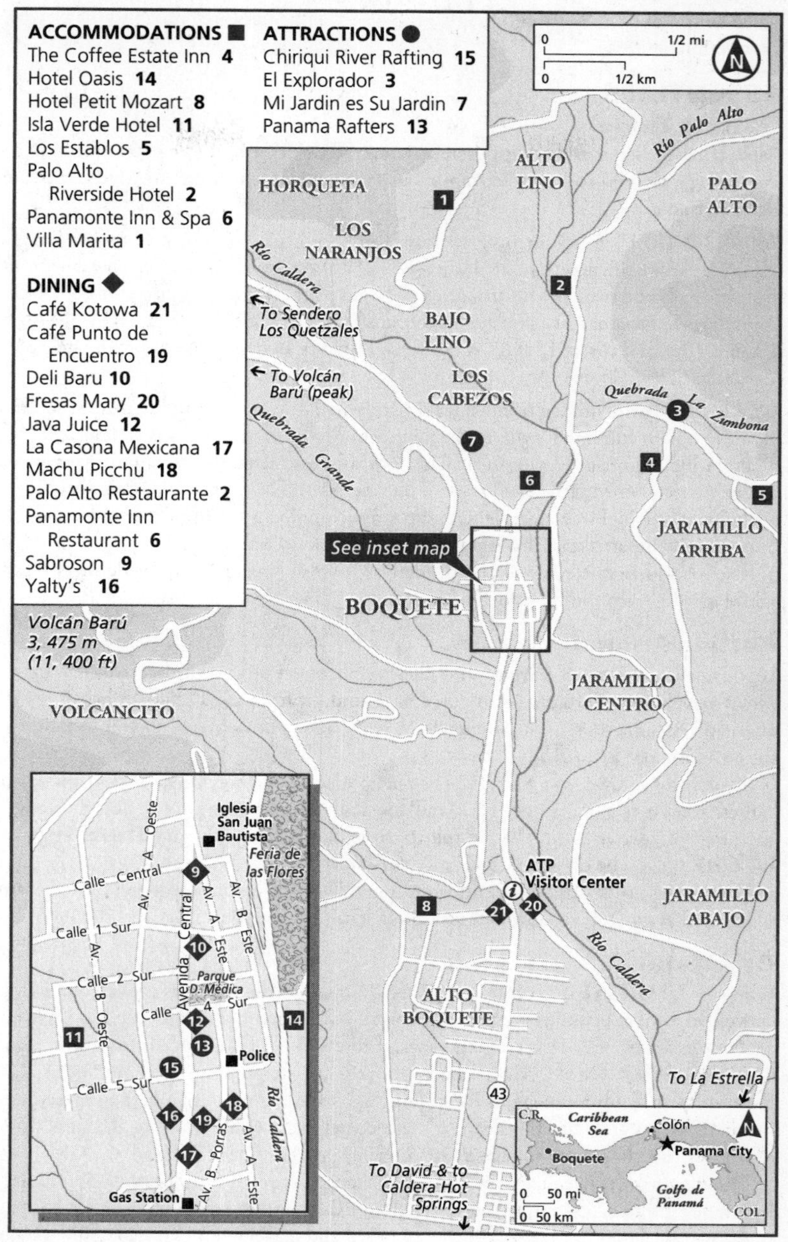
ACCOMMODATIONS
The Coffee Estate Inn 4
Hotel Oasis 14
Hotel Petit Mozart 8
Isla Verde Hotel 11
Los Establos 5
Palo Alto Riverside Hotel 2
Panamonte Inn & Spa 6
Villa Marita 1
ATTRACTIONS
Chiriqui River Rafting 15
El Explorador 3
Mi Jardin es Su Jardin 7
Panama Rafters 13
DINING
Café Kotowa 21
Café Punto de Encuentro 19
Deli Baru 10
Fresas Mary 20
Java Juice 12
La Casona Mexicana 17
Machu Picchu 18
Palo Alto Restaurante 2
Panamonte Inn Restaurant 6
Sabroson 9
Yalty's 16
0 1/2 mi
0 1/2 km
N
Río Palo Alto
ALTO LINO
PALO ALTO
HORQUETA
LOS NARANJOS
Río Caldera
To Sendero Los Quetzales
BAJO LINO
To Volcán Barú (peak)
LOS CABEZOS
Quebrada La Zumbona
Quebrada Grande
JARAMILLO ARRIBA
See inset map
BOQUETE
Volcán Barú 3, 475 m (11, 400 ft)
JARAMILLO CENTRO
VOLCANCITO
Iglesia San Juan Bautista
Feria de las Flores
Calle Central
Av. A Oeste
Avenida Central
Av. A Este
Av. B Este
Calle 1 Sur
Calle 2 Sur
Parque D. Médica
Calle 4 Sur
Av. B Oeste
Police
Calle 5 Sur
Río Caldera
Av. B. Porras
Av. A Este
Gas Station
ATP Visitor Center
JARAMILLO ABAJO
Río Caldera
ALTO BOQUETE
To La Estrella
43
To David & to Caldera Hot Springs
C.R.
Caribbean Sea
Colón
Boquete
Panama City
0 50 mi
0 50 km
Golfo de Panamá
COL.

charm and offers a bounty of activities for travelers. Recently Boquete has climbed the charts to become one of the top-five retirement destinations in the world, and large-scale gated communities have begun their spread on the city's outskirts, much to the chagrin of longtime residents.

ESSENTIALS

Getting There

Most hotels either provide transportation from the David airport (see p. 643 for info) or can arrange for you to be picked up by an independent taxi driver for the 45-minute drive to Boquete.

BY BUS & TAXI Buses for Boquete leave from the David bus terminal every 25 minutes, take approximately 1 hour, and cost $1 (50p) one-way. You can catch a bus from Boquete to David from the north side of the main plaza. If you're coming from Bocas del Toro or from Panama City, you'll need to transfer in David. It takes 7 hours by bus from Panama City, and costs $12 (£6). A taxi from David to Boquete costs approximately $15 to $20 (£7.50–£10) one-way.

BY CAR If you're driving from Panama City, you'll turn right on the signed turnoff for Boquete before entering David, at the intersection next to the Shell gas station.

From the airport in David, turn right onto the main road and drive until you arrive at the intersection with the Shell station, then turn left. Drive until you reach a stop sign at the four-lane highway, turn right, and continue until you reach the intersection at the Super Barú supermarket. Turn left and continue onward to Boquete.

The road to Boquete is well paved; there are two side roads that provide shortcuts if you're driving from the Bocas del Toro area.

Getting Around

If you're a do-it-yourself traveler who likes to explore at your own pace, you'll want to rent a vehicle to get around—but you'll have to do it from the David airport (p. 643); alternatively, some hotels can arrange for a rental car to be delivered to you in Boquete for an additional $30 (£15).

Taxis around town cost $1 to $2 (50p–£1); unless your hotel is located in the town center, you'll need one to get back and forth. If you're looking for a fluent English-speaking taxi driver for a half- or full-day tour around Boquete, try **Daniel Higgins** (✆ **6617-0570**); he charges $15 (£7.50) per hour.

Local buses cruise Avenida Central and the hilly roads around Boquete, but taxis are so cheap that you'll invariably end up hailing a cab before a bus.

Orientation

Boquete's **CEFATI visitor center** (✆ **720-4060;** daily 9am–6pm) is the large building on your right just before you enter town. With its location high above the Río Caldera, the visitor center provides sweeping views of town. You'll find **Café Kotowa** here, too, with a small shop. On the center's second floor is an interpretive display (in Spanish) of the history and anthropology of the region. Ask for a representative here to give you a quick tour and translate the displays. The center isn't within walking distance from downtown, so you'll need to take a cab ($1/50p) or a local bus (25¢/15p).

The main street, Avenida Central, runs the length of town from north to south, and businesses and transportation services are clustered around the main plaza on streets that run east-west. From downtown, a series of paved and gravel roads climb the hilly terrain surrounding Boquete.

Isla Coiba

Once the haunt of pirates, and in recent times an island feared by convicted criminals who were sent there, **Isla Coiba ★★★** (**© 998-4271;** www.coibanationalpark.com) is now a treasured national park, UNESCO World Heritage Site, and nature lover's, fisherman's, and scuba-diver's dream destination. Given Isla Coiba's astounding natural diversity, rich sea life, and rare species, it is frequently referred to as the Galápagos of Central America. Isla Coiba is the largest island in Panama, but the national park spreads beyond the main island, encompassing 38 islands and islets and marine waters for a total of 270,128 hectares (667,500 acres). The area is home to the second-largest coral reef in the eastern Pacific, at Bahía Damas, and its waters teem with huge schools of colorful fish, hammerhead and nurse sharks, dolphins, manta rays, tuna, turtles, whales, and other gigantic marine species. Onshore, there are 36 species of mammals and 39 species of reptiles, including saltwater crocodiles. Beyond these impressive numbers, Coiba is one of the last places on earth where it is possible to see a scarlet macaw in the wild. Indeed, few places in the Americas are as wild, remote, and full of life as Isla Coiba National Park.

Hiking, fishing, snorkeling, and diving opportunities abound here, which might make roughing the park's rustic cabins worthwhile. ANAM only allows catch-and-release fishing within a mile of the boundary of the national park-protected area, so you'll have to go a little farther if you'd like to keep what you catch. Most of the tour operators listed on p. 684 offer fishing excursions of Isla Coiba, but you may also want to check out the following: **Coiba Adventure** (**© 999-8108** or 800/800-0907 in the U.S.; www.coibadventure.com), the **M/V Coral Star** (**© 866/924-2837** in the U.S.; www.coralstar.com), and **Pesca Panama** (**© 800/946-3474** in the U.S.; www.pescapanama.com). Those looking for snorkeling and diving opportunities should book an excursion with **Panama Divers** (**© 314-0817** or 6613-4405; www.panamadivers.com), the country's most respected diving and snorkeling outfitter.

The park is administered by ANAM, which has a **ranger station** (**© 998-0615**) and the only lodging on the island, consisting of several basic air-conditioned cabins on a glorious white-sand and turquoise-water beach. The cost to visit Coiba National Park is $10 (£5) per person. The cabins are used by fishing, diving, and snorkeling tour outfitters (or by those with a private boat). Day visits to Coiba go through operators in nearby Santa Catalina. There is a landing strip on Coiba, but it's for charter flights only.

Visitor Information

Boquete Safari Tours (**© 6742-6614;** www.boquetemountainsafaritours.com), known for their bright yellow jeeps, offer about a half-dozen half-day and full-day excursions of Boquete and the surrounding area. All tour guides are bilingual, and hotel pickup is available. They are currently offering a new coffee-tasting tour that allows you to sample different types of coffees from several farms. The tour is a based on Napa Valley wine-tasting tours, and is one of the more interesting coffee tours available in Boquete.

FAST FACTS For the **police,** dial ✆ **104;** for the **fire department,** dial ✆ **720-1224.** The **Centro Médico San Juan Bautista,** on Avenida Central, 2 blocks up the road past the Hotel Panamonte, has English-speaking doctors (✆ **720-1881**); for serious health problems, you'll need to head to the hospital in David. The **post office** is located on the plaza, and is open Monday to Friday 8am to 5:45pm, and Saturday 8am to 4:45pm; for fast service go to **Mail Boxes Etc.** (✆ **720-2684**) on Avenida Central, in front of the Almacén Reina.

Twenty-four-hour ATMs can be found at **Banco Nacional** and **Global Bank,** which lie across from each other on Avenida Central and Calle 5 Sur. Most hotels have a computer with Internet access for their guests, or try **Java Juice** on Avenida Central.

WHAT TO SEE & DO

The **Bajo Mono Loop** takes you high above the town along a newly asphalted road for panoramic vistas and beautiful forest scenery. This is a good drive from which to get your bearings and see why everyone's gone wild about living in Boquete. To get here, follow the main road past the church and head left at the fork, passing Café Ruiz and staying left until you see the sign for BAJO MONO. Just as pretty is the **Volcancito Loop**—to get here, follow the main road out of town and when you see the CEFATI visitor center, turn right and follow the loop until you arrive back at town. You can bike these loops as well. (See "Biking," below.)

One of the most beautiful drives in Panama heads to **Finca Suiza** (✆ **6615-3774;** www.panama.net.tc) on the main road to the Atlantic Coast, in the Bocas del Toro province. The scenic drive to this property winds through mountain forests and open fields with sweeping views, and farther down to the lush lowlands and rainforest of Bocas province. Take the left turn to Caldera 16km (10 miles) south of Boquete and continue along paved/gravel road, until you hit the major road to Bocas. You can also take a completely paved, easier-to-follow road by heading toward David and turning left toward Gualaca.

Hiking & Bird-Watching Outfitters/Guides

The reputable Panama City–based adventure company **Ecocircuitos,** on Avenida Central next to Chiriquí Rafting Company (✆ **720-1506;** www.ecocircuitos.com) is a one-stop shop for short adventures in the Chiriquí area. Another company, **Coffee Adventures,** offers guided excursions around Boquete, even though they are more commonly called upon for their popular tours of the Kotowa coffee estate (see "Coffee Tours," below). Coffee Adventures offers cultural excursions to a Ngöbe-Buglé community near the Caribbean coast, guided hikes on Los Quetzales Trail from Boquete to Cerro Punta (or vice versa), and low-key excursions like bird-watching and trips to the Caldera Hot Springs.

Feliciano González is a local guide with more than 20 years of experience in the Boquete area (✆ **6632-8645** or 6624-9940; www.geocities.com/boquete_tours). He has a 4WD vehicle, speaks basic English, and can customize tours of Boquete as well as day hikes on the Quetzales Trail, the Pianista Trail, and the full-day hike to the summit of Volcano Barú ($100/£50 for up to four people). Based in Volcán, **Nariño Aizpurua** (✆ **6704-4251;** westernwindnature@yahoo.com) is a fun and friendly guide who specializes in bird-watching; he is a recommended guide for Los Quetzales Trail if you plan to start on that side.

For birding, you can't beat local guide **Santiago "Chago" Caballero** (✆ **6626-2200;** santiagochagotours@hotmail.com) or one of his protégés. Want to see a quetzal? If you're here from December to May, Santiago can guarantee that you will—the reason he is such a valued guide in the region. Santiago typically takes birders to Finca Lérida but can customize tours, including searches for wild orchids in the rainforest.

Exploring El Parque Nacional Volcán Barú ★

As the name states, this national park is centered around the 3,475m (11,500-ft.) extinct **Barú Volcano,** the highest point in the country and the beloved center of adventurous outdoor pursuits for bird-watchers, hikers, rafters, and nature lovers. This rainforest provides a home to nearly 250 species of birds, the most notable of which is the **resplendent quetzal,** whose extraordinary beauty puts the bird in the number-one spot on many a bird-watching list. It's a wonderful place to hike and immerse yourself in wild beauty, but come prepared with waterproof outerwear and shoes and a dry change of clothes just in case. In this national park, temperatures average 50° to 60°F (10°–16°C).

Volcán Barú National Park is administered by ANAM, which has ranger stations at the Los Quetzales trail heads in both Boquete (Alto Chiquero) and Cerro Punta (El Respingo), and charges a $5 (£2.50) per-person entrance fee. Both ranger stations have a handful of truly rustic bunks with shared bathrooms, which cost $5 (£2.50) per bed. There's not much ambience at the Boquete station to encourage even the hardiest of nature lovers to lodge there, however. A taxi to the ranger station, about 8km (5 miles) from Boquete, costs $3 (£1.50).

HIKING By any measure, the most popular trail is **Sendero Los Quetzales (The Quetzales Trail) ★★**, a superb, short-haul day hike—regarded as the best in Panama by most visitors to the country. The rainforest here is thick, lush, and dazzling with its array of colorful birds, panoramic lookout points, and crystalline streams rushing across velvety moss-covered rocks. Most important, and most unique, is the fact that the trail connects Cerro Punta (and Guadalupe) with Boquete, allowing hikers to have their baggage sent from one town to the other, and to arrive by foot at their next destination. If you're physically up to it, I recommend the entire trek as one of the region's highlights; otherwise, a shorter hike should do.

The Quetzales Trail from Boquete begins with a 45-minute walk from the ranger station on a semipaved road. After the sign for the trail head, the trail continues for about 2 hours before heading up into a steep ascent. Midway up the ascent is a picnic area with tables. Farther up, about halfway along the trail, is a sweeping lookout point, with a roofed eating area and a couple of campsites.

From the Cerro Punta ranger station, a rutted road requiring a 4WD heads downhill for almost 3km (2 miles) until it reaches the paved road to Cerro Punta. Tour operators and taxis with 4WD traction can make it up and down this road, but few seem willing—so prepare yourself to walk this portion. The total number of trail miles is anyone's guess, as park signs, rangers, and tour guides all disagree on the distance; it's estimated that the trail is about 9.7km (6 miles). From station to station, plan on 6 to 7 hours if walking uphill, and 4½ hours if walking downhill, plus another 45 minutes to 1 hour for the last leg of the Cerro Punta ranger station to the road.

Serious adventurers might be interested in the trail to the **volcano's summit,** a very arduous climb that puts visitors at the highest point in Panama and offers electrifying views from the Caribbean Sea to the Pacific Ocean. Although this trail can be reached from the Cerro Punta side, the trail from the Boquete side is far easier and better marked. You don't want to get lost on the volcano and spend the night freezing in the wet rainforest. This is but one of the serious considerations you must make when attempting to summit the volcano. The trail, an old service road, is ragged and rough, and even the most agile hikers often slip and fall on the slick downhill trip. Second, the trail is confusing in some areas, so it's highly recommended that you hire a guide. Lastly, the peak is shrouded in thick clouds with such frequency that the chances of seeing the view are not particularly good; but even on good-weather days you'll want to begin the hike at the crack of dawn to increase your chances of clear skies. The trail takes between 5 and 6 hours to climb, and about 4 to 5 hours to descend.

Or, you can call Will Holiday at ✆ **6613-5444** (wh@pocketmail.com), an American bush pilot and adventurer, and have him drive you to the top of the summit in his sturdy 4WD. The trail is so steep and treacherous at times that Will must use a winch to pull his jeep up.

River Rafting & Kayaking

Tours run by **Chiriquí River Rafting,** on Avenida Central (✆ **720-1505** or 6618-0846; www.panama-rafting.com), cost between $85 and $150 (£43–£75), and require a minimum of four guests (a few trips require only three guests); trips include all gear, transportation, and lunch. Note that Chiriquí River Rafting offers accommodations at **El Bajareque Lodge,** a hostel-like spot with dynamite views, simple bunks, and communal meals.

Panama Rafters (✆ **720-2712;** www.panamarafters.com), with offices next to Java Juice on Avenida Central, offers beginning and intermediate kayaking instruction. Rafting trips cost an average of $75 (£38) for a half-day trip, $90 (£45) for a full-day trip—which includes transportation, gear, and lunch. Check out their website or contact them for multiple-day rafting packages with outdoors camping.

Other Outdoor Activities in the Area

BIKING For bike rental, check out Panama Rafters on Avenida Central (see above) or Boquete Tree Trek (see "Canopy Tours," below). The cost to rent is $3 (£1.50) per hour. A half-day bike tour around Boquete is also now being offered by **Aventurist** (✆ **720-1635;** www.aventurist.com).

CANOPY TOURS Canopy tours, the adventure fad of zipping through the treetops suspended by a harness attached to a cable, are available through **Boquete Tree Trek** at Avenida Central (✆ **720-1635;** www.canopypanama.com).

HOT SPRINGS The **Caldera Hot Springs** comprises four undeveloped pools in natural surroundings, with mineral water in varying temperature grades. It's worth a stop if you're a huge fan of hot springs, are already in the area, or are looking for a pretty low-key activity. To get here, you'll need to be part of a tour, or have a 4WD (you might make it in a regular car, but just barely). Head south from Boquete, and 11km (7 miles) later, turn left at the sign for Caldera; once you arrive in Caldera keep driving until you see a sign for the hot springs. Follow a rather brutal dirt road to the end and then walk about 10 minutes to the hot springs.

HORSEBACK RIDING **Eduardo Caño** (✆ **720-1750** or 6629-0814), a local guide from Boquete, is the man to go to for horseback riding tours of 2 to 5 hours, loping along trails on the outskirts of Boquete in areas such as Volcancito and Jaramillo. The views of Boquete and the surrounding area are simply splendid, but Eduardo speaks limited English, so unless you know Spanish, you'll need your hotel to call and make arrangements. Sample prices for two are $40 (£20) for 2 hours, $60 (£30) for 3 hours. Also, contact **Ecocircuitos** (see "Hiking & Bird-Watching Outfitters/Guides," above) for horseback

Spanish-Language Classes in Boquete

Habla Ya Language Center, on Avenida Central above the Global Bank (✆ **720-1294;** www.hablayapanama.com), offers intensive "survival" Spanish courses, as well as more advanced conversational and fluency courses. Beginner survival courses are ideal for the traveling monolinguals with little time in Boquete but who'd love to speak enough to get around. Weekly group classes cost $46 (£23) for 5 hours, $170 (£85) for 20 hours; weekly private courses cost $75 (£38) for 5 hours and $260 (£140) for 20 hours. If you plan to spend a lot of time in Boquete, note that the institute offers dance classes and other activities.

riding or to hire an English-speaking nature guide to accompany you and Eduardo on your ride.

Coffee Tours

Café Ruiz ★★ offers an ideal tour for those interested in seeing large-scale coffee production as opposed to a boutique operation. Tours, led by a jovial and bilingual Ngöbe-Buglé Indian guide, are offered Monday through Saturday from 9am to noon, or from 1 to 4pm; the cost is $14 (£7) per person. Alternatively, you can visit the roasting facility for a 1-hour informational session and cupping. Café Ruiz, by the way, sells to Peet's Coffee.

Café Kotowa ★★ (✆ **720-4060;** www.kotowacoffee.com) is a boutique coffee farm founded nearly a century ago by a Scottish immigrant, and it's still run by the same family. The tour is led by Hans, of **Coffee Adventures** (✆ **720-3852;** www.coffeeadventures.net), who pioneered coffee tours in Boquete, and who is animated and amusing. Tours are Monday to Saturday at 9am and cost $20 (£10) per person, which includes transportation from Boquete to their farm in Palo Alto. Children must be 10 or older, unless they're part of a private tour. Private tours cost $30 (£15) per person but can be scheduled at any time, including Sundays.

Finca Lérida ★★★ (✆ **720-2285;** www.fincalerida.com; open daily sunrise–sunset) is a lovely 324-hectare (800-acre) coffee plantation and nature reserve located 10 minutes from Boquete in the lofty alpine setting of Alto Quiel. The *finca* is widely regarded as one of the most important bird-watching sites in Panama, not only because of the sheer numbers of species on view here but because it is a hot spot for seeing the resplendent quetzal, among other rare birds. You can book a 2-hour coffee tour for $25 (£13) per person, and take to the trails following the tour. For the complete (and somewhat pricey) package, a full-day tour includes a guide, bird-watching, coffee tour, gourmet lunch, transportation to and from Boquete, and access to trails for $310 (£155) for two guests.

Attractions in & Around Town

Mi Jardín es Su Jardín ★★, or "My Garden Is Your Garden," refers to the lavish private gardens of the González family, who live on the property but have opened their grounds to the public. These gardens are some of the most exquisite in Panama, with hundreds of varieties of flowers expertly tended and cared for. To get here, head up the main street past the church, and stay left at the fork and continue until you see the gardens on your right-hand side.

One of the more curious attractions in Boquete is **El Explorador** gardens (**© 720-1989**), which provide visitors with splendid panoramic views enhanced by classical background music. But what's really the attraction here are the eccentric gardens sprinkled with vernacular, artlike recycled items: old television sets, a sewing machine, boots used as planters, shopping carts, old bottles, and more. There is a cafe here with snacks, fresh fruit juices, and coffee. El Explorador costs $1 (50p) per person, and is open daily from 9am to 6pm. To get here, stay right at the fork on the main road and follow the signs.

SHOPPING

Coffee is the local product you won't want to leave Boquete without, and bagged beans are sold all around town in cafes and grocery stores. **Café Kotowa** (**© 720-4060**), at the visitor center just before town, sells top-rated blends and souvenir and gift packs. No stores in the Tocumen International airport sell coffee, so don't put off until the last minute buying a few bags of Panama's best. The **Harmony Gift Shop** on Avenida Central, in front of the Boquete Country Inn, has arts and crafts, jewelry, and other gift items for sale. **Souvenir El Cacique,** on Avenida Central at the plaza, has indigenous handicrafts made by the Ngöbe-Buglé, Kuna, and Emberá indigenous groups, plus handicrafts from indigenous groups around Central America.

WHERE TO STAY

Travelers can opt to stay in town and be close to services and restaurants, or outside of the town center in a more forested setting. It's a good idea to book ahead of time in Boquete. Besides the places listed below, **Los Establos** (**© 720-2685;** Jaramillo Arriba), which has doubles from $120 to $150 (£60–£75) and suites from $200 to $250 (£100–£125), and the historic **Panamonte Inn and Spa** (**© 720-1327;** www.panamonteinnandspa.com), which has doubles for $60 (£30) and cabins for $150 (£75), also offer excellent, high-end accommodations.

For budget options, check out **Hotel Oasis** (**© 720-1586**), with doubles from $45 to $55 (£23–£28) or **Hotel Petit Mozart** (**© 720-3764**), with doubles from $30 to $40 (£15–£20). You'll need a taxi from both to get into town.

Finca Lerida (**© 720-2285;** www.fincalerida.com) also recently opened its B&B, a charming, renovated farmhouse, and can rent out the entire house or individual rooms.

Very Expensive

Palo Alto Riverside Hotel ★★ Opened in 2006, this boutique hotel is sophisticated and gives discriminating travelers the highest level of accommodations available in Boquete. Each room's design is slightly different from the next, both in shape and adornment, but the standard decor consists of exposed wooden beams, stark walls, Indonesian teak furniture, arching windows, and luxurious bathrooms. The Getzemani suite and Bonsai junior suite have a balcony and a panoramic view; the Guayacan junior suite has a bedroom plus a loftlike sleeping area with additional beds. All rooms have king-size beds with Egyptian cotton sheets. There are plenty of common areas in which to sit and read or chat—my favorite is the glass-enclosed balcony, with cozy chairs and a large-screen TV, which looks out into the forested greenery.

Palo Alto. **© 720-1076.** www.paloaltoriverside.com. 6 units. $165 (£83) double; $225 (£113) suite. AE, MC, V. **Amenities:** Restaurant; bar; laundry service; sauna; Wi-Fi. *In room:* A/C, TV, DVD player, minibar, whirlpool tubs.

Expensive

The Coffee Estate Inn ★★★ Finds Cozy yet spacious accommodations with all the trimmings, gorgeous views of Volcán Barú, and truly personalized service are the hallmarks of the Coffee Estate Inn, which is 2.5km (1½ miles) from downtown Boquete, on a very steep slope overlooking the lush valley below. Three contemporary and cheery cabins contain a bedroom for two to three guests, a living area, a fully stocked kitchen, and an outdoor terrace. I particularly like the "Jewel" cabin for its secluded, romantic location and for its stunning views of the volcano.

The owners grow and roast their own coffee; guests of 2 nights or more receive a free tour of the property to learn about coffee production and native flora. Note that children must be at least 9 years old to stay here.

Jaramillo Arriba. ✆ **720-2211.** www.coffeeestateinn.com. 5 units. $110 (£55) double; $30 (£15) for an additional guest. MC, V. **Amenities:** Restaurant; cooking classes; Wi-Fi in lobby. *In room:* TV (in 2 cabins only), dehumidifier, hair dryer, fully stocked kitchen.

Moderate

Isla Verde Hotel ★★ Kids This is an excellent choice for travelers who seek a peaceful setting and leafy surroundings, but within walking distance of town. Half the cabins are for four guests, and half are quite spacious with a capacity for up to six guests (though they're ideal for a group of just four). There is a queen-size bed on the ground floor (but not separate from the living area), and a loft with a double bed; the additional "beds" for the six-person units are two fold-out futon chairs, which look uncomfortable even for young kids. Brand-new at the Isla Verde are four contemporary and fetching suites for couples, each with a terrific outdoor patio that offers forest views, especially from the second-floor units, which are more expensive. The suites have a bedroom and independent living area, and kitchenettes; the cabins have full kitchens. European travelers make up the bulk of guests here, which is apropos because the decor is simple and decidedly European, especially their open-air geodesic dome eating area; there is also an on-site New Age spa.

Calle 5a Sur and Av. B Oeste. ✆ **720-2533** or 6677-4009. www.islaverdehotel.com. 8 units. Prices based on double occupancy: $80 (£40) small roundhouse; $100 (£50) big roundhouse; $60–$90 (£30–£45) suite. Children 4 and under free in parent's room; children 5–18 $5 (£2.50); extra adult $10 (£5). MC, V. **Amenities:** Bar; Internet service; laundry service; limited spa services (massage and facials). *In room:* TV (some rooms), kitchenette, no phone.

Villa Marita ★ Perched high on a plateau above a twisting road 3.5km (2 miles) from town, this hotel is strong in panoramic views of Volcán Barú and the river valley below. It's too far to walk to town, so if you don't mind taking a taxi or driving, the reasonably priced cabins here are an attractive lodging option. There are six mustard-colored cabins, for up to four guests (one bedroom and a sofa bed), which are outfitted with hardwood furnishings and a country decor (and a refrigerator). French doors open onto a patio with the dynamite view. There are also three newer and comfortable hotel rooms in the main building, which is a converted home with a lived-in and homey ambience. Families might be interested in their "Big House" unit that sleeps six to eight guests and has a huge kitchen, but no view. There is a grill and deck for your own outdoor barbecue. The friendly, knowledgeable host and his wife will gladly serve you a home-cooked meal with ingredients from their on-site organic greenhouse.

Alto Lino. ✆ **720-2165.** www.villamarita.com. 10 units. $40 (£20) double hotel room; $60 (£30) cabin; $110 (£35) family house. AE, MC, V. **Amenities:** Restaurant; outdoor grill; Wi-Fi. *In room:* TV, fridge (except in hotel rooms), no phone.

Central Panama in Brief

For the most part, Central Panama is not yet on the radar for most foreign travelers. However, there are a few destinations here worth mentioning. The easiest way to get to and around Central Panama is by renting a car, but if you don't wish to rent a car, **Pasantez Tours** (✆ **263-8771** or 223-5374; www.pesantez-tours.com) offers rides to all the Pacific beaches as well as the Valle de Anton, or you can hire a taxi to Valle de Anton or the Pacific beaches. (This will cost you $60–$180/£30–£90 round-trip depending on where you are going.)

The Pacific beaches are popular with Panama City dwellers looking for a bit of weekend relaxation. These are definitely not the most attractive beaches in Panama, though, and are really only worth a visit if your travels to Panama won't take you to any of the better beaches or you're part of an all-inclusive resort package. The **Intercontinental Playa Bonita Resort and Spa** (Playa Kobbe, Punta Bruja; ✆ **211-8600,** or 800/424-6835 in the U.S.; www.ichotelsgroup.com), just a half-hour away, is the closest beach resort from Panama City. The **Corondado Gulf and Beach Resort** (Av. Punta Prieta, Coronado; ✆ **264-3164** or 240-4444; www.coronadoresort.com) on Playa Coronado is the oldest resort on the Pacific, and a longtime favorite with golfers. **Playa Blanca Resort** (✆ **264-6444;** www.playablancaresort.com) and the gargantuan **Royal Decameron Beach Resort, Golf, Spa & Casino** (Playa Blanca; ✆ **206-5324;** www.decameron.com) offer all-inclusive packages if you wish to stay on Playa Blanca, about a 2-hour drive from Panama City.

The Valle de Anton, a picturesque mountain village 2 hours from Panama City, is also popular with wealthy Panamanians because of its cooler weather. El Valle, as it is popularly known, offers a number of canopy, hiking, and bird-watching activities, and is definitely worth a stop if you don't have a chance to

WHERE TO DINE

Given that many of Boquete's residents are retired folks who tend to dine in or not stay out too late, the restaurants mentioned below can unexpectedly close early or for the night during the low season, from May to November.

Worth a stop is the locally famous **Fresas Mary** (✆ **720-3394;** daily 9:30am–7pm), which you'll find on the left side of the road to Volcancito, reached by turning onto the road opposite the CEFATI visitor center. The specialties here are *batidos,* or fresh fruit drinks, made with strawberries and local fruits such as *guanábana* (soursop); they also make fresh yogurt and frozen fruit sherbet. Sandwiches and hamburgers go for $1.50 (75p). Another spot popular with locals is the German-style bakery and pastry shop **Café Alemana,** south past the CEFATI building (no phone; Thurs–Mon 11am–8pm), which serves delicious apple and pineapple pies, and other sweets.

The **Deli Barú** (✆ **720-2619;** Tues–Sun 9am–8pm) is a gourmet deli with sandwiches, soups, and salads, and a market with an excellent selection of cheeses, cold cuts, wine, fresh bread, and specialty goodies. For fresh fruit juices and cheap sandwiches in town, try **Java Juice** on Avenida Central, next to Panama Rafters (✆ **720-2502;** daily visit Boquete or the Chiriquí highlands. The best hotels here are **Los Mandarinos** (Calle El Ciclo; ✆ **983-6645;** www.losmandarinos.com), **The Park Eden Bed and Breakfast** (Calle Espavé; ✆ **983-6167** or 6695-6190; www.parkeden.com), and the **Anton Valley Hotel** (Av. Principal; ✆ **983-6097**), which is good for more budget-oriented travelers. Most hotels will be happy to book or provide information about adventure opportunities.

Lastly, the Peninsula de Azuero is Panama's most traditional province and home to a number of picturesque colonial-style towns, the most notable being Pedasi, a quiet place where life hasn't changed much in the last hundred years. The Azuero peninsula is famous for its beautiful and ornate Carnaval processions, subsequently making these pre-Lent festivities the most popular and expensive time to visit the Azuero peninsula. I recommend renting a car if you decide to visit the Azuero peninsula, as most attractions are spread out from each other, and bus service is sporadic at best. The best hotels here are **Los Guayacanes** (✆ **996-9758;** www.losguayacanes.com) in Chitre, the capital of the Azuero peninsula; **Hotel la Villa** (✆ **966-8201**) in La Villa de los Santos; and the basic but comfortable **Dim's Hostal** (✆ **995-2303;** mirely@iname.com) in charming Pedasi.

If you are looking for something a bit more luxurious, head to the coast and check out **Posada los Destiladores** (Los Destiladores; ✆ **6675-9715**); **Villa Camilla** (Los Destiladores; ✆ **232-6721**) on Playa los Destiladores; or **Villa Marina** (Playa Venado; ✆ **211-2277;** www.playavenado.com) on Playa Venado, all of which are consistently rated among the best small resort hotels in Panama.

10am–10pm). A mango smoothie and hamburger here cost less than $2 (£1). **Café Punto de Encuentro** (✆ **720-2123;** daily 7am–noon), on Calle 6A S, near Avenida Belisario Porras, and often referred to as "Olga's Place," is *the* spot for breakfast; omelets, fruit pancakes, and fresh coffee can all be savored on their pleasant outdoor patio.

If you're in town on a Sunday, do not miss **Yalty's** at the Boquete Country Inn, on Avenida Central (✆ **720-2470**). Yalty makes the best ribs in town—probably in the entire Chiriquí Province—and every Sunday she hosts an all-you-can-eat night from 6 to 10pm for $17 (£8.50) per person. (She donates $1/50p per person to a needy-children's fund.) Apart from her tasty ribs, she serves pasta, fish, and salads, and often puts on folkloric dance performances. Yalty's is BYOB. Call during the low season (mid-Apr to Nov) to verify that her Sunday nights are happening. **Machu Picchu** ★★ (✆ **264-9308;** Av. Belisario Porras) is considered one of the best restaurants in town. Try the sea bass with black butter and capers or the creamy jumbo prawns. The **Palo Alto Restaurante** ★★ (✆ **720-1076;** road to Palo Alto) is a refined, Mediterranean-style eatery where you can dine on juicy rib-eye or New York steak.

The **Panamonte Inn Restaurant** ★★★ (✆ **720-1324;** Av. Central) is hands-down the best restaurant in Boquete. Try the wild-mushroom polenta, pork chops with onion ragout, and veal stock wine sauce or seafood stew.

For cheaper dining options, head to **La Casona Mexicana** (✆ **720-1274;** Av. Central) at the edge of town. There are hearty burritos, fajitas, and chimichangas here. **Sabroson** (✆ **720-2147;** Av. Central near the church) is as typical as it gets in Boquete. The cafeteria-style restaurant is far from fancy, but the food is filling and tasty.

BOQUETE AFTER DARK

Most Boquete residents are tucked into bed by 11pm, but there are a couple of places for a nightcap or a night out. **Zanzíbar,** on Avenida Central on the right side past the church (no phone), is a bar attractively decorated with African odds and ends. It's a cozy place for a cocktail. **Las Cabanas** (no phone) is the newest bar/club in town, and can be reached by taking the road to the Coffee Estate Inn and bearing right instead of turning left. This place doesn't usually get started until Zanzibar closes down.

7 BOCAS DEL TORO ARCHIPELAGO ★

The Bocas del Toro Archipelago is a scattering of seven islands and more than 200 islets off the northwestern coast of Panama, near the border with Costa Rica. The region has all the trappings of a Caribbean fantasy: dreamy beaches, thatched-roofed huts, aquamarine sea, thick rainforest, and soft ocean breeze. Add to that a funky, carefree ambience and a large English-speaking population, and it's easy to see why Bocas del Toro is quickly emerging as an ecotourism hot spot faster than any other part of Panama.

The principal island in the region is Isla Colón, 62 sq. km (24 sq. miles) and home to **Bocas Town,** the regional capital and the center of activity in the archipelago.

Bocas can hold its own against nearby Costa Rica when it comes to adventure travel in the Caribbean. The diving and snorkeling are outstanding in this region—Bocas is home to some of the best-preserved hard and soft coral on the planet—but make sure your tour operator is willing to take you to the finest examples instead of bleached-out coral in "typical" tourist spots. Your options include sailing tours, boat tours to deserted islands and visits to Indian communities, hiking through luxuriant rainforest in Isla Bastimentos Park, and riding waves in what is largely considered the surfing epicenter of the southwest Caribbean.

Historically there has always been a rough, end-of-the-line feel to Bocas del Toro, which is perceptible even today. But underneath this are the rumblings of an upcoming boom in tourism, with multimillion-dollar hotels, gated residential communities, and waterfront condominiums either in the works or already breaking ground. Still, the laid-back friendliness that characterizes Bocas del Toro endures.

ISLA COLÓN: BOCAS TOWN ★

30 min. by boat from Almirante; 1 hr. by boat from Changuinola; 1 hr. by plane from Panama City

Essentials

Getting There

There are two ways to get to Bocas del Toro: via a land/sea combination, or by air. Considering the cheap price of air travel in Panama and the short flight (1 hr. from Panama City), most travelers opt to fly. If crossing into Bocas del Toro from Costa Rica by land, travelers

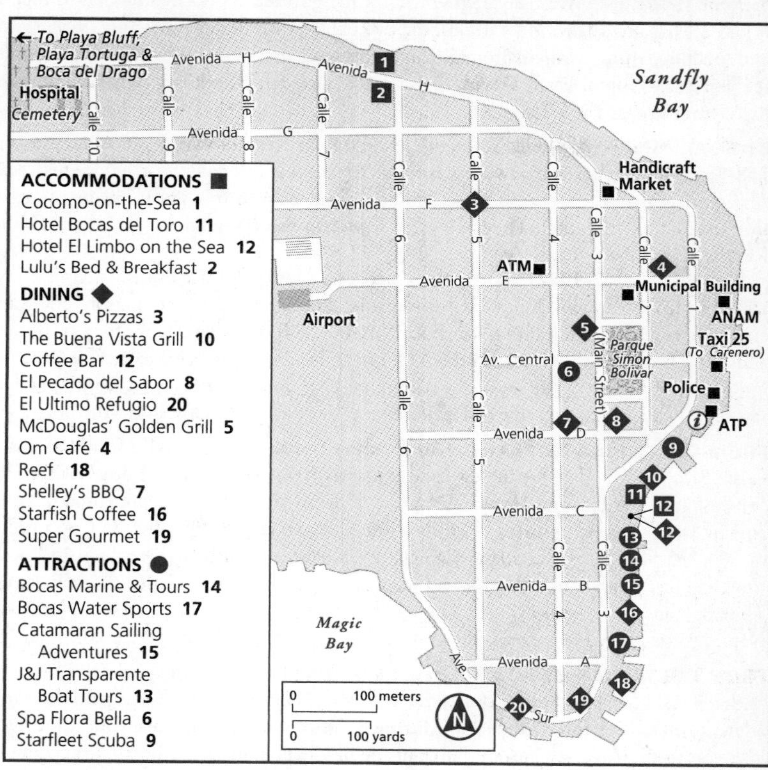

head to Changuinola, where they can grab a boat shuttle to Bocas (1 hr.) or hop over on a small plane from Changuinola (10 min.). ***Tip:*** If traveling from Costa Rica, remember that Costa Rica is **1 hour ahead** of Panama. The route between Changuinola or Almirante is one of the most beautiful in Panama, so if the thought of a large bus speeding through the mountains doesn't scare you, the hours-long bus ride is well worth it.

BY PLANE The basic but spruce **Bocas International Airport** (**BOC; ✆ 757-9208**) is serviced by daily flights from Panama City, David, Changuinola, and Costa Rica.

Air Panama (**✆ 315-0439;** www.flyairpanama.com) has service to Bocas del Toro from Panama City, David, and San José, Costa Rica (for Costa Rica flights, see "From Costa Rica by Plane," below). From Panama City, there are two or three daily flights leaving at 6:45am (Mon–Sat); 8am (Sun); 7:15am (Mon, Wed, Fri); and 3:15pm (daily). Return flights from Bocas to Panama City leave at 8am (Mon–Sat); 9:15am (Sun); 1:45pm (Mon, Wed, Fri); and 4:30pm (daily). From David, there is one flight on Mondays, Wednesdays, and Fridays only, leaving at 1pm; the flight from Bocas to David leaves at 8:35am. **Aeroperlas** (**✆ 315-7500;** www.aeroperlas.com) offers two daily flights from **Panama City** to Bocas, weekdays at 6:25am and 3pm; Saturdays at 8:05am and 3:05pm; and Sundays at 6:30am and 3:05pm. The return trip to Panama City leaves weekdays 10:30am and 5pm; Saturday 10:15am and 5:15pm; and Sunday at 8:40am and 5:15pm. There are three daily flights from **Changuinola** to Bocas, Monday through Friday at 8:05am, 10am, and 4:40pm; the two daily return flights leave Bocas at 7:50am and 4:20pm; Saturday flights from Changuinola are at 9:50am and 4:50pm; Sundays at 8:15am and 4:50pm. From **David,** flights leave once daily, weekdays only, at 9am; the flight from Bocas is at 8:25am.

BY BOAT **Bocas Marine & Tours** (✆ **757-9033** in Bocas, 758-4085 in Almirante, or 758-9859 in Changuinola; www.bocasmarinetours.com) has daily boat service between Almirante and Bocas every 30 to 40 minutes, from 6am to 6:30pm (6:30am–6:30pm from Bocas to Almirante). They also offer service from Changuinola (see "From Costa Rica by Road," below).

Taxi 25 (✆ **757-9028**) also operates between Almirante and Bocas, leaving every half-hour from 6am to 6:30pm. Both companies charge $3 (£1.50) per person, one-way, and leave from the Almirante dock; Bocas Marine & Tours is on Main Street in Bocas, and Taxi 25 can be found next to the ATP office. If you have a vehicle, there is parking for $3 (£1.50) a day at the lot at the Almirante boat dock. To get to the Almirante bus station for the 4-hour bus ride to David, take a $1 (50p) taxi that waits at the port.

FROM COSTA RICA BY PLANE **Air Panama** (see above) has service from San José, Costa Rica, on Monday, Wednesday, and Friday at 10am; service from Bocas del Toro to San José leaves at 8:35am. **Nature Air,** a Costa Rican airline that is represented in Panama by **Bocas Air Adventures** (✆ **656-0460** in Panama, 506/299-6000 in Costa Rica, or 800/235-9272 in the U.S. and Canada; www.natureair.com) has one flight to Bocas from San José (with connections from Quepos, Liberia, and Puerto Jiménez) on Tuesday, Thursday, and Saturday, leaving at 8am and returning from Bocas at 10:30am. Note that Nature Air is known to increase prices during the high season (Dec 1–Apr 20).

FROM COSTA RICA BY ROAD Travelers entering Panama from Costa Rica by road at the Sixaola-Guabito border can take a taxi (about $15/£7.50) to **Changuinola,** then a boat to Bocas del Toro with **Bocas Marine & Tours** (see above). Have your taxi driver take you to the dock at Finca 60, just outside of Changuinola. The boat journey passes through the San San Pond Sak wetlands and an old banana plantation canal, and is so scenic it could be considered a low-price tour. From Changuinola, boats leave daily at 8am, 9:30am, 11am, 12:30pm, 2pm, 3:30pm, and 5pm. From Bocas Town to Changuinola, boats leave at 7am, 8am, 9:30am, 11am, 12:30pm, 2pm, 3:30pm, and 4:30pm. The cost is $5 (£2.50) per person one-way. ***Note:*** Owing to the increase in fuel cost, Bocas Marine & Tours operates with a minimum of six passengers; this means that when business is slow they might not leave promptly on schedule.

Orientation

Bocas is the only town on Isla Colón, centered around a bustling Main Street (Calle 3) and Simon Bolívar Plaza. There are fewer than two dozen streets in Bocas, and most are unpaved. The airport is just a couple of blocks away from the main plaza, meaning you could walk to your hotel if you felt like it. Calles 1 through 10 run west-east and avenidas A to H run north-south. There is no "downtown," but most hotels and restaurants are concentrated on the south end where Calle 1 meets Main Street. Internet cafes and shops are along Main Street between avenidas E and D.

Getting Around

Everything in Bocas Town is within walking distance, but collective taxis are plentiful if you need one. Most hotels arrange pickup and drop-off for guests arriving by air, but there are also taxis waiting for every arrival at the airport. If arriving by boat, find out where your hotel is in relation to the dock—you may already be close enough to walk. Taxis cost between 50¢ and $1 (25p–50p). There are two principal roads on the island: One runs along the coast and ends at Playa Bluff; the other crosses the island to Boca del Drago.

There are **bicycle** rentals on Main Street across from the plaza; all charge $1 (50p) an hour, or $5 to $8 (£2.50–£4) a day. Informal **water taxis** are available at the dock next to the ATP office, with service to neighboring Isla Carenero ($1/50p one-way) and Isla Bastimentos ($7/£3.50 one-way to Red Frog Beach). Hours are irregular, with service generally running from 7am to 9pm. Most people visit Isla Bastimentos as part of a day tour; resorts on that island include round-trip transportation in the price and an extra charge for additional trips.

For beaches outside of Bocas Town, see "What to See & Do," below.

Visitor Information

There is an **ATP visitor center** (✆ **757-9642;** Mon–Fri 8:30am–4:30pm) in a barn-size yellow building on the waterfront at Calle 1, near the police station. It appears that ATP blew its budget on this sparkling new office, because English-speaking, trained information officers, maps, and brochures are all in short supply. Around lunchtime, you'll be lucky to find anyone staffing the desk, though on the second floor you'll find a display on the natural history of Bocas, and there are public bathrooms here, too. For additional information about Bocas, try the Web portal **www.bocas.com**, which has links to hotels, tourism services, transportation information, and more.

FAST FACTS There is a 24-hour ATM at **Banco Nacional de Panama,** at the corner of Calle 4 and Avenida Principal, and an ATM in the Expreso Taxi 25 building, but bring extra cash in case both are down, which can happen, especially during high season.

You'll find FedEx and DHL services at Bravo Center on Main Street between avenidas 2 and 3 (✆ **757-9229;** bravocenter@bocasmail.com).

For an ambulance, call ✆ **757-9814;** for fire, dial ✆ **103;** for police, dial ✆ **104** or 757-9217. There is a basic **hospital clinic** in Bocas, at Calle 10 and Avenida G (✆ **757-9201**), with a 24-hour emergency room. However, service is limited and those with more serious health problems will need to seek medical care in Panama City.

Bravo Center on Main Street has Wi-Fi service (daily 10am–7pm) or try **Internet Bocas Café** (daily 8am–10pm) and **Don Chicho's** (daily 8am–9pm), both on Main Street. All cybercafés charge around $2 (£1) per hour.

There are coin-operated machines and drop-off laundry services including pickup and delivery at **Bubbles** on Avenida C at Main Street (✆ **6591-3814;** Mon–Sat 8am–6pm).

The post office is at Calle A and Avenida 2. It's run by a no-nonsense woman who maintains hours Monday through Friday from 8am to noon and 2 to 4pm (some days 3–4pm and Sat 8am–noon).

What to See & Do

Despite its location in the warm, cerulean Caribbean Sea, Bocas offers poor swimming conditions because of strong riptides. The closest decent beach to Bocas Town (Bluff Beach) is an 8km (5-mile) bike or taxi ride away, and the beaches on Isla Bastimentos can only be reached by boat, followed by a short to medium-long walk. During the calm-water months (early Sept to early Nov), it's possible to arrive directly by boat at the beaches of Isla Bastimentos.

If you don't have an all-inclusive package with your hotel, or if your hotel simply does not offer trips, there are plenty of tour agencies to fulfill your excursion needs. Bocas is a good base for exploring the archipelago—nearly every kind of excursion and destination can be reached from here, including spots for watersports and cultural visits. Trips to Isla Bastimentos and the Zapatilla Cays are better, with fast boats that offer flexible itineraries. If you have a group or can afford a private-boat rental, do so because it offers you the freedom to plan your own itinerary.

Beaches & Other Natural Attractions

BOCA DEL DRAGO BEACH & SWAN'S CAY ★★ Boca del Drago is the best beach on Isla Colón for swimming, and when the sea is calm, visitors can snorkel from the shore here. Though often there isn't much beach to speak of—just a couple of feet or so for throwing down a towel or beach chair—it's still a lovely spot. The beach is on the north shore of Isla Colón. Tour companies include Boca del Drago as part of their standard day tour, including a visit to nearby **Swan's Cay,** a picturesque rocky outcrop and bird sanctuary that attracts nesting boobies, frigates, and the magnificent red-billed tropic bird. You can also get to Boca del Drago from Bocas Town by road in a taxi, which costs $25 (£13) round-trip and takes 30 minutes. There is an excellent restaurant here called **Restaurant Yasinori** that also rents snorkel gear, but I recommend renting gear in Bocas and taking it with you.

BLUFF BEACH ★ This gorgeous, golden-sand beach would be perfect if it weren't for a light sprinkling of trash. It's still the prettiest beach close to town for catching some rays—but don't plan on getting more than your feet wet here because the ocean is fraught with riptides. The beach is about 8km (5 miles) from the city center and can be reached by taxi for $10 (£5) one-way. Some drivers are willing to hang around if you plan on staying an hour or two; if not, you'll need to arrange for pickup later. In this case, negotiate to pay when the driver returns (to make sure that he comes back). You can also rent a bicycle and pedal there, which is quite a pleasant ride if you're up to it. Rain can wreak havoc on the road, so be prepared for lots of puddles.

SAN SAN POND SAK WETLANDS ★★★ The San San Pond Sak Wetlands, covering nearly 16,187 hectares (40,000 acres), are on the coast about 4.8km (3 miles) north of Changuinola. The wetlands are home to sloths, white-faced capuchin monkeys, and caimans, but more importantly, San San is the natural habitat of the manatee, an aquatic, elephant-like mammal that weighs between 363 and 544 kilograms (800–1,200 lb.). Previously it was difficult to visit San San, but **Starfleet Scuba** (see "Scuba Diving & Snorkeling," below) now offers a full-day excursion (7am–5pm) that provides for an out-of-the-ordinary experience. Because there is so little human traffic in this region, your chances of spotting a manatee are very good, but please note that manatees are protected animals. Do not chase, pet, or harass these magnificent creatures—and report anyone who does. The Starfleet tour takes visitors to the coast, where they are transported by minibus to the put-in site for the *cayuco* (dugout canoe) to paddle quietly through the wetlands. There is also an easy nature trail for getting out and stretching your legs. The cost includes a full lunch, park entrance fees, guides, and transportation; contact Starfleet for prices.

Fun in the Water

SCUBA DIVING & SNORKELING Scuba diving and snorkeling are among the most popular activities in Bocas del Toro, owing to well-preserved displays of hard and soft coral, mangrove swamps, volcanic-rock walls, and underwater caves. You might also see colorful sponges, and there is even an underwater landing craft that was sunk to create

Isla Bastimentos

Those looking for a more exotic beach experience may want to consider visiting **Isla Bastimentos ★★★**, which is perfect for honeymooners with its dense jungles and lovely beaches—it's perhaps the best beach in Bocas del Toro, and only 30 minutes by boat from Isla Colón. Hotels here tend to offer packages including lodging, three meals a day, transportation to and from the Isla Colón airport, and some excursions. Getting such a package deal is really your best option since you will have a hard time finding food or arranging transport on your own in this remote region. Most of the tour companies listed under Bocas del Toro also offer day trips to the beaches and national parks of Isla Bastimentos, and you can find out more about these tours by visiting individual companies during your stay on Isla Colón.

One of the best hotels on the Isla is **Tranquilo Bay** (✆ **713/589-6952** in the U.S., or 380-0721 in Panama; www.tranqilobay.com), with packages starting at $995 (£498) per person for 3 nights including transportation from Panama City. This beautiful ecolodge offers modern, brightly decorated cottages with air-conditioning, and the American expat owners offer serious personal attention. Another great option if you are looking for something a little bit more rustic is **La Loma Jungle Lodge** (✆ **6619-5364;** www.thejunglelodge.com), which is set against a backdrop of pristine tropical forest. The Jungle Lodge also functions as a chocolate farm, and although the three cabins are not air-conditioned, the lack of such an amenity is part of the experience—there is no better place to feel at one with nature. Rates start at $100 (£50) a night.

an artificial reef. Recommended snorkeling and diving sites are **Crawl Cay** (or Coral Cay), with shallow waters and some of the best coral formations in the area; **Hospital Point,** just a 10-minute boat ride from Bocas and easy to reach by water taxi; **Polo Beach,** a shallow system of caves suitable for snorkelers but reachable only 6 months of the year; **Swan's Cay,** with interesting rock formations created by battering waves and also a migratory-bird site; and **Cayos Zapatillas,** two delicate islands with white-sand beaches surrounded by an extensive reef system that attracts lots of tropical fish. Cayos Zapatillas, it should be noted, has currents and is for strong swimmers only.

Divers also head to **Buoy Line** near Isla Solarte, which is a deepwater channel where pelagic and larger marine species can be seen; the same is true of **Tiger Rock,** an offshore site and rocky outcrop whose long distance from Bocas Town keeps the crowds away. Adventurous divers and snorkelers really looking to get away from other travelers might consider visiting **Isla Escudo de Veraguas,** which is a full-day trip and a fairly large undertaking (available usually only Sept–Oct). The beaches here are generally considered to be the loveliest in the entire region.

The principal shortcoming of Bocas del Toro as a diving and snorkeling destination is the **unpredictability of the weather,** with spontaneous downpours and wind gusts that can churn up the sea and cloud visibility. If the focus of your trip is diving and snorkeling, come from September to early November, when the sea is tranquil and flat. Other months with better visibility are March and April, but rain and wind can occur at any time during these months. Dive sites with deeper water and larger species (mostly offshore sites such as Tiger Rock) can be visited only during these more tranquil months.

Bocas Water Sports on Main Street (© **757-9541;** www.bocaswatersports.com) is the oldest operation in town, recently bought by a friendly American. Dive trips include all gear; a two-dive trip is $50 (£25) per person, a one-dive trip is $40 (£20) per person. Trips last 3 hours and must be taken before 2pm. Dives to Tiger Rock and Cayos Zapatillas are $75 (£38) per person and only available during calm months. Night dives from 6:30 to 8:30pm are $50 (£25) per person. Snorkeling tours are $17 to $20 (£8.50–£10) for a full day, not including lunch.

Starfleet Scuba, at Calle 1A (© **757-9630;** www.starfleetscuba.com), has a spotless record and a brand-new British owner who last ran diving operations in Indonesia. Starfleet has three boats plus a new, 81kmph (50-mph) inflatable Zodiac boat that gives the company the edge in terms of more quickly getting to remote destinations like Tiger Rock ($90/£45 for minimum of four people; lunch included). Two-tank dives cost $50 (£25), a one-tank dive $35 (£18); snorkeling tours are $20 (£10) per person. Starfleet works in conjunction with the U.K.-based **Ocean Pulse,** a marine-research group that offers 2-week "ecoventures" to travelers with advanced diving experience. Participants accompany marine biologists exploring new dive sites to monitor for conservation, and are treated to lectures and presentations about species and habitats throughout the day. Packages vary depending on accommodations requirements, so it's best to contact them for prices (© **0175/220-2101** in the U.K.; www.oceanpulse.co.uk).

J & J Transparente Boat Tours offers trips to all the islands, but they're garden-variety. Tours cost $17 to $22 (£8.50–£11) per person, and suffer from a get-'em-in and get-'em-out mentality. However, J & J is the company to call for charter-boat rentals, which cost $200 (£100) for a full day, not including lunch.

Catamaran Sailing Adventures at Main Street (© **757-9710** or 6625-8610; www.bocassailing.com) has a 12m (40-ft.) catamaran for laid-back and enjoyable full-day snorkeling trips to Bocas del Drago or around Isla Bastimentos for $30 (£15) per person (4-person minimum, 18 maximum), including a sack lunch. Charter rentals cost $250 (£125) a day. The catamaran has little protection from the sun, so bring sunscreen and a hat.

WATERSPORTS **Bocas Water Sports** (see above) offers water-skiing for $45 (£23) for 1 hour, gear included, using their 7.6m (25-ft.) tour boat (maximum four people). There are many mangrove-fringed canals in the area that provide for glassy water year-round. Full-day water-skiing trips can be arranged; contact the company for price information. Bocas Water Sports also rents one-person kayaks that cost $3 (£1.50) per hour, or $10 (£5) half-day. During bad-weather days, you'll only be able to navigate around mangrove swamps and the coast, but on calm days experienced kayakers can make it all the way to Hospital Point.

BOATING & SAILING For catamaran tours, see **Catamaran Sailing Adventures,** under "Scuba Diving & Snorkeling," above. **Boteros Bocatoreños** (© **757-9760;** boterosbocas@yahoo.com) is a group of local boatmen who have banded together in the face of encroaching competition—they can provide custom tours at slightly lower prices than outfitters. Most speak at least some English, and have local knowledge. Another good source for boatmen is **Ancon Expeditions** (p. 640). **Sailing Explore** has a 9.1m (30-ft.) sloop for day-sailing excursions and overnight trips to Boca del Drago, Crawl Cay, and as far as Isla Escudo de Veraguas (Sept–Oct). For overnight trips, the sailboat fits four people (it can fit up to six if you're really willing to squeeze in, or if you have kids), and costs $150 (£125) per person for 1 night and $240 (£120) per person for 2 nights, including meals, kayaks and snorkeling gear. Day excursions leave at 9am and return at 6pm, costing $30 (£15) per person (four-person minimum), which includes lunch, soft drinks, and snorkel and kayak equipment.

SURFING Bocas experiences the largest and most consistent swells from December to March, and during June and July, with reef point breaks, beach breaks, and huge, challenging waves recommended only for experienced surfers. The waves in Bocas are more suitable for shortboarding and bodyboarding; if you're bringing your own board, check with your airline about requirements because some smaller planes may not accept a long board. **Del Toro Surf** (✆ **6570-8277;** deltorosurf@yahoo.com.ar) offers surf lessons and board rentals to clients participating in lessons. **Rancho Paraíso** (✆ **757-9415;** www.ranchoparaiso.biz) offers lessons, board rentals, and multiple-day packages with transportation to various surf sites; they also offer all-inclusive packages with stays at their pleasant surf hostel located on the road to Bluff Beach. To rent a surfboard, try **Tropix** (✆ **757-9415**), on Main Street across from the plaza, or **Flow** surf shop (no phone) on Avenida H below the Om Restaurant. All offer tips and maps to the best surf spots in the area, as well as information on how to get there.

Other Activities in Bocas Town

SCIENTIFIC VISITS The **Smithsonian Tropical Research Institute** has a base in Bocas del Toro, and is open to the public every Friday from 3 to 5pm. If you're lucky, you'll be around for one of their monthly chats led by a scientist who highlights the center's work and discoveries in the region. Contact the institute at ✆ **212-8000,** or visit their site, www.stri.org, for information about upcoming lectures.

SPA If you're winding down from a day of activity (and a hammock isn't doing the trick), try **Spa Flora Bella** (✆ **6591-3814;** www.spaflorabella.com), which offers deep-tissue massages, reflexology, and hot-stone treatments, as well as an assortment of beauty services such as hair cuts and facials. The spa is located behind Bubbles Laundry at Calle 4 and Avenida Central. Several massage therapists provide in-hotel services; try **Therapueutic Body Work** at ✆ **6632-6269; Bocas Delight Massage** at ✆ **6577-9915;** or **Holistic Alternative Therapy** at ✆ **6686-0235,** which has Zen-Shiatsu massage and Thai foot massages.

Shopping

High-quality handicrafts and fashionable beachwear can be found at **Pachamana,** located on Main Street on the waterfront next to Starfish Coffee at Avenida B (Tues–Sat 9am–12:30pm and 3–6pm). **Artesanía Bri-Bri Emanuel,** at Main Street and Avenida B (Mon–Sat 10am–8pm), specializes in indigenous handicrafts from around Panama. A varied and ultracool selection of beachwear, flip-flops, and surf gear can be found at **Flow** (daily 10am–5pm) at Avenida H, below the Om restaurant. You'll find a good selection of handicrafts, including Kuna Indian–made *molas,* at the compact **open-air market** at the end of Main Street and Avenida H; it's open daily from 10am to 6pm, though it may close for rain.

Where to Stay

Easygoing travelers enjoy the laid-back Caribbean vibe in Bocas Town, and its proximity to restaurants, bars, and shopping, not to mention people-watching and cultural encounters. But loud music and other street noise is a factor, and travelers seeking peaceful isolation will do better lodging elsewhere. Neighboring Isla Carenero is close enough that you can occasionally hear music on loud party nights in Bocas, but it still gives travelers an option for being near Bocas without actually staying in it.

Expensive

Hotel El Limbo on the Sea ★ This oceanfront hotel, conveniently located near most restaurants, tour operators, and water taxis, is virtually identical to the neighboring Hotel Bocas del Toro (see below). Hotel Limbo has the edge, with brighter rooms, but the service here can run from inattentive to unfriendly. Guest rooms are not luxurious, but they are neat as a pin and attractively decorated in a nautical style, with cooling blues and whites, polished wood floors, and wood paneling. This is one of the only hotels in town with a bathtub. The best rooms are the two with balconies that overlook the water; they provide particularly relaxing places to have drinks or order meals in, but if you can't get one, instead take advantage of the Limbo's good restaurant and bar on the first floor.

Calle 1 at Main St. ✆ **757-9062.** www.ellimbo.com. 15 units. $90 (£45) double standard; $125 (£63) city front room; $180 (£90) oceanview room. Rates include breakfast. AE, MC, V. **Amenities:** Restaurant; bar; room service. *In room:* A/C, TV w/DVD player, hair dryer, minibar, whirlpool.

Playa Tortuga Resort ★ Kids A newcomer on the Bocas scene, the Playa Tortuga resort is really more a medium-size hotel with lots of amenities and services than a full-fledged resort. Located about 3.2km (2 miles) from Bocas town, the Playa Tortuga fronts an attractive, relatively calm beach and is perfect for families and those looking for comfort and convenience. The lobby is a bit dim and unwelcoming, but the cheerful, friendly (and bilingual) staff makes up for this. Rooms have a familiar, chainlike decor, but all have their own balcony, complete with a hammock and sitting area, many with great ocean views. The best things about the Playa Tortuga Resort are its impressive, cascading pool, complete with a pool bar and restaurant. The hotel's service desk offers snorkeling, fishing, and wildlife excursions for those looking for a little bit of adventure. Though it may not provide a five-star resort experience, there's really else like it on the island, and it will suffice for those who don't want to rough it in dingy backpacker hostels or cramped bed-and-breakfasts.

Big Creek Beach, on the road to Playa Bluff. ✆ **302-5424.** www.hotelplayatortuga.com. 117 units. $170–$200 (£85–£100) double; $225–$275 (£113–£138) junior suite; $250–$300 (£125–£150) suite. AE, MC, V. **Amenities:** Restaurant; 2 bars; room service. *In room:* A/C, satellite TV, minibar.

Moderate

Cocomo-on-the-Sea ★ The Cocomo is a pleasant little hotel tucked away behind a white picket fence and a lush garden, about a 5-minute walk to the central part of town. The hotel sits on the waterfront, and feels cool and fresh even on a muggy day. There are only four rooms, all pretty close to each other but bright and airy; each comes with a double bed and a twin. The bathrooms are clean but small. There is a spacious deck, with hammocks and lounge chairs, which is partially covered in case of rain. The hotel staff are friendly, and the American owner can help you plan any tour in the area—although he's not around very much, so try to grab him when you can. Rates include a good, hearty breakfast, and they have kayaks for guest use.

Av. Norte at 6A St. ✆/fax **757-9259.** www.panamainfo.com/cocomo. 4 units. $70 (£35) double. MC, V. **Amenities:** Bar; laundry; watersports equipment. *In room:* A/C, no phone.

Hotel Bocas del Toro ★ With its full-service restaurant (equipped with free Wi-Fi) and dock furnished with lounge chairs, this place is virtually identical to Hotel El Limbo on the Sea. Hotel Bocas del Toro features beautiful wood craftsmanship and a fresh, nautical decor, but some of the standard doubles that do not face the water or the street are dark and small; "premium" rooms have balconies. The third-floor "Luxury Room" is a misnomer, but it is one of the best rooms in town for its ample size, long balcony, and water view; it also has a queen-size and a double bed for up to three guests. Like the Limbo, this is not a particularly loud hotel, but a lot of action in the area means it's not whisper-quiet, either.

Calle 1 at Main St. ✆ **757-9018** or 757-9771. www.hotelbocasdeltoro.com. 11 units. $56–$70 (£28–£35) double standard; $68–$85 (£34–£43) double with street view; $88–$110 (£44–£55) room with sea view; $108–$135 (£54–£68) luxury room. AE, MC, V. **Amenities:** Restaurant; bar; Wi-Fi. *In room:* A/C, TV.

Inexpensive

Lula's Bed & Breakfast ★ This American-run B&B fronts the Cocomo-on-the-Sea and is across a dirt street from the waterfront, about a 5-minute walk to town. The B&B offers simple, squeaky-clean guest rooms notable for their polished wood floors and wall paneling. The most appealing aspect of Lula's is its "Turtle Deck" balcony, which receives cool breezes—try to get a room that opens onto the balcony (both triples do). In general, guest rooms are on the small side, but not so small as to seem cramped, and the friendly service here makes guests feel at home. The owner grew up in Bocas and can provide in-depth information and excursion-planning information about the area. A continental breakfast is included in the price.

Av. H at Calle 6. ✆ **757-9057.** www.lulabb.com. 6 units. $42 (£21) double; $66 (£33) triple. No credit cards. *In room:* A/C, no phone.

Where to Dine

Believe it or not, tiny Bocas is home to one of the few gourmet supermarkets in the country, **Super Gourmet** (✆ **757-9357;** Mon–Sat 9am–7pm), with imported foods, vegetarian and organic products, and very expensive produce. Super Gourmet, which has a full-service delicatessen, is next to the Hotel Bahía on the south end of Main Street. You'll find good coffee drinks and lots of reading material at **Starfish Coffee** on Main Street next to El Encanto bar, and good breakfasts on a waterfront dock at the **Coffee Bar** inside Hotel El Limbo on the Sea (see "Where to Stay," above). For cheap, tourist-style fast food, try **McDouglas' Golden Grill** (daily 7:30am–11pm) on Main Street across from the plaza. For pizzas, you can't beat **Alberto's Pizzas** (✆ **756-9066;** Mon–Sat 11am–3pm and 5–11pm), made fresh to order by an Italian who knows his stuff. It's on Calle 5 at Avenida F, but the building was for sale at press time. **Guari Guari ★★★** (✆ **6575-5513**) just outside of town, is conceptually similar to Manolo Caracol in Panama City. It's open for dinner only, and reservations are required. For $16 (£8), you get a 6- to 12-course meal including whatever the chef feels like serving that day. **El Ultimo Refugio** (✆ **6568-8927**), also just outside town, is one of the area's most atmospheric places to dine, with dishes such as grilled tuna and Cajun-style chicken. Reservations are recommended here, too.

Right in town, **El Pecado del Sabor** (✆ **6597-0296;** Main Street at the Plaza) serves Thai, Mexican, Lebanese, and Panamanian food, but while the food is good, the building itself feels like it's on the verge of collapse. **Om Café ★★** (✆ **6587-6757**) is considered one of the top in-town dining options, and serves up delicious Indian food and a funky, mellow vibe that is pure Bocas.

The **Buena Vista Grill** (✆ **757-9035;** Calle 1 at Calle 2) offers typical American fare such as BLT and hot Reuben sandwiches. **Reef** (Main St. on the south end of town) is a local dive serving ultra-fresh Panamanian seafood in a rough-and-tumble, saltwater ambience. **Shelley's**

The San Blas Islands

The very adventurous will not want to miss out on the rustic and wonderfully undiscovered **San Blas Islands** ★★★ on the Caribbean coast bordering Colombia. Home to the Kuna Indians, who have not allowed foreign or even Panamanian investment or megaresorts to infringe upon the islands, this is the perfect kind of place to spend a couple of days sleeping in a hammock and swimming in the clear blue sea. There is not much else to do here, but you do have an opportunity to interact with the Kuna community and eat tasty if simple Kuna meals. The hotels in this region are all-inclusive, and are quite a bit cheaper than those found on Isla Bastimentos (see above), mostly due to the rustic accommodations. For a truly customized tour of the Kuna Yala Islands, contact guide Gilberto Alemancia, director of local communities at the **Panamanian Institute of Tourism** (✆ **6688-4623;** gilbert04@yahoo.com). Gilberto has coordinated expeditions for National Geographic, Photo Safari, PhotoAdventure, Discovery Channel Adventure, and the BBC, and is the go-to guy for all things Kuna. Fully bilingual and U.S. educated, Gilberto is himself a Kuna, and extremely knowledgeable about that culture's history and customs. He can organize specialized tours, set up boat transportation to and from different islands, organize camping trips, or even accompany visitors to the Comarca, which can even include a stay at a traditional Kuna hut on his home island. Call for prices and information.

If you decide to get here on your own, there are frequent flights here between Panama City and El Porvenir or other parts of the Comarca Kuna Yala; you should check **Aeroperlas** (www.aeroperlas.com) and **Air Panama** (www.flyairpanama.com) for more information about these flights.

BBQ (✆ **757-9779;** corner of Calle 4 and Av. D) is a hole-in-the-wall Mexican rotisserie, but a delicious one at that. Try their outstanding tacos and quesadillas.

Bocas Town After Dark

Bocas Town is Party Central for the archipelago, but there are plenty of low-key venues for a quiet drink, and the town's laid-back, friendly atmosphere creates an environment that encourages meeting fellow travelers and locals. **Iguana Bar and Surf Club,** on Calle 1, is the best all-around bar, with a cool surfer theme and a wood-hewn, comfy ambience that's good for conversation and suitable for all ages, though the party can pick up late in the evening. **Buena Vista** (see above) is an old-school expat hangout, with a long wooden bar, lapping seafront, and decent cocktails. The open-air waterfront bar **Barco Hundido (Shipwreck Bar),** on Calle 1, is the all-out party zone with late nights and dancing that culminate with one or two drunk guys jumping into the water on a dare. The bar often has live DJs or bands with a cover charge. **Mondo Taitu,** on Avenida G, caters to 20-something surfers and backpackers, and has cheap drinks and good music late into the night. The awful-sounding **Blue Nasty Mermaid,** on Main Street at Avenida A, has a happy hour from 4 to 6pm and, to keep you going, another from 10 to 11pm; they also have open-mic nights and a sand-floor seating area over the water.

Appendix: Fast Facts, Toll-Free Numbers & Websites

1 FAST FACTS: CENTRAL AMERICA

AMERICAN EXPRESS See individual chapters for info.

AREA CODES See individual chapters for info.

ATM NETWORKS & CASHPOINTS See "Money," throughout individual destination chapters for info.

BUSINESS HOURS See individual chapters for info.

CAR RENTALS See "Toll-Free Numbers & Websites," p. 707.

DRINKING LAWS The legal drinking age throughout Central America is 18 (except in Honduras, where you have to be 21 to drink, but 18 to purchase alcohol), although it is often not enforced. Beer, wine, and liquor are all sold in most supermarkets and small convenience stores from Monday through Saturday. No liquor is sold on Good Friday or Easter Sunday or election days. If you're caught possessing, using, or trafficking drugs anywhere in the region, expect severe penalties, including long jail sentences and large fines.

DRIVING RULES See "Getting There" and "Getting Around" info throughout this book.

ELECTRICITY Central American countries run on 110 volts, 60 Hz, the same as the United States and Canada. However, three-prong grounded outlets are not universally available. It's helpful to bring a three-to-two prong adapter. European and Asian travelers should bring adapters with any accompanying appliances. Be prepared for frequent blackouts, and bring surge protectors.

EMBASSIES & CONSULATES See individual chapters for info.

EMERGENCIES See individual chapters for info.

HOLIDAYS See "Calendar of Events," in the "Planning Your Trip to Central America" chapter.

INTERNET ACCESS Internet access is easy to find in the region, as even the smallest towns usually have at least one Internet center. Access usually costs 50¢ to $1 (25p–50p) per hour. Nearly every hotel has at least one computer with Internet access; some have dataports or Wi-Fi (usually in the hotel lobby or business center). See "Fast Facts" throughout the country chapters for specific locations.

INSURANCE **Medical Insurance** For travel overseas, most U.S. health plans (including Medicare and Medicaid) do not provide coverage, and the ones that do often require you to pay for services upfront and reimburse you only after you return home.

As a safety net, you may want to buy travel medical insurance, particularly if you're traveling to a remote or high-risk area where emergency evacuation might be necessary. If you require additional medical insurance, try **MEDEX Assistance** (✆ **410/453-6300;** www.medexassist.com) or **Travel Assistance International** (✆ **800/821-2828;** www.travelassistance.com; for general information on services, call the company's **Worldwide Assistance Services, Inc.,** at ✆ **800/777-8710.**

Canadians should check with their provincial health plan offices or call **Health Canada** (✆ **866/225-0709;** www.hc-sc.gc.ca) to find out the extent of their coverage and what documentation and receipts they must take home in case they are treated overseas.

Travelers from the U.K. should carry their **European Health Insurance Card (EHIC),** which replaced the E111 form as proof of entitlement to free/reduced cost medical treatment abroad (✆ **0845/606-2030;** www.ehic.org.uk). Note, however, that the EHIC only covers "necessary medical treatment," and for repatriation costs, lost money, baggage, or cancellation, travel insurance from a reputable company should always be sought (www.travelinsuranceweb.com).

Travel Insurance The cost of travel insurance varies widely, depending on the destination, the cost and length of your trip, your age and health, and the type of trip you're taking, but expect to pay between 5% and 8% of the vacation itself. You can get estimates from various providers through **InsureMyTrip.com.** Enter your trip cost and dates, your age, and other information, for prices from more than a dozen companies.

U.K. citizens and their families who make more than one trip abroad per year may find an annual travel insurance policy works out cheaper. Check **www.moneysupermarket.com**, which compares prices across a wide range of providers.

Most big travel agents offer their own insurance and will probably try to sell you their package when you book a holiday. Think before you sign. **Britain's Consumers' Association** recommends that you insist on seeing the policy and reading the fine print before buying travel insurance. The **Association of British Insurers** (✆ **020/7600-3333;** www.abi.org.uk) gives advice by phone and publishes *Holiday Insurance,* a free guide to policy provisions and prices. You might also shop around for better deals: Try **Columbus Direct** (✆ **0870/033-9988;** www.columbusdirect.net).

Trip-Cancellation Insurance Trip-cancellation insurance will help retrieve your money if you have to back out of a trip or depart early, or if your travel supplier goes bankrupt. Trip cancellation traditionally covers such events as sickness, natural disasters, and State Department advisories. The latest news in trip-cancellation insurance is the availability of **expanded hurricane coverage** and the **"any-reason"** cancellation coverage—which costs more but covers cancellations made for any reason. You won't get back 100% of your prepaid trip cost, but you'll be refunded a substantial portion. **TravelSafe** (✆ **888/885-7233;** www.travelsafe.com) offers both types of coverage. Expedia also offers any-reason cancellation coverage for its air-hotel packages. For details, contact one of the following recommended insurers: **Access America** (✆ 866/807-3982; www.accessamerica.com); **Travel Guard International** (✆ 800/826-4919; www.travelguard.com); **Travel Insured International** (✆ 800/243-3174; www.travelinsured.com); and **Travelex Insurance Services** (✆ 888/457-4602; www.travelex-insurance.com).

LANGUAGE Spanish is by far the dominant language in the region, except in Belize, where English is spoken. You will also hear English spoken in the Bay Islands in Honduras, the Canal Zone in Panama, and more touristy destinations. The Caribbean coast has its own form of lilting creole that has West Indian roots. A number of indigenous languages have survived, most notably Mayan. See the individual destination chapters throughout this book for more info. It is also advisable to learn some basic Spanish before you travel here; we recommend picking up a copy of the *Frommer's Spanish PhraseFinder & Dictionary*.

LOST & FOUND Be sure to tell all of your credit card companies the minute you discover your wallet has been lost or stolen and file a report at the nearest police precinct. See individual chapters for more info.

If you need emergency cash, you can have money wired to you via **Western Union** (✆ **800/325-6000;** www.westernunion.com).

MAIL Every country in Central America varies regarding the price, efficiency, and speed of its mail service (known as *correo*). In general, expect it to take 2 weeks for your letter or postcard to reach home. If you're sending a parcel, a Customs officer may have to inspect it first. Theft is a common problem. Always try and send mail from a main post office and insist the envelope is stamped in front of you. It's wise to send things via registered post, though often the letter can be tracked as far as the border and no more. Private courier services are everywhere but most are expensive. See the individual chapters throughout this book for specifics.

MEASUREMENTS See the chart on the inside front cover of this book for details on converting metric measurements to nonmetric equivalents.

NEWSPAPERS & MAGAZINES ***The Miami Herald*** (www.miamiherald.com) is probably the most widely available English-language paper about the region. The Costa Rican based ***Tico Times*** (www.ticotimes.net) is another. You can find both in most capital city downtown kiosks and airport newsstands. See individual chapters for each country's major newspapers.

PASSPORTS The websites listed below provide downloadable passport applications as well as the current fees for processing applications. For an up-to-date, country-by-country listing of passport requirements around the world, go to the "International Travel" tab of the U.S. State Department at **http://travel.state.gov**.

For Residents of Australia You can pick up an application from your local post office or any branch of Passports Australia, but you must schedule an interview at the passport office to present your application materials. Call the **Australian Passport Information Service** at ✆ **131-232,** or visit the government website at www.passports.gov.au.

For Residents of Canada Passport applications are available at travel agencies throughout Canada or from the central **Passport Office,** Department of Foreign Affairs and International Trade, Ottawa, ON K1A 0G3 (✆ **800/567-6868;** www.ppt.gc.ca). ***Note:*** Canadian children who travel must have their own passport. However, if you hold a valid Canadian passport issued before December 11, 2001, that bears the name of your child, the passport remains valid for you and your child until it expires.

For Residents of Ireland You can apply for a 10-year passport at the **Passport Office,** Setanta Centre, Molesworth Street, Dublin 2 (✆ **01/671-1633;** www.irlgov.ie/iveagh). Those 17 and under, or 66 and older, must apply for a 3-year passport.

You can also apply at 1A South Mall, Cork (✆ **21/494-4700**) or at most main post offices.

For Residents of New Zealand You can pick up a passport application at any New Zealand Passports Office or download it from their website. Contact the **Passports Office** at ✆ **0800/225-050** in New Zealand, or 04/474-8100, or log on to www.passports.govt.nz.

For Residents of the United Kingdom To pick up an application for a standard 10-year passport (5-year passport for children 15 and under), visit your nearest passport office, major post office, or travel agency or contact the **United Kingdom Passport Service** at ✆ **0870/521-0410,** or search its website at www.ukpa.gov.uk.

For Residents of the United States: Whether you're applying in person or by mail, you can download passport applications from the U.S. State Department website at **http://travel.state.gov**. To find your regional passport office, either check the U.S. State Department website or call the **National Passport Information Center** toll-free number (✆ **877/487-2778**) for automated information.

POLICE See individual chapters for info.

SMOKING Except for Panama, which recently banned smoking in all restaurants and bars, there are no government smoking bans in Central America at the moment. Private companies do not allow smoking in places like cinemas or long-distance buses, however. The region's better hotels and restaurants have nonsmoking rooms and areas, but in general you can still puff wherever you want.

TAXES VAT and Customs duties differ from country to country. See individual chapters for info.

TELEPHONES See p. 80 in "Planning Your Trip to Central America," along with the "Telephone Dialing Info at a Glance" boxes throughout this guide for info.

TIME All of Central America is 6 hours behind Greenwich Mean Time, except Panama, which is 5 hours behind. No countries observe daylight saving time.

TIPPING Ten percent is the general rule for tipping in restaurants, though tips are sometimes included in bills. In hotels, tip **bellhops** at least $1 (50p) per bag ($2–$3/£1–£1.50 if you have a lot of luggage) and tip the **chamber staff** $1 to $2 (50p–£1) per day. See individual chapters for more info.

TOILETS These are known as *sanitarios, servicios sanitarios,* or *baños.* They are marked *damas* (women) and *hombres* or *caballeros* (men). Throughout Central America, public restrooms are hard to come by. You will almost never find a public restroom in a city park or downtown area. In the towns and cities, it gets much trickier. One must count on the generosity of some hotel or restaurant. Same goes for most beaches. Most restaurants, and, to a lesser degree, hotels, will let you use their facilities, especially if you buy a soft drink or something. Bus and gas stations often have restrooms, but many of these are pretty grim. Don't flush toilet paper; put it in the trash bin.

WATER The water in most major cities and tourist destinations throughout Central America is ostensibly safe to drink. However, many travelers react adversely to water in foreign countries, and it is probably best to drink bottled water and avoid ice or food washed with tap water throughout your visit to the region. See p. 70 in "Planning Your Trip to Central America" for more info.

2 TOLL-FREE NUMBERS & WEBSITES

AIRLINES

Aeroméxico
✆ 800/237-6639 (in the U.S.)
✆ 020/7801-6234 (in the U.K., information only)
www.aeromexico.com

Air Canada
✆ 888/247-2262 (in the U.S. and Canada)
www.aircanada.com

Air New Zealand
✆ 800/262-1234 (in the U.S.)
✆ 800/663-5494 (in Canada)
✆ 0800/028-4149 (in the U.K.)
www.airnewzealand.com

American Airlines
✆ 800/433-7300 (in the U.S. and Canada)
✆ 020/7365-0777 (in the U.K.)
www.aa.com

British Airways
✆ 800/247-9297 (in the U.S. and Canada)
✆ 087/0850-9850 (in the U.K.)
www.british-airways.com

Continental Airlines
✆ 800/523-3273 (in the U.S. and Canada)
✆ 084/5607-6760 (in the U.K.)
www.continental.com

Copa Air
✆ 800/265-2672 (in the U.S. and Canada)
www.copaair.com

Delta Air Lines
✆ 800/221-1212 (in the U.S. and Canada)
✆ 084/5600-0950 (in the U.K.)
www.delta.com

Frontier Airlines
✆ 800/432-1359 (in the U.S. and Canada)
www.frontierairlines.com

Iberia Airlines
✆ 800/722-4642 (in the U.S. and Canada)
✆ 087/0609-0500 (in the U.K.)
www.iberia.com

Lan Airlines
✆ 866/435-9526 (in the U.S.)
✆ 305/670-9999 (in other countries)
www.lan.com

Martin Air
✆ 305/704-9800 (in the U.S.)
www.martinair.com

Mexicana
✆ 800/531-7921
www.mexicana.com

Northwest Airlines
✆ 800/225-2525 (in the U.S.)
✆ 870/0507-4074 (in the U.K.)
www.nwa.com

Qantas Airways
✆ 800/227-4500 (in the U.S.)
✆ 084/5774-7767 (in the U.K. or Canada)
✆ 13 13 13 (in Australia)
www.qantas.com

Spirit Airlines
✆ 800/772-7117
www.spiritair.com

TACA
✆ 800/535-8780 (in the U.S.)
✆ 800/722-TACA (8222) (in Canada)
✆ 087/0241-0340 (in the U.K.)
www.taca.com

United Airlines
✆ 800/864-8331 (in the U.S. and Canada)
✆ 084/5844-4777 (in the U.K.)
www.united.com

US Airways
✆ 800/428-4322 (in the U.S. and Canada)
✆ 084/5600-3300 (in the U.K.)
www.usairways.com

Virgin Atlantic Airways
✆ 800/821-5438 (in the U.S. and Canada)
✆ 087/0574-7747 (in the U.K.)
www.virgin-atlantic.com

CAR-RENTAL AGENCIES

Alamo
© 800/GO-ALAMO (800/462-5266)
www.alamo.com

Avis
© 800/331-1212 (in the U.S. and Canada)
© 084/4581-8181 (in the U.K.)
www.avis.com

Budget
© 800/527-0700 (in the U.S.)
© 087/0156-5656 (in the U.K.)
© 800/268-8900 (in Canada)
www.budget.com

Dollar
© 800/800-4000 (in the U.S.)
© 800/848-8268 (in Canada)
© 080/8234-7524 (in the U.K.)
www.dollar.com

Hertz
© 800/645-3131
© 800/654-3001 (international)
www.hertz.com

National
© 800/CAR-RENT (800/227-7368)
www.nationalcar.com

Thrifty
© 800/367-2277
© 918/669-2168 (international)
www.thrifty.com

MAJOR HOTEL & MOTEL CHAINS

Best Western International
© 800/780-7234 (in the U.S. and Canada)
© 0800/393-130 (in the U.K.)
www.bestwestern.com

Clarion Hotels
© 800/252-7466 or 877/424-6423 (in the U.S. and Canada)
© 0800/444-444 (in the U.K.)
www.choicehotels.com

Comfort Inns
© 800/228-5150
© 0800/444-444 (in the U.K.)
www.comfortinn.com

Courtyard by Marriott
© 888/236-2427 (in the U.S.)
© 0800/221-222 (in the U.K.)
www.marriott.com/courtyard

Crowne Plaza Hotels
© 888/303-1746
www.ichotelsgroup.com/crowneplaza

Days Inn
© 800/329-7466 (in the U.S.)
© 0800/280-400 (in the U.K.)
www.daysinn.com

Doubletree Hotels
© 800/222-TREE (800/222-8733) (in the U.S. and Canada)
© 087/0590-9090 (in the U.K.)
www.doubletree.com

Econo Lodges
© 800/55-ECONO (800/552-3666)
www.choicehotels.com

Embassy Suites
© 800/EMBASSY (800/362-2779)
www.embassysuites.hilton.com

Four Seasons
© 800/819-5053 (in the U.S. and Canada)
© 0800/6488-6488 (in the U.K.)
www.fourseasons.com

Hampton Inn
© 800/HAMPTON (800/426-4766)
www.hamptoninn.hilton.com

Hilton Hotels
© 800/HILTONS (800/445-8667) (in the U.S. and Canada)
© 087/0590-9090 (in the U.K.)
www.hilton.com

Holiday Inn
✆ 800/315-2621 (in the U.S. and Canada)
✆ 0800/405-060 (in the U.K.)
www.holidayinn.com

Howard Johnson
✆ 800/446-4656 (in the U.S. and Canada)
www.hojo.com

InterContinental Hotels & Resorts
✆ 800/424-6835 (in the U.S. and Canada)
✆ 0800/1800-1800 (in the U.K.)
www.ichotelsgroup.com

Marriott
✆ 877/236-2427 (in the U.S. and Canada)
✆ 0800/221-222 (in the U.K.)
www.marriott.com

Quality
✆ 877/424-6423 (in the U.S. and Canada)
✆ 0800/444-444 (in the U.K.)
www.QualityInn.ChoiceHotels.com

Ramada Worldwide
✆ 888/2-RAMADA (888/272-6232) (in the U.S. and Canada)
✆ 080/8100-0783 (in the U.K.)
www.ramada.com

Residence Inn by Marriott
✆ 800/331-3131
✆ 800/221-222 (in the U.K.)
www.marriott.com

Rodeway Inns
✆ 877/424-6423
www.RodewayInn.ChoiceHotels.com

Wyndham Hotels & Resorts
✆ 877/999-3223 (in the U.S. and Canada)
✆ 050/6638-4899 (in the U.K.)
www.wyndham.com

INDEX